D0954139

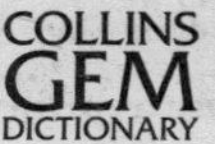

LATIN · ENGLISH
ENGLISH · LATIN

D. A. Kidd MA

Professor of Classics
University of Canterbury
New Zealand

Collins
London and Glasgow
Harper & Row
New York

first published 1957

latest reprint 1990

ISBN 0 00 458644 1

General Editor
W. T. McLeod

Contents

Printed in Great Britain by
Collins Clear-Type Press

FOREWORD

This dictionary is a new publication in a series which has hitherto been confined to the modern languages. Its purpose is to some extent different from that of the others, in so far as the uses of Latin differ from those of French, German, Italian and Spanish. There are two main reasons for learning Latin: one is to read the best in the literature of the Romans; the other is to understand the Latin basis which underlies the structure of many modern languages and the extensive Latin element which still survives in the terminology of historians, lawyers, scientists and other professional writers.

The vocabulary is drawn mostly from the authors that are commonly read in schools and in pass classes at the universities, covering the three centuries from about 180 *B.C.* to *A.D.* 120: Terence, Cicero, Caesar, Lucretius, Catullus, Sallust, Nepos, Virgil, Horace, Propertius, Tibullus, Ovid, Livy, Quintilian, Tacitus, the younger Pliny, and Juvenal. In addition there are many words included from the more familiar plays of Plautus, and at the other end of the Classical era there is a small selection of common ecclesiastical and political terms from later Latin usage, *e.g.* **abbās**.

Latin is a language with a relatively small vocabulary, and many words have to carry a wide range of meanings. Particular care has been taken in distinguishing the most important of these by indicating wherever possible the context of each meaning by a bracketed word in italics before it. See for example the verb **dūcō**. Occasionally, where the range of meanings is unusually complicated, these have been arranged in groups, numbered 1, 2, 3, etc., as for example in the case of the noun **ratiō**. To illustrate special idioms, as many as possible of the commonest phrases have been included under the key word.

Particular attention has been paid to bringing the English renderings of Latin words up to date. There is always a tendency for obsolescent words to linger on in Latin vocabularies, *e.g.* "seek" as a translation of **petō**. These should be avoided unless a stilted or archaic manner is deliberately being affected. The modern idiom is the only live one, and translation into English requires as much care and artistry as translation into Latin.

The Latin vocabulary in the English-Latin section is based on the usage of the prose writers, esp. Cicero, Caesar and Livy, though words of a technical nature are also included even if they are extant only in poets or later prose authors. Latin renderings have also been given for a large number of idiomatic English phrases, many of which are not to be found in other Latin dictionaries of this size.

As in the first section, much thought has been given to distinguishing the various meanings of words by inserting a suggestive reference to their context. Nevertheless the English-

Latin section should be used with great care, and any unfamiliar word selected should be checked against the meanings assigned to it in the Latin-English section. If fuller information is desired about a word it will have to be looked up in any large Latin dictionary which quotes examples of its usage in the Classical authors.

D. A. KIDD.

ABBREVIATIONS

a.	adjective
abl.	ablative
acc.	accusative
ad.	adverb
agr.	agriculture
arch.	architecture
art.	article
astr.	astronomy
aug.	augury
bus.	business
circs.	circumstances
colloq.	colloquial
comp.	comparative
conj.	conjunction
cpd.	compound
dat.	dative
def.	defective
eccl.	ecclesiastical
esp.	especially
exclam.	exclamatory
f.	feminine
fig.	figurative
fut.	future
gen.	genitive
geog.	geography
gram.	grammar
imp.	imperative
impers.	impersonal
impf.	imperfect
indecl.	indeclinable
indic.	indicative
inf.	infinitive
interj.	interjection
interrog.	interrogative
lit.	literature
loc.	locative
m.	masculine
math.	mathematics
med.	medicine
mil.	military
mod.	modern
n.	neuter (after Latin words)
	noun (after English words)
naut.	nautical
neg.	negative
nom.	nominative
num.	numeral
occ.	occasionally
p.	participle
pass.	passive
perf.	perfect
perh.	perhaps
pers.	person
philos.	philosophy
pl.	plural
pol.	politics
ppa.	perfect participle active
ppp.	perfect participle passive
pr.	preposition
pres.	present
pro.	pronoun
prop.	properly
prov.	proverb
rel.	relative
rhet.	rhetoric
s.	singular
sim.	similarly
subj.	subjunctive
sup.	superlative
theat.	theatre
univ.	university
usu.	usually
vi.	intransitive verb
voc.	vocative
vt.	transitive verb
vt. & i.	transitive and intransitive verb

ALPHABET

The Latin alphabet is the one which has been almost universally adopted by the modern languages of Europe and America. In the Classical period it had 23 letters, viz. the English alphabet without **j**, **v** and **w**. The symbol **v** was the capital form of the letter **u**, but in a later age the small **v** came into use to represent the consonantal **u**, and as it is commonly so employed in modern editions of Latin authors, it has been retained in this dictionary for convenience as a distinct letter. Similarly the symbol **j** came to be used as the consonantal **i**, and is found in older editions of the Classics, but as it has been almost entirely discarded in modern texts, it is not used in this dictionary, and words found spelt with a **j** must therefore be looked up under **i**. The letter **w** may be seen in the Latinised forms of some modern names, *e.g.* **Westmonasterium**, Westminster. The letters **y** and **z** occur only in words of Greek origin.

PRONUNCIATION

The ancient pronunciation of Latin has been established with a fair degree of certainty from the evidence of ancient authorities and inscriptions and inferences from the modern Romance languages. It is not possible, of course, to recapture the precise nuances of Classical Latin speech, but what follows is now generally accepted and generally understood as a reasonably accurate guide to the sounds of Latin as spoken by educated Romans during the two centuries from Cicero to Quintilian.

Vowels

Vowels are pure and should not be diphthongized as in certain sounds of Southern English. They may be long or short. Throughout this Dictionary all vowels known or believed by the best authorities to be long are marked with a line above them; those unmarked are either known to be short or of uncertain quantity.

Short **a** is pronounced as *a* in *rat*
Long **ā** „ „ *a* in *rather*
Short **e** „ „ *e* in *pen*
Long **ē** „ „ *ay* in *pay*
Short **i** „ „ *i* in *kin*
Long **ī** „ „ *ee* in *keen*
Short **o** „ „ *o* in *rob*
Long **ō** „ „ *o* in *robe*
Short **u** „ „ *u* in *full*
Long **ū** „ „ *oo* in *fool*

y is a Greek sound and is pronounced (both short and long) as **u** in French.

Diphthongs

ae	is pronounced as	*y* in *try*
au	" "	*ow* in *town*
ei	" "	*ayee* in *payee*
eu	" "	*ay-oo*, with the accent on the first sound
oe	" "	*oy* in *toy*
ui	" "	*oui* in *Louis*.

Consonants

b	is pronounced as	in English, except that
bs	" "	*ps* in *apse*, and
bt	" "	*pt* in *apt*
c	" "	c in *car*
ch	" "	*ch* in *sepulchre*
d	" "	in English
f	" "	in English
g	" "	*g* in *go*
h	" "	*h* in *hand*, but faintly
i	" "	*y* in *yes*
k	" "	in English
l	" "	*l* in *let*
m	" "	*m* in *man*; but final *m* was hardly sounded, and may have simply nasalized the preceding vowel
n	" "	in English
ng	" "	*ng* in *finger*
p	" "	*p* in *apt*
ph	" "	*p* in *pill*
qu	" "	*qu* in *quite*
r	" "	*r* in *brae* (Scottish)
s	" "	*s* in *sister* (*never* as in *rose*)
t	" "	*t* in *stop*
th	" "	*t* in *take*
u, v	" "	*w* in *win*
x	" "	*x* in *six* (as *ks*, not *gs*)
z	" "	*z* in *zero*

Double consonants prolong the sound of the consonant, as in Italian.

ACCENT

The Latin accent in the Classical period was a weak stress, perhaps with an element of pitch in it. It falls, as in English, on the second last syllable of the word, if that syllable is long, and on the third last syllable if the second last is short. Disyllabic words take the accent on the first syllable, unless they have already lost a final syllable, *e.g.* **illī'c(e)**.

Inflected words are commonly learned with the accent wrongly placed on the last syllable, for convenience in memorising the inflexions. But it is advisable to get the accent as

well as the ending right. In this dictionary the accent of each word is shown in the main entry and also, where appropriate, in the inflected parts quoted. It is also included in the tables of Declensions and Conjugations. The correct accent of other parts can easily be found by noting carefully the quantity of the second last syllable and then accenting the word as in English, according to the rule given above. Thus **fuē'runt** is accented on the second last syllable because the **e** is long, whereas **fu'erant** is accented on the third last, because the **e** is short.

DECLENSIONS OF NOUNS

1st Declension

	mainly f.		*m.*	
Sing.				
Nom.	te'rra	cra'mbē	Aenē'ās	Anchī'sēs
Voc.	te'rra	cra'mbē	Aenē'ā	Anchī's/ā, -ē
Acc.	te'rram	cra'mbēn	Aenē'/am, -ān	Anchī's/am, -ēn
Gen.	te'rrae	cra'mbes	Aenē'ae	Anchī'sae
Dat.	te'rrae	cra'mbae	Aenē'ae	Anchī'sae
Abl.	te'rra	cra'mbā	Aenē'ā	Anchī'sā
Plural				
Nom.	te'rrae	cra'mbae		
Voc.	te'rrae	cra'mbae		
Acc.	te'rrās	cra'mbās		
Gen.	terrā'rum	crambā'rum		
Dat.	te'rrīs	cra'mbīs		
Abl.	te'rrīs	cra'mbīs		

2nd Declension

	mainly m.					**n.**
Sing.						
Nom.	mo'dus	Lū'cius	Dē'los(*f*)	pu'er	li'ber	dō'num
Voc.	mo'de	Lū'ci	Dē'le	pu'er	li'ber	dō'num
Acc.	mo'dum	Lū'cium	Dē'lon	pu'erum	li'brum	dō'num
Gen.	mo'dī	Lū'cī	Dē'lī	pu'erī	li'brī	dō'nī
Dat.	mo'dō	Lū'ciō	Dē'lō	pu'erō	li'brō	dō'nō
Abl.	mo'dō	Lū'ciō	Dē'lō	pu'erō	li'brō	dō'nō
Plural						
Nom.	mo'dī			pu'erī	li'brī	dō'na
Voc.	mo'dī			pu'erī	li'brī	dō'na
Acc.	mo'dōs			pu'erōs	li'brōs	dō'na
Gen.	modō'rum			puerō'-rum	librō'-rum	dōnō'-rum
Dat.	mo'dīs			pu'erīs	li'brīs	dō'nīs
Abl.	mo'dīs			pu'erīs	li'brīs	dō'nīs

3rd Declension

Group I: *Vowel stems, with gen. pl. in* -ium

	m. and f.		*n.*	
Sing.				
Nom.	clā'dēs	nā'vis	rē'te	a'nimal
Voc.	clā'dēs	nā'vis	rē'te	a'nimal
Acc.	clā'dem	nā'v/em, (-im)	rē'te	a'nimal
Gen.	clā'dis	nā'vis	rē'tis	animā'lis
Dat.	clā'dī	nā'vī	rē'tī	animā'lī
Abl.	clā'de	nā'v/e, -ī	rē'tī	animā'lī
Plural				
Nom.	clā'dēs	nā'vēs	rē'tia	animā'lia
Voc.	clā'dēs	nā'vēs	rē'tia	animā'lia
Acc.	clā'd/ēs, -īs	nā'v/ēs, -īs	rē'tia	animā'lia
Gen.	clā'dium	nā'vium	rē'tium	animā'lium
Dat.	clā'dibus	nā'vibus	rē'tibus	animā'libus
Abl.	clā'dibus	nā'vibus	rē'tibus	animā'libus

Group II: *Consonant stems, some with gen. pl. in* -ium, *some in* -um *and some in either. Monosyllabic nouns ending in two consonants* (e.g. **urbs** *below*) *regularly have* -ium.

	m. and f.			*f.*	*n.*
Sing.					
Nom.	u'rbs	a'māns	lau's	ae'tās	o's
Voc.	u'rbs	a'māns	lau's	ae'tās	o's
Acc.	u'rbem	ama'ntem	lau'dem	aetā'tem	o's
Gen.	u'rbis	ama'ntis	lau'dis	aetā'tis	o'ssis
Dat.	u'rbī	ama'ntī	lau'dī	aetā'tī	o'ssī
Abl.	u'rbe	ama'nte	lau'de	aetā'te	o'sse
Plural					
Nom.	u'rbēs	ama'ntēs	lau'dēs	aetā'tēs	o'ssa
Voc.	u'rbēs	ama'ntēs	lau'dēs	aetā'tēs	o'ssa
Acc.	u'rbēs	ama'ntēs	lau'dēs	aetā'tēs	o'ssa
Gen.	u'rbium	ama'nt/ium, -um	lau'd/um, -ium	aetāt/um, -ium	o'ssium
Dat.	u'rbibus	ama'ntibus	lau'dibus	aetā'tibus	o'ssibus
Abl.	u'rbibus	ama'ntibus	lau'dibus	aetā'tibus	o'ssibus

Group III: *Consonant stems, with gen. pl. in* -um

	m. and f.			*n.*	
Sing.					
Nom.	mō's	ra'tiō	pa'ter	nō'men	o'pus
Voc.	mō's	ra'tiō	pa'ter	nō'men	o'pus
Acc.	mō'rem	ratiō'nem	pa'trem	nō'men	o'pus
Gen.	mō'ris	ratiō'nis	pa'tris	nō'minis	o'peris
Dat.	mō'rī	ratiō'nī	pa'trī	nō'minī	o'perī
Abl.	mō're	ratiō'ne	pa'tre	nō'mine	o'pere

Plural					
Nom.	mō'rēs	ratiō'nēs	pa'trēs	nō'mina	o'pera
Voc.	mō'rēs	ratiō'nēs	pa'trēs	nō'mina	o'pera
Acc.	mō'rēs	ratiō'nēs	pa'trēs	nō'mina	o'pera
Gen.	mō'rum	ratiō'num	pa'trum	nō'minum	o'perum
Dat.	mō'ribus	ratiō'nibus	pa'tribus	nōmi'nibus	ope'ribus
Abl.	mō'ribus	ratiō'nibus	pa'tribus	nōmi'nibus	ope'ribus

Group IV: ***Greek nouns***

	m.			*f.*	*n.*
Sing.					
Nom.	ā'ēr	hē'rōs	Pe'riclēs	Nai'as	poē'ma
Voc.	ā'ēr	hē'rōs	Pe'riclē	Nai'as	poē'ma
Acc.	ā'era	hērō'a	Pe'riclem, Peri'clea	Nai'ada	poē'ma
Gen.	ā'eris	hērō'is	Pe'ricl/is,-ī	Nai'ad/is,-os	poē'matis
Dat.	ā'erī	hērō'ī	Pe'riclī	Nai'adī	poē'matī
Abl.	ā'ere	hērō'e	Pe'riclē	Nai'ade	poē'mate
Plural					
Nom.	ā'eres	hērō'es		Nai'ades	poē'mata
Voc.	ā'eres	hērō'es		Nai'ades	poē'mata
Acc.	ā'eras	hērō'as		Nai'adas	poē'mata
Gen.	ā'erum	hērō'um		Nai'adum	poēmatō'-rum
Dat.	āe'ribus	hērō'ibus		Naia'dibus	poē'matis
Abl.	āe'ribus	hērō'ibus		Naia'dibus	poē'matis

	4th Declension		**5th Declension**	
	mainly m.	***n.***	***mainly f.***	
Sing.				
Nom.	po'rtus	ge'nū	di'ēs	rē's
Voc.	po'rtus	ge'nū	di'ēs	rē's
Acc.	po'rtum	ge'nū	di'em	re'm
Gen.	po'rtūs	ge'nūs	diē'ī	re'ī
Dat.	po'rtuī	ge'nū	diē'ī	re'ī
Abl.	po'rtū	ge'nū	di'ē	rē'
Plural				
Nom.	po'rtūs	ge'nua	di'ēs	rē's
Voc.	po'rtūs	ge'nua	di'ēs	rē's
Acc.	po'rtūs	ge'nua	di'ēs	rē's
Gen.	po'rtuum	ge'nuum	diē'rum	rē'rum
Dat.	po'rt/ibus, -ubus	ge'n/ibus, -ubus	diē'bus	rē'bus
Abl.	po'rt/ibus, -ubus	ge'n/ibus, -ubus	diē'bus	rē'bus

CONJUGATIONS OF VERBS

First	Second	Third	Fourth
parāre, prepare	**habēre, have**	**sūmere, take**	**audīre, hear**

PRESENT TENSE

Indicative Active

pa'rō	ha'beō	sū'mō	au'diō
pa'rās	ha'bēs	sū'mis	au'dīs
pa'rat	ha'bet	sū'mit	au'dit
parā'mus	habē'mus	sū'mimus	aud'īmus
parā'tis	habē'tis	sū'mitis	audī'tis
pa'rant	ha'bent	sū'munt	au'diunt

Indicative Passive

pa'ror	ha'beor	sū'mor	au'dior
parā'ris	habē'ris	sū'meris	audī'ris
parā'tur	habē'tur	sū'mitur	audī'tur
parā'mur	habē'mur	sū'mimur	audī'mur
parā'minī	habē'minī	sūmi'minī	audī'minī
para'ntur	habe'ntur	sūmu'ntur	audiu'ntur

Subjunctive Active

pa'rem	ha'beam	sū'mam	au'diam
pa'rēs	ha'beās	sū'mās	au'diās
pa'ret	ha'beat	sū'mat	au'diat
parē'mus	habeā'mus	sūmā'mus	audiā'mus
parē'tis	habeā'tis	sūmā'tis	audiā'tis
pa'rent	ha'beant	sū'mant	au'diant

Subjunctive Passive

pa'rer	ha'bear	sū'mar	au'diar
parē'ris	habeā'ris	sūmā'ris	audiā'ris
parē'tur	habeā'tur	sūmā'tur	audiā'tur
parē'mur	habeā'mur	sūmā'mur	audiā'mur
parē'minī	habeā'minī	sumā-minī	audiā'minī
pare'ntur	habea'ntur	sūna'ntur	audia'ntur

IMPERFECT TENSE

Indicative Active

parā'bam	habē'bam	sūmē'bam	audiē'bam
parā'bās	habē'bās	sūmē'bās	audiē'bās
parā'bat	habē'bat	sūmē'bat	audiē'bat
parābā'mus	habēbā'mus	sūmēbā'mus	audiēbā'mus
parābā'tis	habēbā'tis	sūmēbā'tis	audiēbā'tis
parā'bant	habē'bant	sūmē'bant	audiē'bant

Indicative Passive

parā'bar	habē'bar	sūmē'bar	audiē'bar
parābā'ris	habēbā'ris	sūmēbā'ris	audiēbā'ris
parābā'tur	habēbā'tur	sūmēbā'tur	audiēbā'tur
parābā'mur	habēbā'mur	sūmēbā'mur	audiēbā'mur
parābā'mini	habēmā'mini	sūmēbā'mini	audiēbā'mini
parābā'ntur	habēba'ntur	sūmēba'ntur	audiēba'ntur

Subjunctive Active

parā'rem	habē'rem	sū'merem	audī'rem
parā'rēs	habē'rēs	sū'merēs	audī'rēs
parā'ret	habē'ret	sū'meret	audī'ret
parārē'mus	habērē'mus	sūmerē'mus	audīrē'mus
parārē'tis	habērē'tis	sūmerē'tis	audīrē'tis
parā'rent	habē'rent	sū'merent	audī'rent

Subjunctive Passive

parā'rer	habē'rer	sū'merer	audī'rer
parārē'ris	habērē'ris	sūmerē'ris	audīrē'ris
parārē'tur	habērē'tur	sūmerē'tur	audīrē'tur
parārē'mur	habērē'mur	sūmerē'mur	audīrē'mur
parārē'mini	habērē'mini	sūmerē'mini	audīrē'mini
parāre'ntur	habēre'ntur	sūmere'ntur	audīre'ntur

FUTURE TENSE

Indicative Active

parā'bō	habē'bō	sū'mam	au'diam
parā'bis	habē'bis	sū'mēs	au'diēs
parā'bit	habē'bit	sū'met	au'diet
parā'bimus	habē'bimus	sūmē'mus	audiē'mus
parā'bitis	habē'bitis	sūmē'tis	audiē'tis
parā'bunt	habē'bunt	sū'ment	au'dient

Indicative Passive

parā'bor	habē'bor	sū'mar	au'diar
parā'beris	habē'beris	sūmē'ris	audiē'ris
parā'bitur	habē'bitur	sūmē'tur	audiē'tur
parā'bimur	habē'bimur	sūmē'mur	audiē'mur
parābi'mini	habēbi'mini	sūmē'mini	audiē'mini
parābu'ntur	habēbu'ntur	sūme'ntur	audie'ntur

Subjunctive Active

parātū'r/us habitū'r/us sūmptū'r/us auditū'r/us, -a, -um

	sim	*or* e'ssem
	sī's	e'ssēs
	sī't	e'sset
-ī, -ae, -a	sī'mus	essē'mus
	sī'tis	essē'tis
	si'nt	e'ssent

PERFECT TENSE

Indicative Active

parā'vī	ha'buī	sū'mpsī	audī'vī
parāvi'stī	habuī'stī	sūmpsi'stī	audīvi'stī
parā'vit	ha'buit	sū'mpsit	audī'vit
parā'vimus	habu'imus	sū'mpsimus	audī'vimus
parāvi'stis	habuī'stis	sūmpsi'stis	audīvi'stis
parāvē'r/unt, -e	habuē'r/unt, -e	sūmpsē'r/unt, -e	audīvē'r/unt, -e

Indicative Passive

parā't/us ha'bit/us sū'mpt/us audī't/us, -a, -um su'm
e's, *etc.*

Subjunctive Active

parā'verim	habu'erim	sū'mpserim	audī'verim
parā'veris	habu'eris	sū'mpseris	audī'veris
parā'verit	habu'erit	sū'mpserit	audī'verit
parāve'rimus	habue'rimus	sūmpse'rimus	audīve'rimus
parāve'ritis	habue'ritis	sūmpse'ritis	audīve'ritis
parā'verint	habu'erint	sū'mpserint	audī'verint

Subjunctive Passive

parā't/us ha'bit/us sū'mpt/us audī't/us, -a, -um si'm
sī's, *etc.*

PLUPERFECT TENSE

Indicative Active

parā'veram	habu'eram	sū'mpseram	audī'veram
parā'verās	habu'erās	sū'mpserās	audī'verās
parā'verat	habu'erat	sū'mpserat	audī'verat
parāverā'mus	habuerā'mus	sūmpserā'mus	audīverā'mus
parāverā'tis	habuerā'tis	sūmpserā'tis	audīverā'tis
parā'verant	habu'erant	sū'mpserant	audī'verant

Indicative Passive

parā't/us ha'bit/us sū'mpt/us audī't/us, -a, -um e'ram
e'rās, *etc.*

Subjunctive Active

parāvi'ssem	habuī'ssem	sūmpsi'ssem	audīvi'ssem
parāvi'ssēs	habuī'ssēs	sūmpsi'ssēs	audīvi'ssēs
parāvi'sset	habuī'sset	sūmpsi'sset	audīvi'sset
parāvissē'mus	habuissē'mus	sūmpsissē'mus	audīvissē'mus
parāvissē'tis	habuissē'tis	sūmpsissē'tis	audīvissē'tis
parāvi'ssent	habuī'ssent	sūmpsi'ssent	audīvi'ssent

Subjunctive Passive

parā't/us ha'bit/us sū'mpt/us audī't/us, -a, -um e'ssem
e'ssēs *etc.*

FUTURE-PERFECT TENSE

Indicative Active

parā'verō	habu'erō	sū'mpserō	audī'verō
parā'veris	habu'eris	sū'mpseris	audī'veris
parā'verit	habu'erit	sū'mpserit	audī'verit
parāve'rimus	habue'rimus	sūmpse'rimus	audīve'rimus
parāve'ritis	habue'ritis	sūmpse'ritis	audīve'ritis
parā'verint	habu'erint	sū'mpserint	audī'verint

Indicative Passive

parā't/us ha'bit/us sū'mpt/us audī't/us, -a, -um e'rō e'ris, *etc.*

IMPERATIVE

Present Active

Sing.	pa'rā	ha'bē	sū'me	au'dī
Plural	parā'te	habē'te	sū'mite	audī'te

Present Passive

Sing.	parā're	habē're	sū'mere	audī're
Plural	parā'minī	habē'minī	sūmi'minī	audī'minī

Future Active

Sing.	2 parā'tō	habē'tō	sū'mitō	audī'tō
	3 parā'tō	habē'tō	sū'mitō	audī'tō
Plural	2 parātō'te	habētō'te	sūmitō'te	audītō'te
	3 para'ntō	habe'ntō	sūmu'ntō	audiu'ntō

Future Passive

Sing.	2 parā'tor	habē'tor	sū'mitor	audī'tor
	3 parā'tor	habē'tor	sū'mitor	audī'tor
Plural	3 para'ntor	habe'ntor	sūmu'ntor	audiu'ntor

INFINITIVE

Present Active

parā're habē're sū'mere audī're

Present Passive

parā'rī habē'rī sū'mī audī'rī

Perfect Active

parāvi'sse habui'sse sūmpsi'sse audīvi'sse

Perfect Passive

parā't/us ha'bit/us sū'mpt/us audī't/us, -a, -um, e'sse

Future Active

parātū'r/us habitū'r/us sūmptū'r/us audītū'r/us, -a, -um, e'sse

Future Passive

parā'tum ī'ri	ha'bitum ī'ri	sū'mptum ī'ri	audī'tum ī'ri

VERBAL NOUNS AND ADJECTIVES

Present Participle Active

pa'rāns	ha'bēns	sū'mēns	au'diēns

Perfect Participle Passive

parā'tus	ha'bitus	sū'mptus	audī'tus

Future Participle Active

parātū'rus	habitū'rus	sūmptū'rus	audītū'rus

Gerund (*acc., gen., dat. and abl.*)

para'nd/um -ī -ō habe'nd/um -ī -ō sūme'nd/um -ī -ō audie'nd/um -ī -ō

Gerundive

para'ndus	habe'ndus	sūme'ndus	audie'ndus

Supines

1st parā'tum	ha'bitum	sū'mptum	audī'tum
2nd parā'tū	ha'bitū	sū'mptū	audī'tū

Note. *Some verbs of the 3rd conjugation have the present indicative ending in* **-io**; e.g. **capio.** *I capture.*

PRESENT TENSE

Indicative		Subjunctive	
Active	**Passive**	**Active**	**Passive**
cap'io	ca'pior	ca'piam	ca'piar
ca'pis	ca'peris	ca'pias	capiā,ris
ca'pit	ca'pitur	ca'piat	capiā'tur
ca'pimus	ca'pimur	capiā'mus	capiā'mur
ca'pitis	capi'minī	capiā'tis	capiā'minī
cap'iunt	capiu'ntur	ca'piant	capia'ntur

IMPERFECT TENSE

capiē'bam *etc.* capiē'bar *etc.* ca'perem *etc.* ca'perer *etc.*

FUTURE TENSE

ca'piam	ca'piar
capiēs *etc.*	ca'piēris *etc.*

INFINITIVE MOOD

Present Active ca'pere
Present Passive ca'pī

PRESENT IMPERATIVE

Active		Passive	
ca'pe	ca'pite	ca'pere	capi'minī

PARTICIPLE		GERUND	GERUNDIVE
Pres.	ca'piēns	capie'ndum	capie'ndus, -a, -um

In all other tenses and moods *capere* is similiar to *sumere.*

IRREGULAR VERBS

Esse, be	**Posse,** be able	**Velle,** wish	**Īre,** go
	Present Indicative		
sum	possum	volō	eō
es	potes	vīs	īs
est	potest	vult, volt	it
sumus	possumus	volumus	īmus
estis	potestis	vultis, voltis	ītis
sunt	possunt	volunt	eunt
	Present Subjunctive		
sim	possim	velim	eam
sīs	possīs	velīs	eās
sit	possit	velit	eat
sīmus	possīmus	velīmus	eāmus
sītis	possītis	velītis	eātis
sint	possint	velint	eant
	Imperfect Indicative		
eram	poteram	volēbam	ībam
	Imperfect Subjunctive		
essem	possem	vellem	īrem
	Future Indicative		
erō	poterō	volam	ībō
	Future Subjunctive		
futūr/us, -a, -um sim *or* essem	—	—	itūr/us, -a, -um sim *or* essem

		Perfect Indicative		
fuī		potuī	voluī	īvī, iī
		Perfect Subjunctive		
fuerim		potuerim	voluerim	īverim, ierim
		Pluperfect Indicative		
fueram		potueram	volueram	īveram, ieram
		Pluperfect Subjunctive		
fuissem		potuissem	voluissem	īvissem, iissem
		Future-Perfect Indicative		
fuerō		potuerō	voluerō	īverō, ierō
		Present Imperative		
Sing.	es	——	——	ī
Plural	este	——	——	īte
		Future Imperative		
Sing.	estō	——	——	ītō
Plural	estōte	——	——	ītōte
		Infinitives		
Pres.	esse	posse	velle	īre
Perf.	fuisse	potuisse	voluisse	īvisse, iisse
Fut.	futūr/us -a,-um, esse			itūr/us, -a, -um, esse
		Participles		
Pres.	—	—	—	iēns euntis
Fut.	futūrus	—	—	itūrus
		Gerund and Supine		
Gerund	—	—	—	eundum
Supine	—	—	—	itum

MONEY

Roman: 2¼ assēs = 1 sēstertius (*or* nummus)
4 sēstertii = 1 dēnārius
25 dēnārii = 1 aureus

The sesterce is represented by a symbol for 2½, *properly* II S(ēmis), *usually standardized in the form* HS. *The n.pl.* sēstertia *with the distributive numeral denotes thousands of sesterces, and the numeral adverb with the gen. pl.* sēstertium (*understanding* centena milia) *means hundred thousands, e.g.*

10,000 sesterces = dēna sēstertia = HS $\overline{X}$
1,000,000 " = deciēs sēstertium = HS $|\overline{X}|$

MONEY

It is impossible to give exact equivalents in modern money, but it may be useful to think of the sesterce as being worth about 6d. *to-day*, and 1000 sesterces about £25.

Greek:	100 drachumae	=	1 mina
	60 minae	=	1 talentum

In the comedies of Plautus and Terence the talent may be thought of as being worth about £600 *to-day*, and the mina about £10.

MEASURES

Length:	12 ūnciae	=	1 pēs
	5 pedēs	=	1 passus
	125 passūs	=	1 stadium
	8 stadia	=	mille passūs

The Roman mile was about 1620 *yards.*

Area:	100 pedēs quadrātī	=	1 scrīpulum
	144 scrīpula	=	1 āctus quadrātus
	2 āctūs quadrātī	=	1 iugerum
	2 iugera	=	1 hērēdium
	100 hērēdia	=	1 centuria

The iugerum *was about* $\frac{5}{8}$ *acre.*

Capacity:	4 cochleāria	=	1 cyathus
	12 cyathī	=	1 sextārius
(*liquid*)	6 sextāriī	=	1 congius
	8 congiī	=	1 amphora
	20 amphorae	=	1 culleus
(*dry*)	8 sextāriī	=	1 sēmodius
	2 sēmodiī	=	1 modius

The sextārius *was about a pint, the* modius *about a peck.*

Weight:	4 scrīpula	=	1 sextula
	6 sextulae	=	1 ūncia
	12 ūnciae	=	1 lībra

The Roman lb. was about $11\frac{1}{2}$ *oz. avoirdupois, and the* ūncia *was therefore about an ounce. The twelfths of the* lībra *have the following names, which are also used to denote fractions generally, e.g.* hērēs ex triente, *heir to a third of an estate.*

$\frac{1}{12}$ ūncia	$\frac{5}{12}$ quīncūnx	$\frac{3}{4}$ dōdrāns
$\frac{1}{6}$ sextāns	$\frac{1}{2}$ sēmis	$\frac{5}{6}$ dextāns
$\frac{1}{4}$ quadrāns	$\frac{7}{12}$ septūnx	$\frac{11}{12}$ deūnx
$\frac{1}{3}$ triēns	$\frac{2}{3}$ bēs	

NUMERALS

		Cardinal	Ordinal	Distributive	Adverb
1	I	ūnus	prīmus	singulī	semel
2	II	duo	secundus, alter	bīnī	bis
3	III	trēs	tertius	ternī, (trīnī)	ter
4	IV	quattuor	quārtus	quaternī	quater
5	V	quīnque	quīntus	quīnī	quīnquiēs
6	VI	sex	sextus	sēnī	sexiēs
7	VII	septem	septimus	septēnī	septiēs
8	VIII	octō	octāvus	octōnī	octiēs
9	IX	novem	nōnus	novēnī	noviēs
10	X	decem	decimus	dēnī	deciēs
11	XI	undecim	undecimus	undēnī	undeciēs
12	XII	duodecim	duodecimus	duodēnī	duodeciēs
13	XIII	tredecim	tertius decimus	ternī dēnī	ter deciēs
14	XIV	quattuordecim	quārtus decimus	quaternī dēnī	quattuordeciēs
15	XV	quīndecim	quīntus decimus	quīnī dēnī	quīndeciēs
16	XVI	sēdecim	sextus decimus	sēnī dēnī	sēdeciēs
17	XVII	septendecim	septimus decimus	septēnī dēnī	septiēs deciēs
18	XVIII	duodēvīgintī	duodēvīcēsimus	duodēvīcēnī	duodēvīciēs
19	XIX	ūndēvīgintī	ūndēvīcēsimus	ūndēvīcēnī	ūndēvīciēs
20	XX	vīgintī	vīcēsimus	vīcēnī	vīciēs
21	XXI	vīgintī ūnus	vīcēsimus prīmus	vīcēnī singulī	semel et vīciēs
28	XXVIII	duodētrīgintā	duodētrīcēsimus	duodētrīcēnī	duodētrīciēs
29	XXIX	ūndētrīgintā	ūndētrīcēsimus	ūndētrīcēnī	ūndētrīciēs
30	XXX	trīgintā	trīcēsimus	trīcēnī	trīciēs
40	XL	quadrāgintā	quadrāgēsimus	quadrāgēnī	quadrāgiēs
50	L	quīnquāgintā	quīnquāgēsimus	quīnquāgēnī	quīnquāgiēs
60	LX	sexāgintā	sexāgēsimus	sexāgēnī	sexāgiēs
70	LXX	septuāgintā	septuāgēsimus	septuāgēnī	septuāgiēs
80	LXXX	octōgintā	octōgēsimus	octōgēnī	octōgiēs
90	XC	nōnāgintā	nōnāgēsimus	nōngēnī	nōnāgiēs

100	C	centum	centēsimus	centēnī	centiēs
101	CI	centum et ūnus	centēsimus prīmus	centēnī singulī	semel et centiēs
122	CXXII	centum vīgintī duo	centēsimus vīcēsimus alter	centēnī vīcēnī bīnī	centiēs vīciēs bis
200	CC	ducentī	ducentēsimus	ducēnī	ducentiēs
300	CCC	trecentī	trecentēsimus	trecēnī	trecentiēs
400	CCCC	quadringentī	quadringentēsimus	quadringēnī	quadringentiēs
500	D	quīngentī	quīngentēsimus	quīngēnī	quīngentiēs
600	DC	sēscentī	sēscentēsimus	sexcēnī	sexcentiēs
700	DCC	septingentī	septingentēsimus	septingēnī	septingentiēs
800	DCCC	octingentī	octingentēsimus	octingēnī	octingentiēs
900	DCCCC	nōngentī	nōngentēsimus	nōngēnī	nōngentiēs
1000	M	mīlle	mīllēsimus	singula mīlia	mīlliēs
1001	MI	mīlle et ūnus	mīllēsimus prīmus	singula mīlia singulī	semel et mīlliēs
1102	MCII	mīlle centum duo	mīllēsimus centēsimus alter	singula mīlia centēnī bīnī	mīlliēs centiēs bis
3000	MMM	tria mīlia	ter mīllēsimus	trīna mīlia	ter mīlliēs
5000	IↃↃ	quīnque mīlia	quīnquiēs mīllēsimus	quīna mīlia	quīnquiēs mīlliēs
10,000	CCIↃↃ	decem mīlia	deciēs mīllēsimus	dēna mīlia	deciēs mīlliēs
100,000	CCCIↃↃↃ	centum mīlia	centiēs mīllēsimus	centēna mīlia	centiēs mīlliēs
1,000,000	CCCCIↃↃↃↃ	deciēs centēna mīlia	deciēs centiēs mīllēsimus	deciēs centēna mīlia	mīlliēs mīlliēs

FAMILY TREE

tritavus = tritavia
(*great-great-great-great-grandfather*) (*great-great-great-great-grandmother*)

atavus = atavia
(*great-great-great-grandfather*) (*great-great-great-grandmother*)

patruus māximus (*great-great grand-uncle*) · amita māxima (*great-great-grand-aunt*) · abavus (*great-great grandfather*) = abavia (*great-great grandmother*) · avunculus māximus (*great-great grand-uncle*) · mātertera māxima (*great-great-grand-aunt*)

patruus māior (*great-grand-uncle*) · amita māior (*great-grand-aunt*) · proavus (*great-grandfather*) = proavia (*great-grandmother*) · avunculus māior (*great-grand-uncle*) · mātertera māior (*great-grand-aunt*)

patruus māgnus (*grand-uncle*) · amita māgna (*grand-aunt*) · avus (*grand-father*) = avia (*grand-mother*) · avunculus māgnus (*grand-uncle*) · mātertera māgna (*grand-aunt*) · prōsocer (*grand-father-in-law*) = prōsocrus (*grand-mother-in-law*)

patruus (*uncle*) · amita (*aunt*) · noverca (*step mother*) = pater (*father*) = māter (*mother*) = vītricus (*step-father*) · avunculus (*uncle*) · mātertera (*aunt*) · socer (*father-in-law*) = socrus (*mother-in-law*)

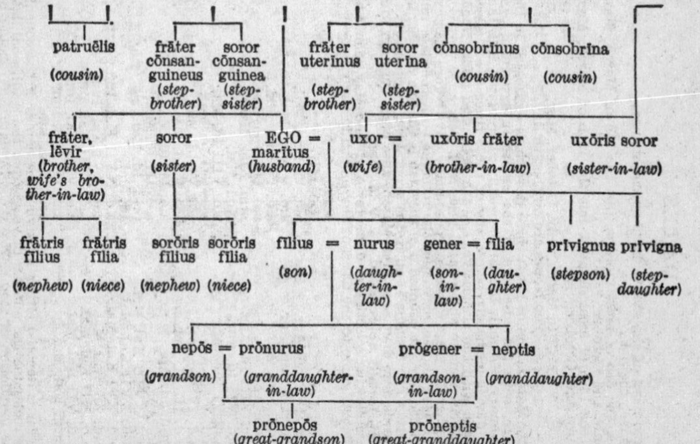

Note.—This is the Family Tree of the man designated EGO in the fourth generation from the end.

DATES

Three days of the month have special names:
Kalendae, the 1st;
Nōnae, the 5th of most months, but the 7th of March, May, July and October;
Idūs, the 13th of most months, but the 15th of March, May, July and October.

> "In March, July, October, May,
> The Nones are on the 7th day."

If the date is one of these three days, it is expressed in the ablative, with the adjective of the month in agreement, *e.g.* 1st January, **Kalendīs Iānuāriīs**, usually abbreviated **Kal. Ian.**

The day immediately before any of these three is expressed by **prīdiē** with the accusative, *e.g.* 4th February, **prīdiē Nōnās Februāriās**, usually abbreviated **prid. Non. Feb.**

All other dates are expressed as so many days before the next named day, and in reckoning the interval both the date and the named day are counted, *e.g.* the 11th is the 5th day before the 15th. The formula is all in the accusative, beginning with the words **ante diem**, *e.g.* 11th March, **ante diem quintum Idūs Martiās**, usually abbreviated **a.d. V Id. Mar.**

The following selection of dates for April and May should be a sufficient guide to the dates of any month in the year:—

	APRIL	MAY
1	Kal. Apr.	Kal. Mai.
2	a.d. IV Non. Apr.	a.d. VI Non. Mai.
3	a.d. III Non. Apr.	a.d. V Non. Mai.
4	prid. Non. Apr.	a.d. IV Non. Mai.
5	Non. Apr.	a.d. III Non. Mai.
6	a.d. VIII Id. Apr.	prid. Non. Mai.
7	a.d. VII Id. Apr.	Non. Mai.
8	a.d. VI Id. Apr.	a.d. VIII Id. Mai.
9	a.d. V Id. Apr.	a.d. VII Id. Mai.
10	a.d. IV Id. Apr.	a.d. VI Id. Mai.
11	a.d. III Id. Apr.	a.d. V Id. Mai.
12	prid. Id. Apr.	a.d. IV Id. Mai.
13	Id. Apr.	a.d. III Id. Mai.
14	a.d. XVIII Kal. Mai.	prid. Id. Mai.
15	a.d. XVII Kal. Mai.	Id. Mai.
16	a.d. XVI Kal. Mai.	a.d. XVII Kal. Iun.
17	a.d. XV Kal. Mai.	a.d. XVI Kal. Iun.
20	a.d. XII Kal. Mai.	a.d. XIII Kal. Iun.
25	a.d. VII Kal. Mai.	a.d. VIII Kal. Iun.
30	prid. Kal. Mai.	a.d. III Kal. Iun.
31		prid. Kal. Iun.

A year is denoted either by giving the names of the consuls or by reckoning the number of years from the traditional date of the foundation of Rome, 753 B.C. (A date B.C. should be subtracted from 754, a date A.D. should be added to 753.)

E.g. "**In the** *year* **218** B.C.," *either* **P. Cornelio Scipione Ti. Sempronio Longo coss.** *or* **a. u. c. DXXXVI.**

QUANTITY

Both vowels and syllables in Latin may be described as long or short. A long vowel or syllable is one on which the voice dwells for a longer time than on a short one, in much the same way as a minim is long compared with a crotchet in musical notation.

A syllable is long if the vowel in it is either long in itself or followed by two or more consonants. The letter **x** counts as a double consonant, the letter **h** not at all, and the following pairs of consonants occurring in the same word after a short vowel do not necessarily make the syllable long: **br, cr, dr, fr, gr, pr, tr; fl, gl, pl.**

A syllable is short if its vowel is a short one and not followed by two or more consonants (except for the groups noted in the preceding paragraph).

Examples:—In **dūcō** both the vowels are long (" by nature ") and therefore the two syllables are long.

In **deus** both the vowels are short, neither is followed by more than one consonant, and therefore the two syllables are short; but if a word beginning with a consonant follows, then the syllable **-us** will become long.

In **adsunt** both the vowels are short, but they are both followed by two consonants, and the two syllables are therefore " long by position."

This long or short characteristic of Latin vowels and syllables is called " Quantity." To determine the quantities of vowels no general rules can be given, and some of them are now not known for certain. The vowel-quantities of words will have to be learned when the words are learned, or else looked up when the need arises. In final syllables, however, there is a certain regularity to be found, and the following table shows the commonest of these:

Ending	Long	Short
-a	*1st decl. abl. s.* *1st conj. imp. s.* *numerals and most adverbs*	*1st decl. nom. and voc. s.* *all nom. and acc. n. pl.* **ita, quia**
-e	*5th decl. abl. s.* *2nd conj. imp. s.* *most adverbs* *Greek nouns*	*all other noun and verb endings* **bene, male** *enclitics*
-i	*all endings, except*	**quasi, nisi**; *and sometimes* **mihi, tibi, sibi, ibi, ubi**
-o	*all endings, except*	*sometimes iambic words, esp.* **cito, duo, ego, homo, modo, puto, rogo, scio**

-u	*all endings*	
-as	*all endings, except*	*Greek nouns*
-es	*all endings, except*	*3rd decl. nom. s. with short* **-e-** *in stem* es, "be," *and compounds* penes
-is	*1st and 2nd decl. dat. and abl. pl.* *3rd decl. acc. pl.* *4th conj. 2nd pers. s.* vis, sīs, velīs	*all others*
-os	*all endings, except*	*2nd decl. nom. s.* os, "bone" compos, impos
-us	*3rd decl. nom. s. with long* **u** *in stem* *4th decl. gen. s. and nom. and acc. pl.*	*all others*

METRES

Latin Verse is a pattern of long and short syllables, grouped together in Feet or in lyric lines.

Feet

The commonest Feet employed in Latin metres are:

Anapaest	(short—short—long) ⏑ ⏑ —
Dactyl	(long—short—short) — ⏑ ⏑
Iambus	(short—long) ⏑ —
Proceleusmatic	(short—short—short—short) ⏑ ⏑ ⏑ ⏑
Spondee	(long—long) — —
Tribrach	(short—short—short) ⏑ ⏑ ⏒
Trochee	(long—short). — ⏑

Caesura and Diaeresis

The longer lines usually have a regular break near the middle, occurring either in the middle of a foot (Caesura) or at the end of a foot (Diaeresis). This break need not imply a pause in the sense of the words, but merely the end of a word, provided that it does not go too closely with the word following, as in the case of a preposition before a noun. *See* examples on pages xxv and xxvi where the caesura is marked †, and the diaeresis //.

Elision

A vowel or a vowel followed by **m** at the end of a word ("open vowel") is regularly elided before a vowel at the beginning of the next word in the same line. In reciting, the elided syllable should not be dropped entirely, but slurred into the following vowel. An open vowel at the end of a line does not elide before a vowel at the beginning of the next line.

Final Syllables

Where the metre requires the final syllable in a line to be long, this syllable may in fact be a short one. This position in the line is commonly called a *syllaba anceps*, and marked down as being either long or short. It is perhaps better to regard this syllable, when the vowel is short, as long by position, since metrical length is a matter of duration, and the end of a line calls naturally for a slight pause in reading, even if the sense runs on to the next line. In the metrical schemes which follow, a long final syllable should be understood in this sense: it may in itself be a short one.

Latin metres fall into three fairly distinct categories, associated with three different genres of verse: 1. *Dactylic*; 2. *Iambic and Trochaic*; 3. *Lyric*.

1. Dactylic Verse

The Dactylic metres are the **Hexameter** and the **Pentameter**. The Hexameter is the medium of epic, didactic and pastoral poetry, of satires and epistles, and other examples of occasional verse. In conjunction with the Pentameter it forms the **Elegiac Couplet**, the metre most commonly used for love poetry, occasional pieces, and the epigram.

DACTYLIC HEXAMETER

The first four feet may be either dactyls or spondees, the 5th is regularly a dactyl, the 6th always a spondee. In Virgil and later poets the last word is either disyllabic or trisyllabic. A Caesura normally occurs in either the 3rd or the 4th foot, and pastoral poetry often has the "Bucolic Diaeresis" at the end of the 4th foot. In Virgilian and later usage there is a tendency for words and feet to overlap in the first four feet and to coincide in the last two. Similarly in the first part of the line the metrical ictus and the normal accent of the spoken word tend to fall on different syllables, whereas they regularly coincide in the last two feet.

Example:

— —/— ⌣⌣/—† ⌣⌣/— —/— ⌣ ⌣/— —
Class(em) aptent taciti sociosqu(e) ad litora torquent
(Virgil, *Aen.* 4, 289)

Occasional lines will be found in the poets, which deliberately violate the above rules for the sake of obtaining some special effect, *e.g.* (a) the echo of a Greek hexameter in

— —/— ⏑ ⏑ /— ⏑ † ⏑ / — —/— ⏑ ⏑/— —
per conubia nostra, per inceptos hymenaeos
(*Aen.* 4, 316)

where the final word is Greek and has four syllables, and the caesura comes between the two short syllables of the dactyl in the 3rd foot; (b) the solemn, archaic touch, suggesting a line of Ennius, in

— ⏑ ⏑/— —/— ⏑ † ⏑/— ⏑ ⏑ / — — / — —
cum sociis natoque penatibus et magnis dis
(*Aen.* 3, 12)

where the 5th foot is a spondee, and the last word is monosyllabic; (c) the comic effect of the monosyllabic ending in

— ⏑ ⏑/— —/— † —/— — / — ⏑ ⏑/— —
parturient montes, nascetur ridiculus mus
(*Hor. A. P.* 139)

DACTYLIC PENTAMETER

This line has two equal parts of 2½ feet each. The two feet in the first part may be either dactyls or spondees, those in the second part are always dactylic. The two half-feet are long (though the final syllable may be a short one), and there is always a diaeresis between the two parts of the line. In Ovid and later poets the last word in the line is regularly disyllabic. *Example*:

— —/— ⏑ ⏑/— // — ⏑ ⏑/— ⏑ ⏑/—
Aenean animo noxque diesque refert
(*Ovid, Her.* 7, 26)

Scansion

The following procedure may assist beginners to scan a normal hexameter or pentameter correctly:—

1. Mark off elisions.
2. Mark the first syllable long, and (Hexameter) the last five dactyl and spondee, or (Pentameter) the last seven syllables two dactyls and a long syllable.
3. Mark all diphthongs long.
4. Mark all syllables that are long by position, omitting any doubtful cases.
5. Mark any other syllables known to be long
6. Mark any syllables known to be short.
7. Fill in the few (if any) remaining syllables, and identify the principal caesura.
8. Read the line aloud.

2. Iambic and Trochaic Verse

The Iambic and Trochaic metres occur mainly in dramatic verse, but some are found elsewhere, as in the lyrics of Catullus and Horace. The principal Iambic metres are the Senarius, the

Septenarius, and the Octonarius; the principal Trochaic metres are the Septenarius and Octonarius.

IAMBIC SENARIUS

Basically this line consists of six iambic feet, but in practice such a line is very rare, e.g. Catullus's

⏑ — / ⏑ — / ⏑ — / ⏑ — / ⏑ — / ⏑ —
Phasellus ille quem videtis, hospites (*Cat.* 4, 1).

In drama the last foot is always iambic, and the 5th regularly a spondee. The spondee is also very common in the first four feet, the dactyl and the tribrach are frequent, occasionally the anapaest is found, and, more rarely, the proceleusmatic. There is usually a caesura in either the third or the fourth foot.

Example:

⏑ — / ⏑ ⏑ — / ⏑ ⏑ ⏑ — — / — — / ⏑ —
In hac habitasse platea dictumst Chrysidem
(*Ter., And.* 796)

IAMBIC SEPTENARIUS

This line consists of seven and a half feet, basically iambic, but allowing the same variations as in the Senarius. The 4th foot is regularly an Iambus, and is usually followed by a diaeresis: this is an aid to identifying the line.

Example:

— — / — — / — — / ⏑ — / — — / ⏑ — / —
N(am) idcirc(o) accersor nupti as quod m(i) adparari
— / —
sen/sit (*Ter. And.* 690).

IAMBIC OCTONARIUS

This line has eight iambic feet, with the same variations as in the other iambic lines. The 4th and 8th feet are regularly iambic, and a diaeresis follows the 4th foot.

Example:

— — / ⏑ — / — ⏑ ⏑ / ⏑ — / ⏑ ⏑ — / ⏑ — / — — / ⏑ —
Curabitur. sed p a t e r ad e st. cave t(e) es se tr i stem sentiat
(*Ter. And.* 403).

TROCHAIC SEPTENARIUS

Apart from drama, this line is common in popular verses, and comes into its own in later Latin poetry. It consists of seven and a half trochees, but in practice only the seventh foot is regularly trochaic, while the others may be spondee, dactyl, tribrach, or (more rarely) anapaest. There is usually a diaeresis after the 4th foot.

Example:

— ⌣/— —/— ⌣/— — / — ⌣/— — /— ⌣/—
Cras amet qui nunqu(am) amavit, quiqu(e) amavit cras amet
(*Pervigilium Veneris*).

TROCHAIC OCTONARIUS

This is a line of eight trochees, allowing the same variations as above. There is a diaeresis after the 4th foot.
Example:

— — / — ⌣ ⌣/— ⌣ / — — / — — / — —
Proin tu sollicitudin(em) istam falsam quae t(e) ex-
⌣ ⌣⌣ / — —
cruciat mittas (*Ter., Heaut.* 177).

3. Lyric Verse

In most lyric metres the line is not to be subdivided into feet, but is itself the unit of scansion, and has a fixed number of syllables. The commonest, which are those used by Catullus and Horace, are the **Hendecasyllabic**, the **Asclepiads**, the **Glyconic** and the **Pherecratic**, which occur either singly or in combinations to form either couplets or stanzas of four lines. Beside these groupings there are the **Alcaic** and **Sapphic stanzas.** Elisions occur much more rarely than in the other metres.

HENDECASYLLABIC

This is Catullus's favourite line. It consists of eleven syllables in the pattern — — — ⌣ ⌣ — ⌣ — ⌣ — — Either the first or the second syllable may occasionally be short, and there is usually a caesura after the 5th syllable.
Example:

— — — ⌣⌣ — ⌣ — ⌣ — —
Vivamus, mea Lesbi(a), atqu(e) amemus (*Cat.* 5, 1).

ASCLEPIADS

There are two Asclepiad lines, of which the Lesser is by far the commoner. It has twelve syllables, in the following pattern — — — ⌣ ⌣ — — ⌣ ⌣ — ⌣ — There is a caesura after the 6th syllable.
Example:

— — — ⌣⌣— —⌣⌣ —⌣—
Maecenas, atavis edite regibus (*Hor. Od.* 1, 1, 1).
The Greater Asclepiad is formed by adding a choriambus — ⌣ ⌣ — after the 6th syllable with a diaeresis both before and after it.

Example:

— —　　— ⌣　⌣ —　— ⌣　⌣ —　— ⌣ ⌣ — ⌣ —
Nullam, Vare, sacra vite prius severis arborem
(*Hor. Od.* 1, 18, 1)

GLYCONIC

The Glyconic occurs by itself in Catullus, but more usually it is found in combination with the Lesser Asclepiad or the Pherecratic. It consists of eight syllables (— — — ⌣ ⌣ — ⌣ —), so that it is like a Lesser Asclepiad minus the choriambus. It has no regular caesura.
Example:

— —　— ⌣　⌣ —　⌣ —
Donec gratus eram tibi　(*Hor. Od. III*, 9, 1).

PHERECRATIC

The Pherecratic is a Glyconic minus the second last (short) syllable. It is found only in combination with other lines.
Example:

— — — ⌣　⌣ — —
Suspendisse potenti　(*Hor. Od.* 1, 5, 11).

ALCAIC STANZA

The Alcaic stanza has four lines, of which the first two have the same pattern — — ⌣ — — — ⌣ ⌣ — ⌣ — In these there is a regular caesura after the 5th syllable. The third line is — — ⌣ — — — ⌣ — — and the 4th — ⌣ ⌣ — ⌣ ⌣ — ⌣ — — Neither of the last two lines has a regular break in it.
Example:

— — ⌣ — —　—　⌣ ⌣　— ⌣ —
Nunc est bibendum, nunc pede libero

— — ⌣　— —　—　⌣ ⌣ — ⌣ —
pulsanda tellus, nunc Saliaribus

— — ⌣　— — —　⌣ — —
ornare pulvinar deorum

— ⌣　⌣ —　⌣ ⌣ —　⌣ — —
tempus erat dapibus, sodales.　(*Hor. Od. I*, 37, 1-4).

SAPPHIC STANZA

The Sapphic stanza has also four lines, of which the first three are the same — ⏑ — — — ⏑ ⏑ — ⏑ — — As in the Alcaic there is a caesura after the 5th syllable. The last line is a short Adonic — ⏑ ⏑ — —
Example:

Integer vitae scelerisque purus

non eget Mauris iaculis neque arcu

nec venenatis gravida sagittis,

Fusce, pharetra. (*Hor. Od. I*, 22, 1-4).

LATIN-ENGLISH DICTIONARY

A

ā, ab, abs *pr.* (*with abl.*) from; after, since; by; in respect of. **ab epistulīs, ā manū** secretary. **ab hāc parte** on this side. **ab integrō** afresh. **ā nōbīs** on our side. **ā tergō** in the rear. **cōpiōsus ā frūmentō** rich in corn. **usque ab** ever since.
ā, āh *interj.* ah!
abā'ctus *ppp.* abigō.
a'bac/us -ī *m.* tray; sideboard; gaming-board; panel; counting-table.
abaliē'n/ō -ā're -ā'vī -ā'tum *vt.* dispose of; remove estrange.
A'b/ās -a'ntis *m.* a king of Argos. **-anti'adēs** *m.* Acrisius or Perseus.
a'bav/us -ī *m.* great-great-grandfather.
a'bb/ās -ā'tis *m.* abbot. **-ā'tia** *f.* abbey. **-āti'ssa** *f.* abbess.
Abdē'r/a -ō'rum or **-ae** *n.pl.* or *f.s.* a town in Thrace. **-ītā'nus** *a.* **-ī'tēs** *m.* Democritus or Protagoras.
abdicā'ti/ō -ō'nis *f.* disowning, abdication.
a'bdic/ō -ā're -ā'vī -ā'tum *vt.* disown; resign. **sē —** abdicate.
abd/ī'cō -ī'cere -ī'xī -i'ctum *vt.* (*aug.*) be unfavourable to.
a'bditus *ppp.* abdō.
a'bd/ō -ere -idī -itum *vt.* hide; remove.
abdō'm/en -inis *n.* paunch, belly; gluttony.
abd/ū'cō -ū'cere -ū'xī -u'ctum *vt.* lead away, take away; seduce.
abdu'ctus *ppp.* abdūcō.
abecedā'r/ium -iī *n.* alphabet.
abē'gī *perf.* abigō.
a'b/eō -ī're -iī -itum *vi.* go away, depart; pass away; be changed; retire (from an office). **sīc —** turn out like this.
abe'quit/ō -ā're -ā'vī -ā'tum *vi.* ride away.
aberrā'ti/ō -ō'nis *f.* relief (from trouble).
abe'rr/ō -ā're -ā'vī -ā'tum *vi.* stray; deviate; have respite.
a'bfore *fut. inf.* absum.
a'bfuī *perf.* absum.
abfutū'rus *fut.p.* absum.
abhi'nc *ad.* since, ago.
abho'rr/eō -ē're -uī *vi.* shrink from; differ; be inconsistent.
ab/i'ciō -i'cere -iē'cī -ie'ctum *vt.* throw away throw down; abandon, degrade.
abie'ctus *ppp.* abiciō. *a.* despondent; contemptible.
abiē'gnus *a.* of fir.
a'b/iēns -eu'ntis *pres.p.* abeō.
a'bi/ēs -etis *f.* fir; ship.
a'b/igō -i'gere -ē'gī -ā'ctum *vt.* drive away.
a'bit/us -ūs *m.* departure; exit.
abiū'dic/ō -ā're -ā'vī -ā'tum *vt.* take away (by judicial award).
abiū'nctus *ppp.* abiungō.
abiū'n/gō -u'ngere -ū'nxī -ū'nctum *vt.* unyoke; detach.
abiū'r/ō -ā're -ā'vī -ā'tum *vt.* deny on oath.
ablā'tus *ppp.* auferō.
ablēgā'ti/ō -ō'nis *f.* sending away.

ablēg/ō -ā're -ā'vī -ā'tum *vt.* send out of the way.
abligu'rr/iō -ī're -ī'vī -ī'tum *vt.* spend extravagantly.
a'bloc/ō -ā're -ā'vī -ā'tum *vt.* let (a house).
ablū'/dō -dere -sī -sum *vi.* be unlike.
a'bl/uō -u'ere -uī -ū'tum *vt.* wash clean; remove.
a'bneg/ō -ā're -ā'vī -ā'tum *vt.* refuse.
a'bnep/ōs -ō'tis *m.* great-great-grandson. **-tis** *f.* great-great-granddaughter
abno'ct/ō -ā're *vi.* stay out all night.
abnō'rmis *a.* unorthodox.
a'bn/uō -u'ere -uī -ū'tum *vt.* refuse; deny.
abo'l/eō -ē're -ē'vī -itum *vt.* abolish. [vanish.
abol/ē'scō -ē'scere -ē'vī *vi.*
aboli'ti/ō -ō'nis *f.* cancelling.
abo'll/a -ae *f.* great-coat.
abō'min/or -ā'rī -ā'tus *vt.* deprecate; detest. **-ā'tus** *a.* accursed.
Aborī'gin/ēs -um *m.pl.* original inhabitants.
abo'r/ior -ī'rī -tus *vi.* miscarry.
abo'rti/ō -ō'nis *f.* miscarriage.
abortī'vus *a.* born prematurely.
abo'rt/us -ūs *m.* miscarriage.
abrā'/dō -dere -sī -sum *vt.* scrape off, shave.
abrā/sus *ppp.* abrādō.
abre'ptus *ppp.* abripiō.
abr/i'piō -i'pere -i'puī -e'ptum *vt.* drag away, carry off.
abrogā'ti/ō -ō'nis *f.* repeal.
a'brog/ō -ā're -ā'vī -ātum *vt.* annul.
abro'ton/um -ī *n.* southernwood.
abr/u'mpō -u'mpere -ū'pī -u'ptum *vt.* break off.
abru'ptus *ppp.* abrumpō *a.* steep; abrupt, disconnected.
abs, *see* **ā, ab.**
absc/ē'dō -ē'dere -e'ssī -e'ssum *vi.* depart, withdraw; cease.
abscī'/dō -dere -dī -sum *vt.* cut off.
absci'/ndō -ndere -dī -ssum *vt.* tear off, cut off.
absci'ssus *ppp.* abscindō.
abscī'sus *ppp.* abscīdō. *a.* steep; abrupt.
absco'nd/ō -ere -ī & idī -itum *vt.* conceal; leave behind.
a'bs/ēns -e'ntis *pres.p.* absum. *a.* absent.
abse'nti/a -ae *f.* absence.
absi'l/iō -ī're -iī & uī *vi.* spring away.
absi'milis *a.* unlike.
absi'nth/ium -ī & iī *n.* wormwood. [chancel.
a'bs/is -ī'dis *f.* vault; (*eccl.*)
abs/i'stō -i'stere -titī *vi.* come away; desist.
absolū'ti/ō -ō'nis *f.* acquittal; perfection.
absolū't/us *ppp.* absolvō *a.* complete; (*rhet.*) unqualified. **-ē** *ad.* fully, unrestrictedly.
abso'l/vō -vere -vī -ū'tum *vt.* release, set free; (*law*) acquit; bring to completion, finish off; pay off, discharge.
a'bsonus *a.* unmusical; incongruous. — **ab** not in keeping with.
abso'r/beō -bē're -buī -ptum *vt.* swallow up; monopolize.
absp-, *see* **asp-.**
a'bsque *pr.* (*with*) *abl.* without, but for.
abstē'mius *a.* temperate.
abste'r/geō -gē're -sī -sum *vt.* wipe away; (*fig.*) banish.
abste'rr/eō -ēre -uī -itum *vt.* scare away, deter.
a'bstin/ēns -e'ntis *a.* continent. **-e'nter** *ad.* with restraint.
abstine'nti/a -ae *f.* restraint, self-control; fasting.
abst/i'neō -inē're -i'nuī -e'ntum *vt.* withhold, keep off. *vi.*

abstain, refrain. sē — refrain.
a'bstitī *perf.* absistō.
a'bst/ō -ā're *vi.* stand aloof.
abstra'ctus *ppp.* abstrahō.
a'bstra/hō -here -xī -ctum *vt.* drag away, remove; divert.
abstrū'/dō -dere -sī -sum *vt.* conceal.
abstrū'sus *ppp.* abstrūdō. *a.* deep, abstruse; reserved.
a'bstulī *perf.* auferō.
a'bsum abe'sse ā'fuī *vi.* be away, absent, distant; keep clear of; be different; be missing, fail to assist. **tantum abest ut** so far from. **haud multum āfuit quin** I was (they were, etc.) within an ace of.
absū'm/ō -ere -psī -ptum *vt.* consume; ruin, kill; (*time*) spend.
absu'rd/us *a.* unmusical; senseless, absurd. **-ē** *ad.* out of tune; absurdly. [Medea.
Absy'rt/us -ī *m.* brother of
abu'nd/āns -a'ntis *a.* overflowing; abundant; rich; abounding in. **-a'nter** *ad.* copiously.
abunda'nti/a -ae *f.* abundance, plenty; wealth.
abu'ndē *ad.* abundantly, more than enough.
abu'nd/ō -ā're -ā'vī -ātum *vi.* overflow; abound, be rich in.
abū'si/ō -ō'nis *f.* (*rhet.*) catachresis.
abu'sque *pr.* (*with abl.*) all the way from.
abū'/tor -tī -sus *vi.* (*with abl.*) use up; misuse.
Abȳ'd/os, Abȳ'd/us -ī *m.* a town on Dardanelles. **-ē'nus** *a.*
ac, *see* **atque.**
Acadē'mi/a -ae *f.* Plato's Academy at Athens; Plato's philosophy; Cicero's villa. **-cus** *a.* **-ca** *n.pl.* Cicero's book on the Academic philosophy.
Acadē'm/us -ī *m.* an Athenian hero. [finch.
acala'nthi/s -dis *f.* thistle-
aca'nth/us -ī *m.* bear's-breech.
Acarnā'n/ia -iae *f.* a district of N.W. Greece. **-es -um** *m.pl.* the Acarnanians. **-icus** *a.*
A'cc/a Lare'nti/a -ae -ae *f.* Roman goddess.
acc/ē'dō -ē'dere -e'ssī -e'ssum *vi.* come, go to, approach; attack; be added; agree with; take up (a duty). **ad rem pūblicam** — enter politics. **prope** — **ad** resemble. **-ēdit quod, hūc -ēdit ut** moreover.
acce'ler/ō -ā're -ā'vī -ā'tum *vt.* & *i.* hasten.
acc/e'ndō -e'ndere -e'ndī -ē'nsum *vt.* set on fire, light; illuminate; (*fig.*) inflame, incite. [assign.
accē'ns/eō -ē're -uī -um *vt.*
accē'nsus *ppp.* accendō and accēnseō.
accē'ns/us -ī *m.* officer attending a magistrate. **-ī** *m.pl.* (*mil.*) supernumeraries.
acce'nt/us -ūs *m.* accent.
accē'pī *perf.* accipiō.
acce'pti/ō -ō'nis *f.* receiving.
acce'pt/us *ppp.* accipiō. *a.* acceptable. **-um** *n.* credit side (of ledger). **in — referre** place to one's credit.
acce'rsō, *see* **arcessō.**
acce'ssi/ō -ō'nis *f.* coming, visiting; attack; increase, addition.
acce'ss/us -ūs *m.* approach, visit; flood-tide; admittance, entrance.
acce'stis *for* accessistis.
accī'/dō -dere -dī -sum *vt.* fell, cut into; eat up, impair.
a'ccid/ō -ere -ī *vi.* fall (at, on); strike (senses); befall, happen (*usu.* misfortune).
accī'n/gō -gere -xī -ctum *vt.* gird on, arm; (*fig.*) make ready.
a'cc/iō -ī're -ī'vī -ī'tum *vt.* summon; procure.
acc/i'piō -i'pere -ē'pī -e'ptum

vt. take, receive, accept; treat (a guest); hear (information); interpret, take as; suffer; approve.
acci'pit/er -ris *m.* hawk.
accī'sus *ppp.* accīdō.
accī'tus *ppp.* acciō.
accīt'/us -ūs *m.* summons.
A'cc/ius -ī *m.* Roman tragic poet. **-iā'nus** *a.*
acclāmā'ti/ō -ō'nis *f.* shout (of approval or disapproval).
acclā'm/ō -ā're -ā'vī -ā'tum *vi.* cry out against; hail.
acclā'r/ō -ā're -ā'vī -ā'tum *vt.* make known.
acclī'nis *a.* leaning against; inclined.
acclīn'/ō -ā're -ā'vī -ā'tum *vt.* lean against. sē — incline towards. -ā'tus *a.* sloping.
acclī'vis *a.* uphill.
acclī'vit/ās -ā'tis *f.* gradient.
a'ccol/a -ae *m.* neighbour.
a'cc/olō -o'lere -o'luī -u'ltum *vt.* live near.
accommodā'ti/ō -ō'nis *f.* fitting together; compliance.
acco'mmod/ō -ā're -ā'vī -ā'tum *vt.* fit, put on; adjust, adapt, bring to, apply. sē — devote oneself. -ā'tus *a.* suited. -ā'tē *ad.* suitably.
acco'mmodus *a.* suitable.
accrē'd/ō -ere -idī -itum *vi.* believe.
accr/ē'scō -ē'scere -ē'vī -ē'tum *vi.* increase, be added.
accrē'ti/ō -ō'nis *f.* increasing.
accubi'ti/ō -ō'nis *f.* reclining (at meals).
a'ccub/ō -ā're *vi.* lie near; recline (at meals).
accu'/mbō -mbere -buī -bitum *vi.* recline at table. in sinū — sit next to.
accu'mul/ō -ā're -ā'vī -ā'tum *vt.* pile up, amass; load. -ā'tē *ad.* copiously.
accūrā'ti/ō -ō'nis *f.* exactness.
accū'r/ō -ā're -ā'vī -ā'tum *vt.* attend to. **-ā'tus** *a.* studied. **-ā'tē** *ad.* painstakingly.
accu'/rrō -rrere -currī & -rrī -rsum *vi.* hurry to.
accu'rs/us -ūs *m.* hurrying.
accūsā'bilis *a.* reprehensible.
accūsā'ti/ō -ō'nis *f.* accusation.
accūsā't/or -ō'ris *m.* accuser, prosecutor. **-ō'rius** *a.* of the accuser. **-ō'riē** *ad.* like an accuser.
accū's/ō -ā're -ā'vī -ā'tum *vt.* accuse, prosecute; reproach. ambitūs — prosecute for bribery.
a'cer -is *n.* maple.
ā'c/er -ris *a.* sharp; (*sensation*) keen, pungent; (*emotion*) violent; (*mind*) shrewd; (*conduct*) eager, brave; hasty, fierce; (*circumstances*) severe. **-riter** *ad.*
ace'rbit/ās -ā'tis *f.* bitterness; (*fig.*) harshness, severity; sorrow.
ace'rb/ō -ā're -ā'vī -ā'tum *vt.* aggravate.
ace'rb/us *a.* bitter, sour; harsh; (*fig.*) premature; (*person*) rough, morose, violent; (*things*) troublesome, sad. **-ē** *ad.*
ace'rnus *a.* of maple.
ace'rr/a -ae *f.* incense-box.
acervā'tim *ad.* in heaps.
ace'rv/ō -ā're -ā'vī -ā'tum *vt.* pile up.
ace'rv/us -ī *m.* heap.
acē'sc/ō -ere a'cuī *vi.* turn [sour.
Ace'st/ēs -ae *m.* a mythical Sicilian.
acē't/um -ī *n.* vinegar; (*fig.*) [wit.
Achae'men/ēs -is *m.* first Persian king; type of Oriental wealth.
Achae'us *a.* Greek.
Achā'i/a -ae *f.* a district in W. Greece; Greece; Roman province. **-cus** *a.*
Achā't/ēs -ae *m.* companion of Aeneas.

Achelō'/us -ī *m.* river in N.W. Greece; river-god. **-ius** *a.*

A'cher/ōn -o'ntis *m.* river in [Hades. **-ū'sius** *a.*

Achi'll/ēs -is *m.* Greek epic hero. **-ē'us** *a.*

Achī'vus *a.* Greek.

Acidā'li/a -ae *f.* Venus. **-us** [*a.*

a'cidus *a.* sour, tart; (*fig.*) disagreeable.

a'ci/ēs -ē'ī *f.* sharp edge or point; (*eye*) sight, keen glance, pupil; (*mind*) power, apprehension; (*mil.*) line of troops, battle-order, army, battle; (*fig.*) debate. **prīma** — van. **novissima** — rearguard.

acīnac/ēs -is *m.* scimitar.

a'cin/us -ī *m.*, **a'cin/um** -ī *n.* berry, grape; fruit-seed.

acipē'ns/er -eris. **-is** -is *m.* sturgeon.

a'cly/s -dis *f.* javelin.

aconī't/um -ī *n.* monkshood; poison.

a'c/or -ō'ris *m.* sour taste.

acqui/ē'scō -ē'scere -ē'vī -ē'tum *vi.* rest, die; find pleasure (in); acquiesce.

acquī'/rō -rere -sī'vī -sī'tum *vt.* get in addition, acquire.

A'crag/ās -a'ntis *m.* Agrigentum. [jar.

acrāto'phor/um -ī *n.* wine-

acrē'dul/a -ae *f.* a bird (unidentified).

ācri'culus *a.* peevish.

ācrimō'ni/a -ae *f.* pungent taste; (*speech, action*) briskness, go.

Acri's/ius -ī *m.* father of Danae. **-iōni'ad/ēs** -ae *m.* Perseus.

ā'criter *ad.* ācer.

ācroā'ma -tis *n.* entertainment, entertainer.

ācroā's/is -is *f.* public lecture.

Ācrocerau'ni/a -ō'rum *n.pl.* a promonotory in N.W. Greece.

Ācrocori'nth/us -ī *f.* fortress of Corinth.

a'ct/a -ae *f.* beach.

ā'ct/a -ō'rum *n.pl.* public records, proceedings. — **diurna,** —**pūblica** daily gazette.

Actae'us *a.* Athenian.

ā'cti/ō -ō'nis *f.* action, doing; official duties, negotiations; (*law*) action, suit, indictment, pleading, case, trial; (*rhet.*) delivery; (*drama*) plot. — **grātiārum** expression of thanks **-ōnem intendere īnstituere** bring an action.

ā'ctit/ō -ā're -ā'vī -ā'tum *vt.* plead, act often.

A'ct/ium -ī & iī *n.* a town in N.W. Greece; Augustus's great victory. **-ius**, **-i'acus** *a.*

ācti'vus *a.* of action, practical.

ā'ct/or -ō'ris *m.* driver, performer; (*law*) plaintiff, pleader; (*bus.*) agent; (*rhet.*) orator; (*drama*) actor. — **pūblicus** manager of public property. — **summārum** cashier.

āctuāri'ol/um -ī *m.* small barge.

āctuā'ri/us *a.* fast (ship). **-a** *f.* pinnace. [*ad.*

āctuō's/us *a.* very active. **-ē**

ā'ctus *ppp.* agō.

ā'ct/us -ūs *m.* moving, driving; right of way for cattle or vehicles; performance; (*drama*) playing a part, recital, act of a play.

āctū'tum *ad.* immediately.

a'cuī *perf.* acēscō: *perf.* acuō.

a'cul/a -ae *f.* small stream.

aculeā'tus *a.* prickly; (*words*) stinging; quibbling.

acu'le/us -ī *m.* sting, prickle barb; (*fig.*) sting.

acū'm/en -inis *n.* point, sting; (*fig.*) shrewdness, ingenuity; trickery.

a'c/uō -u'ere -uī -ū'tum *vt.* sharpen; exercise, stimulate (the mind); rouse (to action).

a'c/us -ūs *f.* needle, pin. **acū pingere** embroider. **rem acū tangere** ***hit the nail on the head.***

acū'tulus *a.* rather subtle.
acū't/us *a.* sharp, pointed; (*senses*) keen; (*sound*) high-pitched; severe; intelligent. **-ē** *ad.*
ad *pr.* (*with acc.*) to, towards, against; near, at; until; (*num.*) about; with regard to, according to; for the purpose of, for; compared with; besides. **ad Castoris** to the temple of Castor. **ad dextram** on the right. **ad hōc** besides. **ad locum** on the spot. **ad manum** at hand. **ad rem** to the point. **ad summam** in short. **ad tempus** in time. **ad ūnum omnes** all without exception. **ad urbem esse** wait outside the city gates. **ad verbum** literally. **nīl ad** nothing to do with. **usque ad** right up to.
adā'cti/ō **-ō'nis** *f.* enforcing.
adā'ctus *ppp.* adigō.
adā'ct/us **-ūs** *m.* snapping (of teeth).
adae'quē *ad.* equally.
adae'qu/ō **-ā're -ā'vī -ā'tum** *vt.* make equal, level; equal, match; *vi.* be equal.
a'dam/ās **-a'ntis** *m.* adamant, steel; diamond. **-antē'us, -a'ntinus** *a.*
a'dam/ō **-ā're -ā'vī -ā'tum** *vt.* fall in love with.
adape'r/iō **-ī're -uī -tum** *vt.* throw open.
adape'rtilis *a.* openable.
a'daqu/ō **-ā're -ā'vī -ā'tum** *vt.* water (plants, animals). **-or** *vi.* fetch water.
adau'ct/us **-ūs** *m.* growing.
adau'/geō **-gē're -xī -ctum** *vt.* aggravate; (*sacrifice*) consecrate.
adaugē'sc/ō **-ere** *vi.* grow bigger.
a'dbib/ō **-ere -ī** *vt.* drink; (*fig.*) drink in.
adbī't/ō **-ere** *vi.* come near.
adc-, *see* **acc-.**
a'ddec/et **-ē're** *vt.* it becomes.
addē'ns/eō **-ē're** *vt.* close (ranks).
add/ī'cō **-ī'cere -ī'xī -i'ctum** *vi.* (*aug.*) be favourable; *vt.* (*law*) award; (*auction*) knock down; (*fig.*) sacrifice, devote.
addi'cti/ō **-ō'nis** *f.* award (at law).
addi'ctus *ppp.* addīcō. *m.* bondsman.
addi'/scō **-scere -dicī** *vt.* learn more.
additāme'nt/um **-ī** *n.* increase.
a'dditus *ppp.* addō.
a'dd/ō **-ere -idī -itum** *vt.* add, put to, bring to; impart; increase. — **gradum** quicken pace. **-e quod** besides.
addo'c/eō **-ēre -uī -tum** *vt.* teach new.
addu'bit/ō **-ā're -ā'vī -ā'tum** *vi.* be in doubt. *vt.* question.
add/ū'cō **-ū'cere -ū'xī -u'ctum** *vt.* take, bring to; draw together, pull taut, wrinkle; (*fig.*) induce; (*pass.*) be led to believe.
addu'ctus *ppp.* addūcō. *a.* contracted; (*fig.*) severe.
a'd/edō **-e'dere -ē'dī -ē'sum** *vt.* begin to eat; eat up; use up; wear away.
adē'mī *perf.* adimō.
ade'mpti/ō **-ō'nis** *f.* taking away.
ade'mptus *ppp.* adimō.
a'd/eō **-ī're -iī -itum** *vt.* & *i.* go to, approach; address; undertake, submit to, enter upon.
a'deō *ad.* so; (*after pro.*) just; (*after conj., ad., a.*) indeed, very; generally used to give emphasis; (*adding an explanation*) for in fact, thus; or rather. — **nōn . . . ut** so far from. **atque** —, **sīve** — or rather. **usque** — so far, so long, so much.
a'd/eps **-ipis** *m., f.* fat; corpulence.
ade'pti/ō **-ō'nis** *f.* attainment.
ade'ptus *ppa.* adipīscor.
ade'quit/ō **-ā're -ā'vī -ā'tum** *vi.* ride up (to).

ade'sdum come here!
ade'sse *inf.* adsum.
adē'sus *ppp.* adedō.
adfā'bilis *a.* easy to talk to.
adfābi'lit/ās -ā'tis *f.* courtesy.
a'dfabrē *ad.* ingeniously.
a'dfatim, *ad.* to one's satisfaction, enough, ad nauseam.
adfā'/tur -rī -tus *vt.* (*def.*) speak to.
adfā'tus *ppa.* adfātur.
adfā't/us -ūs *m.* speaking to.
adfectā'ti/ō -ō'nis *f.* aspiring; (*rhet.*) affectation.
adfe'cti/ō -ō'nis *f.* frame of mind, mood; disposition; good-will; (*astr.*) relative position.
adfe'ct/ō -ā're -ā'vī -ā'tum *vt.* aspire to, aim at; try to win over; make pretence of. **viam** — ad try to get to. **-ā'tus** *a.* (*rhet.*) studied.
adfe'ctus *ppp.* adficiō; affected with, experienced (*abl.*); (*person*) disposed; (*things*) weakened; (*undertakings*) well-advanced.
adfe'ct/us -ūs *m.* disposition, mood; fondness; (*pl.*) loved ones.
a'dferō adfe'rre a'ttulī adlā'tum & allā'tum *vt.* bring, carry to; bring to bear, use against; bring news; bring forward (an explanation); contribute (something useful).
adf/i'ciō -i'cere -ē'cī -e'ctum *vt.* affect; endow, afflict with (*abl.*). **exsiliō** — banish. **honōre** — honour; *sim.* with other nouns to express the corresponding verbs.
adfi'ctus *ppp.* adfingō.
adfi'/gō -gere -xi -xum *vt.* fasten, attach; impress (on the mind).
adfi'/ngō -ngere -nxī -ctum *vt.* make, form (as part of); invent.
adfī'n/is -is *m., f.* neighbour; relation (by marriage). *a.* neighbouring; associated with (*dat.* or *gen.*).
adfī'nit/ās -ā'tis *f.* relationship (by marriage). [tion.
adfirmā'ti/ō -ō'nis *f.* declara-
adfi'rm/ō -ā're -ā'vī -ā'tum *vt.* declare; confirm. **-ā'tē** *ad.* with assurance.
adfī'xus *ppp.* adfigō.
adflā't/us -ūs *m.* breath, exhalation; (*fig.*) inspiration.
a'dfl/eō -ē're *vi.* weep (at).
adflīctā'ti/ō -ō'nis *f.* suffering.
adflī'ct/ō -ā're -ā'vī -ā'tum *vt.* harass, distress.
adflī'ct/or -ōris *m.* destroyer.
adflī'ctus *ppp.* adflīgō. *a.* distressed, ruined; dejected; depraved.
adfl/ī'gō -ī'gere -ī'xī -ī'ctum *vt.* dash against, throw down; (*fig.*) impair, crush.
a'dfl/ō -ā're -ā'vī -ā'tum *vt.* & *i.* blow on, breathe upon.
a'dflu/ēns -e'ntis *a.* rich (in). **-e'nter** *ad.* copiously.
adflue'nti/a -ae *f.* abundance.
a'dflu/ō -ere -xī -xum *vi.* flow; (*fig.*) flock in, abound in.
a'dfore *fut.inf.* adsum. **-m** *impf. subj.*
a'dfuī *perf.* adsum.
adfu'l/geō -gē're -sī *vi.* shine on; appear.
adf/u'ndō -u'ndere -ū'dī -ū'sum *vt.* pour in; rush (troops) to. **-ū'sus** *a.* prostrate.
adfutū'rus *fut.p.* adsum.
a'dgem/ō -ere *vi.* groan at.
adglo'mer/ō -ā're *vt.* add on.
adglū'tin/ō -ā're *vt.* stick on.
adgravē'sc/ō -ere *vi.* become worse. [*vt.* aggravate.
a'dgrav/ō -ā're -ā'vī -ā'tum
adgre'/dior -dī -ssus *vt.* approach, accost; attack; undertake, take up (a task).
a'dgreg/ō -ā're -ā'vī -ā'tum *vt.* add, attach.
adgre'ssi/ō -ō'nis *f.* introductory remarks.

adgre'ssus *ppa.* adgredior.
adhae'/reō -rē're -sī -sum *vi.* stick to; (*fig.*) cling to, keep close to
adhaerē'sc/ō -ere *vi.* stick to or in; (*speech*) falter.
adhae'si/ō -ō'nis *f.* clinging.
adhae's/us -ūs *m.* adhering.
adhi'b/eō -ēre -uī -itum *vt.* bring, put, add; summon, consult, treat; use, apply (for some purpose).
adhi'nn/iō -ī're -ī'vī -ī'tum *vi.* neigh to; (*fig.*) go into raptures over.
adhortā'ti/ō -ō'nis *f.* exhortation.
adhortā't/or -ō'ris *m.* encourager.
adho'rt/or -ārī -ā'tus *vt.* encourage, urge.
adhū'c *ad.* so far; as yet, till now; still. — nōn not yet.
adia'c/eō -ē're -uī *vi.* lie near, border on.
ad/i'ciō -i'cere -iē'cī -ie'ctum *vt.* throw to; add; turn (mind, eyes) towards.
adie'cti/ō -ō'nis *f.* addition.
adie'ctus *ppp.* adiciō. [close.
adie'ct/us -ūs *m.* bringing
a'd/igō -i'gere -ē'gī -ā'ctum *vt.* drive (to); compel. iūs iūrandum — put on oath. in verba — force to own allegiance.
a'd/imō -i'mere -ē'mī -e'mptum *vt.* take away (from, *dat.*).
adipā't/us *a.* fatty; (*fig.*) florid. —**um** *n.* pastry.
ad/ipī'scor -ipī'scī -e'ptus *vt.* overtake; attain, acquire.
a'dit/us -ūs *m.* approach, access (to a person); entrance; (*fig.*) avenue.
adiū'dic/ō -ā're -ā'vī -ā'tum *vt.* award (in arbitration); ascribe.
adiūme'nt/um -ī *n.* aid, means of support.
adiū'ncti/ō -ō'nis *f.* uniting; addition; (*rhet.*) proviso; repetition.
adiū'nct/us *ppp.* adiungō. *a.* connected. -**a** *n.pl.* collateral circumstances.
adi/u'ngō -u'ngere -ū'nxī -ūnctum *vt.* yoke; attach; direct (suspicion, etc.); add (a remark).
adiū'r/ō -ā're -ā'vī -ā'tum *vt.* & *i.* swear, swear by.
adiū't/ō -ā're -ā'vī -ā'tum *vt.* help.
adiū't/or -ō'ris *m.* helper; (*mil.*) adjutant; (*pol.*) official; (*theat.*) supporting cast. —**rīx** -rī'cis *f.*
adiū'tus *ppp.* adiuvō.
a'di/uvō -uvā're -ū'vī -ū'tum *vt.* help; encourage.
adj, *see* **adi-.**
adlā'/bor -bī -psus *vi.* fall, move towards, come to.
adlabō'r/ō -ā're -ā'vī -ā'tum *vi.* work hard; improve by taking trouble.
adla'crim/ō -ā're -ā'vī -ā'tum *vi.* shed tears.
adlā'psus *ppa.* adlābor.
adlā'ps/us -ūs *m.* stealthy approach.
adlā'tr/ō -ā're -ā'vī -ā'tum *vt.* bark at; (*fig.*) revile.
adlā'tus *ppp.* adferō.
adlau'd/ō -ā're -ā'vī -ā'tum *vt.* praise highly.
adle'ct/ō -ā're -ā'vī -ā'tum *vt.* entice.
adlē'ctus *ppp.* adlegō.
adle'ctus *ppp.* adliciō.
adlēgā'ti/ō -ō'nis *f.* mission.
adlē'g/ō -ā're -ā'vī -ā'tum *vt.* despatch, commission; mention. -**ā'tī** *m.pl.* deputies.
a'dl/egō -e'gere -ē'gī -ē'ctum *vt.* elect.
adlevāme'nt/um -ī *n.* relief.
adlevā'ti/ō -ō'nis *f.* easing.
a'dlev/ō -ā're -ā'vī -ā'tum *vt.* lift up; comfort; weaken.
adl/i'ciō -i'cere -e'xī -e'ctum *vt.* attract.
adlī'/dō -dere -sī -sum *vt.* dash (against); (*fig.*) hurt.
a'dlig/ō -ā're -ā'vī -ā'tum *vt.*

tie up, bandage; (*fig.*) bind, lay under an obligation.
a'dl/inō -i'nere -ē'vī -itum *vt.* smear; (*fig.*) attach.
adlī'sus *ppp.* adlīdō.
adlocū'ti/ō -ō'nis *f.* address; comforting words.
adlocū'tus *ppa.* adloquor.
adlo'qu/ium -ī & iī *n.* talk; encouragement.
a'dlo/quor -quī -cū'tus *vt.* speak to, address.
adlū'di/ō -ā're -ā'vī -ā'tum *vi.* play (with).
adlū'/dō -dere -sī -sum *vi.* joke, play.
a'dlu/ō -ere -ī *vt.* wash.
adlu'vi/ēs -ē'ī *f.* pool left by flood water. [land.
adlu'vi/ō -ō'nis *f.* alluvial
admātū'r/ō -ā're -ā'vī -ā'tum *vt.* hurry on.
admē'/tior -tī'rī -nsus *vt.* measure out. [*vt.* prop.
admini'cul/or -ā'rī -ā'tus
admini'cul/um -ī *n.* (*agr.*) stake; (*fig.*) support.
admini'st/er -rī *m.* assistant.
administrā'ti/ō -ō'nis *f.* services; management.
administrā't/or -ō'ris *m.* manager.
admini'str/ō -ā're -ā'vī -ā'tum *vt.* manage, govern.
admīrā'bili/s *a.* wonderful, surprising. **-ter** *ad.* admirably; paradoxically.
admirābi'lit/ās -ā'tis *f.* wonderfulness.
admirā'ti/ō -ō'nis *f.* wonder, surprise, admiration.
admī'r/or -ā'rī -ā'tus *vt.* wonder at, admire; be surprised at.
admi'/sceō -scēre -scuī -xtum *vt.* mix in with, add to; (*fig.*) involve. **sē —** interfere.
admissā'r/ius -ī & iī *m.* stallion.
admi'ssus *ppp.* admittō.
adm/i'ttō -i'ttere -ī'sī -i'ssum *vt.* let in, admit; set at a gallop; allow; commit (a crime). **equō -issō** charging. **-i'ssum** *n.* crime.
admi'xti/ō -ō'nis *f.* admixture.
admi'xtus *ppp.* admisceō.
admo'der/or -ā'rī -ā'tus *vt.* restrain. **-ā'tē** *ad.* suitably.
a'dmodum *ad.* very, quite; fully; yes; (*with neg.*) at all.
admo'n/eō -ē're -uī -itum *vt.* remind, suggest, advise, warn.
admoni'ti/ō -ō'nis *f.* reminder, suggestion; admonition.
admo'nit/or -ō'ris *m.*, **-rīx** -rī'cis *f.* admonisher.
admo'nitū at the suggestion, instance.
admo'r/deō -dē're -sum *vt.* bite into; (*fig.*) cheat.
admo'rsus *ppp.* admordeō.
admō'ti/ō -ō'nis *f.* applying.
admō'tus *ppp.* admoveō.
adm/o'veō -ovēre -ō'vī -ō'tum *vt.* move bring up, apply; lend (an ear), direct (the mind).
admurmurā'ti/ō -ō'nis *f.* murmuring.
admu'rmur/ō -ā're -ā'vī -ā'tum *vi.* murmur (of a crowd approving or disapproving).
admu'til/ō -ā're -ā'vī -ā'tum *vt.* clip close; (*fig.*) cheat.
adne'/ctō -ctere -xuī -xum *vt.* connect, tie.
adne'x/us -ūs *m.* connection.
adnī'sus, adnī'xus *ppp.* adnītor.
adnī'/tor -tī -sus & -xus *vi.* lean on; exert oneself.
a'dn/ō -ā're *vt.* & *i.* swim to.
a'dnot/ō -ā're -ā'vī -ā'tum *vt.* comment on.
adnu'mer/ō -ā're -ā'vī -ā'tum *vt.* pay out; reckon along with.
a'dn/uō -u'ere -uī -ū'tum *vi.* nod; assent, promise; indicate.
ad/o'leō -olē're -o'luī -u'ltum *vt.* burn; pile with gifts.

adolēscen-, *see* **adulēscen-**.
adol/ē'scō -ē'scere -ē'vī *vi.* grow up, increase; burn.
Adō'n/is -is & idis *m.* a beautiful youth loved by Venus.
adope'rtus *a.* covered.
adoptā'ti/ō -ō'nis *f.* adopting.
ado'pti/ō -ō'nis *f.* adoption.
adoptī'vus *a.* by adoption.
ado'pt/ō -ā're -ā'vī -ā'tum *vt.* choose; adopt.
a'd/or -ō'ris & oris *n.* spelt. **-ō'reus** *a.* **-ō'rea** *f.* glory.
ado'r/ior -ī'rī -tus *vt.* accost; attack; set about.
adō'rn/ō -ā're -ā'vī -ā'tum *vt.* get ready.
adō'r/ō -ā're ā'vī -ā'tum *vt.* entreat; worship, revere.
ado'rtus *ppa.* adorior.
adp-, *see* **app-**.
adrā'/dō -dere -sī -sum *vt.* shave close. [Argos.
Adra'st/us -ī *m.* a king of
adrā'sus *ppp.* adrādō.
adrē'ctus *ppp.* adrigō. *a.* steep. [creep, steal into.
adrē'p/ō -ere -sī -tum *vi.*
adre'ptus *ppp.* adripiō.
A'dria, etc., *see* **Hadria**, etc.
adrī'/deō -dē're -sī -sum *vt.* & *i.* laugh, smile at; please.
a'dr/igō -i'gere -ē'xī -ē'ctum *vt.* raise; (*fig.*) rouse.
adr/i'piō -i'pere -i'puī -e'ptum *vt.* seize; appropriate; take hold of; learn quickly; (*law*) arrest; satirize.
adrō'/dō -dere -sī -sum *vt.* gnaw, nibble at.
a'drog/āns -a'ntis *a.* arrogant, insolent. **-a'nter** *ad.*
adroga'nti/a -ae *f.* arrogance, presumption, haughtiness.
adrogā'ti/ō -ō'nis *f.* adoption.
a'drog/ō -ā're -ā'vī -ā'tum *vt.* ask; associate; claim, assume; (*fig.*) award.
adsc-, *see* **asc-**.
a'dsecla, *see* **adsecula**.
adsectā'ti/ō -ō'nis *f.* attendance.
adsectā't/or -ō'ris *m.* follower.
adse'ct/or -ā'rī -ā'tus *vt.* attend on follow (*esp.* a candidate).
adse'cul/a -ae *m.* follower (*derogatory*).
adsē'dī *perf.* adsideō; *perf.* adsidō.
adsē'nsi/ō -ō'nis *f.* assent, applause; (*philos.*) acceptance of the evidence of the senses.
adsē'ns/or -ō'ris *m.* one in agreement.
adsē'nsus, *ppa.* adsentior.
adsē'ns/us -ūs *m.* assent, approval; echo; (*philos.*) acceptance of the evidence of the senses.
adsentā'ti/ō -ō'nis *f.* flattery. **-u'ncula** *f.* trivial compliments.
adsentā't/or -ō'ris *m.* **-rīx** -rī'cis *f.* flatterer. **-ō'riē** *ad.* ingratiatingly.
ads/e'ntiō -entī're -ē'nsī -ē'nsum, **-e'ntior** -entī'rī -ē'nsus *vi.* agree, approve.
adse'nt/or -ā'rī -ā'tus *vi.* agree, flatter.
a'dse/quor -quī -cū'tus *vt.* overtake; attain; grasp (by understanding).
a'dser/ō -ere -uī -tum *vt.* (*law*) declare free (*usu. with* manū), liberate (a slave); lay claim to, appropriate. — in servitūtem claim as a slave.
a'ds/erō -e'rere -ē'vī -itum *vt.* plant near.
adse'rti/ō -ō'nis *f.* declaration of status.
adse'rt/or -ō'ris *m.* champion.
adse'rv/iō -ī're *vi.* assist.
adse'rv/ō -ā're -ā'vī -ā'tum *vt.* watch carefully; keep, preserve. [beside.
adse'ssi/ō -ō'nis *f.* sitting
adse'ss/or -ō'ris *m.* counsellor.

adse′ss/us -ūs *m.* sitting beside. [ally

adsevēra′nter *ad.* emphatic-

adsevērā′ti/ō -ō′nis *f.* assertion; earnestness.

adsevēr/ō -ā′re -ā′vī -ā′tum *vt.* do in earnest; assert strongly.

ads/i′deō -idē′re -ē′dī -e′ssum *vi.* sit by; attend, assist; besiege; resemble.

ads/ī′dō -ī′dere -ē′dī *vi.* sit down.

adsidu′it/ās -ā′tis *f.* constant attendance; continuance, frequent recurrence.

adsi′du/us *a.* constantly in attendance, busy; continual, incessant. **–ē, –ō** *ad.* continually.

adsi′du/us -ī *m.* tax-payer.

adsignā′ti/ō -ō′nis *f.* allotment (of land).

adsi′gn/ō -ā′re -ā′vī -ā′tum *vt.* allot (*esp.* land); assign; impute, attribute; consign.

ads/i′liō -ili′re -i′luī -u′ltum *vi.* leap at or on to.

adsi′mili/s *a.* like. **–ter** *ad.* similarly.

adsi′mul/ō -ā′re -ā′vī -ā′tum *vt.* & *i.* compare; pretend, imitate. **–ā′tus** *a.* similar; counterfeit.

ads/i′stō -i′stere -titī *vi.* stand, stand by; defend.

a′dsitus *ppp.* adserō.

adso′l/eō -ē′re *vi.* be usual.

a′dson/ō -ā′re *vi.* respond.

adsp–, *see* **asp–.**

adste′rn/ō -ere *vt.* prostrate.

adstipulā′t/or -ō′ris *m.* supporter.

adsti′pul/or -ā′rī -ā′tus *vi.* agree with. [adstō.

a′dstitī *perf.* adsistō; *perf.*

a′dst/ō -ā′re -itī *vi.* stand near, stand up; assist.

a′dstrep/ō -ere *vi.* roar.

adstri′ct/us *ppp.* adstringō. *a.* tight, narrow; concise; stingy. **–ē** *ad.* concisely.

adstri′/ngō -ngere -nxī -ctum *vt.* draw close, tighten; bind, oblige; abridge.

a′dstru/ō -ere -xī -ctum *vt.* build on; add. [tonished.

adstu′p/eō -ē′re *vi.* be as-

adsuēf/a′ciō -a′cere -ē′cī -a′ctum *vt.* accustom, train.

adsuē′/scō -scere -vī -tum *vi.* accustom, train.

adsuētū′d/ō -inis *f.* habit.

adsuē′tus *ppp.* adsuēscō. *a.* customary.

adsu′lt/ō -ā′re -ā′vī -ā′tum *vi.* jump; attack.

adsul′t/us -ūs *m.* attack.

a′d/sum -e′sse -fuī *vi.* be present; support, assist (*esp.* at law); come; appear before (a tribunal). **animō** — pay attention. **iam aderō** I'll be back soon.

adsū′m/ō -ere -psī -ptum *vt.* take for oneself, receive; take also.

adsū′mpti/ō -ō′nis *f.* taking up; (*logic*) minor premise.

adsūmptī′vus *a.* (*law*) which takes its defence from extraneous circumstances.

adsūmpt/us *ppp.* adsūmō. **–um** -ī *n.* epithet.

a′dsu/ō -ere *vt.* sew on.

adsu′r/gō -gere -rē′xī -rē′ctum *vi.* rise, stand up; swell, increase.

adt–, *see* **att–.**

adulā′ti/ō -ō′nis *f.* fawning (of dogs); servility.

adulā′t/or -ō′ris *m.* sycophant. **–ō′rius** *a.* flattering.

adulē′sc/ēns -e′ntis *m., f.* young man or woman (*usu.* from 15 to 30 years).

adulēsce′nti/a -ae *f.* youth (age 15 to 30).

adulēsce′ntul/a -ae *f.* girl. **–us** -ī *m.* quite a young man.

a′dul/ō -ā′re -ā′vī -ā′tum

a′dul/or -ā′rī -ā′tus *vt.* & *i.* fawn upon, flatter, kow-tow.

adu′lter -ī *m.*, **–a** -ae *f.*

adulterer, adulteress. *a.* adulterous.
adulterī'nus *a.* forged.
adulte'r/ium -ī & iī *n.* adultery.
adu'lter/ō -ā're -ā'vī -ā'tum *vt.* & *i.* commit adultery; falsify.
adu'ltus *ppp.* adolēscō. *a.* adult, mature.
adumbrā'tim *ad.* in outline.
adumbrā'ti/ō -ō'nis *f.* sketch; semblance.
adu'mbr/ō -ā're -ā'vī -ā'tum *vt.* sketch; represent, copy. **-ā'tus** *a.* false.
adu'ncus *a.* hooked, curved.
adu'ncit/ās -ā'tis *f.* curvature.
adu'rg/eō -ē're *vt.* pursue closely.
adū'/rō -rere -ssī -stum *vt.* burn; freeze; (*fig.*) fire.
adu'sque *pr.* (*with acc.*) right up to. *ad.* entirely.
adū'stus *ppp.* adūrō. *a.* brown.
advectī'cius *a.* imported.
adve'ct/ō -ā're *vt.* carry frequently.
adve'ctus *ppp.* advehō.
adve'ct/us -ūs *m.* bringing.
a'dve/hō -here -xī -ctum *vt.* carry, convey; (*pass.*) ride.
advēl/ō -ā're *vt.* crown.
a'dven/a -ae *m., f.* stranger. *a.* foreign.
adv/e'niō -enī're -ē'nī -e'ntum *vi.* arrive come.
adventī'cius *a.* foreign, extraneous; unearned.
adve'nt/ō -ā're -ā'vī -ā'tum *vi.* come nearer and nearer, advance rapidly.
adve'nt/or -ō'ris *m.* visitor.
adve'nt/us -ūs *m.* arrival, approach.
adversā'r/ius -ī & iī *m.* opponent. *a.* opposing. **-ia** *n.pl.* day-book.
adversā'tr/īx -ī'cis *f.* antagonist.
adve'rsi/ō -ō'nis *f.* turning (the attention).
adve'rs/or -ā'rī -ā'tus *vi.* oppose, resist.
adve'rs/us *ppp.* advertō. *a.* opposite, in front; hostile. **-ō** flūmine upstream. **-ae** rēs misfortune. **-um** -ī *n.* opposite; misfortune.
adve'rsus, adve'rsum *pr.* (*with acc.*) towards, against. *ad.* to meet.
adve'r/tō -tere -tī -sum *vt.* turn, direct towards; call attention. animum — notice, perceive; (*with* ad) attend to; (*with* in) punish.
advesperā'/scit -scere -vit *vi.* it is getting dark.
advi'gil/ō -ā're *vi.* keep watch.
advocā'ti/ō -ō'nis *f.* legal assistance, counsel.
advocā't/us -ī *m.* supporter in a law-suit; advocate, counsel.
a'dvoc/ō -ā're -ā'vī -ā'tum *vt.* summon; (*law*) call in the assistance of.
a'dvol/ō -ā're -ā'vī -ā'tum *vi.* fly to, swoop down upon.
advo'l/vō -vere -vī -ū'tum *vt.* roll to; prostrate.
advor-, *see* **adver-**.
a'dyt/um -ī *n.* sanctuary.
Ae'ac/us -ī *m.* father of Peleus, and judge of the dead. **-idēs** -idae *m.* Achilles; Pyrrhus.
Aeae/a -ae *f.* Circe's island. **-us** *a.* of Circe.
ae'd/ēs -is *f.* temple; (*pl.*) house.
aedi'cul/a -ae *f.* shrine; small house, room.
aedificā'ti/ō -ō'nis *f.* building. **-u'ncula** *f.* little house.
aedificā't/or -ō'ris *m.* builder.
aedifi'c/ium -ī & iī *n.* building.
aedi'fic/ō -ā're -ā'vī -ā'tum *vt.* build, construct.
aedīli'cius *a.* aedile's. *m.* ex-aedile.
aedī'l/is -is *m.* aedile.
aedī'lit/ās -ā'tis *f.* aedileship.
ae'd/is -is *see* aedēs.

aedi'tum/us, aedi'tu/us -ī *m.* temple-keeper.
Ae'du/ī -ō'rum *m.pl.* a tribe of central Gaul. [Medea.
Aeē't/ēs -ae *m.* father of
Aegae'/us *a.* Aegean. *n.* Aegean Sea.
Aegā't/ēs -um *f.pl.* islands off Sicily.
ae'g/er -rī *a.* ill, sick; sorrowful; weak.
Aegī'n/a -ae *f.* a Greek island. **-ē'ta** *m.* inhabitant of A.
ae'gi/s -dis *f.* shield of Jupiter or Athena, aegis.
Aegi'sth/us -ī *m.* paramour of Clytemnestra.
aego'cer/ōs -ō'tis *m.* Capricorn.
ae'grē *ad.* painfully; with displeasure; with difficulty; hardly. — ferre be annoyed.
aegrē'sc/ō -ere *vi.* become ill; be aggravated.
aegrimō'ni/a -ae *f.* distress of mind. [sorrow.
aegritū'd/ō -inis *f.* sickness:
ae'gr/or -ō'ris *m.* illness.
aegrōtā'ti/ō -ō'nis *f.* illness, disease.
aegrō't/ō -ā're -ā'vī -ā'tum *vi.* be ill.
aegrō'tus *a.* ill, sick.
Aegy'pt/us -ī *f.* Egypt; *m.* brother of Danaus. **-ius** *a.*
ae'lin/os -ī -on *m.* dirge.
Aemi'l/ius -ī Roman family name. Via -ia road in N. Italy. **-iā'nus** *a. esp.* Scipio, destroyer of Carthage.
aemulā'ti/ō -ō'nis *f.* rivalry (good or bad); jealousy.
aemulā't/or -ō'ris *m.* zealous imitator.
ae'mul/or -ā'rī -ā'tus *vt.* rival, copy; be jealous.
ae'mul/us -ī *m.* rival. *a.* rivalling; jealous.
Aen/ē'ās -ae *m.* Trojan leader and hero of Virgil's epic. **-e'ad/ēs** -ae *m.* Trojan; Roman. **-ē'ius** *a.*

Aenē'/is -idis & idos *f.* Aeneid.
aē'neus *a.* of bronze.
aeni'gma -tis *n.* riddle, mystery.
aen/us *a.* of bronze. **-um** **-ī** *n.* bronze vessel.
Ae'ol/is -idis *f.* Aeolia, N.W. of Asia Minor. **-ius** *a.* **-ēs** *m.pl.* the Aeolians.
Ae'ol/us -ī *m.* king of the winds. **-ia** *f.* Lipari Is. **-idēs** *m.* a descendant of A. **-is** -idis *f.* daughter of A.
aequā'bili/s *a.* equal; consistent, even; impartial. **-ter** *ad.* uniformly.
aequābi'lit/ās -ā'tis *f.* uniformity; impartiality.
aequae'vus *a.* of the same age.
aequā'li/s *a.* equal, like; of the same age, contemporary; uniform. **-ter** *ad.* evenly.
aequālit/ās -ā'tis *f.* evenness; equality (in politics, age), similarity.
aequani'mit/ās -ā'tis *f.* goodwill; calmness. [distribution.
aequā'ti/ō -ō'nis *f.* equal
ae'quē *ad.* equally; just as (*with* ac, atque, et, quam); justly.
Ae'qu/ī -ō'rum *m.pl.* a people of central Italy. **-icus, -i'culus** *a.*
Aequimae'l/ium -ī & iī *n.* an open space in Rome.
aequino'ct/ium -ī & iī *n.* equinox. **-iā'lis** *a.*
aequi'per/ō -ā're -ā'vī -ā'tum *vt.* compare; equal. **-ā'bilis** *a.* comparable.
ae'quit/ās -ā'tis *f.* uniformity; fair dealing, equity; calmness of mind.
ae'qu/ō -ā're -ā'vī -ā'tum *vt.* make equal, level; compare; equal. solō — raze to the ground.
ae'quor -is *n.* a level surface, sea. **-eus** *a.* of the sea.

ae'qu/us *a.* level, equal; favourable, friendly, fair, just; calm. **-um** -ī *n.* plain; justice -ō animō patiently. -ō Marte without deciding the issue. -um est it is reasonable. ex -ō equally.
ā'ēr ā'eris *m.* air, weather; mist.
aerā'ri/us *a.* of bronze; of money. *m.* a citizen of the lowest class at Rome. **-a** *f.* mine. **-um** *n.* treasury. tribūnī -ī paymasters; a wealthy middle class at Rome.
aerā'tus *a.* of bronze.
ae'reus *a.* of copper or bronze.
ae'rifer -ī *a.* carrying cymbals.
ae'rip/ēs -edis *a.* bronze-footed.
āe'rius *a.* of the air; lofty.
aerūg/ō -inis *f.* rust; (*fig.*) envy, avarice.
aeru'mn/a -ae *f.* trouble hardship. **-ō'sus** *a.* wretched.
aes ae'ris *n.* copper, bronze; money; (*pl.*) objects made of copper or bronze, *esp.* statues, instruments, vessels; soldiers' pay. — aliēnum debt. — circumforāneum borrowed money. — grave Roman coin, as.
Ae'schyl/us -ī *m.* Greek tragic poet.
Aesculā'p/ius -ī *m.* god of medicine.
aesculē't/um -ī *n.* oak forest.
ae'scul/us -ī *f.* durmast oak. **-eus** *a.*
Ae's/ōn -onis *m.* father of Jason. **-o'nid/ēs** -ae *m.* Jason.
Aesō'p/us -ī *m.* Greek writer of fables. **-ius** *a.*
ae'st/ās -ā'tis *f.* summer.
ae'stifer -ī *a.* heat-bringing.
aestimā'ti/ō -ō'nis *f.* valuation, assessment. lītis — assessment of damages.
aestimā't/or -ō'ris *m.* valuer.
ae'stim/ō -ā're -ā'vī -ā'tum *vt.* value, estimate the value of. māgnī — think highly of.
aestīv/us *a.* summer. **-a** -ō'rum *n.pl.* summer camp, campaign.
aestuā'r/ium -ī & iī *n.* tidal waters, estuary.
ae'stu/ō -ā're -ā'vī -ā'tum *vi.* boil, burn; (*movement*) heave, toss; (*fig.*) be excited; waver.
aestuō'sus *a.* very hot; agitated.
ae'st/us -ūs *m.* heat; surge of the sea; tide; (*fig.*) passion; hesitation.
ae't/ās -ā'tis *f.* age, life; time. **-ā'tem** *ad.* for life.
aetā'tul/a -ae *f.* tender age.
aete'rnit/ās -ā'tis *f.* eternity.
aete'rn/ō -ā're *vt.* immortalise.
aete'rn/us *a.* eternal, immortal; lasting. in -um for ever. [air.
ae'th/ēr -eris *m.* sky, heaven;
aethe'rius *a.* ethereal, heavenly; of air.
Ae'thiop/s -is *a.* Ethiopian; (*fig.*) stupid.
ae'thr/a -ae *f.* sky.
Ae'tn/a -ae *f.* Etna in Sicily. **-ae'us**, **-ē'nsis** *a.*
Aetō'l/ia -iae *f.* a district of N. Greece. **-us**, **-icus** *a.*
ae'vit/ās -ā'tis *old form of* aetās.
ae'v/um -ī *n.* age, life-time; eternity. in — for ever.
Ā'f/er -rī *a.* African.
a'fore *fut. inf.* absum. [poet.
Āfrā'n/ius -ī *m.* Latin comic
Ā'fric/a -ae *f.* Roman province, now Tunisia. **-ā'nus** *a.* name of two Scipios. **-ā'nae** *f.pl.* panthers. **-us** *a.* African. *m.* south-west wind.
ā'fuī, **āfutū'rus** *perf.*, *fut.p.* absum.
Agame'mn/ōn -onis *m.* leader of Greeks against Troy. **-o'nius** *a.* [on Helicon.
Agani'pp/ē -ēs *f.* a spring

agā's/ō -ō'nis *m.* ostler, footman.
a'ge, a'gedum come on! well then.
age'll/us -ī *m.* plot of land.
Agēn/ōr -oris *m.* father of Europa. **-o'reus** *a.* **-o'rid/ēs** -ae *m.* Cadmus; Perseus.
a'g/ēns -e'ntis *a.* (*rhet.*) effective.
a'g/er -rī *m.* land, field; countryside; territory.
agg-, *see* **adg-**.
a'gger -is *m.* rampart; mound, embankment, any built-up mass.
a'gger/ō -ā're -ā'vī -ā'tum *vt.* pile up; increase.
a'gge/rō -rere -ssī -stum *vt.* carry, bring.
agge'st/us -ūs *m.* accumulation.
a'gilis *a.* mobile; nimble, busy.
agi'lit/ās -ā'tis *f.* mobility.
agitā'bilis *a.* light.
agitā'ti/ō -ō'nis *f.* movement, activity.
agitā't/or -ō'ris *m.* driver, charioteer.
a'git/ō -ā're -ā'vī -ā'tum *vt.* drive (animals); move, chase, agitate; (*fig.*) excite (to action); persecute, ridicule; keep (a ceremony). *vi.* live; deliberate.
a'gm/en -inis *n.* forward movement, procession, train; army on the march. — claudere bring up the rear. novissimum — rearguard. prīmum — van.
a'gn/a -ae *f.* ewe lamb.
agnā'/scor -scī -tus *vi.* be born after.
agnā't/us -ī *m.* relation (by blood on father's side).
agne'll/us -ī *m.* little lamb.
agnī'n/us *a.* of lamb. **-a** *f.* lamb (flesh).
agni'ti/ō -ō'nis *f.* recognition, knowledge.
a'gnitus *ppp.* agnōscō.
agnō'm/en -inis *n.* an extra surname (e.g. Africanus).
agn/ō'scō -ō'scere -ō'vī -itum *vt.* recognize; acknowledge, allow; understand.
a'gn/us -ī *m.* lamb.
a'gō a'gere ē'gī ā'ctum *vt.* drive, lead; plunder; push forward, put forth; (*fig.*) move, rouse, persecute; do, act, perform; (*time*) pass, spend; (*undertakings*) manage, wage; (*public speaking*) plead, discuss; negotiate, treat; (*theat.*) play, act the part of. — cum populō address the people. age come on! well then. age age all right! āctum est dē it is all up with. aliud — not attend. animam — expire. annum quartum — be three years old. causam — plead a cause. hōc age pay attention. id — ut aim at. lēge — go to law. nīl agis it's no use. quid agis? how are you? rēs agitur interests are at stake. sē — go, come.
agrā'ri/us *a.* of public land. **-ī** *m.pl.* the land reform party. lēx **-a** land law.
agre'stis *a.* rustic; boorish, wild, barbarous. *m.* countryman.
agri'col/a -ae *m.* countryman, farmer.
Agri'col/a -ae *m.* a Roman governor of Britain; his biography by Tacitus.
Agrige'nt/um -ī *n.* a town in Sicily. **-ī'nus** *a.*
agri'pet/a -ae *m.* landgrabber.
Agri'pp/a -ae *m.* Roman surname, *esp.* Augustus's minister.
Agrippī'n/a -ae *f.* mother of Nero. **Colōnia -a** or **-ēnsis** Cologne.
Agyī'/eus -eī & eos *m.* Apollo.
āh, ā *interj.* ah! (in sorrow or joy).
a'ha *interj.* expressing reproof or laughter.
ahēn-, *see* **aēn-**.
Ā'i/āx -ā'cis *m.* Ajax, name of two Greek heroes at Troy.

ā'iō *vt.(def.)* say, speak. **ain tū?** ain **vērō?** really? **quid ais?** I say!
ā'l/a -ae *f.* wing; arm-pit; *(mil.)* wing of army.
alaba'st/er -rī *m.* perfume box.
a'lac/er -ris *a.* brisk, cheerful.
ala'crit/ās -ā'tis *f.* promptness, liveliness; joy, rapture.
a'lap/a -ae *f.* slap on the face; a slave's freedom.
ālā'ri/us *a.* *(mil.)* on the wing. **-ī** *m.pl.* allied troops.
ālā'tus *a.* winged.
alau'd/a -ae *f.* lark; name of a legion of Caesar's.
alā'z/ōn -onis *m.* braggart.
A'lba Lo'nga -ae -ae *f.* a Latin town, precursor of Rome.
Albā'nus *a.* Alban. **Lacus—, Mōns —** lake and mountain near Alba Longa.
albā'tus *a.* dressed in white.
a'lb/eō -ē're *vi.* be white; dawn.
albē'sc/ō -ere *vi.* become white; dawn.
a'lbic/ō -ā're *vi.* be white.
a'lbidus *a.* white.
A'lbi/ōn -ō'nis *f.* ancient name for Britain.
albitū'd/ō -inis *f.* whiteness.
A'lbul/a -ae *f.* old name for the Tiber.
a'lbulus *a.* whitish.
Albu'ne/a -ae *f.* a spring at Tibur; a sulphur spring near Alban Lake.
alb/us *a.* white, bright. **-um -ī** *n.* white; records. [poet.
Alcae'/us -ī *m.* Greek lyric
alcē'd/ō -inis *f.* kingfisher. **-ō'nia** *n.pl.* halcyon days.
a'lc/ēs -is *f.* elk.
Alcibi'ad/ēs -is *m.* brilliant Athenian politician.
Alcī'd/ēs -ae *m.* Hercules.
Alci'no/us -ī *m.* king of Phaeacians in the Odyssey.
ā'le/a -ae *f.* gambling, dice; *(fig.)* chance, hazard. **iacta — est** the die is cast. **in -am** dare to risk.
āleā't/or -ō'ris *m.* gambler. **-ō'rius** *a.* in gambling.
ālēc, *see* **allēc**.
ā'le/ō -ō'nis *m.* gambler.
ā'l/es -itis *a.* winged; swift. *m., f.* bird; omen.
alē'sc/ō -ere *vi.* grow up.
Alexa'nd/er -rī *m.* a Greek name; Paris, prince of Troy; Alexander the Great, king of Macedon.
Alexa'ndr/ēa *(later* **-īa)** **-ē'ae** *f.* Alexandria in Egypt.
a'lg/a -ae *f.* sea-weed.
a'l/geō -gē're -sī *vi.* feel cold; *(fig.)* be neglected.
algē'sc/ō -ere *vi.* catch cold.
a'lgidus *a.* cold. **A'lgid/us -ī** *m.* mountain in Latium.
a'lg/or -ōris *m.* cold. **-ū** with cold.
a'liā *ad.* in another way.
a'liās *ad.* at another time; at one time . . . at another.
a'libī *ad.* elsewhere; otherwise; in one place . . . in another.
ali'cubī *ad.* somewhere.
alicu'nde *ad.* from somewhere.
a'lid, *old form of* **aliud.**
aliēnā'ti/ō -ō'nis *f.* transfer; estrangement.
aliēni'gen/a -ae *m.* foreigner. **-us** *a.* foreign; heterogeneous.
aliē'n/ō -ā're -ā'vī -ā'tum *vt.* transfer (property by sale); alienate, estrange; derange (the mind).
aliē'nus *a.* of another, of others; alien, strange; *(with abl. or* ab) unsuited to, different from; hostile. *m.* stranger.
ā'liger -ī *a.* winged.
alime'nt/um -ī *n.* nourishment, food; obligation of children to parents; *(fig.)* support. **-ā'rius** *a.* about food.
alimō'n/ium -ī & iī *n.* nourishment.

a'liō *ad.* in another direction, elsewhere; one way . . . another way.
aliō'quī, aliō'quīn *ad.* otherwise, else; besides.
aliō'rsum *ad.* in another direction; differently. [fleet.
ā'lip/ēs -edis *a.* wing-footed:
alī'pt/ēs -ae *m.* sports trainer.
a'liquā *ad.* some way or other.
a'liquam *ad.* — diū for some time. — multī a considerable number.
aliqua'ndō *ad.* some time, ever; sometimes; once, for once; now at last.
aliquanti'sper *ad.* for a time.
aliqua'ntul/us *a.* quite small. **-um** *n.* a very little. *ad.* somewhat.
aliqua'nt/us *a.* considerable. **-um** *a.* a good deal. *ad.* somewhat. **-ō** *ad.* (*with comp.*) somewhat. [extent.
aliquā'tenus *ad.* to some
a'li/quī -qua -quod *a.* some, any; some other.
a'li/quis -quid *pro.* somebody, something; someone or something important. -quid *ad.* at all.
a'liquō *ad.* to some place, somewhere else.
a'liquot *a.*(*indecl.*) some.
aliquo'tiēns *ad.* several times.
a'liter *ad.* otherwise, differently; in one way . . . in another.
a'litus *ppp.* alō.
ā'l/ium -ī & iī *n.* garlic.
aliu'nde *ad.* from somewhere else.
a'lius, a'lia a'liud *a.* other another; different. alius . . . alius some . . . others. alius ex aliō one after the other. in alia omnia īre oppose a measure. nihil aliud quam only.
all-, *see* **adl-**.
a'llēc -is *n.* fish-pickle.
a'll/ex -icis *m.* big toe.

A'lli/a -ae *f.* tributary of the Tiber, scene of a great Roman defeat. **-ē'nsis** *a.*
Allo'brog/ēs -um *m.pl.* a people of S.E. Gaul. **-icus** *a.*
a'lmus *a.* nourishing; kindly.
a'ln/us -ī *f.* alder.
a'l/ō -ere -uī -tum & -itum *vt.* nourish, rear; increase, promote.
A'lp/ēs -ium *f.pl.* Alps. **-ī'nus** *a.*
Alphē'/us -ī *m.* river of Olympia in S.W. Greece.
a'lsī *perf.* algeō.
a'lsius, a'lsus *a.* cold.
altā'r/ia -ium *n.pl.* altars, altar; altar-top.
a'ltē *ad.* on high, from above; deep; from afar.
a'lter -ī'us *a.* the one, the other (of two); second, the next; fellow-man; different. — ego,—īdem a second self. -um tantum twice as much. ūnus et — one or two.
altercā'ti/ō -ō'nis *f.* dispute, debate.
alte'rc/or -ā'rī -ā'tus *vi.* wrangle, dispute; cross-examine.
alte'rn/ō -ā're -ā'vī -ā'tum *vt.* do by turns, alternate.
alte'rn/us *a.* one after the other, alternate; elegiac (verses). **-īs** *ad.* alternately.
alte'r/uter -īusutrī'us *a.* one or the other.
a'ltilis *a.* fat (*esp.* fowls).
alti'sonus *a.* sounding on high.
alti'tonāns -a'ntis *a.* thundering on high.
altitū'd/ō -inis *f.* height, depth; (*fig.*) sublimity. (*mind*) secrecy. [on high.
alti'volāns -a'ntis *a.* soaring
a'lt/or -ō'ris *m.* foster-father.
altrī'nsecus *ad.* on the other side.
a'ltr/īx -ī'cis *f.* nourisher, foster-mother.

a'lt/us *a.* high, deep; (*fig.*) noble; profound. **-um** **-ī** *n.* heaven; sea (*usu.* out of sight of land). **ex -ō repetītus** farfetched.
ālū'cin/or **-ā'rī** **-ā'tus** *vi.* talk wildly, wander (in mind).
a'luī *perf.* alō.
alu'mn/us **-ī** *m.* foster-child; pupil.
alū't/a **-ae** *f.* soft leather; shoe, purse, face-patch.
alveār/ium **-ī** & **iī** *n.* beehive.
alve'ol/us **-ī** *m.* basin.
a'lv/eus **-eī** *m.* hollow; trough; hold (of ship); bath-tub; river-bed.
a'lv/us **-ī** *f.* bowels; womb; stomach. [**-ter** *ad.*
amā'bili/s *a.* lovely, lovable.
amābi'lit/ās **-ā'tis** *f.* charm.
Amalthē'/a **-ae** *f.* nymph or she-goat. **cornū -ae** horn of plenty. **-um** **-ī** *n.* Atticus's library.
āma'nd/ō **-ā're** **-ā'vī** **-ā'tum** *vt.* send away. **-ā'tiō** *f.* sending away.
a'm/āns **-a'ntis** *a.* fond. *m.* lover. **-a'nter** *ad.* affectionately. [tary.
āmanuē'ns/is **-is** *m.* secre-
amā'rac/us **-ī** *m., f.,* **-um** **-ī** *n.* sweet marjoram. **-inum** **-inī** *n.* marjoram ointment.
amāri'ti/ēs **-ēī** *f.,* **amāritū'd/ō** **-inis** *f.,* **amā'r/or** **-ō'ris** bitterness.
amā'r/us *a.* bitter; (*fig.*) sad; ill-natured. **-ē** *ad.*
amā's/ius **-ī** & **iī** *m.* lover.
A'math/ūs **-ū'ntis** *f.* town in Cyprus. **-ū'sia** *f.* Venus.
amā'ti/ō **-ō'nis** *f.* love-making.
amā't/or **-ō'ris** *m.* lover, paramour. **-ō'rculus** *m.* poor lover. **-rīx** **-rī'cis** *f.* mistress.
amatō'ri/us *a.* of love, erotic. **-ē** *ad.* amorously.
Amāz/ōn **-onis** *f.* Amazon, warrior woman. **-o'nides** *f.pl.* Amazons. **-o'nius** *a.*
ambā'ct/us **-ī** *m.* vassal.
ambā'g/ēs **-is** *f.* windings; (*speech*) circumlocution, quibbling; enigma.
a'mb/edō **-e'dere** **-ē'dī** **-ē'sum** *vt.* consume.
ambē'sus *ppp.* ambedō.
a'mbig/ō **-ere** *vt.* & *i.* wander about; be in doubt; argue; wrangle
ambigu'it/ās **-ā'tis** *f.* ambiguity.
ambi'gu/us *a.* changeable, doubtful, unreliable; ambiguous. **-ē** *ad.* doubtfully.
a'mb/iō **-ī're** **-iī** **-ī'tum** *vt.* go round, encircle; (*pol.*) canvass for votes; (*fig.*) court (for a favour).
ambi'ti/ō **-ō'nis** *f.* canvassing for votes; currying favour; ambition.
ambitiō's/us *a.* winding; ostentatious, ambitious. **-ē** *ad.* ostentatiously.
ambī'tus *ppp.* ambiō.
a'mbit/us **-ūs** *m.* circuit, circumference; circumlocution; canvassing, bribery. **lēx de -ū** a law against bribery.
a'mbō **a'mbae** **a'mbō** *num.* both, two.
Ambra'ci/a **-ae** *f.* district of N.W. Greece. **-ē'nsis**, **-us** *a.*
ambro'si/a **-ae** *f.* food of the gods. **-us** *a.* divine.
ambūbā'i/a **-ae** *f.* Syrian flute-girl.
ambulā'cr/um **-ī** *n.* avenue.
ambulā'ti/ō **-ō'nis** *f.* walk, walking; walk (place). **-u'ncula** *f.* short walk.
a'mbul/ō **-ā're** **-ā'vī** **-ā'tum** *vi.* walk, go; travel.
ambū'/rō **-rere** **-ssī** **-stum** *vt.* burn up; make frost-bitten; (*fig.*) ruin.
ambū'stus *ppp.* ambūrō.
ame'll/us **-ī** *m.* Michaelmas daisy. [frantic; stupid.
ā'm/ēns **-e'ntis** *a.* mad,

āme'nti/a -ae *f.* madness; stupidity.
āme'nt/um -ī *n.* strap (for throwing javelin)
a'm/es -itis *m.* fowler's pole.
amfr-, *see* **anfr-.**
ami'c/iō -ī're -tus *vt.* clothe, cover. [alliance.
amīci'ti/a -ae *f.* friendship;
ami'ctus *ppp.* amiciō.
ami'ct/us -ūs *m.* dress (manner of); clothing.
ami'cul/um -ī *n.* cloak.
amī'cul/us -ī *m.* dear friend.
amīc/us -ī *m.* friend. **-a** -ae *f.* friend; mistress. *a.* friendly, fond. **-iter**, **-ē** *ad.*
āmi'ssi/ō -ō'nis *f.* loss.
āmi'ssus *ppp.* āmittō.
a'mit/a -ae *f.* aunt (on father's side).
ām/i'ttō -i'ttere -ī'sī -i'ssum *vt.* let go, lose.
A'mmōn -is *m.* Egyptian god identified with Jupiter. **-i'acus** *a.*
amni'col/a -ae *m., f.* growing by a river.
a'mn/is -is *m.* river. **-icus** *a.* **-i'culus** *m.* brook.
a'm/ō -ā're -ā'vī -ā'tum *vt.* love, like; (*colloq.*) be obliged to. ita mē dī ament! *bless my soul!* amābō please!
amoe'nit/ās -ā'tis *f.* delightfulness (*esp.* of scenery).
amoe'n/us *a.* delightful.
āmō'l/ior -ī'rī -ī'tus *vt.* remove.
amō'm/um -ī *n.* cardamom.
a'm/or -ō'ris *m.* love; (*fig.*) strong desire; term of endearment; Cupid; (*pl.*) love affairs.
āmō'ti/ō -ō'nis *f.* removal.
āmō'tus *ppp.* āmoveō.
ām/o'veō -ovē're -ō'vī -ō'tum *vt.* remove; banish.
amphibo'li/a -ae *f.* ambiguity.
Amphī'/ōn -onis *m.* musician and builder of Thebes. **-o'nius** *a.*
amphitheā'tr/um -ī *n.* amphitheatre.
Amphitrī't/ē -ēs *f.* sea goddess; the sea.
Amphi'try/ō -ō'nis *m.* husband of Alcmena. **-ōni'adēs** *m.* Hercules.
a'mphor/a -ae *f.* a two-handled jar; liquid measure; (*naut.*) measure of tonnage.
Amphrȳ's/us -ī *m.* river in Thessaly. **-ius** *a.* of Apollo.
ample'/ctor -ctī -xus *vt.* embrace, encircle; (*mind*) grasp; (*speech*) deal with; (*fig.*) cherish. [embrace; love.
ample'x/or -ā'rī -ā'tus *vt.*
ample'xus *ppa.* amplector.
ample'x/us -ūs *m.* embrace, encircling.
amplificā'ti/ō -ō'nis *f.* enlargement; (*rhet.*) a passage elaborated for effect.
ampli'ficē *ad.* splendidly.
ampli'fic/ō -ā're -ā'vī -ā'tum *vt.* increase, enlarge; (*rhet.*) enlarge upon.
a'mpli/ō -ā're -ā'vī -ā'tum *vt.* enlarge; (*law*) adjourn.
amplitū'd/ō -inis *f.* size; (*fig.*) distinction; (*rhet.*) fulness.
a'mplius *ad.* more (*esp.* amount or number), further, longer. — ducentī more than 200. — nōn petere take no further legal action. — prōnūntiāre adjourn a case.
a'mpl/us *a.* large, spacious; great, abundant; powerful, splendid, eminent; (*sup.*) distinguished. **-iter**, **-ē** *ad.*
ampu'll/a -ae a two-handled flask; (*fig.*) high-flown language. **-ā'rius** -ā'rī *m.* flask-maker.
ampu'll/or -ā'rī *vi.* use high-flown language.
amput/ō -ā're -ā'vī -ā'tum *vt.* cut off, prune; (*fig.*) lop off. **-ā'tus** *a.* (*rhet.*) disconnected.
amputā'ti/ō -ō'nis *f.* pruning.

Amū'l/ius -ī *m.* king of Alba Longa, grand-uncle of Romulus. [oil.
amu'rc/a -ae *f.* lees of olive
amussitā'tus *a.* nicely adjusted.
Amȳ'cl/ae -ā'rum *f.pl.* town in S. Greece. **-ae'us** *a.*
amy'gdal/um -ī *n.* almond.
amy'sti/s -dis *f.* emptying a cup at a draught.
an *conj.* or; perhaps; (*with single question*) surely not. haud sciō — I feel sure.
Ana'cre/ōn -o'ntis *m.* Greek lyric poet.
anadē'ma -tis *n.* head-band.
anagnō'st/ēs -ae *m.* reader.
anapae'st/us *a.* — pēs anapaest. **-um** -ī *n.* poem in anapaests.
a'na/s -tis *f.* duck. **-tī'nus** *a.* **-ti'cula** *f.* duckling.
anatoci'sm/us -ī *m.* compound interest.
Anaxa'gor/ās -ae *m.* early Greek philosopher.
Anaxima'nd/er -rī *m.* early Greek philosopher.
a'nc/eps -i'pitis *a.* two-headed; double; wavering doubtful; dangerous. *n.* danger
Anchī's/ēs -ae *m.* father of Aeneas. **-ē'us** *a.* **-i'adēs** *m.* Aeneas.
ancī'l/e -is *n.* oval shield, *esp.* one said to have fallen from heaven in Numa's reign.
anci'll/a -ae *f.* servant. **-ā'ris** *a.* **-ula** *f.* young servant.
ancī'sus *a* cut round.
a'ncor/a -ae *f.* anchor. **-ā'rius** *a.*
ancorā'l/e -is *n.* cable.
A'nc/us Ma'rc/ius -ī -ī *m.* 4th king of Rome.
Ancȳ'r/a -ae *f.* Ankara, capital of Galatia.
anda'bat/a -ae *m.* blindfold gladiator.
andro'gyn/us -ī *m.*, **-ē** -ēs *f.* hermaphrodite.
Andro'mach/ē -ēs *f.* wife of Hector.
Andro'med/a -ae *f.* wife of Perseus, a constellation.
Andro'nic/us -ī *m.* Livius, earliest Latin poet.
A'ndr/os (**-us**) -ī *m.* Aegean island. **-ius** *a.*
āne'll/us -ī *m.* little ring.
anē'th/um -ī *n.* fennel.
ānfrāct/us -ūs *m.* bend, orbit; roundabout way; (*words*) digression, prolixity.
a'ngel/us -ī *m.* angel.
a'ngin/a -ae *f.* quinsy.
angipo'rt/us -ūs *m.*, **-um** -ī *n.* alley.
a'ng/ō -ere *vt.* throttle; (*fig.*) distress torment.
a'ng/or -ō'ris *m.* suffocation; (*fig.*) anguish, torment.
angui'comus *a.* with snakes for hair. [snake.
angui'cul/us -ī *m.* small
a'nguifer -ī *a.* snake-carrying.
angui'gen/a -ae *m.* one born of serpents; Theban.
angui'll/a -ae *f.* eel.
angui'manus *a.* with a trunk. [footed.
a'nguip/ēs -edis *a.* serpent-
a'ngu/is -is *m., f.* snake, serpent; constellation Draco.
Angui'ten/ēns -e'ntis *m.* Ophiuchus.
a'ngul/us -ī *m.* angle, corner; out-of-the-way place. ad parēs -ōs at right angles. **-ā'tus** *a.* angular.
angu'sti/ae -ā'rum *f.pl.* defile, strait; (*time*) shortness; (*means*) want; (*circs.*) difficulty; (*mind*) narrowness; (*words*) subtleties.
angusticlā'vius *a.* wearing a narrow purple stripe.
angu'st/ō -ā're *vt.* make narrow.
angu'st/us *a.* narrow, close; (*time*) short; (*means*) scanty; (*mind*) mean; (*argument*) subtle; (*circs.*) difficult. **-um**

-ī *n.* narrowness; danger. -ē *ad.* close, within narrow limits; concisely.
anhē'lit/us -ūs *m.* panting; breath, exhalation.
anhē'l/ō -ā're -ā'vī -ā'tum *vi.* breathe hard, pant; exhale.
anhē'lus *a.* panting.
ani'cul/a -ae *f.* poor old woman.
Aniē'n/sis, Aniē'n/us *a.* of the river Anio. -us *m.* Anio.
anī'li/s *a.* of an old woman. **-ter** *ad.* like an old woman. **-tās** -tātis *f.* old age.
a'nim/a -ae *f.* wind, air; breath; life; soul, mind; ghost, spirit. -am agere, efflāre expire. -am comprimere hold one's breath.
animadve'rsi/ō -ō'nis *f.* observation; censure, punishment. [observer.
animadve'rs/or -ō'ris *m.*
animadve'r/tō -tere -tī -sum *vt.* pay attention to, notice; realise; censure, punish. — in punish. [living creature.
a'nim/al -ā'lis *n.* animal;
animā'lis *a.* of air; animate.
anim/āns -a'ntis *m., f., n.* living creature; animal.
animā'ti/ō -ō'nis *f.* being.
animā'tus *a.* disposed, in a certain frame of mind; courageous.
a'nim/ō -ā're -ā'vī -ā'tum *vt.* animate; give a certain temperament to.
animō's/us *a.* airy; life-like; courageous, proud. -ē *ad.* boldly, eagerly.
ani'mul/a -ae *f.* little soul. **-us** -ī *m.* darling.
a'nim/us -ī mind, soul; consciousness; reason, thought, opinion, imagination; heart, feelings, disposition; courage, spirit, pride, passion; will, purpose; term of endearment. -ī in mind, in heart. -ī causā for amusement. -ō fingere imagine. -ō male est I am fainting. aequō -ō esse be patient, calm. bonō -ō esse take courage; be well-disposed. ex -ō sincerely. ex -ō effluere be forgotten. in -ō habēre purpose. meō -ō in my opinion.
A'ni/ō -ē'nis *m.* tributary of the Tiber.
A'nn/a Pere'nn/a -ae -ae *f.* Roman popular goddess.
annā'l/is *a.* of a year. lēx — law prescribing ages for public offices. **-ēs** -ium *m.pl.* annals, chronicle.
a'nne, *see* **an.**
anni'culus *a.* a year old.
anniversā'rius *a.* annual.
annō'n or not.
annō'n/a -ae *f.* year's produce; grain; price of corn; the market.
annō'sus *a.* aged.
annō'tinus *a.* last year's.
a'nn/us -ī *m.* year. — māgnus astronomical great year. — solidus a full year.
a'nnuus *a.* a year's; annual.
anquī'/rō -rere -sī'vī -sī'tum *vt.* search for; make inquiries; (*law*) institute an inquiry (dē) or prosecution (*abl.* or *gen.*).
ā'ns/a -ae *f.* handle; (*fig.*) opportunity. **-ā'tus** *a.* with a handle; (*comedy*) with arms akimbo.
ā'nser -is *m.* goose. **-ī'nus** *a.*
a'nte *pr.* (*with acc.*) before (in time, place, comparison). *ad.* (*place*) in front; (*time*) before. **-quam** *conj.* before.
a'nteā *ad.* before, formerly.
antec/a'piō -a'pere -ē'pī -e'ptum *vt.* take beforehand, anticipate.
antec/ē'dō -ē'dere -e'ssī -essum *vt.* precede; surpass.
antece'll/ō -ere *vi.* excel, be superior.
antece'ptus *ppp.* antecapiō.
antece'ssi/ō -ō'nis *f.* preceding; antecedent cause.

antece'ss/or -ō'ris *m.* forerunner.
antecu'rs/or -ō'ris *m.* forerunner, pioneer.
ante/e'ō -ī're -iī *vi.* precede; surpass.
ante'/ferō -fe'rre -tuli -lā'tum *vt.* carry before; prefer; anticipate.
antefī'x/us *a.* attached (in front). *n.pl.* ornaments on roofs of buildings. [precede.
antegre'/dior -dī -ssus *vt.*
anteha'b/eō -ē're *vt.* prefer.
antehā'c *ad.* formerly, previously.
antelā'tus *ppp.* anteferō.
antelūcā'nus *a.* before dawn.
antemerīdiā'nus *a.* before noon.
antem/i'ttō -i'ttere -ī'sī -issum *vt.* send on in front.
ante'nn/a -ae *f.* yard-arm.
antepīlā'n/ī -ō'rum *m.pl.* (*mil.*) the front ranks.
antep/ō'nō -ō'nere -o'suī -o'situm *vt.* set before; prefer.
a'ntequam *conj.* before.
A'nter/ōs -ō'tis *m.* avenger of slighted love.
a'nt/ēs -ium *m.pl.* rows.
antesignā'n/us -ī *m.* (*mil.*) leader; (*pl.*) defenders of the standards.
a'ntest/ō, a'ntist/ō -ā're -etī *vi.* excel, distinguish oneself.
ante'st/or -ā'rī -ā'tus *vi.* call a witness.
antev/e'niō -enī're -ē'nī -e'ntum *vt.* & *i.* anticipate; surpass.
anteve'r/tō -tere -tī -sum *vt.* precede; anticipate; prefer.
anticipā'ti/ō -ō'nis *f.* foreknowledge.
anti'cip/ō -ā're -ā'vī -ā'tum *vt.* take before, anticipate.
antī'cus *a.* in front.
Anti'gon/ē -ēs *f.* daughter of Oedipus.
Anti'gon/us -ī *m.* name of Macedonian kings.
Antioch/ī'a -ī'ae *f.* Antioch, capital of Syria. **-ē'nsis** *a.*
Anti'och/us -ī *m.* name of kings of Syria.
antīquā'r/ius -ī & iī *m.* antiquary.
antī'quit/ās -ā'tis *f.* antiquity, the ancients; integrity.
antī'quitus *ad.* long ago, from ancient times.
antī'qu/ō -ā're -ā'vī -ā'tum *vt.* vote against (a bill).
antī'qu/us *a.* ancient, former, old; good old-fashioned, honest, illustrious. -ior more important. -issimus most important. **-ē** *ad.* in the old style.
anti'st/ēs -itis *m., f.* high-priest, chief priestess; (*fig.*) master (in any art).
Anti'sthen/ēs -is & ae *m.* founder of Cynic philosophy.
anti'stit/a -ae *f.* chief priestess.
a'ntistō, *see* **antestō.**
anti'thet/on -ī *n.* (*rhet.*) antithesis.
Antōnī'n/us -ī *m.* name of Roman emperors, *esp.* Pius and Marcus Aurelius.
Antō'n/ius -ī *m.* Roman name, *esp.* the famous orator, and Mark Antony.
antr/um -ī *n.* cave, hollow.
ā'nul/us -ī *m.* ring; equestrian rank. **-ā'rius** *m.* ringmaker. **-ā'tus** *a.* with rings on.
ā'n/us -ī *m.* rectum; ring. [old.
a'n/us -ūs *f.* old woman. *a.*
anxi'et/ās -ā'tis *f.* anxiety, trouble (of the mind).
a'nxifer -ī *a.* disquieting.
a'nxi/us *a.* troubled (in mind); disquieting. **-ē** *ad.*
anxitū'd/ō -inis *f.* anxiety.
Ā'on/es -um *a.* Boeotian. **-ia** *f.* part of Boeotia. **-ius** *a.* of Boeotia, of Helicon.
Ao'rn/os -ī *m.* lake Avernus.
a'page *interj.* away with! go away!

apēliō't/ēs -ae *m.* east wind.
Ape'll/ēs -is *m.* Greek painter.
a'p/er -rī *m.* boar.
ape'r/iō -īre uī -tum *vt.* uncover, disclose, open; open up (a country); (*fig.*) unfold, explain, reveal.
ape'rt/us *ppp.* aperiō. *a.* open, exposed; clear, manifest; (*person*) frank. **–um** -ī *n.* open space. in -ō esse be well known; be easy. -ē *ad.* clearly, openly.
ape'ruī *perf.* aperiō.
a'p/ex -icis *m.* summit; crown, priest's cap; (*fig.*) crown.
aphra'ct/us -ī *f.* a long open boat.
apiā'r/ius -ī & iī *m.* beekeeper.
Apī'c/ius -ī *m.* Roman epicure.
api'cul/a -ae *f.* little bee.
a'p/is -is *f.* bee.
ap/ī'scor -ī'scī -tus *vt.* catch, get, attain.
a'p/ium -ī & iī *n.* celery.
aplu'str/e -is *n.* decorated stern of a ship.
apoclē't/ī -ō'rum *m.pl.* committee of the Aetolian League.
apodytē'r/ium -ī & iī *n.* dressing-room.
Apo'll/ō -inis *m.* Greek god of music, archery, prophecy, flocks and herds, and often identified with the sun. **–ināris, –i'neus** *a.* lūdī -inārēs Roman games in July.
apo'log/us -ī *m.* narrative, fable.
apophorē't/a -ō'rum *n.pl.* presents for guests to take home.
apoproē'gmen/a -ō'rum *n.pl* (*philos.*) what is rejected.
apo'stol/us -ī *m.* (*eccl.*) apostle. **–icus** *a.*
apothē'c/a -ae *f.* storehouse, wine-store.
apparā'ti/ō -ō'nis *f.* preparation.
apparā't/us *a.* ready, well-supplied, sumptuous. -ē *ad.*
apparā't/us -ūs *m.* preparation; equipment, munitions; pomp, ostentation.
appā'r/eō -ē're -uī -itum *vi.* come in sight, appear; be seen, show oneself; wait upon (an official). -et it is obvious.
appāri'ti/ō -ō'nis *f.* service; domestic servants.
appā'rit/or -ō'ris *m.* attendant.
a'ppar/ō -ā're -ā'vī -ā'tum *vt.* prepare, provide.
appellā'ti/ō -ō'nis *f.* accosting, appeal; title; pronunciation.
appellā't/or -ō'ris *m.* appellant.
appellitā'tus *a.* usually called.
appe'll/ō -ā're -ā'vī -ā'tum *vt.* speak to; appeal to; dun (for money), sue (at law); call, name; pronounce.
app/e'llō -e'llere -ulī -u'lsum *vt.* drive, bring (to); (*naut.*) bring to land.
appendi'cul/a -ae *f.* small addition.
appe'nd/ix -icis *f.* supplement.
app/e'ndō -endere -endī- ēnsum *vt.* weigh, pay.
a'ppet/ēns -e'ntis *a.* eager; greedy. **–e'nter** *ad.*
appete'nti/a -ae *f.* craving.
appetī'ti/ō -ō'nis *f.* grasping, craving.
appetī'tus *ppp.* appetō.
appetī't/us -ūs *m.* craving; natural desire (as opposed to reason).
a'ppet/ō -ere -ī'vī -ī'tum *vt.* grasp, try to get at; attack; desire. *vi.* approach.
appi'ng/ō -ere *vt.* paint (in); (*colloq.*) write more.
A'pp/ius -ī *m.* Roman praenomen. Via -ia main road from Rome to Capua and Brundisium.

applau'/dō -dere -sī -sum *vt.* strike, clap. *vi.* applaud.
applicā'ti/ō -ō'nis *f.* applying (of the mind). iūs -ōnis the right of a patron to inherit a client's effects.
applic/ā'tus & **-itus** *ppp.* applicō.
a'pplic/ō -ā're -ā'vī & uī -ā'tum & itum *vt.* attach, place close (to); (*naut.*) steer, bring to land; sē, animum — devote self, attention (to).
applō'r/ō -ā're *vt.* deplore.
app/ō'nō -ō'nere -o'suī -o'situm *vt.* put (to, beside), serve (meal); add, appoint; reckon. [near by.
apporrē'ctus *a.* stretched
appo'rt/ō -ā're -ā'vī -ā'tum *vt.* bring, carry (to). [also.
appo'sc/ō -ere *vt.* demand
appo'sit/us *ppp.* appōnō. *a.* situated near; (*fig.*) bordering on; suitable. **-ē** *ad.* suitably.
appo'suī *perf.* appōnō.
appō'tus *a.* drunk.
a'pprec/or -ā'rī -ā'tus *vt.* pray to.
appreh/e'ndō -endere -endī -ēnsum *vt.* take hold of; (*mil.*) occupy; bring forward (an argument).
apprī'mē *ad.* especially.
a'ppr/imō -i'mere -e'ssī -e'ssum *vt.* press close.
approbā'ti/ō -ō'nis *f.* acquiescence; proof. [prove.
approbā't/or -ō'ris *m.* ap-
a'pprobē *ad.* very well.
a'pprob/ō -ā're -ā'vī -ā'tum *vt.* approve; prove; perform to someone's satisfaction.
apprōmi'tt/ō -ere *vt.* promise also.
appro'per/ō -ā're -ā'vī -ā'tum *vt.* hasten. *vi.* hurry up.
appropinquā'ti/ō -ō'nis *f.* approach.
appropi'inqu/ō -ā're -ā'vī -ā'tum *vi.* approach.
appu'gn/ō -ā're *vt.* attack.
appu'lsus *ppp.* appellō.
appu'ls/us -ūs *m.* landing; approach.
aprīcā'ti/ō -ō'nis *f.* basking.
aprī'c/or -ā'rī *vi.* bask.
aprī'c/us *a.* sunny; basking. in -um prōferre bring to light.
Aprī'lis *a.* April, of April.
aprū'gnus *a.* of the wild boar.
aps-, *see* **abs-**.
a'pt/ō -ā're -ā'vī -ā'tum *vt.* fit, put on; (*fig.*) adapt; prepare, equip.
a'pt/us *a.* attached, joined together, fitted (with); suitable. **-ē** *ad.* closely; suitably, rightly.
a'pud, a'put *pr.* (*with acc.*). *With persons*; beside, by, with, at the house of, among, in the time of; (*speaking*) in the presence of, to; (*judgment*) in the opinion of; (*influence*) with; (*faith*) in; in (authors). *With places*; near, at, in. est — mē I have. sum — mē I am in my senses.
Apū'l/ia -iae *f.* district of S.E. Italy. **-us** *a.*
a'qu/a -ae *f.* water. — mihī haeret I am in a fix. — intercus dropsy. -m adspergere revive. -m praebēre entertain. -m et terram petere demand submission. -ā et ignī interdīcere outlaw. -ae *f.pl.* medicinal waters, spa.
aquaedu'ct/us -ūs *m.* aqueduct; right of leading water.
aquā'l/is -is *m., f.* washbasin. **-i'culus** *m.* belly.
aquā'rius *a.* of water. *m.* water-carrier, water-inspector; a constellation.
aquā'ticus *a.* aquatic; humid.
aquā'tilis *a.* aquatic.
aquā'ti/ō -ō'nis *f.* fetching water; watering-place.
aquā't/or -ō'ris *m.* water-carrier.
a'quil/a -ae *f.* eagle; standard

of a legion; (*arch.*) gable; a constellation. **-ae senectūs** a vigorous old age.
Aquilei'/a -ae *f.* town in N. Italy. **-ē'nsis** *a.*
aqui'lifer -ī *m.* chief standard-bearer.
aquilī'nus *a.* eagle's.
a'quil/ō -ō'nis *m.* north wind; north.
aquilō'nius *a.* northerly.
a'quilus *a.* swarthy.
Aquī'n/um -ī *n.* town in Latium. **-ā's -ā'tis** *a.*
Aquitā'n/ia -iae *f.* district of S.W. Gaul. **-us** *a.*
a'qu/or -ā'rī -ā'tus *vi.* fetch water.
aquō'sus *a.* humid, rainy.
a'quul/a -ae *f.* little stream
ā'r/a -ae *f.* altar; (*fig.*) refuge; a constellation. **-ae et foci** hearth and home.
araba'rch/ēs -ae *m.* customs officer in Egypt.
Ara'b/ia -iae *f.* Arabia. **-icus, -s, -us** *a.* **-icē** *ad.* with all the perfumes of Arabia.
Ara'chnē -s *f.* Lydian woman changed into a spider.
arā'ne/a -ae *f.* spider; cobweb. **-ola** *f.*, **-olus** *m.* small spider.
arāneō'sus *a.* full of spiders' [webs.
arā'ne/us -ī *m.* spider. *a.* of spiders. **-um -ī** *n.* spider's web.
A'rar -is *m.* river Saône.
arā'ti/ō -ō'nis *f.* ploughing, farming; arable land. **-u'ncula** *f.* small plot.
arā'/tor -ō'ris *m.* ploughman, farmer; (*pl.*) cultivators of public land.
arā'tr/um -ī *n.* plough.
Arā't/us -ī *m.* Greek astronomical poet. **-ē'us** *a.*
Ara'x/ēs -is *m.* river in Armenia.
a'rbit/er -rī *m.* witness; arbiter, judge, umpire; controller. — **bibendī** president of a drinking party.
a'rbitr/a -ae *f.* witness.
arbitrā'ri/us *a.* uncertain. **-ō** *ad.* with some uncertainty.
arbitrā't/us -ūs *m.* decision. **meō -ū** in my judgment.
arbi'tr/ium -ī & iī *n.* decision (of an arbitrator), judgment; mastery, control.
a'rbitr/or -ā'rī -ā'tus *vt.* & *i.* be a witness of; testify; think, suppose.
a'rb/or, a'rb/ōs -oris *f.* tree; ship, mast, oar. — **īnfēlix** gallows.
arbo'reus *a.* of trees, like a [tree.
arbu'st/um -ī *n.* plantation, orchard; (*pl.*) trees.
arbu'stus *a.* wooded.
arbu'teus *a.* of the strawberry-tree.
a'rbut/us -ī *f.* strawberry-tree. **-um -ī** *n.* fruit of same.
a'rc/a -ae *f.* box; money-box, purse; coffin; prison-cell. **ex -ā absolvere** pay cash.
Arca'd/ia -iae *f.* district of S. Greece. **-es -um** *m.pl.* Arcadians. **-icus, -ius** *a.*
arcā'n/us *a.* secret; able to keep secrets. **-um -ī** *n.* secret, mystery. **-ō** *ad.* privately.
a'rc/eō -ē're -uī -tum *vt.* enclose; keep off, prevent.
arcessī'tū at the summons.
arcessī'tus *ppp.* arcessō. *a.* far-fetched.
arce'ss/ō -ere -ī'vī -ī'tum *vt.* send for, fetch; (*law*) summon, accuse; (*fig.*) derive.
arche'typ/us -ī *m.* original.
Archi'loch/us -ī *m.* Greek iambic and elegiac poet.
archimagī'r/us -ī *m.* chief cook.
Archimē'd/ēs -is *m.* famous mathematician of Syracuse.
archipīrā't/a -ae *m.* pirate chief.

archite'ct/ōn -onis *m.* master builder; master in cunning.
archite'ct/or -ā'rī -ā'tus *vt.* construct; (*fig.*) devise.
architectū'r/a -ae *f.* architecture.
archite'ct/us -ī *m.* architect; (*fig.*) author.
a'rch/ōn -o'ntis *m.* Athenian magistrate.
A'rchyt/ās -ae *m.* Pythagorean philosopher of Tarentum.
arci'ten/ēns -e'ntis *a.* archer. *m.* Apollo. [Boōtes.
Arcto'phyla/x -cis *m.*
a'rct/os -ī *f.* Great Bear, Little Bear; north, north wind; night.
Arctū'r/us -ī *m.* brightest star in Boōtes.
a'rctus etc., *see* **artus** etc.
a'rcuī *perf.* arceō.
a'rcul/a -ae *f.* casket; (*rhet.*) ornament. [curve.
a'rcu/ō -ā're -ā'vī -ā'tum *vt.*
a'rc/us -ūs *m.* bow; rainbow; arch, curve; (*math.*) arc.
a'rde/a -ae *f.* heron.
A'rde/a -ae *f.* town in Latium. **-ā's** -ā'tis **-ātī'nus** *a.*
arde'li/ō -ō'nis *m.* busybody.
ā'rd/ēns -e'ntis *a.* hot, glowing, fiery; (*fig.*) eager, ardent. **-enter** *ad.* passionately.
ā'r/deō -dē're -sī -sum *vi.* be on fire, burn, shine; (*fig.*) be fired, burn.
ārdē'sc/ō -ere *vi.* catch fire, gleam; (*fig.*) become inflamed, wax hotter.
ā'rd/or -ō'ris *m.* heat, brightness; (*fig.*) ardour, passion.
a'rdu/us *a.* steep, high; difficult, troublesome. **-um** -ī *n.* steep slope; difficulty.
ā're/a -ae *f.* vacant site, open space, playground; threshing-floor; (*fig.*) scope (for effort).
āref/a'ciō -a'cere -ē'cī -a'ctum *vt.* dry.
arē'na, *see* **harēna.**

ā'r/eō -ē're *vi.* be dry. **-ēns** -e'ntis *a.* arid; thirsty.
āre'ol/a -ae *f.* small open space.
Arēo'pag/us -ī *m.* Mars' Hill in Athens, a criminal court. **-ī'tēs** *m.* member of the court. [war.
A'r/ēs -is *m.* Greek god of
ārē'sc/ō -ere *vi.* dry, dry up.
Aresto'rid/ēs -ae *m.* Argus.
aretā'log/us -ī *m.* braggart.
Arethū's/a -ae *f.* spring near Syracuse. **-is** *a.* Syracusan.
Argē'/ī -ō'rum *m.pl.* sacred places in Rome; effigies thrown annually into the Tiber.
argentā'ri/us *a.* of silver of money. *m.* banker. **-a** -ae *f.* bank, banking; silver-mine.
argentā'tus *a.* silver-plated; backed with money.
arge'nteus *a.* of silver, adorned with silver; silvery (in colour); of the silver age.
arge'nt/um -ī *n.* silver, silver plate; money.
Argīlē't/um -ī *n.* part of Rome, noted for book-shops. **-ā'nus** *a.*
argi'll/a -ae *f.* clay.
A'rg/ō -ūs *f.* Jason's ship. **-ō'us** *a.*
Argonau't/ae -ā'rum *m.pl.* Argonauts. **-icus** *a.*
A'rg/os *n.*, **-ī** -ō'rum *m.pl.* town in S.E. Greece. **-olis** -o'lidis *f.* district about Argos. **-ē'us, -ī'vus, -o'licus** *a.* Argive; Greek.
argūmentā'ti/ō -ō'nis *f.* adducing proofs.
argūme'nt/or -ā'rī -ā'tus *vt.* & *i.* prove, adduce as proof; conclude.
argūme'nt/um -ī *n.* evidence, proof; (*lit.*) subject-matter, theme, plot (of a play); (*art*) subject, motif.
a'rg/uō -u'ere -uī -ū'tum *vt.* prove, make known; accuse, blame, denounce.

A'rg/us -ī *m.* monster with many eyes.
argū'ti/ae -ā'rum *f.pl.* nimbleness, liveliness; wit, subtlety, slyness.
argū't/or -ā'rī -ā'tus *vi.* chatter.
argū'tulus *a.* rather subtle.
argū't/us *a.* (*sight*) clear, distinct, graceful; (*sound*) clear, melodious, noisy; (*mind*) acute, witty, sly. —ē *ad.* subtly.
argyra'spi/s -dis *a.* silver-shielded.
Aria'dn/a -ae *f.* daughter of Minos of Crete. **—ae'us** *a.*
ări'dulus *a.* rather dry.
ă'rid/us *a.* dry, withered; meagre; (*style*) flat. -um -ī *n.* dry land.
a'ri/ēs -etis *m.* ram; 1st sign of Zodiac; battering-ram; beam used as a breakwater.
ari'et/ō -ā're *vt.* & *i.* butt, strike hard.
Arī'/ōn -onis *m.* early Greek poet and musician. **—o'nius** *a.*
ari'st/a -ae *f.* ear of corn.
Aristae'/us -ī *m.* legendary founder of beekeeping.
Arista'rch/us -ī *m.* Alexandrian scholar; a severe critic.
Aristī'd/ēs -is *m.* Athenian statesman noted for integrity.
Aristi'pp/us -ī *m.* Greek hedonist philosopher. **—ē'us** *a.*
aristolo'chi/a -ae *f.* birthwort.
Aristo'phan/ēs -is *m.* Greek comic poet. **—ē'us, —ī'us** *a.*
Aristo'tel/ēs -is *m.* Aristotle, founder of Peripatetic school of philosophy. **—ē'us, —ī'us** *a.*
arithmē'tic/a -ō'rum *n.pl.* arithmetic.
ăritū'd/ō -inis *f.* dryness.
Ariū'sius *a.* of Ariusia in Chios.
a'rm/a -ō'rum *n.pl.* armour, shield; arms, weapons (of close combat only); warfare, troops; (*fig.*) defence, protection; implements, ship's gear.
armāme'nt/a -ō'rum *n.pl.* implements, ship's gear.
armāmentā'r/ium -ī & iī *n.* arsenal.
armāri'ol/um -ī *n.* small chest.
armā'r/ium -ī & iī *n.* chest, safe.
armā'tū *m. abl.* armour. gravī —with heavy-armed troops.
armātū'r/a -ae *f.* armour, equipment. levis — light-armed troops.
Arme'ni/a -ae *f.* Armenia. **—us** *a.* **—aca** -acae *f.* apricot tree. **—acum** -acī *n.* apricot.
armentā'lis *a.* of the herd.
armentā'r/ius -ī & iī *m.* cattle-herd.
arme'nt/um -ī *n.* cattle (for ploughing), herd (of cattle, horses, or other animals).
a'rmifer -ī *a.* armed.
a'rmiger -ī *m.* armour-bearer. *a.* armed; productive of warriors.
armi'll/a -ae *f.* bracelet. **—ā'tus** *a.* wearing a bracelet.
armi'pot/ēns -e'ntis *a.* strong in battle.
armi'sonus *a.* resounding with arms.
a'rm/ō -ā're -ā'vī -ā'tum *v.t.* arm, equip; rouse to arms (against).
a'rm/us -ī *m.* shoulder (*esp.* of animals).
A'rn/us -ī *m.* river Arno. **—iē'nsis** *a.*
a'r/ō -ā're -ā'vī -ā'tum *vt.* plough, cultivate; live by farming; (*fig.*) furrow (the sea, the brow).
Arpī'n/um -ī *n.* town in Latium, birthplace of Cicero. **—ā's** -ā'tis *a.*
arquā'tus *a.* jaundiced.
a'rrab/ō -ō'nis *m.* earnest-money.

arr–, *see* **adr–**.
ars a'rtis *f.* skill (in any craft); the art (of any profession); science, theory; handbook; work of art; moral quality, virtue; artifice, fraud.
ā'rsī *perf.* ārdeō.
ā'rsus *ppp.* ārdeō.
artē'ri/a -ae *f.* windpipe; artery. **–a -ō'rum** *n.pl.* trachea.
arthrī'ticus *a.* gouty.
articulā'tim *ad.* joint by joint; (*speech*) distinctly.
arti'cul/ō -ā're -ā'vī -ā'tum *vt.* articulate.
articulō'sus *a.* minutely subdivided.
arti'cul/us -ī *m.* joint, knuckle; limb; (*words*) clause; (*time*) point, turning-point. **in ipsō -ō temporis** in the nick of time.
a'rtif/ex -icis *m.* artist, craftsman, master; (*fig.*) maker, author. *a.* ingenious, artistic, artificial.
artificiō's/us *a.* ingenious, artistic, artificial. **–ē** *ad.* skilfully.
artifi'c/ium -ī & iī *n.* skill, workmanship; art, craft; theory, rule of an art; ingenuity, cunning.
a'rt/ō -ā're *vt.* compress, curtail.
artola'gan/us -ī *m.* kind of cake.
arto'pt/a -ae *m.* baker; baking-tin.
a'rt/us *a.* close, narrow, tight; (*sleep*) deep; (*fig.*) strict, straitened. **–ē** *ad.* closely, soundly, briefly.
a'rt/us -ūs *m.* joint; (*pl.*) limbs, body; (*fig.*) strength.
ā'rul/a -ae *f.* small altar.
aru'ndō *etc.*, *see* **harundō** etc.
arvī'n/a -ae *f.* grease.
a'rv/us *a.* ploughed. **–um -ī** *n.* field; land, country, plain.
arx a'rcis *f.* fortress, castle; height, summit; (*fig.*) bulwark, stronghold. **arcem facere ē cloācā** *make a mountain out of a mole-hill.*
ās a'ssis *m.* (*weight*) pound; (*coin*) bronze unit, of low value; (*inheritance*) the whole, subdivided into 12 parts. **ad assem** to the last farthing. **hērēs ex asse** sole heir.
Ascā'n/ius -ī *m.* son of Aeneas.
asc/e'ndō -e'ndere -e'ndī -ē'nsum *vt.* & *i.* go up, climb, embark; (*fig.*) rise.
ascēn'si/ō -ō'nis *f.* ascent; (*fig.*) sublimity.
ascē'ns/us -ūs *m.* ascent, rising; way up.
a'sci/a -ae *f.* axe; mason's trowel.
a'sc/iō -īre *vt.* admit.
asc/ī'scō -ī'scere -ī'vī -ī'tum *vt.* receive with approval; admit (to some kind of association); appropriate, adopt (*esp.* customs); arrogate to oneself. **–ī'tus** *a.* acquired, alien.
A'scr/a -ae *f.* birthplace of Hesiod in Boeotia. **–ae'us** *a.* of Ascra; of Hesiod; of Helicon.
ascrī'/bō -bere -psī -ptum *vt.* add (in writing); attribute, ascribe; apply (an illustration); enrol include.
ascrīptī'cius *a.* enrolled.
ascrī'pti/ō -ō'nis *f.* addition (in writing).
ascrīptī'vus *a.* (*mil.*) supernumerary.
ascrī'pt/or -ō'ris *m.* supporter.
ascrī'ptus *ppp.* ascribō.
ase'll/a -ae *f.* **ase'll/us -ī** *m.* young ass.
Ā'si/a -ae *f.* Roman province; Asia Minor; Asia. **–us, –ā'nus, –ā'ticus** *a.*
asī'l/us -ī *m.* gad-fly.
a'sin/us -ī *m.* ass; fool.
Ā'si/s -dis *f.* Asia.
Āsō'p/us -ī *m.* river in Boeotia.

asō't/us -ī *m.* libertine.
aspa'rag/us -ī *m.* asparagus.
aspargō, *see* **aspergō**.
aspectā'bilis *a.* visible.
aspe'ct/ō -ā're *vt.* look at, gaze at; pay heed to; (*places*) face.
aspe'ctus *ppp.* aspiciō.
aspe'ct/us -ūs *m.* look, sight; glance, sense of sight; aspect, appearance.
aspe'll/ō -ere *vt.* drive away.
a'sper -ī *a.* rough; (*taste*) bitter; (*sound*) harsh; (*weather*) severe; (*style*) rugged; (*person*) violent, exasperated, unkind, austere; (*animal*) savage; (*circs.*) difficult. **-ē** *ad.*
aspe'r/gō -gere -sī -sum *vt.* scatter, sprinkle; bespatter, besprinkle. **aquam** — revive.
aspe'rg/ō -inis *f.* sprinkling; spray.
aspe'rit/ās -ā'tis *f.* roughness, unevenness, harshness, severity; (*fig.*) ruggedness, fierceness; trouble, difficulty.
aspernā'ti/ō -ō'nis *f.* disdain.
aspe'rn/or -ā'rī -ā'tus *vt.* reject, disdain.
a'sper/ō -ā're -ā'vī -ā'tum *vt.* roughen, sharpen; exasperate.
aspe'rsi/ō -ō'nis *f.* sprinkling.
aspe'rsus *ppp.* aspergō.
asp/i'ciō -i'cere -e'xī -e'ctum *vt.* catch sight of, look at; (*places*) face; (*fig.*) examine, consider.
aspīrā'ti/ō -ō'nis *f.* breathing (on); evaporation; pronouncing with an aspirate.
aspī'r/ō -ā're -ā'vī -ā'tum *vi.* breathe, blow; favour; aspire, attain (to). *vt.* blow, instil.
a'spi/s -dis *f.* asp.
asportā'ti/ō -ō'nis *f.* removal.
aspo'rt/ō -ā're *vt.* carry off.
asprē't/a -ō'rum *n.pl.* rough country.
Assa'rac/us -ī *m.* Trojan ancestor of Aeneas.
ass-, *see* **ads-**.
a'sser -is *m.* pole, stake.
a'ssul/a -ae *f.* splinter. **-ā'tim** *ad.* in splinters.
ā'ss/us *a.* roasted. **-um** -ī *n.* roast; (*pl.*) sweating-bath.
Assy'ri/a -ae *f.* country in W. Asia. **-us** *a.* Assyrian; oriental.
ast *conj.* (*laws*) and then; (*vows*) then; (*strong contrast*) and yet.
ast-, *see* **adst-**.
Astrae'/a -ae *f.* goddess of Justice.
Astrae'/us -ī *m.* father of winds. -ī frātrēs the winds.
astrolo'gi/a -ae *f.* astronomy.
astro'log/us -ī *m.* astronomer; astrologer.
a'str/um -ī *n.* star, heavenly body, constellation; a great height; heaven, immortality, glory.
a'stu *n.* (*indecl.*) city, *esp.* [Athens.
a'st/us -ūs *m.* cleverness, cunning. [cunning.
astū'ti/a -ae *f.* slyness,
astū't/us *a.* artful, sly. **-ē** *ad.* cleverly.
Asty'ana/x -ctis *m.* son of Hector and Andromache.
a'sȳl/um -ī *n.* sanctuary.
asy'mbolus *a.* with no contribution.
at *conj.* (*adversative*) but, on the other hand; (*objecting*) but it may be said; (*limiting*) at least, but at least; (*continuing*) then, thereupon; (*transitional*) now; (*with passionate appeals*) but oh! look now! — **enim** yes but. — **tamen** nevertheless.
Atā'bul/us -ī *m.* sirocco.
ata't, atta't *interj.* (*expressing fright, pain, surprise*) oh!
a'tav/us -ī *m.* great-great-great-grandfather; ancestor.
Ate'll/a -ae *f.* Oscan town in Campania. **-ā'nus** *a.* fābula **-āna** kind of comic show popular in Rome. **-ā'nius**, **-ā'nicus** *a.*

ā't/er -rī *a.* black, dark; gloomy, dismal; malicious. diēs -rī unlucky days.
A'tham/ās -a'ntis *m.* king of Thessaly, who went mad. **-antē'us** *a.* **-anti'adēs** *m.* Palaemon. **-a'ntis** *f.* Helle.
Athē'n/ae -ā'rum *f.pl.* Athens. **-ae'us**, **-iē'nsis** *a.*
a'the/os -ī *m.* atheist.
athlē't/a -ae *m.* wrestler, athlete.
athlē'ticē *ad.* athletically.
A'th/os *dat.* -ō, *acc.* -ō, -on, -ō'nem *m.* mount Athos in Macedonia.
A'tl/ās -a'ntis *m.* giant supporting the sky; Atlas mountains. **-antē'us**, **-a'nticus** *a.* mare -anticum Atlantic Ocean. **-anti'adēs** *m.* Mercury. **-a'ntis** *f.* lost Atlantic island; a Pleiad.
a'tom/us -ī *m.* atom.
a'tque, ac *conj.* (*connecting words*) and, and in fact; (*connecting clauses*) and moreover, and then, and so, and yet; (*in comparison*) as, than, to, from. — adeō and that too; or rather. — nōn and not rather. — sī as if. alius — different from. contrā — opposite to. īdem — same as. plūs — more than.
a'tquī *conj.* (*adversative*) and yet, nevertheless, yes but; (*confirming*) by all means; (*minor premiss*) now. — sī if now.
ātrāme'nt/um -ī *n.* ink; blacking.
ātrā'tus *a.* in mourning.
A'tr/eus -eī *m.* son of Pelops, king of Argos. **-ī'dēs** *m.* Agamemnon; Menelaus.
ātriē'ns/is -is *m.* steward, major-domo.
ātri'ol/um -ī *n.* ante-room.
ā'tr/ium -ī & iī *n.* hall, open central room in Roman house; forecourt of a temple; hall (in other buildings).
atrō'cit/ās -ā'tis *f.* hideousness; (*mind*) brutality; (*philos.*) severity.
A'trop/os -ī *f.* one of the Fates.
a'tr/ōx -ō'cis *a.* hideous, dreadful; fierce, brutal, unyielding. **-ō'citer** *ad.* savagely.
attā'ctus *ppp.* attingō.
attā'ct/us -ūs *m.* contact.
a'ttagēn -is *m.* heath-cock.
A'ttal/us -ī *m.* king of Pergamum, who bequeathed his kingdom to Rome. **-icus** *a.* of Attalus; of Pergamum; ornamented with gold cloth. **-ica** *n.pl.* garments of woven gold.
a'ttamen *conj.* nevertheless.
atta't, *see* **atat**.
atte'gi/a -ae *f.* hut.
attemperā'tē *ad.* opportunely
atte'n/dō -dere -dī -tum *vt.* direct (the attention); attend to, notice.
atte'nti/ō -ō'nis *f.* attentiveness.
atte'nt/ō, **atte'mpt/ō** -ā're -ā'vī -ā'tum *vt.* test, try; tamper with (loyalty); attack.
atte'n/tus *ppp.* attendō. *a.* attentive, intent; businesslike, careful (*esp.* about money) **-ē** *ad.* carefully.
atte'ntus *ppp.* attineō.
attenuā't/us *a.* weak; (*style*) brief; refined; plain. **-ē** *ad.* simply.
atte'nu/ō -ā're -ā'vī -ā'tum *vt.* weaken, reduce; diminish; humble.
a'tt/erō -e'rere -rī'vī -rī'tum *vt.* rub; wear away; (*fig.*) impair, exhaust.
atte'st/or -ā'rī -ā'tus *vt.* confirm.
atte'x/ō -ere -uī -tum *vt.* weave on; (*fig.*) add on.
A'tthi/s -dis *f.* Attica.
A'ttic/a -ae *f.* district of Greece about Athens. **-icus** *a.* Attic, Athenian; (*rhet.*) of a plain and direct style. **-ē**

ad. in the Athenian manner. **–i'ssō** *vi.* speak in the Athenian manner.
a'ttigī *perf.* attingō.
a'ttigō, *see* **attingō**.
att/i'neō -inē're -i'nuī -e'ntum *vt.* hold fast detain; guard; reach for. *vi.* concern, pertain, be of importance, avail.
att/i'ngō -i'ngere -igī -ā'ctum *vt.* touch; strike, assault; arrive at; border on; affect; mention; undertake; concern, resemble.
A'tti/s -dis *m.* Phrygian priest of Cybele.
A'tt/ius, A'cc/ius -ī *m.* Latin tragic poet. **–iā'nus** *a.*
atto'll/ō -ere *vt.* lift up, erect; (*fig.*) exalt, extol.
att/o'ndeō -ondē're -o'ndī -ō'nsum shear, prune, crop; (*fig.*) diminish; (*comedy*) fleece.
atto'nitus *a.* thunderstruck, terrified, astonished; inspired.
a'tton/ō -ā're -uī -itum *vt.* stupefy.
attō'nsus *ppp.* attondeō.
atto'rqu/eō -ē're *vt.* hurl upwards.
attra'ctus *ppp.* attrahō.
a'ttra/ho -here -xi -ctum *vt.* drag by force, attract; (*fig.*) draw, incite
attre'ct/ō -ā're *vt.* touch, handle; appropriate. [along.
attre'pid/ō -ā're *vi.* hobble
attri'b/uō -u'ere -uī -ū'tum *vt.* assign, bestow; add; impute, attribute; lay as a tax.
attribū'ti/ō -ō'nis *f.* assignment (of money); (*gram.*) predicate.
attribū't/us *ppp.* attribuō *a.* subject. **–um -ī** *n.* (*gram.*) predicate.
attrī'tus *ppp.* atterō. *a.* worn; bruised; (*fig.*) impudent.
attulī *perf.* adferō.
au *interj.* (*expressing pain, surprise*) oh !
au'c/eps -upis *m.* fowler; (*fig.*) eavesdropper; a pedantic critic.
auctā'r/ium -ī & iī *n.* extra.
aucti'ficus *a.* increasing.
au'cti/ō -ō'nis *f.* increase; auction sale.
auctiōnā'ri/us *a.* auction. tabulae **-ae** catalogues.
auctiō'n/or -ā'rī -ā'tus *vi.* hold an auction.
au'ctit/ō -ā're *vt.* greatly increase.
au'ct/ō -ā're *vt.* increase.
au'ct/or -ō'ris *m., f.* 1. originator; (*of families*) progenitor; (*of buildings*) founder; (*of deeds*) doer. 2. composer; (*of writings*) author, historian; (*of knowledge*) investigator, teacher; (*of news*) informant. 3. instigator; (*of action*) adviser; (*of measures*) promoter; (*of laws*) proposer, supporter; ratifier. 4. person of influence; (*in public life*) leader; (*of conduct*) model; (*of guarantees*) witness, bail; (*of property*) seller; (*of women and minors*) guardian; (*of others' welfare*) champion. **mē -ōre** at my suggestion.
auctōrāme'nt/um -ī *n.* contract; wages.
auctōrā'tus *a.* bound (by a pledge); hired out (for wages).
auctō'rit/ās -ā'tis *f.* 1. source; lead, responsibility. 2. judgment; opinion; advice, support; bidding, guidance; (*of senate*) decree; (*of people*) will. 3. power; (*person*) influence, authority, prestige; (*things*) importance, worth; (*conduct*) example; (*knowledge*) warrant, document, authority; (*property*) right of possession.
auctumn–, *see* **autumn–**.
au'ctus *ppp.* augeō. *a.* enlarged, great.
au'ct/us -ūs *m.* growth, increase.
aucu'p/ium -ī & iī *n.* fowl-

ing; birds caught; (*fig.*) hunting (after), quibbling.

au'cup/ō -ā're *vt.* watch for. **-or** -ā'rī -ā'tus *vi.* go fowling. *vt.* chase; (*fig.*) try to catch.

audā'ci/a -ae *f.* daring, courage; audacity, impudence; (*pl.*) deeds of daring.

au'd/āx -ā'cis *a.* bold, daring; rash, audacious; proud. **-ā'cter, ā'citer** *ad.*

au'd/ēns -e'ntis *a.* bold, brave. **-e'nter** *ad.*

aude'nti/a -ae *f.* boldness, courage.

au'/deō -dē're -sus *vt.* & *i.* dare, venture; be brave.

au'di/ēns -e'ntis *m.* hearer. *a.* obedient.

audie'nti/a -ae *f.* hearing. -m facere gain a hearing.

au'd/iō -ī're -ī'vī & -iī -ī'tum *vt.* hear; learn, be told; be called; listen, attend to, study under (a teacher); examine a case; agree with; obey, heed. **bene, male** — have a good, bad reputation.

audī'ti/ō -ō'nis *f.* listening; hearsay, news. [pupil.

audī't/or -ō'ris *m.* hearer;

auditō'r/ium -ī & iī *n.* lecture-room, law-court; audience.

audī't/us -ūs *m.* (sense of) hearing; a hearing; rumour.

au'ferō aufe'rre a'bstulī ablā'tum *vt.* take away, carry away; mislead, lead into a digression; take by force, steal; win, obtain (as the result of effort). **aufer** away with !

Au'fid/us -ī *m.* river in Apulia.

auf/u'giō -u'gere -ū'gī *vi.* run away. *vt.* flee from.

Augē'/ās -ae *m.* king of Elis, whose stables Hercules cleaned.

au'/geō -gē're -xī -ctum *vt.* increase; enrich, bless (with); praise, worship. *vi.* increase.

augē'sc/ō -ere *vi.* begin to grow increase.

au'gm/en -inis *n.* growth.

au'gur -is *m., f.* augur; prophet, interpreter.

augurā'l/is *a.* augur's. **-e** -is *n.* part of camp where auspices were taken.

augurā'ti/ō -ō'nis *f.* soothsaying. [augur.

augurā't/us -ūs *m.* office of

augu'r/ium -ī & iī *n.* augury; an omen; prophecy, interpretation; presentiment.

augu'rius *a.* of augurs.

au'gur/ō -ā're *vt.* & *i.* take auguries; consecrate by auguries; forebode. **-ātō** after taking auspices.

au'gur/or -ā'rī -ā'tus *vt.* & *i.* take auguries; foretell by omens; predict, conjecture.

Augu'st/a -ae *f.* title of the emperor's wife, mother, daughter or sister.

Augustā'l/is *a.* of Augustus. **lūdī** -ēs games in October. **praefectus** -is governor of Egypt. **sodālēs** -ēs priests of deified Augustus.

augu'st/us *a.* venerable, august, majestic. **-ē** *ad.*

Augu'st/us -ī *m.* title given to C. Octavius, first Roman emperor, and so to his successors. *a.* imperial; (*month*) August, of August.

au'l/a -ae *f.* court-yard of a Greek house; hall of a Roman house; palace, royal court; courtiers; royal power.

au'la, *see* **olla.**

aulae'/um -ī *n.* embroidered hangings, canopy, covering; (*theat.*) curtain (let down at the beginning, raised at the end of a performance).

au'lic/us *a.* of the court. **-ī** -ō'rum *m.pl.* courtiers.

Au'l/is -idis & is *f.* port in Boeotia from which the Greeks sailed for Troy.

auloe'd/us -ī *m.* singer accompanied by flute.
au'r/a -ae *f.* breath of air, breeze, wind; air upper world; vapour, odour, sound, gleam; (*fig.*) winds (of public favour), breeze (of prosperity), air (of freedom), daylight (of publicity).
aurā'ri/us *a.* of gold. **-a -ae** *f.* gold mine.
aurā'tus *a.* gilt, ornamented with gold; gold.
Aurē'l/ius -ī *m.* Roman name. **lēx -ia** law on the composition of juries. **via -ia** main road running N.W. from Rome. [splendid.
aure'olus *a.* gold; beautiful,
au'reus *a.* gold, golden; gilded; (*fig.*) beautiful, splendid. *m.* gold coin.
auricha'lc/um -ī *n.* a precious metal.
auri'comus *a.* golden-leaved.
auri'cul/a -ae *f.* the external ear; ear.
au'rifer -ī *a.* gold-producing.
au'rif/ex -icis *m.* goldsmith.
aurī'g/a -ae *m.* charioteer driver; groom; helmsman; a constellation.
auri'gen/a -ae *a.* gold-begotten.
au'riger -ī *a.* gilded.
aurī'g/ō -ā're *vi.* compete in the chariot-race.
au'r/is -is *f.* ear; (*rhet.*) judgment; (*agr.*) earth-board (of a plough). **ad -em admonēre** whisper. **in utramvis -em dormīre** sleep soundly.
aurī'tul/us -ī *m.* "Long-Ears." [tive.
aurī'tus *a.* long-eared; atten-
aurō'r/a -ae *f.* dawn, morning; goddess of dawn; the East.
au'r/um -ī *n.* gold; gold plate, jewelry, bit, fleece, etc.; money; lustre; the Golden Age.
auscultā'ti/ō -ō'nis *f* obedience.
auscultā't/or -ō'ris *m.* listener.
auscu'lt/ō -ā're -ā'vī -ā'tum *vt.* listen to; overhear. *vi.* (*of servants*) wait at the door; obey.
au'sim *subj.* audeō.
Au'son/es -um *m.pl.* indigenous people of central Italy. **-ia** *f.* Italy. **-ius, -is** *a.* Italian. **-idae** *m.pl.* Italians.
au'sp/ex -icis *m.* augur, soothsayer; patron, commander; witness of a marriage contract.
auspicā'tō *ad.* after taking auspices; at a lucky moment.
auspicā'tus *a.* consecrated; auspicious lucky.
auspi'c/ium -ī & iī *n.* augury, auspices; right of taking auspices; power, command; omen. — **facere** give a sign.
au'spic/ō -ā're *vi.* take the auspices.
au'spic/or -ā'rī -ā'tus *vi.* take the auspices; make a beginning. *vt.* begin, enter upon. [south.
au'st/er -rī *m.* south wind;
austē'rit/ās -ā'tis *f.* severity.
austē'r/us *a.* severe, serious; gloomy, irksome. **-ē** *ad.*
austrā'lis *a.* southern.
austrī'nus *a.* from the south.
au's/us *ppa.* audeō. **-um -ī** *n.* enterprise.
aut *conj.* or; either . . . or; or else or at least, or rather.
au'tem *conj.* (*adversative*) but, on the other hand; (*in transitions, parentheses*) moreover, now, and; (*in dialogue*) indeed
authe'ps/a -ae *f.* stove.
auto'graphus *a.* written with his own hand.
Auto'lyc/us -ī *m.* a robber.
auto'mat/us *a.* spontaneous. **-on -ī** *n.* automaton.

Auto'med/ōn -o'ntis *m.* a charioteer.
autumnā'lis *a.* autumn, autumnal.
autu'mn/us -ī *m.* autumn. *a.* autumnal.
au'xī *perf.* augeō.
au'tum/ō -ā're *vt.* assert.
auxiliā'ris *a.* helping, auxiliary; of the auxiliaries. *m.pl.* auxiliary troops.
auxiliā'rius *a.* helping; auxiliary.
auxiliā't/or -ō'ris *m.* helper.
auxiliā't/us -ūs *m.* aid.
auxi'li/or -ā'rī -ā'tus *vi.* aid, support.
auxi'l/ium -ī & iī *n.* help, assistance. **-ia** -iō'rum *n.pl.* auxiliary troops; military force.
avāri'ti/a -ae *f.* greed, selfishness.
avāri'ti/ēs -ē'ī *f.* avarice.
avā'r/us *a.* greedy, covetous; eager. **-ē, -iter** *ad.*
a'vē, avē'te, avē'tō *imp.* hail! farewell!
ā've/hō -here -xī -ctum *vt.* carry away; (*pass.*) ride away.
āv/e'llō -e'llere -e'llī & u'lsī (olsī) -u'lsum (olsum) *vt.* pull away, tear off; take away (by force), remove.
avē'n/a -ae *f.* oats; (*music*) reed, shepherd's pipe.
Aventī'n/us -ī *m.* Aventine hill in Rome. *a.* of Aventine. **-um** -ī *n.* Aventine hill.
a'v/eō -ē're *vt.* desire, long for. **-ēns** -e'ntis *a.* eager.
Ave'rn/us -ī *m.* lake near Cumae, said to be an entrance to the lower world; the lower world. *a.* birdless; of Avernus; infernal. **-ā'lis** *a.* of lake Avernus.
āverru'nc/ō -ā're *vt.* avert.
āversā'bilis *a.* abominable.
āve'rs/or -ā'rī -ā'tus *vi.* turn away. *vt.* repulse, decline.
āve'rs/or -ō'ris *m.* embezzler.
āve'rs/us *ppp.* āvertō. *a.* in the rear, behind, backwards; hostile, averse. **-ūm** -ī *n.* back.
āve'r/tō -tere -tī -sum *vt.* turn aside, avert; divert; embezzle; estrange. *vi.* withdraw.
a'vi/a -ae *f.* grandmother.
aviā'ri/us *a.* of birds. **-um** -ī *n.* aviary, haunt of birds.
avi'dit/ās -ā'tis *f.* eagerness, longing; avarice.
a'vid/us *a.* eager, covetous; avaricious, greedy; hungry; vast. **-ē** *ad.*
a'v/is -is *f.* bird; omen. — alba a rarity.
avī'tus *a.* of a grandfather; ancestral.
ā'vi/us *a.* out of the way, lonely, untrodden; wandering, astray. **-a** -ō'rum *n.pl.* wilderness.
āvocāme'nt/um -ī *n.* relaxation.
āvocā'ti/ō -ō'nis *f.* diversion.
ā'voc/ō -ā're *vt.* call off; divert, distract; amuse.
ā'vol/ō -ā're *vi.* fly away, hurry away; depart, vanish.
āvo'lsus, avulsus *ppp.* avellō.
avu'ncul/us -ī *m.* uncle (on mother's side). — **māgnus** great-uncle.
a'v/us -ī *m.* grandfather; ancestor.
A'xen/us -ī *m.* Black Sea.
axi'ci/a, axi'ti/a -ae *f.* scissors.
āxi'll/a -ae *f.* arm-pit.
a'xis -is *m.* axle, chariot; axis, pole, sky, clime; plank.
azȳ'mus *a.* unleavened.

B

babae' *interj.* (*expressing wonder or joy*) oho!
Ba'byl/ōn -ō'nis *f.* ancient city on the Euphrates.. **-ō'nia** *f.* the country under Babylon.

-ō'nius *a.* Babylonian, Chaldaean, versed in astrology.
-ō'nicus, -ōniē'nsis *a.*
bā'c/a -ae *f.* berry; olive; fruit; pearl.
bācā'tus *a.* of pearls.
ba'cca, *see* **bāca**.
ba'ccar -is *n.* cyclamen.
Ba'cch/a -ae *f.* Bacchante.
Bacchā'n/al -ā'lis *n.* place consecrated to Bacchus; (*pl.*) festival of Bacchus.
bacchā'ti/ō -ō'nis *f.* revel.
Bacchi'ad/ae -ā'rum *m.pl.* kings of Corinth, founders of Syracuse.
ba'cch/or -ā'rī -ā'tus *vi.* celebrate the festival of Bacchus; revel, rave; rage.
Ba'cch/us -ī *m.* god of wine, vegetation, poetry, and religious ecstasy; vine, wine.
-ē'us -icus, -ius *a.*
bā'cifer -ī *a.* olive-bearing.
baci'll/um -ī *n.* stick, lictor's staff.
Ba'ctr/a -ō'rum *n.pl.* capital of Bactria in central Asia, *mod.* Balkh. **-iā'nus, -ius** *a.* **-iā'na** *f.* Bactria.
ba'cul/um -ī *n.* **-us** -ī *m.* stick, staff.
Bae't/is -is *m.* river in Spain. *mod.* Guadalquivir. **-icus** *a.* **-ica** *f.* Roman province. *mod.* Andalusia.
Ba'grad/a -ae *m.* river in Africa, *mod.* Mejerdah.
Bā'i/ae -ā'rum *f.pl.* Roman spa on Bay of Naples. **-ā'nus** *a.* [thing heavy).
bā'iul/ō -ā're *vt.* carry (some-
bā'iul/us -ī *m.* porter.
bālae'n/a -ae *f.* whale.
ba'lan/us -ī *f.* balsam (from an Arabian nut); a shell-fish.
ba'latr/ō -ō'nis *m.* jester.
bālā't/us -ūs *m.* bleating.
ba'lbus *a.* stammering.
balbū't/iō -ī're *vt.* & *i.* stammer, speak indistinctly; (*fig.*) speak obscurely.

Baliā'r/ēs -ium *f.pl.* Balearic islands. **-is, -icus** *a.*
bali'neum etc., *see* **balneum** etc.
balli'st/a -ae *f.* (*mil.*) catapult for shooting stones and other missiles; (*fig.*) weapon.
ballistā'r/ium -ī & iī *n.* catapult. [baths.
ba'lne/ae -ā'rum *f.pl.* bath,
balneā'ri/us *a.* of the baths. **-a** -ō'rum *n.pl.* bath room.
balneā't/or -ō'ris *m.* bath superintendent.
balne'ol/um -ī *n.* small bath.
ba'lne/um -ī *n.* bath.
bā'l/ō -ā're *vi.* bleat.
ba'lsam/um -ī *n.* balsam, balsam-tree.
ba'lte/us -ī *m.*, **-a** -ō'rum *n.pl.* belt, *esp.* sword-belt; woman's girdle; strapping.
Bandu'si/a -ae *f.* spring near Horace's birthplace.
bapti'sma -tis *n.* baptism.
bapti'z/ō -ā're *vt.* (*eccl.*) baptize.
ba'rathr/um -ī *n.* abyss; the lower world; (*fig.*) a greedy person.
ba'rb/a -ae *f.* beard.
ba'rbarē *ad.* in a foreign language, in Latin; in an uncivilized way; roughly, cruelly.
barba'ri/a -ae **-ēs** *acc.* **-em** *f.* a foreign country, outside Greece or Italy; (*words*) barbarism; (*manners*) rudeness, stupidity.
barba'ricus *a.* foreign, outlandish; Italian.
ba'rbarus *a.* foreign, barbarous; (*to a Greek*) Italian; rude, uncivilized; savage, barbarous. *m.* foreigner, barbarian. [beard.
barbā'tulus *a.* with a little
barbā'tus *a.* bearded, adult; ancient (Romans); of philosophers.
ba'rbiger -ī *a.* bearded.

ba'rbit/os *acc.* **-on** *m.* lyre, lute.
ba'rbul/a **-ae** *f.* little beard.
Ba'rc/ās **-ae** *m.* ancestor of Hannibal. **-ī'nus** *a.*
ba'rdus *a.* dull, stupid.
ba'rd/us **-ī** *m.* Gallic minstrel.
bā'r/ō **-ō'nis** *m.* dunce.
ba'rr/us **-ī** *m.* elephant.
bascau'd/a **-ae** *f.* basket (for the table).
bāsiā'ti/ō **-ō'nis** *f.* kiss.
basi'lic/a **-ae** *f.* public building used as exchange and law-court.
basi'lic/us *a.* royal, magnificent. *m.* highest throw at dice. **-ē** *ad.* royally, in magnificent style. **-um -ī** *n.* regal robe.
bā'si/ō **-ā're** *vt.* kiss.
ba's/is **-is** *f.* pedestal, base.
bā's/ium **-ī** & **iī** *n.* kiss.
Ba'ssar/eus **-eī** *m.* Bacchus.
Batā'v/ī **-ō'rum** *m.pl.* people of Batavia, *mod.* Holland.
bati'll/um **-ī** *n.* fire-pan.
Batti'ad/ēs **-ae** *m.* Callimachus.
bā'tu/ō **-ere** **-ī** *vt.* beat.
bau'b/or **-ā'rī** *vi.* (*of dogs*) howl.
Bau'c/is **-idis** *f.* wife of [Philemon.
beā'tit/ās **-ā'tis** *f.* happiness.
beātitū'd/ō **-inis** *f.* happiness.
beā'tul/us **-ī** *m.* the blessed man.
beā't/us *a.* happy; prosperous, well-off; rich, abundant. **-ē** *ad.*
Bēdriā'c/um **-ī** *n.* village in N. Italy. **-ē'nsis** *a.*
Be'lg/ae **-ā'rum** *m.pl.* people of N. Gaul, *mod.* Belgium.
Bē'lid/es **-um** *f.pl.* Danaids.
bellā'ri/a **-ō'rum** *n.pl.* dessert, confectionery.
bellā't/or **-ō'ris** *m.* warrior, fighter. *a.* warlike.
bellātō'rius *a.* aggressive.
bellā'tr/īx **-ī'cis** *f.* warrioress. *a.* warlike.
Belle'roph/ōn **-o'ntis** *m.* slayer of Chimaera, rider of Pegasus. **-ontē'us** *a.*
bellicō'sus *a.* warlike.
be'llic/us *a.* of war, military. **-um canere** give the signal for marching or attack.
be'lliger **-ī** *a.* martial.
belli'ger/ō **-ā're** **-ā'vī** **-ā'tum** *vi.* wage war. [in war.
belli'pot/ēns **-e'ntis** *a.* strong
be'll/ō **-ā're** **-ā'vī** **-ā'tum** *vi.* fight, wage war. **-or -ā'rī** *vi.* fight. [war.
Bellō'n/a **-ae** *f.* goddess of
be'llulus *a.* pretty.
be'll/um **-ī** *n.* war, warfare; battle. **-ī** in war.
be'll/us *a.* pretty, handsome; pleasant, nice. **-ē** *ad.* well, nicely. **— habēre** be well (in health).
bē'lu/a **-ae** *f.* beast, monster (*esp.* large and fierce); any animal; (*fig.*) brute. **— Gaetula** **India** elephant.
bēluā'tus *a.* embroidered with animals.
bēluō'sus *a.* full of monsters.
Bē'l/us **-ī** *m.* Baal; an oriental king. **-ī'dēs** **-ī'dae** *m.* Danaus, Aegyptus, Lynceus. **-ides** **-idum** *f.pl.* Danaids.
Bēnā'c/us **-ī** *m.* lake in N. Italy, *mod.* Garda.
be'ne *ad.* (*comp.* **melius** *sup.* **optimē**) well; correctly; profitably; very. *interj.* bravo! good! **— dīcere** speak well; speak well of, praise. **—emere** buy cheap. **—est tibi** you are well off. **— facere** do well; do good to. **— facis** thank you. **rem — gerere** be successful. **— sē habēre** have a good time. **— habet** all is well, it's all right. **— merērī dē** do a service to. **— partum** honestly acquired. **— tē!** your health! **— vēndere** sell at a high price. **— vīvere** live a happy life.

bened/ī'co -ī'cere ī'xī -ī'ctum *vt.* speak well of, praise; (*eccl.*) bless.
benedi'cti/ō -ō'nis *f.* (*eccl.*) blessing.
benefice'nti/a -ae *f.* kindness.
beneficiā'ri/ī -ō'rum *m.pl.* privileged soldiers.
benefi'c/ium -ī & iī *n.* benefit, favour; (*pol., mil.*) promotion. -ō tuō thanks to you.
bene'ficus *a.* generous, obliging.
Beneve'nt/um -ī *n.* town in S. Italy, *mod.* Benevento. -ā'nus *a.*
bene'vol/ēns -e'ntis *a.* kind-hearted.
benevole'nti/a -ae *f.* goodwill, friendliness.
bene'vol/us *a.* kindly, friendly; (*of servants*) devoted. -ē *ad.*
beni'gnē *ad.* willingly, courteously; generously; (*colloq.*) no thank you. — facere do a favour.
beni'gnit/ās -ā'tis *f.* kindness; liberality, bounty.
beni'gnus *a.* kind, friendly; favourable; liberal, lavish; fruitful, bounteous.
be'/ō -ā're -ā'vī -ā'tum *vt.* gladden, bless, enrich.
Berecy'nt/us -ī *m.* mountain in Phrygia sacred to Cybele. **-ius** *a.* of Berecyntus; of Cybele. -ia *f.* Cybele.
Bereni'c/ē -ēs *f.* a queen of Egypt. coma -ēs a constellation.
bēry'll/us -ī *m.* beryl.
bēs be'ssis *m.* two-thirds of the as; two-thirds.
bē'sti/a -ae *f.* beast; wild animal for the arena.
bēstiā'rius *a.* of beasts. *m.* beast-fighter in the arena.
bēsti'ol/a -ae *f.* small animal.
bē't/a -ae *f.* beet.
bē'ta *n.* *indecl.* Greek letter beta.
bi'bī *perf.* bibō.
bibliopō'l/a -ae *m.* bookseller.
bibliothē'c/a -ae, -ē -ēs *f.* library.
bi'b/ō -ere -ī *vt.* drink; live on the banks of (a river); drink in, absorb; (*fig.*) listen attentively, be imbued. — aquas be drowned. Graecō mōre — drink to one's health.
bi'bulus *a.* fond of drink, thirsty; (*things*) thirsty.
Bi'bul/us -ī *m.* consul with Caesar in 59 B.C.
bi'c/eps -i'pitis *a.* two-headed.
bicli'n/ium -ī & iī *n.* dining-couch for two.
bi'col/or -ō'ris *a.* two-coloured.
bico'rniger -ī *a.* two-horned.
bico'rnis *a.* two-horned, two-pronged; (*rivers*) two-mouthed.
bico'rpor -is *a.* two-bodied.
bi'd/ēns -e'ntis *a.* with two teeth or prongs. *m.* hoe. *f.* sheep, or other sacrificial animal.
bide'nt/al -ā'lis *n.* a place struck by lightning.
bi'du/um -ī *n.* two days.
bie'nn/ium -ī & iī *n.* two years.
bifā'riam *ad.* in two parts, twice.
bi'fer -ī *a.* flowering twice a year.
bi'fidus *a.* split in two.
bi'foris *a.* double-doored; double.
bifōrmā'tus, bifō'rmis *a.* with two forms.
bi'fr/ōns -o'ntis *a.* two-headed.
bifu'rcus *a.* two-pronged, forked.
bī'g/ae -ā'rum *f.pl.* chariot and pair.
bīgā'tus *a.* stamped with a chariot and pair.
bi'iugis, bi'iug/us *a.* yoked. -ī -ō'rum *m.pl.* two horses

yoked abreast; chariot with two horses.
bili'br/a -ae *f.* two pounds. **-is** *a.* holding two pounds.
bili'nguis *a.* double-tongued; bilingual; deceitful.
bī'l/is -is *f.* bile, gall; (*fig.*) anger, displeasure. — ātra, nigra melancholy; madness.
bil/īx -ī'cis *a.* double-stranded.
bilū'stris *a.* ten years.
bi'maris *a.* between two seas.
bimarī't/us -ī *m.* bigamist.
bimā't/er -ris *a.* having two mothers.
bime'mbris *a.* half man, half beast; (*pl.*) Centaurs.
bimē'stris *a.* of two months, two months old.
bī'mulus *a.* only two years old.
bī'mus *a.* two years old, for two years.
bī'nī bī'nae bī'na *num.* two each, two by two; a pair; (*with pl. nouns having s. meaning*) two.
bino'ct/ium -ī & iī *n.* two nights.
binō'minis *a.* with two names.
Bi'/ōn -ō'nis *m.* satirical philosopher. **-ōnē'us** *a.* satirical.
bipa'lmis *a.* two spans long.
bipartī't/us *a.* divided in two. **-ō** *ad.* in two parts, in two directions.
bi'pat/ēns -e'ntis *a.* double-[opening.
bipedā'lis *a.* two feet long broad or thick.
bipe'nnifer -ī *a.* wielding a battle-axe.
bipe'nnis *a.* two-edged. *f.* battle-axe.
bipertī'tō, *see* **bipartītō**.
bi'p/ēs -edis *a.* two-footed. *m.* biped.
birē'mis *a.* two-oared; with two banks of oars. *f.* two-oared skiff; galley with two banks of oars.

bis *ad.* twice, double. — ad eundem make the same mistake twice. — diē, in diē twice a day. —tantō, tantum twice as much. — terque frequently. — terve seldom.
bisse'xt/us -ī *m.* intercalary day after 24th Feb.
Bi'ston/es -um *m.pl.* people of Thrace. **-ius** *a.* Thracian. **-is** *f.* Thracian woman, Bacchante.
bisulcili'ngu/a -ae *a.* fork-tongued, deceitful.
bisu'lcus *a.* cloven.
Bīthȳ'n/ia -iae *f.* province of Asia Minor. **-icus, -ius, -us** *a.*
bī't/ō -ere *vi.* go.
bitū'm/en -inis *n.* bitumen, a kind of pitch. **-i'neus** *a.*
bi'vi/us *a.* two-way. **-um** *n.* two ways.
blae'sus *a.* lisping, indistinct.
blandi'dicus *a.* fair-spoken.
blandiloque'nti/a -ae *f.* attractive language.
blandi'loqu/us, -e'ntulus *a.* fair spoken.
blandīme'nt/um -ī *n.* compliment, allurement.
bla'nd/ior -ī'ri -ī'tus *vi.* coax, caress; flatter, pay compliments; (*things*) please, entice.
blandi'ti/a -ae *f.* caress, flattery; charm, allurement.
blandī'tim *ad.* caressingly.
bla'nd/us *a.* smooth-tongued, flattering, fawning; charming, winsome. **-ē** *ad.*
bla'ter/ō -ā're *vi.* babble.
bla't/iō -ī're *vt.* babble.
bla'tt/a -ae *f.* cockroach.
ble'nn/us -ī *m.* idiot.
bli'teus *a.* silly.
bli't/um -ī *n.* kind of spinach.
boā'ri/us *a.* of cattle. forum -um cattle market in Rome.
Bodo'tri/a -ae *f.* Firth of Forth.
Boeō't/ia -iae *f.* district of

central Greece. **-ius, -us** *a.* **-a'rchēs** *m.* chief magistrate of Boeotia.
boi'/ae -ā'rum *f.pl.* collar.
Boi'/ī -ō'rum *m.pl.* people of S.E. Gaul.
Boiohae'm/ī -ō'rum *m.pl.* Bohemians.
bōlē't/us -ī *m.* mushroom.
bo'lu/s -ī *m.* (*dice*) throw; (*net*) cast; (*fig.*) haul, piece of good luck; titbit.
bo'mb/us -ī *m.* booming, humming, buzzing.
bombȳ'cinus *a.* of silk.
bo'mb/ȳx -ȳcis *m.* silkworm; silk.
Bo'n/a De'/a -ae -ae *f.* goddess worshipped by women.
bo'nit/ās -ā'tis *f.* goodness; honesty, integrity; kindness, affability.
Bonō'ni/a -ae *f.* town in N. Italy, *mod.* Bologna. **-ē'nsis** *a.*
bo'n/um -ī *n.* a moral good; advantage, blessing; (*pl.*) property. **cui -ō?** who was the gainer?
bo'n/us *a.* (*comp.* melior *sup.* optimus) good; kind; brave; loyal; beneficial; lucky. *m.pl.* upper class party, conservatives. **-a aetās** prime of life. **-ō animō** of good cheer; well-disposed. **-ae artēs** integrity; culture, liberal education. **-a dicta** witticisms. **-a fidēs** good faith. **-ī mōrēs** morality. **-ī nummī** genuine money. **-a pars** large part; conservative party. **-ae rēs** comforts, luxuries; prosperity; morality. **-ā veniā** with kind permission. **-a verba** words of good omen; well-chosen diction. **-a vōx** loud voice.
bo'ō -ā're *vi.* cry aloud.
Boō't/ēs -ae *n.* constellation containing Arcturus.
Bo're/ās -ae *m.* north wind; north. **-us** *a.*
Bory'sthen/ēs -is *m.* river Dnieper. **-ius** *a.* **-idae** *m.pl.* dwellers near the Dnieper.
bōs bo'vis *m., f.* ox, cow; kind of turbot. — **Lūca** elephant. **bovī clītellās impōnere** *put a round peg in a square hole.*
Bo'spor/us -ī *m.* strait from Black Sea to Sea of Marmora. **-ius** *a.* — **Cimme'rius** strait from Sea of Azov to Black Sea. **-ā'nus** *a.*
Boudi'cc/a -ae *f.* British queen, falsely called Boadicea.
bovā'rius, *see* **boārius**.
Bovi'll/ae -ā'rum *f.pl.* ancient Latin town. **-ā'nus** *a.*
bovi'llus *a.* of oxen.
brā'c/ae -ā'rum *f.pl.* trousers.
brācā'tus *a.* trousered; barbarian, *esp.* of tribes beyond the Alps.
bracchiā'lis *a.* of the arm.
bracchi'ol/um -ī *n.* dainty arm.
bra'cch/ium -ī & iī *n.* arm, fore-arm; (*shell-fish*) claw; (*tree*) branch; (*sea*) arm; (*naut.*) yard-arm; (*mil.*) outwork, mole. **levī, mollī bracchiō** casually.
bra'ctea, *see* **brattea**.
bra'ssic/a -ae *f.* cabbage.
bra'tte/a -ae *f.* gold leaf.
bratte'ol/a -ae *f.* very fine gold leaf.
Bre'nn/us -ī *m.* Gallic chief who defeated the Romans.
breviā'r/ium -ī & iī *n.* summary, statistical survey, official report.
brevi'culus *a.* shortish.
brevi'loqu/ēns -ē'ntis *a.* brief.
bre'v/is *a.* short, small, shallow; brief, short-lived; concise. **-ī** *ad.* shortly, soon; briefly, in a few words. **-iter** *ad.* concisely. **-ia -ium** *n.pl.* shoals.
bre'vit/ās -ā'tis *f.* shortness,

smallness; brevity, conciseness.
Briga'nt/ēs -um *m.pl.* British tribe in N. England. **-icus** *a.*
Brīsē'/is -idos *f.* captive of Achilles.
Brita'nn/ia -iae *f.* Britain; the British Isles. **-us**, **-icus** *a.* -icus *m.* son of emperor Claudius.
Bro'm/ius -ī & iī *m.* Bacchus.
brū'm/a -ae *f.* winter solstice, midwinter; winter.
brūmā'lis *a.* of the winter solstice; wintry. — flexus tropic of Capricorn.
Brundi's/ium -ī & iī *n.* port in S.E. Italy. *mod.* Brindisi. **-ī'nus** *a.*
Bru'tti/ī -ō'rum *m.pl.* people of the toe of Italy. -us *a.*
brū'tus *a.* heavy, unwieldy; stupid, irrational.
Brū't/us -ī *m.* liberator of Rome from kings; murderer of Caesar.
bubī'l/e -is *n.* stall.
bū'b/ō -ō'nis *m., f.* owl.
bubu'lcit/or -ā'rī *vi.* drive oxen.
bubu'lc/us -ī *m.* ploughman.
bū'bul/us *a.* of cattle. **-a** -ae *f.* beef.
bū'caed/a -ae *m.* flogged slave.
bu'cc/a -ae *f.* cheek; mouth; ranter.
bu'cc/ō -ō'nis *m.* babbler.
bu'ccul/a -ae *f.* visor.
bucculе'ntus *a.* fat-cheeked.
bū'cerus *a.* horned.
bū'cin/a -ae *f.* shepherd's horn; military trumpet; night watch.
būcinā't/or -ō'ris *m.* trumpeter.
būco'lic/a -ō'rum *n.pl.* pastoral poetry.
bū'cul/a -ae *f.* young cow.
bū'f/ō -ō'nis *m.* toad.
bu'lb/us -ī *m.* bulb; onion.
bū'l/ē -es *f.* Greek senate. **-eu'ta** *m.* senator. **-eutē'rium** *n.* senate-house.

bu'll/a -ae *f.* bubble; knob, stud; gold charm worn round the neck by children of noblemen.
bullā'tus *a.* wearing the bulla; still a child.
būma'st/us -ī *f.* kind of vine.
bū'r/is -is *m.* plough-beam.
Bu'rrus, old form of Pyrrhus.
Busī'r/is -idis *m.* Egyptian king killed by Hercules.
busti'rap/us -ī *m.* grave-robber.
bustuā'rius *a.* at a funeral.
bu'st/um -ī *n.* funeral place; tomb, grave.
bu'xifer -ī *a.* famed for its box-trees.
bu'x/um -ī *n.* box-wood; flute, top, comb, tablet.
bu'x/us -ī *f.* box-tree; flute.
Byza'nt/ium -ī & iī *n.* city on Bosporus, later Constantinople, *mod.* Istanbul. **-ius** *a.*

C

caballī'nus *a.* horse's.
caba'll/us -ī *m.* horse.
cachinnā'ti/ō -ō'nis *f.* loud laughter.
cachi'nn/ō -ā're *vi.* laugh, guffaw.
cachi'nn/ō -ō'nis *m.* scoffer.
cachi'nn/us -ī *m.* laugh, derisive laughter; (*waves*) plashing.
ca'c/ō -ā're *vi.* evacuate the bowels. -ā'tus *a.* impure.
cacoē'th/es -is *n.* (*fig.*) itch.
ca'cul/a -ae *m.* soldier's slave.
cacū'm/en -inis *n.* extremity, point, summit, tree-top; (*fig.*) height, limit.
cacū'min/ō -ā're *vt.* make pointed.
Cā'c/us -ī *m.* giant robber, son of Vulcan.
cadā'ver -is *n.* corpse, carcass. **-ō'sus** *a.* ghastly.
Ca'dm/us -ī *m.* founder of Thebes. **-ē'is**, **-ē'ius**, **-ē'us**

a. of Cadmus; Theban. **-ē'a -ē'ae** *f.* fortress of Thebes. **-ē'is -ē'idis** *f.* Agave; Ino; Semele.

ca'd/ō -ere ce'cidī cā'sum *vi.* fall; droop, die, be killed; (*astr.*) set; (*dice*) be thrown; (*events*) happen, turn out; (*money*) be due; (*strength, speech, courage*) diminish, cease, fail; (*wind, rage*) subside; (*words*) end. — in suit, agree with; come under. — sub be exposed to. animis — be disheartened. causā — lose one's case.

cādūceā't/or -ō'ris *m.* officer with flag of truce.

cādū'ce/us -ī *m.* herald's staff; Mercury's wand. [staff.

cādū'cifer -ī *a.* with herald's

cadū'c/us *a.* falling, fallen; (*fig.*) perishable, fleeting, vain; (*law*) without an heir. *n.* property without an heir.

Cadu'rc/ī -ō'rum *m.pl.* Gallic tribe. **-um** -ī *n.* linen coverlet. [for wine); urn.

ca'd/us -ī *m.* jar, flask (*esp.*

caeci'genus *a.* born blind.

Caeci'l/ius -ī *m.* Roman name, *esp.* early Latin comic poet. **-iā'nus** *a.*

cae'cit/ās -ā'tis *f.* blindness.

cae'c/ō -ā're -ā'vī -ā'tum *vt.* blind; make obscure.

Cae'cub/um -ī *n.* choice wine from the Ager Caecubus in S. Latium.

cae'c/us *a.* blind; invisible, secret; dark, obscure; (*fig.*) aimless, unknown, uncertain. appāret -ō *it's as clear as daylight.* domus -a a house with no windows. -ā diē emere buy on credit. -um corpus the back.

cae'd/ēs -is *f.* murder, massacre; gore; the slain.

cae'd/ō -ere ceci'dī cae'sum *vt.* cut; strike; kill, cut to pieces; (*animals*) sacrifice.

caelā'm/en -inis *n.* engraved work.

caelā't/or -ō'ris *m.* engraver.

caelātū'r/a -ae *f.* engraving in bas-relief.

cae'l/ebs -ibis *a.* unmarried (bachelor or widower); (*trees*) with no vine trained on.

cae'l/es -itis *a.* celestial. *m.pl.* the gods.

caele'st/is -is *a.* of the sky, heavenly; divine; glorious. *m.pl.* the gods. *n.pl.* the heavenly bodies.

caelibā't/us -ūs *m.* celibacy.

caeli'col/a -ae *m.* god. [sky.

cae'lifer -ī *a.* supporting the

Cae'l/ius -ī *m.* Roman name; Roman hill. **-iā'nus** *a.*

cae'l/ō -ā're -ā'vī -ā'tum *vt.* engrave (in relief on metals), carve (on wood); (*fig.*) compose. [chisel.

cae'l/um -ī *n.* engraver's

cae'l/um -ī *n.* sky, heaven; air, climate, weather; (*fig.*) height of success, glory. -um ac terrās miscēre create chaos. ad -um ferre extol. dē -ō dēlāpsus a messiah. dē -ō servāre watch for omens. dē -ō tangī be struck by lightning. digitō -um attingere *be in the seventh heaven.* in -ō esse be overjoyed.

caeme'nt/um -ī *n.* quarry-stone, rubble.

caenō'sus *a.* muddy.

cae'n/um -ī *n.* mud, filth.

cae'p/a -ae *f.*, **cae'p/e** -is *n.* onion.

Cae'r/e *n.indecl.* (*gen.* -itis *abl.* -ē'te *f.*) ancient Etruscan town. **-es** -itis & ē'tis *a.* -ite cērā dignī like the disfranchised masses.

caerimō'ni/a -ae *f.* sanctity; veneration (for gods); religious usage, ritual.

caeru'leus, cae'rulus *a.* blue, dark blue, dark green, dusky. *n.pl.* the sea.

Cae'sar -is *m.* Julius, great Roman soldier, statesman, author; Augustus; the emperor. **-eus, -iā'nus, -ī'nus** *a.*
caesariā'tus *a.* bushy-haired.
caesa'ri/ēs -ēī *f.* hair.
caesī'cius *a.* bluish.
cae'sim *ad.* with the edge of the sword; (*rhet.*) in short clauses.
cae'sius *a.* bluish grey, blue-eyed.
cae'sp/es -itis *m.* sod, turf; mass of roots.
cae'st/us -ūs *m.* boxing-glove.
cae'sus *ppp.* caedō.
cae'tr/a -ae *f.* targe. **-ā'tus** *a.* armed with a targe.
Caī'c/us -ī *m.* river in Asia Minor.
Cāiē't/a -ae, -ē -ēs *f.* town in Latium.
Cā'ius, *see* **Gaius.**
Ca'lab/er -rī *a.* Calabrian. **-ria** *f.* S.E. peninsula of Italy.
Ca'lam/is -idis *m.* Greek sculptor.
calami'st/er -rī *m.*, **-rum** -rī *n.* curling-iron; (*rhet.*) flourish. **-rā'tus** *a.* curled; foppish.
cala'mit/ās -ā'tis *f.* disaster; (*mil.*) defeat; (*agr.*) damage, failure.
calamitō's/us *a.* disastrous, ruinous; blighted, unfortunate. **-ē** *ad.*
ca'lam/us -ī *m.* reed; stalk; pen, pipe, arrow, fishing-rod.
calathi'sc/us -ī *m.* small basket.
ca'lath/us -ī *m.* wicker basket; bowl, cup.
calā't/or -ō'ris *m.* servant.
calcā'ne/um -ī *n.* heel.
ca'lc/ar -ā'ris *n.* spur.
calceāme'nt/um -ī *n.* shoe.
calceā'tus *ppp.* shod.
calceolā'r/ius -ī & iī *m.* shoemaker.
calce'ol/us -ī *m.* small shoe.
ca'lce/us -ī *m.* shoe.
Ca'lch/ās -a'ntis *m.* Greek prophet at Troy.
ca'lcitr/ō -ā're *vi.* kick; (*fig.*) resist.
ca'lc/ō -ā're -ā'vī -ā'tum *vt.* tread, trample on; (*fig.*) spurn.
ca'lcul/us -ī *m.* pebble, stone; draughtsman, counting-stone, reckoning; voting-stone. **-um** **redūcere** take back a move. **-ōs subdūcere** compute. **ad -ōs vocāre** subject to a reckoning.
caldā'rius *a.* with warm water.
ca'ldus, *see* **calidus.**
Calēdo'ni/a -ae *f.* the Scottish Highlands. **-us** *a.*
cale/fa'ciō, cal/fa'cio -fa'cere -fē'cī -fa'ctum *vt.* warm, heat; (*fig.*) provoke, excite.
calefa'ct/ō -ā're *vt.* warm.
Cale'ndae, *see* **Kalendae.**
ca'l/eō -ē're *vi.* be warm, be hot, glow; (*mind*) be inflamed; (*things*) be pursued with enthusiasm; be fresh.
Ca'l/ēs -ium *f.pl.* town in Campania. **-ē'nus** *a.* of Cales. *n.* wine of Cales.
calē'sc/ō -uī -ere *vi.* get hot; (*fig.*) become inflamed.
ca'lid/us, ca'ld/us *a.* warm, hot; (*fig.*) fiery, eager; hasty; prompt. *f.* warm water. *n.* warm drink. **-ē** *ad.* promptly.
calie'ndr/um -ī *n.* headdress of hair.
ca'lig/a -ae *f.* soldier's boot. **-ā'tus** *a.* heavily shod.
cālīginōsus *a.* misty, obscure.
cālī'g/ō -inis *f.* mist, fog; dimness, darkness; (*mind*) obtuseness; (*circs.*) trouble.
cālī'g/ō -ā're *vi.* be misty, be dim; cause dizziness.
Cali'gul/a -ae *m.* emperor Gaius.
ca'li/x -cis *m.* wine-cup; cooking-pot.
ca'll/eō -ē're *vi.* be thick-skinned; (*fig.*) be unfeeling; be wise, be skilful. *vt.* know, understand.

calli'dit/ās -ā'tis *f.* skill; cunning.
ca'llid/us *a.* skilful, clever; crafty. **-ē** *ad.*
Calli'mach/us -ī *m.* Greek poet of Alexandria.
Calli'op/ē **-ēs, -ē'a** -ē'ae *f.* Muse of epic poetry.
ca'll/is -is *m.* foot-path, mountain track; pass; hill-pastures.
Calli'st/ō -ūs *f.* daughter of Lycaon, the constellation Great Bear. [solid.
callō'sus *a.* hard-skinned;
ca'll/um -ī *n.* hard or thick skin; firm flesh; (*fig.*) callousness.
ca'l/ō -ā're -ā'vī -ā'tum *vt.* convoke.
cā'l/ō -ō'nis *m.* soldier's servant; drudge.
ca'l/or -ō'ris *m.* warmth, heat; (*fig.*) passion, love.
Ca'lp/ē -ēs *f.* Rock of Gibraltar.
Calpu'rn/ius -ī *m.* Roman name. **-iā'nus** *a.*
ca'lth/a -ae *f.* marigold.
ca'lthul/a -ae *f.* yellow dress.
ca'luī *perf.* calēscō.
calu'mni/a -ae *f.* chicanery, sharp practice; subterfuge; misrepresentation; (*law*) dishonest accusation, blackmail; being convicted of malicious prosecution. -am iūrāre swear that an action is brought in good faith.
calumniā't/or -ō'ris *m.* legal trickster, slanderer.
calu'mni/or -ā'rī -ā'tus *vt.* misrepresent, slander; (*law*) bring an action in bad faith. sē — depreciate oneself.
ca'lv/a -ae *f.* bald head.
calvi't/ium -ī & -iī *n.* baldness.
ca'lv/or -ā'rī *vt.* deceive.
ca'lvus *a.* bald.
ca'l/x -cis *f.* heel; foot. -ce petere, ferīre kick. adversus stimulum -cēs *kicking against the pricks.*
ca'l/x -cis *f.* pebble; lime, chalk; finishing-line, end. ad carceres ā -ce revocārī have to begin all over again.
Ca'lyd/ōn -ō'nis *f.* town in Aetolia. **-ō'nis, -ō'nius** *a.* Calydonian. *f.* Deianira. -ōnius amnis Achelous — hērōs Meleager. -ōnia rēgna Daunia in S. Italy.
Caly'ps/ō -ūs (*acc.* -ō) *f.* nymph who detained Ulysses in Ogygia.
camēlīnus *a.* camel's.
came'll/a -ae *f.* wine-cup.
camē'l/us -ī *m.* camel.
Camē'n/a -ae *f.* Muse; poetry.
ca'mer/a -ae *f.* arched roof.
Camerī'n/um -ī *n.* town in Umbria.
Ca'mer/s -tis, **-tī'nus** *a.* of Camerinum.
Cami'll/us -ī *m.* Roman hero, who saved Rome from the Gauls.
camī'n/us -ī *m.* furnace, fire; forge. oleum addere -ō *add fuel to the flames.*
ca'mmar/us -ī *m.* lobster.
Campā'n/ia -iae *f* district of W. Italy. **-icus, -ius, -us** *a.* Campanian, Capuan.
ca'mp/ē -ēs *f.* evasion.
campe'st/er -ris *a.* of the plain; of the Campus Martius. *n.* loin-cloth. *n.pl.* level ground.
ca'mp/us -ī *m.* plain; sports field; any level surface; (*fig.*) theatre, arena (of action, debate). — Martius level ground by the Tiber, used for assemblies, sports, military drills.
Camulodū'n/um -ī *n.* town of Trinobantes, *mod.* Colchester.
ca'mur -ī *a.* crooked.
canā'l/is -is *m.* pipe, conduit, canal.

cance'll/ī -ō'rum *m.pl.* grating, enclosure; barrier (in public places), bar of law-court.
ca'nc/er -rī *m.* crab; constellation Cancer; south, tropical heat; (*med.*) cancer.
candefa'c/iō -ere *vt.* make dazzlingly white.
candē'l/a -ae *f.* taper, tallow-candle; waxed cord. -am appōnere valvīs set the house on fire.
candēlā'br/um -ī *n.* candlestick, chandelier, lamp-stand.
ca'nd/ēns -e'ntis *a.* dazzling white; white-hot.
ca'nd/eō -ē're *vi.* shine, be white; be white hot.
candē'sc/ō -ere *vi.* become white; grow white-hot.
candidā't/us *a.* dressed in white. *m.* candidate for office. **-ō'rius** *a.* of a candidate.
candi'dulus *a.* pretty white.
ca'ndid/us *a.* white, bright; radiant, beautiful; clothed in white; (*style*) clear; (*mind*) candid, frank; (*circs.*) happy. -a sententia acquittal. **-ē** *ad.* in white; sincerely.
ca'nd/or -ō'ris *m.* whiteness, brightness, beauty; (*fig.*) brilliance; sincerity.
cā'n/eō -ē're -uī *vi.* be grey, be white. -ēns -e'ntis *a.* white.
cānē'sc/ō -ere *vi.* grow white; grow old. [star, Sirius.
canī'cul/a -ae *f.* bitch; Dog-
canī'nus *a.* dog's, canine; snarling, spiteful. — littera letter R.
ca'n/is -is *m., f.* dog, bitch; (*fig.*) shameless or angry person; hanger-on; (*dice*) lowest throw; (*astr.*) Canis Major, Canis Minor; (*myth*) Cerberus.
cani'str/um -ī *n.* wicker basket.
cāni'ti/ēs -ē'ī *f.* greyness; grey hair; old age.
ca'nn/a -ae *f.* reed; pipe; gondola.
ca'nnab/is -is *f.* hemp.
Ca'nn/ae -ā'rum *f.pl.* village in Apulia, scene of great Roman defeat by Hannibal. **-ē'nsis** *a.*
ca'nō ca'nere ce'cinī *vt.* & *i.* sing; play; sing about, recite, celebrate; prophesy; (*mil.*) sound; (*birds*) sing, crow.
ca'n/or -ō'ris *m.* song, tune, sound.
canō'r/us *a.* musical, melodious; sing-song. *n.* melodiousness.
Ca'ntab/er -rī *m.* Cantabrian. **-ria** -riae *f.* district of N. Spain. **-ricus** *a.*
cantā'm/en -inis *n.* charm.
ca'nthar/is -idis *f.* beetle; Spanish fly.
ca'nthar/us -ī *m.* tankard.
canthē'r/ius -ī & iī *m.* gelding. **-ī'nus** *a.* of a horse.
ca'ntic/um -ī *n.* aria in Latin comedy; song.
cantilē'n/a -ae *f.* old song, gossip. -am eandem canere keep harping on the same theme.
ca'nti/ō -ō'nis *f.* song; charm.
ca'ntit/ō -ā're -ā'vī -ā'tum *vt.* sing or play often.
Ca'nt/ium -ī & iī *n.* Kent.
cantiu'ncul/ae -ā'rum *f.pl.* fascinating strains.
ca'nt/ō -ā're -ā'vī -ā'tum *vt.* & *i.* sing; play; sing about, recite, celebrate; proclaim, harp on; use magic spells; sound; drawl.
ca'nt/or -ō'ris *m.*,**-rīx** -rī'cis *f.* singer, musician, poet; actor.
ca'nt/us -ūs *m.* singing, playing, music; prophecy; magic spell.
cā'nus *a.* white, grey, hoary; old. *m.pl.* grey hairs.
Canu's/ium -ī *n.* town in Apulia, famous for wool. **-ī'nus** *a.* [ness.
capā'cit/ās -ā'tis *f.* spacious-

ca'p/āx -ā'cis *a.* capable of holding, spacious, roomy; capable, able, fit.
capē'd/ō -inis *f.* sacrificial dish. **-u'ncula** *f.* small dish.
cape'll/a -ae *f.* she-goat; (*astr.*) bright star in Auriga.
Capē'n/a -ae *f.* old Etruscan town. **-ā's, -us** *a.* **Porta -a** Roman gate leading to the Via Appia. [the arm-pits.
ca'p/er -rī *m.* goat; odour of
cape'rr/ō -ā're *vi.* wrinkle.
cape'ss/ō -ere -ī'vī -ī'tum *vt.* seize, take hold of, try to reach, make for; take in hand, engage in. **rem pūblicam** — go in for politics.
capillā'tus *a.* long-haired; ancient.
capi'll/us -ī *m.* hair (of head or beard); a hair.
ca'p/iō -ere cē'pī ca'ptum *vt.* take, seize; catch, capture; (*mil.*) occupy, take prisoner; (*naut.*) make, reach (a goal); (*fig.*) captivate, charm, cheat; (*pass.*) be maimed, lose the use of; choose; assume (appearance), cultivate (habit) undertake (duty), conceive, form (ideas), experience (feeling), suffer (harm); receive, get, inherit; contain, hold; (*fig.*) bear, (*mind*) grasp. **cōnsilium** — come to a decision. **impetum** — gather momentum. **initium** — start. **oculō capī** lose an eye. **mente captus** insane. **cupidō eum cēpit** he felt a desire.
ca'pi/s -dis *f.* sacrificial bowl with one handle.
capistrā'tus *a.* haltered.
capi'str/um -ī *n.* halter, muzzle.
ca'pit/al -ā'lis *n.* capital crime.
capitā'lis *a.* mortal, deadly, dangerous; (*law*) capital; important, excellent.
ca'pit/ō -ō'nis *m.* big-head.
Capitō'l/ium -ī *n.* Roman hill with temple of Jupiter. **-ī'nus** *a.* of the Capitol; of Jupiter.
capitulā'tim *ad.* summarily.
capi'tul/um -ī *n.* small head; person, creature.
Cappado'ci/a -ae *f.* country of Asia Minor.
ca'pr/a -ae *f.* she-goat; odour of arm-pits; (*astr.*) Capella.
ca'pre/a -ae *f.* roe.
Ca'pre/ae -ā'rum *f.pl.* island of Capri.
capre'ol/us -ī *m.* roebuck; (*pl.*) cross-beams.
Caprico'rn/us -ī *m.* constellation Capricorn, associated with midwinter.
caprifī'c/us -ī *f.* wild fig-tree.
capri'genus *a.* of goats.
caprimu'lg/us -ī *m.* goatherd, rustic.
caprī'nus *a.* of goats.
ca'prip/ēs -edis *a.* goat-footed.
ca'ps/a -ae *f.* box (*esp.* for papyrus rolls).
ca'psō *archaic fut.* capiō.
ca'psul/a -ae *f.* small box. **dē -ā tōtus** *out of a bandbox.*
Ca'pt/a -ae *f.* Minerva.
captā'ti/ō -ō'nis *f.* catching at.
captā't/or -ō'ris *m.* one who courts; legacy-hunter.
ca'pti/ō -ō'nis *f.* fraud; disadvantage; (*argument*) fallacy, sophism.
captiō's/us *a.* deceptive; dangerous; captious. **-ē** *ad.*
captiu'ncul/a -ae *f.* quibble.
captī'vit/ās -ā'tis *f.* captivity; capture.
captī'vus *a.* captive, captured; of captives; *m., f.* prisoner of war.
ca'pt/ō -ā're -ā'vī -ā'tum *vt.* try to catch, chase; try to win, court, watch for; deceive, trap.
ca'ptus *ppp.* capiō. *m.* prisoner.
ca'pt/us -ūs *m.* grasp, notion.

Ca'pu/a -ae *f.* chief town of Campania.
capulā'ris *a.* due for a coffin.
ca'pul/us -ī *m.* coffin; handle, hilt.
ca'p/ut -itis *n.* head; top, extremity; (*rivers*) source, (more rarely) mouth; person, individual; life; civil rights; (*person*) chief, leader; (*towns*) capital; (*money*) principal; (*writing*) substance, chapter; principle, main point, the great thing. — cēnae main dish. -itis accūsāre charge with a capital offence. -itis damnāre condemn to death. -itis dēminūtiō loss of political rights. -itis poena capital punishment. -ita cōnferre confer in secret. in -ita per head. suprā -ut esse be imminent.
carba'seus *a.* linen, canvas.
ca'rbas/us -ī *f.* (*pl.* –a -ō'rum *n.*) Spanish flax, fine linen; garment, sail, curtain.
ca'rb/ō -ō'nis *m.* charcoal, embers.
carbōnā'r/ius -ī & iī *m.* charcoal-burner.
carbu'ncul/us -ī *m.* small coal; precious stone.
ca'rcer -is *m.* prison; jail-bird; barrier, starting-place (for races). ad -ēs ā calce revocārī have to begin all over again.
carcerā'rius *a.* of a prison.
carchē's/ium -ī & iī *n.* drinking-cup; (*naut.*) mast-head.
cardi'ac/us -ī *m.* dyspeptic.
ca'rd/ō -inis *m.* hinge; (*astr.*) pole, axis, cardinal point; (*fig.*) juncture, critical moment.
ca'rdu/us -ī *m.* thistle.
cāre'ct/um -ī *n.* sedge.
că'r/eō -ē're -uī *vi.* (*with abl.*) be free from, not have, be without; abstain from, be absent from; want, miss.
că'r/ex icis *f.* sedge.
Că'ri/a -ae *f.* district of S.W. Asia Minor. **Cār** -is *m.* Carian. **Că'ricus** *a.* Carian. *f.* dried fig. [dry rot.
ca'ri/ēs (*acc.* -em *abl.* -ē) *f.*
carī'n/a -ae *f.* keel; ship.
Carī'n/ae -ā'rum *f.pl.* district of Rome.
carinā'r/ius -ī & iī *m.* dyer of yellow.
cariō'sus *a.* crumbling; (*fig.*) withered.
că'r/is -idis *f.* kind of crab.
că'rit/ās -ā'tis *f.* dearness, high price; esteem, affection.
ca'rm/en -inis *n.* song, tune; poem, poetry, verse; prophecy; formula (in law, religion); moral text.
Carme'nt/is -is, –a -ae *f.* prophetess, mother of Evander. –ā'lis *a.*
carnā'r/ium -ī & iī *n.* flesh-hook; larder.
Carne'ad/ēs -is *m.* Greek philosopher, founder of the New Academy. –ē'us *a.*
ca'rnif/ex -icis *m.* executioner, hangman; scoundrel; murderer.
carnificī'n/a -ae *f.* execution; torture. -am facere be an executioner.
carni'fic/ō -ā're *vt.* behead, mutilate.
carnuf–, *see* **carnif–**.
ca'r/ō -nis *f.* flesh.
că'r/ō -ere *vt.* card.
Ca'rpath/us -ī *f.* island between Crete and Rhodes. –ius *a.* [shoe.
carpa'tin/a -ae *f.* leather
carpe'nt/um -ī *n.* two-wheeled coach.
ca'rp/ō -ere -sī -tum *vt.* pick, pluck, gather; tear off; browse, graze on; (*wool*) card; (*fig.*) enjoy, snatch; carp at, slander; weaken, wear down; divide up; (*journey*) go, travel.
ca'rptim *ad.* in parts; at

different points; at different times.
ca'rpt/or -ō'ris *m.* carver.
ca'rptus *ppp.* carpō.
ca'rr/us -ī *m.* waggon.
Carthā'g/ō -inis *f.* Carthage, near Tunis. **-iniē'nsis** *a.* — Nova town in Spain, *mod.* Cartagena.
caru'ncul/a -ae *f.* piece of flesh.
cā'r/us *a.* dear, costly; dear, beloved. **-ē** *ad.*
Cary'st/os -ī *f.* town in Euboea, famous for marble. **-ē'us** *a.*
ca's/a -ae *f.* cottage, hut.
ca'scus *a.* old.
cāse'ol/us -ī *m.* small cheese.
cā'se/us -ī *m.* cheese.
ca'si/a -ae *f.* cinnamon; spurge laurel.
Ca'spius *a.* Caspian.
Cassa'ndr/a -ae *f.* Trojan princess and prophetess, doomed never to be believed.
ca'ss/ēs -ium *m.pl.* net, snare; spider's web.
ca'ssid/a -ae *f.* helmet.
Cassi'op/ē -ēs, **Cassiepē'/a** -ae *f.* mother of Andromeda, a constellation.
ca'ss/is -idis *f.* helmet.
Ca'ss/ius -ī *m.* Roman family name. **-iā'nus** *a.*
ca'ss/ō -ā're *vi.* shake.
ca'ss/us *a.* empty; devoid of, without (*abl.*); vain, useless. — lūmine dead. in -um in vain.
Casta'li/a -ae *f.* spring on Parnassus, sacred to Apollo and the Muses. **-us, -s** *a.* **-des** -dum *f.pl.* Muses.
casta'ne/a -ae *f.* chestnut-tree; chestnut.
castellā'nus *a.* of a fortress. *m.pl.* garrison.
castellā'tim *ad.* in different fortresses.
caste'll/um -ī *n.* fortress, castle; (*fig.*) defence, refuge.
castē'ri/a -ae *f.* rowers' quarters.
castīgā'bilis *a.* punishable.
castīgāti/ō -ō'nis *f.* correction, reproof.
castīgā't/or -ō'ris *m.* reprover.
castī'g/ō -ā're -ā'vī -ā'tum *vt.* correct, punish; reprove; restrain. **-ā'tus** *a.* small, slender.
castimō'ni/a -ae *f.* purity, morality; chastity, abstinence.
ca'stit/ās -ā'tis *f.* chastity.
ca'st/or -oris *m.* beaver.
Ca'st/or -oris *m.* twin brother of Pollux, patron of sailors; star in Gemini.
casto're/um -ī *n.* odorous secretion of the beaver.
ca'str/a -ō'rum *n.pl.* camp; day's march; army life; (*fig.*) party, sect. — movēre strike camp. — mūnīre construct a camp. — pōnere pitch camp. bina — two camps.
castrē'nsis *a.* of the camp, military.
ca'str/ō -ā're *vt.* castrate; (*fig.*) weaken.
ca'str/um -ī *n.* fort.
ca'st/us *a.* clean, pure, chaste, innocent; holy, pious. **-ē** *ad.*
ca'sul/a -ae *f.* little cottage.
cā's/us -ūs *m.* fall, downfall; event, chance, accident; misfortune, death; opportunity; (*time*) end; (*gram.*) case. **-ū** by chance.
Catadū'p/a -ō'rum *n.pl.* Nile cataract near Syene.
cata'graphus *a.* painted.
Catamī't/us -ī *m.* Ganymede.
cataphra'ct/ēs -ae *m.* coat of mail. **-us** *a.* wearing mail.
ca'tapl/us -ī *m.* ship arriving.
catapu'lt/a -ae *f.* (*mil.*) catapult; (*fig.*) missile. **-ā'rius** *a.* thrown by catapult.
catara'ct/a -ae *f.* waterfall; sluice; drawbridge.
cata'st/a -ae *f.* stage, scaffold.
catē'i/a -ae *f.* javelin.

cate'll/us -ī *m.*, **-a** -ae *f.* puppy. [small chain.
catĕ'll/us -ī *m.*, **-a** -ae *f.*
catē'n/a -ae *f.* chain; fetter; (*fig.*) bond, restraint; series.
catēnā'tus *a.* chained, fettered.
cate'rv/a -ae *f.* crowd, band; flock; (*mil.*) troop, body; (*theat.*) company.
catervā'tim *ad.* in companies.
ca'thedr/a -ae *f.* arm-chair. sedan chair; teacher's chair.
catho'licus *a.* (*eccl.*) orthodox, universal.
Catilī'n/a -ae *m.* Catiline, conspirator suppressed by Cicero. **-ā'rius** *a.*
catī'll/o -ā're *vt.* lick a plate.
catī'll/us -ī *m.* small dish.
catī'n/us -ī *m.* dish, pot.
Ca't/ō -ō'nis *m.* famous censor and author, idealised as the pattern of an ancient Roman; famous Stoic and republican leader against Caesar. **-ōni-ā'nus** *a.* **-ōnī'nī** *m.pl.* Cato's supporters.
catō'n/ium -ī & ii *n.* the lower world.
Catu'll/us -ī *m.* Latin lyric poet. **-iā'nus** *a.*
ca'tul/us -ī *m.* puppy; cub, young of other animals.
ca't/us *a.* clever, wise; sly, cunning. **-ē** *ad.*
Cau'cas/us -ī *m.* Caucasus mountains. **-ius** *a.*
cau'd/a -ae *f.* tail. **-am** iactāre fawn. **-am** trahere be made a fool of.
cau'deus *a.* wooden.
cau'd/ex, cō'd/ex -icis *m.* trunk; block of wood; book, ledger; (*fig.*) blockhead.
caudicā'lis *a.* of wood-cutting.
Cau'd/ium -ī *n.* Samnite town. **-ī'nus** *a.*
cau'l/ae -ā'rum *f.pl.* opening; sheep-fold.
cau'l/is -is *m.* stalk; cabbage.
Cau'n/us -ī *f.* town in Caria. **-eus** *a.* Caunian. *f.pl.* dried figs. [innkeeper.
cau'p/ō -ō'nis *m.* shopkeeper,
caupō'n/a -ae *f.* shop, inn. **-ius** *a.*
caupō'n/or -ā'rī *vt.* trade in.
caupō'nul/a -ae *f.* tavern.
Cau'r/us, Cō'r/us -ī *m.* north-west wind.
cau's/a, cau'ss/a -ae *f.* cause, reason; purpose, sake; excuse, pretext; opportunity; connection, case, position; (*law*) case, suit; (*pol.*) cause, party; (*rhet.*) subject-matter. **-am agere, ōrāre** plead a case. **-am dēfendere** speak for the defence. **-am dīcere** defend oneself. **-ā** for the sake of. **cum -ā** with good reason. **quā dē -ā** for this reason. **in -ā esse** be responsible. **per -am** under the pretext.
causā'rius *a.* (*mil.*) unfit for service. [hat.
cau'si/a -ae *f.* Macedonian
causi'dic/us -ī *m.* advocate.
causi'fic/or -ā'rī *vi.* make a pretext.
cau's/or -ā'rī -ā'tus *vt.* & *i.* pretend, make an excuse of.
cau'ssa, *see* **causa.**
cau'sul/a -ae *f.* petty law-suit; slight cause.
cautē'l/a -ae *f.* caution.
cau't/ēs -is *f.* rock, crag.
cau'tim *ad.* warily.
cau'ti/ō -ō'nis *f.* caution, wariness; (*law*) security, bond, bail. **mihi — est** I must take care. **mea — est** I must see to it.
cau't/or -ō'ris *m.* wary person; surety.
cau't/us *ppp.* caveō. *a.* wary, provident; safe, secure. **-ē** *ad.* carefully, cautiously; with security.
cavae'd/ium -ī & -iī *n.* inner court of a house.
ca've/a -ae *f.* cage, stall, coop,

hive; (*theat.*) auditorium; theatre. prīma — upper class seats. ultima — lower class seats.
ca'v/eō -ē're cā'vī cau'tum *vt.* beware of, guard against. *vi.* (*with* ab *or abl.*) be on one's guard against; (*with dat.*) look after; (*with* nē) take care that . . . not; (*with* ut) take good care that; (*with subj. or inf.*) take care not to, do not; (*law*) stipulate, decree; (*bus.*) get a guarantee, give a guarantee, stand security. **cavē !** look out !
cave'rn/a -ae *f.* hollow, cave, vault; (*naut.*) hold.
cavi'll/a -ae *f.* jeering.
cavillā'ti/ō -ō'nis *f.* jeering, banter; sophistry.
cavillā't/or -ō'ris *m.* scoffer.
cavi'll/or -ā'rī -ā'tus *vt.* scoff at. *vi.* jeer, scoff; quibble.
ca'v/ō -ā're -ā'vī -ā'tum *vt.* hollow, excavate.
ca'vus *a.* hollow, concave, vaulted; (*river*) deep-channelled. *n.* cavity, hole.
Cay'str/os, -us -ī *m.* river in Lydia, famous for swans.
-ce *demonstrative particle* appended to pronouns and adverbs.
Cē'/a -ae, Ce'/ōs *acc.* **-ō** *f.* Aegean island, birthplace of Simonides. **-us** *a.*
ce'cidī *perf.* cadō.
cecī'dī *perf.* caedō.
ce'cinī *perf.* canō.
Ce'crop/s -is *m.* ancient king of Athens. **-ius** *a.* Athenian. *f.* Athens. **-idēs -idae** *m.* Theseus; Athenian. **-is -idis** *f.* Aglauros; Procne; Philomela; Athenian, Attic.
cē'd/ō -ere ce'ssī ce'ssum *vi.* go, walk; depart, withdraw, retreat; pass away, die; (*events*) turn out; be changed (into); accrue (to); yield, be inferior (to). *vt.* give up, concede, allow. — **bonis, possessiōne** make over property (to). — **forō** go bankrupt. — **locō** leave one's post. — **memoriā** be forgotten.
ce'do (*pl.* ce'tte) *imp.* give me, bring here; tell me; let me; look at !
ce'dr/us -ī *f.* cedar, perfumed juniper; cedar-oil.
Celae'n/ō -ūs *f.* a Harpy; a Pleiad.
ce'leb/er -ris *a.* crowded, populous; honoured, famous; repeated. [celebration.
celebrā'ti/ō -ō'nis *f.* throng;
cele'brit/ās -ā'tis *f.* crowd; celebration; fame.
ce'lebr/ō -ā're -ā'vī -ā'tum *vt.* crowd, frequent; repeat, practise; celebrate, keep (a festival); advertise, glorify. **-ā'tus** *a.* full, much used; festive; famous.
ce'ler -is *a.* quick, swift, fast; hasty. **-iter** *ad.*
Ce'ler/ēs -um *m.pl.* royal bodyguard. [footed.
cele'rip/ēs -edis *a.* swift-
cele'rit/ās -ā'tis *f.* speed, quickness.
ce'ler/ō -ā're *vt.* quicken. *vi.* make haste.
ce'll/a -ae *f.* granary, stall, cell; garret, hut, small room; sanctuary of a temple.
cellā'rius *a.* of the storeroom. *m.* steward.
ce'llul/a -ae *f.* little room.
cē'l/ō -ā're -ā'vī -ā'tum *vt.* hide, conceal, keep secret. id mē -at he keeps me in the dark about it. **-ā'ta** *n.pl.* secrets.
ce'l/ōx -ō'cis *a.* swift. *f.* fast ship, yacht.
ce'lsus *a.* high, lofty; (*fig.*) great, eminent; haughty.
Ce'lt/ae -ā'rum *m.pl.* Celts, *esp.* of central Gaul. **-icus** *a.* Celtic. *n.* the Celtic nation.

Celtibē'r/ī -ō'rum *m.pl.* people of central Spain. **-ia** -iae *f.* their country. **-icus** *a.*

cē'n/a -ae *f.* dinner, the principal Roman meal. inter -am at table.

cēnā'cul/um -ī *n.* dining-room; upper room, garret.

cēnā'ticus *a.* of dinner.

cēnā'ti/ō -ō'nis *f.* dining-room.

Ce'nchre/ae -ā'rum *f.pl.* harbour of Corinth.

cē'nit/ō -ā're *vi.* be accustomed to dine.

cē'n/ō -ā're -ā'vī -ā'tum *vi.* dine. *vt.* eat, dine on. -ā'tus *ppa.* having dined, after dinner. *ppp.* spent in feasting.

cē'ns/eō -ē're -uī -um *vt.* (*census*) assess, rate, take a census, make a property return; (*fig.*) estimate, appreciate, celebrate; (*senate or other body*) decree, resolve; (*member*) express an opinion, move, vote; advise; judge, think, suppose, consider. **cēnsuī** -endō for census purposes.

cē'nsi/ō -ō'nis *f.* punishment; expression of opinion.

cē'ns/or -ō'ris *m.* censor; (*fig.*) severe judge, critic.

cēnsō'rius *a.* of the censors, to be dealt with by the censors; (*fig.*) severe. **homō** — an ex-censor. [criticism.

cēnsū'r/a -ae *f.* censorship;

cē'ns/us *ppp.* **cēnseō.** **capite** -ī the poorest class of Roman citizens.

cē'ns/us -ūs *m.* register of Roman citizens and their property, census; registered property; wealth. **-um agere, habēre** hold a census. **sine -ū** poor.

centaurē'/um -ī *n.* centaury.

Centau'r/us -ī *m.* Centaur, half-man half-horse. **-ē'us** *a.*

centē'n/ī -um *num.* a hundred each, a hundred.

centē'sim/us *a.* hundredth. *f.* hundredth part; (*interest*) 1 per cent monthly (12 per cent per annum).

ce'nticeps *a.* hundred-headed.

ce'nti/ēns -ēs *ad.* a hundred times. [handed.

centi'manus *a.* hundred-

ce'nt/ō -ō'nis *m.* patch-work. -ōnēs sarcīre *tell tall stories.*

ce'ntum *num.* a hundred.

centumge'minus *a.* hundred-fold. [fold.

centu'mplex *a.* hundred-

centumpo'nd/ium -ī & iī *n.* a hundred pounds.

centumvirā'lis *a.* of the centumviri.

centu'mvir/ī -ō'rum *m.pl.* a bench of judges who heard special civil cases in Rome.

centu'ncul/us -ī *m.* piece of patchwork, saddle-cloth.

centu'ri/a -ae *f.* (*mil.*) company; (*pol.*) century, a division of the Roman people according to property.

centuriā'tim *ad.* by companies, by centuries.

centuriā't/us *a.* divided by centuries. **comitia -a** assembly which voted by centuries.

centuriā't/us -ūs *m.* division into centuries; rank of centurion.

centu'ri/ō -ā're -ā'vī -ā'tum *vt.* (*mil.*) assign to companies; (*pol.*) divide by centuries.

centu'ri/ō -ō'nis *m.* (*mil.*) captain, centurion.

centu'ss/is -is *m.* a hundred asses.

cē'nul/a -ae *f.* little dinner.

Ce'ōs, *see* **Cea.**

Cē'ph/eus -eī (*acc.* -ea) *m.* king of Ethiopia, father of Andromeda. **-ē'is** *f.* Andromeda. **-ē'ius** *a.* of Cepheus. **-ē'us** *a.* Ethiopian.

Cēphī's/us -ī *m.* river in central Greece. **-is** *a.* **-ius** *m.* Narcissus.

cē'pī *perf.* capiō.
cē'r/a -ae *f.* wax; honey cells; writing-tablet, note-book; seal; portrait of an ancestor. prīma — first page.
Ceramī'c/us -ī *m.* Athenian cemetery.
cērā'r/ium -ī & iī *n.* seal-duty.
cera'st/ēs -ae *m.* a horned [serpent.
ce'ras/us -ī *f.* cherry-tree; cherry.
cērā'tus *a.* waxed.
Cerau'ni/ī, Cerau'ni/a -ō'rum *m., n.* mountains in Epirus.
Ce'rber/us -ī *m.* three-headed watch-dog of Hades. **-eus** *a.*
cercopithē'c/us -ī *m.* monkey.
cercū'r/us -ī *m.* Cyprian type of ship.
ce'rd/ō -ō'nis *m.* tradesman.
Cereā'l/is *a.* of Ceres; of corn, of meal. **-ia** -ium *n.pl.* festival of Ceres.
cerebrō'sus *a.* hot-headed.
ce'rebr/um -ī *n.* brain; understanding; quick temper.
Ce'r/ēs -eris *f.* goddess of agriculture; (*fig.*) grain, bread.
cē'reus *a.* waxen; wax-coloured; (*fig.*) supple, easily led. *m.* taper.
cēriā'ri/a -ae *f.* taper-maker.
cēri'nth/a -ae *f.* honey-wort.
cē'rin/a -ō'rum *n.pl.* wax-coloured clothes.
ce'rn/ō -ere crē'vī crē'tum *vt.* see, discern; understand, perceive; decide, determine; (*law*) decide to take up (an inheritance).
ce'rnuus *a.* face downwards.
cērō'm/a -atis *n.* wrestlers' ointment. **-a'ticus** *a* smeared. with wax-ointment.
cerrī'tus *a.* crazy.
certā'm/en -inis *n.* contest, match; battle, combat; (*fig.*) struggle, rivalry.
certā'tim *ad.* emulously.
certā'ti/ō -ō'nis *f.* contest; debate; rivalry.
ce'rtē *ad.* assuredly, of course; at least.
ce'rtō *ad.* certainly, really.
ce'rt/ō -ā're -ā'vī -ā'tum *vi.* contend, compete; (*mil.*) fight it out; (*law*) dispute; (*with inf.*) try hard.
ce'rt/us *a.* determined, fixed, definite; reliable, unerring; sure, certain. mihi -um est I have made up my mind. -um scīre, prō -ō habēre know for certain, be sure. -iōrem facere inform.
cē'rul/a -ae *f.* piece of wax. — miniāta red pencil.
cēru'ss/a -ae *f.* white-lead. **-ā'tus** *a.* painted with white-lead.
ce'rv/a -ae *f.* hind, deer.
cervī'c/al -ā'lis *n.* pillow.
cervī'cul/a -ae *f.* slender neck.
cervī'nus *a.* deer's.
ce'rv/īx -ī'cis *f.* neck. in -īcibus esse be a burden (to), threaten.
ce'rv/us -ī *m.* stag, deer; (*mil.*) palisade.
cessā'ti/ō -ō'nis *f.* delaying; inactivity, idleness.
cessā't/or -ō'ris *m.* idler.
ce'ssī *perf.* cēdō.
ce'ssi/ō -ō'nis *f.* giving up.
ce'ss/ō -ā're -ā'vī -ā'tum *vi.* be remiss, stop; loiter, delay; be idle, rest, do nothing; (*land*) lie fallow; err.
ce'strosphe'ndon/ē -ēs *f.* (*mil.*) engine for shooting stones.
ce'st/us -ī *m.* girdle (*esp.* of Venus).
cētā'r/ium -ī & iī *n.* fish-[pond.
cētā'r/ius -ī & iī *m.* fish-monger.
cē'ter/ī -ō'rum *a.* the rest, the others; (*s.*) the rest of. **-a** *ad.* in other respects. **-um** *ad.* for the rest, otherwise; but for all that; besides.

cēterō'quī, -n *ad.* otherwise.
Cethē'g/us -ī *m.* a conspirator with Catiline.
cētr-, *see* **caetr-.**
ce'tte, *see* **cedo.**
cē't/us -ī *m.* (**-ē** *n.pl.*) sea-monster, whale.
ceu *ad.* just as, as if.
Cē'/ȳx - ȳ'cis *m.* husband of Alcyone, changed to a kingfisher.
Cha'lci/s -dis *f.* chief town of Euboea. **-dē'nsis, -dicus** *a.*
Chald/ae'ī -aeō'rum *m.pl.* Chaldeans; astrologers. **-ā'icus** *a.*
chalybē'ius *a.* of steel.
Cha'lyb/es -um *m.pl.* a people of Pontus, famous as iron-workers.
cha'lyb/s -is *m.* steel.
Chā'on/es -um *m.pl.* a people of Epirus. **-ia -iae** *f.* their country. **-ius, -is** *a.*
Cha'/os (*abl.* **-ō**) *n.* empty space, the lower world, chaos.
cha'r/a -ae *f.* an unidentified vegetable.
chari'sti/a -ō'rum *n.pl.* a Roman family festival.
Cha'rit/es -um *f.pl.* the Graces.
Cha'r/ōn -o'ntis *m.* Charon, ferryman of Hades.
cha'rt/a -ae *f.* sheet of papyrus, paper; writing.
cha'rtul/a -ae *f.* piece of paper.
Chary'bd/is -is *f.* monster personifying a whirlpool in the Straits of Messina; (*fig.*) peril.
Cha'tt/ī -ō'rum *m.pl.* a people of central Germany.
Chē'l/ae -ā'rum *f.pl.* (*astr.*) the Claws (of Scorpio), Libra.
chely'dr/us -ī *m.* water-snake. [lyre.
che'l/ys (*acc.* **-yn**) *f.* tortoise;
chera'gr/a -ae *f.* gout in the hands.
Cherronē's/us, Chersonē's/us -ī *f.* Gallipoli peninsula; Crimea.
chīlia'rch/us -ī *m.* officer in charge of 1000 men; chancellor of Persia.
Chimae'r/a -ae *f.* fire-breathing monster formed of lion, goat and serpent. **-i'ferus** *a.* birthplace of C.
Chī'/os -ī *f.* Aegean island famous for wine. **Chī'us** *a.* Chian. *n.* Chian wine; Chian cloth.
chīro'graph/um -ī *n.* handwriting; document.
Chī'r/ōn -ō'nis *m.* a learned Centaur, tutor of heroes.
chīro'nom/os -ī *m., f.,* **-ōn -untis** *m.* mime actor.
chīrū'rgi/a -ae *f.* surgery; (*fig.*) violent measures.
chlamydā'tus *a.* wearing a military cloak.
chla'my/s -dis *f.* Greek military cloak. [Greek poet.
Choe'ril/us -ī *m.* inferior
chorā'g/ium -ī & iī *n.* producing of a chorus.
chorā'g/us -ī *m.* one who finances a chorus.
chorau'l/ēs -ae *m.* flute-player accompanying a chorus.
cho'rd/a -ae *f.* string (of an instrument); rope.
chorē'/a -ae *f.* dance.
chorē'/us -ī *m.* trochee.
cho'r/us -ī *m.* choral dance; chorus, choir of singers or dancers; band, troop.
Chri'st/us -ī *m.* Christ. **-iā'nus** *a.* Christian. **-iāni'sm/us -ī** *m.* Christianity.
Chrȳ's/ēs -ae *m.* priest of Apollo in the Iliad. **-ē'is -ē'idis** *f.* daughter of C.
Chrȳsi'pp/us -ī *m.* Stoic philosopher. **-ē'us** *a.*
chrȳso'lith/os -ī *m., f.* topaz.
chrȳ's/os -ī *m.* gold.
cibā'rius *a.* food-; common. *n.pl.* rations.
cibā't/us -ūs *m.* food.

cibō'r/ium -ī & iī *n.* kind of drinking-cup.
ci'b/us -ī *m.* food, fodder, nourishment.
cicā'd/a -ae *f.* cicala.
cicātrīcō'sus *a.* scarred.
cicātr/īx -ī'cis *f.* scar; (*plants*) mark of an incision. [pip.
ci'cc/us -ī *m.* pomegranate
ci'cer -is *n.* chick-pea.
Ci'cer/ō -ō'nis *m.* great Roman orator and author. **-ōniā'nus** *a.*
cichorē'/um -ī *n.* chicory.
Ci'con/es -um *m.pl.* people of Thrace.
cicō'ni/a -ae *f.* stork.
ci'cur -is *a.* tame.
cicū't/a -ae *f.* hemlock; pipe.
ci'eō ciē're cī'vī ci'tum *vt.* move stir, rouse; call, invoke; (*fig.*) give rise to, produce. **calcem** — make a move (in chess).
Cili'ci/a -ae *f.* country in S. Asia Minor, famous for piracy. **-ē'nsis**, **-us**.
Ci'li/x -cis **-ssa** *a.* Cilician. *a.* Cilician. *n.* goats' hair garment.
Cimbr/ī -ō'rum *m.pl.* people of N. Germany. **-icus** *a.*
cī'm/ex -icis *m.* bug.
Cimme'ri/ī -ō'rum *m.pl.* people of the Crimea; mythical race in caves near Cumae. **-us** *a.*
cinae'dius *a.* lewd.
cinae'd/us -ī *m.* sodomite; lewd dancer. [hair.
cincinnā'tus *a.* with curled
Cincinnā't/us -ī *m.* ancient Roman dictator.
cinci'nn/us -ī *m.* curled hair; (*fig.*) rhetorical ornament.
Ci'nc/ius -ī *m.* Roman tribune; Roman historian.
cincti'cul/us -ī *m.* small girdle.
ci'nctus *ppp.* **cingō.**
ci'nct/us -ūs *m.* girding. **— Gabīnus** a ceremonial style of wearing the toga.
cinctū'tus *a.* girded.
cinefa'ctus *a.* reduced to ashes.
cinerā'r/ius -ī & iī *m.* hair-curler.
ci'n/gō -gere -xī -ctum *vt.* surround, enclose; gird, crown; (*mil.*) besiege, fortify; cover, escort. **ferrum** -or I put on my sword.
ci'ngul/a -ae *f.* girth (of animals).
ci'ngul/um -ī *n.* belt.
ci'ngul/us -ī *m.* zone.
cinī'fl/ō -ō'nis *m.* hair-curler.
ci'n/is -eris *m.* ashes; (*fig.*) ruin.
Ci'nn/a -ae *m.* colleague of Marius; poet friend of Catullus.
cinnamō'm/um, **ci'nnam/-um** -ī *n.* cinnamon.
ci'nxī *perf.* **cingō.**
Cīny'phius *a.* of the Cinyps, river of N. Africa; African.
Ci'nyr/ās -ae *m.* father of Adonis. **-ē'ius** *a.*
ci'pp/us -ī *m.* tombstone; (*pl.*) palisade.
ci'rcā *ad.* around, round about. *pr.* (*with acc.*) (*place*) round, in the vicinity of, in; (*time, number*) about; with regard to.
circamoe'r/ium -ī & iī *n.* space on both sides of a wall.
Ci'rc/ē -ēs & ae *f.* goddess with magic powers living in Aeaea. **-ae'us** *a.*
circē'ns/is *a.* of the Circus. **-ēs** -ium *m.pl.* the games.
ci'rcin/ō -ā're *vt.* circle through. [passes.
ci'rcin/us -ī *m.* pair of com-
ci'rciter *ad* (*time, number*) about. *pr.* (*with acc.*) about, near.
circu'/eō, **circu'm/eō** -ī're -ī'vī & i'ī -itum *vt.* & *i.* go round, surround; (*mil.*) encircle; visit, go round canvassing; deceive.
circui'ti/ō, **circumi'ti/ō**

-ō'nis *f.* (*mil.*) rounds; (*speech*) evasiveness.
circu'itus *ppp.* circueō.
circu'it/us, circu'mit/us -ūs *m.* revolution; way round, circuit; (*rhet.*) period, periphrasis.
circulā't/or -ō'ris *m.* pedlar.
ci'rcul/or -ā'rī *vi.* collect in crowds.
ci'rcul/us -ī *m.* circle; orbit; ring; social group.
ci'rcum *ad* round about. *pr.* (*with acc.*) round, about; near. — insulās mittere send to the islands round about.
circu'm/agō -a'gere -ē'gī -ā'ctum *vt.* turn, move in a circle, wheel. *pass.* (*time*) pass; (*mind*) be swayed.
circu'mar/ō -ā're *vt.* plough round. [outline.
circumcaesū'r/a -ae *f.*
circumcī'/dō -dere -dī -sum *vt.* cut round, trim; cut down, abridge. -sus *a.* precipitous.
circumci'rcā *ad.* all round.
circumcī'sus *ppp.* circumcīdō.
circumclū'/dō -dere -sī -sum *vt.* shut in, hem in.
circu'mcol/ō -ere *vt.* live round about.
circumcu'rs/ō -ā're *vi.* run about.
circu'md/ō -are -edī -atum *vt.* put round; surround, enclose.
circumd/ū'cō -ū'cere -ū'xī -u'ctum *vt.* lead round, draw round; cheat; (*speech*) prolong, drawl. [dūcō.
circumdu'ctus *ppp.* circum-
circu'meō, *see* **circueō**.
circume'quit/ō -ā're *vt.* ride round.
circu'm/ferō -fe'rre -tulī -lā'tum *vt.* carry round, pass round; spread, broadcast; purify; (*pass.*) revolve.
circumfle'/ctō -ctere -xī -xum *vt.* wheel round.
circu'mfl/ō -ā're *vt.* (*fig.*) buffet.
circu'mflu/ō -ere -xī *vt.* & *i.* flow round; (*fig.*) overflow, abound.
circu'mfluus *a.* flowing round; surrounded (by water).
circumforā'neus *a.* itinerant; (*money*) borrowed.
circumf/u'ndō -u'ndere -ū'dī -ū'sum *vt.* pour round, surround; (*fig.*) crowd round, overwhelm; (*pass.*) flow round.
circu'mgem/ō -ere *vt.* growl round. [about.
circumge'st/ō -ā're *vt.* carry
circumgre'/dior -dī -ssus *vt.* & *i.* make an encircling move, surround.
circumia'c/eō -ē're *vi.* be adjacent.
circum/i'ciō -i'cere -iē'cī -ie'ctum *vt.* throw round, put round; surround. **-ie'ctus** *a.* surrounding. *n.pl.* neighbourhood.
circumie'ct/us -ūs *m.* enclosure; embrace.
circumit-, *see* **circuit-**.
circumlā'tus *ppp.* circumferō.
circu'mlig/ō -ā're -ā'vī -ā'tum *vt.* tie to, bind round.
circu'mli/nō -nere -tum *vt.* smear all over, bedaub.
circu'mlu/ō -ere *vt.* wash.
circumlu'vi/ō -ō'nis *f.* alluvial land.
circumm/i'ttō -i'ttere -ī'sī -i'ssum *vt.* send round.
circummoe'n/iō, circummū'n/iō -ī're -ī'vī -ī'tum *vt.* fortify. [investing.
circummūnī'ti/ō -ō'nis *f.*
circumpadā'nus *a.* of the Po valley.
circumpe'nd/eō -ē're *vi.* hang round.
circumplau'd/ō -ere *vt.* applaud on all sides.
circumple'/ctor -ctī -xus *vt.* embrace, surround.

circu'mplic/ō -ā're -ā'vī -ā'tum *vt.* wind round.
circump/ō'nō -ō'nere -o'suī -o'situm *vt.* put round.
circumpōtā'ti/ō -ō'nis *f.* passing drinks round.
circumrē't/iō -ī're -ī'vī -ī'tum *vt.* ensnare.
circumrō'd/ō -ere *vt.* nibble round about; (*fig.*) slander.
circumsae'p/iō -ī're -sī -tum *vt.* fence round.
circumsci'nd/ō -ere *vt.* strip.
circumscrī'/bō -bere -psī -ptum *vt.* draw a line round; mark the limits of; restrict, circumscribe; set aside; defraud. **-ptus** *a.* restricted; (*rhet.*) periodic. **-ptē** *ad.* in periods.
circumscrī'pti/ō -ō'nis *f.* circle, contour; fraud; (*rhet.*) period.
circumscrī'pt/or -ō'ris *m.* defrauder.
circumscrī'ptus *ppp.* circumscrībō. [round.
circu'msec/ō -ā're *vt.* cut
circums/e'dcō -edē're -ē'dī -e'ssum *vt.* blockade, beset.
circumsē'piō, *see* circumsaepiō.
circumse'ssi/ō -ō'nis *f.* siege.
circumse'ssus *ppp.* circumsedeō.
circumsī'd/ō -ere *vt.* besiege.
circumsi'l/iō -ī're *vi.* hop about; (*fig.*) be rampant.
circums/i'stō -i'stere -tetī surround.
circu'mson/ō -ā're *vi.* resound on all sides. *vt.* fill with sound.
circu'msonus *a.* noisy.
circumspectā'tr/īx -ī'cis *f.* spy.
circumspe'cti/ō -ō'nis *f.* caution.
circumspe'ct/ō -ā're *vt.* & *i.* look all round, search anxiously, be on the look-out.
circumspe'ctus *ppp.* circumspiciō. *a.* carefully considered, cautious.
circumspe'ct/us -ūs *m.* consideration; view.
circumsp/i'ciō -i'cere -e'xī -e'ctum *vi.* look all round; be careful. *vt.* survey; (*fig.*) consider, search for.
circu'mstetī *perf.* circumsistō: *perf.* circumstō.
circu'mst/ō -ā're -etī *vt.* & *i.* stand round; besiege; (*fig.*) encompass. **-a'ntēs** -a'ntium *m.pl.* by-standers.
circu'mstrep/ō -ere *vt.* make a clamour round.
circumsu'rg/ēns -e'ntis *pres.p.* rising on all sides.
circumten'tus *ppp.* covered tightly. [round.
circu'mter/ō -ere *vt.* crowd
circumte'xtus *ppp.* embroidered round the edge.
circu'mton/ō -ā're -uī *vt.* thunder about.
circumvā'/dō -dere -sī *vt.* assail on all sides.
circu'mvagus *a.* encircling.
circumva'll/ō -ā're -ā'vī -ā'tum *vt.* blockade, beset.
circumve'cti/ō -ō'nis *f.* carrying about; (*sun*) revolution.
circumve'ct/or -ā'rī travel round, cruise round; (*fig.*) describe.
circu'mve/hor -hī -ctus *vt.* & *i.* ride round, sail round; (*fig.*) describe.
circumvē'l/ō -ā're *vt.* envelop.
circumv/e'niō -enī're -ē'nī -e'ntum *vt.* surround, beset; oppress; cheat.
circumve'rt/ō, **circumvo'rt/ō** -ere *vt.* turn round.
circumve'st/iō -ī're *vt.* envelop. [about.
circumvi'nc/iō -ī're *vt.* lash
circumvī's/ō -ere *vt.* look at all round.
circumvo'lit/ō -ā're -ā'vī -ā'tum *vt.* & *i.* fly round; hover around.

circu'mvol/ō -ā're *vt.* fly round. [round.
circumvo'l/vō -vere *vt.* roll
ci'rc/us -ī *m.* circle; the Circus Maximus, famous Roman race-course; a race-course.
Ci'rrh/a -ae *f.* town near Delphi, sacred to Apollo. **-ae'us** *a.* [fringe.
ci'rr/us -ī *m.* curl of hair;
cis *pr.* (*with acc.*) on this side of; (*time*) within.
Cisalpī'nus *a.* on the Italian side of the Alps, Cisalpine.
ci's/ium -ī & iī *n.* two-wheeled carriage.
Cissē'i/s -dis *f.* Hecuba.
ci'st/a -ae *f.* box, casket; ballot-box.
ciste'll/a -ae *f.* small box.
cistellā'tr/īx -ī'cis *f.* keeper of the money-box.
ciste'llul/a -ae *f.* little box.
ciste'rn/a -ae *f.* reservoir.
cisto'phor/us -ī *m.* an Asiatic coin.
ci'stul/a -ae *f.* little box.
cit/e'rior (*sup.* -imus) *a.* on this side, nearer.
Cithae'r/ōn -ō'nis *m.* mountain range between Attica and Boeotia.
ci'thar/a -ae *f.* lute.
cithari'st/a -ae *m.*, **cithari'stri/a** -ae *f.* lute-player.
cithari'z/ō -ā're *vi.* play the lute.
citharoe'd/us -ī *m.* a singer who accompanies himself on the lute.
ci'timus *a.* nearest.
ci't/o (*com.* -ius *sup.* -i'ssimē) *ad.* quickly, soon. **nōn —** not easily.
ci't/ō -ā're -ā'vī -ā'tum *vt.* set in motion, rouse; call (by name), appeal to, cite, mention. **-ā'tus** *a.* quick, impetuous.
ci'trā *ad.* on this side, this way, not so far. *pr.* (*with acc.*) on this side of, short of; (*time*) before, since; apart from. **— quam** before.
ci'treus *a.* of citrus-wood.
ci'trō *ad.* hither, this way. **ultrō -que** to and fro.
ci'tr/us -ī *f.* citrus-tree; citron-tree.
ci'tus *ppp.* cieō. *a.* quick.
cī'vic/us *a.* civic, civil. **corōna -a** civic crown for saving a citizen's life in war.
cīvī'l/is *a.* of citizens, civil; political, civilian; courteous, democratic. **iūs -e** civil rights; Civil Law; code of legal procedure. **-iter** *ad.* like citizens; courteously.
cīvī'lit/ās -ā'tis *f.* politics; politeness.
cī'v/is -is *m. f.* citizen, fellow-citizen.
cī'vit/ās -ā'tis *f.* citizenship; community state; city. **-āte dōnāre** naturalize.
clā'd/ēs -is *f.* damage, disaster, ruin; defeat; (*fig.*) scourge. **dare -em** make havoc.
clam *ad.* secretly; unknown *pr.* (*with acc.*) unknown to **— mē habēre** keep from me.
clāmā't/or -ō'ris *m.* bawler.
clāmitā'ti/ō -ō'nis *f.* bawling.
clā'mit/ō -ā're -ā'vī -ā'tum *vt.* & *i.* bawl, screech cry out.
clā'm/ō -ā're -ā'vī -ā'tum *vt.* & *i.* shout, cry out; call upon, proclaim.
clā'm/or -ō'ris *m.* shout, cry; acclamation.
clāmō'sus *a.* noisy.
cla'nculum *ad.* secretly. *pr.* (*with acc.*) unknown to.
clandestī'n/us *a.* secret. **-ō** *ad.* [noise.
cla'ng/or -ō'ris *m.* clang,
clā'r/eō -ē're *vi.* be bright, be clear; be evident; be renowned.
clārē'sc/ō -ere **clā'ruī** *vi.* brighten, sound clear; become obvious; beome famous.
clārigā'ti/ō -ō'nis *f.* formal

ultimatum to an enemy; fine for trespass.
clā'rig/ō -ā're *vi.* deliver a formal ultimatum.
clāri'sonus *a.* loud and clear.
clā'rit/ās -ā'tis *f.* distinctness; (*rhet.*) lucidity; celebrity.
clāritū'd/ō -inis *f.* brightness; (*fig.*) distinction.
clā'r/ō -ā're *vt.* illuminate; explain; make famous.
Cla'r/os -ī *f.* town in Ionia, famous for worship of Apollo. -**ius** *a.* of Claros. *m.* Apollo.
clā'r/us *a.* (*sight*) bright; (*sound*) loud; (*mind*) clear; (*person*) distinguished. — intonāre thunder from a clear sky. vir -issimus a courtesy title for eminent men. -ē *ad.* brightly, loudly, clearly, with distinction.
classiā'rius *a.* naval. *m.pl.* marines.
classi'cul/a -ae *f.* flotilla.
cla'ssic/us *a.* of the first class; naval. *m.pl.* marines. -**um** -ī *n.* battle-signal; trumpet.
cla'ss/is -is *f.* a political class; army; fleet. [*m.pl.* cage.
clā'thr/ī, **clā'tr/ī** -ō'rum
clātrā'tus *a.* barred.
clau'd/eō -ē're, **clau'd/ō** -ere *vi.* limp; (*fig.*) be defective.
claudicā'ti/ō -ō'nis *f.* limping.
clau'dic/ō -ā're *vi.* be lame; waver, be defective.
Clau'd/ius -ī *m.* patrician family name, *esp.* Appius Claudius Caecus, famous censor; the Emperor Claudius. -**ius**, -**iā'nus**, -**iā'lis** *a.*
clau'/dō -dere -sī -sum *vt.* shut, close; cut off, block; conclude; imprison, confine, blockade. agmen — bring up the rear.
clau'dō, *see* **claudeō**.
clau'dus *a.* lame, crippled; (*verse*) elegiac; (*fig.*) wavering.
clau'sī *perf.* claudō.
clau'str/a -ō'rum *n.pl.* bar, bolt, lock; barrier, barricade, dam.
clau'sul/a -ae *f.* conclusion; (*rhet.*) ending of a period.
clau's/us *ppp.* claudō. -**um** -ī *n.* enclosure.
clāv'/a -ae *f.* club, knotty branch; (*mil.*) foil.
clāvā'r/ium -ī & iī *n.* money for buying shoe-nails.
clāvā't/or -ō'ris *m.* cudgel-bearer.
clāvi'cul/a -ae *f.* vine-tendril.
clā'viger -ī *m.* (*Hercules*) club-bearer; (*Janus*) key-bearer.
clā'v/is -is *f.* key.
clā'v/us -ī *m.* nail; tiller, rudder; purple stripe on the tunic, broad for senators, narrow for equites. -um anni movēre reckon the beginning of the year. [philosopher.
Clea'nth/ēs -is *m.* Stoic
clē'm/ēns -e'ntis *a.* mild, gentle, merciful; (*weather, water*) mild, calm. -**e'nter** *ad.* gently, indulgently; gradually.
clēme'nti/a -ae *f.* mildness, forbearance, mercy.
Cleopa'tr/a -ae *f.* queen of Egypt.
cle'p/ō -ere -sī -tum *vt.* steal.
clepsy'dr/a -ae *f.* water-clock used for timing speakers. -am dare give leave to speak. -am petere ask leave to speak.
cle'pt/a -ae *m.* thief.
cli'/ēns -e'ntis *m.* client, dependent; follower; vassal-state.
clie'nt/a -ae *f.* client.
clientē'l/a -ae *f.* clientship, protection; clients.
clien'tul/us -ī *m.* insignificant client.
clīnā'm/en -inis *n.* swerve.
clīnā'tus *a.* inclined.
Cli'/ō -ūs *f.* Muse of history.
clipeā'tus *a.* armed with a shield.

cli'pe/us -ī *m.*, **-um** -ī *n.* round bronze shield; disc; medallion on a metal base.
clite'll/ae -ā'rum *f.pl.* pack-saddle, attribute of an ass.
clitellā'rius *a.* carrying pack-saddles. [Umbria.
Clitu'mn/us -ī *m.* river in
clīvō'sus *a.* hilly.
clī'v/us -ī *m.* slope, hill. — sacer part of the Via Sacra.
cloā'c/a -ae *f.* sewer, drain.
Cloācī'n/a -ae *f.* Venus.
Clō'd/ius -ī *m.* Roman plebeian name, *esp.* the tribune, enemy of Cicero.
Cloe'li/a -ae *f.* Roman girl hostage, who escaped by swimming the Tiber.
Clō'th/ō (*acc.* -ō) *f.* one of the Fates.
clu'/eō -ē're, **-eor** -ē'rī *vi.* be called, be famed.
clū'n/is -is *m.*, *f.* buttock.
clūrī'nus *a.* of apes.
Clū's/ium -ī *n.* old Etruscan town, *mod.* Chiusi. **-ī'nus** *a.*
Clū's/ius -ī *m.* Janus.
Clytaemnē'str/a -ae *f.* wife of Agamemnon, whom she murdered.
Cni'd/us -ī *f.* town in Caria, famous for worship of Venus. **-ius** *a.*
coacervā'ti/ō -ō'nis *f.* accumulation. [accumulate.
coace'rv/ō -ā're *vt.* heap,
coac/ē'scō -ē'scere -uī *vi.* become sour.
coā'ct/ō -ā're *vt.* force.
coā'ct/or -ō'ris *m.* collector (of money). **-ōrēs agminis** rearguard.
coā'ctus *ppp.* cōgō.
coā'ct/us -ūs *m.* compulsion.
coaedi'fic/ō -ā're -ā'tum *vt.* build on.
coae'qu/ō -ā're -ā'vī -ā'tum *vt.* make equal, bring down to the same level.
coagmentā'ti/ō -ō'nis *f.* combination.
coagme'nt/ō -ā're -ā'vī -ā'tum *vt.* glue, join together.
coagme'nt/um -ī *n.* joining, joint.
coā'gul/um -ī *n.* rennet.
coal/ē'scō -ē'scere -uī -itum *vi.* grow together; (*fig.*) agree together; flourish.
coangu'st/ō -ā're *vt.* restrict.
coarct-, *see* **coart-**.
coa'rgu/ō -ere -ī *vt.* convict, prove conclusively.
coartā'ti/ō -ō'nis *f.* crowding together.
coa'rt/ō -ā're -ā'vī -ā'tum *vt.* compress, abridge.
cocci'neus, **co'ccinus** *a.* scarlet.
co'cc/um -ī *n.* scarlet.
co'cle/a, **co'chle/a** -ae *f.* snail.
cocleā'r/e -is *n.* spoon.
co'cl/es -itis *m.* man blind in one eye; surname of Horatius who defended the bridge.
co'ctilis *a.* baked; of bricks.
co'ctus *ppp.* coquō. *a.* (*fig.*) well considered.
co'cus, *see* **coquus**.
Cōcȳ't/os, **-us** -ī *m.* river in the lower world. **-ius** *a.*
cō'da, *see* **cauda**.
cō'dex, *see* **caudex**.
cōdici'll/ī -ō'rum *m.pl.* letter, note, petition; codicil.
Co'dr/us -ī *m.* last king of Athens.
coē'gī *perf.* cōgō.
coel-, *see* **cael-**.
co'/emō -e'mere -ē'mī -e'mptum *vt.* buy up.
coe'mpti/ō -ō'nis *f.* a form of Roman marriage; mock sale of an estate.
coemptiōnā'lis *a.* used in a mock sale; worthless.
coen-, *see* **cēn-** or **caen-**.
co'/eō -ī're -ī'vī & iī -itum *vi.* meet, assemble; encounter; combine, mate; (*wounds*) close; agree, conspire. *vt.* — **societā-tem** make a compact.

coe'p/iō -ere -ī -tum *vt.* & *i.* begin (*esp. in perf. tenses*). rēs agī **-tae sunt** things began to be done.
coe'pt/ō -ā're -ā'vī -ā'tum *vt.* & *i.* begin, attempt.
coe'pt/us *ppp.* coepiō. **-um -ī** *n.* beginning, undertaking.
coe'pt/us -ūs *m.* beginning.
coepulō'n/us -ī *m.* fellow-banqueter.
coerā'tor, *see* **cūrātor**.
coe'rc/eō -ē're -uī -itum *vt.* enclose; confine, repress; (*fig.*) control, check, correct.
coerci'ti/ō -ō'nis *f.* coercion, punishment.
coe't/us, co'it/us -ūs *m.* meeting, joining together; assembly, crowd.
cōgitā'ti/ō -ō'nis *f.* thought, reflection; idea, plan; faculty of thought, imagination.
cō'git/ō -ā're -ā'vī -ā'tum *vt.* & *i.* think, ponder, imagine; feel disposed; plan, intend. **-ā'tus** *a.* deliberate. *n.pl.* ideas. **-ā'tē** *ad.* deliberately.
cognā'ti/ō -ō'nis *f.* relationship (by blood); kin, family; (*fig.*) affinity, resemblance.
cognā't/us -ī *m.*, **-a -ae** *f.* relation. *a.* related; (*fig.*) connected, similar.
cogni'ti/ō -ō'nis *f.* acquiring of knowledge, knowledge; idea, notion; (*law*) judicial inquiry; (*comedy*) recognition.
co'gnit/or -ō'ris *m.* (*law*) attorney; witness of a person's identity; (*fig.*) defender.
co'gnitus *ppp.* cognōscō.
cognō'm/en -inis *n.* surname (*e.g.* Cicero); name.
cognōme'nt/um -ī *n.* surname, name.
cognō'minis *a.* with the same name.
cognō'min/ō -ā're -ā'vī -ā'tum *vt.* give a surname to. verba **-āta** synonyms.
cogn/ō'scō -ō'scere -ō'vī -itum *vt.* get to know, learn, understand; know, recognize, identify; (*law*) investigate; (*mil.*) reconnoitre. **-itus** *a.* acknowledged.
cō'g/ō -ere coē'gī coā'ctum *vt.* collect, gather together; (*liquids*) thicken, curdle; contract, confine; compel, force; infer. agmen — bring up the rear. senātum — call a meeting of the senate. **coā'ctus** *a.* forced.
coā'ct/um -ī *n.* thick coverlet. [ence.
cohaere'nti/a -ae *f.* coher-
cohae'/reō -rē're -sī -sum *vi.* stick together, cohere; cling to; (*fig.*) be consistent, harmonize; agree, be consistent with.
cohaerē'sc/ō -ere *vi.* stick together.
cohae'sus *ppp.* cohaereō.
cohē'r/ēs -ē'dis *m.*, *f.* co-heir.
cohi'b/eō -ē're -uī -itum *vt.* hold together, encircle; hinder, stop; (*fig.*) restrain, repress.
cohone'st/ō -ā're *vt.* do honour to.
cohorr/ē'scō -ē'scere -uī *vi.* shudder all over.
co'hor/s -tis *f.* court-yard; (*mil.*) cohort (about 600 men); retinue, *esp.* of the praetor in a province; (*fig.*) company.
cohortā'ti/ō -ō'nis *f.* encouragement. [cohort.
cohorti'cul/a -ae *f.* small
coho'rt/or -ā'rī -ā'tus *vt.* encourage, urge.
coi'ti/ō -ō'nis *f.* encounter; conspiracy.
co'itus, *see* **coetus**.
co'laph/us -ī *m.* blow with the fist, box.
Co'lch/is -idis *f.* Medea's country, at the E. end of the Black Sea. **-is, -us, -icus** *a.* Colchian.
cō'leus, *see* **culleus**.
cō'lis, *see* **caulis**.

collabā'sc/ō -ere *vi.* waver also.
collabefa'ct/ō -ā're *vt.* shake violently.
collabe/fī'ō -fi'erī -fa'ctus *vi.* be destroyed.
collā'/bor -bī -psus *vi.* fall in ruin, collapse. [pieces.
collacerā'tus *a.* torn to
collacrimā'ti/ō -ō'nis *f.* weeping.
colla'cte/a -ae *f.* foster-sister.
collā'psus *ppa.* collābor.
collā'r/e -is *n.* neck-band.
Collā't/ia -iae *f.* ancient town near Rome. **–ī'nus** *a.* of Collatia. *m.* husband of Lucretia.
collā'ti/ō -ō'nis *f.* bringing together, combination; (*money*) contribution; (*rhet.*) comparison; (*philos.*) analogy.
collā't/or -ō'ris *m.* contributor.
collā'tus *ppp.* cōnferō.
collaudā'ti/ō -ō'nis *f.* praise.
collau'd/ō -ā're -ā'vī -ā'tum *vt.* praise highly.
colla'x/ō -ā're *vt.* make porous.
collē'ct/a -ae *f.* money contribution.
collēctī'cius *a.* hastily gathered.
collē'cti/ō -ō'nis *f.* gathering up; (*rhet.*) recapitulation.
collē'ctus *ppp.* colligō.
collē'ct/us -ūs *m.* accumulation. [associate.
collē'g/a -ae *m.* colleague;
collē'gī *perf.* colligō.
collē'g/ium -ī & iī *n.* association in office; college, guild (of magistrates, etc.).
collībe'rt/us -ī *m.* fellow-freedman.
co'llib/et, co'llub/et -uit & itum est *vi.* it pleases.
collī'/dō -dere -sī -sum *vt.* beat together, strike, bruise; (*fig.*) bring into conflict.
colligā'ti/ō -ō'nis *f.* connection.
co'llig/ō -ā're -ā'vī -ā'tum *vt.* fasten, tie up; (*fig.*) combine; restrain, check.
co'll/igō -i'gere -ē'gī -ē'ctum *vt.* gather, collect; compress, draw together; check; (*fig.*) acquire; think about; infer, conclude. **animum, mentem** — recover, rally. **sē** — crouch; recover one's courage. **vāsa** — (*mil.*) pack up.
Collī'na Po'rta gate in N.E. of Rome. [straight.
collī'ne/ō -ā're *vt.* & *i.* aim
co'll/inō -i'nere -ē'vī -itum *vt.* besmear; (*fig.*) deface.
colliquefa'ctus *a.* dissolved.
co'll/is -is *m.* hill, slope.
collī'si *perf.* collīdō.
collī'sus *ppp.* collīdō.
co'llitus *ppp.* collinō.
collocā'ti/ō -ō'nis *f.* arrangement; giving in marriage.
co'lloc/ō -ā're -ā'vī -ā'tum *vt.* place, station, arrange; give in marriage; (*money*) invest; (*fig.*) establish; occupy, employ. [enrich.
collocuplē't/ō -ā're -ā'vī *vt.*
collocū'ti/ō -ō'nis *f.* conversation.
collo'qu/ium -ī & iī *n.* conversation, conference.
co'llo/quor -quī -cū'tus *vi.* converse, hold a conference. *vt.* talk to.
co'llubet, *see* **collibet.**
collū'c/eō -ē're *vi.* shine brightly; (*fig.*) be resplendent.
collū'/dō -dere -sī -sum *vi.* play together or with; practise collusion.
co'll/um -ī *n.* neck. — torquēre, obtorquēre, obstringere arrest.
co'll/uō -u'ere -uī -ū'tum *vt.* rinse, moisten.
co'llus, *see* **collum.**
collū'si/ō -ō'nis *f.* secret understanding.
collū's/or -ō'ris *m.* playmate, fellow-gambler.

collū'str/ō -ā're -ā'vī -ā'tum *vt.* light up; survey.
collu'vi/ō -ō'nis, -ēs -em -ē *f.* sweepings, filth; (*fig.*) dregs, rabble.
co'llyb/us -ī *m.* money exchange, rate of exchange.
collȳ'r/a -ae *f.* vermicelli. **-icus** *a.* [lotion.
collȳ'r/ium -ī & iī *n.* eye
co'l/ō -ere -uī cu'ltum *vt.* (*agr.*) cultivate, work; (*place*) live in; (*human affairs*) cherish, protect, adorn; (*qualities, pursuits*) cultivate, practise; (*gods*) worship; (*men*) honour, court. **vītam —** live.
colocā'si/a -ae *f.*, **-a -ō'rum** *n.pl.* Egyptian bean, caladium.
colō'n/a -ae *f.* countrywoman.
colō'ni/a -ae *f.* settlement, colony; settlers.
colō'nicus *a.* colonial.
colō'n/us -ī *m.* crofter, farmer; settler, colonist.
co'l/or (co'lōs) -ō'ris *m.* colour; complexion; beauty, lustre; (*fig.*) outward show; (*rhet.*) style, tone; colourful excuse. **-ōrem mūtāre** blush, go pale. **homō nullīus -ōris** an unknown person.
colō'r/ō -ā're -ā'vī -ā'tum *vt.* colour, tan; (*fig.*) give a colour to. **-ā'tus** *a.* healthily tanned.
colo'ss/us -ī *m.* gigantic statue, *esp.* that of Apollo at Rhodes.
colo'str/a, colu'str/a -ae *f.* beestings.
co'lub/er -rī *m.* snake.
colu'br/a -ae *f.* snake.
colu'brifer -ī *a.* snaky.
colubrī'nus *a.* wily.
co'luī *perf.* **colō.**
cō'l/um -ī *n.* strainer.
colu'mb/a -ae *f.* dove, pigeon. [collar.
colu'mb/ar -ā'ris *n.* kind of
columbā'r/ium -ī & iī *n.* dove-cote.
columbī'nus *a.* pigeon's. *m.* little pigeon.
colu'mb/us -ī *m.* dove, cock-pigeon.
colume'll/a -ae *f.* small pillar.
co'lum/en -inis *n.* height, summit; pillar; (*fig.*) chief; prop.
colu'mn/a -ae *f.* column, pillar; a pillory in the Forum Romanum; water-spout. **-ā'tus** *a.* pillared.
columnā'r/ium -ī & iī *n.* pillar-tax.
columnā'r/ius -ī *m.* criminal.
colu'rnus *a.* made of hazel.
co'l/us -ī & ūs *f.* (*occ. m.*) distaff. [of athletes.
cōlȳ'phi/a -ō'rum *n.pl.* food
co'm/a -ae *f.* hair (of the head); foliage.
co'm/āns -a'ntis *a.* hairy, plumed; leafy. [master.
cōma'rch/us -ī *m.* burgo-
comā'tus *a.* long-haired; leafy. **Gallia —** Transalpine Gaul.
co'mbib/ō -ere -ī *vt.* drink to the full, absorb.
co'mbib/ō -ō'nis *m.* fellow-drinker.
combū'/rō -rere -ssī -stum *vt.* burn up; (*fig.*) ruin.
combūstus *ppp.* **combūrō.**
co'm/edō -ē'sse -ē'dī -ē'sum & -ē'stum *vt.* eat up, devour; (*fig.*) waste, squander. **sē —** pine away.
co'm/es -itis *m., f.* companion, partner; attendant, follower; one of a magistrate's or emperor's retinue; (*medieval title*) count.
co'mēs, co'mēst *pres. tense* **comedō.**
comē'stus, comē'sus *ppp.* **comedō.**
comē't/ēs -ae *m.* comet.
cō'mic/us -ī *m.* comedy actor, comedy writer. *a.* of comedy, comic. **-ē** *ad.* in the manner of comedy.

cō′m/is *a.* courteous, friendly. **-iter** *ad.* [ing.
cōmissābu′ndus *a.* carous-
cōmissā′ti/ō -ō′nis *f.* Bacchanalian revel.
cōmissā′t/or -ō′ris *m.* reveller.
cōmi′ss/or -ā′rī -ā′tus *vi.* carouse, make merry.
cō′mit/ās -ā′tis *f.* kindness, affability.
comitā′t/us -ūs *m.* escort, retinue; company.
comitiā′lis *a.* of the elections. — morbus epilepsy.
comitiā′t/us -ūs *m.* assembly at the elections.
comi′t/ium -ī & iī *n.* place of assembly. **-ia** -iō′rum *n.pl.* assembly for the election of magistrates and other business, *esp.* the —centuriāta; elections.
co′mit/ō -ā′re -ā′vī -ā′tum *vt.* accompany.
co′mit/or -ā′rī -ā′tus *vt.* & *i.* attend, follow.
comma′cul/ō -ā′re -ā′vī -ā′tum *vt.* stain, defile.
commanipulā′r/is -is *m.* soldier in the same company.
commeā′t/us -ūs *m.* passage; leave, furlough; convoy (of troops or goods); (*mil.*) lines of communication, provisions, supplies.
comme′dit/or -ā′rī *vt.* practise.
comme′min/ī -i′sse *vt.* & *i.* remember perfectly.
commemorā′bilis *a.* memorable.
commemorā′ti/ō -ō′nis *f.* recollection, recounting.
comme′mor/ō -ā′re -a′vī -ā′tum *vt.* recall, remind; mention, relate.
commendā′bilis *a.* praiseworthy.
commendātī′cius *a.* of recommendation or introduction.
commendā′ti/ō -ō′nis *f.* recommendation; worth, excellence.
commendā′t/or -ō′ris *m.*, **-rīx** -rī′cis *f.* commender.
comme′nd/ō -ā′re -ā′vī -ā′tum *vt.* entrust, commit, commend (to one's care or charge); recommend, set off to advantage. **-ā′tus** *a.* approved, valued. [mētior.
commē′nsus *ppa.* com-
commentāri′ol/um -ī *n.* short treatise.
commentā′r/ius -ī & iī *m.*, **-ium** -ī & iī *n.* note-book; commentary, memoir; (*law*) brief.
commentā′ti/ō -ō′nis *f.* studying, meditation.
commentī′cius *a.* fictitious, imaginary; false.
comme′nt/or -ā′rī -ā′tus *vt.* & *i.* study think over, prepare carefully; invent, compose, write. [ventor.
comme′nt/or -ō′ris *m.* in-
comme′nt/us *ppa.* comminīscor. *a.* feigned, fictitious. **-um** -ī *n.* invention, fiction; contrivance.
co′mme/ō -ā′re *vi.* pass to and fro; go or come often.
comme′rc/ium -ī & iī *n.* trade, commerce; right to trade; dealings, communication.
comme′rc/or -ā′rī -ā′tus *vt.* buy up.
comme′r/eō -ē′re -uī -itum, **-eor** -ē′rī -itus *vt.* deserve; be guilty of.
commē′/tior -tī′rī -nsus *vt.* measure.
commē′t/ō -ā′re *vi.* go often.
commi′ctus *ppp.* commingō.
commi′gr/ō -ā′re-ā′vī -ā′tum *vi.* remove, migrate.
commīli′t/ium -ī & iī *n.* service together.
commī′lit/ō -ō′nis *m.* fellow-soldier.

comminā'ti/ō -ō'nis *f.* threat.
commi'ngō -i'ngere -i'nxī -i'ctum *vt.* pollute.
comminī'sc/or -ī comme'ntus *vt.* devise, contrive.
co'mmin/or -ā'rī -ā'tus *vt.* threaten.
commi'n/uō -u'ere -uī -ū'tum *vt.* break up, smash; diminish; impair.
co'mminus *ad.* hand to hand; near at hand.
commi'/sceō -scē're -scuī -xtum *vt.* mix together, join together.
commiserā'ti/ō -ō'nis *f.* (*rhet.*) passage intended to arouse pity.
commiserē'sc/ō -ere *vt.* pity.
commi'ser/or -ā'rī *vt.* bewail. *vi.* (*rhet.*) try to excite pity.
commi'ssi/ō -ō'nis *f.* start (of a contest).
commissū'r/a -ae *f.* joint, connection.
commi'ss/us *ppp.* committō. **-um** -ī *n.* enterprise; offence, crime; secret.
comm/i'ttō -i'ttere -ī'sī -i'ssum *vt.* join, connect, bring together; begin, undertake; (*battle*) join, engage in; (*offence*) commit, be guilty of; (*punishment*) incur, forfeit; entrust, trust. **sē urbī —** venture into the city.
commi'xtus *ppp.* commisceō.
commo'dit/ās -ā'tis *f.* convenience, ease, fitness; advantage; (*person*) kindliness; (*rhet.*) apt expression.
co'mmod/ō -ā're -ā'vī -ā'tum *vt.* adjust, adapt; give, lend, oblige with; (*with dat.*) oblige.
commo'dul/ē, -um *ad.* conveniently.
co'mmod/um -ī *n.* convenience; advantage, interest; pay, salary; loan. **-ō tuō** at your leisure. **-a vītae** the good things of life.
co'mmodum *ad.* opportunely; just.
co'mmod/us *a.* proper, fit, full; suitable, easy, opportune; (*person*) pleasant, obliging. **-ē** *ad.* properly, well; aptly, opportunely; pleasantly.
commō'l/ior -ī'rī *vt.* set in motion.
commone/fa'ciō -fa'cere -fē'cī -fa'ctum *vt.* remind, recall.
commo'n/eō -ē're -uī -itum *vt.* remind, impress upon. [out.
commō'nstr/ō -ā're *vt.* point
commorā'ti/ō -ō'nis *f.* delay, residence; (*rhet.*) dwelling (on a topic).
co'mmor/or -ā'rī -ā'tus *vi.* sojourn, wait; (*rhet.*) dwell. *vt.* detain.
commō'ti/ō -ō'nis *f.* excitement. **-u'ncula** *f.* slight indisposition.
commō'tus *ppp.* commoveō. *a.* excited, emotional.
comm/o'veō -ovē're -ō'vī -ō'tum *vt.* set in motion, move, dislodge, agitate; (*mind*) unsettle, shake, excite, move, affect; (*emotions*) stir up, provoke.
commūnicā'ti/ō -ō'nis *f.* imparting; (*rhet.*) making the audience appear to take part in the discussion.
commū'nic/ō -ā're -ā'vī -ā'tum *vt.* share (by giving or receiving); impart, communicate. **cōnsilia — cum** make common cause with.
commū'n/iō -ī're -ī'vī & iī -ī'tum *vt.* build (a fortification); fortify, strengthen.
commū'ni/ō -ō'nis *f.* sharing in common, communion.
commū'n/is *a.* common, general, universal; (*person*) affable, democratic. **-ia loca** public places. **-ēs locī** general

topics. **-is** sēnsus popular sentiment. aliquid **-e** habēre have something in common. **-e -is** *n.* common property; state. in **-e** for a common end; equally; in general. **-iter** *ad.* in common, jointly.
commū'nit/ās -ā-tis *f.* fellowship; sense of fellowship; affability.
commūnī'ti/ō -ō'nis *f.* preparing the way.
commu'rmur/or -ā'rī -ā'tus *vi.* mutter to oneself.
commūtā'bilis *a.* changeable.
commūtā't/iō -iō'nis *f.*, **-us** -ūs *m.* change.
commū't/ō -ā're -ā'vī -ā'tum *vt.* change, exchange, interchange.
cō'm/ō -ere -psī -ptum *vt.* arrange, dress, adorn.
cōmoe'di/a -ae *f.* comedy.
cōmoe'dicē *ad.* as in comedy.
cōmoe'd/us -ī *m.* comic actor.
comō'sus *a.* shaggy.
compā'cti/ō -ō'nis *f.* joining together.
compā'ctus *ppp.* compingō.
compā'g/ēs -is, **-ō** -inis *f.* joint, structure, framework.
co'mp/ār -aris *m., f.* comrade, husband, wife. *a.* equal.
comparā'bilis *a.* comparable.
comparā'ti/ō -ō'nis *f.* comparison; (*astr.*) relative positions; agreement; preparation, procuring.
comparātī'vus *a.* based on comparison.
compā'r/eō -ē're *vi.* be visible; be present, be realised.
co'mpar/ō -ā're -ā'vī -ā'tum *vt.* couple together, match; compare; (*pol.*) agree (about respective duties); prepare, provide; (*custom*) establish; procure, purchase, get. **-ā'tē** *ad.* by bringing in a comparison.
compā'sc/ō -ere *vt.* put (cattle) to graze in common.
compā'scuus *a.* for common pasture.
compec/ī'scor -ī'scī -tus *vi.* come to an agreement. **-tum** -tī *n.* agreement.
compe'd/iō -ī're -ī'tum *vt.* fetter.
compē'gī *perf.* compingō.
compellā'ti/ō -ō'nis *f.* reprimand.
compe'll/ō -ā're -ā'vī -ā'tum *vt.* call, address; reproach; (*law*) arraign.
comp/e'llō -e'llere -ulī -u'lsum *vt.* drive, bring together, concentrate; impel, compel.
compendiā'rius *a.* short.
compe'nd/ium -ī & iī *n.* saving; abbreviating; short cut. **-ī** facere save; abridge. **-ī** fierī be brief.
compēnsā'ti/ō -ō'nis *f.* (*fig.*) compromise.
compē'ns/ō -ā're -ā'vī -ā'tum *vt.* balance (against), make up for.
compe'r/cō -cere -sī *vt.* & *i.* save; refrain.
comperendinā't/iō -iō'nis *f.*, **-us** -ūs *m.* adjournment for two days.
compere'ndin/ō -ā're *vt.* adjourn for two days.
compe'r/iō -ī're -ī -tum (*occ.* **-ior**) *vt.* find out, learn. **-tus** detected; found guilty. **-tum** habēre know for certain.
co'mp/ēs -edis *f.* fetter, bond.
compē'sc/ō -ere -uī *vt.* check, suppress.
competī't/or -ō'ris *m.*, **-rīx** -rī'cis *f.* rival candidate.
co'mpet/ō -ere -ī'vī & iī -ī'tum *vi.* coincide, agree; be capable.
compīlā'ti/ō -ō'nis *f.* plundering; compilation.
compī'l/ō -ā're -ā'vī -ā'tum *vt.* pillage.
comp/i'ngō -i'ngere -ē'gī

-ā'ctum *vt.* put together, compose; lock up, hide away.

compitāli'cius *a.* of the Compitalia.

compitā'l/is *a.* of cross-roads. **-ia -ium & iō'rum** *n.pl.* festival in honour of the Lares Compitales.

co'mpit/um -ī *n.* cross-roads.

compla'c/eō -ē're -uī & itus sum *vi.* please (someone else) as well, please very much.

complā'n/ō -ā're *vt.* level, raze to the ground.

comple'/ctor -ctī -xus *vt.* embrace, clasp; enclose; (*speech, writing*) deal with, comprise; (*mind*) grasp, comprehend; honour, be fond of.

complēme'nt/um -ī *n.* complement.

co'mpl/eō -ē're -ē'vī -ē'tum *vt.* fill, fill up; (*mil.*) man, make up the complement of; (*time, promise, duty*) complete, fulfil, finish. **-ē'tus** *a.* perfect.

comple'xi/ō -ō'nis *f.* combination; (*rhet.*) period; (*logic*) conclusion of an argument; dilemma.

comple'x/us -ūs *m.* embrace; (*fig.*) affection, close combat; (*speech*) connection.

co'mplic/ō -ā're *vt.* fold up.

complōrā't/iō -iō'nis *f.*, **-us -ūs** *m.* loud lamentation.

complō'r/ō -ā're -ā'vī -ā'tum *vt.* mourn for.

complū'r/ēs -ium *a.* several, very many.

complū'riēns *ad.* several [times.

complū'scul/ī -ō'rum *a.* quite a few.

complu'v/ium -ī & iī *n.* roof-opening in a Roman house.

comp/ō'nō -ō'nere -o'suī -o'situm *vt.* put together, join; compose, construct; compare, contrast; match, oppose; put away, store up, stow; (*dead*) lay out, inter; allay, quieten, reconcile; adjust, settle, arrange; devise, prepare. *vi.* make peace.

compo'rt/ō -ā're *vt.* collect, bring in.

co'mpo/s -tis *a.* in control, in possession; sharing. **vōtī —** having got one's wish.

composi'ti/ō -ō'nis *f.* compounding, system; (*words*) arrangement; reconciliation; matching (of fighters).

compo'sit/or -ō'ris *m.* arranger.

compositū'r/a -ae *f.* con-[nection.

compo'sit/us *ppp.* compōnō. *a.* orderly, regular; adapted, assumed, ready; calm, sedate; (*words*) compound. **-ō, ex -ō** as agreed. **-ē** *ad.* properly, in a polished manner.

compōtā'ti/ō -ō'nis *f.* drinking-party.

compo't/iō -ī're *vt.* put in possession (of).

compō't/or -ō'ris *m.*, **-rīx -rī'cis** *f.* fellow-drinker.

comprā'ns/or -ō'ris *m.* fellow-guest.

comprecā'ti/ō -ō'nis *f.* public supplication.

co'mprec/or -ā'rī -ā'tus *vt.* & *i.* pray to; pray for.

compreh/e'ndō, compr/e'ndō -en'dere -e'ndī -ē'nsum *vt.* grasp, catch; seize, arrest catch in the act; (*words*) comprise, recount; (*thought*) grasp, comprehend; hold in affection. **numerō —** count.

comprehēnsi'bilis *a.* conceivable.

comprehē'nsi/ō -ō'nis *f.* grasping, seizing; perception, idea; (*rhet.*) period.

comprehē'nsus, comprē'nsus *ppp.* comprehendō.

compre'ndō, *see* **comprehendō.**

compre'ssī *perf.* comprimō.

compre'ssi/ō -ō'nis *f.* embrace; (*rhet.*) compression.

compre'ssus *ppp.* comprimō.
compre'ss/us -ūs *m.* compression, embrace.
co'mpr/imō -i'mere -e'ssī -e'ssum *vt.* squeeze, compress; check, restrain; suppress, withhold. animam — hold one's breath. -essīs manibus with hands folded, idle.
comprobā'ti/ō -ō'nis *f.* approval. [supporter.
comprobā't/or -ō'ris *m.*
co'mprob/ō -ā're -ā'vī ā'tum *vt.* prove, make good; approve.
comprōmi'ss/um -ī *n.* mutual agreement to abide by an arbitrator's decision.
comprōm/i'ttō -i'ttere -ī'sī -i'ssum *vt.* undertake to abide by an arbitrator's decision.
cō'mpsī *perf.* cōmō.
cō'mptus *ppp.* cōmō. *a.* elegant. [union.
cō'mpt/us -ūs *m.* coiffure;
co'mpulī *perf.* compellō.
compu'lsus *ppp.* compellō.
comp/u'ngō -u'ngere -ū'nxī -ū'nctum *vt.* prick, sting, tattoo.
compu't/ō -ā're -ā'vī -ā'tum *vt.* reckon, number.
Cō'm/um -ī *n.* town in N. Italy, also Novum Cōmun *mod.* Como. **-ē'nsis, Novocōmē'nsis** *a.*
cōnā'm/en -inis *n.* effort; support.
cōnā't/a -ō'rum *n.pl.* undertaking, venture.
cōnā't/us -ūs *m.* effort; endeavour; inclination, impulse.
concae'd/ēs -ium *f.pl.* barricade of felled trees.
concale/fa'ciō -fa'cere -fē'cī -fa'ctum *vt.* warm well.
conca'l/eō -ē're *vi.* be hot.
concal/ē'scō -ē'scere -uī *vi.* become hot, glow.
concall/ē'scō -ē'scere -uī *vi.* become shrewd; become unfeeling.
concastī'g/ō -ā're *vt.* punish severely.
co'ncav/ō -ā're *vt.* curve.
co'ncavus *a.* hollow; vaulted, bent.
conc/ē'dō -ē'dere -e'ssī -e'ssum *vi.* withdraw, depart; disappear, pass away, pass; yield, submit, give precedence, comply. *vt.* give up, cede; grant, allow; pardon, overlook.
conce'lebr/ō -ā're -ā'vī -ā'tum *vt.* frequent, fill, enliven; (*study*) pursue eagerly; celebrate; make known.
concēnā'ti/ō -ō'nis *f.* dining together.
conce'nti/ō -ō'nis *f.* chorus.
concentu'ri/ō -ā're *vt.* marshal.
conce'nt/us -ūs *m.* chorus, concert; (*fig.*) concord, harmony.
conce'pti/ō -ō'nis *f.* conception; drawing up legal formulae. [movable.
conceptī'vus *a.* (*holidays*)
conce'ptus *ppp.* concipiō.
conce'pt/us -ūs *m.* conception.
conce'rp/ō -ere -sī -tum *vt.* tear up; (*fig.*) abuse.
concertā'ti/ō -ō'nis *f.* controversy.
concertā't/or -ō'ris *m.* rival.
concertātō'rius *a.* controversial.
conce'rt/ō -ā're -ā'vī -ā'tum *vi.* fight; dispute.
conce'ssi/ō -ō'nis *f.* grant, permission; (*law*) pleading guilty and asking indulgence.
conce'ss/ō -ā're *vi.* stop, loiter.
conce'ssus *ppp.* concēdō.
conce'ss/us -ūs *m.* permission.
co'nch/a -ae *f.* mussel, oyster, murex; mussel-shell, oyster-shell, pearl; purple dye; trumpet, perfume-dish.
co'nch/is -is *f.* kind of bean.

conchī't/a -ae *m.* catcher of shell-fish.
conchȳliā'tus *a.* purple.
conchȳ'l/ium -ī & iī *n.* shell-fish, oyster, murex; purple.
co'ncid/ō -ere -ī *vi.* fall, collapse; subside, fail, perish.
concī'/dō -dere -dī -sum *vt.* cut up, cut to pieces, kill; (*fig.*) ruin, strike down; (*rhet.*) dismember, enfeeble. **-sus** *a.* broken up, concise.
conc/i'eō -iē're -ī'vī -itum, **co'nc/iō** -ī're -ī'tum *vt.* rouse, assemble; stir up, shake; (*fig.*) rouse, provoke.
conciliā'bul/um -ī *n.* place for public gatherings.
conciliā'ti/ō -ō'nis *f.* union; winning over (friends, hearers); (*philos.*) inclination.
conciliā't/or -ō'ris *m.* promoter.
conciliā'tr/īx -ī'cis, **-ī'cul/a** -ae *f.* promoter, match-maker.
conciliā't/us -ūs *m.* combination.
conci'li/ō -ā're -ā'vī -ā'tum *vt.* unite; win over, reconcile; procure, purchase, bring about, promote. **-ā'tus** *a.* beloved; favourable.
conci'l/ium -ī & iī *n.* gathering, meeting; council; (*things*) union.
conci'nnit/ās -ā'tis, **-ū'dō** -ū'dinis *f.* (*rhet.*) rhythmical style.
conci'nn/ō -ā're -ā'vī -ā'tum *vt.* arrange; bring about, produce; (*with a.*) make.
conci'nnus *a.* symmetrical, beautiful; (*style*) polished, rhythmical; (*person*) elegant, courteous; (*things*) suited, pleasing. **-ē** *ad.*
co'ncin/ō -ere -uī *vi.* sing, play, sound together; (*fig.*) agree, harmonize. *vt.* sing about, celebrate, prophesy.
co'nciō, *see* **concieō**.
concio-, *see* **contio-**.
conc/i'piō -i'pere -ē'pī -e'ptum *vt.* take to oneself, absorb; (*women*) conceive; (*senses*) perceive; (*mind*) conceive, imagine, understand; (*feelings, acts*) harbour, foster, commit; (*words*) draw up, intimate formally.
concī'si/ō -ō'nis *f.* breaking up into short clauses.
concī'sus *ppp.* concīdō.
concitā'ti/ō -ō'nis *f.* acceleration; (*mind*) excitement, passion; riot.
concitā't/or -ō'ris *m.* agitator.
concitā't/us *ppp.* concitō. *a.* fast; excited. **-ē** *ad.*
co'ncit/ō -ā're -ā'vī -ā'tum *vt.* move rapidly, bestir, hurl; urge, rouse, impel; stir up, occasion.
co'ncit/or -ō'ris *m.* instigator.
co'ncitus, concī'tus *ppp.* concieō, conciō.
conclāmā'ti/ō -ō'nis *f.* great shout.
conclā'mit/ō -ā're *vi.* keep on shouting.
conclā'm/ō -ā're -ā'vī -ā'tum *vt.* & *i.* shout, cry out; call to help; (*mil.*) give the signal; (*dead*) call by name in mourning. vāsa — give the order to pack up. **-ātum est** it's all over.
conclā'v/e -is *n.* room.
conclū'/dō -dere -sī -sum *vt.* shut up, enclose; include, comprise; end, conclude, round off (*esp.* with a rhythmical cadence); (*philos.*) infer, demonstrate.
conclū'si/ō -ō'nis *f.* (*mil.*) blockade; end, conclusion; (*rhet.*) period, peroration; (*logic*) conclusion.
conclūsiu'ncul/a -ae *f.* quibble.
conclū's/us *ppp.* conclūdō. **-um** -ī *n.* logical conclusion. **-ē** *ad.* with rhythmical cadences.

conco'ctus *ppp.* concoquō.
co'ncol/or -ō'ris *a.* of the same colour.
concomitā'tus *a.* escorted.
co'nco/quō -quere -xī -ctum *vt.* boil down; digest; (*fig.*) put up with, stomach; (*thought*) consider well, concoct.
conco'rdi/a -ae *f.* friendship, concord, union; goddess of Concord.
conco'rd/ō -ā're *vi.* agree, be in harmony.
co'ncor/s -dis *a.* concordant, united, harmonious. **—diter** *ad.* amicably.
concrēbr/ē'scō -ē'scere -uī *vi.* gather strength.
concrē'd/ō -ere -idī -itum *vt.* entrust.
co'ncrem/ō -ā're -ā'vī -ā'tum *vt.* burn.
co'ncrep/ō -ā're -uī -itum *vi.* rattle, creak, clash, snap (fingers). *vt.* beat.
concrē'/scō -scere -vī -tum *vi.* harden, curdle, congeal, clot; grow, take shape.
concrē'ti/ō -ō'nis *f.* condensing; matter.
concrē't/us *ppa.* concrēscō. *a.* hard, thick, stiff, congealed; compounded. **—um** -ī *n.* solid matter, hard frost.
concrī'min/or -ā'rī -ā'tus *vi.* bring a complaint.
concru'ci/ō -ā're *vt.* torture.
concubī'n/a -ae *f.*, **—us** -ī *m.* concubine.
concubīnā't/us -ūs *m.* concubinage.
concu'bit/us -ūs *m.* reclining together (at table); sexual union.
concu'b/ius *a.* -iā nocte during the first sleep. *n.* the time of the first sleep.
concu'lc/ō -ā're *vt.* trample under foot, treat with contempt.
concu'/mbō -mbere -buī -bitum *vi.* lie together, lie with.
concup/ī'scō -ī'scere -ī'vī -ī'tum *vt.* covet long for, aspire to.
concū'r/ō -ā're *vt.* take care of.
concu'r/rō -rere -rī -sum *vi.* flock together, rush in; (*things*) clash, meet; (*mil.*) join battle, charge; (*events*) happen at the same time, concur.
concursā'ti/ō -ō'nis *f.* running together, rushing about; (*mil.*) skirmishing; (*dreams*) coherent design.
concursā't/or -ō'ris *m.* skirmisher.
concu'rsi/ō -ō'nis *f.* meeting, concourse; (*rhet.*) repetition for emphasis.
concu'rs/ō -ā're *vi.* collide; rush about, travel about; (*mil.*) skirmish. *vt.* visit, go from place to place.
concu'rs/us -ūs *m.* concourse, gathering, collision; uproar; (*fig.*) combination; (*mil.*) assault, charge.
concu'ssī *perf.* concutiō.
concu'ssus *ppp.* concutiō.
concu'ss/us -ūs *m.* shaking.
concu'/tiō -tere -ssī -ssum *vt.* strike, shake, shatter; (*weapons*) hurl; (*power*) disturb, impair; (*person*) agitate, alarm; (*self*) search, examine; rouse. [ring.
conda'l/ium -ī & iī *n.* slave's
co'ndec/et -ē're *vt.impers.* it becomes.
conde'cor/ō -ā're *vt.* enhance.
condemnā't/or -ō'ris *m.* accuser.
conde'mn/ō -ā're -ā'vī -ā'tum *vt.* condemn, sentence; urge the conviction of; blame, censure. **ambitūs** — convict of bribery. **capitis** — condemn to death. **vōtī** -ā'tus obliged to fulfil a vow.
condē'ns/ō -ā're, **—eō** -ē're

vt. compress, move close together.
condē'nsus *a.* very dense, close, thick.
condi'ci/ō -ō'nis *f.* arrangement, condition, terms; marriage contract, match; situation, position, circumstances; manner, mode. eā -ōne ut on condition that. sub -ōne conditionally. hīs -ōnibus on these terms. vītae — way of life.
cond/ī'cō -ī'cere -ī'xī -i'ctum *vt.* & *i.* talk over, agree upon, promise. ad cēnam — have a dinner engagement.
co'ndidī *perf.* condō.
condi'gn/us *a.* very worthy. -ē *ad.*
condime'nt/um -ī *n.* spice, seasoning.
co'nd/iō -ī're -ī'vī -ī'tum *vt.* pickle, preserve, embalm; season; (*fig.*) give zest to, temper. -ī'tus *a.* savoury; (*fig.*) polished.
condisci'pul/us -ī *m.* schoolfellow.
condi'/scō -scere -dicī *vt.* learn thoroughly learn by heart.
condi'tiō, *see* **condiciō**.
condī'ti/ō -ō'nis *f.* preserving, seasoning.
co'ndit/or -ō'ris *m.* founder, author, composer.
conditō'r/ium -ī & iī *n.* coffin, urn, tomb.
co'nditus *ppp.* condō.
condī'tus *ppp.* condiō.
co'nd/ō -ere -idī -itum *vt.* 1. build, found; (*arts*) make, compose, write; (*institutions*) establish. 2. put away for keeping, store up; (*fruit*) preserve; (*person*) imprison; (*dead*) bury; (*memory*) lay up; (*time*) pass, bring to a close. 3. put out of sight, conceal; (*eyes*) close; (*sword*) sheathe, plunge; (*troops*) place in ambush.
condocefa'c/iō -ere *vt.* train.
condo'c/eō -ē're -uī -tum *vt.* train.
condol/ē'scō -ē'scere -uī *vi.* begin to ache, feel very sore.
condōnā'ti/ō -ō'nis *f.* giving away.
condō'n/ō -ā're -ā'vī -ā'tum *vt.* give, present, deliver up; (*debt*) remit; (*offence*) pardon, let off.
condorm/ī'sco -ī'scere -ī'vī *vi.* fall fast asleep.
condūci/bilis *a.* expedient.
cond/ū'cō -ū'cere -ū'xī -u'ctum *vt.* bring together, assemble, connect; hire, rent, borrow; (*public work*) undertake, get the contract for; (*taxes*) farm. *vi.* be of use, profit.
conductī'cius *a.* hired.
condu'cti/ō -ō'nis *f.* hiring, farming.
condu'ct/or -ō'ris *m.* hirer, tenant; contractor.
condu'ct/us *ppp.* condūcō. -ī -ō'rum *m.pl.* hirelings, mercenaries. -um -ī *n.* anything hired or rented.
condu'plic/ō -ā're *vt.* double.
condū'r/ō -ā're *vt.* make very hard.
co'nd/us -ī *m.* steward.
cōne'/ctō -ctere -xuī -xum *vt.* tie, fasten, link, join; (*logic*) state a conclusion.
cōne'x/us *ppp.* cōnectō. *a.* connected; (*time*) following. -um -ī *n.* logical inference.
cōne'x/us -ūs *m.* combination.
cōnfā'bul/or -ā'rī -ā'tus *vi.* talk (to), discuss.
cōnfarreā'ti/ō -ō'nis *f.* the most solemn of Roman marriage ceremonies.
cōnfa'rre/ō -ā're -ā'tum *vt.* marry by confarreatio.
cōnfātā'lis *a.* bound by the same destiny.
confē'cī *perf.* cōnficiō.
cōnfe'cti/ō -ō'nis *f.* making, completion; (*food*) chewing.

cōnfe'ct/or -ō'ris *m.* maker, finisher; destroyer.
cōnfe'ctus *ppp.* cōnficiō.
cōnfe'r/ciō -cī're -tum *vt.* stuff, cram, pack closely.
cō'n/ferō -fe'rre -tulī -lā'tum *vt.* gather together, collect; contribute; confer, talk over; (*mil.*) oppose, engage in battle; compare; (*words*) condense; direct, transfer; transform (into), turn (to); devote, bestow; ascribe, assign, impute; (*time*) postpone. capita — put heads together, confer. gradum — cum walk beside. sē — go, turn (to). sermōnēs — converse. signa — join battle.
cōnfe'rtim *ad.* in close order.
cōnfe'rtus *ppp.* cōnferciō. *a.* crowded, full; (*mil.*) in close order.
cōnfer/vē'scō -vē'scere -buī *vi.* boil up, grow hot.
cōnfe'ssi/ō -ō'nis *f.* acknowledgement, confession.
cōnfe'ss/us *ppa.* cōnfiteor. *a.* acknowledged, certain. in -ō esse, in -um venīre be generally admitted.
cōnfe'stim *ad.* immediately.
cōnf/i'ciō -i'cere -ē'cī -e'ctum *vt.* make, effect, complete, accomplish; get together, procure; wear out, exhaust, consume, destroy. (*bus.*) settle; (*space*) travel; (*time*) pass, complete; (*philos.*) be an active cause; (*logic*) deduce; (*pass.*) it follows.
cōnfi'cti/ō -ō'nis *f.* fabrication.
cōnfi'ctus *ppp.* cōnfingō.
cōnfī'd/ēns -e'ntis *pres.p.* cōnfīdō. *a.* self-confident, bold, presumptuous. **-e'nter** *ad.* fearlessly, insolently.
cōnfīde'nti/a -ae *f.* confidence, self-confidence; impudence.
cōnfīdenti'loquus *a.* outspoken.
cōnfī'/dō -dere -sus sum *vi.* trust, rely, be sure. sibi — be confident.
cōnfī'/gō -gere -xī -xum *vt.* fasten together; pierce, shoot; (*fig.*) paralyse.
cōnf/i'ngō -i'ngere -i'nxī -i'ctum *vt.* make, invent, pretend.
cōnfī'nis *a.* adjoining; (*fig.*) akin.
cōnfī'n/ium -ī *n.* common boundary; (*pl.*) neighbours; (*fig.*) close connection, borderland between.
cōn/fī'ō -fi'erī *occ. pass.* cōnficiō.
cōnfirmā'ti/ō -ō'nis *f.* establishing; (*person*) encouragement; (*fact*) verifying; (*rhet.*) adducing of proofs.
cōnfirmā't/or -ō'ris *m.* guarantor (of money).
cōnfi'rm/ō -ā're -ā'vī -ā'tum *vt.* strengthen reinforce; (*decree*) confirm, ratify; (*mind*) encourage; (*fact*) corroborate, prove, assert. sē — recover; take courage. **-ā'tus** *a.* resolute; proved, certain.
cōnfi'sc/ō -ā're *vt.* keep in a chest; confiscate.
cōnfī'si/ō -ō'nis *f.* assurance.
cōnfī'sus *ppa.* cōnfīdō.
cōnf/i'teor -itē'rī -e'ssus *vt.* & *i.* confess, acknowledge; reveal.
cōnfī'xus *ppp.* cōnfīgō.
cōnfla'gr/ō -ā're -ā'vī -ā'tum *vi.* burn, be ablaze.
cōnflī'cti/ō -ō'nis *f.* conflict.
cōnflī'ct/ō -ā're -ā'vī -ā'tum *vt.* strike down, contend (with); (*pass.*) fight, be harassed, be afflicted.
cōnflī'ct/us -ūs *m.* striking together.
cōnflī'/gō -gere -xī -ctum *vt.* dash together; (*fig.*) contrast. *vi.* fight, come into conflict.
cō'nfl/ō -ā're -ā'vī -ā'tum *vt.* ignite; (*passion*) inflame; melt down; (*fig.*) produce, procure, occasion.

cō'nflu/ō -ere -xī *vi.* flow together; (*fig.*) flock together, pour in. **–ēns** -e'ntis, **–e'ntēs** e'ntium *m.* confluence of two rivers.
cōnf/o'diō -o'dere -ō'dī -o'ssum *vt.* dig; stab.
cō'nfore *fut.inf.* cōnsum.
cōnfōrmā'ti/ō -ō'nis *f.* shape, form; (*words*) arrangement; (*voice*) expression; (*mind*) idea; (*rhet.*) figure.
cōnfō'rm/ō -ā're -ā'vī -ā'tum *vt.* shape, fashion.
cōnfo'ssus *ppp.* cōnfodiō. *a.* full of holes.
cōnfrā'ctus *ppp.* cōnfringō.
cōnfragō'sus *a.* broken, rough; (*fig.*) hard.
cōnfrēgī *perf.* cōnfringō.
cō'nfrem/ō -ere -uī *vi.* murmur aloud.
cō'nfric/ō -ā're *vt.* rub well.
cōnfr/i'ngō -i'ngere -ē'gī -ā'ctum *vt.* break in pieces, wreck; (*fig.*) ruin.
cōnf/u'giō -u'gere -ū'gī *vi.* flee for help (to), take refuge (with); (*fig.*) have recourse (to). [refuge.
cōnfu'g/ium -ī & iī *n.*
cōnf/u'ndō -u'ndere -ū'dī -ū'sum *vt.* mix, mingle, join; mix up, confuse, throw into disorder; (*mind*) perplex, bewilder; diffuse, spread over.
cōnfū'si/ō -ō'nis *f.* combination; confusion, disorder. ōris — going red in the face.
cōnfū's/us *ppp.* cōnfundō. *a.* confused, disorderly, troubled. **–ē** *ad.* confusedly.
cōnfū't/ō -ā're -ā'vī -ā'tum *vt.* keep from boiling over; repress; silence, confute.
co'ngel/ō -ā're -ā'vī -ā'tum *vt.* freeze, harden. *vi.* freeze over, grow numb.
conge'min/ō -ā're -ā'vī -ā'tum *vt.* double.
co'ngem/ō -ere -uī *vi.* groan, sigh. *vt.* lament.
co'ng/er -rī *m.* sea-eel.
conge'ri/ēs -ēī *f.* heap, mass, accumulation.
co'nge/rō -rere -ssī -stum *vt.* collect, accumulate, build; (*missiles*) shower; (*speech*) comprise; (*fig.*) heap (upon), ascribe.
co'nger/ō -ō'nis *m.* thief.
conge'rr/ō -ō'nis *m.* companion in revelry.
congestī'cius *a.* piled up.
conge'stus *ppp.* congerō.
conge'st/us -ūs *m.* accumulating; heap, mass.
congiā'r/ium -ī & iī *n.* gift of food to the people, gratuity to the army.
co'ng/ius -ī & iī *m.* Roman liquid measure, about 6 pints. **–iā'lis** *a.* holding a congius.
congla'ci/ō -ā're *vi.* freeze up.
conglī'sc/ō -ere *vi.* blaze up.
conglobā'ti/ō -ō'nis *f.* mustering.
con'glob/ō -ā're -ā'vī -ā'tum *vt.* make round; mass together.
conglo'mer/ō -ā're *vt.* roll up.
conglūtinā'ti/ō -ō'nis *f.* gluing, cementing; (*fig.*) combination.
conglū'tin/ō -ā're -ā'vī -ā'tum *vt.* glue, cement; (*fig.*) join, weld together; contrive.
congrae'c/ō -ā're *vt.* squander on luxury. [congratulate.
congrā'tul/or -ā'rī -ā'tus *vi.*
congre'/dior -dī -ssus *vt.* & *i.* meet, accost; contend, fight.
congregā'bilis *a.* gregarious.
congregā'ti/ō -ō'nis *f.* union, society.
co'ngreg/ō -ā're -ā'vī -ā'tum *vt.* collect, assemble, unite.
congre'ssi/ō -ō'nis *f.* meeting conference.
congre'ssus *ppa.* congredior.
congre'ss/us -ūs *m.* meeting, association, union; encounter, fight.

co'ngru/ēns -e'ntis *a.* suitable, consistent, proper; harmonious. **-e'nter** *ad.* in conformity.
co'ngru/ō -ere -ī *vi.* coincide; correspond, suit; agree, sympathize.
co'ngruus *a.* agreeable.
con/i'ciō -i'cere -iē'cī -ie'ctum *vt.* throw together; throw, hurl; put, fling, drive, direct; infer, conjecture; (*augury*) interpret. sē — rush, fly; devote oneself.
conie'cti/ō -ō'nis *f.* throwing; conjecture, interpretation.
conie'ct/ō -ā're *vt.* infer, conjecture, guess.
conie'ct/or -ō'ris *m.*, **-rīx** -rī'cis *f.* interpreter, diviner.
coniectū'r/a -ae *f.* inference, conjecture, guess; interpretation.
coniectūrā'lis *a.* (*rhet.*) involving a question of fact.
conie'ctus *ppp.* coniciō.
conie'ct/us -ūs *m.* heap, mass, concourse; throwing, throw, range; (*eyes, mind*) turning, directing.
cō'nifer, cō'niger -ī *a.* cone-bearing.
cōnī'/tor -tī -sus & xus *vi.* lean on; strive, struggle on; labour. [conjugal.
coniugā'lis *a.* of marriage,
coniugā'ti/ō -ō'nis *f.* etymological relationship.
coniugā't/or -ō'ris *m.* uniter.
coniugiā'lis *a.* marriage-.
coniu'g/ium -ī & iī *n.* union, marriage, husband, wife.
co'niug/ō -ā're *vt.* form (a friendship). -āta verba words related etymologically.
coniū'nctim *ad.* together, jointly.
coniū'ncti/ō -ō'nis *f.* union, connection, association; (*minds*) sympathy, affinity; (*gram.*) conjunction.
coniū'nct/us *ppp* coniungō. *a.* near; connected, agreeing, conforming; related, friendly, intimate. **-um** -ī *n.* (*rhet.*) connection; (*philos.*) inherent property (of a body). **-ē** *ad.* jointly; on familiar terms; (*logic*) hypothetically.
coni/u'ngō -ū'ngere -ū'nxī -ū'nctum *vt* yoke, join together, connect; (*war*) join forces in; unite in love, marriage, friendship; continue without a break.
co'ni/ūnx -ugis *m., f.* consort, wife, husband, bride.
coniūrā'ti/ō -ō'nis *f.* conspiracy, plot; alliance.
coniūrā't/ī -ō'rum *m.pl.* conspirators.
coniū'r/ō -ā're -ā'vī -ā'tum *vi.* take an oath; conspire, plot. -ā'tus (*mil.*) after taking the oath.
co'niux, *see* **coniūnx**.
cōnī'/veō -vē're -vī & xī *vi.* shut the eyes, blink; (*fig.*) be asleep; connive at.
conj-, *see* **coni-**.
conl-, *see* **coll-**.
conm-, *see* **comm-**.
conn-, *see* **cōn-**.
Co'nōn -is *m.* Athenian commander; Greek astronomer.
cōnōp/ē'um (-eum) -ē'ī *n.* mosquito-net.
cō'n/or -ā'rī -ā'tus *vt.* try, attempt, venture.
conp-, *see* **comp-**.
conquassā'ti/ō -ō'nis *f.* severe shaking.
conqua'ss/ō -ā're -ā'tum *vt.* shake, upset, shatter.
co'nque/ror -rī -stus *vt. & i.* complain bitterly of, bewail.
conque'sti/ō -ō'nis *f.* complaining; (*rhet.*) appeal to pity.
conque'stus *ppa.* conqueror.
conque'st/us -ūs *m.* outcry.
conquiē'/scō -scere -vī -tum *vi.* rest, take a respite; (*fig.*) be at peace, find recreation; (*things*) stop, be quiet.

conquinī'sc/ō -ere *vi.* cower, squat, stoop down.
conquī'/rō -rere -sī'vī -sī'tum *vt.* search for, collect.
conquīsī'ti/ō -ō'nis *f.* search; (*mil.*) levy.
conquīsī't/or -ō'ris *m.* recruiting officer; (*theatre*) claqueur.
conquīsī't/us *ppp.* conquīrō. *a.* select, costly. **-ē** *ad.* carefully.
conr-, *see* **corr-**.
cōnsae'p/iō -ī're -sī -tum *vt.* enclose, fence round. **-tum** **-tī** *n.* enclosure.
cōnsalūtā'ti/ō -ō'nis *f.* mutual greeting.
cōnsalūt/ō -ā're -ā'vī -ā'tum *vt.* greet, hail.
cōnsān/ē'scō -ē'scere -uī *vi.* heal up.
cōnsangui'neus *a.* brother, sister, kindred. *m.pl.* relations.
cōnsangui'nit/ās -ā'tis *f.* relationship.
cōnsce'ler/ō -ā're -ā'vī -ā'tum *vt.* disgrace. **-ā'tus** *a.* wicked.
cōnsc/e'ndō -e'ndere -e'ndī -ē'nsum *vt.* & *i.* climb, mount, embark.
cōnscē'nsi/o -ō'nis *f.* embarkation.
cōnscē'nsus *ppp.* cōnscendō.
cōnscie'nti/a -ae *f.* joint knowledge, being in the know; consciousness, sense (of); moral sense, conscience, guilty conscience.
cōnsci'/ndō -ndere -dī -ssum *vt.* tear to pieces; (*fig.*) abuse.
cō'nsc/iō -ī're *vt.* be conscious of guilt.
cōnscī'/scō -scere -vī & iī -ī'tum *vt.* decide on publicly; inflict on oneself. **mortem** (sibi) — commit suicide.
cōnsci'ssus *ppp.* cōnscindō.
cōnscī'tus *ppp.* cōnscīscō.
cō'nscius *a.* sharing knowledge, privy, in the know; aware, conscious (of); conscious of guilt. *m.*, *f.* confederate, confidant.
cō'nscre/or -ā'rī *vi.* clear the throat.
cōnscrī'/bō -bere -psī -ptum *vt.* enlist, enrol; write, compose, draw up, prescribe.
cōnscrī'pti/ō -ō'nis *f.* document, draft.
cōnscrī'pt/us *ppp.* cōnscrībō. **patrēs -ī** (*prop.* patrician and elected plebeian members) senators.
cō'nsec/ō -ā're -uī -tum *vt.* cut up.
cōnsecrā'ti/ō -ō'nis *f.* consecration, deification.
cō'nsecr/ō -ā're -ā'vī -ā'tum *vt.* dedicate, consecrate, deify; (*fig.*) devote; immortalise. **caput** — doom to death.
cōnsectā'rius *a.* logical, consequent. *n.pl.* inferences.
cōnsectā'ti/ō -ō'nis *f.* pursuit.
cōnsectā'tr/īx -ī'cis *f.* (*fig.*) follower.
cōnse'cti/ō -ō'nis *f.* cutting up.
cōnse'ct/or -ā'rī -ā'tus *vt.* follow, go after, try to gain; emulate, imitate; pursue, chase.
cōnsecū'ti/ō -ō'nis *f.* (*philos.*) consequences, effect; (*rhet.*) sequence.
cōnsēd'ī *perf.* cōnsīdō.
cōnsen/ē'scō -ē'scere -uī *vi.* grow old, grow old together; (*fig.*) fade, pine, decay, become obsolete.
cōnsē'nsi/ō -ō'nis *f.* agreement, accord; conspiracy, plot.
cōnsē'nsus *ppp.* cōnsentiō.
cōnsē'ns/us -ūs *m.* agreement, concord; conspiracy; (*philos.*) common sensation; (*fig.*) harmony. **-ū** unanimously.
cōnsentā'ne/us *a.* agreeing, in keeping with. **-um est** it is reasonable.
cōns/e'ntiō -entī're -ē'nsī -ē'nsum *vi.* agree, determine together; plot, conspire; (*philos.*)

have common sensations; (*fig.*) harmonize, suit, be consistent (with). **bellum** — vote for war.

cō'nsequ/ēns -e'ntis *pres.p.* cōnsequor. *a.* coherent, reasonable; logical, consequent *n.* consequence.

cō'nse/quor -quī -cū'tus *vi.* follow, pursue; overtake, reach; (*time*) come after; (*example*) follow, copy; (*effect*) result, be the consequence of; (*aim*) attain, get; (*mind*) grasp, learn; (*events*) happen to, come to; (*standard*) equal, come up to; (*speech*) do justice to.

cō'ns/erō -e'rere -ē'vī -itum *vt.* sow, plant; (*ground*) sow with, plant with; (*fig.*) cover, fill.

cō'nser/ō -ere -uī -tum *vt.* join, string together, twine; (*mil.*) join battle. **manum, manūs** — engage in close combat. **ex iūre manum** — lay claim to (in an action for possession).

cōnse'rt/us *ppp.* cōnserō. -ē *ad.* connectedly.

cōnse'rv/a -ae *f.* fellow-slave.

cōnservā'ti/ō -ō'nis *f.* preserving.

cōnservā't/or -ō'ris *m.* preserver.

cōnservi't/ium -ī & iī *n.* being fellow-slaves.

cōnse'rv/ō -ā're -ā'vī -ā'tum *vt.* preserve, save, keep.

cōnse'rv/us -ī *m.* fellow-slave.

cōnse'ss/or -ō'ris *m.* companion at table, fellow-spectator; (*law*) assessor.

cōnse'ss/us -ūs *m.* assembly; (*law*) court.

cōnsē'vī *perf.* cōnserō.

cōnsīderā'ti/ō -ō'nis *f.* contemplation.

cōnsī'der/ō -ā're -ā'vī -ā'tum *vt.* look at, inspect; consider, contemplate. **-ā'tus** *a.* (*person*) circumspect; (*things*) well-considered. **-ā'tē** *ad.* cautiously, deliberately.

cōns/ī'dō -ī'dere -ē'dī -e'ssum *vi.* sit down, take seats; (*courts*) be in session; (*mil.*) take up a position; (*residence*) settle; (*places*) subside, sink; (*fig.*) sink, settle down, subside.

cōnsi'gn/ō -ā're -ā'vī -ā'tum *vt.* seal, sign; attest, vouch for; record, register.

cōnsilē'sc/ō -ere *vi.* calm down.

cōnsiliā'r/ius -ī & iī *m.* adviser, counsellor; spokesman. *a.* counselling.

cōnsiliā't/or -ō'ris *m.* counsellor.

cōnsi'li/or -ā'rī -ā'tus *vi.* consult; (*with dat.*) advise.

cōnsi'l/ium -ī & iī *n.* deliberation, consultation; deliberating body, council; decision, purpose; plan, measure, stratagem; advice, counsel; judgment, insight, wisdom. **-ium capere, inīre** come to a decision, resolve. **-ī esse** be an open question. **-iō** intentionally. **eō -iō ut** with the intention of. **prīvātō -iō** for one's own purposes.

cōnsi'milis *a.* just like.

cōnsi'p/iō -ere *vi.* be in one's senses.

cōns/i'stō -i'stere -titī *vi.* stand, rest, take up a position; consist (of), depend (on); exist, be; (*fig.*) stand firm, endure; (*liquid*) solidify, freeze; stop, pause, halt, come to rest; (*fig.*) come to a standstill, come to an end.

cōnsi'ti/ō -ō'nis *f.* sowing, planting. [planter.

cō'nsit/or -ō'ris *m.* sower,

cō'nsitus *ppp.* cōnserō.

cōnsōbrī'n/us -ī *m.*, -a -ae *f.* cousin.

cōnsociā'ti/ō -ō'nis *f.* society.

cōnso'ci/ō -ā're -ā'vī -ā'tum *vt.* share, associate, unite.
cōnsōlā'bilis *a.* consolable.
cōnsōlā'ti/ō -ō'nis *f.* comfort, encouragement, consolation.
cōnsōlā't/or -ō'ris *m.* comforter.
cōnsōlātō'rius *a.* of consolation.
cōnsō'l/or -ā'rī -ā'tus *vt.* console, comfort, reassure; (*things*) relieve, mitigate.
cōnso'mni/ō -ā're *vt.* dream about.
cō'nson/ō -ā're -uī *vi.* resound; (*fig.*) accord.
cō'nsonus *a.* concordant; (*fig.*) suitable.
cōnsō'p/iō -ī're -ī'tum *vt.* put to sleep.
cō'nsor/s -tis *a.* sharing in common; (*things*) shared in common. *m., f.* partner, colleague.
cōnso'rti/ō -ō'nis *f.* partnership, fellowship.
cōnso'rt/ium -ī & iī *n.* society, participation.
cōnspe'ctus *ppp.* **cōnspiciō.** *a.* visible; conspicuous.
cōnspe'ct/us -ūs *m.* look, view, sight; appearing on the scene; (*fig.*) mental picture, survey. **in -um venīre** come in sight, come near.
cōnspe'r/gō -gere -sī -sum *vt.* besprinkle; (*fig.*) spangle.
cōnsp/i'ciō -i'cere -e'xī -e'ctum *vt.* observe, catch sight of; look at (*esp.* with admiration), contemplate; (*pass.*) attract attention, be conspicuous, be notorious; (*mind*) see, perceive. **-icie'ndus** *a.* noteworthy, distinguished.
cō'nspic/or -ā'rī -ā'tus *vt.* observe, see, catch sight of.
cōnspi'cuus *a.* visible; conspicuous, distinguished.
cōnspīrā'ti/ō -ō'nis *f.* concord, unanimity; plotting, conspiracy.
cōnspī'r/ō -ā're -ā'vī -ā'tum *vi.* agree, unite; plot, conspire; (*music*) sound together.
cōnspō'ns/or -ō'ris *m.* coguarantor.
cō'nspu/ō -ere *vt.* spit upon.
cōnspu'rc/ō -ā're *vt.* pollute.
cōnspū't/ō -ā're *vt.* spit upon (with contempt).
cōnstabi'l/iō -ī're -ī'vī -ī'tum *vt.* establish.
cō'nst/āns -a'ntis *pres.p.* **cōnstō.** *a.* steady, stable, constant; consistent; faithful, steadfast. **-a'nter** *ad.* steadily, firmly, calmly; consistently.
cōnsta'nti/a -ae *f.* steadiness, firmness; consistency, harmony; self-possession, constancy.
cōnsternā'ti/ō -ō'nis *f.* disorder, tumult; (*horses*) stampede; (*mind*) dismay, alarm.
cōnst/e'rnō -e'rnere -rā'vī -rā'tum *vt.* spread, cover, thatch, pave. **-rāta nāvis** decked ship.
cōnste'rn/ō -ā're -ā'vī -ā'tum *vt.* startle, stampede; alarm, throw into confusion.
cōnstī'p/ō -ā're *vt.* crowd together.
cō'nstitī *perf.* **cōnsistō.**
cōnsti't/uō -u'ere -uī -ū'tum *vt.* put, place, set down; (*mil.*) station, post, halt; establish, build, create; settle, arrange, organize; appoint, determine, fix; resolve, decide. **bene -ūtum corpus** a good constitution. **-ū'tum -ū'tī** *n.* agreement.
cōnstitū'ti/ō -ō'nis *f.* state, condition; regulation, decree; definition, point at issue.
cō'nst/ō -ā're -itī -ā'tum *vi.* stand together; agree, correspond, tally; stand firm, remain constant; exist, be; consist (of), be composed (of); (*facts*) be established, be well-known;

(*bus.*) cost. **sibi —** be consistent. **inter omnēs -at** it is common knowledge. **mihi -at** I am determined. **ratiō -at** the account is correct.
cōnstrā'tus *ppp.* cōnsternō.
-um -ī *n.* flooring, deck.
cōnstr/i'ngō -i'ngere -i'nxī -i'ctum *vt.* tie up, bind, fetter; (*fig.*) restrain, restrict; (*speech*) compress, condense.
cōnstru'cti/ō -ō'nis *f.* building up; (*words*) arrangement, sequence.
cō'nstru/ō -ere -xī -ctum *vt.* heap up; build, construct.
cōnstuprā't/or -ō'ris *m.* debaucher. [rape.
cōnstu'pr/ō -ā're *vt.* debauch,
cōnsuā'd/eō -ē're *vi.* advise strongly.
Cōnsuā'l/ia -ium *n.pl.* festival of Consus.
cōnsuā's/or -ō'ris *m.* earnest adviser.
cōnsū'd/ō -ā're *vi.* sweat profusely.
cōnsuē/fa'ciō -fa'cere -fē'cī -fa'ctum *vt.* accustom.
cōnsuē'/scō -scere -vī -tum *vt.* accustom, inure. *vi.* get accustomed; cohabit (with); (*perf. tenses*) be accustomed, be in the habit of.
cōnsuētū'd/ō -inis *f.* custom, habit; familiarity, social intercourse; love affair; (*language*) usage, idiom. **-ine, ex -ine** as usual. **epistulārum —** correspondence.
cōnsuē'tus *ppp.* cōnsuēscō. *a.* customary, usual.
cōnsuē'vī *perf.* cōnsuēscō.
cō'nsul -is *m.* consul. **— dēsignātus** consul elect. **— ōrdinārius** regular consul. **— suffectus** successor to a consul who has died during his term of office. **— iterum, tertium** consul for the second, third time. **-em creāre, dīcere, facere** elect to the consulship. **L. Domitiō App. Claudiō -ibus** in the year 54 B.C.
cōnsulā'r/is *a.* consular, consul's; of consular rank. *m.* ex-consul. **-iter** *ad.* in a manner worthy of a consul.
cōnsulā't/us -ūs *m.* consulship. **-um petere** stand for the consulship.
cō'nsul/ō -ere -uī -tum *vi.* deliberate, take thought; (*with dat.*) look after, consult the interests of; (*with* dē *or* in) take measures against, pass sentence on. *vt.* consult, ask advice of; consider; advise (something); decide. **bonī, optimī —** take in good part, be satisfied with.
cōnsultā'ti/ō -ō'nis *f.* deliberation; inquiry; case.
cōnsu'lt/ō *ad.* deliberately.
cōnsu'lt/ō -ā're -ā'vī -ā'tum *vt. & i.* deliberate, reflect; consult; (*with dat.*) consult the interests of.
cōnsu'lt/or -ō'ris *m.* counsellor; consulter, client.
cōnsu'ltr/īx -ī'cis *f.* protectress.
cōnsu'lt/um -ī *n.* decree (*esp.* of the Senate); consultation; response (from an oracle).
cōnsu'lt/us *ppp.* cōnsulō. *a.* considered; experienced, skilled. *m.* lawyer. **iūris -us** lawyer. **-ē** *ad.* deliberately.
cōnsu'luī *perf.* cōnsulō.
(cō'n/sum) -futū'rum -fore *vi.* be all right.
cōnsu'mm/ō -ā're *vt.* sum up; complete, perfect. **-ā'tus** *a.* perfect.
cōnsū'm/ō -ere -psī -ptum *vt.* consume, use up, eat up; waste, squander; exhaust, destroy, kill; spend, devote.
cōnsū'mpti/ō -ō'nis *f.* wasting. [destroyer.
cōnsū'mpt/or -ō'ris *m.*
cōnsū'mptus *ppp.* cōnsūmō

cō'ns/uō -u'ere -uī -ū'tum *vt.* sew up; (*fig.*) contrive.
cōnsu'r/gō -gere -rē'xī -rē'c-tum *vi.* rise, stand up; be roused (to); spring up, start.
cōnsurrē'cti/ō -ō'nis *f.* standing up.
Cō'ns/us -ī *m.* ancient Roman god, connected with harvest.
cōnsusu'rr/ō -ā're *vi.* whisper together.
cōnsū'tus *ppp.* cōnsuō.
contābefa'c/iō -ere *vt.* wear out. [waste away.
contāb/ē'scō -ē'scere -uī *vi.*
contabulā'ti/ō -ō'nis *f.* flooring, storey.
conta'bul/ō -ā're -ā'vī -ā'tum *vt.* board over, build in storeys.
contā'ctus *ppp.* contingō.
contā'ct/us -ūs *m.* touch, contact; contagion, infection.
contā'g/ēs -is *f.* contact, touch.
contā'gi/ō -ō'nis *f.*, **contā'-g/ium** -ī & iī *n.* contact; contagion, infection; (*fig.*) contamination, bad example.
contā'min/ō -ā're -ā'vī -ā'tum *vt.* defile; (*fig.*) mar, spoil. **-ā'tus** *a.* impure, vicious.
conte'chn/or -ā'rī -ā'tus *vi.* think out plots.
co'nt/egō -e'gere -e'xī -ē'ctum *vt.* cover up cover over; protect; hide.
conte'mer/ō -ā're *vt.* defile.
conte'm/nō -nere -psī -ptum *vt.* think light of, have no fear of, despise, defy; disparage.
contemplā'ti/ō -ō'nis *f.* contemplation, surveying.
contemplā't/or -ō'ris *m.* observer.
contemplā't/us -ūs *m.* contemplation.
conte'mpl/ō -ā're -ā'vī -ā'tum, **-or** -ā'rī -ā'tus *vt.* look at, observe, contemplate.
contempsī *perf.* contemnō.
conte'mptim *ad.* contemptuously, slightingly.
conte'mpti/ō -ō'nis *f.* disregard, scorn, despising.
conte'mpt/or -ō'ris *m.*, **-rīx** -rī'cis *f.* despiser, defier.
conte'mptus *ppp.* contemnō. *a.* contemptible.
conte'mpt/us -ūs *m.* despising, scorn; being slighted. **-uī esse** be despised.
conte'n/dō -dere -dī -tum *vt.* stretch, draw, tighten; (*instrument*) tune; (*effort*) strain, exert, (*argument*) assert, maintain; (*comparison*) compare, contrast; (*course*) direct. *vi.* exert oneself, strive; hurry; journey, march; contend, compete, fight; entreat, solicit.
conte'nti/ō -ō'nis *f.* straining, effort; striving (after); struggle, competition, dispute; comparison, contrast, antithesis.
conte'nt/us *ppp.* contendō. *a.* strained, tense; (*fig.*) intent. **-ē** *ad.* earnestly, intensely.
conte'nt/us *ppp.* contineō. *a.* content, satisfied. **-ē** *ad.* closely.
conte'rminus *a.* bordering, neighbouring.
co'nt/erō -e'rere -rī'vī -rī'tum *vt.* grind, crumble; wear out, waste; (*time*) spend, pass; (*fig.*) obliterate.
conte'rr/eō -ē're -uī -itum *vt.* terrify.
conte'st/or -ā'rī -ā'tus *vt.* call to witness. **lītem** — open a lawsuit by calling witnesses. **-ā'tus** *a.* proved.
conte'x/ō -ere -uī -tum *vt.* weave, interweave; devise, construct; (*recital*) continue. **-tus** *a.* connected. **-tē** *ad.* in a connected fashion.
conte'xt/us -ūs *m.* connection, coherence.
contic/ē'sco (-ī'sco) -ē'scere

-uī *vi.* become quiet, fall silent; (*fig.*) cease, abate.
co'ntigī *perf.* contingō.
contignā'ti/ō -ō'nis *f.* floor, storey.
conti'gn/ō -ā're *vt.* floor.
conti'guus *a.* adjoining, near; within reach.
co'ntin/ēns -e'ntis *pres.p.* contineō. *a.* bordering, adjacent; unbroken, continuous; (*time*) successive, continual, uninterrupted; (*person*) temperate, continent. *n.* mainland, continent; essential point (in an argument). **-e'nter** *ad.* (*place*) in a row; (*time*) continuously; (*person*) temperately.
contine'nti/a -ae *f.* moderation, self-control.
cont/i'neō -inē're -i'nuī -e'ntum *vt.* hold, keep together; confine, enclose; contain, include, comprise; (*pass.*) consist of, rest on; control, check, repress.
cont/i'ngō -i'ngere -igī -ā'ctum *vt.* touch, take hold of, partake of; be near, border on; reach, come to; contaminate; (*mind*) touch, affect, concern. *vi.* happen, succeed.
conti'ng/ō -ere *vt.* moisten, smear.
continuā'ti/ō -ō'nis *f.* unbroken, succession, series; (*rhet.*) period.
conti'nuī *perf.* contineō.
conti'nuō *ad.* immediately, without delay; (*argument*) necessarily.
conti'nu/ō -ā're -ā'vī -ā'tum *vt.* join together, make continuous; continue without a break. **verba —** form a sentence.
conti'nu/us *a.* joined (to); continuous, successive, uninterrupted. **-ā nocte** the following night. **triduum -um** three days running.
cō'nti/ō -ō'nis *f.* public meeting; speech, address; rostrum. **-ōnem habēre** hold a meeting; deliver an address. **prō -ōne** in public.
cōntiōnābu'ndus *a.* delivering a harangue, playing the demagogue.
cōntiōnā'lis *a.* suitable for a public meeting, demagogic.
cōntiōnā'rius *a.* fond of public meetings.
cōntiōnā't/or -ō'ris *m.* demagogue.
cōntiō'n/or -ā'rī -ā'tus *vi.* address a public meeting, harangue; declare in public; come to a meeting.
cōntiu'ncul/a -ae *f.* short speech.
conto'r/queō -quē're -sī -tum *vt.* twist, turn; (*weapons*) throw, brandish; (*words*) deliver forcibly.
conto'rti/ō -ō'nis *f.* intricacy.
conto'rt/or -ō'ris *m.* perverter.
conto'rtulus *a.* somewhat complicated.
conto'rtuplicā'tus *a.* very complicated.
conto'rt/us *ppp.* contorqueō. *a.* vehement; intricate. **-ē** *ad.* intricately.
co'ntrā *ad.* (place) opposite, face to face; (*speech*) in reply; (*action*) to fight, in opposition, against someone; (*result, with* esse) adverse, unsuccessful; (*comparison*) the contrary, conversely, differently; (*argument*) on the contrary, on the other hand. **— atque, quam** contrary to what, otherwise than. *pr.* (*with acc.*) facing, opposite to; against; contrary to, in violation of.
contra'cti/ō -ō'nis *f.* contracting; shortening; despondency.
contractiu'ncul/a -ae *f.* slight despondency.
contra'ctus *ppp.* contrahō.

a. contracted, narrow; short; in seclusion.
contrā/dī'cō -dī'cere -dī'xī -di'ctum (*usu.* two words) *vt.* & *i.* oppose, object; (*law*) be counsel for the other side.
contrādi'cti/ō -ō'nis *f.* objection.
co'ntra/hō -here -xī -ctum *vt.* draw together, assemble; bring about, achieve; (*bus.*) contract, make a bargain; shorten, narrow; limit, depress; (*blame*) incur; (*brow*) wrinkle; (*sail*) shorten; (*sky*) overcast.
contrā'ri/us *a.* opposite, from opposite; contrary; hostile, harmful. *n.* opposite, reverse. ex -ō on the contrary. -ē *ad.* differently.
contrectābi'liter *ad.* so as to be felt. [touching.
contrectā'ti/ō -ō'nis *f.*
contre'ct/ō -ā're -ā'vī -ā'tum *vt.* touch, handle; (*fig.*) consider.
contrem/ī'scō -ī'scere -uī *vi.* tremble all over; (*fig.*) waver. *vt.* be afraid of.
co'ntrem/ō -ere *vi.* quake.
contri'b/uō -u'ere -uī -ū'tum *vt.* bring together, join, incorporate.
contri'st/ō -ā're -ā'vī -ā'tum *vt.* sadden, darken, cloud.
contrī'tus *ppp.* conterō. *a.* trite, well-worn.
contrōve'rsi/a -ae *f.* dispute, argument, debate, controversy.
contrōversiō'sus *a.* much disputed. [questionable.
contrōve'rsus *a.* disputed,
contrucī'd/ō -ā're -ā'vī -ā'tum *vt.* massacre.
contrū'/dō -dere -sī -sum *vt.* crowd together.
contru'nc/ō -ā're *vt.* hack to pieces.
contrū'sus *ppp.* contrūdō.
contubernā'l/is -is *m., f.* tent-companion; junior officer serving with a general; (*fig.*) companion, mate.
contube'rn/ium -ī & iī *n.* service in the same tent, mess; service as junior officer with a general; common tent; slaves' home.
contu'/eor -ē'rī -itus *vt.* look at, consider, observe.
contu'it/us, contū't/us -ūs *m.* observing, view.
co'ntulī *perf.* cōnferō.
contumā'ci/a -ae *f.* obstinacy, defiance.
co'ntum/āx -ā'cis *a.* stubborn, insolent, pig-headed. -ā'citer *ad.*
contumē'li/a -ae *f.* (*verbal*) insult, libel, invective; (*physical*) assault, ill-treatment.
contumēliō's/us *a.* insulting, outrageous. -ē *ad.* insolently.
contu'mul/ō -ā're *vt.* bury.
cont/u'ndō -u'ndere -udī -ū'sum *vt.* pound, beat, bruise; (*fig.*) suppress, destroy.
co'ntuor, *see* **contueor.**
conturbā'ti/ō -ō'nis *f.* confusion, mental disorder.
contu'rb/ō -ā're -ā'vī -ā'tum *vt.* throw into confusion; (*mind*) derange, disquiet; (*money*) embarrass. -ā'tus *a.* distracted, diseased.
co'nt/us -ī *m.* pole.
contū'sus *ppp.* contundō.
contū'tus, *see* **contuitus.**
cōnūbiā'lis *a.* conjugal.
cōnū'b/ium -ī & iī *n.* marriage. iūs -ī right of inter-marriage. [apex.
cō'n/us -ī *m.* cone; (*helmet*)
co'nvad/or -ā'rī -ā'tus *vt.* (*law*) bind over.
conval/ē'scō -ē'scere -uī *vi.* recover, get better; (*fig.*) grow stronger, improve.
conva'll/is -is *f.* valley with hills on all sides.
convā's/ō -ā're *vt.* pack up.
conve'ct/ō -ā're *vt.* bring home.

conve'ct/or -ō'ris *m.* fellow-passenger.
co'nve/hō -here -xī -ctum *vt.* bring in, carry.
conv/e'llō -e'llere -e'llī -u'lsum & o'lsum *vt.* wrench, tear away; break up; (*fig.*) destroy, overthrow. signa — decamp.
co'nven/a -ae *a.* meeting. -ae -ā'rum *m., f.* crowd of strangers, refugees.
conve'ni/ēns -e'ntis *pres.p.* conveniō. *a.* harmonious, consistent; fit, appropriate. **-e'nter** *ad.* in conformity (with), consistently; aptly.
convenie'nti/a -ae *f.* conformity, harmony.
conv/e'niō enī're -ē'nī -e'ntum *vi.* meet, assemble; (*events*) combine, coincide; (*person*) agree, harmonize; (*things*) fit, suit; (*impers.*) be suitable, be proper. *vt.* speak to, interview.
conventī'c/ius *a.* visiting regularly. **-ium** -ī & iī *n.* payment for attendance at assemblies.
conventi'cul/um -ī *n.* gathering; meeting-place.
conve'nti/ō -ō'nis *f.* agreement.
conve'nt/um -ī *n.* agreement.
conve'ntus *ppp.* conveniō.
conve'nt/us -ūs *m.* meeting; (*law*) local assizes; (*bus.*) corporation; agreement. -ūs agere hold the assizes.
conve'r/rō (**convo'rrō**) -rere -rī -sum *vt.* sweep up, brush together; (*comedy*) give a good beating to.
conversā'ti/ō -ō'nis *f.* associating (with).
conve'rsi/ō -ō'nis *f.* revolution, cycle; change over; (*rhet.*) well-rounded period; verbal repetition at end of clauses.
conve'rs/ō -ā're *vt.* turn round.
conve'rsus *ppp.* converrō; *ppp.* convertō.
conve'r/tō (**convo'rtō**) -tere -tī -sum *vt.* turn round, turn back; (*mil.*) wheel; turn, direct; change, transform; (*writings*) translate. *vi.* return, turn, change.
conve'st/iō -ī're -ī'vī -ī'tum *vt.* clothe, encompass.
conve'xus *a.* vaulted, rounded; hollow; sloping. *n.* vault, hollow.
convīciā't/or -ō'ris *m.* slanderer.
convī'ci/or -ā'rī -ā'tus *vt.* revile.
convī'c/ium -ī & iī *n.* loud noise, outcry; invective, abuse; reproof, protest.
convī'cti/o -ō'nis *f.* companionship.
convī'ct/or -ō'ris *m.* familiar friend.
convī'ctus *ppp.* convincō.
convī'ct/us -ūs *m.* community life, intercourse; entertainment.
conv/i'ncō -i'ncere -ī'cī -i'ctum *vt.* refute, convict, prove wrong; prove, demonstrate.
convī's/ō -ere *vt.* search, examine; pervade.
convī'tium, *see* **convīcium**.
convī'v/a -ae *m., f.* guest.
convīvā'lis *a.* festive, convivial.
convīvā't/or -ō'ris *m.* host.
convī'v/ium -ī & iī *n.* banquet, entertainment; guests.
convī'v/or -ā'rī -ā'tus *vi.* feast together, carouse.
convocā'ti/ō -ō'nis *f.* assembling.
co'nvoc/ō -ā're -ā'vī -ā'tum *vt.* call a meeting of, muster.
convo'lnerō, *see* **convulnerō**.
co'nvol/ō -ā're -ā'vī -ā'tum *vi.* flock together.
convo'lsus, *see* **convulsus**.
convo'l/vō -vere -vī -ū'tum *vt.* roll up, coil up; intertwine.

co'nvom/ō -ere *vt.* vomit over.
convo'rtō, *see* **convertō.**
convu'lner/ō -ā're *vt.* wound seriously.
convu'lsus *ppp.* convellō.
coope'r/iō -ī're -uī -tum *vt.* cover over, overwhelm.
cooptā'ti/ō -ō'nis *f.* electing, nominating (of new members).
coo'pt/ō -ā're -ā'vī -ā'tum *vt.* elect (as a colleague).
coo'r/ior -ī'rī -tus *vi.* rise appear; break out, begin.
coo'rt/us -ūs *m.* originating.
cō'p/a ae *f.* barmaid.
co'phin/us -ī *m.* basket.
cō'pi/a ae *f.* abundance, plenty, number; resources, wealth, prosperity; (*mil.*, *usu. pl.*) troops, force; (*words, thought*) richness, fulness, store; (*action*) opportunity, facility, means, access. prō -ā according to one's resources, as good as possible considering.
cōpi'ol/ae -ā'rum *f.pl.* small force.
cōpiō's/us *a.* abounding, rich, plentiful; (*speech*) eloquent, fluent. **-ē** *ad.* abundantly fully, at great length.
cō'pis *a.* rich.
cō'pul/a -ae *f.* rope, leash, grapnel; (*fig.*) bond.
cōpulā'ti/ō -ō'nis *f.* coupling, union.
cō'pul/ō -ā're ā'vī ā'tum *vt.* couple, join; (*fig.*) unite, associate. **-ā'tus** *a.* connected, binding.
co'qu/a -ae *f.* cook.
coquī'n/ō -ā're *vi.* be a cook.
coquī'nus *a.* of cooking.
co'/quō -quere -xī -ctum *vt.* cook, boil, bake; parch, burn; (*fruit*) ripen; (*stomach*) digest; (*thought*) plan, concoct; (*care*) disquiet, disturb.
co'qu/us (**co'cus**) -ī *m.* cook.
cor co'rdis *n.* heart; (*feeling*) heart, soul; (*thought*) mind, judgment. cordī esse please, be agreeable.
cō'ram *ad.* in one's presence; in person. *pr.* (*with abl.*) in the presence of, before.
co'rb/is -is *m.*, *f.* basket.
corbī't/a -ae *f.* slow boat.
co'rbul/a -ae *f.* little basket.
co'rcul/um -ī *n.* dear heart.
Corcȳ'r/a -ae *f.* island off W. coast of Greece, *mod.* Corfu. **-ae'us** *a.*
cordā't/us *a.* wise. **-ē** *ad.*
cordo'l/ium -ī & iī *n.* sorrow.
Corfī'n/ium -ī *n.* town in central Italy. **-iē'nsis** *a.*
coria'ndr/um -ī *n.* coriander.
Cori'nth/us -ī *f.* Corinth. **-i'acus**, **-iē'nsis** **-ius** *a.* -ium aes Corinthian brass, an alloy of gold, silver and copper.
co'r/ium (**corius** *m.*) -ī & iī *n.* hide, skin; leather, strap.
Cornē'l/ius -ī *m.* famous Roman family name, *esp.* Scipios, Gracchi, Sulla. -ia -iae *f.* mother of the Gracchi. **-iā'nus**, **-ius** *a.* lēgēs -iae Sulla's laws.
corne'olus *a.* horny.
co'rneus *a.* of horn.
co'rneus *a.* of the cornel-tree, of cornel-wood.
co'rnic/en -cinis *m.* horn-blower.
cornī'cul/a -ae *f.* little crow.
corniculā'r/ius -ī & iī *m.* adjutant.
corni'cul/um -ī *n.* a horn-shaped decoration.
co'rniger -ī *a.* horned.
co'rnip/ēs -edis *a.* horn-footed.
co'rn/īx -ī'cis *f.* crow.
co'rn/ū -ūs, **-um** -ī *n.* horn; anything horn-shaped; (*army*) wing, (*bay*) arm, (*book*) roller-end, (*bow*) tip, (*helmet*) crest-socket, (*land*) tongue, spit, (*lyre*) arm, (*moon*) horn, (*place*) side, (*river*) branch, (*yard-arm*) point; anything made of horn;

bow, funnel, lantern, (*music*) horn, (*oil*) cruet; anything like horn: beak, hoof, wart; (*fig.*) strength, courage. — cōpiae Amalthea's horn, symbol of plenty.
co'rn/um -ī *n.* cornelian cherry.
co'rnum, *see* **cornū.**
co'rn/us -ī *f.* cornelian cherry-tree; javelin.
corō'll/a -ae *f.* small garland.
corōllā'r/ium -ī & iī *n.* garland for actors; present, gratuity.
corō'n/a -ae *f.* garland, crown; (*astr.*) Corona Borealis; (*people*) gathering, bystanders; (*mil.*) cordon of besiegers or defenders. sub -ā vēndere, vēnīre sell, be sold as slaves.
corōnā'rium au'rum gold collected in the provinces for a victorious general.
Corōn/ē'a ē'ae *f.* town in central Greece. **-ae'us, -ē'us, -ē'nsis** *a.*
corō'n/ō -ā're -ā'vī -ā'tum *vt.* put a garland on, crown; encircle. [flesh.
corpo'reus *a.* corporeal; of
corpule'ntus *a.* corpulent.
co'rp/us -oris *n.* body; substance, flesh; corpse; trunk, torso; person, individual; (*fig.*) structure, corporation, body politic.
corpu'scul/um -ī *n.* particle; term of endearment.
corrā'/dō -dere -sī -sum *vt.* scrape together, procure.
corrē'cti/ō -ō'nis *f.* amending, improving. [critic.
corrē'ct/or -ō'ris *m.* reformer,
corrē'ctus *ppp.* corrigō.
corrē'p/ō -ere -sī *vi.* creep, slink, cower.
corre'pt/us *ppp.* corripiō. **-ē** *ad.* briefly. [aloud.
corrī'd/eō -ē're *vi.* laugh
corri'gi/a -ae *f.* shoe-lace.
co'rr/igō -i'gere -ē'xī -ē'ctum *vt.* make straight; put right improve, correct.
corr/i'piō -i'pere -i'puī -e'ptum *vt.* seize, carry off, get along quickly; (*speech*) reprove, reproach, accuse; (*passion*) seize upon, attack; (*time, words*) cut short. sē gradum, viam — hasten, rush.
corrō'bor/ō -ā're -ā'vī -ā'tum *vt.* make strong, invigorate.
corrō'/dō -dere -sī -sum *vt.* nibble away.
co'rrog/ō -ā're *vt.* gather by requesting.
corrū'g/ō -ā're *vt.* wrinkle.
corr/u'mpō -u'mpere -ū'pī -u'ptum *vt.* break up, ruin, waste; mar, adulterate, falisfy; (*person*) corrupt, seduce, bribe.
co'rru/ō -ere -ī *vi.* fall, collapse. *vt.* overthrow, heap up.
corruptē'l/a -ae *f.* corruption, bribery; seducer.
corru'pti/ō -ō'nis *f.* bribing, seducing; corrupt state.
corru'pt/or -ō'ris *m.*, **-rīx** -rī'cis *f.* corrupter, seducer.
corru'pt/us *ppp.* corrumpō. *a.* spoiled, corrupt, bad. **-ē** *ad.* perversely; in a lax manner.
Co'rsus *a.* Corsican.
co'rt/ex -icis *m., f.* bark, rind; cork.
cortī'n/a -ae *f.* kettle, cauldron; tripod of Apollo; (*fig.*) vault, circle.
Cōrus, *see* **Caurus.**
coru'sc/ō -ā're *vt.* butt; shake, brandish. *vi.* flutter, flash, quiver.
coru'scus *a.* tremulous, oscillating; shimmering, glittering.
co'rv/us -ī *m.* raven; (*mil.*) grapnel.
Coryba'nt/ēs -ium *m.pl.* priests of Cybele. **-ius** *a.*
cō'ryc/us -ī *m.* punch-ball.
corylē't/um -ī *n.* hazel-copse.
co'ryl/us, **corul/us** -ī *f.* hazel.

cory'mb/us -ī *m.* cluster, *esp.* of ivy-berries. **-ifer** Bacchus.
coryphae'/us -ī *m.* leader.
cō'ryt/os, -us -ī *m.* quiver.
cōs, cō'tis *f.* hard rock, flint; grindstone.
Cōs, Co'us Co'ī *f.* Aegean island, famous for wine and weaving. **Cō'us** *a.* Coan. *n.* Coan wine. *n.pl.* Coan clothes.
cosmē't/a -ae *m.* master of the wardrobe.
co'st/a -ae *f.* rib; side, wall.
co'st/um -ī *n.* an aromatic plant, perfume. [tragic.
cothurnā'tus *a.* buskined,
cothu'rn/us -ī *m.* buskin, hunting-boot; tragedy, elevated style.
cotīd-, *see* **cottīd-.**
co'ttab/us -ī *m.* game of throwing drops of wine.
co'ttan/a -ōrum *n.pl.* Syrian figs.
cottīdiā'n/us *a.* daily; everyday, ordinary. **-ō** *ad.* daily.
cottī'diē *ad.* every day, daily.
cotu'rn/īx -ī'cis *f.* quail.
Coty'tti/a -ōrum *n.pl.* festival of Thracian goddess Cotytto.
Co'us, *see* **Cōs.**
covinnā'r/ius -ī & iī *m.* chariot-fighter.
covi'nn/us -ī *m.* war-chariot; coach. [*f.* hip.
co'x/a -ae, **coxe'nd/īx** -ī'cis
co'xī *perf.* coquō.
crā'br/ō -ō'nis *m.* hornet.
cra'mb/ē -ēs *f.* cabbage. — repetita stale repetitions.
Cra'nt/or -oris *m.* Greek Academic philosopher.
crā'pul/a -ae *f.* intoxication, hangover.
crāpulā'rius *a.* for intoxication.
crās *ad.* to-morrow.
crassitū'd/ō -inis *f.* thickness, density.
cra'ss/us *a.* thick, gross dense; (*fig.*) dull, stupid. **-ē** *ad.* grossly, dimly.
Cra'ss/us -ī *m.* famous orator; wealthy politician, triumvir with Caesar and Pompey. **-iā'nus** *a.*
crā'stin/us *a.* of to-morrow. diē -ī to-morrow. **-um** -ī *n.* the morrow.
crā'tēr -is *m.*, **-a** -ae *f.* bowl, *esp.* for mixing wine and water; crater; a constellation.
crā't/is -is *f.* wicker-work, hurdle; (*agr.*) harrow, (*mil.*) faggots for lining trenches, (*shield*) ribs; (*fig.*) frame, joints.
creā'ti/ō -ō'nis *f.* election.
creā't/or -ō'ris *m.*, **-rīx** -rī'cis *f.* creator, father, mother.
crē'b/er -rī *a.* dense, thick, crowded; numerous, frequent; (*fig.*) prolific, abundant. **-rō** *ad.* repeatedly.
crēbr/ē'scō -ē'scere -uī *vi.* increase, become frequent.
crē'brit/ās -ā'tis *f.* frequency.
crēdi'bili/s *a.* credible. **-ter** *ad.*
crē'dit/or -ō'ris *m.* creditor.
crē'd/ō -ere -idī -itum *vt.* & *i.* entrust, lend; trust, have confidence in; believe; think, suppose. -erēs one would have thought. **-itum** -itī *n.* loan.
crēdu'lit/ās -ā'tis *f.* credulity.
crē'dulus *a.* credulous, trusting.
cre'm/ō -ā're -ā'vī -ā'tum *vt.* burn, cremate.
Cremō'n/a -ae *f.* town in N. Italy. **-ē'nsis** *a.*
cre'm/or -ō'ris *m.* juice, broth.
cre'/ō -ā're -ā'vī -ā'tum *vt.* create, produce, beget, elect (to an office); cause, occasion. -ātus (*with abl.*) son of.
cre'per -ī *a.* dark; doubtful.
cre'pid/a -ae *f.* sandal. nē

sūtor suprā -am *let the cobbler stick to his last.* [sandals.
crepidā'tus *a.* wearing
crepī'd/ō -inis *f.* pedestal, base; bank, pier, dam.
crepi'dul/a -ae *f.* small sandal.
crepitāci'll/um -ī *n.* rattle.
cre'pit/ō -ā're *vi.* rattle, chatter, rustle, creak.
cre'pit/us -ūs *m.* rattling, chattering, rustling, creaking.
cre'p/ō -ā're -uī -itum *vi.* rattle, creak, snap (fingers). *vt.* make rattle, clap; chatter about.
crepu'ndi/a -ō'rum *n.pl.* rattle, babies' toys.
crepu'scul/um -ī *n.* twilight, dusk; darkness.
Cr/ēs -ē'tis *m.*, **Crē'ss/a** -ae *f.*, **Crē'sius** *a.* Cretan.
crē'/scō -scere -vī -tum *vi.* arise, appear, be born; grow up, thrive, increase, multiply; prosper, be promoted, rise in the world. -tus descended, born.
Crē't/a -ae *f.* Crete. **-ae'us**, **-ē'nsis**, **-icus**, **-is** -idis *a.*
crē't/a -ae *f.* chalk; good mark.
crētā'tus *a.* chalked, dressed in white.
Crē'tē, *see* **Crēta.**
crē'teus *a.* of chalk, of clay.
crē'ti/ō -ō'nis *f.* declaration of accepting an inheritance.
crētō'sus *a.* chalky, clayey.
crē'tul/a -ae *f.* white clay for sealing. [crēscō.
crē'tus *ppp.* cernō; *ppa.*
Creū's/a -ae *f.* wife of Jason; wife of Aeneas.
crē'vī *perf.* cernō; *perf.* crēscō.
crī'br/um -ī *n.* sieve.
crī'm/en -inis *n.* accusation, charge, reproach; guilt, crime; cause of offence. esse in -ine stand accused.
crīminā'ti/ō -ō'nis *f.* complaint, slander. [accuser.
crīminā't/or -ō'ris *m.*
crī'min/ō -ā're *vt.* accuse.
crī'min/or -ā'rī -ā'tus accuse, impeach; (*things*) complain of, charge with.
crīminō's/us *a.* reproachful, slanderous. **-ē** *ad.* accusingly, slanderously.
crīnā'lis *a.* for the hair, hair-. *n.* hair-pin. [tail.
crī'n/is -is *m.* hair; (*comet*)
crīnī't/us *a.* long-haired; crested. stēlla -a comet.
crī'sp/ō -ā're *vt.* curl, swing, wave. **-āns** -a'ntis *a.* wrinkled.
crī'spus *a.* curled; curly-headed; wrinkled; tremulous.
cri'st/a -ae *f.* cock's comb, crest; plume.
cristā'tus *a.* crested, plumed.
cri'tic/us -ī *m.* critic.
cro'ceus *a.* of saffron, yellow.
cro'cinus *a.* yellow. *n.* saffron-oil.
crō'c/iō -ī're *vi.* croak.
crocodī'l/us -ī *m.* crocodile.
crocōtā'rius *a.* of saffron clothes. [dress.
crocō'tul/a -ae *f.* saffron
cro'c/us -ī *m.*, **-um** -ī *n.* saffron; yellow.
Croe's/us -ī *m.* king of Lydia, famed for wealth.
crotali'stri/a -ae *f.* castanet-dancer. [castanet.
cro'tal/um -ī *n.* rattle,
cruciābi'lit/ās -ā'tis *f.* torment. [ture.
cruciāme'nt/um -ī *n.* tor-
cruciā't/us -ūs *m.* torture; instrument of torture; (*fig.*) ruin, misfortune.
cru'ci/ō -ā're -ā'vī -ā'tum *vt.* torture; torment.
crūdē'l/is *a.* hard-hearted, cruel. **-iter** *ad.*
crūdē'lit/ās -ā'tis *f.* cruelty, severity.
crūd/ē'scō -ē'scere -uī *vi.* grow violent, grow worse.
crū'dit/ās -ā'tis *f.* indigestion.
crū'dus *a.* bleeding; (*food*)

raw, undigested; (*person*) dyspeptic; (*leather*) raw-hide; (*fruit*) unripe; (*age*) immature, fresh; (*voice*) hoarse; (*fig.*) unfeeling, cruel, merciless.
crue'nt/ō -ā're *vt.* stain with blood, wound.
crue'ntus *a.* bloody, gory; blood-thirsty, cruel; blood-red. [money.
crumē'n/a -ae *f.* purse;
crumi'll/a -ae *f.* purse.
cru'/or -ō'ris *m.* blood; bloodshed.
cruppellā'ri/ī -ō'rum *m.pl.* mail-clad fighters.
crūrifra'g/ius -ī & iī *m.* broken-shins.
cr/ūs -ū'ris *n.* leg, shin.
crū'st/a -ae *f.* hard surface, crust; stucco, embossed or inlaid work. [pastry.
crū'stul/um -ī *n.* small
crū'st/um -ī *n.* pastry.
cr/ux -u'cis *f.* gallows, cross; (*fig.*) torment. **abī in malam -cem** *go and be hanged!*
cry'pt/a -ae *f.* underground passage, grotto.
cryptopo'rtic/us -ūs *f.* covered walk.
crystalli'nus *a.* of crystal. *n.pl.* crystal vases.
crysta'll/um -ī *n.*, **-us -ī** *m.* crystal.
cubiculā'ris, cubiculā'rius *a.* of the bed-room. *m.* valet de chambre.
cubi'cul/um -ī *n.* bed-room.
cubī'l/e -is *n.* bed, couch; (*animals*) lair, nest; (*fig.*) den.
cu'bit/al -ā'lis *n.* cushion.
cubitā'lis *a.* a cubit long.
cu'bit/ō -ā're *vi.* lie (in bed).
cu'bit/um -ī *n.* elbow; cubit.
cu'bit/us -ūs *m.* lying in bed.
cu'b/ō -ā're -uī -itum *vi.* lie in bed; recline at table; (*places*) lie on a slope.
cucu'll/us -ī *m.* hood, cowl.
cucū'l/us -ī *m.* cuckoo.
cu'cum/is -eris *m.* cucumber.
cucu'rbit/a -ae *f.* gourd; cupping-glass.
cucu'rrī *perf.* **currō.**
cū'd/ō -ere *vt.* beat, thresh; (*metal*) forge; (*money*) coin.
cui'cuimo'dī of whatever kind, whatever like.
cuiā'/s -tis *pro.* of what country? of what town?
cū'ius *pro.* (*interrog.*) whose? (*rel.*) whose.
cu'lcit/a -ae *f.* mattress, pillow; eye-patch.
cū'leus, *see* **culleus.**
cu'l/ex -icis *m., f.* gnat.
culī'n/a -ae *f.* kitchen; food.
cu'lle/us, cū'le/us -ī *m.* leather bag for holding liquids; a fluid measure.
cu'lm/en -inis *n.* stalk; top, roof, summit; (*fig.*) height, acme.
cu'lm/us -ī *m.* stalk, straw.
cu'lp/a -ae *f.* blame, fault; mischief. **in -ā sum, mea -a est** I am at fault, to blame.
cu'lpit/ō -ā're *vt.* find fault with.
cu'lp/ō -ā're -ā'vī -ā'tum *vt.* blame, reproach. **-ā'tus** *a.* blameworthy.
culte'll/us -ī *m.* small knife.
cu'lt/er -rī *m.* knife, razor.
cu'lti/ō -ō'nis *f.* cultivation.
cu'lt/or -ō'ris *m.* cultivator, planter, farmer; inhabitant; supporter, upholder; worshipper.
cu'ltr/īx -ī'cis *f.* inhabitant; (*fig.*) nurse, fosterer.
cultū'r/a -ae *f.* cultivation, agriculture; (*mind*) care, culture; (*person*) courting.
cu'lt/us *ppp.* **colō.** *a.* cultivated; (*dress*) well-dressed; (*mind*) polished, cultured. *n.pl.* cultivated land. **-ē** *ad.* in a refined manner.
cu'lt/us -ūs *m.* cultivation, care; (*mind*) training, culture; (*dress*) style, attire; (*way of life*) refinement, civilisation;

(*gods*) worship; (*men*) honouring.
culu'll/us -ī *m.* goblet.
cū'l/us -ī *m.* buttocks.
cum *pr.* (*with abl.*) with, *denoting* accompaniment, resulting circumstances, means, dealings, comparison, possession. — **decimō** tenfold. — **eō quod, ut** with the proviso that. — **prīmīs** especially. — **māgnā calamitāte cīvitātis** to the great misfortune of the community. — **perīculō suō** at one's own peril.
cum, quom *conj.* (*time*) when, whenever, while, as, after, since; (*cause*) since, as, seeing that; (*concession*) although; (*condition*) if; (*contrast*) while, whereas. **multī annī sunt — in aere meō est** for many years now he has been in my debt. **aliquot sunt annī — vōs dēlēgī** it is now some years since I chose you. — **māximē** just when; just then, just now. — **prīmum** as soon as. — . . . **tum** not only . . . but also, both . . . and.
Cū'm/ae -ā'rum *f.pl.* town near Naples, famous for its Sibyl. **-ae'us, -ā'nus** *a.* **-ā'num** -ā'nī *n.* Cicero's Cumaean residence.
cu'mb/a, cy'mb/a -ae *f.* boat, skiff.
cu'mer/a -ae *f.* grain-chest.
cumī'n/um -ī *n.* cumin.
cu'mque, cu'nque, quo'mque *ad.* -ever, -soever; at any time.
cu'mul/ō -ā're -ā'vī -ā'tum *vt.* heap up; amass, increase; fill up, overload; (*fig.*) fill, overwhelm, crown, complete. **-ā'tus** *a.* increased; complete. **-ā'tē** *ad.* fully, abundantly.
cu'mul/us -ī *m.* heap, mass; crowning addition, summit.
cūnā'bul/a -ō'rum *n.pl.* cradle.
cū'n/ae -ā'rum *f.pl.* cradle.
cunctābu'ndus *a.* hesitant, dilatory.
cu'nct/āns -a'ntis *a.* dilatory, reluctant; sluggish, tough. **-a'nter** *ad.* slowly.
cunctā'ti/ō -ō'nis *f.* delaying, hesitation.
cunctā't/or -ō'ris *m.* loiterer; one given to cautious tactics, *esp.* Q. Fabius Maximus.
cu'nct/or -ā'rī -ā'tus *vi.* linger, delay, hesitate; move slowly.
cū'nctus *a.* the whole of; (*pl.*) all together, all.
cuneā'tim *ad.* in the form of a wedge.
cuneā'tus *a.* wedge-shaped.
cu'ne/us -ī *m.* wedge; (*mil.*) wedge-shaped formation of troops; (*theatre*) block of seats.
cunī'cul/us -ī *m.* rabbit; underground passage; (*mil.*) mine.
cu'nque, *see* **cumque**.
cū'p/a -ae *f.* vat, tun.
cupi'dit/ās -ā'tis *f.* desire, eagerness, enthusiasm; passion lust; avarice, greed; ambition; partisanship.
cupī'd/ō -inis *f.* desire, eagerness; passion, lust; greed.
Cupī'd/ō -inis *m.* Cupid, son of Venus. **-i'neus** *a.*
cu'pid/us *a.* desirous, eager; fond, loving; passionate, lustful; greedy, ambitious; partial. **-ē** *ad.* eagerly, passionately.
cu'pi/ēns -ē'ntis *pres.p.* cupiō. *a.* eager, desirous. **-e'nter** *ad.*
cu'p/iō -ere -ī'vī & iī -ī'tum *vt.* wish, desire, long for; (*with dat.*) wish well.
cupī't/or -ō'ris *m.* desirer.
cupī'tus *ppp.* cupiō.
cuppē'di/a -ae *f.* fondness for delicacies. **-a** -ō'rum *n.pl.* delicacies.
cuppēdinā'r/ius -ī *m.* confectioner.

cuppē'd/ō -inis *f.* longing, passion.
cu'ppe/s -dis *a.* fond of delicacies. [grove.
cupressē't/um -ī *n.* cypress-
cupre'sseus *a.* of cypress-wood. [bearing.
cupre'ssifer -ī *a.* cypress-
cupre'ss/us -ī *f.* cypress.
cūr, quor *ad.* why? (*indirect*) why, the reason for.
cū'r/a -ae *f.* care, trouble, pains (bestowed); anxiety, concern, sorrow (felt); attention (to), charge (of) concern (for); (*med.*) treatment, cure; (*writing*) work; (*law*) trusteeship; (*poet*) love; (*person*) mistress, guardian. — est I am anxious. -ae esse be attended to, looked after.
cūrā'bilis *a.* troublesome.
cūra'l/ium -ī & iī *n.* red coral.
cūrā'ti/ō -ō'nis *f.* charge, management; office; treatment, healing.
cūrā't/or -ō'ris *m.* manager, overseer; (*law*) guardian.
cūrātū'r/a -ae *f.* dieting.
curcu'li/ō -ō'nis *m.* weevil.
curculiu'ncul/us -ī *m.* little weevil.
Cu'r/ēs -ium *m.pl.* ancient Sabine town. **-ē'nsis** *a.*
Cūrē't/ēs -um *m.pl.* attendants of Jupiter in Crete. **-is** -idis *a.* Cretan.
cū'ri/a -ae *f.* earliest division of the Roman people; meeting-place of a curia; senate-house; senate. [a curia.
cūriā'l/is -is *m.* member of
cūriā'tim *ad.* by curiae.
cūriā't/us *a.* of the curiae. comitia -a earliest Roman assembly.
cū'ri/ō -ō'nis *m.* president of a curia. — **māximus** head of all the curiae.
cū'ri/ō -ō'nis *a.* emaciated.
cūriō'sit/ās -ā'tis *f.* curiosity.
cūriō's/us *a.* careful, thoughtful, painstaking; inquiring, inquisitive, officious; care-worn. **-ē** *ad.* carefully; inquisitively.
cu'r/is, qui'r/is -itis *f.* spear.
cū'r/ō -ā're -ā'vī -ā'tum *vt.* take care of, attend to; bother about; (*with gerundive*) get something done; (*with inf.*) take the trouble; (*with* ut) see to it that; (*public life*) be in charge of, administer; (*med.*) treat, cure; (*money*) pay, settle up. aliud -ā never mind. corpus, cutem — take it easy. prōdigia — avert portents. **-ā'tus** *a.* cared for; earnest, anxious. **-ā'tē** *ad.* carefully.
curri'cul/um -ī *n.* running, race; course, lap; (*fig.*) career. -ō at full speed.
cu'rr/ō -ere cucu'rrī cu'rsum *vi.* run; hasten, fly. *vt.* run through, traverse. -entem incitāre *spur a willing horse.*
cu'rr/us -ūs *m.* car, chariot; triumph; team of horses; plough-wheels.
cu'rsim *ad.* quickly, at the double.
cu'rsit/ō -ā're *vi.* run about, fly hither and thither.
cu'rs/ō -ā're *vi.* run about.
cu'rs/or -ō'ris *m.* runner, racer; courier.
cursū'r/a -ae *f.* running.
cu'rs/us -ūs *m.* running, speed; passage, journey; course, direction; (*things*) movement, flow; (*fig.*) rapidity, flow, progress. — honōrum succession of magistracies. — rērum course of events. -um tenēre keep on one's course. -ū at a run. māgnō -ū at full speed.
cu'rt/ō -ā're *vt.* shorten.
cu'rtus *a.* short, broken off; incomplete.

curū′lis *a.* official, curule. aedīlis — patrician aedille. sella — magistrates' chair. equī — horses provided for the games by the state.
curvā′m/en -inis *n.* bend.
curvātū′r/a -ae *f.* curve.
cu′rv/ō -ā′re -ā′vī -ā′tum *vt.* curve, bend, arch; (*fig.*) move.
cu′rvus *a.* bent, curved, crooked; (*person*) aged; (*fig.*) wrong.
cu′spi/s -dis *f.* point; spear, javelin, trident, sting.
custōdē′l/a -ae *f.* care, guard.
custō′di/a -ae *f.* watch, guard, care; (*person*) sentry, guard; (*place*) sentry's post, guard-house; custody, confinement, prison. lībera — confinement in one's own house.
custō′d/iō -ī′re -ī′vī & iī -ī′tum *vt.* guard, defend; hold in custody, keep watch on; keep, preserve, observe.
cu′st/ōs -ō′dis *m., f.* guard, body-guard, protector, protectress; jailer, warder; (*mil.*) sentry, spy; container.
cutī′cul/a -ae *f.* skin.
cu′t/is -is *f.* skin. -em cūrāre *take it easy.*
cyathi′ss/ō -ā′re *vi.* serve wine.
cy′ath/us -ī *m.* wine-ladle; (*measure*) one-twelfth of a pint.
cybae′/a -ae *f.* kind of merchant ship.
Cy′bel/ē (**Cybē′bē**) -ēs *f.* Phrygian mother-goddess, Magna Mater. **-ē′ius** *a.*
Cy′clad/es -um *f.pl.* group of Aegean islands.
cy′cl/as -adis *f.* formal dress with a border.
cy′clicus *a.* of the traditional epic stories.
Cy′clōp/s -is *m.* one-eyed giant, *esp.* Polyphemus. **-ius** *a.*
cycnē′us *a.* of a swan, swan's.
cy′cn/us -ī *m.* swan.
Cydō′nius *a.* Cretan. *n.pl.* quinces.
cy′gnus, *see* **cycnus.**
cyli′ndr/us -ī *m.* cylinder; roller.
Cyllē′n/ē -ēs & ae *f.* mountain in Arcadia. **-ē′us, -is, -ius** *a.* **-ius** -ī *m.* Mercury.
cy′mba, *see* **cumba.**
cy′mbal/um -ī *n.* cymbal.
cy′mb/ium -ī & iī *n.* cup.
Cy′nic/us -ī *m.* a Cynic philosopher, *esp.* Diogenes. *a.* Cynic. **-ē** *ad.* like the Cynics.
cynoce′phal/us -ī *m.* dog-headed ape.
Cynosū′r/a -ae *f.* constellation of Ursa Minor. **-is** -idis *a.*
Cy′nth/us -ī *m.* hill in Delos, birth-place of Apollo and Diana. **-ius** -ī *m.* Apollo. **-ia** -iae *f.* Diana.
cypari′ss/us -ī *f.* cypress.
Cy′pr/is -idis *f.* Venus.
Cy′pr/us -ī *f.* island of Cyprus, famed for its copper and the worship of Venus. **-ius** *a.* Cyprian; copper.
Cyrē′n/ē -ēs *f.* **-ae** -ā′rum *f.pl.* town and province of N. Africa. **-ae′us, -a′icus, -ē′nsis** *a.* **-ae′ī, -a′icī** *m.pl.* followers of Aristippus.
Cyrnē′us *a.* Corsican.
Cȳ′r/us -ī *m.* Persian king.
Cytae′/is -idis *f.* Medea.
Cythē′r/a -ae *f.* island S. of Greece, famed for its worship of Venus. **Cyther/ē′us, -ē′ius, -ē′ias, Cythēri′-acus** *a.* Cytherean; of Venus.
Cyther/ē′a -ē′ae, **-ē′ia** -ē′iae, **-ē′is** -ē′idis *f.* Venus.
cy′tis/us -ī *m., f.* cytisus, a kind of clover.
Cy′zic/um -ī *n.*, **-us, -os** -ī *f.* town on Sea of Marmora. **-ē′nus** *a.*

D

Dā'c/ī -ō'rum *m.pl.* Dacians, a people on the lower Danube. **-ia -iae** *f.* their country, *mod.* Rumania. **-icus -icī** *m.* gold coin of Domitian's reign.
dacty'licus *a.* dactylic.
da'ctyl/us -ī *m.* dactyl.
dae'dalus *a.* artistic, skilful in creating; skilfully made, variegated.
Dae'dal/us -ī *m.* mythical Athenian craftsman and inventor. **-ē'us** *a.*
Da'lmat/ae, De'lmat/ae -ā'rum *m.pl.* Dalmatians, a people on the E. coast of the Adriatic. **-ia -iae** *f.* Dalmatia **-icus** *a.*
dā'm/a, da'mm/a -ae *f.* deer; venison.
Dama'sc/us -ī *f.* Damascus. **-ē'nus** *a.*
damnā'ti/ō -ō'nis *f.* condemnation.
damnātō'rius *a.* condemnatory.
damni'ficus *a.* pernicious.
da'mn/ō -ā're -ā'vī -ā'tum *vt.* condemn, sentence; procure the conviction of; (*heirs*) oblige; censure. **capitis, capite** — condemn to death. **māiestātis, dē māiestāte** — condemn for treason. **vōtī** — oblige to fulfil a vow. **-ā'tus** *a.* criminal; miserable.
damnō's/us *a.* harmful, ruinous; spendthrift; wronged. **-ē** *ad.* ruinously.
da'mn/um -ī *n.* loss, harm, damage; (*law*) fine, damages. — **facere** suffer loss.
Da'na/ē -ēs *f.* mother of Perseus. **-ē'ius** *a.*
Da'na/us -ī *m.* king of Argos and father of 50 daughters. — *a.* Greek. **-ī -ō'rum & um** *m.pl.* the Greeks. **-ides -idum** *f.pl.* daughters of Danaus.
danī'st/a -ae *m.* moneylender.
danī'sticus *a.* money-lending.
da'nō, *see* **dō.**
Dānu'v/ius -ī *m.* upper Danube.
Da'phn/ē -ēs *f.* nymph changed into a laurel-tree.
Da'phn/is -idis (*acc.* -im & in) *m.* mythical Sicilian shepherd.
da'pin/ō -ā're *vt.* serve (food).
daps da'pis *f.* religious feast; meal, banquet.
da'psilis *a.* sumptuous, abundant.
Da'rdan/us -ī *m.* son of Jupiter and ancestor of Trojan kings. **-us, -ius, -is -idis** *a.* Trojan. **-ia -iae** *f.* Troy. **-idēs -idae** *m.* Trojan, *esp.* Aeneas.
Darē'/us -ī *m.* Persian king.
datā'rius *a.* to give away.
datā'tim *ad.* passing from one to the other.
da'ti/ō -ō'nis *f.* right to give away; (*laws*) making.
da't/ō -ā're *vt.* be in the habit of giving.
da't/or -ō'ris *m.* giver; (*sport*) bowler.
Dau'li/s -dis *f.* town in central Greece, noted for the story of Procne and Philomela. **-as -adis** *a.*
Dau'n/us -ī *m.* legendary king of Apulia, ancestor of Turnus. **-ius** *a.* Rutulian; Italian. **-ias -i'adis** *f.* Apulia.
dē *pr.* (*with abl.*) (*movement*) down from, from; (*origin*) from, of, out of; (*time*) immediately after, in; (*thought, talk, action*) about, concerning; (*reason*) for, because of; (*imitation*) after, in accordance with. — **industriā** on purpose. — **integrō** afresh. — **nocte** during the night. **diem — diē** from day to day.
de'/a -ae *f.* goddess.
dea'lb/ō -ā're *vt.* whitewash, plaster.

deambulā'ti/o -ō'nis *f.* walk.
dea'mbul/ō -ā're -ā'vī -ā'tum *vi.* go for a walk.
de'am/ō -ā're -ā'vī -ā'tum *vt.* be in love with; be much obliged to.
dearmā'tus *a.* disarmed.
dea'rtu/ō -ā're -ā'vī -ā'tum *vt.* dismember, ruin.
dea'sci/ō -ā're *vt.* smooth with an axe; (*fig.*) cheat.
dēba'cch/or -ā'rī -ā'tus *vi.* rage furiously. [queror.
dēbellā't/or -ō'ris *m.* con-
dēbe'll/ō -ā're -ā'vī -ā'tum *vi.* bring a war to an end. *vt.* subdue; fight out.
dē'b/eō -ē're -uī -itum *vt.* owe; (*with inf.*) be bound, ought, should, must; have to thank for, be indebted for; (*pass.*) be destined.
dē'bilis *a.* frail, weak, crippled.
dēbi'lit/ās -ā'tis *f.* weakness, infirmity. [ening.
dēbilitā'ti/ō -ō'nis *f.* weak-
dēbi'lit/ō -ā're -ā'vī -ā'tum *vt.* cripple, disable; (*fig.*) paralyse, unnerve.
dēbi'ti/ō -ō'nis *f.* owing.
dē'bit/or -ō'ris *m.* debtor.
dē'bit/um -ī *n.* debt.
dēbla'ter/ō -ā're *vt.* blab.
dēca'nt/ō -ā're -ā'vī -ā'tum *vt.* keep on repeating. *vi.* stop singing.
dēc/ē'dō -ē'dere -e'ssī -e'ssum *vi.* withdraw, depart; retire from a province (after term of office); abate, cease, die; (*rights*) give up, forgo; (*fig.*) go wrong, swerve (from duty). dē viā — get out of the way.
de'cem *num.* ten.
Dece'mb/er -ris *a.* of December. *m.* December.
dece'mped/a -ae *f.* ten-foot rule.
decempedā't/or -ō'ris *m.* surveyor.
dece'mpl/ex -icis *a.* tenfold.
decemprī'm/ī -ō'rum *m.pl.* civic chiefs of Italian towns.
decemsca'lmus *a.* ten-oared.
decemvirā'lis *a.* of the decemviri.
decemvirā't/us -ūs *m.* office of decemvir.
dece'mvir/ī -ō'rum & um *m.pl.* commission of ten men (for public or religious duties).
dece'nnis *a.* ten years'.
de'c/ēns -e'ntis *a.* seemly, proper; comely, handsome. **-e'nter** *ad.* with propriety.
dece'nti/a -ae *f.* comeliness.
dēce'ptus *ppp.* dēcipiō.
dēc/e'rnō -e'rnere -rē'vī -rē'tum *vt.* decide, determine; decree; fight it out, decide the issue.
dēce'rp/ō -ere -sī -tum *vt.* pluck off, gather; (*fig.*) derive, enjoy.
dēcertā'ti/ō -ō'nis *f.* deciding the issue.
dēce'rt/ō -ā're -ā'vī -ā'tum *vi.* fight it out, decide the issue.
dēce'ssi/ō -ō'nis *f.* departure; retirement (from a province); deduction, disappearance.
dēce'ss/or -ō'ris *m.* retiring magistrate.
dēce'ss/us -ūs *m.* retirement (from a province); death; (*tide*) ebbing.
de'c/et -ē're -uit *vt.* & *i.* it becomes, suits; it is right, proper.
dē'cid/ō -ere -ī *vi.* fall down, fall off; die; (*fig.*) fail, come down.
dēcī'/dō -dere -dī -sum *vt.* cut off; settle, put an end to.
de'ciēns, de'ciēs *ad.* ten times.
de'cim/us, de'cum/us *a.* tenth. **cum -ō** tenfold. **-um** for the tenth time.
dēc/i'piō -i'pere -ē'pī -e'ptum *vt.* ensnare; deceive, beguile, disappoint.
dēcī'si/ō -ō'nis *f.* settlement.
dēcī'sus *ppp.* dēcīdō.

De'cius -ī *m.* Roman plebeian name, *esp.* P. Decius Mus, father and son, who devoted their lives in battle. **-ius, -iā'nus** *a.*

dēclāmā'ti/ō -ō'nis *f.* loud talking; rhetorical exercise on a given theme.

dēclāmā't/or -ō'ris *m.* apprentice in public speaking.

dēclāmātō'rius *a.* rhetorical.

dēclā'mit/ō -ā're *vi.* practise rhetoric; bluster. *vt.* practise pleading.

dēclā'm/ō -ā're -ā'vī -ā'tum *vi.* practise public speaking, declaim; bluster.

dēclārā'ti/ō -ō'nis *f.* expression, making known.

dēclā'r/ō -ā're -ā'vī -ā'tum *vt.* make known; proclaim, announce, reveal, express, demonstrate.

dēclīnā'ti/ō -ō'nis *f.* swerving; avoidance; (*rhet.*) digression; (*gram.*) inflection.

dēclī'n/ō -ā're -ā'vī -ā'tum *vt.* turn aside, deflect; (*eyes*) close; evade, shun. *vi.* turn aside, swerve; digress.

dēclī'vis *a.* sloping, steep, downhill. *n.* slope, decline.

dēclī'vit/ās -ā'tis *f.* sloping ground.

dēco'ct/or -ō'ris *m.* bankrupt.

dēco'ct/us *ppp.* dēcoquō. *a.* (*style*) ripe, elaborated. **-a -ae** *f.* a cold drink.

dēcō'l/ō -ā're *vi.* run out; (*fig.*) fail.

dē'col/or -ō'ris *a.* discoloured, faded. — aetās a degenerate age.

dēcolōrā'ti/ō -ō'nis *f.* discolouring.

dēcolō'r/ō -ā're -ā'vī -ā'tum *vt.* discolour, deface.

dē'co/quō -quere -xī -ctum *vt.* boil down; cook. *vi.* go bankrupt.

de'c/or -ō'ris *m.* comeliness, ornament, beauty.

de'cor/ō -ā're -ā'vī -ā'tum *vt.* adorn, embellish; (*fig.*) distinguish, honour.

decō'r/us *a.* becoming, proper; beautiful, noble; adorned. **-um -ī** *n.* propriety. **-ē** *ad.* becomingly, beautifully.

dēcre'pitus *a.* decrepit.

dēcrē'/scō -scere -vī -tum *vi.* decrease, wane, wear away; disappear.

dēcrēt/us *ppp.* dēcernō. **-um -ī** *n.* decree, resolution; (*philos.*) doctrine.

dēcrē'vī *perf.* dēcernō; *perf.* dēcrēscō.

de'cum/a -ae *f.* tithe; provincial land-tax; largess.

decumān/us *a.* paying tithes; (*mil.*) of the 10th cohort or legion. *m.* collector of tithes. **-a -ae** *f.* wife of a tithe-collector. **-ī -ōrum** *m.pl.* men of the 10th legion. porta **-a** main gate of a Roman camp.

decumā't/ēs -ium *a. pl.* subject to tithes.

dēcu'/mbo -mbere -bui *vi.* lie down; recline at table; fall (in fight).

de'cumus, *see* **decimus.**

decu'ri/a -ae *f.* group of ten; panel of judges; social club.

decuriā'ti/ō -ō'nis *f.*, **decuriā't/us -ūs** *m.* dividing into decuriae.

decu'ri/ō -ā're -ā'vī -ā'tum *vt.* divide into decuriae or groups.

decu'ri/ō -ō'nis *m.* head of a decuria; (*mil.*) cavalry officer; senator of a provincial town or colony.

dēcu'/rrō -rrere -cu'rrī & rrī -rsum *vt.* & *i.* run down, hurry, flow, sail down; traverse; (*mil.*) parade, charge; (*time*) pass through; (*fig.*) have recourse to.

dēcu'rsi/ō -ō'nis *f.* military manoeuvre.

dēcu'rsus *ppp.* dēcurrō.

dēcu'rs/us -ūs *m.* descent.

downrush; (*mil.*) manoeuvre, attack; (*time*) career.
dēcurtā'tus *a.* mutilated.
de'c/us -oris *n.* ornament, glory, beauty; honour, virtue; (*pl.*) heroic deeds.
dēcu'ss/ō -ā're *vt.* divide crosswise.
dēcu'/tiō -tere -ssī -ssum *vt.* strike down, shake off.
dē'dec/et -ē're -uit *vt.* it is unbecoming to, is a disgrace to.
dēde'cor/ō -ā're *vt.* disgrace.
dēdecō'rus *a.* dishonourable.
dē'dec/us -oris *n.* disgrace, shame; vice, crime.
de'dī *perf.* dō.
dēdicā'ti/o -ō'nis *f.* consecration.
dē'dic/ō -ā're -ā'vī -ā'tum *vt.* consecrate, dedicate; declare (property in a census return).
dē'didī *perf.* dēdō.
dēdi'gn/or -ā'rī -ā'tus *vt.* scorn, reject.
dēdi'/scō -scere -dicī *vt.* unlearn, forget.
dēditī'c/ius -ī & iī *m.* one who has capitulated.
dēdi'ti/ō -ō'nis *f.* surrender, capitulation.
dē'dit/us *ppp.* dēdō. *a.* addicted, devoted. -ā operā intentionally.
dē'd/ō -ere -idī -itum *vt.* give up, yield, surrender; devote.
dēdo'c/eō -ē're *vt.* unteach, teach not to.
dēdo'l/eō -ē're -uī *vi.* cease grieving.
dēd/ū'co -ū'cere -ū'xī -u'ctum *vt.* bring down, lead away, deflect; (*mil.*) lead, withdraw; (*bride*) bring home; (*colony*) settle; (*hair*) comb out; (*important person*) escort; (*law*) evict, bring to trial; (*money*) subtract; (*sail*) unfurl; (*ship*) launch; (*thread*) spin out; (*writing*) compose; (*fig.*) bring, reduce, divert, derive.
dēdu'cti/ō -ō'nis *f.* leading off; settling a colony; reduction; eviction; inference.
dēdu'ct/or -ō'ris *m.* escort.
dēdu'ctus *ppp.* dēdūcō. *a.* finely spun.
dee'rr/ō -ā're -ā'vī -ā'tum *vi.* go astray.
dee'sse *inf.* dēsum.
dēfae'c/ō -ā're -ā'vī -ā'tum *vt.* clean; (*fig.*) make clear, set at ease.
dēfatīgā'ti/ō -ō'nis *f.* tiring out; weariness.
dēfatī'g/ō -ā're -ā'vī -ā'tum *vt.* tire out, exhaust.
dēfatī'scor, *see* **dēfetī'scor**.
dēfe'cti/ō -ō'nis *f.* desertion; failure, faintness; (*astr.*) eclipse.
dēfe'ct/or -ō'ris *m.* deserter, rebel.
dēfe'ctus *ppp.* dēficiō. *a.* weak, failing. [eclipse.
dēfe'ct/us -ūs *m.* failure;
dēfe'n/dō -dere -dī -sum *vt.* avert, repel; defend, protect; (*law*) speak in defence, urge, maintain; (*theatre*) play (a part). crīmen — answer an accusation.
dēfē'nsi/ō -ō'nis *f.* defence, speech in defence. [often.
dēfē'nsit/ō -ā're *vt.* defend
dēfē'ns/ō -ā're *vt.* defend.
dēfē'ns/or -ō'ris *m.* averter; defender, protector, guard.
dē'/ferō -fe'rre -tulī -lā'tum *vt.* bring down, bring, carry; bear away; (*power, honour*) offer, confer; (*information*) report; (*law*) inform against, indict; recommend (for public services). ad cōnsilium — take into consideration.
dēfer/vē'scō -vē'scere -vī & buī *vi.* cool down, calm down.
dēfe'ssus *a.* tired, exhausted.
dēfetī'gō, *see* **dēfatīgō**.
dēfe/tī'scor -tī'scī -ssus *vi.* grow weary.
dēf/i'ciō -i'cere -ē'cī -e'ctum *vt.* & *i* desert, forsake, fail; be lacking, run short, cease;

(*astr.*) be eclipsed. animō — lose heart.
dēfī'/gō -gere -xī -xum *vt.* fix firmly; drive in, thrust; (*eyes, mind*) concentrate; (*fig.*) stupefy, astound; (*magic*) bewitch. [portray.
dēfi'ng/ō -ere *vt.* make,
dēfī'n/iō -ī're -ī'vī -ī'tum *vt.* mark the limit of, limit; define, prescribe; restrict; terminate. **-ī'tus** *a.* precise. **-ī'tē** *ad.* precisely.
dēfīnī'ti/ō -ō'nis *f.* limiting, prescribing; definition.
dēfīnītī'vus *a.* explanatory.
dēf/ī'ō -i'erī *vi.* fail.
dēflagrā'ti/ō -ō'nis *f.* conflagration.
dēfla'gr/ō -ā're -ā'vī -ā'tum *vi.* be burned down, perish; cool down, abate. *vt.* burn down.
dēfle'/ctō -ctere -xī -xum *vt.* bend down, turn aside; (*fig.*) pervert. *vi.* turn aside, deviate.
dē'fl/eō -ē're -ē'vī -ē'tum *vt.* lament bitterly, bewail. *vi.* weep bitterly.
dēfle'xus *ppp.* dēflectō.
dēflōr/ē'scō -ē'scere -uī *vi.* shed blooms; (*fig.*) fade.
dē'flu/ō -ere -xī -xum *vi.* flow down, float down; fall, drop, droop. (*fig.*) come from, be derived; flow past; (*fig.*) pass away, fail.
dēf/o'diō -o'dere -ō'dī -o'ssum *vt.* dig, dig out; bury; (*fig.*) hide away.
dē'fore *fut.inf.* dēsum.
dēfō'rmis *a.* misshapen, disfigured, ugly; shapeless; (*fig.*) disgraceful, disgusting.
dēfō'rmit/ās -ā'tis *f.* deformity, hideousness; baseness.
dēfō'rm/ō -ā're -ā'vī -ā'tum *vt.* form, sketch; deform, disfigure; describe; mar, disgrace.
dēfo'ssus *ppp.* dēfodiō.
dēfrau'd/ō, dēfrū'd/ō -ā're *vt.* cheat, defraud. genium — deny oneself.
dēfrēnā'tus *a.* unbridled.
dē'fric/ō -ā're -uī -ā'tum & tum *vt.* rub down; (*fig.*) satirize.
dēfr/i'ngō -i'ngere -ē'gī -ā'ctum *vt.* break off, break down.
dēfrū'dō, *see* **dēfraudō.**
dē'frut/um -ī *n.* new wine boiled down.
dēf/u'giō -u'gere -ū'gī *vt.* run away from, shirk. *vi.* flee.
dē'fuī *perf.* dēsum.
dēfū'nctus *ppa.* dēfungor. *a.* discharged; dead.
dēf/u'ndō -u'ndere -ū'dī -ū'sum *vt.* pour out.
dēf/u'ngor -ungī -ūnctus *vi.* (*with abl.*) discharge, have done with; die.
dēfutū'rus *fut.p.* dēsum.
dē'gener -is *a.* degenerate, unworthy, base.
dēge'ner/ō -ā're -ā'vī -ā'tum *vi.* degenerate, deteriorate. *vt.* disgrace. **-ā'tum -ā'tī** *n.* degenerate character.
dē'ger/ō -ere *vt.* carry off.
dē'g/ō -ere -ī *vt.* (*time*) pass, spend, (*war*) wage. *vi.* live.
dēgra'ndinat it is hailing heavily.
dē'grav/ō -ā're *vt.* weigh down, overpower.
dēgre'/dior -dī -ssus *vi.* march down, descend, dismount. [hard.
dēgru'nn/iō -ī're *vi.* grunt
dēgu'st/ō -ā're *vt.* taste touch; (*fig.*) try, experience.
dehi'nc *ad.* from here; from now, henceforth; then, next.
dehī'sc/ō -ere *vi.* gape, yawn.
dehonestāme'nt/um -ī *n.* disfigurement.
dehone'st/ō -ā're *vt.* disgrace.
deho'rt/or -ā'rī -ā'tus *vt.* dissuade, discourage.
Dēianī'r/a -ae *f.* wife of Hercules.

dē/i'ciō -i'cere -iē'cī -ie'ctum *vt.* throw down, hurl, fell; overthrow, kill; (*eyes*) lower, take off; (*law*) evict; (*mil.*) dislodge; (*ship*) drive off its course; (*hopes, honours*) foil, disappoint.
dēie'cti/ō -ō'nis *f.* eviction.
dēie'ctus *ppp.* dēiciō. *a.* low-lying; disheartened.
dēie'ct/us -ūs *m.* felling; steep slope. [swear solemnly.
dē'ier/ō -ā're -ā'vī -ā'tum *vi.*
de'in, *see* **deinde.**
de'inceps *ad.* successively, in order.
de'inde, de'in *ad.* from there, next; then, thereafter; next in order.
Dēio'tar/us -ī *m.* king of Galatia, defended by Cicero.
Dēi'phob/us -ī *m.* son of Priam, second husband of Helen.
dēiu'ng/ō -ere *vt.* sever.
dē'iuv/o -ā're *vt.* not help.
dej-, *see* **dei-.**
dēlā'/bor -bī -psus *vi.* fall down, fly down, sink; (*fig.*) come down, fall into.
dēla'cer/ō -ā're *vt.* tear to pieces. [bitterly for.
dēlāme'nt/or -ā'rī *vt.* mourn
dēlā'psus *ppa.* dēlābor.
dēla'ss/ō -ā're *vt.* tire out.
dēlā'ti/ō -ō'nis *f.* accusing, informing.
dēlā't/or -ō'ris *m.* informer, denouncer.
dēlectā'bilis *a.* enjoyable.
dēlectāme'nt/um -ī *n.* amusement.
dēlectā'ti/ō -ō'nis *f.* delight.
dēle'ct/ō -ā're *vt.* charm, delight, amuse.
dēlē'ctus *ppp.* dēligō.
dēlē'ct/us -ūs *m.* choice. (*See also* **dīlēctus.**)
dēlēgā'ti/ō -ō'nis *f.* assignment.
dēlē'gī *perf.* dēligō.
dē'lēg/ō -ā're -ā'vī -ā'tum *vt.* assign, transfer, make over; ascribe.
dēlēni'ficus *a.* charming.
dēlēnīme'nt/um -ī *n.* solace, allurement.
dēlē'n/iō -ī're -ī'vī -ī'tum *vt.* soothe, solace; seduce, win over.
dēlēnī't/or -ō'ris *m.* cajoler.
dē'l/eō -ē're -ē'vī -ē'tum *vt.* destroy, annihilate; efface, blot out. [*a.* of Delos.
Dē'li/a -ae *f.* Diana. **-acus**
dēlīberābu'ndus *a.* deliberating.
dēlīberā'ti/ō -ō'nis *f.* deliberating, consideration.
dēlīberātī'vus *a.* deliberative. [sulter.
dēlīberā't/or -ō'ris *m.* con-
dēlī'ber/ō -ā're -ā'vī -ā'tum *vt.* & *i.* consider, deliberate, consult; resolve, determine. **-ārī** potest it is in doubt. **-ā'tus** *a.* determined.
dēlī'b/ō -ā're -ā'vī -ā'tum *vt.* taste, sip; pick, gather; detract from, mar.
dē'libr/ō -ā're *vt.* strip the bark off.
dēli'b/uō -u'ere -uī -ū'tum smear, steep.
dēlicā't/us *a.* delightful; tender, soft; voluptuous, spoiled, effeminate; fastidious. **-ē** *ad.* luxuriously.
dēli'ci/ae -ā'rum *f.pl.* delight, pleasure; whimsicalities, sport; (*person*) sweetheart, darling.
dēlici'ol/ae -ā'rum *f.pl.* darling.
dēli'c/ium -ī & **iī** *n.* favourite.
dē'lic/ō -ā're *vt.* explain.
dēli'ct/um -ī *n.* offence, wrong.
dēli'cuus *a.* lacking.
dē'l/igō -i'gere -ē'gī -ē'ctum *vt.* select, gather; set aside.
de'lig/ō -ā're -ā'vī -ā'tum *vt.* tie up, make fast.
dēli'ng/ō -ere *vt.* have a lick of.

dēlīni-, *see* **dēlēni-**.
dēl/i'nquō -i'nquere -ī'quī -i'ctum *vi.* fail, offend, do wrong.
dēli/quē'scō -quē'scere -cuī *vi.* melt away; (*fig.*) pine away.
dēli'qui/ō -ō'nis *f.* lack.
dēlīrāme'nt/um -ī *n.* nonsense.
dēlīrā'ti/ō -ō'nis *f.* dotage.
dēlī'r/ō -ā're *vi.* be crazy, drivel.
dēlī'rus *a.* crazy.
dēlit/ē'scō -ē'scere -uī *vi.* hide away, lurk; (*fig.*) skulk, take shelter under.
dēlī'tig/ō -ā're *vi.* scold.
Delmat-, *see* **Dalmat-**.
Dē'l/os -ī *f.* sacred Aegean island, birthplace of Apollo and Diana. **-ius**, **-i'acus** *a.*
De'lph/ī -ō'rum *m.pl.* town in central Greece famous for its oracle of Apollo; the Delphians. **-icus** *a.*
delphī'n/us -ī, **de'lphīn** -is *m.* dolphin.
Deltō't/on -ī *n.* constellation Triangulum. [temple.
dē'lubr/um -ī *n.* sanctuary,
dēlu'ct/ō -ā're, **-or** -ā'rī *vi.* wrestle. [fun of.
dēlūdi'fic/ō -ā're *vt.* make
dēlū'/dō -dere -sī -sum *vt.* dupe, delude.
dēlu'mbis *a.* feeble.
dēlu'mb/ō -ā're *vt.* enervate.
dēmad/ē'scō -ē'scere -uī *vi.* be drenched. [commit.
dēma'nd/ō -ā're *vt.* entrust
dēma'rch/us -ī *m.* demarch, chief of a village in Attica.
dē'm/ēns -e'ntis *a.* mad, foolish. **-e'nter** *ad.*
dēmē'ns/us *ppa.* **dēmētior.** **-um** -ī *n.* ration.
dēme'nti/a -ae *f.* madness, folly.
dēme'nt/iō -ī're *vi.* rave.
dēme'r/eō -ē're -uī -itum, **-eor** -ē'rī *vt.* earn, deserve; do a service to.
dēme'r/gō -gere -sī -sum *vt.* submerge, plunge, sink; (*fig.*) overwhelm.
dēme'ssus *ppp.* dēmetō.
dēmē'/tior -tī'rī -nsus *vt.* measure out.
dē'me/tō -tere -ssuī -ssum *vt.* reap, harvest; cut off.
dēmigrā'ti/ō -ō'nis *f.* emigration.
dē'migr/ō -ā're *vi.* move, emigrate.
dēmi'n/uō -u'ere -uī -ū'tum *vt.* make smaller, lessen, detract from. capite — deprive of citizenship.
dēminū'ti/ō -ō'nis *f.* decrease, lessening; (*law*) right to transfer property. capitis — loss of political rights.
dēmī'r/or -ā'rī -ā'tus *vt.* marvel at, wonder.
dēmissī'cius *a.* flowing.
dēmi'ssi/ō -ō'nis *f.* letting down; (*fig.*) dejection.
dēmi'ss/us *ppp.* dēmittō. *a.* low-lying; drooping; humble, unassuming; dejected; (*origin*) descended. **-ē** *ad.* modestly, meanly. [milder.
dēmī'tig/ō -ā're *vt.* make
dēm/i'ttō -i'ttere -ī'sī -i'ssum *vt.* let down, lower, sink; send down, plunge; (*beard*) grow; (*ship*) bring to land; (*troops*) move down; (*fig.*) cast down, dishearten, reduce, impress. sē — stoop; descend; be disheartened.
dēmiū'rg/us -ī *m.* chief magistrate in a Greek state.
dē'm/ō -ere -psī -ptum *vt.* take away, subtract.
Dēmo'crit/us -ī *m.* Greek philosopher, author of the atomic theory. **-icus**, **-ius**, **-ē'us** *a.*
dēmō'l/ior -ī'rī *vt.* pull down destroy. [down.
dēmōlī'ti/ō -ō'nis *f.* pulling
dēmōnstrā'ti/ō -ō'nis *f.* pointing out, explanation.

dēmōnstrātī'vus *a.* (*rhet.*) for display.
dēmōnstrā't/or -ō'ris *m.* indicator.
dēmō'nstr/ō -ā're -ā'vī -ā'tum *vt.* point out; explain, represent, prove.
dēmo'r/ior -ī -tuus *vi.* die, pass away. *vt.* be in love with.
dē'mor/or -ā'rī -ā'tus *vi.* wait. *vt.* detain, delay.
dēmo'rtuus *ppa.* dēmorior.
Dēmo'sthen/ēs -is *m.* greatest Athenian orator.
dēm/o'veō -ovē're -ō'vī -ō'tum *vt.* remove, turn aside, dislodge.
dē'mpsī *perf.* dēmō.
dē'mptus *ppp.* dēmō.
dēmūgī'tus *a.* filled with lowing. [stroke.
dēmu'l/ceō -cē're -sī *vt.*
dē'mum *ad.* (*time*) at last, not till; (*emphasis*) just, precisely. ibi — just there. modo — only now. nunc — now at last. post — not till after. tum — only then.
dēmu'rmur/ō -ā're *vt.* mumble through.
dēmūtā'ti/ō -ō'nis *f.* change.
dēmū't/ō -ā're *vt.* change, make worse. *vi.* change one's mind.
dēnā'r/ius -ī & iī *m.* Roman silver coin.
dēnā'rr/ō -ā're *vt.* relate fully.
dēnā's/ō -ā're *vt.* take the nose off.
dē'nat/ō -ā're *vi.* swim down.
dē'neg/ō -ā're -ā'vī -ā'tum *vt.* deny, refuse, reject. *vi.* say no.
dē'n/ī -ō'rum *a.* ten each, in tens; ten; tenth.
dēnicā'lis *a.* for purifying after a death.
dē'nique *ad.* at last, finally; (*enumerating*) lastly, next; (*summing up*) in short, briefly; (*emphasis*) just, precisely.
dēnō'min/ō -ā're *vt.* designate.
dēnō'rm/ō -ā're *vt.* make irregular.
dē'not/ō -ā're -ā'vī -ā'tum *vt.* point out, specify; observe.
dēns de'ntis *m.* tooth; ivory; prong, fluke.
dē'ns/ō -ā're -ā'vī -ā'tum, **dē'ns/eō** -ē're *vt.* thicken; (*ranks*) close.
dē'ns/us *a.* thick, dense, close; frequent; (*style*) concise. **-ē** *ad.* repeatedly. [beam.
dentā'l/ia -ium *n.pl.* plough-
dentā'tus *a.* toothed; (*paper*) polished.
de'nt/iō -ī're *vi.* cut one's teeth, (*teeth*) grow.
dēnū'/bō -bere -psī -ptum *vi.* marry, marry beneath one.
dēnū'd/ō -ā're -ā'vī -ā'tum *vt.* bare, strip, (*fig.*) disclose.
dēnūntiā'ti/ō -ō'nis *f.* intimation, warning.
dēnū'nti/ō -ā're -ā'vī -ā'tum *vt.* intimate, give notice of, declare; threaten, warn; (*law*) summon as witness.
dē'nuō *ad.* afresh, again, once more.
deo'ner/ō -ā're *vt.* unload.
deo'rsum, deo'rsus *ad.* downwards.
deō'scul/or -ā'rī *vt.* kiss warmly. [scor.
dēpacī'scor, *see* **dēpecī-**
dēpā'ctus *a.* driven in firmly.
dēpā'/scō -scere -vī -stum, **-scor** -scī *vt.* feed on, eat up; (*fig.*) devour, destroy, prune away.
dēpec/ī'scor -ī'scī -tus *vt.* bargain for, agree about.
dēpe'/ctō -ctere -xum *vt.* comb; (*comedy*) flog.
dēpe'ctus *ppa.* dēpecīscor.
dēpecūlā't/or -ō'ris *m.* embezzler. [plunder.
dēpecū'l/or -ā'rī -ā'tus *vt.*
dēp/e'llō -e'llere -ulī -u'lsum *vt.* expel, remove, cast down;

(*mil.*) dislodge; (*infants*) wean; (*fig.*) deter, avert.
dēpe'nd/eō -ē're *vi.* hang down, hang from; depend on; be derived.
dēp/e'ndō -e'ndere -e'ndī -ē'nsum *vt.* weigh, pay up.
dēpe'rd/ō -ere -idī -itum *vt.* lose completely, destroy, ruin.
dēpe'r/eō -ī're -iī *vi.* perish, be completely destroyed; be undone; *vt.* be hopelessly in love with.
dēpe'xus *ppp.* dēpectō.
dēp/i'ngō -i'ngere -i'nxī -i'ctum *vt.* paint; (*fig.*) portray, describe.
dēpla'n/gō -gere -xī *vt.* bewail frantically.
dēple'xus *a.* grasping.
dēplōrābu'ndus *a.* weeping bitterly.
dēplō'r/ō -ā're -ā'vī -ā'tum *vi.* weep bitterly. *vt.* bewail bitterly, mourn; despair of.
dē'plu/it -ere *vi.* rain down.
dēp/ō'nō -ō'nere -o'suī -o'situm *vt.* lay down; set aside, put away, get rid of; wager; deposit, entrust, commit to the care of; (*fig.*) give up.
dēpopulā'ti/ō -ō'nis *f.* ravaging.
dēpopulā't/or -ō'ris *m.* marauder.
dēpo'pul/or -ā'rī -ā'tus, -ō -ā're *vt.* ravage, devastate; (*fig.*) waste, destroy.
dēpo'rt/ō -ā're -ā'vī -ā'tum *vt.* carry down, carry off; bring home (from a province); (*law*) banish for life; (*fig.*) win.
dēpo'/scō -scere -po'scī *vt.* demand, require, claim.
dēpo'sit/us *ppp.* dēpōnō. *a.* dying, dead, despaired of. **-um -ī** *n.* trust, deposit.
dēprāvā'ti/ō -ō'nis *f.* distorting.
dēprā'v/ō -ā're -ā'vī -ā'tum *vt.* distort; (*fig.*) pervert, corrupt. **-ā'tē** *ad.* perversely.
dēprecābu'ndus *a.* imploring.
dēprecā'ti/ō -ō'nis *f.* averting by prayer; imprecation, invocation; plea for indulgence.
dēprecā't/or -ō'ris *m.* intercessor.
dē'prec/or -ā'rī -ā'tus *vt.* avert (by prayer); deprecate, intercede for.
dēpreh/e'ndō, dēpr/e'ndō -e'ndere -e'ndī -ē'nsum *vt.* catch, intercept; overtake, surprise; catch in the act, detect; (*fig.*) perceive, discover.
dēprehē'nsi/ō -ō'nis *f.* detection. [*ppp.* dēprehendō.
dēprehē'nsus, dēprē'nsus
dēpre'ssī *perf.* dēprimō.
dēpre'ssus *ppp.* dēprimō. *a.* low.
dē'pr/imō -i'mere -e'ssī -e'ssum *vt.* press down, weigh down; dig deep; (*ship*) sink; (*fig.*) suppress, keep down.
dēproe'li/or -ā'rī *vi.* fight it out.
dēprō'm/ō -ere -psī -ptum *vt.* fetch, bring out, produce.
dēpro'per/ō -ā're *vi.* hurry up. *vt.* hurry and make.
de'ps/ō -ere *vt.* knead.
dē'pud/et -ē're -uit *v.impers.* not be ashamed.
dēpūgis *a.* thin-buttocked.
dēpu'gn/ō -ā're -ā'vī -ā'tum *vi.* fight it out, fight hard.
dē'pulī *perf.* dēpellō.
dēpu'lsi/ō -ō'nis *f.* averting; defence. [of the way.
dēpu'ls/ō -ā're *vt.* push out
dēpu'ls/or -ō'ris *m.* repeller.
dēpu'lsus *ppp.* dēpellō.
dēpū'rg/ō -ā're *vt.* clean.
dē'put/ō -ā're *vt.* prune; consider, reckon.
dēpȳ'gis, *see* **dēpūgis.**
dē'que *ad.* down.
dērē'ct/us *ppp.* dērigō. *a.* straight, upright, at right angles; straightforward. **-ā. -ē, -ō** *ad.* straight.

dēreli′cti/ō -ō′nis *f.* disregarding.
dērel/i′nquō -i′nquere -ī′quī -i′ctum *vt.* abandon, forsake.
dērepe′nte *ad.* suddenly.
dērē′p/ō -ere *vi* creep down.
dēre′ptus *ppp.* dēripiō.
dērī′/deō -dē′re -sī -sum *vt.* laugh at, deride.
dērīdi′cul/us *a.* laughable. **-um** -ī *n.* mockery, absurdity; object of derision.
dērig/ē′scō -ē′scere -uī *vi.* stiffen, curdle.
dē′r/igō -i′gere -ē′xī -ē′ctum *vt.* turn, aim, direct; (*fig.*) regulate.
dēr/i′piō -i′pere -i′puī -e′ptum *vt.* tear off, pull down.
dērī′s/or -ō′ris *m.* scoffer.
dērī′sus *ppp.* dērīdeō.
dērī′s/us -ūs *m.* scorn, derision.
dērīvā′ti/ō -ō′nis *f.* diverting.
dērī′v/ō -ā′re -ā′vī -ā′tum *vt.* lead off, draw off.
dē′rog/ō -ā′re *vt.* (*law*) propose to amend; (*fig.*) detract from.
dērō′sus *a.* gnawed away.
dēru′ncin/ō -ā′re *vt.* plane off; (*comedy*) cheat.
dē′ru/ō -ere -ī *vt.* demolish.
dēru′ptus *a.* steep. *n.pl.* precipice.
dēsae′v/iō -ī′re *vi.* rage furiously; cease raging.
dēsc/e′ndō -e′ndere -e′ndī -ē′nsum *vi.* come down, go down, descend, dismount; (*mil.*) march down; (*things*) fall, sink, penetrate; (*fig.*) stoop (to), lower oneself.
dēscē′nsi/ō -ō′nis *f.* going down.
dēscē′ns/us -ūs *m.* way down.
dēsc/ī′scō -ī′scere -ī′vī & iī -ī′tum *vi.* desert, revolt; deviate, part company.
dēscrī′/bō -bere -psī -ptum *vt.* copy out; draw, sketch; describe. (*See also* **dīscrībō**.)
dēscrī′pti/ō -ō′nis *f.* copy; drawing, diagram; description.
dēscrī′ptus *ppp.* dēscrībō. (*See also* **dīscrīptus**.)
dē′sec/ō -ā′re -uī -tum *vt.* cut off.
dē′ser/ō -ere -uī -tum *vt.* desert, abandon, forsake; (*bail*) forfeit.
dēse′rt/or -ō′ris *m.* deserter.
dēse′rt/us *ppp.* dēserō. *a.* desert, uninhabited. *n.pl.* deserts.
dēse′rv/iō -ī′re *vi.* be a slave (to), serve.
dē′s/es -idis *a.* idle, inactive.
dēsi′cc/ō -ā′re *vt.* dry, drain.
dēs/i′deō -idē′re -ē′dī *vi.* sit idle.
dēsīderā′bilis *a.* desirable.
dēsīderā′ti/o -ō′nis *f.* missing.
dēsīde′r/ium -ī & iī *n.* longing, sense of loss; want; petition. **mē** — tenet urbis I miss Rome.
dēsī′der/ō -ā′re -ā′vī -ā′tum *vt.* feel the want of, miss; long for, desire; (*casualties*) lose.
dēsi′di/a -ae *f.* idleness, apathy.
dēsidiō′s/us *a.* lazy, idle; relaxing. **-ē** *ad.* idly.
dēs/ī′dō -ī′dere -ē′dī *vi.* sink, settle down; (*fig.*) deteriorate.
dēsignā′ti/ō -ō′nis *f.* specifying; election (of magistrates).
dēsignā′tor, *see* **dissignātor**.
dēsi′gn/ō -ā′re -ā′vī -ā′tum *vt.* trace out; indicate, define; (*pol.*) elect; (*art*) depict. **-ā′tus** *a.* elect.
dē′siī *perf.* dēsinō.
dēs/i′liō -ilī′re -i′luī -u′ltum *vi.* jump down, alight.
dē′si/nō -nere -ī *vt.* leave off, abandon. *vi.* stop, desist; end (in).
dēsipie′nti/a -ae *f.* folly.
dēsi′p/iō -ere *vi.* be stupid, play the fool. **-iēns** -ie′ntis *a.* silly.

dēs/i'stō -i'stere -titī -titum *vi.* stop, leave off, desist.
dē'situs *ppp.* dēsinō.
dēsō'l/ō -ā're -ā'vī -ā'tum *vt.* leave desolate, abandon.
dēspe'ct/ō -ā're *vt.* look down on, command a view of; despise.
dēspe'ctus *ppp.* dēspiciō. *a.* contemptible.
dēspe'ct/us -ūs *m.* view, prospect.
dēspērā'nter *ad.* despairingly.
dēspērā'ti/ō -ō'nis *f.* despair.
dēspē'r/ō -ā're -ā'vī -ā'tum *vt.* & *i.* despair, give up hope of. **-ā'tus** *a.* despaired of, hopeless; desperate, reckless.
dēspe'xī *perf.* dēspiciō.
dēspicā'ti/ō -ō'nis *f.* contempt.
de'spicā'tus *a.* despised, contemptible.
dēspicā't/us -ūs *m.* contempt.
dēspicie'nti/a -ae *f.* contempt.
dēsp/i'ciō -i'cere -e'xī -e'ctum *vt.* look down on; despise. *vi.* look down.
dēspoliā't/or -ō'ris *m.* robber.
dēspo'li/ō -ā're *vt.* rob, plunder.
dēsp/o'ndeō -ondē're -o'ndī & opo'ndī -ō'nsum *vt.* pledge, promise; betroth; devote; give up, despair of. animum — despond.
dēspū'm/ō -ā're *vt.* skim off.
dē'spu/ō -ere *vi.* spit on the ground. *vt.* reject.
dēsquā'm/ō -ā're *vt.* scale, peel.
dēsti'll/ō -ā're *vi.* drop down. *vt.* distil.
dēsti'mul/ō -ā're *vt.* run through.
dēstinā'ti/ō -ō'nis *f.* resolution, appointment.
dē'stin/ō -ā're -ā'vī -ā'tum *vt.* make fast; appoint, determine, resolve; (*archery*) aim at; (*fig.*) intend to buy. **-ā'tus** *a.* fixed, decided. *n.* mark; intention. **-ātum** est mihi I have decided.
dē'stitī *perf.* dēsistō.
dēsti't/uō -u'ere -uī -ū'tum *vt.* set apart, place; forsake, leave in the lurch.
dēstitū'ti/ō -ō'nis *f.* defaulting.
dēstitū'tus *ppp.* dēstituō.
dēstri'ctus *ppp.* dēstringō. *a.* severe.
dēstr/i'ngō -i'ngere -i'nxī -i'ctum *vt.* (*leaves*) strip, (*body*) rub down, (*sword*) draw; graze, skim; (*fig.*) censure.
dē'stru/ō -ere -xī -ctum *vt.* demolish; destroy.
dēsu'bitō *ad.* all of a sudden.
dēsūdā'sc/ō -ere *vi.* sweat all over.
dēsū'd/ō -ā're *vi.* exert oneself.
dēsuēfa'ctus *a.* unaccustomed.
dēsuē'tus *a.* unaccustomed, unused.
dēsuētū'd/ō -inis *f.* disuse.
dēsu'lt/or -ō'ris *m.* circus-rider; (*fig.*) fickle lover.
dēsultū'r/a -ae *f.* jumping down.
dē'/sum dee'sse -fuī *vi.* be missing, fail, fail in one's duty.
dēsū'm/ō -ere -psī -ptum *vt.* select, choose.
dē'super *ad.* from above.
dēsu'rg/ō -ere *vi.* rise.
dē't/egō -e'gere -ē'xī -ē'ctum *vt.* uncover, disclose; (*fig.*) reveal, detect.
dēt/e'ndō -e'ndere -ē'nsum *vt.* (*tent*) strike.
dēte'ntus *ppp.* dētineō.
dēte'r/gō -gere -sī -sum *vt.* wipe away, clear away; clean; break off.
dēte'ri/or -ō'ris *a.* lower; inferior, worse. **-us** *ad.* worse.
dētermina'ti/ō -ō'nis *f.* boundary, end.
dēte'rmin/ō -ā're -ā'vī -ā'tum *vt.* bound, limit; settle.
dē't/erō -e'rere -rī'vī -rī'tum

vt. rub, wear away; (*style*) polish; (*fig.*) weaken.
dēte'rr/eō -ē're -uī -itum *vt.* frighten away; deter, discourage, prevent.
dēte'rsus *ppp.* **dētergeō.**
dētestā'bilis *a.* abominable.
dētestā'ti/ō -ō'nis *f.* execration, curse; averting.
dēte'st/or -ā'rī -ā'tus *vt.* invoke, invoke against; curse, execrate; avert, deprecate.
dēte'x/ō -ere -uī -tum *vt.* weave, finish weaving; (*comedy*) steal; (*fig.*) describe.
dēt/i'neō -inē're -i'nuī -e'ntum *vt.* hold back, detain; keep occupied.
dēt/o'ndeō -ondē're -o'ndī -ō'nsum *vt.* shear off, strip.
dē'ton/ō -ā're -uī *vi.* cease thundering.
dēto'r/queō -quē're -sī -tum *vt.* turn aside, direct; distort, misrepresent.
dētra'cti/ō -ō'nis *f.* removal, departure.
dētra'ctō, *see* **dētrectō.**
dētra'ctus *ppp.* **dētrahō.**
dē'tra/hō -here -xī -ctum *vt.* draw off, take away, pull down; withdraw, force to leave; detract, disparage.
dētractā'ti/ō -ō'nis *f.* declining.
dētrectā't/or -ō'ris *m.* disparager.
dētre'ct/ō -ā're -ā'vī -ā'tum *vt.* decline, shirk; detract from, disparage.
dētrīmentō'sus *a.* harmful.
dētrīme'nt/um -ī *n.* loss, harm; (*mil.*) defeat. — capere suffer harm.
dētrī'tus *ppp.* **dēterō.**
dētrū'/dō -dere -sī -sum *vt.* push down, thrust away; dislodge, evict; postpone; (*fig.*) force.
dētru'nc/ō -ā're -ā'vī -ā'tum *vt.* cut off, behead, mutilate.
dētrū'sus *ppp.* **dētrūdō.**
dētu'rb/ō -ā're -ā'vī -ā'tum *vt.* dash down, pull down; (*fig.*) cast down, deprive.
Deuca'li/ōn -ō'nis *m.* son of Prometheus, survivor of the Flood. -ōnē'us *a.*
de'ūn/x -cis *m.* eleven twelfths.
deū'/rō -rere -ssī -stum *vt.* burn up; frost.
de'/us -ī (*voc.* de'us *pl.* dī de'os de'um dīs) *m.* god. dī meliōra! Heaven forbid! dī tē ament! bless you!
deū'stus *ppp.* **deūrō.**
deū't/or -ī *vi.* maltreat.
dēva'st/ō -ā're *vt.* lay waste.
dē've/hō -here -xī -ctum *vt.* carry down, convey; (*pass.*) ride down, sail down.
dēv/e'llō -e'llere -e'llī & o'lsī -u'lsum *vt.* pluck, pull out.
dēvē'l/ō -ā're *vt.* unveil.
dēve'ner/or -ā'rī *vt.* worship; avert by prayers.
dēv/e'niō -enī're -ē'nī -e'ntum *vi.* come, reach, fall into.
dēve'rber/ō -ā're -ā'vī -ā'tum *vt.* thrash soundly.
dēve'rs/or -ā'rī *vi.* lodge, stay (as guest).
dēve'rs/or -ō'ris *m.* guest.
dēversōri'ol/um -ī *n.* small lodging.
dēversō'r/ius *a.* for lodging. **-ium** -ī & iī *n.* inn, lodging.
dēverti'cul/um -ī *n.* by-road, by-pass; digression; lodging-place; (*fig.*) refuge.
dēve'r/tō, dēvo'r/tō -tere -tī -sum, **-tor** -tī *vi.* turn aside, put up; have recourse to; digress.
dēve'xus *a.* sloping, going down, steep.
dēvi'n/ciō -cī're -xī -ctum *vt.* tie up; (*fig.*) bind, lay under an obligation.
dēv/i'ncō -i'ncere -ī'cī -i'ctum *vt.* defeat completely, win the day.
dēvītā'ti/ō -ō'nis *f.* avoiding.
dēvī't/ō -ā're *vt.* avoid.
dē'vius *a.* out of the way, devious; (*person*) solitary,

wandering off the beaten track; (*fig.*) inconstant.
dē'voc/ō -ā're -ā'vī -ā'tum *vt.* call down, fetch; entice away.
dē'vol/ō -ā're *vi.* fly down.
dēvo'l/vō -vere -vī -ū'tum *vt.* roll down, fall; (*wool*) spin off.
dē'vor/ō -ā're -ā'vī -ā'tum *vt.* swallow, gulp down; engulf, devour; (*money*) squander; (*tears*) repress; (*trouble*) endure patiently.
dēvors-, **dēvort-**, *see* **dē-vers-**, **dēvert-**.
dēvo'rti/a -ō'rum *n.pl.* by-ways.
dēvō'ti/ō -ō'nis *f.* devoting; (*magic*) spell.
dēvō't/ō -ā're *vt.* bewitch.
dēvō'tus *ppp.* dēvoveō. *a.* faithful; accursed.
dēv/o'veō -ovē're -ō'vī -ō'tum *vt.* devote, vow, dedicate; give up; curse; bewitch.
dēvu'lsus *ppp.* dēvellō.
dexte'll/a -ae *f.* little right hand.
de'xt/er -erī & rī *a.* right, right-hand; handy, skilful; favourable. *f.* right hand, right-hand side; hand; pledge of friendship. **-rā** *pr.* (*with acc.*) on the right of. **-rē** (*comp.* **-e'rius**) *ad.* adroitly.
dexte'rit/ās -ā'tis *f.* adroitness.
dextrō'/rsum, **-rsus**, **-vo'rsum** *ad.* to the right.
dī *pl.* deus.
diabathrā'r/ius -ī & iī *m.* slipper-maker.
dia'bol/us -ī *m.* devil.
diā'con/us -ī *m.* (*eccl.*) deacon.
diadē'ma -tis *n.* royal headband, diadem.
diae't/a -ae *f.* diet; living-room.
diale'ctic/us *a.* dialectical. *m.* logician. **-a** -ae, **-ē** -ēs *f.* dialectic, logic. *n.pl.* logical questions. **-ē** *ad.* dialectically.
Diā'lis *a.* of Jupiter. *m.* high-priest of Jupiter.
dia'log/us -ī *m.* dialogue, conversation.
Diā'n/a -ae *f.* virgin goddess of hunting, also identified with the moon and Hecate, and patroness of child-birth. **-ius** *a.* *n.* sanctuary of Diana.
diā'ri/a -ō'rum *n.pl.* daily allowance of food or pay.
di'baph/us -ī *f.* Roman state-robe.
di'c/a -ae *f.* lawsuit.
dicā'cit/ās -ātis *f.* raillery, repartee.
dicā'culus *a.* pert.
dicā'ti/ō -ō'nis *f.* declaration of citizenship.
di'c/āx -ā'cis *a.* witty, smart.
dichorē'/us -ī *m.* double trochee.
di'ci/ō -ō'nis *f.* power, sway, authority.
di'cis cau'sā for the sake of appearance.
di'c/ō -ā're -ā'vī -ā'tum *vt.* dedicate, consecrate; deify; devote, give over.
dī'/cō -cere -xī di'ctum *vt.* say, tell; mention, mean, call, name; pronounce; (*rhet.*) speak, deliver; (*law*) plead; (*poetry*) describe, celebrate; (*official*) appoint; (*time, place*) settle, fix. *vi.* speak (in public). causam — plead. iūs — deliver judgment. sententiam — vote. -cō namely. -xī I have finished. dictum factum no sooner said than done.
di'crot/um -ī *n.* bireme.
dicta'mn/us -ī *f.* dittany, a kind of wild marjoram.
dictā't/a -ō'rum *n.pl.* lessons, rules.
dictā't/or -ō'ris *m.* dictator. **-ō'rius** *a.* dictator's.
dictātū'r/a -ae *f.* dictatorship.
Di'ct/ē -ēs *f.* mountain in Crete, where Jupiter was brought up. **-ae'us** *a.* Cretan.
di'cti/ō -ō'nis *f.* speaking, declaring; style, expression, oratory; (*oracle*) response.

di'ctit/ō -ā're *vt.* keep saying, assert; plead often.
di'ct/ō -ā're -ā'vī -ā'tum *vt.* say repeatedly; dictate; compose.
di'ct/us *ppp.* dīcō. —um -ī *n.* saying, word; proverb; bon mot, witticism; command.
Dicty'nn/a -ae *f.* Britomartis; Diana. —ae'us *a.*
di'dicī *perf.* discō.
dī'd/ō -ere -idī -itum *vt.* distribute, broadcast.
Dī'd/ō -ūs & -ō'nis (*acc.* -ō) *f.* Queen of Carthage.
dīd/ū'cō -ū'cere -ū'xī -u'ctum *vt.* separate, split, open up; (*mil.*) disperse; (*fig.*) part, divide.
diē'cul/a -ae *f.* one little day.
diērē'ctus *a.* crucified. abī — go and be hanged.
di'/ēs -ē'ī *m.*, *f.* day; set day (*usu. fem.*); a day's journey; (*fig.*) time. — meus my birthday. -em dīcere impeach. -em obīre die. -em dē -ē, -em ex -ē from day to day. in -em to a later day; for to-day. in -ēs daily.
Diē'spit/er -ris *m.* Jupiter.
diffā'm/ō -ā're -ā'vī -ā'tum *vt.* divulge; malign.
differe'nti/a -ae *f.* difference, diversity; species.
diffe'rit/ās -ā'tis *f.* difference.
di'ff/erō -e'rre di'stulī dīlā'tum *vt.* disperse; divulge, publish; (*fig.*) distract, disquiet; (*time*) put off, delay. *vi.* differ, be distinguished.
diffe'rtus *a.* stuffed, crammed.
diffi'c/ilis *a.* difficult; (*person*) awkward, surly. —u'lter, -i'liter *ad.* with difficulty.
difficu'lt/ās -ā'tis *f.* difficulty, distress, hardship; surliness.
diffī'd/ēns -e'ntis *a.* nervous. —e'nter *ad.* without confidence.
diffīde'nti/a -ae *f.* mistrust, diffidence.
diffī'/dō -dere -sus *vi.* distrust, despair.
diffi'/ndō -ndere -dī -ssum *vt.* split, open up; (*fig.*) break off.
diffi'ng/ō -ere *vt.* remake.
diffi'ssus *ppp.* diffindō.
diffī'sus *ppa.* diffīdō.
diffi't/eor -ē'rī *vt.* disown.
di'fflu/ō -ere *vi.* flow away; melt away; (*fig.*) wallow. -ēns -e'ntis *a.* (*rhet.*) loose.
diffri'ng/ō -ere *vt.* shatter.
diff/u'giō -u'gere -ū'gī *vi.* disperse, disappear.
diffu'g/ium -ī & iī *n.* dispersion.
diffu'ndit/ō -ā're *vt.* pour out, waste.
diff/u'ndō -u'ndere -ū'dī -ū'sum *vt.* pour off; spread, diffuse; cheer, gladden.
diffū'silis *a.* diffusive.
diffū's/us *ppp.* diffundō. *a.* spreading; (*writing*) loose. -ē *ad.* expansively.
Dīge'nti/a -ae *f.* tributary of the Anio, near Horace's villa.
dī'ge/rō -rere -ssī -stum *vt.* divide, distribute; arrange, set out; interpret.
dīge'sti/ō -ō'nis *f.* (*rhet.*) enumeration.
dīge'stus *ppp.* dīgerō.
digi'tul/us -ī *m.* little finger.
di'git/us -ī *m.* finger; toe; inch; (*pl.*) skill in counting. -um porrigere, prōferre take the slightest trouble. -um trānsversum nōn discēdere not swerve a finger's breadth. attingere caelum -ō reach the height of happiness. licērī -ō bid at an auction. mōnstrārī -ō be a celebrity. extrēmī, summī -ī the finger-tips. concrepāre -īs snap the fingers.
dīgla'di/or -ā'rī *vi.* fight fiercely.
dignā'ti/ō -ō'nis *f.* honour, dignity.
di'gnit/ās -ā'tis *f.* worth,

worthiness; dignity, rank, position; political office.
di'gn/ō -ā're *vt.* think worthy. **-or** -ā'rī *vt.* think worthy; deign.
dīgnō'sc/ō, dīnō'sc/ō -ere *vt.* distinguish.
di'gn/us *a.* worth, worthy; (*things*) fitting, proper. **-ē** *ad.*
dīgre'/dior -dī -ssus *vi.* separate, part; deviate, digress.
dīgre'ssi/ō -ō'nis *f.* parting; deviation, digression.
dīgre'ssus *ppa.* dīgredior.
dīgre'ss/us -ūs *m.* parting.
diiūdicā'ti/ō -ō'nis *f.* decision.
diiū'dic/ō -ā're *vt.* decide; discriminate.
diiun-, *see* **disiun-**.
dīlā'/bor -bī -psus *vi.* dissolve, disintegrate; flow away; (*troops*) disperse; (*fig.*) decay, vanish.
dīla'cer/ō -ā're *vt.* tear to pieces.
dīlā'min/ō -ā're *vt.* split in two.
dīla'ni/ō -ā're -ā'vī -ā'tum *vt.* tear to shreds.
dīla'pid/ō -ā're *vt.* demolish.
dīlā'psus *ppa.* dīlābor.
dīla'rg/ior -ī'rī *vt.* give away liberally.
dīlā'ti/ō -ō'nis *f.* putting off, adjournment.
dīlā't/ō -ā're -ā'vī -ā'tum *vt.* expand, (*pronunciation*) broaden.
dīlā't/or -ō'ris *m.* procrastinator.
dīlā'tus *ppp.* differō.
dīlau'd/ō -ā're *vt.* praise extravagantly.
dīlē'ctus *ppp.* dīligō. *a.* beloved.
dīlē'ct/us -ūs *m.* selection, picking; (*mil.*) levy. **-um habēre** hold a levy, recruit.
dīlē'xī *perf.* dīligō.
dī'lig/ēns -e'ntis *a.* painstaking, conscientious, attentive (to); thrifty. **-e'nter** *ad.*
dīlige'nti/a -ae *f.* carefulness, attentiveness; thrift.
dī'l/igō -i'gere -ē'xī -ē'ctum *vt.* prize especially, esteem, love.
dīlōrī'c/ō -ā're *vt.* tear open.
dīlū'c/eō -ē're *vi.* be evident.
dīlū/cē'scit -cē'scere -xit *vi.* dawn, begin to grow light.
dīlū'cid/us *a* clear, distinct. **-ē** *ad.*
dīlū'cul/um -ī *n.* dawn.
dīlū'd/ium -ī & iī *n.* interval.
dī'l/uō -u'ere -uī -ū'tum *vt.* wash away, dissolve, dilute; explain; (*fig.*) weaken, do away with.
dīlu'v/iēs -iē'ī *f.*, **-ium** -ī & iī *n.* flood, deluge.
dīlu'vi/ō -ā're *vt.* inundate.
dīmā'n/ō -ā're *vi.* spread abroad.
dīmē'nsi/ō -ō'nis *f.* measuring.
dīmē'/tior -tī'rī -nsus *vt.* measure out. **-nsus** *a.* measured.
dīmē't/ō -ā're, **-or** -ā'rī *vt.* mark out.
dīmicā'ti/ō -ō'nis *f.* fighting, struggle.
dī'mic/ō -ā're -ā'vī -ā'tum *vi.* fight. struggle, contend.
dīmidiā'tus *a.* half, halved.
dīmi'dius *a.* half. *n.* half.
dīmi'ssi/ō -ō'nis *f.* sending away; discharging.
dīmi'ssus *ppp.* dīmittō.
dīm/i'ttō -i'ttere -ī'sī -i'ssum *vt.* send away, send round; let go, lay down; (*meeting*) dismiss; (*mil.*) disband, detach; (*fig.*) abandon, forsake.
dimmi'nu/ō -ere *vt.* dash to pieces.
dīm/o'veō -ovē're -ō'vī -ō'tum *vt.* part, separate; disperse; entice away.
Di'ndym/us -ī *m.* mountain in Mysia, sacred to Cybele. **-ē'nē** -ē'nēs *f.* Cybele.
dīnōscō, *see* **dīgnōscō**.
dīnumerā'ti/ō -ō'nis *f.* reckoning up.

dīnu'mer/ō -ā're *vt.* count, reckon up; pay out.
diōbolā'ris *a.* costing two obols. [(*eccl.*) diocese.
dioecē's/is -is *f.* district;
dioecē't/ēs -ae *m.* treasurer.
Dio'gen/ēs -is *m.* famous Cynic philosopher; a Stoic philosopher.
Diomē'd/ēs -is *m.* Greek hero at the Trojan War. **-ē'us** *a.*
Diō'n/ē -ēs, **-a** -ae *f.* mother of Venus; Venus. **-ae'us** *a.*
Dionȳ's/ius -ī *m.* tyrant of Syracuse.
Dionȳ's/us -ī *m.* Bacchus. **-ia** -iō'rum *n.pl.* Greek festival of Bacchus.
diō't/a -ae *f.* a two-handled wine-jar.
diplō'ma -tis *n.* letter of recommendation.
Di'pyl/on -ī *n.* Athenian gate.
Di'rc/ē -ēs *f.* famous spring in Boeotia. **-ae'us** *a.* Boeotian.
dīrē'ctus *ppp.* dīrigō. *a.* straight; straightforward, simple (*See also* **dērēctus.**)
dirē'mī *perf.* dirimō.
dire'mptus *ppp.* dirimō.
dire'mpt/us -ūs *m.* separation.
dīre'pti/ō -ō'nis *f.* plundering.
dīre'pt/or -ō'ris *m.* plunderer.
dīre'ptus *ppp.* dīripiō.
dīrē'xī *perf.* dīrigō.
dīri'b/eō -ē're *vt.* sort out (votes taken from ballot-boxes).
dīribi'ti/ō -ō'nis *f.* sorting.
dīri'bit/or -ō'ris *m.* ballot-sorter.
dī'r/igō -i'gere -ē'xī -ē'ctum *vt.* put in line, arrange. (*See also* **dērigō.**)
di'r/imō -i'mere -ē'mī -e'mptum *vt.* part, divide; interrupt, break off; put an end to.
dīr/i'piō -i'pere -i'puī -e'ptum *vt.* tear in pieces; plunder, ravage; seize; (*fig.*) distract.
dī'rit/ās -ā'tis *f.* mischief, cruelty.
dīr/u'mpō, disr/u'mpō -u'mpere -ū'pī -u'ptum *vt.* burst, break in pieces; (*fig.*) break off; (*pass.*) burst (with passion).
dī'ru/ō -ere -ī -tum *vt.* demolish; scatter. **-tus** *a.* bankrupt. aere **-tus** having one's pay stopped.
dīru'ptus *ppp.* dīrumpō.
dī'rus *a.* ominous, fearful; (*pers.*) dread, terrible. *f.pl.* bad luck; the Furies. *n.pl.* terrors.
dī'rutus *ppp.* dīruō.
dīs dī'tis *a.* rich.
Dī's Dī'tis *m.* Pluto.
disc/ē'dō -ē'dere -e'ssī -e'ssum *vi.* go away, depart; part, disperse; (*mil.*) march away; (*result of battle*) come off; (*pol.*) go over (to a different policy); pass away, disappear; leave out of consideration. ab signīs — break the ranks. victor — come off best.
disceptā'ti/ō -ō'nis *f.* discussion, debate.
disceptā't/or -ō'ris *m.*, **-rīx** -rī'cis *f.* arbitrator.
disce'pt/ō -ā're *vt.* debate, discuss; (*law*) decide.
disc/e'rnō -e'rnere -rē'vī -rē'tum *vt.* divide, separate; distinguish between.
disce'rp/ō -ere -sī -tum *vt.* tear apart, disperse; (*fig.*) revile.
disce'ssi/ō -ō'nis *f.* separation, departure; (*senate*) division.
disce'ss/us -ūs *m.* parting; departure; marching away.
disci'd/ium -ī & iī *n.* disintegration; separation, divorce; discord.
discī'd/ō -ere *vt.* cut in pieces.
disci'nctus *ppp.* discingō. *a.* ungirt; negligent; dissolute.
disci'/ndō -ndere -dī -ssum *vt.* tear up, cut open.

disci'n/gō -gere -xi -ctum *vt.* ungird.
discipli'n/a -ae *f.* teaching, instruction; learning, science, school, system; training, discipline; habits.
disci'pul/us -ī *m.*, -a -ae *f.* pupil, apprentice.
disci'ssus *ppp.* discindō.
disclū'/dō -dere -sī -sum *vt.* keep apart, separate out.
di'sc/ō -ere di'dicī *vt.* learn, be taught, be told.
di'scol/or -ō'ris *a.* of a different colour; variegated; different. [while.
discondū'cit it is not worth
disconve'n/iō -ī're *vi.* disagree, be inconsistent.
discordā'bilis *a.* disagreeing.
disco'rdi/a -ae *f.* discord, disagreement.
discordiō'sus *a.* seditious.
disco'rd/ō -ā're *vi.* disagree, quarrel; be unlike.
di'scor/s -dis *a.* discordant, at variance; inconsistent.
discrepa'nti/a -ae *f.* disagreement.
discrepā'ti/ō -ō'nis *f.* dispute.
discre'pit/ō -ā're *vi.* be quite different.
di'screp/ō -ā're -uī *vi.* be out of tune; disagree, differ; be disputed.
discrē'tus *ppp.* discernō.
discrī'/bō -bere -psī -ptum *vt.* distribute, apportion, classify.
discrī'm/en -inis *n.* interval, dividing-line; distinction difference; turning point, critical moment; crisis, danger.
discrī'min/ō -ā're *vt.* divide.
discrī'pti/ō -ō'nis *f.* apportioning, distributing.
discrī'pt/us *ppp.* discrībō. *a.* secluded; well-arranged. -ē *ad.* in good order.
discru'ci/ō -ā're *vt.* torture; (*fig.*) torment, trouble.
discu'/mbō -mbere -buī -bitum *vi.* recline at table; go to bed.
discu'p/iō -ere *vi.* long.
discu'/rrō -rrere -currī & rrī -rsum *vi.* run about, run different ways.
discu'rs/us -ūs *m.* running hither and thither.
di'sc/us -ī *m.* quoit.
discu'ssus *ppp.* discutiō.
discu'/tiō -tere -ssī -ssum *vt.* dash to pieces, smash; scatter, dispel.
dise'rt/us *a.* fluent, eloquent; explicit. -ē, -im *ad.* distinctly; eloquently.
dis/i'ciō -i'cere -iē'cī -ie'ctum *vt.* scatter, cast asunder; break up, destroy; (*mil.*) rout.
disie'ct/ō -ā're *vt.* toss about.
disie'ctus *ppp.* disiciō.
disie'ct/us -ūs *m.* scattering.
disiū'ncti/ō -ō'nis *f.* separation, differing; (*logic*) statement of alternatives; (*rhet.*) a sequence of short co-ordinate clauses.
disiū'nct/us *ppp.* disiungō. *a.* distinct, distant, removed; (*speech*) disjointed; (*logic*) opposite. -ius *ad.* rather in the manner of a dilemma.
disi/u'ngō -u'ngere -ū'nxī -ū'nctum *vt.* unyoke; separate, remove. [noised abroad.
dispālē'sc/ō -ere *vi.* be
disp/a'ndō (**dispe'nnō**) ā'-ndere -ā'nsum & -e'ssum *vt.* spread out. [equal.
di'sp/ār -aris *a.* unlike, un-
dispa'rilis *a.* dissimilar.
di'spar/ō -ā're -ā'vī -ā'tum *vt.* segregate.
dispart-, *see* **dispert-**.
dispe'ctus *ppp.* dispiciō.
disp/e'llō -e'llere -ulī -u'lsum *vt.* scatter, dispel.
dispend/ium -ī & iī *n.* expense, loss.
dispe'nnō, *see* **dispandō**.
dispēnsā'ti/ō -ō'nis *f.* management, stewardship.

dispēnsā't/or -ō'ris *m.* steward, treasurer.
dispē'ns/ō -ā're -ā'vī -ā'tum *vi.* weigh out, pay out; manage, distribute; (*fig.*) regulate.
dispercu't/iō -ere *vt.* dash out.
dispe'rd/ō -ere -idī -itum *vt.* ruin, squander.
dispe'r/eō -ī're -iī *vi.* go to ruin, be undone.
dispe'r/gō -gere -sī -sum *vt.* disperse, spread over, space out.
dispe'rs/us *ppp.* dispergō. -ē *ad.* here and there.
dispe'rt/iō -ī're -ī'vī -ī'tum, -ior -ī'rī *vt.* apportion, distribute.
disperti'ti/ō -ō'nis *f.* division.
dispe'ssus *ppp.* dispandō.
disp/i'ciō -i'cere -e'xī -e'ctum *vt.* see clearly, see through; distinguish, discern; (*fig.*) consider.
displi'c/eō -ē're *vi.* (*with dat.*) displease. sibi — be in a bad humour.
displō'/dō -dere -sum *vt.* burst with a crash.
disp/ō'nō -ō'nere -o'suī -o'situm *vt.* set out, arrange; (*mil.*) station.
disposi'ti/ō -ō'nis *f.* arrangement.
dispositū'r/a -ae *f.* arrangement.
dispo'sit/us *ppp.* dispōnō. *a.* orderly. -ē *ad.* methodically.
dispo'sit/us -ūs *m.* arranging.
di'spud/et -ē're -uit *v.impers.* be very ashamed.
dispu'lsus *ppp.* dispellō.
disputā'ti/ō -ō'nis *f.* argument.
disputā't/or -ō'ris *m.* debater.
di'sput/ō -ā're -ā'vī -ā'tum *vt.* calculate; examine, discuss.
disquī'r/ō -ere *vt.* investigate.
disquīsī'ti/ō -ō'nis *f.* inquiry.
disru'mpo, *see* **dīrumpō**.
dissae'p/iō -ī're -sī -tum *vt.* fence off, separate off.
dissae'pt/um -ī *n.* partition.
dissā'vi/or -ā'rī *vt* kiss passionately.
dissē'dī *perf.* dissideō.
dissē'min/ō -ā're *vt.* sow, broadcast.
dissē'nsi/ō -ō'nis *f.* disagreement, conflict.
dissē'ns/us -ūs *m.* dissension.
dissentā'neus *a.* contrary.
diss/e'ntiō -entī're -ē'nsī -ē'nsum *vi.* disagree, differ; be unlike, be inconsistent.
dissēp-, *see* **dissaep-**.
disserē'n/ō -ā're *vi.* clear up.
di'ss/erō -e'rere -ē'vī -itum *vt.* sow, plant at intervals.
di'sser/ō -ere -uī -tum *vt.* set out in order, arrange; examine, discuss.
disse'rp/ō -ere *vi.* spread imperceptibly.
disse'rt/ō -ā're *vt.* discuss, dispute.
diss/i'deō -idē're -ē'dī -e'ssum *vi.* be distant; disagree, quarrel; differ, be unlike, be uneven.
dissignā'ti/ō -ō'nis *f.* arrangement.
dissignā't/or -ō'ris *m.* master of ceremonies; undertaker.
dissi'gn/ō -ā're *vt.* arrange, regulate. (*See also* **dēsignō**.)
dissi'l/iō -ī're -uī *vi.* fly apart, break up.
dissi'mil/is *a.* unlike, different. -iter *ad.* differently.
dissimilitū'd/ō -inis *f.* unlikeness.
dissimula'nter *ad.* secretly.
dissimula'nti/a -ae *f.* dissembling.
dissimulā'ti/ō -ō'nis *f.* disguising, dissembling; Socratic irony.
dissimulā't/or -ō'ris *m.* dissembler.
dissi'mul/ō -ā're -ā'vī -ā'tum *vt.* dissemble, conceal, pretend that . . . not, ignore.
dissipā'bilis *a.* diffusible.

dissipā'ti/ō -ō'nis *f.* scattering, dispersing.
di'ssip/ō, di'ssup/ō -ā're -ā'vī -ā'tum *vt.* scatter, disperse; spread, broadcast; squander, destroy; (*mil.*) put to flight.
di'ssitus *ppp.* disserō.
dissociā'bilis *a.* disuniting; incompatible.
dissociā'ti/ō -ō'nis *f.* separation.
disso'ci/ō -ā're -ā'vī -ā'tum *vt.* disunite, estrange.
dissolū'bilis *a.* dissoluble.
dissolū'ti/ō -ō'nis *f.* breaking up, destruction; looseness; (*law*) refutation; (*person*) weakness.
dissolū't/us *ppp.* dissolvō. *a.* loose; lax, careless; licentious. **-um** -ī *n.* asyndeton **-ē** *ad.* loosely, negligently.
disso'l/vō -vere -vī -ū'tum *vt.* unloose, dissolve; destroy, abolish; refute; pay up, discharge (debt); free, release.
di'ssonus *a.* discordant, jarring; disagreeing, different.
di'ssor/s -tis *a.* not shared.
dissuā'/deō -dē're -sī -sum *vt.* advise against, oppose.
dissuā'si/ō -ō'nis *f.* advising against.
dissuā's/or -ō'ris *m.* opposer.
dissu'lt/ō -ā're *vi.* fly asunder.
di'ssu/ō -ere *vt.* undo, open up.
di'ssupō, *see* **dissipō**.
distae'd/et -ē're *v.impers.* loathe.
dista'nti/a -ae *f.* diversity.
diste'n/dō (**-nō**) -dere -dī -tum *vt.* stretch out, swell.
diste'ntus *ppp.* distendō. *a* full. *ppp.* distineō. *a.* busy.
diste'rmin/ō -ā're *vt.* divide, limit.
di'stich/on -ī *n.* couplet.
disti'ncti/ō -ō'nis *f.* differentiating, difference; (*gram.*) punctuation; (*rhet.*) distinction between words.
disti'nct/us *ppp.* distinguō. *a.* separate, distinct; ornamented, set off; lucid. **-ē** *ad.* distinctly, lucidly.
disti'nct/us -ūs *m.* difference.
disti'neō -inē're -i'nuī -e'ntum *vt.* keep apart, divide; distract; detain, occupy; prevent.
disti'n/guō -guere -xī -ctum *vt.* divide, distinguish, discriminate; punctuate; adorn, set off.
di'st/ō -ā're *vi.* be apart, be distant; be different.
disto'r/queō -quē're -sī -tum *vt.* twist, distort.
disto'rti/ō -ō'nis *f.* contortion.
disto'rtus *ppp.* distorqueō. *a.* deformed. [variance.
distra'cti/ō -ō'nis *f.* parting,
distra'ctus *ppp.* distrahō. *a.* separate.
di'stra/hō -here -xī -ctum *vt.* tear apart, separate, estrange; sell piecemeal, retail; (*mind*) distract, perplex. aciem — break up a formation. contrōversiās — end a dispute. vōcēs — leave a hiatus.
distri'b/uō -u'ere -uī -ū'tum *vt.* distribute, divide. **-ū'tē** *ad.* methodically.
distribū'ti/ō -ō'nis *f.* distribution, division.
distri'ctus *ppp.* distringō. *a.* busy, occupied; perplexed; severe.
distri'/ngō -ngere -nxī -ctum *vt.* draw apart; engage, distract; (*mil.*) create a diversion against. [two.
distru'nc/ō -ā're *vt.* cut in
di'stulī *perf.* differō.
distu'rb/ō -ā're -ā'vī -ā'tum *vt.* throw into confusion; demolish; frustrate, ruin.
dītē'sc/ō -ere *vi.* grow rich.
dīthyra'mbicus *a.* dithyrambic. [ramb.
dīthyra'mb/us -ī *m.* dithy-

dī'ti/ae -ā'rum *f.pl.* wealth.
ditiō, *see* **diciō**.
dī't/ō -ā're *vt.* enrich.
di'ū (*comp.* diū'tius *sup.* diūti'ssimē) *ad.* long, a long time; long ago; by day.
diu'rn/us *a.* daily, for a day; by day, day-. **-um** -ī *n.* day-book. ācta -a Roman daily gazette.
dī'us *a.* divine, noble.
diū'tin/us *a.* long, lasting. **-ē** *ad.* long. [diū.
diū't/ius, **-i'ssimē**, *see*
diūtu'rnit/ās -ā'tis *f.* long time, long duration.
diūtu'rnus *a.* long, lasting.
dī'v/a -ae *f.* goddess.
dīvā'ric/ō -ā're *vt.* spread.
dīv/e'llō -e'llere -e'llī -u'lsum *vt.* tear apart, tear in pieces; (*fig.*) tear away, separate estrange.
dīvē'nd/ō -ere -itum *vt.* sell in lots.
dīve'rber/ō -ā're *vt.* divide, cleave.
dīve'rb/ium -ī & iī *n.* (*comedy*) passage in dialogue.
dīve'rsit/ās -ā'tis *f.* contradiction, disagreement, difference.
dīve'rs/us, **dīvo'rs/us** *ppp.* divertō. *a.* in different directions, apart; different; remote; opposite, conflicting; hostile. *m.pl.* individuals **-ē** *ad.* in different directions, variously.
dīve'r/tō -tere -tī -sum *vi.* turn away; differ.
dī'v/es -itis *a.* rich.
dīve'x/ō -ā're *vt.* pillage.
dīvi'di/a -ae *f.* worry, concern.
dī'v/idō -i'dere -ī'sī -ī'sum *vt.* divide, break open; distribute, apportion; separate, keep apart; distinguish; (*jewel*) set off. **sententiam** — take the vote separately on the parts of a motion.
dīvi'duus *a.* divisible; divided.
dīvīnā'ti/ō -ō'nis *f.* foreseeing the future, divination; (*law*) inquiry to select the most suitable prosecutor.
dīvī'nit/ās -ā'tis *f.* divinity; divination; divine quality.
dīvī'nitus *ad.* from heaven, by divine influence; excellently.
dīvī'n/ō -ā're -ā'vī -ā'tum *vt.* foresee, prophesy.
dīvī'n/us *a.* divine, of the gods; prophetic; superhuman, excellent. *m.* soothsayer. *n.* sacrifice; oath. rēs -a religious service, sacrifice. -a hūmānaque all things in heaven and earth. -ī crēdere believe on oath. **-ē** *ad.* by divine influence; prophetically; admirably.
dīvī'sī *perf.* dīvidō.
dīvī'si/ō -ō'nis *f.* division; distribution.
dīvī's/or -ō'ris *m.* distributor; bribery agent.
dīvī'sus *ppp.* dīvidō. *a.* separate.
dīvī's/us -ūs *m.* division.
dīvi'ti/ae -ā'rum *f.pl.* wealth; (*fig.*) richness.
dīvor-, *see* **dīver-**.
dīvo'rt/ium -ī & iī *n.* separation; divorce (by consent); road fork, watershed.
dīvu'lg/ō -ā're -ā'vī -ā'tum *vt.* publish, make public. -ā'tus *a.* widespread.
dīvu'lsus *ppp.* divellō.
dī'v/um -ī *n.* sky. sub -ō in the open air. [*m.* god.
dī'vus *a.* divine; deified.
dī'xī *perf.* dīcō.
dō da're de'dī da'tum *vt.* give; permit, grant; put, bring, cause, make; give up, devote; tell; impute. **fābulam** — produce a play. **in fugam** — put to flight. **litterās** — post a letter. **manūs** — surrender. **nōmen** — enlist. **operam**— take pains, do one's best **poenās** — pay the penalty

vēla — set sail. verba — cheat.
do′c/eō -ē′re -uī -tum *vt.* teach; inform, tell. fābulam — produce a play.
do′chm/ius -ī & iī *m.* dochmiac foot.
do′cilis *a.* easily trained, [docile.
doci′lit/ās -ā′tis *f.* aptness for being taught.
do′ct/or -ō′ris *m.* teacher, instructor.
doctrī′n/a -ae *f.* instruction, education, learning; science.
do′ct/us *ppp.* doceō. *a.* learned, skilled; cunning, clever. **-ē** *ad.* skilfully, cleverly.
docume′nt/um -ī *n.* lesson, example, proof.
Dōdō′n/a -ae *f.* town in Epirus, famous for its oracle of Jupiter. **-ae′us, -is** -idis *a.*
dō′dr/āns -a′ntis *m.* three-fourths. [fourths.
do′gma -tis *n.* philosophical doctrine.
dolā′br/a -ae *f.* pick-axe.
do′l/ēns -e′ntis *pres.p.* doleō. *a.* painful. **-e′nter** *ad.* sorrowfully.
do′l/eō -ē′re -uī -itum *vt.* & *i.* be in pain, be sore; grieve, lament, be sorry (for); pain. cuī -et meminit *once bitten, twice shy.*
dōliā′ris *a.* tubby.
dōli′ol/um -ī *n.* small cask.
dō′l/ium -ī & iī *n.* large wine jar.
do′l/ō -ā′re -ā′vī -ā′tum *vt.* hew, shape with an axe.
do′l/ō -ō′nis *m.* pike; sting; fore-topsail.
Do′lop/es -um *m.pl.* people of Thessaly. **-ia** -iae *f.* their country.
do′l/or -ō′ris *m.* pain, pang; sorrow, trouble; indignation, resentment; (*rhet.*) pathos.
dolō′s/us *a.* deceitful, crafty. **-ē** *ad.*
do′l/us -ī *m.* deceit, guile, trick. — malus wilful fraud.
domā′bilis *a.* tameable.
dome′sticus *a.* domestic, household; personal, private; of one's own country, internal. *m.pl.* members of a household. bellum — civil war.
do′mī *ad.* at home.
domici′l/ium -ī & iī *n.* dwelling.
do′min/a -ae *f.* mistress, lady of the house; wife, mistress; (*fig.*) lady.
do′min/āns -a′ntis *pres.p.* dominor. *a.* (*words*) literal. *m.* tyrant. [tyranny.
dominā′ti/ō -ō′nis *f* mastery,
dominā′t/or -ō′ris *m.* lord. **-rīx** -rī′cis *f.* queen.
dominā′t/us -ūs *m.* mastery, sovereignty. [Lord's.
domi′nicus *a.* (*eccl.*) the
domi′n/ium -ī & iī *n.* absolute ownership; feast.
do′min/or -ā′rī -ā′tus *vi.* rule, be master; (*fig.*) lord it.
do′min/us -ī *m.* master, lord; owner; host; despot; (*eccl.*) the Lord.
Domi′t/ius -ī *m.* Roman plebeian name, *esp.* with surname Ahenobarbus. **-iā′nus** *a. m.* Roman Emperor.
do′mit/ō -ā′re *vt.* break in.
do′mit/or -ō′ris *m.*, **-rīx** -rī′cis *f.* tamer; conqueror.
do′mitus *ppp.* domō.
do′mit/us -ūs *m.* taming.
do′m/ō -ā′re -uī -itum *vt.* tame, break in; conquer.
do′m/us -ūs & ī *f.* house (*esp.* in town); home, native place; family; (*philos.*) sect. -ī at home; in peace. -ī habēre have of one's own, have plenty of. -um home-(wards). -ō from home.
dōnā′bilis *a.* deserving a present.
dōnā′r/ium -ī & iī *n.* offering; altar, temple.

dōnā'ti/ō -ō'nis *f.* presenting.
dōnātī'v/um -ī *n.* largess gratuity.
dō'nec (**dōnicum, dōnique**) *conj.* until; while, as long as.
dō'n/ō -ā're -ā'vī -ā'tum *vt.* present, bestow; remit, condone (for another's sake); (*fig.*) sacrifice.
dō'n/um -ī *n.* gift; offering.
do'rca/s -dis *f.* gazelle.
Dō'r/ēs -um *m.pl.* Dorians, mostly the Greeks of the Peloponnese. **-icus** *a.* Dorian; Greek. [the sea.
Dō'ri/s -dis *f.* a sea-nymph;
do'rm/iō -ī're -ī'vī -ī'tum *vi.* sleep, be asleep.
dormītā't/or -ō'ris *m.* dreamer. [nod.
dormī't/ō -ā're *vi.* be drowsy,
do'rs/um -ī *n.* back; mountain-ridge.
dōs dō'tis *f.* dowry; (*fig.*) gift, talent. [clown.
Dossē'n/us -ī *m.* hunchback,
dōtā'lis *a.* dowry-, dotal.
dō't/ō -ā're *vt.* endow. **-ā'tus** *a.* richly endowed.
dra'chm/a (**dra'chuma**) -ae *f.* a Greek silver coin.
dra'c/ō -ō'nis *m.* serpent, dragon; (*astr.*) Draco.
dracōni'gen/a -ae *a.* sprung from dragon's teeth. [slave.
drā'pet/a -ae *m.* runaway
Dre'pan/um -ī, -a -ō'rum *n.* town in W. Sicily.
dro'ma/s -dis *m.* dromedary.
dro'm/os -ī *m.* race-course at Sparta. [*m.pl.* Druids.
Dru'id/ēs -um, -ae -ā'rum
Drū's/us -ī *m.* Roman surname, *esp.* famous commander in Germany under Augustus. **-iā'nus** *a.*
Dry'ad/es -um *f.pl.* wood-nymphs, Dryads.
Dry'op/es -um *m.pl.* a people of Epirus.
dubitā'bilis *a.* doubtful.
dubita'nter *ad.* doubtingly, hesitatingly.
dubitā'ti/ō -ō'nis *f.* wavering, uncertainty, doubting; hesitancy, irresolution; (*rhet.*) misgiving.
du'bit/ō -ā're -ā'vī -ā'tum *vt.* & *i.* waver, be in doubt, wonder, doubt; hesitate, stop to think.
du'bi/us *a.* wavering, uncertain; doubtful, indecisive; precarious; irresolute. *n.* doubt. **-ē** *ad.* doubtfully. **in -um vocāre** call in question. **in -um venīre** be called in question. **sine -ō, haud -ē** undoubtedly.
ducē'n/ī -ō'rum *a.* 200 each.
ducentē'sim/a -ae *f.* one-half per cent.
duce'nt/ī -ō'rum *num.* two hundred. **-iēs, -iēns** *ad.* 200 times.
dū'/cō -cere -xī du'ctum *vt.* lead, guide, bring take; draw, draw out; reckon, consider; (*mil.*) lead, march, command; (*breath*) inhale; (*ceremony*) conduct; (*changed aspect*) take on, receive; (*dance*) perform; (*drink*) quaff; (*metal*) shape, beat out; (*mind*) attract, induce, deceive; (*oars*) pull; (*origin*) derive, trace; (*time*) prolong, put off, pass; (*udders*) milk; (*wool*) spin; (*a work*) construct, compose, make; (*bus.*) calculate. **īlia** — become broken-winded. **in numerō hostium** — regard as an enemy. **ōs** — make faces. **parvī** — think little of. **ratiōnem** — have regard for. **uxōrem** — marry.
du'ctim *ad.* in streams.
du'ctit/ō -ā're *vt.* lead on, deceive; marry.
du'ct/ō -ā're *vt.* lead, draw; take home; cheat.
du'ct/or -ō'ris *m.* leader, commander; guide, pilot.

du'ctus *ppp.* dūcō.
du'ct/us -ūs *m.* drawing, drawing off; form; command, generalship.
dū'dum *ad.* a little while ago, just now; for long. **haud** — not long ago. **iam** — **adsum** I have been here a long time. **quam**— how long.
due'llum, *see* **bellum.**
Dui'll/ius -ī *m.* consul who defeated the Carthaginians at sea.
du'im *pres. subj.* dō.
dulcē'd/ō -inis *f.* sweetness; pleasantness, charm.
dulcē'sc/ō -ere *vi.* become sweet.
dulci'culus *a.* rather sweet.
du'lcifer -ī *a.* sweet.
du'lc/is *a.* sweet; pleasant, lovely; kind, dear. **-e**, **-iter** *ad.*
dulcitū'd/ō -inis *f.* sweetness.
dū'licē *ad.* like a slave.
Dūli'ch/ium -ī *n.* island in the Ionian Sea near Ithaca. **-ius** *a.* of Dulichium; of Ulysses.
dum *conj* while, as long as; provided that, if only; until. *ad.* (*enclitic*) now a moment; (*with neg.*) yet.
dūmē't/um -ī *n.* thicket, thorn-bushes. [that.
du'mmodo *conj.* provided
dūmō'sus *a.* thorny.
dumta'xat *ad.* at least; only, merely.
dū'm/us -ī *m.* thorn-bush.
du'o, **du'ae** **du'o** *num.* two.
duode'ci/ēns, **-ēs** *ad.* twelve times.
duo'decim *num.* twelve.
duode'cimus *a.* twelfth.
duodē'n/ī -ō'rum *a.* twelve each, in dozens.
duodēquadrāgē'simus *a.* thirty-eighth.
duodēquadrāgi'ntā *num.* thirty-eight.
duodēquīnquāgē'simus *a.* forty-eighth.
duodētrī'ciēns *ad.* twenty-eight times.
duodētrīgi'ntā *num.* twenty-eight.
duodēvīcē'nī *a.* eighteen each.
duodēvīgi'ntī *num.* eighteen.
duoetvīcē'sim/us *a.* twenty-second. **-ā'nī** -ānō'rum *m.pl.* soldiers of the 22nd legion.
duo'vir/ī, **duu'mvir/ī** -ō'rum *m.pl.* a board of two men; colonial magistrates. — **nāvālēs** naval commissioners (for supply and repair). — **sacrōrum** keepers of the Sibylline Books.
du'pl/ex -icis *a.* double, twofold; both; (*person*) false. **-i'citer** *ad.* doubly, on two accounts.
duplicā'r/ius -ī & iī *m.* soldier receiving double pay.
du'plic/ō -ā're -ā'vī -ā'tum *vt.* double, increase; bend.
du'plus *a.* double, twice as much. *n.* double. *f.* double the price.
dupo'nd/ius -ī & iī *m.* coin worth two asses.
dūrā'bilis *a.* lasting.
dūrā'm/en -inis *n.* hardness.
dūra'teus *a.* wooden.
dūr/ē'scō -ē'scere -uī *vi.* harden.
dū'rit/ās -ā'tis *f.* harshness.
dūri'ti/a -ae, **-ēs** -em *f.* hardness; hardiness; severity; want of feeling.
dū'r/ō -ā're -ā'vī -ā'tum *vt.* harden, stiffen; make hardy, inure; (*mind*) dull. *vi.* harden; be patient, endure; hold out, last; (*mind*) be steeled.
dū'ruī *perf.* dūrēscō.
dū'r/us *a.* hard, harsh, rough; hardy, tough; rude, uncultured; (*character*) severe, unfeeling, impudent, miserly; (*circs.*) hard, cruel. **-ē**, **-iter**

ad. stiffly; hardily; harshly, roughly.
duu'mvirī, *see* **duovirī**.
dux du'cis *m.* leader, guide; chief, head; (*mil.*) commander, general.
dū'xī *perf.* dūcō.
Dy'm/ās -a'ntis *m.* father of Hecuba. **-a'ntis** -a'ntidis *f.* Hecuba.
dy'nam/is -is *f.* plenty.
dyna'st/ēs -ae *m.* ruler, prince.
Dyrrha'ch/ium (**Dyrrachium**) -ī *n.* Adriatic port, *mod.* Durazzo. **-ī'nus** *a.*

E

ē *pr.*, *see* **ex**.
e'a *f.* is. **-dem** *f.* idem. **-pse** *f.* ipse.
e'ā *ad.* there, that way. **-dem** *ad.* the same way; at the same time. **-tenus** *ad.* so far.
e'benus, *see* **hebenus**.
ē'bib/ō -ere -ī *vt.* drink up, drain; squander; absorb.
ēbla'nd/ior -ī'rī *vt.* coax out, obtain by flattery. **-ī'tus** obtained by flattery.
Eborā'c/um, **Eburā'c/um** -ī *n.* York.
ēbri'et/ās ā'tis *f.* drunkenness.
ēbri'olus *a.* tipsy.
ēbriō'sit/ās -ā'tis *f* addiction to drink. [juicy.
ēbriō'sus *a.* drunkard; (*berry*)
ē'brius *a.* drunk; full; (*fig.*) intoxicated.
ēbu'll/iō -ī're *vi.* bubble up. *vt.* brag about.
e'bul/us -ī *m.*, **-um** -ī *n.* danewort, dwarf elder.
e'bur -is *n.* ivory; ivory work.
eburā'tus *a.* inlaid with ivory.
eburne'olus *a.* of ivory.
ebu'rneus, **ebu'rnus** *a.* of ivory; ivory-white.

ēca'stor *interj.* by Castor!
e'cc/e *ad.* look! here is! there is!; lo and behold! **-a**, **-am**, **-illam**, **-istam** here she is! **-um**, **-illum** here he is! **-ōs**, **-ās** here they are!
e'ccerē *interj.* there now!
eccheu'ma -tis *n.* pouring out.
ecclē'si/a -ae *f.* a Greek assembly; (*eccl.*) congregation, church.
e'ccum *etc.*, *see* **ecce**.
e'cdic/us -ī *m.* civic lawyer.
ecf-, *see* **eff-**.
echi'dn/a -ae *f.* viper. — Lernaea hydra.
echī'n/us -ī *m.* sea-urchin; hedgehog; a rinsing-bowl.
Echī'ōn -onis *m.* Theban hero. **-o'nius** *a.* Theban. **-o'nidēs** *m.* Pentheus.
Ē'ch/ō -us *f.* wood-nymph; echo.
e'clog/a -ae *f.* selection; eclogue.
ecqua'ndō *ad.* ever.
e'cqu/ī -ae -od *a.* (*interrog.*) any.
e'cqu/is -id *pro.* (*interrog.*) anyone, anything. **-id** -ī *ad.* whether. **-ō** *ad.* anywhere.
ecu'le/us -ī *m.* foal; rack.
edā'cit/ās -ā'tis *f.* gluttony.
e'd/āx -ā'cis *a.* gluttonous; (*fig.*) devouring, carking.
ēde'nt/ō -ā're *vt.* knock the teeth out of.
ēde'ntulus *a.* toothless; old.
edepo'l *interj.* by Pollux, indeed.
ē'dī *perf.* edō.
ēd/ī'cō -ī'cere -ī'xī -i'ctum *vt.* declare; decree, publish an edict.
ēdi'cti/ō -ō'nis *f.* decree.
ēdi'ct/ō -ā're *vt.* proclaim.
ēdi'ct/um -ī *n.* proclamation, edict (*esp.* a praetor's).
ē'didī *perf.* ēdō.
ēdi'sc/ō -ere ēdi'dicī *vt.* learn well, learn by heart.

ēdi'sser/ō -ere -uī -tum *vt.* explain in detail.
ēdisse'rt/ō -ā're *vt.* explain fully.
ēditī'cius *a.* chosen by the [plaintiff.
ēdi'ti/ō -ō'nis *f.* publishing, edition; statement; (*law*) designation of a suit.
ē'ditus *ppp.* ēdō. *a.* high; descended. *n.* height; order.
e/dō e'dere & ē'sse ē'dī ē'sum *vt.* eat; (*fig.*) devour.
ē'd/ō -ere -idī -itum *vt.* put forth, discharge; emit; give birth to, produce; (*speech*) declare, relate, utter; (*action*) cause, perform; (*book*) publish; (*pol.*) promulgate. **lūdōs —** put on a show. **tribūs —** nominate tribes of jurors.
ēdo'c/eō -ere -uī -ctum *vt.* instruct clearly, teach thoroughly.
ē'dom/ō -ā're -uī -itum *vt.* conquer, overcome.
Ēdō'nus *a.* Thracian.
ēdo'rm/iō -ī're *vi.* have a good sleep. *vt.* sleep off.
ēdormī'sc/ō -ere *vt.* sleep off.
ēducā'ti/ō -ō'nis *f.* bringing up, rearing.
ēducā't/or -ō'ris *m.* foster-father, tutor.
ēducā'tr/īx -ī'cis *f.* nurse.
ē'duc/ō -ā're -ā'vī -ā'tum *vt.* bring up, rear, train; produce.
ēd/ū'cō -ū'cere -ū'xī -u'ctum *vt.* draw out, bring away; raise up, erect; (*law*) summon; (*mil.*) lead out, march out; (*ship*) put to sea; (*young*) hatch, rear, train.
edū'lis *a.* edible.
ēdū'r/ō -ā're *vi.* last out.
ēdū'rus *a.* very hard.
effa'rciō, *see* **effercio.**
effā'tus *ppa.* effor. *a.* solemnly pronounced, declared. *n.* axiom; (*pl.*) predictions.
effe'cti/ō -ō'nis *f.* performing; efficient cause.
effe'ct/or -ō'ris *m.*, **-rīx -rī'cis** *f.* producer, author.
effe'ctus *ppp.* efficiō.
effe'ct/us -ūs *m.* completion, performance; effect.
effē'min/ō -ā're -ā'vī -ā'tum *vt.* make a woman of; enervate. **-ā'tus** *a.* effeminate. **-ā'tē** *ad.*
effe'r/ciō -cīre -tum *vt.* cram full.
effe'rit/ās -ā'tis *f.* wildness.
e'ffer/ō -ā're -ā'vī -ā'tum *vt.* make wild; (*fig.*) exasperate. **-ā'tus** *a.* savage.
e'ffer/ō, e'cfer/ō -re e'xtulī ēlā'tum *vt.* bring out, carry out; lift up, raise; (*dead*) carry to the grave; (*emotion*) transport; (*honour*) exalt; (*news*) spread abroad; (*soil*) produce; (*trouble*) endure to the end. **sē —** rise; be conceited.
effe'rtus *ppp.* effercio. *a.* full, bulging.
e'fferus *a.* savage.
effer/vē'scō -vē'scere -buī *vi.* boil over; (*fig.*) rage.
effe'rv/ō -ere *vi.* boil up.
effē'tus *a.* exhausted.
efficā'cit/ās -ā'tis *f.* power.
e'ffic/āx -ā'cis *a.* capable, effective. **-ā'citer** *ad.* effectually.
effi'ci/ēns -e'ntis *pres. p.* efficiō. *a.* effective, efficient. **-e'nter** *ad.* efficiently.
efficie'nti/a -ae *f.* power, efficacy.
eff/i'ciō -i'cere -ē'cī -e'ctum *vt.* make, accomplish; cause, bring about; (*numbers*) amount to; (*soil*) yield; (*theory*) make out, try to prove.
effi'ctus *ppp.* effingō.
effi'gi/ēs -ē'ī, -a -ae *f.* likeness, copy; ghost; portrait, statue; (*fig.*) image, ideal.
effi'/ngō -ngere -nxī -ctum *vt.* form, fashion; portray, represent; wipe clean; fondle.

efflāgitā'ti/ō -ō'nis *f.* urgent demand.
efflāgitā't/us -ūs *m.* urgent request.
efflā'git/ō -ā're *vt.* demand urgently.
efflī'ctim *ad.* desperately.
efflī'ct/ō -ā're *vt.* strike dead.
efflī'/gō -gere -xī -ctum *vt.* exterminate.
e'ffl/ō -ā're -ā'vī -ā'tum *vt.* breathe out, blow out. *vi.* billow out. animam — expire.
efflōr/ē'scō -ē'scere -uī *vi.* blossom forth.
efflu/ō -ere -xī *vi.* run out, issue, emanate; (*fig.*) pass away, vanish; (*rumour*) get known. ex animō — become forgotten.
efflu'v/ium -ī & iī *n.* outlet.
eff/o'diō (**ecfo'diō**) -o'dere -ō'dī -ossum *vt.* dig up; (*eyes*) gouge out; (*house*) ransack.
e'ff/or -ā'rī -ā'tus *vt.* speak, utter; (*augury*) ordain; (*logic*) state a proposition.
effo'ssus *ppp.* effodiō.
effrēnā'ti/ō -ō'nis *f.* impetuousness.
effrēnā't/us *a.* unbridled, violent, unruly. -ē *ad.*
effrē'nus *a.* unbridled.
effr/i'ngō -i'ngere -ē'gī -ā'ctum *vt.* break open, smash.
eff/u'giō -u'gere -ū'gī *vi.* run away, escape. *vt.* flee from, escape; escape the notice of.
effu'g/ium -ī & iī *n.* flight, escape; means of escape.
effu'l/geō -gēre -sī *vi.* shine out, blaze.
effu'ltus *a.* supported.
eff/u'ndō -u'ndere -ū'dī -ū'sum *vt.* pour forth, pour out; (*crops*) produce in abundance; (*missiles*) shoot; (*rider*) throw; (*speech*) give vent to; (*effort*) waste; (*money*) squander; (*reins*) let go. sē —, -undī rush out; indulge (in).
effū'si/ō -ō'nis *f.* pouring out, rushing out; profusion, extravagance; exuberance.
effū's/us *ppp.* effundō. *a.* vast, extensive; loose, straggling; lavish, extravagant. -ē *ad.* far and wide; lavishly, extravagantly.
effū't/iō -ī're *vt.* blab, chatter.
ēge'lidus *a.* mild, cool.
e'g/ēns -e'ntis *pres.p.* egeō. *a.* needy.
egē'nus *a.* destitute.
e'g/eō -ē're -uī *vi.* be in want; (*with abl. or gen.*) need, want.
Ēge'ri/a -ae *f.* nymph who taught Numa.
ē'ge/rō -rere -ssī -stum *vt.* carry out; discharge, emit.
ege'st/ās -ā'tis *f.* want, poverty.
ēge'stus *ppp.* ēgerō.
ēgī *perf.* agō.
e'go *pro.* I. **-met** I (*emphatic*).
ēgre'/dior -dī -ssus *vi.* go out, come out; go up, climb; (*mil.*) march out; (*naut.*) disembark, put to sea; (*speech*) digress. *vt.* go beyond, quit; (*fig.*) overstep, surpass.
ēgre'gi/us *a.* outstanding, surpassing; distinguished, illustrious. -ē *ad.* uncommonly well, singularly.
ēgre'ssus *ppa.* ēgredior.
ēgre'ss/us -ūs *m.* departure; way out; digression; (*naut.*) landing; (*river*) mouth.
e'guī *perf.* egeō.
ēgu'rgit/ō -ā're *vt.* lavish.
e'hem *interj.* (*expressing surprise*) ha! so!
ē'heu *interj.* (*expressing pain*) alas!
e'ho *interj.* (*expressing rebuke*) look here!
e'ī *dat.* is.
ei' *interj.* (*expressing alarm*) [oh!
ei'a, hei'a *interj.* (*expressing delight, playful remonstrance encouragement*) aha! come now! come on!
ēia'cul/or -ā'rī *vt.* shoot out.

ē/i'ciō -i'cere -iē'cī -ie'ctum *vt.* throw out, drive out, put out; (*joint*) dislocate; (*mind*) banish; (*naut.*) bring to land, run aground wreck; (*rider*) throw; (*speech*) utter; (*theat.*) hiss off. **sē** — rush out, break out. [refuse.
ēiectāme'nt/a -ō'rum *n.pl.*
ēie'cti/ō -ō'nis *f.* banishment.
ēie'ct/ō -ā're *vt.* throw up.
ēie'ctus *ppp.* **ēiciō.** *a.* shipwrecked.
ēie'ct/us -ūs *m.* emitting.
ē'ier/ō, ēiū'r/ō -ā're *vt.* abjure, reject on oath, forswear; (*office*) resign. **bonam cōpiam** — declare oneself bankrupt.
ēiulā'ti/ō -ō'nis *f.*, **ēiulā't/us -ūs** *m.* wailing.
ē'iul/ō -ā're *vi.* wail, lament.
ē'ius *pro.* his, her, its. **-modī** such.
ej-, *see* **ei-.**
ēlā'/bor -bī -psus *vi.* glide away, slip off; escape, get off; pass away.
ēlabō'r/ō -ā're -ā'vī -ā'tum *vi.* exert oneself, take great pains. *vt.* work out, elaborate. **-ā'tus** *a.* studied.
ēlāmentā'bilis *a.* very mournful.
ēlangu/ē'scō -ē'scere -ī *vi.* grow faint; relax.
ēlā'psus *ppa.* **ēlābor.**
ēlā'ti/ō -ō'nis *f.* ecstasy, exaltation.
ēlā'tr/ō -ā're *vt.* bark out.
ēlā't/us *ppp.* **efferō.** *a.* high; exalted. **-ē** *ad.* proudly.
ē'l/avō -avā're -ā'vī -au'tum & **-ō'tum** *vt.* wash clean; (*comedy*) rob.
E'le/a -ae *f.* town in S. Italy, birthplace of Parmenides. **-ā'tēs, -ā'ticus** *a.*
ēle'cebr/a ae *f.* snare.
ēlē'ctilis *a.* choice.
ēlē'cti/ō -ō'nis *f.* choice, option.
ēle'ct/ō -ā're *vt.* coax out.
ēlē'ct/ō -ā're *vt.* select.
Ēle'ctr/a -ae *f.* a Pleiad, daughter of Atlas; sister of Orestes.
ēle'ctr/um -ī *n.* amber; an alloy of gold and silver.
ēlē'ct/us *ppp.* **ēligō.** *a.* select, choice. **-ē** *ad.* choicely.
ēlē'ct/us -ūs *m.* choice.
ē'le/gāns -a'ntis *a.* tasteful, refined, elegant; fastidious; (*things*) fine, choice. **-a'nter** *ad.* with good taste.
ēlega'nti/a -ae *f.* taste, finesse, elegance; fastidiousness.
ēlē'gī *perf.* **ēligō.** [verses.
e'leg/ī -ō'rum *m.pl.* elegiac
elegī'/a -ae *f.* elegy.
E'lel/eus -eī *m.* Bacchus. **-e'ides -e'idum** *f.pl.* Bacchantes.
eleme'nt/um -ī *n.* element; (*pl.*) first principles, rudiments; beginnings; letters (of alphabet).
ele'nch/us -ī *m.* a pear-shaped pearl.
elephanto'mach/a -ae *m.* fighter mounted on an elephant.
elepha'nt/us -ī, e'leph/ās -a'ntis *m.* elephant; ivory.
Eleu'sīn -is *f.* Eleusis, Attic town famous for its mysteries of Demeter. **-us** *a.*
eleuthe'ri/a -ae *f.* liberty.
ē'lev/ō -ā're *vt.* lift raise; alleviate; make light of, lessen, disparage.
ēli'c/iō -ere -uī -itum *vt.* lure out, draw out; (*god*) call down; (*spirit*) conjure up; (*fig.*) elicit, draw.
ēlī'/dō -dere -sī -sum *vt.* dash out, squeeze out; drive out; crush, destroy.
ē'l/igō -i'gere -ē'gī -ē'ctum *vt.* pick, pluck out; choose.
ēlī'min/ō -ā're *vt.* carry outside. [perfect.
ēlī'm/ō -ā're *vt.* file; (*fig.*)

ēli'nguis *a.* speechless; not eloquent.
ēli'ngu/ō -ā're *vt.* tear the tongue out of.
Ē'l/is -idis *f.* district and town in W. Peloponnese, famous for Olympia. **-ē'us, -ius, -ias** *a.* Elean; Olympian.
Eli'ss/a -ae *f.* Dido.
ēli'sus *ppp.* ēlīdō.
ēli'xus *a.* boiled.
elleborō'sus *a.* quite mad.
elle'bor/us -ī *m.*, **-um** -ī *n.* hellebore.
e'llum, e'llam there he (she) is!
ē'loc/ō -ā're *vt.* lease, farm out.
ēlocū'ti/ō -ō'nis *f.* delivery, style.
ēlocū'tus *ppa.* ēloquor.
ēlo'g/ium -ī & iī *n.* short saying; inscription; (*will*) clause.
ē'loqu/ēns -e'ntis *a.* eloquent. **-e'nter** *ad.*
ēloque'nti/a -ae *f.* eloquence.
ēlo'qu/ium -ī & iī *n.* eloquence.
ē'lo/quor -quī -cū'tus *vt.* & *i.* speak out, speak eloquently.
ēlū'/ceō -cē're -xī *vi.* shine out, glitter.
ēlu'ct/or -ā'rī -ā'tus *vi.* struggle, force a way out. *vt.* struggle out of, surmount.
ēlū'cubr/ō -ā're, **-or** -ā'rī -ā'tus *vt.* compose by lamplight.
ēlūdi'fic/or -ā'rī -ā'tus *vt.* cheat, play up.
ēlū'/dō -dere -sī -sum *vt.* parry, ward off, foil; win off at play; outplay, outmanoeuvre; cheat, make fun of. *vi.* finish one's sport. [for.
ēlū'/geō -gē're -xī *vt.* mourn
ēlu'mbis *a.* feeble.
ē'l/uō -u'ere -uī -ū'tum *vt.* wash clean; (*money*) squander; (*fig.*) wash away, get rid of.
ēlū'sus *ppp.* ēlūdō.
ēlū'tus *ppp.* ēluō. *a.* insipid.
ēlu'vi/ēs -em -ē *f.* discharge; overflowing.
ēlu'vi/ō -ō'nis *f.* deluge.
Ēly's/ium -ī *n.* Elysium. **-ius** *a.* Elysian.
em *interj.* there you are!
ēmancipā'ti/ō -ō'nis *f.* giving a son his independence; conveyance of property.
ēma'ncip/ō -ā're *vt.* declare independent; transfer, give up, sell.
ēmā'n/ō -ā're -ā'vī -ā'tum *vi.* flow out; spring (from); (*news*) leak out, become known.
Ēma'thi/a -ae *f.* district of Macedonia; Macedonia, Thessaly. **-us** *a.* Macedonian, Pharsalian. **-des** -dum *f.pl.* Muses.
ēmātūr/ē'scō -ē'scere -uī *vi.* soften.
e'm/āx -ā'cis *a.* fond of buying.
emblē'ma -tis *n.* inlaid work, mosaic.
embo'l/ium -ī & iī *n.* interlude.
ēmendā'bilis *a.* corrigible.
ēmendā'ti/ō -ō'nis *f.* correction
ēmendā't/or -ō'ris *m.*, **-rīx** -rī'cis *f.* corrector. [-ē *ad.*
ēmendā't/us *a.* faultless.
ēme'nd/ō -ā're -ā'vī -ā'tum *vt.* correct improve.
ēmē'nsus *ppa.* ēmētior. *ppp.* traversed.
ēme'nt/ior -ī'rī -ī'tus *vi.* tell lies. *vt.* pretend, fabricate. -ī'tus pretended.
ēme'rc/or -ā'rī *vt.* purchase.
ēme'r/eō -ē're -uī -itum, **-eor** -ē'rī *vt.* earn fully, deserve; lay under an obligation; complete one's term of service.
ēme'r/gō -gere -sī -sum *vt.* raise out; (*fig.*) extricate. *vi.* rise, come up, emerge; (*fig.*) get clear, extricate oneself; (*impers.*) it becomes evident.

ēme'ritus *ppa.* ēmereor. *a.* superannuated, worn out. *m.* veteran.
ēme'rsus *ppp.* ēmergō.
eme'tic/a -ae *f.* emetic.
ēmē'/tior -tī'rī -nsus *vt.* measure out; traverse, pass over; (*time*) live through; (*fig.*) impart.
ē'met/ō -ere *vt.* harvest.
ēmī *perf.* emō.
ē'mic/ō -ā're -uī -ā'tum *vi.* dart out, dash out, flash out; (*fig.*) shine.
ē'migr/ō -ā're -ā'vī -ā'tum *vi.* remove, depart.
ē'min/ēns -e'ntis *pres.p.* ēmineō. *a.* high, projecting; (*fig.*) distinguished, eminent.
ēmine'nti/ā -ae *f.* prominence; (*painting*) light.
ēmi'n/eō -ē're -uī *vi.* stand out, project; be prominent, be conspicuous, distinguish oneself.
ē'min/ōr -ā'rī *vi.* threaten.
ē'minus *ad.* at or from a distance.
ēmī'r/or -ā'rī *vt.* marvel at.
ēmissā'r/ium -ī & iī *n.* outlet.
ēmissā'r/ius -ī & iī *m.* scout.
ēmissī'cius *a.* prying.
ēmi'ssi/ō -ō'nis *f.* letting go, discharge.
ēmi'ssus *ppp.* ēmittō.
ēmi'ss/us -ūs *m.* emission.
ēm/i'ttō -i'ttere -ī'sī -i'ssum *vt.* send out, let out; let go, let slip; (*missile*) discharge; (*person*) release, free; (*sound*) utter; (*writing*) publish.
e'm/ō -ere ē'mī e'mptum *vt.* buy, procure; win over. bene — buy cheap. male — buy dear. in diem — buy on credit.
ēmo'der/or -ā'rī *vt.* give expression to.
ēmo'dul/or -ā'rī *vt.* sing through.
ēmō'l/ior -ī'rī *vt.* accomplish.
ēmo'll/iō -ī're -iī -ī'tum *vt.* soften; mollify; enervate.
ēmolume'nt/um -ī *n.* profit advantage. [advise.
ēmo'n/eō -ē're *vt.* strongly
ēmo'r/ior -ī -tuus *vi.* die; (*fig.*) pass away.
ēmortuā'lis *a.* of death.
ēm/o'veō -ovē're -ō'vī -ō'tum *vt.* remove, drive away.
Empe'docl/ēs -is *m.* Sicilian philosopher. **—ē'us** *a.*
empī'ric/us -ī *m.* empirical doctor.
empo'r/ium -ī & iī *n.* market, market-town.
e'mpti/ō -ō'nis *f.* buying; a purchase.
e'mptit/ō -ā're *vt.* often buy.
e'mpt/or -ō'ris *m.* purchaser.
e'mptus *ppp.* emō
ēmu'lg/eō -ē're *vt.* drain.
ēmu'nctus *ppp.* ēmungō. *a.* discriminating.
ēmu'n/gō -gere -xī -ctum *vt.* blow the nose of; (*comedy*) cheat.
ēmū'n/iō -ī're -ī'vī -ī'tum *vt.* strengthen, secure; build up; make roads through.
ēn *interj.* (*drawing attention*) look! see! (*excited question*) really, indeed; (*command*) come now!
ēnārrā'bilis *a.* describable.
ēnā'rr/ō -ā're -ā'vī -ā'tum *vt.* describe in detail.
ēnā'/scor -scī -tus *vi.* sprout, grow.
ē'nat/ō -ā're *vi.* swim ashore; (*fig.*) escape.
ēnā'tus *ppa.* ēnāscor.
ēnā'vig/ō -ā're *vi.* sail clear, clear. *vt.* sail over.
Ence'lad/us -ī *m.* giant under Etna. [wrap.
e'ndromi/s -dis *f.* sports
Endy'mi/ōn -ō'nis *m.* a beautiful youth loved by the Moon, and doomed to lasting sleep.
ē'nec/ō, ē'nic/ō -ā're -uī &

ā'vī -tum & ā'tum *vt.* kill; wear out; torment.
ēne'rvis *a.* enfeebled.
ēne'rv/ō -ā're -ā'vī -ā'tum *vt.* weaken, unman. **-ā'tus** *a.* limp.
ē'nicō, *see* **ēnecō**.
e'nim *conj.* (*affirming*) yes, truly, in fact; (*explaining*) for, for instance, of course. at — but it will be objected. quid — well? sed — but actually.
enimvē'rō *conj.* certainly yes indeed.
Enī'p/eus -eī *m.* river in Thessaly.
ēnī'sus *ppa.* ēnītor.
ēni't/eō -ē're -uī *vi.* shine, brighten up; (*fig.*) be brilliant distinguish oneself.
ēnit/ē'scō -ē'scere -uī *vi.* shine, be brilliant.
ēnī'/tor -tī -sus & xus *vi.* struggle up, climb; strive, make a great effort. *vt.* give birth to; climb.
ēnī'x/us *ppa.* ēnītor. *a.* strenuous. **-ē** *ad.* earnestly.
E'nn/ius -ī *m.* greatest of the early Latin poets. **-iā'nus** *a.*
Ennosigae'/us -ī *m.* Earth-shaker, Neptune.
ē'n/ō -ā're -ā'vī *vi.* swim out, swim ashore; fly away.
ēnōdā'ti/ō -ō'nis *f.* unravelling. [plain.
ēnō'dis *a.* free from knots;
ēnō'd/ō -ā're -ā'vī -ā'tum *vt.* elucidate. **-ā'tē** *ad.* lucidly.
ēnō'rmis *a.* irregular; immense.
ēnōt/ē'scō -ē'scere -uī *vi* get known. [note of.
ē'not/ō -ā're *vt.* make a
ēnsi'cul/us -ī *m.* little sword.
ē'nsiger -ī *a.* with his sword.
ē'ns/is -is *m.* sword. [ment.
enthȳmē'ma -tis *n.* argu-
ēnū'/bō -bere -psī *vi.* marry out of one's station; marry and go away.
ēnu'cle/ō -ā're *vt.* elucidate. **-ā'tus** *a.* (*style*) straightforward; (*votes*) honest. **-ā'tē** *ad.* plainly.
ēnumerā'ti/ō -ō'nis *f.* enumeration; (*rhet.*) recapitulation.
ēnu'mer/ō -ā're *vt.* count up; pay out; relate.
ēnūntiā'ti/ō -ō'nis *f.* proposition.
ēnūntiā't/um -ī *n.* proposition.
ēnū'nti/ō -ā're *vt.* disclose, report; express; pronounce.
ēnū'pti/ō -ō'nis *f.* marrying out of one's station. [up.
ēnū'tr/iō -ī're *vt.* feed, bring
e'ō ī're ī'vī & iī i'tum *vi.* go; (*mil.*) march; (*time*) pass; (*event*) proceed, turn out. in alia omnia — vote against a bill. in sententiam — support a motion. sīc eat so may he fare! ī (*mocking*) go on!
e'ō *ad.* (*place*) thither, there; (*purpose*) with a view to; (*degree*) so far, to such a pitch; (*time*) so long; (*cause*) on that account, for the reason, (*with comp.*) the. accēdit eō besides. rēs erat eō locī such was the state of affairs. eō magis all the more.
eō'dem *ad.* to the same place, purpose, or person. — locī in the same place.
Ē'ōs *f.* dawn. **Ēō'us** *a.* at dawn, eastern. *m.* morning-star; Oriental.
Ēpamīnō'nd/ās -ae *m.* Theban general.
ēpā'stus *a.* eaten up.
ephē'b/us -ī *m.* youth (18 to 20).
ephē'mer/is -idis *f.* diary.
E'phes/us -ī *f.* Ionian town in Asia Minor. **-ius** *a.*
ephippiā'tus *a.* riding a saddled horse.
ephi'pp/ium -ī & iī *n.* saddle.
e'phor/us -ī *m.* a Spartan magistrate, ephor.

E'phyr/a -ae, -ē -ēs *f.* Corinth. **-ē'ius** *a.*
Epicha'rm/us -ī *m.* Greek philosopher and comic poet.
epi'chys/is -is *f.* kind of jug.
epicō'pus *a.* rowing.
Epicū'r/us -ī *m.* famous Greek philosopher. **-ē'us** *a.*
e'picus *a.* epic.
Epidau'r/us -ī *f.* town in E. Peloponnese. **-ius** *a.*
epidī'cticus *a.* (*rhet.*) for display.
epigra'mma -tis *n.* inscription; epigram.
epi'log/us -ī *m.* peroration.
epimē'ni/a -ō'rum *n.pl.* a month's rations.
Epimē'thi/s -dis *f.* Pyrrha daughter of Epimetheus.
epirē'd/ium -ī & iī *n.* trace.
Ēpī'r/us, -os -ī *f.* district of N.W. Greece. **-ō'tēs** -ō'tae *m.* native of Epirus. **-ō'ticus -ē'nsis** *a.*
epi'scop/us -ī *m.* bishop.
epis'tol/ium -ī & iī *n.* short note.
epi'stul/a -ae *f.* letter. ab -īs secretary.
epita'ph/ium -ī & iī *n.* funeral oration.
epithē'c/a -ae *f.* addition.
epi'tom/a -ae, -ē -ēs *f.* abridgement.
epitȳ'r/um -ī *n.* olive-salad.
e'pop/s -is *m.* hoopoe.
e'p/os (*pl.* -ē) *n.* epic.
ēpō't/ō -ā're -ā'vī -um *vt.* drink up, drain; waste in drink; absorb.
e'pul/ae -ā'rum *f.pl.* dishes; feast, banquet.
epulā'ris *a.* at a banquet.
e'pul/ō -ō'nis *m.* guest at a feast; priest in charge of religious banquets.
e'pul/or -ā'rī -ā'tus *vi.* be at a feast. *vt.* feast on.
e'pul/um -ī *n.* banquet.
e'qu/a -ae *f.* mare.
e'qu/es -itis *m.* horseman, trooper; (*pl.*) cavalry; knight, member of the equestrian order.
eque'st/er -ris *a.* equestrian; cavalry-.
e'quidem *ad.* (*affirming*) indeed, of course, for my part; (*concessive*) to be sure.
equī'nus *a.* horse's.
equī'ri/a -ō'rum *n.pl.* horse-races.
equitā't/us -ūs *m.* cavalry.
e'quit/ō -ā're *vi.* ride.
equu'leus, *see* **eculeus**.
e'quul/us -ī *m.* colt.
e'qu/us -ī *m.* horse; (*astr.*) Pegasus. — bipēs sea-horse. -ō merēre serve in the cavalry. -īs virīsque with might and main.
e'r/a -ae *f.* mistress (of the house); (*goddess*) Lady.
ērādī'c/ō -ā're *vt.* root out, destroy.
ērā'/dō -dere -sī -sum *vt.* erase, obliterate.
E'ratō *f.* Muse of lyric poetry.
Erato'sthen/ēs -is *m.* famous Alexandrian geographer.
E'reb/us -ī *m.* god of darkness; the lower world. **-ē'us** *a.*
Ere'chth/eus -eī *m.* legendary king of Athens. **-ē'us** *a.* **-ī'dae** *m.pl.* Athenians. **-is** -idis *f.* Orithyia; Procris.
ērē'ctus *ppp.* ērigō. *a.* upright, lofty; noble, haughty; alert, tense; resolute.
ērē'p/ō -ere -sī *vi.* creep out, clamber up. *vt.* crawl over, climb.
ēre'pti/ō -ō'nis *f.* seizure, robbery.
ēre'pt/or -ō'ris *m.* robber.
ēre'ptus *ppp.* ēripiō.
e'rga *pr.* (*with acc.*) towards; against.
erga'stul/um -ī *n.* prison (*esp.* for slaves); (*pl.*) convicts.
e'rgō *ad.* therefore, consequently; (*questions, commands*) then, so; (*resuming*)

well then; (*with gen.*) for the sake of, because of.
Erichtho'n/ius -ī *m.* a king of Troy; a king of Athens. *a.* Trojan; Athenian.
ēri'c/ius -ī & iī *m.* hedgehog; (*mil.*) beam with iron spikes.
Ēri'dan/us -ī *m.* mythical name of river Po. [slave.
eri'fug/a -ae *m.* runaway
ē'r/igō -i'gere -ē'xī -ē'ctum *vt.* make upright, raise up, erect; excite; encourage.
Ēri'gon/ē -ēs *f.* constellation Virgo. **-ē'ius** *a.*
erī'lis *a.* the master's, the mistress's.
Erī'n/ȳs -yos *f.* Fury; (*fig.*) curse, frenzy.
Eriphȳ'l/a -ae *f.* mother of Alcmaeon, who killed her.
ēr/i'piō -i'pere -i'puī -e'ptum *vt.* tear away, pull away, take by force; rob; rescue. **sē —** escape.
ērogā'ti/ō -ō'nis *f.* paying out.
ēro'git/ō -ā're *vt.* enquire.
ē'rog/ō -ā're -ā'vī -ā'tum *vt.* pay out, expend; bequeath.
errābu'ndus *a.* wandering.
errā'ticus *a.* roving, shifting.
errā'ti/ō -ō'nis *f.* wandering, roving.
errā't/um -ī *n.* mistake, error.
errā't/us -ūs *m.* wandering.
e'rr/ō ā're -ā'vī -ā'tum *vi.* wander, stray, lose one's way; waver; make a mistake err. *vt.* traverse. **stēllae -antēs** planets.
e'rr/ō -ō'nis *m.* vagabond.
e'rr/or -ō'ris *m.* wandering; meander, maze; uncertainty; error, mistake, delusion; deception.
ērub/ē'scō -ē'scere -uī *vi.* blush; feel ashamed. *vt.* blush for, be ashamed of; respect.
ērū'c/a -ae *f.* colewort.
ēru'ct/ō -ā're *vt.* belch, vomit; talk drunkenly about; throw up.
ēru'd/iō -ī're -iī -ī'tum *vt.* educate, instruct.
ērudī'ti/ō -ō'nis *f.* education, instruction; learning, knowledge.
ērudī'tulus *a.* somewhat skilled.
ērudī't/us *ppp.* ērudiō. *a.* learned, educated, accomplished. **-ē** *ad.* learnedly.
ēr/u'mpō -u'mpere -ū'pī -u'ptum *vt.* break open; make break out. *vi.* burst out, break through; end (in).
ē'ru/ō -ere -ī -tum *vt.* uproot, tear out; demolish, destroy; elicit, draw out; rescue.
ēru'pti/ō -ō'nis *f.* eruption; (*mil.*) sally.
ēru'ptus *ppp.* ērumpō.
e'r/us -ī *m.* master (of the house); owner.
ē'rutus *ppp.* ēruō.
e'rv/um -ī *n.* vetch.
Erycī'nus, *see* **Eryx.**
Eryma'nth/us -ī *m.* mountain range in Arcadia, where Hercules killed the bear. **-ius, -is** *a.*
E'ry/x -cis *m.* town and mountain in the extreme W. of Sicily. **-cī'nus** *a.* of Eryx; of Venus; Sicilian. *f.* Venus.
e'sc/a -ae *f.* food, tit-bits; bait.
escā'rius *a.* of food; of bait. *n.pl.* dishes.
ēsc/e'ndō -e'ndere -e'ndī -ē'nsum *vi.* climb up, go up. *vt.* mount.
ēscē'nsi/ō -ō'nis *f.* raid (from the coast); disembarkation.
escule'ntus *a.* edible, tasty.
Esqui'l/iae -iā'rum *f.pl.* Esquiline hill in Rome. **-ī'nus** *a.* Esquiline. *f.* Esquiline gate.
essedā'r/ius -ī & iī *m.* chariot-fighter.
e'ssed/um -ī *n.* war-chariot.
e'ssit/ō -ā're *vt.* usually eat.

ē'st *pres.* edō.
ē'str/īx -ī'cis *f.* glutton.
ēsuriā'lis *a.* of hunger.
ēsu'r/iō -ī're -ī'tum *vi.* be hungry. *vt.* hunger for.
ēsurī'ti/ō -ō'nis *f.* hunger.
ē'sus *ppp.* edō.
et *conj.* and; (*repeated*) both . . . and; (*adding emphasis*) in fact, yes; (*comparing*) as, than. *ad.* also, too; even.
e'tenim *conj.* (*adding an explanation*) and as a matter of fact, in fact.
etē'si/ae -ā'rum *f.pl.* Etesian winds. **-us** *a.*
ētho'log/us -ī *m.* mimic.
e'tiam *ad.* also, besides; (*emphatic*) even, actually; (*affirming*) yes, certainly; (*indignant*) really! (*time*) still, as yet; again. — **atque** — again and again. — **cavēs?** do be careful! **nihil** — nothing at all.
etia'mdum *ad.* still, as yet.
etia'm/nunc, -num *ad.* still, till now, till then; besides.
etia'msī *conj.* even if, although.
etia'm/tum -tunc *ad.* till then, still.
Etrūri/a -ae *f.* district of Italy N. of Rome. **Etru'scus** *a.* Etruscan.
e'tsī *conj.* even if, though; and yet.
etymolo'gi/a -ae *f.* etymology.
eu' *interj* well done! bravo!
Eu'an, Eu'han *m.* Bacchus.
Eua'nd/er -rus -rī *m.* Evander, ancient king on the site of Rome. **-rius** *a.*
eu'ax *interj.* hurrah!
Eub/oe'a -oe'ae *f.* Greek island. **-o'icus** *a.* Euboean.
eu'ge, -pae' *interj.* bravo! cheers!
eu'h/āns -a'ntis *a.* shouting the Bacchic cry.
Eu'h/ius, Eu'/ius -ī *m.* Bacchus. **-ias** *f.* Bacchante.
eu'hoe, eu'oe *interj.* ecstatic cry of Bacchic revellers.
Eume'nid/es -um *f.pl.* Furies.
eunū'ch/us -ī *m.* eunuch.
Euphrā't/ēs -is *m.* river Euphrates.
Eu'poli/s -dis *m.* Athenian comic poet.
Eurī'pid/ēs -is *m.* Athenian tragic poet. **-ē'us** *a.*
Eurī'p/us -ī *m.* strait between Euboea and mainland; a channel, conduit.
Eurō'p/a -ae, **-ē** -ēs *f.* mythical princess of Tyre who was carried by a bull to Crete; continent of Europe. **-ae'us** *a.*
Eurō't/ās -ae *m.* river of Sparta.
Eu'r/us -ī *m.* E. wind. S.E. wind. **-ō'us** *a.* eastern.
Eury'dic/ē -ēs *f.* wife of Orpheus.
Eury'sth/eus -eī *m.* king of Mycenae who imposed the labours on Hercules.
euschē'mē *ad.* gracefully.
Eute'rp/ē -ēs *f.* Muse of music.
Euxī'nus *a.* the Black (Sea).
ēvā'/dō -dere -sī -sum *vi* come out; climb up; escape; turn out, result, come true. *vt.* pass, mount; escape from.
ē'vag/or -ā'rī -ā'tus *vi.* (*mil.*) manoeuvre; (*fig.*) spread. *vt.* stray beyond.
ēvalē'scō -ē'scere -uī *vi.* grow, increase; be able; come into vogue.
Ēva'nder, *see* **Euander**.
ēvān/ē'scō -ē'scere -uī *vi.* vanish, die away, lose effect.
ēvange'l/ium -ī & iī *n.* (*eccl.*) Gospel.
ēvā'nidus *a.* vanishing.
ēvāsī *perf.* ēvādō.
ēva'st/ō -ā're *vt.* devastate.
ē've/hō -here -xī -ctum *vt.* carry out; raise up, exalt;

spread abroad; (*pass.*) ride, sail, move out.
ēv/e'llō -e'llere -e'llī -u'lsum *vt.* tear out, pull out; eradicate.
ēv/e'niō -enī're -ē'nī -e'ntum *vi.* come out; turn out, result; come to pass, happen, befall.
eve'nt/um -ī *n.* result, issue occurrence, event; fortune, experience.
eve'nt/us -ūs *m.* result, issue; success; fortune, fate.
ēve'rber/ō -ā're *vt.* beat violently.
ēverri'cul/um -ī *n.* drag-net.
ēve'r/rō -rere -rī -sum *vt.* sweep out, clean out.
ēve'rsi/ō -ō'nis *f.* overthrow, destruction.
ēve'rs/or -ō'ris *m.* destroyer.
ēve'rsus *ppp.* ēverrō; *ppp.* ēvertō.
ēve'r/tō -tere -tī -sum *vt.* turn out eject; turn up, overturn; overthrow, ruin, destroy.
ēvestīgā'tus *a.* tracked down.
ēvi'ctus *ppp.* ēvincō.
ē'vid/ēns -e'ntis *a.* visible plain, evident. **-e'nter** *ad.*
ēvide'nti/a -ae *f.* distinctness.
ēvi'gil/ō -ā're -ā'vī -ā'tum *vi.* be wide awake. *vt.* compose carefully.
ēvīlē'sc/ō -ere *vi.* become [worthless.
ēvi'n/ciō -cī're -xī -ctum *vt.* garland, crown.
ēv/i'nco -i'ncere -ī'cī -i'ctum *vt.* overcome, conquer; prevail over; prove.
ē'vir/ō -ā're *vt.* castrate.
ēvi'scer/ō -ā're *vt.* disembowel, tear to pieces.
ēvītā'bilis *a.* avoidable.
ēvī't/ō -ā're -ā'vī -ā'tum *vt.* avoid, clear.
ēvocā't/ī -ō'rum *m.pl.* veteran volunteers.
ēvocā't/or -ō'ris *m.* enlister.
ē'voc/ō -ā're -ā'vī -ā'tum *vt.* call out, summon; challenge; call up; call forth, evoke.
ē'vol/ō -ā're -ā'vī -ā'tum *vi.* fly out, fly away; rush out; (*fig.*) rise, soar.
ēvolū'ti/ō -ō'nis *f.* unrolling (a book).
ēvo'l/vō -vere -vī -ū'tum *vt.* roll out, roll along; unroll, unfold; (*book*) open, read; (*fig.*) disclose, unravel, disentangle.
ē'vom/ō -ere -uī -itum *vt.* vomit up, disgorge.
ēvu'lg/ō -ā're -ā'vī -ā'tum *vt.* divulge, make public.
ēvu'lsi/ō -ō'nis *f.* pulling out.
ēvu'lsus *ppp.* ēvellō.
ex, ē *pr.* (*with abl.*) (*place*) out of, from, down from; (*person*) from; (*time*) after, immediately after, since; (*change*) from being; (*source, material*) of; (*cause*) by reason of through; (*conformity*) in accordance with. **ex itinere** on the march. **ex parte** in part. **ex quō** since. **ex rē, ex ūsū** for the good of. **ē rē pūblicā** constitutionally. **ex sententiā** to one's liking. **aliud ex aliō** one thing after another. **ūnus ex** one of.
exace'rb/ō -ā're *vt.* exasperate.
exā'cti/ō -ō'nis *f.* expulsion; supervision; tax; (*debts*) calling in.
exā'ct/or -ō'ris *m.* expeller; superintendent; tax-collector.
exā'ctus *ppp.* exigō. *a.* precise, exact.
exa'c/uō -u'ere -uī -ū'tum *vt.* sharpen; (*fig.*) quicken, inflame.
exadve'rs/um, -us *ad., pr.* (*with acc.*) right opposite.
exaedificā'ti/ō -ō'nis *f.* construction.
exaedi'fic/ō -ā're *vt.* build up; finish the building of.
exaequā'ti/ō -ō'nis *f.* levelling.
exae'qu/ō -ā're -ā'vī -ā'tum

vt. level out; compensate; put on an equal footing; equal.
exae'stu/ō -ā're *vi.* boil up.
exaggerā'ti/ō -ō'nis *f.* exaltation.
exa'gger/ō -ā're -ā'vī -ā'tum *vt.* pile up; (*fig.*) heighten, enhance.
exagitā't/or -ō'ris *m.* critic.
exa'git/ō -ā're -ā'vī -ā'tum *vt.* disturb, harass; scold, censure; excite, incite.
exagō'g/a -ae *f.* export.
exalb/ē'scō -ē'scere -uī *vi.* turn quite pale.
exā'm/en -inis *n.* swarm, crowd; tongue of a balance; examining.
exa'min/ō -ā're -ā'vī -ā'tum *vt.* weigh; consider, test.
examu'ssim *ad.* exactly, perfectly.
exa'ncl/ō -ā're *vt.* drain; endure to the end.
exanimā'lis *a.* dead; deadly.
exanimā'ti/ō -ō'nis *f.* panic.
exa'nimis, exa'nimus *a.* lifeless, breathless; terrified.
exa'nim/ō -ā're -ā'vī -ā'tum *vt.* wind; kill; terrify, agitate; (*pass.*) be out of breath.
exa'nimus, *see* **exanimis.**
exār/dē'scō -dē'scere -sī -sum *vi.* catch fire, blaze up; (*fig.*) be inflamed, break out.
exār/ē'scō -ē'scere -uī *vi.* dry, dry up.
exa'rm/ō -ā're *vt.* disarm.
e'xar/ō -ā're -ā'vī -ā'tum *vt.* plough up; cultivate, produce; (*brow*) furrow; (*writing*) pen.
exā'rsī *perf.* exārdēscō.
exasciā'tus *a.* hewn out.
exa'sper/ō -ā're -ā'vī -ā'tum *vt.* roughen; (*fig.*) provoke.
exauctō'r/ō -ā're -ā'vī -ā'tum *vt.* (*mil.*) discharge, release; cashier.
exau'd/iō -ī're -ī'vī -ī'tum *vt.* hear clearly; listen to; obey.
exau'g/eō -ē're *vt.* increase.
exaugurā'ti/ō -ō'nis *f.* desecrating.
exau'gur/ō -ā're *vt.* desecrate.
exau'spic/ō -ā're *vi.* take an omen.
e'xbibō, *see* **ēbibō.**
excae'c/ō -ā're *vt.* blind; (*river*) block up.
excandēsce'nti/a -ae *f.* growing anger.
excand/ē'scō -ē'scere -uī *vi.* burn, be inflamed.
exca'nt/ō -ā're *vt.* charm out, spirit away.
excarni'fic/ō -ā're *vt.* tear to pieces.
e'xcav/ō -ā're *vt.* hollow out.
exc/ē'dō -ē'dere -e'ssī -e'ssum *vi.* go out, go away; die, disappear; advance, proceed (to); digress. *vt.* leave; overstep, exceed.
exce'll/ēns -e'ntis *pres.p.* excellō. *a.* outstanding, excellent. **-e'nter** *ad.*
excelle'nti/a -ae *f.* superiority, excellence.
exce'll/ō -ere *vi.* be eminent, excel.
exce'lsit/ās -ā'tis *f.* loftiness.
exce'ls/us *a.* high, elevated; eminent, illustrious. **-um** -ī *n.* height. **-ē** *ad.* loftily.
exce'pti/ō -ō'nis *f.* exception, restriction; (*law*) objection.
exce'pt/ō -ā're *vt.* catch, take out.
exce'ptus *ppp.* excipiō.
exc/e'rnō -e'rnere -rē'vī -rē'tum *vt.* sift out, separate.
exce'rp/ō -ere -sī -tum *vt.* take out; select, copy out extracts; leave out, omit.
exce'ss/us -ūs *m.* departure, death.
e'xcetr/a -ae *f.* snake.
exci'di/ō -ō'nis *f.* destruction.
exci'd/ium -ī & iī *n.* overthrow, destruction.
e'xcid/ō -ere -ī *vi.* fall out, fall; (*speech*) slip out, escape; (*memory*) get forgotten, escape

(*person*) fail, lose; (*things*) disappear, be lost.
exci'/dō -dere -dī -sum *vt.* cut off, hew out, fell; raze; (*fig.*) banish.
e'xc/iō -ī're -ī'vī & iī -itum & ī'tum, -i'eō -iē're *vt.* call out, rouse, summon; occasion, produce; excite.
exc/i'piō -i'pere -ē'pī -e'ptum *vt.* take out, remove; exempt, make an exception of, mention specifically; take up, catch, intercept, overhear; receive, welcome, entertain; come next to, follow after, succeed.
excī'si/ō -ō'nis *f.* destroying.
excī'sus *ppp.* excī'dō.
e'xcit/ō -ā're -ā'vī -ā'tum *vt.* rouse, wake up, summon; raise, build; call on (to stand up); (*fig.*) encourage, revive, excite. **-ā'tus** *a.* loud, strong.
e'xcitus, excī'tus *ppp.* exciō.
exclāmā'ti/ō -ō'nis *f.* exclamation.
exclā'm/ō -ā're -ā'vī -ā'tum *vi.* cry out, shout. *vt.* exclaim, call.
exclū'/dō -dere -sī -sum *vt.* shut out, exclude; shut off, keep off; (*egg*) hatch out; (*eye*) knock out; (*fig.*) prevent, except.
exclū'si/ō -ō'nis *f.* shutting out.
exclū'sus *ppp.* exclūdō.
exco'ctus *ppp.* excoquō.
excōgitā'ti/ō -ō'nis *f.* thinking out, devising.
excō'git/ō -ā're -ā'vī -ā'tum *vt.* think out, contrive.
e'xc/olō -o'lere -o'luī -u'ltum *vt.* work carefully; perfect, refine.
e'xco/quō -quere -xī -ctum *vt.* boil away; remove with heat, make with heat; dry up.
e'xcor/s -dis *a.* senseless, stupid.
excrēme'nt/um -ī *n.* excretion.
e'xcreō, *see* **exscreō**.
excrē'/scō -scere -vī -tum *vi.* grow, rise up.
excrē'tus *ppp.* excernō.
excru'ci/ō -ā're -ā'vī -ā'tum *vt.* torture, torment.
excu'bi/ae -ā'rum *f.pl.* keeping guard, watch; sentry.
excu'bit/or -ō'ris *m.* sentry.
e'xcub/ō -ā're -uī -itum *vi.* sleep out of doors; keep watch; (*fig.*) be on the alert.
excū'/dō -dere -dī -sum *vt.* strike out, hammer out; (*egg*) hatch; (*fig.*) make, compose.
excu'lc/ō -ā're *vt.* beat, tramp down.
excu'ltus *ppp.* excolō.
excu'/rrō -rrere -cu'rrī & rrī -rsum *vi.* run out, hurry out; make an excursion; (*mil.*) make a sortie; (*place*) extend, project; (*fig.*) expand.
excu'rsi/ō -ō'nis *f.* raid, sortie; (*gesture*) stepping forward; (*fig.*) outset.
excu'rs/or -ō'ris *m.* scout.
excu'rs/us -ūs *m.* excursion, raid, charge.
excūsā'bilis *a.* excusable.
excūsā'ti/ō -ō'nis *f.* excuse, plea.
excū's/ō -ā're -ā'vī -ā'tum *vt.* excuse; apologize for; plead as an excuse. **-ā'tē** *ad.* excusably.
excu'ssus *ppp.* excutiō.
excū'sus *ppp.* excūdō.
excu'/tiō -tere -ssī -ssum *vt.* shake out, shake off; knock out, drive out, cast off; (*fig.*) discard, banish; examine, inspect.
exdo'rsu/ō -ā're *vt.* fillet.
exec-, *see* **exsec-**.
e'x/edō -ē'sse -ē'dī -ē'sum *vt.* eat up; wear away, destroy; (*feelings*) prey on.
e'xedr/a -ae *f.* hall, lecture-room.
exe'dr/ium -ī & iī *n.* sitting-room.
exē'mī *perf.* eximō.
exe'mpl/ar -ā'ris *n.* copy;

likeness; model, ideal. **-ā'rēs** *m.pl.* copies.
exe'mpl/um -ī *n.* copy; example, sample, precedent, pattern; purport, nature; warning, object-lesson. **— dare** set an example. **-ī causā, gratiā** for instance.
exe'mptus *ppp.* **eximō.**
exe'nter/ō -ā're *vt.* (*comedy*) empty, clean out; torture.
e'x/eō -ī're -iī -itum *vi.* go out, leave; come out, issue; (*mil.*) march out; (*time*) expire; spring up, rise. *vt.* pass beyond; avoid. **— ex potestāte** lose control.
exeq-, *see* **exseq-.**
exe'rc/eō -ē're -uī -itum *vt.* keep busy, supervise; (*ground*) work, cultivate; (*mil.*) drill, exercise; (*mind*) engage, employ; (*occupation*) practise, follow, carry on; (*trouble*) worry, harass. **sē —** practise, exercise.
exercitā'ti/ō -ō'nis *f.* practice, exercise, experience.
exercitā'tus *a.* practised, trained, versed; troubled.
exerci't/ium -ī & iī *n.* exercising.
exe'rcit/ō -ā're *vt.* exercise.
exe'rcit/or -ō'ris *m.* trainer.
exe'rcitus *ppp.* **exerceō.** *a.* disciplined; troubled; troublesome.
exe'rcit/us -ūs *m.* army, *esp.* the infantry; assembly; troop, flock; exercise.
e'xerō, *see* **exserō.**
exē's/or -ō'ris *m.* corroder.
exē'sus *ppp.* **exedō.**
exhālā'ti/ō -ō'nis *f.* vapour.
exhā'l/ō -ā're *vt.* exhale, breathe out. *vi.* steam; expire.
exhau'/riō -rī're -sī -stum *vt.* drain off, empty; take away, remove; (*fig.*) exhaust, finish; (*trouble*) undergo, endure to the end.
exhērē'd/ō -ā're *vt.* disinherit.
exhē'r/ēs -ē'dis *a.* disinherited.
exhi'b/eō -ere -uī -itum *vt.* hold out, produce (in public); display, show; cause, occasion.
exhilarā'tus *a.* delighted.
exhorr/ē'scō -ē'scere -uī *vi.* be terrified. *vt.* be terrified at.
exhortā'ti/ō -ō'nis *f.* encouragement. [encourage.
exho'rt/or -ā'rī -ā'tus *vt.*
e'x/igō -i'gere -ē'gī -ā'ctum *vt.* drive out, thrust; (*payment*) exact, enforce; demand, claim; (*goods*) dispose of; (*time*) pass, complete; (*work*) finish; (*news*) ascertain; test, examine, consider.
exigu'it/ās -ā'tis *f.* smallness, meagreness.
exi'gu/us *a.* small, short, meagre. *n.* a little bit. **-ē** *ad.* briefly, slightly, hardly.
exi'liō, *see* **exsiliō.**
exī'li/s *a.* thin, small, meagre; poor; (*style*) flat, insipid. **-ter** *ad.* feeble.
exī'lit/ās -ā'tis *f.* thinness, meagreness.
exi'lium, *see* **exsilium.**
e'xim, *see* **exinde.**
exi'mi/us *a.* exempt; select; distinguished, exceptional. **-ē** *ad.* exceptionally.
e'x/imō -i'mere -ē'mī -e'mptum *vt.* take out, remove; release, free; exempt; (*time*) waste; (*fig.*) banish.
e'xin, *see* **exinde.**
exinā'n/iō -ī're, -iī -ī'tum *vt.* empty; pillage.
exi'nde, e'xin, e'xim *ad.* (*place*) from there, next; (*time*) then, thereafter, next; (*measure*) accordingly.
exīstimā'ti/ō -ō'nis *f.* opinion, judgment; reputation, character; (*money*) credit.
exīstimā't/or -ō'ris *m.* judge, critic.
exī'stim/ō, exī'stum/ō -ā're -ā'vī -ā'tum *vt.* value, estimate, judge, think, consider.

exi'stō, *see* **exsistō**.
exitiā'bilis *a.* deadly, fatal.
exitiā'lis *a.* deadly.
exitiō'sus *a.* pernicious, fatal.
exi't/ium -ī & iī *n.* destruction, ruin.
e'xit/us -ūs *m.* departure; way out, outlet; conclusion, end; death; outcome, result.
e'xl/ēx -ē'gis *a.* above the law, lawless.
exo'cul/ō -ā're *vt.* knock the eyes out of.
exo'd/ium -ī & iī *n.* afterpiece.
exolē'/scō -scere -vī -tum *vi.* decay, become obsolete.
exolē'tus *a.* full-grown.
exo'ner/ō -ā're -ā'vī -ā'tum *vt.* unload, discharge; (*fig.*) relieve, exonerate.
exo'pt/ō -ā're -ā'vī -ā'tum *vt.* long for, desire. **-ā'tus** *a.* welcome.
exōrā'bilis *a.* sympathetic.
exōrā't/or -ō'ris *m.* successful pleader.
exō'r/dior -dī'rī -sus *vt.* lay the warp; begin.
exō'rd/ium -ī & iī *n.* beginning; (*rhet.*) introductory section.
exo'r/ior -ī'rī -tus *vi.* spring up, come out, rise; arise, appear, start.
exōrnā'ti/ō -ō'nis *f.* embellishment.
exōrnā't/or -ō'ris *m.* embellisher.
exō'rn/ō -ā're -ā'vī -ā'tum *vt.* equip, fit out; embellish, adorn.
exō'r/ō -ā're -ā'vī -ā'tum *vt.* prevail upon, persuade; obtain, win by entreaty.
exō'rsus *ppa.* exōrdior. *a.* begun. *n.pl.* preamble.
exō'rs/us -ūs *m.* beginning.
exo'rtus *ppa.* exorior.
exo'rt/us -ūs *m.* rising; east.
e'x/os -os'sis *a.* boneless.
exō'scul/or -ā'rī -ā'tus *vt.* kiss fondly.
exo'ss/ō -ā're *vt.* bone.
exō'str/a -ae *f.* stage mechanism; (*fig.*) public.
exō'sus *a.* detesting.
exō'ticus *a.* foreign.
expall/ē'scō -ē'scere -uī *vi.* turn pale, be afraid.
expa'lp/ō -ā're *vt.* coax out.
expa'nd/ō -ere *vt.* unfold.
e'xpatr/ō -ā're *vt.* squander.
expavē'sc/ō -ere expā'vī *vi.* be terrified. *vt.* dread.
expect-, *see* **exspect-**.
expe'd/iō -ī're -ī'vī & iī -ī'tum *vt.* free, extricate, disentangle; prepare, clear (for action); put right, settle; explain, relate; (*impers.*) it is useful, expedient.
expedī'ti/ō -ō'nis *f.* (*mil.*) expedition, enterprise.
expedī't/us *ppp.* expediō. *a.* light-armed; ready, prompt; at hand. *m.* light-armed soldier. **in -ō** esse, habēre be, have in readiness. **-ē** *ad.* readily, freely.
exp/e'llō -e'llere -ulī -u'lsum *vt.* drive away, eject, expel; remove, repudiate.
exp/e'ndō -e'ndere -e'ndī -ē'nsum *vt.* weigh out; pay out; (*penalty*) suffer; (*mind*) ponder, consider, judge.
expē'ns/um -ī *n.* payment, expenditure.
expergē/fa'ciō -fa'cere -fē'cī -fa'ctum *vt.* rouse, excite.
exper/gī'scor -gī'scī -rē'ctus *vi.* wake up; bestir oneself.
expe'rg/ō -ere -ī -itum *vt.* awaken.
expe'ri/ēns -e'ntis *pres.p.* experior. *a.* enterprising.
experie'nti/a -ae *f.* experiment; endeavour; experience, practice.
experīme'nt/um -ī *n.* proof, test; experience.
expe'r/ior -ī'rī -tus *vt.* test, make trial of; attempt, experience; (*law*) go to law; (*perf. tenses*) know from experience.

experrē'ctus *ppa.* expergīscor.
e'xper/s -tis *a.* having no part in, not sharing; free from, without.
expe'rtus *ppa.* experior. *a.* proved, tried; experienced.
expete'ss/ō -ere *vt.* desire.
e'xpet/ō -ere -ī'vī & iī -ī'tum *vt.* aim at, tend towards; desire, covet; attack; demand, require. *vi.* befall, happen.
expiā'ti/ō -ō'nis *f.* atonement.
expi'ctus *ppp.* expingō.
expīlā'ti/ō -ō'nis *f.* pillaging.
expīlā't/or -ō'ris *m.* plunderer.
expī'l/ō -ā're -ā'vī -ā'tum *vt.* rob, plunder.
exp/i'ngō -i'ngere -i'nxī -i'ctum *vt.* portray.
e'xpi/ō -ā're -ā'vī -ā'tum *vt.* purify; atone for, make amends for; avert (evil).
expī'rō, *see* **exspīrō**.
expi'sc/or -ā'rī -ā'tus *vt.* try to find out, ferret out.
explānā'ti/ō -ō'nis *f.* explanation.
explānā't/or -ō'ris *m.* interpreter.
explā'n/ō -ā're -ā'vī -ā'tum *vt.* state clearly, explain; pronounce clearly. -ā'tus *a.* distinct. -ā'tē *ad.*
explau'dō, *see* **explōdō**.
explēme'nt/um -ī *n.* filling.
e'xpl/eō -ē're -ē'vī -ē'tum *vt.* fill up; complete; (*desire*) satisfy, appease; (*duty*) perform, discharge; (*loss*) make good; (*time*) fulfil, complete.
explē'ti/ō -ō'nis *f.* satisfying.
explē'tus *ppp.* expleō. *a.* complete.
explicā'ti/ō -ō'nis *f.* uncoiling; expounding, analysing.
explicā't/or -ō'ris *m.*, -rīx -rī'cis *f.* expounder.
explicā't/us -ūs *m.* explanation.
e'xplic/ō -ā're -ā'vī & uī -ā'tum & itum *vt.* unfold, undo, spread out; (*book*) open; (*mil.*) deploy, extend; (*difficulty*) put in order, settle; (*speech*) develop, explain; set free. -ā'tus *a.* spread out; plain, clear. -itus *a.* easy. -ā'tē *ad.* plainly.
explō'/dō -dere -sī -sum *vt.* hiss off, drive away; (*fig.*) reject.
explōrā'ti/ō -ō'nis *f.* spying.
explōrā't/or -ō'ris *m.* spy, scout.
explō'r/ō -ā're -ā'vī -ā'tum *vt.* investigate, reconnoitre; ascertain; put to the test. -ā'tus *a.* certain, sure. -ā'tē *ad.* with certainty.
explō'sī *perf.* explōdō.
explō'si/ō -ō'nis *f.* driving off (the stage).
explō'sus *ppp.* explōdō.
expo'l/iō -ī're -ī'vī -ī'tum *vt.* smooth off, polish; (*fig.*) refine, embellish.
expolī'ti/ō -ō'nis *f.* smoothing off; polish, finish.
exp/ō'nō -ō'nere -o'suī -o'situm *vt.* set out, put out; (*child*) expose; (*naut.*) disembark; (*money*) offer; (*fig.*) set forth, expose, display; (*speech*) explain, expound.
expo'rr/igō -i'gere -ē'xī -ē'ctum *vt.* extend, smooth out.
exportā'ti/ō -ō'nis *f.* exporting.
expo'rt/ō -ā're -ā'vī -ā'tum *vt.* carry out, export.
expo'sc/ō -ere expopo'scī *vt.* implore, pray for; demand.
expositī'cius *a.* foundling.
exposi'ti/ō -ō'nis *f.* narration, explanation.
expo'situs *ppp.* expōnō. *a.* open, affable; vulgar.
expostulā'ti/ō -ō'nis *f.* complaint.
expo'stul/ō -ā're -ā'vī -ā'tum *vt.* demand urgently; complain of, expostulate.
expō'tus *ppp.* ēpōtō.
expre'ssus *ppp.* exprimō. *a.* distinct, prominent.

e'xpr/imō -i'mere -e'ssī -e'ssum *vt.* squeeze out, force out; press up; (*fig.*) extort, wrest; (*art*) mould, model; (*words*) imitate, portray, translate, pronounce. [proach.
exprobrā'ti/ō -ō'nis *f.* re-
expro'br/ō -ā're -ā'vī -ā'tum *vt.* reproach, cast up.
exprō'm/ō -ere -psī -ptum *vt.* bring out, fetch out; (*acts*) exhibit, practise; (*feelings*) give vent to; (*speech*) disclose, state.
expugnā'bilis *a.* capable of being taken by storm.
expugnā'ti/ō -ō'nis *f.* storming, assault.
expugnā't/or -ō'ris *m.* stormer.
expugnā'ci/or -ō'ris *a.* more effective.
expu'gn/ō -ā're -ā'vī -ā'tum *vt.* storm, reduce; conquer; (*fig.*) overcome, extort.
e'xpulī *perf.* expellō.
expu'lsi/ō -ō'nis *f.* expulsion.
expu'ls/or -ō'ris *m.* expeller.
expu'lsus *ppp.* expellō.
expu'ltr/īx -ī'cis *f.* expeller.
exp/u'ngō -u'n-gere -ū'nxī -ū'nctum *vt.* prick out, cancel.
expūrgā'ti/ō -ō'nis *f.* excuse.
expū'rg/ō -ā're *vt.* purify; justify.
e'xput/ō -ā're *vt.* consider, comprehend.
exquī'/rō -rere -sī'vī -sī'tum *vt.* search out, investigate; inquire; devise.
exquīsī't/us *ppp.* exquīrō. *a.* well thought out, choice. **–ē** *ad.* with particular care.
exsae'v/iō -ī're *vi.* cease raging. [feeble.
exsa'nguis *a.* bloodless, pale;
exsa'r/ciō (**exse'rciō**) -cī're -tum *vt.* repair.
exsa'ti/ō -ā're *vt.* satiate, satisfy.
exsaturā'bilis *a.* appeasable.
exsa'tur/ō -ā're *vt.* satiate.
exsce–, *see* **esce–**.
exsci'/ndō -ndere -dī -ssum *vt.* extirpate.
e'xscre/ō -ā're *vt.* cough up.
exscrī'/bō -bere -psī -ptum *vt.* copy out; note down.
exscu'lp/ō -ere -sī -tum *vt.* carve out; erase; (*fig.*) extort.
e'xsec/ō -ā're -uī -tum *vt.* cut out; castrate. [deadly.
exsecrā'bilis *a.* cursing,
exsecrā'ti/ō -ō'nis *f.* curse; solemn oath'
e'xsecr/or -ā'rī -ā'tus *vt.* curse; take an oath. **–ā'tus** *a.* accursed.
exse'cti/ō -ō'nis *f.* cutting out.
exsecū'ti/ō -ō'nis *f.* management; discussion.
exsecū'tus *ppa.* exsequor.
exse'qui/ae -ā'rum *f.pl.* funeral, funeral rites.
exsequiā'lis *a.* funeral.
e'xse/quor -quī -cū'tus *vt.* follow, pursue; follow to the grave; (*duty*) carry out, accomplish; (*speech*) describe, relate; (*suffering*) undergo; (*wrong*) avenge, punish.
e'xser/ō -ere -uī -tum *vt.* put out, stretch out; reveal.
exse'rt/ō -ā're *vt.* stretch out repeatedly.
exse'rtus *ppp.* exserō. *a.* protruding.
exsī'bil/ō -ā're *vt.* hiss off.
exsi'cc/ō -ā're -ā'vī -ā'tum *vt.* dry up; drain. **–ā'tus** *a.* (*style*) uninteresting.
e'xsicō, *see* **exsecō**.
exsi'gn/ō -ā're *vt.* write down in detail.
exsi'l/iō -ī're -uī *vi.* jump up, spring out; start.
exsi'l/ium -ī & iī *n.* banishment, exile; retreat.
exs/i'stō -i'stere -titī -titum *vi.* emerge, appear; arise, spring (from); be, exist.
exso'l/vō -vere -vī -ū'tum *vt.* undo, loosen, open; release, free; get rid of, throw off;

(*debt, promise*) discharge, fulfil, pay up; (*words*) explain.
exso'mnis *a.* sleepless, watchful.
exso'rb/eō -ē're -uī *vt.* suck, drain; devour, endure.
e'xsor/s -tis *a.* chosen, special; free from.
exspa'rgō, *see* **exspergō**.
exspa'ti/or -ā'rī -ā'tus *vi.* go off the course. [pected.
exspectā'bilis *a.* to be ex-
exspectā'ti/ō -ō'nis *f.* waiting, expectation.
exspe'ct/ō -ā're -ā'vī -ā'tum *vt.* wait for, till, to see; expect; hope for, dread; require. **-ā'tus** *a.* looked for, welcome.
exspe'r/gō -gere -sum *vt.* scatter; diffuse.
e'xspēs *a.* despairing.
exspīrā'ti/ō -ō'nis *f.* exhalation.
exspī'r/ō -ā're -ā'vī -ā'tum *vt.* breathe out, exhale; emit. *vi.* rush out; expire, come to an end.
exsplendē'sc/ō -ere *vi.* shine.
exspo'li/ō -ā're *vt.* pillage.
e'xsp/uō -u'ere -uī -ū'tum *vt.* spit out, eject; (*fig.*) banish.
exste'rn/ō -ā're *vt.* terrify.
exsti'll/ō -ā're *vi.* drip.
exstimulā't/or -ō'ris *m.* instigator.
exsti'mul/ō -ā're *vt.* goad on; excite. [hilation.
exsti'ncti/ō -ō'nis *f.* anni-
exsti'nct/or -ō'ris *m.* extinguisher; destroyer.
exsti'n/guō -guere -xī -ctum *vt.* put out, extinguish; kill, destroy, abolish.
exsti'rp/ō -ā're *vt.* root out, eradicate.
e'xstitī *perf.* **exsistō.**
e'xst/ō -ā're *vi.* stand out, project; be conspicuous, be visible; be extant, exist, be.
exstru'cti/ō -ō'nis *f.* erection.
e'xstru/ō -ere -xī -ctum *vt.* heap up; build up, construct.
exsū'd/ō -ā're *vi.* come out in sweat. *vt.* (*fig.*) toil through.
exsū'/gō -gere -xī -ctum *vt.* suck out.
e'xsul, e'xul -is *m., f.* exile.
e'xsul/ō -ā're -ā'vī -ā'tum *vi.* be an exile. [rejoicing.
exsultā'ti/ō -ō'nis *f.* great
exsu'ltim *ad.* friskily.
exsu'lt/ō -ā're -ā'vī -ā'tum *vi.* jump up, prance; (*fig.*) exult, run riot, boast; (*speech*) range at will.
exsuperā'bilis *a.* superable.
exsupera'nti/a -ae *f.* superiority.
exsu'per/ō -ā're -ā'vī -ā'tum *vi.* mount up; gain the upper hand, excel. *vt.* go over; surpass; overpower.
exsu'rd/ō -ā're *vt.* deafen; (*fig.*) dull.
exsu'r/gō -gere -rē'xī -rē'ctum *vi.* rise, stand up; recover.
exsu'scit/ō -ā're *vt.* wake up; (*fire*) fan; (*mind*) excite.
e'xt/a -ō'rum *n.pl.* internal organs.
extāb/ē'scō -ē'scere -uī *vi.* waste away; vanish.
extā'ris *a.* sacrificial.
exte'mplō *ad.* immediately, on the spur of the moment. quom — as soon as.
extemporā'lis *a.* extempore.
exte'mpulō, *see* **extemplō**.
exte'n/dō -dere -dī -tum & extē'nsum *vt.* stretch out, spread, extend; enlarge, increase; (*time*) prolong. sē — exert oneself. īre per -tum fūnem walk the tight-rope.
extē'nsus *ppp.* **extendō.**
exte'nt/ō -ā're *vt.* strain, exert. [broad.
exte'ntus *ppp.* **extendō.** *a.*
extenuā'ti/ō -ō'nis *f.* (*rhet.*) diminution.
exte'nu/ō -ā're -ā'vī -ā'tum *vt.* thin out, rarefy; diminish, weaken.

e'xter, e'xterus *a.* from outside; foreign.
exte'rebr/ō -ā're *vt.* bore out; extort.
exte'r/geō -gē're -sī -sum *vt.* wipe off, clean; plunder.
exte'ri/or -ō'ris *a.* outer, exterior. **–us** *ad.* on the outside.
exte'rmin/ō -ā're *vt.* drive out, banish; (*fig.*) put aside.
exte'rnus *a.* outward, external; foreign, strange.
e'xt/erō -e'rere -rī'vī -rī'tum *vt.* rub out, wear away.
exte'rr/eō -ē're -uī -itum *vt.* frighten.
exte'rsus *ppp.* extergeō.
e'xterus, *see* **exter.**
exte'x/ō -ere *vt.* unweave; (*fig.*) cheat.
extim/ē'scō -ē'scere -uī *vi.* be very frightened. *vt.* be very afraid of. [farthest.
e'xtimus *a.* outermost,
extin–, *see* **exstin–.**
exti'sp/ex -icis *m.* diviner.
exto'll/ō -ere *vt.* lift up, raise; (*fig.*) exalt, beautify; (*time*) defer.
exto'r/queō -quē're -sī -tum *vt.* wrench out, wrest; dislocate; (*fig.*) obtain by force, extort.
exto'rris *a.* banished, in exile.
exto'rt/or -ō'ris *m.* extorter.
exto'rtus *ppp.* extorqueō.
e'xtrā *ad.* outside. **— quam** except that, unless. *pr.* (*with acc.*) outside, beyond; free from; except.
e'xtra/hō -here -xī -ctum *vt.* draw out, pull out; extricate, rescue; remove; (*time*) prolong, waste.
extrā'ne/us -ī *m.* stranger. *a.* external, foreign.
extraōrdinā'rius *a.* special, unusual.
extrā'rius *a.* external; unrelated. *m.* stranger.
extrē'mit/ās -ā'tis *f.* extremity, end.
extrē'm/us *a.* outermost, extreme; last; utmost, greatest, meanest. **–um** -ī *n.* end. **ad -um** at last. **–um** *ad.* for the last time.
extrī'c/ō -ā're -ā'vī -ā'tum *vt.* disentangle, extricate; clear up.
extrī'nsecus *ad.* from outside, from abroad; on the outside.
extrī'tus *ppp.* exterō.
extrū'/dō -dere -sī -sum *vt.* drive out; keep out; (*sale*) push.
extulī *perf.* efferō.
extu'm/eō -ē're *vi.* swell up.
ext/u'ndō -u'ndere -udī -ū'sum *vt.* beat out, hammer out; (*comedy*) extort; (*fig.*) form, compose.
extu'rb/ō -ā're -ā'vī -ā'tum *vt.* drive out, throw out, knock out; (*wife*) put away; (*fig.*) banish, disturb.
exū'ber/ō -ā're *vi.* abound.
e'xul, *see* **exsul.**
exu'lcer/ō -ā're -ā'vī -ā'tum *vt.* aggravate.
exu'lul/ō -ā're *vi.* howl wildly. *vt.* invoke with cries.
exū'nctus *ppp.* exungō.
exu'nd/ō -ā're *vi.* overflow; be washed up. [liberally.
exu'ng/ō -ere *vt.* anoint
e'x/uō -u'ere -uī -ū'tum *vt.* draw out, put off; lay aside; strip.
exū'/rō -rere -ssī -stum *vt.* burn up; dry up; burn out; (*fig.*) inflame. [tion.
exū'sti/ō -ō'nis *f.* conflagra-
exū'tus *ppp.* exuō.
exu'vi/ae -ā'rum *f.pl.* clothing, arms; hide; spoils.

F

fa'b/a -ae *f.* bean. **–ā'lis** *a.* bean-. [fable; play.
fābe'll/a -ae *f.* short story,
fa'b/er -rī *m.* craftsman (in

metal, stone, wood), tradesman, smith; (*mil.*) artisan. — **ferrārius** blacksmith. — **tignārius** carpenter. *a.* skilful. **-rē** *ad.* skilfully.
Fa'b/ius -ī *m.* Roman family name, *esp.* Q. F. Maximus Cunctator, dictator against Hannibal. **-ius**, **-iā'nus** *a.*
fa'brē/fa'ciō -fa'cere -fē'cī -fa'ctum *vt.* make, build, forge.
fa'bric/a -ae *f.* art, trade; work of art; workshop; (*comedy*) trick.
fabricā'ti/ō -ō'nis *f.* structure.
fabricā't/or -ō'ris *m.* artificer.
Fabri'c/ius -ī *m.* Roman family name, *esp.* C. F. Luscinus, incorruptible commander against Pyrrhus. **-ius**, **-iā'nus** *a.*
fa'bric/or -ā'rī -ā'tus, -ō -ā're *vt.* make, build, forge.
fabrī'lis *a.* artificer's. *n.pl.* tools.
fā'bul/a -ae *f.* story; common talk; play, drama; fable. **-ae!** nonsense! **lūpus in -ā** *talk of the devil!*
fā'bul/or -ā'rī -ā'tus *vi.* talk, converse. *vt.* say, invent.
fābulō'sus *a.* legendary.
face'ss/ō -ere -ī'vī -ī'tum *vt.* perform, carry out; cause (trouble). *vi.* go away, retire.
facē'ti/ae -ā'rum *f.pl.* wit, clever talk, humour.
facē't/us *a.* witty, humorous; fine, genteel, elegant. **-ē** *ad.* humorously; brilliantly.
fa'ci/ēs -ē'ī *f.* form, shape; face, looks; appearance, aspect, character.
fa'cil/is *a.* easy; well-suited; ready, quick; (*person*) good-natured, approachable; (*fortune*) prosperous. **-e** *ad.* easily; unquestionably; readily; pleasantly.
faci'lit/ās -ā'tis *f.* ease, readiness; (*speech*) fluency; (*person*) good nature, affability.
facinorō'sus *a.* criminal.
fa'cin/us -oris *n.* deed, action; crime.
fa'c/iō -ere fē'cī fa'ctum (*imp.* **fac**, *pass.* **fīō**) *vt.* make, create, compose, cause; do, perform; (*profession*) practise; (*property*) put under; (*value*) regard, think of; (*words*) represent, pretend, suppose. *vi.* do, act; (*religion*) offer sacrifice; (*with* ad or dat.) be of use. **cōpiam** — afford an opportunity. **damnum** — suffer loss. **metum** — excite fear. **proelium** — join battle. **rem** — make money. **verba** — talk. **māgnī** — think highly of. **quid tibi faciam?** how am I to answer you? **quid tē faciam?** what am I to do with you? **fac sciam** let me know. **fac potuisse** suppose one could have.
fa'cti/ō -ō'nis *f.* making, doing; group, party, faction (*esp.* in politics and chariot-racing).
factiō'sus *a.* factious, oligarchical.
fa'ctit/ō -ā're -ā'vī -ā'tum *vt.* keep making or doing; practise; declare (to be).
fa'ct/or -ō'ris *m.* (*sport*) batsman.
fa'ct/us *ppp.* **faciō**. **-um -ī** *n.* deed, exploit.
fa'cul/a -ae *f.* little torch.
facu'lt/ās -ā'tis *f.* means, opportunity; ability; abundance, supply, resources.
fācu'ndi/a -ae *f.* eloquence.
fācu'nd/us *a.* fluent, eloquent. **-ē** *ad.*
fae'ceus *a.* impure.
fae'cul/a -ae *f.* wine-lees.
fae'nebris *a.* of usury.
faenerā'ti/ō -ō'nis *f.* usury.
faenerā'tō *ad.* with interest.
faenerā't/or -ō'ris *m.* money-lender.
fae'ner/or -ā'rī -ā'tus, -ō -ā're *vt.* lend at interest; ruin with usury; (*fig.*) trade in.

faenī'li/a -um *n.pl.* hay-loft.
fae'n/um -ī *n.* hay. — habet in cornū he is dangerous.
fae'n/us -oris *n.* interest; capital lent at interest; (*fig.*) profit, advantage.
faenu'scul/um -ī *n.* a little interest.
Fae'sul/ae -ā'rum *f.pl.* town in Etruria, *mod.* Fiesole. **-ā'nus** *a.*
faex fae'cis *f.* sediment, lees; brine (of pickles); (*fig.*) dregs.
fāgi'neus, fā'ginus *a.* of beech.
fā'g/us -ī *f.* beech.
fa'l/a -ae *f.* siege-tower, used in assaults; (*Circus*) pillar.
falā'ric/a -ae *f.* a missile, fire-brand.
falcā'r/ius -ī & iī *m.* sickle-maker. [shaped.
falcā'tus *a.* scythed; sickle-
fa'lcifer -ī *a.* scythe-carrying.
Fale'rnus *a.* Falernian, of a district in N. Campania famous for its wine. *n.* Falernian wine.
Fali'sc/ī -ō'rum *m.pl.* a people of S.E. Etruria, with chief town Falerii. **-us** *a.*
fallā'ci/a -ae *f.* trick, deception.
fa'll/āx -ā'cis *a.* deceitful, deceptive. **-ā'citer** *ad.*
fa'l/lō -lere fefe'llī -sum *vt.* deceive, cheat, beguile; disappoint, fail, betray; (*promise*) break; escape the notice of, be unknown to; (*pass.*) be mistaken. **mē -lit** I am mistaken; I do not know.
falsi'dicus *a.* lying.
falsi'ficus *a.* deceiving.
falsiiū'rius *a.* perjurious.
falsi'loquus *a.* lying.
falsi'par/ēns -e'ntis *a.* with a pretended father.
fa'ls/us *ppp.* fallō. *a.* false, mistaken; deceitful; forged, falsified; sham, fictitious. *n.* falsehood, error. **-ō, -ē** *ad.* wrongly, by mistake; fraudulently.
falx fa'lcis *f.* sickle, scythe; pruning-hook; (*mil.*) siege hook.
fā'm/a -ae *f.* talk, rumour, tradition; public opinion; reputation, fame; infamy.
famē'licus *a.* hungry.
fa'm/ēs -is *f.* hunger; famine; (*fig.*) greed; (*rhet.*) poverty of expression.
fāmigerā'ti/ō -ō'nis *f.* rumour. [tale.
fāmigerā't/or -ō'ris *m.* tell-
fami'li/a -ae *f.* domestics, slaves of a household; family property, estate; family, house; school, sect. **pater -ās** master of a household. **-am dūcere** be head of a sect, company, etc.
familiā'ri/s *a.* domestic, household, family; intimate, friendly; (*entrails*) relating to the sacrificer. *m.* servant; friend. **-ter** *ad.* on friendly terms.
familiā'rit/ās -ā'tis *f.* intimacy, friendship.
fāmō'sus *a.* celebrated; infamous; slanderous.
fa'mul/a -ae *f.* maid-servant, handmaid.
famulā'ris *a.* of servants.
famulā't/us -ūs *m.* slavery.
fa'mul/or -ā'rī *vi.* serve.
fa'mul/us -ī *m.* servant, attendant. *a.* serviceable.
fānā'ticus *a.* inspired; frantic, frenzied.
fa'ndī *gerund* for.
fā'n/um -ī *n.* sanctuary temple.
fār fa'rris *n.* spelt; corn; meal.
fa'r/ciō -cī're -sī -tum *vt.* stuff, fill full.
farī'n/a -ae *f.* meal, flour.
farrā'g/ō -inis *f.* mash, hotchpotch; medley.
farrā'tus *a.* of corn; filled with corn.

fa'rsī *perf.* farciō.
fa'rt/em -im *f.acc.* filling; mincemeat. [poulterer.
fa'rt/or -ō'ris *m.* fattener,
fa'rtus *ppp.* farciō.
fās *n.* divine law; right. — est it is lawful, possible.
fa'sci/a -ae *f.* band, bandage; streak of cloud.
fasci'cul/us -ī *m.* bundle, packet.
fa'scin/ō -ā're *vt.* bewitch, *esp.* with the evil eye.
fa'scin/um -ī *n.*, **-us** -ī *m.* charm.
fasci'ol/a -ae *f.* small bandage.
fa'sc/is -is *m.* bundle, faggot; soldier's pack, burden; (*pl.*) rods and axe carried before the highest magistrates; high office, *esp.* the consulship.
fa'ssus *ppa.* fateor.
fā'st/ī -ō'rum *m.pl.* register of days for legal and public business; calendar; registers of magistrates and other public records.
fastī'd/iō -ī're -iī -ī'tum *vt.* loathe, dislike, despise. *vi.* feel squeamish, be disgusted; be disdainful.
fastīdiō's/us *a.* squeamish, disgusted; fastidious, nice; disagreeable. **-ē** *ad.* squeamishly; disdainfully.
fastī'd/ium -ī & iī *n.* squeamishness, distaste; disgust, aversion; disdain, pride.
fastīgā't/ē *ad.* in a sloping position. **-us** *a.* sloping up or down.
fastī'g/ium -ī & iī *n.* gable, pediment; slope; height, depth; top, summit; (*fig.*) highest degree, acme, dignity; (*speech*) main headings.
fā'stus *a.* lawful for public business.
fa'st/us -ūs *m.* disdain, pride.
fātā'li/s *a.* fateful, destined; fatal, deadly. **-ter** *ad.* by fate.
fa'/teor -tē'rī -ssus *vt.* confess, acknowledge; reveal, bear witness to.
fāti'c/anus, **-inus** *a.* prophetic.
fāti'dicus *a.* prophetic. *m.* prophet.
fā'tifer -ī *a.* deadly.
fatīgā'ti/ō -ō'nis *f.* weariness.
fatī'g/ō -ā're -ā'vī -ā'tum *vt.* tire, exhaust; worry, importune; wear down, torment.
fāti'loqu/a -ae *f.* prophetess.
fatī'sc/ō -ere, **-or** -ī *vi.* crack, split; (*fig.*) become exhausted.
fatu'it/ās -ātis *f.* silliness.
fā't/um -ī *n.* divine word, oracle; fate, destiny; divine will; misfortune, doom, death. **-ō obīre** die a natural death. **Fāta** *pl.* the Fates.
fā'tur, **fā'tus** 3rd *pers.*, *ppa.* for. [*m.* fool.
fa'tuus *a.* silly; unwieldy.
fau'c/ēs -ium *f.pl.* throat; pass, narrow channel, chasm; (*fig.*) jaws.
Fau'n/us -ī *m.* father of Latinus, god of forests and herdsmen, identified with Pan; (*pl.*) woodland spirits, Fauns.
fau'stit/ās -ā'tis *f.* good fortune, fertility.
fau'st/us *a.* auspicious, lucky. **-ē** *ad.*
fau't/or -ō'ris *m.* supporter, patron.
fau'tr/īx -ī'cis *f.* protectress.
fa've/a -ae *f.* pet slave.
fa'veō -ē're fā'vī fau'tum *vi.* (*with dat.*) favour, befriend, support. — **linguīs** keep silence.
favi'll/a -ae *f.* embers, ashes; (*fig.*) spark.
fa'vitor, *see* **fautor**.
Favō'n/ius -ī *m.* west wind, zephyr.
fa'v/or -ō'ris *m.* favour, support; applause.
favōrā'bilis *a.* in favour; pleasing.

fa'v/us -ī *m.* honeycomb.
fax fa'cis *f.* torch, wedding-torch, funeral-torch; marriage, death; (*astr.*) meteor; (*fig.*) flame, fire, instigator; guide. facem praeferre act as guide.
fa'xim, **fa'xō** *old subj. and fut.* faciō.
febrī'cul/a -ae *f.* slight fever.
fe'br/is -is *f.* fever.
Februā'r/ius -ī *m.* February. *a.* of February.
fe'bru/um -ī *n.* purification. Fe'brua *pl.* festival of purification in February.
fē'cī *perf.* faciō.
fēcu'ndit/ās -ā'tis *f.* fertility; (*style*) exuberance.
fēcu'nd/ō -ā're *vt.* fertilise.
fēcu'ndus *a.* fertile, fruitful; fertilising; (*fig.*) abundant, rich, prolific.
fefe'llī *perf.* fallō.
fel fe'llis *n.* gall-bladder, bile; poison; (*fig.*) animosity.
fē'l/ēs -is *f.* cat.
fēlī'cit/ās -ā'tis *f.* happiness, good luck.
fē'l/īx -ī'cis *a.* fruitful; auspicious, favourable; fortunate, successful. **-ī'citer** *ad.* abundantly; favourably; happily.
fēme'll/a -ae *f.* girl.
fē'min/a -ae *f.* female, woman.
fēmi'neus *a.* woman's, of women; unmanly.
fe'm/ur -oris & inis *n.* thigh.
fēn-, *see* **faen-**.
fene'str/a -ae *f.* window; (*fig.*) loop-hole.
fe'r/a -ae *f.* wild beast.
fērā'lis *a.* funereal; of the Feralia; deadly. *n.pl.* festival of the dead in February.
fe'r/āx -ā'cis *a.* fruitful, productive. **-ā'cius** *ad.* more fruitfully.
fe'rbuī *perf.* ferveō.
fe'rcul/um -ī *n.* litter, barrow; dish, course.
fe'rē, **fe'rmē** *ad.* almost, nearly, about; quite, just; usually, generally, as a rule; (*with neg.*) hardly. nihil — hardly anything.
ferentā'r/ius -ī & iī *m.* a light-armed soldier.
Fere'tr/ius -ī *m.* an epithet of Jupiter.
fere'tr/um -ī *n.* bier.
fē'ri/ae -ā'rum *f.pl.* festival, holidays; (*fig.*) peace, rest.
fēriā'tus *a.* on holiday, idle.
ferī'nus *a.* of wild beasts. *f.* game.
fe'r/iō -ī're *vt.* strike, hit; kill, sacrifice; (*comedy*) cheat. foedus — conclude a treaty.
fe'rit/ās -ā'tis *f.* wildness, savagery.
fe'rmē, *see* **ferē**.
ferme'nt/um -ī *n.* yeast; beer; (*fig.*) passion, vexation.
fe'rō fe'rre tu'lī lā'tum *vt.* carry, bring, bear; bring forth, produce; move, stir, raise; carry off, sweep away, plunder; (*pass.*) rush, hurry, fly, flow, drift; (*road*) lead; (*trouble*) endure, suffer, sustain; (*feelings*) exhibit, show; (*speech*) talk about, give out, celebrate; (*book-keeping*) enter; (*circs.*) allow, require. sē — rush, move; profess to be, boast. condiciōnem, lēgem — propose terms, a law. iūdicem — sue. sententiam, suffrāgium — vote. signa — march; attack. aegrē, graviter — be annoyed at. laudibus — extol. in oculīs — be very fond of. prae sē — show, declare. fertur, ferunt it is said, they say. ut mea fert opīniō in my opinion.
ferō'ci/a -ae *f.* courage, spirit; pride, presumption.
ferō'cit/ās -ā'tis *f.* high spirits, aggressiveness; presumption.
Fērō'ni/a -ae *f.* old Italian goddess.
fe'r/ōx -ō'cis *a.* warlike, spirited, daring; proud, in-

solent. **-ō'citer** *ad* bravely; insolently.
ferrāme'nt/um **-ī** *n.* tool, implement.
ferrā'rius *a.* of iron. faber — blacksmith. *f.* iron-mine, iron-works.
ferrā'tus *a.* iron-clad, iron-shod. *m.pl.* men in armour.
fe'rreus *a.* of iron, iron; (*fig.*) hard, cruel; strong, unyielding.
ferrūgi'neus *a.* rust-coloured, dark.
ferrū'g/ō **-inis** *f.* rust; dark colour; gloom.
fe'rr/um **-ī** *n.* iron; sword; any iron implement; force of arms. — et ignis devastation.
fe'rtilis *a.* fertile, productive; fertilising.
ferti'lit/ās **-ā'tis** *f.* fertility.
fe'rul/a **-ae** *f.* fennel; staff, rod. [cruel. *m.* beast.
fe'rus *a.* wild; uncivilised,
fervēfa'c/iō **-ere** **-tum** *vt.* boil.
fe'rv/ēns **-e'ntis** *pres.p.* ferveō. *a.* hot; raging; (*fig.*) impetuous, furious. **-e'nter** *ad.* hotly.
fe'r/veō **-vē're** **-buī**, **-vō** **-vere** **-vī** *vi.* boil, burn; (*fig.*) rage, bustle, be agitated.
fervē'sc/ō **-ere** *vi.* boil up, grow hot.
fe'rvidus *a.* hot, raging; (*fig.*) fiery, violent.
fe'rv/or **-ō'ris** *m.* seething; heat; (*fig.*) ardour, passion.
Fescennī'nus *a.* Fescennine, a kind of ribald song, perhaps from Fescennium in Etruria.
fe'ssus *a.* tired, worn out.
festīna'nter *ad.* hastily.
festīnā'ti/ō **-ō'nis** *f.* haste, hurry.
festī'n/ō **-ā're** *vi.* hurry, be quick. *vt.* hasten, accelerate.
festī'nus *a.* hasty, quick.
fēstī'vit/ās **-ā'tis** *f.* gaiety, merriment; humour, fun.
fēstī'v/us *a.* gay, jolly; delightful; (*speech*) humorous. **-ē** *ad.* gaily; humorously.
festū'c/a **-ae** *f.* rod with which slaves were manumitted.
fē'stus *a.* festal, on holiday. *n.* holiday; feast.
fētiā'l/is **-is** *m.* priest who carried out the ritual in making war and peace.
fētū'r/a **-ae** *f.* breeding; brood.
fē'tus *a.* pregnant; newly delivered; (*fig.*) productive, full of.
fē't/us **-ūs** *m.* breeding, bearing, producing; brood, young; fruit, produce; (*fig.*) production.
fi'b/er **-rī** *m.* beaver.
fi'br/a **-ae** *f.* fibre; section of lung or liver; entrails.
fī'bul/a **-ae** *f.* clasp, brooch; clamp.
fice'dul/a **-ae** *f.* fig-pecker.
fi'ctilis *a.* clay, earthen. *n.* jar; clay figure.
fi'ct/or **-ō'ris** *m.* sculptor; maker, inventor.
fi'ctr/īx **-ī'cis** *f.* maker.
fictū'r/a **-ae** *f.* shaping, invention.
fi'ct/us *ppp.* fingō. *a.* false, fictitious. *n.* falsehood. **-ē** *ad.* falsely.
ficu'lnus *a.* of the fig-tree.
fī'c/us **-ī** & **ūs** *f.* fig-tree; fig.
fidē'li/a **-ae** *f.* pot, pail. dē eādem -ā duōs parietēs dealbāre *kill two birds with one stone.*
fidē'l/is *a.* faithful, loyal; trustworthy, sure. **-iter**, **-e** *ad.* faithfully, surely firmly.
fidē'lit/ās **-ā'tis** *f.* faithfulness, loyalty.
Fīdē'n/ae **-ā'rum** *f.pl.* ancient Latin town. **-ā's** **-ā'tis** *a.*
fī'd/ēns **-e'ntis** *pres.p.* fīdō. *a.* bold, resolute. **-e'nter** *ad.*
fīde'nti/a **-ae** *f.* self-confidence.
fi'd/ēs **-ĕī** *f.* trust, faith, belief; trustworthiness, honour, loyalty, truth; promise, assurance, word; guarantee, safe-

conduct, protection; (*bus.*) credit; (*law*) good faith. — mala dishonesty. rēs —que entire resources. -em facere convince. -em servāre erga keep faith with. dī vostram -em! for Heaven's sake! ex fidē bonā in good faith.
fi'd/ēs -is *f.* (*usu. pl.*) stringed instrument, lyre, lute; (*astr.*) Lyra.
fi'dī *perf.* findō.
fi'dic/en -inis *m.* musician; lyric poet.
fidi'cin/a -ae *f.* music-girl.
fidi'cul/a -ae *f.* small lute.
Fi'd/ius -ī *m.* an epithet of Jupiter.
fi'/dō -dere -sus *vi.* (*with dat. or abl.*) trust, rely on.
fidū'ci/a -ae *f.* confidence, assurance; self-confidence; (*law*) trust, security.
fidūciā'rius *a.* to be held in trust.
fi'dus *a.* trusty, reliable; sure, safe.
fi'/gō -gere -xī -xum *vt.* fix, fasten, attach; drive in, pierce; (*speech*) taunt.
figulā'ris *a.* a potter's.
fi'gul/us -ī *m.* potter; builder.
figū'r/a -ae *f.* shape, form; nature, kind; phantom; (*rhet.*) figure of speech.
figū'r/ō -ā're *vt.* form, shape.
filā'tim *ad.* thread by thread.
fi'li/a -ae *f.* daughter.
filicā'tus *a.* with fern patterns.
fili'ol a -ae *f.* little daughter.
fili'ol/us -ī *m.* little son.
fī'l/ius -ī & iī *m.* son. terrae — a nobody.
fi'li/x -cis *f.* fern.
fī'l/um -ī *n.* thread; band of wool, fillet; string, shred, wick; contour, shape; (*speech*) texture, quality. [end.
fi'mbri/ae -ā'rum *f.pl.* fringe,
fi'm/us -ī *m.* dung; dirt.
fi'/ndō -ndere -dī -ssum *vt.* split, divide; burst.
fi'ng/ō -ere fi'nxī fi'ctum *vt.* form, shape, make; mould, model; dress, arrange; train; (*mind, speech*) imagine, suppose, represent, sketch; invent, fabricate. vultum — compose the features.
fī'n/iō -ī're -ī'vī -ī'tum *vt.* bound, limit; restrain; prescribe, define, determine; end, finish, complete. *vi.* finish, die.
fī'n/is -is *m.*(*occ. f.*) boundary, border; (*pl.*) territory; bound, limit; end; death; highest point, summit; aim, purpose. — bonōrum the chief good. quem ad -em? how long? -e genūs up to the knee.
fīnī't/imus, -umus *a.* neighbouring, adjoining; akin, like. *m.pl.* neighbours.
fīnī't/or -ō'ris *m.* surveyor.
fīnī't/us *ppp.* finiō. *a.* (*rhet.*) well-rounded. -ē *ad.* within limits.
fi'nxī *perf.* fingō.
fi'ō fi'erī fa'ctus *vi.* become, arise; be made, be done; happen. quī fit ut how is it that. ut fit as usually happens. quid mē fiet? what will become of me?
firmā'm/en -inis *n.* support.
firmāme'nt/um -ī *n.* support, strengthening; (*fig.*) mainstay.
firmā't/or -ō'ris *m.* establisher.
fi'rmit/ās -ā'tis *f.* firmness, strength; steadfastness, stamina. [stability.
firmitū'd/ō -inis *f.* strength,
fi'rm/ō -ā're -ā'vī -ā'tum *vt.* strengthen, support, fortify; (*mind*) encourage, steady; (*fact*) confirm, prove, assert.
fi'rm/us *a.* strong, stable, firm; (*fig.*) powerful, constant, sure, true. -ē, -iter *ad.* powerfully, steadily.
fisce'll/a -ae *f.* wicker basket.
fi'scin/a -ae *f.* wicker basket.

fi'sc/us -ī *m.* purse, money-box; public exchequer; imperial treasury, the emperor's privy purse.
fi'ssilis *a.* easy to split.
fi'ssi/ō -ō'nis *f.* dividing.
fi'ssus *ppp.* findō. *n.* slit, fissure.
fistū'c/a -ae *f.* rammer.
fi'stul/a -ae *f.* pipe, tube; Pan-pipes; (*med.*) ulcer.
fistulā't/or -ō'ris *m.* Pan-pipe player.
fi'sus *ppa.* fidō.
fi'xī *perf.* figō.
fi'xus *ppp.* figō. *a.* fixed, fast, permanent.
flābelli'fer/a -ae *f.* fan-bearer.
flābe'll/um -ī *n.* fan.
flā'bilis *a.* airy.
flā'br/a -ō'rum *n.pl.* blasts, gusts; wind.
fla'cc/eō -ē're *vi.* flag, lose heart.
flaccē'sc/ō -ere *vi.* flag, droop.
fla'ccidus *a.* flabby, feeble.
fla'ccus *a.* flap-eared.
Fla'cc/us -ī *m.* surname of Horace.
flage'll/ō -ā're *vt.* whip, lash.
flage'll/um -ī *n.* whip, lash; strap, thong; (*vine*) shoot; (*polypus*) arm; (*feelings*) sting.
flāgitā'ti/ō -ō'nis *f.* demand.
flāgitā't/or -ō'ris *m.* demander, dun.
flāgitiō's/us *a.* disgraceful, profligate. **-ē** *ad.* infamously.
flāgi't/ium -ī & iī *n.* offence, disgrace, shame; scoundrel.
flā'git/ō -ā're -ā'vī -ā'tum *vt.* demand, importune, dun; (*law*) summon.
fla'gr/āns -a'ntis *pres.p.* flagrō. *a.* hot, blazing; brilliant; passionate. **-a'nter** *ad.* passionately.
flagra'nti/a -ae *f.* blazing; (*fig.*) shame.
fla'gr/ō -ā're *vi.* blaze, burn, be on fire; (*feelings*) be excited, be inflamed; (*ill-will*) be the victim of.
fla'gr/um -ī *n.* whip, lash.
flā'm/en -inis *m.* priest of a particular deity.
flā'm/en -inis *n.* blast, gale, wind.
flāmi'nic/a -ae *f.* wife of a priest.
Flāminī'n/us -ī *m.* Roman surname, *esp.* the conqueror of Philip V of Macedon.
flāmi'n/ium -ī & iī *n.* priesthood.
Flāmi'n/ius -ī *m.* Roman family name, *esp.* the consul defeated by Hannibal. **–ius, –iā'nus** *a.* Via -ia road from Rome N.E. to Ariminum.
fla'mm/a -ae *f.* flame, fire; torch, star; fiery colour; (*fig.*) passion; danger, disaster.
flamme'ol/um -ī *n.* bridal veil.
flammē'sc/ō -ere *vi.* become fiery.
fla'mmeus *a.* fiery, blazing; flame-coloured. *n.* bridal veil.
fla'mmifer -ī *a.* fiery.
fla'mm/ō -ā're -ā'vī -ā'tum *vi.* blaze. *vt.* set on fire, burn; (*fig.*) inflame, incense.
fla'mmul/a -ae *f.* little flame.
flā't/us -ūs *m.* blowing, breath; breeze; (*fig.*) arrogance.
flā'v/ēns -e'ntis *a.* yellow, golden.
flāvē'sc/ō -ere *vi.* turn yellow.
Flā'v/ius -ī *m.* Roman family name, *esp.* the emperors Vespasian, Titus and Domitian. **–iā'nus** *a.*
flā'vus *a.* yellow, golden.
flē'bili/s *a.* lamentable; tearful, mournful. **–ter** *ad.*
fle'/ctō -ctere -xī -xum *vt.* bend, turn; turn aside, wheel; (*promontory*) round; (*mind*) direct, persuade, dissuade. *vi.* turn, march.
fl/e'ō -ē're -ē'vī -ē'tum *vi.* weep, cry. *vt.* lament, mourn for.
flē't/us -ūs *m.* weeping, tears.
flexa'nimus *a.* moving.

fle'xī *perf.* flectō.
flexi'bilis *a.* pliant, flexible; fickle.
fle'xilis *a.* pliant.
flexi'loquus *a.* ambiguous.
fle'xi/ō -ō'nis *f.* bending, winding, (*voice*) modulation.
fle'xip/ēs -edis *a.* twining.
flexuō'sus *a.* tortuous.
flexū'r/a -ae *f.* bending.
fle'xus *ppp.* flectō. *a.* winding.
fle'x/us -ūs *m.* winding, bending; change.
flī'ct/us -ūs *m.* collision.
fl/ō -ā're -ā'vī -ā'tum *vt.* & *i.* blow; (*money*) coin.
flo'cc/us -ī *m.* bit of wool; triviality. **-ī nōn faciō** *I don't care a straw for.*
Flō'r/a -ae *f.* goddess of flowers. **-ā'lis** *a.*
flō'r/ēns -e'ntis *pres.p.* flōreō. *a.* in bloom; bright; prosperous, flourishing.
flō'r/eō -ē're -uī *vi.* blossom, flower; (*age*) be in one's prime; (*wine*) froth; (*fig.*) flourish prosper; (*places*) be gay with.
flōrē'sc/ō -ere *vi.* begin to flower; grow prosperous.
flō'reus *a.* of flowers, flowery.
flōri'dulus *a.* pretty little.
flō'ridus *a.* of flowers, flowery; fresh, pretty; (*style*) florid, ornate.
flō'rifer -ī *a.* flowery.
flōri'legus *a.* flower-sipping.
flō'rus *a.* beautiful.
fl/ōs -ō'ris *m.* flower, blossom; (*wine*) bouquet; (*age*) prime, heyday; (*youth*) downy beard, youthful innocence; (*fig.*) crown, glory; (*speech*) ornament.
flō'scul/us -ī *m.* little flower; (*fig.*) pride, ornament.
flūcti'fragus *a.* surging.
flūctuā'ti/ō -ō'nis *f.* wavering.
flū'ctu/ō -ā're *vi.* toss, wave; (*fig.*) rage, swell, waver.
flūctuō'sus *a.* stormy.
flū'ct/us -ūs *m.* wave; flowing. flood; (*fig.*) disturbance. **-ūs** (*pl.*) **in simpulō** *a storm in a teacup.*
flu'/ēns -e'ntis *pres.p.* fluō. *a.* lax, loose, enervated; (*speech*) fluent. **-e'nter** *ad.* in a flowing manner.
flue'nt/a -ō'rum *n.pl.* stream, flood.
fluenti'sonus *a.* wave-echoing.
flu'idus, flū'vidus *a.* flowing, fluid; lax, soft; relaxing.
flu'it/ō -ā're *vi.* flow, float about; wave, flap, move unsteadily; (*fig.*) waver.
flū'm/en -inis *n.* stream, river; (*fig.*) flood, flow, fluency. **adversō -ine** up-stream. **secundō -ine** down-stream.
flūmi'neus *a.* river-
flu'/ō -ere -xī -xum *vi.* flow; overflow, drip; (*fig.*) fall in, fall away, vanish; (*speech*) run evenly, (*circs.*) proceed, tend.
flū'tō, *see* **fluitō**.
fluviā'lis *a.* river-.
fluviā'tilis *a.* river-.
flū'vidus, *see* **fluidus**.
flu'v/ius -ī & iī *m.* river, stream.
flu'xi *perf.* fluō.
flu'xus *a.* flowing, loose, leaky; (*person*) lax, dissolute; (*thing*) frail, fleeting, unreliable.
fōcā'l/e -is *n.* scarf.
fo'cul/us -ī *m.* stove, fire.
fo'c/us -ī *m.* hearth, fire-place; pyre, altar; (*fig.*) home.
fo'dic/ō -ā're *vt.* nudge, jog.
fo'd/iō -ere fō'dī fo'ssum *vt.* dig; prick, stab; (*fig.*) goad.
foederā'tus *a.* confederated.
foedi'fragus *a.* perfidious.
foe'dit/ās -ā'tis *f.* foulness, hideousness.
foe'd/ō -ā're -ā'vī -ā'tum *vt.* mar, disfigure; disgrace, sully.
foe'd/us *a.* foul, hideous, revolting; vile, disgraceful. **-ē** *ad.*
foe'd/us -eris *n.* treaty, league; agreement, compact; law.

foen-, *see* **faen-**.
foe't/eō -ē're *vi.* stink.
foe'tidus *a.* stinking.
foe't/or -ō'ris *m.* stench.
foetu-, *see* **fētu-**.
foliā't/um -ī *n.* nard-oil.
fo'l/ium -ī & iī *n.* leaf.
folli'cul/us -ī *m.* small bag; egg-shell.
fo'll/is -is *m.* bellows; punch-ball; purse.
fōme'nt/um -ī *n.* poultice, bandage; (*fig.*) alleviation.
fō'm/es -itis *m.* tinder, kindling.
fōns **fo'ntis** *m.* spring, source; water; (*fig.*) origin, fountain-head.
fontā'nus *a.* spring-.
fonti'cul/us -ī *m.* little spring.
for **fā'rī** **fā'tus** *vt.* & *i.* speak, utter. **fa'nd/um** -ī *n.* right.
forā'bilis *a.* penetrable.
forā'm/en -inis *n.* hole, opening.
fo'rās *ad.* out, outside.
fo'rc/eps -ipis *m., f.* tongs, forceps.
fo'rd/a -ae *f.* cow in calf.
fo're, **fo'rem** *fut.inf.*, *imperf. subj.* sum.
forē'nsis *a.* public, forensic; of the market-place.
fo'r/is -is *f.* (*usu. pl.*) door; (*fig.*) opening, entrance.
fo'rīs *ad.* out of doors, outside, abroad; from outside, from abroad. — cēnāre dine out.
fō'rm/a -ae *f.* form, shape, appearance; mould, stamp, last; (*person*) beauty; (*fig.*) idea, nature, kind.
fōrmāme'nt/um -ī *n.* shape.
fōrmātū'r/a -ae *f.* shaping.
Fo'rmi/ae -ā'rum *f.pl.* town in S. Latium. **-ā'nus** *a.* of Formiae. *n.* villa at Formiae.
formī'c/a -ae *f.* ant.
formī'cinus *a.* crawling.
formīdā'bilis *a.* terrifying.
formī'd/ō -ā're -ā'vī -ā'tum *vt.* & *i.* fear, be terrified.
formī'd/ō -inis *f.* terror, awe, horror; scarecrow.
formīdolō's/us *a.* fearful, terrifying; afraid. **-ē** *ad.*
fō'rm/ō -ā're -ā'vī -ā'tum *vt.* shape, fashion, form.
fōrmō'sit/ās -ā'tis *f.* beauty.
fōrmō'sus *a.* beautiful, handsome.
fō'rmul/a -ae *f.* rule, regulation; (*law*) procedure, formula; (*philos.*) principle.
fornā'cul/a -ae *f.* small oven.
fo'rn/āx -ā'cis *f.* furnace, oven, kiln.
fornicā'tus *a.* arched.
fo'rn/ix -icis *m.* arch, vault; brothel.
fo'r/ō -ā're *vt.* pierce.
fors **fo'rtis** *f.* chance, luck. *ad.* perchance. **-te** by chance, as it happened; perhaps. **nē -te** in case. **sī -te** if perhaps; in the hope that.
fo'rsan, **fo'rsit**, **fo'rsitan** *ad.* perhaps.
forta'ss/e, **-is** *ad.* perhaps, possibly; (*irony*) very likely.
forti'culus *a.* quite brave.
fo'rti/s *a.* strong, sturdy; brave, manly, resolute. **-ter** *ad.* vigorously; bravely.
fortitū'd/ō -inis *f.* courage, resolution; strength.
fortuī't/us *a.* casual, accidental. **-ō** *ad.* by chance.
fortū'n/a -ae *f.* chance, luck, fortune; good luck, success; misfortune; circumstances, lot; (*pl.*) possessions. **-ae fīlius** Fortune's favourite. **-am habēre** be successful.
fortūnā't/us *a.* happy, lucky; well off, rich, blessed. **-ē** *ad.*
fortū'n/ō -ā're *vt.* bless, prosper.
fo'rul/ī -ō'rum *m.pl.* book-case.
fo'r/um -ī *n.* public place, market; market-town; Roman Forum between the Palatine and Capitol; public affairs, law-courts, business. — boār-

ium cattle-market. — **olitōrium** vegetable-market. — **piscātōrium** fish-market. — **agere** hold an assize. — **attingere** enter public life. **cēdere -ō** go bankrupt. **utī -ō** take advantage of a situation.
Fo'r/um Iū'li colony in S. Gaul, *mod.* Fréjus. **-oiūliē'nsis** *a.*
fo'r/us -ī *m.* gangway; block of seats; (*bees*) cell frame.
fo'ss/a -ae *f.* ditch, trench.
fo'ssi/ō -ō'nis *f.* digging.
fo'ss/or -ō'ris *m.* digger.
fo'ssus *ppp.* fodiō.
fō'tus *ppp.* foveō.
fo've/a -ae *f.* pit, pitfall.
fo'v/eō -ē're fō'vī fō'tum *vt.* warm, keep warm; (*med.*) foment; fondle, keep; (*fig.*) cherish, love, foster, pamper, encourage. **castra —** remain in camp.
frā'ctus *ppp.* frangō. *a.* weak, faint.
frā'g/a -ō'rum *n.pl.* strawberries.
fra'gilis *a.* brittle, fragile; frail, fleeting.
fragi'lit/ās -ā'tis *f.* frailness.
fra'gm/en -inis *n.* (*pl.*) fragments, ruins, wreck.
fragme'nt/um -ī *n.* fragment, remnant.
fra'g/or -ō'ris *m.* crash, din; disintegration.
fragō'sus *a.* crashing, roaring, breakable; rough.
frā'gr/āns -a'ntis *a.* fragrant.
fra'me/a -ae *f.* German spear.
fr/a'ngō -a'ngere -ē'gī -ā'ctum *vt.* break, shatter, wreck; crush, grind; (*fig.*) break down, weaken, humble; (*emotion*) touch, move. **cervicem —** strangle.
frā't/er -ris *m.* brother; cousin; (*fig.*) friend, ally.
frāte'rcul/us -ī *m.* brother.
frāte'rnit/ās -ā'tis *f.* brotherhood.
frāte'rn/us *a.* brotherly, a brother's, fraternal. **-ē** *ad.* like a brother.
frātricī'd/a -ae *m.* fratricide.
frauda'ti/ō -ō'nis *f.* deceit, fraud.
fraudā't/or -ō'ris *m.* swindler.
frau'd/ō -ā're -ā'vī -ā'tum *vt.* cheat, defraud; steal, cancel.
fraudule'ntus *a.* deceitful, fraudulent.
fr/aus -au'dis *f.* deceit, fraud; delusion, error; offence, wrong; injury, damage. **lēgī -dem facere** evade the law. **in -dem incidere** be disappointed. **sine -de** without harm.
fraxi'neus, fra'xinus *a.* of ash. [ashen spear.
fra'xin/us -ī *f.* ash-tree;
Frege'll/ae -ā'rum *f.pl.* town in S. Latium. **-ā'nus** *a.*
frē'gī *perf.* frangō.
fremebu'ndus *a.* roaring.
fre'mit/us -ūs *m.* roaring, snorting, noise.
fre'm/ō -ere -uī -itum *vi.* roar, snort, grumble. *vt.* shout for complain.
fre'm/or -ō'ris *m.* murmuring.
fre'nd/ō -ere *vi.* gnash the teeth.
frē'n/ō -ā're -ā'vī -ā'tum *vt.* bridle; (*fig.*) curb, restrain.
frē'n/um -ī *n.* (*pl.* **-a -ō'rum** *n.*, **-ī -ōrum** *m.*) bridle, bit; (*fig.*) curb, check. **-ōs dare** give vent to. **-um mordēre** *take the bit between one's teeth.*
fre'qu/ēns -e'ntis *a.* crowded, numerous, populous; regular, repeated, frequent. **— senatus** a crowded meeting of the senate. **-e'nter** *ad.* in large numbers; repeatedly, often.
frequentā'ti/ō -ō'nis *f.* accumulation.
freque'nti/a -ae *f.* full attendance, throng, crowd.
freque'nt/ō -ā're -ā'vī -ā'tum *vt.* crowd, populate; visit repeatedly, frequent; repeat; (*festival*) celebrate, keep.

fre't/um -ī *n.* strait; sea; (*fig.*) violence. — Siciliēnse Straits of Messina. **-ē'nsis** *a.* of the Straits of Messina.
fre't/us -ūs *m.* strait.
frē'tus *a.* relying, confident.
fri'c/ō -ā're -uī -tum *vt.* rub, rub down.
frī'ctus *ppp.* frīgō.
frīgefa'ct/ō -ā're *vt.* cool.
frī'g/eō -ē're *vi.* be cold; (*fig.*) be lifeless, flag; be coldly received, fall flat.
frī'gerāns *a.* cooling.
frīgē'sc/ō -ere *vi.* grow cold; become inactive. [faint.
frīgi'dulus *a.* rather cold,
frī'gid/us *a.* cold, cool; chilling; (*fig.*) dull, torpid; (*words*) flat, uninteresting. **-a** -ae *f.* cold water. **-ē** *ad.* feebly.
frī'/gō -gere -xī -ctum *vt.* roast, fry.
frī'g/us -oris *n.* cold; cold weather, winter; death; (*fig.*) dullness, inactivity; coldness, indifference.
frigu'tt/iō -ī're *vi.* stammer.
fri'/ō -are *vt.* crumble.
friti'll/us -ī *m.* dice-box.
frī'volus *a.* empty, paltry.
frī'xī *perf.* frīgō.
frondā't/or -ō'ris *m.* vine-dresser, pruner.
fro'nd/eō -ē're *vi.* be in leaf.
frondē'sc/ō -ere *vi.* become leafy, shoot.
fro'ndeus *a.* leafy.
fro'ndifer -ī *a.* leafy.
frondō'sus *a.* leafy.
fr/ōns -o'ndis *f.* leaf, foliage; garland of leaves.
fr/ōns -o'ntis *f.* forehead, brow; front, facade; (*fig.*) look, appearance, exterior. **-ontem contrahere** frown. **ā -onte** in front. **in -onte** in breadth.
frontā'li/a -um *n.pl.* frontlet.
fro'nt/ō -ō'nis *m.* a broad-browed man.
frūctuā'rius *a.* productive; paid for out of produce.
frūctuō'sus *a.* productive; profitable.
frū'ctus *ppa.* fruor.
frū'ct/us -ūs *m.* enjoyment; revenue, income; produce, fruit; (*fig.*) consequence, reward. **-uī esse** be an asset (to). **-um percipere** reap the fruits (of).
frūgā'li/s *a.* thrifty, worthy. **-ter** *ad.* temperately.
frūgā'lit/ās -ā'tis *f.* thriftiness, restraint.
frū'gēs, *see* **frūx.**
frū'gī *a.(indecl.)* frugal, temperate, honest; useful.
frū'gifer -ī *a.* fruitful, fertile.
frūgi'fer/ēns -e'ntis *a.* fruitful. [ing.
frūgi'legus *a.* food-gather-
frūgi'parus *a.* fruitful.
frūmentā'ri/us *a.* of corn, corn-. *m.* corn-dealer. **lēx -a** law about the distribution of corn. **rēs -a** commissariat.
frūmentā'ti/ō -ō'nis *f.* foraging.
frūmentā't/or -ō'ris *m.* corn-merchant, forager.
frūme'nt/or -ā'rī -ā'tus *vi.* go foraging.
frūme'nt/um -ī *n.* corn, grain, (*pl.*) crops.
frūnī'sc/or -ī *vt.* enjoy.
fr/u'or -u'ī -ū'ctus *vt.* & *i.* (*usu. with abl.*) enjoy, enjoy the company of; (*law*) have the use and enjoyment of.
frūstillā'tim *ad.* in little bits.
frū'strā *ad.* in vain, for nothing; groundlessly; in error. — esse be deceived. — habēre foil. [tion.
frūstrā'm/en -inis *n.* decep-
frūstrā'ti/ō -ō'nis *f.* deception, frustration.
frū'str/or -ā'rī -ā'tus, **-ō** -ā're *vt.* deceive, trick.
frūstule'ntus *a.* full of crumbs.

frū'st/um -ī *n.* bit, scrap.
fru't/ex -icis *m.* bush, shrub; (*comedy*) blockhead.
fruticē't/um -ī *n.* thicket.
fru'tic/or -ārī *vi.* sprout.
fruticō'sus *a.* bushy.
frū'/x -ū'gis *f.*, *esp.* **-ū'gēs** -ū'gum *pl.* fruits of the earth, produce; (*fig.*) reward, success; virtue. **sē ad -ūgem bonam** recipere reform.
fu'am *old pres.subj.* sum.
fū'c/ō -ā're -ā'vī -ā'tum *vt.* paint dye (*esp.* red). **-ā'tus** *a.* counterfeit, artificial.
fūcō'sus *a.* spurious.
fū'c/us -ī *m.* red dye, rouge; bee-glue; (*fig.*) deceit, pretence.
fū'c/us -ī *m.* drone.
fū'dī *perf.* fundō.
fu'g/a -ae *f.* flight, rout; banishment; speed, swift passing; refuge; (*fig.*) avoidance, escape. **-am facere, in -am dare** put to flight.
fu'g/āx -ā'cis *a.* timorous, shy, fugitive; swift, transient; (*with gen.*) avoiding. **-ā'cius** *ad.* more timidly.
fū'gī *perf.* fugiō.
fu'gi/ēns -e'ntis *pres.p.* fugiō. *a.* fleeting, dying; averse (to).
fu'g/iō -ere fū'gī -itum *vi.* flee, run away, escape; go into exile; (*fig.*) vanish, pass swiftly. *vt.* flee from, escape from; shun, avoid; (*fig.*) escape, escape notice of. **-e quaerere** do not ask. **mē -it** I do not notice or know.
fugitī'v/us -ī *m.* runaway slave, truant, deserter. *a.* fugitive.
fu'git/ō -ā're *vt.* flee from, shun.
fu'g/ō -ā're -ā'vī -ā'tum *vt.* put to flight; banish; rebuff.
fulcī'm/en -inis *n.* support.
fu'l/ciō -cī're -sī -tum *vt.* prop, support; strengthen, secure; (*fig.*) sustain, bolster up.
fu'lcr/um -ī *n.* bed-post; couch.
fu'l/geō -gē're -sī *vi.* flash, lighten; shine; (*fig.*) be illustrious.
fu'lgidus *a.* flashing.
fu'lgō, *see* **fulgeō**.
fu'lg/or -ō'ris *m.* lightning; flash, brightness; (*fig.*) splendour.
fu'lgur -is *n.* lightning; thunder-bolt; splendour.
fulgurā'lis *a.* on lightning as an omen.
fulgurā't/or -ō'ris *m.* interpreter of lightning.
fulgurī'tus *a.* struck by lightning.
fu'lgur/ō -ā're *vi.* lighten.
fu'lic/a -ae (**fu'li/x** -cis) *f.* coot.
fūlī'g/ō -inis *f.* soot; black [paint.
fu'll/ō -ō'nis *m.* fuller.
fullō'nius *a.* fuller's.
fu'lm/en -inis *n.* thunderbolt; (*fig.*) disaster.
fulme'nt/a -ae *f.* heel of a [shoe.
fulmi'neus *a.* of lightning; (*fig.*) deadly.
fu'lmin/ō -ā're *vi.* lighten; (*fig.*) threaten.
fu'lsī *perf.* fulciō; *perf.* **fulgeō.**
fultū'r/a -ae *f.* support.
fu'ltus *ppp.* fulciō.
Fu'lv/ius -ī *m.* Roman family name. **-ia -iae** *f.* wife of M. Antony.
fu'lvus *a.* yellow, tawny, dun.
fū'meus *a.* smoking.
fū'midus *a.* smoky, smoking.
fū'mifer -ī *a.* smoking.
fūmi'fic/ō -ā're *vi.* burn incense.
fūmi'ficus *a.* steaming.
fū'm/ō -ā're *vi.* smoke, steam.
fūmō'sus *a.* smoky, smoked.
fū'm/us -ī *m.* smoke, steam.
fūnā'l/e -is *n.* cord; wax torch; chandelier.
fūna'mbul/us -ī *m.* tightrope walker.
fū'ncti/ō -ō'nis *f.* performance.

fū'nctus *ppa.* fungor.
fū'nd/a -ae *f.* sling; drag-net.
fundā'm/en -inis *n.* foundation.
fundāme'nt/um -ī *n.* foundation. **-a agere, iacere** lay the foundations.
fundā't/or -ō'ris *m.* founder.
Fu'nd/ī -ō'rum *m.pl.* coast town in Latium. **-ā'nus** *a.*
fu'ndit/ō -ā're *vt.* sling.
fu'ndit/or -ō'ris *m.* slinger.
fu'nditus *ad.* utterly, completely; at the bottom.
fu'nd/ō -ā're -ā'vī -ā'tum *vt.* found; secure; (*fig.*) establish, make secure.
fu'nd/ō -ere fū'dī fū'sum *vt.* pour shed, spill; (*metal*) cast; (*solids*) hurl, scatter, shower; (*mil.*) rout; (*crops*) produce in abundance; (*speech*) utter; (*fig.*) spread, extend.
fu'nd/us -ī *m.* bottom; farm, estate; (*law*) authorizer.
fū'nebris *a.* funeral-; murderous.
fūnerā'tus *a.* killed.
fūne'reus *a.* funeral-; fatal.
fūne'st/ō -ā're *vt.* pollute with murder, desecrate.
fūno'stus *a.* deadly, fatal; sorrowful, in mourning.
fungī'nus *a.* of a mushroom.
fu'n/gor -gī fūnctus *vt.* & *i.* (*usu. with abl.*) perform, discharge, do; be acted on.
fu'ng/us -ī *m.* mushroom, fungus; (*candle*) clot on the wick.
fūni'cul/us -ī *m.* cord.
fū'n/is -is *m.* rope, rigging. **-em dūcere** be the master.
fū'n/us -eris *n.* funeral; death; corpse; ruin, destruction.
fūr fū'ris *m.* thief; slave.
fū'r/āx -ā'cis *a.* thieving. **-āci'ssimē** *ad.* most thievishly. [shaped pole; pillory.
fu'rc/a -ae *f.* fork; fork-
fu'rcifer -ī *m.* gallows-rogue.
furci'll/a -ae *f.* little fork.
furci'll/ō -ā're *vt.* prop up.
fu'rcul/a -ae *f.* forked prop. **-ae Caudīnae** Pass of Caudium.
fure'nter *ad.* furiously.
fu'rfur -is *m.* bran; scurf.
Fu'ri/a -ae *f.* Fury, avenging spirit; madness, frenzy, rage.
furiā'li/s *a.* of the Furies; frantic, fearful; infuriating. **-ter** *ad.* madly.
furibu'ndus *a.* mad, frenzied.
fu'ri/ō -ā're -ā'vī -ā'tum *vt.* madden.
furiō's/us *a.* mad, frantic. **-ē** *ad.* in a frenzy.
fu'rn/us -ī *m.* oven.
fu'r/ō -ere *vi.* rave, rage, be mad, be crazy.
fū'r/or -ā'rī -ā'tus *vt.* steal; pillage; impersonate.
fu'r/or -ō'ris *m.* madness, frenzy, passion.
fūrti'ficus *a.* thievish.
fū'rtim *ad.* by stealth, secretly.
fūrtī'v/us *a.* stolen; secret, furtive. **-ē** *ad.* secretly.
fū'rt/um -ī *n.* theft, robbery; (*pl.*) stolen goods; (*fig.*) trick, intrigue. **-ō** *ad.* secretly.
fūru'ncul/us -ī *m.* pilferer.
fu'rvus *a.* black, dark.
fu'scin/a -ae *f.* trident.
fu'sc/ō -ā're *vt.* blacken.
fu'scus *a.* dark, swarthy; (*voice*) husky, muffled.
fū'silis *a.* molten, softened.
fū'si/ō -ō'nis *f.* outpouring.
fū'st/is -is *m.* stick, club, cudgel; (*mil.*) beating to death.
fūstuā'r/ium -ī & iī *n.* beating to death.
fū's/us *ppp.* fundō. *a.* broad, diffuse; copious. **-ē** *ad.* diffusely.
fū's/us -ī *m.* spindle.
fu'ttil/is *a.* brittle; worthless. **e-** *ad.* in vain.
futti'lit/ās -ā'tis *f.* futility.
futū'r/us *fut.p.* sum. *a.* future, coming. **-um** -ī *n.* future.

G

Ga'b/iī -iō'rum *m.pl.* ancient town in Latium. **–ī'nus** *a.*
Gabi'n/ius -ī *m.* Roman family name, *esp.* Aulus, tribune 67 B.C. **-ius**, **–iā'nus** *a.* lēx -ia law giving Pompey command against the pirates.
Gā'd/ēs -ium *f.pl.* town in Spain *mod.* Cadiz. **–itā'nus** *a.*
gae's/um -ī *n.* Gallic javelin.
Gaetū'l/ī -ō'rum *m.pl.* African people N. of Sahara. **–us**, **–icus** *a.* Gaetulian; African.
Gā'/ius -ī *m.* Roman praenomen, *esp.* emperor Caligula. **-ius**, **-ia** (*wedding ceremony*) bridegroom, bride
Ga'lat/ae -ā'rum *m.pl.* Galatians of Asia Minor. **–ia** -iae *f.* Galatia.
Ga'lb/a -ae *m.* Roman surname, *esp.* emperor 68-9.
galba'neus *a.* of galbanum, a Syrian plant.
ga'lbinus *a.* greenish-yellow. *n.pl.* pale green clothes.
ga'le/a -ae *f.* helmet.
galeā'tus *a.* helmeted.
galērī'tus *a.* rustic.
galē'r/um -ī *n.*, **–us** -ī *m.* leather hood cap; wig.
ga'll/a -ae *f.* oak-apple.
Ga'll/ī -ō'rum *m.pl.* Gauls, people of *mod.* France and N. Italy. **–ia** -iae *f.* Gaul, **–icus** *a.* Gallic. *f.* a Gallic shoe. **–icā'nus** *a.* of Italian Gaul.
gallī'n/a -ae *f.* hen. -ae albae filius fortune's favourite.
gallīnā'ceus *a.* of poultry.
gallīnā'r/ius -ī & iī *m.* poultry-farmer.
Gallograe'c/ī -ō'rum *m.pl.* Galatians. **–ia** -iae *f.* Galatia.
ga'll/us -ī *m.* cock.
Ga'll/us -ī *m.* Gaul; Roman surname, *esp.* the lyric poet; priest of Cybele.
ga'ne/a -ae *f.*, **–um** -ī *n* low eating-house.
ga'ne/ō -ō'nis *m.* profligate.
Ga'ng/ēs -is *m.* river Ganges. **–ē'ticus** *a.* **–a'rid/ae** -ā'rum *m.pl.* a people on the Ganges.
ga'nn/iō -ī're *vi.* yelp; (*fig.*) grumble.
gannī't/us -ūs *m.* yelping.
Ganymē'd/ēs -is *m.* Ganymede, cup-bearer in Olympus.
Garama'nt/es -um *m.pl.* N. African tribe. **–is** -idis *a.*
Gargā'n/us -ī *m.* mountain in E. Italy.
ga'rr/iō -ī're *vi.* chatter.
garru'lit/ās -ā'tis *f.* chattering. [bling.
ga'rrulus *a.* talkative, babbling.
ga'r/um -ī *n.* fish sauce.
Garu'mn/a -ae *f.* river Garonne.
gau'd/eō -ē're gāvī'sus *vt.* & *i.* rejoice, be pleased, delight (in). in sē, in sinū — be secretly pleased.
gau'd/ium -ī & iī *n.* joy, delight, enjoyment.
gau'l/us -ī *m.* bucket.
gau'sap/e -is *n.*, **–a** -ō'rum *pl.* a woollen cloth, frieze.
gāvī'sus *ppa.* gaudeō.
gā'z/a -ae *f.* treasure, riches.
ge'lid/us *a.* cold, frosty; stiff, numb; chilling. *f.* cold water. **–ē** *ad.* feebly.
ge'l/ō -ā're *vt.* freeze.
Gelō'n/ī -ō'rum *m.pl.* Scythian tribe, *mod.* Ukraine.
ge'l/ū -ūs *n.* frost, cold; chill.
gemebu'ndus *a.* groaning.
gemelli'par/a -ae *f.* mother of twins.
geme'llus *a.* twin, double; alike. *m.* twin.
geminā'ti/ō -ō'nis *f.* doubling.
ge'min/ō -ā're -ā'vī -ā'tum *vt.* double, bring together; repeat. *vi.* be double.
ge'minus *a.* twin, double, both; similar. *m.pl.* twins, *esp.* Castor and Pollux.

ge'mit/us -ūs *m.* groan, sigh; moaning sound.
ge'mm/a -ae *f.* bud, precious stone, jewel; jewelled cup, signet.
gemmā'tus *a.* bejewelled.
ge'mmeus *a.* jewelled; sparkling. [ducing.
ge'mmifer -ī *a.* gem-pro-
ge'mm/ō -ā're *vi.* bud, sprout; sparkle.
ge'm/ō -ere -uī -itum *vi.* sigh, groan, moan. *vt.* bewail.
Gemō'ni/ae -ā'rum *f.pl.* steps in Rome on which bodies of criminals were thrown.
ge'n/ae -ā'rum *f.pl.* cheeks; eyes, eye-sockets. [alogist.
geneā'log/us -ī *m.* gene-
ge'ner -ī *m.* son-in-law
generā'li/s *a.* of the species; universal. -**ter** *ad.* generally.
generā'sc/ō -ere *vi.* be produced.
generā'tim *ad.* by species, in classes; in general.
generā't/or -ō'ris *m.* producer.
ge'ner/ō -ā're -ā'vī -ā'tum *vt.* breed, procreate.
generō'sus *a.* high-born, noble; well-stocked; generous, chivalrous; (*things*) noble honourable.
ge'nes/is -is *f.* birth; horoscope.
genethli'ac/on -ī *n.* birthday poem.
geneti'vus *a.* native, inborn.
ge'netr/īx -ī'cis *f.* mother.
geniā'li/s *a.* nuptial; joyful, genial. -**ter** *ad* merrily.
geniculā'tus *a.* jointed.
geni'st/a -ae *f.* broom.
genitā'bilis *a.* productive.
genitā'li/s *a.* fruitful generative; of birth. -**ter** *ad.* fruitfully.
ge'nit/or -ō'ris *m.* father, creator.
ge'nitus *ppp.* gignō.
ge'n/ius -ī & iī *m.* guardian spirit; enjoyment, inclination; talent. -iō indulgēre enjoy oneself.
gēns ge'ntis *f.* clan family, stock, race; tribe, people, nation; descendant; (*pl.*) foreign peoples. minimē gentium by no means. ubi gentium where in the world.
ge'nticus *a.* national.
gentīli'cius *a.* family.
gentī'lis *a.* family, hereditary; national. *m.* kinsman.
gentī'lit/ās -ā'tis *f.* clan relationship.
ge'n/ū -ūs *n.* knee.
genuā'li/a -um *n.pl.* garters.
ge'nuī *perf.* gignō.
genuī'nus *a.* natural.
genuī'nus *a.* of the cheek. *m.pl.* back teeth.
ge'n/us -eris *n.* birth, descent, noble birth, descendant race; kind, class, species, respect, way; (*logic*) genus, general term. id — of that kind. in omnī -ere in all respects.
geōgra'phi/a -ae *f.* geography.
geōme'tr/ēs -ae *m.* geometer.
geōme'tri/a -ae *f* geometry.
geōme'tricus *a.* geometrical. *n.pl.* geometry.
Germā'n/ī -ō'rum *m.pl.* Germans. -**ia** -iae *f.* Germany. -**icus** *a.* *m.* cognomen of Nero Claudius Drusus and his son.
germā'nit/ās -ā'tis *f.* brotherhood, sisterhood; relation of sister colonies.
germā'n/us *a.* of the same parents full (brother, sister); genuine, true *m.* full brother. *f.* full sister. -**ē** *ad.* sincerely.
ge'rm/en -inis *n.* bud, shoot; embryo; (*fig*) germ.
ge'/rō -rere -ssī -stum *vt.* carry, wear; bring; (*plants*) bear, produce; (*feelings*) entertain, show; (*activity*) conduct, manage, administer, wage.

(*time*) spend. mōrem — comply, humour. persōnam — play a part. sē — behave. sē medium — be neutral. prae sē — exhibit. rēs -stae exploits.
ge'r/ō -ō'nis *n.* carrier.
ge'rr/ae -ā'rum *f.pl.* trifles, nonsense.
ge'rr/ō -ō'nis *m.* idler.
ge'rul/us -ī *m.* carrier.
Gē'ry/ōn -onis *m.* mythical three-bodied king killed by Hercules.
ge'ssī *perf.* gerō.
gestā'm/en -inis *n.* arms, ornaments, burden; litter, carriage.
ge'sti/ō -ō'nis *f.* performance.
ge'st/iō -ī're *vi.* jump for joy, be excited; be very eager.
ge'stit/ō -ā're *vt.* always wear or carry.
ge'st/ō -ā're *vt.* carry about, usually wear; fondle; blab; (*pass.*) go for a ride, drive, sail.
ge'st/or -ō'ris *m.* tell-tale.
ge'stus *ppp.* gerō.
ge'st/us -ūs *m.* posture, gesture, gesticulation.
Ge't/ae -ā'rum *m.pl.* Thracian tribe on the lower Danube. **-icus** *a* Getan, Thracian.
gi'bb/us -ī *m.* hump.
Giga'nt/es -um *m.pl.* Giants, sons of Earth. **-ē'us** *a.*
gi'gn/ō -ere ge'nuī ge'nitum *vt.* beget, bear produce; cause.
gi'lvus *a.* pale yellow dun.
gingī'v/a -ae *f.* gum.
gla'b/er -rī *a.* smooth, bald. *m.* favourite slave.
glaciā'lis *a.* icy.
gla'ci/ēs -ē'ī *f.* ice.
gla'ci/ō -ā're *vt.* freeze.
gladiā't/or -ō'ris *m.* gladiator; (*pl.*) gladiatorial show.
gladiātō'rius *a.* of gladiators. *n.* gladiators' pay.
gladiātū'r/a -ae *f.* gladiator's profession.
gla'd/ius -ī & iī *m.* sword; (*fig.*) murder, death. -ium stringere draw the sword. suō sibī -iō iugulāre *beat at his own game.*
glae'b/a -ae *f.* sod, clod of earth; soil; lump.
glae'bul/a -ae *f.* small lump; small holding.
glae'sum, *see* **glēsum**.
gla'ndifer -ī *a.* acorn-bearing.
gla'nd/ium -ī & iī *n.* glandule (in meat). [bullet.
gl/āns -a'ndis *f.* acorn, nut;
glā're/a -ae *f.* gravel.
glāreō'sus *a.* gravelly.
glau'cum/a -ae *f.* cataract. -am ob oculōs obicere *throw dust in the eyes of.*
glau'cus *a.* bluish grey.
glē'ba, *see* **glaeba**.
glē's/um -ī *n.* amber.
gl/īs -ī'ris *m.* dormouse.
glī'sc/ō -ere *vi.* grow, swell, blaze up.
globō'sus *a.* spherical.
glo'b/us -ī *m.* ball, sphere; (*mil.*) troop; mass crowd, cluster.
glomerā'm/en -inis *n.* bell.
glo'mer/ō -ā're -ā'vī -ā'tum *vt.* form into a ball, gather, accumulate.
glo'm/us -eris *n.* ball of thread, clue.
glō'ri/a -ae *f.* glory, fame; ambition, pride, boasting; (*pl.*) glorious deeds.
glōriā'ti/ō -ō'nis *f.* boasting.
glōri'ol/a -ae *f.* a little glory.
glō'ri/or -ā'rī -ā'tus *vt.* & *i.* boast, pride oneself.
glōriō's/us *a.* famous, glorious; boastful. **-ē** *ad.*
glū't/en -inis *n.* glue.
glūtinā't/or -ō'ris *m.* bookbinder.
glu'tt/iō -ī're *vt.* gulp down.
gnā'rus, **gnā'ruris** *a.* knowing, expert; known.
gnā'tus, *see* **nātus**.
gnā'vus, *see* **nāvus**.

Gnō′s/us -ī *f.* Cnossos, ancient capital of Crete. **-ius, -i′acus, -ias, -is** *a.* of Cnossos, Cretan. *f.* Ariadne.
gō′b/ius -ī & iī, **gō′bi/ō** -ō′nis *m.* gudgeon.
Go′rgi/ās -ae *m.* Sicilian sophist and teacher of rhetoric.
Go′rg/ō -ōnis *f.* mythical monster capable of turning men to stone, Medusa. **-o′-neus** *a.* equus — Pegasus. lacus — Hippocrene.
Gortȳ′n/a -ae *f.* Cretan town. **-ius, -i′acus** *a.* Gortynian, Cretan.
gōrȳ′t/os -ī *m.* quiver.
grabā′t/us -ī *m.* camp-bed, low couch.
Gra′cch/us -ī *m.* Roman surname, *esp.* the famous tribunes Tiberius and Gaius. **-ā′nus** *a.*
gra′cilis *a.* slender, slight, meagre, poor; (*style*) plain.
graci′lit/ās -ā′tis *f.* slimness, leanness; (*style*) simplicity.
grā′cul/us -ī *m.* jackdaw.
gradā′tim *ad.* step by step, gradually. [climax.
gradā′ti/ō -ō′nis *f.* (*rhet.*)
gr/a′dior -a′dī -e′ssus *vi.* step, walk.
Grādī′v/us -ī *m.* Mars.
gra′d/us -ūs *m.* step, pace; stage, step towards; firm stand, position, standing; (*pl.*) stair, steps; (*hair*) braid; (*math.*) degree; (*fig.*) degree, rank. citātō, plēnō -ū at the double. suspēnsō -ū on tiptoe. dē -ū deicī be disconcerted.
Grae′c/ia -iae *f.* Greece. Māgna — S. Italy. **-us** *a.* Greek. **-ē** *ad.* in Greek. **-ulus** *a.* (*contemptuous*) Greek. [Greeks.
graeci′ss/ō -ā′re *vi.* ape the
grae′c/or -ā′rī *vi.* live like Greeks.
Grāiu′gen/a -ae *m.* Greek.
Grā′ius *a.* Greek.
grallā′t/or -ō′ris *m.* stilt-walker.
grā′m/en -inis *n.* grass; herb.
grāmi′neus *a.* grassy; of cane.
gramma′ticus *a.* literary, grammatical. *m.* teacher of literature and language. *f., n.pl.* grammar, literature, philology.
grānā′ri/a -ō′rum *n.pl.* granary. [old.
grandae′vus *a.* aged, very
grandē′sc/ō -ere *vi.* grow.
grandi′culus *a.* quite big.
gra′ndifer -ī *a.* productive.
grandi′loqu/us -ī *m.* grand speaker; boaster.
gra′ndin/at -ā′re *vi.* it hails.
gra′ndis *a.* large, great, tall; old; stong; (*style*) grand, sublime. — nātū old.
gra′ndit/ās -ā′tis *f.* grandeur.
gra′nd/ō -inis *f.* hail.
grā′nifer -ī *a.* grain-carrying.
grā′n/um -ī *n.* seed, grain.
gra′phic/us *a.* fine, masterly. **-ē** *ad.* nicely. [pen.
gra′ph/ium -ī & iī *n.* stilus,
grassā′t/or -ō′ris *m.* vagabond; robber, foot-pad.
gra′ss/or -ā′rī -ā′tus *vi.* walk about, prowl, loiter; (*action*) proceed; (*fig.*) attack, rage against.
grā′tēs *f.pl.* thanks.
grā′ti/a -ae *f.* charm, grace; favour, influence, regard, friendship; kindness, service; gratitude, thanks. -am facere excuse. -am referre return a favour. in -am redīre cum be reconciled to. -ās agere thank. -ās habēre feel grateful. -ā (*with gen.*) for the sake of. eā -ā on that account. -īs, for nothing.
Grā′ti/ae -ā′rum *f.pl.* the three Graces.
grātificā′ti/ō -ō′nis *f.* obligingness.
grāti′fic/or -ā′rī *vi.* do a

favour, oblige. *vt.* make a present of.
grā'tiīs, grā'tīs *ad.* for nothing.
grātiō'sus *a.* in favour popular; obliging.
grā't/or -ā'rī -ā'tus *vi.* rejoice, congratulate.
grātuī't/us *a.* free, gratuitous. **-ō** *ad.* for nothing.
grātulābu'n/dus *a.* congratulating.
grātulā'ti/ō -ō'nis *f.* rejoicing; congratulation; public thanksgiving.
grā'tul/or -ā'rī -ā'tus *vt.* & *i.* congratulate; give thanks.
grā't/us *a.* pleasing, welcome, dear; grateful, thankful; (*acts*) deserving thanks. **-um** facere do a favour. **-ē** *ad.* with pleasure; gratefully.
gravā'tim *ad.* unwillingly.
gravēdinō'sus *a.* liable to colds. [head.
gravē'd/ō -inis *f.* cold in the
grave'ol/ēns -e'ntis *a.* strong-smelling.
gravē'sc/ō -ere *vi.* become heavy; grow worse.
gravi'dit/ās -ā'tis *f.* pregnancy.
gra'vid/ō -ā're *vt.* impregnate.
gra'vidus *a.* pregnant; loaded, full.
gra'vi/s *a.* heavy; loaded, pregnant; (*smell*) strong, offensive; (*sound*) deep, bass; (*body*) sick; (*food*) indigestible; (*fig.*) oppressive, painful, severe; important, influential, dignified. **-ter** *ad.* heavily; strongly, deeply; severely, seriously, violently; gravely, with dignity. — ferre be vexed at.
gra'vit/ās -ā'tis *f.* weight, severity, sickness; importance, dignity, seriousness. annōnae — high price of corn.
gra'v/ō -ā're *vt.* load, weigh down; oppress, aggravate.
-or -ā'rī *vt.* & *i.* feel annoyed, object to, disdain. **-ā'tē** *ad.* reluctantly, grudgingly.
gregā'lis *a.* of the herd, common. *m.* comrade.
gregā'rius *a.* common; (*mil.*) private.
gregā'tim *ad.* in crowds.
gre'm/ium -ī *n.* bosom, lap.
gre'ssus *ppa.* gradior.
gre'ss/us -ūs *m.* step; course.
gr/ex -e'gis *m.* flock, herd; company, troop.
gru'nn/iō -ī're *vi.* grunt.
grunnī't/us -ūs *m.* grunting.
gr/ūs -u'is *f.* crane.
gr/ȳps -ypis *m.* griffin.
gubernā'cul/um (gubernā'clum) **-ī** *n.* rudder, tiller; helm, government.
gubernā'ti/ō -ō'nis *f.* steering, management.
gubernā't/or -ō'ris *m.* steersman, pilot, governor.
gubernā'tr/īx -ī'cis *f.* directress.
gube'rn/ō -ā're -ā'vī -ā'tum *vt.* steer, pilot; manage, govern.
gu'l/a -ae *f.* gullet, throat; gluttony, palate.
gulō'sus *a.* dainty.
gu'rg/es -itis *m.* abyss, deep water, flood; (*person*) spendthrift. [windpipe.
gurgu'li/ō -ō'nis *f.* gullet,
gurgu'st/ium -ī & iī *n.* hovel, shack.
gustā't/us -ūs *m.* sense of taste; flavour.
gu'st/ō -ā're -ā'vī -ā'tum *vt.* taste; have a snack; (*fig.*) enjoy, overhear. prīmīs labrīs — have a superficial knowledge of. [liminary dish.
gu'st/us -ūs *m.* tasting; pre-
gu'tt/a -ae *f.* drop; spot, speck.
guttā'tim *ad.* drop by drop.
gu'ttur -is *n.* throat gluttony.
gū't/us -ī *m.* flask.
Gy'/ās -ae *m.* giant with a hundred arms.

Gȳ'g/ēs -is & ae *m.* king of Lydia, famed for his magic ring. -ae'us *a.*
gymnasia'rch/us -ī *m.* master of a gymnasium.
gymna's/ium -ī & ii *n.* sports ground, school.
gymna'sticus, gy'mnicus *a.* gymnastic.
gynaec/ē'um -ē'-ī, **-ī'um** -ī'ī *n.* women's quarters.
gypsā'tus *a.* coated with plaster.
gy'ps/um -ī *n.* plaster of Paris; a plaster figure.
gȳ'r/us -ī *m.* circle, coil, ring; course.

H

ha, hahae', hahahae' *interj.* (*expressing joy or laughter*) hurrah ! ha ha !
habē'n/a -ae *f.* strap; (*pl.*) reins; (*fig.*) control, **-ās** dare, immittere allow to run freely.
ha'b/eō -ē're -uī -itum *vt.* have, hold; keep, contain, possess; (*fact*) know; (*with inf.*) be in a position to; (*person*) treat, regard, consider; (*action*) make, hold, carry out. *vi.* have possessions. **ōrātiōnem** — make a speech. **in animō** — intend. **prō certō** — be sure. **sē** — find oneself, be. **sibi, sēcum** — keep to oneself. (*fight*) **-et** a hit ! **bene -et** it is well. **sīc -et** so it is. **sīc -ētō** be sure of this.
ha'bilis *a.* manageable, handy; suitable, nimble, expert.
habi'lit/ās -ā'tis *f.* aptitude.
habitā'bilis *a.* habitable.
habitā'ti/ō -ō'nis *f.* dwelling, house.
habitā't/or -ō'ris *m.* tenant, inhabitant.
ha'bit/ō -ā're -ā'vī -ā'tum *vt.* inhabit. *vi.* live, dwell; remain, be always (in).
habitū'd/ō -inis *f.* condition.
ha'bitus *ppp.* habeō. *a.* stout; in a humour.
ha'bit/us -ūs *m.* condition, appearance; dress; character, quality; disposition, feeling.
hāc *ad.* this way.
hā'ctenus *ad.* thus far, so far; till now.
Ha'dri/a -ae *f.* town in N. Italy; Adriatic Sea. **-ā'ticus, -ā'nus, -acus** *a.* **-ā'nus** -ānī *m.* emperor Hadrian.
haedi'li/a -ae *f.*', **hae'dul/us** -ī *m.* little kid.
haedi'nus *a.* kid's.
hae'd/us -ī *m.* kid; (*astr., usa. pl.*) the Kids, a cluster in Auriga.
Haemo'ni/a -ae *f.* Thessaly. -us *a.* Thessalian.
Hae'm/us -ī *m.* mountain range in Thrace.
hae'reō -rē're -sī -sum *vi.* cling, stick, be attached; (*nearness*) stay close, hang on; (*continuance*) linger, remain (*a'*); (*stoppage*) stick fast, come to a standstill, be at a loss.
haerē'sc/ō -ere *vi.* adhere.
hae'res/is -is *f.* sect.
hae'sī *perf.* haereō.
haesita'nti/a -ae *f.* stammering.
haesitā'ti/ō ō'nis *f.* stammering; indecision.
hae'sit/ō -ā're *vi.* get stuck; stammer; hesitate, be uncertain.
hahae', hahahae', *see* **ha.**
halyae'et/os -ī *m.* osprey.
hā'lit/us -ūs *m.* breath, vapour.
ha'll/ex -icis *m.* big toe.
hallūc-, hālūc-, *see* **ālūc-.**
hā'l/ō -ā're *vi.* be fragrant, *vt.* exhale.
ha'm/a -ae *f.* water-bucket.
Hamā'dry/as -adis *f.* wood-nymph.
hāmā'tilis *a.* with hooks.
hāmā'tus *a.* hooked.

Ha'milcar -is *m.* father of Hannibal.
hā'm/us -ī *m.* hook; talons.
Ha'nnibal -is *m.* famous Carthaginian general in 2nd Punic War.
ha'r/a -ae *f.* stye, pen.
harē'n/a -ae *f.* sand; desert, sea-shore; arena (in the amphitheatre).
harēnō'sus *a.* sandy.
hari'ol/or -ā'rī *vi.* prophesy; talk nonsense.
hari'ol/us -ī *m.*, **-a** -ae *f.* soothsayer.
harmo'ni/a -ae *f.* concord, melody; (*fig.*) harmony.
ha'rpag/ō -ā're *vt.* steal.
ha'rpag/ō -ō'nis *m.* grappling-hook; (*person*) robber.
ha'rp/ē -ēs *f.* scimitar.
Harpȳ'i/ae -ā'rum *f.pl.* Harpies, mythical monsters, half woman, half bird.
haru'ndifer -ī *a.* reed-crowned.
harundi'neus *a.* reedy.
harundinō'sus *a.* abounding in reeds.
haru'nd/ō -inis *f.* reed, cane; fishing-rod; shaft, arrow; (*fowling*) limed twig; (*music*) pipe, flute; (*toy*) hobby-horse; (*weaving*) comb; (*writing*) pen.
haru'sp/ex -icis *m.* diviner (from entrails); prophet.
haru'spic/a -ae *f.* soothsayer.
haruspicī'nus *a.* of divination by entrails. *f.* art of such divination. [divination.
haruspi'c/ium -ī & iī *n.*
Ha'sdrubal -is *m.* brother of Hannibal.
ha'st/a -ae *f.* spear, pike; sign of an auction sale. sub -ā vēndere put up for auction.
hastā'tus *a.* armed with a spear. *m.pl.* first line of Roman army in battle. **prīmus** — 1st company of hastati.
hastī'l/e -is *n.* shaft, spear, javelin; vine-prop.

haud, haut, hau *ad.* not, not at all.
hau'ddum *ad.* not yet.
haudquā'quam *ad.* not at all, not by any means.
hau'/riō -rī're -sī -stum *vt.* draw, draw off, derive; drain, empty, exhaust; take in, drink, swallow, devour.
hau'stus *ppp.* hauriō.
hau'st/us -ūs *m.* drawing (water); drinking; drink, draught.
haut, *see* **haud.**
he'bdoma/s -dis *f.* week.
Hē'b/ē -ēs *f.* goddess of youth, cup-bearer to the gods.
he'ben/us -ī *f.* ebony.
he'b/eō -ē're *vi.* be blunt, dull, sluggish.
he'be/s -tis *a.* blunt, dull, sluggish; obtuse, stupid.
hebē'sc/ō -ere *vi.* grow dim or dull. [dim.
he'bet/ō -ā're *vt.* blunt, dull,
He'br/us -ī *m.* Thracian river, *mod.* Maritza.
He'cat/ē -ēs *f.* goddess of magic, and often identified with Diana. **-ē'ius, -ē'is** *a.*
hecato'mb/ē -ēs *f.* hecatomb.
He'ctor -is *m.* son of Priam, chief warrior of the Trojans against the Greeks. **-eus** *a.* of Hector; Trojan.
He'cub/a -ae, **-ē** -ēs *f.* wife of Priam.
he'der/a -ae *f.* ivy.
hede'riger -ī *a.* wearing ivy.
hederō'sus *a.* covered with ivy. [perfume.
hēdy'chr/um -ī *n.* a cosmetic
hei, hei'a, *see* **ei, eia.**
He'len/a -ae, **-ē** -ēs *f.* Helen, wife of Menelaus, abducted by Paris.
He'len/us -ī *m.* son of Priam, with prophetic powers.
Hēli'ad/es -um *f.pl.* daughters of the Sun, changed to poplars or alders, and their tears to amber.

He'lic/ē -ēs *f.* the Great Bear.
He'lic/ōn -ō'nis *m.* mountain in Greece sacred to Apollo and the Muses. **-ō'nius** *a.* **-ōni'ad/es** -um *f.pl.* the Muses.
He'lla/s -dis *f.* Greece.
He'll/ē -ēs *f.* mythical Greek princess, carried by the golden-fleeced ram, and drowned in the Hellespont.
Hellēspo'nt/us -ī *m.* Hellespont, *mod.* Dardanelles. **-ius, -i'acus** *a.*
he'llu/ō -ō'nis *m.* glutton.
he'llu/or -ā'rī *vi.* be a glutton.
helve'll/a -ae *f.* a savoury herb.
Helvē'ti/ī -ō'rum *m.pl.* people of E. Gaul, *mod.* Switzerland. **-us, -cus** *a.*
hem *interj* (*expressing surprise*) eh? well well!
hēmero'drom/us -ī *m.* express courier.
hēmici'll/us -ī *m.* mule.
hēmicy'cl/ium -ī & iī *n.* semi-circle with seats.
hēmī'n/a -ae *f.* half a pint.
he'ndecasy'llab/ī -ō'rum *m.pl.* hendecasyllabics, verses of eleven syllables.
heptē'r/is -is *f.* ship with seven banks of oars.
he'ra, *see* **era**.
Hē'r/a -ae *f.* Greek goddess identified with Juno. **-ae'a** -aeō'rum *n.pl.* festival of Hera.
Hēraclī't/us -ī *m.* early Greek philosopher.
he'rb/a -ae *f.* blade, young plant; grass, herb, weed.
herbē'sc/ō -ere *vi.* grow into blades.
he'rbeus *a.* grass-green.
he'rbidus *a.* grassy.
he'rbifer -ī *a.* grassy.
herbō'sus *a.* grassy, made of turf; made of herbs.
he'rbul/a -ae *f.* little herb.
hercī'sc/ō -ere *vt.* divide an inheritance.
he'rcle *interj.* by Hercules!
he'rct/um -ī *n.* inheritance.
He'rcul/ēs -is & ī *m.* mythical Greek hero, later deified. **-e** *interj.* by Hercules! **-eus** *a.* arbor — poplar. urbs — Herculaneum.
he're, *see* **herī**.
hērēditā'rius *a.* inherited; about an inheritance.
hērē'dit/ās -ā'tis *f.* inheritance. — sine sacris a gift without awkward obligations.
hērē'd/ium -ī & iī *n.* inherited estate.
hē'r/ēs -ēdis *m.*, *f.* heir, heiress; (*fig.*) master, successor.
he'rī, he're *ad.* yesterday.
herī'lis, *see* **erilis**.
He'rm/ēs -ae *m.* Greek god identified with Mercury; Hermes-pillar.
He'rnic/ī -ō'rum *m.pl.* people of central Italy. **-us** *a.*
Hēro'dot/us -ī *m.* first Greek historian.
hērō'icus *a.* heroic, epic.
hērōī'n/a -ae *f.* demi-goddess.
hērō'i/s -dis *f.* demi-goddess.
hē'rō/s -is *m.* demi-god, hero.
hērō'us *a.* heroic, epic.
he'rus, *see* **erus**.
Hēsi'od/us -ī *m.* Hesiod, Greek didactic poet. **-ē'us, -ī'us** *a.*
He'sper/us -ī *m.* evening star. **-ius, -is** *a.* western. **-ia** -iae *f.* Italy; Spain. **-ides** -idum *f.pl.* keepers of a garden in the far West.
heste'rnus *a.* of yesterday.
heu *interj.* (*expressing dismay or pain*) oh! alas!
heus *interj.* (*calling attention*) ho! hallo!
hexa'met/er -rī *m.* hexameter verse.
hexē'r/is -is *f.* ship with six banks of oars.
hiā't/us -ūs *m.* opening, abyss; open mouth, gaping; (*gram.*) hiatus.

Hibē'r/es -um *m.pl.* Spaniards. **-us, -icus** *a.* Spanish. **-ia** -iae *f.* Spain. **-us** -ī *m.* river Ebro.
hībe'rn/a -ō'rum *n.pl.* winter quarters.
hībernā'cul/a -ō'rum *n.pl.* winter tents.
Hibe'rni/a -ae *f.* Ireland.
hībe'rn/ō -ā're *vi.* winter, remain in winter quarters.
hībe'rnus *a.* winter, wintry.
hibi'sc/um -ī *n.* marsh mallow.
hi'brid/a, hy'brid/a -ae *m., f.* mongrel, half-breed.
hīc, haec, hōc *pro., a.* this; he, she, it; my, the latter, the present. **hīc homō** I. **hōc magis** the more. **hōc est** that is.
hīc *ad.* here; herein; (*time*) at this point.
hī'ce, hae'ce hō'ce; **hī'cine**, hae'cine hō'cine *emphatic forms of* **hīc haec hōc.**
hiemā'lis *a.* winter, stormy.
hi'em/ō -ā're *vi.* pass the winter; be wintry, stormy.
hi'em/s (hiemps) -is *f.* winter; stormy weather, cold.
Hierō'nym/us -ī *m.* Jerome.
Hieroso'lym/a -ō'rum *n.pl.* Jerusalem. **-ā'rius** *a.*
hi'et/ō -ā're *vi.* yawn.
hi'lari/s *a.* cheerful, merry. **-e** *ad.*
hila'rit/ās -ā'tis *f.* cheerfulness.
hilaritū'd/ō -inis *f.* merriment.
hi'lar/ō -ā're *vt.* cheer, gladden.
hila'rulus *a.* a gay little thing.
hi'larus, *see* **hilaris.**
hī'll/ae -ā'rum *f.pl.* smoked sausage.
Hīlō't/ae -ā'rum *m.pl.* Helots (of Sparta).
hī'l/um -ī *n.* something, a whit.
hinc *ad.* from here, hence; on this side; from this source, for this reason; (*time*) henceforth.
hi'nn/iō -ī're *vi.* neigh.
hinnī't/us -ūs *m.* neighing.
hinnu'le/us -ī *m.* fawn.
hi'/ō -ā're *vi.* be open, gape, yawn; (*speech*) be disconnected, leave a hiatus. *vt.* sing.
hippagō'g/ī -ō'rum *f.pl.* cavalry transports.
hippocentau'r/us -ī *m.* centaur.
hippo'drom/os -ī *m.* racecourse.
Hippo'lyt/us -ī *m.* son of Theseus, slandered by stepmother Phaedra.
hippo'man/es -is *n.* mare's fluid; membrane on foal's forehead.
Hippōna/x -ctis *m.* Greek satirist. **-ctē'us** *a.* of Hipponax. *m.* iambic verse used by him.
hippoto'xot/ae -ā'rum *m.pl.* mounted archers.
hī'r/a -ae *f.* the empty gut.
hircī'nus *a.* of a goat.
hircō'sus *a.* goatish.
hi'rc/us -ī *m.* he-goat; goatish smell.
hi'rne/a -ae *f.* jug.
hirq-, *see* **hirc-.**
hirsū'tus *a.* shaggy, bristly; uncouth.
hi'rtus *a.* hairy, shaggy; rude.
hirū'd/ō -inis *f.* leech.
hirundinī'nus *a.* swallows'.
hiru'nd/ō -inis *f.* swallow.
hī'sc/ō -ere *vi.* gape; open the mouth. *vt.* utter.
Hispā'n/ia -iae *f.* Spain. **-iē'nsis, -us** *a.* Spanish.
hi'spidus *a.* hairy, rough.
Hi'st/er -rī *m.* lower Danube.
histo'ri/a -ae *f.* history, inquiry; story.
histo'ricus *a.* historical. *m.* historian.
hi'stricus *a.* of the stage.
hi'stri/ō -ō'nis *m.* actor.
histriōnā'lis of an actor.
histriō'ni/a -ae *f.* acting.
hiu'lc/ō -ā're *vt.* split open.

hiu'lc/us *a.* gaping, open; (*speech*) with hiatus. **-ē** *ad.* with hiatus.
ho'diē *ad.* to-day; nowadays, now; up to the present.
hodie'rnus *a.* to-day's.
ho'lit/or **-ō'ris** *m.* market-gardener.
holitō'rius *a.* for market-gardeners.
ho'l/us **-eris** *n.* vegetables.
holu'scul/um **-ī** *n.* small cabbage.
Homē'r/us **-ī** *m.* Greek epic poet, Homer. **-icus** *a.*
homicī'd/a **-ae** *m.* killer, murderer.
homicī'd/ium **-ī & iī** *n.* murder.
ho'm/ō **-inis** *m., f.* human being, man; (*pl.*) people, the world; (*derogatory*) fellow, creature. **inter -inēs esse** be alive; see the world.
homu'll/us **-ī, homu'nci/ō** **-ō'nis, homu'ncul/us** **-ī** *m.* little man, poor creature, mortal.
hone'st/ās **-ā'tis** *f.* good character, honourable reputation; sense of honour, integrity; (*things*) beauty.
hone'st/ō **-ā're** *vt.* honour, dignify, embellish.
hone'st/us *a.* honoured, respectable; honourable, virtuous; (*appearance*) handsome. *m.* gentleman. *n.* virtue, good; beauty. **-ē** *ad.* decently, virtuously.
ho'n/or, ho'n/ōs **-ō'ris** *m.* honour, esteem; public office, position, preferment; award, tribute, offering; ornament, beauty. **-ōris causā** out of respect; for the sake of. **-ōrem praefārī** apologize for a remark. [respect.
honōrā'bilis *a.* a mark of
honōrā'rius *a.* done out of respect, honorary.
honōri'fic/us *a.* complimentary. **-ē** *ad.* in complimentary terms.
honō'r/ō **-ā're -ā'vī -ā'tum** *vt.* do honour to, embellish. **-ā'tus** *a.* esteemed distinguished; in high office; complimentary. **-ā'tē** *ad.* honourably.
honō'rus *a.* complimentary.
ho'nōs, *see* **honor**.
hō'r/a **-ae** *f.* hour; time, season; (*pl.*) clock. **in -ās** hourly. **in -am vīvere** *live from hand to mouth.*
hōrae'/um **-ī** *n.* pickle.
Horā't/ius **-ī** *m.* Roman family name, *esp.* the defender of Rome against Porsenna; the lyric poet Horace. **-ius** *a.*
ho'rde/um **-ī** *n.* barley.
ho'ri/a **-ae** *f.* fishing-smack.
hōrnō'tinus *a.* this year's.
hō'rn/us *a.* this year's. **-ō** *ad.* this year.
hōrolo'g/ium **-ī & iī** *n.* clock.
horre'ndus *a.* fearful, terrible; awesome.
ho'rr/ēns **-e'ntis** *pres.p.* horreō. *a.* bristling, shaggy.
ho'rr/eō **-ē're -uī** *vi.* stand stiff, bristle; shiver shudder, tremble; *vt.* dread; be afraid, be amazed.
horrē'sc/ō **-ere** *vi.* stand on end, become rough; begin to quake; start, be terrified. *vt.* dread.
ho'rre/um **-ī** *n.* barn, granary, store. [amazing.
horri'bilis *a.* terrifying;
horri'dulus *a.* protruding a little; unkempt; (*fig.*) uncouth.
ho'rrid/us *a.* bristling, shaggy rough, rugged; shivering; (*manners*) rude, uncouth; frightening. **-ē** *ad.*
ho'rrifer **-ī** *a.* chilling; terrifying.
horri'fic/ō **-ā're** *vt.* ruffle; terrify.
horri'fic/us *a.* terrifying. **-ē** *ad.* in awesome manner.

horri'sonus *a.* dread-sounding.
ho'rr/or -ō'ris *m.* bristling; shivering, ague; terror, fright, awe, a terror.
hō'rsum *ad.* this way.
hortā'm/en -inis *n.* encouragement.
hortāme'nt/um -ī *n.* encouragement.
hortā'ti/ō -ō'nis *f.* harangue, encouragement.
hortā't/or -ō'ris *m.* encourager.
hortā't/us -ūs *m.* encouragement.
Hortē'ns/ius -ī *m.* Roman family name, *esp.* an orator in Cicero's time.
ho'rt/or -ā'rī -ā'tus *vt.* urge, encourage, exhort, harangue.
ho'rtul/us -ī *m.* little garden.
ho'rt/us -ī *m.* garden; (*pl.*) park.
ho'sp/es -itis *m.*, **ho'spit/a** -ae *f.* host, hostess; guest, friend; stranger, foreigner. *a.* strange.
hospitā'li/s *a.* host's, guest's; hospitable. **-ter** *ad.* hospitably.
hospitā'lit/ās -ā'tis *f.* hospitality.
hospi't/ium -ī & iī *n.* hospitality, friendship; lodging, inn.
ho'sti/a -ae *f.* victim, sacrifice.
hostiā'tus *a.* provided with victims.
ho'sticus *a.* hostile; strange. *n.* enemy territory.
hostī'li/s *a.* of the enemy, hostile. **-ter** *ad.* in hostile manner.
hostīme'nt/um -ī *n.* recompense.
ho'st/iō -ī're *vt.* requite.
ho'st/is -is *m., f.* enemy.
hūc *ad.* hither, here; to this, to such a pitch. — **illūc** hither and thither.
hui *interj.* (expressing surprise) ho! my word!
hūiu'smodī such.
hūmā'nit/ās -ā'tis *f.* human nature, mankind; humanity, kindness, courtesy; culture, refinement.
hūmā'nitus *ad.* in accordance with human nature: kindly.
hūmā'n/us *a.* human, humane, kind, courteous; cultured, refined, well-educated. **-ō** māior superhuman. **-ē**, **-iter** *ad.* humanly; gently, politely.
humā'ti/ō -ō'nis *f.* burying.
hūme-, **hūmi-**, *see* **ūme-**, **ūmi-**.
hu'mili/s *a.* low, low-lying, shallow; (*condition*) lowly, humble, poor; (*language*) commonplace; (*mind*) mean, base. **-ter** *ad.* meanly, humbly.
humi'lit/ās -ā'tis *f.* low position, smallness, shallowness; lowliness, insignificance; meanness, baseness.
hu'm/ō ā're -ā'vī -ā'tum *vt.* bury.
hu'm/us -ī *f.* earth, ground; land. **-ī** on the ground.
hyaci'nthinus *a.* of the hyacinthus.
hyaci'nth/us -ī *m.* iris, lily.
Hy'ad/es -um *f.pl.* Hyads, a group of stars in Taurus.
hyae'n/a -ae *f.* hyena.
hy'al/us -ī *m.* glass.
Hy'bl/a -ae *f.* mountain in Sicily, famous for bees. **-ae'us** *a.*
hy'brida, *see* **hibrida**.
Hyda'sp/ēs -is *m.* tributary of river Indus, *mod.* Jelum.
Hȳ'dr/a -ae *f.* hydra, a mythical dragon with seven heads.
hydrau'l/us -ī *m.* water-organ.
hy'dri/a -ae *f.* ewer.
Hydro'cho/us -ī *m.* Aquarius.
hydrō'picus *a.* suffering from dropsy.
hy'drōp/s -is *m.* dropsy.
hy'dr/us -ī *m.* serpent.
Hy'l/ās -ae *m.* a youth loved by Hercules.
Hy'm/ēn -enis, **Hymen-**

ae'/us -ī *m.* god of marriage; wedding-song; wedding.
Hyme'tt/us -ī *m.* mountain near Athens, famous for honey and marble. **-ius** *a.*
Hy'pan/is -is *m.* river of Sarmatia, *mod.* Bug.
Hyperbo're/ī -ō'rum *m.pl.* fabulous people in the far North. **-us** *a.*
Hyperī'/ōn -onis *m.* father of the Sun; the Sun.
hypodida'scul/us -ī *m.* assistant teacher.
hypomnē'ma -tis *n.* memorandum.
Hyrcā'n/ī -ō'rum *m.pl.* people on the Caspian Sea. **-us** *a.* Hyrcanian.

I

Ia'cch/us -ī *m.* Bacchus; wine.
ia'c/eō -ē're -uī *vi.* lie; be ill, lie dead; (*places*) be situated, be flat or low-lying, be in ruins; (*dress*) hang loose; (*fig.*) be inactive, be downhearted; (*things*) be dormant, neglected, despised.
ia'c/iō -ere iē'cī ia'ctum *vt.* throw; lay, build; (*seed*) sow; (*speech*) cast, let fall, mention.
ia'ct/āns -a'ntis *pres.p.* iactō. *a.* boastful. **-a'nter** *ad.* ostentatiously.
iacta'nti/a -ae *f.* boasting, ostentation.
iactā'ti/ō -ō'nis *f.* tossing, gesticulation; boasting, ostentation — populāris publicity.
iactā't/us -ūs *m.* waving.
ia'ctit/ō -ā're *vt.* mention, bandy.
ia'ct/ō -ā're -ā'vī -ā'tum *vt.* throw, scatter; shake, toss about; (*mind*) disquiet; (*ideas*) consider, discuss, mention; (*speech*) boast of. sē — waver, fluctuate; behave ostentatiously, be officious.
iactū'r/a -ae *f.* throwing overboard; loss, sacrifice.
ia'ctus *ppp.* iaciō.
ia'ct/us -ūs *m.* throwing, throw. intrā tēlī iactum within spear's range.
ia'cuī *perf.* iaceō.
iaculā'bilis *a.* missile.
iaculā't/or -ō'ris *m.* thrower, shooter; light-armed soldier.
iaculā'tr/īx -ī'cis *f.* huntress.
ia'cul/or -ā'rī -ā'tus *vt.* throw, hurl, shoot; throw the javelin; shoot at, hit; (*fig.*) aim at, attack. [fishing-net.
ia'cul/um -ī *n.* javelin;
iāien-, *see* **iēn-**.
iam *ad.* (*past*) already, by then; (*present*) now, already; (*future*) directly, very soon; (*emphasis*) indeed, precisely; (*inference*) therefore, then surely; (*transition*) moreover, next. iam dūdum for a long time, long ago; immediately. iam iam right now, any moment now. iam . . . iam at one time . . . at another. iam nunc just now. iam pridem long ago, for a long time. iam tum even at that time. sī iam supposing for the purpose of argument.
iambē'us *a.* iambic.
ia'mb/us -ī *m.* iambic foot; iambic poetry.
Iāni'cul/um -ī *n.* Roman hill across the Tiber.
iā'nit/or -ō'ris *m.* door-keeper, porter. [(*fig.*) key.
iā'nu/a -ae *f.* door; entrance;
Iānuā'rius *a.* of January. *m.* January.
Iā'n/us -ī *m.* god of gateways and beginnings; archway, arcade. **-ā'lis** *a.*
Ia'pet/us -ī *m.* a Titan, father of Atlas and Prometheus. **-io'nid/ēs** -ae *m.* Atlas.
Iā'py/x -gis *a.* Iapygian; Apulian. *m.* W.N.W. wind from Apulia.

Iā'sl/ōn -onis *m.* Jason, leader of Argonauts, husband of Medea. **-o'nius** *a.*
ia'spi/s -dis *f.* jasper.
Ībēr-, *see* **Hibēr-**.
i'bi *ad.* there; then; in this, [at it.
ibī'dem *ad.* in the same place; at that very moment.
ī'b/is -is & idis *f.* ibis.
Ī'car/us -ī *m.* son of Daedalus, drowned in the Aegean. **-ius** *a.* **-ium** -ī *n.* Icarian Sea.
ī'c/ō -ere -ī i'ctum *vt.* strike. foedus — make a treaty.
icte'ricus *a.* jaundiced.
i'cti/s -dis *f.* weasel.
i'ctus *ppp.* īcō.
i'ct/us -ūs *m.* stroke, blow; wound; (*metre*) beat.
Ī'd/a -ae, -ē -ēs *f.* mountain in Crete; mountain near Troy. **-ae'us** *a.* Cretan; Trojan.
idci'rcō *ad.* for that reason; for the purpose.
ī'dem, e'adem, i'dem *pro.* the same; also, likewise.
ide'ntidem *ad.* repeatedly, again and again.
i'deō *ad.* therefore, for this reason, that is why.
idiō't/a -ae *m.* ignorant person, layman.
īdō'l/on -ī *n.* apparition.
idō'ne/us *a.* fit, proper, suitable, sufficient. **-ē** *ad.*
Ī'd/ūs -uum *f.pl.* Ides, the 15th March, May, July, October, the 13th of other months.
iē'cī *perf.* iaciō.
ie'c/ur -oris & i'noris *n.* liver; (*fig.*) passion.
iecu'scul/um -ī *n.* small liver.
iēiūniō'sus *a.* hungry.
iēiū'nit/ās -ā'tis *f.* fasting; (*fig.*) meagreness.
iēiū'n/ium -ī & iī *n.* fast; hunger; leanness.
iēiū'n/us *a.* fasting, hungry; (*things*) barren, poor, meagre; (*style*) feeble.
iēntā'cul/um -ī *n.* breakfast.
i'gitur *ad.* therefore, then, so.
ignā'rus *a.* ignorant, unaware; unknown.
ignā'vi/a -ae *f.* idleness, laziness; cowardice.
ignā'v/us *a.* idle, lazy, listless; cowardly; relaxing. **-ē, -iter** *ad.* without energy.
ignē'sc/ō -ere *vi.* take fire, [burn.
i'gneus *a.* burning, fiery.
igni'cul/us -ī *m.* spark; (*fig.*) fire, vehemence.
i'gnifer -ī *a.* fiery.
igni'gen/a -ae *m.* the fire-born (Bacchus).
i'gnip/ēs -edis *a.* fiery-footed.
igni'pot/ēns -e'ntis *a* fire-working (Vulcan).
i'gn/is -is *m.* fire, a fire; firebrand, lightning; brightness, redness; (*fig.*) passion, love.
ignō'bilis *a.* unknown, obscure; low-born.
ignōbi'lit/ās -ā'tis *f.* obscurity; low birth.
ignōmi'ni/a -ae *f.* dishonour, [disgrace.
ignōminiō'sus *a.* (*person*) degraded, disgraced; (*things*) shameful.
ignōrā'bilis *a.* unknown.
ignōra'nti/a -ae *f.* ignorance.
ignōrā'ti/ō -ō'nis *f.* ignorance.
ignō'r/ō -ā're -ā'vī -ā'tum *vt.* not know, be unacquainted with; disregard.
ignō'/scō -scere -vī -tum *vt.* & *i.* forgive. pardon.
ignō'tus *a.* unknown; low-born; ignorant.
ī'l/ex -icis *f.* holm-oak.
ī'li/a -um *n.pl.* groin; entrails. — dūcere become broken-winded.
Ī'li/a -ae *f.* mother of Romulus and Remus. **-adēs** -adae *m.* son of Ilia; Trojan.
Ī'lia/s -dis *f.* the Iliad; a Trojan woman.
ī'licet *ad.* it's all over, let us go; immediately.
ī'licō *ad.* on the spot; instantly,

Ili'gnus *a.* of holm-oak.
Īlīthyi'/a -ae *f.* Greek goddess of childbirth.
Ī'li/um, -on -ī *n.*, **-os -ī** *f.* Troy. **-us, -acus** *a.* Trojan.
i'llā *ad.* that way.
illābefa'ctus *a.* unbroken.
illā'/bor -bī -psus *vi.* flow into, fall down.
illabō'r/ō -ā're *vi.* work (at).
illā'c *ad.* that way.
illacessī'tus *a.* unprovoked.
illacrimā'bilis *a.* unwept; inexorable.
illa'crim/ō -ā're, **-or** -ā'rī *vi.* weep over, lament; weep.
illae'sus *a.* unhurt.
illaetā'bilis *a.* cheerless.
illā'psus *ppa.* illābor.
illa'que/ō -ā're *vt.* ensnare.
illā'tus *ppp.* inferō.
illaudā'tus *a.* wicked.
i'll/e -a -ud *pro.* & *a.* that, that one; he, she, it; the famous; the former, the other. ex -ō since then.
ille'cebr/a -ae *f.* attraction, lure, bait, decoy-bird.
illecebrō'sus *a.* seductive.
ille'ctus *ppp.* illiciō.
illē'ctus *a.* unread.
ille'pid/us *a.* inelegant, churlish. **-ē** *ad.*
i'll/ex -icis *m.*, *f.* lure.
i'll/ēx -ē'gis *a.* lawless.
ille'xī *perf.* illiciō.
illībā'tus *a.* unimpaired.
illīberā'li/s *a.* ungenerous, mean, disobliging. **-ter** *ad.*
illīberā'lit/ās -ā'tis *f.* meanness.
ill/i'c, -ae'c -ū'c *pro.* he, she, it; that.
illī'c *ad.* there, yonder; in that matter.
ill/i'ciō -i'cere -e'xī -e'ctum *vt.* seduce, decoy, mislead.
illicitā't/or -ō'ris *m.* sham bidder (at an auction).
illi'citus *a.* unlawful.
illī'/dō -dere -sī -sum *vt.* strike, dash against.
i'llig/ō -ā're -ā'vī -ā'tum fasten on, attach; connect; impede, encumber, oblige.
i'llim *ad.* from there.
illī'mis *a.* clear.
illi'nc *ad.* from there; on that side.
i'll/inō -i'nere -ē'vī -itum *vt.* smear over, cover, bedaub.
illiquefa'ctus *a.* melted.
illī'sī *perf.* illīdō.
illī'sus *ppp.* illīdō.
illitterā'tus *a.* uneducated, uncultured.
i'llitus *ppp.* illinō.
i'llō *ad.* (to) there; to that end.
illō'tus *a.* dirty.
illū'c *ad.* (to) there; to that; to him, her.
illū'c/eō -ē're *vi.* blaze.
illū/cē'scō -cē'scere -xī *vi.* become light, dawn.
illū'/dō -dere -sī -sum *vt.* & *i.* play, amuse oneself; abuse; jeer at, ridicule.
illū'min/ō -ā're -ā'vī -ā'tum *vt.* light up; enlighten; embellish. **-ā'tē** *ad.* luminously.
illū'si/ō -ō'nis *f.* irony.
illū'stris *a.* bright, clear; distinct, manifest; distinguished, illustrious.
illū'str/ō -ā're -ā'vī -ā'tum *vt.* illuminate; make clear, explain; make famous.
illū'sus *ppp.* illūdō.
illu'vi/ēs -ē'ī *f.* dirt, filth; floods.
Illy'ri/ī -ō'rum *m.pl.* people E. of the Adriatic. **-a** -ae *f.*, **-cum** -cī *n.* Illyria. **-cus, -us** *a.*
I'lv/a -ae *f.* Italian island, *mod.* Elba.
imāginā'rius *a.* fancied.
imāginā'ti/ō -ō'nis *f.* fancy.
imā'gin/or -ā'rī *vt.* picture to oneself.
imā'g/ō -inis *f.* likeness, picture, statue; portrait of ancestor; apparition, ghost; echo, mental picture, idea; (*fig.*) semblance, mere shadow; (*rhet.*) comparison.

imbēci'llit/ās -ā'tis *f.* weakness, helplessness.
imbēci'll/us *a.* weak, frail; helpless. **-ē** *ad.* faintly.
imbe'llis *a.* non-combatant; peaceful; cowardly.
i'mb/er -ris *m.* rain, heavy shower; water; (*fig.*) stream, shower.
imbe'rbis, imbe'rbus *a.* beardless.
i'mbib/ō -ere -ī *vt.* (*mind*) conceive; resolve.
i'mbr/ex -icis *f.* tile.
i'mbricus *a.* rainy.
i'mbrifer -ī *a.* rainy.
i'mb/uō -u'ere -uī -ū'tum *vt.* wet, steep, dip; (*fig.*) taint, fill; inspire, accustom, train; begin, be the first to explore.
imitā'bilis *a.* imitable.
imitā'm/en -inis *n.* imitation; likeness. [pretence.
imitāme'nt/a -ō'rum *n.pl.*
imitā'ti/ō -ō'nis *f.* imitation.
imitā't/or -ō'ris *m.*, **-rīx** -rī'cis *f.* imitator.
i'mit/or -ā'rī -ā'tus *vt.* copy, portray; imitate, act like. -ā'tus *a.* copied.
immad/ē'scō -ē'scere -uī *vi.* become wet.
immā'n/is *a.* enormous, vast; monstrous, savage, frightful. **-e** *ad.* savagely.
immā'nit/ās -ā'tis *f.* vastness; savageness, barbarism.
immānsuē'tus *a.* wild.
immātū'rit/ās -ā'tis *f.* over-eagerness.
immātū'rus *a.* untimely.
immedicā'bilis *a.* incurable.
i'mmemor -is *a.* unmindful, forgetful, negligent.
immemorā'bilis *a.* indescribable, not worth mentioning. [untold.
immemorā'tus *a.* hitherto
immē'nsit/ās -ā'tis *f.* immensity.
immē'ns/us *a.* immeasurable, vast, unending. **-um** -ī *n.* infinity, vast extent. **-um** *ad.* exceedingly. [deserving.
i'mmer/ēns -e'ntis *a.* un-
imme'r/gō -gere -sī -sum *vt.* plunge, immerse.
imme'rit/us *a.* undeserving, innocent; undeserved. **-ō** *ad.* unjustly.
immērsā'bilis *a.* never foundering.
immē'rsus *ppp.* immergō.
immētā'tus *a.* unmeasured.
i'mmigr/ō -ā're -ā'vī- ā'tum *vi.* move (into).
immi'n/eō -ē're -ui *vi.* overhang, project; be near, adjoin, impend; threaten, be a menace to; long for grasp at.
immi'n/uō -u'ere -uī -ū'tum *vt.* lessen shorten; impair; encroach on, ruin.
imminū'ti/ō -ō'nis *f.* mutilation; (*rhet.*) understatement.
immi'/sceō -scē're -scuī -xtum *vt.* intermingle, blend. **sē** — join, meddle with.
immiserā'bilis *a.* unpitied.
immise'ricor/s -dis *a.* pitiless. **-diter** *ad.* unmercifully.
immi'ssi/ō -ō'nis *f.* letting grow.
immi'ssus *ppp.* immittō.
immī'tis *a.* unripe; severe, inexorable.
imm/i'ttō -i'ttere -ī'sī -i'ssum *vt.* let in, put in; graft on; let go, let loose, let grow; launch, throw; incite, set on.
immi'xtus *ppp.* immisceō.
i'mmo *ad.* (*correcting preceding words*) no, yes; on the contrary, or rather. — **sī** ah, if only.
immō'bilis *a.* motionless; immovable. [cess.
immoderā'ti/ō -ō'nis *f.* ex-
immoderā't/us *a.* limitless; excessive, unbridled. **-ē** *ad.* extravagantly.
immode'sti/a -ae *f.* license.
immode'st/us *a.* immoderate. **-ē** *ad.* extravagantly.

immo'dic/us *a.* excessive, extravagant, unruly. **-ē** *ad.*
immodulā'tus *a.* unrhythmical.
immolā'ti/ō **-ō'nis** *f.* sacrifice.
immolā't/or **-ō'ris** *m.* sacrificer.
immōlī'tus *a.* erected.
i'mmol/ō **-ā're** **-ā'vī** **-ā'tum** *vt.* sacrifice; slay.
immo'r/ior **-ī** **-tuus** *vi.* die upon; waste away.
immo'rsus *a.* bitten; (*fig.*) stimulated.
immortā'l/is *a.* immortal, everlasting. **-iter** *ad.* infinitely.
immortā'lit/ās **-ā'tis** *f.* immortality; lasting fame.
immō'tus *a.* motionless, unmoved, immovable.
immū'g/iō **-ī're** **-iī** *vi.* roar (in).
immu'lg/eō **-ēre** *vt.* milk.
immu'ndus *a.* unclean, dirty.
immū'n/iō **-ī're** **-ī'vī** *vt.* strengthen.
immū'nis *a.* with no public obligations, untaxed, free from office; exempt, free (from).
immū'nit/ās **-ā'tis** *f.* exemption, immunity, privilege.
immūnī'tus *a.* undefended; (*roads*) unmetalled.
immu'rmur/ō **-ā're** *vi.* murmur (at).
immūtā'bilis *a.* unalterable.
immūtābi'lit/ās **-ā'tis** *f.* immutability.
immūtā'ti/ō **-ō'nis** *f.* exchange, (*rhet.*) metonymy.
immūtā'tus *a.* unchanged.
immū't/ō **-ā're** **-ā'vī** **-ā'tum** *vt.* change; (*words*) substitute by metonymy.
impācā'tus *a.* aggressive.
impā'ctus *ppp.* impingō.
i'mp/ār **-aris** *a.* unequal, uneven, unlike; no match for, inferior; (*metre*) elegiac. **-a'riter** *ad.* unequally.
imparā'tus *a.* unprepared, unprovided.
impā'stus *a.* hungry.
impa'ti/ēns **-e'ntis** *a.* unable to endure, impatient. **-e'nter** *ad.* intolerably.
impatie'nti/a **-ae** *f.* want of endurance.
impa'vid/us *a.* fearless, undaunted. **-ē** *ad.*
impedīme'nt/um **-ī** *n.* hindrance, obstacle; (*pl.*) baggage, luggage, supply train.
impe'd/iō **-ī're** **-ī'vī** & **iī** **-ī'tum** *vt.* hinder, entangle; encircle; (*fig.*) embarrass, obstruct, prevent. **-ī'tus** *a.* (*mil.*) hampered with baggage, in difficulties; (*place*) difficult, impassable; (*mind*) busy, obsessed.
impedī'ti/ō **-ō'nis** *f.* obstruction.
impē'gī *perf.* impingō.
imp/e'llō **-e'llere** **-ulī** **-u'lsum** *vt.* strike, drive; set in motion, impel, shoot; incite, urge on; (*fig.*) overthrow, ruin.
impe'nd/eō **-ē're** *vi.* overhang; be imminent, threaten.
impe'nd/ium **-ī** & **iī** *n.* expense, outlay; interest on a loan. **-iō** very much.
imp/e'ndō **-e'ndere** **-e'ndī** **-ē'nsum** *vt.* weigh out, pay out, spend; (*fig.*) devote.
impenetrā'bilis *a.* impenetrable.
impē'ns/a **-ae** *f.* expense, outlay.
impē'ns/us *ppp.* impendō. *a.* (*cost*) high, dear; (*fig.*) great, earnest. **-ē** *ad.* very much; earnestly.
imperā't/or **-ō'ris** *m.* commander-in-chief, general; emperor; chief, master.
imperātō'rius *a.* of a general; imperial.
imperā't/um **-ī** *n.* order.
imperce'ptus *a.* unknown.
impercu'ssus *a.* noiseless.
impe'rditus *a.* not slain.
imperfe'ctus *a.* unfinished, imperfect.

imperfo'ssus *a.* not stabbed.
imperiō'sus *a.* powerful, imperial; tyrannical.
imperī'ti/a -ae *f.* inexperience.
impe'rit/ō -ā're *vt.* & *i.* rule, command.
imperī't/us *a.* inexperienced, ignorant. **-ē** *ad.* awkwardly.
impe'r/ium -ī & iī *n.* command, order; mastery, sovereignty, power; military command, supreme authority; empire; (*pl.*) those in command, the authorities.
impermi'ssus *a.* unlawful.
i'mper/ō -ā're -ā'vī -ā'tum *vt.* & *i.* order, command; requisition, demand; rule, govern, control; be emperor.
imperte'rritus *a.* undaunted.
impe'rt/iō -ī're -ī'vī & iī -ī'tum *vt.* share, communicate, impart.
imperturbā'tus *a.* unruffled.
impe'rvius *a.* impassable.
impeti'bilis *a.* intolerable.
i'mpet/is (*gen.*) -e (*abl.*) *m.* force; extent.
impetrā'bilis *a.* attainable; successful.
impetrā'ti/ō -ō'nis *f.* favour.
impe'tr/iō -ī're *vt.* succeed with the auspices.
i'mpetr/ō -ā're -ā'vī -ā'tum *vt.* achieve; obtain, secure (a request).
i'mpet/us -ūs *m.* attack, onset; charge; rapid motion, rush; (*mind*) impulse, passion.
impe'xus *a.* unkempt.
impi'et/ās -ā'tis *f.* impiety, disloyalty, unfilial conduct.
i'mpig/er -rī *a.* active, energetic. **-rē** *ad.*
impi'grit/ās -ā'tis *f.* energy.
imp/i'ngō -i'ngere -ē'gī -ā'ctum *vt.* dash, force against; force upon; (*fig.*) bring against, drive.
'mpi/ō -ā're *vt.* make sinful.
'mpi/us *a.* (*to gods*) impious, (*to parents*) undutiful, (*to country*) disloyal; wicked, unscrupulous. **-ē** *ad.* wickedly.
implācā'bili/s *a.* implacable. **-ter** *ad.*
implācā'tus *a.* unappeased.
impla'cidus *a.* savage.
i'mpl/eō -ē're -ē'vī -ē'tum *vt.* fill; satisfy; (*time, number*) make up, complete; (*duty*) discharge, fulfil.
imple'xus *a.* entwined; involved.
implicā'ti/ō -ō'nis *f.* entanglement.
i'mplic/ō -ā're -ā'vī & uī -ā'tum & itum *vt.* entwine, enfold, clasp; (*fig.*) entangle, involve; connect closely, join. **-ā'tus** *a.* complicated, confused. **-ite** *ad.* intricately.
implōrā'ti/ō -ō'nis *f.* beseeching.
implō'r/ō -ā're -ā'vī -ā'tum *vt.* invoke, entreat, appeal to.
implū'mis *a.* unfledged.
i'mplu/ō -ere *vi.* rain upon.
implu'v/ium -ī & iī *n.* roof-opening of the Roman atrium; rain-basin in the atrium.
impolī't/us *a.* unpolished, inelegant. **-ē** *ad.* without ornament.
impollū'tus *a.* unstained.
imp/ō'nō -ō'nere -o'suī -o'situm *vt.* put in, lay on, place; embark; (*fig.*) impose, inflict, assign; put in charge; (*tax*) impose; (*with dat.*) impose upon, cheat.
impo'rt/ō -ā're -ā'vī -ā'tum *vt.* bring in, import; (*fig.*) bring upon, introduce.
importū'nit/ās -ā'tis *f.* insolence, ill nature.
importū'n/us *a.* unsuitable; troublesome; ill-natured, uncivil, bullying. **-ē** *ad.*
importuō'sus *a.* without a harbour.
i'mpo/s -tis *a.* not master (of).
impo'situs, impo'stus *ppp.* impōnō.

i'mpot/ēns -e'ntis *a.* powerless, weak; with no control over; headstrong, violent. -e'**nter** *ad.* weakly; violently.
impote'nti/a -ae *f.* poverty; want of self-control, violence.
impraesentiā'rum *ad.* at present.
imprā'nsus *a.* fasting, without breakfast.
i'mprec/or -ā'rī *vt.* invoke.
impre'ssi/ō -ō'nis *f.* (*mil.*) thrust, raid; (*mind*) impression; (*speech*) emphasis; (*rhythm*) beat.
impre'ssus *ppp.* imprimō.
imprī'mīs *ad.* especially.
i'mpr/imō -i'mere -e'ssī -e'ssum *vt.* press upon, impress, imprint, stamp.
improbā'ti/ō -ō'nis *f.* blame.
impro'bit/ās -ā'tis *f.* badness, dishonesty.
i'mprob/ō -ā're -ā'vī -ā'tum *vt.* disapprove, condemn reject. [presumptuous.
impro'bulus *a.* a little
i'mprob/us *a.* bad, inferior (in quality); wicked, perverse, cruel; unruly, persistent, rebellious. -ē *ad.* badly, wrongly; persistently.
imprōcē'rus *a.* undersized.
imprōdi'ctus *a.* not postponed. [slow.
imprō'mptus *a.* unready,
improperā'tus *a.* lingering.
impro'sper -ī *a.* unsuccessful. -ē *ad.* unfortunately.
imprō'vid/us *a.* unforeseeing, thoughtless. -ē *ad.*
imprōvī's/us *a.* unexpected. -ō, de -ō, ex -ō unexpectedly.
imprū'd/ēns -e'ntis *a.* unforeseeing, not expecting; ignorant, unaware. -e'**nter** *ad.* thoughtlessly; unawares.
imprūde'nti/a -ae *f.* thoughtlessness; ignorance; aimlessness.
impū'b/ēs -eris & **is** *a.* youthful; chaste.
i'mpud/ēns -e'ntis *a.* shameless, impudent. -e'**nter** *ad.*
impude'nti/a -ae *f.* impudence.
impudīci'ti/a -ae *f.* lewdness.
impudī'cus *a.* shameless; immodest.
impugnā'ti/ō -ō'nis *f.* assault.
impu'gn/ō -ā're -ā'vī -ā'tum *vt.* attack; (*fig.*) oppose, impugn.
i'mpulī *perf.* impellō.
impu'lsi/ō -ō'nis *f.* pressure; (*mind*) impulse.
impu'ls/or -ō'ris *m.* instigator.
impu'lsus *ppp.* impellō.
impu'ls/us -ūs *m.* push, pressure, impulse; (*fig.*) instigation.
impū'ne *ad.* safely, with impunity.
impū'nit/ās -ā'tis *f.* impunity.
impūnī't/us *a.* unpunished. -ē *ad.* with impunity.
impūrā'tus *a.* vile.
impū'rit/ās -ā'tis *f.* uncleanness.
impū'r/us *a.* unclean; infamous, vile. -ē *ad.*
imputā'tus *a.* unpruned.
i'mput/ō -ā're -ā'vī -ā'tum *vt.* put to one's account; ascribe, credit, impute.
ī'mulus *a.* little tip of.
ī'mus *a.* lowest, deepest, bottom of; last.
in *pr.* (*with abl.*) in, on, at; among; in the case of; (*time*) during. (*with acc.*) into, on to, to, towards; against; (*time*) for, till; (*purpose*) for. — **armīs** under arms. — **equō** on horseback. — **eō esse ut** be in the position of; be on the point of. — **hōrās** hourly. — **modum** in the manner of. — **rem** of use. — **universum** in general. [able.
inacce'ssus *a.* unapproach-
inacē'sc/ō -ere *vi.* turn sour.

Ī'nach/us -ī *m.* first king of Argos. **-ius** *a.* of Inachus, Argive, Greek. **-idēs** -idae *m.* Perseus; Epaphus. **-is** -idis *f.* Io.
inadsuē'tus *a.* unaccustomed.
inadū'stus *a.* unsinged.
inaedi'fic/ō -ā're -ā'vī -ā'tum *vt.* build on, erect; wall up, block up.
inaequā'bilis *a.* uneven.
inaequā'li/s *a.* uneven; unequal; capricious. **-ter** *ad.*
inaequā'tus *a.* unequal.
inae'qu/ō -ā're *vt.* level up.
inaestimā'bilis *a.* incalculable; invaluable; valueless.
inae'stu/ō -ā're *vi.* rage in.
inamā'bilis *a.* hateful.
inamārē'sc/ō -ere *vi.* become bitter.
inambitiō'sus *a.* unambitious.
inambulā'ti/ō -ō'nis *f.* walking about.
ina'mbul/ō -ā're *vi.* walk up and down.
inamoe'nus *a.* disagreeable.
ina'nimus *a.* lifeless, inanimate.
inā'n/iō -ī're *vt.* make empty.
inā'n/is *a.* empty, void; poor, unsubstantial; useless, worthless, vain, idle. *n.* (*philos.*) space; (*fig.*) vanity. **-iter** *ad.* idly, vainly.
inā'nit/ās -ā'tis *f.* empty space; inanity.
inarā'tus *a.* fallow.
inār/dē'scō -dē'scere **-sī** *vi.* be kindled, flare up.
inass-, *see* **inads-**.
inattenuā'tus *a.* undiminished.
inau'd/āx -ā'cis *a.* timorous.
inau'd/iō -ī're *vt.* hear of, learn.
inaudī'tus *a.* unheard of, unusual; without a hearing.
inau'gur/ō -ā're *vi.* take auspices. *vt.* consecrate, inaugurate. **-ā'tō** after taking the auspices.
inau'r/ēs -ium *f.pl.* ear-rings.
inau'r/ō -ā're -ā'vī -ā'tum *vt.* gild; (*fig.*) enrich.
inauspicā't/us *a.* done without auspices. **-ō** *ad.* without taking the auspices.
inau'sus *a.* unattempted.
incae'duus *a.* uncut.
incal/ē'scō -ē'scere **-uī** *vi.* grow hot; (*fig.*) warm, glow.
incalfa'c/iō -ere *vt.* heat.
inca'llid/us *a.* stupid, simple. **-ē** *ad.* unskilfully.
incand/ē'scō -ē'scere **-uī** *vi.* become hot; turn white.
incān/ē'scō -ē'scere **-uī** *vi.* grow grey.
incantā'tus *a.* enchanted.
incā'nus *a.* grey.
inca'ssum *ad.* in vain.
incastīgā'tus *a.* unrebuked.
incau't/us *a.* careless, heedless; unforeseen, unguarded. **-e** *ad.* negligently.
inc/ē'dō -ē'dere -e'ssī -e'ssum *vi.* walk, parade, march; (*mil.*) advance; (*feelings*) come upon.
incelebrā'tus *a.* not made known.
incēnā'tus *a.* supperless.
incendiā'r/ius -ī & iī *m.* incendiary.
ince'nd/ium -ī & iī *n.* fire, conflagration; heat; (*fig.*) fire, vehemence, passion.
ince'nd/ō -ere -ī **incē'nsum** *vt.* set fire to, burn; light, brighten; (*fig.*) inflame, rouse, incense.
incē'nsi/ō -ō'nis *f.* burning.
incē'nsus *ppp.* incendō.
incē'nsus *a.* not registered.
incē'pī *perf.* incipiō.
ince'pti/ō -ō'nis *f.* undertaking.
ince'pt/ō -ā're *vt.* begin, attempt.
ince'pt/or -ō'ris *m.* originator.
ince'pt/us *ppp.* incipiō. **-um** -ī *n.* beginning, undertaking, attempt.
incē'r/ō -ā're *vt.* cover with wax.
ince'rt/us *a.* uncertain, doubt-

ful, unsteady. *n.* uncertainty. **-ō** *ad.* not for certain.
ince'ss/ō -ere -ī'vī *vt.* attack; (*fig.*) assail.
ince'ss/us -ūs *m.* gait, pace, tramp; invasion; approach.
ince'st/ō -ā're *vt.* pollute, dishonour.
ince'st/us *a.* sinful; unchaste, incestuous. *n.* incest. **-ē** *ad.*
ince'st/us -ūs *m.* incest.
incho-, *see* **incoh-**.
i'nc/idō -i'dere -idī -ā'sum *vi.* fall upon, fall into; meet, fall in with, come across; befall occur, happen. in mentem — occur to one.
incī'/dō -dere -dī -sum *vt.* cut open, cut up; engrave, inscribe; interrupt, cut short.
incī'l/e -is *n.* ditch.
incī'l/ō -ā're *vt.* rebuke.
inci'n/gō -gere -xī -ctum *vt.* gird, wreathe; surround.
i'ncin/ō -ere *vt.* sing, play.
inc/i'piō -i'pere -ē'pī -e'ptum *vt.* & *i.* begin.
incipi'ss/ō -ere *vt.* begin.
incī'sim *ad.* in short clauses.
incī'si/ō -ō'nis *f.* clause.
incī's/us *ppp.* incīdō. **-um** -ī *n.* clause. **-ē** *ad.* in short clauses.
incitāme'nt/um -ī *n.* incentive.
incitā'ti/ō -ō'nis *f.* inciting; rapidity.
incitā't/us *ppp.* incitō. *a.* swift, rapid. equō -ō at a gallop. **-ē** *ad.* impetuously.
i'ncit/ō -ā're -ā'vī -ā'tum *vt.* urge on, rush; rouse, encourage, excite; inspire; increase. sē — rush. currentem — *spur a willing horse.*
i'ncitus *a.* swift.
i'ncit/us *a.* immovable. ad -ās, -a redigere bring to a standstill.
inclā'm/ō -ā're *vt.* & *i.* call out, cry out to; scold abuse.
inclār/ē'scō -ē'scere -uī *vi.* become famous.
inclē'm/ēns -e'ntis *a.* severe. **-e'nter** *ad.* harshly.
inclēme'nti/a -ae *f.* severity.
inclīnā'ti/ō -ō'nis *f.* leaning, slope; (*fig.*) tendency, inclination, bias; (*circs.*) change; (*voice*) modulation.
inclī'n/ō -ā're -ā'vī -ā'tum *vt.* bend, turn; turn back; (*fig.*) incline, direct, transfer; change. *vi.* bend, sink; (*mil.*) give way; (*fig.*) change, deteriorate; incline, tend, turn in favour. **-ā'tus** *a.* inclined, prone; falling; (*voice*) deep.
i'nclitus, *see* **inclutus.**
inclū'/dō -dere -sī -sum *vt.* shut in, keep in, enclose; obstruct, block; (*fig.*) include; (*time*) close, end.
inclū'si/ō -ō'nis *f.* imprisonment.
inclū'sus *ppp.* inclūdō.
i'nclutus, i'nclitus *a.* famous, glorious.
inco'ctus *ppp.* incoquō.
inco'ctus *a.* uncooked, raw.
incōgitā'bilis *a.* thoughtless.
incō'git/āns -a'ntis *a.* thoughtless.
incōgita'nti/a -ae *f.* thoughtlessness.
incō'git/ō -ā're *vt.* contrive.
inco'gnitus *a.* unknown unrecognised; (*law*) untried.
i'ncoh/ō -ā're -ā'vī -ā'tum *vt.* begin, start. **-ā'tus** *a.* unfinished.
i'ncol/a -ae *f.* inhabitant, resident.
i'ncol/ō -ere -uī *vt.* live in, inhabit. *vi.* live, reside.
inco'lumis *a.* safe and sound, unharmed.
incolu'mit/ās -ā'tis *f.* safety.
incomitā'tus *a.* unaccompanied.
incommendā'tus *a.* unprotected.
incommo'dit/ās -ā'tis *f.* inconvenience, disadvantage.
inco'mmod/ō -ā're *vi.* be inconvenient, annoy.
inco'mmod/us *a.* incon-

venient, troublesome. **-um -ī** *n.* inconvenience, disadvantage, misfortune. **-ē** *ad.* inconveniently, unfortunately.
incommūtā'bilis *a.* unchangeable.
incompe'rtus *a.* unknown.
incompo'sit/us *a.* in disorder, irregular. **-ē** *ad.*
incō'mptus *a.* undressed, inelegant.
inconce'ssus *a.* forbidden.
inconci'li/ō **-ā're** *vt.* win over (by guile); trick, inveigle, embarrass.
inconci'nnus *a.* inartistic, awkward.
inconcu'ssus *a.* unshaken, stable.
inco'ndit/us *a.* undisciplined, not organised; (*language*) artless. **-ē** *ad.* confusedly.
incōnsīderā't/us *a.* thoughtless, ill-advised. **-ē** *ad.*
incōnsōlā'bilis *a.* incurable.
incō'nst/āns **-a'ntis** *a.* fickle, inconsistent. **-a'nter** *ad.* inconsistently.
incōnsta'nti/a **-ae** *f.* fickleness, inconsistency.
incōnsu'lt/us *a.* indiscreet, ill-advised; unanswered; not consulted. **-ē** *ad.* indiscreetly.
incōnsu'ltū without consulting.
incōnsū'mptus *a.* unconsumed.
incontāminā'tus *a.* untainted.
inconte'ntus *a.* untuned.
inco'ntin/ēns **-e'ntis** *a.* intemperate. **-e'nter** *ad.* without self-control.
incontine'nti/a **-ae** *f.* lack of self-control.
inconve'ni/ēns **-e'ntis** *a.* ill-matched.
i'nco/quō **-quere** **-xī** **-ctum** *vt.* boil; dye.
incorrē'ctus *a.* unrevised.
incorru'pt/us *a.* unspoiled; uncorrupted, genuine. **-ē** *ad.* justly.
incrēbr/ē'scō, **incrēb/ē'scō** **-ē'scere** **-uī** *vi.* increase, grow, spread.
incrēdi'bili/s *a.* incredible, extraordinary. **-ter** *ad.*
incrē'dulus *a.* incredulous.
incrēme'nt/um **-ī** *n.* growth, increase; addition; offspring.
incre'pit/ō **-ā're** *vt.* rebuke; challenge.
i'ncrep/ō **-ā're** **-uī** **-itum** *vi.* make a noise, sound; (*news*) be noised abroad. *vt.* cause to make a noise; exclaim against, rebuke.
incrē'/scō **-scere** **-vī** *vi.* grow in, increase.
incrē'tus *a.* sifted in.
incruentā'tus *a.* unstained with blood.
incrue'ntus *a.* bloodless, without bloodshed.
incrū'st/ō **-ā're** *vt.* encrust.
i'ncub/ō **-ā're** **-uī** **-itum** *vi.* lie in or on; (*fig.*) brood over.
incu'buī *perf.* **incubō**: *perf.* **incumbō**.
incu'lc/ō **-ā're** **-ā'vī** **-ā'tum** *vt.* force in; force upon, impress on.
inculpā'tus *a.* blameless.
incu'lt/us *a.* uncultivated; (*fig.*) neglected, uneducated, rude. **-ē** *ad.* uncouthly.
incu'lt/us **-ūs** *m.* neglect, squalor.
incu'/mbō **-mbere** **-buī** **-bitum** *vi.* lean, recline on; fall upon, throw onself upon; oppress, lie heavily upon; (*fig.*) devote attention to, take pains with; incline.
incūnā'bul/a **-ō'rum** *n.pl.* swaddling-clothes; (*fig.*) cradle, infancy, birthplace, origin.
incūrā'tus *a.* neglected.
incū'ri/a **-ae** *f.* negligence.
incūriō's/us *a.* careless, indifferent. **-ē** *ad.* carelessly.
incu'/rrō **-rrere** **-rrī** & **cu'rrī** **-rsum** *vi.* run into, rush, attack; invade; meet with,

get involved in; (*events*) occur, coincide.
incu'rsi/ō -ō'nis *f.* attack; invasion, raid; collision.
incu'rs/ō -ā're *vt.* & *i.* run into, assault; frequently invade; (*fig.*) meet, strike.
incu'rs/us -ūs *m.* assault, striking; (*mind*) impulse.
incu'rv/ō -ā're *vt.* bend, crook.
incu'rvus *a.* bent, crooked.
i'nc/ūs -ū'dis *f.* anvil.
incūsā'ti/ō -ō'nis *f.* blaming.
incū's/ō -ā're -ā'vī -ā'tum *vt.* find fault with, accuse.
incu'ssī *perf.* incutiō.
incu'ssus *ppp.* incutiō.
incu'ss/us -ūs *m.* shock.
incustōdī'tus *a.* unguarded, unconcealed.
incū'sus *a.* forged.
incu'/tiō -tere -ssī -ssum *vt.* strike, dash against; throw; (*fig.*) strike into, inspire with.
indāgā'ti/ō -ō'nis *f.* search.
indāgā't/or -ō'ris *m.*, **-rīx** -rī'cis *f.* explorer.
indā'g/ō -ā're *vt.* track down; (*fig.*) trace, investigate.
indā'g/ō -inis *f.* (*hunt*) drive, encirclement.
indau'diō, *see* **inaudiō**.
i'nde *ad.* from there, from that, from them; on that side; from then, ever since; after that, then.
indē'bitus *a.* not due.
indēclīnā'tus *a.* constant.
in'decor -is *a.* dishonourable, a disgrace.
inde'cor/ō -ā're *vt.* disgrace.
indecō'r/us *a.* unbecoming, unsightly. **-ē** *ad.* indecently.
indēfē'nsus *a.* undefended.
indēfe'ssus *a.* unwearied tireless.
indēflē'tus *a.* unwept.
indēie'ctus *a.* undemolished.
indēlē'bilis *a.* imperishable.
indēlībā'tus *a.* unimpaired.
indemnā'tus *a.* unconvicted.
indēplōrā'tus *a.* unlamented.
indēprē'nsus *a.* undetected.
inde'ptus *ppa.* indipīscor.
indēse'rtus *a.* unforsaken.
indēstri'ctus *a.* unscathed.
indētō'nsus *a.* unshorn.
indēvītā'tus *a.* unerring.
i'nd/ex -icis *m.* forefinger; witness, informer; (*book, art*) title, inscription; (*stone*) touchstone; (*fig.*) indication, pointer, sign.
I'nd/ia -iae *f.* India. **-us** -ī *m.* Indian; Ethiopian; mahout. **-us**, **-icus** *a.*
indicā'ti/ō -ō'nis *f.* value.
indīce'nte mē without my telling.
indi'c/ium -ī & iī *n.* information, evidence; reward for information; indication, sign, proof. — **profitērī, offerre** *turn King's evidence.* — **postulāre,** dare ask, grant permission to give evidence.
i'ndic/ō -ā're -ā'vī -ā'tum *vt.* point out; disclose, betray; give information, give evidence; put a price on.
ind/ī'cō -ī'cere -ī'xī -i'ctum *vt.* declare, proclaim, appoint.
indī'ctus *ppp.* indīcō.
indi'ct/us *a.* not said, unsung. causā **-ā** without a hearing.
i'ndidem *ad.* from the same place or thing.
i'ndidī *perf.* indō.
indi'ffer/ēns -e'ntis *a.* neither good nor bad.
indi'gen/a -ae *m.* native. *a.* native.
indige'nti/a -ae *f.* need; craving.
indi'g/eō -ē're -uī *vi.* (*with abl.*) need, want, require; crave. **-ēns** -e'ntis *a.* needy.
i'ndig/es -etis *m.* national deity.
indīge'stus *a.* confused.
indignābu'ndus *a.* enraged.
indignā'ti/ō -ō'nis *f* indignation.
indi'gnit/ās -ā'tis *f.* un-

worthiness, enormity; insulting treatment; indignation.
indi'gn/or -ā'rī -ā'tus *vt.* be displeased with, be angry at. **-āns -a'ntis** *a.* indignant.
indi'gn/us *a.* unworthy, undeserving; shameful, severe; undeserved. **-ē** *ad.* unworthily; indignantly.
i'ndigus *a.* in want.
indī'lig/ēns -e'ntis *a.* careless. **-e'nter** *ad.*
indīlige'nti/a -ae *f.* carelessness.
indipī'sc/or -ī inde'ptus *vt.* obtain, get, reach.
indīre'ptus *a.* unplundered.
indiscrē'tus *a.* closely connected, indiscriminate, indistinguishable.
indise'rt/us *a.* not eloquent. **-ē** *ad.* without eloquence.
indispo'situs *a.* disorderly.
indissolū'bilis *a.* imperishable.
indisti'nctus *a.* confused, obscure.
i'nditus *ppp.* **indō.**
indīvi'duus *a.* indivisible; inseparable. *n.* atom.
i'nd/ō -ere -idī -itum *vt.* put in or on; introduce; impart, impose.
indo'cilis *a.* difficult to teach, hard to learn; untaught.
indo'ct/us *a.* untrained, illiterate, ignorant. **-ē** *ad.* unskilfully.
indole'nti/a -ae *f.* freedom from pain.
i'ndol/ēs -is *f.* nature, character, talents.
indol/ē'scō -ē'scere -uī *vi.* feel sorry.
indo'mitus *a.* untamed, wild; ungovernable.
indo'rm/iō -ī're *vi.* sleep on; be careless.
indōtā'tus *a.* with no dowry; unhonoured; (*fig.*) unadorned.
indu'bit/ō -ā're *vi.* begin to doubt.
indu'bius *a.* undoubted.
ind/ū'cō -ū'cere -ū'xī -u'ctum *vt.* bring in, lead on; introduce; overlay, cover over; (*fig.*) move, persuade, seduce; (*bookkeeping*) enter; (*dress*) put on; (*public show*) exhibit; (*writing*) erase. **animum, in animum** — determine, imagine.
indu'cti/ō -ō'nis *f.* leading, bringing on; (*mind*) purpose, intention; (*logic*) induction.
indu'ctus *ppp.* **indūcō.**
indugre'dior, *see* **ingredior.**
i'nduī *perf.* **induō.**
indu'lg/ēns -e'ntis *pres.p.* **indulgeō.** *a.* indulgent, kind. **-e'nter** *ad.* indulgently.
indulge'nti/a -ae *f.* indulgence, gentleness.
indu'l/geō -gē're -sī *vi.* (*with dat.*) be kind to, indulge, give way to; indulge in. *vt.* concede. **sibi** — take liberties.
i'nd/uō -u'ere -uī -ū'tum *vt.* (*dress*) put on; (*fig.*) assume, entangle.
indup-, *see* **imp-.**
indūr/ē'scō -ē'scere -uī *vi.* harden.
indū'r/ō -ā're *vt.* harden.
indu'stri/a -ae *f.* diligence. **dē, ex -ā** on purpose.
indu'stri/us *a.* diligent, painstaking. **-ē** *ad.*
indū'ti/ae -ā'rum *f.pl.* truce, armistice.
indū'tus *ppp.* **induō.**
indū't/us -ūs *m.* wearing.
indu'vi/a -ā'rum *f.pl.* clothes.
indū'xī *perf.* **indūcō.**
inē'bri/ō -ā're *vt.* intoxicate; (*fig.*) saturate.
ine'di/a -ae *f.* starvation.
inē'ditus *a.* unpublished.
inē'leg/āns -a'ntis *a.* tasteless. **-a'nter** *ad.* without taste.
inēluctā'bilis *a.* inescapable.
inēmo'r/ior -ī *vi.* die in.
ine'mptus *a.* unpurchased.
inēnārrā'bilis *a.* indescribable.
inēnōdā'bilis *a.* inexplicable.
i'n/eō -ī're -ī'vī & iī -itum *vi.*

go in, come in; begin. *vt.* enter; begin, enter upon, form, undertake. cōnsilium — form a plan. grātiam — win favour. numerum — enumerate. ratiōnem — calculate, consider, contrive. suffrāgium — vote. viam — find out a way.
ine'pti/a -ae *f.* stupidity; (*pl.*) nonsense. [fool.
ine'pt/iō -ī're *vi.* play the
ine'pt/us *a.* unsuitable; silly, tactless, absurd. -ē *ad.*
ine'rmis, ine'rmus *a.* unarmed, defenceless; harmless.
ine'rr/āns -a'ntis *a.* fixed.
ine'rr/ō -ā're *vi.* wander about in.
i'ner/s -tis *a.* unskilful; inactive, indolent, timid; insipid.
ine'rti/a -ae *f.* lack of skill; idleness, laziness.
inērudī'tus *a.* uneducated.
ine'sc/ō -ā're *vt.* entice, deceive.
inēve'ctus *a.* mounted.
inēvītā'bilis *a.* inescapable.
inexcī'tus *a.* peaceful.
inexcūsā'bilis *a.* with no excuse.
inexercitā'tus *a.* untrained.
inexhau'stus *a.* unexhausted.
inexōrā'bilis *a.* inexorable; (*things*) severe. [ened.
inexperrē'ctus *a.* unawak-
inexpe'rtus *a.* inexperienced; untried.
inexpiā'bilis *a.* inexpiable; implacable.
inexplē'bilis *a.* insatiable.
inexplē'tus *a.* incessant.
inexplicā'bilis *a.* inexplicable; impracticable, unending.
inexplōrā't/us *a.* unreconnoitred. -ō without making a reconnaissance.
inexpugnā'bilis *a.* impregnable, safe. [pected.
inexspectā'tus *a.* unex-
inexsti'nctus *a.* unextinguished; insatiable, imperishable.
inexsuperā'bilis *a.* insurmountable. [able.
inextrīcā'bilis *a.* inextric-
ī'nfabrē *ad.* unskilfully.
infabricā'tus *a.* unfashioned.
infacē'tus *a.* not witty, crude.
infācu'ndus *a.* ineloquent.
infā'mi/a -ae *f.* disgrace, scandal.
infā'mis *a.* infamous, disreputable.
infā'm/ō -ā're -ā'vī -ā'tum *vt.* disgrace, bring into disrepute.
infa'ndus *a.* unspeakable, atrocious.
ī'nf/āns -a'ntis *a.* mute, speechless; young, infant; tongue-tied; childish. *m., f.* infant, child.
infa'nti/a -ae *f.* inability to speak; infancy; lack of eloquence.
infa'tu/ō -ā're *vt.* make a fool of.
infau'stus *a.* unlucky.
infe'ct/or -ō'ris *m.* dyer.
infe'ctus *ppp.* inficiō.
infe'ct/us *a.* undone, unfinished. rē -ā without achieving one's purpose.
infēcu'ndit/ās -ā'tis *f.* infertility.
infēcu'ndus *a.* unfruitful.
infēlī'cit/ās -ā'tis *f.* misfortune. [happy.
infēlī'c/ō -ā're *vt.* make un-
infē'l/īx -ī'cis *a.* unfruitful; unhappy, unlucky. -ī'citer *ad.*
infe'ns/ō -ā're *vt.* make dangerous, make hostile.
infe'ns/us *a.* hostile, dangerous. -ē *ad.* aggressively.
infe'rc/iō -ī're *vt.* cram in.
infe'ri/ae -ā'rum *f.pl.* offerings to the dead.
infe'ri/or -ō'ris *comp.* inferus. -us *comp.* infrā.
infe'rn/us *a.* beneath; of the lower world, infernal. *m.pl.* the shades. *n.pl.* the lower world. -ē *ad.* below.

I'nfer/ō -re i'ntulī illā'tum *vt.* carry in, bring to, put on; move forward; (*fig.*) introduce, cause; (*book-keeping*) enter; (*logic*) infer. bellum — make war (on). pedem — advance. sē — repair, rush, strut about. signa — attack, charge.
I'nfer/us (*comp.* -ior *sup.* ī'nfimus) *a.* lower, below. *m.pl.* the dead, the lower world. *comp.* lower; later; inferior. *sup.* lowest, bottom of; meanest, humblest.
Infer/vē'scō -vē'scere -buī *vi.* boil.
Infe'st/ō -ā're *vt.* attack.
Infe'st/us *a.* unsafe; dangerous, aggressive. -ē *ad.* aggressively.
Inficēt-, *see* **Infacēt-**.
Inf/i'ciō -i'cere -ē'cī -e'ctum *vt.* dip, dye, discolour; taint, infect; (*fig.*) instruct, corrupt, poison.
Infidē'li/s *a.* faithless. -ter *ad.* treacherously. [loyalty.
Infidē'lit/ās -ā'tis *f.* dis-
Infī'dus *a.* unsafe, treacherous.
Infī'/gō -gere -xī -xum *vt.* thrust, drive in; (*fig.*) impress, imprint.
I'nfimus *sup.* **inferus.**
Infi'nd/ō -ere *vt.* cut into, plough.
Infī'nit/ās -ā'tis *f.* boundless extent, infinity.
Infinī'ti/ō -ō'nis *f.* infinity.
Infinī't/us *a.* boundless, endless, infinite; indefinite. -ē *ad.* without end.
Infirmā'ti/ō -ō'nis *f.* invalidating, refuting.
Infī'rmit/ās -ā'tis *f.* weakness; infirmity, sickness.
Infī'rm/ō -ā're *vt.* weaken; invalidate, refute.
Infī'rm/us *a.* weak, indisposed; weak-minded; (*things*) trivial. -ē *ad.* feebly.
I'nfit *vi.* (*def.*) begins.
Infī'tiās e'ō deny.

Infitiā'lis *a.* negative.
Infitiā'ti/ō -ō'nis *f.* denial.
Infitiā't/or -ō'ris *m.* denier (of a debt). [repudiate.
Infī'ti/or -ā'rī -ā'tus *vt.* deny,
Infī'xus *ppp.* **infīgō.**
Inflammā'ti/ō -ō'nis *f.* (*fig.*) exciting.
Infla'mm/ō -ā're -ā'vī -ā'tum *vt.* set on fire, light; (*fig.*) inflame, rouse.
Inflā'ti/ō -ō'nis *f.* flatulence.
Inflā't/us -ūs *m.* blow; inspiration.
Infle'/ctō -ctere -xī -xum *vt.* bend, curve; change; (*voice*) modulate; (*fig.*) affect, move.
Inflē'tus *a.* unwept.
Infle'xi/ō -ō'nis *f.* bending.
Infle'xus *ppp.* **inflectō.**
Inflī'/gō -gere -xī -ctum *vt.* dash against, strike; inflict.
I'nfl/ō -ā're -ā'vī -ā'tum *vt.* blow, inflate; (*fig.*) inspire, puff up. -ā'tus *a.* blown up, swollen; (*fig.*) puffed up, conceited; (*style*) turgid. -ē *ad.* pompously.
I'nflu/ō -ere -xī -xum *vi.* flow in; (*fig.*) stream, pour in.
Inf/o'diō -o'dere -ō'dī -o'ssum *vt.* dig in, bury.
Infōrmā'ti/ō -ō'nis *f.* sketch, idea. [eous.
Infō'rmis *a.* shapeless; hid-
Infō'rm/ō -ā're -ā'vī -ā'tum *vt.* shape, fashion; sketch; educate.
Infortūnā'tus *a.* unfortunate.
Infortū'n/ium -ī & iī *n.* misfortune.
Info'ssus *ppp.* **infodiō.**
I'nfrā (*comp.* infe'rius) *ad.* underneath, below. *comp.* lower down. *pr.* (*with acc.*) below, beneath, under; later than.
Infrā'cti/ō -ō'nis *f.* weakening.
Infrā'ctus *ppp.* **infringō.**
Infra'gilis *a.* strong.
I'nfrem/ō -ere -uī *vi.* growl.
Infrēnā'tus *ppp.* **infrēnō.**

infrēnā'tus *a.* without a bridle.
infre'nd/ō -ere *vi.* gnash.
infrē'n/is, -us *a.* unbridled.
infrē'n/ō -ā're -ā'vī -ā'tum *vt.* put a bridle on, harness; (*fig.*) curb.
i'nfrequ/ēns -e'ntis *a.* not crowded, infrequent; badly attended.
infreque'nti/a -ae *f.* small number; emptiness.
infr/i'ngō -i'ngere -ē'gī -ā'ctum *vt.* break, bruise; (*fig.*) weaken, break down, exhaust.
i'nfr/ōns -o'ndis *a.* leafless.
infūcā'tus *a.* showy.
i'nful/a -ae *f.* woollen band, fillet, badge of honour.
i'nfumus, *see* **infimus.**
inf/u'ndō -u'ndere -ū'dī -ū'sum *vt.* pour in or on; serve; (*fig.*) spread.
infu'sc/ō -ā're *vt.* darken; spoil, tarnish.
infū'sus *ppp.* **infundō.**
inge'min/ō -ā're *vt.* redouble. *vi.* be redoubled.
ingem/ī'scō -ī'scere -uī *vi.* groan, sigh. *vt* sigh over.
i'ngem/ō -ere -uī *vt.* & *i.* sigh for mourn.
inge'ner/ō -ā're -ā'vī -ā'tum *vt.* engender, produce, create.
ingeniā'tus *a.* with a natural talent.
ingeniō's/us *a.* talented, clever; (*things*) naturally suited. **-ē** *ad.* cleverly.
inge'nitus *ppp.* **ingignō.** *a* inborn, natural.
inge'n/ium -ī & iī *n.* nature; (*disposition*) bent, character; (*intellect*) ability, talent, genius; (*person*) genius.
i'ng/ēns -e'ntis *a.* huge, mighty, great.
ingenu'it/ās -ā'tis *f.* noble birth, noble character.
inge'nu/us *a.* native innate; free-born; noble frank; delicate. **-ē** *ad.* liberally, frankly.
i'ngo/rō -rere -ssī -stum *vt.* carry in; heap on; throw, hurl; (*fig.*) press, obtrude.
ing/i'gnō -i'gnere -e'nuī -e'nitum *vt.* engender, implant.
inglō'rius *a.* inglorious.
inglu'vi/ēs -ē'ī *f.* maw; gluttony.
ingrā'tiīs, ingrā'tīs *ad.* against one's will.
ingrā't/us *a.* disagreeable, unwelcome; ungrateful thankless. **-ē** *ad.* unwillingly; ungratefully.
ingravē'sc/ō -ere *vi.* grow heavy, become worse, increase.
i'grav/ō -ā're *vt.* weigh heavily on; aggravate.
ingre'/dior -dī -ssus *vt.* & *i.* go in, enter; walk, march; enter upon, engage in; commence, begin to speak.
ingre'ssi/ō -ō'nis *f.* entrance; beginning; pace.
ingre'ss/us -ūs *m.* entrance; (*mil.*) inroad; beginning; walking, gait. [assail.
i'ngru/ō -ere -ī *vi.* fall upon,
i'ngu/en -inis *n.* groin.
ingu'rgit/ō -ā're *vt.* pour in. **sē** — gorge oneself; (*fig.*) be absorbed in.
ingustā'tus *a.* untasted.
inha'bilis *a.* unwieldy awkward; unfit. [able.
inhabitā'bilis *a.* uninhabit-
inha'bit/ō -ā're *vt.* inhabit.
inhae'/reō -rē're -sī -sum *vi.* stick in, cling to; adhere, be closely connected with, be always in.
inhaerē'sc/ō -ere *vi.* take hold, cling fast.
inhā'l/ō -ā're *vt.* breathe on.
inhi'b/eō -ē're -uī -itum *vt.* check, restrain; use, practise. — **rēmis, nāvem** back water.
inhibi'ti/ō -ō'nis *f.* backing water.
i'nhi/ō -ā're *vi.* gape. *vt.* gape at, covet. [honour.
inhone'st/ō -ā're *vt.* dis-

inhone'st/us *a.* dishonourable, inglorious; ugly. **-ē** *ad.*
inhonōrā'tus *a.* unhonoured; unrewarded.
inhonō'rus *a.* defaced.
inho'rr/eō -ē're -uī *vi.* stand erect, bristle.
inhorr/ē'scō -ē'scere -uī *vi.* bristle up; shiver, shudder, tremble.
inhospitā'lis *a.* inhospitable.
inhospitā'lit/ās -ā'tis *f.* inhospitality.
inho'spitus *a.* inhospitable.
inhūmā'nit/ās -ā'tis *f.* barbarity; discourtesy, churlishness, meanness.
inhūmā'n/us *a.* savage, brutal; ill-bred, uncivil, uncultured. **-ē, -iter** *ad.* savagely; uncivilly.
inhumā'tus *a.* unburied.
i'nibi *ad.* there, therein; about to happen.
in/i'ciō -i'cere -iē'cī -ie'ctum *vt.* throw into, put on; (*fig.*) inspire, cause; (*speech*) hint, mention. **manum —** take possession.
inie'ct/us -ūs *m.* putting in, throwing over. [feud.
inimīci'ti/a -ae *f.* enmity,
inimī'c/ō -ā're *vt.* make enemies.
inimī'c/us *a.* unfriendly, hostile; injurious. *m., f.* enemy. **-i'ssimus** greatest enemy. **-ē** *ad.* hostilely.
inī'quit/ās -ā'tis *f.* unevenness; difficulty; injustice, unfair demands.
inī'qu/us *a.* unequal, uneven; adverse, unfavourable injurious; unfair, unjust; excessive; impatient, discontented. *m.* enemy. **-ē** *ad.* unequally, unjustly.
ini'ti/ō -ā're *vt.* initiate.
ini't/ium -ī & iī *n.* beginning; (*pl.*) elements, first principles; holy rites, mysteries.
i'nitus *ppp.* ineō.
i'nit/us -ūs *m.* approach; beginning.
iniūcu'ndit/ās -ā'tis *f.* unpleasantness.
iniūcu'nd/us *a.* unpleasant. **-ē** *ad.*
ini/u'ngō -u'ngere -ū'nxī -ū'nctum *vt.* join, attach; (*fig.*) impose, inflict.
iniūrā'tus *a.* unsworn.
iniū'ri/a -ae *f.* wrong, injury, injustice; insult, outrage; severity, revenge; unjust possession. **-ā** unjustly.
iniūriō's/us *a.* unjust, wrongful; harmful. **-ē** *ad.* wrongfully.
iniū'rius *a* wrong, unjust.
iniū'ssū without orders (from).
iniū'ssus *a.* unbidden.
iniūsti'ti/a -ae *f.* injustice, severity.
iniū'st/us *a.* unjust, wrong; excessive, severe. **-ē** *ad.*
inl-, *see* **ill-**.
inm-, *see* **imm-**.
innā'bilis *a.* that none may swim.
innā'/scor -scī -tus *vi.* be born in, grow up in.
i'nnat/ō -ā're *vt.* swim in, float on; swim, flow into.
innā'tus *ppa.* innāscor. *a.* innate, natural. [able.
innāvigā'bilis *a.* unnavig-
inne'/ctō -ctere -xuī -xum *vt.* tie, fasten together, entwine; (*fig.*) connect; contrive.
innī'/tor -tī -xus & sus *vi.* rest, lean on; depend.
i'nn/ō -ā're *vi.* swim in, float on, sail on.
i'nnoc/ēns -e'ntis *a.* harmless; innocent; upright, unselfish. **-e'nter** *ad.* blamelessly.
innoce'nti/a -ae *f.* innocence; integrity, unselfishness.
inno'cu/us *a.* harmless; innocent; unharmed. **-ē** *ad.* innocently.
innōt/ē'scō -ē'scere -uī *vi.* become known.

i'nnov/ō -ā're *vt.* renew. sē — return.
in'noxius *a.* harmless, safe; innocent; unharmed.
innū'bilus *a.* cloudless.
i'nnub/a -ae *a.* unmarried.
innū'/bō -bere -psī *vi.* marry into.
innumerā'bili/s *a.* countless. **-ter** *ad.* innumerably.
innumerābi'lit/ās -ā'tis *f.* countless number.
innumerā'lis *a.* numberless.
innu'merus *a.* countless.
i'nnu/ō -ere -ī *vi.* give a nod.
innū'pt/a -ae *a.* unmarried.
Ī'n/ō -ūs *f.* daughter of Cadmus. **-ōus** *a.*
inoblī'tus *a.* unforgetful.
ino'brutus *a.* not overwhelmed.
inobservā'bilis *a.* unnoticed.
inobservā'tus *a.* unobserved.
inoffē'nsus *a.* without hindrance, uninterrupted.
inofficiō'sus *a.* irresponsible; disobliging.
i'nol/ēns -e'ntis *a.* odourless.
inolē'/scō -scere -vī *vi.* grow in.
inōminā'tus *a.* inauspicious.
ino'pi/a -ae *f.* want, scarcity, poverty; helplessness.
inopī'n/āns -a'ntis *a.* unaware.
inopīnā't/us *a.* unexpected; off one's guard. **-ō** *ad.* unexpectedly.
inopī'nus *a.* unexpected.
inopiō'sus *a.* in want.
i'nop/s -is *a.* destitute, poor, in need (of); helpless, weak; (*speech*) poor in ideas.
inōrā'tus *a.* unpleaded.
inōrdinā'tus *a.* disordered irregular.
inōrnā'tus *a.* unadorned, plain; uncelebrated.
inp-, *see* **imp-**.
i'nquam *vt.* (*def.*) say; (*emphatic*) I repeat, maintain.
i'nqui/ēs -ē'tis *a.* restless.
inquiē't/ō -ā're *vt.* unsettle, make difficult.
inquiē'tus *a.* restless, unsettled.
inquilī'n/us -ī *m.* inhabitant, tenant.
i'nquin/ō -ā're -ā'vī -ā'tum *vt.* defile, stain, contaminate. **-ā'tus** *a.* filthy, impure. **-ā'tē** *ad.* filthily.
inquī'/rō -rere -sī'vī -sī'tum *vt.* search for, inquire into; (*law*) collect evidence.
inquīsī'ti/ō -ō'nis *f.* searching, inquiry, (*law*) inquisition.
inquīsī't/or -ō'ris *m.* searcher, spy; investigator.
inquīsī'tus *ppp.* inquīrō.
inquīsī'tus *a.* not investigated.
inr-, *see* **irr-**.
īnsalūtā'tus *a.* ungreeted.
īnsānā'bilis *a.* incurable.
īnsā'ni/a -ae *f.* madness; folly, mania, poetic rapture.
īnsā'n/iō -ī're -ī'vī -ī'tum *vi.* be mad, rave; rage; be inspired.
īnsā'nit/ās -ā'tis *f.* unhealthiness.
īnsā'n/us *a.* mad; frantic, furious; outrageous. **-ē** *ad.* madly. **-um** *ad.* (*slang*) frightfully.
īnsatiā'bili/s *a.* insatiable; never cloying. **-ter** *ad.*
īnsati'et/ās -ā'tis *f.* insatiateness.
īnsaturā'bili/s *a.* insatiable. **-ter** *ad.*
īnsc/e'ndō -e'ndere -e'ndī -ē'nsum *vt.* & *i.* climb up, mount, embark, board.
īnscē'nsi/ō -ō'nis *f.* going on board.
īnscē'nsus *ppp.* īnscendō.
ī'nsci/ēns -e'ntis *a.* unaware; stupid. **-e'nter** *ad.* ignorantly.
īnscie'nti/a -ae *f.* ignorance, inexperience; neglect.
īnscī'ti/a -ae *f.* ignorance, stupidity, inattention.
īnscī't/us *a.* ignorant, stupid. **-ē** *ad.* clumsily.

I'nscius *a.* unaware, ignorant.
Inscrī'/bō -bere -psī -ptum *vt.* write on, inscribe; ascribe, assign; (*book*) entitle; (*for sale*) advertise.
Inscrī'pti/ō -ō'nis *f.* inscribing, title.
Inscrī'ptus *ppp.* inscrībō.
Inscu'lp/ō -ere -sī -tum *vt.* carve in, engrave on.
Insectā'ti/ō -ō'nis *f.* hot pursuit; (*words*) abusing, persecution.
Insectā't/or -ō'ris *m.* persecutor.
Inse'ct/or -ā'rī -ā'tus, -ō -ā're *vt.* pursue, attack, criticise.
Inse'ctus *a.* notched.
Insēdābi'liter *ad.* incessantly
Insē'dī *perf.* insidō.
Insen/ē'scō -ē'scere -uī *vi.* grow old in.
Insē'nsilis *a.* imperceptible.
Insepu'ltus *a.* unburied.
I'nsequ/ēns -e'ntis *pres.p.* insequor. *a.* the following.
I'nse/quor -quī -cū'tus *vt.* follow, pursue hotly; proceed; (*time*) come after, come next; (*fig.*) attack, persecute.
I'ns/erō -e'rere -ē'vī -itum *vt.* graft; (*fig.*) implant.
I'nser/ō -ere -uī -tum *vt.* let in, insert; introduce, mingle, involve.
Inse'rt/ō -ā're *vt.* put in.
Inse'rtus *ppp.* inserō.
Inse'rv/iō -ī're -iī -ī'tum *vt.* & *i.* be a slave (to); be devoted, submissive (to).
Inse'ssus *ppp.* insidō.
Insī'bil/ō -ā're *vi.* whistle in.
Insi'd/eō -ē're *vi.* sit on or in; remain fixed. *vt.* hold, occupy.
Insi'di/ae -ā'rum *f.pl.* ambush; (*fig.*) trap, trickery.
Insidiā't/or -ō'ris *n.* soldier in ambush; (*fig.*) waylayer, plotter.
Insi'di/or -ā'rī -ā'tus *vi.* lie in ambush; (*with dat.*) lie in wait for, plot against.
Insidiō's/us *a.* artful, treacherous. **-ē** *ad.* insidiously.
Ins/ī'dō -ī'dere -ē'dī -e'ssum *vi.* settle on; (*fig.*) become fixed, rooted in. *vt.* occupy.
Insi'gn/e -is *n.* distinguishing mark, badge, decoration; (*pl.*) insignia, honours; (*speech*) purple passages.
Insi'gn/iō -ī're *vt.* distinguish. **-ī'tē** *ad.* remarkably.
Insi'gni/s *a.* distinguished, conspicuous. **-ter** *ad.* markedly.
Insi'li/a -um *n.pl.* treadle (of a loom).
Insi'l/iō -ī're -uī *vi.* jump into or on to.
Insimulā'ti/ō -ō'nis *f.* accusation.
Insi'mul/ō -ā're -ā'vī -ā'tum *vt.* charge, accuse, allege (*esp.* falsely).
Insincē'rus *a.* adulterated.
Insinuā'ti/ō -ō'nis *f.* ingratiating.
Insi'nu/ō -ā're -ā'vī -ā'tum *vt.* bring in, introduce stealthily. *vi.* creep in, worm one's way in, penetrate. **sē** — ingratiate oneself; make one's way into.
Insi'pi/ēns -e'ntis *a.* senseless, foolish. **-e'nter** *ad.* foolishly.
Insipie'nti/a -ae *f.* folly.
Ins/i'stō -i'stere -titī *vi.* stand on, step on; stand firm, halt, pause; tread on the heels, press on, pursue; enter upon, apply oneself to, begin; persist, continue.
Insi'ti/ō -ō'nis *f.* grafting; grafting-time.
Insitī'vus *a.* grafted; (*fig.*) spurious.
I'nsit/or -ō'ris *m.* grafter.
I'nsitus *ppp.* inserō. *a.* innate; incorporated.
Insociā'bilis *a.* incompatible.
Insōlābi'liter *ad.* unconsolably.
I'nsol/ēns -e'ntis *a.* unusual

unaccustomed; excessive, extravagant, insolent. **-e'nter** *ad.* unusually; immoderately, insolently.
īnsole'nti/a -ae *f.* inexperience, novelty, strangeness; excess, insolence.
īnsolē'sc/ō -ere *vi.* become insolent, elated.
īnso'lidus *a.* soft.
īnso'litus *a.* unaccustomed, unusual.
īnso'mni/a -ae *f.* sleeplessness.
īnso'mnis *a.* sleepless.
īnso'mn/ium -ī & iī *n.* dream.
ī'nson/ō -ā're -uī *vi.* resound, sound; make a noise.
ī'ns/ōns -o'ntis *a.* innocent; harmless.
īnsōpī'tus *a.* sleepless.
īnspe'ct/ō -ā're *vt.* look at.
īnspe'ctus *ppp.* īnspiciō.
īnspē'r/āns -a'ntis *a.* not expecting.
īnspērā't/us *a.* unexpected. -ō, ex -ō unexpectedly.
īnspe'r/gō -gere -sī -sum *vt.* sprinkle on.
īnsp/i'ciō -i'cere -e'xī -e'ctum *vt.* look into; examine, inspect; (*mil.*) review; (*mind*) consider, get to know.
īnspī'c/ō -ā're *vt.* sharpen.
īnspī'r/ō -ā're -ā'vī -ā'tum *vt.* & *i.* blow on breathe into.
īnspoliā'tus *a.* unpillaged.
īnspū't/ō -ā're *vt.* spit on.
īnstā'bilis *a.* unsteady, not firm; (*fig.*) inconstant.
ī'nst/āns -a'ntis *pres.p.* īnstō. *a.* present; urgent, threatening. **-a'nter** *ad.* vehemently.
īnsta'nti/a -ae *f* presence; vehemence.
ī'nstar *n.* (*indecl.*) likeness, appearance; as good as, worth.
īnstaurā'ti/ō -ō'nis *f.* renewal.
īnstaurā'tīvus *a.* renewed.
īnstau'r/ō -ā're -ā'vī -ā'tum *vt.* renew, restore; celebrate; requite.
īnst/e'rnō -e'rnere -rā'vī -rā'tum *vt.* spread over, cover.
īnstīgā't/or -ō'ris *m.*, **-rīx** -rī'cis *f.* instigator.
īnstī'g/ō -ā're *vt.* goad, incite, instigate.
īnsti'll/ō -ā're *vt.* drop on, instil.
īnstimulā't/or -ō'ris *m.* instigator.
īnsti'mul/ō -ā're *vt.* urge on.
īnsti'nct/or -ō'ris *m.* instigator.
īnsti'nctus *a.* incited, inspired.
īnsti'nct/us -ūs *m.* impulse, inspiration.
īnsti'pul/or -ā'rī -ā'tus *vi.* bargain for.
ī'nstit/a -ae *f.* flounce of a lady's tunic.
ī'nstitī *perf.* īnsistō.
īnsti'ti/ō -ō'nis *f.* stopping.
ī'nstit/or -ō'ris *m.* pedlar.
īnsti't/uō -u'ere -uī -ū'tum *vt.* set, implant; set up, establish, build, appoint; marshal, arrange, organize; teach, educate; undertake, resolve on.
īnstitū'ti/ō -ō'nis *f.* custom; arrangement; education, (*pl.*) principles of education.
īnstitū't/um -ī *n.* way of life, tradition, law; stipulation, agreement; purpose; (*pl.*) principles.
ī'nst/ō -ā're -itī *vi.* stand on or in; be close, be hard on the heels of, pursue; (*events*) approach, impend; (*fig.*) press on, work hard at; (*speech*) insist, urge.
īnstrā'tus *ppp.* īnsternō.
īnstrē'nuus *a.* languid, slow.
ī'nstrep/ō -ere *vi.* creak.
īnstru'cti/ō -ō'nis *f.* building; setting out.
īnstru'ct/or -ō'ris *m.* preparer.
īnstru'ct/us *ppp.* īnstruō. *a.* provided, equipped; prepared, versed. **-ius** *ad.* in better style.

instru'ct/us -ūs *m.* equipment.
instrūme'nt/um -ī *n.* tool, instrument; equipment, furniture, stock; (*fig.*) means, provision; dress, embellishment.
i'nstru/ō -ere -xī -ctum *vt.* erect, build up; (*mil.*) marshal, array; equip, provide, prepare; (*fig.*) teach, train.
insuā's/um -ī *n.* a dark colour.
insuā'vis *a.* disagreeable.
insū'd/ō -ā're *vi.* perspire on.
insuēfa'ctus *a.* accustomed.
insuē'/scō -scere -vī -tum *vt.* train, accustom. *vi.* become accustomed.
insuē'tus *ppp.* insuēscō.
insuē'tus *a.* unaccustomed, unused; unusual.
i'nsul/a -ae *f.* island; block of houses.
insulā'n/us -ī *m.* islander.
insu'lsit/ās -ā'tis *f.* lack of taste, absurdity.
insu'ls/us *a.* tasteless, absurd, dull. **-ē** *ad.*
insu'lt/ō -ā're *vt.* & *i.* jump on, leap in; (*fig.*) exult, taunt, insult.
insultū'r/a -ae *f.* jumping on.
i'n/sum ine'sse i'nfuī *vi.* be in or on; belong to.
insū'm/ō -ere -psī -ptum *vt.* spend, devote.
i'ns/uō -u'ere -uī -ū'tum *vt.* sew in, sew up in.
i'nsuper *ad.* above, on top; besides, over and above. (*pr. with abl.*) besides.
insuperā'bilis *a.* unconquerable, impassable.
insu'r/gō -gere -rē'xī -rē'ctum *vi.* stand up, rise to; rise, grow, swell; rise against.
insusu'rr/ō -ā're *vt.* & *i.* whisper.
insū'tus *ppp.* insuō.
intāb/ē'scō -ē'scere -uī *vi.* melt away, waste away.
intā'ctilis *a.* intangible.
intā'ctus *a.* untouched, intact; untried; undefiled, chaste.
intāminā'tus *a* unsullied.
intē'ctus *ppp.* integō.
intē'ctus *a.* uncovered, unclad; frank. [pure.
intege'llus *a.* fairly whole or
i'nteg/er -rī *a.* whole, complete, unimpaired, intact; sound, fresh, new; (*mind*) unbiassed, free; (*character*) virtuous, pure, upright; (*decision*) undecided, open. **in -rum restituere** restore to a former state. **ab, dē, ex -rō** afresh. **-rum est mihi** I am at liberty (to). **-rē** *ad.* entirely; honestly; correctly.
i'nt/egō -e'gere -ē'xī -ē'ctum *vt.* cover over; protect.
integrā'sc/ō -ere *vi.* begin all over again.
integrā'ti/ō -ō'nis *f.* renewing.
inte'grit/ās -ā'tis *f.* completeness, soundness; integrity, honesty; (*language*) correctness.
i'ntegr/ō -ā're *vt.* renew, replenish, repair; (*mind*) refresh.
integume'nt/um -ī *n.* cover, covering, shelter.
intellē'ctus *ppp.* intellegō.
intellē'ct/us -ūs *m.* understanding; (*word*) meaning.
inte'lleg/ēns -e'ntis *pres.p.* intellegō. *a.* intelligent, a connoisseur. **-e'nter** *ad.* intelligently.
intellege'nti/a -ae *f.* discernment, understanding; taste.
inte'll/egō -e'gere -ē'xī -ē'ctum *vt.* understand, perceive, realise; be a connoisseur.
intemerā'tus *a.* pure, undefiled.
inte'mper/āns -a'ntis *a.* immoderate, extravagant; incontinent. **-a'nter** *ad.* extravagantly.
intempera'nti/a -ae *f.* excess, extravagance; arrogance.

intemperā't/us *a.* excessive. **-ē** *ad.* dissolutely.
intempe'ri/ae **-ā'rum** *f.pl.* inclemency; madness.
intempe'ri/ēs **-ē'ī** *f.* inclemency, storm; (*fig.*) fury.
intempestī'v/us *a.* unseasonable, untimely. **-ē** *ad.* inopportunely.
intempe'stus *a.* (*night*) the dead of; unhealthy.
intempta'tus *a.* untried.
inte'n/dō **-dere** **-dī** **-tum** *vt.* stretch out, strain, spread; (*weapon*) aim; (*tent*) pitch; (*attention, course*) direct, turn, (*fact*) increase, exaggerate, (*speech*) maintain; (*trouble*) threaten. *vi.* make for, intend. animō — purpose. sē — exert oneself.
inte'nti/ō **-ō'nis** *f.* straining, tension; (*mind*) exertion, attention; (*law*) accusation.
inte'nt/ō **-ā're** *vt.* stretch out, aim; (*fig.*) threaten with, attack.
inte'nt/us *ppp.* **intendō.** *a.* taut; attentive, intent; strict; (*speech*) vigorous. **-ē** *ad.* strictly. [out.
inte'nt/us **-ūs** *m.* stretching
inte'p/eō **-ē're** *vi.* be warm.
intep/ē'scō **-ē'scere** **-uī** *vi.* be warmed.
i'nter *pr.*(*with acc.*) between, among, during, in the course of; in spite of. — **haec** meanwhile. — **manūs** within reach. — **nōs** confidentially. — **sē** mutually one another. — **sicāriōs** in the murder court. — **viam** on the way.
interāme'nt/a **-ō'rum** *n.pl.* ship's timbers.
intera'ptus *a.* joined together. [away.
interārē'sc/ō **-ere** *vi.* wither
inte'rbib/ō **-ere** *vi.* drink up.
interbī't/ō **-ere** *vi.* fall through.
intercalā'ris *a.* intercalary.
intercalā'rius *a.* intercalary.
inte'rcal/ō **-ā're** *vt.* intercalate.
intercapē'd/ō **-inis** *f.* interruption, respite.
interc/ē'dō **-ē'dere** **-e'ssī** **-e'ssum** *vi.* come between, intervene; occur; become surety; interfere, obstruct; (*tribune*) protest, veto.
interce'pti/ō **-ō'nis** *f.* taking away.
interce'pt/or **-ō'ris** *m.* embezzler.
interce'ptus *ppp.* **intercipiō.**
interce'ssi/ō **-ō'nis** *f.* (*law*) becoming surety; (*tribune*) veto.
interce'ss/or **-ō'ris** *m.* mediator, surety; interposer of the veto; obstructor.
inte'rcid/ō **-ere** **-ī** *vi.* fall short, happen in the meantime; get lost, become obsolete, be forgotten.
intercī'/dō **-dere** **-dī** **-sum** *vt.* cut through, sever.
inte'rcin/ō **-ere** *vt.* sing between.
interc/i'piō **-i'pere** **-ē'pī** **-e'ptum** *vt* intercept; embezzle, steal; cut off, obstruct.
intercī's/us *ppp* **intercīdō.** **-ē** *ad.* piecemeal.
interclū'/dō **-dere** **-sī** **-sum** *vt.* cut off, block, shut off, prevent. animam — suffocate.
interclū'si/ō **-ō'nis** *f.* stoppage.
interclū'sus *ppp.* **interclūdō.**
intercolu'mn/ium **-ī** & **iī** *n.* space between two pillars.
intercu'rr/ō **-ere** *vi.* mingle with; intercede; hurry in the meantime.
intercu'rs/ō **-ā're** *vi.* crisscross; attack between the lines.
intercu'rs/us **-ūs** *m.* intervention. [dropsy.
inte'rcu/s **-tis** *a.* aqua —
interd/ī'cō **-ī'cere** **-ī'xī** **-i'ctum**

vt. & *i.* forbid, interdict; (*praetor*) make a provisional order. aquā et ignī — banish.
interdi'cti/ō -ō'nis *f.* prohibiting, banishment.
interdi'ct/um -ī *n.* prohibition; provisional order (by a praetor).
inte'rdiū *ad.* by day.
inte'rd/ō -a're *vt.* make at intervals; distribute. nōn -uim I wouldn't care.
interdu'ct/us -ūs *m.* punctuation.
inte'rdum *ad.* now and then, occasionally.
inte'reā *ad.* meanwhile, in the meantime; nevertheless.
interē'mī *perf.* interimō.
intere'mptus *ppp.* interimō.
inte'r/eō -ī're -iī -itum *vi.* be lost, perish, die.
intere'quit/ō -ā're *vt.* & *i.* ride between.
intere'sse *inf.* intersum.
interfā'ti/ō -ō'nis *f.* interruption.
interf/ā'tur -ā'rī -ā'tus *vi.* interrupt.
interfe'cti/ō -ō'nis *f.* killing.
interfe'ct/or -ō'ris *m.*, -rīx -rī'cis *f.* murderer, murderess.
interfe'ctus *ppp.* interficiō.
interf/i'ciō -i'cere -ē'cī -e'ctum *vt.* kill, destroy.
interf/ī'ō -i'erī *vi.* pass away.
inte'rflu/ō -ere -xī *vt.* & *i.* flow between.
interfo'd/iō -ere *vt.* pierce.
interfu'g/iō -ere *vi.* flee among.
inte'rfuī *perf.* intersum.
interfu'lg/eō -ē're *vi.* shine amongst.
interfū'sus *ppp.* lying between; marked here and there.
interia'c/eō -ē're *vi.* lie between.
inte'ribi *ad.* in the meantime.
inter/i'ciō -i'cere -iē'cī -ie'ctum *vt.* put amongst or between, interpose, mingle. annō -iectō after a year.
interie'ct/us -ūs *m.* coming in between; interval.
inte'riī *perf.* intereō.
i'nterim *ad.* meanwhile, in the meantime; sometimes; all the same.
inte'r/imō -i'mere -ē'mī -e'mptum *vt.* abolish, destroy, kill.
inte'ri/or -ō'ris *a.* inner, interior; nearer, on the near side; secret, private; more intimate, more profound. -us *ad.* inwardly; too short.
interi'ti/ō -ō'nis *f.* ruin.
inte'rit/us -ūs *m.* destruction, ruin, death.
interiū'nctus *a.* joined together.
interlā'b/or -ī *vi* glide between.
inte'rleg/ō -ere *vt.* pick here and there.
inte'rl/inō -i'nere -ē'vī -itum *vt.* smear in parts; erase here and there.
inte'rlo/quor -quī -cū'tus *vi.* interrupt.
interlū'/ceō -cē're -xī *vi.* shine through, be clearly seen.
interlū'ni/a -ō'rum *n.pl.* new moon.
inte'rlu/ō -ere *vt.* wash, flow between.
intermē'nstruus *a.* of the new moon. *n.* new moon.
interminā'tus *ppa.* interminor. *a.* forbidden.
interminā'tus *a.* endless.
inte'rmin/or -ā'rī -ā'tus *vi.* threaten; forbid threateningly.
intermi'/sceō -scē're -scuī -xtum *vt.* mix, intermingle.
intermi'ssi/ō -ō'nis *f.* interruption.
interm/i'ttō -i'ttere -ī'sī -i'ssum *vt.* break off; interrupt; omit, neglect; allow to elapse. *vi.* cease, pause.
intermi'xtus *ppp.* intermisceō.
intermo'r/ior -ī -tuus *vi.*

die suddenly. **-tuus** falling unconscious.
intermu'ndi/a -ō'rum *n.pl.* space between worlds.
intermūrā'lis *a.* between two walls.
internā'tus *a.* growing among.
interneci'nus, interneci'vus *a.* murderous, of extermination.
interne'ci/ō -ō'nis *f.* massacre, extermination.
interne'ct/ō -ere *vt.* enclasp.
internō'di/a -ō'rum *n.pl.* space between joints.
internō'/scō -scere -vī -tum *vt.* distinguish between.
internū'nti/ō -ā're *vi.* exchange messages.
internū'nt/ius -ī & iī *m.*, **-ia -iae** *f.* messenger, mediator, go-between.
inte'rnus *a.* internal, civil. *n.pl.* domestic affairs.
i'nt/erō -e'rere -rī'vī -rī'tum *vt.* rub in; (*fig.*) concoct.
interpellā'ti/ō -ō'nis *f.* interruption.
interpellā't/or -ō'ris *m.* interrupter.
interpe'll/ō -ā're -ā'vī -ā'tum *vt.* interrupt; disturb, obstruct.
inte'rpolis *a.* made up.
inte'rpol/ō -ā're *vt.* renovate, do up; (*writing*) falsify
interp/ō'nō -ō'nere -o'suī -o'situm *vt.* put between or amongst insert; (*time*) allow to elapse; (*person*) introduce, admit; (*pretext, etc.*) put forward, interpose. **fidem —** pledge one's word. **sē —** interfere, become involved.
interposi'ti/ō -ō'nis *f.* introduction.
interpo'situs *ppp.* **interpōnō.**
interpo'sit/us -ūs *m.* obstruction.
inte'rpre/s -tis *m., f.* agent, negotiator; interpreter explainer, translator.
interpretā'ti/ō -ō'nis *f.* interpretation, exposition, meaning.
inte'rpret/or -ā'rī -ā'tus *vt.* interpret, explain, translate, understand. **-ā'tus** *a.* translated.
inte'rpr/imō -i'mere -e'ssī -e'ssum *vt.* squeeze.
interpū'ncti/ō -ō'nis *f.* punctuation.
interpū'nctus *a.* well-divided. *n.pl.* punctuation.
interquiē'/scō -scere -vī *vi.* rest awhile.
interrē'gn/um -ī *n.* regency, interregnum; interval between consuls.
inte'rr/ēx -ē'gis *m.* regent; deputy-consul. [unafraid.
inte'rritus *a.* undaunted,
interrogā'ti/ō -ō'nis *f.* question; (*law*) cross-examination; (*logic*) syllogism.
interrogātiu'ncul/a -ae *f.* short argument.
inte'rrog/ō -ā're -ā'vī -ā'tum *vt.* ask, put a question; (*law*) cross-examine, bring to trial.
interr/u'mpō -u'mpere -ū'pī -u'ptum *vt.* break up, sever; (*fig.*) break off, interrupt. **-u'ptē** *ad.* interruptedly.
intersae'p/iō -ī're -sī -tum *vt.* shut off, close.
intersci'/ndō -ndere -dī -ssum *vt.* cut off, break down.
inte'rs/erō -e'rere -ē'vī -itum *vt.* plant at intervals.
inte'rser/ō -ere -uī -tum *vt.* interpose.
inte'rsitus *ppp.* **interserō.**
interspīrā'ti/ō -ō'nis *f.* pause for breath.
intersti'n/guō -guere -ctum *vt.* mark, spot; extinguish.
interstri'ng/ō -ere *vt.* strangle.
inte'r/sum -e'sse -fuī *vi.* be between; be amongst, be present at; (*time*) elapse. **-est** there is a difference; it is of importance, it concerns.

it matters. **meā -est** it is important for me.
interte'xtus *a.* interwoven.
inte'rtra/hō -here -xī *vt.* take away.
intertrīme'nt/um -ī *n.* wastage; loss, damage. [fusion.
interturbā'ti/ō -ō'nis *f.* con-
interva'll/um -ī *n.* space, distance, interval; (*time*) pause, interval, respite; difference.
interve'll/ō -ere *vt.* pluck out; tear apart.
interv/e'niō -enī're -ē'nī -e'ntum *vi.* come on the scene, intervene; interfere (with), interrupt; happen, occur.
interve'nt/or -ō'ris *m.* intruder.
interve'nt/us -ūs *m.* appearance, intervention; occurence.
interve'r/tō (intervo'rtō) -tere -tī -sum *vt.* embezzle; rob, cheat.
intervī's/ō -ere -ī -um *vt.* have a look at, look and see; visit occasionally.
intervo'lit/ō -ā're *vi.* fly about amongst.
inte'rvom/ō -ere *vt.* throw up (amongst). [wicked.
intestā'bilis *a.* infamous,
intestā't/us *a.* intestate; not convicted by witnesses. **-ō** *ad.* without making a will.
intestī'nus *a.* internal. *n.* & *n.pl.* intestines, entrails.
inte'x/ō -ere -uī -tum *vt.* inweave embroider, interlace.
i'ntib/um -ī *n.* endive.
i'ntim/us *a.* innermost; deepest, secret; intimate. *m.* most intimate friend. **-ē** *ad.* most intimately, cordially.
inti'n/gō (inti'nguō) -gere -xī -ctum *vt.* dip in.
intolerā'bilis *a.* unbearable; irresistible.
intolera'ndus *a.* intolerable.
into'ler/āns -a'ntis *a.* impatient; unbearable. **-a'nter** *ad.* excessively.
intolera'nti/a -ae *f.* insolence.
i'nton/ō -ā're -uī -ā'tum *vi.* thunder, thunder out.
intō'nsus *a.* unshorn, unshaven; long-haired, bearded; uncouth.
into'r/queō -quē're -sī -tum *vt.* twist, wrap round; hurl at.
into'rtus *ppp.* intorqueō. *a.* twisted, curled; confused.
i'ntrā *ad.* inside, within. *pr.*(*with acc.*) inside, within; (*time*) within, during; (*amount*) less than, within the limits of.
intrā'bilis *a.* navigable.
intractā'bilis *a.* formidable.
intractā'tus *a.* not broken in; unattempted.
intrem/ī'scō -ī'scere -uī *vi.* begin to shake.
i'ntrem/ō -ere *vi.* tremble.
intre'pid/us *a.* calm, brave; undisturbed. **-ē** *ad.*
intrī'c/ō -ā're *vt.* entangle.
intrī'nsecus *ad.* on the inside.
intrī'tus *a.* not worn out.
intrīvī *perf.* interō.
i'ntrō *ad.* inside, in.
i'ntr/ō -ā're -ā'vī -ā'tum *vt.* & *i.* go in, enter; penetrate.
intrōd/ū'cō -ū'cere -ū'xī -u'ctum *vt.* bring in, introduce, escort in; institute.
intrōdu'cti/ō -ō'nis *f.* bringing in.
intro'/eō -ī're -iī -itum *vi.* go into, enter.
intrō'/ferō -fe'rre -tulī -lā'tum *vt.* carry inside.
intrōgre'/dior -dī -ssus *vi.* step inside.
intro'it/us -ūs *m.* entrance; beginning.
intrōlā'tus *ppp.* intrōferō.
intrōm/i'ttō -i'ttere -ī'sī -i'ssus *vt.* let in, admit.
intrō'rsum, intrō'rsus *ad.* inwards, inside.
intrōru'mp/ō -ere *vi.* break into. [in at.
intrōspe'ct/ō -ā're *vt.* look
intrōsp/i'ciō -i'cere -e'xī

-e'ctum *vt.* look inside; look at, examine.
i'ntubum, *see* **intibum.**
intu'/eor -ē'rī -itus *vt.* look at, watch; contemplate, consider; admire.
intum/ē'scō -ē'scere -uī *vi.* begin to swell, rise; increase; become angry.
intumulā'tus *a.* unburied.
in'tuor, *see* **intueor.**
intu'rbidus *a.* undisturbed; quiet.
i'ntus *ad.* inside, within, in; from within.
intū'tus *a.* unsafe; unguarded.
i'nul/a -ae *f.* elecampane.
inu'ltus *a.* unavenged; unpunished.
inu'mbr/ō -ā're *vt.* shade; cover.
inu'nd/ō -ā're -ā'vī -ā'tum *vt.* & *i.* overflow, flood.
in/u'nguō -u'nguere -ū'nxī -ū'nctum *vt.* anoint.
inurbā'n/us *a.* rustic, unmannerly, unpolished. **-ē** *ad.*
inu'rg/eō -ē're *vi.* push, butt.
inū'/rō -rere -ssī -stum *vt.* brand; (*fig.*) brand, inflict.
inūsitā't/us *a.* unusual, extraordinary. **-ē** *ad.* strangely.
inū'stus *ppp.* inūrō.
inū'tili/s *a.* useless; harmful. **-ter** *ad.* unprofitably.
inūti'lit/ās -ā'tis *f.* uselessness, harmfulness.
invā'/dō -dere -sī -sum *vt.* & *i.* get in, make one's way in; enter upon; fall upon, attack, invade; seize, take possession of.
inval/ē'scō -ē'scere -uī *vi.* grow stronger.
inva'lidus *a.* weak; inadequate.
invā'sī *perf.* invādō.
inve'cti/ō -ō'nis *f.* importing; invective.
inve'ctus *ppp.* invehō.
i'nve/hō -here -xī -ctum *vt.* carry in, bring in. **sē —** attack. **-hor** -hī -ctus *vi.* ride, drive, sail in or into, enter; attack; inveigh against.
invēndi'bilis *a.* unsaleable.
inv/e'niō -enī're -ē'nī -e'ntum *vt.* find, come upon; find out, discover; invent, contrive; win, get.
inve'nti/ō -ō'nis *f.* invention; (*rhet.*) compiling the subject-matter.
inve'nt/or -ō'ris *m.*, **-rīx** -rī'cis *f.* inventor, discoverer.
inve'ntus *ppp.* inveniō. *n.* invention, discovery.
invenu'stus *a.* unattractive; unlucky in love.
inverēcu'ndus *a.* immodest, shameless.
inve'rg/ō -ere *vt.* pour upon.
inve'rsi/ō -ō'nis *f.* transposition; irony.
inve'rsus *ppp.* invertō. *a.* upside down, inside out; perverted.
inve'r/tō -tere -tī -sum *vt.* turn over, invert; change, pervert.
invesperā'sc/it -ere *vi.* it is dusk.
investīgā'ti/ō -ō'nis *f.* search.
investīgā't/or -ō'ris *m.* investigator.
investī'g/ō -ā're -ā'vī -ā'tum *vt.* follow the trail of; (*fig.*) track down, find out.
inveterā'/scō -scere -vī *vi.* grow old (in); become established, fixed, inveterate; grow obsolete.
inveterā'ti/ō -ō'nis *f.* chronic illness.
inveterā'tus *a.* of long standing, inveterate.
inve'xī *perf.* invehō.
i'nvicem *ad.* in turns, alternately; mutually, each other.
invi'ctus *a.* unbeaten; unconquerable.
invide'nti/a -ae *f.* envy.
inv/i'deō -idē're -ī'dī -ī'sum *vt.* & *i.* cast an evil eye on; (*with dat.*) envy, grudge; begrudge.

invi'di/a -ae *f.* envy, jealousy, ill-will; unpopularity.
invidiō's/us *a.* envious, spiteful; enviable; invidious, hateful. **-ē** *ad.* spitefully.
i'nvidus *a.* envious, jealous, hostile.
invi'gil/ō -ā're *vi.* be awake over; watch over, be intent on.
inviolā'bilis *a.* invulnerable; inviolable.
inviolā't/us *a.* unhurt; inviolable. **-ē** *ad.* inviolately.
invīsitā'tus *a.* unseen, unknown, strange.
invī's/ō -ere -ī -um *vt.* go and see, visit, have a look at; inspect. [hostile.
invī'sus *a.* hateful, detested;
invī'sus *a.* unseen.
invītāme'nt/um -ī *n.* attraction, inducement.
invītā'ti/ō -ō'nis *f.* invitation; entertainment.
invītā't/us -ūs *m.* invitation.
invī't/ō -ā're -ā'vī -ā'tum *vt.* invite; treat, entertain; summon; attract, induce.
invī't/us *a.* against one's will, reluctant. **-ē** *ad.* unwillingly.
i'nvius *a.* trackless, impassable; inaccessible.
invocā'tus *ppp.* invocō.
invocā'tus *a.* unbidden, uninvited.
i'nvoc/ō -ā're -ā'vī -ā'tum *vt.* call upon, invoke; appeal to; call.
involā't/us -ūs *m.* flight.
invo'lit/ō -ā're *vi.* play upon.
i'nvol/ō -ā're *vi.* fly at, pounce on, attack.
involū'cr/e -is *n.* napkin.
involū'cr/um -ī *n.* covering, case.
involū'tus *ppp.* involvō. *a.* complicated.
invo'lv/ō -vere -vī -ū'tum *vt.* roll on; wrap up, envelop, entangle.
invo'lvol/us -ī *m.* caterpillar.
invulnerā'tus *a.* unwounded.

iō *interj.* (*joy*) hurrah! (*pain*) oh! (*calling*) ho there!
Iōa'nn/ēs -is *m.* John.
iocā'ti/ō -ō'nis *f.* joke.
io'c/or -ā'rī -ā'tus *vt.* & *i.* joke, jest.
iocō's/us *a.* humorous, playful. **-ē** *ad.* jestingly.
ioculā'ris *a.* laughable, funny. *n.pl.* jokes.
ioculā'rius *a.* ludicrous.
ioculā't/or -ō'ris *m.* jester.
io'cul/or -ā'rī *vi.* joke.
io'cul/us -ī *m.* a bit of fun.
io'c/us -ī *m.* (*pl.* -a -ō'rum *n.*) joke, jest. **extrā -um** joking apart. **per -um** for fun.
Iō'n/es -um *m.pl.* Ionians. **-ia** -iae *f.* Ionia. coastal district of Asia Minor. **-ius, -icus** *a.* Ionian. **-ium** -ī *n.* Ionian Sea, W. of Greece.
iō'ta *n.*(*indecl.*) Greek letter I.
Io'vis *gen.* Iuppiter.
Īphiana'ss/a -ae *f.* Iphigenia.
Īphigenī'/a -ae *f.* daughter of Agamemnon, who sacrificed her at Aulis to Diana.
i'ps/e, -a, -um -ī'us *pr.* self, himself, etc.; in person, for one's own part, of one's own accord, by oneself; just, precisely, very; the master, the host. **-i'ssimus** his very own self. **nunc -um** right now.
ī'r/a -ae *f.* anger, rage; object of indignation.
īrācu'ndi/a -ae *f.* irascibility, quick temper; rage, resentment.
īrācu'nd/us *a.* irascible, choleric; resentful. **-ē** *ad.* angrily.
īrā'sc/or -ī *vi.* be angry, get furious. [-ē *ad.*
īrā't/us *a.* angry, furious.
ī're *inf.* eō.
Ī'ri/s -dis (*acc.* -m) *f.* messenger of the gods; the rainbow.
īrōnī'/a -ae *f.* irony.
irrā'sus *a.* unshaven.

irrau/cē'scō -cē'scere -sī *vi.* become hoarse.
irredivī'vus *a.* irreparable.
irreligā'tus *a.* not tied.
irreligiō's/us *a.* impious. **-ē** *ad.*
irremeā'bilis *a.* from which there is no returning.
irreparā'bilis *a.* irretrievable.
irrepe'rtus *a.* undiscovered.
irrē'p/ō -ere -sī *vi.* steal into, insinuate oneself into.
irreprehē'nsus *a.* blameless.
irrequiē'tus *a.* restless.
irrese'ctus *a.* unpared.
irresolū'tus *a.* not slackened.
irrē't iō -ī're -iī -ī'tum *vt.* ensnare, entangle.
irreto'rtus *a.* not turned back.
irrevere'nti/a -ae *f.* disrespect.
irrevocā'bilis *a.* irrevocable; implacable.
irrevocā'tus *a.* without an encore.
irrī'/deō -dē're -sī -sum *vi.* laugh, joke. *vt.* laugh at, ridicule.
irrīdi'culē *ad.* unwittily.
irrīdi'cul/um -ī *n.* laughing-stock.
irrigā'ti/ō -ō'nis *f.* irrigation.
i'rrig/ō -ā're -ā'vī -ā'tum *vt.* water, irrigate; inundate; (*fig.*) shed over, flood, refresh.
irri'guus *a.* well-watered, swampy; refreshing.
irrī'si/ō -ō'nis *f.* ridicule, mockery.
irrī's/or -ō'ris *m.* scoffer.
irrī'sus *ppp.* irrīdeō.
irrī's us -ūs *m.* derision.
irrītā'bilis *a.* excitable.
irrītā'm/en -inis *n.* excitement, provocation.
irrītā'ti/ō -ō'nis *f.* incitement, irritation.
irrī't/ō -ā're -ā'vī -ā'tum *vt.* provoke, incite, enrage.
i'rrit us *a.* invalid, null and void; useless, vain, ineffective; (*person*) unsuccessful. **ad -um cadere** come to nothing.
irrogā'ti/ō -ō'nis *f.* imposing.
i'rrog/ō -ā're *vt.* propose (a measure) against; impose.
irrō'r/ō -ā're *vt.* bedew.
irr/u'mpō -u'mpere -ū'pī -u'ptum *vt.* & *i.* rush in, break in; intrude, invade.
i'rru/ō -ere -ī *vi.* force a way in, rush in, attack; (*speech*) make a blunder.
irru'pti/ō -ō'nis *f.* invasion, raid.
irru'ptus *ppp.* irrumpō.
irru'ptus *a.* unbroken.
is, e'a, id *pro.* he, she, it; this, that, the; such. **nōn is sum quī** I am not the man to. **id** (*with vi.*) for this reason. **id quod** what. **ad id** hitherto; for the purpose; besides. **in eō est** it has come to this; one is on the point of; it depends on this.
I'smar/us -ī *m.*, **-a -ō'rum** *n.pl.* Mt. Ismarus in Thrace. **-ius** *a.* Thracian.
Īso'crat/ēs -is *m.* Athenian orator and teacher of rhetoric.
istā'c *ad.* that way.
i'st/e, -a, -ud -ī'us *pro.* that of yours; (*law*) your client, the plaintiff, the defendant; (*contemptuous*) the fellow; that, such.
I'sthm/us (-os) -ī *m.* Isthmus of Corinth. **-ius** *a.* *n.pl.* the Isthmian Games.
ist/i'c, -ae'c, -u'c & o'c *pro.* that of yours, that.
istī'c *ad.* there; in this, on this occasion.
isti'nc *ad.* from there; of that.
istiu'smodī such, of that kind.
i'stō, istō'c *ad.* to you, there, yonder.
istō'rsum *ad.* in that direction.
istū'c *ad.* (to) there, to that.
i'ta *ad.* thus, so; as follows; yes; accordingly. **itane?** really? **nōn ita** not so very. **ita ut** just as. **ita . . . ut** so, to such an extent that; on condition that; only in so far

as. **ita . . . ut nōn** without. **ut . . . ita** just as . . . so; although . . . . nevertheless.
I'tal/ī -ō'rum *m.pl.* Italians; **-ia** -iae *f.* Italy. **-icus**, **-is**, **-us** *a.* Italian.
i'taque *conj.* and so, therefore, accordingly.
i'tem *ad.* likewise, also.
i't/er -i'neris *n.* way, journey, march; a day's journey or march; route, road, passage; (*fig.*) way, course. **— mihi est** I have to go to. **— dare** grant a right of way. **ex, in -inere** on the way, on the march. **māgnīs -ineribus** by forced marches.
iterā'ti/ō -ō'nis *f.* repetition.
i'ter/ō -ā're -ā'vī -ā'tum *vt.* repeat, renew; plough again.
i'terum *ad.* again, a second time. **— atque —** repeatedly.
I'thac/a -ae, **-ē** -ēs *f.* island W. of Greece, home of Ulysses. **-ē'nsis**, **-us** *a.* Ithacan. **-us** -ī *m.* Ulysses.
i'tidem *ad.* in the same way similarly.
i'ti/ō -ō'nis *f.* going.
i't/ō -ā're *vi.* go. [departure.
i't/us -ūs *m.* going, movement,
iu'b/a -ae *f.* mane; crest.
Iu'b/a -ae *m.* king of Numidia, supporter of Pompey.
iu'bar -is *n.* brightness, light.
iubā'tus *a.* crested.
iu'/beō -bē're -ssī -ssum *vt.* order, command, tell; (*greeting*) bid; (*med.*) prescribe; (*pol.*) decree, ratify, appoint.
iūcu'ndit/ās -ā'tis *f.* delight, enjoyment.
iūcu'nd/us *a.* delightful, pleasing. **-ē** *ad.* agreeably.
Iūdae'/a -ae *f.* Judaea, Palestine. **-us** -ī *m.* Jew. **-us**, **Iūda'icus** *a.* Jewish.
iū'd/ex -icis *m.* judge; (*pl.*) panel of jurors; (*fig.*) critic.
iūdicā'ti/ō -ō'nis *f.* judicial inquiry; opinion.
iūdicā't/um -ī *n.* judgment, precedent.
iūdicā't/us -ūs *m.* office of judge.
iūdiciā'lis *a.* judicial, forensic.
iūdiciā'rius *a.* judiciary.
iūdi'c/ium -ī & iī *n.* trial; court of justice; sentence; judgment, opinion; discernment, taste, tact. **in — vocāre**, **-ō arcessere** sue, summon.
iū'dic/ō -ā're -ā'vī -ā'tum *vt.* judge, examine, sentence, condemn; form an opinion of, decide; declare.
iugā'lis *a.* yoked together; nuptial.
iugā'ti/ō -ō'nis *f.* training (of a vine)
iū'ger/um -ī *n.* a land measure (240 x 120 feet).
iū'gis *a.* perpetual, never-failing.
iū'gl/āns -a'ndis *f.* walnut-tree.
iu'g/ō -ā're -ā'vī -ā'tum *vt.* couple, marry.
iugō'sus *a.* hilly. [Belt.
Iu'gul/ae -ā'rum *f.pl.* Orion's
iu'gul/ō -ā're -ā'vī -ā'tum *vt.* cut the throat of, kill, murder.
iu'gul/um -ī *n.*, **-us** -ī *m.* throat.
iu'g/um -ī *n.* (*animals*) yoke, collar; pair, team; (*mil.*) yoke of subjugation; (*mountain*) ridge, height, summit; (*astr.*) Libra, (*loom*) cross-beam; (*ship*) thwart; (*fig.*) yoke, bond.
Iugu'rth/a -ae *m.* king of Numidia, rebel against Rome. **-ī'nus** *a.*
Iū'l/ius -ī *m.* Roman family name, *esp.* Caesar; (*month*) July **-ius**, **-iā'nus** *a.*
Iū'l/us -ī *m.* son of Aeneas, Ascanius. **-ē'us** *a.* of Iulus; of Caesar; of July.
iūme'nt/um -ī *n.* beast of burden, pack-horse.
iu'nceus *a.* of rushes; slender.
iuncō'sus *a.* rushy.

iū'ncti/ō -ō'nis *f.* union.
iūnctū'r/a -ae *f.* joint; combination; relationship.
iū'nctus *ppp.* iungō. *a.* connected, attached.
iu'nc/us -ī *m.* rush.
iu'n/gō -gere iū'nxī iū'nctum *vt.* join together, unite; yoke, harness; mate; (*river*) span, bridge; (*fig.*) bring together, connect, associate; (*agreement*) make; (*words*) compound.
iū'ni/or -ō'ris *a.* younger.
iūni'per/us -ī *f.* juniper.
Iū'n/ius -ī *m.* Roman family name; (*month*) June. **-ius** *a.* of June.
Iū'n/ō -ō'nis *f.* Roman goddess, wife of Jupiter, patroness of women and marriage. **-ō'nius, -ōnā'lis** *a.* **-ōni'col/a** -ae *m.* worshipper of Juno. **-ōni'gen/a** -ae *m.* Vulcan.
Iu'ppiter Io'vis *m.* Jupiter, king of the gods, god of sky and weather. — **Stygius** Pluto. **sub Iove** in the open air.
iūrā't/or -ō'ris *m.* sworn judge.
iū'recōnsu'ltus, *see* **iūriscōnsultus.**
iūreiū'r/ō -ā're *vi.* swear.
iū'reperī'tus, *see* **iūrisperītus.** [brawl.
iū'rg/ium -ī & iī *n.* quarrel,
iū'rg/ō -ā're *vi.* quarrel, squabble. *vt.* scold.
iūridiciā'lis *a.* of law, juridical. [lawyer.
iū'riscōnsu'lt/us -ī *m.*
iū'risdi'cti/ō -ō'nis *f.* administration of justice; authority. [the law.
iū'risperī't/us *a.* versed in
iū'r/ō -ā're -ā'vī -ā'tum *vi.* & *t.* swear, take an oath; conspire. **in nōmen** — swear allegiance to. **in verba** — take a prescribed form of oath **-ātus** having sworn, under oath.
iūs iū'ris *n.* broth, soup.
iūs iū'ris *n.* law, right, justice; law-court; jurisdiction, authority. — **gentium** international law. — **pūblicum** constitutional law. **summum** — the strict letter of the law. — **dīcere** administer justice. **suī iūris** independent. **iūre** rightly, justly. [*n.* oath.
iūsiūra'ndum iūrisiūra'ndī
iu'ssī *perf.* iubeō.
iu'ssū *abl.m.* by order.
iu'ssus *ppp.* iubeō. *n.* order, command, prescription.
iūsti'ficus *a.* just-dealing.
iūsti'ti/a -ae *f.* justice, uprightness, fairness.
iūsti't/ium -ī & iī *n.* cessation of legal business.
iū'st/us *a.* just, fair; lawful, right; regular, proper. *n.* right. *n.pl.* rights; formalities, obsequies. **-ē** *ad.* duly, rightly.
iū'tus *ppp.* iuvō.
iuvenā'li/s *a.* youthful. *n.pl.* youthful games. **-ter** *ad.* vigorously, impetuously.
Iuvenā'l/is -is *m.* Juvenal, Roman satirist.
iuve'nc/a -ae *f.* heifer; girl.
iuve'nc/us -ī *m.* bullock; young man. *a.* young.
iuven/ē'scō -ē'scere -uī *vi.* grow up; grow young again.
iuvenī'li/s *a.* youthful. **-ter** *ad.*
iu'venis *a.* young. *m., f.* young man or woman (20-45 years), man, warrior.
iu'ven/or -ā'rī *vi.* behave indiscreetly.
iuve'nt/a -ae *f.* youth.
iuve'nt/ās -ā'tis *f.* youth.
iuve'nt/ūs -ū'tis *f.* youth, manhood; men, soldiers.
iu'v/ō -ā're iū'vī iū'tum *vt.* help, be of use to; please, delight. **-at mē** I am glad.
iu'xtā *ad.* near by, close; alike, just the same. *pr.* (*with*

acc.) close to, hard by; next to; very like, next door to. — ac, cum, quam just the same as.
iu'xtim *ad.* near; equally.
ī'vī *perf.* eō.
Ixī'/ōn -onis *m.* Lapith king, bound to a revolving wheel in Tartarus. **–o'neus** *a.* **–o'nid/ēs** -ae *m.* Pirithous. **–o'nid/ae** -ā'rum *m.pl.* Centaurs.

J, *see* **I**

K

Kale'nd/ae -ā'rum *f.pl.* Kalends, first day of each month.
Karthā'gō, *see* **Carthāgō.**

L

labā'sc/ō -ere *vi.* totter, waver.
lābē'cul/a -ae *f.* aspersion.
labe/fa'ciō -fa'cere -fē'cī -fa'ctum (*pass.* **–fī'ō** -fi'erī) *vt.* shake; (*fig.*) weaken, ruin.
labefa'ct/ō -ā're -ā'vī -ā'tum *vt.* shake; (*fig.*) weaken, destroy.
labe'll/um -ī *n.* lip.
lābe'll/um -ī *n.* small basin.
Labe'r/ius -ī *m.* Roman family name, *esp.* a writer of mimes.
lā'b/ēs -is *f.* sinking, fall; ruin, destruction.
lā'b/ēs -is *f.* spot, blemish; disgrace, stigma; (*person*) blot.
la'b/ia -iae *f.*, **–ium** -ī & iī *n.* lip.
Labiē'n/us -ī *m.* Roman surname, *esp.* Caesar's officer who went over to Pompey.
labiō'sus *a.* large-lipped.
la'bium, *see* **labia.**
la'b/ō -ā're *vi.* totter, be unsteady, give way; waver, hesitate, collapse.
lā'/bor -bī -psus *vi.* slide, glide; sink, fall; slip away, pass away; (*fig.*) fade, decline, perish; be disappointed, make a mistake.
la'b/or (**–ōs**) -ō'ris *m.* effort, exertion, labour; work, task; hardship, suffering, distress; (*astr.*) eclipse.
labō'rifer -ī *a.* sore afflicted.
labōriō's/us *a.* troublesome, difficult; industrious. **–ē** *ad.* laboriously, with difficulty.
labō'r/ō -ā're -ā'vī -ā'tum *vi.* work, toil, take pains; suffer, be troubled (with), be in distress; be anxious, worried. *vt.* work out, make, produce.
la'bōs, *see* **labor.**
la'br/um -ī *n.* lip; edge, rim. primis -īs gustāre acquire a smattering of.
lā'br/um -ī *n.* tub, vat; bath.
lābru'sc/a -ae *f.* wild vine.
lābru'sc/um -ī *n.* wild grape.
labyri'nth/us -ī *m.* labyrinth, maze, *esp.* that of Cnossos in Crete. **–eus** *a.* labyrinthine.
lac la'ctis *n.* milk.
Lacae'n/a -ae *f.* Spartan woman. *a.* Spartan.
Lacedae'm/ōn (**–ō**) -onis (*acc.* -ona) *f.* Sparta. **–o'nius** *a.* Spartan.
la'cer -ī *a.* torn, mangled, lacerated; tearing.
lacerā'ti/ō -ō'nis *f.* tearing.
laco'rn/a -ae *f.* cloak (worn in cold weather).
lacernā'tus *a.* cloaked.
la'cer/ō -ā're -ā'vī -ā'tum *vt.* tear, lacerate, mangle; (*ship*) wreck; (*speech*) slander, abuse; (*feeling*) torture, distress; (*goods, time*) waste, destroy.
lace'rt/a -ae *f.*, **–us** -ī *m.* lizard; a sea-fish.
lacertō'sus *a.* brawny.
lace'rt/us -ī *m.* upper arm, arm; (*pl.*) brawn, muscle.
lace'rtus, *see* **lacerta.**
lace'ss/ō -ere -ī'vī & iī -ī'tum

vt. strike, provoke, challenge; (*fig.*) incite, exasperate.
La'ches/is -is *f.* one of the Fates.
laci'ni/a -ae *f.* flap, corner (of dress).
Laci'n/ium -ī *n.* promontory in S. Italy, with a temple of Juno. **-ius** *a.*
La'c/ō (-ōn) -ō'nis *m.* Spartan; Spartan dog. **-ō'nicus** *a.* Spartan. *n.* sweating-bath. [gum-drop.
la'crim/a -ae *f.* tear; (*plant*)
lacrimā'bilis *a.* mournful.
lacrimābu'ndus *a.* bursting into tears.
la'crim/ō -ā're -ā'vī -ā'tum *vt.* & *i.* weep, weep for.
lacrimō'sus *a.* tearful; lamentable.
lacri'mul/a -ae *f.* tear, crocodile tear.
lacrum-, *see* **lacrim-**.
la'ct/āns -a'ntis *a.* giving milk; sucking.
lactā'ti/ō -ō'nis *f.* allurement.
la'ct/ēns -e'ntis *a.* sucking; milky, juicy.
lacte'olus *a.* milk-white.
la'ct/ēs -ium *f.pl.* guts, small intestines. [milk.
lactē'sc/ō -ere *vi.* turn to
la'cteus *a.* milky, milk-white.
la'ct/ō -ā're *vt.* dupe, wheedle.
lactū'c/a -ae *f.* lettuce.
lacū'n/a -ae *f* hole, pit; pool, pond; (*fig.*) deficiency.
lacū'n/ar -ā'ris *n.* panel-ceiling.
lacū'n/ō -ā're *vt.* panel.
lacūnō'sus *a.* sunken.
la'c/us -ūs *m.* vat, tank; lake; reservoir, cistern.
lae'/dō -dere -sī -sum *vt.* hurt, strike, wound; (*fig.*) offend, annoy, break.
Lae'l/ius -ī *m.* Roman family name, *esp.* the friend of Scipio.
lae'n/a -ae *f.* a lined cloak.
Lāē'rt/ēs -ae *m.* father of Ulysses. **-ius** *a.* **-i'adēs** *m.* Ulysses.
lae'sī *perf.* laedō.
lae'si/ō -ō'nis *f.* attack.
Laestry'gon/ēs -um *m.pl.* fabulous cannibals of Campania, founders of Formiae. **-ius** *a.*
lae'sus *ppp.* laedō.
laetā'bilis *a.* joyful.
laeti'fic/ō -ā're *vt.* gladden.
laeti'ficus *a.* glad, joyful.
laeti'ti/a -ae *f.* joy, delight, exuberance.
lae't/or -ā'rī -ā'tus *vi.* rejoice, be glad.
lae't/us *a.* glad, cheerful; delighting (in); pleasing, welcome; (*growth*) fertile, rich; (*style*) exuberant. **-ē** *ad.* gladly.
lae'v/us *a.* left; stupid; ill-omened, unfortunate; (*augury*) lucky, favourable. *f.* left hand. **-ē** *ad.* awkwardly.
la'gan/um -ī *n.* a kind of oil-cake.
lagē'/os -ī *f.* a Greek vine.
lagoe'n/a (lagō'na) -ae *f.* flagon. [grouse.
lagō'/is -idis *f.* a kind of
Lā'/ius -ī *m.* father of Oedipus. **-i'ad/ēs -ae** *m.* Oedipus.
la'll/ō -ā're *vi.* sing a lullaby.
lā'm/a -ae *f.* bog. [pieces.
la'mber/ō -ā're *vt.* tear to
la'mb/ō -ere -ī *vt.* lick, touch; (*river*) wash.
lāme'nt/a -ō'rum *n.pl.* lamentation.
lāmentā'bilis *a.* mournful, sorrowful.
lāmentā'rius *a.* sorrowful.
lāmentā'ti/ō -ō'nis *f.* weeping, lamentation.
lāme'nt/or -ā'rī -ā'tus *vi.* weep, lament. *vt.* weep for, bewail.
la'mi/a -ae *f.* witch.
lā'min/a (la'mmina, lāmna) -ae *f.* plate, leaf (of metal, wood); blade; coin.

la'mpa/s -dis *f.* torch; brightness, day. [king.
La'm/us -ī *m.* Laestrygonian
lā'n/a -ae *f.* wool.
lānā'r/ius -ī & ii *m.* woolworker.
lānā'tus *a.* woolly.
la'nce/a -ae *f.* spear, lance.
la'ncin/ō -ā're *vt.* tear up; squander.
lā'neus *a.* woollen.
languefa'c/iō -ere *vt.* make weary.
la'ngu/eō -ē're *vi.* be weary, be weak, droop; be idle, dull.
langu/ē'scō -ē'scere -uī *vi.* grow faint, droop.
langui'dulus *a.* languid.
la'nguid/us *a.* faint, languid, sluggish; listless, feeble. -ē *ad.*
la'ngu/or -ō'ris *m.* faintness, fatigue, weakness; dullness, apathy.
laniā't/us -ūs *m.* mangling; (*mind*) anguish.
laniē'n/a -ae *f.* butcher's shop.
lānifi'c/ium -ī & ii *n.* woolworking.
lāni'ficus *a.* wool-working.
lā'niger -ī *a.* fleecy. *m., f.* ram, sheep.
la'ni/ō -ā're -ā'vī -ā'tum *vt.* tear to pieces, mangle.
lani'st/a -ae *m.* trainer of gladiators, fencing-master; (*fig.*) agitator.
lāni't/ium -ī & ii *n.* woolgrowing.
la'n/ius -ī & ii *m.* butcher.
lante'rn/a -ae *f.* lamp.
lanternā'r/ius -ī & ii *m.* guide. [ness.
lānū'g/ō -inis *f.* down, woolli-
Lānu'v/ium -ī *n.* Latin town on the Appian Way. -ī'nus *a.*
lanx la'ncis *f.* dish, platter; (*balance*) scale.
Lāo'med/ōn-o'ntis *m.* king of Troy, father of Priam. -ontē'us, -o'ntius *a.* Trojan. -onti'ad/ēs -ae *m.* son of L.; (*pl.*) Trojans.

la'path/um -ī *n.*, -us -ī *f.* sorrel.
lapicī'd/a -ae *m.* stonecutter.
lapicīdī'n/ae -ā'rum *f.pl.* quarries.
lapidā'rius *a.* stone-.
lapidā'ti/ō -ō'nis *f.* throwing of stones. [thrower.
lapidā't/or -ō'ris *m.* stone-
lapi'deus *a.* of stones, stone-.
la'pid/ō -ā're *vt.* stone. *vi.* rain stones. [stone.
lapidō'sus *a.* stony; hard as
lapi'll/us -ī *m.* stone, pebble; precious stone, mosaic piece.
la'pi/s -dis *m.* stone; milestone, boundary-stone, tombstone; precious stone; marble; auctioneer's stand; (*abuse*) blockhead. bis ad eundem (offendere) *make the same mistake twice.* Juppiter — the Jupiter stone.
La'pith/ae -ā'rum & um *m.pl.* Lapiths, mythical people of Thessaly. -ae'us, -ē'ius *a.*
la'pp/a -ae *f.* goose-grass.
lā'psi/ō -ō'nis *f.* tendency.
lā'ps/ō -ā're *vi.* slip, stumble.
lā'psus *ppa.* lābor.
lā'ps/us -ūs *m.* fall, slide, course, flight; error, failure.
laqueā'r/ia -ium *n.pl.* panelled ceiling.
laqueā'tus *a.* panelled, with a panelled ceiling.
la'que/us -ī *m.* noose, snare, halter; (*fig.*) trap.
Lār La'ris *m.* tutelary deity, household god; hearth, home.
lā'rdum, *see* **lāridum**.
largi'ficus *a.* bountiful.
largi'fluus *a.* copious.
largi'loquus *a.* talkative.
la'rg/ior -ī'rī -ī'tus *vt.* give freely, lavish; bestow, confer. *vi.* give largesses.
la'rgit/ās -ā'tis *f.* liberality, abundance.
largī'ti/ō -ō'nis *f.* giving freely, distributing; bribery.

largī'tor -ō'ris *m.* liberal giver, dispenser; spendthrift; briber.
la'rg/us *a.* copious, ample; liberal, bountiful. **-ē, -iter** *ad.* plentifully, generously, very much. [bacon fat.
lā'rid/um (**lā'rdum**) -ī *n.*
Lāri'ss/a (**Lārī'sa**) -ae *f.* town in Thessaly. **-ae'us, -ē'nsis** *a.*
Lā'r/ius -ī *m.* lake Como.
la'ri/x -cis *f.* larch.
la'rv/a -ae *f.* ghost; mask.
larvā'tus *a.* bewitched.
la'san/um -ī *n.* pot.
lasarpī'cifer -ī *a.* producing asafoetida.
lascī'vi/a -ae *f.* playfulness; impudence, lewdness.
lascī'v/iō -ī're *vi.* frolic, frisk; run wild, be irresponsible.
lascī'vus *a.* playful, frisky; impudent, lustful.
laserpī'c/ium -ī & iī *n.* silphium.
lassitū'd/ō -inis *f.* fatigue, heaviness.
la'ss/ō -ā're *vt.* tire, fatigue.
la'ssulus *a.* rather weary.
la'ssus *a.* tired, exhausted.
lā'tē *ad.* widely, extensively. longē —que far and wide, everywhere.
la'tebr/a -ae *f.* hiding-place, retreat; (*fig.*) loophole, pretext.
latebri'col/a -ae *a.* low-living.
latebrō's/us *a.* secret, full of coverts; porous. **-ē** *ad.* in hiding.
la't/ēns -e'ntis *pres.p.* lateō. *a.* hidden, secret. **-e'nter** *ad.* in secret.
la't/eō -ē're -uī *vi.* lie hid, lurk, skulk; be in safety, live a retired life; be unknown, escape notice.
la'ter -is *m.* brick, tile. **-em** lavāre *waste one's time.*
laterā'm/en -inis *n.* earthenware.
late'rcul/us -ī *m.* small brick, tile; kind of cake.
lateri'cius *a.* of bricks. *n.* brickwork.
lāte'rna, *see* **lanterna.**
latē'sc/ō -ere *vi.* hide oneself.
la't/ex -icis *m.* water; any other liquid.
lati'bul/um -ī *n.* hiding-place, den, lair.
lāticlā'vius *a.* with a broad purple stripe. *m.* senator, patrician. [large estate.
lātifu'nd/ium -ī & iī *n.*
Latī'nit/ās -ā'tis *f.* good Latin, Latinity; Latin rights.
Latī'n/us *a.* Latin. *m.* legendary king of the Laurentians. **-ē** *ad.* in Latin, into Latin. — loquī speak Latin, speak plainly, speak correctly. — reddere translate into Latin.
lā'ti/ō -ō'nis *f.* bringing; proposing.
la'tit/ō -ā're *vi.* hide away, lurk, keep out of the way.
lātitū'd/ō -inis *f.* breadth, width; size; broad pronunciation.
La't/ium -ī *n.* district of Italy including Rome; Latin rights. **-ius, -ī'nus, -iā'ris** *a.* Latin. **-iar** -iā'ris *n.* festival of Jupiter Latiaris.
lātom-, *see* **lautum-.**
Lātō'n/a -ae *f.* mother of Apollo and Diana. **-ius** *a.* *f.* Diana. **-i'gen/ae** -ā'rum *pl.* Apollo and Diana.
lā't/or -ō'ris *m.* proposer.
Lātō'/us *a.* of Latona. *m.* Apollo. **-ius, -is** *a.* **-is** -idis *f.* Diana.
lātrā't/or -ō'ris *m.* barker.
lātrā't/us -ūs *m.* barking.
lā'tr/ō -ā're *vi.* bark; rant, roar. *vt.* bark at; clamour for.
la'tr/ō -ō'nis *m.* mercenary soldier; bandit, brigand; (*chess*) man.
latrōci'n/ium -ī & iī *n.* highway robbery, piracy.

latrō'cin/or -ā'rī -ā'tus *vi.* serve as a mercenary; be a brigand or pirate.
latru'ncul/us -ī *m.* brigand; (*chess*) man.
lātu'miae, *see* **lautumiae**.
lā'tus *ppp.* ferō.
lā'tus *a.* broad, wide; extensive; (*pronunciation*) broad; (*style*) diffuse.
la't/us -eris *n.* side, flank; lungs; body. — dare expose oneself. — tegere walk beside. -eris dolor pleurisy. ab -ere on the flank.
latu'scul/um -ī *n.* little side.
laudā'bili/s *a.* praiseworthy. **-ter** *ad.* laudably.
laudā'ti/ō -ō'nis *f.* commendation, eulogy; panegyric, testimonial.
laudā't/or -ō'ris *m.*, **-rīx** -rī'cis *f.* praiser, eulogizer; speaker of a funeral oration.
lau'd/ō -ā're -ā'vī -ā'tum *vt.* praise, commend, approve; pronounce a funeral oration over; quote, name. **-ā'tus** *a.* excellent.
laureā'tus *a.* crowned with bay; (*despatches*) victorious.
Laure'nt/ēs -um *m.pl.* Laurentians, people of ancient Latium. **-ius** *a.*
laure'ol/a -ae *f.* triumph.
lau're/us *a.* of bay. **-a** **-ae** *f.* bay-tree; crown of bay; triumph.
lauri'comus *a.* bay-covered.
lau'riger -ī *a.* crowned with bay.
lau'r/us -ī *f.* bay-tree; bay crown; victory, triumph.
laus lau'dis *f.* praise, approval; glory, fame; praiseworthy act, merit, worth.
lau'ti/a -ō'rum *n.pl.* State [banquet.
lauti'ti/a -ae *f.* luxury.
lautu'mi/ae -ā'rum *f.pl.* stone-quarry; prison.
lau't/us *ppp.* lavō. *a.* neat, elegant, sumptuous; fine, grand, distinguished. **-ē** *ad.* elegantly, splendidly; excellently.
lavā'br/um -ī *n.* bath.
lavā'ti/ō -ō'nis *f.* washing, bath; bathing gear.
Lāvī'n/ium -ī *n.* town of ancient Latium. **-ius** *a.*
la'v/ō -ā're lā'vī lau'tum (lavā'tum & lō'tum) *vt.* wash, bathe; wet, soak, wash away.
laxāme'nt/um -ī *n.* respite, relaxation.
la'xit/ās -ā'tis *f.* roominess.
la'x/ō -ā're -ā'vī -ā'tum *vt.* extend, open out; undo; slacken; (*fig.*) release, relieve; relax, abate. *vi.* (*price*) fall off.
la'x/us *a.* wide, loose, roomy; (*time*) deferred; (*fig.*) free, easy. **-ē** *ad.* loosely, freely.
le'/a -ae *f.* lioness.
leae'n/a -ae *f.* lioness.
Lea'nd/er -rī *m.* Hero's lover, who swam the Hellespont.
le'b/ēs -ē'tis *m.* basin, pan, cauldron.
lectī'c/a -ae *f.* litter, sedan [chair.
lecticā'r/ius -ī & iī *m.* litter-bearer.
lectī'cul/a -ae *f.* small litter; [bier.
lē'cti/ō -ō'nis *f.* selecting; reading, calling the roll.
lectisterniā't/or -ō'ris *m.* arranger of couches.
lectiste'rn/ium -ī & iī *n.* religious feast.
le'ctit/ō -ā're *vt.* read frequently.
lēctiu'ncul/a -ae *f.* light reading.
lē'ct/or -ō'ris *m.* reader.
le'ctul/us -ī *m.* couch, bed.
le'ct/us -ī *m.* couch, bed; bier.
lē'ctus *ppp.* legō. *a.* picked; choice, excellent.
Lē'd/a -ae, **-ē** -ēs *f.* mother of Castor, Pollux, Helen and Clytemnestra. **-ae'us** *a.*
lēgā'ti/ō -ō'nis *f.* mission, embassy; members of a mission; (*mil.*) staff appoint-

ment, command of a legion. **libera** — free commission (to visit provinces). **vōtīva** — free commission for paying a vow in a province.
lēgā't/or -ō'ris *m.* testator.
lēgā't/um -ī *n.* legacy, bequest.
lēgā't/us -ī *m.* delegate, ambassador; deputy, lieutenant; commander (of a legion).
lē'gifer -ī *a.* law-giving.
le'gi/ō -ō'nis *f.* legion (up to 6000 men); (*pl.*) troops, army.
legiōnā'r/ius *a.* legionary.
lēgi'rup/a -ae, **-iō** -iō'nis *m.* law-breaker.
lēgi'tim/us *a.* lawful, legal; right, proper. **-ē** *ad.* lawfully, properly.
legiu'ncul/a -ae *f.* small [legion.
lē'g/ō -ā're -ā'vī -ā'tum *vt.* send, charge, commission; appoint as deputy or lieutenant; (*will*) leave, bequeath.
le'g/ō -ere lē'gī lē'ctum *vt.* gather, pick; choose, select; (*sail*) furl; (*places*) traverse, pass, coast along; (*view*) scan; (*writing*) read, recite. **senātum** — call the roll of the senate.
lēgulē'/ius -ī & iī *m.* pettifogging lawyer.
legū'm/en -inis *n.* pulse, [bean.
le'mb/us -ī *m.* pinnace, cutter.
lēmniscā'tus *a.* beribboned.
lēmni'sc/us -ī *m.* ribbon (hanging from a victor's crown).
Lē'mn/os (-us) -ī *f.* Aegean island, abode of Vulcan. **-ius** *a.* **-ias** *f.* Lemnian woman. **-i'col/a** -ae *m.* Vulcan.
Le'mur/ēs -um *m.pl.* ghosts.
lē'n/a -ae *f.* procuress; seductress.
Lēnae'us *a.* Bacchic. *m.* Bacchus.
lēnī'm/en -inis *n.* solace, comfort.
lēnīme'nt/um -ī *n.* sop.
lē'n/iō -ī're -ī'vī & iī -ī'tum *vt.* soften, soothe, heal, calm.
lē'ni/s *a.* soft, smooth, mild, gentle, calm. **-ter** *ad.* softly, gently; moderately, halfheartedly.
lē'nit/ās -ā'tis *f.* softness, smoothness, mildness, tenderness.
lēnitū'd/ō -inis *f.* smoothness, [mildness.
lē'n/ō -ō'nis *m.* pander, brothel-keeper; go-between.
lēnōci'n/ium -ī & iī *n.* pandering; allurement; meretricious ornament.
lēnō'cin/or -ā'rī -ā'tus *vi.* pay court to; promote.
lēnō'nius *a.* pander's.
lēns le'ntis *f.* lentil.
lentē'sc/ō -ere *vi.* become sticky, soften; relax.
lenti'scifer -ī *a.* bearing mastic-trees.
lenti'sc/us -ī *f.* mastic-tree.
lentitū'd/ō -inis *f.* slowness, dullness, apathy.
le'nt/ō -ā're *vt.* bend.
le'ntulus *a.* rather slow.
le'nt/us *a.* sticky, sluggish; pliant; slow, lasting, lingering; (*person*) calm, at ease, indifferent. **-ē** *ad.* slowly; calmly, coolly.
lēnu'ncul/us -ī *m.* skiff.
le'/ō -ō'nis *m.* lion.
Leō'nid/ās -ae *m.* Spartan king who fell at Thermopylae.
leōnī'nus *a.* lion's.
Leontī'n/ī -ō'rum *m.pl.* town in Sicily. **-us** *a.*
le'pa/s -dis *f.* limpet.
le'pid/us *a.* pleasant, charming, neat, witty. **-ē** *ad.* neatly, charmingly; (*reply*) very well, splendidly.
le'p/ōs (**le'por**) -ō'ris *m.* pleasantness, charm; wit.
le'p/us -oris *m.* hare.
lepu'scul/us -ī *m.* young hare.
Le'rn/a -ae, **-ē** -ēs *f.* marsh near Argos, where Hercules

killed the Hydra. **-ae'us** *a.* Lernaean.
Le'sb/os (-us) **-ī** *f.* Aegean island, home of Alcaeus and Sappho. **-ius, -ō'us, -is** *a.* **-ias** -i'adis *f.* Lesbian woman.
lētā'lis *a.* deadly.
lētha'rgic/us **-ī** *m.* lethargic person.
lētha'rg/us **-ī** *m.* drowsiness.
Lē'th/ē **-ēs** *f.* river in the lower world, which caused forgetfulness. **-ae'us** *a.* of Lethe; infernal; soporific.
lē'tifer **-ī** *a.* fatal.
lē't/ō **-ā're** *vt.* kill.
lē't/um **-ī** *n.* death; destruction.
Leu'ca/s **-dis, -dia** **-diae** *f.* island off W. Greece. **-dius** *a.*
Leuco'the/a **-ae, -ē** **-ēs** *f.* Ino, a sea-goddess.
Leu'ctr/a **-ō'rum** *n.pl.* battlefield in Boeotia. **-icus** *a.*
levā'm/en -inis *n.* alleviation, comfort.
levāme'nt/um **-ī** *n.* mitigation, consolation.
levā'ti/ō **-ō'nis** *f.* relief; diminishing.
lē'vī *perf.* linō.
levi'culus *a.* rather vain.
levidē'nsis *a.* slight.
le'vip/ēs **-edis** *a.* light-footed.
le'vi/s *a.* (*weight*) light; (*mil.*) light-armed; (*fig.*) easy, gentle; (*importance*) slight, trivial; (*motion*) nimble, fleet; (*character*) fickle unreliable. **-ter** *ad.* lightly; slightly; easily.
lē'vis *a.* smooth; (*youth*) beardless, delicate.
leviso'mnus *a.* light-sleeping.
le'vit/ās **-ā'tis** *f.* lightness; nimbleness; fickleness, frivolity. [fluency.
lē'vit/ās **-ā'tis** *f.* smoothness;
le'v/ō **-ā're** *vt.* lighten, ease; (*fig.*) alleviate, lessen; comfort, relieve; impair; (*danger*) avert. **sē** — rise.
lē'v/ō **-ā're** *vt.* smooth, polish.
lē'v/or **-ō'ris** *m.* smoothness.
lēx **lē'gis** *f.* law, statute; bill; rule, principle; contract, condition. **lēgem ferre** propose a bill. **lēgem perferre** carry a motion. **lēge agere** proceed according to law. **sine lēge** out of control. [libation.
lībā'm en -inis *n.* offering,
lībāme'nt/um **-ī** *n.* offering, libation.
lībā'ti/ō **-ō'nis** *f.* libation.
lībe'll/a **-ae** *f.* small coin, as; level. **ad -am** exactly. **ex -ā** sole heir.
libe'll/us **-ī** *m.* small book; note-book, diary, letter; notice, programme, handbill; petition, complaint; lampoon.
li'b/ēns **-e'ntis** *a.* willing, glad. **-e'nter** *ad.* willingly, with pleasure.
li'b/er **-rī** *m.* inner bark (of a tree); book; register.
Lī'ber **-ī** *m.* Italian god of fertility, identified with Bacchus. **-ā'lia** **-ā'lium** *n.pl.* festival of Liber in March.
lī'ber **-ī** *a.* free, open, unrestricted, undisturbed; (*with abl.*) free from; (*speech*) frank; (*pol.*) free, not slave, democratic. **-ē** *ad.* freely, frankly, boldly.
Lī'ber/a **-ae** *f.* Proserpine; Ariadne.
līberā'li/s *a.* of freedom, of free citizens, gentlemanly, honourable; generous, liberal; handsome. **-ter** *ad.* courteously, nobly; generously.
līberā'lit/ās **-ā'tis** *f.* courtesy, kindness; generosity; bounty.
līberā'ti/ō **-ō'nis** *f.* delivery, freeing; (*law*) acquittal.
līberā't/or **-ō'ris** *m.* liberator, deliverer.
lī'ber/ī **-ō'rum** *m.pl.* children.
lī'ber/ō **-ā're** **-ā'vī** **-ā'tum** *vt.* free, set free, release; exempt; (*law*) acquit; (*slave*) give

freedom to. fidem — keep one's promise. nōmina — cancel debts.
līibe'rt/a -ae f. freedwoman.
lībe'rt/ās -ā'tis f. freedom, liberty; status of a freeman; (pol.) independence; freedom of speech, outspokenness.
lībertī'nus a. of a freedman, freed. m. freedman. f. freedwoman.
lībe'rt/us -ī m. freedman.
li'b/et (lu'bet) -ē're -uit & -itum est vi.(impers.) it pleases. mihi — I like. ut — as you please.
libīdinō's/us a. wilful, arbitrary, extravagant; sensual, lustful. -ē ad. wilfully.
libī'd/ō (lubī'dō) -inis f. desire, passion; wilfulness, caprice; lust. [fancy.
libit/a -ō'rum n.pl. pleasure,
Libitī'n/a -ae f. goddess of burials.
lī'b/ō -ā're -ā'vī -ā'tum vt. taste, sip, touch; pour (a libation), offer; extract, take out; impair.
lī'br/a -ae f. pound; balance, pair of scales. ad -am of equal size.
lībrāme'nt/um -ī n. level surface, weight (to give balance or movement); (water) fall.
librā'ri/a -ae f. head spinner.
librāri'ol/us -ī m copyist.
librā'r/ium -ī & iī n. bookcase. [copyist.
librā'rius a. of books. m.
lībrī'lis a. weighing a pound.
lī'brit/or -ō'ris m. slinger.
lī'br/ō -ā're -ā'vī -ā'tum vt. poise, hold balanced; swing, hurl. -ā'tus a.level; powerful.
lī'b/um -ī n. cake.
Libu'rn/ī -ō'rum m.pl. people of Illyria. -us a. Liburnian. -a -ae f. a fast galley, frigate.
Li'by/a -ae, -ē -ēs f. Africa. -cus, -ssus, -stinus, -stis a. African. -es -um m.pl. Libyans, people in N. Africa.
li'c/ēns -e'ntis a. free, bold, unrestricted. -e'nter ad. freely, lawlessly.
lice'nti/a -ae f. freedom, license; lawlessness, licentiousness.
li'c/eō -ē're -uī vi. be for sale, value at.
li'c/eor -ē'rī -itus vt. & i. bid (at an auction), bid for.
li'c/et -ē're -uit & -itum est vi.(impers.) it is permitted, it is lawful; (reply) all right; (conj.) although. mihi — I may.
Lici'n/ius -ī m. Roman family name, esp. with surname Crassus. -ius a.
licitā'ti/ō -ō'nis f. bidding (at a sale).
li'cit/or -ā'rī vi. make a bid.
li'citus a. lawful.
lī'c/ium -ī & iī n. thread.
lī'ct/or -ō'ris m. lictor, an attendant with fasces preceding a magistrate.
li'cuī perf. liceō; perf. liquēscō.
li'/ēn -ē'nis m. spleen.
ligā'm/en -inis n. band, bandage.
ligāme'nt/um -ī n. bandage.
Li'ger -is m. river Loire.
lignā'r/ius -ī & iī m. carpenter. [wood.
lignā'ti/ō -ō'nis f. fetching
lignā't/or -ō'ris m. woodcutter.
ligne'olus a. wooden.
li'gneus a. wooden.
li'gn/or -ā'rī vi. fetch wood.
li'gn/um -ī n. wood, firewood, timber. in silvam -a ferre carry coals to Newcastle.
li'g/ō -ā're -ā'vī -ā'tum vt. tie up, bandage; (fig.) unite.
li'g/ō -ō'nis m. mattock, hoe.
li'gul/a -ae f. shoe-strap.
Li'gu/r, Li'gu/s -ris m., f. Ligurian. -ria -riae f.

district of N.W. Italy. **-sticus, -stĭ'nus** *a.*
ligū'r/iō (ligu'rriō) -ī're *vt.* lick; eat daintily; (*fig.*) feast on, lust after.
ligūrī'ti/ō -ō'nis *f.* daintiness.
Li'gus, *see* **Ligur.**
ligu'str/um -ī *n.* privet.
lī'l/ium -ī & iī *n.* lily; (*mil.*) spiked pit.
lī'm/a -ae *f.* file; (*fig.*) revision.
limā'tulus *a.* refined.
limā'tius *ad.* more elegantly.
lī'm/āx -ā'cis *f.* slug, snail.
lī'mb/us -ī *m.* fringe, hem.
lī'm/en -inis *n.* threshold, lintel; doorway, entrance; house, home; (*fig.*) beginning.
lī'm/es -itis *m.* path between fields, boundary; path, track, way; frontier, boundary-line.
lī'm/ō -ā're -ā'vī -ā'tum *vt.* file; (*fig.*) polish, refine; file down, investigate carefully; take away from.
līmō'sus *a.* muddy.
li'mpidus *a.* clear, limpid.
lī'mus *a.* sidelong, askance.
lī'm/us -ī *m.* mud, slime, dirt.
lī'm/us -ī *m.* ceremonial apron.
lī'ne/a -ae *f.* line, string; plumb-line; boundary. ad -am, rectā -ā vertically. **extrēmā -ā amāre** love at a distance.
līneāme'nt/um -ī *n.* line; feature; outline.
līneus *a.* flaxen, linen.
li'ng/ō -ere *vt.* lick.
li'ngu/a -ae *f.* tongue; speech, language; tongue of land. — Latīna Latin.
li'ngul/a -ae *f.* tongue of land.
lī'niger -ī *a.* linen-clad.
li'n/ō -ere lē'vī li'tum *vt.* daub, smear; overlay; (*writing*) rub out; (*fig.*) befoul.
li'nqu/ō -ere lī'quī *vt.* leave, quit; give up, let alone; (*pass.*) faint, swoon. **-itur ut** it remains to.
linteā'tus *a.* canvas.
li'nte/ō -ō'nis *m.* linen-weaver.
li'nt/er -ris *f.* boat; trough.
li'nte/um -ī *n.* linen cloth, canvas; sail.
li'nteus *a.* linen.
lintri'cul/us -ī *m.* small boat.
lī'n/um -ī *n.* flax; linen; thread, line, rope; net.
Li'par/a -ae, -ē -ēs *f.* island N. of Sicily, *mod.* Lipari. **-ae'us, -ē'nsis** *a.*
li'pp/iō -ī're *vi.* have sore eyes.
lippitū'd/ō -inis *f.* inflammation of the eyes.
li'ppus *a.* blear-eyed, with sore eyes; (*fig.*) blind.
lique/fa'ciō -fa'cere -fē'cī -fa'ctum (*pass.* -fī'ō) *vt.* melt, dissolve; decompose; (*fig.*) enervate. [clear.
li'qu/ēns -e'ntis *a.* fluid,
liquē'sc/ō -ere li'cuī *vi.* melt; clear; (*fig.*) grow soft, waste away.
li'qu/et -ē're li'cuit *vi.* (*impers.*) it is clear, it is evident. **nōn** — not proven.
lī'quī *perf.* linquō.
li'quid/us *a.* fluid, liquid, flowing; clear, transparent, pure; (*mind*) calm, serene. *n.* liquid water. **-ō** *ad.* clearly.
li'qu/ō -ā're *vt.* melt; strain.
lī'qu/or -ī *vi.* flow; (*fig.*) waste away.
li'qu/or -ō'ris *m.* fluidity; liquid, the sea.
Lī'r/is -is *m.* river between Latium and Campania.
līs lī'tis *f.* quarrel, dispute; lawsuit; matter in dispute. **lītem aestimāre** assess damages.
litā'ti/ō -ō'nis *f.* favourable sacrifice.
lī'tera, *see* **littera.**
lītigā't/or -ō'ris *m.* litigant.
lītigiō'sus *a.* quarrelsome, contentious; disputed.
līti'g/ium -ī & iī *n.* quarrel.
lī'tig/ō -ā're *vi.* quarrel; go to law.
li't/ō -ā're -ā'vī -ā'tum *vi*

offer an acceptable sacrifice, obtain favourable omens; (*with dat.*) propitiate. *vt.* offer successfully.
lītorā'lis *a.* of the shore.
lītoʹreus *a.* of the shore.
liʹtter/a -ae *f.* letter (of the alphabet). **-ae -ā'rum** *f.pl.* writing; letter, dispatch; document, ordinance; literature; learning, scholarship. **-ās** discere learn to read and write. homō trium **-ārum** thief (*i.e.* fur). sine **-īs** uncultured.
litterā'rius *a.* of reading and writing.
litterā't/or -ō'ris *m.* grammarian.
litterātū'r/a -ae *f.* writing, alphabet.
litterā't/us *a.* with letters on it, branded; educated, learned. **-ē** *ad.* in clear letters; literally;
litteʹrul/a -ae *f.* small letter; short note; (*pl.*) studies.
litū'r/a -ae *f.* correction, erasure, blot.
liʹtus *ppp.* linō.
lī't/us -oris *n.* shore, beach, coast; bank. — arāre labour in vain.
liʹtu/us -ī *m.* augur's staff; trumpet; (*fig.*) starter.
lī'v/ēns -e'ntis *pres.p.* līveō. *a.* bluish, black and blue.
lī'v/eō -ē're *vi.* be black and blue; envy.
līvē'sc/ō -ere *vi.* turn black and blue.
līvi'dulus *a.* a little jealous.
lī'vidus *a.* bluish, black and blue; envious, malicious.
Lī'v/ius -ī Roman family name, *esp.* the first Latin poet; the famous historian, Livy. **-ius, -ia'nus** *a.*
lī'v/or -ō'ris *m.* bluish colour; envy, malice.
li'x/a -ae *m.* sutler, camp-follower.
locā'ti/ō -ō'nis *f.* leasing; lease, contract.
locātō'rius *a.* concerned with leases.
lo'cit/ō -ā're *vt.* let frequently.
lo'c/ō -ā're -ā'vī -ā'tum *vt.* place, put; give in marriage; let, lease, hire out; contract for; (*money*) invest.
lo'cul/us -ī *m.* little place; (*pl.*) satchel, purse.
lo'cupl/ēs -ē'tis *a.* rich, opulent; reliable, responsible.
locuplē't/ō -ā're *vt.* enrich.
lo'c/us -ī *m.* (*pl.* -ī *m.* & -a *n.*) place, site, locality, region; (*mil.*) post; (*theatre*) seat; (*book*) passage; (*speech*) topic, subject, argument; (*fig.*) room, occasion; situation, state; rank, position. **-ī** individual spots. **-a** regions, ground. **-ī** commūnēs general arguments. **-ō** (*with gen.*) instead of. in **-ō** opportunely. eō **-ī** in the position. intereā **-ī** meanwhile.
locu'st/a -ae *f.* locust.
locū'ti/ō -ō'nis *f.* speech; pronunciation.
locū'tus *ppa.* loquor.
lō'd/īx -ī'cis *f.* blanket.
lo'gic/a -ō'rum *n.pl.* logic.
lo'g/os (-us) -ī *m.* word; idle talk; witticism.
lōlīg-, *see* **lollīg-**.
lo'l/ium -ī & iī *n.* darnel.
lollī'g/ō -inis *f.* cuttle-fish.
lōme'nt/um -ī *n.* face-cream.
Londi'n/ium -ī *n.* London.
longae'vus *a.* aged.
longē *ad.* far, far off; (*time*) long; (*comp.*) by far, very much. — esse be far away, of no avail. — latēque everywhere.
longi'nquit/ās -ā'tis *f.* length: distance; duration.
longi'nquus *a.* distant, remote; foreign, strange; lasting, wearisome; (*hope*) long deferred.
longitū'd/ō -inis *f.* length; duration. in **-inem** lengthwise.
longiu'sculus *a.* rather long.
lo'ngul/us *a.* rather long. **-ē** *ad.* rather far.

longu'r/ius -ī & ii *m.* long pole.

lo'ng/us *a.* long; vast; (*time*) long, protracted, tedious; (*hope*) far-reaching. **-a nāvis** warship. **-um est** it would be tedious. **nē -um faciam** *to cut a long story short.*

loquā'cit/ās -ā'tis *f.* talkativeness.

loquā'culus *a.* somewhat talkative.

lo'qu/āx -ā'cis *a.* talkative, chattering. **-ā'citer** *ad.*

loque'll/a -ae *f.* language, words.

lo'/quor -quī cū'tus *vt.* & *i.* speak, talk, say; talk about, mention; (*fig.*) indicate. **rēs -quitur ipsa** the facts speak for themselves.

lōrā'r/ius -ī & ii *m.* flogger.

lōrā'tus *a.* strapped.

lō'reus *a.* of leather strips.

lōrī'c/a -ae *f.* breastplate; parapet.

lōrīcā'tus *a.* mailed.

lō'rip/ēs -edis *a.* bandy-legged.

lō'r/um -ī *n.* strap; whip, lash; leather charm; (*pl.*) reins.

lō't/os (-us) -ī *f.* lotus.

lō'tus *ppp.* lavō.

lu'bēns, lu'bet, lubī'dō, *see* **libēns, libet, libīdō.**

lube'nti/a -ae *f.* pleasure.

lū'bric/ō -ā're *vt.* make slippery.

lū'bricus *a.* slippery, slimy; gliding, fleeting; (*fig.*) dangerous, hazardous.

Lū'ca bōs *f.* elephant.

Lūca'n/ia -iae *f.* district of S. Italy. **-us** *a.* Lucanian. *m.* the epic poet Lucan. **-ica** *f.* kind of sausage.

lū'c/ar -ā'ris *n.* forest-tax.

luce'll/um -ī *n.* small gain.

lū'/ceō -cē're -xī *vi.* shine, be light; (*impers.*) dawn, be daylight; (*fig.*) shine, be clear. meridiē nōn -cēre (*argue*) *that black is white.*

Lū'cer/ēs -um *m.pl.* a Roman patrician tribe.

Lūce'r/ia -iae *f.* town in Apulia. **-ī'nus** *a.*

luce'rn/a -ae *f.* lamp; (*fig.*) *midnight oil.*

lūcē'sc/ō (**lūcī'scō**) -ere *vi.* begin to shine, get light, dawn.

lū'cid/us *a.* bright, clear; (*fig.*) lucid. **-ē** *ad.* clearly.

lū'cifer -ī *a.* light-bringing. *m.* morning-star, Venus; day.

lūci'fugus *a.* shunning the light.

Lūcī'l/ius -ī *m.* Roman family name, *esp.* the first Latin satirist.

Lūcī'n/a -ae *f.* goddess of childbirth.

lūcī'scō, *see* **lūcēscō.**

Lucrē't/ius -ī *m.* Roman family name, *esp.* the philosophic poet. **-ia** -iae *f.* wife of Collatinus, ravished by Tarquin.

lucri'fug/a -ae *m.* non-profiteer.

Lucrī'n/us -ī *m.* lake near Baiae, famous for oysters. **-us, -ē'nsis** *a.*

lu'cr/or -ā'rī -ā'tus *vt.* gain, win, acquire.

lucrō'sus *a.* profitable.

lu'cr/um -ī *n.* profit, gain; greed; wealth. **-ī facere** gain, get the credit of. **-ō esse** be of advantage. **in -īs pōnere** count as gain.

luctā'm/en -inis *n.* struggle, exertion.

luctā'ti/ō -ō'nis *f.* wrestling; fight, contest.

luctā't/or -ō'ris *m.* wrestler.

lūcti'ficus *a.* baleful.

lūcti'sonus *a.* mournful.

lu'ct/or -ā'rī -ā'tus *vi.* wrestle; struggle, fight.

lūctuō'sus *a.* sorrowful, lamentable.

lū'ct/us -ūs *m.* mourning, lamentation; mourning (dress).

lūcubrā'ti/ō -ō'nis *f.* work by lamplight, nocturnal study.
lū'cubr/ō -ā're -ā'vī -ā'tum *vi.* work by night. *vt.* compose by night.
lūculе'nt/us *a.* bright; (*fig.*) brilliant, excellent, rich, fine. **-ē** *ad.* splendidly, right. **-er** *ad.* very well.
Lūcu'll/us -ī *m.* Roman surname, *esp.* the conqueror of Mithridates.
Lu'cum/ō (**Lu'cmō**) -ō'nis *m.* Etruscan prince or priest.
lū'c/us -ī *m.* grove; wood.
lū'di/a -ae *f.* woman gladiator.
lūdi'br/ium -ī & iī *n.* mockery, derision; laughing-stock; sport, play. **-iō** habēre make fun of.
lūdibu'ndus *a.* playful; safely, easily.
lū'dic/er -rī *a.* playful; theatrical. **-um** -ī *n.* public show, play; sport.
lūdificā'ti/ō -ō'nis *f.* ridicule; tricking.
lūdificā't/or -ō'ris *m.* mocker.
lūdi'fic/ō -ā're, **-or** -ā'rī -ā'tus *vt.* make a fool of, ridicule; delude, thwart.
lū'di/ō -ō'nis *m.* actor.
lū'd/ius -ī & iī *m.* actor; gladiator.
lū'/dō -dere -sī -sum *vi.* play; sport, frolic; dally, make love. *vt.* play at; amuse oneself with; mimic, imitate; ridicule, mock; delude.
lū'd/us -ī *m.* game, sport, play; (*pl.*) public spectacle, games; school; (*fig.*) child's play; fun, jest; (*love*) dalliance. **-um** dare humour. **-ōs** facere put on a public show; make fun of.
lue'll/a -ae *f.* atonement.
lu'/ēs -is *f.* plague, pest; misfortune.
Lugdū'n/um -ī *n.* town in E.Gaul, *mod.* Lyons. **-ē'nsis** *a.*
lū'/geō -gē're -xī *vt.* & *i.* mourn; be in mourning.
lū'gubris *a.* mourning; disastrous; (*sound*) plaintive. *n.pl.* mourning dress.
lu'mb/ī -ō'rum *m.pl.* loins.
lumbrī'c/us -ī *m.* worm.
lū'm/en -inis *m.* light; lamp, torch; day; eye; life; (*fig.*) ornament, glory; clarity.
lūminā'r/e -is *n.* window.
lūminō'sus *a.* brilliant.
lū'n/a -ae *f.* moon; month; crescent.
lūnā'ris *a.* of the moon.
lūnā'tus *a.* crescent-shaped.
lū'n/ō -ā're *vt.* bend into a crescent.
lu'/ō -ere -ī *vt.* pay; atone for; avert by expiation.
lu'p/a -ae *f.* she-wolf; prostitute.
lupā'n/ar -ā'ris *n.* brothel.
lupā'tus *a.* toothed. *m.* & *n.pl.* curb.
Lupe'rc/us -ī *m.* Pan; priest of Pan. **-al** -ā'lis *n.* a grotto sacred to Pan. **-ā'lia** -ā'lium *n.pl.* festival of Pan in February.
lupī'nus *a.* wolf's.
lupī'n/us -ī *m.*, **-um** -ī *n.* lupin; sham money, counters.
lu'p/us -ī *m.* wolf; (*fish*) pike; toothed bit; grapnel. — in fābulā *talk of the devil.*
lū'ridus *a.* pale yellow, ghastly pallid.
lū'r/or -ō'ris *m.* yellowness.
lūsci'ni/a -ae *f.* nightingale.
luscitiō'sus *a.* purblind.
lu'scus *a.* one-eyed.
lū'si/ō -ō'nis *f.* play.
Lūsitā'n/ia -iae *f.* part of W. Spain, including *mod.* Portugal. **-us** *a.*
lū'sit/ō -ā're *vi.* play.
lū's/or -ō'ris *m.* player; humorous writer.
lūstrā'lis *a.* lustral, propitiatory; quinquennial.
lūstrā'ti/ō -ō'nis *f.* purification; roving.
lū'str/ō -ā're -ā'vī -ā'tum *vt.*

purify; (*motion*) go round, encircle, traverse; (*mil.*) review; (*eyes*) scan, survey; (*mind*) consider; (*light*) illuminate. [brothels.
lu'str/or -ā'rī *vi.* frequent
lu'str/um -ī *n.* den, lair; (*pl.*) wild country; (*fig.*) brothels, debauchery.
lū'str/um -ī *n.* purificatory sacrifice; (*time*) five years.
lū'sus *ppp.* lūdō.
lū's/us -ūs *m.* play, game, sport; dalliance.
lūte'olus *a.* yellow.
Lute'ti/a -ae *f.* town in N. Gaul, *mod.* Paris.
lū'teus *a.* yellow, orange.
lu'teus *a.* of clay; muddy, dirty, (*fig.*) vile.
lu'tit/ō -ā're *vt.* throw mud at.
lutule'ntus *a.* muddy, filthy; (*fig.*) foul. [yellow.
lū't/um -ī *n.* dyer's weed;
lu't/um -ī *n.* mud, mire; clay.
lūx lū'cis *f.* light; daylight; day; life; (*fig.*) public view; glory, encouragement, enlightenment. lūce in the daytime. prīmā lūce at daybreak. lūce carentēs the dead.
lū'xī *perf.* lūceō; *perf.* lūgeō.
lu'x/or -ā'rī *vi.* live riotously.
luxu'ri/a -ae, **–ēs** -ē'ī *f.* rankness profusion; extravagance, luxury.
luxu'ri/ō -ā're, **–or** -ā'rī *vi.* grow to excess, be luxuriant; (*fig.*) be exuberant, run riot.
luxuriō's/us *a.* luxuriant; excessive, extravagant; voluptuous. **–ē** *ad.* voluptuously.
lu'x/us -ūs *m.* excess, debauchery pomp.
Lyae'/us -ī *m.* Bacchus; wine.
Lycae'/us -ī *m.* mountain in Arcadia, sacred to Pan.
Lycā'/ōn -onis *m.* father of Callisto, the Great Bear. **–o'nius** *a.*
Lycē'/um (**Lycī'um**) -ī *n.* Aristotle's school at Athens.
lychnū'ch/us -ī *m.* lampstand.
ly'chn/us -ī *m.* lamp.
Ly'ci/a -ae *f.* country in S.W. Asia Minor. **–us** *a.* Lycian.
Ly'ctius *a.* Cretan.
Lycu'rg/us -ī *m.* Thracian king killed by Bacchus; Spartan lawgiver; Athenian orator.
Lȳ'd/ia -iae *f.* country of Asia Minor. **–us** -ī *m.* Lydian. **–ius** *a.* Lydian; Etruscan.
ly'mph/a -ae *f.* water.
lymphā'ticus *a.* crazy, frantic.
lymphā'tus *a.* distracted.
Ly'nc/eus -eī *m.* keen-sighted Argonaut.
lynx ly'ncis *m., f.* lynx.
ly'r/a -ae *f.* lyre; lyric poetry.
ly'ricus *a.* of the lyre, lyrical.
Ly'si/ās -ae *m.* Athenian orator.

M

Ma'ced/ō -onis *m.* Macedonian. **–o'nia** *f.* Macedonia. **–o'nius**, **–o'nicus** *a.*
mace'll/um -ī *n.* market.
ma'c/eō -ē're *vi.* be lean.
ma'c/er -rī *a.* lean, meagre; poor.
māce'ri/a -ae *f.* wall.
mā'cer/ō -ā're *vt.* soften; (*body*) enervate; (*mind*) distress.
macē'sc/ō -ere *vi.* grow thin.
machae'r/a -ae *f.* sword.
machaero'phor/us -ī *m.* soldier armed with a sword.
Machā'/ōn -onis *m.* legendary Greek surgeon. **–o'nius** *a.*
mā'chin/a -ae *f.* machine, engine; (*fig.*) scheme, trick
māchināme'nt/um -ī *n.* engine.
māchinā'ti/ō -ō'nis *f.* mechanism, machine; (*fig.*) contrivance.

măchinā't/or -ō'ris *m.* engineer; (*fig.*) contriver.
mā'chin/or -ā'rī -ā'tus *vt.* devise, contrive; (*fig.*) plot, scheme.
ma'ci/ēs -ē'ī *f.* leanness, meagreness; poorness.
macile'ntus *a.* thin.
macrē'sc/ō -ere *vi.* grow thin.
macritū'd/ō -inis *f.* leanness.
macroco'll/um -ī *n.* large size of paper.
mactā'bilis *a.* deadly.
mactā't/us -ūs *m.* sacrifice
ma'cte blessed; well done !
ma'ct/ō -ā're -ā'vī -ā'tum *vt.* sacrifice; punish, kill.
ma'ct/ō -ā're *vt.* glorify.
ma'cul/a -ae *f.* spot, stain; (*net*) mesh; (*fig.*) blemish, fault. [stain, defile.
ma'cul/ō -ā're -ā'vī -ā'tum *vt.*
maculō'sus *a.* dappled, mottled; stained, polluted.
made/fa'ciō -fa'cere -fē'cī -fa'ctum (*pass.* **-fī'ō** -fi'erī) *vt.* wet, soak.
ma'd/eō -ē're *vi.* be wet, be drenched; be boiled soft; (*comedy*) be drunk; (*fig.*) be steeped in.
madē'sc/ō -ere *vi.* get wet, become moist.
ma'didus *a.* wet, soaked; sodden; drunk.
madu'ls/a -ae *m.* drunkard.
Maea'nd/er (**-ros**) -rī *m.* a winding river of Asia Minor; winding, wandering.
Maecēn/ā's -ā'tis *m.* friend of Augustus, patron of poets.
mae'n/a -ae *f.* sprat.
Mae'na/s -dis *f.* Bacchante.
Mae'nal/us (**-os**) -ī *m.*, **-a** -ō'rum *n.pl.* mountain range in Arcadia. **-ius**, **-is** *a.* of Maenalus; Arcadian.
Mae'n/ius -ī *m.* Roman family name. -ia columna whipping-post in the Forum. -iā'num *n.* balcony.
Maeo'ni/a -ae *f.* Lydia. **-dēs** -dae *m.* Homer. **-us**, **-s** *a.* Lydian; Homeric; Etruscan.
Maeō'ti/s -dis *f.* Sea of Azov. **-cus**, **-us** *a.* Scythian, Maeotic. [be sad.
mae'r/eō -ē're *vi.* mourn,
mae'r/or -ō'ris *m.* mourning, sorrow, sadness.
maesti'ti/a -ae *f.* sadness, melancholy.
mae'st/us *a.* sad, sorrowful; gloomy; mourning. **-iter** *ad.*
măgā'li/a -um *n.pl.* huts.
ma'ge, *see* **magis**.
ma'gicus *a.* magical.
ma'gis (**ma'ge**) *ad.* more. eō — the more, all the more.
magi'st/er -rī *m.* master, chief, director, (*school*) teacher; (*fig.*) instigator. — equitum chief of cavalry, second in command to a dictator. — mōrum censor. — sacrōrum chief priest.
magiste'r/ium -ī & ii *n.* presidency, tutorship.
magi'str/a -ae *f.* mistress, instructress.
magistrā't/us -ūs *m.* magistracy, office; magistrate, official.
māgnani'mit/ās -ā'tis *f.* greatness. [brave.
māgna'nimus *a.* great,
Ma'gn/ēs -ē'tis *m.* Magnesian; magnet. **-ē'sia** *f.* district of Thessaly. **-ē'sius**, **-ē'ssus**, **-ē'tis** *a.*
māgni'dicus *a.* boastful.
māgnifice'nti/a -ae *f.* greatness, grandeur; pomposity.
māgni'fic/ō -ā're *vt.* esteem highly.
māgni'fic/us (*comp.* -e'ntior *sup.* -enti'ssimus) *a.* great, grand, splendid; pompous. **-ē** *ad.* grandly; pompously.
māgniloque'nti/a -ae *f.* elevated language; pomposity.
māgni'loquus *a.* boastful.
māgnitū'd/ō -inis *f.* great-

ness, size, large amount; dignity. [much.
māgno'pere *ad.* greatly, very
mā'gn/us (*comp.* mā'ior *sup.* mā'ximus) *a.* great, large, big, tall; (*voice*) loud; (*age*) advanced; (*value*) high, dear; (*fig.*) grand, noble, important. avunculus — great-uncle. -a loquī boast. -ī aestimāre think highly of. -ī esse be highly esteemed. -ō stāre cost dear. -ō opere very much.
ma'g/us -ī *m.* wise man; magician. *a.* magic.
Mā'i/a -ae *f.* mother of Mercury. **-us** -ī *m.* May. *a.* of May
māie'st/ās -ā'tis *f.* greatness, dignity, majesty; treason. -ātem laedere, minuere offend against the sovereignty of. lēx -ātis law against treason.
mā'i/or -ō'ris *comp.* māgnus. — nātū older, elder. **-ō'rēs** -ō'rum *m.pl.* ancestors. in -us crēdere, ferre exaggerate.
māiu'sculus *a.* somewhat greater; a little older.
mā'l/a -ae *f.* cheek, jaw.
mala'ci/a -ae *f.* dead calm.
ma'lacus *a.* soft.
ma'le (*comp.* pēius, *sup.* pessimē) *ad.* badly, wrongly, unfortunately; not; (*with words having bad sense*) very much. — est animō I feel ill. — sānus insane. — dīcere abuse, curse. — facere harm.
maledi'cti/ō -ō'nis *f.* abuse.
maledi'ct/um -ī *n.* curse.
male'dic/us *a.* scurrilous. **-ē** *ad.* abusively.
malefa'ct/um -ī *n.* wrong.
malefi'c/ium -ī & iī *n.* misdeed, wrong, mischief.
male'fic/us *a.* wicked. *m.* criminal. **-ē** *ad.*
malesuā'dus *a.* seductive.
male'vol/ēns -e'ntis *a.* spiteful.
malevole'nti/a -ae *f.* ill-will.
male'volus *a.* ill-disposed, malicious.
mā'lifer -ī *a.* apple-growing.
mali'gnit/ās -ā'tis *f.* malice; stinginess.
mali'gn/us *a.* unkind, ill-natured, spiteful; stingy; (*soil*) unfruitful; (*fig.*) small, scanty. **-ē** *ad.* spitefully; grudgingly.
mali'ti/a -ae *f.* badness, malice; roguishness.
malitiō's/us *a.* wicked, crafty. **-ē** *ad.*
maliv-, *see* **malev-**.
mā'lle *inf.* mālō.
malle'ol/us -ī *m.* hammer; (*mil.*) fire-brand.
ma'lle/us -ī *m.* hammer, mallet, maul.
mā'l/ō -le -uī *vt.* prefer, would rather.
māloba'thr/um -ī *n.* an oriental perfume.
mā'luī *perf.* mālō.
mā'l/um -ī *n.* apple, fruit.
mā'l/us -ī *f.* apple-tree.
mā'l/us -ī *m.* mast, pole.
ma'l/us (*comp.* pē'ior *sup.* pe'ssimus) *a.* bad, evil, harmful; unlucky; ugly. ī in -am rem go to hell! **-um** -ī *n.* evil, wrong, harm, misfortune; (*interj.*) mischief.
ma'lv/a -ae *f.* mallow.
Mā'mer/s -tis *m.* Mars. **-tī'n/ī** -ō'rum *m.pl.* mercenary troops who occupied Messana.
mammi'll/a ae *f.* breast.
ma'mm/a -ae *f.* breast; teat.
mānā'bilis *a.* penetrating.
ma'nc/eps -ipis *m.* purchaser; contractor.
manci'p/ium -ī & iī *n.* formal purchase; property; slave. [deliver up.
ma'ncip/ō -ā're *vt.* sell,
mancup-, *see* **mancip-**.
ma'ncus *a.* crippled.
mandā't/um -ī *n.* commission, command; (*law*) contract.

mandā'tus -ūs *m.* command.
ma'nd/ō -ā're -ā'vī -ā'tum *vt.* entrust, commit; commission, command.
ma'nd/ō -ere -ī mā'nsum *vt.* chew, eat, devour.
ma'ndr/a -ae *f.* drove of cattle.
mandū'c/us -ī *m.* masked figure of a glutton.
mā'ne *n.*(*indecl.*) morning. *ad.* in the morning, early.
ma'n/eō -ē're mā'nsī mā'nsum *vi.* remain; stay, stop; last, abide, continue. *vt.* wait for, await. in condiciōne — abide by an agreement.
Mā'n/ēs -ium *m.pl.* ghosts, shades of the dead; the lower world; bodily remains.
ma'ng/ō -ō'nis *m.* dealer.
ma'nic/ae -ā'rum *f.pl.* sleeves, gloves; handcuffs.
manicā'tus *a.* with long sleeves.
mani'cul/a -ae *f.* little hand.
manife'st/ō -ā're *vt.* disclose.
manife'st/us *a.* clear, obvious; convicted, caught. -ō *ad.* clearly, evidently.
manipl-, *see* **manipul-**.
manipulā'ris *a.* of a company. *m.* private, in the ranks; fellow-soldier.
manipulā'tim *ad* by companies.
mani'pul/us -ī *m.* bundle (*esp.* of hay); (*mil.*) company.
Ma'nl/ius -ī *m.* Roman family name, *esp.* the saviour of the Capitol from the Gauls; a severe disciplinarian. -**ius**, -**iā'nus** *a.*
ma'nn/us -ī *m.* Gallic horse.
mā'n/ō -ā're -ā'vī -ā'tum *vi.* flow, drip, stream; (*fig.*) spread, emanate.
mā'nsī *perf.* maneō.
mā'nsi/ō -ō'nis *f.* remaining, stay.
mā'nsit/ō -ā're *vi.* stay on.
mānsuē/fa'ciō -fa'cere -fē'cī -fa'ctum (*pass.* -fī'ō -fi'erī) *vt.* tame.
mānsuē'/scō -scere -vī -tum *vt.* tame. *vi.* grow tame, grow mild.
mānsuētū'd/ō -inis *f.* tameness; gentleness.
mānsuē't/us *ppp.* mānsuēscō. *a.* tame; mild, gentle. -ē *ad.*
mā'nsus *ppp.* mandō; *ppp.* maneō.
mantē'l/e -is *n.* napkin, towel.
mantē'l/um -ī *n.* cloak.
ma'ntic/a -ae *f.* knapsack.
manti'cin/or -ā'rī -ā'tus *vi.* be a prophet.
ma'nt/ō -ā're *vi.* remain, wait.
Ma'ntu/a -ae *f.* birthplace of Vergil in N. Italy.
manuā'lis *a.* for the hand.
manu'bi/ae -ā'rum *f.pl.* money from sale of booty.
manū'br/ium -ī & iī *n.* handle, haft.
manuleā'tus *a.* with long sleeves.
manūmi'ssi/ō -ō'nis *f.* emancipation (of a slave).
manūm/i'ttō -i'ttere -ī'sī -i'ssum *vt.* emancipate, make free.
manupre't/ium -ī & iī *n.* pay, wages, reward.
ma'n/us -ūs *f.* hand; corps, band, company; (*elephant*) trunk; (*art*) touch; (*work*) handiwork, handwriting; (*war*) force, valour, hand to hand fighting; (*fig.*) power. — extrēma finishing touch. — ferrea grappling-iron. -um dare give up, yield. -ū artificially. -ū mittere emancipate. ad -um at hand. in -ū obvious; subject. in -ūs venīre come to hand. in -ibus well known; at hand. in -ibus habēre be engaged on; fondle. per -ūs forcibly. per -ūs trādere hand down.
mapā'li/a -um *n.pl.* huts.
ma'pp/a -ae *f.* napkin, cloth.
Ma'rath/ōn -ō'nis *f.* Attic

village famous for Persian defeat. -ō'nius *a.*

Marce'll/us -ī *m.* Roman surname. *esp.* the captor of Syracuse. -ia -iō'rum *n.pl.* festival of the Marcelli.

ma'rc/eō -ē're *vi.* droop. be faint.

marcē'sc/ō -ere *vi.* waste away. grow feeble.

ma'rcidus *a.* withered; enervated.

Ma'rc/ius -ī *m.* Roman family name. *esp.* Ancus. fourth kind. -ius, -iā'nus *a.*

ma'r/e -is *n.* sea. — nostrum Mediterranean. — inferum Tyrrhenian Sea. — superum Adriatic.

Mareō'ticus *a.* Mareotic; Egyptian.

margarī't/a -ae *f.* pearl.

ma'rgin/ō -ā're *vt.* put a border or kerb on.

ma'rg/ō -inis *m., f.* edge. border. boundary. — cēnae side-dishes.

Marī'c/a -ae *f.* nymph of Minturnae.

marī'nus *a.* of the sea.

maritā'lis *a.* marriage-.

marī'timus *a.* of the sea. maritime. coastal. *n.pl.* coastal area.

marī't/ō -ā're *vt.* marry.

marī't/us -ī *m.* husband. *a.* nuptial.

Ma'r/ius -ī *m.* Roman family name. *esp.* the victor over Jugurtha and the Teutons. **-ius, -iā'nus** *a.*

ma'rmor -is *n.* marble; statue. tablet; sea.

marmo'reus *a.* of marble; like marble.

Ma'r/ō -ō'nis *m.* surname of Vergil.

ma'rr/a -ae *f.* kind of hoe.

Mars Ma'rtis *m.* god of war. father of Romulus; war. conflict; planet Mars. aequō Marte on equal terms. suō Marte by one's own exertions.

Ma'rti/us *a.* of Mars; of March; warlike **-ā'lis** *a.* of Mars

Ma'rs/ī -ō'rum *m.pl.* people of central Italy. famous as fighters **-us**, **-icus** *a.* Marsian.

marsu'pp/ium -ī & iī *n.* purse.

Martī'col/a -ae *m.* worshipper of Mars.

Martī'gen/a -ae *m.* son of Mars.

mās ma'ris *m.* male. man. *a.* male; manly.

mā'sculus *a.* male. masculine; manly.

Masinī'ss/a -ae *m.* king of Numidia.

ma'ss/a -ae *f.* lump. mass.

Ma'ssic/us -ī *m.* mountain in Campania, famous for vines. **-um** -ī *n.* Massic wine.

Massi'li/a -ae *f.* Greek colony in Gaul. *mod.* Marseilles. **-ē'nsis** *a.*

mastī'gi/a -ae *n.* scoundrel.

mastrū'c/a -ae *f.* sheepskin. **-ā'tus** *a.* wearing sheepskin.

ma'tar/a -ae, **-is** -is *f.* Celtic javelin.

mate'lli/ō ō'nis *m.* pot.

mā't/er -ris *f.* mother. Māgna — Cybele.

māte'rcul/a -ae *f.* poor mother.

māte'ri/a -ae, **-ēs** -ē'ī *f.* matter. substance; wood. timber; (*fig.*) subject-matter. theme; occasion. opportunity; (*person*) ability. character.

māteriā'r/ius -ī & iī *m.* timber-merchant.

māte'riēs, *see* **māteria.**

māteriā'tus *a.* timbered.

māte'ri/or -ā'rī *vi.* fetch wood.

māte'rnus *a.* mother's.

māte'rter/a -ae *f.* aunt (maternal).

mathēma'tic/us -ī *m.* mathematician; astrologer.
mātricī'd/a -ae *m.* matricide.
mātricī'd/ium -ī & iī *n.* a mother's murder.
mātrimō'n/ium -ī & iī *n.* marriage.
mā'trimus *a.* whose mother is still alive.
mātrō'n/a -ae *f.* married woman, matron, lady.
mātrōnā'lis *a.* a married woman's.
ma'tul/a -ae *f.* pot.
mātūr/ē'scō -ē'scere -uī *vi.* ripen.
mātū'rit/ās -ā'tis *f.* ripeness; (*fig.*) maturity, perfection, height.
mātū'r/ō -ā're -ā'vī -ā'tum *vt.* bring to maturity; hasten, be too hasty with. *vi.* make haste.
mātū'r/us *a.* ripe, mature; timely, seasonable; early. **-ē** *ad.* at the right time; early, promptly.
Mātū't/a -ae *f.* goddess of dawn.
mātūtī'nus *a.* morning, early.
Mau'r/us -ī *m.* Moor. *a.* Moorish, African. **-itā'ni/a** -ae *f.* Mauretania, *mod.* Morocco. **-ū'sius** *a.* [a.
Mā'vor/s -tis *m.* Mars. **-tius**
maxi'll/a -ae *f.* jaw.
mā'ximē *ad.* most, very much, especially; precisely, just; certainly, yes. cum — just as. quam — as much as possible.
māxi'mit/ās -ā'tis *f.* great size.
mā'ximus *sup.* māgnus.
māxum-, *see* **māxim-**.
māzo'nom/us -ī *m.* dish.
mea'pte my own.
meā't/us -ūs *m.* movement, course.
mēca'stor *interj.* by Castor!
mē'cum with me.
Mēdē'/a -ae *f.* Colchian wife of Jason, expert in magic. **-is** *a.* magical.
me'd/eor -ē'rī *vi.* (*with dat.*) heal, remedy. **-entēs** -entum *m.pl.* doctors.
me'ddix tu'ticus *m.* senior Oscan magistrate.
mediastī'n/us -ī *m.* drudge.
mē'dic/a -ae *f.* lucern (kind of clover).
medicā'bilis *a.* curable.
medicā'm/en -inis *n.* drug, medicine; cosmetic; (*fig.*) remedy.
medicāme'nt/um -ī *n.* drug, medicine; potion, poison; (*fig.*) relief; embellishment.
medicā't/us -ūs *m.* charm.
medicī'n/a -ae *f.* medicine; cure; (*fig.*) remedy, relief.
me'dic/ō -ā're -ā'vī -ā'tum *vt.* cure; steep, dye.
me'dic/or -ā'rī *vt.* & *i.* cure.
me'dicus *a.* healing. *m.* doctor.
medi'et/ās -ā'tis *f.* mean.
medi'mn/um -ī *n.*, **-us** -ī *m.* bushel.
medio'cri/s *a.* middling, moderate, average. **-ter** *ad.* moderately, not particularly; calmly.
medio'crit/ās -ā'tis *f.* mean, moderation; mediocrity.
Mediolā'n/um -ī *n.* town in N. Italy, *mod.* Milan. **-ē'nsis** *a.* [preparation, drill.
meditāme'nt/um -ī *n.*
meditā'ti/ō -ō'nis *f.* thinking about; preparation, practice.
mediterrā'neus *a.* inland.
me'dit/or -ā'rī -ā'tus *vt.* & *i.* think over, contemplate, reflect; practise, study. **-ā'tus** *a.* studied.
me'di/us *a.* middle, the middle of; intermediate; intervening; middling, moderate; neutral. *n.* middle; public. *m.* mediator. **-um complecti** clasp round the waist. **-um**

sē gerere be neutral. -ō midway. -ō temporis meanwhile. in -um for the common good. in -um prōferre publish. dē -ō tollere do away with. ē -ō abīre die, disappear. in -ō esse be public. in -ō positus open to all. in -ō relinquere leave undecided.
me'dius fi'dius *interj.* by Heaven!
me'dix, *see* **meddix.**
medu'lli/a -ae *f.* marrow, pith. [heart.
medu'llitus *ad.* from the
medu'llul/a -ae *f.* marrow.
Mē'd/us -ī *m.* Mede, Persian. **-us, -icus** *a.*
Medū's/a -ae *f.* Gorgon, whose look turned everything to stone. **-ae'us** *a.* — equus Pegasus.
Megalē'nsi/a (**Megalē'sia**) -um *n.pl.* festival of Cybele in April.
Me'gar/a -ae *f.*, -ō'rum *n.pl.* town in Greece near the Isthmus. **-ē'us, -icus, -us** *a.* Megarean.
megistā'n/es -um *m.pl.* grandees.
mehe'rcules, mehe'rcule, mehe'rcle *interj.* by Hercules!
mē'i/ō -ere *vi.* make water.
mel me'llis *n.* honey. [choly.
melancho'licus *a.* melan-
me'lē *pl.* melos.
Mele'ag/er (**-ros**) -rī *m.* prince of Calydon.
me'licus *a.* musical; lyrical.
melilō't/os -ī *f.* kind of clover.
melimē'l/a -ō'rum *n.pl.* honey-apples.
Mēli'n/um -ī *n.* Melian white.
me'li/or -ō'ris *a.* better.
melisphy'll/um -ī *n.* balm.
Me'lit/a -ae *f.* Malta. **-ē'nsis** *a.* Maltese.
me'lius *n.* melior. *ad.* better.
meliu'scul/us *a.* rather better. **-ē** *ad.* fairly well.
me'llifer -ī *a.* honey-making.
mellī'tus *a.* honeyed; sweet.
me'l/os -ī *n.* tune, song.
Melpo'men/ē -ēs *f.* Muse of tragedy.
membrā'n/a -ae *f.* skin, membrane, slough; parchment.
membrā'nul/a -ae *f.* piece of parchment.
membrā'tim *ad.* limb by limb; piecemeal; in short sentences.
me'mbr/um -ī *n.* limb, member; part, division; clause.
mē'met *emphatic form of* **mē.**
me'min/ī -isse *vi* (*with gen.*) remember, think of; mention.
Me'mn/ōn -onis *m.* Ethiopian king, killed at Troy. **-o'nius** *a.*
me'mor -is *a.* mindful, remembering; in memory (of). **-iter** *ad.* from memory; accurately.
memorā'bilis *a.* memorable, remarkable.
memora'ndus *a.* noteworthy.
memorā't/us -ūs *m.* mention.
memo'ri/a -ae *f.* memory, remembrance; time, life-time; history. haec — our day. -ae prōdere hand down to posterity. post hominum -am since the beginning of history.
memori'ol/a -ae *f.* weak memory.
me'mor/ō -ā're -ā'vī -ā'tum *vt.* mention, say, speak. **-ā'tus** *a.* famed.
Me'mph/is -is & idos *f.* town in middle Egypt. **-ī'tēs, -ī'tis, -ī'ticus** *a.* of Memphis; Egyptian.
Mena'nd/er (**-ros**) -rī *m.* Greek writer of comedy. **-rē'us** *a.*
me'nd/a -ae *f.* fault.
mendā'c/ium -ī & iī *n.* lie.
mendāciu'ncul/um -ī *n.* fib.

me'nd/āx -ā'cis *a.* lying; deceptive, unreal. *m.* liar.
mendī'cit/ās -ā'tis *f.* beggary.
mendī'c/ō -ā're, -or -ā'rī *vi.* beg, go begging.
mendī'cus *a.* beggarly, poor. *m.* beggar.
medō's/us *a.* faulty; wrong, mistaken. **-ē** *ad.*
me'nd/um -ī *n.* fault, blunder.
Menelā'/us -ī *m.* brother of Agamemnon, husband of Helen. **-ē'us** *a.* [clus.
Menoeti'ad/ēs -ae *m.* Patro-
mēns me'ntis *f.* mind, understanding; feelings, heart; idea, plan, purpose; courage. **venit in mentem** it occurs. **mente captus** insane. **eā mente ut** with the intention of.
mē'ns/a -ae *f.* table; meal, course; counter, bank. **secunda —** dessert.
mēnsā'r/ius -ī & iī *m.* banker.
mē'nsi/ō -ō'nis *f.* (*metre*) quantity.
mē'ns/is -is *m.* month.
mē'ns/or -ō'ris *m.* measurer, surveyor.
mēnstruā'lis *a.* for a month.
mē'nstruus *a.* monthly; for a month. *n.* a month's provisions.
mē'nsul/a -ae *f.* little table.
mēnsū'r/a -ae *f.* measure, measurement; standard, standing; amount, size, capacity.
mē'nsus *ppa.* mētior.
me'nt/a -ae *f.* mint.
me'nti/ō -ō'nis *f.* mention, hint.
me'nt/ior -ī'rī -ī'tus *vi.* lie, deceive. *vt.* say falsely; feign, imitate. **-iēns** -ie'ntis *m.* fallacy. **-ī'tus** *a.* lying, false.
Me'ntor -is *m.* artist in metalwork; ornamental cup. **-eus** *a.*
me'nt/um -ī *n.* chin.
me'/ō -ā're *vi.* go, pass.
mephī't/is -is *f.* noxious vapour, malaria.
merā'cus *a.* pure.
mercā'bilis *a.* buyable.
mercā't/or -ō'ris *m.* merchant, dealer.
mercātū'r/a -ae *f.* commerce; purchase; goods.
mercā't/us -ūs *m.* trade, traffic; market, fair.
mercē'dul/a -ae *f.* poor wages, small rent.
mercēnnā'rius *a.* hired, mercenary. *m.* servant.
me'rc/ēs -ē'dis *f.* pay, wages, fee; bribe; rent; (*fig.*) reward, retribution, cost.
mercimō'n/ium -ī & iī *n.* wares, goods.
me'rc/or -ā'rī -ā'tus *vt.* trade in, purchase.
Mercu'r/ius -ī *m.* messenger of the gods, god of trade, thieves, speech and the lyre. **stēlla -ī** planet Mercury. **-iā'lis** *a.*
me'rd/a -ae *f.* dung.
mere'nd/a -ae *f.* lunch.
me'r/eō -ē're -uī, -eor -ē'rī -itus *vt.* & *i.* deserve; earn, win, acquire; (*mil.*) serve. **bene — dē** do a service to, serve well. **— equō** serve in the cavalry.
meretrī'cius *a.* a harlot's.
meretrī'cul/a -ae *f.* pretty harlot.
me'retr/īx -ī'cis *f.* harlot.
me'rg/ae -ā'rum *f.pl.* pitchfork.
me'rg/es -itis *f.* sheaf.
me'r/gō -gere -sī -sum *vt.* dip, immerse, sink; (*fig.*) bury, plunge, drown.
me'rg/us -ī *m.* (*bird*) diver.
merīdiā'nus *a.* midday; southerly.
merīdiā'ti/ō -ō'nis *f.* siesta.
merī'di/ēs -ē'ī *f.* midday, noon; south. [siesta.
merī'di/ō -ā're *vi.* take a
me'rit/ō -ā're *vt.* earn.
meritō'rius *a.* money-earning. *n.pl.* lodgings.

me'rit/us *ppp.* mereō. *a.* deserved, just. **-um** -ī *n.* service, kindness, merit; blame. **-ō** *ad.* deservedly.
me'rop/s -is *f.* bee-eater.
me'rsī *perf* mergō.
me'rs/ō -ā're *vt.* immerse, plunge; overwhelm.
me'rsus *ppp.* mergō.
me'rul/a -ae *f.* blackbird.
me'r/um -ī *n.* wine.
me'rus *a.* pure, undiluted; bare, mere.
merx me'rcis *f.* goods, wares.
Messa'll/a -ae *m.* Roman surname *esp.* — **Corvīnus** Augustan orator, soldier and literary patron. **-ī'na** -ī'nae *f.* wife of emperor Claudius; wife of Nero.
Mess'n/a -ae *f.* Sicilian town, *mod.* Messina.
me'ssis -is *f.* harvest.
me'ssor -ō'ris *m.* reaper.
messō'rius *a.* a reaper's.
mess'uī *perf.* metō.
me'ssus *ppp.* metō.
mē't/a -ae *f.* pillar at each end of the Circus course; turning-point, winning-post; (*fig.*) goal, end, limit.
meta'll/um -ī *n.* mine, quarry; metal.
mētā't/or -ō'ris *m.* surveyor.
Metau'r/us -ī *m.* river in Umbria, famous for the defeat of Hasdrubal.
Mete'll/us -ī *m.* Roman surname *esp.* the commander against Jugurtha.
Mēthy'mn/a -ae *f.* town in Lesbos. **-ae'us** *a.*
mē'/tior -tī'rī -nsus *vt.* measure, measure out; traverse; (*fig.*) estimate, judge.
me'/tō -tere -ssuī -ssum *vt.* reap, gather; mow, cut down.
mē't/or -ā'rī -ā'tus *vt.* measure off, lay out.
metrē't/a -ae *f.* liquid measure (about 9 gallons).
metuculō'sus *a.* frightful.
me't/uō -u'ere -uī -ū'tum *vt.* fear, be apprehensive.
me't/us -ūs *m.* fear, alarm, anxiety.
me'us *a.* my, mine.
mī *dat.* ego; *voc.* & *m.pl.* **meus.**
mī'c/a -ae *f.* crumb, grain.
mi'c/ō -ā're -uī *vi.* quiver, flicker, beat, flash, sparkle.
Mi'd/ās -ae *m.* Phrygian king whose touch turned everything to gold.
migrā'ti/ō -ō'nis *f.* removal, change.
mi'gr/ō -ā're -ā'vī -ā'tum *vi.* remove, change, pass away. *vt.* transport, transgress.
mī'l/es -itis *m.* soldier, infantryman; army troops.
Mīlē'/tus -tī *f.* town in Asia Minor. **-sius** *a.*
mī'li/a -um *n.pl.* thousands. — passuum miles.
mīliā'r/ium (**milliā'rium**) -ī & iī *n.* mile-stone.
mīlitā'ri/s *a.* military, a soldier's. **-ter** *ad.* in a soldierly fashion.
mīli'ti/a -ae *f.* military service, war; the army. **-ae** on service. **domī -aeque** at home and abroad.
mī'lit/ō -ā're *vi.* serve, be a soldier.
mi'l/ium -ī & iī *n.* millet.
mī'l/le (*pl.* -ia) *num.* a thousand. — **passūs** a mile.
mīll/ē'simus, **-ē'nsimus** *a.* thousandth.
mīllia, *see* **mīlia.**
mīlliā'rium, *see* **mīliārium.**
mī'lli/ēns, **-ēs** *ad.* a thousand times.
Mi'l/ō -ō'nis *m.* tribune who killed Clodius and was defended by Cicero. **-ōniā'nus** *a.*
Milti'ad/ēs -is *m.* Athenian general, victor at Marathon.
mīluī'nus *a.* resembling a kite; rapacious.
mī'lu/us (**mī'lvus**) -ī *m.* kite; gurnard.
mī'm/a -ae *f.* actress.

Mima'lloni/s -dis *f.* Bacchante.
mī'mic/us *a.* farcical. **–ē** *ad.*
Mimne'rm/us -ī *m.* Greek elegiac poet.
mī'mul/a -ae *f.* actress.
mī'm/us -ī *m.* actor; mime, farce.
mi'n/a -ae *f.* Greek silver coin.
mi'n/ae -ā'rum *f.pl.* threats; (*wall*) pinnacles.
minā'ti/ō -ō'nis *f.* threat.
mi'n/āx -ā'cis *a.* threatening; projecting. **–ā'citer** *ad.*
Mine'rv/a -ae *f.* goddess of wisdom and arts, *esp.* weaving; (*fig.*) talent, genius; working in wool. sūs -am "*teach your grandmother!*"
miniā'nus *a.* red-leaded.
miniā'tulus *a.* painted red.
mi'nimē *ad.* least, very little; (*reply*) no, not at all.
mi'nimus *a.* least, smallest, very small; youngest.
mi'ni/ō -ā're -ā'vī -ā'tum *vt.* colour red.
mini'st/er -rī *m.*, **–ra** -rae *f.* attendant, servant; helper, agent, tool.
ministe'r/ium -ī & iī *n.* service, office, duty; retinue.
ministrā't/or -ō'ris *m.*, **–rīx** -rī'cis *f.* assistant, handmaid.
mini'str/ō -ā're *vt.* serve, supply; manage.
minitābu'ndus *a.* threatening.
mi'nit/or -ā'rī, **–ō** -ā're *vt.* & *i.* threaten.
mi'n/ium -ī & iī *n.* vermilion, red lead.
mi'n/or -ā'rī -ā'tus *vt.* & *i.* threaten; project. **–a'nter** *ad.* threateningly.
mi'n/or -ō'ris *a.* smaller, less, inferior; younger; (*pl.*) descendants.
Mīnō/s -is *m.* king of Crete, judge in the lower world. **–ius**, **–us** *a.* **–is** -idis *f.* Ariadne.
Mīnōtau'r/us -ī *m.* monster of the Cretan labyrinth, half bull, half man.
Mintu'rn/ae -ā'rum *f.pl.* town in S. Latium. **–ē'nsis** *a.*
minum–, *see* **minim–**.
mi'n/uō -u'ere -uī -ū'tum *vt.* make smaller, lessen; chop up; reduce, weaken. *vi.* (*tide*) ebb.
mi'nus *n.* minor. *ad.* less; not, not at all. quō — (*prevent*) from.
minu'sculus *a.* smallish.
minū't/al -ā'lis *n.* mince.
minūtā'tim *ad.* bit by bit.
minū't/us *ppp.* minuō. *a.* small; paltry. **–ē** *ad.* in a petty manner.
mīrā'bili/s *a.* wonderful, extraordinary. **–ter** *ad.*
mīrābu'ndus *a.* astonished.
mīrācul/um -ī *n.* marvel, wonder; amazement.
mīr'andus *a.* wonderful.
mīrā'ti/ō -ō'nis *f.* wonder.
mīrā't/or -ō'ris *m.* admirer.
mīrā'tr/īx -ī'cis *a.* admiring.
mīri'fic/us *a.* wonderful. **–ē** *ad.*
mirmi'llō, *see* **murmillō**.
mī'r/or -ā'rī -ā'tus *vt.* wonder at, be surprised at, admire. *vi.* wonder, be surprised.
mī'r/us *a.* wonderful, strange. -um quam, quantum extraordinarily. **–ē** *ad.*
miscellā'ne/a -ō'rum *n.pl.* (*food*) hotch-potch.
mi'/sceō -scē're -scuī -xtum *vt.* mix, mingle, blend; join, combine; confuse, embroil.
mise'llus *a.* poor little.
Mīsē'n/um -ī *n.* promontory and harbour near Naples. **–ē'nsis** *a.*
mi'ser -ī *a.* wretched, poor, pitiful, sorry. **–ē** *ad.*
miserā'bili/s *a.* pitiable, sad, plaintive. **–ter** *ad.*
misera'ndus *a.* deplorable.
miserā'ti/ō -ō'nis *f.* pity, compassion, pathos.
mise'r/eō -ē're -uī, **–eor**

-ērī -itus *vt.* & *i.* (*with gen.*) pity, sympathise with. **-et mē** I pity, I am sorry.
miserē'sc/ō -ere *vi.* feel pity.
mise'ri/a -ae *f.* misery, trouble, distress.
miserico'rdi/a -ae *f.* pity, sympathy, mercy.
mise'ricor/s -dis *a.* sympathetic, merciful.
mise'riter *ad.* sadly.
mi'ser/or -ārī -ā'tus *vt.* deplore; pity.
mī'sī *perf.* mittō.
mi'ss/a -ae *f.* (*eccl.*) mass.
mi'ssilis *a.* missile.
mi'ssi/ō -ō'nis *f.* sending; release; (*mil.*) discharge; (*gladiators*) quarter; (*events*) end. **sine -ōne** to the death.
mi'ssit/ō -ā're *vt.* send repeatedly.
mi'ssus *ppp.* mittō.
mi'ss/us -ūs *m.* sending; throwing. **— sagittae** bowshot.
mite'll/a -ae *f.* turban.
mītē'sc/ō -ere *vi.* ripen; grow mild.
Mithridā't/ēs -is *m.* king of Pontus, defeated by Pompey. **-ē'us, -icus** *a.*
mītigā'ti/ō -ō'nis *f.* soothing.
mī'tig/ō -ā're -ā'vī -ā'tum *vt.* ripen, soften; calm, pacify.
mī'tis *a.* ripe, mellow; soft, mild; gentle.
mi'tr/a -ae *f.* turban.
mi'tt/ō -ere mī'sī mi'ssum *vt.* send, dispatch; throw, hurl; let go, dismiss; emit, utter; (*news*) send word; (*gift*) bestow; (*event*) end; (*speech*) omit, stop. **sanguinem —** bleed. **ad cēnam —** invite to dinner. **missum facere** forgo.
mī'tul/us -ī *m.* mussel.
mi'xtim *ad.* promiscuously.
mixtū'r/a -ae *f.* mingling.
Mnēmo'syn/ē -ēs *f.* mother of the Muses. [enir.
mnēmo'syn/on -ī *n.* souv-
mō'bili/s *a.* movable; nimble, fleet; excitable, fickle. **-ter** *ad.* rapidly.
mōbi'lit/ās -ā'tis *f.* agility, rapidity; fickleness. [rapid.
mōbi'lit/ō -ā're *vt.* make
moderā'bilis *a.* moderate.
moderā'm/en -inis *n.* control; government.
modera'nter *ad.* with control.
moderā'tim *ad.* gradually.
moderā'ti/ō -ō'nis *f.* control, government; moderation; rules.
moderā't/or -ō'ris *m.* controller, governor.
moderā'tr/īx -ī'cis *f.* mistress, controller.
moderā't/us *a.* restrained, orderly. **-ē** *ad.* with restraint.
mo'der/or -ā'rī -ā'tus *vt.* & *i.* (*with dat.*) restrain, check; (*with acc.*) manage, govern, guide.
mode'sti/a -ae *f.* temperate behaviour, discipline; humility.
mode'st/us *a.* sober, restrained; well-behaved, disciplined; modest, unassuming. **-ē** *ad.* with moderation; humbly.
modiā'lis *a.* holding a peck.
mo'dic/us *a.* moderate; middling, small, mean. **-ē** *ad.* moderately; slightly.
modificā'tus *a.* measured.
mo'd/ius -ī & iī *m.* corn measure, peck.
mo'do *ad.* only; at all, in any way; (*with imp.*) just; (*time*) just now, a moment ago, in a moment. *conj.* if only. **nōn —** not only; not only . . . not. **— nōn** all but, almost. **— . . . —** sometimes . . . sometimes. **— . . . tum** at first . . . then. [sician.
modulā't/or -ō'ris *m.* mu-
mo'dul/or -ā'rī -ā'tus *vt.* modulate, play, sing. **-ā'tus** played, measured. **-ā'tē** *ad.* melodiously.

mo'dul/us -ī *m.* measure.
mo'd/us -ī *m.* measure; size; metre, music; way, method; limit, end. ēius -ī such. -ō, in -um like.
moe'ch/a -ae *f.* adulteress.
moe'ch/or -ā'rī *vi.* commit adultery.
moe'ch/us -ī *m.* adulterer.
moe'nera, *see* **mūnus.**
moe'ni/a -um *n.pl.* defences, walls; town, stronghold.
moe'niō, *see* **mūniō.**
Moe's/ī -ō'rum *m.pl* people on lower Danube, *mod.* Bulgaria.
mo'l/a -ae *f.* mill-stone, mill; grains of spelt.
molā'r/is -is *m.* mill-stone; (*tooth*) molar.
mō'l/ēs -is *f.* mass, bulk, pile; dam, pier, massive structure; (*fig.*) greatness, weight, effort, trouble.
mole'sti/a -ae *f.* trouble, annoyance, worry; (*style*) affectation.
mole'st/us *a.* irksome, annoying; (*style*) laboured. **-ē** *ad.*
mōlī'm/en -inis *n.* exertion, labour; importance.
mōlīme'nt/um -ī *n.* great effort.
mō'l/ior -ī'rī -ī'tus *vt.* labour at, work, build; wield, move, heave; undertake, devise, occasion. *vi.* exert oneself, struggle. [work.
mōlī'ti/ō -ō'nis *f.* laborious
mōlī't/or -ō'ris *m.* builder.
mollē'sc/ō -ere *vi.* soften, become effeminate.
molli'culus *a.* tender.
mo'll/iō -ī're -ī'vī -ī'tum *vt.* soften, make supple; mitigate, make easier; demoralise.
mo'lli/s *a.* soft, supple; tender, gentle; (*character*) sensitive, weak, unmanly; (*poetry*) amatory; (*opinion*) changeable; (*slope*) easy. **-ter** *ad.* softly, gently; calmly; voluptuously.
molli'ti/a -ae, **-ēs** -ē'ī *f.* softness, suppleness; tenderness, weakness, effeminacy.
mollitū'd/ō -inis *f.* softness; susceptibility.
mo'l/ō -ere *vt.* grind.
Molo'ss/ī -ō'rum *m.pl.* Molossians, people in Epirus. **-is** -idis *f.* their country. **-us** -ī *m.* Molossian hound. **-icus, -us** *a.*
mō'ly -os *n.* a magic herb.
mō'm/en -inis *n.* movement, momentum.
mōme'nt/um -ī *n.* movement; change; (*time*) short space, moment; (*fig.*) cause, influence, importance. **nullīus** -ī unimportant.
momo'rdī *perf.* mordeō.
Mo'n/a -ae *f.* Isle of Man; Anglesey.
mo'nach/us -ī *m.* monk.
monē'dul/a -ae *f.* jackdaw.
mo'n/eō -ē're -uī -itum *vt.* remind, advise, warn; instruct, foretell.
monē'r/is -is *f.* galley with one bank of oars.
monē'rula, *see* **monēdula.**
monē't/a -ae *f.* mint; money; stamp. [collar.
monī'l/e -is *n.* necklace,
monim-, *see* **monum-.**
moni'ti/ō -ō'nis *f.* admonishing.
mo'nit/or -ō'ris *m.* admonisher; prompter; teacher.
mo'nit/um -ī *n.* warning; prophecy.
mo'nit/us -ūs *m.* admonition; warning.
monogra'mmus *a.* shadowy.
monopo'd/ium -ī & iī *n.* table with one leg.
mōns mo'ntis *m.* mountain.
mōnstrā't/or -ō'ris *m.* shower, inventor.
mō'nstr/ō -ā're -ā'vī -ā'tum *vt.* point out, show; inform, instruct; appoint; denounce. **-ā'tus** *a.* distinguished.

mō'nstr/um -ī *n.* portent, marvel; monster. [-ē *ad.*
mōnstruō's/us *a.* unnatural.
montā'nus *a.* mountainous; mountain-, highland.
monti'col/a -ae *m.* highlander. [roving.
monti'vagus *a.* mountain-
montuō'sus, montō'sus *a.* mountainous.
monume'nt/um -ī *n.* memorial, monument; record.
Mopso'pius *a.* Athenian.
mo'r/a -ae *f.* delay, pause; hindrance; space of time, sojourn. -am facere put off.
mo'r/a -ae *f.* division of the Spartan army.
mōrā'lis *a.* moral.
morā't/or -ō'ris *m.* delayer.
mōrā'tus *a.* mannered, of a nature; (*writing*) in character.
mo'rbidus *a.* unwholesome.
mo'rb/us -ī *m.* illness, disease; distress.
mo'rd/āx -ā'cis *a.* biting, sharp, pungent; (*fig.*) snarling, carking. **-ā'citer** *ad.*
mo'r/deō -dē're momo'rdī -sum *vt.* bite; bite into, grip; (*cold*) nip; (*words*) sting, hurt, mortify.
mo'rdicus *ad.* with a bite; (*fig.*) doggedly.
mō'rēs *pl.* mōs.
morē't/um -ī *n.* salad.
moribu'ndus *a.* dying, mortal; deadly.
mōri'ger/or -ā'rī -ā'tus *vi.* (*with dat.*) gratify, humour.
mōri'gerus *a.* obliging, obedient.
mo'r/ior -ī -tuus *vi.* die; decay, fade.
moritū'rus *fut.p.* morior.
mōro'logus *a.* foolish.
mo'r/or -ā'rī -ā'tus *vi.* delay, stay, loiter. *vt.* detain, retard; entertain; (*with neg.*) heed, object. nihil, nīl — have no objection to; not care for; withdraw a charge against.
mōrō'sit/ās -ā'tis *f.* peevishness.
mōrō's/us *a.* peevish, difficult. -ē *ad.*
Mo'rph/eus -eos *m.* god of dreams.
mors mo'rtis *f.* death; corpse. mortem sibi cōnsciscere commit suicide. mortis poena capital punishment.
morsiu'ncul/a -ae *f.* little kiss.
mo'rsus *ppp.* mordeō. *n.pl.* little bits.
mo'rs/us -ūs *m.* bite; grip; (*fig.*) sting, vexation.
mortā'lis *a.* mortal; transient; man-made. *m.* human being.
mortā'lit/ās -ā'tis *f.* mortality, death.
mortā'r/ium -ī & iī *n.* mortar.
mo'rtifer -ī *a.* fatal.
mo'rtuus *ppa.* morior. *a.* dead. *m.* dead man.
mō'r/um -ī *n.* blackberry, mulberry. [tree.
mō'r/us -ī *f.* black mulberry
mō'rus *a.* foolish. *m.* fool.
mōs mō'ris *m.* nature, manner; humour, mood; custom, practice, law; (*pl.*) behaviour, character, morals. — māiōrum national tradition. mōrem gerere oblige, humour. mōre, in mōrem like.
Mo's/a -ae *m.* river Meuse.
Mō's/ēs, Mō'ys/ēs -is *m.* Moses.
mō'ti/ō -ō'nis *f.* motion.
mō't/ō -ā're *vt.* keep moving.
mō'tus *ppp.* moveō.
mō't/us -ūs *m.* movement; dance, gesture; (*mind*) impulse, emotion; (*pol.*) rising, rebellion. terrae — earthquake.
mo'v/ēns -e'ntis *pres.p.* moveō. *a.* movable. *n.pl.* motives.
mo'v/eō -ē're mō'vī mō'tum *vt.* move, set in motion; disturb; change; dislodge,

expel; occasion, begin; *(opinion)* shake; *(mind)* affect, influence, provoke. *vi.* move. castra — strike camp. sē — budge; dance.
mox *ad.* presently, soon, later on; next.
Mō'ysēs, *see* **Mōsēs**.
mū'cidus *a.* snivelling; mouldy.
Mū'c/ius -ī *m.* Roman family name, *esp.* Scaevola, who burned his right hand before Porsena. [sword.
mū'cr/ō -ō'nis *m.* point, edge;
mū'c/us -ī *m.* mucus.
mū'gil/is -is *m.* mullet.
mu'gin/or -ā'rī *vi.* hesitate.
mū'g/iō -ī're *vi.* bellow, groan.
mūgī't/us -ūs *m.* lowing, roaring.
mū'l/a -ae *f.* she-mule.
mu'l/ceō -cē're -sī -sum *vt.* stroke, caress; soothe, alleviate, delight.
Mu'lciber -is & ī *m.* Vulcan.
mu'lc/ō -ā're -ā'vī -ā'tum *vt.* beat, ill-treat damage.
mu'lctr/a -ae *f.*, **-ā'rium** -ā'rī & āriī, **-um** -ī *n.* milk-pail.
mu'lg/eō -ēre **mu'lsī** *vt.* milk.
mulie'bri/s *a.* woman's, feminine; effeminate. **-ter** *ad.* like a woman; effeminately.
mu'lier -is *f.* woman; wife.
mulierā'rius *a.* woman's.
mulie'rcul/a -ae *f.* girl.
mulierō'sit/ās -ā'tis *f.* fondness for women.
mulierō'sus *a.* fond of women.
mūlī'nus *a.* mulish.
mū'li/ō -ō'nis *m.* mule-driver.
mūliō'nius *a.* mule-driver's.
mu'lsī *perf.* **mulceō**; *perf.* **mulgeō**.
mu'll/us -ī *m.* red mullet.
mu'lsus *ppp.* **mulceō**.
mu'lsus *a.* honeyed, sweet. *n.* honey-wine, mead. [loss.
mu'lt/a -ae *f.* penalty, fine;
multa'ngulus *a.* many-angled.
multātī'cius *a.* fine-.
multā'ti/ō -ō'nis *f.* fining.
multē'simus *a.* very small.
multi'cavus *a.* many-holed.
multī'ci/a -ō'rum *n.pl.* transparent garments. [places.
multifā'riam *ad.* in many
multi'fidus *a.* divided into many parts. [forms.
multifō'rmis *a.* of many
multi'forus *a.* many-holed.
multige'n/eris, **-us** *a.* of many kinds.
multi'iug/is, **-us** *a.* yoked together; complex.
multilo'qu/ium -ī & iī *n.* talkativeness.
multi'loquus *a.* talkative.
multi'modīs *ad.* variously.
mu'ltipl/ex -icis *a.* with many folds, tortuous; many-sided, manifold, various; *(comparison)* far greater; *(character)* fickle, sly.
multi'plic/ō -ā're -ā'vī -ā'tum *vt.* multiply, enlarge.
multi'pot/ēns -e'ntis *a.* very powerful.
multitū'd/ō -inis *f.* great number, multitude, crowd.
multi'volus *a.* longing for much
mu'lt/ō -ā're -ā'vī -ā'tum *vt.* punish, fine.
mu'lt/us *(comp.* **plūs** *sup.* **plūrimus**) *a.* much, many; *(speech)* lengthy, tedious; *(time)* late. **-ā** nocte late at night. nē **-a** *to cut a long story short.* **-um** *ad.* much, very, frequently. **-ō** *ad.* much, far, by far; *(time)* long.
mū'l/us -ī *m.* mule.
Mu'lvius *a.* Mulvian, a Tiber bridge above Rome.
mundā'n/us -ī *m.* world-citizen.
mundi'ti/a -ae, **-ēs** -ē'ī *f.* cleanness; neatness, elegance.
mu'nd/us *a.* clean, neat,

elegant. in -ō esse be in readiness.
mu'nd/us -ī *m.* toilet gear; universe, world, heavens; mankind.
mūnerige'rul/us -ī *m.* bringer of presents.
mū'ner/ō -ā're, **-or** -ā'rī *vt.* present, reward. [duties.
mū'ni/a -ō'rum *n.pl.* official
mū'nic/eps -ipis *m., f.* citizen (of a municipium), fellow-citizen.
mūnicipā'lis *a.* provincial.
mūnici'p/ium -ī & iī *n.* provincial town, burgh.
mūnifice'nti/a -ae *f.* liberality.
mūni'fic/ō -ā're *vt.* treat generously.
mūni'fic/us *a.* liberal. **-ē** *ad.*
mūnī'm/en -inis *n.* defence.
mūnīme'nt/um -ī *n.* defence-work, protection.
mū'n/iō -ī're -iī -ī'tum *vt.* fortify, secure, strengthen; (*road*) build; (*fig.*) protect.
mū'nis *a.* ready to oblige.
mūnī'ti/ō -ō'nis *f.* building; fortification; (*river*) bridging.
mūnī't/ō -ā're *vt.* (*road*) open up.
mūnī't/or -ō'ris *m.* sapper, builder.
mū'n/us -eris *n.* service, duty; gift; public show; entertainment; tax; (*funeral*) tribute; (*book*) work.
mūnu'scul/um -ī *n.* small present.
mūrae'n/a -ae *f.* a fish.
mūrā'lis *a.* wall-, mural, for fighting from or attacking walls.
mū'r/ex -icis *m.* purple-fish; purple dye, purple; jagged rock.
mu'ri/a -ae *f.* brine.
murmi'll/ō -ō'nis *m.* kind of gladiator.
mu'rmur -is *n.* murmur, hum, rumbling, roaring.
murmuri'll/um -ī *n.* low murmur.
mu'rmur/ō -ā're *vi.* murmur, rumble; grumble.
mu'rr/a -ae *f.* myrrh.
mu'rreus *a.* perfumed; made of the stone called murra.
mu'rrin/a -ae *f.* myrrh-wine.
mu'rrin/a -ō'rum *n.pl.* murrine vases.
murt-, *see* **myrt-**.
mū'r/us -ī *m.* wall; dam; defence.
mūs mū'ris *m., f.* mouse, rat.
Mū's/a -ae *f.* goddess inspiring an art; poem; (*pl.*) studies.
mūsae'us *a.* poetic, musical.
mu'sc/a -ae *f.* fly.
mūsci'pul/a -ae *f.*, **-um** -ī *n.* mouse-trap.
mūscō'sus *a.* mossy.
mū'scul/us -ī *m.* mouse; muscle; (*mil.*) shed.
mū'sc/us -ī *m.* moss.
mū'sic/us *a.* of music, of poetry. *m.* musician. *f.* music, culture. *n.pl.* music. **-ē** *ad.* very pleasantly.
mu'ssit/ō -ā're *vi.* say nothing; mutter. *vt.* bear in silence.
mu'ss/ō -ā're *vt.* & *i.* say nothing, brood over; mutter, murmur.
mustā'ce/us -ī *m.*, **-um** -ī *n.* wedding-cake.
mūstē'l/a -ae *f.* weasel.
mu'st/um -ī *n.* unfermented wine, must; vintage.
mūtā'bilis *a.* changeable, fickle. [ness.
mūtābi'lit/ās -ā'tis *f.* fickle-
mūtā'ti/ō -ō'nis *f.* change, alteration; exchange.
mu'til/ō -ā're -ā'vī -ā'tum *vt.* cut off, maim; diminish.
mu'tilus *a.* maimed.
Mu'tin/a -ae *f.* town in N. Italy. **-ē'nsis** *a.* *mod.* Modena.
mū'tiō, *see* **muttiō**.
mū't/ō -ā're -ā'vī -ā'tum *vt.* shift; change, alter; exchange,

barter. *vi.* change. **-āta verba** figurative language.
mu'tt/iō -ī're *vi.* mutter, mumble. [ing.
mūtuā'ti/ō -ō'nis *f.* borrow-
mūtu'it/ō -ā're *vt.* try to borrow.
mū'tu/or -ā'ri -ā'tus *vt.* borrow. [still.
mū'tus *a.* dumb, mute; silent,
mū'tu/us *a.* borrowed, lent; mutual, reciprocal. **-um** dare lend. **-um** sūmere borrow. **-um** facere return like for like. **–um** -ī *n.* loan. **–ē, –ō** *ad.* mutually, in turns.
Mycē'n/ae -ā'rum *f.pl.* Agamemnon's capital in S. Greece. **–ae'us, –ē'nsis** *a.* **–is** -idis *f.* Iphigenia.
Mygdo'nius *a.* Phrygian.
myo'par/ō -ō'nis *m.* pirate galley.
myrī'c/a -ae *f.* tamarisk.
Myrmi'don/es -um *m.pl.* followers of Achilles.
My'r/ōn -ō'nis *m.* famous Greek sculptor.
myropō'l/a -ae *m.* perfumer.
myropō'l/ium -ī & ii *n.* perfumer's shop.
myrothē'c/ium -ī & ii *n.* perfume-box.
myrrh-, *see* **murr-**.
myrtē't/um -ī *n.* myrtle-grove.
my'rteus *a.* myrtle-.
Myrtō'um mare Sea N.W. of Crete.
my'rt/um -ī *n.* myrtle-berry.
my'rt/us -ī & ūs *f.* myrtle.
Mȳ's/ia -iae *f.* country of Asia Minor. **–us, –ius** *a.*
my'st/a -ae *m.* priest of mysteries.
mystagō'g/us -ī *m.* initiator.
mystē'r/ium -ī & ii *n.* secret religion, mystery; secret.
my'sticus *a.* mystic.
Mytilē'n/ē -ēs *f.*, **–ae** -ā'rum *f.pl.* capital of Lesbos. **–ae'us –ē'nsis** *a.*

N

na'bl/ium -ī & ii *n.* kind of harp.
na'ctus *ppa.* nanciscor.
nae, *see* **nē**.
nae'nia, *see* **nēnia**.
Nae'v/ius -ī *m.* early Latin poet. **–iā'nus** *a.*
nae'v/us -ī *m.* mole (on the body).
Nā'i/as -adis, **–s** -dis *f.* water-nymph, Naiad. **–cus** *a.*
nam *conj.* (*explaining*) for; (*illustrating*) for example; (*transitional*) now; (*interrog.*) but; (*enclitic*) *an emphatic particle.*
na'mque *conj.* for, for indeed, for example.
nancī'sc/or -ī na'ctus & na'nctus *vt.* obtain, get; come upon, find.
nā'n/us -ī *m.* dwarf.
Napae'/ae -ā'rum *f.pl.* dell-nymphs.
nā'p/us -ī *m.* turnip.
Na'rb/ō -ō'nis *m.* town in S. Gaul. **–ōnē'nsis** *a.*
narci'ss/us -ī *m.* narcissus.
na'rd/us -ī *f.*, **–um** -ī *n.* nard, nard-oil.
nā'r/is -is *f.* nostril; (*pl.*) nose; (*fig.*) sagacity, scorn.
nārrā'bilis *a.* to be told.
nārrā'ti/ō -ō'nis *f.* narrative.
nārrā't/or -ō'ris *m.* story-teller, historian.
nārrā't/us -ūs *m.* narrative.
nā'rr/ō -ā're -ā'vī -ā'tum *vt.* tell, relate, say. male — bring bad news.
narthē'c/ium -ī & ii *n.* medicine-chest.
nā'/scor -scī -tus *vi.* be born; originate, grow, be produced.
Nā's/ō -ō'nis *m.* surname of Ovid.
na'ss/a -ae *f.* wicker basket for catching fish; (*fig.*) snare.
nastu'rt/ium -ī & ii *n.* cress.
nā's/us -ī *m.* nose.

nāsū'tus *a.* big-nosed; satirical. **-ē** *ad.* sarcastically.
nā't/a -ae *f.* daughter.
nātāli'cius *a.* of one's birthday, natal. *f.* birthday party.
nātā'lis *a.* of birth, natal. *m.* birthday. *m.pl.* birth, origin.
natā'ti/ō -ō'nis *f.* swimming.
natā't/or -ō'ris *m.* swimmer.
nā'ti/ō -ō'nis *f.* tribe, race; breed, class.
na't/is -is *f.* (*usu. pl.*) buttocks.
nātī'vus *a.* created; inborn, native, natural.
na't/ō -ā're *vi.* swim, float; flow, overflow; (*eyes*) swim, fail; (*fig.*) waver.
nā'tr/īx -ī'cis *f.* water-snake.
nā'tū *abl. m.* by birth, in age. grandis —, māgnō — quite old. **māior** — older. **māximus** — oldest.
nātū'r/a -ae *f.* birth; nature, quality, character; natural order of things; the physical world; (*physics*) element. rērum — Nature.
nātūrā'li/s *a.* by birth; by nature, natural. **-ter** *ad.* by nature.
nā'tus *ppa.* **nāscor.** *m.* son. *a.* born, made (for); old, of age. **prō, ē rē nātā** under the circumstances, as things are. annōs vīgintī — 20 years old.
naua'rch/us -ī *m.* captain.
nau'cī nōn esse, facere, habēre be, consider worthless.
nauclē'ricus *a.* skipper's.
nauclē'r/us -ī *m.* skipper.
naufra'g/ium -ī & iī *n.* shipwreck, wreck. — **facere** be shipwrecked.
nau'fragus *a.* shipwrecked, wrecked; (*sea*) dangerous to shipping. *m.* shipwrecked man; (*fig.*) ruined man.
nau'l/um -ī *n.* fare.
nauma'chi/a -ae *f.* mock sea-fight.
nau'se/a -ae *f.* sea-sickness.
nau'se/ō -ā're *vi.* be sick; (*fig.*) disgust.
nause'ol/a -ae *f.* squeamishness.
nau't/a (nā'vita) -ae *m.* sailor, mariner.
nau'ticus *a.* nautical, sailors'. *m.pl.* seamen.
nāvā'lis *a.* naval, of ships. *n.* & *n.pl.* dockyard; rigging.
nāvi'cul/a -ae *f.* boat.
nāviculā'ri/a -ae *f.* shipping business.
nāviculā'r/ius -ī & iī *m.* ship-owner.
nāvi'fragus *a.* dangerous.
nāvigā'bilis *a.* navigable.
nāvigā'ti/ō -ō'nis *f.* voyage.
nā'viger -ī *a.* ship-carrying.
nāvi'g/ium -ī & iī *n.* vessel, ship.
nā'vig/ō -ā're -ā'vī -ā'tum *vi.* sail, put to sea. *vt* sail across, navigate.
nā'v/is -is *f.* ship. — **longa** warship. — **mercātōria** merchant-man. — **onerāria** transport. — **praetōria** flagship. **-em dēdūcere** launch. **-em solvere** set sail. **-em statuere** heave to. **-em subdūcere** beach. **-ibus atque quadrīgīs** with might and main.
nā'vita, *see* **nauta.**
nā'vit/ās -ā'tis *f.* energy.
nā'viter *ad.* energetically; absolutely.
nā'v/ō -ā're *vt.* perform energetically. **operam** — be energetic; come to the assistance (of).
nā'vus (gnā'vus) *a.* energetic.
Na'x/os -ī *f.* Aegean island, famous for wines and the story of Ariadne.
nē *interj.* truly, indeed.
nē *ad.* not. *conj.* that not, lest; (*fear*) that; (*purpose*) so that . . not, to avoid, to prevent.

-ne *enclitic* (*introducing a question*).
Neā'pol/is -is *f.* Naples. **-ītā'nus** *a.* [cloud.
ne'bul/a -ae *f.* mist, vapour,
ne'bul/ō -ō'nis *m.* idler, good-for-nothing.
nebulō'sus *a.* misty, cloudy.
nec, *see* **neque**.
ne'cdum *ad.* and not yet.
necessā'ri/us *a.* necessary, inevitable; indispensable; (*kin*) related. *m., f.* relative. *n.pl.* necessities. **-ē**, **-ō** *ad.* of necessity, unavoidably.
nece'sse *a.*(*indecl.*) necessary, inevitable; needful.
nece'ssit/ās -ā'tis *f.* necessity, compulsion; requirement, want; relationship, connection.
necessitū'd/ō -inis *f.* necessity, need, want; connection, friendship; (*pl.*) relatives.
nece'ssum, *see* **necesse**.
ne'cne *ad.* or not.
ne'cnōn *ad.* also, besides.
ne'c/ō -ā're -ā'vī -ā'tum *vt.* kill, murder.
necopī'n/āns -a'ntis *a.* unaware. [**-ō** *ad.*
necopīnā't/us *a.* unexpected.
necopī'nus *a.* unexpected; unsuspecting.
ne'ctar -is *n.* nectar, the drink of the gods.
necta'reus *a.* of nectar.
ne'/ctō- ctere **-xī** & **xuī** **-xum** *vt.* tie, fasten, connect; weave; (*fig.*) bind, enslave (*esp.* for debt); contrive, frame.
nē'cubi *conj.* so that nowhere.
nēcu'nde *conj.* so that from nowhere.
nē'dum *ad.* much less, much more.
nefa'ndus *a.* abominable, impious.
nefā'ri/us *a.* heinous, criminal. **-ē** *ad.*
ne'fās *n.*(*indecl.*) wickedness, sin, wrong; (*interj.*) horror! shame!
nefā'stus *a.* wicked; unlucky; (*days*) closed to public business.
negā'ti/ō -ō'nis *f.* denial.
ne'git/ō -ā're *vt.* deny, refuse.
neglē'cti/ō -ō'nis *f.* neglect.
neglē'ctus *ppp.* neglegō.
neglē'ct/us -ūs *m.* neglecting.
ne'gleg/ēns -e'ntis *pres.p.* neglegō. *a.* careless, indifferent. **-e'nter** *ad.* carelessly.
neglege'nti/a -ae *f.* carelessness, neglect, coldness.
ne'gl/egō -e'gere -ē'xī -ē'ctum *vt.* neglect, not care for; slight, disregard; overlook.
ne'g/ō -ā're -ā'vī -ā'tum *vt.* & *i.* say no; say not, deny; refuse, decline.
negōtiā'lis *a.* business-
negō'ti/āns -a'ntis *m.* business man.
negōtiā'ti/ō -ō'nis *f.* banking business.
negōtiā't/or -ō'ris *m.* business man, banker.
negōti'ol/um -ī *n.* trivial matter.
negō'ti/or -ā'rī -ā'tus *vi.* do business, trade.
negōtiō'sus *a.* busy.
negō't/ium -ī & iī *n.* business, work; trouble; matter, thing. quid est -ī? what is the matter?
Nē'l/eus -eī *m.* father of Nestor. **-ē'ius**, **-ē'us** *a.*
Ne'me/a -ae *f.* town in S. Greece, where Hercules killed the lion. **-ae'us** *a.* Nemean. **-a** -ō'rum *n.pl.* Nemean Games.
nē'm/ō -inis *m., f.* no one, nobody. *a.* no. — nōn everybody. nōn — many. — ūnus not a soul.
nemorā'lis *a.* sylvan.
nemorē'nsis *a.* of the grove.
nemoricu'ltr/īx -ī'cis *f.* forest-dweller.
nemori'vagus *a.* forest-roving.

nemorō'sus *a.* well-wooded; leafy.
ne'mpe *ad.* (*confirming*) surely, of course, certainly; (*in questions*) do you mean?
ne'm/us -oris *n.* wood, grove.
nē'ni/a -ae *f.* dirge; incantation; song, nursery rhyme.
ne'ō ne're nē'vī nē'tum *vt.* spin; weave.
Neopto'lem/us -ī *m.* Pyrrhus, son of Achilles.
ne'p/a -ae *f.* scorpion.
ne'p/ōs -ō'tis *m.* grandson; descendant; spendthrift.
nepōtī'n/us -ī *m.* little grandson.
ne'pt/is -is *f.* grand-daughter.
Neptū'n/us -ī *m.* Neptune, god of the sea; sea. **-ius** *a.* — hērōs Theseus. [bad.
nē'quam *a.*(*indecl.*) worthless,
nēquā'quam *ad.* not at all, by no means.
ne'que, nec *ad.* not. *conj.* and not, but not; neither, nor. — . . . et not only not . . . but also.
ne'qu/eō -ī're -ī'vī -ī'tum *vi.* be unable, cannot.
nēquī'quam *ad.* fruitlessly, for nothing; without good reason.
nē'quior, nēqui'ssimus *comp., sup.* nēquam.
nē'quiter *ad.* worthlessly, wrongly.
nēqui'ti/a -ae, **-ēs** *f.* worthlessness, badness.
Nē'r/eus -eī *m.* a sea-god; the sea. **-ē'ius** *a.* **-ē'is** -ē'idis *f.* Nereid, sea-nymph.
Nē'rit/os -ī *m.* island near Ithaca. **-ius** *a.* of Neritos; Ithacan.
Ne'r/ō -ō'nis *m.* Roman surname, *esp.* the emperor. **-ōniā'nus** *a.*
nervō's/us *a.* sinewy, vigorous. **-ē** *ad.* vigorously.
ne'rvul/ī -ō'rum *m.pl.* energy.
ne'rv/us -ī *m.* sinew; string; fetter, prison; (*shield*) leather; (*pl.*) strength, vigour, energy.
ne'sc/iō -ī're -ī'vī & iī -ī'tum *vt.* not know be ignorant of; be unable. — **quis, quid** somebody, something. — **an** probably.
ne'scius *a.* ignorant, unaware; unable; unknown.
Ne'st/or -oris *m.* Greek leader at Troy, famous for his great age and wisdom.
neu, *see* **nēve.**
neu't/er -rī *a.* neither; neuter. **-rō** *ad.* neither way.
neu'tiquam *ad.* by no means, certainly not.
nē've, neu *conj.* and not; neither, nor.
nē'vī *perf.* neō.
nex ne'cis *f.* murder, death.
ne'xilis *a.* tied together.
ne'x/um -ī *n.* personal enslavement.
ne'xus *ppp.* nectō.
ne'x/us -ūs *m.* entwining, grip; (*law*) bond, obligation, *esp.* enslavement for debt.
nī' *ad.* not. *conj.* if not, unless; that not. **quid nī?** why not?
nīcētē'r/ium -ī & iī *n.* prize.
ni'ct/ō -ā're *vi.* wink
nīdāme'nt/um -ī *n.* nest.
nī'd/or -ō'ris *m.* steam, smell.
nī'dul/us -ī *m.* little nest.
nī'd/us -ī *m.* nest; (*pl.*) nestlings; (*fig.*) home.
ni'g/er -rī *a.* black, dark; dismal, ill-omened; (*character*) bad.
ni'gr/āns -a'ntis *a.* black, dusky.
nigrē'sc/ō -ere *vi.* blacken, grow dark.
ni'gr/ō -ā're *vi.* be black.
ni'gr/or -ō'ris *m.* blackness.
ni'hil, nīl *n.*(*indecl.*) nothing. *ad.* not. — **ad nōs** it has nothing to do with us. — **est** it's no use. — **est quod** there is no reason why. — **nisi**

nothing but, only. — nōn everything. nōn — something.
ni'hil/um (**nī'lum**) -ī *n.* nothing. -ī esse be worthless. -ō minus none the less.
nīl, nī'lum *see* **nihil, nihilum.**
Nī'l/us -ī *m.* Nile; conduit. **-i'acus** *a.* of the Nile; Egyptian.
ni'mbifer -ī *a.* stormy.
nimbō'sus *a.* stormy.
ni'mb/us -ī *m.* cloud, rain, storm. [course.
nimī'rum *ad.* certainly, of
ni'mis *ad.* too much, very much. nōn — not very.
ni'mi/us *a.* too great, excessive; very great. *n.* excess. **-ō** *ad.* much, far. **-um** *ad.* too, too much; very, very much. [it snows.
ni'ng/it, ni'ngu/it -ere *vi.*
ni'ngu/ēs -ium *f.pl.* snow.
Ni'ob/a -ae, **-ē** -ēs *f.* daughter of Tantalus, changed to a weeping rock. **-ē'us** *a.*
Nī'r/eus -eī & eos *m.* handsomest of the Greeks at Troy.
ni'si *conj.* if not, unless; except, but.
nī'sus *ppa.* nītor.
nī's/us -ūs *m.* pressure, effort; striving, soaring.
Nī's/us -ī *m.* father of Scylla. **-ae'us, -ē'ius** *a.* **-ē'is** -ē'idis *f.* Scylla.
nitē'dul/a -ae *f.* dormouse.
ni't/ēns -e'ntis *pres.p.* niteō. *a.* bright; brilliant, beautiful.
ni't/eō -ē're *vi.* shine, gleam; be sleek, be greasy; thrive, look beautiful.
nitē'sc/ō -ere ni'tuī *vi.* brighten, shine, glow.
nitidiu'scul/us *a.* a little shinier. **-ē** *ad.* rather more finely.
ni'tid/us *a.* bright, shining; sleek; blooming; smart, spruce; (*speech*) refined. **-ē** *ad.* magnificently.
ni't/or -ō'ris *m.* brightness, sheen; sleekness, beauty; neatness, elegance.
nī/tor -tī -sus & xus *vi.* rest on, lean on; press, stand firmly; press forward, climb; exert oneself, strive, labour; depend on.
ni'tr/um -ī *n.* soda.
nivā'lis *a.* snowy.
ni'veus *a.* of snow, snowy, snow-white.
nivō'sus *a.* snowy.
nix ni'vis *f.* snow.
nī'x/or -ā'rī *vi.* rest on; struggle.
nī'xus *ppa.* nītor.
nī'x/us -ūs *m.* pressure; labour. [sail, fly.
nō nā're nā'vī *vi.* swim, float;
nō'bilis *a.* known, noted, famous, notorious; noble, high-born; excellent.
nō'bilit/ās -ā'tis *f.* fame; noble birth; the nobility; excellence.
nōbi'lit/ō -ā're -ā'vī -ā'tum *vt.* make famous or notorious.
no'c/ēns -e'ntis *pres.p.* noceō. *a.* harmful; criminal, guilty.
no'c/eō -ē're -uī -itum *vi.* (*with dat.*) harm, hurt.
nocī'vus *a.* injurious.
no'ctifer -ī *m.* evening star.
noctilū'c/a -ae *f.* moon.
nocti'vagus *a.* night-wandering.
no'ctū *ad.* by night.
no'ctu/a -ae *f.* owl.
noctuābu'ndus *a.* travelling by night. [turnal.
noctu'rnus *a.* night-, noc-
nō'd/ō -ā're -ā'vī -ā'tum *vt.* knot, tie.
nōdō'sus *a.* knotty.
nō'd/us -ī *m.* knot; knob; girdle; (*fig.*) bond, difficulty.
nō'l/ō -le -uī *vt.* & *i.* not wish, be unwilling, refuse. -ī, -ī'te do not.
No'ma/s -dis *m., f.* nomad; Numidian.

nō'm/en -inis *n.* name; title; (*bus.*) demand, debt; (*gram.*) noun; (*fig.*) reputation, fame; account, pretext. — dare, profitērī enlist. — dēferre accuse. -ina facere enter the items of a debt.
nōmenclā't/or -ō'ris *m.* slave who told his master the names of people.
nōminā'tim *ad.* by name, one by one.
nōminā'ti/ō -ō'nis *f.* nomination.
nōmi'nit/ō -ā're *vt.* usually name.
nō'min/ō -ā're -ā'vī -ā'tum *vt.* name, call; mention; make famous; nominate; accuse, denounce.
nomi'sma -tis *n.* coin.
nōn *ad.* not; no.
Nō'n/ae -ā'rum *f.pl.* Nones, 7th day of March, May, July, October, 5th of other months.
nōnāgē'simus *a.* ninetieth.
nōnā'gi/ēns, -ēs *ad.* ninety times.
nōnāgin'tā *num.* ninety.
nōnā'nus *a.* of the ninth legion.
nō'ndum *ad.* not yet.
nōnge'nt/ī -ō'rum *num.* nine hundred.
no'nn/a -ae *f.* nun.
nō'nne *ad.* do not? is not? etc.; (*indirect*) whether not.
nōnnu'llus *a.* some.
nōnnu'nquam *ad.* sometimes.
nō'nus *a.* ninth. *f.* ninth hour.
nōnusde'cimus *a.* nineteenth.
Nō'ric/um -ī *n.* country between the Danube and the Alps. -us *a.*
nō'rm/a -ae *f.* rule.
nō's *pro.* we, us; I, me. -met (*emphatic*).
nō'scit/ō -ā're *vt.* know, recognise; observe, examine.
nō'/scō -scere -vī -tum *vt.* get to know, learn; examine; recognise, allow; (*perf.*) know.
no'st/er -rī *a.* our, ours; for us; my; (*with names*) my dear, good old. *m.* our friend. *m.pl.* our side, our troops. -rī, -rum of us.
nostr/ā's -ā'tis *a.* of our country, native.
no't/a -ae *f.* mark, sign, note; (*writing*) note, letter; (*pl.*) memoranda, shorthand, secret writing; (*books*) critical mark, punctuation; (*wine, etc.*) brand, quality; (*gesture*) sign; (*fig.*) sign, token; (*censor's*) black mark; (*fig.*) stigma, disgrace.
notā'bili/s *a.* remarkable; notorious. -ter *ad.* perceptibly.
notā'r/ius -ī & iī *m.* shorthand-writer; secretary.
notā'ti/ō -ō'nis *f.* marking; choice; observation; (*censor*) stigmatizing; (*words*) etymology.
nōtē'sc/ō -ere nō'tuī *vi.* become known.
no'thus *a.* bastard; counterfeit.
nō'ti/ō -ō'nis *f.* (*law*) cognisance, investigation; (*philos.*) idea.
nōti'ti/a -ae, -ēs -ēī *f.* fame; acquaintance; (*philos.*) idea, preconception.
no't/ō -ā're -ā'vī -ā'tum *vt.* mark, write; denote; observe; brand, stigmatize.
nō'tuī *perf.* nōtēscō.
nō'tus *ppp.* nōscō. *a.* known, familiar; notorious. *m.pl.* acquaintances.
No't/us (-os) -ī *m.* south wind.
novā'cul/a -ae *f.* razor.
novā'l/is -is *f.*, -e -is *n.* fallow land; field; crops.
novā'tr/īx -ī'cis *f.* renewer.
nove'llus *a.* young, fresh, new.
no'vem *num.* nine.
Nove'mb/er -ris *a.* of November. *m.* November.

nove'ndecim *num.* nineteen.
novendiā'lis *a.* nine days'; on the ninth day.
Novē'nsil/ēs -ium *m.pl.* new gods. [nine.
novē'nī -ō'rum *a.* in nines;
nove'rc/a -ae *f.* step-mother.
novercā'lis *a.* step-mother's.
nō'vī *perf.* nōscō.
novī'cius *a.* new.
no'vi/ēns, -ēs *ad.* nine times.
no'vit/ās -ā'tis *f.* newness, novelty; strangeness.
no'v/ō -ā're -ā'vī -ā'tum *vt.* renew, refresh; change; (*words*) coin. **rēs** — effect a revolution.
no'v/us *a.* new, young, fresh, recent; strange, unusual; inexperienced. — **homō** upstart, first of his family to hold curule office. **-ae rēs** revolution. **-ae tabulae** cancellation of debts. **quid -ī** what news? **-i'ssimus** latest, last, rear. **-ē** *ad.* unusually. **-i'ssimē** lately; last of all.
nox no'ctis *f.* night; darkness, obscurity. **nocte, noctū** by night. **dē nocte** during the night.
no'x/a -ae *f.* hurt, harm; offence, guilt; punishment.
no'xi/us *a.* harmful; guilty. **-a -ae** *f.* harm, damage; guilt, fault.
nūbē'cul/a -ae *f.* cloudy look.
nū'b/ēs -is *f.* cloud; (*fig.*) gloom; veil.
nū'bifer -ī *a.* cloud-capped; cloudy.
nūbi'gen/a -ae *m.* cloud-born, Centaur.
nū'bilis *a.* marriageable.
nū'bilus *a.* cloudy; gloomy, sad. *n.pl.* clouds.
nū'/bō -bere -psī -ptum *vi.* (*women*) be married.
nu'cle/us -ī *m.* nut, kernel.
nū'dius day since, days ago. — **tertius** the day before yesterday.
nū'd/ō -ā're -ā'vī -ā'tum *vt.* bare, strip, expose; (*mil.*) leave exposed; plunder; (*fig.*) disclose, betray.
nū'd/us *a.* naked, bare; exposed, defenceless; wearing only a tunic; (*fig.*) destitute, poor; mere; unembellished, undisguised. **vestīmenta dētrahere -ō** *draw blood from a stone.*
nū'g/ae -ā'rum *f.pl.* nonsense, trifles; (*person*) waster.
nūgā't/or -ō'ris *m.* silly creature, liar.
nūgātō'rius *a.* futile.
nū'g/āx -ā'cis *a.* frivolous.
nū'g/or -ā'rī -ā'tus *vi.* talk nonsense; cheat.
nu'll/us -ī'us (*dat.* **-ī**) *a.* no, none; not, not at all; non-existent, of no account. *m., f.* nobody.
num *interrog. particle* surely not? (*indirect*) whether, if.
Nu'm/a -ae *m.* second king of Rome.
nū'm/en -inis *n.* nod, will; divine will, power; divinity, god.
numerā'bilis *a.* easy to count.
nu'mer/ō -ā're -ā'vī -ā'tum *vt.* count, number; (*money*) pay out; (*fig.*) reckon, consider as. **-ā'tus** *a.* in cash. *n.* ready money.
numerō's/us *a.* populous; rhythmical. **-ē** *ad.* rhythmically.
nu'mer/us -ī *m.* number; many, numbers; (*mil.*) troop; (*fig.*) a cipher; (*pl.*) mathematics; rank, category, regard; rhythm, metre, verse. **in -ō esse, habērī** be recokoned as. **nullō -ō** of no account. **-ō** *ad.* just now, quickly, too soon.
Nu'mid/ae -ā'rum *m.pl.* Numidians, people of N. Africa. **-ia -iae** *f.* their country. **-a, -icus** *a.*

Nu'mit/or -ō'ris *m.* king of Alba, grandfather of Romulus.
nummā'rius *a.* money-, financial; mercenary.
nummā'tus *a.* moneyed.
nu'mmul/ī -ō'rum *m.pl.* some money, cash.
nu'mm/us -ī *m.* coin, money, cash; (*Roman coin*) sestertius; (*Greek coin*) two-drachma piece. [**num.**
nu'mnam, nu'mne, *see*
nu'mquam, nu'nquam *ad.* never. — nōn always. nōn — sometimes.
nu'mquid (*question*) do you? does he? etc.; (*indirect*) whether.
nunc *ad.* now; at present, nowadays; but as it is. — . . . — at one time . . . at another.
nuncupā'ti/ō -ō'nis *f.* pronouncing.
nu'ncup/ō -ā're -ā'vī -ā'tum *vt.* call, name; pronounce formally.
nū'ndin/ae -ā'rum *f.pl.* market-day; market; trade.
nūndinā'ti/ō -ō'nis *f.* trading.
nū'ndin/or -ā'rī *vi.* trade, traffic; flock together. *vt.* buy.
nū'ndin/um -ī *n.* market-time. trīnum — 17 days.
nunq-, *see* **numq-.**
nūntiā'ti/ō -ō'nis *f.* announcing.
nū'nti/ō -ā're -ā'vī -ā'tum *vt.* announce, report, tell.
nū'ntius *a.* informative, speaking. *m.* messenger; message, news; injunction; notice of divorce. *n.* message.
nū'per *ad.* recently, lately.
nū'psī *perf.* nūbō.
nū'pt/a -ae *f.* bride, wife.
nū'pti/ae -ā'rum *f.pl.* wedding, marriage.
nūptiā'lis *a.* wedding-, nuptial.
nu'r/us -ūs *f.* daughter-in-law; young woman.
nū'squam *ad.* nowhere; in nothing, for nothing.
nū't/ō -ā're *vi.* nod; sway, totter, falter.
nūtrī'c/ius -ī *m.* tutor.
nūtrī'c/ō -ā're, **-or** -ā'rī *vt.* nourish, sustain.
nūtrī'cul/a -ae *f.* nurse.
nūtrī'm/en -inis *n.* nourishment.
nūtrīme'nt/um -ī *n.* nourishment, support.
nū'tr/iō -ī're -ī'vī -ī'tum *vt.* suckle, nourish, rear, nurse.
nū'tr/īx -ī'cis *f.* nurse, foster-mother.
nū't/us -ūs *m.* nod; will, command; (*physics*) gravity.
nux **nu'cis** *f.* nut; nut-tree, almond-tree.
Nyctē'/is -idis *f.* Antiopa.
ny'mph/a -ae, -ē -ēs *f.* bride; nymph; water.
Ny's/a -ae *f.* birthplace of Bacchus. **-ae'us, -ē'is -ius** *a.*

O

ō *interj.* (*expressing joy, surprise, pain, etc.*) oh! (*with voc.*) O!
ob *pr.*(*with acc.*) in front of; for, on account of, for the sake of. quam — rem accordingly. debtor.
obaerā'tus *a.* in debt. *m.*
oba'mbul/ō -ā're *vi.* walk past, prowl about.
oba'rm/ō -ā're *vt.* arm (against).
o'bar/ō -ā're *vt.* plough up.
obc-, *see* **occ-.**
o'bd/ō -ere -idī -itum *vt.* shut; expose.
obdorm/ī'scō -ī'scere -ī'vī *vi.* fall asleep. *vt.* sleep off.
obd/ū'cō -ū'cere -ū'xī -u'ctum *vt.* draw over, cover; bring up; (*drink*) swallow; (*time*) pass.
obdu'cti/ō -ō'nis *f.* veiling.

obdu'ct/ō -ā're *vt.* bring as a rival.
obdu'ctus *ppp.* obdūcō.
obdūr/ē'scō -ē'scere -uī *vi.* harden; become obdurate.
obdū'r/ō -ā're *vi.* persist, stand firm.
o'b/eō -ī're -ī'vī & iī -itum *vi.* go to, meet; die; (*astr.*) set. *vt.* visit, travel over; survey, go over; envelop; (*duty*) engage in, perform; (*time*) meet. diem — die; (*law*) appear on the appointed day.
obe'quit/ō -ā're *vi.* ride up to.
obe'rr/ō -ā're *vi.* ramble about; make a mistake.
obē'sus *a.* fat, plump; coarse.
ō'b/ex -icis *m., f.* bolt, bar, barrier.
obf-, *see* **off-**.
obg-, *see* **ogg-**.
obhae/rē'scō -rē'scere -sī *vi.* stick fast.
obia'c/eō -ē're *vi.* lie over against.
ob/i'ciō -i'cere -iē'cī -ie'ctum *vt.* throw to, set before; (*defence*) put up, throw against; (*fig.*) expose, give up; (*speech*) taunt, reproach.
obiectā'ti/ō -ō'nis *f.* reproach.
obie'ct/ō -ā're *vt.* throw against; expose, sacrifice; reproach; (*hint*) let on.
obie'ctus *ppp.* obiciō. *a.* opposite, in front of; exposed. *n.pl.* accusations.
obie'ct/us -ūs *m.* putting in the way, interposing.
obīrā'tus *a.* angered.
o'biter *ad.* on the way; incidentally.
o'bitus *ppp.* obeō.
o'bit/us -ūs *m.* death, ruin; (*astr.*) setting; visit.
obiūrgā'ti/ō -ō'nis *f.* reprimand.
obiūrgā't/or -ō'ris *m.* reprover. [ful.
obiūrgātō'rius *a.* reproach-
obiū'rgit/ō -ā're *vt.* keep on reproaching.
obiū'rg/ō -ā're -ā'vī -ā'tum *vt.* scold, rebuke; deter by reproof.
oblangu/ē'scō -ē'scere -uī *vi.* become feeble.
oblātrā'tr/īx -ī'cis *f.* nagging woman.
oblā'tus *ppp.* offerō.
oblectāme'nt/um -ī *n.* amusement.
oblectā'ti/ō -ō'nis *f.* delight.
oble'ct/ō -ā're -ā'vī -ā'tum *vt.* delight, amuse, entertain; detain; (*time*) spend pleasantly. sē — enjoy oneself.
oblī'/dō -dere -sī -sum *vt.* crush, strangle.
obligā'ti/ō -ō'nis *f.* pledge.
o'blig/ō -ā're -ā'vī -ā'tum *vt.* tie up, bandage; put under an obligation, embarrass; (*law*) render liable, make guilty; mortgage. [mud.
oblī'm/ō -ā're *vt.* cover with
o'bl/inō -i'nere -ē'vī -itum *vt.* smear over; defile; (*fig.*) overload. [veer.
oblī'qu/ō -ā're *vt.* turn aside,
oblī'qu/us *a.* slanting, downhill; from the side, sideways; (*look*) askance, envious; (*speech*) indirect. -ē *ad.* sideways; indirectly.
oblī'sus *ppp.* oblīdō.
oblitē'sc/ō -ere *vi.* hide away.
obli'tter/ō -ā're -ā'vī -ā'tum *vt.* erase, cancel; (*fig.*) consign to oblivion.
o'blitus *ppp.* oblinō.
oblī'tus *ppa.* oblīvīscor.
oblī'vi/ō -ō'nis *f.* oblivion, forgetfulness.
oblīviō'sus *a.* forgetful.
oblī/vī'scor -vī'scī -tus *vt.* & *i.* forget.
oblī'v/ium -ī & iī *n.* forgetfulness, oblivion.
oblocū't/or -ō'ris *m.* contradicter.
oblo'ngus *a.* oblong.

o'blo/quor -quī -cū'tus *vi.* contradict, interrupt; abuse; (*music*) accompany.
oblu'ct/or -ā'rī *vi.* struggle against.
obmō'l/ior -ī'rī *vt.* throw up (as a defence).
obmu'rmur/ō -ā're *vi.* roar in answer.
obmūt/ē'scō -ē'scere -uī *vi.* become silent; cease.
obnā'tus *a.* growing on.
obnī'/tor -tī -xus *vi.* push against, struggle; stand firm, resist.
obnī'x/us *ppa.* obnītor. *a.* steadfast. **-ē** *ad.* resolutely.
obnoxiō'sus *a.* submissive.
obno'xi/us *a.* liable, addicted; culpable; submissive, slavish; under obligation, indebted; exposed (to danger). **-ē** *ad.* slavishly.
obnū'/bō -bere -psī -ptum *vt.* veil, cover.
obnūntiā'ti/ō -ō'nis *f.* announcement of an adverse omen.
obnū'nti/ō -ā're *vt.* announce an adverse omen.
oboe'di/ēns -e'ntis *pres.p.* oboediō. *a.* obedient. **-e'nter** *ad.* readily.
oboedie'nti/a -ae *f.* obedience.
oboe'd/iō -ī're *vi.* listen; obey, be subject to.
obo'l/eō -ē're -uī *vt.* smell of.
obo'r/ior -ī'rī -tus *vi.* arise, spring up.
obp-, *see* **opp-.**
obrē'p/ō -ere -sī -tum *vt.* & *i.* creep up to, steal upon, surprise; cheat.
obrē't/iō -ī're *vt.* entangle.
obrig/ē'scō -ē'scere -uī *vi.* stiffen.
o'brog/ō -ā're -ā'vī -ā'tum *vt.* invalidate (by making a new law).
o'bru/ō -ere -ī -tum *vt.* cover over, bury, sink; overwhelm, overpower. *vi.* fall in ruin.
obru'ss/a -ae *f.* test, touchstone.
o'brutus *ppp.* obruō.
obsae'p/iō -ī're -sī -tum *vt.* block, close.
obsa'tur/ō -ā're *vt.* sate, glut.
obscaen-, *see* **obscen-.**
obscē'nit/ās -ā'tis *f.* indecency.
obscē'n/us *a.* filthy; indecent; ominous. **-ē** *ad.* indecently.
obscūrā'ti/ō -ō'nis *f.* darkening, disappearance.
obscū'rit/ās -ā'tis *f.* darkness; (*fig.*) uncertainty; (*rank*) lowliness.
obscū'r/ō -ā're -ā'vī -ā'tum *vt.* darken; conceal, suppress; (*speech*) obscure; (*pass.*) become obsolete.
obscū'r/us *a.* dark, shady, hidden; (*fig.*) obscure, indistinct; unknown, ignoble; (*character*) reserved. **-ē** *ad.* secretly.
obsecrā'ti/ō -ō'nis *f.* entreaty; public prayer.
o'bsecr/ō -ā're *vt.* implore, appeal to.
obsecu'nd/ō -ā're *vi.* comply with, back up.
obsē'dī *perf.* obsideō.
obsēp-, *see* **obsaep-.**
o'bsequ/ēns -e'ntis *pres.p.* obsequor. *a.* compliant; (*gods*) gracious. **-e'nter** *ad.* compliantly.
obseque'nti/a -ae *f.* complaisance.
obsequiō'sus *a.* complaisant.
obse'qu/ium -ī & iī *n.* compliance, indulgence; obedience, allegiance.
o'bse/quor -quī -cū'tus *vi.* comply with, yield to, indulge.
o'bser/ō -ā're *vt.* bar close.
o'bs/erō -e'rere -ē'vī -itum *vt.* sow, plant; cover thickly.
obse'rv/āns -a'ntis *pres.p.* observō. *a.* attentive, respectful.
observa'nti/a -ae *f.* respect.

observā'ti/ō -ō'nis *f.* watching; caution.
obse'rvit/ō -ā're *vt.* observe carefully.
obse'rv/ō -ā're -ā'vī -ā'tum *vt.* watch, watch for; guard; (*laws*) keep, comply with; (*person*) pay respect to.
o'bs/es -idis *m., f.* hostage; guarantee.
obse'ssi/ō -ō'nis *f.* blockade.
obse'ss/or -ō'ris *m.* frequenter; besieger.
obse'ssus *ppp.* obsideō.
obs/i'deō -idē're -ē'dī -e'ssum *vt.* sit at, frequent; (*mil.*) blockade, besiege; block, fill, take up; guard, watch for. *vi.* sit.
obsi'di/ō -ō'nis *f.* siege, blockade; (*fig.*) imminent danger.
obsi'd/ium -ī & iī *n.* siege, blockade; hostageship.
obsī'd/ō -ere *vt.* besiege, occupy.
obsignā't/or -ō'ris *m.* sealer; witness.
obsi'gn/ō -ā're -ā'vī -ā'tum *vt.* seal up; sign and seal; (*fig.*) stamp.
obs/i'stō -i'stere -titī -titum *vi.* put oneself in the way, resist.
o'bsitus *ppp.* obserō.
obsole/fī'ō -fi'erī *vi.* wear out, become degraded.
obsolē'/scō -scere -vī -tum *vi.* wear out, become out of date.
obsolē't/us *ppa.* obsolēscō. *a.* worn out, shabby; obsolete; (*fig.*) ordinary, mean. **-ius** *ad.* more shabbily.
obsōnā't/or -ō'ris *m.* caterer.
obsōnā't/us -ūs *m.* marketing.
obsō'n/ium -ī & iī *n.* food eaten with bread, *usu.* fish.
obsō'n/ō -ā're, -or -ā'rī *vi.* cater, buy provisions; provide a meal.
o'bson/ō -ā're *vi.* interrupt.
obso'rb/eō -ē're *vt.* swallow, bolt.
obsta'nt/ia -ium *n.pl.* obstructions.
obste'tr/īx -ī'cis *f.* midwife.
obstinā'ti/ō -ō'nis *f.* determination, stubbornness.
obstinā't/us *a.* firm, resolute; stubborn. **-ē** *ad.* firmly, obstinately.
o'bstin/ō -ā're *vi.* be determined, persist.
obstipē'scō, *see* **obstupēscō**.
obstī'pus *a.* bent, bowed, drawn back.
o'bstitī *perf.* obsistō; *perf.* obstō.
o'bst/ō -ā're -itī *vi.* stand in the way; obstruct, prevent.
o'bstrep/ō -ere -uī -itum *vi.* make a noise; shout against, cry down, molest. *vt.* drown (in noise); fill with noise.
obstri'ctus *ppp.* obstringō.
obstr/i'ngō -i'ngere -i'nxī -i'ctum *vt.* bind up, tie round; (*fig.*) confine, hamper; lay under an obligation.
obstru'cti/ō -ō'nis *f.* barrier.
obstru'ctus *ppp.* obstruō.
obstrū'/dō (**obtrū'dō**) -dere -sī -sum *vt.* force on to; gulp down.
o'bstru/ō -ere -xī -ctum *vt.* build up against, block; shut, hinder.
obstupe/fa'ciō -fa'cere -fē'cī -fa'ctum (*pass.* -fī'ō -fi'erī) *vt.* astound, paralyse.
obstup/ē'scō (**obstipē'scō**) -ē'scere -uī *vi.* be astounded, paralysed.
obstu'pidus *a.* stupefied.
o'b/sum -e'sse -fuī *vi.* be against, harm.
o'bs/uō -u'ere -uī -ū'tum *vt.* sew on, sew up.
obsurd/ē'scō -ē'scere -uī *vi.* grow deaf; turn a deaf ear.
obsū'tus *ppp.* obsuō.
o'bt/egō -e'gere -ē'xī -ē'ctum *vt.* cover over; conceal.

obtemperā'ti/ō -ō'nis *f.* obedience.
obte'mper/ō -ā're -ā'vī -ā't-um *vi.* (*with dat.*) comply with, obey.
obte'n/dō -dere -dī -tum *vt.* spread over, stretch over against; conceal; make a pretext of.
obte'ntus *ppp.* obtendō; *ppp.* obtineō. [pretext.
obte'nt/us -ūs *m.* screen;
o'bt/erō -e'rere -rī'vī -rī'tum *vt.* trample on, crush; disparage.
obtestā'ti/ō -ō'nis *f.* adjuring; supplication.
obte'st/or -ā'rī -ā'tus *vt.* call to witness; entreat. [spread.
obte'x/ō -ere -uī *vt.* over-
obti'c/eō -ē're *vi.* be silent.
obtic/ē'scō -ē'scere -uī *vi.* be struck dumb.
o'btigī *perf.* obtingō.
o'btigō, *see* **obtegō.**
obt/i'neō -inē're -i'nuī -e'n-tum *vt.* hold, possess; maintain; gain, obtain. *vi.* prevail, continue.
obti'/ngō -ngere -gī *vi.* fall to one's lot; happen.
obtorp/ē'scō -ē'scere -uī *vi.* become numb, lose feeling.
obto'r/queō -quē're -sī -tum *vt.* twist about, wrench.
obtrectā'ti/ō -ō'nis *f.* disparagement.
obtrectā't/or -ō'ris *m.* disparager.
obtre'ct/ō -ā're *vt.* & *i.* detract, disparage.
obtrī'tus *ppp.* obterō.
obtrū'dō, *see* **obstrūdō.**
obtru'nc/ō -ā're *vt.* cut down, slaughter.
obtu'/eor -ē'rī, -or -ī *vt.* gaze at, see clearly.
o'btulī *perf.* offerō.
obt/u'ndō -u'ndere -udī -ū'sum & -ū'nsum *vt.* beat, thump; blunt; (*speech*) deafen, annoy.
obtu'rb/ō -ā're *vt.* throw into confusion; bother, distract.
obturgē'sc/ō -ere *vi.* swell up.
obtū'r/ō -ā're *vt.* stop up, close.
obtū'sus, obtū'nsus *ppp.* obtundō. *a.* blunt; (*fig.*) dulled, blurred, unfeeling.
obtū't/us -ūs *m.* gaze.
obu'mbr/ō -ā're *vt.* shade, darken; (*fig.*) cloak, screen.
obu'ncus *a.* hooked.
obū'stus *a.* burnt, hardened in fire.
obvallā'tus *a.* fortified.
obv/e'niō -enī're -ē'nī -e'ntum *vi.* come up; fall to; occur.
obve'rs/or -ā'rī *vi.* move about before; (*visions*) hover.
obve'rsus *ppp.* obvertō. *a.* turned towards. *m.pl.* enemy.
obve'r/tō -tere -tī -sum *vt.* direct towards, turn against.
o'bviam *ad.* to meet, against.
o'bvius *a.* in the way, to meet; opposite, against; at hand, accessible; exposed.
obvo'l/vō -vere -vī -ū'tum *vt.* wrap up, muffle up; (*fig.*) cloak.
occae'c/ō -ā're -ā'vī -ā'tum *vt.* blind, obscure, conceal; benumb.
occall/ē'scō -ē'scere -uī *vi.* grow a thick skin; become hardened.
o'ccan/ō -ere *vi.* sound the attack.
occā'si/ō -ō'nis *f.* opportunity, convenient time; (*mil.*) surprise.
occāsiu'ncul/a -ae *f.* opportunity.
occā's/us -ūs *m.* setting; west; downfall, ruin.
occā'ti/ō -ō'nis *f.* harrowing.
occā't/or -ō'ris *m.* harrower.
occē'd/ō -ere *vi.* go up to.
occe'nt/ō -ā're *vt.* & *i.* serenade; sing a lampoon.
occē'pī *perf.* occipiō.
occe'psō *archaic fut.* occipiō.
occe'pt/ō -ā're *vt.* begin.

o'ccid/ēns -e'ntis *pres.p.* occidō. *m.* west.
occī'di/ō -ō'nis *f.* massacre. -ōne occidere annihilate.
occī/dō -dere -dī -sum *vt.* fell; cut down, kill; pester.
o'cc/idō -i'dere -idī -ā'sum *vi.* fall; set; die, perish, be ruined. [failing.
occi'duus *a.* setting; western;
o'ccin/ō -ere -uī *vi.* sing inauspiciously.
occ/i'piō -i'pere -ē'pī -e'ptum *vt.* & *i.* begin.
occipi't/ium -ī & iī *n.* back of the head.
occī'si/ō -ō'nis *f.* massacre.
occī's/or -ō'ris *m.* killer.
occī'sus *ppp.* occidō.
occlā'mit/ō -ā're *vi.* bawl.
occlū'/dō -dere -sī -sum *vt.* shut up; stop.
o'cc/ō -ā're *vt.* harrow.
o'ccub/ō -ā're *vi.* lie.
occu'lc/ō -ā're *vt.* trample down.
o'ccul/ō -ere -uī -tum *vt.* cover over, hide.
occultā'ti/ō -ō'nis *f.* concealment.
occultā't/or -ō'ris *m.* hider.
occu'lt/ō -ā're -ā'vī -ā'tum *vt.* conceal secrete.
occu'lt/us *ppp.* occulō. *a.* hidden, secret; (*person*) reserved, secretive. *n.* secret, hiding. **-ē** *ad.* secretly.
occu'/mbō -mbere -buī -bitum *vi.* fall, die.
occupā'ti/ō -ō'nis *f.* taking possession; business; engagement.
o'ccup/ō -ā're -ā'vī -ā'tum *vt.* take possession of, seize; occupy, take up; surprise, anticipate; (*money*) lend invest **-ā'tus** *a.* occupied, busy.
occu'r/rō -rere -rī -sum *vi.* run up to, meet; attack; fall in with; hurry to; (*fig.*) obviate, counteract; (*words*) object; (*thought*) occur, suggest itself.
occursā'ti/ō -ō'nis *f.* fussy welcome.
occu'rs/ō -ā're *vi.* run to meet, meet; oppose; (*thought*) occur.
occu'rs/us -ūs *m.* meeting.
Ōce'an/us -ī *m.* Ocean a stream encircling the earth; the Atlantic. **-ī'tis** -ī'tidis *f.* daughter of Ocean.
oce'll/us -ī *m.* eye; darling, gem.
ō'ci/or -ō'ris *a.* quicker, swifter.
ō'cius *ad.* more quickly; sooner, rather; quickly.
o'cre/a -ae *f.* greave.
ocreā'tus *a.* greaved.
Octā'v/ius -ī *m.* Roman family name, *esp.* the emperor Augustus; his father. **-iā'nus** *a.* of Octavius. *m.* Octavian, a surname of Augustus.
octā'v/us *a.* eighth. *f.* eighth hour. **-um** *ad.* for the eighth time. [eenth.
octāvusde'cimus *a.* eight-
o'cti/ēns, **-ēs** *ad.* eight times.
octingentē'simus *a.* eight hundredth.
octinge'nt/ī -ō'rum *num.* eight hundred.
o'ctip/ēs -edis *a.* eight-footed.
o'ctō *num.* eight.
Octō'b/er -ris *a.* of October. *m.* October. [each.
octōgē'n/ī -ō'rum *a.* eighty
octōgē'simus *a.* eightieth.
octō'giēns, **-ēs** *ad.* eighty times.
octōgi'ntā *num.* eighty.
octō'iugis *a.* eight together.
octō'n/ī -ō'rum *a.* eight at a time, eight each.
octō'phoros *a.* (*litter*) carried by eight bearers.
octuplicā'tus *a.* multiplied by eight.
octu'plus *a.* eight-fold.
octu'ss/is -is *m.* eight asses.

oculā't/us *a.* with eyes; visible. **-ā** diē vēndere sell for cash.
o'cul/us **-ī** *m.* eye; sight; (*plant*) bud; (*fig.*) darling, jewel. **-ōs** adicere ad glance at, covet. ante **-ōs** pōnere imagine. ex **-īs** out of sight. esse in **-īs** be in view; be a favourite.
ō'd/ī -i'sse *vt.* hate, dislike.
odiō's/us *a.* odious, unpleasant. **-ē** *ad.*
o'd/ium **-ī** & **iī** *n.* hatred, dislike, displeasure; insolence. **-iō** esse be hateful, be disliked.
o'd/or (**-ōs**) **-ō'ris** *m.* smell, perfume, stench; (*fig.*) inkling, suggestion.
odōrā'ti/ō **-ō'nis** *f.* smelling.
odōrā'tus *a.* fragrant, perfumed.
odōrā't/us **-ūs** *m.* sense of smell; smelling.
odō'rifer **-ī** *a.* fragrant; perfume-producing.
odō'r/ō **-ā're** *vt.* perfume.
odō'r/or **-ā'rī** **-ā'tus** *vt.* smell, smell out; (*fig.*) search out; aspire to; get a smattering of.
odō'rus *a.* fragrant; keen-scented.
o'dōs, *see* **odor.**
Odry'sius *a.* Thracian.
Odyssē'/a **-ae** *f.* Odyssey.
Oea'grius *a.* Thracian.
Oe'bal/us **-ī** *m.* king of Sparta. **-ius** *a.* Spartan. **-ia** -iae *f.* Tarentum. **-idēs** -idae *m.* Castor, Pollux. **-is** -idis *f.* Helen.
Oe'dip/ūs **-odis** & **ī** *m.* king of Thebes; solver of riddles.
oeno'phor/um **-ī** *n.* wine-basket.
Oeno'pi/a **-ae** *f.* Aegina.
Oeno'tri/a **-ae** *f.* S.E. Italy. **-us** *a.* Italian.
oe'str/us **-ī** *m.* gad-fly; (*fig.*) frenzy.
Oe't/a **-ae**, **-ē** **-ēs** *f.* mountain range in Thessaly, associated with Hercules. **-ae'us** *a.*
ofe'll/a **-ae** *f.* morsel.
o'ff/a **-ae** *f.* pellet, lump; swelling.
offe'ctus *ppp.* officiō.
off/e'ndō -e'ndere -e'ndī -ē'nsum *vt.* hit; hit on, come upon; offend, blunder; take offence; fail, come to grief.
offē'ns/a **-ae** *f.* displeasure, enmity; offence, injury.
offē'nsi/ō **-ō'nis** *f.* stumbling; stumbling-block; misfortune, indisposition; offence, displeasure.
offēnsiu'ncul/a **-ae** *f.* slight displeasure; slight check.
offē'ns/ō **-ā're** *vt.* & *i.* dash against.
offē'nsus *ppp.* offendō. *a.* offensive; displeased. *n.* offence. [offence.
offē'ns/us **-ūs** *m.* shock;
o'ffer/ō **-re obtulī oblātum** *vt.* present, show; bring forward, offer; expose; occasion inflict. sē — encounter.
offerume'nt/a **-ae** *f.* present.
officī'n/a **-ae** *f.* workshop factory.
off/i'ciō **-i'cere** **-ē'cī** **-e'ctum** *vi.* obstruct, interfere with; hurt, prejudice.
officiō's/us *a* obliging; dutiful. **-ē** *ad.* courteously.
offi'c/ium **-ī** & **iī** *n.* service, attention; ceremonial; duty, sense of duty; official duty, function. [in.
offī'g/ō **-ere** *vt.* fasten, drive
offi'rm/ō **-ā're** *vt.* & *i.* persevere in. **-ā'tus** *a.* determined.
offle'ct/ō **-ere** *vt.* turn about.
offrēnā'tus *a.* checked.
offū'ci/a **-ae** *f* (*cosmetic*) paint; (*fig.*) trick. [on.
offu'l/geō **-gē're** **-sī** *vi.* shine
off/u'ndō **-u'ndere** **-ū'dī** **-ū'sum** *vt.* pour out to; pour over, spread; cover, fill.

offū'sus *ppp.* offundō.
ogga'nn/iō -ī're *vi.* growl at.
o'gger/ō -ere *vt.* bring, give.
Ōgy'gius *a.* Theban.
oh *interj.* (*expressing surprise, joy, grief*) oh !
o'hē *interj.* (*expressing surfeit*) stop ! enough !
oi *interj.* (*expressing complaint, weeping*) oh ! oh dear !
oi'ei *interj.* (*lamenting*) oh dear!
Oī'l/eus -eī *m.* father of the less famous Ajax.
o'le/a -ae *f.* olive; olive-tree.
oleā'ginus *a.* of the olive-tree.
oleā'rius *a.* oil-. *m.* oil-seller.
olea'st/er -rī *m.* wild olive.
o'l/ēns -e'ntis *pres.p.* oleō. *a.* fragrant; stinking, musty.
o'l/eō -ē're -uī *vt.* & *i.* smell, smell of; (*fig.*) betray.
o'le/um -ī *n.* olive-oil oil; wrestling-school. — et operam perdere waste time and trouble.
ol/fa'ciō fa'cere -fē'cī -fa'ctum *vt.* smell, scent.
olfa'ct/ō -ā're *vt.* smell at.
o'lidus *a.* smelling, rank.
ō'lim *ad.* once, once upon a time; at the time, at times; for a good while; one day (in the future).
olit-, *see* **holit-**.
olī'v/a -ae *f.* olive, olive-tree; olive-branch, olive-staff.
olīvē't/um -ī *n.* olive-grove.
olī'vifer -ī *a.* olive-bearing.
olī'v/um -ī *n.* oil; wrestling-school; perfume.
o'll/a -ae *f.* pot, jar.
o'lle, **o'llus**, *see* **ille**.
o'l/or -ō'ris *m.* swan.
olōrī'nus *a.* swan's.
o'lus, *see* **holus**.
Oly'mpi/a -ae *f.* site of the Greek games in Elis. **-acus**, **-cus**, **-us** *a.* Olympic. **-a** -ō'rum *n.pl.* Olympic Games. **-as** -adis *f.* Olympiad, period of four years.
Olympionī'c/ēs -ae *m.* Olympic winner.
Oly'mp/us -ī *m.* mountain in N. Greece, abode of the gods; heaven.
omā's/um -ī *n.* tripe; paunch.
ō'm/en -inis *n.* omen, sign; solemnity.
ōme'nt/um -ī *n.* bowels.
ō'min/or -ā'rī -ā'tus *vt.* forebode, prophesy.
ōmi'ssus *ppp.* ōmittō. *a.* remiss.
ōm/i'ttō -i'ttere -ī'sī -i'ssum *vt.* let go; leave off, give up; disregard, overlook; (*speech*) pass over, omit.
o'mnifer -ī *a.* all-sustaining.
omni'genus *a.* of all kinds.
omni'modīs *ad.* wholly.
omnī'nō *ad.* entirely, altogether, at all; in general; (*concession*) to be sure, yes; (*number*) in all, just. — nōn not at all.
omni'par/ēns -e'ntis *a.* mother of all.
omni'pot/ēns -e'ntis *a.* almighty.
o'mnis *a.* all, every, any; every kind of; the whole of. *n.* the universe. *m.pl.* everybody. *n.pl.* everything.
omni'tu/ēns -e'ntis *a.* all-seeing.
omni'vagus *a.* roving everywhere.
omni'volus *a.* willing every-[thing.
o'nag/er -rī *m.* wild ass.
onerā'rius *a.* (*beast*) of burden; (*ship*) transport.
o'ner/ō -ā're -ā'vī -ā'tum *vt.* load, burden; (*fig.*) overload, oppress; aggravate.
onerō'sus *a.* heavy, burdensome, irksome.
o'n/us -eris *n.* load, burden, cargo; (*fig.*) charge, difficulty.
onu'stus *a.* loaded, burdened; (*fig.*) filled.
o'ny/x -chis *m.*, *f.* onyx; onyx-box.

opā'cit/ās -ā'tis *f.* shade.
opā'c/ō -ā're *vt.* shade.
opā'cus *a.* shady; dark.
o'pe *abl.* ops.
ope'll/a -ae *f.* light work, small service.
o'per/a -ae *f.* exertion, work; service; care, attention; leisure, time; (*person*) workman, hired rough. -am dare pay attention; do one's best. -ae pretium worth while. -ā meā thanks to me.
operā'rius *a.* working. *m.* workman.
ope'rcul/um -ī *n.* cover, lid.
operīme'nt/um -ī *n.* covering.
ope'r/iō -ī're -uī -tum *vt.* cover; close; (*fig.*) overwhelm, conceal.
o'per/or -ā'rī -ā'tus *vi.* work, take pains, be occupied.
operō's/us *a.* active, industrious; laborious, elaborate. -ē *ad.* painstakingly.
ope'rtus *ppp.* operiō. *a.* covered, hidden. *n.* secret.
o'pēs *pl.* ops.
o'picus *a.* barbarous, boorish.
o'pifer -ī *a.* helping.
o'pif/ex -icis *m., f.* maker; craftsman, artisan.
ōpi'li/ō -ō'nis *m.* shepherd.
opī'mit/ās -ā'tis *f.* abundance.
opī'm/us *a.* rich, fruitful, fat; copious, sumptuous; (*style*) overloaded. spolia -a spoils of an enemy commander killed by a Roman general.
opīnā'bilis *a.* conjectural.
opīnā'ti/ō -ō'nis *f.* conjecture.
opīnā't/or -ō'ris *m.* conjecturer.
opīnā't/us -ūs *m.* supposition.
opī'ni/ō -ō'nis *f.* opinion, conjecture, belief; reputation, esteem; rumour. contrā, praeter -ōnem contrary to expectation.
opīniō'sus *a.* dogmatic.
opī'n/or -ā'rī -ā'tus *vi.* think, suppose, imagine. *a.* imagined.
opi'par/us *a.* rich, sumptuous. -ē *ad.*
opi'tul/or -ā'rī -ā'tus *vi.* (*with dat.*) help.
opo'rt/et -ē're -uit *vt.*(*impers.*) ought, should.
oppē'd/ō -ere *vi.* insult.
oppe'r/ior -ī'rī -tus *vt.* & *i.* wait, wait for.
o'ppet/ō -ere -ī'vī -ī'tum *vt.* encounter; die.
oppidā'nus *a.* provincial. *m.pl.* townsfolk.
o'ppidō *ad.* quite, completely, exactly.
oppi'dul/um -ī *n.* small town.
o'ppid/um -ī *n.* town.
oppi'gner/ō -ā're *vt.* pledge.
oppī'l/ō -ā're *vt.* stop up.
o'ppl/eō -ē're -ē'vī -ē'tum *vt.* fill, choke up.
opp/ō'nō -ō'nere -o'suī -o'situm *vt.* put against, set before; expose; present; (*argument*) adduce, reply, oppose; (*property*) pledge, mortgage.
opportū'nit/ās -ā'tis *f.* suitableness, advantage; good opportunity.
opportū'n/us *a.* suitable, opportune; useful; exposed. -ē *ad.* opportunely.
opposi'ti/ō -ō'nis *f.* opposing.
oppo'situs *ppp.* oppōnō. *a.* against, opposite.
oppo'sit/us -ūs *m.* opposing.
oppo'suī *perf.* oppōnō.
oppre'ssi/ō -ō'nis *f.* violence; seizure; overthrow.
oppre'ssus *ppp.* opprimō.
oppre'ss/us -ūs *m.* pressure.
o'ppr/imō -i'mere -e'ssī -e'ssum *vt.* press down, crush; press together, close; suppress, overwhelm, overthrow; surprise, seize.
oppro'br/ium -ī & iī *n.* reproach, disgrace, scandal.
oppro'br/ō -ā're *vt.* taunt.

oppugnā'ti/ō -ō'nis *f.* attack, assault.
oppugnā't/or -ō'ris *m.* assailant.
oppu'gn/ō -ā're -ā'vī -ā'tum *vt.* attack, assault.
op/s -o'pis *f.* power, strength; help. **o'p/ēs** -um *f.pl.* resources, wealth. **Ops** goddess of plenty.
ops–, *see* **obs–**.
optā'bilis *a.* desirable.
optā'ti/ō -ō'nis *f.* wish.
optim/ā's -ā'tis *a.* aristocratic. *m.pl.* the nobility.
o'ptimē *ad.* best, very well; just in time.
o'ptim/us *a.* best, very good; excellent. -ō iūre deservedly.
o'pti/ō -ō'nis *f.* choice. *m.* assistant.
optī'vus *a.* chosen.
o'pt/ō -ā're -ā'vī -ā'tum *vt.* choose; wish for. **–ā'tus** *a.* longed for. *n.* wish. -ā'tō according to one's wish.
optum–, *see* **optim–**.
o'pul/ēns -e'ntis *a.* rich.
opule'nti/a -ae *f.* wealth; power.
opule'nt/ō -ā're *vt.* enrich.
opule'nt/us *a.* rich, sumptuous powerful. **–ē**, **–er** *ad.* sumptuously.
o'p/us -eris *n.* work, workmanship; (*art*) work, building, book; (*mil.*) siege-work; (*colloq.*) business; (*with* esse) need. virō — est a man is needed. māgnō -ere much, greatly.
opu'scul/um -ī *n.* little work.
ō'r/a -ae *f.* edge, boundary; coast; country, region; (*naut.*) hawser.
ōrā'cul/um -ī *n.* oracle, prophecy.
ōrā'ti/ō -ō'nis *f.* speech, language; a speech, oration; eloquence; prose; emperor's message. -ōnem habēre deliver a speech.
ōrātiu'ncul/a -ae *f.* short speech.
ōrā't/or -ō'ris *m.* speaker, spokesman, orator. [–ē *ad.*
ōrātō'ri/us *a.* oratorical.
ōrā'tr/īx -ī'cis *f.* suppliant.
ōrā't/us -ūs *m.* request.
orbā't/or -ō'ris *m.* bereaver.
orbiculā'tus *a.* round.
o'rb/is -is *m.* circle, ring, disc, orbit; world; (*movement*) cycle, rotation; (*style*) rounding off. — lacteus Milky Way. — signifer Zodiac. — fortūnae wheel of Fortune. — terrārum the earth, world. in -em cōnsistere form a circle. in -em īre go the rounds.
o'rbit/a -ae *f.* rut, track, path.
o'rbit/ās -ā'tis *f.* childlessness, orphanhood, widowhood.
orbitō'sus *a.* full of ruts.
o'rb/ō -ā're -ā'vī -ā'tum *vt.* bereave, orphan, make childless. [childless; destitute.
o'rbus *a.* bereaved, orphan,
o'rc/a -ae *f.* vat.
O'rcad/es -um *f.pl.* Orkneys.
o'rcha/s -dis *f.* kind of olive.
orchē'str/a -ae *f.* senatorial seats (in the theatre).
O'rc/us -ī *m.* Pluto; the lower world; death.
ōrdinā'rius *a.* regular.
ōrdinā'tim *ad.* in order, properly.
ōrdinā'ti/ō -ō'nis *f.* orderly arrangement.
ō'rdin/ō -ā're -ā'vī -ā'tum *vt.* arrange, regulate, set in order. -ā'tus *a.* appointed.
ō'r/dior -dī'rī -sus *vt.* & *i.* begin, undertake.
ō'rd/ō -inis *m.* line, row, series; order, regularity, arrangement; (*mil.*) rank, line, company, (*pl.*) captains; (*building*) course, layer; (*seats*) row; (*pol.*) class, order, station. ex -ine in order, in one's turn; one after the other. extrā -inem irregularly, unusually.

Orē'a/s -dis *f.* mountain-nymph.
Ore'st/ēs -is & ae *m.* son of Agamemnon, whom he avenged by killing his mother. **-ē'us** *a.*
ore'x/is -is *f.* appetite.
o'rgan/um -ī *n.* instrument, organ.
o'rgi/a -ō'rum *n.pl.* Bacchic revels; orgies.
oricha'lc/um -ī *n.* copper ore, brass.
ōrici'll/a -ae *f.* lobe.
o'ri/ēns -e'ntis *pres.p.* orior. *m.* morning; east.
orī'g/ō -inis *f.* beginning, source; ancestry, descent; founder.
Ōrī'/ōn -onis & -ō'nis *m.* mythical hunter and constellation.
o'r/ior -ī'rī -tus *vi.* rise; spring, descend.
oriu'ndus *a.* descended, sprung.
ōrnāme'nt/um -ī *n.* equipment, dress; ornament, decoration; distinction, pride of.
ōrnā't/us *ppp.* ōrnō. *a.* equipped, furnished; embellished, excellent. **-ē** *ad.* elegantly.
ōrnā't/us -ūs *m.* preparation; dress, equipment; embellishment.
ō'rn/ō -ā're -ā'vī -ā'tum *vt.* fit out, equip, dress, prepare; adorn, embellish, honour.
o'rn/us -ī *f.* manna ash.
ō'r/ō -ā're -ā'vī -ā'tum *vt.* speak, plead; beg, entreat; pray.
Oro'nt/ēs -is & ī *m.* river of Syria. **-ē'us** *a.* Syrian.
O'rph/eus -eī & eos (*acc.* -ea) *m.* legendary Thracian singer, who went down to Hades for Eurydice. **-ē'us**, **-icus** *a.*
ō'rsus *ppa.* ōrdior. *n.pl.* beginning; utterance.
ō'rs/us -ūs *m.* beginning.
o'rtus *ppa.* orior. *a.* born, descended.
o'rt/us -ūs *m.* rising; east; origin, source.
Orty'gi/a -ae, -ē -ēs *f.* Delos. **-us** *a.*
o'ry/x -gis *m.* gazelle.
ory'z/a -ae *f.* rice.
os o'ssis *n.* bone; (*fig.*) very soul.
ōs ō'ris *n.* mouth; face; entrance, opening; effrontery. ūnō ōre unanimously. in ōre esse be talked about. quō ōre redībō how shall I have the face to go back?
o'sc/en -inis *m.* bird of omen.
ōsci'll/um -ī *n.* little mask.
ō'scit/āns -a'ntis *pres.p.* ōscitō. *a.* listless, drowsy. **-a'nter** *ad.* half-heartedly.
ō'scit/ō -ā're, **-or** -ā'rī *vi.* yawn, be drowsy.
ōsculā'ti/ō -ō'nis *f.* kissing.
ō'scul/or -ā'rī -ā'tus *vt.* kiss; make a fuss of.
ō'scul/um -ī *n.* sweet mouth; kiss.
O'scus *a.* Oscan.
Osī'r/is -is & idis *m.* Egyptian god, husband of Isis.
O'ss/a -ae *f.* mountain in Thessaly.
o'sseus *a.* bony.
ossi'frag/a -ae *f.* osprey.
oste'n/dō -dere -dī -tum *vt.* hold out, show, display; expose; disclose, reveal; (*speech*) say, make known.
ostentā'ti/ō -ō'nis *f.* display; showing off, ostentation; pretence.
ostentā't/or -ō'ris *m.* displayer, boaster.
oste'nt/ō -ā're *vt.* hold out, proffer, exhibit; show off, boast of; make known, indicate.
oste'nt/us *ppp.* ostendō. **-um** -ī *n.* portent.
oste'nt/us -ūs *m.* display, appearance; proof.
Ō'sti/a -ae *f.*, -ō'rum *n.pl.*

port at the Tiber mouth. **-ē'nsis** *a.*
ōstiā'r/ium -ī & ii *n.* door-tax. [door.
ōstiā'tim *ad.* from door to
ŏ'st/ium -ī & ii *n.* door; entrance, mouth.
o'stre/a -ae *f.*, **-um** -ī *n.* oyster.
ostreō'sus *a.* rich in oysters.
o'strifer -ī *a.* oyster-producing.
ostrī'nus *a.* purple.
o'str/um -ī *n.* purple; purple dress or coverings. [ōdī.
ō'sus, ōsū'rus *ppa.* & *fut.p.*
O'th/ō -ō'nis *m.* author of a law giving theatre seats to Equites; Roman emperor after Galba. **-ōniā'nus** *a.*
ōti'ol/um -ī *n.* bit of leisure.
ō'ti/or -ā'rī *vi.* have a holiday, be idle.
ōtiō's/us *a.* at leisure, free; out of public affairs; neutral, indifferent; quiet, unexcited; (*things*) free, idle. *m.* private citizen, civilian. **-ē** *ad.* leisurely; quietly; fearlessly.
ŏ't/ium -ī & ii *n.* leisure, time (for); idleness, retirement; peace, quiet.
ovā'ti/ō -ō'nis *f.* minor triumph.
ovī'l/e -is *n.* sheep-fold, goat-fold.
ovi'llus *a.* of sheep.
o'v/is -is *f.* sheep.
o'v/ō -ā're *vi.* rejoice; celebrate a minor triumph.
ō'v/um -ī *n.* egg.

P

pābulā'ti/ō -ō'nis *f.* foraging.
pābulā't/or -ō'ris *m.* forager.
pā'bul/or -ā'rī *vi.* forage.
pā'bul/um -ī *n.* food, fodder.
pācā'lis *a.* of peace.
Pachy̆'n/um -ī *n.* S.E. point of Sicily, *mod.* Cape Passaro.

pā'cifer -ī *a.* peace-bringing.
pācificā'ti/ō -ō'nis *f.* peace-making.
pācificā't/or -ō'ris *m.* peace-maker. **-ō'rius** *a.* peace-making.
pāci'fic/ō -ā're *vi.* make a peace. *vt.* appease.
pāci'ficus *a.* peace-making.
pac/ī'scor -ī'scī -tus *vi.* make a bargain, agree. *vt.* stipulate for; barter.
pā'c/ō -ā're -ā'vī -ā'tum *vt.* pacify, subdue. **-ā'tus** *a.* peaceful, tranquil. *n.* friendly country.
pa'cti/ō -ō'nis *f.* bargain, agreement, contract; collusion; (*words*) formula.
Pactō'l/us -ī *m.* river of Lydia, famous for its gold.
pa'ct/or -ō'ris *m.* negotiator.
pa'ct/us *ppa.* pacīscor. *a.* agreed, settled; betrothed. **-um** -ī *n.* agreement, contract. [poet.
Pācu'v/ius -ī *m.* Latin tragic
Pa'd/us -ī *m.* river Po.
pae'/ān -ā'nis *m.* healer, epithet of Apollo; hymn of praise, shout of joy; (*metre*) paeon.
paedagō'g/us -ī *m.* slave who took children to school.
pae'd/or -ō'ris *m.* filth.
pae'l/ex -icis *f.* mistress, concubine.
paelicā't/us -ūs *m.* concubinage.
Paeli'gn/ī -ō'rum *m.pl.* people of central Italy. **-us** *a.*
pae'ne *ad.* almost, nearly.
paenī'nsul/a -ae *f.* peninsula.
paenite'ndus *a.* regrettable.
paenite'nti/a -ae *f.* repentance.
pae'nit/et -ē're -uit *vt.* & *i.*(*impers.*) repent, regret, be sorry; be dissatisfied. an **-et** is it not enough?
pae'nul/a -ae *f.* travelling cloak.

paenulā'tus *a.* wearing a cloak.
pae'/ōn -ō'nis *m.* metrical foot of one long and three short syllables.
paeō'nius *a.* healing.
Pae'st/um -ī *n.* town in S. Italy. **-ā'nus** *a.*
pae'tulus *a.* with a slight cast in the eye.
pae'tus *a.* with a cast in the eye.
pāgā'nus *a.* rural. *m.* villager, yokel.
pāgā'tim *ad.* in every village.
pāge'll/a -ae *f.* small page.
pā'gin/a -ae *f.* (*book*) page, leaf.
pāgi'nul/a -ae *f.* small page.
pā'g/us -ī *m.* village, country district; canton.
pā'l/a -ae *f.* spade; (*ring*) bezel.
palae'str/a -ae *f.* wrestling-school, gymnasium; exercise, wrestling; (*rhet.*) exercise, training.
palae'stric/us *a.* of the wrestling-school. **-ē** *ad.* in gymnastic fashion.
palaestrī't/a -ae *m.* head of a wrestling-school.
pa'lam *ad.* openly, publicly, well-known. *pr.*(*with abl.*) in the presence of.
Palā't/ium -ī *n.* Palatine Hill in Rome; palace. **-ī'nus** *a.* Palatine; imperial.
palā't/um -ī *n.* palate; taste, judgment.
pa'le/a -ae *f.* chaff.
paleā'r/ia -ium *n.pl.* dewlap.
Pa'l/ēs -is *f.* goddess of shepherds. **-ī'lis** *a.* of Pales. *n.pl.* festival of Pales.
palimpsē'st/us -ī *m.* palimpsest.
Palinū'r/us -ī *m.* pilot of Aeneas; promontory in S. Italy.
paliū'r/us -ī *m.* Christ's thorn.
pa'll/a -ae *f.* woman's robe; tragic costume.
Pa'lla/s -dis & dos *f.* Athene, Minerva; oil; olive-tree. **-dius** *a.* of Pallas. **-dium** -dī *n.* image of Pallas.
Pa'll/ās -a'ntis *m.* ancestor or son of Evander. **-antē'us** *a.*
pa'll/ēns -e'ntis *pres.p.* palleō. *a.* pale; greenish.
pa'll/eō -ē're -uī *vi.* be pale or yellow; fade; be anxious.
pall/ē'scō -ē'scere -uī *vi.* turn pale, turn yellow.
palliā'tus *a.* wearing a Greek cloak.
palli'dulus *a.* palish.
pa'llidus *a.* pale, pallid, greenish; in love.
palli'ol/um -ī *n.* small cloak, cape, hood.
pa'll/ium -ī & iī *n.* coverlet; Greek cloak.
pa'll/or -ō'ris *m.* paleness, fading; fear.
pa'lm/a -ae *f.* (*hand*) palm, hand; (*oar*) blade; (*tree*) palm, date; branch; (*fig.*) prize, victory, glory.
palmā'ris *a.* excellent.
palmā'rius *a.* prize-winning.
palmā'tus *a.* palm-embroidered.
pa'lm/es -itis *m.* pruned shoot, branch.
palmē't/um -ī *n.* palm-grove.
pa'lmifer -ī *a.* palm-bearing.
palmō'sus *a.* palm-clad.
pa'lmul/a -ae *f.* oar-blade.
pā'l/or -ā'rī -ā'tus *vi.* wander about, straggle.
palpā'ti/ō -ō'nis *f.* flatteries.
palpā't/or -ō'ris *m.* flatterer.
palpe'br/a -ae *f.* eyelid.
pa'lpit/ō -ā're *vi.* throb, writhe.
pa'lp/ō -ā're, -or -ā'rī *vt.* stroke; coax, flatter.
pa'lp/us -ī *m.* coaxing.
palūdāme'nt/um -ī *n.* military cloak.
palūdā'tus *a.* in a general's cloak.

palūdō'sus *a.* marshy.
palu'mb/ēs -is *m., f.* wood-pigeon.
pā'l/us -ī *m.* stake, pale.
pa'l/ūs -ū'dis *f.* marsh, pool, lake.
palū'st/er -ris *a.* marshy.
pampi'neus *a.* of vine-shoots.
pa'mpin/us -ī *m.* vine-shoot.
P/ān -ā'nos (*acc.* -ā'na) *m.* Greek god of shepherds, hills and woods, *esp.* associated with Arcadia.
panacē'/a -ae *f.* a herb supposed to cure all diseases.
Panae't/ius -ī *m.* Stoic philosopher.
Panchā'/ia -iae *f.* part of Arabia. **-ae'us, -ā'ius** *a.*
panchrē'stus *a.* good for everything.
pancra't/ium -ī & iī *n.* all-in boxing and wrestling match.
pandi'cul/or -ā're *vi.* stretch oneself.
Pandī'/ōn -onis *m.* king of Athens, father of Procne and Philomela. **-o'nius** *a.*
pa'nd/ō -ere -ī pā'nsum & pa'ssum *vt.* spread out, stretch, extend; open; (*fig.*) disclose, explain.
pa'ndus *a.* curved, bent.
pa'ng/ō -ere pa'nxī & pe'pigī pā'ctum *vt.* drive in, fasten; make, compose; agree, settle.
pāni'cul/a -ae *f.* tuft.
pā'nic/um -ī *n.* Italian millet.
pā'n/is -is *m.* bread, loaf.
Pāni'sc/us -ī *m.* little Pan.
panni'cul/us -ī *m.* rag.
Panno'ni/a -ae *f.* country on the middle Danube. **-us** *a.*
pannō'sus *a.* ragged.
pa'nn/us -ī *m.* piece of cloth, rag, patch.
Pano'rm/us -ī *f.* town in Sicily, *mod.* Palermo.
pā'nsa *a.* splay-foot.
pā'nsus *ppp.* pandō.
panthē'r/a -ae *f.* panther.
Pa'nth/ūs -ī *m.* priest of Apollo at Troy. **-o'id/ēs** -ae *m.* Euphorbus.
pa'ntic/ēs -um *m.pl.* bowels; sausages.
pa'nxī *pref.* pangō.
papae' *interj.* (*expressing wonder*) ooh!
pā'p/as -ae *m.* tutor. [*a.*
papā'ver -is *n.* poppy. **-eus**
Pa'ph/os -ī *f.* town in Cyprus, sacred to Venus. **-ius** *a.*
pāpi'li/ō -ō'nis *m.* butterfly.
papi'll/a -ae *f.* teat, nipple; breast.
pa'pp/us -ī *m.* woolly seed.
pa'pul/a -ae *f.* pimple.
papȳ'rifer -ī *a.* papyrus-bearing.
papȳ'r/us -ī *m., f.,* **-um** -ī *n.* papyrus; paper.
pār pa'ris *a.* equal, like; a match for; proper, right. *m.* peer, partner, companion. *n.* pair. **pār parī respondēre** return like for like. **parēs cum paribus facillimē congregantur** *birds of a feather flock together.* **lūdere pār impār** play at evens and odds.
parā'bilis *a.* easy to get.
parasī't/a -ae *f.* woman parasite.
parasīta'st/er -rī *m.* sorry parasite.
parasī'ticus *a.* of a parasite.
parasī't/us -ī *m.* parasite, sponger.
parā'ti/ō -ō'nis *f.* trying to get.
paratragoe'd/ō -ā're *vi.* talk theatrically.
parā't/us *ppp.* parō. *a.* ready; equipped; experienced. **-ē** *ad.* with preparation; carefully; promptly.
parā't/us -ūs *m.* preparation, equipment.
Pa'rc/a -ae *f.* Fate.
pa'r/cō -cere pepe'rcī -sum *vt.* & *i.* (*with dat.*) spare, economize; refrain from, forgo; (*with inf.*) forbear, stop.

pa'rc/us *a.* sparing, thrifty; niggardly, scanty; chary. **-ē** *ad.* frugally; moderately.
pa'rd/us -ī *m.* panther.
pā'r/ēns -e'ntis *pres.p.* pāreō. *a.* obedient. *m.pl.* subjects.
pa'r/ēns -e'ntis *m., f.* parent, father, mother; ancestor; founder.
parentā'lis *a.* parental. *n.pl.* festival in honour of dead ancestors and relatives.
pare'nt/ō -ā're *vi.* sacrifice in honour of dead parents or relatives; avenge (with the death of another).
pā'r/eō -ē're -uī -itum *vi.* be visible, be evident; (*with dat.*) obey, submit to, comply with. -et it is proved.
pa'ri/ēs -etis *m.* wall.
parie'tin/ae -ā'rum *f.pl.* ruins.
Parī'l/ia -ium *n.pl.* festival of Pales.
parī'lis *a.* equal.
pa'r/iō -ere pe'perī -tum *vt.* give birth to; produce, create, cause; procure.
Pa'ri/s -dis *m.* son of Priam, abducter of Helen.
pa'riter *ad.* equally, alike; at the same time, together.
pa'rit/ō -ā're *vt.* get ready.
pa'rm/a -ae *f.* shield, buckler.
parmā'tus *a.* armed with a buckler.
pa'rmul/a -ae *f.* little shield.
Parnā's/us -ī *m.* mount Parnassus in central Greece, sacred to the Muses. **-ius, -is** -idis *a.* Parnassian.
pa'r/ō -ā're -ā'vī -ā'tum *vt.* prepare, get ready, provide; intend, set about; procure, get, buy; arrange.
pa'roch/a -ae *f.* provision of necessaries (to officials travelling). [host.
pa'roch/us -ī *m.* purveyor;
paro'psi/s -dis *f.* dish.
Pa'r/os -ī *f.* Aegean island, famous for white marble. **-ius** *a.*
pa'rr/a -ae *f.* owl.
Pa'rrhas/is -idis, **-ius** *a.* Arcadian.
parricī'd/a -ae *m.* parricide, assassin; traitor.
parricī'd/ium -ī & iī parricide, murder; high treason.
par/s -tis *f.* part, share, fraction; party, side; side, direction; respect, degree; (*with pl. verb*) some; (*pl.*) stage part, role; duty, function. māgna — the majority. māgnam -tem largely. in eam -tem in that direction, on that side, in that sense. nullā -te not at all. omnī -te entirely. ex -te partly. ex alterā -te on the other hand. ex māgnā -te to a large extent. prō -te to the best of one's ability. -tēs agere play a part. duae -tēs two-thirds. trēs -tēs three-fourths. multīs -ibus a great deal.
parsimō'ni/a -ae *f.* thrift, frugality.
parthe'nic/ē -ēs *f.* a plant.
Parthe'nop/ē -ēs *f.* old name of Naples. **-ē'ius** *a.*
Pa'rth/ī -ō'rum *m.pl.* Parthians, Rome's great enemy in the East. **-us, -icus** *a.*
pa'rtic/eps -ipis *a.* sharing, partaking. *m.* partner.
parti'cip/ō -ā're *vt.* share, impart, inform.
parti'cul/a -ae *f.* particle.
pa'rtim *ad.* partly, in part; mostly; some . . . others.
pa'rt/iō -ī're -ī'vī -ī'tum, **-ior** -ī'rī *vt.* share, distribute, divide.
partī'tē *ad.* methodically.
partī'ti/ō -ō'nis *f.* distribution, division.
partu'r/iō -ī're *vi.* be in labour; (*fig.*) be anxious. *vt.* teem with, be ready to produce; (*mind*) brood over.

pa'rtus *ppp.* pariō. *n.pl.* possessions.
pa'rt/us -ūs *m.* birth; young.
pa'rum *ad.* too little, not enough; not very, scarcely.
paru'mper *ad.* for a little while.
pa'rvit/ās -ā'tis *f.* smallness.
pa'rvulus, parvolus *a.* very small, slight; quite young. *m.* child.
pa'rv/us (*comp.* minor *sup.* minimus) *a.* small, little, slight; (*time*) short; (*age*) young. -ī esse be of little value.
Pa'sch/a -ae *f.* Easter.
pā'/scō -scere -vī -stum *vt.* feed, put to graze; keep, foster; (*fig.*) feast, cherish. *vi.* graze, browse.
pā'scuus *a.* for pasture. *n.* pasture.
Pāsi'pha/ē -ēs *f.* wife of Minos, mother of the Minotaur.
pa'sser -is *m.* sparrow; (*fish*) plaice. — marīnus ostrich.
passe'rcul/us -ī *m.* little sparrow.
pa'ssim *ad.* here and there, at random; indiscriminately.
pa'ss/um -ī *n.* raisin-wine.
pa'ssus *ppp.* pandō. *a.* spread out, dishevelled; dried.
pa'ssus *ppa.* patior.
pa'ss/us -ūs *m.* step, pace; footstep. mille -ūs mile. mīlia -uum miles.
pasti'll/us -ī *m.* lozenge.
pā'st/or -ō'ris *m.* shepherd.
pāstōrā'lis *a.* shepherd's pastoral.
pāstōri'cius, pāstō'rius *a.* shepherd's.
pā'stus *ppp.* pāscō.
pā'st/us -ūs *m.* pasture, food.
Pa'tar/a -ae *f.* town in Lycia, with oracle of Apollo. **-ae'us, -ā'nus, -eus** *a.*
Pata'v/ium -ī *n.* birthplace of Livy, *mod.* Padua. **-ī'nus** *a.*
pate/fa'ciō -fa'cere -fē'cī -fa'ctum (*pass.* -fī'ō -fi'erī) *vt.* open, open up; disclose.
patefa'cti/ō -ō'nis *f.* disclosing.
patefī'ō, *see* **patefaciō**.
pate'll/a -ae *f.* small dish, plate.
pa't/ēns -e'ntis *pres.p.* pateō. *a.* open, accessible, exposed; broad; evident. **-e'nter** *ad.* clearly.
pa't/eō -ē're -uī *vi.* be open, accessible, exposed; extend; be evident, known.
pa't/er -ris *m.* father; (*pl.*) forefathers; senators.
pa'ter/a -ae *f.* dish, saucer, bowl.
paterfami'liās patrisfamiliās *m.* master of the house.
pate'rnus *a.* father's, paternal; native.
patē'sc/ō -ere *vi.* open out; extend; become evident.
pati'bilis *a.* endurable; sensitive.
patibulā'tus *a.* pilloried.
pati'bul/um -ī *n.* fork-shaped yoke, pillory.
pa'ti/ēns -e'ntis *pres.p.* patior. *a.* able to endure; patient; unyielding. **-e'nter** *ad.* patiently.
patie'nti/a -ae *f.* endurance, stamina; forbearance; submissiveness.
pa'tin/a -ae *f.* dish, pan.
pa'/tior -tī -ssus *vt.* suffer, experience; submit to; allow, put up with. facile — be well pleased with. aegrē — be displeased with.
Pa'tr/ae -ā'rum *f.pl.* Greek seaport, *mod* Patras. **-ē'nsis** *a.*
patrā't/or -ō'ris *m.* doer.
patrā'tus *a.* pater — officiating priest.
pa'tri/a -ae *f.* native land, native town, home.
patri'cius *a.* patrician. *m.* aristocrat.

patrimō'n/ium -ī & iī *n.* inheritance, patrimony.
pa'trimus *a.* having a father living.
patri'ss/ō -āre *vi.* take after one's father.
patrī'tus *a.* of one's father.
pa'trius *a.* father's; hereditary, native.
pa'tr/ō -āre -āvī -ātum *vt.* achieve, execute, complete.
patrōci'n/ium -ī & iī *n.* patronage, advocacy, defence.
patrō'cin/or -ārī *vi.* (*with dat.*) defend, support.
patrō'n/a -ae *f.* patron goddess; protectress, safeguard.
patrō'n/us -ī *m.* patron, protector; (*law*) advocate, counsel.
patruē'lis *a.* cousin's. *m.* cousin.
pa'tru/us -ī *m.* (paternal) uncle. *a.* uncle's.
pa'tulus *a.* open; spreading, broad.
pau'cit/ās -ātis *f.* small number, scarcity.
pau'culus *a.* very few.
pau'cus *a.* few, little. *m.pl.* a few, the select few. *n.pl.* a few words.
paulā'tim *ad.* little by little, gradually.
pauli'sper *ad.* for a little while.
pau'lulus *a.* very little. *n.* a little bit.
pau'l/us *a.* little. **–ō, –um** *ad.* a little, somewhat.
Pau'l/us, Pau'll/us -ī *m.* Roman surname, *esp.* victor of Pydna.
pau'per -is *a.* poor; meagre. *m.pl.* the poor.
paupe'rculus *a.* poor.
paupe'ri/ēs -ēī *f.* poverty.
pau'per/ō -āre *vt.* impoverish; rob.
paupe'rt/ās -ātis *f.* poverty, moderate means.
pau's/a -ae *f.* stop, end.
pauxillā'tim *ad.* bit by bit.
pauxi'llulus *a.* very little.
pauxi'llus *a.* little.
pavefa'ctus *a.* frightened.
pa'v/eō -ēre pāvī *vi.* be terrified, quake. *vt.* dread, be scared of.
pavē'sc/ō -ere *vt.* & *i.* become alarmed (at).
pā'vī *perf.* pāscō.
pa'vid/us *a.* quaking, terrified. **–ē** *ad.* in a panic.
pavīmentā'tus *a.* paved.
pavīme'nt/um -ī *n.* pavement, floor.
pa'v/iō -īre *vt.* strike.
pa'vit/ō -āre *vi.* be very frightened; shiver.
pā'v/ō -ōnis *m.* peacock.
pa'v/or -ōris *m.* terror, panic.
pāx pācis *f.* peace; (*gods*) grace; (*mind*) serenity; (*interj.*) enough! **pāce tuā** by your leave.
peccā't/um -ī *n.* mistake, fault, sin.
pe'cc/ō -āre -āvī -ātum *vi.* make a mistake, go wrong, offend.
pecorō'sus *a.* rich in cattle.
pe'ct/en -inis *m.* comb; (*fish*) scallop; (*loom*) reed; (*lyre*) plectrum.
pe'/ctō -ctere -xī -xum *vt.* comb.
pe'ct/us -oris *n.* breast; heart, feeling; mind, thought.
pe'cū *n.* flock of sheep; (*pl.*) pastures.
pecuā'rius *a.* of cattle. *m.* cattle-breeder. *n.pl.* herds.
pecūlā't/or -ōris *m.* embezzler.
pecūlā't/us -ūs *m.* embezzlement.
pecūliā'ris *a.* one's own; special.
pecūliā'tus *a.* provided with money.
pecūliō'sus *a.* with private property.
pecū'l/ium -ī & iī *n.* small savings, private property.

pecū'ni/a -ae *f.* property; money.
pecūniā'rius *a.* of money.
pecūniō'sus *a.* moneyed, well off.
pe'c/us -oris *n.* cattle, herd, flock; animal.
pe'c/us -udis *f.* sheep, head of cattle, beast.
pedā'lis *a.* a foot long.
pedā'rius *a.* (*senator*) without full rights.
pe'd/es -itis *m.* foot-soldier, infantry. *a.* on foot.
pede'st/er -ris *a.* on foot, pedestrian; infantry-; on land; (*writing*) in prose, prosaic.
pedete'mptim *ad.* step by step, cautiously.
pe'dic/a -ae *f.* fetter, snare.
pe'd/is -is *m.* louse.
pedi'sequ/us -ī *m.*, **-a** -ae *f.* attendant, lackey, handmaid.
peditā't/us -ūs *m.* infantry.
pe'd/um -ī *n.* crook.
Pē'gas/us -ī *m.* mythical winged horse, associated with the Muses. **-eus**, **-is** -idis *a.* Pegasean.
pē'gma -tis *n.* book-case; stage elevator. [oneself.
pē'ier/ō -ā're *vi.* perjure
pē'i/or -ō'ris *comp.* malus. **-us** *ad.* worse.
pela'gius *a.* of the sea.
pe'lag/us -ī (*pl.* -ē) *n.* sea, open sea.
pe'lamy/s -dis *f.* young tunny-fish.
Pela'sg/ī -ō'rum *m.pl.* Greeks. **-ias**, **-is**, **-us** *a.* Grecian.
Pē'l/eus -eī & eos (*acc.* -ea) *m.* king of Thessaly, father of Achilles. **-ī'dēs** -ī'dae *m.* Achilles; Neoptolemus.
Pe'li/ās -ae *m.* uncle of Jason.
Pē'li/on -ī *n.* mountain in Thessaly. **-i'acus**, **-ias**, **-ius** *a.*
Pe'll/a -ae, **-ē** -ēs *f.* town of Macedonia, birthplace of Alexander. **-ae'us** *a.* of Pella; Alexandrian; Egyptian.
pellā'ci/a -ae *f.* attraction.
pe'll/āx -ā'cis *a.* seductive.
pellē'cti/ō -ō'nis *f.* reading through.
pelle'ctus *ppp.* pelliciō.
pell/i'ciō -i'cere -e'xī -e'ctum *vt.* entice, inveigle.
pelli'cul/a -ae *f.* skin, fleece.
pe'lli/ō -ō'nis *m.* furrier.
pe'll/is -is *f.* skin, hide; leather, felt; tent.
pellī'tus *a.* wearing skins, with leather coats.
pe'll/ō -ere pe'pulī pu'lsum *vt.* push, knock, drive; drive off, rout, expel; (*lyre*) play; (*mind*) touch, affect; (*feeling*) banish.
pellūc-, *see* **perlūc-**.
Peloponnē's/us -ī *f.* Peloponnese, S. Greece. **-i'acus**, **-ius** *a.*
Pe'lop/s -is *m.* son of Tantalus, grandfather of Agamemnon. **-ō'ias**, **-ē'is**, **-ē'ius**, **-ē'us** *a.* **-idae** -idā'rum *m.pl.* house of Pelops.
pelō'r/is -idis *f.* a large mussel.
pe'lt/a -ae *f.* light shield.
pelta'st/ae -ā'rum *m.pl.* peltasts. [pelta.
peltā'tus *a.* armed with the
Pēlū's/ium -ī *n.* Egyptian town at the E. mouth of the Nile. **-i'acus**, **-ius** *a.*
pe'lv/is -is *f.* basin.
penā'rius *a.* provision-.
Penā't/ēs -ium *m.pl.* spirits of the larder, household gods; home. [home gods.
penā'tiger -ī *a.* carrying his
pe'nd/eō -ē're pepe'ndī *vi.* hang; overhang, hover; hang down, be flabby; (*fig.*) depend; gaze, listen attentively; (*mind*) be in suspense, be undecided.
pe'nd/ō -ere pepe'ndī pē'nsum *vt.* weigh; pay; (*fig.*) ponder, value. *vi.* weigh. [doubt.
pe'ndulus *a.* hanging; in

Pēne'lop/ē -ēs, **-a** -ae *f.* wife of Ulysses, famed for her constancy. **-ē'us** *a.*
pe'nes *pr.* (*with acc.*) in the power or possession of; in the house of, with.
penetrā'bilis *a.* penetrable; piercing.
penetrā'lis *a.* penetrating; inner, inmost. *n.pl.* inner room, interior, sanctuary; remote parts.
pe'netr/ō -ā're -ā'vī -ā'tum *vt.* & *i.* put into, penetrate, enter.
Pēnē'/us -ī *m.* chief river of Thessaly. **-ē'is, -ē'ius, -ē'us** *a.*
pēnici'lli/us -ī *m.* painter's brush, pencil. [sponge.
pēni'cul/us -ī *m.* brush;
pē'n/is -is *m.* penis.
pe'nitē *ad.* inwardly.
pe'nitus *ad.* inside, deep within; deeply, from the depths; utterly, thoroughly.
pe'nn/a, pi'nn/a -ae *f.* feather, wing; flight.
pennā'tus *a.* winged.
pe'nniger -ī *a.* feathered.
penni'pot/ēns -e'ntis *a.* winged.
pe'nnul/a -ae *f.* little wing.
pē'nsilis *a.* hanging, pendent.
pē'nsi/ō -ō'nis *f.* payment, instalment.
pē'nsit/ō -ā're *vt.* pay; consider.
pē'ns/ō -ā're -ā'vī -ā'tum *vt.* weight out; compensate, repay; consider, judge.
pē'ns/um -ī *n.* spinner's work; task, duty; weight, value. **-ī esse** be of importance. **-ī habēre** care at all about.
pē'nsus *ppp.* pendō.
pentē'r/is -is *f.* quinquereme.
Pe'nth/eus -eī & eos *m.* king of Thebes, killed by Bacchantes.
pēnū'ri/a -ae *f.* want, need.
pe'n/us -ūs & ī *m., f.,* **-um** -ī, **-us** -oris *n.* provisions, store of food. [pendō.
pepe'ndī *perf.* pendeō; *perf.*
pepe'rcī *perf.* parcō.
pe'perī *perf.* pariō.
pe'pigī *perf.* pangō.
pe'pl/um -ī *n.,* **-us** -ī *m.* state robe of Athena.
pe'pulī *perf.* pellō.
per *pr.* (*with acc.*) (*space*) through, all over; (*time*) throughout, during; (*means*) by, by means of; (*cause*) by reason of, for the sake of. — **īram** in anger. — **manūs** from hand to hand. — **mē** as far as I am concerned. — **vim** forcibly. — **ego tē deōs ōrō** in Heaven's name I beg you.
pē'r/a -ae *f.* bag.
perabsu'rdus *a.* very absurd.
peraccommodā'tus *a.* very convenient.
perā'c/er -ris *a.* very sharp.
perace'rbus *a.* very sour.
perac/ē'scō -ē'scere -uī *vi.* get vexed.
perā'cti/ō -ō'nis *f.* last act.
perā'ctus *ppp.* peragō.
peracū't/us *a.* very sharp, very clear. **-ē** *ad.* very acutely.
peradulē'sc/ēns -e'ntis *a.* very young.
perae'quē *ad.* quite equally, uniformly.
peragitā'tus *a.* harried.
pe'r/agō -a'gere -ē'gī -ā'ctum *vt.* carry through, complete; pass through, pierce; disturb; (*law*) prosecute to a conviction; (*words*) go over, describe.
peragrā'ti/ō -ō'nis *f.* travelling.
pera'gr/ō -ā're -ā'vī -ā'tum *vt.* travel through, traverse.
pe'ram/āns -a'ntis *a.* very fond. **-ā'nter** *ad.* devotedly.
pera'mbul/ō -ā're *vt.* walk through, traverse.

peramoe'nus *a.* very pleasant.
pera'mplus *a.* very large.
perangu'st/us *a.* very narrow. **-ē** *ad.*
perantī'quus *a.* very old.
perappo'situs *a.* very suitable.
pera'rduus *a.* very difficult.
perargū'tus *a.* very witty.
pe'rar/ō **-ā're** *vt.* furrow; write (on wax).
peratte'nt/us *a.* very attentive. **-ē** *ad.*
peraudie'ndus *a.* to be heard to the end.
perba'cch/or **-ā'rī** *vt.* carouse through.
perbeā'tus *a.* very happy.
perbe'llē *ad.* very nicely.
pe'rbene *ad.* very well.
perbene'volus *a.* very friendly.
perbeni'gnē *ad.* very kindly.
pe'rbib/ō **-ere** **-ī** *vt.* drink up, imbibe.
perbī't/ō **-ere** *vi.* perish.
perbla'ndus *a.* very charming.
pe'rbonus *a.* very good.
pe'rbrevi/s *a.* very short. **-ter** *ad.* very briefly.
pe'rc/a **-ae** *f.* perch.
percalefa'ctus *a.* quite hot.
percal/ē'scō **-ē'scere** **-uī** *vi.* become quite hot.
percall/ē'scō **-ē'scere** **-uī** *vi.* become quite hardened. *vt.* become thoroughly versed in.
percā'rus *a.* very dear.
percau'tus *a.* very cautious.
perce'lebr/ō **-ā're** *vt.* talk much of.
pe'rceler **-is** *a.* very quick. **-iter** *ad.*
perc/e'llō **-e'llere** **-ulī** **-u'lsum** *vt.* knock down, upset; strike; (*fig.*) ruin, overthrow; discourage, unnerve.
percē'ns/eō **-ē're** **-uī** *vt.* count over; (*place*) travel through; (*fig.*) review.
perce'pti/ō **-ō'nis** *f.* harvesting; understanding, idea.
perce'ptus *ppp.* **percipiō.**
perc/i'eō **-iē're,** **-iō** **-ī're** *vt.* rouse, excite.
perc/i'piō **-i'pere** **-ē'pī** **-e'ptum** *vt.* take, get hold of; gather in; (*senses*) feel; (*mind*) learn, grasp, understand.
pe'rcitus *ppp.* **percieō.** *a.* roused, excited; excitable.
perco'ctus *ppp.* **percoquō.**
pe'rcol/ō **-ā're** *vt.* filter through.
pe'rc/olō **-o'lere** **-o'luī** **-u'ltum** *vt.* embellish; honour.
percō'mis *a.* very friendly.
perco'mmod/us *a.* very suitable. **-ē** *ad.* very conveniently.
percontā'ti/ō **-ō'nis** *f.* asking questions.
percontā't/or **-ō'ris** *m.* inquisitive person.
perco'nt/or **-ā'rī** **-ā'tus** *vt.* question, inquire.
perco'ntumāx **-ā'cis** *a.* very obstinate.
pe'rco/quō **-quere** **-xī** **-ctum** *vt.* cook thoroughly, heat, scorch, ripen.
percrēb/ē'scō, percrēbr/ē'scō **-ē'scere** **-uī** *vi.* be spread abroad.
pe'rcrep/ō **-ā're** **-uī** *vi.* resound.
pe'rculī *perf* **percellō.**
percu'lsus *ppp.* **percellō.**
percu'ltus *ppp.* **percolō.**
percunct-, *see* **percont-.**
percu'pidus *a.* very fond.
percu'p/iō **-ere** *vi.* wish very much.
percūriō'sus *a.* very inquisitive.
percū'r/ō **-ā're** *vt.* heal completely.
percu'/rrō **-rrere** **-currī & rrī** **-rsum** *vt.* run through, hurry over; (*fig.*) run over, look over. *vi.* run along; pass.
percursā'ti/ō **-ō'nis** *f.* travelling through.

percu'rsi/ō -ō'nis *f.* running over. [about.

percu'rs/ō -ā're *vi.* rove

percu'rsus *ppp.* percurrō.

percu'ssi/ō -ō'nis *f.* beating; (*fingers*) snapping; (*music*) time.

percu'ss/or -ō'ris *m.* assassin.

percu'ssus *ppp.* percutiō.

percu'ss/us -ūs *m.* striking.

percu'/tiō -tere -ssī -ssum *vt.* strike, beat; strike through, kill; (*feeling*) shock, impress, move; (*colloq.*) trick.

perdēlī'rus *a.* quite crazy.

pe'rdidī *perf.* perdō.

perdiffi'cili/s *a.* very difficult. **-ter** *ad.* with great difficulty.

perdi'gnus *a.* most worthy.

perdī'lig/ēns -e'ntis *a.* very diligent. **-e'nter** *ad.*

perdi'/scō -scere -dicī *vt.* learn by heart.

perdise'rtē *ad.* very eloquently.

pe'rdit/or -ō'ris *m.* destroyer.

pe'rdit/us *ppp.* perdō. *a.* desperate, ruined; abandoned, profligate. **-ē** *ad.* desperately; recklessly. [time.

pe'rdiū *ad.* for a very long

perdiūtu'rnus *a.* protracted.

perdī'v/es -itis *a.* very rich.

pe'rd/īx -ī'cis *m., f.* partridge.

pe'rd/ō -ere -idī -itum *vt.* destroy, ruin; squander, waste; lose. **dī tē -uint** curse you!

perdo'c/eō -ē're -uī -tum *vt.* teach thoroughly.

perdol/ē'scō -ē'scere -uī *vi.* take it to heart.

pe'rdom/ō -ā're -uī -itum *vt.* subjugate, tame completely.

perdormī'sc/ō -ere *vi.* sleep on.

perd/ū'cō -ū'cere -ū'xī -u'ctum *vt.* bring, guide to; induce, seduce; spread over; prolong, continue.

perdu'ct/ō -ā're *vt.* guide.

perdu'ct/or -ō'ris *m.* guide; pander.

perdu'ctus *ppp.* perdūcō.

perdue'llī/ō -ō'nis *f.* treason.

perdue'll/is -is *m.* enemy.

pe'rduint *archaic subj.* perdō.

perdū'r/ō -ā're *vi.* endure, hold out.

pe'r/edō -e'dere -ē'dī -ē'sum *vt.* consume, devour.

pe'regrē *ad.* away from home, abroad; from abroad. [ling.

peregrīnābu'ndus *a.* travel-

peregrīnā'ti/ō -ō'nis *f.* living abroad, travel.

peregrīnā't/or -ō'ris *m.* traveller.

peregrī'nit/ās -ā'tis *f.* foreign manners.

peregrī'n/or -ā'rī -ā'tus *vi.* be abroad, travel; be a stranger.

peregrī'nus *a.* foreign, strange. *m.* foreigner, alien.

perē'leg/āns -a'ntis *a.* very polished. **-a'nter** *ad.* in a very polished manner.

perē'loqu/ēns -e'ntis *a.* very eloquent.

perē'mī *perf.* perimō.

pere'mn/ia -ium *n.pl.* auspices taken on crossing a river.

pere'mptus *ppp.* perimō.

pere'ndiē *ad.* the day after to-morrow.

pere'ndinus *a.* (the day) after to-morrow.

pere'nnis *a.* perpetual, unfailing.

pere'nnit/ās -ā'tis *f.* continuance.

pere'nn/ō -ā're *vi.* last a long time.

pe'r/eō -ī're -iī -itum *vi.* be lost, pass away, perish, die; (*fig.*) be wasted, be in love, be undone.

pere'quit/ō -ā're *vt. & i.* ride up and down.

pere'rr/ō -ā're -ā'vī -ā'tum *vt.* roam over, cover.

perērudī'tus *a.* very learned.

perē'sus *ppp.* peredō.

perexce'lsus *a.* very high.

perexi'gu/us *a.* very small, very short. **-ē** *ad.* very meagrely.
perfacē't/us *a.* very witty. **-ē** *ad.* very wittily.
perfa'cil/is *a.* very easy; very courteous. **-e** *ad.* very easily.
perfamiliā'ris *a.* very intimate. *m.* very close friend.
perfe'cti/ō -ō'nis *f.* completion, perfection.
perfe'ct/or -ō'ris *m.* perfecter.
perfe'ct/us *ppp.* perficiō. *a.* complete, perfect. **-ē** *ad.* fully.
pe'r/ferō -fe'rre -tulī -lā'tum *vt.* carry through, bring, convey; bear, endure, put up with; (*work*) finish, bring to completion, (*law*) get passed. (*message*) bring news.
perf/i'ciō -i'cere -ē'cī -e'ctum *vt.* carry out, finish, complete; perfect; cause, make.
pe'rficus *a.* perfecting.
perfidē'lis *a.* very loyal.
perfi'di/a -ae *f.* treachery, dishonesty.
perfidiō's/us *a.* treacherous, dishonest. **-ē** *ad.* [less.
pe'rfidus *a.* treacherous, faith-
perfī'/gō -gere -xī -xum *vt.* pierce.
perflā'bilis *a.* that can be blown through.
perflāgitiō'sus *a.* very wicked.
pe'rfl/ō -ā're *vt.* blow through, blow over.
perflu'ctu/ō -ā're *vt.* flood through.
pe'rflu/ō -ere -xī *vi.* run out, leak.
perf/o'diō -o'dere -ō'dī -o'ssum *vt.* dig through, excavate, pierce.
pe'rfor/ō -ā're -āvī -ā'tum *vt.* bore through, pierce.
perfo'rtiter *ad.* very bravely.
perfo'ss/or -ō'ris *m.* — parietum burglar.
perfo'ssus *ppp.* **perfodiō.**
perfrā'ctus *ppp.* perfringō.
perfrēgī *perf.* perfringō.
pe'rfrem/ō -ere *vi.* snort along.
pe'rfrequ/ēns -e'ntis *a.* much frequented.
pe'rfric/ō -ā're -uī -tum & ā'tum *vt.* rub all over. ōs — put on a bold face.
perfrīgefa'c/iō -ere *vt.* make shudder.
perfrī/gē'scō -gē'scere -xī *vi.* catch a bad cold.
perfrī'gidus *a.* very cold.
perfr/i'ngō -i'ngere -ē'gī -ā'ctum *vt.* break through, fracture, wreck; (*fig.*) violate; affect powerfully.
perfrī'xī *perf.* perfrīgēscō.
perfrū'ctus *ppa.* perfruor.
pe'rfr/uor -uī -ū'ctus *vi.* (*with abl.*) enjoy to the full; fulfil.
pe'rfug/a -ae *m.* deserter.
perf/u'giō -u'gere -ū'gī *vi.* flee for refuge, desert to.
perfu'g/ium -ī & iī *n.* refuge, shelter. [forming.
perfū'ncti/ō -ō'nis *f.* per-
perfū'nctus *ppa.* perfungor.
perf/u'ndō -u'ndere -ū'dī -ū'sum *vt.* pour over, drench, besprinkle; dye; (*fig.*) flood, fill.
perfu'n/gor -gī perfūnctus *vi.* (*with abl.*) perform, discharge; undergo.
pe'rfur/ō -ere *vi.* rage furiously.
perfū'sus *ppp.* perfundō.
Pe'rgam/a -ō'rum *n.pl.* Troy. **-eus** *a.* Trojan.
Pe'rgam/um -ī *n.* town in Mysia, famous for its library. **-ē'nus** *a.*
pergau'd/eō -ē're *vi.* be very glad.
pe'r/gō -gere -rē'xī -rē'ctum *vi.* proceed, go on, continue. *vt.* go on with, continue.
pergrae'c/or -ā'rī *vi.* have a good time.

pergra'ndis *a.* very large; very old.
pergra'phicus *a.* very artful.
pergrā'tus *a.* very pleasant.
pe'rgravi/s *a.* very weighty. **-ter** *ad.* very seriously.
pe'rgul/a -ae *f.* balcony; school; brothel.
perhi'b/eō -ē're -uī -itum *vt.* assert, call, cite.
perhī'lum *ad.* very little.
perhonōri'fic/us *a.* very complimentary. **-ē** *ad.* very respectfully.
perhorr/ē'scō -ē'scere -uī *vi.* shiver, tremble violently. *vt.* have a horror of.
perho'rridus *a.* quite horrible.
perhūmā'n/us *a.* very polite. **-iter** *ad.*
Pe'ricl/ēs -is & ī *m.* famous Athenian statesman and orator.
periclitā'ti/ō -ō'nis *f.* experiment.
perī'clit/or -ā'rī -ā'tus *vt.* test, try; risk, endanger. *vi.* attempt, venture; run a risk, be in danger.
perīculō's/us *a.* dangerous, hazardous. **-ē** *ad.*
perī'cul/um (**perī'clum**) **-ī** *n.* danger, risk; trial, attempt; (*law*) lawsuit, writ.
peridō'neus *a.* very suitable.
pe'riī *perf.* pereō.
perillū'stris *a.* very notable; highly honoured.
perimbēci'llus *a.* very weak.
pe'r/imō -i'mere -ē'mī -e'mptum *vt.* destroy, prevent, kill.
perinco'mmod/us *a.* very inconvenient. **-ē** *ad.*
peri'nde *ad.* just as, exactly as.
perindu'lg/ēns -e'ntis *a.* very tender.
perinfi'rmus *a.* very feeble.
peringeniō'sus *a.* very clever.
perinī'quus *a.* very unfair; very discontented.
perinsi'gnis *a.* very conspicuous.
perinvī'tus *a.* very unwilling.
peri'od/us -ī *f.* sentence, period.
Peripatē'tic/ī -ō'rum *m.pl.* Peripatetics, followers of Aristotle.
peripeta'smat/a -um *n.pl.* curtains.
perīrā'tus *a.* very angry.
peri'sceli/s -dis *f.* anklet.
peristrō'm/a -atis *n.* coverlet.
peri'styl/um -ī *n.* colonnade, peristyle.
perī'ti/a -ae *f.* practical knowledge, skill.
perī't/us *a.* experienced, skilled, expert. **-ē** *ad.* expertly.
periūcu'nd/us *a.* very enjoyable. **-ē** *ad.*
periū'r/ium -ī & iī *n.* perjury.
periū'rō, *see* **pēierō**.
periū'rus *a.* perjured, lying.
perlā'/bor -bī -psus *vi.* glide along or through, move on.
perlae'tus *a.* very glad.
perlā'psus *ppa.* perlābor.
perlā'tē *ad.* very extensively.
perla't/eō -ē're *vi.* lie quite hidden.
perlā'tus *ppp.* perferō.
pe'rl/egō (**pe'llegō**) **-e'gere -ē'gī -ē'ctum** *vt.* survey; read through.
pe'rlevi/s *a.* very slight. **-ter** *ad.*
pe'rlib/ēns (**pe'rlubēns**) **-e'ntis** *a.* very willing. **-e'nter** *ad.*
perlīberā'li/s *a.* very genteel. **-ter** *ad.* very liberally.
pe'rlib/et (**pe'rlubet**) **-ē're** *vi.*(*impers.*) (I) should very much like.
perli'ciō, *see* **pelliciō**.
pe'rlit/ō -ā're -ā'vī -ā'tum *vi.* sacrifice with auspicious results.
perlo'ng/us *a.* very long,

very tedious. **-ē** *ad.* very far.
perlub-, *see* **perlib-**.
perlū'/ceō (pellū'ceō) -cē're -xī *vi.* shine through, be transparent; (*fig.*) be quite intelligible.
perlūci'dulus *a.* transparent.
perlū'cidus *a.* transparent; very bright.
perlūctuō'sus *a.* very mournful.
pe'rlu/ō -ere *vt.* wash thoroughly; (*pass.*) bathe.
perlū'str/ō -ā're *vt.* traverse; (*fig.*) survey.
permā'gnus *a.* very big, very great.
permāna'nter *ad.* by flowing through.
permānā'sc/ō -ere *vi.* penetrate.
perm/a'neō -anē're -ā'nsī -ā'nsum *vi.* last, persist, endure to the end.
permā'n/ō -ā're -ā'vī -ā'tum *vi.* flow or ooze through, penetrate.
permā'nsi/ō -ō'nis *f.* continuing, persisting.
permarī'nus *a.* of sea-faring.
permātūr/ē'scō -ē'scere -uī *vi.* ripen fully.
permedio'cris *a.* very moderate.
permē'nsus *ppa.* permētior.
pe'rme/ō -ā're *vt.* & *i.* pass through, penetrate.
permē'/tior -tī'rī -nsus *vt.* measure out; traverse.
permī'rus *a.* very wonderful.
permi'/sceō -scē're -scuī -xtum *vt.* mingle, intermingle; throw into confusion.
permi'ssi/ō -ō'nis *f.* unconditional surrender; permission.
permi'ssus *ppp.* permittō.
permi'ss/us -ūs *m.* leave, permission.
permitiā'lis *a.* destructive.
permi'ti/ēs -ē'ī *f.* ruin.
perm/i'ttō -i'ttere -ī'sī -i'ssum *vt.* let go, let pass; hurl; give up, entrust, concede; allow, permit.
permi'xti/ō -ō'nis *f.* mixture; disturbance.
permi'xt/us *ppp.* permisceō. *a.* promiscuous, disordered. **-ē** *ad.*
permode'stus *a.* very moderate.
permole'st/us *a.* very troublesome. **-ē** *ad.* with much annoyance.
permō'ti/ō -ō'nis *f.* excitement; emotion.
permō'tus *ppp.* permoveō.
perm/o'veō -ovē're -ō'vī -ō'tum *vt.* stir violently; (*fig.*) influence, induce; excite, move deeply.
permu'l/ceō -cē're -sī -sum *vt.* stroke, caress; (*fig.*) charm, flatter; soothe, appease.
permu'lsus *ppp.* permulceō.
permu'ltus *a.* very much, very many.
permū'n/iō -ī're -ī'vī -ī'tum *vt.* finish fortifying; fortify strongly.
permūtā'ti/ō -ō'nis *f.* change, exchange.
permū't/ō -ā're -ā'vī -ā'tum *vt.* change completely; exchange; (*money*) remit by bill of exchange.
pe'rn/a -ae *f.* ham.
pernecessā'rius *a.* very necessary; very closely related.
pernece'sse *a.* indispensable.
pe'rneg/ō -ā're *vi.* deny flatly.
perniciā'bilis *a.* ruinous.
perni'ci/ēs -ē'ī *f.* destruction, ruin, death.
perniciō's/us *a.* ruinous. **-ē** *ad.*
pernī'cit/ās -ā'tis *f.* agility, swiftness.
pernī'citer *ad.* nimbly.
perni'mius *a.* much too much.
pe'rn/īx -ī'cis *a.* nimble, agile, swift.
pernō'bilis *a.* very famous.
perno'ct/ō -ā're *vi.* stay all night.

pernō'/scō -scere -vī -tum *vt.* examine thoroughly; become fully acquainted with, know thoroughly.
pernōt/ē'scō -ē'scere -uī *vi.* become generally known.
pernō'tus *ppp.* pernōscō.
pe'rn/ox -o'ctis *a.* all night long. [up.
pernu'mer/ō -ā're *vt.* count
pē'r/ō -ō'nis *m.* raw-hide boot.
perobscū'rus *a.* very obscure.
perodiō'sus *a.* very troublesome.
perofficiō'sē *ad.* very attentively.
pero'l/eō -ē're *vi.* give off a strong smell.
peropportū'n/us *a.* very timely. -**ē** *ad.* very opportunely.
peroptā'tō *ad.* very much to one's wish.
pe'ropus est it is most essential.
perōrā'ti/ō -ō'nis *f.* peroration.
perōrnā'tus *a.* very ornate.
perō'rn/ō -ā're *vt.* give great distinction to.
perō'r/ō -ā're -ā'vī -ā'tum *vt.* plead at length; (*speech*) bring to a close; conclude.
perō'sus *a.* detesting.
perpā'c/ō -ā're *vt.* quieten completely.
perpa'rcē *ad.* very stingily.
perpa'rvulus *a.* very tiny.
perpa'rvus *a.* very small.
perpā'stus *a.* well fed.
perpau'culus *a.* very very few.
perpau'cus *a.* very little, very few.
perpau'l/um -ī *n.* a very little.
perpau'per -is *a.* very poor.
perpauxi'll/um -ī *n.* a very little.
perp/e'llō -e'llere -ulī -u'lsum *vt.* urge, force, influence.
perpendi'cul/um -ī *n.* plumb-line. **ad —** perpendicularly.
perp/e'ndō -e'ndere -e'ndī -ē'nsum *vt.* weigh carefully, judge. [falsely.
pe'rperam *ad.* wrongly,
pe'rp/es -etis *a.* continuous.
perpe'ssi/ō -ō'nis *f.* suffering, enduring.
perpe'ssus *ppa.* perpetior.
perpe'/tior -tī -ssus *vt.* endure patiently, allow.
pe'rpetr/ō -ā're -ā'vī -ā'tum *vt.* perform, carry out.
perpetu'it/ās -ā'tis *f.* continuity, uninterrupted duration.
perpe'tuō *ad.* without interruption, forever, utterly.
perpe'tu/ō -ā're *vt.* perpetuate preserve.
perpe'tu/us *a.* continuous, entire; universal. **in -um** forever.
perpla'c/eō -ē're *vi.* please greatly.
perple'x/or -ā'rī *vi.* cause confusion.
perple'x/us *a.* confused, intricate, obscure. -**ē** *ad.* obscurely.
perplicā'tus *a.* interlaced.
pe'rplu/ō -ere *vi.* let the rain through, leak.
perpo'l/iō -ī're -ī'vī -ī'tum *vt.* polish thoroughly. -**ī'tus** *a.* finished, refined.
perpo'pul/or -ā'rī -ā'tus *vt.* ravage completely.
perpōtā'ti/ō -ō'nis *f.* drinking-bout.
perpō't/ō -ā're *vi.* drink continuously. *vt.* drink off.
pe'rprim/ō -ere *vt.* lie on.
perpu'gn/āx -ā'cis *a.* very pugnacious.
perpu'lch/er -rī *a.* very beautiful.
pe'rpulī *perf.* perpellō.
perpū'rg/ō -ā're -ā'vī -ā'tum *vt.* make quite clean; explain.
perpusi'llus *a.* very little.

pe'rquam *ad.* very, extremely.
perquī'/rō -rere -sī'vī -sī'tum *vt.* search for, inquire after; examine carefully. [rately.
perquīsī'tius *ad.* more accu-
perră'r/us *a.* very uncommon. -ō *ad.* very seldom.
perreco'nditus *a.* very abstruse.
perrĕ'p/ō -ere *vt.* crawl over.
perrĕ'pt/ō -ā're -ā'vī -ā'tum *vt.* & *i.* creep about or through.
perrĕ'xī *perf.* pergō.
perrīdi'cul/us *a.* very laughable. -ē *ad.*
perrogā'ti/ō -ō'nis *f.* passing (of a law).
pe'rrog/ō -ā're *vt.* ask one after another.
perr/u'mpō -u'mpere -ū'pī -u'ptum *vt.* & *i.* break through, force a way through; (*fig.*) break down.
perru'ptus *ppp.* perrumpō.
Pe'rs/ae -ā'rum *m.pl.* Persians. -ēs -ae *m.* Persian. -is -idis *f.* Persia. -icus *a.* Persian. *f.* peach-tree. *n.* peach.
persae'pe *ad.* very often.
persa'ls/us *a.* very witty. -ē *ad.*
persalūtā'ti/ō -ō'nis *f.* greeting everyone in turn.
persalū't/ō -ā're *vt.* greet in turn.
persa'nctē *ad.* most solemnly.
persa'pi/ēns -e'ntis *a.* very wise. -e'nter *ad.*
perscie'nter *ad.* very discreetly.
persci'/ndō -ndere -dī -ssum *vt.* tear apart.
perscī'tus *a.* very smart.
perscrī'/bō -bere -psī -ptum *vt.* write in full; describe, report; (*record*) enter; (*money*) make over in writing.
perscrī'pti/ō -ō'nis *f.* entry; assignment.
perscrī'pt/or -ō'ris *m.* writer.
perscrī'ptus *ppp.* perscrībō.
perscrū't/or -ā'rī -ā'tus *vt.* search, examine thoroughly.
pe'rsec/ō -ā're -uī -tum *vt.* dissect; do away with.
perse'ct/or -ā'rī *vt.* investigate.
persecū'ti/ō -ō'nis *f.* (*law*) prosecution.
persecū'tus *ppa.* persequor.
pers/e'deō -edē're -ē'dī -e'ssum *vi.* remain sitting.
perse'gnis *a.* very slow.
pers/e'ntiō -entī're -ē'nsī *vt.* see clearly; feel deeply.
persentī'sc/ō -ere *vi.* begin to see; begin to feel. [pine.
Perse'phon/ē -ēs *f.* Proser-
pe'rse/quor -quī -cū'tus *vt.* follow all the way; pursue, chase, hunt after; overtake; (*pattern*) be a follower of, copy; (*enemy*) proceed against, take revenge on; (*action*) perform, carry out; (*words*) write down, describe.
Pe'rs/ēs -ae *m.* last king of Macedonia.
Pe'rs/eus -eī & eos (*acc.* -ea) *m.* son of Danae, killer of Medusa, rescuer of Andromeda. -ē'us, -ē'ius *a.*
persevĕ'r/āns -a'ntis *pres.p.* persevērō. *a.* persistent. -a'nter *ad.* [sistence.
persevērā'nti/a -ae *f.* per-
persevĕ'r/ō -ā're -ā'vī -ā'tum *vi.* persist. *vt.* persist in.
persevĕ'rus *a.* very strict.
Pe'rsicus *a.* Persian; of Perses.
pers/ī'dō -ī'dere -ē'dī -e'ssum *vi.* sink down into.
persi'gn/ō -ā're *vt.* record.
persi'milis *a.* very like.
persi'mpl/ex -icis *a.* very simple.
pers/i'stō -i'stere -titī *vi.* persist.
persō'lus *a.* one and only.
persolū'tus *ppp.* persolvō.
perso'l/vō -vere -vī -ū'tum *vt.* pay, pay up; explain.

persō'n/a -ae *f.* mask; character, part; person, personality.
persōnā'tus *a.* masked; in an assumed character.
pe'rson/ō -ā're -uī -itum *vi.* resound, ring (with); play. *vt.* make resound; cry aloud.
perspe'ct/ō -ā're *vt.* have a look through.
perspe'ct/us *ppp.* perspiciō. *a.* well-known. -ē *ad.* intelligently. [noitre.
perspe'cul/or -ā'rī *vt.* recon-
perspe'r/gō -gere -sī -sum *vt.* besprinkle.
pe'rspic/āx -ā'cis *a.* sharp, shrewd.
perspicie'nti/a -ae *f.* full understanding.
persp/i'ciō -i'cere -e'xī -e'ctum *vt.* see through; examine, observe.
perspicu'it/ās -ā'tis *f.* clarity.
perspi'cu/us *a.* transparent; clear, evident. -ē *ad.* clearly.
perst/e'rnō -e'rnere -rā'vī -rā'tum *vt.* pave all over.
persti'mul/ō -ā're *vt.* rouse violently.
pe'rstitī *perf.* persistō: *perf.* perstō.
pe'rst/ō -ā're -itī -ā'tum *vi.* stand fast; last; continue, persist.
perstrā'tus *ppp.* persternō.
pe'rstrep/ō -ere *vi.* make a lot of noise.
perstri'ctus *ppp.* perstringō.
perstr/i'ngō -i'ngere -i'nxī -i'ctum *vt.* graze, touch lightly; (*words*) touch on, belittle, censure; (*senses*) dull, deaden.
perstudiō's/us *a.* very fond. -ē *ad.* very eagerly.
persuā'/deō -dē're -sī -sum *vi.* (*with dat.*) convince, persuade. -sum habeō, mihi -sum est I am convinced.
persuā'si/ō -ō'nis *f.* convincing. [sion.
persuā's/us -ūs *m.* persua-
persubtī'lis *a.* very fine.
persu'lt/ō -ā're *vt.* & *i.* prance about, frisk over.
pertae'/det -dē're -sum est *vt.* (*impers.*) be weary of, be sick of.
pe'rt/egō -e'gere -ē'xī -ē'ctum *vt.* cover over.
perte'mpt/ō -ā're *vt.* test carefully; consider well; pervade, seize.
perte'nd/ō -ere -ī *vi.* push on, persist. *vt.* go on with.
perte'nuis *a.* very small, very slight. [through.
perte'rebr/ō -ā're *vt.* bore
perte'r/geō -gē're -sī -sum *vt.* wipe over; touch lightly.
perterrefa'c/iō -ere *vt.* scare thoroughly.
perte'rr/eō -ē're -uī -itum *vt.* frighten thoroughly.
perterri'crepus *a.* with a terrifying crash.
perte'x/ō -ere -uī -tum *vt.* accomplish.
pe'rtic/a -ae *f.* pole, staff.
pertimefa'ctus *a.* very frightened.
pertim/ē'scō -ē'scere -uī *vt.* & *i.* be very alarmed, be very afraid of.
pertinā'ci/a -ae *f.* perseverance, stubbornness.
pe'rtin/āx -ā'cis *a.* very tenacious; unyielding, stubborn. -ā'citer *ad.*
perti'n/eō -ē're -uī *vi.* extend, reach; tend, lead to, concern; apply, pertain, belong. quod -et ad as far as concerns.
perti'ng/ō -ere *vi.* extend.
perto'ler/ō -ā're *vt.* endure to the end.
perto'rqu/eō -ē're *vt.* distort.
pertractā'tē *ad.* in a hackneyed fashion. [ling.
pertractā'ti/ō -ō'nis *f.* hand-
pertra'ct/ō -ā're *vt.* handle, feel all over; (*fig.*) treat, study.
pertra'ctus *ppp.* pertrahō.
pe'rtra/hō -here -xī -ctum

vt. drag across, take forcibly; entice.
pertrect-, *see* **pertract-**.
pertri'stis *a.* very sad, very morose.
pe'rtulī *perf.* perferō.
pretumultuō'sē *ad.* very excitedly.
pert/u'ndō -u'ndere -udī -ū'sum *vt.* perforate.
perturbā'ti/ō -ō'nis *f.* confusion, disturbance; emotion.
perturbā'tr/īx -ī'cis *f.* disturber.
perturbā't/us *ppp.* perturbō. *a.* troubled; alarmed. **-ē** *ad.* in confusion.
pertu'rb/ō -ā're -ā'vī -ā'tum *vt.* throw into disorder, upset, alarm.
pertu'rpis *a.* scandalous.
pertū'sus *ppp.* pertundō. *a.* in holes, leaky.
per/u'ngō -ungere -ūnxī -ūnctum *vt.* smear all over.
perurbā'nus *a.* very refined; over-fine.
perū'/rō -rere -ssi -stum *vt.* burn up,scorch; inflame, chafe; freeze, nip.
Peru's/ia -iae *f.* Etruscan town, *mod.* Perugia. -ī'nus *a.*
perū'stus *ppp.* perūrō.
perū'tilis *a.* very useful.
pervā'/dō -dere -sī -sum *vt.* & *i.* pass through, spread through; penetrate, reach.
pe'rvag/or -ā'rī -ā'tus *vi.* range, rove about; extend, spread. *vt.* pervade. **-ā'tus** *a.* wide-spread, well-known; general.
pe'rvagus *a.* roving.
perva'riē *ad.* very diversely.
perva'st/ō -ā're -ā'vī -ā'tum *vt.* devastate.
pervā'sus *ppp.* pervādō.
perve'ctus *ppp.* pervehō.
pe'rve/hō -here -xī -ctum *vt.* carry, convey, bring through; (*pass.*) ride, drive, sail through; attain.
perve'll/ō -ere -ī *vt.* pull, twitch, pinch; stimulate; disparage.
perv/e'niō -enī're -ē'nī -e'ntum *vi.* come to, arrive, reach; attain to.
pervē'n/or -ā'rī *vi.* chase through. [verseness.
perve'rsit/ās -ā'tis *f.* per-
perve'rs/us (**pervo'rsus**) *ppp.* pervertō. *a.* awry, squint; wrong, perverse. **-ē** *ad.* perversely.
perve'r/tō (**pervo'rtō**) -tere -tī -sum *vt.* overturn, upset; overthrow, undo; (*speech*) confute.
perve'sperī *ad.* very late.
pervestīgā'ti/ō -ō'nis *f.* thorough search.
pervestī'g/ō -ā're -ā'vī -ā'tum *vt.* track down; investigate.
pe'rvet/us -eris *a.* very old.
pervetu'stus *a.* antiquated.
pervicā'ci/a -ae *f.* obstinacy; firmness.
pe'rvic/āx -ā'cis *a.* obstinate, wilful; dogged. **-ā'citer** *ad.*
pervi'ctus *ppp.* pervincō.
perv/i'deō -idē're -ī'dī -ī'sum *vt.* look over, survey; consider; discern.
pervi'g/eō -ē're -uī *vi.* continue to flourish. [ful.
pe'rvigil -is *a.* awake, watch-
pervigilā'ti/ō -ō'nis *f.* vigil.
pervigi'l/ium -ī & iī *n.* vigil.
pervi'gil/ō -ā're -ā'vī -ā'tum *vt.* & *i.* stay awake all night, keep vigil.
pervī'lis *a.* very cheap.
perv/i'ncō -i'ncere -ī'cī -i'ctum *vt.* & *i.* conquer completely; outdo, surpass; prevail upon, effect; (*argument*) carry a point, maintain, prove.
pervī'v/ō -ere *vi.* survive.
pe'rvius *a.* passable, accessible.
pervo'lgō, *see* **pervulgō**.
pervo'lit/ō -ā're *vt.* & *i.* fly about.

pe'rvol/ō -ā're -ā'vī -ā'tum *vt.* & *i.* fly through or over, fly to.

pe'rv/olō -e'lle -o'luī *vi.* wish very much.

pervolū't/ō -ā're *vt.* (*books*) read through.

pervo'l/vō -vere -vī -ū'tum *vt.* tumble about; (*book*) read through; (*pass.*) be very busy (with).

pervor-, *see* **perver-**.

pervu'lg/ō -ā're -ā'vī -ā'tum *vt.* make public, impart; haunt. **-ā'tus** *a.* very common.

pē's pe'dis *m.* foot; (*length*) foot; (*verse*) foot, metre, (*sail-rope*) sheet. **pedem cōnferre** come to close quarters. **pedem referre** go back. **ante pedēs** self-evident. **pedibus** on foot, by land. **pedibus īre in sententiam** take sides. **pedibus aequīs** (*naut.*) with the wind right aft. **servus ā pedibus** footman.

pe'ssim/us *sup.* **malus. -ē** *sup.* male.

pe'ssul/us -ī *m.* bolt.

pe'ssum *ad.* to the ground, to the bottom. — **dare** put an end to, ruin, destroy. — **īre** sink, perish.

pe'stifer -ī *a.* pestilential; baleful, destructive.

pe'stil/ēns -e'ntis *a.* unhealthy; destructive.

pestile'nti/a -ae *f.* plague, pest; unhealthiness.

pesti'lit/ās -ā'tis *f.* plague.

pe'st/is -is *f.* plague, pest; ruin, destruction.

petasā'tus *a.* wearing the petasus.

petasu'ncul/us -ī *m.* small leg of pork.

pe'tas/us -ī *m.* broad-brimmed hat.

pete'ss/ō -ere *vt.* be eager for.

petī'ti/ō -ō'nis *f.* thrust, attack; request, application; (*office*) candidature, standing for; (*law*) civil suit, right of claim. [plaintiff.

petī't/or -ō'ris *m.* candidate;

petītu'r/iō -ī're *vt.* long to be a candidate.

petī'tus *ppp.* **petō.**

petī't/us -ūs *m.* falling to.

pe't/ō -ere -ī'vī & iī -ī'tum *vt.* aim at, attack; (*place*) make for, go to; seek, look for, demand, ask; go and fetch; (*law*) sue; (*love*) court; (*office*) stand for.

peto'rrit/um -ī *n.* carriage.

pe'tr/ō -ō'nis *m.* yokel.

Petrō'n/ius -ī *m.* arbiter of fashion under Nero.

pe'tul/āns -a'ntis *a.* pert, impudent, lascivious. **-a'nter** *ad.* [impudence.

petula'nti/a -ae *f.* pertness,

petu'lcus *a.* butting.

pe'xus *ppp.* **pectō.**

Phaeā'/ces -cum *m.pl.* fabulous islanders in the Odyssey. **-x** -cis, **-cius**, **-cus** *a.* Phaeacian.

Phae'dr/a -ae *f.* step-mother of Hippolytus.

Phae'dr/us -ī *m.* pupil of Socrates; writer of Latin fables.

Pha'eth/ōn -o'ntis *m.* son of the Sun, killed while driving his father's chariot. **-o'nteus** *a.* **-onti'ad/es** -um *f.pl.* sisters of Phaethon.

phala'ng/ae -ā'rum *f.pl.* wooden rollers.

phalangī't/ae -ā'rum *m.pl.* soldiers of a phalanx.

pha'lan/x -gis *f.* phalanx; troops, battle-order.

Pha'lari/s -dis *m.* tyrant of Agrigentum.

pha'ler/ae -ā'rum *f.pl.* medallions, badges; (*horse*) trappings.

phalerā'tus *a.* wearing medallions; ornamented.

Phalē'r/um -ī *n.* harbour of Athens. **-eus**, **-icus** *a.*

pha'retr/a -ae *f.* quiver.

pharetrā'tus *a.* wearing a quiver.
pharmaceu'tri/a -ae *f.* sorceress.
pharmacopō'l/a -ae *m.* quack doctor.
Pharsā'l/us (-os) -ī *f.* town in Thessaly, where Caesar defeated Pompey. **-icus, -ius** *a.*
Pha'r/us (-os) -ī *f.* island off Alexandria with a famous lighthouse; lighthouse. **-ius** *a.*
phasē'l/us -ī *m., f.* French beans; (*boat*) pinnace.
Phā'si/s -dis & dos *m.* river of Colchis. **-s, -acus** *a.* Colchian. **-ā'nus, -ā'na** *m., f.* pheasant.
pha'sma -tis *n.* ghost.
Phe'r/ae -ā'rum *f.pl.* town in Thessaly, home of Admetus. **-ae'us** *a.*
phi'al/a -ae *f.* saucer.
Phī'di/ās -ae *m.* famous Athenian sculptor. **-acus** *a.*
philē'ma -tis *n.* kiss.
Phili'pp/ī -ō'rum *m.pl.* town in Macedonia, where Brutus and Cassius were defeated.
Phili'pp/us -ī *m.* king of Macedonia; gold coin. **-ē'us, -icus** *a.* **-icae** *f.pl.* Cicero's speeches against Antony.
phili'ti/a (**phīdi'tia**) -ō'rum *n.pl.* public meals at Sparta.
Phi'l/ō (-ōn) -ō'nis *m.* Academic philosopher, teacher of Cicero.
Philoctē't/ēs -ae *m.* Greek archer who gave Hercules poisoned arrows.
philolo'gi/a -ae *f.* study of literature. [literary.
philo'logus *a.* scholarly,
Philomē'l/a -ae *f.* sister of Procne; nightingale.
philoso'phi/a -ae *f.* philosophy.
philo'soph/or -ā'rī -ā'tus *vi.* philosophize.
philo'soph/us -ī *m.* philosopher. *a.* philosophical. **-ē** *ad.*
phi'ltr/um -ī *n.* love-philtre.
phi'lyr/a -ae *f.* inner bark of the lime-tree.
phī'm/us -ī *m.* dice-box.
Phle'geth/ōn -o'ntis *m.* a river of Hades. **-o'ntis** *a.*
Phlī'/ūs -ū'ntis *f.* town in Peloponnese. **-ā'sius** *a.*
phō'c/a -ae *f.* seal.
Phō'c/is -idis *f.* country of central Greece. **-ē'us, -ius, -a'icus** *a.*
Phoe'b/ē -ēs *f.* Diana, the moon.
Phoebi'gen/a -ae *m.* son of Phoebus, Aesculapius.
Phoe'b/us -ī *m.* Apollo; the sun. **-ē'ius, -ē'us** *a.* **-as** -adis *f.* prophetess.
Phoenī'/cē -cēs *f.* Phoenicia. **-ces** -cum *m.pl.* Phoenicians. **-ssus** *a.* Phoenician. *f.* Dido.
phoenīco'pter/us -ī *m.* flamingo.
Phoe'n/īx -ī'cis *m.* friend of Achilles.
phoe'n/īx -ī'cis *m.* phoenix.
Pho'rc/us -ī *m.* son of Neptune, father of Medusa. **-is** -idos, **-ȳ'nis** -ȳ'nidos *f.* Medusa. [Parthia.
Phraā't/ēs -ae *m.* king of
phrenē's/is -is *f.* delirium.
phrenē'ticus *a.* mad, delirious.
Phri'x/us -ī *m.* Helle's brother, who took the ram with the golden fleece to Colchis. **-ē'us** *a.*
Phry'g/es -um *m.pl.* Phrygians; Trojans. **-ia** -iae *f.* Phrygia, country of Asia Minor; Troy. **-ius** *a.* Phrygian, Trojan.
Phthī'/a -ae *f.* home of Achilles in Thessaly. **-ō'ta, -ō'tēs** -ō'tae *m.* native of Phthia. **-us** *a.*
phthi's/is *f.* consumption.
phy *interj.* bah!

phy'lac/a -ae *f.* prison.
phyla'rch/us -ī *m.* chieftain.
phy'sic/a -ae, -ē -ēs *f.* physics.
phy'sic/us *a.* of physics, natural. *m.* natural philosopher. *n.pl.* physics. -ē *ad.* scientifically.
physiognō'm/ōn -onis *m.* physiognomist.
physiolo'gi/a -ae *f.* natural philosophy, science.
piā'bilis *a.* expiable.
piāculā'ris *a.* atoning. *n.pl.* sin-offerings.
piā'cul/um -ī *n.* sin-offering; victim; atonement, punishment; sin, guilt.
piā'm/en -inis *n.* atonement.
pī'c/a -ae *f.* magpie.
picā'ri/a -ae *f.* pitch-hut.
pi'ce/a -ae *f.* pine.
Pī'c/ēns -e'ntis, -ē'nus *a.* of Picenum in E. Italy. -ē'num -ē'nī *n.*
pi'ceus *a.* pitch-black; of pitch.
pi'ct/or -ō'ris *m.* painter.
pictū'r/a -ae *f.* painting; picture.
pictūrā'tus *a.* painted; embroidered.
pi'ctus *ppp.* pingō. *a.* coloured, tattooed; (*style*) ornate; (*fear*) unreal.
pī'c/us -ī *m.* woodpecker.
pi'ē *ad.* religiously, dutifully.
Pī'eri/s -dis *f.* Muse. -us *a.* of the Muses, poetic.
pi'et/ās -ā'tis *f.* sense of duty (to gods, family, country), piety, filial affection, love, patriotism.
pi'g/er -rī *a.* reluctant, slack, slow; numbing, dull.
pi'g/et -ē're -uit *vt.* (*impers.*) be annoyed, dislike; regret, repent.
pigmentā'r/ius -ī & iī *m.* dealer in paints.
pigme'nt/um -ī *n.* paint, cosmetic; (*style*) colouring.
pignerā't/or -ō'ris *m.* mortgagee.
pi'gner/ō -ā're *vt.* pawn, mortgage.
pi'gner/or -ā'rī -ā'tus *vt.* claim, accept.
pi'gn/us -oris & eris *n.* pledge, pawn, security; wager, stake; (*fig.*) assurance, token; (*pl.*) children, dear ones.
pigri'ti/a -ae, -ēs -ē'ī *f.* sluggishness, indolence.
pi'gr/ō -ā're, -or -ā'rī *vi.* be slow, be slack.
pī'l/a -ae *f.* mortar.
pī'l/a -ae *f.* pillar; pier.
pi'l/a -ae *f.* ball, ball-game.
pīlā'n/us -ī *m.* soldier of the third line.
pīlā'tus *a.* armed with javelins.
pīle'nt/um -ī *n.* carriage.
pilleā'tus *a.* wearing the felt cap.
pille'ol/us -ī *m.* skull-cap.
pi'lle/us -ī *m.*, -um -ī *n.* felt cap presented to freed slaves; (*fig.*) liberty.
pilō'sus *a.* hairy.
pī'l/um -ī *n.* javelin.
pī'l/us -ī *m.* division of triarii. prīmus — chief centurion.
pi'l/us -ī *m.* hair; a whit.
Pimplē'/a -ae, -is -idis *f.* Muse. -us *a.* of the Muses.
Pi'ndar/us -ī *m.* Pindar, Greek lyric poet. -icus *a.*
Pi'nd/us -ī *m.* mountain range in Thessaly.
pīnē't/um -ī *n.* pine-wood.
pī'neus *a.* pine-.
pi'ng/ō -ere pi'nxī pi'ctum *vt.* paint, embroider; colour; (*fig.*) embellish, decorate.
pinguē'sc/ō -ere *vi.* grow fat, become fertile.
pi'nguis *a.* fat, rich, fertile; (*mind*) gross, dull; (*ease*) comfortable, calm; (*weather*) thick. *n.* grease.
pī'nifer -ī, **pī'niger** -ī *a.* pine-clad.

pi'nn/a -ae *f.* feather; wing, arrow; battlement; (*fish*) fin.
pinnā'tus *a.* feathered, winged.
pi'nniger -ī *a.* winged; finny.
pi'nnip/ēs -edis *a.* wing-footed.
pinni'rap/us -ī *m.* plume-snatcher.
pi'nnul/a -ae *f.* little wing.
pīnotē'r/ēs -ae *m.* hermit-crab.
pī'ns/ō -ere *vt.* beat, pound.
pī'n/us -ūs & ī *f.* stone pine, Scots fir; ship, torch, wreath.
pi'nxī *perf.* pingō.
pi'/ō -ā're *vt.* propitiate, worship; atone for, avert; avenge.
pi'per -is *n.* pepper.
pī'pil/ō -ā're *vi.* chirp.
Pīrae'/eus, -us -ī *m.,* **-a -ō'rum** *n.pl.* Piraeus, port of Athens. **-us** *a.*
pīrā't/a -ae *m.* pirate.
pīrā'ticus *a.* pirate. *f.* piracy.
Pīrē'n/ē -ēs *f.* spring in Corinth. **-is -idis** *a.*
Pīri'tho/us -ī *m.* king of the Lapiths.
pi'r/um -ī *n.* pear.
pi'r/us -ī *f.* pear-tree.
Pī's/a -ae *f.* Greek town near the Olympic Games site. **-ae'us** *a.*
Pī's/ae -ā'rum *f.pl.* town in Etruria, *mod* Pisa. **-ā'nus** *a.*
piscā'rius *a.* fish-, fishing-.
piscā't/or -ō'ris *m.* fisherman.
piscātō'rius *a.* fishing-.
piscā't/us -ūs *m.* fishing; fish; catch, haul.
pisci'cul/us -ī *m.* little fish.
piscī'n/a -ae *f.* fish-pond; swimming-pool.
piscīnā'r/ius -ī & iī *m.* person keen on fish-ponds.
pi'sc/is -is *m.* fish; (*astr.*) Pisces.
pi'sc/or -ā'rī -ā'tus *vi.* fish.
piscō'sus *a.* full of fish.
piscule'ntus *a.* full of fish.
Pīsi'strat/us -ī *m.* tyrant of Athens. **-idae -idā'rum** *m.pl.* his sons.
pisti'll/um -ī *n.* pestle.
pi'st/or -ō'ris *m.* miller; baker.
pistri'll/a -ae *f.* little mortar.
pistrī'n/um -ī *n.* mill, bakery, drudgery.
pi'str/is -is, -īx -ī'cis *f.* sea monster, whale; swift ship.
pithē'c/ium -ī & iī *n.* little ape.
pītuī't/a -ae *f.* phlegm; catarrh, cold in the head.
pītuītō'sus *a.* phlegmatic.
pi'us *a.* dutiful, conscientious; godly, holy; filial, affectionate; patriotic; good, upright. *m.pl.* the blessed dead.
pix pi'cis *f.* pitch.
plācā'bilis *a.* easily appeased.
plācābi'lit/ās -ā'tis *f.* readiness to condone.
plācā'm/en -inis, plācāme'nt/um -ī *n.* peace-offering.
plācā'ti/ō -ō'nis *f.* propitiating.
plācā't/us *ppp.* plācō. *a.* calm, quiet, reconciled. **-ē** *ad.* calmly.
place'nt/a -ae *f.* cake.
Place'nt/ia -iae *f.* town in N. Italy, *mod.* Piacenza. **-ī'nus** *a.*
pla'c/eō -ē're -uī -itum *vi.* (*with dat.*) please, satisfy. **-et** it seems good, it is agreed, resolved. mihi **-eō** I am pleased with myself.
pla'cid/us *a.* calm, quiet, gentle. **-ē** *ad.* peacefully, gently.
pla'cit/us *ppa.* placeō. *a.* pleasing; agreed on. **-um -ī** *n.* principle, belief.
plā'c/ō -ā're -ā'vī -ā'tum *vt.* calm, appease, reconcile.
plā'g/a -ae *f.* blow, stroke, wound.
pla'g/a -ae *f.* region, zone.
pla'g/a -ae *f.* hunting-net, snare, trap.

plagiā'r/ius -ī & iī *m.* plunderer, kidnapper.
plāgige'rulus *a.* much flogged.
plāgō'sus *a.* fond of punishing.
pla'gul/a -ae *f.* curtain.
pla'nct/us -ūs *m.* beating the breast, lamentation.
plā'nē *ad.* plainly, clearly; completely, quite; certainly.
pla'n/gō -gere -xī -ctum *vt.* & *i.* beat noisily; beat in grief; lament loudly, bewail.
pla'ng/or -ō'ris *m.* beating; loud lamentation.
plā'nip/ēs -edis *m.* ballet-dancer.
plā'nit/ās -ā'tis *f.* perspicuity.
plāni'ti/ēs -ē'ī (-a -ae) *f.* level ground, plain.
pla'nt/a -ae *f.* shoot, slip; sole, foot.
plantā'r/ia -ium *n.pl.* slips, young trees.
plā'n/us *a.* level, flat; plain, clear. *n.* level ground. dē -ō easily.
pla'n/us -ī *m.* impostor.
platа'le/a -ae *f.* spoonbill.
pla'te/a -ae *f.* street.
Pla't/ō -ō'nis *m.* Plato, founder of the Academic school of philosophy. **-ō'nicus** *a.*
plau'/dō -dere -sī -sum *vt.* clap, beat, stamp. *vi.* clap, applaud; approve, be pleased with.
plausi'bilis *a.* praiseworthy.
plau's/or -ō'ris *m.* applauder.
plau'str/um -ī *n.* waggon, cart; (*astr.*) Great Bear. — percellere *upset the apple-cart.*
plau'sus *ppp.* plaudō.
plau's/us -ūs *m.* flapping; clapping, applause.
Plau't/us -ī *m.* early Latin comic poet. **-ī'nus** *a.*
plēbē'cul/a -ae *f.* rabble.
plēbē'ius *a.* plebeian; common, low.
plēbi'col/a -ae *m.* friend of the people.
plēbīscī't/um -ī *n.* decree of the people.
plē'b/s (**plē'bēs**) -is *f.* common people, plebeians; lower classes, masses.
plē'ct/ō -ere *vt.* punish.
plē'ctr/um -ī *n.* plectrum; lyre, lyric poetry.
Plē'ia/s -dis *f.* Pleiad; (*pl.*) the Seven Sisters.
plē'n/us *a.* full, filled; (*fig.*) sated; (*age*) mature; (*amount*) complete; (*body*) stout, plump; (*female*) pregnant; (*matter*) solid; (*style*) copious; (*voice*) loud. ad **-um** abundantly. **-ē** *ad.* fully, entirely.
plēr/u'sque *a.* a large part, most; (*pl.*) the majority, the most; very many. **-u'mque** *ad.* generally, mostly.
ple'xus *a.* plaited, interwoven.
Plī'as, *see* **Plēias**.
plicā'tr/īx -ī'cis *f.* clothes-folder.
pli'c/ō -ā're -ā'vī & uī -ā'tum & itum *vt.* fold, coil.
Plī'n/ius -ī *m.* Roman family name, *esp.* Pliny the Elder, who died in the eruption of Vesuvius; Pliny the Younger, writer of letters.
plōrā't/us -ūs *m.* wailing.
plō'r/ō -ā're -ā'vī -ā'tum *vi.* wail, lament. *vt.* weep for, bewail.
plōste'll/um -ī *n.* cart.
plo'xen/um -ī *n.* cart-box.
plu'/it -ere -it *vi.*(*impers.*) it is raining.
plū'm/a -ae *f.* soft feather, down.
plu'mbeus *a.* of lead; (*fig.*) heavy, dull, worthless.
plu'mb/um -ī *n.* lead; bullet, pipe, ruler. — album tin.
plū'meus *a.* down, downy.
plū'mip/ēs -edis *a.* feather-footed.
plūmō'sus *a.* feathered.
plū'rimus *sup.* multus.
pl/ūs -ū'ris *comp.* multus. *ad.* more.

plū'sculus *a.* a little more.
plu'te/us -ī *m.* shelter, penthouse; parapet; couch; bookcase.
Plū't/ō -ō'nis *m.* king of the lower world. **-ō'nius.**
plu'vi/a -ae *f.* rain.
pluviā'lis *a.* rainy.
plu'vius *a.* rainy, rain-.
pōci'll/um -ī *n.* small cup.
pō'cul/um -ī *n.* cup; drink, potion.
poda'gr/a -ae *f.* gout.
podagrō'sus *a.* gouty.
po'd/ium -ī & iī *n.* balcony.
poē'ma -tis *n.* poem.
poe'n/a -ae *f.* penalty, punishment.
Poe'n/ī -ō'rum *m.pl.* Carthaginians. **-us, Pūnicus** *a.* Punic.
poē's/is -is *f.* poetry, poem.
poē't/a -ae *m.* poet.
poē'tic/us *a.* poetic. *f.* poetry. **-ē** *ad.* poetically.
poē'tri/a -ae *f.* poetess.
pol *interj.* by Pollux ! truly.
pole'nt/a -ae *f.* pearl barley.
po'l/iō -ī're -ī'vī -ī'tum *vt.* polish; improve, put in good order. **-ī'tus** *a.* polished, refined, cultured. **-ī'tē** *ad.* elegantly.
polītī'/a -ae *f.* Plato's Republic.
poli'ticus *a.* political.
po'll/en -inis *n.*, **-is** -inis *m., f.* fine flour, meal.
po'll/ēns -e'ntis *pres.p.* polleō. *a.* powerful, strong.
polle'nti/a -ae *f.* power.
po'll/eō -ē're *vi.* be strong, be powerful.
po'll/ex -icis *m.* thumb.
polli'c/eor -ē'rī -itus *vt.* promise, offer. [ise.
pollicitā'ti/ō -ō'nis *f.* prom-
polli'cit/or -ā'rī -ā'tus *vt.* promise.
polli'cit/um -ī *n.* promise.
Po'lli/ō -ō'nis *m.* Roman surname, *esp.* C. Asinius, soldier, statesman and literary patron under Augustus.
po'llis, *see* **pollen.**
pollūcibi'liter *ad.* sumptuously.
pollū'ctus *a.* offered up. *n.* offering.
po'll/uō -u'ere -uī -ū'tum *vt.* defile, pollute, dishonour.
Po'll/ūx -ū'cis *m.* twin brother of Castor, famous as a boxer. [sky.
po'l/us -ī *m.* pole, North pole;
Polyhy'mni/a -ae *f.* a Muse.
Polyphē'm/us -ī *m.* one-eyed Cyclops.
pō'lyp/us -ī *m.* polypus.
pōmā'r/ius -ī & iī *m.* fruiterer.
pōmā'r/ium -ī & iī *n.* orchard.
pōmerīdiā'nus *a.* afternoon.
pōmē'r/ium (pōmoe'rium) -ī & iī *n.* free space round the city boundary.
pō'mifer -ī *a.* fruitful.
pōmoe'rium, *see* **pōmērium.**
pōmō'sus *a.* full of fruit.
po'mp/a -ae *f.* procession; retinue, train; ostentation.
Pompei'/ī -ō'rum *m.pl.* Campanian town buried by an eruption of Vesuvius. **-ā'nus** *a.*
Pompei'/us -ī *m.* Roman family name, *esp.* Pompey the Great. **-us, -ā'nus** *a.*
Pompi'l/ius -ī *m.* Numa, second king of Rome. **-ius** *a.*
Pomptī'nus *a.* Pomptine, name of marshy district in S. Latium.
pō'm/um -ī *n.* fruit; fruit-tree.
pō'm/us -ī *f.* fruit-tree.
po'nder/ō -ā're *vt.* weigh; consider, reflect on.
ponderō'sus *a.* heavy, weighty.
po'ndō *ad.* in weight; pounds.
po'nd/us -eris *n.* weight; mass, burden; (*fig.*) import-

ance, authority; (*character*) firmness; (*pl.*) balance.
pō'ne *ad.* behind.
pō'n/ō -ere po'suī po'situm *vt.* put, place, lay, set; lay down, lay aside; (*fig.*) regard, reckon; (*art*) make, build; (*camp*) pitch; (*corpse*) lay out, bury; (*example*) take; (*food*) serve; (*hair*) arrange; (*hope*) base, stake; (*hypothesis*) suppose, assume; (*institution*) lay down, ordain; (*money*) invest; (*sea*) calm; (*theme*) propose; (*time*) spend, devote; (*tree*) plant; (*wager*) put down. *vi* (*wind*) abate.
pōns po'ntis *m.* bridge; drawbridge; (*ship*) gangway, deck.
ponti'cul/us -ī *m.* small bridge. [pontiff.
po'ntif/ex -icis *m.* high-priest,
pontificā'lis *a.* pontifical.
pontificā't/us -ūs *m.* high-priesthood.
pontifi'cius *a.* pontiff's.
po'nt/ō -ō'nis *m.* ferry-boat.
po'nt/us -ī *m.* sea.
Po'nt/us -ī *m.* Black Sea; kingdom of Mithridates in Asia Minor. **-icus** *a.*
po'p/a -ae *m.* minor priest.
po'pan/um -ī *n.* sacrificial cake.
pope'll/us -ī *m.* mob.
popī'n/a -ae *f.* eating-house, restaurant.
popī'n/ō -ō'nis *m.* glutton.
po'pl/es -itis *m.* knee.
popl-, *see* **pūbl-**.
popo'scī *perf.* poscō.
poppy'sma -tis *n.* clicking of the tongue.
populā'bilis *a.* destroyable.
populābu'ndus *a.* ravaging.
populā'ri/s *a.* of, from, for the people; popular, democratic; native. *m.* fellow-countryman. *m.pl.* the people's party, the democrats. **-ter** *ad.* vulgarly; democratically.
populā'rit/ās -ā'tis *f.* courting popular favour.
populā'ti/ō -ō'nis *f.* plundering; plunder.
populā't/or -ō'ris *m.* ravager.
pōpu'leus *a.* poplar-.
pōpu'lifer -ī *a.* rich in poplars.
po'pul/or -ā'rī -ā'tus, -ō -ā're *vt.* ravage, plunder; destroy, ruin.
po'pul/us -ī *m.* people, nation; populace, the public; large crowds; district.
pō'pul/us -ī *f.* poplar-tree.
po'rc/a -ae *f.* sow.
porce'll/a -ae *f.*, **-us -ī** *m.* little pig.
porcīnā'r/ius -ī & iī *m.* pork-seller.
porcī'n/a -ae *f.* pork.
Po'rc/ius -ī *m.* family name of Cato. **-ius** *a.*
po'rcul/us -ī *m.* porker.
po'rc/us -ī *m.* pig, hog.
po'rgō, *see* **porrigō**.
Porphy'ri/ōn -ō'nis *m.* a Giant.
porrē'cti/ō -ō'nis *f.* extending.
porrē'ct/us *ppp.* porrigō. *a.* long, protracted; dead.
porrē'xī *perf.* porrigō.
porri'c/iō -ere *vt.* make an offering of. **inter caesa et porrēcta** *at the eleventh hour.*
po'rr/igō -i'gere -ē'xī -ē'ctum *vt.* stretch, spread out, extend; offer, hold out.
porrī'g/ō -inis *f.* scurf, dandruff.
po'rrō *ad.* forward, a long way off; (*time*) in future, long ago; (*sequence*) next, moreover, in turn.
po'rr/um -ī *n.* leek.
Po'rsen/a, Porse'nn/a, Porsi'nn/a -ae *f.* king of Clusium in Etruria.
po'rt/a -ae *f.* gate; entrance, outlet.
portā'ti/ō -ō'nis *f.* carrying.
porte'n/dō -dere -dī -tum *vt.* denote, predict.
portenti'ficus *a.* marvellous.

portentō'sus *a.* unnatural.
porte'nt/um -ī *n.* omen, unnatural happening; monstrosity, monster; (*story*) marvel.
po'rthm/eus -eī & eos *m.* ferryman.
porti'cul/a -ae *f.* small [gallery.
po'rtic/us -ūs *m.* portico, colonnade; (*mil.*) gallery; (*philos.*) Stoicism.
po'rti/ō -ō'nis *f.* share, instalment. prō -ōne proportionally.
po'rtit/or -ō'ris *m.* customs-officer.
po'rtit/or -ō'ris *m.* ferryman.
po'rt/ō -ā're -ā'vī -ā'tum *vt.* carry, convey, bring.
portō'r/ium -ī & iī *n.* customs duty, tax.
po'rtul/a -ae *f.* small gate.
portuō'sus *a.* well off for harbours.
po'rt/us -ūs *m.* harbour, port; (*fig.*) safety, haven.
pō'sc/a -ae *f.* a vinegar drink.
po'sc/ō -ere popo'scī *vt.* ask, require, demand; call on.
Posīdō'n/ius -ī *m.* Stoic philosopher, teacher of Cicero.
posi'ti/ō -ō'nis *f.* position, climate.
po'sit/or -ō'ris *m.* builder.
positū'r/a -ae *f.* position; formation.
po'situs *ppp.* pōnō. *a.* situated.
posse *inf.* possum.
possē'dī *perf.* possideō ; *perf.* possīdō.
posse'ssi/ō -ō'nis *f.* seizing; occupation; possession, property. [estate.
possessiu'ncul/a -ae *f.* small
posse'ss/or -ō'ris *m.* occupier, possessor.
posse'ssus *ppp.* possideō & possīdō.
poss/i'deō -idē're -ē'dī -e'ssum *vt.* hold, occupy; have, possess.
poss/ī'dō -ī'dere -ē'dī -e'ssum *vi.* take possession of.
po'/ssum -sse -tuī *vi.* be able, can; have power, avail.
post *ad.* (*place*) behind; (*time*) after; (*sequence*) next. *pr.* (*with acc.*) behind; after, since. paulō — soon after. — urbem conditam since the foundation of the city.
po'steā *ad.* afterwards, thereafter; next, then. — quam *conj.* after.
poste'ri/or -ō'ris *a.* later, next; inferior, less important. -us *ad.* later.
poste'rit/ās -ā'tis *f.* posterity, the future.
po'sterus *a.* next, following. *m.pl.* posterity.
po'stfer/ō -re *vt.* put after, sacrifice.
postge'nit/ī -ō'rum *m.pl.* later generations.
postha'b/eō -ē're -uī -itum *vt.* put after, neglect.
posthā'c *ad.* hereafter, in future.
po'stibi *ad.* then, after that.
postī'cul/um -ī *n.* small back building.
postī'cus *a.* back-, hind-. *n.* back-door.
posti'deā *ad.* after that.
posti'llā *ad.* afterwards.
po'st/is -is *m.* door-post, door.
postlīmi'n/ium -ī & iī *n.* right of recovery.
postmerīdiā'nus *a.* in the afternoon.
po'stmodo, po'stmodum *ad.* shortly, presently.
postp/ō'nō -ō'nere -o'suī -o'situm *vt.* put after, disregard.
po'stput/ō -ā're *vt.* consider less important.
po'stquam *conj.* after, when.
postrē'm/us *a.* last, rear; lowest, worst. -ō *ad.* finally.
postrī'diē *ad.* next day, the day after.
postscae'n/ium -ī & iī *n.* behind the scenes.

postscrī'b/ō -ere *vt.* write after.
postulā'ti/ō -ō'nis *f.* demand, claim; complaint.
postulā't/um -ī *n.* demand, claim.
postulā't/us -ūs *m.* claim.
po'stul/ō -ā're -ā'vī -ā'tum *vt.* demand, claim; (*law*) summon, prosecute; apply for a writ (to prosecute).
po'stumus *a.* last, last-born.
po'stus, *see* **positus**.
po'suī *perf.* pōnō.
pōtā'ti/ō -ō'nis *f.* drinking.
pōtā't/or -ō'ris *m.* toper.
po'te, *see* **potis**.
po't/ēns -e'ntis *a.* able, capable; powerful, strong, potent; master of, ruling over; successful in carrying out. **-e'nter** *ad.* powerfully; competently. [power.
potentā't/us -ūs *m.* political
pote'nti/a -ae *f.* power, force, efficacy; tyranny.
potē'r/ium -ī & iī *n.* goblet.
pote'sse *archaic inf.* possum.
pote'st/ās -ā'tis *f.* power, ability; control, sovereignty, authority; opportunity, permission; (*person*) magistrate; (*things*) property. **-ātem suī** facere allow access to oneself.
po'tin can (you)? is it possible?
pō'ti/ō -ō'nis *f.* drink, draught, philtre. [power of.
po't/iō -ī're *vt.* put into the
po't/ior -ī'rī -ī'tus *vi.* (*with gen.* & *abl.*) take possession of, get hold of, acquire; be master of. [ferable.
po'ti/or -ō'ris *a.* better, pre-
po'tis, **po'te** *a.*(*indecl.*) able; possible.
poti'ssim/us *a.* chief, most important. **-um** *ad.* especially.
pō'tit/ō -ā're *vt.* drink much.
po'tius *ad.* rather, more.
pō't/ō -ā're -ā'vī -ā'tum & um *vt.* drink.
pō't/or -ō'ris *m.* drinker.
pō'tr/īx -ī'cis *f.* woman tippler.
po'tuī *perf.* possum.
pōtule'nt/a -ō'rum *n.pl.* drinks.
pō'tus *ppp.* pōtō. *a.* drunk.
pō't/us -ūs *m.* drink.
prae *ad.* in front, before; in comparison. *pr.*(*with abl.*) in front of; compared with; (*cause*) because of, for. — **sē** openly. — **sē ferre** display. — **manū** to hand.
praeacū'tus *a.* pointed.
praeaa'ltus *a.* very high, very deep.
prae'b/eō -ē're -uī -itum *vt.* hold out, proffer; give, supply; show, represent. **sē—** behave, prove.
prae'bib/ō -ere -ī *vt.* toast.
prae'bit/or -ō'ris *m.* purveyor.
praeca'lidus *a.* very hot.
praecā'nus *a.* prematurely grey.
praecau'tus *ppp.* praecaveō.
praec/a'veō -avē're -ā'vī -au'tum *vt.* guard against. *vi.* beware, take precautions.
praecē'/dō -dere -ssī -ssum *vt.* go before; surpass. *vi.* lead the way; excel.
praece'll/ō -ere *vi.* excel, be distinguished. *vt.* surpass.
praece'lsus *a.* very high.
praece'nti/ō -ō'nis *f.* prelude.
praece'nt/ō -ā're *vi.* sing an incantation for.
prae'c/eps -i'pitis *a.* head first, headlong; going down, precipitous; rapid, violent, hasty; inclined (to); dangerous. *n.* edge of an abyss, precipice; danger. *ad.* headlong; into danger.
praece'pti/ō -ō'nis *f.* previous notion; precept.
praece'pt/or -ō'ris *m.*, **-rīx** -rī'cis *f.* teacher.
praece'pt/um -ī *n.* maxim, precept; order.

praece'ptus *ppp.* praecipiō.
praece'rp/ō -ere -sī -tum *vt.* gather prematurely; forestall.
praecī'/dō -dere -dī -sum *vt.* cut off, damage; (*fig.*) cut short, put an end to.
praeci'nctus *ppp.* praecingō.
praec/i'ngō -i'ngere -i'nxī -i'nctum *vt.* gird in front; surround.
prae'c/inō -i'nere -i'nuī -e'ntum *vi.* play before; chant a spell. *vt.* predict.
praec/i'piō -i'pere -ē'pī -ē'ptum *vt.* take beforehand, get in advance; anticipate; teach, admonish, order.
praecipita'nter *ad.* at full speed.
praeci'pitem *acc.* praeceps.
praeci'pit/ō -ā're -ā'vī -ā'tum *vt.* throw down, throw away, hasten; (*fig.*) remove, carry away, ruin. *vi.* rush headlong, fall; be hasty.
praeci'pu/us *a.* special; principal, outstanding. **-ē** *ad.* especially, chiefly.
praecī's/us *ppp.* praecīdō. *a.* steep. **-ē** *ad.* briefly; absolutely.
praeclā'r/us *a.* very bright; beautiful, splendid; distinguished, noble. **-ē** *ad.* very clearly; excellently.
praeclū'/dō -dere -sī -sum *vt.* close, shut against; close to, impede.
prae'c/ō -ō'nis *m.* crier, herald; auctioneer.
praecō'git/ō -ā're *vt.* premeditate.
praeco'gnitus *a.* foreseen.
prae'c/olō -o'lere -o'luī -u'ltum *vt.* cultivate early.
praecompo'situs *a.* studied.
praecō'n/ius *a.* of a public crier. **-ium** -ī & iī *n.* office of a crier; advertisement; commendation.
praecōnsū'm/ō -ere -ptum *vt.* use up beforehand.
praecontre'ct/ō -ā're *vt.* consider beforehand.
praeco'rdi/a -ō'rum *n.pl.* midriff; stomach; breast, heart; mind.
praecorr/u'mpō -u'mpere -ū'pī -u'ptum *vt.* bribe beforehand.
prae'co/x -cis *a.* early, premature.
praecu'ltus *ppp.* praecolō.
praecu'/rrō -rrere -cu'rrī & rrī -rsum *vi.* hurry on before, precede; excel. *vt.* anticipate; surpass. **-rre'nt/ia** -ium *n.pl.* antecedents.
praecu'rsi/ō -ō'nis *f.* previous occurrence; (*rhet.*) preparation.
praecu'rs/or -ō'ris *m.* advance-guard; scout.
praecu't/iō -ere *vt.* brandish before.
prae'd/a -ae *f.* booty, plunder; (*animal*) prey; (*fig.*) gain.
praedābu'ndus *a.* plundering.
praeda'mn/ō -ā're *vt.* condemn beforehand.
praedā'ti/ō -ō'nis *f.* plundering.
praedā't/or -ō'ris *m.* plunderer.
praedātō'rius *a.* marauding.
praedēla'ss/ō -ā're *vt.* weaken beforehand.
praedē'stin/ō -ā're *vt.* predetermine.
praediā't/or -ō'ris *m.* buyer of landed estates.
praediātō'rius *a.* relating to the sale of estates.
praedicā'bilis *a.* laudatory.
praedicā'ti/ō -ō'nis *f.* proclamation; commendation.
praedicā't/or -ō'ris *m.* eulogist.
prae'dic/ō -ā're -ā'vī -ā'tum *vt.* proclaim, make public; declare; praise, boast.
praed/ī'cō -ī'cere -ī'xī -i'ctum *vt.* mention beforehand, prearrange; foretell; warn, command.
praedi'cti/ō -ō'nis *f.* foretelling.

praedi'ct/us *ppp.* praedīcō. **–um** -ī *n.* prediction; command; prearrangement.
praedi'ol/um -ī *n.* small estate.
praedi'sc/ō -ere *vt.* learn beforehand.
praedispo'situs *a.* arranged beforehand.
prae'ditus *a.* endowed, provided.
prae'd/ium -ī & iī *n.* estate.
praedī'v/es -itis *a.* very rich.
prae'd/ō -ōnis *m.* robber, pirate.
prae'd/or -ārī -ātus *vt.* & *i.* plunder, rob; (*fig.*) profit.
praed/ū'cō -ū'cere -ū'xī -u'ctum *vt.* draw in front.
praedu'lcis *a.* very sweet.
praedū'rus *a.* very hard, very tough.
praeēmi'n/eō -ē're *vt.* surpass.
prae'/eō -ī're -ī'vī & iī -itum *vi.* lead the way, go first; (*formula*) dictate, recite first. *vt.* precede, outstrip.
praeesse *inf.* praesum.
praefā'ti/ō -ōnis *f.* formula; preface.
praefā'tus *ppa.* praefor.
praefectū'r/a -ae *f.* superintendence; governorship; Italian town governed by Roman edicts, prefecture; district, province.
praefe'ctus *ppp.* praeficiō. *m.* overseer, director, governor, commander. — classis admiral. — legiōnis colonel. — urbis or urbī city prefect (of Rome).
prae'/ferō -fe'rre -tulī -lā'tum *vt.* carry in front, hold out; prefer; show display; anticipate; (*pass.*) hurry past, outflank.
prae'fer/ōx -ō'cis *a.* very impetuous, very insolent.
praefe'rvidus *a.* very hot.
praefestī'n/ō -ā're *vi.* be too hasty; hurry past.
prae'fic/a -ae *f.* hired mourner.
praef/i'ciō -i'cere -ē'cī -e'ctum *vt.* put in charge, give command over.
prae'fīd/ēns -e'ntis *a.* overconfident.
prae'fī/gō -gere -xī -xum *vt.* fasten in front, set up before; tip, point; transfix.
praefī'n/iō -ī're -ī'vī & iī -ī'tum *vt.* determine, prescribe.
praefi'scin/e, **–ī** *ad.* without offence.
praeflō'r/ō -ā're *vt.* tarnish.
prae'flu/ō -ere *vt.* & *i.* flow past.
prae'foc/ō -ā're *vt.* choke.
praef/o'diō -o'dere -ō'dī *vt.* dig in front of; bury beforehand.
prae'f/or -ā'rī -ā'tus *vt.* & *i.* say in advance, preface; pray beforehand; predict.
praefrā'ct/us *ppp.* praefringō. *a.* abrupt; stern. **–ē** *ad.* resolutely.
praefrī'gidus *a.* very cold.
praefr/i'ngō -i'ngere -ē'gī -ā'ctum *vt.* break off, shiver.
prae'fuī *perf.* praesum.
praefu'l/ciō -cī're -sī -tum *vt.* prop up; use as a prop.
praef/u'lgeō -ulgē're -ulsī *vt.* shine conspicuously; outshine.
praege'lidus *a.* very cold.
praege'st/iō -ī're *vi.* be very eager.
prae'gn/āns -a'ntis *a.* pregnant; full.
praegra'cilis *a.* very slim.
praegra'ndis *a.* very large, very great.
prae'gravis *a.* very heavy; very wearisome.
prae'grav/ō -ā're *vt.* weigh down; eclipse.
praegre'/dior -dī -ssus *vt.* & *i.* go before; go past; surpass.
praegre'ssi/ō -ōnis *f.* precession, precedence.
praegustā't/or -ō'ris *m.* taster.

praegu'st/ō -ā're *vt.* taste beforehand. [give.
praehi'b/eō -ē're *vt.* offer,
praeia'c/eō -ē're *vt.* lie in front of.
praeiūdi'c/ium -ī & iī *n.* precedent, example; prejudgment.
praeiū'dic/ō -ā're -ā'vī -ā'tum *vt.* prejudge, decide beforehand.
prae'iuv/ō -ā're *vt.* give previous assistance to.
prael..'/bor -bī -psus *vt.* & *i.* move past, move along. [first.
praela'mb/ō -ere *vt.* lick
praelā'tus *ppp.* praeferō.
prae'leg/ō -ere *vt.* coast along.
prae'lig/ō -ā're *vt.* bind, tie up. [very tall.
praelo'ngus *a.* very long,
prae'lo/quor -quī -cū'tus *vi.* speak first.
praelū'/ceō -cē're -xī *vi.* light, shine; outshine.
praelū'stris *a.* very magnificent.
praema'nd/ō -ā're -ā'vī -ā'tum *vt.* bespeak. -ā'ta *n.pl.* warrant of arrest.
praematū'r/us *a.* too early, premature. -ē *ad.* too soon.
praemedicā'tus *a.* protected by charms.
praemeditā'ti/ō -ō'nis *f.* thinking over the future.
praeme'dit/or -ā'rī -ā'tus *vt.* think over, practise. -ā'tus *a.* premeditated. [iously.
praemetue'nter *ad.* anx-
praeme'tu/ō -ere *vi.* be anxious. *vt.* fear the future.
praemi'ssus *ppp.* praemittō.
praem/i'ttō -i'ttere -ī'sī -i'ssum *vt.* send in advance.
prae'm/ium -ī & iī *n.* prize, reward. [hension.
praemole'sti/a -ae *f.* appre-
praemō'l/ior -ī'rī *vt.* prepare thoroughly.
praemo'n/eō -ē're -uī -itum *vt.* forewarn, foreshadow.
praemo'nit/us -ūs *m.* premonition. [guide.
praemōnstrā't/or -ō'ris *m.*
praemō'nstr/ō -ā're *vt.* guide; predict. [off; pilfer.
praemo'rd/eō -ē're *vt.* bite
praemo'r/ior -ī -tuus *vi.* die too soon.
praemū'n/iō -ī're -ī'vī -ī'tum *vt.* fortify, strengthen, secure.
praemūnī'ti/ō -ō'nis *f.* (*rhet.*) preparation.
praenā'rr/ō -ā're *vt.* tell beforehand.
prae'nat/ō -ā're *vt.* flow past.
Praene'st/e -is *n.*, *f.* Latin town, *mod.* Palestrina. -ī'nus *a.* [more attractive.
praeni't/eō -ē're -uī *vi.* seem
praenō'm/en -inis *n.* first name.
praenō'sc/ō -ere *vt.* foreknow.
praenō'ti/ō -ō'nis *f.* preconceived idea.
praenū'bilus *a.* very gloomy.
praenū'nti/ō -ā're *vt.* foretell.
praenū'nt/ius -ī & iī *m.*, -ia -iae *f.* harbinger.
praeo'ccup/ō -ā're -ā'vī -ā'tum *vt.* take first, anticipate.
prae'olit mihi I get a hint of.
praeo'pt/ō -ā're -ā'vī -ā'tum *vt.* choose rather, prefer.
praepa'nd/ō -ere *vt.* spread out; expound.
praeparā'ti/ō -ō'nis *f.* preparation.
prae'par/ō -ā're -ā'vī -ā'tum *vt.* prepare, prepare for. ex -ātō by arrangement.
praepe'd/iō -ī're -ī'vī -ī'tum *vt.* shackle, tether; hamper.
praepe'nd/eō -ē're *vi.* hang down in front.
prae'p/es -etis *a.* swift, winged; of good omen. *f.* bird.
praepilā'tus *a.* tipped with a ball.
praepi'nguis *a.* very rich.
praepo'll/eō -ē're *vi.* be very powerful, be superior.

praepo'nder/ō -ā're *vt.* outweigh.
praep/ō'nō -ō'nere -o'suī -o'situm *vt.* put first, place in front; put in charge, appoint commander; prefer.
praepo'rt/ō -ā're *vt.* carry before.
praeposi'ti/ō -ō'nis *f.* preference; (*gram.*) preposition.
praepo'situs *ppp.* praepōnō. *m.* overseer, commander.
praepo'/ssum -sse -tuī *vi.* gain the upper hand.
praepo'ster/us *a.* inverted, perverted; absurd. **-ē** *ad.* the wrong way round.
prae'pot/ēns -e'ntis *a.* very powerful.
praepropera'nter *ad.* too hastily.
praepro'per/us *a.* overhasty, rash. **-ē** *ad.* too hastily.
praepū't/ium -ī & iī *n.* foreskin.
prae'quam *ad.* compared [with.
praeque'stus *a.* complaining beforehand.
praera'di/ō -ā're *vt.* outshine.
praera'pidus *a.* very swift.
praere'ptus *ppp.* praeripiō.
praerig/ē'scō -ē'scere -uī *vi.* become very stiff.
praer/i'piō -i'pere -i'puī -e'ptum *vt.* take before, forestall; carry off prematurely; frustrate.
praerō'/dō -dere -sum *vt.* bite the end of, nibble off.
praerogātī'v/us *a.* voting first. **-a** -ae *f.* tribe or century with the first vote, the first vote; previous election; omen, sure token.
praerō'sus *ppp.* praerōdō.
praer/u'mpō -u'mpere -ū'pī -u'ptum *vt.* break off.
praeru'ptus *ppp.* praerumpō. *a.* steep, abrupt; headstrong.
pr/aes -ae'dis *m.* surety; property of a surety.
praesaep-, *see* **praesēp-**.
praesā'g/iō -ī're *vt.* have a presentiment of, forebode.
praesāgī'ti/ō -ō'nis *f.* foreboding.
praesā'g/ium -ī & iī *n.* presentiment; prediction.
praesā'gus *a.* foreboding, prophetic.
prae'sc/iō -ī're -iī *vt.* know before.
praescī'sc/ō -ere *vt.* find out beforehand.
prae'scius *a.* foreknowing.
praescrī'/bō -bere -psī -ptum *vt.* write first; direct, command; dictate, describe; put forward as a pretext.
praescrī'pti/ō -ō'nis *f.* preface, heading; order, rule; pretext.
praescrī'pt/us *ppp.* praescrībō. **-um** -ī *n.* order, rule.
prae'sec/ō -ā're -uī -tum & -ā'tum *vt.* cut off, pare.
prae's/ēns -e'ntis *a.* present, in person; (*things*) immediate, ready, prompt; (*mind*) resolute; (*gods*) propitious. *n.pl.* present state of affairs. **in** **-ēns** for the present. **in rē** **-enti** on the spot.
praesē'nsi/ō -ō'nis *f.* foreboding; preconception.
praesē'nsus *ppp.* praesentiō.
praesentā'rius *a.* instant, ready.
praese'nti/a -ae *f.* presence; effectiveness.
praes/e'ntiō -entī're -ē'nsī -ē'nsum *vt.* presage, have a foreboding of.
prasē'p/e -is *n.*, **-is**, **-ēs** -is *f.* stable, fold, pen; hovel; hive. [barricade.
praesē'p/iō -ī're -sī -tum *vt.*
praese'rtim *ad.* especially.
praese'rv/iō -ī're *vi.* serve as a slave.
prae's/es -idis *m.* guardian, protector; chief, ruler.
praes/i'deō -idē're -ē'dī *vi.*

guard, defend; preside over, direct.
praesidiā'rius *a.* garrison-.
praesi'd/ium -ī & iī *n.* defence, protection; support, assistance; guard, garrison, convoy; defended position, entrenchment.
praesigni'fic/ō -ā're *vt.* foreshadow.
praesi'gnis *a.* conspicuous.
prae'son/ō -ā're -uī *vi.* sound before. [before.
praespa'rg/ō -ere *vt.* strew
praestā'bilis *a.* outstanding; preferable.
prae'st/āns -a'ntis *pres.p.* praestō. *a.* outstanding, preeminent.
praesta'nti/a -ae *f.* preeminence. [guardian.
prae'st/es -itis *a.* presiding,
praesti'gi/ae -ā'rum *f.pl.* illusion, sleight of hand.
praestigiā't/or -ō'ris *m.*, **-rīx** -rī'cis *f.* conjurer, cheat.
prae'stin/ō -ā're *vt.* buy.
prae'stitī *perf.* praestō.
praesti't/uō -u'ere -uī -ū'tum *vt.* prearrange, prescribe.
prae'stitus *ppp.* praestō.
prae'stō *ad.* at hand, ready.
prae'st/ō -ā're -itī -itum & ā'tum *vi.* be outstanding, be superior; (*impers.*) it is better. *vt.* excel; be responsible for, answer for; (*duty*) discharge, perform; (*quality*) show, prove; (*things*) give, offer, provide. sē— behave, prove.
praestō'l/or -ā'rī -ā'tus *vt.* & *i.* wait for, expect.
praestri'ctus *ppp.* praestringō.
praestr/i'ngō -i'ngere -i'nxī -i'ctum *vt.* squeeze; blunt, dull; (*eyes*) dazzle.
prae'stru/ō -ere -xī -ctum *vt.* block up; build beforehand.
prae'sul -is *n.* public dancer.
praesultā't/or -ō'ris *m.* public dancer.
praesu'lt/ō -ā're *vi.* dance before.
prae'/sum -e'sse -fuī *vi.* (*with dat.*) be at the head of, be in command of; take the lead; protect.
praesū'm/ō -ere -psī -ptum *vt.* take first; anticipate; take for granted.
praesū'tus *a.* sewn over at the point.
praete'mpt/ō -ā're *vt.* feel for, grope for; test in advance.
praete'n/dō -dere -dī -tum *vt.* hold out, put before, spread in front of; give as an excuse, allege. [tō.
praete'ntō, *see* **praetemp-**
praete'ntus *ppp.* praetendō. *a.* lying over against.
praete'p/eō -ē're -uī *vi.* glow before.
prae'ter *ad.* beyond; excepting. *pr.*(*with acc.*) past, along; except, besides; beyond, more than, in addition to, contrary to. [past.
praete'rag/ō -ere *vt.* drive
praeterbi't/ō -ere *vt.* & *i.* pass by. [past.
praeterdū'c/ō -ere *vt.* lead
praete'reā *ad.* besides; moreover; henceforth.
praete'r/eō -ī're -iī -itum *vi.* go past. *vt.* pass, overtake; escape, escape the notice of; omit, leave out, forget, neglect; reject, exclude; surpass; transgress.
praetere'quit/āns -a'ntis *a.* riding past.
praete'rflu/ō -ere *vt.* & *i.* flow past.
praetergre'/dior -dī -ssus *vt.* pass, march past; surpass.
praeterhā'c *ad.* further, more.
praete'ritus *ppp.* praetereō. *a.* past, gone by. *n.pl.* the past.
praeterlā'/bor -bī -psus *vt.* flow past, move past. *vi.* slip away.

praeterlā'tus *a.* driving, flying past. [by.
praete'rme/ō -ā're *vi.* pass
praetermi'ssi/ō -ō'nis *f.* omission, passing over.
praeterm/i'ttō -i'ttere -ī'sī -i'ssum *vt.* let pass; omit, neglect; make no mention of; overlook. [besides.
prae'terquam *ad.* except,
praeterve'cti/ō -ō'nis *f.* passing by.
praete'rve/hor -hī -ctus *vt.* & *i.* ride past, sail past; march past; pass by, pass over.
praete'rvol/ō -ā're *vt.* & *i.* fly past; escape.
praete'x/ō -ere -uī -tum *vt.* border, fringe; adorn; pretend, disguise.
praetextā'tus *a.* wearing the toga praetexta, under age.
praete'xt/us *ppp.* praetexō. *a.* wearing the toga praetexta. *f.* toga with a purple border; Roman tragedy. *n.* pretext.
praete'xt/us -ūs *m.* splendour; pretence.
praeti'm/eō -ē're *vi.* be afraid in advance.
praeti'nctus *a.* dipped beforehand.
prae't/or -ō'ris *m.* chief magistrate, commander; praetor; propraetor, governor.
praetōriā'nus *a.* of the emperor's bodyguard.
praetō'r/ium -ī & iī *n.* general's tent, camp headquarters; governor's residence; council of war; palace, grand building; emperor's bodyguard.
praetō'r/ius *a.* praetor's, praetorian; of a propraetor; of the emperor's bodyguard. *m.* ex-praetor. -ia cohors bodyguard of general or emperor. porta -ia camp gate facing the enemy.
praeto'rqu/eō -ē're *vt.* strangle first.
praetre'pid/āns -a'ntis *a.* very impatient.
praetru'nc/ō -ā're *vt.* cut off.
prae'tulī *perf.* praeferō.
praetū'r/a -ae *f.* praetorship.
praeu'mbr/āns -a'ntis *a.* obscuring.
praeū'stus *a.* hardened at the point; frost-bitten.
prae'ut *ad.* compared with.
praeva'l/eō -ē're -uī *vi.* be very powerful, have most influence, prevail.
praeva'lidus *a.* very strong, very powerful; too strong.
praevāricā'ti/ō -ō'nis *f.* collusion.
praevāricā't/or -ō'ris *m.* advocate guilty of collusion.
praevā'ric/or -ā'rī -ā'tus *vi.* (*with dat.*) favour by collusion.
prae've/hor -hī -ctus *vi.* ride, fly in front, flow past.
praev/e'niō -enī're -ē'nī -e'ntum *vt.* & *i.* come before; anticipate, prevent.
praeve'rr/ō -ere *vt.* sweep before.
praeve'rt/ō -ere -ī, -or -ī *vt.* put first, prefer; turn to first, attend first to; outstrip; anticipate, frustrate, prepossess.
praev/i'deō -idē're -ī'dī -ī'sum *vt.* foresee. [beforehand.
praevi'ti/ō -ā're *vt.* taint
prae'vius *a.* leading the way.
prae'vol/ō -ā're *vi.* fly in front.
pragma'ticus *a.* of affairs. *m.* legal expert.
pra'nd/eō -ē're -ī *vi.* take lunch. *vt.* eat.
pra'nd/ium -ī & iī *n.* lunch.
prā'ns/or -ō'ris *m.* guest at lunch. [fed.
prā'nsus *a.* having lunched,
pra'sinus *a.* green.
prātē'nsis *a.* meadow.
prā'tul/um -ī *n.* small meadow.

prā't/um -ī *n.* meadow; grass.
prā'vit/ās -ā'tis *f.* irregularity; perverseness, depravity.
prā'v/us *a.* crooked, deformed; perverse, bad, wicked. **-ē** *ad.* wrongly, badly.
Prāxi'tel/ēs -is *m.* famous Greek sculptor. **-i'us** *a.*
precā'ri/us *a.* obtained by entreaty. **-ō** *ad.* by request.
precā'ti/ō -ō'nis *f.* prayer.
precā't/or -ō'ris *m.* intercessor.
pre'ces *pl.* **prex.**
pre'ci/ae -ā'rum *f.pl.* kind of vine.
pre'c/or -ā'rī -ā'tus *vt.* & *i.* pray, beg, entreat; wish (well), curse.
preh/e'ndō (pre'ndō) -endere -e'ndī -e'nsum *vt.* take hold of, catch; seize, detain; surprise; (*eye*) take in; (*mind*) grasp.
prehē'nsō, *see* **prēnsō.**
prehē'nsus *ppp.* **prehendō.**
prē'l/um -ī *n.* wine-press, oil-press.
pre'/mō -mere -ssī -ssum *vt.* press, squeeze; press together, compress, (*eyes*) close, (*reins*) tighten, (*trees*) prune; press upon, lie, sit, stand on, cover, conceal, surpass; press hard on, follow closely, (*coast*) hug; press down, lower, burden; (*fig.*) overcome, rule, (*words*) disparage; press in, sink, stamp, plant; press back, repress, check, stop.
pre'ndō, *see* **prehendō.**
prēnsā'ti/ō -ō'nis *f.* canvassing.
prē'ns/ō (prehēnsō) -ā're -ā'vī -ā'tum *vt.* clutch at, take hold of, buttonhole.
prē'nsus *ppp.* **prehendō.**
pre'sbyter -ī *m.* (*eccl.*) elder.
pre'ssī *perf.* **premō.**
pre'ssi/ō -ō'nis *f.* fulcrum.
pre'ss/ō -ā're *vt.* press.
pre'ss/us *ppp.* **premō.** *a.* (*style*) concise, compressed; (*pace*) slow; (*voice*) subdued. **-ē** *ad.* concisely, accurately, simply.
pre'ss/us -ūs *m.* pressure.
prē'st/ēr -ē'ris *m.* waterspout.
pretiō's/us *a.* valuable, expensive; extravagant. **-ē** *ad.* expensively.
pre't/ium -ī & iī *n.* price, value; worth; money, fee, reward. **māgnī** -ī, in -iō valuable. **operae** — worth while.
pr/ex -e'cis *f.* request, entreaty; prayer; good wish; curse.
Pri'am/us -ī *m.* king of Troy. **-ē'ius** *a.* **-idēs** -idae *m.* son of Priam. **-ē'is** -ē'idis *f.* Cassandra.
Priā'p/us -ī *m.* god of fertility and of gardens.
prī'dem *ad.* long ago, long.
prī'diē *ad.* the day before.
prīmae'vus *a.* youthful.
prīmā'n/ī -ō'rum *m.pl.* soldiers of the 1st legion.
prīmā'rius *a.* principal, first-rate.
primi'genus *a.* original.
prīmipīlā'r/is -is *m.* chief centurion.
prīmipī'l/us -ī *m.* chief centurion. [fruits.
prīmi'ti/ae -ā'rum *f.pl.* first-
prī'mitus *ad.* originally.
prī'mō *ad.* at first; firstly.
prīmō'rd/ium -ī & iī *n.* beginning. -ia rērum atoms.
prīmō'ris *a.* first, foremost, tip of; principal. *m.pl.* nobles; (*mil.*) front line.
prī'mul/us *a.* very first. **-um** *ad.* first.
prī'mum *ad.* first, to begin with, in the first place; for the first time. cum, ubi, ut — as soon as. quam — as soon as possible. — dum in the first place.

prī'm/us *a.* first, foremost, tip of; earliest; principal, most eminent. — **veniō** I am the first to come. **-ō mēnse** at the beginning of the month. **-īs digitīs** with the finger-tips. **-ās agere** play the leading part. **-ās dare** give first place to. **in -īs** in the front line; especially.

prī'nc/eps **-ipis** *a.* first, in front, chief, most eminent. *m.* leader, chief; first citizen, emperor; (*mil.*) company, captain, captaincy; *pl.* (*mil.*) the second line.

prīncipā'lis *a.* original; chief; the emperor's.

prīncipā't/us **-ūs** *m.* first place; post of commander-in-chief; emperorship.

prīncipiā'lis *a.* from the beginning.

prīnci'p/ium **-ī & iī** *n.* beginning, origin; first to vote. *pl.* first principles; (*mil.*) front line; camp headquarters.

pri'/or **-ō'ris** (*n.* **-us**) *a.* former, previous, first, better, preferable. *m.pl.* forefathers.

prī'sc/us *a.* former, ancient, old-fashioned. **-ē** *ad.* strictly.

prī'stinus *a.* former, original; of yesterday.

pri'us *ad.* previously, before; in former times. — **quam** before, sooner than.

prīvā'tim *ad.* individually, privately; at home.

prīvā'ti/ō **-ō'nis** *f.* removal.

prīvā'tus *a.* individual, private; not in public office. *m.* private citizen.

Prīve'rn/um **-ī** *n.* old Latin town. **-ā's** **-ā'tis** *a.*

prīvī'gn/a **-ae** *f.* step-daughter.

prīvī'gn/us **-ī** *m.* step-son. *pl.* step-children.

prīvilē'g/ium **-ī & iī** *n.* law in favour of or against an individual.

prī'v/ō **-ā're** **-ā'vī** **-ā'tum** *vt.* deprive, rob; free.

prī'vus *a.* single, one each; own, private.

prō *ad.* (*with* **ut** *and* **quam**) in proportion (as). *pr.* (*with abl.*) in front of, on the front of; for, on behalf of, instead of, in return for; as, as good as; according to, in proportion to, by virtue of. — **eō ac** just as. — **eō quod** just because. — **eō quantum, ut** in proportion as.

prō *interj.* (*expressing wonder or sorrow*) O! alas!

proā'gor/us **-ī** *m.* chief magistrate (in Sicilian towns).

proavī'tus *a.* ancestral.

pro'av/us **-ī** *m.* great-grand-father, ancestor.

probā'bili/s *a.* laudable; credible probable. **-ter** *ad.* credibly.

probābi'lit/ās **-ā'tis** *f.* credibility.

probā'ti/ō **-ō'nis** *f.* approval; testing.

probā't/or **-ō'ris** *m.* approver.

pro'bit/ās **-ā'tis** *f.* goodness, honesty.

pro'b/ō **-ā're** **-ā'vī** **-ā'tum** *vt.* approve, approve of; appraise; recommend; prove, show. **-ā'tus** *a.* tried, excellent; acceptable.

probrō'sus *a.* abusive; disgraceful.

pro'br/um **-ī** *n.* abuse, reproach; disgrace; infamy, unchastity.

pro'b/us *a.* good, excellent; honest, upright. **-ē** *ad.* well, properly; thoroughly, well done!

procā'cit/ās **-ā'tis** *f.* impudence.

pro'c/āx **-ā'cis** *a.* bold, forward, insolent. **-ā'citer** *ad.* insolently

prōc/ē'dō **-ē'dere** **-e'ssī** **e'ssum** *vi.* go forward, advance; go out, come forth; (*time*) go on, continue; (*fig.*) make

progress, get on; (*events*) turn out, succeed.
proce'll/a -ae *f.* hurricane, storm; (*mil.*) charge.
procellō'sus *a.* stormy.
pro'cer -is *m.* chief, noble, prince. [length.
prōcē'rit/ās -ā'tis *f.* height;
prōcē'rus *a.* tall; long.
prōce'ssi/ō -ō'nis *f.* advance.
prōce'ss/us -ūs *m.* advance, progress.
prō'cid/ō -ere -ī *vi.* fall forwards, fall down.
prōci'nct/us -ūs *m.* readiness (for action). [bawler.
prōclāmā't/or -ō'ris *m.*
prōclā'm/ō -ā're *vi.* cry out.
prōclī'n/ō -ā're *vt.* bend. **-ā'tus** *a.* tottering.
prōclī'v/is, -us *a.* downhill, steep; (*mind*) prone, willing; (*act*) easy. in -ī easy. **-e** *ad.* downwards; easily.
prōclī'vit/ās -ā'tis *f.* descent; tendency.
prōclī'vus, *see* **proclīvis.**
Pro'cn/ē -ēs *f.* wife of Tereus, changed to a swallow; swallow.
prōcō'nsul -is *m.* proconsul, governor.
prōcōnsulā'ris *a.* proconsular.
prōcōnsulā't/us -ūs *m.* proconsulship.
prōcrāstinā'ti/ō -ō'nis *f.* procrastination.
prōcrā'stin/ō -ā're *vt.* put off from day to day.
prōcreā'ti/ō -ō'nis *f.* begetting. [parent.
prōcreā't/or -ō'ris *m.* creator,
prōcreā'tr/īx -ī'cis *f.* mother.
prō'cre/ō -ā're *vt.* beget, produce.
prōcrē'sc/ō -ere *vi.* be produced, grow up.
Procrū'st/ēs -ae *m.* Attic highwayman, who tortured victims on a bed.
prō'cub/ō -ā're *vi.* lie on the ground.
prōcū'/dō -dere -dī -sum *vt.* forge; produce.
pro'cul *ad.* at a distance, far, from afar. [down.
prōcu'lc/ō -ā're *vt.* trample
prōcu'/mbō -mbere -buī -bitum *vi.* fall forwards, bend over; sink down, be broken down.
prōcūrā'ti/ō -ō'nis *f.* management; (*religion*) expiation.
prōcūrā't/or -ō'ris *m.* administrator, financial agent; (*province*) governor. [ness.
prōcūrā'tr/īx -ī'cis *f.* gover-
prōcū'r/ō -ā're -ā'vī -ā'tum *vt.* take care of, manage; expiate. *vi.* be a procurator.
prōcu'/rrō -rrere -cu'rrī & rrī -rsum *vi.* rush forward; jut out.
prōcursā'ti/ō -ō'nis *f.* charge.
prōcursā't/or -ō'ris *m.* skirmisher. [sally.
prōcu'rs/ō -ā're *vi.* make a
prōcu'rs/us -ūs *m.* charge.
prōcu'rvus *a.* curving forwards.
pro'c/us -ī *m.* nobleman.
pro'c/us -ī *m.* wooer, suitor.
Pro'cy/ōn -ō'nis *m.* Lesser Dog-star.
prōdea'mbul/ō -ā're *vi.* go out for a walk.
prō'd/eō -ī're -iī -itum *vi.* come out, come forward, appear; go ahead, advance; project.
prōde'sse *inf.* prōsum.
prōd/ī'cō -ī'cere -ī'xī -i'ctum *vt.* appoint, adjourn.
prōdictā't/or -ō'ris *m.* vice-dictator.
prōdige'nti/a -ae *f.* profusion. [ally.
prōdigiā'liter *ad.* unnatur-
prōdigiō'sus *a.* unnatural, marvellous.
prōdi'g/ium -ī & iī *n.* portent; unnatural deed; monster.
prō'd/igō -i'gere -ē'gī -ā'ctum *vt.* squander.

prō'dig/us *a.* wasteful; lavish, generous. **-ē** *ad.* extravagantly.
prōdi'ti/ō -ō'nis *f.* betrayal.
prō'dit/or -ō'ris *m.* traitor.
prō'ditus *ppp.* prōdō.
prō'd/ō -ere -idī -itum *vt.* bring forth, produce; make known, publish; betray, give up; (*tradition*) hand down.
prōdo'c/eō -ē're *vt.* preach.
pro'drom/us -ī *m.* forerunner.
prōd/ū'cō -ū'cere -ū'xī -u'ctum *vt.* bring forward, bring out; conduct; drag in front; draw out, extend; (*acting*) perform; (*child*) beget, bring up; (*fact*) bring to light; (*innovation*) introduce; (*rank*) promote; (*slave*) put up for sale; (*time*) prolong, protract, put off; (*tree*) cultivate; (*vowel*) lengthen. [ening.
prōdu'cti/ō -ō'nis *f.* length-
prōdu'ct/ō -ā're *vt.* spin out.
prōdu'ct/us *ppp.* prōdūcō. *a.* lengthened, long. **-ē** *ad.* long.
proē'gmen/on -ī *n.* a preferred thing.
proeliā't/or -ō'ris *m.* fighter.
proe'li/or -ā'rī -ā'tus *vi.* fight, join battle.
proe'l/ium -ī & iī *n.* battle, conflict.
profā'n/ō -ā're *vt.* desecrate.
profā'nus *a.* unholy, common; impious; ill-omened.
profā'tus *ppa.* profor.
profe'cti/ō -ō'nis *f.* departure; source.
profe'ctō *ad.* really, certainly.
profe'ctus *ppa.* proficiscor.
prōfe'ctus *ppp.* prōficiō.
prōfe'ct/us -ūs *m.* growth, progress, profit.
prō'/ferō -fe'rre -tulī -lā'tum *vt.* bring forward, forth or out; extend, enlarge; (*time*) prolong, defer; (*instance*) mention, quote; (*knowledge*) publish, reveal. **pedem —** proceed. **signa —** advance.
profe'ssi/ō -ō'nis *f.* declaration; public register; profession.
profe'ss/or -ō'ris *m.* teacher.
professō'rius *a.* authoritative.
profe'ssus *ppa.* profiteor.
profē'stus *a.* not holiday, working.
prōf/i'ciō -i'cere -ē'cī -e'ctum *vi.* make progress, profit; be of use.
prof/icī'scor -icī'scī -e'ctus *vi.* set out, start; originate, proceed.
prof/i'teor -itē'rī -e'ssus *vt.* declare, profess; make an official return of; promise, volunteer. [thrift.
prōfligā't/or -ō'ris *m.* spend-
prōflī'g/ō -ā're -ā'vī -ā'tum *vt.* dash to the ground; destroy, overthrow; bring almost to an end; degrade. **-ā'tus** *a.* dissolute.
prō'fl/ō -ā're *vt.* breathe out.
prō'flu/ēns -e'ntis *pres.p.* prōfluō. *a.* flowing; fluent. *f.* running water. **-e'nter** *ad.* easily.
prōflue'nti/a -ae *f.* fluency.
prō'flu/ō -ere -xī *vi.* flow on, flow out, (*fig.*) proceed. [ing.
prōflu'v/ium -ī & iī *n.* flow-
pro'f/or -ā'rī -ā'tus *vi.* speak, give utterance.
prof/u'giō -u'gere -ū'gī *vi.* flee, escape; take refuge (with). *vt.* flee from.
pro'fugus *a.* fugitive; exiled; nomadic.
prō'fuī *perf.* prōsum.
prof/u'ndō -u'ndere -ū'dī -ū'sum *vt.* pour out, shed; bring forth, produce; prostrate; squander. **sē —** burst forth, rush out.
profu'ndus *a.* deep, vast, high; infernal; (*fig.*) profound, immoderate. *n.* depths, abyss.

profū's/us *ppp.* profundō. *a.* lavish; excessive. **-ē** *ad.* in disorder, extravagantly. [law.
prō'gener **-ī** *m.* grandson-in-
prōge'ner/ō **-ā're** *vt.* beget.
prōge'ni/ēs **-ē'ī** *f.* descent; offspring, descendants.
prōge'nit/or **-ō'ris** *m.* ancestor.
prōg/i'gnō **-i'gnere** **-e'nuī** **-e'nitum** *vt.* beget, produce.
prōgnā'tus *a.* born, descended. *m.* son, descendant.
Pro'gnē, *see* **Procnē**.
prognō'stic/a **-ō'rum** *n.pl.* weather signs.
prōgre'/dior **-dī** **-ssus** *vi.* go forward, advance; go out.
prōgre'ssi/ō **-ō'nis** *f.* advancing, increase; (*rhet.*) climax.
prōgre'ssus *ppa.* prōgredior.
prōgre'ss/us **-ūs** *m.* advance, progress; (*events*) march.
prōh, *see* **prō** *interj.*
prohi'b/eō **-ē're** **-uī** **-itum** *vt.* hinder, prevent; keep away, protect; forbid. [ding.
prohibi'ti/ō **-ō'nis** *f.* forbid-
prō/i'ciō **-i'cere** **-iē'cī** **-ie'ctum** *vt.* throw down, fling forwards; banish; (*building*) make project; (*fig.*) discard, renounce; forsake; (*words*) blurt out; (*time*) defer **sē**—rush forward, run into danger; fall prostrate.
prōie'cti/ō **-ō'nis** *f.* forward stretch.
prōie'ctus *ppp.* prōiciō. *a.* projecting, prominent; abject, useless; downcast; addicted (to). [out.
prōie'ct/us **-ūs** *m.* jutting
pro'inde, **pro'in** *ad.* consequently, therefore; just (as).
prōlā'/bor **-bī** **-psus** *vi.* slide, move forward; fall down; (*fig.*) go on, come to; slip out; fail, fall, sink into ruin.
prōlā'psi/ō **-ō'nis** *f.* falling.
prōlā'psus *ppa.* prōlābor.
prōlā'ti/ō **-ō'nis** *f.* extension; postponement; adducing.
prōlā't/ō **-ā're** *vt.* extend; postpone.
prōlā'tus *ppp.* prōferō.
prōle'ct/ō **-ā're** *vt.* entice.
prō'l/ēs **-is** *f.* offspring child; descendants, race.
prōlētā'r/ius **-ī** & **iī** *m.* citizen of the lowest class.
prōli'/ciō **-cere** **-xī** *vt.* entice.
prōli'x/us *a.* long, wide, spreading; (*person*) obliging; (*circs.*) favourable. **-ē** *ad.* fully, copiously, willingly.
prō'log/us **-ī** *m.* prologue.
prō'lo/quor **-quī** **-cū'tus** *vt.* speak out. [clination.
prōlu'b/ium **-i** & **iī** *n.* in-
prōlū'/dō **-dere** **-sī** **-sum** *vi.* practise.
prō'l/uō **-u'ere** **-uī** **-ū'tum** *vt.* wash out, wash away.
prōlū'si/ō **-ō'nis** *f.* prelude.
prōlu'vi/ēs **-ē'ī** *f.* flood; excrement.
prōme'r/eō **-ē're** **-uī**, **prōme'r/eor** **-ē'rī** **-itus** *vt.* deserve, earn.
prōme'rit/um **-ī** *n.* desert, merit, guilt.
Promē'th/eus **-eī** & **eos** *m.* demi-god who stole fire from the gods. **-ē'us** *a.*
prō'min/ēns **-e'ntis** *pres.p.* prōmineō. *a.* projecting. *n.* headland, spur.
prōmi'n/eō **-ē're** **-uī** *vi.* jut out, overhang; extend.
prōmi'sc/am, **-ē**, **-uē** *ad.* indiscriminately.
prōmi'scuus (**prōmi'scus**) *a.* indiscrimate, in common; ordinary; open to all.
prōmī'sī *perf.* prōmittō.
prōmi'ssi/ō **-ō'nis** *f.* promise.
prōmi'ss/or **-ō'ris** *m.* promiser.
prōmi'ss/um **-ī** *n.* promise.
prōmi'ssus *ppp.* prōmittō. *a.* long.
prōm/i'ttō **-i'ttere** **-ī'sī** **-i'ssum** *vt.* let grow; promise, give promise of.

prō'm/ō -ere -psī -ptum *vt.* bring out, produce; disclose.
prōmont-, *see* **prōmunt-**.
prōmō't/us *ppp.* prōmoveō. *n.pl.* preferable things.
prōm/o'veō -ovē're -ō'vī -ō'tum *vt.* move forward, advance; enlarge; postpone; disclose.
prō'mpsī *perf.* prōmō.
prō'mpt/ō -ā're *vt.* distribute.
prō'mptū *abl. m.* in — at hand, in readiness; obvious, in evidence; easy.
prō'mpt/us *ppp.* prōmō. *a.* at hand, ready; prompt, resolute; easy. **-ē** *ad.* readily; easily. [mulgating.
prōmulgā'ti/ō -ō'nis *f.* pro-
prōmu'lg/ō -ā're -ā'vī -ā'tum *vt.* make public, publish.
prōmu'ls/is -idis *f.* hors d'oeuvre.
prōmuntu'r/ium -ī & iī *n.* headland, promontory, ridge.
prō'm/us -ī *m.* cellarer, butler.
prōmū'tuus *a.* as a loan in advance. [grandson.
pro'nep/ōs -ō'tis *m.* great-
pronoe'/a -ae *f.* providence.
prōnō'm/en -inis *n.* pronoun.
prō'nub/a -ae *f.* matron attending a bride.
prōnūntiā'ti/ō -ō'nis *f.* declaration; (*rhet.*) delivery; (*logic*) proposition.
prōnūntiā't/or -ō'ris *m.* narrator.
prōnū'nti/ō -ā're -ā'vī -ā'tum *vt.* declare publicly, announce; recite, deliver; narrate; nominate. **-ā'tum** -ā'tī *n.* proposition.
prō'nur/us -ūs *f.* granddaughter-in-law.
prō'nus *a.* leaning forward; headlong, downwards; sloping, sinking; (*fig.*) inclined, disposed, favourable; easy.
prooe'm/ium -ī & iī *n.* prelude, preface.
propāgā'ti/ō -ō'nis *f.* propagating; extension. [larger.
propāgā't/or -ō'ris *m.* en-
propā'g/ō -ā're -ā'vī -ā'tum *vt.* propagate; extend; prolong.
propā'g/ō -inis *f.* (*plant*) layer, slip; (*men*) offspring, posterity.
prō'palam *ad.* openly, known.
prōpa'tul/us *a.* open. **-um** -ī *n.* open space.
pro'pe *ad.* (*comp.* pro'pius, *sup.* pro'ximē) near; nearly. *pr.* (*with acc.*) near, not far from.
prope'diem *ad.* very soon.
prōp/e'llō -e'llere -ulī -u'lsum *vt.* drive, push forward, impel; drive away, keep off.
pro'pemod/um, **-o** *ad.* almost.
prōp/e'ndeō -endē're -e'ndī -ē'nsum *vi.* hang down; preponderate; be disposed (to).
prōpē'nsi/ō -ō'nis *f.* inclination.
propē'ns/us *a.* inclining; inclined, well-disposed; important. **-ē** *ad.* willingly.
propera'nter *ad.* hastily, quickly.
propera'nti/a -ae *f.* haste.
properā'ti/ō -ō'nis *f.* haste.
prope'rip/ēs -edis *a.* swift-footed.
pro'per/ō -ā're -ā'vī -ā'tum *vt.* hasten, do with haste. *vi.* make haste, hurry. **-ā'tus** *a.* speedy. **-ā'tō** *ad.* quickly.
Prope'rt/ius -ī *m.* Latin elegiac poet.
pro'per/us *a.* quick, hurrying. **-ē** *ad.* quickly. [forward.
prōpe'xus *a.* combed
propī'n/ō -ā're *vt.* drink as a toast; pass on (a cup).
propi'nquit/ās -ā'tis *f.* nearness; relationship, friendship.
propi'nqu/ō -ā're *vi.* approach. *vt.* hasten.
propi'nquus *a.* near, neighbouring; related. *m., f.* relation. *n.* neighbourhood.

pro'pi/or -ō'ris *a.* nearer; more closely related, more like; (*time*) more recent. **-us** *ad.* nearer, more closely.
propi'ti/ō -ā're *vt.* appease.
propi'tius *a.* favourable, gracious.
propō'l/a -ae *f.* retailer.
prōpo'llu/ō -ere *vt.* defile further.
prōp/ō'nō -ō'nere -o'suī -o'situm *vt.* set forth, display; publish, declare; propose, resolve; imagine; expose; (*logic*) state the first premise. ante oculōs — picture to oneself.
Propo'nt/is -idis & idos *f.* Sea of Marmora. **-i'acus** *a.*
prōpo'rrō *ad.* furthermore; utterly. [metry, analogy.
prōpo'rti/ō -ō'nis *f.* sym-
prōposi'ti/ō -ō'nis *f.* purpose; theme; (*logic*) first premise.
propo'sit/us *ppp.* prōpōnō. **-um** -ī *n.* plan, purpose; theme; (*logic*) first premise.
prōprae't/or -ō'ris *m.* propraetor, governor; vice-praetor.
propri'et/ās -ā'tis *f.* peculiarity, property.
proprī'tim *ad.* properly.
pro'pri/us *a.* one's own, peculiar; personal, characteristic; permanent; (*words*) literal, regular. **-ē** *ad.* properly, strictly; particularly.
pro'pter *ad.* near by. *pr.*(*with acc.*) near, beside; on account of; by means of.
propte'reā *ad.* therefore.
prōpu'd/ium -ī & iī *n.* shameful act; villain.
prōpugnā'cul/um -ī *n.* bulwark, tower; defence.
prōpugnā'ti/ō -ō'nis *f.* defence.
prōpugnā't/or -ō'ris *m.* defender, champion.
prōpu'gn/ō -ā're *vi.* make a sortie; fight in defence.
prōpulsā'ti/ō -ō'nis *f.* repulse.
prōpu'ls/ō -ā're -ā'vī -ā'tum *vt.* repel, avert.
prōpu'lsus *ppp.* prōpellō.
Propylae'/a -ō'rum *n.pl.* gateway to the Acropolis of Athens.
prō quaestō're *m.* proquaestor.
prō'quam *conj.* according as.
prō'r/a -ae *f.* prow, bows; ship.
prōrē'p/ō -ere -sī -tum *vi.* crawl out.
prōrē't/a -ae *m.* man at the prow. [prow.
prō'r/eus -eī *m.* man at the
prōr/i'piō -i'pere -i'puī -e'ptum *vt.* drag out; hurry away. sē — rush out, run away.
prōrogā'ti/ō -ō'nis *f.* extension; deferring.
prō'rog/ō -ā're -ā'vī -ā'tum *vt.* extend, prolong, continue; defer. [absolutely.
prō'rsum *ad.* forwards;
prō'rsus *ad.* forwards; absolutely; in short.
prōr/u'mpō -u'mpere -ū'pī -u'ptum *vt.* fling out; (*pass.*) rush forth. *vi.* break out, burst forth.
prō'ru/ō -ere -ī -tum *vt.* throw down, demolish. *vi.* rush forth.
prōru'ptus *ppp.* prōrumpō.
prōsā'pi/a -ae *f.* lineage.
proscae'n/ium -ī & iī *n.* stage.
prosci'/ndō -ndere -dī -ssum *vt.* plough up; (*fig.*) revile.
prōscrī'/bō -bere -psī -ptum *vt.* publish in writing; advertise; confiscate; proscribe, outlaw.
prōscrī'pti/ō -ō'nis *f.* advertisement; proscription.
prōscrīptu'r/iō -ī're *vi.* want to have a proscription.
prōscrī'ptus *ppp.* prōscrībō. *m.* outlaw.

prŏ'sec/ō -ā're -uī -tum *vt.* cut off (for sacrifice).
prōsē'min/ō -ā're *vt.* scatter; propagate.
prōs/e'ntiō -entī're -ē'nsī *vt.* see beforehand.
prŏ'se/quor -quī -cū'tus *vt.* attend, escort; pursue, attack; honour (with); (*words*) proceed with, continue.
Prose'rpin/a -ae *f.* Proserpine, daughter of Ceres and wife of Pluto.
proseu'ch/a -ae *f.* place of prayer.
prōsi'l/iō -ī're -uī *vi.* jump up, spring forward; burst out, spurt.
prŏ'socer -ī *m.* wife's grandfather.
prōspe'ct/ō -ā're *vt.* look out at, view; look forward to, await; (*place*) look towards.
prōspe'ctus *ppp.* prōspiciō.
prōspe'ct/us -ūs *m.* sight, view, prospect; gaze.
prōspe'cul/or -ā'rī *vi.* look out, reconnoitre. *vt.* watch for.
pro'sper, pro'sper/us *a.* favourable, successful. **-ē** *ad.*
prospe'rit/ās -ā'tis *f.* good fortune.
pro'sper/ō -ā're *vt.* make successful, prosper.
pro'sperus, *see* **prosper.**
prōspicie'nti/a -ae *f.* foresight.
prōsp/i'ciō -i'cere -e'xī -e'ctum *vi.* look out, watch; see to, take precautions. *vt.* descry, watch for; foresee; provide; (*place*) command a view of.
prōst/e'rnō -e'rnere -rā'vī -rā'tum *vt.* throw in front prostrate; overthrow, ruin. **sē —** fall prostrate; demean oneself.
prōsti'bul/um -ī *n.* prostitute.
prōsti't/uō -u'ere -uī -ū'tum *vt.* put up for sale, prostitute.
prŏ'st/ō -ā're -itī *vi.* project; be on sale; prostitute oneself.
prōstrā'tus *ppp.* prōsternō.
prōsu'big/ō -ere *vt.* dig up.
prō'/sum -de'sse -fuī *vi.* (*with dat.*) be useful to, benefit.
Prōta'gor/ās -ae *m.* Greek sophist, native of Abdera.
prōtē'ctus *ppp.* prōtegō.
prō't/egō -e'gere -ē'xī -ē'ctum *vt.* cover over, put a projecting roof on; (*fig.*) shield, protect.
prōtē'l/ō -ā're *vt.* drive off.
prōtē'l/um -ī *n.* team of oxen; (*fig.*) succession.
prōte'n/dō -dere -dī -tum *vt.* stretch out, extend.
prōte'ntus *ppp.* prōtendō.
prō't/erō -e'rere -rī'vī -rī'tum *vt.* trample down, crush; overthrow.
prōte'rr/eō -ē're -uī -itum *vt.* scare away.
prote'rvit/ās -ā'tis *f.* forwardness, insolence.
prote'rv/us *a.* forward, insolent, violent. **-ē** *ad.* insolently; boldly.
Prōtesilā'/us -ī *m.* first Greek killed at Troy. **-ē'us** *a.*
Prō't/eus -eī & eos *m.* sea-god with power to assume many forms.
prothȳ'mē *ad.* gladly.
prō'tinam *ad.* immediately.
prō'tinus *ad.* forward, onward; continuously; right away, forthwith.
prōto'll/ō -ere *vt.* stretch out; put off.
prōtra'ctus *ppp.* prōtrahō.
prō'tra/hō -here -xī -ctum *vt.* draw on (to); drag out; bring to light, reveal.
prōtrī'tus *ppp.* prōterō.
prōtrū'/dō -dere -sī -sum *vt.* thrust forward, push out; postpone.
prō'tulī *perf.* prōferō.
prōtu'rb/ō -ā're -ā'vī -ā'tum *vt.* drive off; overthrow.
pro'ut *conj.* according as.
prōve'ctus *ppp.* prōvehō. *a.* advanced.

prō've/hō -here -xī -ctum *vt.* carry along, transport; promote, advance, bring to; (*speech*) prolong; (*pass.*) drive, ride, sail on.
prōv/e'niō -enī're -ē'nī -e'ntum *vi.* come out, appear; arise, grow; go on, prosper, succeed.
prōve'nt/us -ūs *m.* increase; result, success.
prōve'rb/ium -ī & iī *n.* saying, proverb.
prō'vid/ēns -e'ntis *pres.p.* prōvideō. *a.* prudent. **-e'nter** *ad.* with foresight.
prōvide'nti/a -ae *f.* foresight, forethought.
prōv/i'deō -idē're -ī'dī -ī'sum *vi.* see ahead; take care, make provision. *vt.* foresee; look after, provide for; obviate.
prō'vidus *a.* foreseeing, cautious, prudent; provident.
prōvi'nci/a -ae *f.* sphere of action, duty, province.
prōvinciā'lis *a.* provincial. *m.pl.* provincials.
prōvī'si/ō -ō'nis *f.* foresight; precaution.
prōvī's/ō -ere *vi.* go and see.
prōvī's/or -ō'ris *m.* foreseer; provider.
prōvī's/us *ppp.* prōvideō. **-ō** *ad.* with forethought.
prōvī's/us -ūs *m.* looking forward; foreseeing; providing providence.
prōvī'/vō -vere -xī *vi.* live on.
prōvocā'ti/ō -ō'nis *f.* challenge; appeal.
prōvocā't/or -ō'ris *m.* kind of gladiator.
prō'voc/ō -ā're -ā'vī -ā'tum *vt.* challenge, call out; provoke; bring about. *vi.* appeal.
prō'vol/ō -ā're *vi.* fly out, rush out.
prōvo'l/vō -vere -vī -ū'tum *vt.* roll forward, tumble over; (*pass.*) fall down, humble oneself, be ruined. **sē —** wallow.
prō'vom/ō -ere *vt.* belch forth.
pro'ximē *ad.* next, nearest; (*time*) just before or after; (*with acc.*) next to, very close to, very like.
proxi'mit/ās -ā'tis *f.* nearness; near relationship; similarity.
pro'ximus *a.* nearest, next; (*time*) previous, last, following, next; most akin, most like. *m.* next of kin. *n.* next door.
proxum-, *see* **proxim-**.
prū'd/ēns -e'ntis *a.* foreseeing, aware, wise, prudent, circumspect; skilled, versed (in). **-e'nter** *ad.* prudently; skilfully.
prūde'nti/a -ae *f.* prudence, discretion; knowledge.
pruī'n/a ae. *f.* hoar-frost.
pruīnō'sus *a.* frosty.
prū'n/a -ae *f.* live coal.
prūni'tius *a.* of plum-tree wood.
prū'n/um -ī *n.* plum.
prū'n/us -ī *f.* plum-tree.
prū'r/iō -ī're *vi.* itch.
prytanē'/um -ī *n.* Greek town hall.
pry'tan/is -is *m.* Greek chief magistrate.
psa'll/ō -ere *vi.* play the lyre or lute.
psaltē'r/ium -ī & iī *n.* kind of lute.
psa'ltri/a -ae *f.* girl musician.
pse'c/as -adis *f.* slave who perfumed the lady's hair.
psēphi'sma -tis *n.* decree of the people.
Pseudo'cat/ō -ō'nis *m.* sham Cato.
pseudo'men/os -ī *m.* sophistical argument.
pseudo'thyr/um -ī *n.* back door.
psi'thius *a.* psithian (kind of Greek vine).
psi'ttac/us -ī *m.* parrot.
psychomantē'/um (-īum) -ī *n.* place of necromancy.

-pte *enclitic* (*to pronouns*) self, own. [gruel.
ptisanā'r/ium -ī & iī *n.*
Ptolemae'/us -ī *m.* Ptolemy, name of Egyptian kings. **-ē'us, -us** *a.*
pū'b/ēns -e'ntis *a.* full-grown; (*plant*) juicy.
pūbe'rt/ās -ā'tis *f.* manhood; signs of puberty.
pū'b/ēs (pū'ber) -eris *a.* grown up, adult; (*plant*) downy.
pū'b/ēs -is *f.* hair at age of puberty; groin; youth, men, people.
pūb/ē'scō -ē'scere -uī *vi.* grow to manhood, become mature; become clothed.
pūblicā'nus *a.* of public revenue. *m.* tax-farmer.
pūblicā'ti/ō -ō'nis *f.* confiscation.
pūbli'citus *ad.* at the public expense; in public.
pū'blic/ō -ā're -ā'vī -ā'tum *vt.* confiscate; make public.
Pūbli'col/a -ae *m.* P. Valerius, an early Roman consul.
pū'blic/us *a.* of the State, public, common. *m.* public official. **-um** -ī *n.* State revenue; State territory; public. **-a causa** criminal trial. **rēs -a** the State. **dē -ō** at the public expense. **in -ō** in public. **-ē** *ad.* by or for the State, at the public expense; all together. [praenomen.
Pu'bl/ius -ī *m.* Roman
pude'ndus *a.* shameful.
pu'd/ēns -e'ntis *a.* bashful, modest. **-e'nter** *ad.* modestly.
pu'd/et -ē're -uit & itum est *vt.* (*impers.*) shame, be ashamed.
pudibu'ndus *a.* modest.
pudīci'ti/a -ae *f.* modesty, chastity. [**-ē** *ad.*
pudī'c/us *a.* modest, chaste.
pu'd/or -ō'ris *m.* shame, modesty, sense of honour; disgrace.
pue'll/a -ae *f.* girl; sweetheart, young wife.
puellā'ris *a.* girlish, youthful.
pue'llul/a -ae *f.* little girl.
pue'll/us -ī *m.* little boy.
pu'er -ī *m.* boy, child; son; slave.
puerī'li/s *a.* boyish, child's; childish, trivial. **-ter** *ad.* like a child; childishly.
pueri'ti/a (pue'rtia) -ae *f.* childhood, youth.
puerpe'r/ium -ī & iī *n.* childbirth.
pue'rperus *a.* to help childbirth. *f.* woman in labour.
pue'rtia, *see* **pueritia**.
pue'rul/us -ī *m.* little boy, slave.
pu'gil -is *m.* boxer.
pugilā't/iō -iō'nis *f.* **-us** -ūs *m.* boxing.
pugillā'ris *a.* that can be held in the hand. *m.pl.*, *n.pl.* writing-tablets. [punch-ball.
pugillātō'rius *a.* follis —
pu'gi/ō -ō'nis *m.* dirk, dagger.
pugiu'ncul/us -ī *m.* small dagger.
pu'gn/a -ae *f.* fight, battle.
pugnā'cit/ās -ā'tis *f.* fondness for a fight.
pugnā'cul/um -ī *n.* fortress.
pugnā't/or -ō'ris *m.* fighter.
pu'gn/āx -ā'cis *a.* fond of a fight, aggressive; obstinate. **-ā'citer** *ad.* aggressively.
pu'gneus *a.* with the fist.
pu'gn/ō -ā're -ā'vī -ā'tum *vi.* fight; disagree; struggle. **sēcum —** be inconsistent. **-ātum est** the battle was fought.
pu'gn/us -ī *m.* fist.
pulche'llus *a.* pretty little.
pu'lch/er -rī *a.* beautiful, handsome; fine, glorious. **-rē** *ad.* excellently; well done!
pulchritū'd/ō -inis *f.* beauty, excellence.
pūlē'/ium, pūle'g/ium -ī & iī *n.* pennyroyal.

pū'l/ex -icis *m.* flea.
pullā'r/ius -ī & iī *m.* keeper of the sacred chickens.
pullā'tus *a.* dressed in black.
pu'llul/ō -ā're *vi.* sprout.
pu'll/us -ī *m.* young (of animals), chicken.
pullus *a.* dark-grey; mournful. *n.* dark-grey clothes.
pullment/ā'rium -ā'rī & -ā'riī, **-um** -ī *n.* relish; food.
pu'lm/ō -ō'nis *m.* lung.
pulmō'neus *a.* of the lungs.
pu'lp/a -ae *f.* fleshy part.
pulpāme'nt/um -ī *n.* titbits.
pu'lpit/um -ī *n.* platform, [stage.
puls pu'ltis *f.* porridge.
pulsā'ti/ō -ō'nis *f.* beating.
pu'ls/ō -ā're -ā'vī -ā'tum *vt.* batter, knock, strike.
pu'lsus *ppp.* pellō.
pu'ls/us -ūs *m.* push, beat, blow; impulse.
pulti'phag/us -ī *m.* porridge-eater.
pu'lt/ō -ā're *vt.* beat, knock at.
pulve'reus *a.* of dust, dusty fine as dust; raising dust.
pulverule'ntus *a.* dusty; laborious.
pulvi'll/us -ī *m.* small cushion.
pulvī'n/ar -ā'ris *n.* sacred couch; seat of honour.
pulvī'n/us -ī *m.* cushion, pillow.
pu'lv/is -eris *m.* dust, powder; arena; effort.
pulvi'scul/us -ī *m.* fine dust.
pū'm/ex -icis *m.* pumice-stone; stone, rock.
pūmi'ceus *a.* of soft stone.
pū'mic/ō -ā're *vt.* smooth with pumice-stone.
pūmi'li/ō -ō'nis *m., f.* dwarf, pygmy.
pū'nctim *ad.* with the point.
pū'nct/um -ī *n.* point, dot; vote; (*time*) moment; (*speech*) short section.
pū'nctus *ppp.* pungō.
pu'ng/ō -ere pu'pugī pū'nctum *vt.* prick, sting, pierce; (*fig.*) vex.
Pūnicā'nus *a.* in the Carthaginian style.
pūni'ceus *a.* reddish, purple.
Pū'nic/us *a.* Punic, Carthaginian; purple-red. **-um** -ī *n.* pomegranate. **-ē** *ad.* in Punic.
pū'n/iō (**poe'niō**) -ī're, **-ior** -ī'rī *vt.* punish; avenge.
pūnī't/or -ō'ris *m.* avenger.
pū'p/a -ae *f.* doll.
pūpi'll/a -ae *f.* ward; (*eye*) pupil. [an orphan.
pūpillā'ris *a.* of a ward, of
pūpi'll/us -ī *m.* orphan, ward.
pu'pp/is -is *f.* after part of a ship, stern; ship.
pu'pugī *perf.* pungō.
pū'pul/a -ae *f.* (*eye*) pupil.
pū'pul/us -ī *m.* little boy.
pūrgā'm/en -inis *n.* sweepings, dirt; means of expiation.
pūrgāme'nt/um -ī *n.* refuse, dirt.
pūrgā'ti/ō -ō'nis *f.* purging; justification.
pū'rg/ō -ā're -ā'vī -ā'tum *vt.* cleanse, purge, clear away; exculpate, justify; purify.
pū'riter *ad.* cleanly, purely.
pu'rpur/a -ae *f.* purple-fish, purple; purple cloth; finery, royalty.
purpurā'tus *a.* wearing purple. *m.* courtier.
purpu'reus *a.* red, purple, black; wearing purple; bright, radiant. [of rouge.
purpuri'ss/um -ī *n.* kind
pū'r/us *a.* clear, unadulterated, free from obstruction or admixture; pure, clean; plain, unadorned; (*moral*) pure, chaste. *n.* clear sky. **-ē** *ad* cleanly, brightly; plainly, simply, purely, chastely.
pūs pū'ris *n.* pus; (*fig.*) malice.
pusi'llus *a.* very little; petty, paltry.

pū'si/ō -ō'nis *m.* little boy.
pū'stul/a -ae *f.* pimple, blister.
putā'm/en -inis *n.* peeling, shell, husk.
putā'ti/ō -ō'nis *f.* pruning.
putā't/or -ō'ris *m.* pruner.
pu'te/al -ā'lis *n.* low wall round a well or sacred place.
puteā'lis *a.* well-.
pū't/eō -ē're *vi.* stink.
Pute'ol/ī -ō'rum *m.pl.* town on the Canpanian coast. **-ā'nus** *a.*
pu't/er, pu't/ris -ris *a.* rotten, decaying; crumbling, flabby.
put/ē'scō -ē'scere -uī *vi.* become rotten.
pu'te/us -ī *m.* well; pit.
pūtidiu'sculus *a.* somewhat nauseating.
pū'tid/us *a.* rotten, stinking; (*speech*) affected, nauseating. **-ē** *ad.*
pu't/ō -ā're -ā'vī -ā'tum *vt.* think, suppose; think over; reckon, count; (*money*) settle; (*tree*) prune.
pū't/or -ō'ris *m.* stench.
putre/fa'ciō -fa'cere -fē'cī -fa'ctum *vt.* make rotten; make crumble. [moulder.
putrē'sc/ō -ere *vi.* rot,
pu'tridus *a.* rotten, decayed; withered.
pu'tris, *see* **puter.**
pu'tus *a.* perfectly pure.
pu't/us -ī *m.* boy.
py'ct/a, -ēs -ae *m.* boxer.
Py'dn/a -ae *f.* town in Macedonia. **-ae'us** *a.*
pȳ'g/a -ae *f.* buttocks.
Pygmae'us *a.* Pygmy.
Py'lad/ēs -ae & is *m.* friend of Orestes. **-ē'us** *a.*
Py'l/ae -ā'rum *f.pl.* Thermopylae. **-a'icus** *a.*
Py'l/os -ī *f.* Pylus, Peloponnesian town, home of Nestor. **-ius** *a.*
py'r/a -ae *f.* funeral pyre.
pȳ'ram/is -idis *f.* pyramid.
Pȳ'ram/us -ī *m.* lover of Thisbe. [**-ae'us** *a.*
Pȳrē'n/ē -ēs *f.* Pyrenees.
pyre'thr/um -ī *n.* Spanish camomile.
Py'rg/ī -ō'rum *m.pl.* ancient town in Etruria. **-ē'nsis** *a.*
pyrō'p/us -ī *m.* bronze.
Py'rrh/a -ae, -ē -ēs *f.* wife of Deucalion. **-ae'us** *a.*
Py'rrh/ō -ō'nis *m.* Greek philosopher, founder of the Sceptics. **-ōnē'us** *a.*
Py'rrh/us -ī *m.* son of Achilles; king of Epirus, enemy of Rome.
Pȳtha'gor/ās -ae *m.* Greek philosopher who founded a school in S. Italy. **-ē'us, -icus** *a.* Pythagorean.
Pȳ'th/ō -ūs *f.* Delphi. **-ius, -icus** *a.* Pythian, Delphic. *m.* Apollo. *f.* priestess of Apollo. *n.pl.* Pythian Games.
Pȳ'th/ōn -ō'nis *m.* serpent killed by Apollo.
pȳti'sma -tis *n.* what is spit out. [wine.
pȳti'ss/ō -ā're *vi.* spit out
py'xi/s -dis *f.* small box, toilet-box.

Q

quā *ad.* where, which way; whereby; as far as; partly . . . partly.
quācu'mque *ad.* wherever; anyhow.
quā'dam tenus *ad.* only so far.
qua'dr/a -ae *f.* square; morsel; table.
quadrāgē'n/ī -ō'rum *a.* forty each.
quadrāgē'simus *a.* fortieth. *f.* 2½ per cent tax.
quadrā'gi/ēns, -ēs *ad.* forty times.
quadrāgi'ntā *num.* forty.

qua'dr/āns -a'ntis *m.* quarter; (*coin*) quarter as.
quadrantā'rius *a.* of a quarter.
quadrā't/us *ppp.* quadrō. *a.* square. -ō agmine in battle order. **-um** -ī *n.* square; (*astr.*) quadrature.
quadri'du/um -ī *n.* four days.
quadrie'nn/ium -ī & iī *n.* four years.
quadrifā'riam *ad.* in four [parts.
quadri'fidus *a.* split in four.
quadrī'g/ae -ā'rum *f.pl.* team of four; chariot.
quadrīgā'r/ius -ī & iī *m.* chariot-racer.
quadrīgā'tus *a.* stamped with a chariot.
quadrī'gul/ae -ā'rum *f.pl.* little four-horse team.
quadri'iug/is, -us *a.* of a team of four. **-ī** -ō'rum *m.pl.* team of four.
quadrilī'bris *a.* weighing four pounds. [old.
quadrī'mulus *a.* four years
quadrī'mus *a.* four years old.
quadringēnā'rius *a.* of four hundred each.
quadringē'n/ī -ō'rum *a.* four hundred each.
quadringentē'simus *a.* four-hundredth.
quadringe'nt/ī -ō'rum *num.* four hundred.
quadringe'nti/ēns, -ēs *ad.* four hundred times.
quadripertī'tus *a.* fourfold.
quadrirē'm/is -is *f.* quadrireme.
quadri'v/ium -ī & iī *n.* cross-roads.
qua'dr/ō -ā're *vt.* make square; complete. *vi.* square, fit, agree.
qua'dr/um -i *n.* square.
quadru'ped/āns -a'ntis *a.* galloping.
qua'drup/ēs -edis *a.* four-footed, on all fours. *m., f.* quadruped.
quadruplā't/or -ō'ris *m.* informer, twister. [fold.
qua'drupl/ex -icis *a.* four-
qua'drupl/um -ī *n.* four times as much.
quae'rit/ō -ā're *vt.* search diligently for; earn (a living); keep on asking.
quae'/rō -rere -sī'vī & siī -sī'tum *vt.* look for, search for; seek, try to get; acquire, earn; (*plan*) think out, work out; (*question*) ask, make inquiries; (*law*) investigate; (*with inf.*) try, wish. quid -ris? in short. sī -ris, -rimus to tell the truth.
quaesī'ti/ō -ō'nis *f.* inquisition.
quaesī't/or -ō'ris *m.* investigator, judge.
quaesī'tus *ppp.* quaerō. *a.* special; far-fetched. *n.* question. *n.pl.* gains.
quaesī'vī *perf.* quaerō.
quae's/ō -ere *vt.* ask, beg.
quaesti'cul/us -ī *m.* slight profit.
quae'sti/ō -ō'nis *f.* seeking, questioning; investigation, research; criminal trial; court. servum in -ōnem ferre take a slave for questioning by torture. -ōnēs perpetuae standing courts.
quaestiu'ncul/a -ae *f.* trifling question.
quae'st/or -ō'ris *m.* quaestor, treasury official.
quaestō'rius *a.* of a quaestor. *m.* ex-quaestor. *n.* quaestor's tent or residence.
quaestuō'sus *a.* lucrative, productive; money-making; wealthy.
quaestū'r/a -ae *f.* quaestorship; public money.
quae'st/us -ūs *m.* profit, advantage; money-making, occupation. -uī habēre make money out of. -um facere make a living.

quā'libet, quā'lubet *ad.* anywhere; anyhow.
quā'li/s *a.* (*interrog.*) what kind of? (*rel.*) such as, even as. **-ter** *ad.* just as.
quālis/cu'mque, -cu'nque *a.* of whatever kind; any whatever.
quā'lit/ās -ā'tis *f.* quality, nature.
quā'l/us -ī *m.* wicker basket.
quam *ad.* (*interrog., exclam.*) how, how much; (*comparison*) as, than; (*with sup.*) as . . . as possible; (*emphatic*) very. dīmidium — quod half of what. quīntō diē — four days after.
qua'mdiū *ad.* how long? as long as.
qua'm/libet, -lubet *ad.* as much as you like, however.
qua'mobrem *ad.* (*interrog.*) why? (*rel.*) why. *conj.* therefore.
qua'mquam *conj.* although; and yet.
qua'mvīs *ad.* however, ever so. *conj.* however much, although.
quā'nam *ad.* what way.
qua'ndō *ad.* (*interrog.*) when? (*rel.*) when; (*with* sī, nē, num) ever. *conj.* when; since.
quandō/cu'mque, -cu'nque *ad.* whenever, as often as; some day.
quandō'que *ad.* whenever; some day. *conj.* seeing that.
quandō quidem *conj.* seeing that, since.
qua'nquam, *see* **quamquam.**
quanti'llus *a.* how little, how much.
quanto'pere *ad.* how much; (*after* tantopere) as.
qua'ntulus *a.* how little, how small.
quantuluscu'mque *a.* however small, however trifling.
qua'ntum *ad.* how much; as much as. **-cumque** as much as ever. **-libet** however much. **-vīs** as much as you like; although.
qua'nt/us *a.* how great; so great as, such as. **-ī** how dear, how highly. **-ō** (*with comp.*) how much; the. in **-um** as far as.
quantuscu'mque *a.* however great, whatever size.
quantu'slibet *a.* as great as you like.
qua'ntus qua'ntus *a.* however great.
qua'ntusvīs *a.* however great.
quāpro'pter *ad.* why; and therefore.
quā'quā *ad.* whatever way.
quā'rē *ad.* how, why; whereby; and therefore.
quartadecumā'n/ī -ō-rum *m.pl.* men of the fourteenth legion.
quartā'nus *a.* every four days. *f.* quartan fever. *m.pl.* men of the fourth legion.
quartā'r/ius -ī & iī *m.* quarter-pint.
qua'rt/us *a.* fourth. **-um, -ō** for the fourth time.
quartusde'cimus *a.* fourteenth.
qua'si *ad.* as if; as it were; (*numbers*) about.
quasi'll/um -ī *n.*, **-us -ī** *m.* wool-basket.
quassā'ti/ō -ō'nis *f.* shaking.
qua'ss/ō -ā're -ā'vī -ā'tum *vt.* shake, toss; shatter, damage.
qua'ssus *ppp.* quatiō. *a.* broken.
quate/fa'ciō -fa'cere -fē'cī *vt.* shake, give a jolt to.
quā'tenus *ad.* (*interrog.*) how far? how long? (*rel.*) as far as; in so far as, since.
qua'ter *ad.* four times. — deciēs fourteen times.
quate'rn/ī -ō'rum *a.* four each, in fours.
qua'/tiō -tere -ssum *vt.* shake, disturb, brandish; strike,

shatter; (*fig.*) agitate, harass.
qua'ttuor *num.* four.
quattuo'rdecim *num.* fourteen.
quattuorvirā't/us -ūs *m.* membership of quattuorviri.
quattuo'rvir/ī -ō'rum *m.pl.* board of four officials.
-que *conj.* and; both . . . and; (*after neg.*) but.
quema'dmodum *ad.* (*interrog.*) how; (*rel.*) just as.
qu/e'ō -ī're -ī/vī & iī -itum *vi.* be able, can.
quercē't/um -ī *n.* oak-forest.
que'rceus *a.* of oak.
que'rc/us -ūs *f.* oak; garland of oak-leaves; acorn.
quere'll/a (**querē'la**) -ae *f.* complaint; plaintive sound.
queribu'ndus *a.* complaining.
querimō'ni/a -ae *f.* complaint; elegy. [much.
que'rit/or -ā'rī *vi.* complain
que'rnus *a.* oak-.
que'/ror -rī -stus *vt.* & *i.* complain, lament; (*birds*) sing.
querquetulā'nus *a.* of oak-woods.
que'rulus *a.* complaining; plaintive, warbling.
que'stus *ppa.* queror.
que'st/us -ūs *m.* complaint, lament.
quī, quae, quod *pro.* (*interrog.*) what, which? (*rel.*) who, which, that; what; and this, he, etc.; (*with* sī, nisi, nē num) any.
quī *ad.* (*interrog.*) how; (*rel.*) with which, whereby; (*indef.*) somehow; (*exclam.*) indeed.
qui'a *conj.* because. -namwhy?
qui'cquam *n.* quisquam.
qui'cque *n.* quisque.
qui'cquid *n.* quisquis.
quī'cum with whom, with which.
quī/cu'mque, -**cu'nque** *pro.* whoever, whatever, all that; every possible.
quid *n.* quis. *ad.* why?
quī'dam, quae'dam, quo'ddam *pro.* a certain, a sort of, a. qui'ddam *n.* something.
qui'dem *ad.* (*emphatic*) in fact; (*qualifying*) at any rate; (*conceding*) it is true; (*alluding*) for instance. nē . . . — not even.
qui'dnam, **qui'dpiam**, **qui'dquam**, **qui'dquid** *n.* quisnam, quispiam, quisquam, quisquis.
quī'dnī *ad.* why not?
quī'/ēs -ē'tis *f.* rest, peace, quiet; sleep, dream, death; neutrality; lair.
quiē'/scō -scere -vī -tum *vi.* rest, keep quiet; be at peace, keep neutral; sleep; (*with acc. & inf.*) stand by and see; (*with inf.*) cease.
quiē't/us *ppa.* quiēscō. *a.* at rest; peaceful, neutral; calm, quiet, asleep. -ē *ad.* peacefully, quietly.
quī'libet, quae'libet, quo'dlibet *pro.* any, anyone at all. qui'dlibet *n.* anything.
quī'n *ad.* (*interrog.*) why not? (*correcting*) indeed, rather. *conj.* who not; but that, but, without; (*preventing*) from, (*doubting*) that.
quī'nam, quae'nam quo'dnam *pro.* which, what?
Quīnct-, *see* **Quīnt-**.
quī'nc/ūnx -ū'ncis *m.* five-twelfths; number five on a dice. in -ūncem dispositī arranged in oblique lines.
quīnde'ci/ēns, -ēs *ad.* fifteen times.
quī'ndecim *num.* fifteen. — prīmī fifteen chief magistrates.
quīndecimvirā'lis *a.* of the council of fifteen.
quīndeci'mvir/ī -ō'rum *m.pl.* council of fifteen.
quīngē'n/ī -ō'rum *a.* five hundred each.

quīngentē'simus *a.* five-hundredth.
quīnge'nt/ī -ō'rum *num.* five hundred.
quīnge'nti/ēns, -ēs *ad.* five hundred times.
quī'n/ī -ō'rum *a.* five each; five. — dēnī fifteen each. — vīcēnī twenty-five each.
quīnquāgē'n/ī -ō'rum *a.* fifty each.
quīnquāgē'simus *a.* fiftieth. *f.* 2 per cent tax.
quīnquāgi'ntā *num.* fifty.
Quīnqā'tr/ūs -uum *f.pl.*, **-ia -iō'rum & ium** *n.pl.* festival of Minerva.
quī'nque *num.* five.
quīnquennā'lis *a.* quinquennial; lasting five years.
quīnque'nnis *a.* five years old; quinquennial.
quīnque'nn/ium -ī & iī *n.* five years.
quīnquepartī'tus *a.* five-fold.
quīnqueprī'm/ī -ō'rum *m.pl.* five leading men.
quīnquerē'mis *a.* five-banked. *f.* quinquereme.
quīnquevirā't/us -ūs *m.* membership of the board of five.
quīnque'vir/ī -ō'rum *m.pl.* board of five.
quī'nqui/ēns, -ēs *ad.* five times.
quīnquī'plic/ō -ā're *vt.* multiply by five.
quīntadecimā'n/ī -ō'rum *m.pl.* men of the fifteenth legion.
quīntā'nus *a.* of the fifth. *f.* street in a camp between the 5th and 6th maniples. *m.pl.* men of the fifth legion.
Quīntiliā'n/us -ī *m.* Quintilian, famous teacher of rhetoric in Rome.
Quīntī'lis (Quīnctī'lis) *a.* of July.
quī'nt/us *a.* fifth. **-um, -ō** *ad.* for the fifth time.
Quī'nt/us -ī *m.* Roman praenomen.
quīntusde'cimus *a.* fifteenth.
qui'ppe *ad.* (*affirming*) certainly, of course. *conj.* (*explaining*) for in fact, because, since. — quī since I, he, etc.
qui'ppiam, *see* **quispiam.**
qui'ppinī *ad.* certainly.
Quirī'n/us -ī *m.* Romulus. *a.* of Romulus. **-ā'lis** *a.* of Romulus; Quirinal (hill).
Qui'r/īs -ī'tis *m.* inhabitant of Cures; Roman citizen; citizen.
quirītā'ti/ō -ō'nis *f.* shriek.
Quirī'tēs *pl.* Quiris.
quirī't/ō -ā're *vi.* cry out, wail.
quis, quid *pro.* who? what? (*indef.*) anyone anything.
quīs *poetic form of* quibus.
qui'snam, quae'nam, qui'dnam *pro.* who, what?
qui'spiam, quae'piam, quo'dpiam & qui'dpiam *pro.* some, some one, something.
qui'squam quae'quam, qui'cquam & qui'd-quam *pro.* any, anyone, anything. nec — and no one.
qui'sque, quae'que, quo'dque *pro.* each, every, every one. qui'dque, qui'cque everything. decimus — every tenth. optimus — all the best. prīmus — the first possible.
quisqui'li/ae -ā'rum *f.pl.* refuse, rubbish.
qui'squis, quae'quae, quo'dquod, qui'dquid & qui'cquid *pro.* whoever, whatever, all.
quī'vīs, quae'vīs, quo'dvīs, qui'dvīs *pro.* any you please, anyone, anything.
quīvīscu'mque, quaevīscum'-que, quodvīscu'mque *pro.* any whatsoever.
quō *ad.* (*interrog.*) where? whither? for what purpose? what for? (*rel.*) where, to which (place), to whom; (*with*

comp.) the (more); (*with* sī) anywhere. *conj.* (*with subj.*) in order that. nōn— not that.
quo'ad *ad.* how far? how long? *conj.* as far as, as long as; until.
quōci'rcā *conj.* therefore.
quōcu'mque *ad.* whithersoever.
quod *conj.* as for, in that, that; because; why. — sī but if.
quō'dam modo *ad.* in a way.
quoi, quō'ius *old forms of* **cui, cūius.**
quō'libet *ad.* anywhere, in any direction.
quom, *see* **cum** *conj.*
quō'minus *conj.* that not, (*preventing*) from.
quō'modo *ad.* (*interrog.*) how? (*rel.*) just as. **-cu'mque** howsoever. **-nam** how?
quō'nam *ad.* where, where to?
quo'ndam *ad.* once, formerly; sometimes; (*fut.*) one day.
quō'niam *conj.* since, seeing that.
quō'piam *ad.* anywhere.
quō'quam *ad.* anywhere.
quo'que *ad.* also, too.
quō'quō *ad.* to whatever place, wherever.
quō'quō modo *ad.* howsoever.
quō'quō ve'rs/us, -um *ad.* in every direction.
quō'rsum, quō'rsus *ad.* where to, in what direction; what for, to what end?
quot *a.* how many; as many as, every.
quota'nnīs *ad.* every year.
quotcu'mque *a.* however many.
quotē'n/ī -ō'rum *a.* how [many.
quotīd-, *see* **cottīd-.**
quo'ti/ēns, -ēs *ad.* how often? (*rel.*) as often as.
quotiēnscu'mque *ad.* however often.
quo'tquot *a.* however many.
quo'tumus *a.* which number, what date.
quo't/us *a.* what number, how many. — quisque how few. -a hōra what time.
quotuscu'mque *a.* whatever number, however big.
quōu'sque *ad.* how long, till when; how far.
quō'vīs *ad.* anywhere.
quum, *see* **cum** *conj.*

R

ra'bid/us *a.* raving, mad; impetuous. **-ē** *ad.* furiously.
ra'bi/ēs -em -ē *f.* madness, rage, fury.
ra'b/iō -ere *vi.* rave.
rabiō'sulus *a.* somewhat rabid.
rabiō's/us *a.* furious, mad. **-ē** *ad.* wildly. [lawyer.
ra'bul/a -ae *m.* wrangling
racē'mifer -ī *a.* clustered.
racē'm/us -ī *m.* stalk of a cluster; bunch of grapes; grape.
radiā'tus *a.* radiant.
rādī'citus *ad.* by the roots; utterly.
rādī'cul/a -ae *f.* small root.
ra'di/ō -ā're *vt.* irradiate. *vi.* radiate, shine.
ra'd/ius -ī & iī *m.* stick, rod; (*light*) beam, ray; (*loom*) shuttle; (*math.*) rod for drawing figures, radius of a circle; (*plant*) long olive; (*wheel*) spoke.
rā'd/īx -ī'cis *f.* root; radish; (*hill*) foot; (*fig.*) foundation, origin.
rā'/dō -dere -sī -sum *vt.* scrape, shave, scratch; erase; touch in passing, graze, pass along.
rae'd/a -ae *f.* four-wheeled carriage.
raedā'r/ius -ī & iī *m.* driver.
Rae't/ī -ō'rum *m.pl.* Alpine

people between Italy and Germany. **-ia -iae** *f.* their country. **-icus, -ius, -us** *a.*
rāmā'l/ia -ium *n.pl.* twigs brushwood. [chips.
rāme'nt/um -ī *n.* shavings
rā'meus *a.* of branches.
rā'm/ex -icis *m.* rupture, blood-vessels of the lungs.
Ra'mn/ēs, Ramnē'ns/ēs -ium *m.pl.* one of the original Roman tribes; a century of equites.
rāmō'sus *a.* branching.
rā'mul/us -ī *m.* twig, sprig.
rā'm/us -ī *m.* branch, bough.
rā'n/a -ae *f.* frog; frog-fish.
ra'nc/ēns -e'ntis *a.* putrid
ranci'dulus *a.* rancid.
ra'ncidus *a.* rank rancid; disgusting.
rānu'ncul/us -ī *m.* tadpole.
rapā'cid/a -ae *m.* son of a thief.
rapā'cit/ās -ā'tis *f.* greed.
ra'p/āx -ā'cis *a.* greedy, grasping, ravenous.
ra'phan/us -ī *m.* radish.
rapi'dit/ās -ā'tis *f.* rapidity.
ra'pid/us *a.* tearing, devouring; swift, rapid; hasty, impetuous. **-ē** *ad.* swiftly, hurriedly.
rapī'n/a -ae *f.* pillage, robbery; booty, prey.
ra'p/iō -ere -uī -tum *vt.* tear, snatch, carry off; seize plunder; hurry, seize quickly.
ra'ptim *ad.* hastily, violently
ra'pti/ō -ō'nis *f.* abduction.
ra'pt/ō -ā're -ā'vī -ā'tum *vt* seize and carry off, drag away, move quickly; plunder, lay waste; (*passion*) agitate.
ra'pt/or -ō'ris *m.* plunderer, robber, ravisher.
ra'ptus *ppp.* rapiō. *n.* plunder
ra'pt/us -ūs *m.* carrying off, abduction; plundering.
rā'pul/um -ī *n.* small turnip.
rā'p/um -ī *n.* turnip.

rārē/fa'ciō -fa'cere -fē'cī -fa'ctum (*pass.* **-fī'ō -fi'erī**) *vt.* rarefy.
rārē'sc/ō -ere *vi.* become rarefied, grow thin; open out.
rā'rit/ās -ā'tis *f.* porousness, open texture; thinness, fewness.
rā'r/us *a.* porous, open in texture; thin, scanty; scattered, straggling, here and there; (*mil.*) in open order; few, infrequent; uncommon, rare. **-ō, -ē** *ad.* seldom.
rā'sī *perf* rādō.
rā'silis *a.* smooth, polished.
rā'str/um -ī *n.* hoe, mattock.
rā'sus *ppp.* rādō.
ra'ti/ō -ō'nis *f.* 1. reckoning: account, calculation; list, register; affair, business. 2. relation: respect, consideration; procedure, method, system, way, kind. 3. reason: reasoning, thought; cause, motive; science, knowledge, philosophy. — **atque ūsus** theory and practice. — **est** it is reasonable. **Stōicōrum** — Stoicism. **-ōnem dūcere, inīre** calculate. **-ōnem habēre** take account of, have to do with, consider. **-ōnem reddere** give an account of. **cum -ōne** reasonably. **meae -ōnēs** my interests. **ā -ōnibus** accountant.
ratiōcinā'ti/ō -ō'nis *f.* reasoning; syllogism.
ratiōcinātī'vus *a.* syllogistic.
ratiōcinā't/or -ō'ris *m.* accountant.
ratiō'cin/or -ā'rī -ā'tus *vt.* & *i.* calculate; consider; argue, infer.
ratiōnā'lis *a.* rational; syllogistic.
ra't/is -is *f.* raft; boat.
ratiu'ncul/a -ae *f.* small calculation; slight reason; petty syllogism.
ra't/us *ppa.* **reor.** *a.* fixed.

settled, sure; valid. prō -ā (parte) proportionally. -um dūcere, facere, habēre ratify.
rauci'sonus *a.* hoarse.
rau'cus *a.* hoarse; harsh, strident.
rau'd/us (**rū'dus**) -eris *n.* copper coin. [money.
raudu'scul/um -ī *n.* bit of
Rave'nn/a -ae *f.* port in N.E. Italy. **-ā's** -ā'tis *a.*
rā'v/is -im *f.* hoarseness.
rā'vus *a.* grey, tawny.
re'/a -ae *f.* defendant, culprit.
reā'pse *ad.* in fact, actually.
Reā't/e -is *n.* ancient Sabine town. **-ī'nus** *a.*
rebellā'ti/ō -ō'nis *f.* revolt.
rebellā'tr/īx -ī'cis *f.* rebellious.
rebe'lli/ō -ō'nis *f.* revolt.
rebe'llis *a.* rebellious. *m.pl.* rebels.
rebe'll/ium -ī & iī *n.* revolt.
rebe'll/ō -ā're *vi.* revolt.
rebī't/ō -ere *vi.* return.
re'bo/ō -ā're *vi.* re-echo. *vt.* make resound.
reca'lcitr/ō -ā're *vi.* kick back.
reca'l/eō -ē're *vi.* be warm again. [again.
recalē'sc/ō -ere *vi.* grow warm
recal/fa'ciō -fa'cere -fē'cī *vt.* warm again.
reca'lvus *a.* bald in front.
recand/ē'scō -ē'scere -uī *vi.* whiten (in response to); glow.
reca'nt/ō -ā're -ā'vī -ā'tum *vt.* recant; charm away.
re'ccidī *perf.* recidō.
rec/ē'dō -ē'dere -e'ssī -e'ssum *vi.* move back, withdraw, depart; (*place*) recede; (*head*) be severed.
rece'll/ō -ere *vi.* spring back.
re'c/ēns -e'ntis *a.* fresh, young, recent; (*writer*) modern; (*with* ab) immediately after. *ad.* newly, just.
recē'ns/eō -ē're -uī -um *vt.* count; review.
recē'nsi/ō -ō'nis *f.* revision.
recē'nsus *ppp.* recēnseō.
recē'pī *perf.* recipiō.
receptā'cul/um -ī *n.* receptacle, reservoir; refuge, shelter.
rece'pt/ō -ā're *vt.* take back; admit, harbour; tug hard at.
rece'pt/or -ō'ris *m.*, **-rīx** -rī'cis *f.* receiver, shelterer.
rece'pt/um -ī *n.* obligation.
rece'ptus *ppp.* recipiō.
rece'pt/us -ūs *m.* withdrawal; retreat; return; refuge. -uī canere sound the retreat.
rece'ssī *perf.* recēdō.
rece'ssim *ad.* backwards.
rece'ss/us -ūs *m.* retreat, departure; recess, secluded spot; (*tide*) ebb.
recidī'vus *a.* resurrected; recurring.
re'c/idō -i'dere -cidī -ā'sum *vi.* fall back; recoil, relapse; (*fig.*) fall, descend.
recī'/dō -dere -dī -sum *vt.* cut back, cut off.
reci'n/gō -gere -ctum *vt.* ungird, loose.
re'cin/ō -ere *vt.* & *i.* re-echo, repeat; sound a warning.
reciper-, *see* **recuper-**.
rec/i'piō -i'pere -ē'pī -e'ptum *vt.* take back, retake; get back, regain, rescue; accept, admit; (*mil.*) occupy; (*duty*) undertake; (*promise*) pledge, guarantee. sē — withdraw, retreat. nōmen — receive notice of a prosecution.
reci'proc/ō -ā're *vt.* move to and fro; (*ship*) bring round to another tack; (*proposition*) reverse. *vi.* (*tide*) rise and fall.
reci'procus *a.* ebbing.
recī'sus *ppp.* recī'dō.
recitā'ti/ō -ō'nis *f.* reading aloud, recital. [reciter.
recitā't/or -ō'ris *m.* reader,
re'cit/ō -ā're -ā'vī -ā'tum *vt.* read out, recite.
reclāmā'ti/ō -ō'nis *f.* outcry (of disapproval).

reclā'mit/ō -ā'-re *vi.* cry out against.
reclā'm/ō -ā're *vi.* cry out, protest; reverberate.
reclī'nis *a.* leaning back.
reclī'n/ō -ā're -ā'vī -ā'tum *vt.* lean back.
reclū'/dō -dere -sī -sum *vt.* open up; disclose.
reclū'sus *ppp.* reclūdō.
reco'ctus *ppp.* recoquō.
recō'git/ō -ā're *vi.* think over, reflect.
rocogni'ti/ō -ō'nis *f.* review.
recogn/ō'scō -ō'scere -ō'vī -itum *vt.* recollect; examine, review.
reco'll/igō -i'gere -ē'gī -ē'c-tum *vt.* gather up; (*fig.*) recover, reconcile.
re'c/olō -o'lere -o'luī -u'ltum *vt.* recultivate; resume; reflect on, contemplate; revisit.
recomminī'sc/or -ī *vi.* recollect.
recompo'situs *a.* rearranged.
reconciliā'ti/ō -ō'nis *f.* restoration, reconciliation.
reconci'li/ō -ā're -ā'vī -ā'tum *vt.* win back again, restore, reconcile.
reconci'nn/ō -ā're *vt.* repair.
reco'nditus *ppp.* recondō. *a.* hidden, secluded; abstruse profound; (*disposition*) reserved.
reco'nd/ō -ere -idī -itum *vt.* store away, stow; hide away, bury.
recō'nfl/ō -ā're *vt.* rekindle.
re'co/quō -quere -xī -ctum *vt.* cook again, boil again; forge again, recast; (*fig.*) rejuvenate. [tion.
recordā'ti/ō -ō'nis *f.* recollec-
reco'rd/or -ā'rī -ā'tus *vt.* & *i.* recall, remember; ponder over.
re'cre/ō -ā're -ā'vī -ā'tum *vt.* remake, reproduce; revive, refresh.
re'crep/ō -ā're *vt.* & *i.* ring, re-echo.
recrē'/scō -scere -vī *vi.* grow again.
recrūd/ē'scō -ē'scere -uī *vi.* (*wound*) open again; (*war*) break out again.
rē'ctā *ad.* straight forward, right on.
rē'ctē *ad.* straight; correctly, properly, well; quite; (*colloq.*) good, all right, no thank you.
rē'cti/ō -ō'nis *f.* government.
rē'ct/or -ō'ris *m.* guide, driver, helmsman; governor, master.
rē'ctus *ppp.* regō. *a.* straight; upright, steep; right, correct, proper; (*moral*) good, virtuous. **-um -ī** *n.* right, virtue.
re'cub/ō -ā're *vi.* lie, recline.
recu'ltus *ppp.* recolō.
recu'/mbō -mbere -buī *vi.* lie down, recline; fall, sink down.
recuperā'ti/ō -ō'nis *f.* recovery.
recuperā't/or -ō'ris *m.* recapturer; (*pl.*) board of justices who tried civil cases requiring a quick decision, *esp.* cases involving foreigners.
recuperātō'rius *a.* of the recuperatores.
recu'per/ō -ā're -ā'vī -ā'tum *vt.* get back, recover, recapture.
recū'r/ō -ā're *vt.* restore.
recu'rr/ō -ere -ī *vi.* run back; return, recur; revert.
recu'rs/ō -ā're *vi.* keep coming back, keep recurring.
recu'rs/us -ūs *m.* return, retreat.
recu'rv/ō -ā're *vt.* bend back, curve.
recu'rvus *a.* bent, curved.
recūsā'ti/ō -ō'nis *f.* refusal, declining; (*law*) objection, counter-plea.
recū's/ō -ā're -ā'vī -ā'tum *vt.* refuse, decline, be reluctant; (*law*) object, plead in defence.
recu'ssus *a.* reverberating.
redā'ctus *ppp.* redigō.

reda'mbul/ō -ā're *vi.* come back.
re'dam/ō -ā're *vt.* love in return.
redārdē'sc/ō -ere *vi.* blaze up again.
reda'rgu/ō -ere -ī *vt.* refute, contradict.
redau'spic/ō -ā're *vi.* take auspices for going back.
re'dditus *ppp.* reddō.
re'dd/ō -ere -idī -itum *vt.* give back, return, restore; give in, response, repay; give up, deliver, pay; (*copy*) represent, reproduce; (*speech*) report, repeat, recite, reply; translate; (*with a.*) make. iūdi'cium — fix the date for a trial. iūs — administer justice.
redē'gī *perf.* redigō.
redē'mī *perf.* redimō.
rede'mpti/ō -ō'nis *f.* ransoming; bribing; (*revenue*) farming.
rede'mpt/ō -ā're *vt.* ransom.
rede'mpt/or -ō'ris *m.* contractor.
redemptū'r/a -ae *f.* contracting.
rede'mptus *ppp.* redimō.
re'd/eō -ī're -iī -itum *vi.* go back, come back, return; (*speech*) revert; (*money*) come in; (*circs.*) be reduced to, come to.
redhā'l/ō -ā're *vt.* exhale.
redhi'b/eō -ē're *vt.* take back.
re'd/igō -i'gere -ē'gī -ā'ctum *vt.* drive back, bring back; (*money*) collect, raise; (*to a condition*) reduce, bring; (*number*) reduce. ad irritum — make useless.
re'diī *perf.* redeō.
redimī'cul/um -ī *n.* band.
redi'm/iō -ī're -iī -ī'tum *vt.* bind, crown, encircle.
re'd/imō -i'mere -ē'mī -e'mptum *vt.* buy back; ransom, redeem; release, rescue; (*good*) procure; (*evil*) avert; (*fault*) make amends for; (*bus.*) undertake by contract, hire.
redi'ntegr/ō -ā're -ā'vī -ā'tum *vt.* restore, renew, refresh.
redipī'sc/or -ī *vt.* get back.
redi'ti/ō -ō' is *f.* returning.
re'dit/us -ūs *m.* return, returning; (*money*) revenue.
redivī'vus *a.* renovated.
redo'l/eō -ē're -uī *vi.* give out a smell. *vt.* smell of, smack of.
redo'mitus *a.* broken in again.
redō'n/ō -ā're *vt.* restore; give up.
red/ū'cō -ū'cere -ū'xī -u'ctum *vt.* draw back; lead back, bring back; escort home; marry again; (*troops*) withdraw; (*fig.*) restore; (*to a condition*) make into.
redu'cti/ō -ō'nis *f.* restoration.
redu'ct/or -ō'ris *m.* man who brings back.
redu'ctus *ppp.* redūcō. *a.* secluded, aloof.
redu'ncus *a.* curved back.
redunda'nti/a -ae *f.* extravagance.
redu'nd/ō -ā're -ā'vī -ā'tum *vi.* overflow; abound, be in excess; (*fig.*) stream.
redu'vi/a -ae *f.* hang-nail.
re'du/x -cis *a.* (*gods*) who brings back; (*men*) brought back, returned.
refe'ctus *ppp.* reficiō.
refe'll/ō -ere -ī *vt.* disprove, rebut.
refe'r/ciō -cī're -sī -tum *vt.* stuff, cram, choke full.
refe'r/iō -ī're *vt.* hit back; reflect.
re'/ferō -fe'rre -ttulī -lā'tum *vt.* bring back, carry back; give back, pay back, repay; repeat, renew; (*authority*) refer to, trace back to; (*blame, credit*) ascribe; (*likeness*) reproduce, resemble; (*memory*) recall; (*news*) report, mention; (*opinion*) reckon amongst; (*record*) enter; (*senate*) lay before, move; (*speech*) reply

say in answer. grātiam — be grateful, requite. pedem, gradum — return; retreat. ratiōnēs — present an account. sē — return.
rē'/fert -fe'rre -tulit *vi.* (*impers.*) it is of importance, it matters, it concerns. meā — it matters to me. [crammed, full.
refe'rtus *ppp.* referciō. *a.*
refe'rv/eō -ē're *vi.* boil over.
refervē'sc/ō -ere *vi.* bubble up.
ref/i'ciō -i'cere -ē'cī -e'ctum *vt.* repair, restore; (*body, mind*) refresh, revive; (*money*) get back, get in return; (*pol.*) re-elect.
refī'/gō -gere -xī -xum *vt.* unfasten, take down; (*fig.*) annul.
refi'ng/ō -ere *vt.* remake.
refī'xus *ppp.* refigō.
reflā'git/ō -ā're *vt.* demand back. [wind.
reflā't/us -ūs *m.* contrary
refle'/ctō -ctere -xī -xum *vt.* bend back, turn back; (*fig.*) bring back. *vi.* give way.
refle'xus *ppp.* reflectō.
re'fl/ō -ā're -ā'vī -ā'tum *vi.* blow contrary. *vt.* breathe out again. [overflow.
re'flu/ō -ere *vi.* flow back,
re'fluus *a.* ebbing.
reformī'd/ō -ā're *vt.* dread; shun in fear.
refō'rm/ō -ā're *vt.* reshape.
refō'tus *ppp.* refoveō.
ref/o'veō -ovē're -ō'vī -ō'tum *vt.* refresh, revive.
refrāctāri'olus *a.* rather stubborn.
refrā'ctus *ppp.* refringō.
refrā'g/or -ā'rī -ā'tus *vi.* (*with dat.*) oppose, thwart.
refrē'gī *perf.* refringō.
refrē'n/ō -ā're *vt.* curb, restrain.
re'fric/ō -ā're -uī -ā'tum *vt.* scratch open; re-open, renew. *vi.* break out again.
refrīgerā'ti/ō -ō'nis *f.* coolness.
refrī'ger/ō -ā're -ā'vī -ā'tum *vi.* cool, cool off; (*fig.*) flag.
refrī/gē'scō -gē'scere -xī *vi.* grow cold; (*fig.*) flag grow stale.
refr/i'ngō -i'ngere -ē'gī -ā'ctum *vt.* break open; break off; (*fig.*) break, check.
refrī'xī *perf.* refrigēscō.
ref/u'giō -u'gere -ū'gī *vi.* run back, flee, shrink. *vt.* run away from, shun.
refu'g/ium -ī & iī *n.* refuge.
re'fugus *a.* fugitive, receding.
refu'l/geō -gē're -sī *vi.* flash back, reflect light.
ref/u'ndō -u'ndere -ū'dī -ū'sum *vt.* pour back, pour out; (*pass.*) overflow.
refū'sus *ppp.* refundō.
refūtā'ti/ō -ō'nis *f.* refutation.
refūtā't/us -ūs *m.* refutation.
refū't/ō -ā're -ā'vī -ā'tum *vt.* check, repress; refute, disprove.
rēgā'li/s *a.* king's, royal, regal. **-ter** *ad.* magnificently; tyranically.
re'ge/rō -rere -ssī -stum *vt.* carry back, throw back.
rē'gi/a -ae *f.* palace; court; (*camp*) royal tent; (*town*) capital.
rēgi'ficus *a.* magnificent.
regi'gn/ō -ere *vt.* reproduce.
Rēgi'll/us -ī *m.* Sabine town; lake in Latium, scene of a Roman victory over the Latins. **-ā'nus, -ē'nsis** *a.*
re'gim/en -inis *n.* guiding, steering; rudder; rule, command, government; ruler.
rēgī'n/a -ae *f.* queen, noblewoman.
re'gi/ō -ō'nis *f.* direction, line; boundary-line; quarter, region; district, ward, territory; (*fig.*) sphere, province. ē -ōne in a straight line; (*with gen.*) exactly opposite.

regiōnā'tim *ad.* by districts.
Rē'g/ium -ī & iī *n.* town in extreme S. of Italy, *mod.* Reggio. -**ī'nus** *a.*
rē'gi/us *a.* king's, kingly, royal; princely, magnificent. -**ē** *ad.* regally; imperiously.
reglū'tin/ō -**ā're** *vt.* unstick.
rēgnā't/or -**ō'ris** *m.* ruler.
rēgnā'tr/īx -**ī'cis** *a.* imperial.
rē'gn/ō -**ā're** -**ā'vī** -**ā'tum** *vi.* be king, rule, reign; be supreme, lord it; (*things*) prevail, predominate. *vt.* rule over.
rē'gn/um -**ī** *n.* kingship, monarchy; sovereignty, supremacy; despotism; kingdom; domain.
re'g/ō -**ere** **rē'xī** **rē'ctum** *vt.* keep straight, guide, steer; manage, direct; control, rule, govern. — **fīnēs** (*law*) mark out the limits.
regre'/dior -**dī** -**ssus** *vi.* go back, come back, return; (*mil.*) retire.
regre'ssus *ppa.* regredior.
regre'ss/us -**ūs** *m.* return; retreat.
rē'gul/a -**ae** *f.* rule, ruler; stick, board; (*fig.*) rule, pattern standard.
rē'gul/us -**ī** *m.* petty king, chieftain; prince.
Rē'gul/us -**ī** *m.* Roman consul taken prisoner by the Carthaginians.
regu'st/ō -**ā're** *vt.* taste again.
rē/i'ciō -**i'cere** -**iē'cī** -**ie'ctum** *vt.* throw back, throw over the shoulder, throw off; drive back, repel; cast off, reject; reject with contempt, scorn; (*jurymen*) challenge, refuse; (*matter for discussion*) refer; (*time*) postpone. **sē** — fling oneself.
rēiectā'neus *a.* to be rejected.
rēic'cti/ō -**ō'nis** *f.* rejection; (*law*) challenging.
rēie'ct/ō -**ā're** *vt.* throw back.
rēie'ctus *ppp.* rēiciō.
relā'/bor -**bī** -**psus** *vi.* glide back, sink back, fall back.
relangu/ē'scō -**ē'scere** -**ī** *vi.* faint; weaken.
relā'ti/ō -**ō'nis** *f.* (*law*) retorting; (*pl.*) magistrate's report; (*rhet.*) repetition.
relā't/or -**ō'ris** *m.* proposer of a motion.
relā'tus *ppp.* referō.
relā't/us -**ūs** *m.* official report; recital.
relaxā'ti/ō -**ō'nis** *f.* easing.
rela'x/ō -**ā're** -**ā'vī** -**ā'tum** *vt.* loosen, open out; (*fig.*) release, ease, relax, cheer.
relē'ctus *ppp.* relegō.
relēgā'ti/ō -**ō'nis** *f.* banishment.
relē'g/ō -**ā're** -**ā'vī** -**ā'tum** *vt.* send away, send out of the way; banish; (*fig.*) reject; refer, ascribe.
re'l/egō -**e'gere** -**ē'gī** -**ē'ctum** *vt.* gather up; (*place*) traverse, sail over again; (*speech*) go over again, reread. [off.
relentē'sc/ō -**ere** *vi.* slacken
relē'vī *perf.* relinō.
re'lev/ō -**ā're** -**ā'vī** -**ā'tum** *vt.* lift up; lighten; (*fig.*) relieve, ease, comfort.
reli'cti/ō -**ō'nis** *f.* abandoning.
reli'ctus *ppp.* relinquō.
rēli'cuus, *see* **reliquus**.
religā'ti/ō -**ō'nis** *f.* tying up.
rēli'gi/ō -**ō'nis** *f.* religious scruple, reverence, awe; religion; superstition; scruples, conscientiousness; holiness, sanctity (in anything); object of veneration, sacred place; religious ceremony, observance.
rēligiō's/us *a.* devout, religious; superstitious; involving religious difficulty; scrupulous, conscientious; (*objects*) holy, sacred. -**ē** *ad.* devoutly; scrupulously, conscientiously.
re'lig/ō -**ā're** -**ā'vī** -**ā'tum** *vt.*

tie up, fasten behind; (*ship*) make fast, moor; (*fig.*) bind.
re'l/inō -i'nere -ē'vī *vt.* unseal.
rel/i'nquō -i'nquere -ī'quī -i'ctum *vt.* leave, leave behind; bequeath; abandon, forsake; (*argument*) allow; (*pass.*) remain.
rēli'qui/ae -ā'rum *f.pl.* leavings, remainder, relics.
re'liqu/us *a.* remaining, left; (*time*) subsequent, future; (*debt*) outstanding. *n.* remainder, rest; arrears. *m.pl.* the rest. -um est it remains, the next point is. -ī facere leave behind, leave over, omit. in -um for the future.
roll-, *see* **rel-**.
relū'/ceō -cē're -xī *vi.* blaze.
relū/cē'scō -cē'scere -xī *vi.* become bright again.
relu'ct/or -ā'rī -ā'tus *vi.* struggle against, resist.
rem/a'neō -anē're -ā'nsī *vi.* remain behind; remain, continue, endure.
remā'n/ō -ā're *vi.* flow back.
remā'nsi/ō -ō'nis *f.* remaining behind.
reme'd/ium -ī & iī *n.* cure, remedy, medicine.
remē'nsus *ppa.* remētior.
re'me/ō -ā're *vi.* come back, go back, return.
remē'/tior -tīrī -nsus *vt.* measure again; go back over.
rē'm/ex -igis *m.* rower, oarsman.
Rē'm/ī -ō'rum *m.pl.* people of Gaul in region of *mod.* Rheims.
rēmigā'ti/ō -ō'nis *f.* rowing.
rēmi'g/ium -ī & iī *n.* rowing; oars; oarsmen.
rē'mig/ō -ā're *vi.* row.
re'migr/ō -ā're *vi.* move back, return (home).
reminī'sc/or -ī *vt.* & *i.* (*usu. with gen.*) remember, call to mind.
remi'/sceō -scē're -xtum *vt.* mix up, mingle.
remi'ssi/ō -ō'nis *f.* release; (*tension*) slackening, relaxing; (*payment*) remission; (*mind*) slackness, mildness, relaxation; (*illness*) abating.
remi'ss/us *ppp.* remittō. *a.* slack; negligent; mild, indulgent, cheerful. -ē *ad.* mildly, gently.
rem/i'ttō -i'ttere -ī'sī -i'ssum *vt.* let go back, send back, release; slacken, loosen, relax; emit, produce; (*mind*) relax, relieve; (*notion*) discard, give up; (*offence, penalty*) let off, remit; (*right*) resign, sacrifice; (*sound*) give back. *vi.* abate.
remi'xtus *ppp.* remisceō.
remō'l/ior -ī'rī -ī'tus *vt.* heave back.
remollē'sc/ō -ere *vi.* become soft again, be softened.
remo'll/iō -ī're *vt.* weaken.
re'mor/a -ae *f.* hindrance.
remorā'min/a -um *n.pl.* hindrances.
remo'r/deō -dē're -sum *vt.* (*fig.*) worry, torment.
re'mor/or -ā'rī -ā'tus *vi.* linger, stay behind. *vt.* hinder, delay, defer.
remo'rsus *ppp.* remordeō.
remō'ti/ō -ō'nis *f.* removing.
remō't/us *ppp.* removeō. *a.* distant, remote; secluded; (*fig.*) far removed, free from. -ē *ad.* far.
rem/o'veō -ovē're -ō'vī -ō'tum *vt.* move back, withdraw, set aside; subtract.
remū'g/iō -ī're *vi.* bellow in answer, re-echo.
remu'l/ceō -cē're -sī *vi.* stroke; (*tail*) droop.
remu'lc/um -ī *n.* tow-rope.
remūnerā'ti/ō -ō'nis *f.* recompense, reward.
remū'ner/or -ā'rī -ā'tus *vt.* repay, reward.
remu'rmur/ō -ā're *vi.* murmur in answer.
rē'm/us -ī *m.* oar.

Re'm/us -ī *m.* brother of Romulus.
renā'rr/ō -ā're *vt.* tell over again.
renā'/scor -scī -tus *vi.* be born again; grow, spring up again.
renā'tus *ppa.* renāscor.
renā'vig/ō -ā're *vi.* sail back.
re'n/eō -ē're *vt.* unspin, undo.
rē'n/ēs -um *m.pl.* kidneys.
renī'd/eō -ē're *vi.* shine back, be bright; be cheerful, smile, laugh.
renīdē'sc/ō -ere *vi.* reflect the gleam of.
renī't/or -ī *vi.* struggle, resist.
re'n/ō -ā're *vi.* swim back.
rē'n/ō (rhēnō) -ō'nis *m.* fur.
renō'd/ō -ā're *vt.* tie back in a knot. [condition.
renovā'm/en -inis *n.* new
renovā'ti/ō -ō'nis *f.* renewal; compound interest.
re'nov/ō -ā're -ā'vī -ā'tum *vt.* renew, restore; repair, revive, refresh; (*speech*) repeat. **faenus** — take compound interest.
renu'mer/ō -ā're *vt.* pay back.
renūntiā'ti/ō -ō'nis *f.* report, announcement.
renū'nti/ō -ā're -ā'vī -ā'tum *vt.* report, bring back word; announce, make an official statement; (*election*) declare elected, return; (*duty*) refuse, call off, renounce.
renū'nt/ius -ī & iī *m.* reporter.
re'nu/ō -ere -ī *vt.* & *i.* deny, decline, refuse. [firmly.
renū't/ō -ā're *vi.* refuse
re'or rē'rī ra'tus *vi.* think, suppose.
repā'gul/a -ō'rum *n.pl.* (*door*) bolts, bars.
repa'ndus *a.* curving back, turned up.
reparā'bilis *a.* retrievable.
repa'rc/ō -ere *vi.* be sparing with, refrain.
re'par/ō -ā're -ā'vī -ā'tum *vt.* retrieve, recover; restore, repair; purchase; (*mind, body*) refresh; (*troops*) recruit.
repastinā'ti/ō -ō'nis *f.* digging up again.
rep/e'llō -e'llere -pulī -u'lsum *vt.* push back, drive back, repulse; remove, reject.
rep/e'ndō -e'ndere -e'ndī -ē'nsum *vt.* return by weight; pay, repay; requite, compensate.
re'p/ēns -e'ntis *a.* sudden; new.
repē'nsus *ppp.* rependō.
repe'nte *ad.* suddenly.
repentī'n/us *a.* sudden, hasty; upstart. -ō *ad.* suddenly.
repe'rcō, *see* **reparcō**.
repercu'ssus *ppp.* repercutiō. [tion, echo.
repercu'ss/us -ūs *m.* reflec-
repercu'/tiō -tere -ssī -ssum *vt.* make rebound, reflect, echo.
repe'r/iō -ī're re'pperī -tum *vt.* find, find out, get, procure; discover, ascertain; devise, invent.
repe'rt/or -ō'ris *m.* discoverer, inventor, author.
repe'rtus *ppp.* reperiō. *n.pl.* discoveries.
repetī'ti/ō -ō'nis *f.* repetition; (*rhet.*) anaphora.
repetī't/or -ō'ris *m.* reclaimer.
repetī'tus *ppp.* repetō. *a.* altē, longē — far-fetched.
re'pet/ō -ere -ī'vī & iī -ī'tum *vt.* go back to, revisit; fetch back, take back; (*mil.*) attack again; (*action, speech*) resume, repeat; (*memory*) recall, think over; (*origin*) trace, derive; (*right*) claim, demand back. **rēs** — demand satisfaction; reclaim one's property. **pecūniae** -undae extortion.
repetu'nd/ae -ā'rum *f.pl.* extortion (by a provincial governor).
repe'xus *a.* combed.

re'pl/eō -ē're -ē'vī -ē'tum *vt.* fill up, refill; replenish, make good, complete; satiate, fill to overflowing. **-ē'tus** *a.* full.
replicā'ti/ō -ō'nis *f.* rolling up.
re'plic/ō -ā're *vt.* roll back, unroll, unfold. [crawl.
rē'p/ō -ere -sī -tum *vi.* creep,
rep/ō'nō -ō'nere -o'suī -o'situm *vt.* put back, replace, restore; bend back; put (in the proper place); (*performance*) repeat; (*something received*) repay; (*store*) lay up, put away; (*task*) lay aside, put down; (*hope*) place, rest; (*with* prō) substitute. in numerō, in numerum — count, reckon among.
repo'rt/ō -ā're -ā'vī -ā'tum *vt.* bring back, carry back; (*prize*) win, carry off; (*words*) report.
repo'sc/ō -ere *vt.* demand back; claim, require.
repo'situs *ppp.* repōnō. *a.* remote.
repo'st/or -ō'ris *m.* restorer.
repo'stus, *see* **repositus**.
repō'ti/a -ō'rum *n.pl.* second drinking.
re'pperī *perf.* reperiō.
re'ppulī *perf.* repellō.
repraesentā'ti/ō -ō'nis *f.* vivid presentation; (*bus.*) cash payment.
repraese'nt/ō -ā're -ā'vī -ā'tum *vt.* exhibit, reproduce; do at once, hasten; (*bus.*) pay cash.
repreh/e'ndō, **repr/e'ndō** -e'ndere -e'ndī -ē'nsum *vt.* hold back, catch, restrain; hold fast, retain; blame, rebuke, censure; refute.
reprehē'nsi/ō -ō'nis *f.* check; blame, reprimand, refutation.
reprehē'ns/ō -ā're *vt.* keep holding back.
reprehē'ns/or -ō'ris *m.* censurer, critic, reviser.
reprehē'nsus *ppp.* reprehendō.
repre'ndō, *see* **reprehendō**.
repre'ss/or -ō'ris *m.* restrainer.
repre'ssus *ppp.* reprimō.
re'pr/imō -i'mere -e'ssī -e'ssum *vt.* keep back, force back; check, restrain, suppress.
reprōmi'ssi/ō -ō'nis *f.* counter-promise.
reprōm/i'ttō -i'ttere -ī'sī -ī'ssum *vt.* promise in return, engage oneself.
rē'pt/ō -ā're *vi.* creep about crawl along. [tion.
repudiā'ti/ō -ō'nis *f.* rejec-
repu'di/ō -ā're -ā'vī -ā'tum *vt.* reject, refuse, scorn; (*wife*) divorce.
repu'd/ium -ī & iī *n.* divorce; repudiation.
repuerā'sc/ō -ere *vi.* become a child again; behave like a child.
repugna'nt/ia -ium *n.pl.* contradictions.
repugna'nter *ad.* reluctantly.
repu'gn/ō -ā're -ā'vī -ā'tum *vi.* oppose, resist; disagree, be inconsistent.
repu'ls/a -ae *f.* refusal, denial, repulse; (*election*) rebuff.
repu'ls/ō -ā're *vi.* throb, reverberate.
repu'lsus *ppp.* repellō.
repu'ls/us -ūs *m.* (*light*) reflection; (*sound*) echoing.
repu'ng/ō -ere *vt.* prod again.
repū'rg/ō -ā're -ā'vī -ā'tum *vt.* clear again, cleanse again; purge away. [over.
reputā'ti/ō -ō'nis *f.* pondering
re'put/ō -ā're -ā'vī -ā'tum *vt.* count back; think over, consider.
re'qui/ēs -ē'tis *f.* rest, relaxation, repose.
requiē'/scō -scere -vī -tum *vi.* rest, find rest; cease. *vt.* stay. **-tus** *a.* rested, refreshed.

requī'rit/ō -ā're *vt.* keep asking after.
requī'/rō -rere -sī'vī & siī -sī'tum *vt.* search for look for; ask, inquire after; (*with* ex *or* ab) question; need, want, call for; miss, look in vain for.
requīsī'tus *ppp.* requīrō.
rēs re'ī *f* thing, object; circumstance, case, matter, affair; business, transaction; fact, truth, reality; possessions, wealth, money; advantage, interest; (*law*) case; (*mil.*) campaign, operations; (*pol.*) politics, power, the State; (*writing*) subject-matter, story, history. — mihi est tēcum I have to do with you. — dīvīna sacrifice. — mīlitāris war. — pūblica public affairs politics, the State, republic — rūstica agriculture. rem facere get rich. rem gerere wage war, fight. ad rem to the point, to the purpose; in rem usefully. ob rem to the purpose. ob eam rem therefore. ī in malam rem go to the devil! contrā rem pūblicam unconstitutionally ē rē pūblicā constitutionally rē vērā in fact, actually eā rē for that reason. tuā rē, ex tuā rē to your advantage ab rē unhelpfully. ē rē (nātā as things are. prō rē according to circumstances. rēs adversae failure, adversity. rēs dubiae danger rēs gestae achievements, career rēs novae revolution. rēs prosperae, secundae success, prosperity rērum māximus greatest in the world. rērum scriptor historian.
re'sacrō, *see* **resecrō**.
resae'v/iō -ī're *vi.* rage again.
resalū't/ō -ā're *vt.* greet in return. [heal up again.
resān/ē'scō -ē'scere -uī *vi*
resa'r/ciō -cī're -tum *vt.* patch up, repair.
resci'/ndō -ndere -dī -ssum *vt.* cut back, cut open, break down; open up; (*law, agreement*) repeal, annul.
resc/ī'scō -ī'scere -ī'vī & iī -ī'tum *vt.* find out, learn.
resci'ssus *ppp.* rescindō.
rescrī'/bō -bere -psī -ptum *vt.* write back, reply; rewrite, revise; (*emperors*) give a decision; (*mil.*) transfer, re-enlist; (*money*) place to one's credit, pay back.
rescrī'ptus *ppp.* rescrībō. *n.* imperial rescript.
re'sec/ō -ā're -uī -tum *vt.* cut back, cut short; curtail. ad vīvum — cut to the quick.
re'secr/ō -ā're *vt.* pray again; free from a curse.
rese'ctus *ppp.* resecō.
resecū'tus *ppa.* resequor.
resē'dī *perf.* resideō; *perf.* resīdō.
resē'min/ō -ā're *vt.* reproduce.
re'se/quor -quī -cū'tus *vt.* answer.
re'ser/ō -ā're -ā'vī -ā'tum *vt.* unbar, unlock; disclose.
rese'rv/ō -ā're -ā'vī -ā'tum *vt.* keep back, reserve; preserve, save.
re's/es -idis *a.* remaining; inactive; idle; calm.
res/i'deō -idē're -ē'dī *vi.* remain behind; be idle, be listless; (*fig.*) remain, rest.
res/ī'dō -ī'dere -ē'dī *vi.* sit down, sink down, settle; subside; (*fig.*) abate, calm down.
resi'duus *a.* remaining, left over; (*money*) outstanding.
resi'gn/ō -ā're *vt.* unseal, open; (*fig.*) reveal; (*bus.*) cancel, pay back.
resi'l/iō -ī're -uī *vi.* spring back; recoil, rebound, shrink.
resī'mus *a.* turned up.
rēsī'n/a -ae *f.* resin.
rēsīnā'tus *a.* smeared with resin. [smack of
resi'p/iō -ere *vt.* savour of

resip/ī'scō -ī'scere -iī & uī *vi.* come to one's senses.
res/i'stō -i'stere -titī *vi.* stand still, stop, halt; resist, oppose; rise again.
resolū'tus *ppp.* resolvō.
reso'l/vō -vere -vī -ū'tum *vt.* unfasten, loosen, open, release; melt, dissolve; relax; (*debt*) pay up; (*difficulty*) banish, dispel; (*tax*) abolish; (*words*) explain.
resonā'bilis *a.* answering.
re'son/ō -ā're *vi.* resound, re-echo. *vt.* echo the sound of; make resound.
re'sonus *a.* echoing.
reso'rb/eō -ē're *vt.* suck back, swallow again.
respe'ct/ō -ā're *vi.* look back; gaze about, watch. *vt.* look back at, look for; have regard for.
respe'ctus *ppp.* respiciō.
respe'ct/us -ūs *m.* looking back; refuge; respect, regard.
respe'r/gō -gere -sī -sum *vt.* besprinkle, splash.
respe'rsi/ō -ō'nis *f.* sprinkling.
respe'rsus *ppp.* respergō.
resp/i'ciō -i'cere -e'xī -e'ctum *vt.* look back at, see behind; (*help*) look to; (*care*) have regard for, consider, respect. *vi.* look back, look.
respīrā'm/en -inis *n.* windpipe.
respīrā'ti/ō -ō'nis *f.* breathing; exhalation; taking breath, pause.
respīrā't/us -ūs *m.* inhaling.
respī'r/ō -ā're -ā'vī -ā'tum *vt.* & *i.* breathe, blow back; breathe again, revive; (*things*) abate.
resple'nd/eō -ē're *vi.* flash back, shine brightly.
resp/o'ndeō -ondē're -o'ndī -ō'nsum *vt.* answer, reply; (*lawyer, priest, oracle*) advise, give a response; (*law-court*) appear; (*pledge*) promise in return; (*things*) correspond, agree, match. **pār pari** — return like for like, give tit for tat.
respō'nsi/ō -ō'nis *f.* answering; refutation.
respō'nsit/ō -ā're *vi.* give advice.
respō'ns/ō -ā're *vt.* & *i.* answer back; defy.
respō'ns/or -ō'ris *m.* answerer.
respō'ns/um -ī *n.* answer, reply; response, opinion, oracle.
rēspū'blica reipū'blicae *f.* public affairs, politics the State, republic.
re'spu/ō -ere -ī *vt.* spit out, eject; reject, refuse.
resta'gn/ō -ā're *vi.* overflow; be flooded.
restau'r/ō -ā're *vt.* repair, rebuild.
resti'cul/a -ae *f.* rope, cord.
resti'ncti/ō -ō'nis *f.* quenching.
resti'nctus *ppp.* restinguō.
resti'n/guō -guere -xī -ctum *vt.* extinguish quench; (*fig.*) destroy.
re'sti/ō -ō'nis *m.* rope-maker.
restipulā'ti/ō -ō'nis *f.* counter-obligation.
resti'pul/or -ā'rī *vt.* stipulate in return.
re'st/is -is *f.* rope.
re'stitī *perf.* resistō; *perf.* restō.
re'stit/ō -ā're *vi.* stay behind, hesitate.
resti't/uō -u'ere -uī -ū'tum *vt.* replace, restore; rebuild, renew; give back, return; (*to a condition*) reinstate; (*decision*) quash, reverse; (*character*) reform.
restitū'ti/ō -ō'nis *f.* restoration; reinstating.
restitū't/or -ō'ris *m.* restorer.
restitū'tus *ppp.* restituō.
re'st/ō -ā're -itī *vi.* stand firm; resist; remain, be left; be in store (for). **quod -at** for the future.

restri'ct/us *ppp.* restringō. *a.* tight, short; niggardly; severe **-ē** *ad.* sparingly; strictly.
restri'/ngō -ngere -nxī -ctum *vt.* draw back tightly, bind fast; (*teeth*) bare; (*fig.*) check.
resu'lt/ō -ā're *vi.* rebound; re-echo.
resū'm/ō -ere -psī -ptum *vt.* take up again, get back, resume.
resupī'n/ō -ā're *vt.* turn back, throw on one's back.
resupī'nus *a.* lying back, face upwards.
resu'r/gō -gere -rē'xī -rē'ctum *vi.* rise again, revive.
resu'scit/ō -ā're *vt.* revive.
retardā'ti/ō -ō'nis *f.* hindering.
reta'rd/ō -ā're -ā'vī -ā'tum *vt.* retard, detain, check.
rē't/e -is *n.* net; (*fig.*) snare.
retē'ctus *ppp.* retegō.
re't/egō -e'gere -ē'xī -ē'ctum *vt.* uncover, open; reveal.
rete'mpt/ō -ā're *vt.* try again.
ret/e'ndō -e'ndere -e'ndī -e'ntum & -ē'nsum *vt.* slacken, relax.
retē'nsus *ppp.* retendō.
rete'nti/ō -ō'nis *f.* holding back. [hold fast.
rete'nt/ō -ā're *vt.* keep back.
rete'ntō, *see* **retemptō.**
rete'ntus *ppp.* retendō; *ppp.* retineō.
retē'xī *perf.* retegō.
rete'x/ō -ere -uī -tum *vt.* unravel; (*fig.*) break up, cancel; renew. [fighter.
rētiā'r/ius -ī & iī *m.* net-
retice'nti/a -ae *f.* saying nothing; pause.
reti'c/eō -ē're -uī *vi.* be silent, say nothing. *vt.* keep secret.
rēti'cul/um -ī *n.* small net, hair-net; net-work bag.
retinā'cul/um -ī *n.* tether, hawser.
re'tin/ēns -e'ntis *pres.p.* retineō. *a.* tenacious, observant.
retine'nti/a -ae *f.* memory.
ret/i'neō -inē're -i'nuī -e'ntum *vt.* hold back, detain, restrain; keep, retain, preserve.
reti'nn/iō -ī're *vi.* ring.
re'ton/ō -ā're *vi.* thunder in answer.
reto'r/queō -quē're -sī -tum *vt.* turn back, twist.
reto'rridus *a.* dried up, wizened.
reto'rtus *ppp.* retorqueō.
retractā'ti/ō -ō'nis *f.* hesitation.
retra'ct/ō (retre'ctō) -ā're -ā'vī -ā'tum *vt.* rehandle, take up again; reconsider, revise; withdraw. *vi.* draw back, hesitate.
retra'ctus *ppp.* retrahō. *a.* remote.
re'tra/hō -here -xī -ctum *vt.* draw back, drag back; withdraw, remove.
retre'ctō, *see* **retractō.**
retri'b/uō -u'ere -uī -ū'tum *vt.* restore, repay.
re'trō *ad.* back, backwards, behind; (*time*) back, past.
retrō'rsum *ad.* backwards, behind; in reverse order.
retrū'/dō -dere -sum *vt.* push back; withdraw.
re'ttulī *perf.* referō.
ret/u'ndō -u'ndere -udī & tudī -ū'sum & ū'nsum *vt.* blunt; (*fig.*) check, weaken.
retū'sus, retū'nsus *ppp.* retundō. *a.* blunt, dull.
re'/us -ī *m.* the accused, defendant; guarantor, debtor, one responsible; culprit, criminal. **vōtī** — one who has had a prayer granted.
reval/ē'scō -ē'scere -uī *vi.* recover.
re've/hō -here -xī -ctum *vt.* carry back, bring back; (*pass.*) ride, drive, sail back.
rev/e'llō -e'llere -e'llī -u'lsum

(o'lsum) *vt.* pull out, tear off; remove. [uncover.
revē'l/ō -ā're *vt.* unveil,
rev/e'niō -enī're -ē'nī -e'ntum *vi.* come back, return.
rēvē'rā *ad.* in fact, actually.
revere'ndus *a.* venerable, awe-inspiring.
re'ver/ēns -e'ntis *pres.p.* revereor. *a.* respectful, reverent. **-e'nter** *ad.* respectfully.
revere'nti/a -ae *f.* respect, reverence, awe.
reve'r/eor -ē'rī -itus *vt.* stand in awe of; respect, revere.
reve'rsi/ō (**revo'rsiō**) -ō'nis *f.* turning back; recurrence.
reve'rsus *ppa.* revertor.
reve'rt/ō -ere -ī, **reve'r/tor** -tī -sus *vi.* turn back, return; revert.
reve'xī *perf.* revehō.
revi'ctus *ppp.* revincō.
revi'n/ciō -cī're -xī -ctum *vt.* tie back, bind fast.
rev/i'ncō -i'ncere -ī'cī -i'ctum *vt.* conquer, repress; (*words*) refute, convict.
revi'nctus *ppp.* revinciō.
revir/ē'scō -ē'scere -uī *vi.* grow green again; be rejuvenated; grow strong again, flourish again. [to, revisit.
revī's/ō -ere *vt.* & *i.* come back
revī/vī'scō (**-vē'scō**) -vī'scere -xī *vi.* come to life again, revive.
revocā'bilis *a.* revocable.
revocā'm/en -inis *n.* recall.
revocā'ti/ō -ō'nis *f.* recalling; (*word*) withdrawing.
re'voc/ō -ā're -ā'vī -ā'tum *vt.* call back, recall; (*action*) revoke; (*former state*) recover, regain; (*growth*) check; (*guest*) invite in return; (*judgment*) apply, refer; (*law*) summon again; (*performer*) encore; (*troops*) withdraw.
re'vol/ō -ā're *vi.* fly back.
revo'lsus, *see* **revulsus**.
revolū'bilis *a.* that may be rolled back.
revolū'tus *ppp.* revolvō.
revo'l/vō -vere -vī -ū'tum *vt.* roll back, unroll, unwind; (*speech*) relate, repeat; (*thought*) think over; (*writing*) read over; (*pass.*) revolve, return, come round.
re'vom/ō -ere -uī *vt.* disgorge.
revor-, *see* **rever-**.
revu'lsus *ppp.* revellō.
rēx rē'gis *m.* king; tyrant, despot; leader; patron, rich man.
rē'xī *perf.* regō.
Rhadama'nth/us -ī *m.* judge in the lower world.
Rhae'ti, *see* **Raetī**.
Rha'mn/ūs -ū'ntis *f.* town in Attica, famous for its statue of Nemesis. **-ū'sius** *a.* **-ū'sis** -ū'sidis *f.* Nemesis.
rhapsō'di/a -ae *f.* a book of Homer.
Rhe'/a -ae *f.* Cybele.
Rhe'/a Si'lvi/a -ae -ae *f.* mother of Romulus and Remus.
Rhē'gium, *see* **Rēgium**.
rhē'nō, *see* **rēnō**.
Rhē'n/us -ī *m.* Rhine. **-ā'nus** *a.* Rhenish.
Rhē's/us -ī *m.* Thracian king killed at Troy.
rhē't/or -oris *m.* teacher of rhetoric; orator.
rhēto'ric/us *a.* rhetorical, on rhetoric. **-a** -ae, **-ē** -ēs *f.* art of oratory, rhetoric. **-ī** -ō'rum *m.pl.* teachers of rhetoric. **-ē** *ad.* rhetorically, in an oratorical manner.
rhīno'cer/ōs -ō'tis *m.* rhinoceros.
rhō *n.*(*indecl.*) Greek letter rho.
Rho'dan/us -ī *m.* Rhone.
Rho'dop/ē -ēs *f.* mountain range in Thrace. **-ē'ius** *a.* Thracian.
Rho'd/os (**Rho'dus**) -ī *f.* island of Rhodes. **-ius** *a.*

Rhoetē'/um -ī *n.* promontory on the Dardanelles, near Troy. **-us** *a.* Trojan.
rho'mb/us -ī *m.* magician's circle; (*fish*) turbot.
rhomphae'/a -ae *f.* long barbarian javelin.
rhy'thmic/us -ī *m.* teacher of prose rhythm.
rhy'thm/os (**-us**) -ī *m.* rhythm, symmetry.
rī'c/a -ae *f.* sacrificial veil.
rīci'n/ium -ī & iī *n.* small cloak with hood.
ri'ct/us -ūs *m.*, **-um** -ī *n.* open mouth, gaping jaws.
rī'/deō -dē're -sī -sum *vi.* laugh, smile. *vt.* laugh at, smile at; ridicule.
rīdibu'ndus *a.* laughing.
rīdiculā'r/ia -ium *n.pl.* jokes.
rīdi'cul/us *a.* amusing, funny; ridiculous, silly. *m.* jester. *n.* joke. **-ē** *ad.* jokingly; absurdly.
ri'g/ēns -e'ntis *pres.p.* rigeō. *a.* stiff, rigid, frozen.
ri'g/eō -ē're *vi.* be stiff.
rig/ē'scō -ē'scere -uī *vi.* stiffen, harden; bristle.
ri'gid/us *a.* stiff, rigid, hard; (*fig.*) hardy, strict, inflexible. **-ē** *ad.* rigorously.
ri'g/ō -ā're *vt.* water, moisten, bedew; convey (water).
ri'g/or -ō'ris *m.* stiffness, hardness; numbness, cold; strictness, severity.
ri'guī *perf.* rigēscō.
ri'guus *a.* irrigating; watered.
rī'm/a -ae *f.* crack, chink.
rī'm/or -ā'rī -ā'tus *vt.* tear open; search for, probe, examine; find out.
rīmō'sus *a.* cracked, leaky.
ri'ng/or -ī *vi.* snarl.
rī'p/a -ae *f.* river bank; shore.
Rīphae'/ī -ō'rum *m.pl.* mountain range in N. Scythia. **-us** *a.*
rī'pul/a -ae *f.* river bank.

ri'sc/us -ī *m.* trunk, chest.
rī'sī *perf.* rīdeō.
rī's/or -ō'ris *m.* scoffer.
rī's/us -ūs *m.* laughter, laugh; laughing-stock.
rī'te *ad.* with the proper formality or ritual; duly, properly, rightly; in the usual manner; fortunately.
rī't/us -ūs *m.* ritual, ceremony; custom, usage. **-ū** after the manner of.
rīvā'l/is -is *m.* rival in love.
rīvā'lit/ās -ā'tis *f.* rivalry in love.
rī'vul/us -ī *m.* brook.
rī'v/us -ī *m.* stream, brook. **ē -ō** **flūmina māgna facere** *make a mountain of a mole-hill.*
ri'x/a -ae *f.* quarrel, brawl, fight. [brawl, squabble.
ri'x/or -ā'rī -ā'tus *vi.* quarrel,
rōbīginō'sus *a.* rusty.
rōbī'g/ō -inis *f.* rust; blight, mould, mildew.
rōbo'reus *a.* of oak.
rō'bor/ō -ā're *vt.* strengthen, invigorate.
rō'b/ur -oris *n.* oak; hard wood; prison, dungeon (at Rome); (*fig.*) strength, hardness, vigour; best part, élite, flower.
rōbu'stus *a.* of oak; strong, hard; robust, mature.
rō'/dō -dere -sī -sum *vt.* gnaw; (*rust*) corrode; (*words*) slander.
rogā'lis *a.* of a pyre.
rogā'ti/ō -ō'nis *f.* proposal, motion, bill; request; (*rhet.*) question.
rogātiu'ncul/a -ae *f.* unimportant bill; question.
rogā't/or -ō'ris *m.* proposer; polling-clerk.
rogā't/us -ūs *m.* request.
ro'git/ō -ā're *vt.* ask for, inquire eagerly.
ro'g/ō -ā're -ā'vī -ā'tum *vt.* ask, ask for; (*bill*) propose, move; (*candidate*) put up for election. **lēgem —, populum**

— introduce a bill. magistrātum populum — nominate for election to an office. militēs sacrāmentō — administer the oath to the troops. mālō emere quam rogāre I'd rather buy it than borrow it.
ro'g/us -ī *m.* funeral pyre.
Rō'm/a -ae *f.* Rome. **-ā'nus** *a.* Roman.
Rō'mul/us -ī *m.* founder and first king of Rome. **-eus, -us** *a.* of Romulus; Roman. **-idae** -idā'rum *m.pl.* the Romans.
rōrā'ri/ī -ō'rum *m.pl.* skirmishers.
rō'ridus *a.* dewy.
rō'rifer -ī *a.* dew-bringing.
rō'r/ō -ā're *vi.* distil dew; drip, trickle. *vt.* bedew, wet.
rōs rō'ris *m.* dew; moisture, water; (*plant*) rosemary. — marīnus rosemary.
ro's/a -ae *f.* rose; rose-bush.
rosā'ri/a -ō'rum *n.pl.* rose-garden.
rō'scidus *a.* dewy; wet.
Ro'sc/ius -ī *m.* L. — Othō, tribune in 67 B.C., whose law reserved theatre seats for the equites; Q. — Gallus, famous actor, defended by Cicero; Sex. — of Ameria, defended by Cicero. **-ius, -iā'nus** *a.*
rosē't/um -ī *n.* rose-bed.
ro'seus *a.* rosy; of roses.
rō'sī *perf.* rōdō.
rōstrā't/us *a.* beaked, curved. columna -a column commemorating a naval victory.
rō'str/um -ī *n.* (*bird*) beak, bill; (*animal*) snout, muzzle; (*ship*) beak, end of prow; (*pl.*) orators' platform in the Forum.
rō'sus *ppp.* rōdō.
ro't/a -ae *f.* wheel; potter's wheel, torture-wheel; car, disc.
ro't/ō -ā're -ā'vī -ā'tum *vt.* turn, whirl, roll; (*pass.*) revolve.
rotu'nd/ō -ā're *vt.* round off.
rotu'nd/us *a.* round, circular, spherical; (*style*) well-turned, smooth. **-ē** *ad.* elegantly.
rube/fa'ciō -fa'cere -fē'cī -fa'ctum *vt.* redden.
ru'b/ēns -e'ntis *pres.p.* rubeō. *a.* red; blushing.
ru'b/eō -ē're *vi.* be red; blush.
ru'b/er -rī *a.* red. mare -rum Red Sea; Persian Gulf. ōceanus — Indian Ocean. Saxa -ra stone quarries between Rome and Veii.
rub/ē'scō -ē'scere **-uī** *vi.* redden, blush.
rubē't/a -ae *f.* toad.
rubē't/a -ō'rum *n.pl.* bramble-bushes.
ru'beus *a.* of bramble.
Ru'bic/ō -ō'nis *m.* stream marking the frontier between Italy and Gaul.
rubicu'ndulus *a.* reddish.
rubicu'ndus *a.* red, ruddy.
rūbīg-, *see* **rōbīg-.**
ru'b/or -ō'ris *m.* redness; blush; bashfulness; shame.
rubrī'c/a -ae *f.* red earth, red ochre.
ru'buī *perf* rubēscō.
ru'b/us -ī *m.* bramble-bush; bramble, blackberry.
ru'ct/ō -ā're, **-or** -ā'rī *vt.* & *i.* belch.
ru'ct/us -us *m.* belching.
ru'd/ēns -e'ntis *pres.p.* rudō. *m.* rope; (*pl.*) rigging.
Ru'd/iae -iā'rum *f.pl.* town in S. Italy, birthplace of Ennius. **-ī'nus** *a.*
rudiā'r/ius -ī & iī *m.* retired gladiator.
rudīme'nt/um -ī *n.* first attempt, beginning.
ru'dis *a.* unwrought, unworked, raw; coarse, rough, badly-made; (*age*) new, young; (*person*) uncultured, unskilled, clumsy; ignorant (of), inexperienced (in).
ru'd/is -is *f.* stick, rod; foil

for fighting practice); (*fig.*) discharge.
ru'd/ō -ere -ī'vī -ī'tum *vi.* roar, bellow, bray; creak.
rū'd/us -eris *n.* rubble, rubbish; piece of copper.
rū'fulus *a.* red-headed.
Rū'ful/ī -ō'rum *m.pl.* military tribunes chosen by the general.
rū'fus *a.* red, red-haired.
rū'g/a -ae *f.* wrinkle, crease.
rū'g/ō -ā're *vi.* become creased.
rūgō'sus *a.* wrinkled, shrivelled, corrugated.
r'uī *perf.* ruō.
ruī'n/a -ae *f.* fall, downfall; collapse, falling in; debris, ruins; destruction, disaster, ruin (*fig.*).
ruīnō'sus *a.* collapsing; ruined.
ru'm/ex -icis *f.* sorrel.
rūmi'fic/ō -ā're *vt.* report.
Rūmī'n/a -ae *f.* goddess of nursing mothers. ficus -ālis the fig-tree of Romulus and Remus, under which the she-wolf suckled them.
rūminā'ti/ō -ō'nis *f.* chewing the cud; (*fig.*) ruminating.
rū'min/ō -ā're *vt.* & *i.* chew the cud.
rū'm/or -ō'ris *m.* noise, cheering; rumour, hearsay; public opinion; reputation.
ru'mpia, *see* **rhomphaea**.
ru'mp/ō -ere rū'pī ru'ptum *vt.* break, burst, tear; break down, burst through; (*activity*) interrupt; (*agreement*) violate, annul; (*delay*) put an end to; (*voice*) give vent to; (*way*) force through.
rūmu'scul/ī -ō'rum *m.pl.* gossip.
rū'n/a -ae *f.* dart.
ru'nc/ō -ā're *vt.* weed.
ru'/ō -ere -ī -tum *vi.* fall down, tumble; rush, run, hurry; come to ruin. *vt.* dash down, hurl to the ground; throw up, turn up.
rū'p/ēs -is *f.* rock, cliff.
rū'pī *perf.* rumpō.
ru'pt/or -ō'ris *m.* violator.
ru'ptus *ppp.* rumpō.
rūri'col/a -ae *a.* rural, country-.
rūri'gen/a -ae *m.* countryman.
rū'rsus, rū'rsum (rū'sum) *ad.* back, backwards; on the contrary, in return; again.
rūs rū'ris *n.* the country, countryside; estate, farm. rūs to the country. rūrī in the country. rūre from the country.
ru'sc/um -ī *n.* butcher's-broom.
ru'ssus *a.* red.
rūsticā'nus *a.* country-, rustic.
rūsticā'ti/ō -ō'nis *f.* country life.
rūsti'cit/ās -ā'tis *f.* country manners, rusticity.
rū'stic/or -ā'rī *vi.* live in the country.
rūsti'cul/us -ī *m.* yokel.
rū'stic/us *a.* country-, rural; simple, rough, clownish. *m.* countryman. **-ē** *ad.* in a countrified manner, awkwardly.
rū'sum, *see* **rūrsus**.
ru'ta cae'sa *n.pl.* minerals and timber on an estate.
rū't/a -ae *f.* (*herb*) rue; (*fig.*) unpleasantness.
ru'til/ō -ā're *vt.* colour red. *vi.* glow red.
ru'tilus *a.* red, auburn.
ru'tr/um -ī *n.* spade, shovel, trowel.
rū'tul/a -ae *f.* little piece of rue.
Ru'tul/ī -ō'rum *m.pl.* ancient Latin people. **-us** *a.* Rutulian.
Rutu'p/iae -iā'rum *f.pl.* seaport in Kent, *mod.* Richborough. **-ī'nus** *a.*
ru'tus *ppp.* ruō.

S

Sa'b/a -ae *f.* town in Arabia Felix. **-ae'us** *a.*

Sabā'z/ius -ī *m.* Bacchus. **-ia** -iō'rum *n.pl.* festival of Bacchus.

sa'bbat/a -ō'rum *n.pl.* Sabbath, Jewish holiday.

Sabe'll/us -ī *m.* Sabine, Samnite. **-us, -icus** *a.*

Sabī'n/ī -ō'rum *m.pl.* Sabines, a people of central Italy. **-us** *a.* Sabine. *f.* Sabine woman. *n.* Sabine estate; Sabine wine. herba -a savin, a kind of juniper.

Sabrī'n/a -ae *f.* river Severn.

sabu'rr/a -ae sand, ballast.

Sa'c/ae -ā'rum *m.pl.* tribe of Scythians.

saccipē'r/ium -ī & iī *n.* purse-pocket.

sa'cc/ō -ā're *vt.* strain, filter.

sa'ccul/us -ī *m.* little bag, purse. [wallet.

sa'cc/us -ī *m.* bag, purse,

sace'll/um -ī *n.* chapel.

sa'c/er -rī *a.* sacred, holy; devoted for sacrifice, forfeited; accursed, criminal, infamous. Mōns — hill to which the Roman plebs seceded. Via -ra street from the Forum to the Capitol. **-rum** -rī *n.* holy thing, sacred vessel; shrine; offering, victim; rite; (*pl.*) sacrifice, worship, religion. -ra facere sacrifice. inter -rum saxumque *with one's back to the wall.* hērēditās sine -rīs a gift with no awkward obligations. [priestess.

sace'rd/ōs -ō'tis *m., f.* priest,

sacerdō't/ium -ī & iī *n.* priesthood.

sacrāme'nt/um -ī *n.* deposit made by parties to a lawsuit; civil lawsuit, dispute; (*mil.*) oath of allegiance, engagement.

sacrā'r/ium -ī & iī *n.* shrine, chapel.

sacri'col/a -ae *m., f.* sacrificing priest or priestess.

sa'crifer -ī *a.* carrying holy things.

sacrificā'lis *a.* sacrificial.

sacrificā'ti/ō -ō'nis *f.* sacrificing. [sacrifice.

sacrifi'c/ium -ī & iī *n.*

sacri'fic/ō -ā're *vt.* & *i.* sacrifice.

sacrifi'cul/us -ī *m.* sacrificing priest. rēx — high-priest.

sacri'ficus *a.* sacrificial.

sacrilē'g/ium -ī & iī *n.* sacrilege.

sacri'legus *a.* sacrilegious; profane, wicked. *m.* temple-robber.

sa'cr/ō -ā're -ā'vī -ā'tum *vt.* consecrate; doom, curse; devote, dedicate; make inviolable; (*poetry*) immortalize. **-ā'tus** *a.* holy, hallowed. -āta lēx a law whose violation was punished by devotion to the infernal gods.

sacrōsa'nctus *a.* inviolable, sacroscant.

sacru'ficō, *see* **sacrificō**.

sae'clum, *see* **saeculum**.

saeculā'ris *a.* centenary; (*eccl.*) secular, pagan.

sae'cul/um -ī *n.* generation, lifetime, age; the age, the times; century. in -a (*eccl.*) for ever.

sae'pe *ad.* often, frequently. **-numerō** very often.

sae'p/ēs -is *f.* hedge, fence.

saepīme'nt/um -ī *n.* enclosure.

sae'p/iō -ī're -sī -tum *vt.* hedge round, fence in, enclose; (*fig.*) shelter, protect.

sae'ptus *ppp.* saepiō. *n.* fence, wall; stake, pale; (*sheep*) fold; (*Rome*) voting area in the Campus Martius.

sae't/a -ae *f.* hair, bristle.

sae'tiger -ī *a.* bristly.

saetō'sus *a.* bristly, hairy.

saevi'dicus *a.* furious.

sae'v/iō -ī're -iī -ī'tum *vi.* rage, rave. [cruelty.
saevi'ti/a -ae *f.* rage; ferocity,
sae'v/us *a.* raging, fierce; cruel, barbarous. **-ē, -iter** *ad.* fiercely, cruelly.
sā'g/a -ae *f.* fortune-teller.
sagā'cit/ās -ā'tis *f.* (*dogs*) keen scent; (*mind*) shrewdness.
sagā'tus *a.* wearing a soldier's cloak.
sa'g/āx -ā'cis *a.* (*senses*) keen, keen-scented; (*mind*) quick, shrewd. **-ā'citer** *ad.* keenly; shrewdly.
sagī'n/a -ae *f.* stuffing, fattening; food, rich food; fatted animal.
sagī'n/ō -are *vt.* cram, fatten; feed, feast. [keenly.
sā'g/iō -ī're *vi.* perceive
sagi'tt/a -ae *f.* arrow.
sagittā'r/ius -ī & **iī** *m.* archer.
sagi'ttifer -ī *a.* armed with arrows.
sa'gm/en -inis *n.* tuft of sacred herbs used as a mark of inviolability.
sa'gul/um -ī *n.* short military cloak.
sa'g/um -ī *n.* military cloak; woollen mantle.
Sagu'nt/um -ī *n.*, **-us (os) -ī** *f.* town in E. Spain. **-ī'nus** *a.*
sā'gus *a.* prophetic.
sāl sa'lis *m.* salt; brine, sea; (*fig.*) shrewdness, wit, humour, witticism; good taste.
sa'lac/ō -ō'nis *m.* swaggerer.
Sa'lam/īs -ī'nis *f.* Greek island near Athens; town in Cyprus. **-ī'nius** *a.*
salapū't/ium -ī & **iī** *n.* manikin.
salā'rius *a.* salt-. *n.* allowance, salary.
sa'l/āx -ā'cis *a.* lustful, salacious. [rut.
sa'lebr/a -ae *f.* roughness,
Saliā'ris *a.* of the Salii; sumptuous.
sali'ct/um -ī *n.* willow plantation.
salie'nt/ēs -ium *f.pl.* springs.
sali'gnus *a.* of willow.
Sa'li/ī -ō'rum *m.pl.* priests of Mars. [cellar.
sali'll/um -ī *n.* little salt-
salī'n/ae -ā'rum *f.pl.* salt-works.
salī'n/um -ī *n.* salt-cellar.
sa'l/iō -ī're -uī -tum *vi.* leap, spring; throb.
saliu'nc/a -ae *f.* Celtic nard.
salī'v/a -ae *f.* saliva, spittle; taste.
sa'l/ix -icis *f.* willow.
Sallu'st/ius -ī *m.* Sallust, Roman historian; his wealthy grand-nephew. **-iā'nus** *a.*
Salmō'n/eus -eos *m.* son of Aeolus, punished in Tartarus for imitating lightning. **-is -idis** *f.* his daughter Tyro.
salsāme'nt/um -ī *n.* brine, pickle; salted fish.
sa'ls/us *a.* salted; salt, briny; (*fig.*) witty. **-ē** *ad.* wittily.
saltā'ti/ō -ō'nis *f.* dancing, dance.
saltā't/or -ō'ris *m.* dancer.
saltātō'rius *a.* dancing-.
saltā'tr/īx -ī'cis *f.* dancer.
saltā't/us -ūs *m.* dance.
sa'ltem *ad.* at least, at all events. **nōn** — not even.
sa'lt/ō -ā're *vt.* & *i.* dance.
saltuō'sus *a.* wooded.
sa'lt/us -ūs *m.* leap, bound.
sa'lt/us -ūs *m.* woodland pasture, glade; pass, ravine.
salū'bri/s (sa'lūber) *a.* health-giving, wholesome; healthy, sound. **-ter** *ad.* wholesomely; beneficially.
salū'brit/ās -ā'tis *f.* healthiness; health.
sa'luī *perf.* saliō.
sa'l/um -ī *n.* sea, high sea.
sa'l/ūs -ū'tis *f.* health; welfare, life; safety; good wish, greeting. **-ūtem dicere** greet; bid farewell.

salūtā'ri/s *a.* wholesome, healthy; beneficial. — littera letter A (for absolvō acquittal). **-ter** *ad.* beneficially.
salūtā'ti/ō -ō'nis *f.* greeting; formal morning visit, levee.
salūtā't/or -ō'ris *m.*, **-rīx** **-rī'cis** *f.* morning caller; courtier.
salū'tifer -ī *a.* health-giving.
salūtige'rulus *a.* carrying greetings.
salū't/ō -ā're -ā'vī -ā'tum *vt.* greet, salute, wish well; call on, pay respects to.
sa'lvē *ad.* well, in good health; all right.
sa'lvē *imp.* salveō.
sa'lv/eō -ē're *vi.* be well, be in good health. -ē, -ētō, -ēte hail! good day! good-bye! -ēre iubeō I bid good day.
sa'lv/us, sa'lv/os *a.* safe, alive, intact, well; without violating; all right. — sīs good day to you! -a rēs est all is well. -ā lēge without breaking the law.
Samarobrī'v/a -ae *f.* Belgian town, *mod.* Amiens.
sambū'c/a -ae *f.* harp.
sambūci'stri/a -ae *f.* harpist.
Sa'm/ē -ēs *f.* old name of the Greek island Cephallenia. **-ao'us** *a.*
Sa'mn/ium -ī & iī *n.* district of central Italy. **-īs** -ī'tis *a.* Samnite.
Sa'm/os (-us) -ī *f.* Aegean island off Asia Minor, famous for its pottery and as the birthplace of Pythagoras. **-ius** *a.* Samian. *n.pl.* Samian pottery.
Samothrā'c/ia -iae, -a -ae *f.* Samothrace, island in the N. Aegean. **-ius** *a.* **-es** -um *m.pl.* Samothracians.
sānā'bilis *a.* curable.
sānā'ti/ō -ō'nis *f.* healing.
sa'n/ciō -cī're -xī -ctum *vt.* make sacred or inviolable; ordain, ratify; enact a punishment against.
sanctimō'ni/a -ae *f.* sanctity; chastity.
sa'ncti/ō -ō'nis *f.* decree, penalty for violating a law.
sa'nctit/ās -ā'tis *f.* sacredness; integrity, chastity.
sanctitū'd/ō -inis *f.* sacredness.
sa'nct/or -ō'ris *m.* enacter.
sa'nct/us *ppp.* sanciō. *a.* sacred, inviolable; holy, venerable; pious, virtuous, chaste. **-ō** *ad.* solemnly, religiously.
sandalige'rul/a -ae *f.* sandal-bearer.
sanda'l/ium -ī & iī *n.* sandal, slipper. [bier.
sanda'pil/a -ae *f.* common
sa'nd/ȳx -ȳ'cis *f.* scarlet.
sā'nē *ad.* sensibly; (*intensive*) very, doubtless; (*ironical*) to be sure, of course; (*concessive*) of course, indeed; (*in answer*) certainly, surely; (*with imp.*) then, if you please. — quam very much. haud — not so very, not quite.
sa'nguen, *see* **sanguis.**
sa'nguin/āns -ā'ntis *a.* bloodthirsty. [thirsty.
sanguinā'rius *a.* blood-
sangui'neus *a.* bloody, of blood; blood-red.
sanguinole'ntus *a.* bloody; blood-red; sanguinary.
sa'ngu/is -inis *m.* blood, bloodshed; descent, family; offspring; (*fig.*) strength, life. -inem dare shed one's blood. -inem mittere let blood.
sa'ni/ēs -em -ē *f.* diseased blood, matter; venom.
sā'nit/ās -ā'tis *f.* (*body*) health, sound condition; (*mind*) sound sense, sanity; (*style*) correctness, purity.
sa'nn/a -ae *f.* grimace, mocking.
sa'nni/ō -ō'nis *m.* clown.
sā'n/ō -ā're -ā'vī -ā'tum *vt.*

cure, heal; (*fig.*) remedy, relieve.
Sanquā'lis avis *f.* osprey.
sā'nus *a.* (*body*) sound, healthy; (*mind*) sane, sensible; (*style*) correct. male — mad, inspired. sānun es ? are you in your senses ?
sa'nxī *perf.* sanciō.
sa'p/a -ae *f.* new wine.
sa'pi/ēns -e'ntis *pres.p.* sapiō. *a.* wise, discreet. *m.* wise man, philosopher; man of taste. -e'nter *ad.* wisely, sensibly.
sapie'nti/a -ae *f.* wisdom, discernment; philosophy; knowledge.
sa'p/iō -ere -ī'vī & uī *vi.* have a flavour or taste; have sense, be wise. *vt.* taste of, smell of, smack of; understand.
sa'p/or -ō'ris *m.* taste, flavour; (*food*) delicacy; (*fig.*) taste, refinement.
Sa'pph/ō -ūs *f.* famous Greek lyric poetess, native of Lesbos. **-icus** *a.*
sa'rcin/a -ae *f.* bundle, burden; (*mil.*) pack.
sarcinā'rius *a.* baggage-.
sarcinā't/or -ō'ris *m.* patcher.
sarci'nul/a -ae *f.* little pack.
sa'r/ciō -cī're -sī -tum *vt.* patch, mend, repair.
sarco'phag/us -ī *m.* sepulchre.
sa'rcul/um -ī *n.* light hoe.
Sa'rd/ēs (-is) -ium *f.pl.* Sardis, capital of Lydia. **-iā'nus** *a.*
Sard/i'nia -i'niae *f.* island of Sardinia. **-us, -ō'us, -iniē'nsis** *a.*
sa'rdony/x -chis *f.* sardonyx.
sa'r/iō -ī're -ī'vī & uī *vt.* hoe, weed.
sarī's/a -ae *f.* Macedonian [lance.
sarīso'phor/us -ī *m.* Macedonian lancer.
Sa'rmat/ae -ā'rum *m.pl.* Sarmatians, a people of S.E. Russia. **-icus, -is** *a.*
sarme'nt/um -ī *n.* twigs, brushwood.
Sarpē'd/ōn -onis *m.* king of Lycia.
Sa'rr/a -ae *f.* Tyre. **-ā'nus** *a.* Tyrian.
sarrā'c/um -ī *n.* cart.
sa'rriō, *see* **sariō.**
sa'rsī *perf.* sarciō.
sartā'g/ō -inis *f.* frying-pan.
sa'rt/or -ō'ris *m.* hoer, weeder.
sa'rtus *ppp.* sarciō.
sat, *see* **satis.**
sa'tag/ō -ere *vi.* have one's hands full, be in trouble; bustle about fuss.
sate'll/es -itis *m., f.* attendant, follower; assistant, accomplice.
sa'ti/ās -ā'tis *f.* sufficiency; satiety. [satiety.
sati'et/ās -ā'tis *f.* sufficiency;
sa'tin, sa'tine *for* **satisne.** *ad.* quite, really.
sa'ti/ō -ā're -ā'vī -ā'tum *vt.* satisfy, appease; fill, saturate; glut, cloy, disgust.
sa'ti/ō -ō'nis *f.* sowing, planting; (*pl.*) fields.
sa'tis, sat *a.* enough, sufficient. *ad.* enough, sufficiently; tolerably, fairly, quite. — accipiō take sufficient bail. — agō, agitō have one's hands full, be harassed. — dō offer sufficient bail. — faciō satisfy; give satisfaction, make amends; (*creditor*) pay. **sa'tius** *comp.* better, preferable.
satisda'ti/ō -ō'nis *f.* giving security.
sati'sdō, *see* **satis dō.**
satisfa'ciō, *see* **satis faciō.**
satisfa'cti/ō -ō'nis *f.* amends, apology.
sa'tius *comp.* satis.
sa't/or -ō'ris *m.* sower, planter; father; promoter.
sa'trap/ēs -is *m.* satrap, Persian governor.
sa'tur -ī *a.* filled, sated; (*fig.*) rich.
sa'tur/a -ae *f.* mixed dish;

medley; (*poem*) satire. per -am confusingly.
saturē'i/a -ō'rum *n.pl.* savory.
satu'rit/ās -ā'tis *f.* repletion; fulness, plenty.
Saturnā'l/ia -ium & iō'rum *n.pl.* festival of Saturn in December.
Saturnī'n/us -ī *m.* revolutionary tribune in 103 and 100 B.C.
Satu'rn/us -ī *m.* Saturn, god of sowing, ruler of the Golden Age; the planet Saturn. **-ius** *a.* **-ia** -iae *f.* Juno.
sa'tur/ō -ā're -ā'vī -ā'tum *vt.* fill, glut, satisfy; disgust.
sa'tus *ppp.* serō. *m.* son. *f.* daughter. *n.pl.* crops.
sa't/us -ūs *m.* sowing, planting; begetting.
satyri'sc/us -ī *m.* little satyr.
sa'tyr/us -ī *m.* satyr.
sauciā'ti/ō -ō'nis *f.* wounding.
sau'ci/ō -ā're *vt.* wound, hurt.
sau'cius *a.* wounded, hurt; ill, stricken.
Sauro'matae, *see* **Sarmatae**.
sāviā'ti/ō -ō'nis *f.* kissing.
sāvi'ol/um -ī *n.* sweet kiss.
sā'vi/or -ā'rī *vt.* kiss.
sā'v/ium -ī & iī *n.* kiss.
saxā'tilis *a.* rock-.
saxē't/um -ī *n.* rocky place.
sa'xeus *a.* of rock, rocky.
saxi'ficus *a.* petrifying.
saxō'sus *a.* rocky, stony.
sa'xul/um -ī *n.* small rock.
sa'x/um -ī *n.* rock, boulder; the Tarpeian Rock.
sca'b/er -rī *a.* rough, scurfy; mangy, itchy.
sca'bi/ēs -em -ē *f.* roughness, scurf; mange, itch.
scabi'll/um -ī *n.* stool; a castenet played with the foot.
sca'b/ō -ere scā'bī *vt.* scratch.
Scae'/a po'rt/a -ae -ae *f.* the west gate of Troy.
scae'n/a -ae *f.* stage, stage setting; (*fig.*) limelight, public life; outward appearance, pretext.
scaenā'lis *a.* theatrical.
scae'nicus *a.* stage-, theatrical. *m.* actor.
Scae'vol/a -ae *m.* early Roman who burned his hand off before Porsenna; famous jurist of Cicero's day.
scae'vus *a.* on the left; perverse. *f.* omen.
scā'l/ae -ā'rum *f.pl.* steps, ladder, stairs.
sca'lm/us -ī *m.* thole-pin.
scalpe'll/um -ī *n.* scalpel, lancet.
sca'lp/ō -ere -sī -tum *vt.* carve, engrave; scratch.
sca'lpr/um -ī *n.* knife, penknife; chisel.
scalpu'rr/iō -ī're *vi.* scratch.
Scama'nd/er -rī *m.* river of Troy, also called Xanthus.
scammō'ne/a -ae *f.* (*plant*) scammony.
sca'mn/um -ī *n.* bench, stool; throne. [mount.
sca'nd/ō -ere *vt.* & *i.* climb,
sca'ph/a -ae *f.* boat, skiff.
sca'ph/ium -ī & iī *n.* a boat-shaped cup.
sca'pul/ae -ā'rum *f.pl.* shoulder-blades; shoulders.
scā'p/us -ī *m.* shaft; (*loom*) yarn-beam.
sca'r/us -ī *m.* (*fish*) scar.
sca'tebr/a -ae *f.* gushing water.
sca't/eō -ē're, -ō -ere *vi.* bubble up, gush out; (*fig.*) abound, swarm. [springs.
scatūrī'gin/ēs -um *f.pl.*
scatū'r/iō -ī're *vi.* gush out; (*fig.*) be full of.
scau'rus *a.* large-ankled.
scelerā't/us *a.* desecrated; wicked, infamous, accursed; pernicious. **-ē** *ad.* wickedly.
sce'ler/ō -ā're *vt.* desecrate.
scelerō'sus *a.* vicious, accursed.
scelo'st/us *a.* wicked, villain-

ous, accursed; unlucky. **-ē** *ad.* wickedly.
sce'l/us -eris *n.* wickedness, crime, sin; (*person*) scoundrel; (*event*) calamity.
scēn-, *see* **scaen-**.
scē'ptrifer -ī *a.* sceptered.
scē'ptr'um -ī *n.* staff, sceptre; kingship, power.
scēptū'ch/us -ī *m.* sceptre-bearer.
sche'da, *see* **scida.**
schē'm/a -ae *f.* form, figure, style.
Schoe'n/eus -eī *m.* father of Atalanta. **-ē'ius** *a.* **-ē'is -ē'idis** *f.* Atalanta. [dancer.
schoeno'bat/ēs -ae *m.* rope-
scho'l/a -ae *f.* learned discussion, dissertation; school; sect, followers.
schola'sticus *a.* of a school. *m.* rhetorician.
sci'd/a -ae *f.* sheet of paper.
sci'/ēns -e'ntis *pres.p.* sciō. *a.* knowing, purposely; versed in, acquainted with. **-e'nter** *ad.* expertly. [skill.
scie'nti/a -ae *f.* knowledge,
scī'licet *ad.* evidently, of course; (*concessive*) no doubt; (*ironical*) I suppose, of course.
sci'lla, *see* **squilla.**
scīn *for* **scīsne.**
sci'/ndō -ndere -dī -ssum *vt.* cut open, tear apart, split, break down; divide, part.
scinti'll/a -ae *f.* spark.
scinti'll/ō -ā're *vi.* sparkle.
scinti'llul/a -ae *f.* little spark.
sc/i'ō -ī're -ī'vī -ī'tum *vt.* know; have skill in; (*with inf.*) know how to. **quod -iam** as far as I know. **-ītō** you may be sure.
Scīpi'ad/ēs -ae *m.* Scipio.
scī'pi/ō -ō'nis *m.* staff.
Scī'pi/ō -ō'nis *m.* famous Roman family name. *esp.* Africanus, the conqueror of Hannibal; Aemilianus, destroyer of Carthage and patron of literature.
scī'rpeus *a.* rush-. *f.* wicker-work frame. [basket.
scirpi'cul/us -ī *m.* rush-
sci'rp/us -ī *m.* bulrush.
scī'scit/or -ā'rī -ā'tus, -ō -ā're *vt.* inquire; question.
scī'/scō -scere -vī -tum *vt.* inquire, learn; (*pol.*) approve, decree, appoint.
sci'ssus *ppp.* scindō. *a.* split; (*voice*) harsh. [dainties.
scītāme'nt/a -ō'rum *n.pl.*
scī't/or -ā'rī -ā'tus *vt.* & *i.* inquire; consult.
scī'tulus *a.* neat, smart.
scī't/um -ī *n.* decree, statute.
scī't/us *ppp.* sciō; *ppp.* scīscō. *a.* clever, shrewd, skilled; (*words*) sensible, witty; (*appearance*) fine, smart. **-ē** *ad.* cleverly, tastefully.
scī't/us -ūs *m.* decree.
sciū'r/us -ī *m.* squirrel.
scī'vī *perf.* sciō; *perf.* scīscō.
sco'b/is -is *f.* sawdust, filings.
sco'mb/er -rī *m.* mackerel.
scō'p/ae -ā'rum *f.pl.* broom.
Sco'p/ās -ae *m.* famous Greek sculptor.
scopulō'sus *a.* rocky.
sco'pul/us -ī *m.* rock, crag, promontory; (*fig.*) danger.
sco'rpi/ō -ō'nis, -us & **os -ī** *m.* scorpion; (*mil.*) a kind of catapult. [cator.
scortā't/or -ō'ris *m.* forni-
sco'rteus *a.* of leather.
sco'rt/or -ā'rī *vi.* associate with harlots.
sco'rt/um -ī *n.* harlot, prostitute.
screā't/or -ō'ris *m.* one who clears his throat noisily.
screā't/us -ūs *m.* clearing the throat.
scrī'b/a -ae *m.* clerk, writer.
scrī'/bō -bere -psī -ptum *vt.* write, draw; write down, describe; (*document*) draw up; (*law*) designate; (*mil.*) enlist.

scrī'n/ium -ī & iī *n.* book-box, letter-case.
scrī'pti/ō -ō'nis *f.* writing; composition; text.
scrī'ptit/ō -ā're -ā'vī -ā'tum *vt.* write regularly, compose.
scrī'pt/or -ō'ris *m.* writer, author; secretary. **rērum** — historian.
scrī'ptul/a -ō'rum *n.pl.* lines of a squared board.
scrī'pt/um -ī *n.* writing, book, work; (*law*) ordinance. **duōdecim** -a Twelve Lines, a game played on a squared board.
scrīptū'r/a -ae *f.* writing; composition; document; (*pol.*) tax on public pastures; (*will*) provision.
scrī'ptus *ppp.* scrībō.
scrī'pt/us -ūs *m.* clerkship.
scrī'pul/um -ī *n.* small weight, scruple. [grave.
scro'b/is -is *f.* ditch, trench;
scrō'f/a -ae *f.* breeding-sow.
scrōfipā'sc/us -ī *m.* pig-breeder.
scrū'peus *a.* stony, rough.
scrūpō'sus *a.* rocky, jagged.
scrūpulō'sus *a.* stony, rough; (*fig.*) precise. [lum.
scrū'pulum, *see* **scrīpu-**
scrū'pul/us -ī *m.* small sharp stone; (*fig.*) uneasiness, doubt, scruple.
scrū'p/us -ī *m.* sharp stone; (*fig.*) uneasiness.
scrū't/a -ō'rum *n.pl.* trash.
scrū't/or -ā'rī -ā'tus *vt.* search, probe into, examine; find out.
scu'lp/ō -ere -sī -tum *vt.* carve, engrave. [clogs.
sculpō'ne/ae -ā'rum *f.pl.*
scu'lptilis *a.* carved.
scu'lpt/or -ō'ris *m.* sculptor.
scu'lptus *ppp.* sculpō.
scu'rr/a -ae *m.* jester; dandy.
scurrī'lis *a.* jeering.
scurrī'lit/ās -ā'tis *f.* scurrility.
scu'rr/or -ā'rī *vi.* play the fool.
scūtā'l/e -is *n.* sling-strap.
scūtā'tus *a.* carrying a shield.
scute'll/a -ae *f.* bowl.
scu'tic/a -ae *f.* whip.
scu'tr/a -ae *f.* flat dish.
scu'tul/a -ae *f.* small dish.
scu'tul/a, **scy'tal/a** -ae *f.* wooden roller; secret letter.
scutulā't/a -ae *f.* a checked garment.
scū'tul/um -ī *n.* small shield.
scū't/um -ī *n.* shield.
Scy'll/a -ae *f.* dangerous rock or sea monster in the Straits of Messina. **-ae'us** *a.*
scy'mn/us -ī *m.* cub.
scy'ph/us -ī *m.* wine-cup.
Scy'r/os, **-us** -ī *f.* Aegean island near Euboea. **-ius**, **-ias** *a.*
scy'tala, *see* **scutula**.
Scy'th/a, **-ēs** -ae *m.* Scythian. **-ia** -iae *f.* Scythia, country N.E. of the Black Sea. **-icus** *a.* **-is** -idis *f.* Scythian woman.
sē, **sēsē** *pro.* himself, herself, itself, themselves; one another. **apud** — at home; in his senses. **inter** — mutually.
sē'b/um -ī *n.* tallow, suet, grease.
sēc/ē'dō -ē'dere -e'ssī -e'ssum *vi.* withdraw, retire; revolt, secede.
sēc/e'rnō -e'rnere -rē'vī -rē'tum *vt.* separate, set apart; dissociate; distinguish.
sēce'ssi/ō -ō'nis *f.* withdrawal; secession.
sēce'ss/us -ūs *m.* retirement, solitude; retreat, recess.
sēclū'/dō -dere -sī -sum *vt.* shut off, seclude; separate, remove. [remote.
sēclū'sus *ppp.* **sēclūdō**. *a.*
se'c/ō -ā're -uī -tum *vt.* cut; injure; divide; (*med.*) operate on; (*motion*) pass through; (*dispute*) decide.

sēcrē'ti/ō -ō'nis *f.* separation.
sēcrē'tō *ad.* apart, in private in secret.
sēcrē't/um -ī *n.* privacy, secrecy; retreat, remote place; secret, mystery.
sēcrē'tus *ppp.* sēcernō. *a.* separate; solitary, remote; secret, private.
se'ct/a -ae *f.* path; method, way of life; (*pol.*) party; (*philos.*) school.
sectā'rius *a.* leading.
sectā't/or -ō'ris *m.* follower, adherent.
se'ctilis *a.* cut; for cutting.
se'cti/ō -ō'nis *f.* auctioning of confiscated goods.
se'ct/or -ō'ris *m.* cutter; buyer at a public sale.
se'ct/or -ā'rī -ā'tus *vt.* follow regularly, attend; chase, hunt.
sectū'r/a -ae *f.* digging.
se'ctus *ppp.* secō.
sēcu'bit/us -ūs *m.* lying alone.
sē'cub/ō -ā're -uī *vi.* sleep by oneself; live alone.
se'cuī *perf.* secō.
sēcul-, *see* **saecul-**.
sē'cum with himself, etc.
secundā'n/ī -ō'rum *m.pl.* men of the second legion.
secundā'rius *a.* second-rate.
secu'ndō *ad.* secondly.
secu'nd/ō -ā're *vt.* favour, make prosper.
secu'ndum *pr.* (*place*) behind, along; (*time*) after; (*rank*) next to; (*agreement*) according to, in favour of. *ad.* behind.
secu'nd/us *a.* following, next, second; inferior; favourable, propitious, fortunate. *f.pl.* (*play*) subsidiary part; (*fig.*) second fiddle. *n.pl.* success, good fortune. -ō flūmine. downstream. rēs -ae prosperity, success.
secūri'cul/a -ae *f.* little axe.
secū'rifer -ī *a.* armed with an axe.
secū'riger -ī *a.* armed with an axe.
secū'r/is -is *f.* axe; (*fig.*) death-blow; (*pol.*) authority, supreme power.
sēcū'rit/ās -ā'tis *f.* freedom from anxiety, composure; negligence; safety, feeling of security.
sēcū'rus *a.* untroubled, unconcerned; carefree, cheerful; careless.
se'cus *n.*(*indecl.*) sex.
se'cus *ad.* otherwise, differently; badly. nōn — even so. sequius, sētius *comp.* otherwise. nihilō — none the less.
secū't/or -ō'ris *m.* pursuer.
sed *conj.* but; but also, but in fact.
sēdā'ti/ō -ō'nis *f.* calming.
sēdā't/us *ppp.* sēdō. *a.* calm, quiet, composed. -ē *ad.* calmly.
sē'decim *num.* sixteen.
sēdē'cul/a -ae *f.* low stool.
sedentā'rius *a.* sitting.
se'd/eō -ē're sē'dī se'ssum *vi.* sit; (*army*) be encamped, blockade; (*magistrates*) be in session; (*clothes*) suit, fit; (*places*) be low-lying; (*heavy things*) settle, subside; (*weapons*) stick fast; (*inactivity*) be idle; (*thought*) be firmly resolved.
sē'd/ēs -is *f.* seat, chair; abode, home; site, ground, foundation.
sē'dī *perf.* sedeō.
sedī'l/e -is *n.* seat, chair.
sēdi'ti/ō -ō'nis *f.* insurrection, mutiny.
sēditiō's/us *a.* mutinous, factious; quarrelsome; troubled. -ē *ad.* seditiously.
sē'd/ō -ā're -ā'vī -ā'tum *vt.* calm, allay, lull.
sēd/ū'cō -ū'cere -ū'xī -u'ctum *vt.* take away, withdraw; divide.
sēdu'cti/ō -ō'nis *f.* taking sides.
sēdu'ctus *ppp.* sēdūcō. *a.* remote.

sēdu'lit/ās -ā'tis *f.* earnestness, assiduity; officiousness.
sēdul/us *a.* busy, diligent, assiduous; officious. **-ō** *ad.* busily, diligently; purposely.
se'g/es -itis *f.* corn-field; crop.
Sege'st/a -ae *f.* town in N.W. Sicily. **-ā'nus** *a.*
segmentā'tus *a.* flounced.
segme'nt/um -ī *n.* brocade.
se'gnip/ēs -edis *a.* slow of foot.
se'gn/is *a.* slow, sluggish, lazy. **-e**, **-iter** *ad.* slowly, lazily.
segni'ti/a -ae, -ēs -em -ē *f.* slowness, sluggishness, sloth.
sē'greg/ō -ā're -ā'vī -ā'tum *vt.* separate, put apart; dissociate.
sēiugā'tus *a.* separated.
sē'iug/is -is *m.* chariot and six.
sēiū'nctim *ad.* separately.
sēiū'ncti/ō -ō'nis *f.* separation.
sēiū'nctus *ppp.* sēiungō.
sēiu'n/gō -gere sēiūnxī sēiūnctum separate, part.
sēlē'cti/ō -ō'nis *f.* choice.
sēlē'ctus *ppp.* sēligō.
Seleu'c/us -ī *m.* king of Syria.
sēlī'br/a -ae *f.* half-pound.
sē'l/igō -i'gere -ē'gī -ē'ctum *vt.* choose, select.
se'll/a -ae *f.* seat, chair, stool, sedan-chair. — cūrūlis chair of office for higher magistrates.
selliste'rni/a -ō'rum *n.pl* sacred banquets to goddesses.
se'llul/a -ae *f.* stool; sedan-chair.
sellulā'r/ius -ī & iī *m.* mechanic.
sēma'nimus, *see* **sēmianimis.**
se'mel *ad.* once; once for all; first; ever. — atque iterum again and again. — aut iterum once or twice.
Se'mel/ē -ēs *f.* mother of Bacchus. **-ē'ius** *a.*
sē'm/en -inis *n.* seed; (*plant*) seedling, slip; (*men*) race, child; (*physics*) particle; (*fig.*) origin, instigator.
sēme'ntifer -ī *a.* fruitful.
sēme'nt/is -is *f.* sowing, planting; young corn.
sēmentī'vus *a.* of seed-time.
sēme'rmis, *see* **sēmiermis.**
sēmē'stris *a.* half-yearly, for six months.
sēmē'sus *a.* half-eaten.
sē'met *pro.* self, selves.
sēmiadape'rtus *a.* half-open.
sēmia'nim/is, **-us** *a.* half-dead.
sēmiape'rtus *a.* half-open.
sē'mib/ōs -ovis *a.* half-ox.
sē'micap/er -rī *a.* half-goat.
sēmicremā'tus, **sēmi'cremus** *a.* half-burned.
sēmicubitā'lis *a.* half a cubit long.
sē'mideus *a.* half-divine. *m.* demigod.
sēmido'ctus *a.* half-taught.
sēmie'rm/is, **-us** *a.* half-armed.
sēmiē'sus *a.* half-eaten.
sēmifa'ctus *a.* half-finished.
sē'mifer -ī *a.* half-beast; half-savage.
sēmigermā'nus *a.* half-German.
sē'migravis *a.* half-overcome.
sē'migr/ō -ā're *vi.* go away.
sē'mihi/āns -a'ntis *a.* half-opened.
sē'mihom/ō -inis *m.* half-man, half-human.
sēmihō'r/a -ae *f.* half an hour.
sē'milacer -ī *a.* half-mangled.
sēmilau'tus *a.* half-washed.
sēmilī'ber -ī *a.* half-free.
sēmili'x/a -ae *m.* not much better than a camp-follower.
sēmimarī'nus *a.* half in the sea.
sē'mim/ās -aris *m.* hermaphrodite, *a.* castrated.
sēmimo'rtuus *a.* half-dead.
sēminā'r/ium -ī & iī *n.* nursery, seed-plot.
sēminā't/or -ō'ris *m.* originator.

sē'minecis *a.* half-dead.
sēmi'n/ium **-ī** & **iī** *n.* procreation; breed.
sē'min/ō **-ā're** *vt.* sow; produce; beget.
sēminū'dus *a.* half-naked; almost unarmed.
sēmipāgā'nus *a.* half-rustic.
sēmiplē'nus *a.* half-full, half-manned.
sēmiputā'tus *a.* half-pruned.
Semī'ram/is **-is** & **idis** *f.* queen of Assyria. **–ius** *a.*
sēmirā'sus *a.* half-shaven.
sēmiredu'ctus *a.* half turned back.
sēmirefe'ctus *a.* half-repaired.
sē'mirutus *a.* half-demolished, half in ruins.
sē'm/is **-i'ssis** *m.* (*coin*) half an as; (*interest*) ½ per cent per month, i.e. 6 per cent per annum; (*area*) half an acre.
sēmisepu'ltus *a.* half-buried.
sēmiso'mnus *a.* half-asleep.
sēmisupī'nus *a.* half lying back.
sē'mit/a **-ae** *f.* path, way.
sēmitā'lis *a.* of by-ways.
sēmitā'rius *a.* frequenting by-ways.
sēmiūst–, *see* **sēmūst–**.
sē'mivir **-ī** *a.* half-man; emasculated; unmanly.
sēmivī'vus *a.* half-dead.
sēmo'd/ius **-ī** & **iī** *m.* half a peck.
sēmō'tus *ppp.* **sēmoveō** *a.* remote; distinct.
sēm/o'veō **-ovē're** **-ō'vī** **-ō'tum** *vt.* put aside, separate.
se'mper *ad.* always, ever, every time.
sempite'rnus *a.* everlasting, life-long.
Semprō'n/ius **-ī** *m.* Roman family name, *esp.* the Gracchi. **–ius**, **–iā'nus** *a.*
sēmū'nci/a **-ae** *f.* half an ounce; a twenty-fourth.
sēmūnciā'rius *a.* (*interest*) at the rate of one twenty-fourth.
sēmūstulā'tus *a.* half-burned.
sēmū'stus *a.* half-burned.
senā'cul/um **-ī** *n.* open-air meeting-place of the Senate.
sēnāri'ol/us **-ī** *m.* little trimeter.
sēnā'r/ius **-ī** & **iī** *m.* (iambic) trimeter.
senā't/or **-ō'ris** *m.* senator.
senātō'rius *a.* senatorial, in the Senate.
senā't/us **-ūs** *m.* Senate; meeting of the Senate. **–ūsconsult/um** **-ī** *n.* decree of the Senate.
Se'nec/a **-ae** *m.* Stoic philosopher, tutor of Nero.
sene'ct/a **-ae** *f.* old age.
sene'ctus *a.* old, aged.
sene'ct/ūs **-ū'tis** *f.* old age; old men.
se'n/eō **-ē're** *vi.* be old.
sen/ē'scō **-ē'scere** **-uī** *vi.* grow old; (*fig.*) weaken, wane, pine away.
se'n/ex **-is** (*comp.* **-ior**) *a.* old (over 45). *m., f.* old man, old woman.
sē'n/ī **-ō'rum** *a.* six each, in sixes; six. **— dēnī** sixteen each.
senī'lis *a.* of an old person, senile.
sē'ni/ō **-ō'nis** *m.* number six on a dice.
se'nior *comp.* **senex.**
se'n/ium **-ī** & **iī** *n.* weakness of age, decline; affliction; peevishness.
Se'non/ēs **-um** *m.pl.* tribe of S. Gaul.
sē'nsī *perf.* **sentiō.**
sē'nsifer **-ī** *a.* sensory.
sē'nsilis *a.* having sensation.
sē'nsim *ad.* tentatively, gradually.
sē'nsus *ppp.* **sentiō.** *n.pl.* thoughts.
sē'ns/us **-ūs** *m.* (*body*) feeling, sensation, sense; (*intellect*) understanding, judgment, thought; (*emotion*) sentiment

attitude, frame of mind; (*language*) meaning, purport, sentence. **commūnis** — universal human feelings, human sympathy, social instinct.
sente'nti/a -ae *f.* opinion, judgment; purpose, will; (*law*) verdict, sentence; (*pol.*) vote, decision; (*language*) meaning, sentence, maxim, epigram. **meā -ā** in my opinion. **dē meā -ā** in accordance with my wishes. **ex meā -ā** to my liking. **ex animī meī -ā** to the best of my knowledge and belief. **in -am pedibus īre** support a motion.
sententi'ol/a -ae *f.* phrase.
sententiō's/us *a.* pithy. **-ē** *ad.* pointedly. [brake.
senticē't/um -ī *n.* thorn-
sentī'n/a -ae *f.* bilge-water; (*fig.*) dregs, scum.
se'nt/iō -ī're -sē'nsī sē'nsum *vt.* (*senses*) feel, see, perceive; (*circs.*) experience, undergo; (*mind*) observe, understand; (*opinion*) think, judge; (*law*) vote, decide.
se'nt/is -is *m.* thorn, brier.
sentī'sc/ō -ere *vt.* begin to perceive.
se'ntus *a.* thorny; untidy.
se'nuī *perf.* senēscō.
seo'rsum, **seo'rsus** *ad.* apart, differently.
sēparā'bilis *a.* separable.
sēparā'tim *ad.* apart, separately. [tion, severing.
sēparā'ti/ō -ō'nis *f.* separa-
sē'par/ō -ā're -ā'vī -ā'tum *vt.* part, separate, divide; distinguish. **-ā'tus** *a.* separate, different. **-ā'tius** *ad.* less closely.
sep/e'liō -elī're -elī'vī & e'liī -u'ltum *vt.* bury; (*fig.*) overwhelm, overcome.
sē'pi/a -ae *f.* cuttle-fish.
Sēpla'si/a -ae *f.* street in Capua where perfumes were sold.
sēp/ō'nō -ō'nere -o'suī -o'situm *vt.* put aside, pick out; reserve; banish; appropriate; separate.
sēpo'situs *ppp.* sēpōnō. *a.* remote; distinct, choice.
sē'pse *pro.* oneself.
se'ptem *num.* seven.
Septe'mb/er -ris *m.* September. *a.* of September.
septe'mdecim, *see* **septendecim.**
septe'mfluus *a.* with seven streams.
septemge'minus *a.* sevenfold. [fold.
septe'mpl/ex -icis *a.* seven-
septe'mtriō, *see* **septentriōnēs.**
septemvirā'lis *a.* of the septemviri. *m.pl.* the septemviri.
septemvirā't/us -ūs *m.* office of septemvir.
septe'mvir/ī -ō'rum *m.pl.* board of seven officials.
septēnā'r/ius -ī & iī *m.* verse of seven feet.
septe'ndecim *num.* seventeen.
septē'n/ī -ō'rum *a.* seven each, in sevens.
septentriōnā'lis *a.* northern. *n.pl.* northern regions.
septentri/ō'nēs -ō'num *m.pl.*, **-ō -ō'nis** *m.* Great Bear, Little Bear; north; north wind. [times.
se'pti/ēns, **-ēs** *ad.* seven
septimā'n/ī -ō'rum *m.pl.* men of the seventh legion.
se'ptim/us (**se'ptumus**) *a.* seventh. **-um** *ad.* for the seventh time. — **decimus** seventeenth.
septingentē'simus *a.* seven hundredth.
septinge'nt/ī -ō'rum *a.* seven hundred.
septuāgē'simus *a.* seventieth.
septuāgi'ntā *a.* seventy.

septue'nnis *a.* seven years old.
se'pt/ūnx -ū'ncis *m.* seven ounces, seven-twelfths.
sepulcrā'lis *a.* funeral.
sepulcrē't/um -ī *n.* cemetery.
sepu'lcr/um -ī *n.* grave, tomb. [funeral.
sepultū'r/a -ae *f.* burial,
sepu'ltus *ppp.* sepeliō.
Sequā'n/a -ae *f.* river Seine. **-ī** -ō'rum *m.pl.* people of N. Gaul.
se'qu/āx -ā'cis *a.* pursuing, following.
se'qu/ēns -e'ntis *pres.p.* sequor. *a.* following, next.
seque'st/er -rī & ris *m.* trustee; agent, mediator. **-rum** -rī *n.* deposit.
sēquius *comp.* secus.
se'/quor -quī -cū'tus *vt.* & *i.* follow; accompany, go with; (*time*) come after, come next, ensue; (*enemy*) pursue; (*objective*) make for, aim at; (*pulling*) come away easily; (*share, gift*) go to, come to; (*words*) come naturally.
se'r/a -ae *f.* door-bolt, bar.
Serā'p/is -is & idis *m.* chief Egyptian god. **-ē'um** -ē'ī *n.* temple of Serapis.
serē'nit/ās -ā'tis *f.* fair weather. [brighten up.
serē'n/ō -ā're *vt.* clear up,
serē'nus *a.* fair, clear; (*wind*) fair-weather; (*fig.*) cheerful, happy. *n.* clear sky, fair weather.
Sē'r/es -um *m.pl.* Chinese. **-icus** *a.* Chinese; silk.
serē'sc/ō -ere *vi.* dry off.
sē'ri/a -ae *f.* tall jar.
sē'ric/a -ō'rum *n.pl.* silks.
se'ri/ēs -em -ē *f.* row, sequence, succession.
sēri'ol/a -ae *f.* small jar.
Serī'ph/us (-os) -ī *f.* Aegean island. **-ius** *a.*
sē'ri/us *a.* earnest, serious. **-ō** *ad.* in earnest, seriously.
sē'rius *comp.* sērō.
se'rm/ō -ō'nis *m.* conversation, talk; learned discussion, discourse; common talk, rumour; language, style; every day language, prose; (*pl.*) Satires (of Horace).
sermō'cin/or -ā'rī *vi*; converse. [rumour.
sermu'ncul/us -ī *m.* gossip,
se'r/ō -ere sē'vī sa'tum *vt.* sow, plant; (*fig.*) produce, sow the seeds of.
se'r/ō -ere -tum *vt.* sew, join, wreathe; (*fig.*) compose, devise, engage in.
sē'r/ō (*comp.* **-ius**) *ad.* late; too late.
se'rp/ēns -e'ntis *m., f.* snake, serpent; (*constellation*) Draco.
serpenti'gen/a -ae *m.* offspring of a serpent.
serpe'ntip/ēs -edis *a.* serpent-footed. [splints.
serpera'str/a -ō'rum *n.pl.*
se'rp/ō -ere -sī -tum *vi.* creep, crawl; (*fig.*) spread slowly.
serpy'll/um -ī *n.* wild thyme.
se'rr/a -ae *f.* saw.
serrā'cum, *see* **sarrācum.**
serrā'tus *a.* serrated, notched.
se'rrul/a -ae *f.* small saw.
Sertō'r/ius -ī *m.* commander under Marius, who held out against Sulla in Spain. **-iā'nus** *a.* [garlands.
se'rtus *ppp.* serō. *n.pl.*
se'r/um -ī *n.* whey, serum.
sē'r/us *a.* late; too late. **-ā** nocte late at night. **-um** **-ī** *n.* late hour.
se'rv/a -ae *f.* maid-servant, slave. [saved.
servā'bilis *a.* that cannot be
servā't/or -ō'ris *m.* deliverer; watcher.
servā'tr/īx -ī'cis *f.* deliverer.
servī'li/s *a.* of slaves, servile. **-ter** *ad.* slavishly.
Servī'l/ius -ī *m.* Roman family name of many consuls. **-ius**, **-ā'nus** *a.*

se'rv/iō -ī're -ī'vī & iī -ī'tum *vi.* be a slave; (*with dat.*) serve, be of use to, be good for; (*property*) be mortgaged.
servi't/ium -ī & iī *n.* slavery, servitude; slaves.
servitū'd/ō -inis *f.* slavery.
se'rvit/ūs -ū'tis *f.* slavery, service; slaves; (*property*) liability.
Se'rv/ius -ī *m.* sixth king of Rome; famous jurist of Cicero's day.
se'rv/ō -ā're -ā'vī -ā'tum *vt.* save, rescue; keep, preserve, retain; store, reserve; watch, observe, guard; (*place*) remain in.
se'rvul/a -ae *f.* servant-girl.
se'rvul/us (se'rvolus) -ī *m.* young slave.
se'rv/us (se'rvos) -ī *m.* slave, servant. *a.* slavish, serving; (*property*) liable to a burden.
sescēnā'ris *a.* a year and a half old.
sescē'n/ī -ō'rum *a.* six hundred each.
sescentē'simus *a.* six hundredth.
sesce'nt/ī -ō'rum *num.* six hundred; an indefinitely large number.
sesce'nti/ēns, -ēs *ad.* six hundred times.
sē'sē, *see* **sē**.
se'sel/is -is *f.* (*plant*) seseli.
se'squi *ad.* one and a half times.
sesquia'lter -ī *a.* one and [a half.
sesquimo'd/ius -ī & iī *m.* a peck and a half.
sesquioctā'vus *a.* of nine to eight.
se'squiop/us -eris *n.* a day and a half's work.
sesquipedā'lis *a.* a foot and a half.
se'squip/ēs -edis *m.* a foot and a half.
sesquiplā'g/a -ae *f.* a blow and a half.
se'squipl/ex -icis *a.* one and a half times. [three.
sesquite'rtius *a.* of four to
se'ssilis *a.* for sitting on.
se'ssi/ō -ō'nis *f.* sitting; seat; session; loitering.
se'ssit/ō -ā're -ā'vī *vi.* sit regularly.
sessiu'ncul/a -ae *f.* small meeting.
se'ss/or -ō'ris *m.* spectator; resident.
sēste'rt/ius -ī & iī *m.* sesterce, a silver coin. **-ium -ī** *n.* 1000 sesterces. **dēna -ia** 10,000 sesterces. **centēna mīlia -ium** 100,000 sesterces. **deciēns -ium** 1,000,000 sesterces.
Se'st/ius -ī *m.* tribune defended by Cicero. **-ius, -iā'nus** *a.* of a Sestius.
Se'st/os (-us) -ī *f.* town on Dardanelles, home of Hero. **-us** *a.*
sēt-, *see* **saet-**.
Sētia -iae *f.* town in S. Latium, famous for wine. **-ī'nus** *a.*
sē'tius *comp.* **secus.**
seu, *see* **sīve**.
sevē'rit/ās -ā'tis *f.* strictness, austerity.
sevē'r/us *a.* strict, stern; severe, austere; grim, terrible. **-ē** *ad.* sternly, severely.
sē'vī *perf.* **serō.**
sē'voc/ō -ā're *vt.* call aside; withdraw, remove.
sē'vum, *see* **sēbum**.
sex *num.* six. [old.
sexāgēnā'rius *a.* sixty years
sexāgē'n/ī -ō'rum *a.* sixty each.
sexāgē'simus *a.* sixtieth.
sexā'gi/ēns, -ēs *ad.* sixty times.
sexāgi'ntā *num.* sixty.
sexa'ngulus *a.* hexagonal.
sexcēnā'rius *a.* of six hundred.
sexcēn-, *see* **sescēn-**.

sexe'nnis *a.* six years old, after six years.
sexe'nn/ium -ī & **iī** *n.* six years.
se'xi/ēns, –ēs *ad.* six times.
sexprī'm/ī -ō'rum *m.pl.* a provincial town, council.
sextadecimā'n/ī -ō'rum *m. pl.* men of the sixteenth legion.
se'xt/āns -a'ntis *m.* a sixth; (*coin, weight*) a sixth of an as.
sextā'r/ius -ī & **iī** *m.* pint.
Sextī'l/is -is *m.* August. *a.* of August.
se'xtul/a -ae *f.* a sixth of an ounce.
se'xt/us *a.* sixth. **–um** *ad.* for the sixth time. — **decimus** sixteenth.
se'x/us -ūs *m.* sex.
sī *conj.* if; if only; to see if. **sī forte** in the hope that. **sī iam** assuming for the moment. **sī minus** if not. **sī quandō** whenever. **sī quidem** if indeed; since. **sī quis** if anyone, whoever. **mīrum sī** surprising that. **quod sī** and if, but if.
sī'bil/ō -ā're *vi.* hiss, whistle. *vt.* hiss at.
sī'bil/us -ī *m.*, **–a -ō'rum** *n.pl.* whistle, hissing.
sī'bilus *a.* hissing.
Siby'll/a (Sibu'lla) -ae *f.* prophetess, Sibyl. **–ī'nus** *a.*
sīc *ad.* so, thus, this way, as follows; as one is, as things are; on this condition; yes.
sī'c/a -ae *f.* dagger.
Sicā'n/ī -ō'rum *m.pl.* ancient people of Italy, later of Sicily. **–us, –ius** *a.* Sicanian, Sicilian. **–ia -iae** *f.* Sicily.
sīcā'r/ius -ī & **iī** *m.* assassin, murderer.
si'ccit/ās -ā'tis *f.* dryness, drought; (*body*) firmness; (*style*) dullness.
si'cc/ō -ā're -ā'vī -ā'tum *vt.* dry; drain, exhaust; (*sore*) heal up.
sicco'culus *a.* dry-eyed.
si'cc/us *a.* dry; thirsty, sober; (*body*) firm, healthy; (*argument*) solid, sound; (*style*) flat, dull. *n.* dry land. **–ē** *ad.* (*speech*) firmly.
Sici'li/a -ae *f.* Sicily. **–ē'nsis, –s -dis** *a.* Sicilian.
sicili'cul/a -ae *f.* little sickle.
sī'cine is this how?
sī'cubi *ad.* if anywhere, wheresoever.
Si'culus *a.* Sicilian.
sī'cunde *ad.* if from anywhere.
sī'cut, sī'cutī *ad.* just as, as in fact; (*comparison*) like, as; (*example*) as for instance; (*with subj.*) as if.
Si'cy/ōn -ō'nis *f.* town in N. Peloponnese. **–ō'nius** *a.*
sīde'reus *a.* starry; (*fig.*) radiant.
Sidicī'n/ī -ō'rum *m.pl.* people of Campania. **–us** *a.*
sī'd/ō -ere -ī *vi.* sit down, settle; sink, subside; stick fast.
Sī'd/ōn -ōnis *f.* famous Phoenician town. **–ō'nius** *a.* Sidonian, Phoenician. **–ōnis -ō'nidis** *a.* Phoenician. *f.* Europa; Dido.
sī'd/us -eris *n.* constellation; heavenly body, star; season, climate, weather; destiny; (*pl.*) sky; (*fig.*) fame, glory.
si'em *archaic subj.* sum.
Siga'mbrī, *see* **Sugambri.**
Sīgē'/um -ī *n.* promontory near Troy. **–us, –ius** *a.* Sigean.
sigi'll/a -ō'rum *n.pl.* little figures; seal.
sigillā'tus *a.* decorated with little figures.
signā't/or -ō'ris *m.* witness (to a document).
si'gnifer -ī *a.* with constellations. — **orbis** Zodiac. *m.* (*mil.*) standard-bearer.
significa'nter *ad.* pointedly, tellingly.
significā'tī/ō -ō'nis *f.* indication, signal, token; sign of

approval; (*rhet.*) emphasis; (*word*) meaning.
signi'fic/ō -ā're -ā'vī -ā'tum *vt.* indicate, show; betoken, portend; (*word*) mean.
si'gn/ō -ā're -ā'vī -ā'tum *vt.* mark, stamp, print; (*document*) seal; (*money*) coin, mint; (*fig.*) impress, designate, note.
si'gn/um -ī *n.* mark, sign, token; (*mil.*) standard; signal, password; (*art*) design, statue; (*document*) seal; (*astr.*) constellation. **-a cōnferre** join battle. **-a cōnstituere** halt. **-a convertere** wheel about. **-a ferre** move camp; attack. **-a īnferre** attack. **-a prōferre** advance. **-a sequī** march in order. **ab -īs discēdere** leave the ranks. **sub -īs īre** march in order.
Sī'l/a -ae *f.* forest in extreme S. Italy.
sīlā'n/us -ī *m.* fountain, jet of water.
si'l/ēns -e'ntis *pres.p.* sileō. *a.* still, silent. *m.pl.* the dead.
sile'nt/ium -ī & iī *n.* stillness, silence; (*fig.*) standstill, inaction.
Sīlē'n/us -ī *m.* old and drunken companion of Bacchus.
si'l/eō -ē're -uī *vi.* be still, be silent; cease. *vt.* say nothing about.
si'ler -is *n.* willow.
silē'sc/ō -ere *vi.* calm down, fall silent.
si'l/ex -icis *m.* flint, hard stone; rock.
silice'rn/ium -ī & iī *n.* funeral feast.
silī'g/ō -inis *f.* winter-wheat; fine flour. [(*pl.*) pulse.
si'liqu/a -ae *f.* pod, husk;
si'llyb/us -ī *m.* label bearing a book's title.
Si'lur/ēs -um *m.pl.* British tribe in S. Wales.
silū'r/us -ī *m.* sheat-fish.
sī'lus *a.* snub-nosed.
si'lv/a -ae *f.* wood, forest; plantation, shrubbery; (*plant*) flowering stem; (*lit.*) material.
Silvā'n/us -ī *m.* god of uncultivated land. [wood.
silvē'sc/ō -ere *vi.* run to
silve'stris *a.* wooded, forest-; wild; pastoral.
silvi'col/a -ae *m., f.* sylvan.
silvicu'ltr/īx -ī'cis *a.* living in the woods.
silvi'fragus *a.* tree-breaking.
silvō'sus *a.* woody.
sī'mi/a -ae *f.* ape.
si'mil/is *a.* like, similar. **— atque** like what. **vērī —** probable. **-e -is** *n.* comparison, parallel. **-iter** *ad.* similarly.
similitū'd/ō -inis *f.* likeness, resemblance; imitation; analogy; monotony; (*rhet.*) simile.
sīmi'ol/us -ī *m.* monkey.
simī'tu *ad.* at the same time, together.
sī'm/ius -ī & iī *m.* ape.
Si'mo/īs -e'ntis *m.* river of Troy.
Simō'nid/ēs -is *m.* Greek lyric poet of Ceos, famous for dirges. **-ē'us** *a.*
si'mpl/ex -icis *a.* single, simple; natural, straightforward; (*character*) frank, sincere. **-i'citer** *ad.* simply, naturally; frankly.
simpli'cit/ās -ā'tis *f.* singleness; frankness, innocence.
si'mpl/um -ī *n.* simple sum.
si'mpul/um -ī *n.* small ladle. **excitāre fluctūs in -ō** *raise a storm in a tea-cup.*
simpu'v/ium -ī & iī *n.* libation-bowl.
si'mul *ad.* at the same time, together, at once; likewise, also; both . . . and. **— ac atque, ut** as soon as. *conj.* as soon as.
simulā'cr/um -ī *n.* likeness, image, portrait, statue; phan-

tom, ghost; (*writing*) symbol; (*fig.*) semblance, shadow.
simulā'm/en -inis *n.* copy.
si'mul/āns -a'ntis *pres.p.* simulō. *a.* imitative.
simulā'tē *ad.* deceitfully.
simulā'ti/ō -ō'nis *f.* pretence, shamming, hypocrisy.
simulā't/or -ō'ris *m.* imitator; pretender, hypocrite.
simula'tque *conj.* as soon as.
si'mul/ō -ā're -ā'vī -ā'tum *vt.* imitate, represent; impersonate; pretend, counterfeit.
simu'lt/ās -ā'tis *f.* feud, quarrel.
sī'mulus *a.* snub-nosed.
sī'mus *a.* snub-nosed.
sīn *conj.* but if. — **aliter, minus** but if not.
sinā'p/i -is *n.*, **-is** -is *f.* mustard.
sincē'rit/ās -ā'tis *f.* integrity.
sincē'r/us *a.* clean, whole, genuine; (*fig.*) pure, sound, honest. **-ē** *ad.* honestly.
sincipitāme'nt/um -ī *n.* half a head.
si'ncip/ut -itis *n.* half a head; brain. [-less.
si'ne *pr.* (*with abl.*) without,
singillā'tim *ad.* singly, one by one.
singulā'r/is *a.* one at a time, single, sole; unique, extraordinary. **-iter** *ad.* separately; extremely.
singulā'rius *a.* single.
si'ngul/ī -ō'rum *a.* one each, single, one.
singu'ltim *ad.* in sobs.
singu'lt/ō -ā're *vi.* sob, gasp, gurgle. *vt.* gasp out.
singu'lt/us -ūs *m.* sob, gasp, death-rattle.
si'ngulus, *see* **singulī**.
sini'st/er -rī *a.* left; (*fig.*) perverse, unfavourable; (*Roman auspices*) lucky; (*Greek auspices*) unlucky. **-ra -rae** *f.* left hand, left-hand side. **-rē** *ad.* badly.
sinistrō'rs/us, -um *ad.* to the left.
si'n/ō -ere sī'vī si'tum *vt.* let, allow; let be. nē dī sirint God forbid!
Sinō'p/ē -ēs *f.* Greek colony on the Black Sea. **-ē'nsis, -eus** *a.*
Sinue'ss/a -ae *f.* town on the borders of Latium and Campania. **-ā'nus** *a.*
sī'num, *see* **sīnus**.
si'nu/ō -ā're -ā'vī -ā'tum *vt.* wind, curve.
sinuō'sus *a.* winding, curved.
si'n/us -ūs *m.* curve, fold; (*fishing*) net; (*geog.*) bay, gulf, valley; (*hair*) curl; (*ship*) sail; (*toga*) fold, pocket, purse; (*person*) bosom; (*fig.*) protection, love, heart, hiding-place. in -ū gaudēre be secretly glad.
sī'n/us -ī *m.* large cup.
sīpa'r/ium -ī & iī *n.* act-curtain.
sī'ph/ō -ō'nis *m.* siphon; fire-engine.
sīqua'ndō *ad.* if ever.
si'quidem *ad.* if in fact. *conj.* since.
sī'quī, sī'quis *pro.* if any, if anyone, whoever.
sire'mpse *a.* the same.
Sī'r/ēn -ē'nis *f.* Siren.
sī'ris, sī'rit *perf. subj.* sinō.
Sī'r/ius -ī *m.* Dog-star. *a.* of Sirius.
si'rp/e -is *n.* silphium.
sī'r/us -ī *m.* corn-pit.
sīs (*for* sī vīs) *ad.* please.
si'st/ō -ere sti'tī sta'tum *vt.* place, set, plant; (*law*) produce in court; (*monument*) set up; (*movement*) stop, arrest, check. *vi.* stand, rest; (*law*) appear in court; (*movement*) stand still, stop, stand firm. sē — appear, present oneself. **tūtum** — see safe. **vadimōnium** — duly appear in court. **-ī nōn potest** the situation is desperate.

si'str/um -ī *n.* Egyptian rattle, cymbal.
sisy'mbr/ium -ī & iī *n.* fragrant herb, *perh.* mint.
Sī'syph/us -ī *m.* criminal condemned in Hades to roll a rock repeatedly up a hill. **-ius** *a.* **-idēs** -idae *m.* Ulysses.
site'll/a -ae *f.* lottery urn.
Sītho'n/ius *a.* Thracian. **-is** -idis *a.* Thracian.
sitīculō'sus *a.* thirsty, dry.
si'ti/ēns -e'ntis *pres.p.* sitiō. *a.* thirsty, dry; parching; (*fig.*) eager. **-e'nter** *ad.* eagerly.
si't/iō -ī're *vi.* be thirsty; be parched. *vt.* thirst for, covet.
si't/is -is *f.* thirst; drought.
si'ttybus, *see* **sillybus.**
si'tul/a -ae *f.* bucket.
si'tus *ppp.* sinō. *a.* situated, lying; founded; (*fig.*) dependent.
si't/us -ūs *m.* situation, site; structure; neglect, squalor, mould; (*mind*) dullness.
sī've, seu *conj.* or if; or; whether . . . or.
sīvī *perf.* sinō.
smara'gd/us -ī *m., f.* emerald.
smī'l/ax -acis *f.* bind-weed.
Smi'nth/eus -eī *m.* Apollo.
Smy'rn/a -ae *f.* Ionian town in Asia Minor. **-ae'us** *a.*
sobol-, *see* **subol-.**
sobrī'n/us -ī *m.*, **-a** -ae *f.* cousin (on the mother's side).
so'bri/us *a.* sober; temperate, moderate; (*mind*) sane, sensible. **-ē** *ad* temperately: sensibly.
so'cc/us -ī *m.* slipper, *esp.* the sock worn by actors in comedy; comedy.
so'cer -ī *m.* father-in-law.
sociā'bilis *a.* compatible.
sociā'l/is *a.* of allies, confederate; conjugal. **-iter** *ad.* sociably.
socie'nn/us *m.* -ī friend.
soci'et/ās -ā'tis *f.* fellowship, association; alliance.
so'ci/ō -ā're -ā'vī -ā'tum *vt.* unite, associate, share.
sociofrau'd/us -ī *m.* deceiver of friends.
so'cius *a.* associated, allied. *m.* friend, companion; partner, ally. [apathy; folly.
sōco'rdi/a -ae *f.* indolence,
sō'cor/s -dis *a.* lazy, apathetic; stupid. **-dius** *ad.* more carelessly, lazily.
Sō'crat/ēs -is *m.* famous Athenian philosopher. **-icus** *a.* of Socrates, Socratic. *m.pl.* the followers of Socrates.
so'cr/us -ūs *f.* mother-in-law.
sodālic/ium -ī & iī *n.* fellowship; secret society.
sodāli'cius *a.* of fellowship.
sodā'l/is -is *m., f.* companion, friend; member of a society, accomplice.
sodā'lit/ās -ā'tis *f.* companionship, friendship; society, club; secret society.
sodāli'tius, *see* **sodālicius.**
sō'dēs *ad.* please.
sōl sō'lis *m.* sun; sunlight, sun's heat; (*poetry*) day; (*myth*) Sun-god. — **oriēns**, -is **ortus** east. — **occidēns**, -is **occāsus** west. [of comfort.
sōlāci'ol/um -ī *n.* a grain
sōlā'c/ium -ī & iī *n.* comfort, consolation, relief.
sōlā'm/en -inis *n.* solace, relief.
sōlā'ris *a.* of the sun.
sōlā'r/ium -ī & iī *n.* sundial; clock; balcony, terrace.
sōlā'tium, *see* **sōlācium.**
sōlā't/or -ō'ris *m.* consoler.
soldū'ri/ī -ō'rum *m.pl.* retainers.
so'ldus, *see* **solidus.**
so'le/a -ae *f.* sandal, shoe; fetter; (*fish*) sole.
soleā'r/ius -ī & iī *m.* sandal-maker.
soleā'tus *a.* wearing sandals

so'l/eō -ē're -itus *vi.* be accustomed, be in the habit, usually do. ut — as usual.
soli'dit/ās -ā'tis *f.* solidity.
so'lid/ō -ā're *vt.* make firm, strengthen.
so'lid/us *a.* solid, firm, dense; whole, complete; (*fig.*) sound, genuine, substantial. *n.* solid matter, firm ground. **-ē** *ad.* for certain.
sōlife'rre/um -ī *n.* an all-iron javelin.
sōli'stimus *a.* (*aug.*) most favourable.
sōlitā'rius *a.* solitary, lonely.
sōlitū'd/ō -inis *f.* solitariness, loneliness; destitution; (*place*) desert.
so'lit/us *ppa.* soleō. *a.* usual, customary. *n.* custom. plūs -ō more than usual.
so'l/ium -ī & iī *n.* seat, throne; tub; (*fig.*) rule.
sōli'vagus *a.* going by oneself; single.
solle'mn/is *a.* annual, regular; religious, solemn; usual, ordinary. **-e** -is *n.* religious rite, festival; usage practice. **-iter** *ad.* solemnly.
so'ller/s -tis *a.* skilled, clever, expert; ingenious. **-ter** *ad.* cleverly. [genuity.
solle'rti/a -ae *f.* skill, in-
sollicitā'ti/ō -ō'nis *f.* inciting.
solli'cit/ō -ā're -ā'vī -ā'tum *vt.* stir up, disturb; trouble, distress, molest; rouse, urge, incite, tempt, tamper with.
sollicitū'd/ō -inis *f.* uneasiness, anxiety.
solli'citus *a.* agitated, disturbed; (*mind*) troubled, worried, alarmed; (*things*) anxious, careful; (*cause*) disquieting.
sollife'rreum, *see* **sōliferreum.** [mus.
solli'stimus, *see* **sōlisti-**
solocci'sm/us -ī *m.* grammatical mistake.

So'l/ōn -ō'nis *m.* famous Athenian law-giver.
sō'l/or -ā'rī -ā'tus *vt.* comfort, console; relieve, ease.
sōlstitiā'lis *a.* of the summer solstice; midsummer.
sōlsti't/ium -ī & iī *n.* summer solstice; midsummer, summer heat.
so'l/um -ī *n.* ground, floor, bottom; soil, land, country; (*foot*) sole; (*fig.*) basis. **-ō** aequāre raze to the ground.
sō'lum *ad.* only, merely.
sō'l/us (*gen.* -ī'us *dat.* -ī) *a.* only alone; lonely, forsaken; (*place*) lonely, deserted.
solū'ti/ō -ō'nis *f.* loosening; payment.
solū't/us *ppp.* solvō. *a.* loose, free; (*from distraction*) at ease, at leisure, merry; (*from obligation*) exempt; (*from restraint*) free, independent, unprejudiced; (*moral*) lax, weak, insolent; (*language*) prose, unrhythmical; (*speaker*) fluent. ōrātiō -a, verba -a prose. **-ē** *ad.* loosely, freely, carelessly, weakly, fluently.
so'l/vō -vere -vī -ū'tum *vt.* loosen, undo; free, release, acquit, exempt; dissolve, break up, separate; relax, slacken, weaken; cancel, remove, destroy; solve, explain; pay, fulfil; (*argument*) refute; (*discipline*) undermine; (*feelings*) get rid of; (*hair*) let down; (*letter*) open; (*sail*) unfurl; (*siege*) raise; (*troops*) dismiss. *vi.* set sail; pay. nāvem — set sail. poenās — be punished. praesēns — pay cash. rem — pay. sacrāmentō — discharge. -vendō esse be solvent.
So'lym/a -ō'rum *n.pl.* Jerusalem. **-us** *a.* of the Jews.
somniculō's/us *a.* sleepy. **-ē** *ad.* sleepily.
so'mnifer -ī *a.* soporific; fatal.

so'mni/ō -ā're *vt.* dream, dream about; talk nonsense.
so'mn/ium -ī & iī *n.* dream; nonsense, fancy.
so'mn/us -ī *m.* sleep; sloth.
sonā'bilis *a.* noisy.
so'nip/ēs -edis *m.* steed.
so'nit/us -ūs *m.* sound, noise.
soni'vius *a.* noisy.
so'n/ō -ā're -uī -itum *vi.* sound, make a noise. *vt.* utter, speak, celebrate; sound like.
so'n/or -ō'ris *m.* sound, noise.
sonō'rus *a.* noisy, loud.
sōns so'ntis *a* guilty.
so'nticus *a.* critical; important. [(*fig.*) tone.
so'n/us -ī *m.* sound, noise;
sophi'st/ēs -ae *m.* sophist.
So'phocl/ēs -is *m.* famous Greek tragic poet. **-ē'us** *a.* of Sophocles, Sophoclean.
so'phus *a.* wise.
sō'p/iō -ī're -ī'vī -ī'tum *vt.* put to sleep; (*fig.*) calm, lull.
so'p/or -ō'ris *m.* sleep; apathy.
sopō'rifer -ī *a.* soporific, drowsy.
sopō'r/ō -ā're *vt.* lull to sleep; make soporific.
sopō'rus *a.* drowsy.
Sōra'ct/e -is *n.* mountain in S. Etruria.
so'rb/eō -ē're -uī *vt.* suck, swallow; (*fig.*) endure.
sorbi'll/ō -ā're *vt.* sip.
sorbi'ti/ō -ō'nis *f.* drink, broth.
so'rb/um -ī *n.* service-berry.
so'rb/us -ī *f.* service-tree.
so'rd/eō -ē're *vi.* be dirty, be sordid; seem shabby, be of no account.
so'rd/ēs -is *f.* dirt, squalor, shabbiness; mourning; meanness, vulgarity; (*people*) rabble.
sordē'sc/ō -ere *vi.* become dirty.
sordidā'tus *a.* shabbily dressed, in mourning.
sordi'dulus *a.* soiled, shabby.
so'rdid/us *a.* dirty, squalid, shabby; in mourning; poor, mean; base, vile. **-ē** *ad.* meanly, vulgarly.
sō'r/ex -icis *m.* shrew-mouse.
sōricī'nus *a.* of the shrew-mouse. [syllogism.
sōrī't/ēs -ae *m.* chain
so'r/or -ō'ris *f.* sister.
sorōricī'd/a -ae *m.* murderer of a sister.
sorō'rius *a.* of a sister.
sors so'rtis *f.* lot; allotted duty; oracle, prophecy; fate, fortune, (*money*) capital, principal.
sō'rsum, *see* **seōrsum**.
sorti'legus *a.* prophetic. *m.* soothsayer.
so'rt/ior -ī'rī -ī'tus *vi.* draw or cast lots. *vt.* draw lots for, allot, obtain by lot; distribute, share; choose; receive.
sortī'ti/ō -ō'nis *f.* drawing lots, choosing by lot.
sortī't/us *ppa.* sortior. *a.* assigned, allotted. -ō by lot.
sortī't/us -ūs *m.* drawing lots.
So's/ius -ī *m.* Roman family name, *esp.* two brothers Sosii, famous booksellers in Rome.
sō'sp/es -itis *a.* safe and sound, unhurt; favourable, lucky.
sō'spit/a -ae *f.* saviour.
sōspitā'lis *a.* beneficial.
sō'spit/ō -ā're *vt.* preserve, prosper.
sō't/ēr -ē'ris *m.* saviour.
spā'd/īx -ī'cis *a.* chestnut-brown.
spa'd/ō -ō'nis *m.* eunuch.
spa'r/gō -gere -sī -sum *vt.* throw, scatter, sprinkle; strew, spot, moisten; disperse, spread abroad. [freckled.
spa'rsus *ppp.* **spargō**. *a.*
Spa'rt/a -ae, **-ē** **-ēs** *f.* famous Greek city. **-ā'nus**, **-icus** *a.* Spartan. **-iā'tēs** -iā'tae *m.* Spartan.
Spa'rtac/us -ī *m.* gladiator who led a revolt against Rome

spa'rt/um -ī *n.* Spanish broom.
spa'rul/us -ī *m.* bream.
spa'r/us -ī *m.* hunting-spear.
spa'th/a -ae *f.* broadsword.
spa'ti/or -ā'rī -ā'tus *vi.* walk; spread.
spatiō's/us *a.* roomy, ample, large; (*time*) prolonged. **-ē** *ad.* greatly; after a time.
spa't/ium -ī & iī *n.* space, room, extent; (*between points*) distance; (*open space*) square, walk, promenade; (*race*) lap, track, course; (*time*) period, interval; (*opportunity*) time, leisure; (*measure*) quantity.
spe'ci/ēs -ē'ī *f.* seeing, sight; appearance, form, outline; (*thing seen*) sight; (*mind*) idea; (*in sleep*) vision, apparition; (*fair show*) beauty, splendour; (*false show*) pretence, pretext; (*classification*) species. in -em for the sake of appearances; like. per -em under the pretence. sub -ē under the cloak.
speci'll/um -ī *n.* probe.
spe'cim/en -inis *n.* sign, evidence, proof; pattern, ideal.
speciō's/us *a.* showy, beautiful; specious, plausible. **-ē** *ad.* handsomely.
spectā'bilis *a.* visible; notable, remarkable.
spectā'cul/um (**spectā'clum**) -ī *n.* sight, spectacle; public show, play; theatre, seats.
spectā'm/en -inis *n.* proof.
spectā'ti/ō -ō'nis *f.* looking; testing.
spectā't/or -ō'ris *m.* onlooker, observer, spectator; critic.
spectā'tr/īx -ī'cis *f.* observer.
spectā'tus *ppp.* spectō. *a.* tried, proved; worthy, excellent.
spe'cti/ō -ō'nis *f.* the right to take auspices.
spe'ct/ō -ā're -ā'vī -ā'tum *vt.* look at, observe, watch; (*place*) face; (*aim*) look to, bear in mind, contemplate, tend towards; (*judging*) examine, test.
spe'ctr/um -ī *n.* spectre.
spe'cul/a -ae *f.* watch-tower, look-out; height.
spē'cul/a -ae *f.* slight hope.
speculābu'ndus *a.* on the look-out. [*n.pl.* window.
speculā'ris *a.* transparent.
speculā't/or -ō'ris *m.* explorer, investigator; (*mil.*) spy, scout.
speculātō'rius *a.* for spying, scouting. *f.* spy-boat.
speculā'tr/īx -ī'cis *f.* watcher.
spe'cul/or -ā'rī -ā'tus *vt.* spy out, watch for, observe.
spe'cul/um -ī *n.* mirror.
spe'c/us -ūs *m., n.* cave; hollow, chasm.
spēlae'/um -ī *n.* cave, den.
spēlu'nc/a -ae *f.* cave, den.
spērā'bilis *a.* to be hoped for.
Sperchē'/us (-os) -ī *m.* river in Thessaly. **-is** -idis *a.*
spe'rn/ō -ere sprē'vī sprē'tum *vt.* remove, reject, scorn.
spē'r/ō -ā're -ā'vī -ā'tum *vt.* hope, hope for, expect; trust; look forward to. **-ā'ta** -ā'tae *f.* bride.
spēs spe'ī *f.* hope, expectation. praeter spem unexpectedly. spē dēiectus disappointed.
Speusi'pp/us -ī *m.* successor of Plato in the Academy.
sphae'r/a -ae *f.* ball, globe, sphere.
Sph/inx -i'ngis *f.* fabulous monster near Thebes.
spī'c/a -ae *f.* (*grain*) ear; (*plant*) tuft; (*astr.*) brightest star in Virgo.
spī'ceus *a.* of ears of corn.
spī'cul/um -ī *n.* point, sting; dart, arrow.
spī'n/a -ae *f.* thorn; prickle, fish-bone; spine, back; (*pl.*) difficulties, subtleties.

spīnē'tum -ī *n.* thorn-hedge.
spī'neus *a.* of thorns.
spī'nifer -ī *a.* prickly.
spīnō'sus *a.* thorny, prickly; (*style*) difficult. [bracelet.
spi'nt/ēr -ē'ris *n.* elastic
spī'n/us -ī *f.* blackthorn, sloe.
spī'r/a -ae *f.* coil; twisted band. [life-giving.
spīrā'bilis *a.* breathable,
spīrā'cul/um -ī *n.* vent.
spīrāme'nt/um -ī *n.* vent, pore; breathing-space.
spī'rit/us -ūs *m.* breath, breathing; breeze, air; inspiration; character, spirit, courage, arrogance.
spī'r/ō -ā're -ā'vī -ā'tum *vi.* breathe, blow; be alive; be inspired. *vt.* emit, exhale; (*fig.*) breathe, express.
spissā'tus *a.* condensed.
spissē'sc/ō -ere *vi.* thicken.
spi'ss/us *a.* thick, compact, crowded; slow; (*fig.*) difficult. –ē *ad.* closely; slowly.
sple'nd/eō -ē're *vi.* be bright, shine; be illustrious.
splendē'sc/ō -ere *vi.* become bright.
sple'ndid/us *a.* bright, brilliant, glittering; (*sound*) clear; (*dress, house*) magnificent; (*person*) illustrious; (*appearance*) showy. –ē *ad* brilliantly, magnificently, nobly.
sple'nd/or -ō'ris *m.* brightness, lustre; magnificence; clearness; nobility.
spoliā'ti/ō -ō'nis *f.* plundering.
spoliā't/or -ō'ris *m.*, –**rīx** -rī'cis *f.* robber.
spo'li/ō -ā're -ā'vī -ā'tum *vt.* strip; rob, plunder.
spo'l/ium -ī & iī *n.* (*beast*) skin; (*enemy*) spoils, booty.
spo'nd/a -ae *f.* bed-frame; bed, couch.
spondā'l/ium -ī & iī *n.* hymn accompanied by the flute.
spo'nd/eō -ē're spopo'ndī spō'nsum *vt.* promise, pledge, vow; (*law*) go bail for; (*marriage*) betroth.
spondē'/us -ī *m.* spondee.
spo'ngi/a -ae *f.* sponge; coat of mail.
spō'ns/a -ae *f.* fiancée, bride.
spōnsā'l/ia -ium *n.pl.* engagement.
spō'nsi/ō -ō'nis *f.* promise, guarantee; (*law*) agreement that the loser in a suit pays the winner a sum; bet.
spō'ns/or -ō'ris *m.* guarantor, surety.
spō'nsus *ppp.* spondeō. *m.* fiancé, bridegroom. *n.* agreement, covenant. [surety.
spō'ns/us -ūs *m.* contract,
spo'nte *f.* (*abl.*) voluntarily, of one's own accord; unaided, by oneself; spontaneously.
spopo'ndī *perf.* spondeō.
sporte'll/a -ae *f.* fruit-basket.
spo'rtul/a -ae *f.* small basket; gift to clients, dole.
sprē'ti/ō -ō'nis *f.* contempt.
sprē't/or -ō'ris *m.* despiser.
sprē'tus *ppp.* spernō.
sprē'vī *perf.* spernō.
spū'm/a -ae *f.* foam, froth.
spūmē'sc/ō -ere *vi.* become frothy.
spū'meus *a.* foaming, frothy.
spū'mifer -ī *a.* foaming.
spū'miger -ī *a.* foaming.
spū'm/ō -ā're *vi.* foam, froth.
spūmō'sus *a.* foaming.
sp/u'ō -u'ere -uī -ū'tum *vi.* spit. *vt.* spit out.
spurci'dicus *a.* obscene.
spurci'ficus *a.* obscene.
spurci'ti/a -ae, –**ēs** -ē'ī *f.* filth, smut.
spu'rc/ō -ā're *vt.* befoul.
spu'rc/us *a.* filthy, nasty, foul. –ē *ad.* obscenely.
spūtāti'licus *a.* despicable.
spūtā't/or -ō'ris *m.* spitter.
spū't/ō -ā're *vt.* spit out.
spū't/um -ī *n.* spit, spittle.
squā'l/eō -ē're -uī *vi.* be rough, stiff, clotted; be

parched; be neglected, squalid, filthy; be in mourning.
squā'lid/us *a.* rough, scaly; neglected, squalid, filthy; (*speech*) unpolished. **-ē** *ad.* rudely.
squā'l/or -ō'ris *m.* roughness; filth, squalor. [armour.
squā'm/a -ae *f.* scale; scale-
squā'meus *a.* scaly.
squā'mifer -ī *a.* scaly.
squā'miger -ī *a.* scaly. *m.pl.* fishes.
squāmō'sus *a.* scaly.
squi'll/a -ae *f.* prawn, shrimp.
st *interj.* sh! [support.
stabilīme'nt/um -ī *n.*
stabi'l/iō -ī're *vt.* make stable; establish.
sta'bilis *a.* firm, steady; (*fig.*) steadfast, unfailing.
stabi'lit/ās -ā'tis *f.* firmness, steadiness, reliability.
sta'bul/ō -ā're *vt.* house, stable. *vi.* have a stall.
sta'bul/um -ī *n.* stall, stable, steading; lodging, cottage; brothel.
sta'ct/a -ae *f.* myrrh-oil.
sta'd/ium -ī & iī *n.* stade, furlong; race-track.
Stagī'r/a -ō'rum *n.pl.* town in Macedonia, birth-place of Aristotle. **-ī'tēs -ī'tae** *m.* Aristotle.
sta'gn/ō -ā're *vi.* form pools; be inundated. *vt.* flood.
sta'gn/um -ī *n.* standing water, pool, swamp; waters.
stā'm/en -inis *n.* warp; thread; (*instrument*) string; (*priest*) fillet.
stāmi'neus *a.* full of threads.
Sta'ta māter Vesta.
statā'rius *a.* standing, stationary, steady; calm. *f.* refined comedy. *m.pl.* actors in this comedy.
statē'r/a -ae *f.* scales.
sta'tim *ad.* steadily; at once, immediately. — **ut** as soon as.
sta'ti/ō -ō'nis *f.* standing still; station, post, residence; (*pl.*) sentries; (*naut.*) anchorage.
Sta't/ius -ī *m.* Caecilius, early writer of comedy; Papinius, epic and lyric poet of the Silver Age.
statī'vus *a.* stationary. *n.pl.* standing camp. [orderly.
sta't/or -ō'ris *m.* attendant,
Sta't/or -ō'ris *m.* the Stayer, epithet of Jupiter.
sta'tu/a -ae *f.* statue.
statū'm/en -inis *n.* (*ship*) rib.
sta't/uō -u'ere -uī -ū'tum *vt.* set up, place; bring to a stop; establish, constitute; determine, appoint; decide, settle; decree, prescribe; (*with inf.*) resolve, propose; (*with acc. and inf.*) judge, consider, conclude; (*army*) draw up; (*monument*) erect; (*price*) fix; (*sentence*) pass; (*tent*) pitch; (*town*) build. **condiciōnem** — dictate (to). **fīnem** — put an end (to). **iūs** — lay down a principle. **modum** — impose restrictions. **apud animum** — make up one's mind. **dē sē** — commit suicide. **gravius** — **in** deal severely with.
statū'r/a -ae *f.* height, stature.
sta'tus *ppp.* **sistō.** *a.* appointed, due.
sta't/us -ūs *m.* posture, attitude; position; (*social*) standing, status, circumstances; (*pol.*) situation, state, form of government; (*nature*) condition. **reī pūblicae** — the political situation; constitution. **dē -ū movēre** dislodge.
statū'tus *ppp.* **statuō.**
ste'g/a -ae *f.* deck. [planet.
stē'll/a -ae *f.* star. — **errāns**
stē'll/āns -a'ntis *a.* starry.
stēllā'tus *a.* starred; set in the sky.
stē'llifer -ī *a.* starry.
stē'lliger -ī *a.* starry.
stē'lli/ō (stēliō) -ō'nis *m.* newt.

ste'mma -tis *n.* pedigree.
sterco'reus *a.* filthy.
ste'rcor/ō -ā're *vt.* manure.
ste'rc/us -oris *n.* dung.
ste'rilis *a.* barren, sterile; bare, empty; unprofitable, fruitless. [ness.
steri'lit/ās -ā'tis *f.* barren-
ste'rn/āx -ā'cis *a.* bucking.
ste'rn/ō -ere strā'vī strā'tum *vt.* spread, cover, strew; smooth, level; stretch out, extend; throw to the ground, prostrate; overthrow; (*bed*) make; (*horse*) saddle; (*road*) pave.
sternūme'nt/um -ī *n.* sneezing. [sneeze.
ste'rnu/ō -ere -ī *vt.* & *i.*
Ste'rop/ē -ēs *f.* a Pleiad.
sterquili'n/ium -ī & iī, **-um** -ī *n.* dung-heap.
ste'rt/ō -ere -uī *vi.* snore.
Stēsi'chor/us -ī *m.* Greek lyric poet.
ste'tī *perf.* stō.
Sthe'nel/us -ī *m.* father of Eurystheus; father of Cycnus. **-ē'ius**, **-ē'is** -ē'idis *a.*
sti'gma -tis *n.* brand. [slave.
stigma'ti/ās -ae *m.* branded
sti'll/a -ae *f.* drop.
stillici'd/ium -ī & iī *n.* dripping water, rain-water from the eaves.
sti'll/ō -ā're -ā'vī -ā'tum *vi.* drip, trickle. *vt.* let fall in drops, distil.
sti'l/us -ī *m.* stake; pen; (*fig.*) writing, composition, style **-um vertere** erase.
stimulā'ti/ō -ō'nis *f.* incentive.
stimulā'tr/īx -ī'cis *f.* provocative woman.
stimu'leus *a.* smarting.
sti'mul/ō -ā're -ā'vī -ā'tum *vt.* goad; trouble, torment; rouse, spur on, excite.
sti'mul/us -ī *m.* goad; (*mil.*) stake; (*pain*) sting, pang; (*incentive*) spur, stimulus.
sti'ngu/ō -ere *vt.* extinguish.
stīpā'ti/ō -ō'nis *f.* crowd, retinue.
stīpā't/or -ō'ris *m.* attendant; (*pl.*) retinue, bodyguard.
stīpendiā'rius *a.* tributary, liable to a money tax; (*mil.*) receiving pay. *m.pl.* tributary peoples.
stīpe'nd/ium -ī & iī *n.* tax tribute; soldier's pay; military service, campaign. — **merēre, merērī** serve. — **ēmererī** complete one's period of service.
stī'p/es -itis *m.* log, trunk; tree; (*insult*) blockhead.
stī'p/ō -ā're -ā'vī -ā'tum *vt.* press, pack together; cram, stuff full; crowd round, accompany in a body.
stips sti'pis *f.* donation, contribution.
sti'pul/a -ae *f.* stalk, blade, stubble; reed. [bargain.
stipulā'ti/ō -ō'nis *f.* promise,
stipulātiu'ncul/a -ae *f.* slight stipulation.
stipulā'tus *a.* promised.
sti'pul/or -ā'rī *vt.* & *i.* demand a formal promise, bargain, stipulate.
stī'ri/a -ae *f.* icicle.
sti'rpēs, *see* **stirps**.
sti'rpitus *ad.* thoroughly.
sti'rp/s (**-ēs**) -is *f.* lower trunk and roots, stock; plant, shoot; family, lineage, progeny; origin. **ab -e** utterly.
stī'v/a -ae *f.* plough-handle.
stlattā'rius *a.* sea-borne.
stō stā're ste'tī sta'tum *vi.* stand; remain in position, stand firm; be conspicuous; (*fig.*) persist, continue; (*battle*) go on; (*hair*) stand on end; (*naut.*) ride at anchor; (*play*) be successful; (*price*) cost; (*with* **ab, cum, prō**) be on the side of, support; (*with* **in**) rest, depend on; (*with* **per**) be the fault of. **stat sententia** one's mind is made up. **per Āfrānium**

stetit quōminus dīmicārētur thanks to Afranius there was no battle.
Stō'ic/us *a.* Stoic. *m.* Stoic philosopher. *n.pl.* Stoicism. **-ē** *ad.* like a Stoic.
sto'l/a **-ae** *f.* long robe, *esp.* worn by matrons.
sto'lid/us *a.* dull, stupid. **-ē** *ad.* stupidly.
sto'mach/or **-ā'rī** **-ā'tus** *vi.* be vexed, be annoyed.
stomachō's/us *a.* angry, irritable. **-ē** *ad.*
sto'mach/us **-ī** *m.* gullet; stomach; taste, liking; dislike, irritation, chagrin.
sto're/a **(sto'ria)** **-ae** *f.* rush-mat, rope-mat.
stra'b/ō **-ō'nis** *m.* squinter.
strā'g/ēs **-is** *f.* heap, confused mass; havoc, massacre.
strā'gulus *a.* covering. *n.* bed-spread, rug. [litter.
strā'm/en **-inis** *n.* straw,
strāme'nt/um **-ī** *n.* straw, thatch; straw-bed; covering, rug. [thatched.
strāmi'neus *a.* straw-,
stra'ngul/ō **-ā're** **-ā'vī** **-ā'tum** *vt.* throttle, choke.
strangū'ri/a **-ae** *f.* difficult discharge of urine.
stratēgē'ma **-tis** *n.* a piece of generalship, stratagem.
stratē'g/us **-ī** *m.* commander, president.
stratiō'ticus *a.* military.
strā't/us *ppp.* sternō. *a.* prostrate. **-um** **-ī** *n.* coverlet, blanket; bed, couch; horse-cloth, saddle; pavement.
strā'vī *perf.* sternō.
strēnu'it/ās **-ā'tis** *f.* energy, briskness.
strē'nu/us *a.* brisk, energetic, busy; restless. **-ē** *ad.* energetically, quickly.
stre'pit/ō **-ā're** *vi.* make a noise, rattle, rustle.
stre'pit/us **-ūs** *m.* din, clatter crashing, rumbling; sound.
stre'p/ō **-ere** **-uī** *vi.* make a noise, clang, roar, rumble, rustle, etc. *vt.* bawl out.
striā't/a **-ae** *f.* scallop.
stri'ctim *ad.* superficially, cursorily. [metal.
strictū'r/a **-ae** *f.* mass of
stri'ctus *ppp.* stringō. *a.* close, tight.
strī'd/eō **-ē're** **-ī,** **-ō** **-ere** **-ī** *vi.* creak, hiss, shriek, whistle.
strī'd/or **-ō'ris** *m.* creaking, hissing, grating.
strī'dulus *a.* creaking, hissing, whistling.
stri'gil/is *f.* scraper, strigil.
stri'g/ō **-ā're** *vi.* stop, jib.
strigō'sus *a.* thin, scraggy; (*style*) insipid.
stri'/ngō **-ngere** **-nxī** **-ctum** *vt.* draw together, draw tight; touch, graze; cut off, prune, trim; (*sword*) draw; (*mind*) affect, pain.
stri'ng/or **-ō'ris** *m.* twinge.
str/ix **-i'gis** *f.* screech-owl.
stro'ph/a **-ae** *f.* trick.
Stro'phad/es **-um** *f.pl.* islands off S. Greece.
strophiā'r/ius **-ī** **&** **iī** *m.* maker of breast-bands.
stro'ph/ium **-ī** **&** **iī** *n.* breast-band; head-band.
stru'ct/or **-ō'ris** *m.* mason, carpenter; (*at table*) server, carver.
structū'r/a **-ae** *f.* construction, structure; works.
stru'ctus *ppp.* struō.
stru'/ēs **-is** *f.* heap, pile.
stru'/ix **-icis** *f.* heap, pile.
strū'm/a **-ae** *f.* tumour.
strūmō'sus *a.* scrofulous.
stru'/ō **-ere** **-xī** **-ctum** *vt.* pile up; build, erect; arrange in order; make, prepare; cause, contrive, plot.
strū'theus *a.* sparrow-.
strūthiocamē'l/us **-ī** *m.* ostrich.
Strȳ'm/ōn **-onis** *m.* river between Macedonia and

Thrace, *mod.* Struma. **-o'nius** *a.* Strymonian, Thracian.
stu'd/eō -ē're -uī *vi.* (*usu. with dat.*) be keen, be diligent, apply oneself to; study; (*person*) be a supporter of.
studiō's/us *a.* (*usu. with gen.*) keen on, fond of, partial to; studious. *m.* student. **-ē** *ad.* eagerly, diligently.
stu'd/ium -ī & iī *n.* enthusiasm, application, inclination; fondness, affection; party spirit, partisanship; study, literary work.
stultiloque'nti/a -ae *f.* foolish talk.
stultilo'qu/ium -ī & iī *n.* foolish talk.
stulti'ti/a -ae *f.* folly, silliness.
stulti'vidus *a.* simple-sighted.
stu'lt/us *a.* foolish, silly. *m.* fool. **-ē** *ad.* foolishly.
stupe/fa'ciō -fa'cere -fē'cī -fa'ctum (*pass.* **-fī'ō** -fī'erī) *vt.* stun, astound.
stu'p/eō -ē're -uī *vi.* be stunned, be astonished; be brought to a standstill. *vt.* marvel at.
stupē'sc/ō -ere *vi.* become amazed.
stū'peus, *see* **stuppeus.**
stupi'dit/ās -ā'tis *f.* senselessness.
stu'pidus *a.* senseless, astounded; dull, stupid.
stu'p/or -ō'ris *m.* numbness, bewilderment; dullness, stupidity.
stu'pp/a -ae *f.* tow.
stu'ppeus *a.* of tow.
stu'pr/ō -ā're -ā'vī -ā'tum *vt.* defile; ravish.
stu'pr/um -ī *n.* debauchery, unchastity.
stu'rn/us -ī *m.* starling.
Sty'gius *a.* of the lower world, Stygian.
sty'lus, *see* **stilus.**
Stympha'l/us -ī *m.*, **-um** -ī *n.* district of Arcadia, famous for birds of prey killed by Hercules. **-icus, -ius, -is** *a.* Stymphalian.
St'yx -y'gis & -y'gos *f.* river of Hades. **-ius** *a.*
suādē'l/a -ae *f.* persuasion.
suā'/deō -dē're -sī -sum *vi.* (*with dat.*) advise, urge, recommend.
suā'si/ō -ō'nis *f.* speaking in favour (of a proposal); persuasive type of oratory.
suā's/or -ō'ris *m.* adviser; advocate.
suā'sus *ppp.* suādeō.
suā's/us -ūs *m.* advice.
suāve'ol/ēns -e'ntis *a.* fragrant.
suāviā'tiō, *see* **sāviātiō.**
suāvi'dicus *a.* charming.
suāvi'loqu/ēns -e'ntis *a.* charming.
suāviloque'nti/a -ae *f.* charm of speech.
suā'vior, *see* **sā'vior.**
suā'v/is *a.* sweet, pleasant, delightful. **-iter** *ad.*
suā'vit/ās -ā'tis *f.* sweetness, pleasantness, charm.
suā'vium, *see* **sā'vium.**
sub *pr.* 1. *with abl.:* (*place*) under, beneath; (*hills, walls*) at the foot of, close to; (*time*) during, at; (*order*) next to; (*rule*) under, in the reign of. 2. *with acc.:* (*place*) under, along under; (*hills, walls*) up to, to; (*time*) up to, just before, just after. — ictum venīre come within range. — manum to hand.
subabsu'rd/us *a.* somewhat absurd. **-ē** *ad.*
subaccū's/ō -ā're *vt.* find some fault with.
subā'cti/ō -ō'nis *f.* working (the soil).
subā'ctus *ppp.* subigō.
subadroga'nter *ad.* a little conceitedly.
subagre'stis *a.* rather boorish.
subalā'ris *a.* carried under the arms.
subamā'rus *a.* rather bitter.

suba'quilus *a.* brownish.
subauscu'lt/ō -ā're *vt.* & *i.* listen secretly, eavesdrop.
subbasilicā'n/us -ī *m.* lounger.
subbla'nd/ior -ī'rī *vi.* (*with dat.*) flirt with.
subc-, *see* **succ-**.
su'bdidī *perf.* subdō.
subdiffi'cilis *a.* rather difficult.
subdiffī'd/ō -ere *vi.* be a little doubtful.
subditī'cius *a.* sham.
subditī'vus *a.* sham.
su'bditus *ppp.* subdō. *a.* spurious.
su'bd/ō -ere -idī -itum *vt.* put under, plunge into; subdue; substitute, forge.
subdo'c/eō -ē're *vt.* teach as an assistant.
su'bdol/us *a.* sly, crafty, underhand. **-ē** *ad.* slily.
subdu'bit/ō -ā're *vi.* be a little undecided.
subd/ū'cō -ū'cere -ū'xī -u'ctum *vt.* pull up, raise; withdraw, remove; take away secretly, steal; (*account*) balance; (*ship*) haul up, beach. sē — steal away, disappear.
subdu'cti/ō -ō'nis *f.* (*ship*) hauling up; (*thought*) reckoning.
subdu'ctus *ppp.* subdūcō.
su'b/edō -e'sse -ē'dī *vt.* wear away underneath.
subē'gī *perf.* subigō.
su'b/eō -ī're -iī -itum *vi.* go under, go in; come up to, climb, advance; come immediately after; come to the assistance; come as a substitute, succeed; come secretly, steal in; come to mind, suggest itself. *vt.* enter, plunge into; climb; approach, attack; take the place of; steal into; submit to, undergo, suffer; (*mind*) occur to.
sū'ber -is *n* cork-tree; cork.
sube'sse *inf.* subsum.

subf-, **subg-**, *see* **suff-**, **sugg-**.
subho'rridus *a.* somewhat uncouth.
subia'c/eō -ē're -uī *vi.* lie under, be close (to); be connected (with).
sub/i'ciō -i'cere -iē'cī -ie'ctum *vt.* put under, bring under; bring up, throw up; bring near; submit, subject, expose; subordinate, deal with under; append, add on, answer; adduce, suggest; substitute forge; suborn. sē — grow up.
subie'cti/ō -ō'nis *f.* laying under; forging.
subie'ct/ō -ā're *vt.* lay under, put to; throw up.
subie'ct/or -ō'ris *m.* forger.
subie'ct/us *ppp.* subiciō. *a.* neighbouring, bordering; subject, exposed. **-ē** *ad.* submissively.
subigitā'ti/ō -ō'nis *f.* lewdness.
subi'git/ō -ā're *vt.* behave improperly to.
su'b/igō -i'gere -ē'gī -ā'ctum *vt.* bring up to; impel, compel; subdue conquer; (*animal*) tame, break in; (*blade*) sharpen; (*boat*) row, propel; (*cooking*) knead; (*earth*) turn up, dig; (*mind*) train.
subiī *perf.* subeō.
subi'mpud/ēns -e'ntis *a.* rather impertinent.
subinā'nis *a.* rather empty.
subi'nde *ad.* immediately after; repeatedly.
subīnsū'lsus *a.* rather insipid.
subinvi'd/eō -ē're *vi.* be a little envious of.
subinvī'sus *a.* somewhat odious.
subinvī't/ō -ā're *vt.* invite vaguely.
subīrā'/scor -scī -tus *vi.* be rather angry.
subīrā'tus *a.* rather angry.
subitā'rius *a.* sudden, emergency-.
su'bitō *ad.* suddenly.

su'bitus *ppp.* subeō. *a.* sudden, unexpected; (*man*) rash; (*troops*) hastily raised. *n.* surprise, emergency.
subiū'nctus *ppp.* subiungō.
subi/u'ngō -ungere -ūnxī -ūnctum *vt.* harness; add, affix; subordinate, subdue.
sublā'/bor -bī -psus *vi.* sink down; glide away.
sublā'psus *ppa.* sublābor.
sublā'ti/ō -ō'nis *f.* elevation.
sublā't/us *ppp.* tollō. *a.* elated. -ē *ad.* loftily.
suble'ct/ō -ā're *vt.* coax.
sublē'ctus *ppp.* sublegō.
su'bl/egō -e'gere -ē'gī -ē'ctum *vt.* gather up; substitute; (*child*) kidnap; (*talk*) overhear.
suble'stus *a.* slight. [tion.
sublevā'ti/ō -ō'nis *f.* allevia-
su'blev/ō -ā're -ā'vī -ā'tum *vt.* lift up, hold up; support, encourage; lighten, alleviate.
su'blic/a -ae *f.* pile, palisade.
subli'cius *a.* on piles.
subligā'cul/um -ī, **su'blig/ar** -ā'ris *n.* loin-cloth.
su'blig/ō -ā're *vt.* fasten on.
sublī'm/is *a.* high, raised high, lifted up; (*character*) eminent, aspiring; (*language*) lofty, elevated. -ē *ad.* aloft, in the air. [ness.
sublī'mit/ās -ā'tis *f.* lofti-
sublī'mus, *see* **sublīmis**.
subli'ngi/ō -ō'nis *m.* scullion.
su'bl/inō -i'nere -ē'vī -itum *vt.* ōs — fool, bamboozle.
su'blitus *ppp.* sublinō.
sublū'c/eō -ē're *vi.* glimmer.
su'blu/ō -ere *vt.* (*river*) flow past the foot of.
sublū'stris *a.* faintly luminous.
sublū'tus *ppp.* subluō.
subm-, *see* **summ-**.
subnā'tus *a.* growing up underneath.
subne'/ctō -ctere -xuī -xum *vt.* tie under, fasten to.
su'bneg/ō -ā're *vt.* half refuse.
subne'xus *ppp.* subnectō.
su'bnig/er -rī *a.* darkish.
subnī'/xus, -sus *a.* supported, resting (on); relying (on).
su'bnub/a -ae *f.* rival.
subnū'bilus *a.* overcast.
su'b/ō -ā're *vi.* be in heat.
subobscē'nus *a.* rather indecent. [obscure.
subobscū'rus *a.* somewhat
subodiō'sus *a.* rather odious.
suboffe'nd/ō -ere *vi.* give some offence.
su'bol/et -ē're *vi.* (*impers.*) there is a faint scent. — mihi I detect, have an inkling.
su'bol/ēs -is *f.* offspring, children.
subolē'sc/ō -ere *vi.* grow up.
subo'r/ior -ī'rī *vi.* spring up in succession.
subō'rn/ō -ā're -ā'vī -ā'tum *vt.* fit out, equip; instigate secretly, suborn.
subo'rt/us -ūs *m.* rising up repeatedly.
subp-, *see* **supp-**.
subra'ncidus *a.* slightly tainted.
subrau'cus *a.* rather hoarse.
subrē'ctus *ppp.* subrigō.
subrē'mig/ō -ā're *vi.* paddle under (water).
subrē'p/ō -ere -sī -tum *vi.* creep along, steal up to.
subre'ptus *ppp.* subripiō.
subrī'/deō -dere -sī *vi.* smile.
subrīdi'culē *ad.* rather funnily. [*vt.* lift, raise.
su'br/igō -i'gere -ē'xī -ē'ctum
subri'ng/or -ī *vi.* make a wry face, be rather vexed.
subr/i'piō -i'pere -i'puī & u'puī -e'ptum *vt.* take away secretly, steal.
su'brog/ō -ā're *vt.* propose as successor.
subrōstrā'n/ī -ō'rum *m.pl.* idlers. [slightly.
subru'b/eō -ē're *vi.* blush
subrū'fus *a.* ginger-haired.

su'bru/ō -ere -ī -tum *vt.* undermine, demolish.
subrū'sticus *a.* rather countrified.
su'brutus *ppp.* subruō.
subscrī'/bō -bere -psī -ptum *vt.* write underneath; (*document*) sign, subscribe; (*censor*) set down; (*law*) add to an indictment, prosecute; (*fig.*) record; (*with dat.*) assent to, approve.
subscrī'pti/ō -ō'nis *f.* inscription underneath; signature; (*censor*) noting down; (*law*) subscription (to an indictment); register.
subscrī'pt/or -ō'ris *m.* subscriber (to an indictment).
subscrī'ptus *ppp.* subscrībō
subsecī'vus, *see* **subsicīvus**.
su'bsec/ō -ā're -uī -ctum *vt.* cut off, clip.
subsē'dī *perf.* subsīdō.
subse'll/ium -ī & iī *n.* bench, seat; (*law*) the bench, the court.
subs/e'ntiō -entī're -ē'nsī *vt.* have an inkling of.
su'bse/quor -quī -cū'tus *vt.* & *i.* follow closely; support; imitate.
subse'rv/iō -ī're *vi.* be a slave; (*fig.*) comply (with).
subsicī'vus *a.* left over; (*time*) spare; (*work*) overtime.
subsidiā'rius *a.* in reserve. *m.pl.* reserves.
subsi'd/ium -ī & iī *n.* reserve ranks, reserve troops; relief, aid, assistance.
subs/ī'dō -ī'dere -ē'dī -e'ssum *vi.* sit down, crouch, squat; sink down, settle, subside; (*ambush*) lie in wait; (*residence*) stay, settle. *vt.* lie in wait for.
subsignā'nus *a.* special reserve (troops).
subsi'gn/ō -ā're *vt.* register; guarantee.
subsi'l/iō -ī're -uī *vi.* leap up.
subs/i'stō -i'stere -titī *vi.* stand still, make a stand; stop halt; remain, continue, hold out; (*with dat.*) resist. *vt.* withstand.
subso'rt/ior -ī'rī -ī'tus *vt.* choose as a substitute by lot.
subsortī'ti/ō -ō'nis *f.* choosing of substitutes by lot.
substa'nti/a -ae *f.* means, wealth.
subst/e'rnō -e'rnere -rā'vī -rā'tum *vt.* scatter under, spread under; (*fig.*) put at one's service.
sub'stitī *perf.* subsistō.
substi't/uō -u'ere -uī -ū'tum *vt.* put next; substitute; (*idea*) present, imagine.
substitū'tus *ppp.* substituō.
su'bst/ō -ā're *vi.* hold out.
substrā'tus *ppp.* substernō.
substri'ctus *ppp.* substringō. *a.* narrow, tight.
substri'/ngō -ngere -nxī -ctum *vt.* bind up; draw close; check.
substru'cti/ō -ō'nis *f.* foundation.
su'bstru/ō -ere -xī -ctum *vt.* lay, pave.
subsu'lt/ō -ā're *vi.* jump up.
su'b/sum -e'sse *vi.* be underneath; be close to, be at hand; (*fig.*) underlie, be latent in.
subsū'tus *a.* fringed at the bottom.
subtē'm/en -inis *n.* woof; thread.
su'bter *ad.* below, underneath. *pr.* (*with acc.* & *abl.*) beneath; close up to.
subterdū'/cō -cere -xī *vt.* withdraw secretly.
subterf/u'giō -u'gere -ū'gī *vt.* escape from, evade.
subterlā'b/or -ī *vt.* & *i.* flow past under; slip away.
subterrā'neus *a.* underground.
subte'x/ō -ere -uī -tum *vt.* weave in; veil, obscure.
subtī'l/is *a.* slender, fine; (*senses*) delicate, nice; (*judgment*) discriminating, precise;

(*style*) plain, direct. **-iter** *ad.* finely; accurately; simply.

subtī'lit/ās -ā'tis *f.* fineness; (*judgment*) acuteness, exactness; (*style*) plainness, directness.

subti'm/eō -ē're *vt.* be a little afraid of.

subtra'ctus *ppp.* subtrahō.

sub'tra/hō -here -xī -ctum *vt.* draw away from underneath; take away secretly; withdraw, remove.

subtri'stis *a.* rather sad.

subturpi'culus *a.* a little bit mean.

subtu'rpis *a.* rather mean.

su'btus *ad.* below, underneath.

subtū'sus *a.* slightly bruised.

subū'cul/a -ae *f.* shirt, vest.

sū'bul/a -ae *f.* awl.

subu'lc/us -ī *m.* swineherd.

Subū'r/a -ae *f.* a disreputable quarter of Rome. **-ā'nus** *a.*

suburbā'nit/ās -ā'tis *f.* nearness to Rome.

suburbā'nus *a.* near Rome. *n.* villa near Rome. *m.pl.* inhabitants of the towns near Rome. [suburb.

subu'rb/ium -ī & iī *n.*

subu'rg/eō -ē're *vt.* drive close (to).

subve'cti/ō -ō'nis *f.* transport.

subve'ct/ō -ā're *vt.* carry up regularly.

subve'ctus *ppp.* subvehō.

subve'ct/us -ūs *m.* transport.

su'bve/hō -here -xī -ctum *vt.* carry up, transport upstream.

subv/e'niō -enī're -ē'nī -e'ntum *vi.* (*with dat.*) come to the assistance of, relieve, reinforce.

subve'nt/ō -ā're *vi.* (*with dat.*) come quickly to help.

subve'r/eor -ē'rī *vi.* be a little afraid. [verter.

subve'rs/or -ō'ris *m.* sub-

subve'rsus *ppp.* subvertō.

subve'r/tō (subvo'rtō) -tere -tī -sum *vt.* turn upside down, upset; overthrow, subvert.

subve'xī *perf.* subvehō.

subve'xus *a.* sloping upwards.

su'bvol/ō -ā're *vi.* fly upwards.

subvo'lv/ō -ere *vt.* roll uphill.

su'ccavus *a.* hollow underneath.

succ/ē'dō -ē'dere -e'ssī -e'ssum *vt.* & *i.* (*with dat.*) go under, pass into, take on; (*with dat., acc.,* in) go up, climb; (*with dat., acc.,* ad, sub) march on, advance to; (*with dat.,* in) come to take the place of, relieve; (*with dat.,* in, ad) follow after, succeed, succeed to; (*result*) turn out, be successful.

succ/e'ndō -e'ndere -e'ndī -ē'nsum *vt.* set fire to, kindle; (*fig.*) fire, inflame.

succē'nseō, *see* **suscēnseō.**

succē'nsus *ppp.* succendō.

succenturiā'tus *a.* in reserve. [centurion.

succentu'ri/ō -ō'nis *m.* under-

succe'ssī *perf.* succēdō. [sion.

succe'ssi/ō -ō'nis *f.* succes-

succe'ss/or -ō'ris *m.* successor.

succe'ssus *ppp.* succēdō.

succe'ss/us -ūs *m.* advance uphill; result, successs.

succī'di/a -ae *f.* leg or side of meat, flitch.

succī'/dō -dere -dī -sum *vt.* cut off, mow down.

su'ccid/ō -ere -ī *vi.* sink, give way.

succi'duus *a.* sinking, failing.

succi'nctus *ppp.* succingō.

succi'n/gō -gere -xī -ctum *vt.* gird up, tuck up; equip, arm.

succi'ngul/um -ī *n.* girdle.

su'ccin/ō -ere *vi.* chime in.

succī'sus *ppp.* succīdō.

succlāmā'ti/ō -ō'nis *f.* shouting, barracking.

succlā'm/ō -ā're -ā'vī -ā'tum *vt.* shout after, interrupt with shouting.

succontumēliō'sē *ad.* somewhat insolently.

succrē'sc/ō -ere *vi.* grow up (from or to).
succri'spus *a.* rather curly.
succu'/mbō -mbere -buī -bitum *vi.* fall, sink under; submit, surrender.
succu'r/rō -rere -rī -sum *vi.* come quickly up; run to the help of, succour; (*idea*) occur.
su'ccus, *see* **sūcus**.
succu'ss/us -ūs *m.* shaking.
succu'st/ōs -ō'dis *m.* assistant keeper.
succu'/tiō -tere -ssī -ssum *vt.* toss up. [plump.
sū'cidus *a.* juicy, fresh,
sū'cin/um -ī *n.* amber.
sū'ctus *ppp.* sūgō.
su'cul/a -ae *f.* winch, windlass.
su'cul/a -ae *f.* piglet; (*pl.*) the Hyads.
sū'c/us -ī *m.* juice, sap; medicine, potion; taste, flavour; (*fig.*) strength, vigour, life.
sūdā'r/ium -ī & iī *n.* handkerchief.
sūdātō'rius *a.* for sweating. *n.* sweating-bath. [spike.
su'd/is -is *f.* stake, pile, pike,
sū'd/ō -ā're -āvī -ā'tum *vi.* sweat, perspire; be drenched with; work hard. *vt.* exude.
sū'd/or -ō'ris *m.* sweat, perspiration; moisture; hard work, exertion.
su'dus *a.* cloudless, clear. *n.* fine weather.
su'/eō -ē're *vi.* be accustomed.
suē'/scō -scere -vī -tum *vi.* be accustomed. *vt.* accustom.
Sue'ss/a -ae *f.* town in Latium.
Suessiō'n/ēs -um *m.pl.* people of Gaul, *mod.* Soissons.
suē'tus *ppp.* suēscō. *a.* accustomed; usual.
Suē'v/ī -ō'rum *m.pl.* people of N.E. Germany.
sū'f/es -etis *m.* chief magistrate of Carthage.
suffarcinā'tus *a.* stuffed full.
suffe'ctus *ppp.* sufficiō. *a.* (*consul*) appointed to fill a vacancy during the regular term of office.
su'ffer/ō -re *vt.* support, undergo, endure.
su'ffes, *see* **sūfes**.
suff/i'ciō -i'cere -ē'cī -e'ctum *vt.* dye, tinge; supply, provide; appoint in place (of another), substitute. *vi.* be adequate, suffice.
suffī'/gō -gere -xī -xum *vt.* fasten underneath, nail on.
suffī'm/en -inis, **suffīme'nt/um** -ī *n.* incense.
su'ff/iō -ī're *vt.* fumigate, perfume.
suffī'xus *ppp.* suffīgō.
sufflā'm/en -inis *n.* brake.
su'ffl/ō -ā're *vt.* blow up; puff up. [stifle.
su'ffoc/ō -ā're *vt.* choke,
suff/o'diō -o'dere -ō'dī -o's-sum *vt.* stab; dig under, undermine.
suffo'ssus *ppp.* suffodiō.
suffrāgā'ti/ō -ō'nis *f.* voting for, support.
suffrāgā't/or -ō'ris *m.* voter, supporter.
suffrāgātō'rius *a.* supporting a candidate.
suffrā'g/ium -ī & iī *n.* vote, ballot; right of suffrage; (*fig.*) judgment, approval. — ferre vote.
suffrā'g/or -ā'rī -ā'tus *vi.* vote for; support, favour.
suffri'ng/ō -ere *vt.* break.
suff/u'giō -u'gere -ū'gī *vi.* run for shelter. *vt.* elude.
suffu'g/ium -ī & iī *n.* shelter, refuge.
suffu'l/ciō -cī're -sī -tum *vt.* prop up, support.
suff/u'ndō -u'ndere -ū'dī -ū'sum *vt.* pour in; suffuse, fill; tinge, colour, blush; overspread.
suffū'r/or -ā'rī *vi.* filch.
suffu'scus *a.* darkish.

suffū'sus *ppp.* suffundō.
Suga'mbr/ī -ō'rum *m.pl.* people of N.W. Germany.
su'gge/rō -rere -ssī -stum *vt.* bring up to, supply; add on, put next.
sugge'st/um -ī *n.* platform.
sugge'stus *ppp.* suggerō.
sugge'st/us -ūs *m.* platform, stage.
suggra'ndis *a.* rather large.
suggre'/dior -dī -ssus *vi.* come up close, approach. *vt.* attack. [ing.
sūgillā'ti/ō -ō'nis *f.* affront-
sūgillā'tus *a.* bruised; insulted.
sū'/gō -gere -xī -ctum *vt.* suck.
su'ī *gen.* sē.
su'ī *perf.* suō.
sui'llus *a.* of pigs.
su'lc/ō -ā're *vt.* furrow, plough.
su'lc/us -ī *m.* furrow; trench; track.
su'lfur, *see* **sulpur.**
Su'll/a -ae *m.* famous Roman dictator. **-ā'nus** *a.*
sullātu'r/iō -ī're *vi.* hanker after being a Sulla.
Su'lm/ō -ō'nis *m.* town in E. Italy, birthplace of Ovid. **-ōnē'nsis** *a.*
su'ltis *ad.* please.
sum e'sse fu'ī *vi.* be, exist. — ab belong to. — ad be designed for. — ex consist of. est, sunt there is, are. est mihi I have. mihi tēcum nīl est I have nothing to do with you. est quod something; there is a reason for. est ubi sometimes. est ut it is possible that. est (*with gen.*) belong to, be the duty of, be characteristic of; (*with inf.*) it is possible, it is permissible. sunt quī some. fuit Īlium Troy is no more. [sow.
sū'm/en -inis *n.* udder, teat;
su'mm/a -ae *f.* main part, chief point, main issue; gist, summary; sum, amount, the whole; supreme power. — rērum the general interest, the whole responsibility. — summārum the universe. ad -am in short, in fact; in conclusion. in -ā in all; after all.
Summā'n/us -ī *m.* god of nocturnal thunderbolts.
summ/ā's -ā'tis *a.* high-born eminent.
summā'tim *ad.* cursorily, summarily. [eignty.
summā't/us -ūs *m.* sover-
su'mmē *ad.* in the highest degree, extremely.
summe'r/gō -gere -sī -sum *vt.* plunge under, sink.
summe'rsus *ppp.* summergō.
summini'str/ō -ā're -ā'vī -ā'tum *vt.* provide, furnish.
summi'ssi/ō -ō'nis *f.* lowering.
summi'ss/us *ppp.* summittō. *a.* low; (*voice*) low, calm; (*character*) mean, grovelling, submissive, humble. **-ē** *ad.* softly; humbly, modestly.
summ/i'ttō -i'ttere -ī'sī -i'ssum *vt.* (*growth*) send up, raise, rear; despatch, supply; let down, lower, reduce, moderate; supersede; send secretly. animum — submit. sē — condescend.
summole'st/us *a.* a little annoying. **-ē** *ad.* with some annoyance.
summo'n/eō -ē're -uī *vt.* drop a hint to. [peevish.
summōrō'sus *a.* rather
summō't/or -ō'ris *m.* clearer.
summō'tus *ppp.* summoveō.
summ/o'veō -ovē're -ō'vī -ō'tum *vt.* move away, drive off; clear away (to make room); withdraw, remove, banish; (*fig.*) dispel.
su'mm/us *a.* highest, the top of, the surface of; last, the end of; (*fig.*) utmost, greatest, most important; (*person*) distinguished, excellent. *m.* head

of the table **-um -ī** *n.* top, surface. **-um** *ad.* at the most.
summū´t/ō -ā´re *vt.* substitute.
sū´m/ō -ere -psī -ptum *vt.* take, take up; assume, arrogate; (*action*) undertake; (*argument*) assume, take for granted; (*dress*) put on; (*punishment*) exact; (*for a purpose*) use, spend.
sū´mpti/ō -ō´nis *f.* assumption.
sūmptuā´rius *a.* sumptuary.
sūmptuō´s/us *a.* expensive, lavish, extravagant. **-ē** *ad.*
sū´mptus *ppp.* sūmō.
sū´mpt/us -ūs *m.* expense, cost.
Sū´n/ium -ī & iī *n.* S.E. promontory of Attica.
su/ō su´ere su´ī sū´tum *vt.* sew, stitch, join together.
suō´met, suō´pte *emphatic abl.* suus.
suovetaurī´l/ia -ium *n.pl.* sacrifice of a pig, sheep and bull.
supe´ll/ex -e´ctilis *f.* furniture, goods, outfit.
su´per *a.*, *see* **superus.**
su´per *ad.* above, on the top; besides, moreover; left, remaining. *pr.* (*with abl.*) upon, above; concerning; besides; (*time*) at. (*with acc.*) over, above, on; beyond; besides, over and above.
su´perā, *see* **suprā.**
superā´bilis *a.* surmountable, conquerable.
supera´dd/ō -ere -itum *vt.* add over and above.
su´per/āns -a´ntis *pres.p.* superō. *a.* predominant.
superā´t/or -ō´ris *m.* conqueror.
supe´rbi/a -ae *f.* arrogance, insolence, tyranny; pride, lofty spirit.
superbiloque´nti/a -ae *f.* arrogant speech.
supe´rb/iō -ī´re *vi.* be arrogant, take a pride in; be superb.
supe´rb/us *a.* arrogant, insolent, overbearing; fastidious; superb, magnificent. **-ē** *ad.* arrogantly, despotically.
superci´l/ium -ī & iī *n.* eyebrow; (*hill*) brow, ridge; (*fig.*) arrogance.
superēmi´n/eō -ē´re *vt.* overtop.
supere´sse *inf.* supersum.
superfi´ci/ēs -ē´ī *f.* surface; (*law*) a building, *esp.* on another's land.
superf/ī´ō -i´erī *vi.* be left over.
superfī´xus *a.* fixed on top.
supe´rflu/ō -ere *vi.* overflow.
supe´rfuī *perf.* supersum.
superf/u´ndō -u´ndere -ū´dī -ū´sum *vt.* & *i.* pour over, shower; (*pass.*) overflow, spread out.
superfū´sus *ppp.* superfundō.
supergre´/dior -dī -ssus *vt.* surpass
super/ia´ciō -ia´cere -iē´cī -ie´ctum & ia´ctum *vt.* throw over, overspread; overtop; (*fig.*) exaggerate.
superie´ctus *ppp.* superiaciō.
superimmi´n/eō -ē´re *vi.* overhang.
superimpe´nd/ēns -e´ntis *a.* overhanging.
superimp/ō´nō -ō´nere -o´suī -o´situm *vt.* place on top.
superimpo´situs *ppp.* superimpōnō.
superi´ncid/ēns -e´ntis *a.* falling from above.
superi´ncub/āns -a´ntis *a.* lying upon.
superincu´mb/ō -ere *vi.* fling oneself down upon.
superi´nger/ō -ere *vt.* pour down.
superi´n/icō -i´cere -iē´cī -ie´ctum *vt.* throw upon, put on top.
superinie´ctus *ppp.* superinicō.

superinste'rn/ō -ere *vt.* lay over.
supe'ri/or -ō'ris *a.* higher, upper; (*time, order*) preceding previous, former; (*age*) older; (*battle*) victorious, stronger; (*quality*) superior, greater.
superlā'ti/ō -ō'nis *f.* exaggeration.
superlā'tus *a.* exaggerated.
supe'rn/us *a.* upper; celestial. –ē *ad.* at the top, from above.
su'per/ō -ā're -ā'vī -ā'tum *vi.* rise above, overtop; have the upper hand; be in excess, be abundant; be left over, survive. *vt.* pass over, surmount go beyond; surpass, outdo; (*mil.*) overcome, conquer; (*naut.*) sail past, double.
supero'bru/ō -ere *vt.* overwhelm. [overhanging.
superpe'nd/ēns -e'ntis *a.*
superp/ō'nō -ō'nere -o'suī -o'situm *vt.* place upon; put in charge of. [pōnō.
superpo'situs *ppp.* super-
supersca'nd/ō -ere *vt.* climb over.
supers/e'deō -edē're -ē'dī -e'ssum *vi.* forbear, desist from.
supe'rst/es -itis *a.* standing over; surviving.
supersti'ti/ō -ō'nis *f.* awful fear, superstition.
superstitiō's/us *a.* superstitious; prophetic. –ē *ad.* superstitiously; scrupulously.
supe'rst/ō -ā're *vt.* & *i.* stand over, stand on.
superstrā'tus *a.* spread over.
supe'rstru/ō -ere -xī -ctum *vt.* build on top.
supe'r/sum -e'sse -fuī *vi.* be left, remain; survive; be in abundance, be sufficient; be in excess.
supe'rteg/ō -ere *vt.* cover over.
superu'rg/ēns -e'ntis *a.* pressing from above.
su'per/us (*comp.* -ior *sup.* suprē'mus, su'mmus) *a.* upper, above. *m.pl.* the gods above; the living. *n.pl.* the heavenly bodies; higher places. mare -um Adriatic Sea.
supervacā'neus *a.* extra, superfluous.
superva'cuus *a.* superfluous, pointless.
supervā'd/ō -ere *vt.* climb over, surmount.
supe'rve/hor -hī -ctus *vt.* ride past, sail past.
superv/e'niō -enī're -ē'nī -e'ntum *vt.* overtake, come on top of. *vi.* come on the scene, arrive unexpectedly
superve'nt/us -ūs *m.* arrival.
supervo'lit/ō -ā're *vt.* fly over. [fly over.
supe'rvol/ō -ā're *vt.* & *i.*
supī'n/ō -ā're -ā'vī -ā'tum *vt.* upturn, lay on its back.
supī'nus *a.* lying back, face up; sloping, on a slope; backwards; (*mind*) indolent, careless.
suppā'ctus *ppp.* suppingō.
suppae'nit/et -ē're *vt.* (*impers.*) be a little sorry.
suppa'lp/or -ā'rī *vi.* coax gently.
su'pp/ār -aris *a.* nearly equal.
supparasī't/or -ā'rī *vi.* flatter gently.
su'ppar/um -ī *n.*, –us -ī *m.* woman's linen garment; topsail. [dance.
suppeditā'ti/ō -ō'nis *f.* abun-
suppe'dit/ō -ā're -ā'vī -ā'tum *vi.* be at hand, be in full supply, be sufficient; be rich in. *vt.* supply, furnish.
suppē'd/ō -ere *vi.* break wind quietly. [ance.
suppe'ti/ae -ā'rum *f.pl.* assist-
suppe'ti/or -ā'rī -ā'tus *vi.* come to the assistance of.
su'ppet/ō -ere -ī'vī & iī -ī'tum *vi.* be available, be in store; be equal to, suffice for.

suppī'l/ō -ā're *vt* steal.
supp/i'ngō -i'ngere -ā'ctum *vt.* fasten underneath.
suppl'ant/ō -ā're *vt.* trip up.
supplēme'nt/um -ī *n.* full complement; reinforcements.
su'ppl/eō -ē're *vt.* fill up, make good, make up to the full complement.
su'ppl/ex -icis *a.* suppliant, in entreaty. **-i'citer** *ad.* in supplication.
supplicā'ti/ō -ō'nis *f.* day of prayer, public thanksgiving.
suppli'c/ium -ī & iī *n.* prayer, entreaty; sacrifice; punishment, execution, suffering. -iō afficere execute.
su'pplic/ō -ā're -ā'vī -ā'tum *vi.* (*with dat.*) entreat, pray to, worship.
supplō'/dō -dere -sī *vt.* stamp.
supplō'si/ō -ō'nis *f.* stamping.
supp/ō'nō -ō'nere -o'suī -o'situm *vt.* put under, apply; subject; add on; substitute, falsify. [transport.
suppo'rt/ō -ā're *vt.* bring up.
suppositī'cius *a.* spurious.
supposi'ti/ō -ō'nis *f.* substitution.
suppo'situs *ppp.* suppōnō.
suppo'suī *perf.* suppōnō.
suppre'ssi/ō -ō'nis *f.* embezzlement.
suppre'ssus *ppp.* supprimō. *a.* (*voice*) low.
su'ppr/imō -i'mere -e'ssī -e'ssum *vt.* sink; restrain, detain, put a stop to; keep secret, suppress.
supprō'm/us -ī *m.* under-butler.
su'ppud/et -ē're *vt.* (*impers.*) be a little ashamed.
suppū'r/ō -ā're *vi.* fester.
su'ppus *a.* head downwards.
su'pput/ō -ā're *vt.* count up.
su'prā *ad.* above, up on top; (*time*) earlier, previously; (*amount*) more. — **quam** beyond what. *pr.* (*with acc.*) over, above; beyond; (*time*) before; (*amount*) more than, over. [mount.
suprāsca'nd/ō -ere *vt.* sur-
suprē'm/us *a.* highest; last, latest; greatest, supreme. *n.pl.* moment of death; funeral rites; testament. **-um** *ad.* for the last time.
sū'r/a -ae *f.* calf (of the leg).
sū'rcul/us -ī *m.* twig, shoot; graft, slip.
surda'st/er -rī *a.* rather deaf.
su'rdit/ās -ā'tis *f.* deafness.
su'rd/us *a.* deaf; silent.
surē'n/a -ae *m.* grand vizier (of the Parthians).
su'rg/ō -ere surrē'xī surrē'ctum *vi.* rise, get up, stand up; arise, spring up, grow
su'rpere *etc. for* **surripere** *etc.*
surr-, *see* **subr-**.
surrē'xī *perf.* surgō.
surru'puī *perf.* subripiō.
surruptī'cius *a.* stolen.
sū'rsum, **sū'rsus** *ad.* upwards, up, high up — **deōrsum** up and down. [sow.
sūs su'is *m.*, *f.* pig, boar, hog,
Sū's/a -ō'rum *n.pl.* ancient Persian capital.
suscē'ns/eō -ē're -uī *vi.* be angry, be irritated.
susce'pti/ō -ō'nis *f.* undertaking.
susce'ptus *ppp.* suscipiō.
susc/i'piō -i'pere -ē'pī -e'ptum *vt.* take up, undertake; receive, catch; (*child*) acknowledge; beget; take under one's protection.
su'scit/ō -ā're -ā'vī -ā'tum *vt.* lift, raise; stir, rouse, awaken; encourage, excite.
suspe'ct/ō -ā're *vt.* & *i.* look up at, watch; suspect, mistrust.
suspe'ctus *ppp.* suspiciō. *a.* suspected, suspicious.
suspe'ct/us -ūs *m.* looking up; esteem.

suspe'nd/ium -ī & iī *n.* hanging.
susp/e'ndō -e'ndere -e'ndī -ē'nsum *vt.* hang, hang up; (*death*) hang; (*building*) support; (*mind*) keep in suspense; (*movement*) check, interrupt; (*pass.*) depend.
suspē'ns/us *ppp.* suspendō. *a.* raised, hanging, poised; with a light touch; (*fig.*) in suspense, uncertain, anxious; dependent. -ō gradū on tiptoe
su'spic/āx -ā'cis *a.* suspicious.
susp/i'ciō -i'cere -e'xī -e'ctum *vt.* look up at, look up to; admire, respect; mistrust.
suspī'ci/ō -ō'nis *f.* mistrust, suspicion.
suspīciō's/us *a.* suspicious. -ē *ad.* suspiciously.
su'spic/or -ā'rī -ā'tus *vt.* suspect; surmise, suppose.
suspīrā't/us -ūs *m.* sigh.
suspī'rit/us -ūs *m.* deep breath, difficult breathing; sigh.
suspī'r/ium -ī & iī *n.* deep breath, sigh.
suspī'r/ō -ā're -ā'vī -ā'tum *vi.* sigh. *vt.* sigh for; exclaim with a sigh.
su'sque dē'que *ad.* up and down.
sustentā'cul/um -ī *n.* prop.
sustentā'ti/ō -ō'nis *f.* forbearance.
suste'nt/ō -ā're -ā'vī -ā'tum *vt.* hold up, support; (*fig.*) uphold, uplift; (*food, means*) sustain, support; (*enemy*) check, hold; (*trouble*) suffer; (*event*) hold back, postpone.
sust/i'neō -inē're -i'nuī -e'ntum *vt.* hold up, support; check, control; (*fig.*) uphold, maintain; (*food, means*) sustain, support; (*trouble*) bear, suffer, withstand; (*event*) put off.
susto'll/ō -ere *vt.* lift up, raise; destroy.
su'stulī *perf.* tollō.
susurrā't/or -ō'ris *m.* whisperer.
susu'rr/ō -ā're *vt.* & *i.* murmur, buzz, whisper.
susu'rr/us -ūs *m.* murmuring, whispering.
susu'rrus *a.* whispering.
sūtē'l/a -ae *f.* trick.
sū'tilis *a.* sewn.
sū't/or -ō'ris *m.* shoemaker. — nē suprā crepidam *let the cobbler stick to his last.*
sūtō'rius *a.* shoemaker's; ex-cobbler.
sūtrī'nus *a.* shoemaker's.
sūtū'r/a -ae *f.* seam.
sū'tus *ppp.* suō.
su'us *a.* his, her, its, their; one's own, proper, due, right. *m.pl.* one's own troops, friends, followers, etc. *n.* one's own property.
Sy'bar/is -is *f.* town in S. Italy, noted for its debauchery. -ī'ta -ī'tae *m.* Sybarite.
Sȳchae'/us -ī *m.* husband of Dido.
sȳcopha'nt/a -ae *m.* slanderer, cheat, sycophant.
sȳcopha'nti/a -ae *f.* deceit.
sȳcophantiō'sē *ad.* deceitfully.
sȳcopha'nt/or -ā'rī *vi.* cheat.
Syē'n/ē -ēs *f.* town in S. Egypt, *mod.* Assuan.
sy'llab/a -ae *f.* syllable.
syllabā'tim *ad.* syllable by syllable.
sy'mbol/a -ae *f.* contribution.
sy'mbol/us -ī *m.* token, symbol.
symphō'ni/a -ae *f.* concord, harmony.
symphōni'acus *a.* choir-.
Symplē'gad/es -um *f.pl.* clashing rocks in the Black Sea.
sy'nedr/us -ī *m.* senator (in Macedonia).
Synephē'b/ī -ō'rum *m.pl.* Youths Together, comedy by Caecilius.
sy'ngraph/a -ae *f.* promissory [note.

sy'ngraph/us -ī *m.* written contract; passport, pass.
Sy'nnad/a -ō'rum *n.pl.* town in Phrygia, famous for marble. **-ē'nsis** *a.*
sy'nod/ūs -o'ntis *m.* bream.
sy'nthes/is -is *f.* dinner service; suit of clothes; dressing-gown.
Sy'ph/āx -ā'cis *m.* king of Numidia.
Syrācū's/ae -ā'rum *f.pl.* Syracuse. **-ā'nus**, **-ius**, **Syrāco'sius** *a.* Syracusan.
Sy'r/ia -iae *f.* country at the E. end of the Mediterranean. **-ius**, **-us**, **-i'acus**, **-i'scus** *a.* Syrian.
sy'rm/a -ae *f.* robe with a train; (*fig.*) tragedy.
Sy'rt/is -is *f.* Gulf of Sidra in N. Africa; sandbank.

T

tabe'll/a -ae *f.* small board, sill; writing-tablet, voting-tablet, votive tablet; picture; (*pl.*) writing, records, dispatches.
tabellā'rius *a.* about voting. *m.* courier. [be wet.
tā'b/eō -ē're *vi.* waste away;
tabe'rn/a -ae *f.* cottage; shop; inn; (*circus*) stalls.
tabernā'cul/um -ī *n.* tent. — capere choose a site (for auspices).
tabernā'ri/ī -ō'rum *m.pl.* shop-keepers.
tā'b/ēs -is *f.* wasting away, decaying, melting; putrefaction; plague, disease.
tāb/ē'scō -ē'scere -uī *vi.* waste away, melt, decay; (*fig.*) pine, languish.
tābi'dulus *a.* consuming.
tā'bidus *a.* melting, decaying; pining; corrupting, infectious.
tābi'ficus *a.* melting, wasting.
ta'bul/a -ae *f.* board, plank; writing-tablet; votive tablet; map; picture; auction; (*pl.*) account-books, records, lists, will. — Sullae Sulla's proscriptions. **XII -ae** Twelve Tables of Roman laws. **-ae** novae cancellation of debts.
tabulā'r/ium -ī & iī *n.* archives. [storey.
tabulā'ti/ō -ō'nis *f.* flooring,
tabulā't/um -ī *n.* flooring, storey; (*trees*) layer, row.
tā'b/um -ī *n.* decaying matter; disease, plague.
ta'c/eō -ē're -uī -itum *vi.* be silent, say nothing; be still, be hushed. *vt.* say nothing about, not speak of.
tacitu'rnit/ās -ā'tis *f.* silence, taciturnity.
tacitu'rnus *a.* silent, quiet.
ta'cit/us *ppp.* taceō. *a.* silent, mute, quiet; secret, unmentioned; tacit, implied. per **-um** quietly. **-ē** *ad.* silently; secretly.
Ta'cit/us -ī *m.* famous Roman historian.
tā'ctilis *a.* tangible.
tā'cti/ō -ō'nis *f.* touching; sense of touch.
tā'ctus *ppp.* tangō.
tā'ct/us -ūs *m.* touch, handling sense of touch; influence.
tae'd/a -ae *f.* pitch-pine, pinewood; torch; plank; (*fig.*) wedding.
tae'd/et -ē're -uit & tae'sum est *vt.* (*impers.*) be weary (of), loathe.
tae'difer -ī *a.* torch-bearing.
tae'd/ium -ī & iī *n.* weariness, loathing.
Tae'nar/us (**-os**) -ī *m.*, *f.*, **-um** (**-on**) -ī *n.* town and promontory in S. Greece, *mod.* Matapan; the lower world. **-ius**, **-is** *a.* of Taenarus; Spartan. **-idēs** -idae *m.* Spartan, *esp.* Hyacinthus.
tae'ni/a -ae *f.* hair-band, ribbon.

tae'sum est *perf.* taedet.
tae't/er -rī *a.* foul, hideous, repulsive. **–rē** *ad.* hideously.
tae'tricus, *see* **te'tricus**.
ta'g/āx -ā'cis *a.* light-fingered.
Ta'g/us -ī *m.* river of Lusitania *mod.* Tagus.
tālā'ris *a.* reaching to the ankles. *n.pl.* winged sandals; a garment reaching to the ankles.
tālā'rius *a.* of dice.
Talā's/ius -ī & iī *m.* god of weddings; wedding-cry.
tā'le/a -ae *f.* rod, stake.
tale'nt/um -ī *n.* talent, a Greek weight about half-cwt.; a large sum of money, *esp.* the Attic talent of 60 minae.
tā'li/ō -ō'nis *f.* retaliation in kind.
tā'lis *a.* such; the following.
ta'lp/a -ae *f.* mole.
tā'l/us -ī *m.* ankle; heel; (*pl.*) knuckle-bones, oblong dice.
tam *ad.* so, so much, so very.
ta'mdiū *ad.* so long, as long.
ta'men *ad.* however, nevertheless, all the same.
Tā'mes/is -is, **–a** -ae *m.* Thames.
tame'tsī *conj.* although.
ta'mquam, ta'nquam *ad.* as, just as, just like. *conj.* as if.
Ta'nagr/a -ae *f.* town in Boeotia.
Ta'na/is -is *m.* river in Sarmatia, *mod.* Don.
Ta'naqu/il -ilis *f.* wife of the elder Tarquin.
ta'ndem *ad.* at last, at length, finally; (*question*) just.
ta'ng/ō -ere te'tigī tā'ctum *vt.* touch, handle; (*food*) taste; (*with force*) hit, strike; (*with liquid*) sprinkle; (*mind*) affect, move; (*place*) reach; border on; (*task*) take in hand; (*by trick*) take in, fool; (*in words*) touch on, mention. **dē caelō tāctus** struck by lightning.
ta'nquam, *see* **tamquam**.
Ta'ntal/us -ī *m.* father of Pelops, condemned to hunger and thirst in Tartarus, or to the threat of an overhanging rock. **–eus** *a.* **–idēs** -idae *m.* Pelops, Atreus, Thyestes or Agamemnon. **–is** -idis *f.* Niobe or Hermione.
tanti'llus *a.* so little, so small.
tanti'sper *ad.* so long, just for a moment.
tanto'pere *ad.* so much.
ta'ntulus *a.* so little, so small.
ta'ntum *ad.* so much, so, as; only, merely. — **modo** only. — **nōn** all but, almost. — **quod** only just.
tantu'mmodo *ad.* only.
tantu'ndem just as much, just so much.
ta'nt/us *a.* so great; so little. *n.* so much; so little. **-ī esse** be worth so much, be so dear, be so important. **-ō** so much, so far; (*with comp.*) so much the. **-ō opere** so much. **in -um** to such an extent. **tria -a** three times as much.
tantu'sdem *a.* just so great.
tapē't/a -ae *m.*, **–ia** -ium *n.pl.* carpet, tapestry, hangings.
Tapro'ban/ē -ēs *f.* Ceylon.
tardē'sc/ō -ere *vi.* become slow, falter.
ta'rdip/ēs -edis *a.* limping.
ta'rdit/ās -ā'tis *f.* slowness, tardiness; (*mind*) dullness.
tardiu'sculus *a.* rather slow.
ta'rd/ō -ā're -ā'vī -ā'tum *vt.* retard, impede. *vi.* delay, go slow.
ta'rd/us *a.* slow, tardy, late; (*mind*) dull; (*speech*) deliberate. **–ē** *ad.* slowly, tardily.
Tare'nt/um -ī *n.* town in S. Italy, *mod.* Taranto. **–ī'nus** *a.* Tarentine.
ta'rm/es -itis *m.* wood-worm.
Tarpē'i/us *a.* Tarpeian. **mōns** — the Tarpeian Rock on the Capitoline Hill from which criminals were thrown.

tarpezī′t/a -ae *m.* banker.
Tarquiʹn/ius -ī *m.* Tarquin, *esp.* Priscus, the fifth king of Rome, and Superbus, the last king. **-iī -iōʹrum** *m.pl.* ancient town in Etruria. **-ius** *a.* of Tarquin. **-iēʹnsis** of Tarquinii.
Tarracīʹn/a -ae *f.*, **-ae -āʹrum** *f.pl.* town in Latium.
Taʹrrac/ō -ōʹnis *f.* town in Spain, *mod.* Tarragona. **-ōnēʹnsis** *a.*
Taʹrs/us -ī *f.* capital of Cilicia. **-ēʹnsis** *a.*
Taʹrtar/us (-os) -ī *m.*, **-a** -ōʹrum *n.pl.* Tartarus, the lower world, *esp.* the part reserved for criminals. **-eus** *a.* infernal.
tat *interj.* hallo there!
Taʹt/ius -ī *m.* Sabine king, who ruled jointly with Romulus. **-ius** *a.*
Taʹ/um -ī *n.* Firth of Tay.
tauʹreus *a.* bull's. *f.* whip of bull's hide.
Tauʹr/ī -ōʹrum *m.pl.* Thracians of the Crimea. **-icus** *a.*
taurifōʹrmis *a.* bull-shaped.
Taurīʹn/ī -ōʹrum *m.pl.* people of N. Italy, *mod.* Turin.
taurīʹnus *a.* bull's.
Tauromeʹn/ium -ī & iī *n.* town in E. Sicily. **-ītāʹnus** *a.*
tauʹr/us -ī *m.* bull.
Tauʹr/us -ī *m.* mountain range in S.E. Asia Minor.
taxāʹti/ō -ōʹnis *f.* valuing.
taʹxeus *a.* of yews.
taxiʹll/us -ī *m.* small dice.
taʹx/ō -āʹre *vt.* value estimate.
taʹx/us -ī *f.* yew.
Tāyʹget/ē -ēʹs *f.* a Pleiad.
Tāyʹget/us -ī *m.*, **-a** -ōʹrum *n.pl.* mountain range in S. Greece.
tē *acc.* & *abl.* **tū.**
-te *suffix for* tū.
Teāʹn/um -ī*n.* town in Apulia; town in Campania. **-ēʹnsis** *a.*
teʹchin/a -ae *f.* trick.
Tecmeʹss/a -ae *f.* wife of Ajax.
tēʹct/or -ōʹris *m.* plasterer.
tēctōriʹol/um -ī *n.* a little plaster. [stucco.
tēctōʹr/ium -ī & iī *n.* plaster,
tēctōʹrius *a.* of a plasterer.
tēʹct/um -ī *n.* roof, ceiling, canopy; house, dwelling, shelter.
tēʹctus *ppp.* **tegō.** *a.* hidden; secret, reserved, close.
tēʹcum with you.
Teʹge/a -ae *f.* town in Arcadia. **-aeʹus** *a.* Arcadian. *m.* the god Pan. *f.* Atalanta. **-āʹtae** -ātāʹrum *m.pl.* Tegeans.
teʹg/es -etis *f.* mat.
tegiʹll/um -ī *n.* hood, cowl.
teʹgim/en (teʹgumen, teʹgmen) -inis *n.* covering.
tegimeʹnt/um (tegumeʹntum, tegmeʹntum) -ī *n.* covering.
tegm-, *see* **tegim-.**
teʹg/ō -ere **tēʹxī tēʹctum** *vt.* cover; hide, conceal; protect, defend; bury. latus — walk by the side of. [roof.
tēʹgul/a -ae *f.* tile; (*pl.*) tiled
tegum- *see* **tegim.**
Tēʹius *a.* of Teos.
tēʹl/a -ae *f.* web; warp; yarn-beam, loom; (*fig.*) plan.
Teʹlam/ōn -ōʹnis *m.* father of Ajax.
Tēleʹgon/us -ī *m.* son of Ulysses and Circe.
Tēleʹmach/us -ī *m.* son of Ulysses and Penelope.
Tēleph/us -ī *m.* king of Mysia, wounded by Achilles' spear.
teʹll/ūs -ūʹris *f.* the earth; earth, ground; land, country.
tēʹl/um -ī *n.* weapon, missile; javelin, sword; (*fig.*) shaft, dart.
temerāʹrius *a.* accidental; rash, thoughtless.
teʹmerē *ad.* by chance, at random; rashly, thoughtlessly.

nōn — not for nothing; not easily; hardly ever.
teme'rit/ās -ā'tis *f.* chance; rashness, thoughtlessness.
te'mer/ō -ā're -ā'vī -ā'tum *vt.* desecrate, disgrace.
tēmē't/um -ī *n.* wine, alcohol.
te'mn/ō -ere *vt.* slight, despise.
tē'm/ō -ō'nis *m.* beam (of plough or carriage); cart; (*astr.*) the Plough.
Te'mpē *n.pl.* famous valley in Thessaly.
temperāme'nt/um -ī *n.* moderation, compromise.
te'mper/āns -a'ntis *pres.p.* temperō. *a.* moderate, temperate. **-a'nter** *ad.* with moderation.
tempera'nti/a -ae *f.* moderation, self-control.
temperā'ti/ō -ō'nis *f.* proper mixture, composition, constitution; organizing power.
temperā't/or -ō'ris *m.* organizer.
temperā't/us *ppp.* temperō. *a.* moderate, sober. **-ē** *ad.* with moderation.
te'mperī *ad.* in time, at the right time.
tempe'ri/ēs -ē'ī *f.* due proportion; temperature, mildness.
te'mper/ō -ā're -ā'vī -ā'tum *vt.* mix in due proportion, blend, temper; regulate, moderate, tune; govern, rule. *vi.* be moderate, forbear, abstain; (*with dat.*) spare, be lenient to.
tempe'st/ās -ā'tis *f.* time, season, period; weather; storm; (*fig.*) storm, shower.
tempestī'vit/ās -ā'tis *f.* seasonableness.
tempestī'v/us *a.* timely, seasonable, appropriate; ripe, mature; early. **-ē** *ad.* at the right time, appropriately.
te'mpl/um -ī *n.* space marked off for taking auspices; open space, region, quarter; sanctuary; temple.
temporā'rius *a.* for the time, temporary.
temptābu'ndus *a.* making repeated attempts.
temptāme'nt/um -ī *n.* trial, attempt, proof.
temptā'min/a -um *n.pl.* attempts, essays.
temptā'ti/ō -ō'nis *f.* trial, proof; attack.
temptā't/or -ō'ris *m.* assailant.
te'mpt/ō -ā're -ā'vī -ā'tum *vt.* feel, test by touching; make an attempt on, attack; try, essay, attempt; try to influence, tamper with, tempt, incite. vēnās— feel the pulse.
te'mp/us -oris *n.* time; right time, opportunity; danger, emergency, circumstance; (*head*) temple; (*verse*) unit of metre; (*verb*) tense. **-ore** at the right time, in time. **ad -us** at the right time; for the moment. **ante -us** too soon. **ex -ore** on the spur of the moment; to suit the circumstances. **in -ore** in time. **in -us** temporarily. **per -us** just in time. **prō -ore** to suit the occasion.
tēmule'ntus *a.* intoxicated.
tenā'cit/ās -ā'tis *f.* firm grip; stinginess.
te'n/āx -ā'cis *a.* gripping, tenacious; sticky; (*fig.*) firm, persistent; stubborn; stingy. **-ā'citer** *ad.* tightly, firmly.
tendi'cul/a -ae *f.* little snare.
te'nd/ō -ere tete'ndī te'ntum & tē'nsum *vt.* stretch, spread; strain; (*arrow*) aim, shoot; (*bow*) bend; (*course*) direct; (*lyre*) tune; (*tent*) pitch; (*time*) prolong; (*trap*) lay. *vi.* encamp go, proceed; aim, tend; (*with inf.*) endeavour, exert oneself.
te'nebr/ae -ā'rum *f.pl.* darkness, night; unconsciousness, death, blindness; (*place*) dun-

geon, haunt, the lower world; (*fig.*) ignorance, obscurity.
tenebricō'sus *a.* gloomy.
tenebrō'sus *a.* dark, gloomy.
Te'ned/os (**-us**) **-ī** *f.* Aegean island near Troy. **-ius** *a.*
tene'llulus *a.* dainty little.
te'n/eō -ē're -uī *vt.* hold, keep; possess, occupy, be master of; attain, acquire; (*argument*) maintain, insist; (*category*) comprise; (*goal*) make for; (*interest*) fascinate; (*law*) bind, be binding on; (*mind*) grasp, understand, remember; (*movement*) hold back, restrain. *vi.* hold on, last, persist; (*rumour*) prevail. **cursum —** keep on one's course. **sē —** remain; refrain.
te'ner -ī *a.* tender, delicate; young, weak; effeminate; (*poet*) erotic. **-ē** *ad.* softly.
tenerā'sc/ō -ere *vi.* grow weak.
tene'rit/ās -ā'tis *f.* weakness.
te'n/or -ō'ris *m.* steady course. **ūnō -ōre** without a break, uniformly.
tē'ns/a -ae *f.* carriage bearing the images of the gods in procession. [strained.
tē'nsus *ppp.* **tendō.** *a.*
tentā-, *see* **temptā-.**
tentī'g/ō -inis *f.* lust.
te'ntō, *see* **temptō.**
tentō'r/ium -ī & iī *n.* tent.
te'ntus *ppp.* **tendō.**
tenui'culus *a.* paltry.
te'nu/is *a.* thin, fine; small, shallow; (*air*) rarefied; (*water*) clear; (*condition*) poor, mean, insignificant; (*style*) refined, direct, precise. **-iter** *ad.* thinly; poorly; with precision; superficially.
tenu'it/as -ā'tis *f.* thinness, fineness; poverty, insignificance; (*style*) precision.
te'nu/ō -ā're -ā'vī -ā'tum *vt.* make thin, attenuate, rarefy; lessen, reduce.
te'nus *pr.* (*with gen. or abl.*) as far as, up to, down to. **verbō —** in name, nominally.
Te'/os -ī *f.* town on coast of Asia Minor, birthplace of Anacreon. **Te'/ius** *a.*
tepe/fa'ciō -fa'cere -fē'cī -fa'ctum *vt.* warm.
te'p/eō -ē're *vi.* be warm, be lukewarm; (*fig.*) be in love.
tep/ē'scō -ē'scere -uī *vi.* grow warm; become lukewarm, cool off.
te'pidus *a.* warm, lukewarm.
te'p/or -ō'ris *m.* warmth; coolness.
ter *ad.* three times, thrice.
terde'ci/ēns, -ēs *ad.* thirteen times. [tree.
terebi'nth/us -ī *f.* turpentine
te'rebr/a -ae *f.* gimlet.
te'rebr/ō -ā're *vt.* bore.
terē'd/ō -inis *f.* grub.
Tere'nt/ius -ī *m.* Roman family name, *esp.* the comic poet Terence. **-ius, -iā'nus** *a.* **-ia -iae** *f.* Cicero's wife.
te'r/es -etis *a.* rounded (*esp.* cylindrical), smooth, shapely; (*fig.*) polished, elegant.
Tē'r/eus -eī & eos *m.* king of Thrace, husband of Procne, father of Itys. [triple.
terge'minus *a.* threefold,
te'r/geō -gē're (**-gō -gere**) **-sī -sum** *vt.* wipe off, scour, clean; rub up, burnish.
tergī'n/um -ī *n.* raw-hide.
tergiversā'ti/ō -ō'nis *f.* refusal, subterfuge.
tergive'rs/or -ā'rī -ā'tus *vi.* hedge, boggle, be evasive.
te'rgō, *see* **tergeō.**
te'rg/um -ī, -us -oris *n.* back; rear; (*land*) ridge; (*water*) surface; (*meat*) chine; (*skin*) hide, leather, anything made of leather. **-a vertere** take to flight. **ā -ō** behind, in the rear.
te'rgus, *see* **tergum.**
te'rm/es -itis *m.* branch

Terminā'l/ia -ium *n.pl.* Festival of the god of Boundaries.
terminā'ti/ō -ō'nis *f.* decision; (*words*) clausula.
te'rmin/ō -ā're -ā'vī -ā'tum *vt.* set bounds to, limit; define, determine; end.
te'rmin/us -ī *m.* boundary-line, limit, bound; god of boundaries. [three.
te'rn/ī -ō'rum *a.* three each;
te'r/ō -ere trī'vī trī'tum *vt.* rub, crush, grind; smooth, sharpen; wear away, use up; (*road*) frequent; (*time*) waste; (*word*) make commonplace.
Terpsi'chor/ē -ēs *f.* Muse of dancing.
te'rr/a -ae *f.* dry land earth, ground, soil; land, country. orbis -ārum the world. ubi -ārum where in the world.
terrē'nus *a.* of earth; terrestrial, land-. *n.* land.
te'rr/eō -ē're -uī -itum *vt.* frighten, terrify; scare away; deter.
terre'stris *a.* earthly, on earth, land-.
terri'bilis *a.* terrifying, dreadful. [bogy.
terri'cul/a -ō'rum *n.pl.* scare,
terri'fic/ō -ā're *vt.* terrify.
terri'ficus *a.* alarming, formidable.
terri'gen/a -ae *m.* earth-born.
terri'loquus *a.* alarming.
te'rrit/ō -ā're *vt.* frighten, intimidate. [territory.
territō'r/ium -ī & iī *n.*
te'rr/or -ō'ris *m.* fright, alarm, terror; a terror.
te'rsī *perf.* tergeō.
te'rsus *ppp.* tergeō. *a.* clean; neat, terse.
tertiadecimā'n/ī -ō'rum *m.pl.* men of the thirteenth legion.
tertiā'nus *a.* recurring every second day. *f.* a fever. *m.pl.* men of the third legion.
te'rti/us *a.* third. **-um** *ad.* for the third time. **-ō** *ad.* for the third time; thirdly. — decimus (decumus) thirteenth.
terū'nc/ius -ī & iī *m.* quarter-as; a fourth; (*fig.*) farthing.
te'squ/a (**te'sca**) -ō'rum *n.pl.* waste ground, desert.
tesse'll/a -ae *f.* cube of mosaic stone.
te'sser/a -ae *f.* cube, dice; (*mil.*) password; token (for mutual recognition of friends); ticket (for doles).
tesserā'r/ius -ī & iī *m.* officer of the watch.
te'st/a -ae *f.* brick, tile; (*earthenware*) pot, jug, sherd; (*fish*) shell, shell-fish.
testāmentā'rius *a.* testamentary. *m.* forger of wills.
testāme'nt/um -ī *n.* will, testament.
testā'ti/ō -ō'nis *f.* calling to witness.
testā'tus *ppa.* testor. *a.* public.
testi'cul/us -ī *m.* testicle.
testificā'ti/ō -ō'nis *f.* giving evidence, evidence.
testi'fic/or -ā'rī -ā'tus *vt.* give evidence, vouch for; make public, bring to light; call to witness.
testimō'n/ium -ī & iī *n.* evidence, testimony; proof.
te'st/is -is *m., f.* witness; eye-witness.
te'st/is -is *m.* testicle.
te'st/or -ā'rī -ā'tus *vt.* give evidence, testify; prove, vouch for; call to witness, appeal to. *vi.* make a will.
te'st/ū (*abl.* -ū), **-um** -ī *n.* earthenware lid, pot.
testūdi'neus *a.* of tortoise-shell, tortoise-.
testū'd/ō -inis *f.* tortoise; tortoise-shell; lyre, lute; (*mil.*) shelter for besiegers, covering of shields; (*building*) vault.
te'stum, *see* **testū**.
tete'ndī *perf.* tendō.

tē'te *emphatic acc.* **tū.**
tē'ter, *see* **taeter.**
Tē'thy/s -os *f.* sea-goddess; the sea.
te'tigī *perf.* tangō.
tetradra'chm/um, tetra'chm/um -ī *n.* four drachmas.
te'tra/ō -ō'nis *m.* black-cock, grouse or capercailzie.
tetra'rch/ēs -ae *m.* tetrarch, ruler.
tetra'rchi/a -ae *f.* tetrarchy.
te'tricus *a.* gloomy, sour.
te'tulī *archaic perf.* ferō.
Teu'c/er -rī *m.* son of Telamon of Salamis; son-in-law of Dardanus. **-rī** -rō'rum *m.pl.* Trojans. **-ria** -riae *f.* Troy.
Teu'ton/ī -ō'rum, **-es** -um *m.pl.* Teutons, a German people. **-icus** *a.* Teutonic, German.
tē'xī *perf.* tegō.
te'x/ō -ere -uī -tum *vt.* weave; plait; build, make; (*fig.*) compose, contrive.
te'xtilis *a.* woven. *n.* fabric.
te'xt/or -ō'ris *m.* weaver.
textrī'n/um -ī *n.* weaving; ship-yard.
textū'r/a -ae *f.* web, fabric.
te'xtus *ppp.* texō. *n.* web, fabric.
te'xt/us -ūs *m.* texture.
te'xuī *perf.* texō. [courtesan.
Thā'/is -idis *f.* an Athenian
tha'lam/us -ī *m.* room, bedroom; marriage-bed; marriage.
thala'ssicus *a.* sea-green.
thala'ssinus *a.* sea-green.
Tha'l/ēs -is & ē'tis *m.* early Greek philosopher, one of the seven wise men.
Tha'li/a -ae *f.* Muse of comedy.
tha'll/us -ī *m.* green bough.
Tha'myr/ās -ae *m.* blinded Thracian poet.
Tha'ps/us (-os) -ī *f.* town in N. Africa, scene of Caesar's victory. **-itā'nus** *a.*
Tha's/us (-os) -ī *f.* Greek island in N. Aegean. **-ius** *a.*
Thauma'ntia/s -dis *f.* Iris.
theātrā'lis *a.* of the theatre, in the theatre.
theā'tr/um -ī *n.* theatre; audience; (*fig.*) theatre, stage.
Thē'b/ae -ā'rum *f.pl.* Thebes, capital of Boeotia; town in Upper Egypt. **-ā'nus** *a.* Theban. **-ais** -a'idis *f.* Theban woman; epic poem by Statius.
thē'c/a -ae *f.* case, envelope.
The'mi/s -dis *f.* goddess of justice.
Themisto'cl/ēs -ī & is *m.* famous Athenian statesman. **-ē'us** *a.* [ure.
thēnsaurā'rius *a.* of treas-
thēnsau'rus, *see* **thēsaurus.**
theo'log/us -ī *m.* theologian.
Theophra'st/us -ī *m.* Greek philosopher, successor to Aristotle.
Theopo'mp/us -ī *m.* Greek historian. **-ē'us**, **-ī'nus** *a.*
the'rm/ae -ā'rum *f.pl.* warm baths.
The'rmōd/ōn -o'ntis *m.* river of Pontus, where the Amazons lived. **-ontē'us**, **-onti'acus** *a.* Amazonian.
thermopō'l/ium *n.* restaurant serving warm drinks.
thermo'pot/ō -ā're *vt.* refresh with warm drinks.
Thermo'pyl/ae -ā'rum *f.pl.* famous Greek pass defended by Leonidas.
thēsau'r/us, thēnsau'r/us -ī *m.* treasure, store; storehouse, treasury.
Thē's/eus -eī & eos *m.* Greek hero, king of Athens. **-ē'us**, **-ē'ius** *a.* **-ī'dēs** -ī'dae *m.* Hippolytus; (*pl.*) Athenians.
The'spi/ae -ā'rum *f.pl.* Boeotian town near Helicon. **-ē'nsis**, **-as** -adis *a.* Thespian.
The'sp/is -is *m.* traditional founder of Greek tragedy.

Thessa'l/ia -iae *f.* Thessaly, district of N. Greece. **-icus, -us, -is** -idis *a.* Thessalian.
The't/is -idis & idos *f.* sea-nymph, mother of Achilles; the sea.
thi'as/us -ī *m.* Bacchic dance.
Tho'/ās -a'ntis *m.* king of Crimea, killed by Orestes; king of Lemnos, father of Hypsipyle. **-antē'us** *a.*
tho'l/us -ī *m.* rotunda.
thō'r/āx -ā'cis *m.* breast plate.
Thrā'c/a -ae, -ē -ēs, -ia -iae *f.* Thrace. **-ius, Thrēi'cius** *a.* Thracian. **Thr/āx** -ā'cis *m.* Thracian; kind of gladiator.
Thra'se/a -ae *m.* Stoic philosopher under Nero.
Thrasy'mach/us -ī *m.* Greek sophist.
Thrē'ss/a -ae, **Thrēi'ss/a** -ae *f.* Thracian woman.
Thr/ēx -ē'cis *m.* kind of gladiator.
Thūcy'did/ēs -is *m.* famous Greek historian. **-ius** *a.* Thucydidean.
Thū'l/ē (**Thȳ'lē**) -ēs *f.* island in the extreme N., *perh.* Shetland.
thu'nnus, *see* **thynnus.**
Thū'r/iī -iō'rum *m.pl.* town in S. Italy. **-ī'nus** *a.*
thūs, thūr-, *see* **tūs, tūr-.**
thȳ'/a (**thȳ'ia**) -ae *f.* citrus-tree.
Thy'br/is -is & idis *m.* river [Tiber.
Thye'st/ēs -ae *m.* brother of Atreus, whose son's flesh he served up to him to eat. **-ē'us** *a.* **-i'adēs** -i'adae *m.* Aegisthus.
Thyi'/as (**Thȳ'as**) -adis *f.* Bacchante.
Thȳ'lē, *see* **Thūlē.**
thy'mbr/a -ae *f.* savory.
thy'm/um -ī *n.* garden thyme.
Thȳ'n/ia -iae *f.* Bithynia. **-us, -i'acus, -ias** *a.* Bithynian.
thy'nn/us -ī *m.* tunny-fish.
Thyō'n/eus -eī *m.* Bacchus.
thy'rs/us -ī *m.* Bacchic wand.
tiā'r/a -ae *f.*, **-ās** -ae *m.* turban.
Ti'ber/is (**Ti'bris**) -is *m.* river Tiber. **-ī'nus, -ī'nis** *a.* **-ī'nus** -ī'nī *m.* Tiber.
Tibe'r/ius -ī *m.* Roman praenomen, *esp.* the second emperor. **-iā'nus** *a.*
ti'bi *dat.* **tū.**
tī'bi/a -ae *f.* shin-bone; pipe, flute.
tībī'c/en -inis *m.* flute-player; pillar.
tībī'cin/a -ae *f.* flute-player.
tībici'n/ium -ī & iī *n.* flute-playing.
Tibu'll/us -ī *m.* Latin elegiac poet.
Tī'bur -is *n.* town on the river Anio, *mod.* Tivoli. **-s** -tis, **-tī'nus, -nus** *a.* Tiburtine.
Tīcī'n/us -ī *m.* tributary of the river Po. [of Nero.
Tigellī'n/us -ī *m.* favourite
tigi'll/um -ī *n.* small log, small beam.
tignā'rius *a.* working in wood. **faber** — carpenter.
ti'gn/um -ī *n.* timber, trunk, log. [Armenia.
Tigrā'n/ēs -is *m.* king of
ti'gr/is -is & idis *f.* tiger.
tī'li/a -ae *f.* lime-tree.
Tīmae'/us -ī *m.* Sicilian historian; Pythagorean philosopher; a dialogue of Plato.
timefa'ctus *a.* frightened.
ti'm/eō -ē're -uī *vt.* & *i.* fear, be afraid.
timi'dit/ās -ā'tis *f.* timidity, cowardice.
ti'mid/us *a.* timid, cowardly. **-ē** *ad.* timidly.
ti'm/or -ō'ris *m.* fear, alarm; a terror.
ti'nctilis *a.* dipped in.
ti'nctus *ppp.* **tingō.**
ti'ne/a -ae *f.* moth, bookworm.

ti'n/gō -gere -xī -ctum *vt.* dip, soak; dye, colour; (*fig.*) imbue.
tinnīme'nt/um -ī *n.* ringing [noise.
ti'nn/iō -ī're *vt.* & *i.* ring, tinkle. [jingle.
tinnī't/us -ūs *m.* ringing,
ti'nnulus *a.* ringing, jingling.
tintinnā'bul/um -ī *n.* bell.
ti'ntin/ō -ā're *vi.* ring.
tī'n/us -ī *m.* a shrub, laurustinus.
ti'nxī *perf.* tingō. [the Argo.
Tī'phy/s -os *m.* helmsman of
ti'ppul/a -ae *f.* water-spider.
Tīre'si/ās -ae *m.* blind soothsayer of Thebes.
Tīridā't/ēs -ae *m.* king of Armenia. [ginner.
tī'r/ō -ō'nis *m.* recruit, be-
Tī'r/ō -ō'nis *m.* Cicero's freedman secretary. **-ōniā'nus** *a.*
tīrōci'n/ium -ī & iī *n.* first campaign; recruits; (*fig.*) first attempt, inexperience.
tīru'ncul/us -ī *m.* young beginner.
Tī'ryn/s -this *f.* ancient town in S.E. Greece, home of Hercules. **-thius** *a.* of Tiryns, of Hercules. *m.* Hercules.
tis *archaic gen.* tū.
Tīsi'phon/ē -ēs *f.* a Fury.
-ē'us *a.* guilty.
Tī't/ān -ā'nis, **-ā'nus** -ā'nī *m.* Titan, an ancient race of gods; the sun. **-ā'nius**, **-āni'acus**, **-ā'nis** *a.*
Tīthō'n/us -ī *m.* consort of Aurora, granted immortality without youth. **-ius** *a.*
tītillā'ti/ō -ō'nis *f.* tickling.
tīti'll/ō -ā're *vt.* tickle.
tituba'nter *ad.* falteringly.
titubā'ti/ō -ō'nis *f.* staggering.
ti'tub/ō -ā're *vi.* stagger, totter, stammer; waver, falter.
ti'tul/us -ī *m.* inscription, label, notice; title of honour; fame; pretext.
Ti'ty/os -ī *m.* giant punished in Tartarus.
Tmō'l/us -ī *m.* mountain in Lydia.
tocu'li/ō -ō'nis *m.* usurer.
tō'f/us -ī *m.* tufa.
to'g/a -ae *f.* toga, dress of the Roman citizen; (*fig.*) peace. — candida dress of election candidates. — picta ceremonial dress of a victor in triumph. —praetexta purple-edged toga of magistrates and children. — pūra, virīlis plain toga of manhood.
togā'tus *a.* wearing the toga. *m.* Roman citizen; client. *f.* drama on a Roman theme.
to'gul/a -ae *f.* small toga.
tolerā'bil/is *a.* bearable, tolerable; patient. **-iter** *ad.* patiently.
to'ler/āns -a'ntis *pres.p.* tolerō. *a.* patient. **-a'nter** *ad.* patiently.
tolera'nti/a -ae *f.* endurance.
tolerā'ti/ō -ō'nis *f.* enduring.
to'ler/ō -ā're -ā'vī -ā'tum *vt.* bear, endure; support, sustain. **-ā'tus** *a.* tolerable.
tollē'n/ō -ō'nis *m.* crane, derrick, lift.
to'll/ō -ere su'stulī sublā'tum *vt.* lift, raise; take away remove; do away with, abolish, destroy; (*anchor*) weigh; (*child*) acknowledge, bring up; (*mind*) elevate, excite, cheer; (*passenger*) take on board. signa — decamp. [**-ā'nus** *a.*
Tolō's/a -ae *f.* Toulouse.
tolū'tim *ad.* at a trot.
tomā'cul/um -ī *n.* sausage.
tōme'nt/um -ī *n.* stuffing, padding.
To'm/is -is *f.* town on the Black Sea, to which Ovid was exiled. **-ītā'nus** *a.*
To'n/āns -a'ntis *m.* Thunderer, epithet of Jupiter.
to'nd/eō -ē're toto'ndī tō'nsum *vt.* shear, clip, shave; crop, reap, mow; graze, browse on; (*fig.*) fleece, rob.

tonitrā'lis *a.* thunderous.
to'nitr/us **-ūs** *m.*, **–ua** **-uō'rum** *n.pl.* thunder.
to'n/ō **-ā're** **-uī** *vi.* thunder. *vt.* thunder out.
tō'ns/a **-ae** *f.* oar.
tōnsi'll/ae **-ā'rum** *f.pl.* tonsils.
tō'ns/or **-ō'ris** *m.* barber.
tōnsō'rius *a.* for shaving.
tōnstri'cul/a **-ae** *f.* barber-girl. [shop.
tōnstrī'n/a **-ae** *f.* barber's
tō'nstr/īx **-ī'cis** *f.* woman barber. [clipping.
tōnsū'r/a **-ae** *f.* shearing,
tō'nsus *ppp.* tondeō.
tō'ns/us **-ūs** *m.* coiffure.
tō'phus, *see* **tōfus**.
topiā'rius *a.* of ornamental gardening. *m.* topiarist. *f.* topiary.
to'pic/ē **-ēs** *f.* the art of finding topics.
to'r/al **-ā'lis** *n.* valance.
to'rcul/ar **-ā'ris**, **–um** **-ī** *n.* press.
toreu'ma **-tis** *n.* embossed work, relief.
torme'nt/um **-ī** *n.* windlass, torsion catapult, artillery; shot; rack, torture; (*fig.*) torment, anguish.
to'rmin/a **-um** *n.pl.* colic.
torminō'sus *a.* subject to colic.
to'rn/ō **-ā're** **-ā'vī** **-ā'tum** *vt.* turn (in a lathe), round off.
to'rn/us **-ī** *m.* lathe.
torō'sus *a.* muscular.
torpē'd/ō **-inis** *f.* numbness, lethargy; (*fish*) electric ray.
to'rp/eō **-ē're** *vi.* be stiff, be numb; be stupefied.
torp/ē'scō **-ē'scere** **-uī** *vi.* grow stiff, numb, listless.
to'rpidus *a.* benumbed.
to'rp/or **-ō'ris** *m.* numbness, torpor, listlessness.
torquā'tus *a.* wearing a neck-chain. [of Manlius.
Torquā't/us **-ī** *m.* surname
to'r/queō **-quē're** **-sī** **-tum** *vt.* turn, twist, bend, wind; (*missile*) whirl, hurl, brandish; (*body*) rack, torture; (*mind*) torment.
to'rqu/ēs, **–is** **-is** *m.*, *f.* neck-chain, necklace, collar.
to'rr/ēns **-e'ntis** *pres.p.* torreō. *a.* scorching, hot; rushing, rapid. *m.* torment.
to'rr/eō **-ē're** **-uī** **to'stum** *vt.* parch, scorch, roast.
torrē'sc/ō **-ere** *vi.* become parched.
to'rridus *a.* parched, dried up; frost-bitten. [brand.
to'rr/is **-is** *m.* brand, fire-
to'rsī *perf.* **torqueō**.
to'rtilis *a.* twisted, winding.
to'rt/or **-ā'rī** *vi.* writhe.
to'rt/or **-ō'ris** *m.* torturer, executioner. [complicated.
tortuō'sus *a.* winding; (*fig.*)
to'rt/us *ppp.* torqueō. *a.* crooked; complicated. **–ē** *ad.* awry.
to'rt/us **-ūs** *m.* twisting, writhing.
to'rul/us **-ī** *m.* tuft (of hair).
to'r/us **-ī** *m.* knot, bulge; muscle, brawn; couch, bed; (*earth*) bank, mound; (*language*) ornament. [grimness.
to'rvit/ās **-ā'tis** *f.* wildness,
to'rvus *a.* wild, grim, fierce.
to'stus *ppp.* torreō.
tot *a.* (*indecl.*) so many, as many.
to'tidem *a.* (*indecl.*) just as many, the same number of.
to'tiēns, **to'tiēs** *ad.* so often, as often.
toto'ndī *perf.* **tondeō**.
tō't/us (*gen.* **-ī'us** *dat.* **-ī**) *a.* entire, the whole, all; entirely, completely taken up with. **ex -ō** totally. **in -ō** on the whole.
to'xic/um **-ī** *n.* poison.
trabā'lis *a.* for beams. **clāvus** — large nail.
tra'be/a **-ae** *f.* ceremonial robe.

trabeā'tus *a.* wearing a ceremonial robe.

tr/abs -a'bis *f.* beam, timber; tree; ship, roof.

Trā'ch/īn -ī'nis *f.* town in Thessaly, where Hercules cremated himself. **-ī'nius** *a.*

tractā'bilis *a.* manageable, tractable. [treatment.

tractā'ti/ō -ō'nis *f.* handling,

tractā't/us -ūs *m.* handling.

tra'ctim *ad.* slowly, little by little.

tra'ct/ō -ā're -ā'vī -ā'tum *vt.* maul; handle, deal with, manage; (*activity*) conduct, perform; (*person*) treat; (*subject*) discuss, consider.

tra'ctus *ppp.* trahō. *a.* fluent.

tra'ct/us -ūs *m.* dragging, pulling, drawing; train, track; (*place*) extent, region, district; (*movement*) course; (*time*) lapse; (*word*) drawling.

trā'didī *perf.* trādō.

trādi'ti/ō -ō'nis *f.* surrender; handing down.

trā'dit/or -ō'ris *m.* traitor.

trā'ditus *ppp.* trādō.

trā'd/ō (trā'nsdō) -ere -idī -itum *vt.* hand over, deliver, surrender; commit, entrust; betray; bequeath, hand down; (*narrative*) relate, record; (*teaching*) propound. **sē** — surrender, devote oneself.

trād/ū'cō (trānsdūcō) -ū'cere -ū'xī -u'ctum *vt.* bring across, lead over, transport across; transfer; parade, make an exhibition of (in public); (*time*) pass, spend.

trādu'cti/ō -ō'nis *f.* transference; (*time*) passage; (*word*) metonymy. [ferrer.

trādu'ct/or -ō'ris *m.* trans-

trādu'ctus *ppp.* trādūcō.

trā'd/ux -ucis *m.* vine-layer.

tragicocōmoe'di/a -ae *f.* tragi-comedy.

tra'gic/us *a.* of tragedy, tragic; in the tragic manner, lofty; terrible, tragic. *m.* writer of tragedy. **-ē** *ad.* dramatically.

tragoe'di/a -ae *f.* tragedy; (*fig.*) bombast.

tragoe'd/us -ī *m.* tragic actor.

trā'gul/a -ae *f.* kind of javelin.

tra'he/a -ae *f.* sledge.

tra'/hō -here -xī -ctum *vt.* draw, drag, pull, take with one; pull out, lengthen; draw together, contract; carry off, plunder; (*liquid*) drink, draw; (*money*) squander; (*wool*) spin; (*fig.*) attract; (*appearance*) take on; (*consequence*) derive, get; (*praise, blame*) ascribe, refer; (*thought*) ponder; (*time*) spin out.

trā/i'ciō (trānsi'ciō) -i'cere -iē'cī -ie'ctum *vt.* throw across, shoot across; (*troops*) get across, transport; (*with weapon*) pierce, stab; (*river, etc.*) cross; (*fig.*) transfer. *vi* cross.

trāie'cti/ō -ō'nis *f.* crossing, passage; (*fig.*) transferring (*rhet.*) exaggeration; (*words*) transposition.

trāie'ctus *ppp.* trāiciō.

trāie'ct/us -ūs *m.* crossing, passage.

trālāt-, *see* **trānslāt-**.

Tra'll/ēs -ium *f.pl.* town in Lydia. **-iā'nus** *a.*

trālū'ceō, *see* **trānslūceō**.

trā'm/a -ae *f.* woof, web.

trā'm/es -itis *m.* foot-path, path.

trāmi'ttō, *see* **trānsmittō**.

trā'natō, *see* **trānsnatō**.

trā'n/ō (trā'nsnō) -ā're -ā'vī -ā'tum *vt.* & *i.* swim across; (*air*) fly through.

tranqui'llit/ās -ā'tis *f.* quietness, calm; (*fig.*) peace, quiet.

tranqui'll/ō -ā're *vt.* calm.

tranqui'll/us *a.* quiet, calm. *n.* calm sea. **-ē** *ad.* quietly.

trāns *pr.* (*with acc.*) across, over, beyond.

trānsa'b/eō -ī're -iī *vt.* pierce.
trānsā'ct/or -ō'ris *m.* manager.
trānsā'ctus *ppp.* trānsigō.
trānsa'dig/ō -ere *vt.* drive through, pierce.
Trānsalpī'nus *a.* Transalpine.
trānsc/e'ndō (**trānssce'ndō**) -e'ndere -e'ndī -ē'nsum *vt.* & *i.* pass over, surmount; overstep, surpass, transgress.
trānscrī'/bō (**transscrībō**) -bere -psī -ptum copy out; (*fig.*) make over, transfer.
trānscu'r/rō -rere -rī -sum *vt.* & *i.* run across, run past, traverse.
trānscu'rs/us -ūs *m.* running through; (*speech*) cursory remark.
trānsd-, *see* **trād-**.
trānsē'gī *perf.* trānsigō.
trānse'nn/a -ae *f.* net, snare; trellis, lattice-work.
trā'ns/eō -ī're -iī -itum *vt.* & *i.* pass over, cross over; pass along or through; pass by; outstrip, surpass, overstep; (*change*) turn into; (*speech*) mention briefly, leave out, pass on; (*time*) pass, pass away.
trā'ns/ferō -fe'rre -tulī -lā'tum *vt.* bring across, transport, transfer; (*change*) transform; (*language*) translate; (*rhet.*) use figuratively; (*time*) postpone; (*writing*) copy.
trānsfī'/gō -gere -xī -xum *vt.* pierce; thrust through.
trānsfī'xus *ppp.* trānsfīgō.
trānsf/o'diō -o'dere -ō'dī -o'ssum *vt.* run through, stab.
trānsfō'rmis *a.* changed in shape.
trānsfō'rm/ō -ā're *vt.* change in shape.
trānsfo'ssus *ppp.* trānsfodiō.
trā'nsfug/a -ae *m., f.* deserter.
trānsf/u'giō -u'gere -ū'gī *vi.* desert, come over.
trānsfu'g/ium -ī & iī *n.* desertion.
trānsf/u'ndō -u'ndere -ū'dī -ū'sum *vt.* decant, transfuse.
trānsfū'si/ō -ō'nis *f.* transmigration.
trānsfū'sus *ppp.* trānsfundō.
trānsgre'/dior -dī -ssus *vt.* & *i.* step across, cross over, cross; pass on; exceed.
trānsgre'ssi/ō -ō'nis *f.* passage; (*words*) transposition.
trānsgre'ssus *ppa.* trānsgredior.
trānsgre'ss/us -ūs *m.* crossing.
trānsi'ciō, *see* **trāiciō**.
trā'ns/igō -i'gere -ē'gī -ā'ctum *vt.* carry through, complete, finish; (*difference*) settle; (*time*) pass, spend; (*with* **cum**) put an end to; (*with* **weapon**) stab.
trā'nsiī *perf.* trānseō.
trānsi'l/iō, **trānssi'l/iō** -ī're -uī *vi.* jump across. *vt.* leap over; (*fig.*) skip, disregard; exceed, [through.
trā'nsit/ō -ā're *vi.* pass
trānsi'ti/ō -ō'nis *f.* passage; desertion; (*disease*) infection.
trā'nsitus *ppp.* trānseō.
trā'nsit/us -ūs *m.* passing over, passage; desertion; passing by; transition.
trānslātī'cius, **trālātī'cius** *a.* traditional, customary, common.
trānslā'ti/ō, **trālā'ti/ō** -ō'nis *f.* transporting, transferring; (*language*) metaphor.
trānslātī'vus *a.* transferable.
trānslā't/or -ō'ris *m.* transferrer.
trānslā'tus *ppp.* trānsferō.
trā'nslegō/ -ere *vt.* read through.
trānslū'c/eō -ē're *vi.* be reflected; shine through.
trānsmarī'nus *a.* oversea.
trā'nsme/ō -ā're *vi.* cross.
trānsmi'gr/ō -ā're *vi.* emigrate.

trānsmi'ssi/ō -ō'nis *f*. crossing.
trānsmi'ssus *ppp*. trānsmittō. [ing.
trānsmi'ss/us -ūs *m*. cross-
trānsm/i'ttō (**trāmi'ttō**) -i'ttere -ī'sī -i'ssum *vt*. send across, put across; let pass through; transfer, entrust, devote; give up, pass over; (*place*) cross over, go through, pass. *vi*. cross.
trānsmontā'nus *a*. beyond the mountains.
trānsm/o'veō -ovē're -ō'vī -ō'tum *vt*. move, transfer.
trānsmū't/ō -ā're *vt*. shift.
trā'nsnat/ō, **trā'nat/ō** -ā're *vi*. swim across. *vt*. swim.
trā'nsnō, *see* **trā'nō**.
Trānspadā'nus *a*. north of the Po.
trānspe'ct/us -ūs *m*. view.
trānspi'c/iō -ere *vt*. look through.
trānsp/ō'nō -ō'nere -o'suī -o'situm *vt*. transfer.
trānspo'rt/ō -ā're *vt*. carry across, transport, remove.
trānspo'situs *ppp*. trānspōnō.
Trānsrhēnā'nus *a*. east of the Rhine.
trānss-, *see* **trāns-**.
Trānstiberī'nus *a*. across the Tiber.
trānsti'n/eō -ē're *vi*. get through.
trā'nstr/um -ī *n*. thwart.
trā'nstulī *perf*. trānsferō.
trānsu'lt/ō -ā're *vi*. jump across.
trānsū'tus *a*. pierced.
trānsve'cti/ō, **trāve'cti/ō** -ō'nis *f*. crossing.
trānsve'ctus *ppp*. trānsvehō.
trā'nsve/hō, **trā've/hō** -here -xī -ctum *vt*. carry across, transport. **-hor** -hī -ctus *vi*. cross, pass over; (*parade*) ride past; (*time*) elapse.
trānsve'rber/ō -ā're *vt*. pierce through, wound.
trānsve'rs/us (**trānsvo'rsus**, **trāve'rsus**) *a*. lying across, crosswise, transverse. digitum -um a finger's breadth. dē -ō unexpectedly. ex -ō sideways. [through.
trānsvo'lit/ō -ā're *vt*. fly
trā'nsvol/ō, **trā'vol/ō** -ā're *vt*. & *i*. fly across, fly through; move rapidly across; fly past, disregard.
trānsvo'rsus, *see* **trānsversus**. [oil-mill.
trapē't/us -ī *m*. olive-mill,
trapezī'ta, *see* **tarpezīta**.
Trape'z/ūs -ū'ntis *f*. Black Sea town, *mod*. Trebizond.
Trasume'nn/us (**Trasimē'nus**) -ī *m*. lake in Etruria, where Hannibal defeated the Romans.
tra'xī *perf*. trahō.
trāv-, *see* **trānsv-**.
trecēn'/ī -ō'rum *a*. three hundred each. [hundredth.
trecentē'simus *a*. three-
trece'nt/ī -ō'rum *num*. three hundred.
trece'nti/ēns, **-ēs** *ad*. three hundred times.
trechedī'pn/a -ō'rum *n.pl*. dinner-shoes (of parasites).
tre'decim *num*. thirteen.
tremebu'ndus *a*. trembling.
treme/fa'ciō -fa'cere -fē'cī -fa'ctum *vt*. shake. [terrible.
treme'ndus *a*. formidable,
tremē'sc/ō (**tremī'scō**) -ere *vi*. begin to shake. *vt*. be afraid of.
tre'm/ō -ere -uī *vi*. tremble, quake, quiver. *vt*. tremble at, dread.
tre'm/or -ō'ris *m*. shaking, quiver, tremor; earthquake.
tre'mulus *a*. trembling, shivering. [agitation.
trepida'nter *ad*. with
trepidā'ti/ō -ō'nis *f*. agitation, alarm, consternation.
tre'pid/ō -ā're -ā'vī -ā'tum *vi*. be agitated, bustle about,

hurry, be alarmed; flicker, quiver. *vt.* start at.
tre'pid/us *a.* restless, anxious, alarmed; alarming, perilous. **–ē** *ad.* hastily, in confusion.
trēs tri'um *num.* three.
trē'ss/is -is *m.* three asses.
trē'svirī triumvirō'rum, *m.pl.* three commissioners, triumvirs.
Trē'ver/ī -ō'rum *m.pl.* people of E. Gaul, about *mod.* Trèves. **–icus** *a.*
tria'ngul/us *a.* triangular. **–um** -ī *n.* triangle.
triā'ri/ī -ō'rum *m.pl.* the third line (in Roman battle-order), the reserves.
tribuā'rius *a.* of the tribes.
tribū'l/is -is *m.* fellow-tribesman. [sledge.
trī'bul/um -ī *n.* threshing-
tri'bul/us -ī *m.* star thistle.
tribū'n/al -ā'lis *n.* platform; judgment-seat; camp platform, cenotaph.
tribūnā't/us -ūs *m.* tribuneship, rank of tribune.
tribūni'cius *a.* of a tribune. *m.* ex-tribune.
tribū'n/us -ī *m.* tribune. — plēbis tribune of the people, a magistrate who defended the rights of the plebeians. — militum or militāris military tribune, an officer under the legatus. -ī aerārii paymasters.
tri'b/uō -u'ere -uī -ū'tum *vt.* assign, allot; give, bestow, pay; concede, allow; ascribe, attribute; (*subject*) divide; (*time*) devote.
tri'b/us -ūs *m.* tribe.
tribūtā'ri/us *a.* **-ae tabellae** letters of credit.
tribū'tim *ad.* by tribes.
tribū'ti/ō -ō'nis *f.* distribution.
tribū't/us *ppp.* tribuō. **–um** -ī *n.* contribution, tribute, tax.
tribū'tus *a.* arranged by tribes. [tricks, vexations.
trī'c/ae -ā'rum *f.pl.* nonsense;
trīcē'n/ī -ō'rum *a.* thirty each, in thirties. [headed.
tri'c/eps -i'pitis *a.* three-
trīcē'simus *a.* thirtieth.
tri'chil/a -ae *f.* arbour, summer-house. [times.
trī'ci/ēns, –ēs *ad.* thirty
trīclī'n/ium -ī & iī *n.* dining-couch; dining-room.
trī'c/ō -ō'nis *m.* mischief-maker.
trī'c/or -ā'rī *vi.* make mischief, play tricks.
trico'rpor -is *a.* three-bodied.
tricu'sp/is -idis *a.* three-pointed.
tri'd/ēns -e'ntis *a.* three-pronged. *m.* trident.
tride'ntifer -ī *a.* trident-wielding.
tride'ntiger -ī *a.* trident-wielding.
tri'du/um -ī *n.* three days.
trie'nn/ia -ium *n.pl.* a triennial festival. [years.
trie'nn/ium -ī & iī *n.* three
tri'/ēns -e'ntis *m.* a third; (*coin*) a third of an as; (*measure*) a third of a pint.
trientā'bul/um -ī *n.* land given by the State as a third of a debt.
trie'ntius *a.* sold for a third.
triēra'rch/us -ī *m.* captain of a trireme.
triē'r/is -is *f.* trireme.
trietē'ricus *a.* triennial. *n.pl.* festival of Bacchus.
trietē'r/is -idis *f.* three years; a triennial festival.
trifā'riam *ad.* in three parts, in three places.
tri'f/aux -au'cis *a.* three-throated.
tri'fidus *a.* three-forked.
trifō'rmis *a.* triple.
tri'f/ūr -ū'ris *m.* arch-thief.
trifu'rcifer -ī *m.* hardened criminal.
trige'minus *a.* threefold, triple. *m.pl.* triplets.
trīgi'ntā *num.* thirty.

tri'g/ōn -ō'nis *m.* a ball game.
trilī'bris *a.* three-pound.
trili'nguis *a.* three-tongued.
tri'l/īx -ī'cis *a.* three-ply, three-stranded.
trimē'stris *a.* of three months.
tri'metr/us -ī *m.* trimeter.
trī'mus *a.* three years old.
Trīna'cr/ia -iae *f.* Sicily. **-ius**, **-is** -idis *a.* Sicilian.
trī'n/ī -ō'rum *a.* three each, in threes; triple.
Trinoba'nt/ēs -um *m.pl.* British tribe in East Anglia.
trinō'dis *a.* three-knotted.
triō'bol/us -ī *m.* half-a-drachma.
Triō'n/ēs -um *m.pl.* the Plough; the Little Bear.
tripartī't/us, **tripertī't/us** *a.* divided into three parts. **-ō** *ad.* in or into three parts.
tripe'ctorus *a.* three-bodied.
tripedā'lis *a.* three-foot.
tripert-, *see* **tripart-**.
tri'p/ēs -edis *a.* three-legged.
tri'pl/ex -icis *a.* triple, threefold. *n.* three times as much. *m.pl.* three-leaved writing tablet.
tri'plus *a.* triple.
Tripto'lem/us -ī *m.* inventor of agriculture, judge in Hades.
tripu'di/ō -ā're *vi.* dance.
tripu'd/ium -ī & iī *n.* ceremonial dance, dance; a favourable omen, when the sacred chickens ate greedily.
tri'p/ūs -odis *f.* tripod; the Delphic oracle.
tri'quetrus *a.* triangular; Sicilian.
trirē'mis *a.* with three banks of oars. *f.* trireme.
trīs, *see* **trēs**. [fooling.
triscu'rri/a -ō'rum *n.pl.* sheer
trī'stī *for* **trīvistī**.
tristi'culus *a.* rather sad.
tristi'ficus *a.* ominous.
tristimō'ni/a -ae *f.* sadness.
tri'st/is *a.* sad, glum, melancholy; gloomy, sombre, dismal; (*taste*) bitter; (*smell*) offensive; (*temper*) severe, sullen, ill-humoured. **-ē** *ad.* sadly; severely.
tristi'ti/a -ae *f.* sadness, sorrow, melancholy; moroseness, severity.
tristi'ti/ēs -ē'ī *f.* sorrow.
trisu'lcus *a.* three-forked.
tri'tav/us -ī *m.* great-great-great-grandfather.
trīti'ceus *a.* of wheat, wheaten.
trī'tic/um -ī *n.* wheat.
Trī't/ōn -ō'nis *m.* sea-god, son of Neptune; African lake, where Minerva was born. **-ō'nius**, **-ōni'acus**, **-ō'nis** *a.* of Lake Triton, of Minerva. *f.* Minerva.
trītū'r/a -ae *f.* threshing.
trī'tus *ppp.* terō. *a.* well-worn; (*judgment*) expert; (*language*) commonplace, trite. [friction.
trī't/us -ūs *m.* rubbing,
triumphā'lis *a.* triumphal. *n.pl.* insignia of a triumph.
triu'mph/ō -ā're -ā'vī -ā'tum *vi.* celebrate a triumph; triumph, exult. *vt.* triumph over, win by conquest.
triu'mph/us -ī *m.* triumphal procession, victory parade; triumph, victory.
triu'mvir -ī *m.* commissioner, triumvir; mayor (of a provincial town).
triumvirā'lis *a.* triumviral.
triumvirā't/us -ūs *m.* office of triumvir, triumvirate.
triu'mvir/ī -ō'rum *m.pl.* three commissioners, triumvirs.
trivenē'fic/a -ae *f.* old witch.
trī'vī *perf.* terō.
Tri'vi/a -ae *f.* Diana.
triviā'lis *a.* common, popular.
tri'v/ium -ī & iī *n.* cross-roads; public street.
tri'vius *a.* of the cross-roads.
Trō'/as -adis *f.* the district of Troy, Troad; Trojan woman. *a.* Trojan.

trochae'/us -ī *m.* trochee; tribrach. [tackle.
tro'chle/a -ae *f.* block and
tro'ch/us -ī *m.* hoop.
Trō'i/a -ae *f.* Troy. **-us, -ā'nus, -cus** *a.* Trojan.
Trōglo'dyt/ae -ā'rum *m.pl.* cave-dwellers of Ethiopia.
Trō'il/us -ī *m.* son of Priam.
Trōiu'gen/a -ae *m. f.* Trojan; Roman.
tropae'/um -ī *n.* victory memorial, trophy; victory; memorial, token.
Tr/ōs -ō'is *m.* king of Phrygia: Trojan.
trucīdā'ti/ō -ō'nis *f.* butchery.
trucī'd/ō -ā're -ā'vī -ā'tum *vt.* slaughter, massacre.
trucule'nti/a -ae *f.* ferocity, inclemency.
trucule'nt/us *a.* ferocious, grim, wild. **-ē** *ad.*
tru'd/is -is *f.* pike.
trū'/dō -dere -sī -sum *vt.* push, thrust, drive; (*buds*) put forth.
tru'll/a -ae *f.* ladle, scoop; wash-basin.
tru'nc/ō -ā're -ā'vī -ā'tum *vt.* lop off, maim, mutilate.
tru'nc/us -ī *m.* (*tree*) trunk, bole; (*human*) trunk, body; (*abuse*) blockhead. *a.* maimed, broken, stripped (of); defective.
trū'sī *perf.* trūdō.
trū'sit/ō -ā're *vt.* keep pushing.
trū'sus *ppp.* trūdō.
tru'tin/a -ae *f.* balance, scales.
tr/ux -u'cis *a.* savage, grim, wild.
trȳgō'n/us -ī *m.* sting-ray.
tū *pro.* you, thou.
tuā'tim *ad.* in your usual fashion.
tu'b/a -ae *f.* trumpet, war-trumpet.
tū'ber -is *n.* swelling, lump; (*food*) truffle.
tu'ber -is *f.* kind of apple-tree.
tu'bic/en -inis *m.* trumpeter.
tubilū'stri/a -ō'rum *n.pl* festival of trumpets.
tubu'rcin/or -ā'rī *vi.* gobble up, guzzle.
tu'b/us -ī *m.* pipe.
tu'dit/ō -ā're *vt.* strike repeatedly.
tu'/eor -ē'rī -itus & tū'tus *vt.* see, watch, look; guard, protect, keep. [cottage.
tugu'r/ium -ī & iī *n.* hut,
tui'ti/ō -ō'nis *f.* defence.
tu'itus *ppa.* tueor.
tu'lī *perf.* ferō.
Tulli'ol/a -ae *f.* little Tullia, Cicero's daughter.
Tu'll/ius -ī & iī *m.* Roman family name, *esp.* the sixth king; the orator Cicero. **-iā'nus** *a.* **-iā'n/um** -ī *n.* State-dungeon of Rome.
Tu'll/us -ī *m.* third king of Rome.
tum *ad.* (*time*) then, at that time; (*sequence*) then, next. *conj.* moreover, besides. — . . . — at one time . . . at another. — . . . **cum** at the time when, whenever. **cum** . . . — not only . . . but. — **dēmum** only then. — **ipsum** even then. — **māximē** just then. — **vērō** then more than ever.
tume/fa'ciō -fa'cere -fē'cī -fa'ctum *vt.* make swell; (*fig.*) puff up.
tu'm/eō -ē're *vi.* swell, be swollen; (*emotion*) be excited; (*pride*) be puffed up; (*language*) be turgid.
tum/ē'scō -ē'scere -uī *vi.* begin to swell, swell up.
tu'midus *a.* swollen, swelling; (*emotion*) excited, enraged; (*pride*) puffed up; (*language*) bombastic.
tu'm/or -ō'ris *m.* swelling, bulge; hillock; (*fig.*) commotion, excitement.
tu'mul/ō -ā're *vt.* bury.
tumulō'sus *a.* hilly.

tumultuā'rius *a.* hasty; (*troops*) emergency.
tumultuā'ti/ō -ō'nis *f.* commotion.
tumu'ltu/ō -ā're, **-or** -ā'rī *vi.* make a commotion, be in an uproar.
tumultuō's/us *a.* uproarious, excited, turbulent. **-ē** *ad.*
tumu'lt/us -ūs *m.* commotion, uproar, disturbance; (*mil.*) rising, revolt, civil war; (*weather*) storm; (*mind*) disorder.
tu'mul/us -ī *m.* mound, hill; burial mound, barrow.
tunc *ad.* (*time*) then, at that time; (*sequence*) then, next. — dēmum only then. — quoque then too; even so.
tu'nd/ō -ere tu'tudī tū'nsum & tū'sum *vt.* beat, thump, hammer; (*grain*) pound; (*speech*) din, importune.
Tū'n/ēs -ē'tis *m.* Tunis.
tu'nic/a -ae *f.* tunic; (*fig.*) skin, husk.
tunicā'tus *a.* wearing a tunic.
tuni'cul/a -ae *f.* little tunic.
tū'nsus *ppp.* tundō.
tu'or, *see* **tueor**.
tu'rb/a -ae *f.* disorder, riot, disturbance; brawl, quarrel; crowd, mob, troop, number.
turbāme'nt/a -ō'rum *n.pl.* propaganda.
turbā'ti/ō -ō'nis *f.* confusion.
turbā't/or -ō'ris *m.* agitator.
turbā't/us *ppp.* turbō. *a.* troubled, disorderly. **-ē** *ad.* in confusion. [row.
turbe'll/ae -ā'rum *f.pl.* stir,
tu'rben, *see* **turbō**.
tu'rbid/us *a.* confused, wild, boisterous; (*water*) troubled, muddy; (*fig.*) disorderly troubled, alarmed, dangerous. **-ē** *ad.* in disorder.
turbi'neus *a.* conical.
tu'rb/ō -ā're -ā'vī -ā'tum *vt.* disturb, throw into confusion; (*water*) trouble, make muddy.
tu'rb/ō -inis *m.* whirl, spiral, rotation; reel, whorl, spindle; (*toy*) top; (*wind*) tornado, whirlwind; (*fig.*) storm.
turbule'nt/us *a.* agitated, confused, boisterous, stormy; trouble-making, seditious. **-ē**, **-er** *ad.* wildly.
tu'rd/us -ī *m.* thrush.
tū'reus *a.* of incense.
tu'r/geō -gē're -sī *vi.* swell, be swollen; (*speech*) be bombastic.
turgē'sc/ō -ere *vi.* swell up, begin to swell; (*fig.*) become enraged.
turgi'dulus *a.* poor swollen.
tu'rgidus *a.* swollen, distended; bombastic.
tūri'bul/um -ī *n.* censer.
tūri'cremus *a.* incense-burning.
tū'rifer -ī *a.* incense-producing. [ing.
tūri'legus *a.* incense-gather-
tu'rm/a -ae *f.* troop, squadron (of cavalry); crowd.
turmā'lis *a.* of a troop; equestrian. [troop.
turmā'tim *ad.* troop by
Tu'rn/us -ī *m.* Rutulian king, chief opponent of Aeneas.
turpi'culus *a.* ugly little; slightly indecent.
turpificā'tus *a.* debased.
turpilucricu'pidus *a.* fond of filthy lucre.
tu'rp/is *a.* ugly, deformed, unsightly; base, disgraceful. *n.* disgrace. **-iter** *ad.* repulsively; shamefully.
turpitū'd/ō -inis *f.* deformity; disgrace, infamy.
tu'rp/ō -ā're *vt.* disfigure, soil.
tu'rriger -ī *a.* turreted.
tu'rr/is -is *f.* tower, turret; siege-tower; (*elephant*) howdah; (*fig.*) mansion.
turrī'tus *a.* turreted; castellated; towering.
tu'rsī *perf.* turgeō.
tu'rtur -is *m.* turtle-dove.

tūs tū'ris *n.* incense, frankincense. [incense.
tū'scul/um -ī *n.* a little
Tu'scul/um -ī *n.* Latin town near Rome. **-ā'nus, -us** *a.* Tusculan. **-ā'num** -ā'nī *n.* villa at Tusculum, *esp.* Cicero's. **-ānē'nsis** *a.* at Tusculum.
Tu'scus *a.* Etruscan.
tu'ss/iō -ī're *vi.* cough, have a cough.
tu'ss/is -is *f.* cough.
tū'sus *ppp.* tundō.
tūtā'm/en -inis *n.* defence.
tūtāme'nt/um -ī *n.* protection.
tū'te *emphatic form* of **tū**.
tū'tē *ad.* safely.
tūtē'l/a -ae *f.* keeping, charge, protection; (*of minors*) guardianship, wardship; (*person*) watcher, guardian; ward, charge.
tū'temet *emphatic form of* **tū**.
tū't/or -ā'rī -ā'tus, **-ō** -ā're *vt.* watch, guard, protect; guard against.
t'ūt/or -ō'ris *m.* protector; (*law*) guardian.
tu'tudī *perf.* tundō.
tū't/us *ppp.* tueō. *a.* safe, secure; cautious. *n.* safety. **-ē, -ō** *ad.* safely, in safety.
tu'us *a.* your, yours, thy, thine; your own, your proper; of you.
Tȳ'd/eus -eī & eos *m.* father of Diomede. **-ī'dēs** -ī'dae *m.* Diomede.
tympano'trīb/a -ae *m.* timbrel-player.
ty'mpan/um (**ty'panum**) -ī *n.* drum, timbrel (*esp.* of the priests of Cybele); (*mechanism*) wheel.
Ty'ndar/eus -eī *m.* king of Sparta, husband of Leda. **-idae** -idā'rum *m.pl.* Castor and Pollux. **-is** -idis *f.* Helen; Clytemnestra.
Typhō'/eus -eos *m.* giant under Etna. **-ius, -is** *a.*
ty'p/us -ī *m.* figure.
tyrannicī'd/a -ae *m.* tyrannicide. [-ē *ad.*
tyra'nnic/us *a.* tyrannical.
tyra'nn/is -idis *f.* despotism, tyranny.
tyranno'cton/us -ī *m.* tyrannicide.
tyra'nn/us -ī *m.* ruler, king; despot, tyrant.
Ty'r/ās -ae *m.* river Dniester.
tȳrotarī'ch/os -ī *m.* dish of salt fish and cheese.
Tyrrhē'n/us *a.* Etruscan, Tyrrhenian. **-ia** -iae *f.* Etruria.
Tyrtae'/us -ī *m.* Spartan war-poet.
Ty'r/us (**-os**) -ī *f.* Tyre, famous Phoenician seaport. **-ius** *a.* Tyrian, Phoenician, Carthaginian; purple.

U

ū'ber -is *n.* breast, teat; (*fig.*) richness.
ū'ber -is *a.* fertile, plentiful, rich (in); (*language*) full, copious.
ūbe'r/ius (*sup.* -rime) *comp.a.* more fully, more copiously.
ūbe'rt/ās -ā'tis *f.* richness, plenty, fertility.
ūbe'rtim *ad.* copiously.
u'bī *ad.* (*interrog.*) where ? (*rel.*) where, in which, with whom; when.
ubīcu'mque *ad.* wherever; everywhere.
U'bi/ī -ō'rum *m.pl.* German tribe on the lower Rhine.
ubī'nam *ad.* where (in fact) ?
ubīquā'que *ad.* everywhere.
ubī'que *ad.* everywhere, anywhere.
u'biubī *ad.* wherever.
ubī'vīs *ad.* anywhere.
ū'dus *a.* wet, damp.
u'lcer/ō -ā're *vt.* make sore, wound.

ulcerō'sus *a.* full of sores; wounded.
ulcī'sc/or -ī **u'ltus** *vt.* take vengeance on, punish; take vengeance for, avenge.
u'lc/us -eris *n.* sore, ulcer. — tangere touch on a delicate subject.
ūlī'g/ō -inis *f.* moisture, marshiness.
Uli'x/ēs -is *m.* Ulysses, Odysseus, king of Ithaca, hero of Homer's Odyssey.
u'll/us (*gen.* -ī'us *dat.* -ī) *a.* any.
u'lmeus *a.* of elm. [rods.
u'lm/us -ī *f.* elm; (*pl.*) elm-
u'ln/a -ae *f.* elbow; arm; (*measure*) ell.
ulte'ri/or -ō'ris *comp.a.* farther, beyond, more remote.
ulte'rius *comp.* ultrā.
u'ltim/us *sup.a.* farthest, most remote, the end of; (*time*) earliest, latest, last; (*degree*) extreme, greatest, lowest. *n.pl.* the end. -um for the last time. ad -um finally.
u'lti/ō -ō'nis *f.* vengeance, revenge.
u'lt/or -ō'ris *m.* avenger, punisher.
u'ltrā *ad.* beyond, farther, besides. *pr.* (*with acc.*) beyond, on the far side of; (*time*) past; (*degree*) over and above.
u'ltr/īx -ī'cis *a.* avenging.
u'ltrō *ad.* on the other side, away; besides; of one's own accord, unasked, voluntarily. — tribūta *n.pl.* State expenditure for public works.
u'ltus *ppa.* ulcīscor.
u'lul/a -ae *f.* screech-owl.
ululā't/us -ūs *m.* wailing, shrieking, yells, whoops.
u'lul/ō -ā're -ā'vī -ā'tum *vi.* shriek, yell, howl. *vt.* cry out to.
u'lv/a -ae *f.* sedge.
umbe'll/a -ae *f.* parasol.
U'mb/er -rī *a.* Umbrian. *m.* Umbrian dog. **-ria** -riae *f.* Umbria, district of central Italy.
umbilī'c/us -ī *m.* navel; (*fig.*) centre; (*book*) roller-end; (*sea*) cockle or pebble.
u'mb/ō -ō'nis *m.* boss (of a shield); shield; elbow.
u'mbr/a -ae *f.* shadow, shade; (*dead*) ghost; (*diner*) uninvited guest; (*fish*) grayling; (*painting*) shade; (*place*) shelter, school, study; (*unreality*) semblance, mere shadow.
umbrā'cul/um -ī *n.* arbour; school; parasol.
umbrāti'col/a -ae *m.* lounger.
umbrā'ticus *a.* fond of idling; in retirement.
umbrā'tilis *a.* in retirement, private, academic.
u'mbrifer -ī *a.* shady.
u'mbr/ō -ā're *vt.* shade.
umbrō'sus *a.* shady.
ūme'ct/ō -ā're *vt.* wet, water.
ūme'ctus *a.* damp, wet.
ū'm/eō -ē're *vi.* be damp, be wet. [shoulder.
u'mer/us -ī *m.* upper arm,
ūmē'sc/ō -ere *vi.* become damp, get wet.
ūmi'dulus *a.* dampish.
ū'mid/us *a.* wet, damp, dank, moist. -ē *ad.* with damp.
ū'm/or -ōris *m.* liquid, fluid, moisture.
u'mquam, u'nquam *ad.* ever, at any time.
ū'nā *ad.* together.
ūna'nim/āns -a'ntis *a.* in full agreement. [cord.
ūnani'mit/ās -ā'tis *f.* con-
ūna'nimus *a.* of one accord, harmonious.
ū'nci/a -ae *f.* a twelfth; (*weight*) ounce; (*length*) inch.
ūnciā'rius *a.* of a twelfth; (*interest*) $8\frac{1}{3}$ per cent.
ūnciā'tim *ad.* little by little.
uncīnā'tus *a.* barbed.
ūnci'ol/a -ae *f.* a mere twelfth.

ū'ncti/ō -ō'nis *f.* anointing.
ū'nctit/ō -ā're *vt.* anoint regularly.
ūnctiu'sculus *a.* rather too unctuous.
ū'nct/or -ō'ris *m.* anointer.
ūnctū'r/a -ae *f.* anointing (of the dead).
ū'nctus *ppp.* **ungō.** *a.* oiled; greasy, resinous; (*fig.*) rich, sumptuous. *n.* sumptuous dinner.
u'nc/us -ī *m.* hook, grappling-iron. [barbed.
u'ncus *a.* hooked, crooked,
u'nd/a -ae *f.* wave, water; (*fig.*) stream, surge.
u'nde *ad.* from where, whence; from whom, from which. — **petitur** the defendant. — **unde** from wherever; somehow or other.
ūnde'ci/ēns, -ēs *ad.* eleven times.
ū'ndecim *num.* eleven.
ūnde'cimus *a.* eleventh.
undecu'mque *ad.* from wherever.
ūndē'n/ī -ō'rum *a.* eleven each, eleven.
ūndēnōnāgi'ntā *num.* eighty-nine.
ūndeoctōgi'ntā *num.* seventy-nine.
ūndēquadrāgi'ntā *num.* thirty-nine.
ūndēquīnquāgē'simus *a.* forty-ninth.
ūndēquīnquāgi'ntā *num.* forty-nine.
ūndēsexāgi'ntā *num.* fifty-nine. [ninth.
ūndētrīcē'simus *a.* twenty-
ūndēvīcēsimā'n/ī -ō'rum *m.pl.* men of the nineteenth legion.
ūndēvīcē'simus *a.* nineteenth.
ūndēvīgi'ntī *num.* nineteen.
u'ndique *ad.* from every side, on all sides, everywhere; completely.
undi'sonus *a.* sea-roaring.
u'nd/ō -ā're *vi.* surge; (*fig.*) roll, undulate.
undō'sus *a.* billowy.
ūnetvīcēsimā'n/ī -ō'rum *m.pl.* men of the twenty-first legion.
ūnetvīcē'simus *a.* twenty-first.
u'n/gō (u'nguō) -gere -ūnxī -ūnctum *vt.* anoint, smear, grease.
u'ngu/en -inis *n.* fat, grease, ointment.
unguentā'r/ius -ī & iī *m.* perfumer.
unguentā'tus *a.* perfumed.
ungue'nt/um -ī *n.* ointment, perfume. [nail.
ungui'cul/us -ī *m.* finger-
u'ngu/is -is *m.* nail (of finger or toe); claw, talon, hoof. **ad -em** with perfect finish. **trānsversum -em** a hair's breadth. **dē tenerō -ī** from earliest childhood.
u'ngul/a -ae *f.* hoof, talon, claw.
u'nguō, *see* **ungō.**
ūni'col/or -ō'ris *a.* all one colour.
ū'nic/us *a.* one and only sole; unparalleled, unique. **-ē** *ad.* solely, extraordinarily.
ūnifō'rmis *a.* simple.
ūni'gen/a -ae *a.* only-begotten, of the same parentage.
ūni'manus *a.* with only one hand.
ū'ni/ō -ō'nis *m.* a single large pearl.
ū'niter *ad.* together in one.
ūniversā'lis *a.* general.
ūnive'rsit/ās -ā'tis *f.* the whole; the universe.
ūnive'rs/us *a.* all taken together, entire, general. *m.pl.* the community as a whole. *n.* the universe. **in -um** in general. **-ē** *ad.* in general.
u'nquam, *see* **umquam.**
ū'n/us *num.* one. *a.* sole,

single, only; one and the same; the outstanding one; an individual. — et alter one or two. — quisque every single one. nēmō — not a single one. ad -um to a man.
ū'nxī *perf.* ungō.
ūpi'li/ō -ō'nis *m.* shepherd.
u'pup/a -ae *f.* hoopoe; crowbar.
Ūra'ni/a -ae, -ē -ēs *f.* Muse of astronomy.
urbā'nit/ās -ā'tis *f.* city life; refinement, politeness; wit.
urbā'n/us *a.* town-, city-; refined, polite; witty, humorous; impertinent. *m.* townsman. -ē *ad.* politely; wittily, elegantly.
urbi'cap/us -ī *m.* taker of cities.
urbs u'rbis *f.* city; Rome.
urce'ol/us -ī *m.* jug.
u'rce/us -ī *m.* pitcher, ewer.
ūrē'd/ō -inis *f.* blight.
u'r/geō -gē're -sī *vt.* & *i.* force on, push forward; press hard on, pursue closely; crowd, hem in; burden, oppress; (*argument*) press, urge; (*work, etc.*) urge on, ply hard follow up.
ūrī'n/a -ae *f.* urine.
ūrīnā't/or -ō'ris *m.* diver.
u'rn/a -ae *f.* water-jar, urn; voting-urn, lottery-urn, cinerary urn, money-jar.
u'rnul/a -ae *f.* small urn.
ū'r/ō -ere ū'ssī ū'stum *vt.* burn; scorch, parch; (*cold*) nip; (*med.*) cauterize; (*rubbing*) chafe, hurt; (*passion*) fire, inflame; (*vexation*) annoy, oppress.
u'rs/a -ae *f.* she-bear, bear; (*astr.*) Great Bear, Lesser Bear.
u'rsī *perf.* urgeō.
ursī'nus *a.* bear's.
u'rs/us -ī *m.* bear.
urtī'c/a -ae *f.* nettle.
ū'r/us -ī *m.* wild ox.
Usi'p/etēs -etum, -iī -iō'rum *m.pl.* German tribe on the Rhine.
ūsitā't/us *a.* usual, familiar. -ē *ad.* in the usual manner.
u'spiam *ad.* anywhere, somewhere.
u'squam *ad.* anywhere; in any way, at all.
u'sque *ad.* all the way (to, from), right on, right up to; (*time*) all the time, as long as continuously; (*degree*) even, as much as. — quāque everywhere; every moment, on every occasion.
ū'ssī *perf.* ūrō.
ū'st/or -ō'ris *m.* cremator.
ū'stul/ō -ā're *vt.* burn.
ū'stus *ppp.* ūrō.
ūsuc/a'piō -a'pere -ē'pī -a'ptum *vt.* acquire ownership of, take over.
ūsuca'pi/ō -ō'nis *f.* ownership by use or possession.
ūsū'r/a -ae *f.* use, enjoyment; interest, usury.
ūsūrā'rius *a.* for use and enjoyment; paying interest.
ūsurpā'ti/ō -ō'nis *f.* making use (of).
ūsu'rp/ō -ā're -ā'vī -ā'tum *vt.* make use of, employ, exercise; (*law*) take possession of, enter upon; (*senses*) perceive, make contact with; (*word*) call by, speak of.
ū'sus *ppa.* ūtor.
ū's/us -ūs *m.* use, enjoyment, practice; experience, skill; usage, custom; intercourse, familiarity; usefulne s, benefit, advantage; need, necessity. — est, venit there is need (of). -uī esse, ex -ū esse be of use, be of service. -ū venīre happen. — (et frūctus use and enjoyment, ufruct.
ut, utī *ad.* h w; (*rel.*) as; (*explaining*) considering how, according as; plce)awheer — in ōrātōre for an orator. *conj.* 1. with *dic.*: (*manner*)

as; (*concessive*) while, though; (*time*) when, as soon as. 2. *with subj.*: (*expressing the idea of a verb*) that, to; (*purpose*) so that, to; (*causal*) seeing that; (*concessive*) granted that, although; (*result*) that, so that; (*fear*) that not. — . . . ita while . . . nevertheless. — nōn without. — quī seeing that I, he, etc. — quisque māximē the more.
utcu'mque (**utcu'nque**) *ad.* however; whenever; one way or another.
ūtē'nsilis *a.* of use. *n.pl.* necessaries.
ū't/er -ris *m.* bag, skin, bottle.
u't/er (*gen.* -rius *dat.* -rī), -ra -rum *pro.* which (of two), the one that; one or the other.
utercu'mque utracu'mque utrumcu'mque *pro.* whichever (of two).
ute'rlibet utra'libet utru'mlibet *pro.* whichever (of the two) you please, either one.
ute'rque, u'traque utru'mque *pro.* each (of two), either, both.
u'ter/us -ī *m.* (-um -ī *n.*) womb; child; belly.
ute'rvīs u'travīs utru'mvīs *pro.* whichever (of two) you please; either.
ū'tī *inf.* ūtor.
u'tī, *see* **ut**.
ūti'bilis *a.* useful, serviceable.
U'tic/a -ae *f.* town near Carthage, where Cato committed suicide. **-ē'nsis** *a.*
ū'til/is *a.* useful, expedient, profitable; fit (for). **-iter** *ad.* usefully, advantageously.
ūti'lit/ās -ā'tis *f.* usefulness, expediency, advantage.
u'tinam *ad.* I wish, would that, if only!
u'tique *ad.* at least, by all means, especially.
ū'tor ū'tī ū'sus *vi.* (*with abl.*) use, employ; possess, enjoy; practise, experience; (*person*) be on intimate terms with, find. ūtendum rogāre borrow.
u'tpote *ad.* inasmuch as, as being.
ūtrā'r/ius -ī & iī *m.* water-carrier.
ūtriculā'r/ius -ī & iī *m.* bagpiper.
utri'mque (**utri'nque**) *ad.* on both sides, on either side.
u'trō *ad.* in which direction.
utrobī'que, *see* **utrubīque**.
utrō'que *ad.* in both directions, both ways.
u'trubī *ad.* on which side.
utrubī'que *ad.* on both sides, on either side.
u'trum *ad.* whether.
u'tut *ad.* however.
ū'v/a -ae *f.* grape, bunch of grapes; vine; cluster.
ūvē'sc/ō -ere *vi.* become wet.
ūvi'dulus *a.* moist.
ū'vidus *a.* wet, damp; drunken.
u'x/or -ō'ris *f.* wife.
uxo'rcul/a -ae *f.* little wife.
uxō'rius *a.* of a wife; fond of his wife.

V

va'c/āns -a'ntis *pres.p.* vacō. *a.* unoccupied; (*woman*) single.
vacā'ti/ō -ō'nis *f.* freedom, exemption; exemption from military service; payment for exemption from service.
va'cc/a -ae *f.* cow.
vaccī'n/ium -ī & iī *n.* hyacinth.
va'ccul/a -ae *f.* heifer.
vacēf/ī'ō -i'erī *vi.* become empty.
vaci'll/ō -ā're *vi.* stagger, totter; waver, be unreliable.
vacī'vit/ās -ā'tis *f.* want.
vacī'v/us (**vocī'vus**) *a.* empty, free. **-ē** *ad.* at leisure.
va'c/ō -ā're -ā'vī -ā'tum *vi.* be empty, vacant, unoccupied; be free, aloof (from); have

time for, devote one's time to. -at there is time.
vacuē/fa'ciō -fa'cere -fē'cī -fa'ctum *vt.* empty, clear.
vacu'it/ās -ā'tis *f.* freedom, exemption; vacancy.
vacuā'tus *a.* empty.
va'cuus *a.* empty, void, wanting; vacant; free (from), clear; disengaged, at leisure; (*value*) worthless; (*woman*) single. *n.* void, space.
vadimō'n/ium -ī & iī *n.* bail, security. — sistere appear in court. — dēserere default.
vā'd/ō -ere *vi.* go, go on, make one's way.
va'd/or -ā'rī -ā'tus *vt.* bind over by bail.
vadō'sus *a.* shallow.
va'd/um -ī *n.* shoal, shallow, ford; water, sea; bottom.
vae *interj.* woe! alas!
va'f/er -rī *a.* crafty, subtle. **-rē** *ad.* artfully.
vāgī'n/a -ae *f.* sheath, scabbard; (*grain*) husk.
vā'g/iō -ī're *vi.* cry.
vāgī't/us -ūs *m.* crying, bleating.
va'g/or -ā'rī -ā'tus *vi.* wander, rove, go far afield; (*fig.*) spread.
vā'g/or -ō'ris *m.* cry.
va'g/us *a.* wandering, unsettled; (*fig.*) fickle, wavering, vague. **-ē** *ad.* far afield.
vah *interj.* (*expressing surprise, joy, anger*) oh! ah!
va'ldē *ad.* greatly, intensely; very. [well.
va'lē, valē'te good-bye, fare-
va'l/ēns -e'ntis *pres.p.* valeō. *a.* strong, powerful, vigorous; well, healthy. **-e'nter** *ad.* strongly.
vale'ntulus *a.* strong.
va'l/eō -ē're -uī -itum *vi.* be strong; be able, have the power (to); be well, fit, healthy; (*fig.*) be powerful, effective, valid; (*force*) prevail; (*money*) be worth; (*word*) mean. — apud have influence over, carry weight with. **-ēre iubeō** say good-bye to. **-ē dīcō** say good-bye. **-eās** away with you! [thrive.
valē'sc/ō -ere *vi.* grow strong,
valētūdinā'r/ium -ī & iī *n.* hospital.
valētū'd/ō -inis *f.* state of health, health; illness.
va'lgus *a.* bow-legged.
va'lid/us *a.* strong, powerful, able; sound, healthy; effective. **-ē** *ad.* powerfully, very.
vallā'ris *a.* (*decoration*) for scaling a rampart.
va'll/ēs, va'll/is -is *f.* valley.
va'll/ō -ā're -ā'vī -ā'tum *vt.* palisade, entrench, fortify.
va'll/um -ī *n.* rampart, palisade, entrenchment.
va'll/us -ī *m.* stake; palisade, rampart; (*comb*) tooth.
va'lv/ae -ā'rum *f.pl.* folding-door.
vānē'sc/ō -ere *vi.* disappear, pass away.
vāni'dic/us -ī *m.* liar.
vāniloque'nti/a -ae *f.* idle talk.
vāni'loquus *a.* untruthful; boastful.
vā'nit/ās -ā'tis *f.* emptiness; falsehood, worthlessness, fickleness; vanity.
vānitū'd/ō -inis *f.* falsehood.
va'nn/us -ī *f.* winnowing-fan.
vā'nus *a.* empty; idle, useless, groundless; false, untruthful, unreliable; conceited.
va'pidus *a.* spoilt, corrupt.
va'p/or -ō'ris *m.* steam, vapour; heat.
vapōrā'r/ium -ī & iī *n.* steam-pipe.
vapō'r/ō -ā're *vt.* steam, fumigate, heat. *vi.* burn.
va'pp/a -ae *f.* wine that has gone flat; (*person*) good-for-nothing.
vā'pul/ō -ā're *vi.* be flogged, beaten; be defeated.

varia'nti/a -ae *f.* diversity.
variā'ti/ō -ō'nis *f.* difference.
vā'ric/ō -ā're *vi.* straddle.
vāricō'sus *a.* varicose.
vā'ricus *a.* with feet wide apart.
vari'et/ās -ā'tis *f.* difference, diversity.
va'ri/ō -ā're -ā'vī -ā'tum *vt.* diversify, variegate; make different, change, vary. *vi.* change colour; differ, vary.
va'ri/us *a.* coloured, spotted, variegated; diverse, changeable, various; (*ability*) versatile; (*character*) fickle. **-ē** *ad.* diversely, with varying success.
Va'r/ius -ī *m.* epic poet, friend of Vergil and Horace.
va'r/ix -icis *f.* varicose vein.
Va'rr/ō -ō'nis *m.* consul defeated at Cannae; antiquarian writer of Cicero's day. **-ōniā'nus** *a.*
vā'rus *a.* knock-kneed; crooked; contrary.
vas va'dis *m.* surety, bail.
vās vā'sis (*pl.* **vā's/a** -ō'rum) *n.* vessel, dish; utensil, implement; (*mil.*) baggage.
vāsā'r/ium -ī & iī *n.* furnishing allowance (of a governor).
vāsculā'r/ius -ī & iī *m.* metal-worker.
vā'scul/um -ī *n.* small dish.
vastā'ti/ō -ō'nis *f.* ravaging.
vastā't/or -ō'ris *m.* ravager.
vasti'ficus *a.* ravaging.
va'stit/ās -ā'tis *f.* desolation, desert; devastation, destruction.
vasti'ti/ēs -ē'ī *f.* ruin.
va'st/ō -ā're -ā'vī -ā'tum *vt.* make desolate, denude; lay waste, ravage.
va'st/us *a.* empty, desolate, uncultivated; ravaged, devastated; (*appearance*) uncouth, rude; (*size*) enormous, vast. **-ē** *ad.* (*size*) enormously; (*speech*) coarsely.
vā'sum, *see* **vās**.
vā't/ēs -is *m., f.* prophet, prophetess; poet, bard.
Vāticā'nus *a.* Vatican (hill on right bank of Tiber).
vāticinā'ti/ō -ō'nis *f.* prophesying, prediction.
vāticinā't/or -ō'ris *m.* prophet.
vāti'cin/or -ā'rī -ā'tus *vt.* & *i.* prophesy; celebrate in verse; rave, rant.
vāti'cinus *a.* prophetic.
-ve *conj.* or; either . . . or.
vēco'rdi/a -ae *f.* senselessness; insanity.
vē'cor/s -dis *a.* senseless, foolish, mad.
vectī'g/al -ā'lis *n.* tax; honorarium (to a magistrate); income.
ve'cti/ō -ō'nis *f.* transport.
ve'ct/is -is *m.* lever, crow-bar; (*door*) bolt, bar.
Ve'ct/is -is *f.* Isle of Wight.
ve'ct/ō -ā're *vt.* carry; (*pass.*) ride.
ve'ct/or -ō'ris *m.* carrier; passenger, rider.
vectō'rius *a.* transport-.
vectū'r/a -ae *f.* transport; (*payment*) carriage, fare.
ve'ctus *ppp.* vehō.
ve'getus *a.* lively, sprightly.
vēgra'ndis *a.* small.
ve'hem/ēns -e'ntis *a.* impetuous, violent; powerful, strong. **-e'nter** *ad.* violently, eagerly; powerfully, very much.
veheme'nti/a -ae *f.* vehemence.
vehi'cul/um -ī *n.* carriage, cart; (*sea*) vessel.
ve'/hō -here -xī -ctum *vt.* carry, convey; (*pass.*) ride, sail, drive.
Vēi/ī -ō'rum *m.pl.* ancient town in S. Etruria. **-ēns** -e'ntis, **-entā'nus**, **-us** *a.*
Vē'iov/is, **Ve'diov/is** -is *m.* ancient Roman god, anti-Jupiter.
vel *conj.* or, or perhaps; or rather; or else; either . . . or

ad. even, if you like; perhaps; for instance. —**māximus** the very greatest.
Vēlā'br/um -ī *n* low ground between Capitol and Palatine hills.
vēlā'm/en -inis *n.* covering, [garment.
vēlāme'nt/um -ī *n.* curtain; (*pl.*) draped olive-branches carried by suppliants.
vēlā'r/ium -ī & iī *n.* awning.
vēlā't/ī -ō'rum *m.pl.* supernumerary troops.
vē'l/es -itis *m.* light-armed soldier, skirmisher.
vē'lifer -ī *a.* carrying sail.
vēlificā'ti/ō -ō'nis *f.* sailing.
vēli'fic/ō -ā're *vi.* sail. *vt.* sail through. —**or** -ā'rī *vi.* sail; (*with dat.*) make an effort to obtain.
Velī'n/us -ī *m.* a Sabine lake.
vēlitā'ris *a.* of the light-armed troops.
vēlitā'ti/ō -ō'nis *f.* skirmishing.
vē'litēs *pl.* vēles.
vē'lit/or -ā'rī *vi.* skirmish.
vēli'volus *a.* sail-winged.
ve'lle *inf.* volō.
ve'llic/ō -ā're *vt.* pinch, pluck, twitch; (*speech*) taunt, disparage.
ve'll/ō -ere **ve'llī** & **vu'lsī** **vu'lsum** *vt.* pluck, pull, pick; pluck out, tear up.
ve'll/us -eris *n.* fleece, pelt; wool; fleecy clouds.
vē'l/ō -ā're -ā'vī -ā'tum *vt.* cover up, clothe, veil; (*fig.*) conceal.
vēlō'cit/ās -ā'tis *f.* speed, rapidity.
vē'l/ōx -ō'cis *a.* fast, quick, rapid. —**ō'citer** *ad.* rapidly.
vē'l/um -ī *n.* sail; curtain, awning. **rēmīs** -**īsque** with might and main. -**a dare** set sail.
ve'lut, ve'lutī *ad.* as, just as; for instance; just as if.
vē'mēns, *see* **ve'hemēns**.
vē'n/a -ae *f.* vein, artery; vein of metal; water-course; (*fig.*) innermost nature of feelings, talent, strength. -**ās temptāre** feel the pulse. -**ās tenēre** have one's finger on the pulse (of).
vēnā'bul/um -ī *n.* hunting-spear.
Venā'fr/um -ī *n.* Samnite town famous for olive-oil. —**ā'nus** *a.*
vēnāli'cius *a.* for sale. *m.* slave-dealer.
vēnā'lis *a.* for sale; bribable. *m.* slave offered for sale.
vēnā'ticus *a.* hunting-.
vēnā'ti/ō -ō'nis *f.* hunting; a hunt; public show of fighting wild beasts; game.
vēnā't/or -ō'ris *m.* hunter.
vēnātō'rius *a.* hunter's.
vēnā'tr/īx -ī'cis *f.* huntress.
vēnātū'r/a -ae *f.* hunting.
vēnā't/us -ūs *m.* hunting.
vēndi'bilis *a.* saleable; (*fig.*) popular.
vēnditā'ti/ō -ō'nis *f.* showing off, advertising.
vēnditā't/or -ō'ris *m.* braggart.
vēndi'ti/ō -ō'nis *f.* sale.
vē'ndit/ō -ā're *vt.* try to sell; praise up, advertise. **sē** — ingratiate onself (with).
vē'ndit/or -ō'ris *m.* seller.
vē'nd/ō (*pass.* **vē'neō**) -ere -idī -itum *vt.* sell; betray; praise up.
venēfi'c/ium -ī & iī *n.* poisoning; sorcery.
venē'ficus *a.* poisonous, magic *m.* sorcerer. *f.* sorceress.
venē'nifer -ī *a.* poisonous.
venē'n/ō -ā're *vt.* poison. —**ā'tus** *a.* poisonous; magic.
venē'n/um -ī *n.* drug, potion, dye; poison; magic charm; (*fig.*) mischief; charm.
vē'n/eō -ī're -iī -itum *vi.* be sold.
venerā'bilis *a.* honoured, venerable.
venerābu'ndus *a.* reverent.

venerā'ti/ō -ō'nis *f.* respect, reverence.
venerā't/or -ō'ris *m.* reverencer.
Vene'reus, Vene'rius *a.* of Venus. *m.* highest throw at dice.
ve'ner/or -ā'rī -ā'tus *vt.* worship, revere, pray to; honour, respect; ask for, entreat.
Ve'net/us *a.* Venetian; (*colour*) blue. **-ia** -iae *f.* district of the Veneti. **-icus** *a.*
vē'nī *perf.* venio.
ve'ni/a -ae *v.* indulgence, favour, kindness; permission, leave; pardon, forgiveness. **bonā tuā -ā** by your leave. **bonā -ā audire** give a fair hearing.
vē'niī *perf.* vēneō.
ve'n/iō -ī're vē'nī ve'ntum *vi.* come; (*fig.*) fall into, incur, go as far as. **in amīcitiam —** make friends (with). **in spem —** entertain hopes.
vē'n/or -ā'rī -ā'tus *vt.* & *i.* hunt, chase.
ve'nt/er -ris *m.* stomach, belly; womb, unborn child.
ventilā't/or -ō'ris *m.* juggler.
ve'ntil/ō -ā're *vt.* fan, wave, agitate.
ve'nti/ō -ō'nis *f.* coming.
ve'ntit/ō -ā're *vi.* keep coming, come regularly.
ventō'sus *a.* windy; like the wind; fickle; conceited.
ventri'cul/us -ī *m.* belly; (*heart*) ventricle.
ventriō'sus *a.* pot-bellied.
ve'ntul/us -ī *m.* breeze.
ve'nt/us -ī *m.* wind.
vēnū'cul/a -ae *f.* kind of grape.
vō'num, vē'nō for sale.
vēnu'md/ō (**vēnu'ndō**) -ā're -edī -atum *vt.* sell, put up for sale.
ve'n/us -eris *f.* charm, beauty; love, mating.
Ve'n/us -eris *f.* goddess of love; planet Venus; highest throw at dice. **-e'reus, -e'rius** *a.*
Venu's/ia -iae *f.* town in Apulia, birthplace of Horace. **-ī'nus** *a.*
venu'st/ās -ā'tis *f.* charm, beauty.
venu'stulus *a.* charming [little.
venu'st/us *a.* charming, attractive, beautiful. **-ē** *ad.* charmingly.
vēpa'llidus *a.* very pale.
veprē'cul/a -ae *f.* little brier-bush.
ve'pr/ēs -is *m.* thorn-bush, bramble-bush.
vēr vē'ris *n.* spring. **— sacrum** offerings of firstlings.
vērā'tr/um -ī *n.* hellebore.
vē'r/āx -ā'cis *a.* truthful.
verbē'n/a -ae *f.* vervain; (*pl.*) sacred boughs carried by heralds or priests.
ve'rber -is *n.* lash, scourge; (*missile*) strap; (*pl.*) flogging, strokes.
verberā'bilis *a.* deserving a flogging.
verberā'ti/ō -ō'nis *f.* punishment.
verbe'reus *a.* deserving a flogging.
ve'rber/ō -ā're -ā'vī -ā'tum *vt.* flog, beat, lash.
ve'rber/ō -ō'nis *m.* scoundrel.
verbō's/us *a.* wordy. **-ē** *ad.* verbosely.
ve'rb/um -ī *n.* word; saying, expression; (*gram.*) verb; (*pl.*) language, talk. **— ē** (dē, prō) **-ō** literally. **ad -um** word for word. **-ī causā** (grātiā) for instance. **-ō** orally; briefly. **-a dare** cheat, fool. **-a facere** talk. **meīs -īs** in my name.
vē'rē *ad.* really, truly, correctly.
verēcu'ndi/a -ae *f.* modesty, shyness; reverence, dread; shame.

verēcu'nd/or -ā'rī *vi.* be bashful, feel shy.
verēcu'nd/us *a.* modest, shy, bashful. **-ē** *ad.*
vere'ndus *a.* venerable.
ve'r/eor -ē'rī -itus *vt.* & *i.* fear, be afraid; revere, respect.
verē'tr/um -ī *n.* the private parts. [Pleiads.
Vergi'li/ae -ā'rum *f.pl.* the
Vergi'l/ius -ī *m.* Vergil, Virgil, famous epic poet.
ve'rg/ō -ere *vt.* turn, incline. *vi.* turn, incline, decline; (*place*) face.
vēri'dicus *a.* truthful.
vē'rī si'milis *a.* probable.
vē'rī similitū'd/ō -inis *f.* probability.
vē'rit/ās -ā'tis *f.* truth, truthfulness; reality, real life; (*character*) integrity; (*language*) etymology.
ve'ritus *ppa.* vereor.
vermiculā'tus *a.* inlaid with wavy lines, mosaic.
vermi'cul/us -ī *m.* grub.
ve'rmin/a -um *n.pl.* stomach pains.
ve'rm/is -is *m.* worm.
ve'rn/a -ae *f.* slave born in his master's home.
vernā'culus *a.* of home-born slaves; native.
vernī'l/is *a.* slavish; (*remark*) smart. **-iter** *ad.* slavishly.
vē'rn/ō -ā're *vi.* bloom, be spring-like; be young.
ve'rnul/a -ae *f.* young home-born slave; native.
vē'rnus *a.* of spring.
vē'rō *ad.* in fact, assuredly; (*confirming*) certainly, yes; (*climax*) indeed; (*adversative*) but in fact. minimē — certainly not.
Vērō'n/a -ae *f.* town in N. Italy, birthplace of Catullus. **-ē'nsis** *a.*
ve'rp/us -ī *m.* circumcised man.
ve'rr/ēs -is *m.* boar.
Ve'rr/ēs -is *m.* praetor prosecuted by Cicero. **-ius**, **-ī'nus** *a.*
verrī'nus *a.* boar's, pork-.
ve'r/rō -rere -rī -sum *vt.* sweep, scour; sweep away, carry off.
verrū'c/a -ae *f.* wart; (*fig.*) slight blemish.
verrūcō'sus *a.* warty.
verru'nc/ō -ā're *vi.* turn out successfully.
versābu'ndus *a.* rotating.
versā'tilis *a.* revolving; versatile.
versi'col/or -ō'ris *a.* of changing or various colours.
versi'cul/us -ī *m.* short line; (*pl.*) unpretentious verses.
versificā't/or -ō'ris *m.* versifier.
versipe'llis *a.* of changed appearance; crafty. *m.* werwolf.
ve'rs/ō (**vo'rsō**) -ā're -ā'vī -ā'tum *vt.* keep turning, wind, twist; (*fig.*) upset, disturb, ruin; (*mind*) ponder, consider.
ve'rs/or (**vo'rsor**) -ā'rī -ā'tus *vi.* live, be, be situated; be engaged (in), be busy (with).
ve'rsum (**vo'rsum**) *ad.* turned, in the direction.
versū'r/a (**vorsū'ra**) -ae *f.* borrowing to pay a debt; loan.
ve'rsus (**vo'rsus**) *ppp.* vertō. *ad.* turned, in the direction.
ve'rs/us (**vo'rsus**) -ūs *m.* line, row; verse; (*dance*) step.
versū'ti/ae -ā'rum *f.pl.* tricks.
versūti'loquus *a.* sly.
versū't/us (**vorsū'tus**) *a.* clever; crafty, deceitful. **-ē** *ad.* craftily.
ve'rt/ex (**vo'rtex**) -icis *m.* whirlpool, eddy; whirlwind; crown of the head, head; top, summit; (*sky*) pole.
verticō'sus *a.* eddying, swirling. [round; dizziness.
vertī'g/ō -inis *f.* turning
ve'r/tō (**vo'rtō**) -tere -tī -sum

vt. turn; turn over, invert; turn round; turn into, change, exchange; (*cause*) ascribe, impute; (*language*) translate; (*war*) overthrow, destroy; (*pass.*) be (in), be engaged (in). *vi.* turn; change; turn out. **in fugam** — put to flight. **terga** — flee. **solum** — emigrate. **vitiō** — blame. **annō -tente** in the course of a year.
Vertu'mn/us -ī *m.* god of seasons.
ve'r/ū -ūs *n.* spit; javelin.
vē'rum *ad.* truly, yes; but actually; but, yet. — **tamen** nevertheless.
vē'r/us *a.* true, real, actual; truthful; right, reasonable. **-um -ī** *n.* truth, reality; right. **-ī similis** probable.
verū't/um -ī *n.* javelin.
verū'tus *a.* armed with the javelin.
ve'rv/ēx -ē'cis *m.* wether.
vēsā'ni/a -ae *f.* madness.
vēsā'ni/ēns -e'ntis *a.* raging.
vēsā'nus *a.* mad, insane; furious, raging.
ve'sc/or -ī *vi.* (*with abl.*) feed, eat; enjoy.
ve'scus *a.* little, feeble; corroding.
vēsī'c/a -ae *f.* bladder; purse, football. [blister.
vēsī'cul/a -ae *f.* small bladder,
ve'sp/a -ae *f.* wasp.
Vespasiā'n/us -ī *m.* Roman emperor.
ve'sper -is & ī *m.* evening; supper; evening-star; west. **-e. -ī** in the evening.
ve'sper/a -ae *f.* evening.
vesperā'sc/ō -ere *vi.* become evening, get late.
vespertī'li/ō -ō'nis *m.* bat.
vespertī'nus *a.* evening-, in the evening; western.
vesperū'g/ō -inis *f.* evening-star.
Ve'st/a -ae *f.* Roman goddess of the hearth. **-ā'lis** *a.* Vestal. *f.* virgin priestess of Vesta.
ve'st/er (vo'ster) -rī *a.* your, yours. [entrance.
vesti'bul/um -ī *n.* fore-court,
vestī'g/ium -ī & iī *n.* footstep, footprint, track; (*fig.*) trace, sign, vestige; (*time*) moment, instant. **ē -iō** instantly.
vestī'g/ō -ā're -ā'vī -ā'tum *vt.* track, trace, search for, discover.
vestīme'nt/um -ī *n.* clothes.
ve'st/iō -ī're -iī -ī'tum *vt.* clothe, dress; cover, adorn.
vesti'pic/a -ae *f.* wardrobe-woman.
ve'st/is -is *f.* clothes, dress; coverlet, tapestry, blanket; (*snake*) slough. **-em mūtāre** change one's clothes; go into mourning.
vesti'spic/a, *see* **vesti'pica.**
vestī't/us -ūs *m.* clothes, dress; covering. **mūtāre -um** go into mourning. **redīre ad suum -um** come out of mourning.
Vesu'v/ius -ī *m.* the volcano Vesuvius.
veterā'nus *a.* veteran.
veterā'/scō -scere -vī *vi.* grow old.
veterā't/or -ō'ris *m.* expert, old hand; sly fox. [**-ē** *ad.*
veterātō'ri/us *a.* crafty.
veterī'nus *a.* of burden. *f.* & *n.pl.* beasts of burden.
veternō'sus *a.* lethargic, drowsy.
vete'rn/us -ī *m.* lethargy, drowsiness. [hibition.
ve'titus *ppp.* **vetō.** *n.* pro-
ve't/ō -ā're -uī -itum *vt.* forbid, prohibit, oppose; (*tribune*) protest.
ve'tulus *a.* little old, poor old.
ve't/us -eris *a.* old, former. *m.pl.* the ancients. *f.pl.* the old shops (in the Forum). *n.pl.* antiquity, tradition.

vetu'st/ās -ā'tis *f.* age, long standing; antiquity; great age, future age.
vetu'stus *a.* old, ancient; old-fashioned.
vexā'm/en -inis *n.* shaking.
vexā'ti/ō -ō'nis *f.* shaking; trouble, distress.
vexā't/or -ō'ris *m.* troubler, opponent.
ve'xī *perf.* **vehō.**
vexillā'r/ius -ī & iī *m.* standard-bearer, ensign; (*pl.*) special reserve of veterans.
vexi'll/um -ī *n.* standard, flag; company, troop. — **prōpōnere** hoist the signal for battle.
ve'x/ō -ā're -ā'vī -ā'tum *vt* shake, toss, trouble, distress, injure, attack.
vi'/a -ae *f.* road, street, way; journey, march; passage; (*fig.*) way, method, fashion; the right way. -ā properly. inter -ās on the way.
viā'lis *a.* of the highways.
viā'rius *a.* for the upkeep of roads.
viāticā'tus *a.* provided with travelling money.
viā'ticus *a.* for a journey. *n.* travelling allowance; (*mil.*) prize-money, savings.
viā't/or -ō'ris *m.* traveller; (*law*) summoner.
vī'b/īx -ī'cis *f.* weal.
vi'br/ō -ā're -ā'vī -ā'tum *vt.* wave, shake, brandish, hurl, launch. *vi.* shake, quiver, vibrate; shimmer, sparkle.
vību'rn/um -ī *n.* wayfaring-tree or guelder rose.
vīcā'nus *a.* village-. *m.pl.* villagers.
Vi'c/a Po't/a -ae -ae *f.* goddess of victory.
vicā'rius *a.* substituted. *m.* substitute, proxy; under-slave.
vīcā'tim *ad.* from street to street; in villages.
vi'ce (*with gen.*) on account of; like.
vi'cem in turn; (*with gen.*) instead of; on account of; like. **tuam** — on your account.
vīcēnā'rius *a.* of twenty.
vīcē'n/ī -ō'rum *a.* twenty each, in twenties.
vi'cēs *pl.* **vicis.**
vīcēsimā'n/ī -ō'rum *m.pl.* men of the twentieth legion.
vīcēsimā'rius *a.* derived from the 5 per cent tax.
vīcē'simus *a.* twentieth. *f.* a 5 per cent tax.
vī'cī *perf* **vincō.**
vi'ci/a -ae *f.* vetch.
vī'ci/ēns, -ēs *ad.* twenty times.
vīcīnā'lis *a.* neighbouring.
vīcī'ni/a -ae *f.* neighbourhood, nearness.
vīcī'nit/ās -ā'tis *f.* neighbourhood, nearness.
vīcī'nus *a.* neighbouring, nearby, similar, kindred. *m., f.* neighbour. *n.* neighbourhood.
vi'c/is *gen.* (*acc.* -em, *abl.* -e) *f.* interchange, alternation, succession; recompense, retaliation; fortune, changing conditions; duty, function, place. **in -em** in turn, mutually.
vici'ssim *ad.* in turn, again.
vicissitū'd/ō -inis *f.* interchange, alternation.
vi'ctim/a -ae *f.* victim, sacrifice.
victimā'r/ius -ī & iī *m.* assistant at sacrifices.
vī'ctit/ō -ā're *vi.* live, subsist.
vi'ct/or -ō'ris *m.* conqueror, victor, winner. *a.* victorious.
victō'ri/a -ae *f.* victory.
victōriā't/us -ūs *m.* silver coin stamped with Victory.
Victōri'ol/a -ae *f.* little statue of Victory.
vi'ctr/īx -ī'cis *f.* conqueror. *a.* victorious.
vi'ctus *ppp.* **vincō.**

vī'ct/us -ūs *m.* sustenance, livelihood; way of life.
vī'cul/us -ī *m.* hamlet.
vī'c/us -ī *m.* (*city*) quarter, street; (*country*) village, estate.
vidē'licet *ad.* clearly, evidently; (*ironical*) of course; (*explaining*) namely.
vi'den for **vidēsne?**
vi'd/eō -ē're vī'dī vi'sum *vt.* see, look at; (*mind*) observe, be aware, know; consider, think over; see to, look out for; live to see; (*pass.*) seem, appear; seem right, be thought proper. mē -ē rely on me. viderit let him see to it. mihi -eor esse I think I am. sī (tibi) vidētur if you like.
vidu'it/ās -ā'tis *f.* bereavement, want; widowhood.
vī'dul/us -ī *m.* trunk, box.
vi'du/ō -ā're *vt.* bereave. **-ā'ta** *a.* widowed.
vi'duus *a.* bereft, bereaved; unmarried; (*with abl.*) without. *f.* widow; spinster.
Vie'nn/a -ae *f.* town in Gaul on the Rhone.
viē'tus *a.* shrivelled.
vi'g/eō -ē're -uī *vi.* thrive, flourish.
vigē'sc/ō -ere *vi.* begin to flourish, become lively.
vīgē'simus, *see* **vīcēsimus.**
vi'gil -is *a.* awake, watching, alert. *m.* watchman, sentinel; (*pl.*) the watch, police.
vi'gil/āns -a'ntis *pres.p.* vigilō. *a.* watchful. **-a'nter** *ad.* vigilantly.
vigila'nti/a -ae *f.* wakefulness; vigilance.
vi'gil/āx -ā'cis *a.* watchful.
vigi'li/a -ae *f.* lying awake, sleeplessness; keeping watch, guard; a watch; the watch, sentries; vigil; vigilance.
vi'gil/ō -ā're -ā'vī -ā'tum *vi.* remain awake; keep watch; be vigilant. *vt.* spend awake, make while awake at night.
vīgi'ntī *num.* twenty.
vīgintīvirā't/us -ūs *m.* membership of a board of twenty.
vīgintī'vir/ī -ō'rum *m.pl.* a board or commission of twenty men.
vi'g/or -ō'ris *m.* energy, vigour.
vī'lic/ō -ā're *vi.* be an overseer.
vī'lic/us -ī *m.* overseer, manager of an estate, steward. **-a** -ae *f.* wife of a steward.
vī'l/is *a.* cheap; worthless, poor, mean, common. **-iter** *ad.* cheaply.
vī'lit/ās -ā'tis *f.* cheapness, low price; worthlessness.
vī'll/a -ae *f.* country-house, villa.
vīllic-, *see* **vīlic-.**
villō'sus *a.* hairy, shaggy.
vī'llul/a -ae *f.* small villa.
vi'll/um -ī *n.* a drop of wine.
vi'll/us -ī *m.* hair, fleece; (*cloth*) nap.
vī'm/en -inis *n.* osier; basket.
vīme'nt/um -ī *n.* osier.
Vīminā'lis *a.* Viminal (hill of Rome).
vīmi'neus *a.* of osiers, wicker.
vīn *for* **vīsne?**
vīnā'ceus *a.* grape-.
Vīnā'l/ia -ium *n.pl.* Wine festival.
vīnā'rius *a.* of wine, wine-. *m.* vintner. *n.* wine-flask.
vinci'bilis *a.* easily won.
vi'n/ciō -cī're -xī -ctum *vt.* bind, fetter; encircle; (*fig.*) confine, restrain, envelop, attach.
vi'nc/ō -ere vī'cī vi'ctum *vt.* conquer, defeat, subdue; win, prevail, be successful; (*fig.*) surpass, excel; (*argument*) convince, refute, prove conclusively; (*life*) outlive.
vi'nctus *ppp.* vinciō.
vi'ncul/um (**vi'nclum**) -ī *n.* bond, fetter, chain; (*pl.*) prison.

vīndē'mi/a -ae *f.* vintage grape-harvest.
vīndēmiā't/or -ō'ris *m.* vintager.
vīndēmi'ol/a -ae *f.* small vintage.
Vīndē'mit/or -ō'ris *m.* the Vintager, a star in Virgo.
vi'nd/ex -icis *m.* champion, protector; liberator; avenger. *a.* avenging.
vindicā'ti/ō -ō'nis *f.* punishment of offences.
vindi'ci/ae -ā'rum *f.pl.* legal claim. **-ās ab lībertāte in servitūtem dare** condemn a free person to slavery.
vi'ndic/ō -ā're -ā'vī -ā'tum *vt.* lay claim to; claim, appropriate; liberate, protect, champion; avenge, punish. **in lībertātem —** emancipate.
vindi'ct/a -ae *f.* rod used in manumitting a slave; defence, deliverance; revenge, punishment.
vī'ne/a -ae *f.* vineyard; vine; (*mil.*) pent-house (for besiegers).
vīnē't/um -ī *n.* vineyard.
vī'nit/or -ō'ris *m.* vine-dresser.
vi'nnulus *a.* delightful.
vīnole'nti/a -ae *f.* wine-drinking.
vīnole'ntus *a.* drunk.
vīnō'sus *a.* fond of wine, drunken.
vī'n/um -ī *n.* wine.
vi'nxī *perf.* **vinciō.**
vi'ol/a -ae *f.* violet; stock.
violā'bilis *a.* vulnerable.
violā'ceus *a.* violet. [bed.
violā'r/ium -ī & iī *n.* violet-
violā'r/ius -ī & iī *m.* dyer of violet.
violā'ti/ō -ō'nis *f.* desecration.
violā't/or -ō'ris *m.* violator, desecrator.
vi'ol/ēns -e'ntis *a.* raging, vehement. **—e'nter** *ad.* violently, furiously.
viole'nti/a -ae *f.* violence, impetuosity.
viole'ntus *a.* violent, impetuous, boisterous.
vi'ol/ō -ā're -ā'vī -ā'tum *vt.* do violence to, outrage, violate; (*agreement*) break.
vī'per/a -ae *f.* viper, adder, snake.
vīpe'reus *a.* snake's, serpent's.
vīperī'nus *a.* snake's, serpent's.
vir vi'rī *m.* man; grown man; brave man, hero; husband; (*mil.*) foot-soldier.
virā'g/ō -inis *f.* heroine, warrior maid.
vire'ct/a -ō'rum *n.pl.* grassy sward.
vi'r/eō -ē're -uī *vi.* be green; (*fig.*) be fresh, flourish.
vī'rēs *pl.* **vīs.**
virē'sc/ō -ere *vi.* grow green.
vi'rg/a -ae *f.* twig; graft; rod, staff, walking-stick, wand; (*colour*) stripe.
virgā't/or -ō'ris *m.* flogger.
virgā'tus *a.* made of osiers; striped. [osiers.
virgē't/um -ī *n.* thicket of
vi'rgeus *a.* of brushwood.
virgidē'mi/a -ae *f.* crop of flogging.
virginā'lis *a.* maidenly, of maids.
virginā'rius *a.* of maids.
virgi'neus *a.* maidenly, virgin, of virgins.
virgi'nit/ās -ā'tis *f.* maidenhood.
vi'rg/ō -inis *f.* maid, virgin; young woman, girl; constellation Virgo; a Roman aqueduct.
vi'rgul/a -ae *f.* wand.
virgu'lt/a -ō'rum *n.pl.* thicket, shrubbery; cuttings, slips.
virgu'ncul/a -ae *f.* little girl.
vi'rid/āns -a'ntis *a.* green.
viridā'r/ium -ī & iī *n.* plantation, garden.
vi'ridis *a.* green; fresh, young, youthful. *n.pl.* greenery.

viri'dit/ās -ā'tis *f.* verdure, greenness; freshness.
vi'rid/or -ā'rī *vi.* become green.
virī'l/is *a.* male, masculine; man's, adult; manly, brave, bold. — pars one's individual part or duty. prō -ī parte, portiōne to the best of one's ability. **-iter** *ad.* manfully.
virī'lit/ās -ā'tis *f.* manhood.
virī'tim *ad.* individually, separately.
virō'sus *a.* slimy; rank.
vi'rt/ūs -ū'tis *f.* manhood, full powers; strength, courage, ability, worth; (*mil.*) valour, prowess, heroism; (*moral*) virtue; (*things*) excellence, worth.
vī'r/us -ī *n.* slime; poison; offensive smell; salt taste.
vīs (*acc.* vim *abl.* vī *pl.* vī'rēs) *f.* power, force, strength; violence, assault; quantity, amount; (*mind*) energy, vigour; (*word*) meaning, import; (*pl.*) strength; (*mil.*) troops. per vim forcibly. dē vī damnārī be convicted of assault. prō vīribus with all one's might.
vīs *2nd pers.* volō.
viscā'tus *a.* limed.
viscerā'ti/ō -ō'nis *f.* public distribution of meat.
vi'sc/ō -ā're *vt.* make sticky.
vi'sc/um -ī *n.* mistletoe; bird-lime.
vi'sc/us -eris (*usu. pl.* **-era -erum**) *n.* internal organs; flesh; womb, child; (*fig.*) heart, bowels.
vī'si/ō -ō'nis *f.* apparition; idea. [visit.
vī'sit/ō -ā're *vt.* see often;
vī's/ō -ere -ī -um *vt.* look at, survey; see to; go and see, visit. **-e'ndus** *a.* worth seeing.
Visu'rg/is -is *m.* river Weser.
vī'sus *ppp.* videō. *n.* vision.
vī's/us -ūs *m.* sight, the faculty of seeing; a sight, vision.
vī't/a -ae *f.* life, livelihood; way of life; career, biography.
vītā'bilis *a.* undesirable.
vītābu'ndus *a.* avoiding, taking evasive action.
vītā'l/is *a.* of life, vital. *n.* subsistence. *n.pl.* vitals. **-iter** *ad.* with life.
vītā'ti/ō -ō'nis *f.* avoidance.
Vite'll/ius -ī *m.* Roman emperor in A.D. 69 **-ius, -iā'nus** *a.*
vite'll/us -ī *m.* little calf; (*egg*) yolk.
vī'teus *a.* of the vine.
vīti'cul/a -ae *f.* little vine.
vīti'genus *a.* produced from the vine.
vitilē'n/a -ae *f.* procuress.
vi'ti/ō -ā're -ā'vī -ā'tum *vt.* spoil, corrupt, violate; falsify.
vitiō'sit/ās -ā'tis *f.* vice.
vitiō's/us *a.* faulty, corrupt; wicked, depraved. — cōnsul a consul whose election had a religious flaw in it. **-ē** *ad.* badly, defectively.
vī't/is -is *f.* vine; vine-branch; centurion's staff, centurionship. [planter.
vīti'sat/or -ō'ris *m.* vine-
vi't/ium -ī & iī *n.* fault, flaw, defect; (*moral*) failing, offence, vice; (*religion*) flaw in the auspices.
vī't/ō -ā're -ā'vī -ā'tum *vt.* avoid, evade, shun.
vī't/or -ō'ris *m.* basket-maker, cooper.
vi'treus *a.* of glass; glassy. *n.pl.* glass-ware.
vī'tric/us -ī *m.* step-father.
vi'tr/um -ī *n.* glass; woad.
vi'tt/a -ae *f.* head-band, sacrificial fillet.
vittā'tus *a.* wearing a fillet.
vi'tul/a -ae *f.* cow-calf.
vitulī'nus *a.* of veal. *f.* veal.
vī'tul/or -ā'rī *vi.* hold a celebration.

vi'tul/us -ī *m.* calf; foal. — marīnus seal.
vituperā'bilis *a.* blameworthy.
vituperā'ti/ō -ō'nis *f.* blame, censure; scandalous conduct.
vituperā't/or -ō'ris *m.* critic.
vitu'per/ō -ā're *vt.* find fault with, disparage; (*omen*) spoil.
vīvā'r/ium -ī & iī *n.* fishpond, game preserve.
vīvā'tus *a.* animated.
vī'v/āx -ā'cis *a.* long-lived; lasting; (*sulphur*) inflammable.
vīvē'sc/ō (**vīvī'scō**) -ere *vi.* grow, become active.
vī'vidus *a.* full of life.; (*art*) true to life, vivid; (*mind*) lively.
vīvirā'd/īx -ī'cis *f.* a rooted cutting, layer.
vīvī'scō, *see* **vīvēscō**.
vī'/vō -vere -xī -ctum *vi.* live, be alive; enjoy life; (*fame*) last, be remembered; (*with abl.*) live on. -ve farewell! -xērunt they are dead.
vī'v/us *a.* alive, living; (*light*) burning; (*rock*) natural; (*water*) running. -ō videntique before his very eyes. mē -ō as long as I live, in my lifetime. ad -um resecāre cut to the quick. dē -ō dētrahere take out of capital.
vix *ad.* with difficulty, hardly, scarcely.
vi'xdum *ad.* hardly as yet.
vī'xet *for* **vīxisset**.
vī'xī *perf.* **vīvō**.
vocā'bul/um -ī *n.* name, designation; (*gram.*) noun.
vōcā'lis *a.* speaking, singing, tuneful. *f.* vowel.
vocā'm/en -inis *n.* name.
vocā'ti/ō -ō'nis *f.* invitation; (*law*) summons. [call.
vocā't/us -ūs *m.* summons,
vōciferā'ti/ō -ō'nis *f.* loud cry, outcry.
vōci'fer/or -ā'rī *vi.* cry out loud, shout.
vo'cit/ō -ā're -ā'vī -ā'tum *vt.* usually call; shout.
vocī'vus, *see* **vacīvus**.
vo'c/ō -ā're -ā'vī -ā'tum *vt.* call, summon; call, name; (*gods*) call upon; (*guest*) invite; (*mil.*) challenge; (*fig.*) bring (into some condition or plight). — dē name after. in dubium — call in question. in iūdicium — call to account.
vō'cul/a -ae *f.* weak voice; soft tone; gossip.
volae'ma *n.pl.* kind of large pear.
Volate'rr/ae -ā'rum *f.pl.* old Etruscan town, *mod.* Volterra. -ā'nus *a.*
volā'ticus *a.* winged; fleeting, inconstant.
volā'tilis *a.* winged; swift; fleeting.
volā't/us -ūs *m.* flight.
Volcā'n/us -ī *m.* Vulcan, god of fire; fire. -ius *a.*
vo'l/ēns -e'ntis *pres.p.* volō. *a.* willing, glad, favourable. mihi -entī est it is acceptable to me.
volg-, *see* **vulg-**.
vo'lit/ō -ā're *vi.* fly about, flutter; hurry, move quickly; (*fig.*) hover, soar; get excited.
voln-, *see* **vuln-**.
vo'l/ō -ā're -ā'vī -ā'tum *vi.* fly; speed.
vo'lō ve'lle vo'luī *vt.* wish, want; be willing; will, purpose, determine; (*opinion*) hold, maintain; (*word, action*) mean. — dīcere I mean. bene — like. male — dislike. ōrātum tē — I beg you. paucīs tē — a word with you! numquid vīs? (*before leaving*) is there anything else? quid sibi vult? what does he mean? what is he driving at? velim faciās please do it. vellem fēcissēs I wish you had done it.
volō'n/ēs -um *m.pl.* volunteers.

vo'lpēs, *see* **vulpēs.**
Vo'lsc/ī -ō'rum *m.pl.* people in S. Latium. –us *a.* Volscian.
volse'll/a -ae *f.* tweezers.
vo'lsus *ppp.* vellō.
volt, vo'ltis *older forms of* **vult, vultis.**
Voltu'mn/a -ae *f.* patron goddess of Etruria.
vo'ltus, *see* **vultus.**
volū'bil/is *a.* spinning, revolving; (*fortune*) fickle; (*speech*) fluent. –iter *ad.* fluently.
volubi'lit/ās -ā'tis *f.* whirling motion; roundness; fluency; inconstancy.
vo'luc/er -ris *a.* winged; flying, swift; fleeting.
vo'lucr/is -is *f.* bird; insect.
volū'm/en -inis *n.* roll, book; coil, eddy, fold.
voluntā'rius *a.* voluntary. *m.pl.* volunteers.
volu'nt/ās -ā'tis *f.* will, wish, inclination; attitude, goodwill; last will, testament. suā -āte of one's own accord. ad -ātem with the consent (of).
vo'lup *ad.* agreeably, to one's satisfaction.
voluptā'bilis *a.* agreeable.
voluptuā'rius *a.* pleasureable, agreeable; voluptuous.
volu'pt/ās -ā'tis *f.* pleasure, enjoyment; (*pl.*) entertainments, sports.
volūtā'br/um -ī *n.* wallowing-place.
volūtā'ti/ō -ō'nis *f.* wallowing.
volū't/ō -ā're *vt.* roll about, turn over; (*mind*) occupy, engross; (*thought*) ponder, think over; (*pass.*) wallow, flounder.
volū'tus *ppp.* volvō.
vo'lv/a (**vu'lva**) -ae *f.* womb; (*dish*) sow's womb.
vo'l/vō -vere -vī -ū'tum *vt.* roll, turn round; roll along; (*air*) breathe; (*book*) open; (*circle*) form; (*thought*) ponder, reflect on; (*time*) roll on; (*trouble*) undergo; (*pass.*) roll, revolve. *vi.* revolve, elapse.
vō'm/er, vō'm/is -eris *m.* ploughshare.
vo'mic/a -ae *f.* sore, ulcer, abscess, boil.
vō'mis, *see* **vōmer.**
vomi'ti/ō -ō'nis *f.* vomiting.
vo'mit/us -ūs *m.* vomiting, vomit.
vo'm/ō -ere -uī -itum *vt.* vomit, throw up; emit, discharge.
vorā'g/ō -inis *f.* abyss, chasm, depth.
vo'r/āx -ā'cis *a.* greedy, ravenous; consuming.
vo'r/ō -ā're -ā'vī -ā'tum *vt.* swallow, devour; (*sea*) swallow up; (*reading*) devour.
vors–, vort–, *see* **vers–, vert–.**
vōs *pro.* you.
Vo'seg/us -ī *m.* Vosges mountains.
vo'ster, *see* **vester.**
vōtī'vus *a.* votive, promised in a vow.
vo'tō, *see* **vetō.**
vō't/um -ī *n.* vow, prayer; votive offering; wish, longing. -ī damnārī have one's prayer granted.
vō'tus *ppp.* voveō.
vo'v/eō -ē're vō'vī vō'tum *vt.* vow, promise solemnly; dedicate; wish.
vōx vō'cis *f.* voice; sound, cry, call; word, saying, expression; accent. unā vōce unanimously.
Vulcā'nus, *see* **Volcānus.**
vulgā'r/is *a.* common, general. –iter *ad.* in the common fashion.
vulgā't/or -ō'ris *m.* betrayer.
vulgi'vagus *a.* roving; inconstant.
vu'lgō *ad.* publicly, commonly, usually, everywhere.
vu'lg/ō -ā're -ā'vī -ā'tum *vt.* make common, spread; publish, divulge, broadcast; prostitute;

level down. **-ā'tus** *a.* common; generally known, notorious.
vu'lg/us -ī *n.* (*occ. m.*) the mass of the people, the public; crowd, herd; rabble, populace.
vulnerā'ti/ō -ō'nis *f.* wounding, injury.
vu'lner/ō -ā're -ā'vī -ā'tum *vt.* wound, hurt; damage.
vulni'ficus *a.* wounding, dangerous.
vu'ln/us -eris *n.* wound, injury; (*things*) damage, hole; (*fig.*) blow, misfortune, pain.
vulpē'cul/a -ae *f.* little fox.
vu'lp/ēs -is *f.* fox; (*fig.*) cunning.
vu'lsī *perf.* vellō.
vu'lsus *ppp.* vellō.
vulti'cul/us -ī *m.* a mere look (from).
vu'ltum, *see* **vultus.**
vultuō'sus *a.* affected.
vu'ltur -is *m.* vulture.
vultu'r/ius -ī & iī *m.* vulture, bird of prey; (*dice*) an unlucky throw.
Vultu'rn/us -ī *m.* river in Campania.
vu'lt/us (**vo'ltus**) -ūs *m.* look, expression (*esp.* in the eyes); face; (*things*) appearance.
vu'lva, *see* **volva.**

X

Xanthi'pp/ē -ēs *f.* wife of Socrates.
Xa'nth/us -ī *m.* river of Troy, identified with Scamander; river of Lycia.
xe'n/ium -ī & iī *n.* present.
Xeno'crat/ēs -is *m.* disciple of Plato.
Xeno'phan/ēs -is *m.* early Greek philosopher.
Xe'noph/ōn -o'ntis *a.* famous Greek historian. **-ontē'us** *a.*
xērampe'lin/ae -ā'rum *f.pl.* dark-coloured clothes.
Xe'rx/ēs -is *m.* Perisan king defeated at Salamis.
xi'phi/ās -ae *m.* swordfish.
xy'st/us -ī *m.*, **-um** -ī *n.* open colonnade, walk, avenue.

Z

Zacyn'th/us (**-os**) -ī *f.* island off W. Greece, *mod.* Zante. **-ius** *a.*
Za'm/a -ae *f.* town in Numidia, where Scipio defeated Hannibal. **-ē'nsis** *a.*
zā'mi/a -ae *f.* harm.
Za'ncl/ē -ēs *f.* old name of Messana. **-ae'us, -ē'ius** *a.*
zēlo'typus *a.* jealous.
Zē'n/ō, -ōn -ō'nis *m.* founder of Stoicism; a philosopher of Elea; an Epicurean teacher of Cicero.
Zephyrī't/is -idis *f.* Arsinoe, queen of Egypt.
Ze'phyr/us -ī *m.* west wind, zephyr; wind.
Zē'th/us -ī *m.* brother of Amphion.
Zeu'x/is -is & idis *m.* famous Greek painter.
zmara'gdus, *see* **smaragdus.**
Zmy'rna, *see* **Smyrna.**
zōdi'ac/us -ī *m.* zodiac.
zō'n/a -ae *f.* belt, girdle; (*geog.*) zone; (*astr.*) Orion's Belt.
zōnā'rius *a.* of belts. **sector** — cutpurse. *m.* belt-maker.
zō'nul/a -ae *f.* little belt.
zōthē'c/a -ae *f.* private room.
zōthē'cul/a -ae *f.* cubicle.

LATIN ABBREVIATIONS

A.	Aulus; (*vote (against a bill)*) antīquō; (*verdict*) absolvō.
a.d.	ante diem.
App.	Appius.
a.u.c.	annō urbis conditae.
C	centum.
C.	Gāius; (*verdict*) condemnō.
Cn.	Gnaius.
D	quīngentī.
D.	Decimus; (*before dates in letters*) dabam.
D.D.	dōnō dedit.
D.D.D.	dat, dicat, dēdicat.
D.O.M.	DeōOptimōMāximō.
f.	fīlius.
HS	sēstertiī, sēstertia.
Id.	Īdus, Īdibus.
Imp.	Imperātor.
I.O.M.	Iovī Optimō Māximō.
K.	Kaesō.
Kal.	Kalendas, Kalendīs.
L	quīnquāgintā.
L.	Lūcius.
M	mīlle.
M.	Marcus.
M'.	Manius.
Mam.	Mamercus.
n.	nepōs.
Non.	Nōnās, Nōnīs.
Num.	Numerius.
P.	Pūblius.
P.C.	Patrēs cōnscrīptī.
P.M.	Pontifex Māximus.
P.P.	Pater Patriae.
Pr.	Praetōr(ēs).
P.R.	Populus Rōmānus.
R.	Rōmānus.
R.P.	Rēs pūblica.
Q.	Quaestor; Quīntus.
S.	Sextus.
S.C.	Senātus cōnsultum.
s.d.	salūtem dīcit.
Ser.	Servius.
Sex.	Sextus.
Sp.	Spurius.
s.p.d.	salūtem plūrimam dīcit.
S.P.Q.R.	Senātus Populusque Rōmānus.
S.v.b.e.e.v.	Sī valēs, bene est; ego valeō.
T.	Titus.
Ti.	Tiberius.
Tr.	Tribūnus.
T.P.	Tribūnicia potestās.
V	quīnque.
X	decem.

NOTE. Users of the English-Latin section are strongly advised to look up any words they may find there in the Latin-English section also, where more detailed information is to be found, both regarding the forms of the Latin word and its precise meaning in English.

ENGLISH-LATIN DICTIONARY

a, an *art. not translated*; (*a certain*) quīdam. **twice — day** bis in diē. **four acres — man** quaterna in singulōs iūgera.
aback *ad.* **taken —** dēprehēnsus. [pōne.
abaft *ad.* in puppī. *pr.* post,
abandon *vt.* relinquere; (*wilfully*) dērelinquere, dēserere; (*to danger*) ōbicere; (*to pleasure*) dēdere; (*hope*) dīmittere; (*plan*) abicere. **-ed** *a.* perditus.
abase *vt.* dēprimere. **— oneself** sē prōsternere.
abash *vt.* perturbāre; rubōrem incutere (*dat.*)
abate *vt.* minuere, imminuere; (*a portion*) remittere. *vi.* (*fever*) dēcēdere; (*passion*) dēfervēscere; (*price*) laxāre; (*storm*) cadere.
abatement *n.* remissiō *f.*, dēminūtiō *f.*
abbess *n.* abbātissa *f.*
abbey *n.* abbātia *f.*
abbot *n.* abbās *m.*
abbreviate *vt.* imminuere.
abbreviation *n.* (*writing*) nota *f.*
abdicate *vt.* sē abdicāre (*abl.*).
abdication *n.* abdicātiō *f.*
abduct *vt.* abripere.
abduction *n.* raptus.
abeam *ad.* ā latere.
aberration *n.* error *m.*
abed *ad.* in lectō.
abet *vt.* adiuvāre, adesse (*dat.*), favēre (*dat.*).
abettor *n.* adiūtor *m.*, minister *m.*, fautor *m.*, socius *m.*
abeyance *n.* **in —** intermissus. **be in —** iacēre.
abhor *vt.* ōdisse, invīsum habēre.
abhorrence *n.* odium *n.*
abhorrent *a.* **—** to aliēnus ab.
abid/e *vi.* (*dwell*) habitāre; (*tarry*) commorārī; (*last*) dūrāre. **— by** stāre (*abl.*), perstāre in (*abl.*). **-ing** *a.* perpetuus, diūturnus.
ability *n.* (*to do*) facultās *f.*, potestās *f.*; (*physical*) vīrēs *f.pl.*; (*mental*) ingenium *n.* **to the best of my —** prō meā parte, prō virīlī parte.
abject *a.* abiectus, contemptus; (*downcast*) dēmissus. **-ly** *ad.* humiliter, dēmissē.
abjure *vt.* ēiūrāre.
ablative *n.* ablātīvus *m.*
ablaze *a.* flagrāns, ardēns.
abl/e *a.* peritus, doctus. **be —** posse, valēre. **— bodied** *a.* rōbustus. **-y** *ad.* perītē, doctē.
ablution *n.* lavātiō *f.*
abnegation *n.* abstinentia *f.*
abnormal *a.* inūsitātus; (*excess*) immodicus. **-ly** *ad.* inūsitātē, praeter mōrem.
aboard *ad.* in nāvī. **go —** nāvem cōnscendere. **put —** impōnere.
abode *n.* domicilium *n.*, sēdes *f.*
abolish *vt.* tollere, ē mediō tollere, abolēre; (*law*) abrogāre.
abolition *n.* dissolūtiō *f.*; (*law*) abrogātiō *f.*
abominabl/e *a.* dētestābilis, nefārius. **-y** *ad.* nefāriē, foedē.
abominate *vt.* dētestārī.
abomination *n.* odium *n.*; (*thing*) nefas *n.*
aborigin/al *a.* prīscus. **-es** *n.* aborīginēs *m.pl.*

abortion *n.* abortus.
abortive *a.* abortīvus; (*fig.*) inritus. be — ad inritum redigī.
abound *vi.* abundāre, superesse. — in abundāre (*abl.*), adfluere (*abl.*). **-ing** *a.* abundāns, adfluēns; cōpiōsus ab.
about *ad.* (*place*) *usu. expressed by cpd. verbs*; (*number*) circiter, ferē, fermē. *pr.* (*place*) circā, circum (*acc.*); (*number*) circā, ad (*acc.*); (*time*) sub (*acc.*); (*concerning*) dē (*abl.*). — to die moritūrus. I am — to go in eō est ut eam.
above *ad.* suprā. from — dēsuper. over and — insuper. *pr.* suprā (*acc.*), (*motion*) super (*acc.*), (*rest*) super (*abl.*) be — (*conduct*) indignārī.
abreast *ad.* (*ships*) aequātis prōris. walk — of latus tegere (*dat.*).
abridge *vt.* contrahere, compendī facere.
abridgement *n.* epitomē *f.*
abroad *ad.* peregrē; (*out of doors*) foris. be — peregrinārī. from — peregrē.
abrogate *vt.* dissolvere; (*law*) abrogāre.
abrupt *a.* subitus, repentīnus; (*speech*) concīsus.
abscess *n.* vomica *f.*
abscond *vi.* aufugere.
absence *n.* absentia. in my — mē absente. leave of — commeātus.
absent *a.* absens. be — abesse. — minded *a.* immemor, parum attentus. — oneself *vi.* deesse, nōn adesse.
absolute *a.* absolūtus, perfectus; (*not limited*) infīnītus; (*not relative*) simplex. — power rēgnum, dominātus. — ruler rēx. **-ly** *ad.* absolūtē, omnīnō.
absolution *n.* venia *f.*
absolve *vt.* absolvere, exsolvere; (*from punishment*) condōnāre.
absorb *vt.* bibere, absorbēre; (*fig.*) distringere. I am **-ed** in tōtus sum in (*abl.*).
absorbent *a.* bibulus.
abstain *vi.* abstinēre, sē abstinēre; (*from violence*) temperāre.
abstemious *a.* sobrius.
abstinence *n.* abstinentia *f.*, continentia *f.*
abstinent *a.* abstinēns, [sobrius.
abstract *a.* mente perceptus, cōgitātiōne comprehēnsus. *n.* epitomē *f.* *vt.* abstrahere, dēmere.
abstraction *n.* (*idea*) nōtiō *f.*; (*inattention*) animus parum attentus.
abstruse *a.* reconditus, obscūrus, abstrūsus.
absurd *a.* ineptus, absurdus. **-ly** *ad.* ineptē, absurdē.
absurdity *n.* ineptiae *f.pl.*, insulsitās *f.*
abundance *n.* cōpia *f.*, abundantia *f.* there is — of abundē est (*gen.*).
abundant *a.* cōpiōsus, abundāns, largus. be — abundāre. **-ly** *ad.* abundē, abundanter, adfātim.
abuse *vt.* abūtī (*abl.*); (*words*) maledīcere (*dat.*). *n.* probra *n.pl.*, maledicta *n.pl.*, convicium *n.*, contumēlia *f.*
abusive *a.* maledicus, contumēliōsus.
abut *vi.* adiacēre. **-ting** on cōnfīnis (*dat.*), fīnitimus (*dat.*).
abysmal *a.* profundus.
abyss *n.* profundum *n.*, vorāgō *f.*; (*water*) gurges *m.*; (*fig.*) barathrum *n.*
academic *a.* scholasticus; (*style*) umbrātilis; (*sect*) Acadēmicus.
academy *n.* schola *f.*; (*Plato's*) Acadēmia *f.*
accede *vi.* adsentīrī. — to accipere.
accelerate *vt.* & *i.* adcelerāre, festīnāre; (*process*) mātūrāre.

accent *n.* vōx *f.*; (*intonation*) sonus *m.*; (*mark*) apex *m.* *vt.* (*syllable*) acuere; (*word*) sonum admovēre (*dat.*).
accentuate *vt.* exprimere.
accept *vt.* accipere.
acceptable *a.* acceptus, grātus, probābilis. be — placēre.
acceptation *n.* significātiō *f.*
access *n.* aditus *m.*; (*addition*) accessiō *f.*; (*illness*) impetus *m.*
accessary *n.* socius *m.*, particeps *m.*
accessible *a.* (*person*) adfābilis, facilis. be — (*place*) patēre; (*person*) facilem sē praebēre.
accession *n.* (*addition*) accessiō *f.*; (*king's*) initium rēgnī. [amitās *f.*
accident *n.* cāsus *m.*, cal-
accidental *a.* fortuitus. **-ly** *ad.* cāsū, fortuītō.
acclaim *vt.* adclāmāre.
acclamation *n.* clāmor *m.*, studium *n.*
acclimatize *vt.* aliēnō caelō adsuēfacere.
accommodate *vt.* accommodāre, aptāre; (*lodging*) hospitium parāre (*dat.*). — oneself to mōrigerārī (*dat.*). **-ing** *a.* facilis.
accommodation *n.* hospitium *n.*
accompany *vt.* comitārī; (*courtesy*) prōsequī; (*to Forum*) dēdūcere; (*music*) concinere (*dat.*).
accomplice *n.* socius *m.* particeps *m.*, cōnscius *m.*
accomplish *vt.* efficere, perficere, patrāre. **-ed** *a.* doctus, peritus.
accomplishment *n.* effectus *m.*, perfectiō *f.*, fīnis *m.*; (*pl.*) artēs *f.pl.*
accord *vi.* inter sē congruere, cōnsentīre. *vt.* dare, praebēre, praestāre. *n.* cōnsēnsus, concordia; (*music*) concentus. of one's own — suā sponte, ultrō. with one — ūnā vōce.
accordance *n.* in — with ex, ē (*abl.*), secundum (*acc.*).
according *ad.* — as prōut. — to ex, ē (*abl.*), secundum (*acc.*), (*proportion*) prō (*abl.*). **-ly** *ad.* itaque, igitur, ergō.
accost *vt.* appellāre, adloquī, compellāre.
account *n.* ratiō *f.*, (*story*) nārrātio *f.*, expositiō *f.* on — of propter (*acc.*), causā (*gen.*). be of no — (*person*) nihilī aestimārī, nēquam esse. on that — idcircō, ideō. on your — tuā grātiā, tuō nōmine. give an — ratiōnem reddere. present an — ratiōnem referre. take — of ratiōnem habēre (*gen.*). put down to my — mihi expēnsum ferre. the -s balance ratiō cōnstat, convenit.
account *vi.* — for ratiōnēs reddere, adferre (*cūr*). that -s for it haec causa est. (*prov.*) hinc illae lacrimae.
accountant *n.* ā ratiōnibus, ratiōcinātor *m.*
account-book *n.* tabulae *f.pl.* cōdex acceptī et expēnsī.
accountable *a.* reus I am — for mihi ratiō reddenda est (*gen.*). [ōrnātus.
accoutred *a.* instructus,
accoutrements *n.* ōrnāmenta *n.pl.*, arma *n.pl.*
accredited *a.* pūblica auctōritāte missus.
accretion *n.* accessiō *f.*
accrue *vi.* (*addition*) cēdere; (*advantage*) redundāre.
accumulate *vt.* cumulāre, congerere, coacervāre. *vi.* crēscere, cumulārī.
accumulation *n.* cumulus *m.*, acervus *m.* [subtīlitās *f.*
accuracy *n.* cūra *f.*, (*writing*)
accurate *a.* (*work*) exāctus, subtīlis; (*worker*) dīligēns. **-ly** *ad.* subtīliter, ad amussim, dīligenter.

accursed *a.* sacer; (*fig.*) exsecrātus, scelestus.
accusation *n.* (*act*) accūsātiō *f.*; (*charge*) crimen *n.*; (*unfair*) īnsimulātiō *f.*; (*false*) calumnia *f.* bring an — against accūsāre; (*to a magistrate*) nōmen dēferre (*gen.*).
accusative *n.* (*case*) accūsātīvus *m.*
accuse *vt.* accūsāre, crīminārī, reum facere; (*falsely*) īnsimulāre the -d reus; (*said by prosecutor*) iste.
accuser *n.* accūsātor *m.*; (*civil suit*) petītor *m.*; (*informer*) dēlātor *m.*
accustom *vt.* adsuēfacere. — oneself adsuēscere, consuēscere. **-ed** *a.* adsuētus. be -ed solēre. become -ed adsuēscere, consuēscere.
ace *n.* ūniō *f.* I was within an — of going minimum āfuit quīn īrem.
acerbity *n.* acerbitās *f.*
ache *n.* dolor *m.* *vi.* dolēre.
achieve *vt.* cōnficere, patrāre; (*win*) cōnsequī, adsequī.
achievement *n.* factum *n.*, rēs gesta.
acid *a.* acidus. *f.*
acknowledge *vt.* (*fact*) agnōscere; (*fault*) fatērī, cōnfitērī; (*child*) tollere, (*service*) grātias agere prō (*abl.*). I have to — your letter of 1st March accēpī litterās tuās Kal. Mart. datās.
acknowledgement *n.* cōnfessiō *f.*; grātia *f.*
acme *n.* fastigium *n.*, flōs *m.*
aconite *n* aconītum *n.*
acorn *n.* glāns *f.*
acoustics *n.* rēs audītōria. *f.*
acquaint *vt.* certiōrem facere, docēre. — oneself with cognōscere. **-ed** with gnārus (*gen.*), peritus (*gen.*).
acquaintance *n.* (*with fact*) cognitiō *f.*, scientia *f.*; (*with person*) familiāritās *f.*, ūsus *m.*; (*person*) nōtus *m.*, familiāris *m.*
acquiesce *vi.* (*assent*) adquiēscere; (*submit*) aequō animō patī.
acquiescence *n.* with your — tē nōn adversante., pāce tuā. [cōnsequī.
acquire *vt.* adquīrere, adipīscī,
acquirements *n.* artēs *f.pl.*
acquisition *n.* (*act*) comparātiō *f.*, quaestus *m.*; (*thing*) quaesitum *n.*
acquisitive *a.* quaestuōsus.
acquit *vt.* absolvere. — oneself sē praestāre, officiō fungī.
acquittal *n.* absolūtiō *f.*
acre *n.* iugerum *n.*
acrid *a.* asper, ācer.
acrimonious *a.* acerbus, truculentus.
acrimony *n.* acerbitās *f.*
acrobat *n.* fūnambulus *m.*
acropolis *n.* arx *f*
across *ad.* trānsversus. *pr.* trāns (*acc.*).
act *n.* factum *n.*, facinus *n.*; (*play*) āctus *m.*; (*pol.*) āctum *n.*, senātus cōnsultum *n.*, dēcrētum *n.* I was in the — of saying in eō erat ut dīcerem. caught in the — dēprehēnsus. *vi.* facere, agere; (*conduct*) sē gerere; (*stage*) histriōnem esse, partēs agere; (*pretence*) simulāre. *vt.* — a part partēs agere, persōnam sustinēre. — the part of agere. — as esse, munere fungī, (*gen.*). — upon (*instructions*) exsequī.
action *n.* (*doing*) āctio *f.*; (*deed*) factum *n.*, facinus *n.*; (*legal*) āctiō *f.* līs *f.*; (*mil.*) proelium *n.*; (*of play*) āctiō *f.*; (*of speaker*) gestus. bring an — against lītem intendere, āctiōnem īnstituere (*dat.*). be in — agere, rem gerere; (*mil.*) pugnāre, in aciē dīmicāre. man of — vir strēnuus.
active *a.* impiger, strēnuus, sēdulus, nāvus. **-ly** *ad.* impigrē, strēnuē, nāviter.
activity *n.* (*motion*) mōtus *m.*;

(*energy*) industria *f.*. sēdulitās *f.*
actor *n.* histriō *m*; (*in comedy*) cōmoedus *m.*; (*in tragedy*) tragoedus *m.*
actress *n.* mīma *f.*
actual *a.* vērus, ipse. **-ly** *ad.* rē vērā.
actuate *vt.* movēre, incitāre.
acumen *n.* acūmen *n.*, ingenī aciēs, argūtiae *f.pl.*
acute *a.* acūtus, ācer. (*pain*) ācer; (*speech*) argūtus, subtīlis. **-ly** *ad.* acūtē, ācriter, argūtē.
acuteness *n.* (*mind*) acūmen *n.*, aciēs *f.*, subtīlitas *f.*
adage *n.* prōverbium *n.*
adamant *n.* adamās *m.* *a.* obstinātus.
adamantine *a.* adamantinus.
adapt *vt.* accommodāre.
adaptable *a.* flexibilis, facile accommodandus.
adaptation *n.* accommodātiō *f.*
add *vt.* addere, adicere, adiungere. be **-ed** accēdere.
adder *n* vīpera *f.*
addicted *a.* dēditus.
addition *n.* adiūnctiō *f.*, accessiō *f.*; additāmentum *n.*, incrēmentum *n.* in — īnsuper, praetereā. in — to praeter (*acc.*).
additional *a.* novus, adiūnctus.
addled *a.* (*egg*) inrītus; (*brain*) inānis.
address *vt.* compellāre, adloquī; (*crowd*) cōntiōnem habēre apud; (*letter*) īnscrībere. — oneself (*to action*) accingī. *n.* adloquium *n.*; (*public*) cōntiō *f.*, ōrātiō *f.*; (*letter*) īnscrīptiō. *f*
adduce *vt.* (*argument*) adferre; (*witness*) prōdūcere.
adept *a.* perītus.
adequate *a.* idōneus, dignus, pār. be — sufficere. **-ly** *ad.* satis, ut pār est.
adhere *vi.* haerēre, adhaerēre. — to inhaerēre (*dat.*), inhaerēscere in (*abl.*); (*agreement*) manēre stāre in (*abl.*).
adherent *n.* adsectātor *m.*; (*of party*) fautor *m.*; (*of person*) cliēns *m.*
adhesive *a.* tenax.
adieu *interj.* valē, valēte. bid — to valēre iubēre.
adjacent *a.* fīnitimus, vīcīnus. be — to adiacēre (*dat.*).
adjoin *vi.* adiacēre (*dat.*). **-ing** *a.* fīnitimus, adiūnctus.
adjourn *vt.* (*short time*) differre; (*longer time*) prōferre; (*case*) ampliāre. *vi.* rem differe, prōferre.
adjournment *n.* dīlātiō *f.*, prōlātiō *f.*
adjudge *vt.* addīcere, adiūdicāre.
adjudicate *vi.* dēcernere.
adjudicator *n.* arbiter *m.*
adjunct *n.* appendix *f.*, accessiō *f.*
adjure *vt.* obtestārī, obsecrāre.
adjust *vt.* (*adapt*) accommodare; (*put in order*) compōnere.
adjutant *n.* (*mil.*) optiō *m.*; (*civil*) adiūtor *m.*
administer *vt.* administrāre, gerere; (*justice*) reddere; (*oath to*) iūreiūrandō adigere; (*medicine*) dare, adhibēre.
adminstration *n.* administratiō *f.*
adminstrator *a.* administrātor *m.*, prōcūrātor *m.*
admirab/le *a.* admīrābilis, ēgregius. **-ly** *ad.* ēgregiē.
admiral *n.* praefectus classis. **-'s** ship nāvis praetōria.
admiralty *n.* praefectī classium.
admiration *n.* admīrātiō *f.*, laus *f.*
admire *vt.* admīrārī.
admirer *n.* laudātor *m.*; amātor *m.*
admissible *a.* aequus.
admission *n.* aditus *m.*; cōnfessiō *f.*
admit *vt.* (*let in*) admittere, recipere, accipere; (*to member-*

ship) adsciscere; (*argument*) concēdere; (*fault*) fatērī. — of patī, recipere.
admittedly *ad.* sānē.
admonish *vt.* admonēre, commonēre, hortārī.
admonition *n.* admonitiō *f.*
ado *n.* negōtium *n.* make much — about nothing fluctūs in simpulō excitāre. without more — prōtinus, sine morā.
adolescence *n.* prima adulēscentia *f.*
adolescent *a.* adulēscēns. *n.* adulēscentulus *m.*
adopt *vt.* (*person*) adoptāre; (*custom*) adsciscere; (*plan*) capere, inīre.
adoption *n.* (*person*) adoptiō *f.*; (*custom*) adsūmptiō *f.* by — adoptīvus.
adoptive *a.* adoptīvus.
adorab/le *a.* amābilis, venustus. **-ly** *ad.* venustē.
adoration *n.* (*of gods*) cultus *m.*; (*of kings*) venerātiō *f.*; (*love*) amor *m.*
adore *vt.* (*worship*) venerārī; (*love*) adamāre.
adorn *vt.* ōrnāre, exōrnāre, decorāre.
adornment *n.* ōrnāmentum *n.*, decus *n.*
adrift *a.* fluctuāns. be — [fluctuāre.
adroit *a.* sollers, callidus. **-ly** *ad.* callidē, scītē.
adroitness *n.* sollertia *f.*, calliditās *f.*
adulation *n.* adūlātiō *f.*, adsentātiō *f.*
adulatory *a.* blandus.
adult *a.* adultus. *n.* (*pl.*) pūberēs.
adulterate *vt.* corrumpere, adulterāre.
adulterer *n.* adulter *m.*
adulteress *n.* adultera *f.*
adulterous *a.* incestus.
adultery *n.* adulterium *n.* commit — adulterāre.
adumbrate *vt.* adumbrāre.
advance *vt.* prōmovēre; (*a cause*) fovēre; (*money*) crēdere; (*opinion*) dīcere; (*to honours*) prōvehere; (*time*) mātūrāre. *vi.* prōcēdere, prōgredī, adventāre; (*mil.*) signa prōferre, pedem inferre; (*progress*) prōficere; (*walk*) incēdere. — to the attack signa inferre. *n.* prōgressus *m.*, prōcessus *m.* (*attack*) impetus *m.*; (*money*) mūtuae pecūniae. in — mātūrius. fix in — praefinīre. get in — praecipere.
advanced *a.* prōvectus. well — (*task*) adfectus. [*m.*
advancement *n.* (*pol.*) honōs
advantage *n.* (*benefit*) commodum *n.*, bonum *n.*, ūsus *m.*; (*of place or time*) opportūnitās *f.*; (*profit*) fructus *m.*; (*superiority*) praestantia *f.* be of — to prōdesse (*dat.*), ūsuī esse (*dat.*). to your — in rem tuam. it is to your — tibi expedit, tuā interest. take — of (*circs.*) ūtī: (*person*) dēcipere, fallere. have an — over praestāre (*dat.*). be seen to — māximē placēre.
advantageous *a.* ūtilis, opportūnus. **-ly** *ad.* ūtiliter, opportūnē.
advent *n.* adventūs *m.*
adventitious *a.* fortuitus.
adventure *n.* (*exploit*) facinus memorābile *n.*; (*hazard*) periculum *n.*
adventurer *n.* vir audāx *m.*; (*social*) parasītus *m.*
adventurous *a.* audāx.
adversary *n.* adversārius *m.*, hostis *m.*
adverse *a.* adversus, contrārius, inimīcus. **-ly** *ad.* contrāriē, inimīcē, male.
adversity *n.* rēs adversae *f.pl.*, calamitās *f.*
advert *vi.* — to attingere.
advertise *vt.* prōscribere; vēnditāre.
advertisement *n.* prōscrīptiō *f.*, libellus *m.*

advice *n.* cōnsilium *n.*; (*pol.*) auctōritās *f.*; (*legal*) respōnsum *n.* ask — of cōnsulere. on the — of Sulla auctōre Sullā.

advisable *a.* ūtilis, operae pretium.

advise *vt.* monēre, suādēre (*dat.*), cēnsēre (*dat.*). —**against** dissuādēre. **-dly** *ad.* cōnsultō.

adviser *n.* auctor *m.*, suāsor [*m.*

advocacy *n.* patrōcinium *n.*

advocate *n.* patrōnus *m.*, causidicus *m.*; (*supporter*) auctor *m.* be an — causam dīcere. *vt.* suādēre, cēnsēre.

adze *n.* ascia *f.*

aedile *n.* aedīlis *m.* **-'s** *a.* aedīlicius.

aedileship *n.* aedīlitās *f.*

aegis *n.* aegis *f.*; (*fig.*) praesidium *n.*

aerial *a.* āerius.

Aeneid *n.* Aenēis *f.*

aesthetic *a.* pulchritūdinis amāns, artificiōsus.

afar *ad.* procul. **from** — procul.

affability *n.* cōmitās *f.*, facilitās *f.*, bonitās *f.*

affab/le *a.* cōmis, facilis, commodus. **-ly** *ad.* cōmiter.

affair *n.* negōtium *n.*, rēs *f.*

affect *vt.* adficere, movēre, commovēre; (*concern*) attingere; (*pretence*) simulāre.

affectation *n.* simulātiō *f.*; (*rhet.*) adfectātiō *f.*; (*in diction*) īnsolentia *f.*; quaesīta *n.pl.*

affected *a.* (*style*) molestus, pūtidus. **-ly** *ad.* pūtidē.

affecting *a.* miserābilis.

affection *n.* amor *m.*, cāritās *f.*, studium *n.*; (*family*) pietās *f.*

affectionate *a.* amāns, pius. **-ly** *ad.* amanter, piē.

affiance *vt.* spondēre.

affidavit *n.* testimōnium *n.*

affinity *n.* affīnitās *f.*, cognātiō *f.* [rāre.

affirm *vt.* adfirmāre, adsevē-

affirmation *n.* adfirmātiō *f.*

affirmative *a.* I reply in the — āiō.

affix *vt.* adfīgere, adiungere.

afflict *vt.* adflīctāre, angere, vexāre.

affliction *n.* miseria *f.*, dolor *m.*, rēs adversae *f.pl.*

affluence *n.* cōpia *f.*, opēs *f.pl.*

affluent *a.* dīves, opulentus, locuplēs.

afford *vt.* praebēre, dare. I cannot — rēs mihi nōn suppetit ad.

affray *n.* rixa *f.*, pugna *f.*

affright *vt.* terrēre. *n.* terror *m.* pavor *m.*

affront *vt.* offendere, contumēliam dīcere (*dat.*). *n.* iniūria *f.*, contumēlia *f.*

afield *ad.* foris. far — peregrē.

afloat *a.* natāns. be — natāre.

afoot *ad.* pedibus. be — gerī.

aforesaid *a.* suprā dictus.

afraid *a.* timidus. **be** — of timēre, metuere.

afresh *ad.* dēnuō, dē integrō.

aft *ad.* in puppī, puppim versus.

after *a.* posterior. *ad.* post, posteā. the day — postrīdiē. *conj.* postquam. the day — postrīdiē quam. *pr.* post (*acc.*); (*in rank*) secundum (*acc.*); (*in imitation*) ad (*acc.*), dē (*abl.*). — all tamen, dēnique. — reading the book librō lēctō. one thing — another aliud ex aliō. immediately — statim ab.

after-ages *n.* posteritās *f.*

aftermath *n.* ēventus *m.*

afternoon *n.* in the — post merīdiem. *a.* postmerīdiānus.

afterthought *n.* posterior cōgitātiō *f.*

afterwards *ad.* post, posteā, deinde.

again *ad.* rūrsus, iterum. — and — etiam atque etiam, identidem. once — dēnuō. (*new point in a speech*) quid? **against** *pr.* contrā (*acc.*)

adversus (*acc.*), in (*acc.*). — the stream adversō flūmine.
agape *a.* hiāns.
age *n.* (*life*) aetās *f.*; (*epoch*) aetās *f.*, saeculum *n.* old — senectūs *f.* he is of — suī iūris est. he is eight years of — octō annōs nātus est, nōnum annum agit. of the same — aequālis.
aged *a.* senex, aetāte prōvectus; (*things*) antīquus.
agency *n.* opera *f.* through the — of per (*acc.*).
agent *n.* āctor *m.*, prōcūrātor *m.*; (*in crime*) minister *m.*
aggrandize *vt.* augēre, amplificāre. [ficātiō *f.*
aggrandizement *n.* ampli-
aggravat/e *vt.* (*wound*) exulcerāre; (*distress*) augēre. become -d ingravēscere. **-ing** *a.* molestus.
aggregate *n.* summa *f.*
aggression *n.* incursiō *f.*, iniūria *f.*
aggressive *a.* ferōx. [*f.*
aggressiveness *n.* ferōcitās
aggressor *n.* oppugnātor *m.*
aggrieved *a.* īrātus. be — indignārī.
aghast *a.* attonitus, stupefactus. stand — obstupēscere.
agile *a.* pernīx, vēlōx.
agility *n.* pernīcitās *f.*
agitate *vt.* agitāre; (*mind*) commovēre, perturbāre.
agitation *n.* commōtiō *f.*, perturbātiō *f.*, trepidātiō *f.*; (*pol.*) tumultus *m.*
agitator *n.* turbātor *m.*, concitātor *m.*
aglow *a.* fervidus *ad.* be — fervēre.
ago *ad.* abhinc. three days — abhinc trēs diēs. long — antīquitus, iamprīdem, iamdūdum. a short time — dūdum.
agog *a.* sollicitus, ērēctus.
agonize *vt.* cruciāre, torquēre.
agonizing *a.* horribilis. [*m.*
agony *n.* cruciātus *m.*, dolor
agrarian *a.* agrārius. — party agrāriī *m.pl.*
agree *vi.* (*together*) cōnsentīre congruere; (*with*) adsentīr (*dat.*), sentīre cum; (*bargain* pacīscī; (*facts*) cōnstāre, con venīre. (*food*) facilem esse a concoquendum. — upon cōn stituere, compōnere.
agreeab/le *a.* grātus, com modus, acceptus. **-ly** *ad* iūcundē.
agreeableness *n.* dulcēdō *f.* iūcunditās *f.*
agreement *n.* (*together*) cōn sēnsus *m.*, concordia *f.*; (*with* adsēnsus *m.*; (*pact*) pactiō *f.* conventum *n.*, foedus *n* according to — compāctō, e: compositō. be in — cōnsentīre congruere. [agrestis
agricultural *a.* rūsticus
agriculture *n.* rēs rūstica *f.* agrī cultūra *f.*
aground *ad.* be — sīdere run — in lītus ēicī, offendere
ague *n.* horror *m.*, febris *f.*
ahead *ad.* ante. go — anteīre praeīre. go- — *a.* impiger ships in line — agmen nāvium
aid *vt.* adiuvāre, succurrer (*dat.*) subvenīre (*dat.*). *n* auxilium *n.*, subsidium *n.*
aide-de-camp *n.* optiō *m.*
ail *vt.* dolēre. *vi.* aegrōtāre labōrāre, languēre. **-ing** *a* aeger, īnfirmus.
ailment *n.* morbus *m.* valētūdō *f.*
aim *vt.* intendere. — a petere; (*fig.*) adfectāre, spec tāre, sequī; (*with verb*) i agere ut. *n.* fīnis *m.*, prō positum *n.*
aimless *a.* ināānis, vānus. **-l** *ad.* sine ratiōne.
aimlessness *n.* vānitās *f.*
air *n.* āēr *m.*; (*breeze*) aura *f.* (*look*) vultus *m.*, speciēs *f.* (*tune*) modus *m.* in the oper — sub dīvō. **-s** fastus *m* give oneself **-s** sē iactāre.

air/y *a.* (*of air*) āerius; (*light*) tenuis; (*place*) apertus; (*manner*) hilaris. **-ily** *ad.* hilare.
aisle *n.* āla *f.*
ajar *a.* sēmiapertus.
akin *a.* cōnsanguineus, cognātus.
alacrity *n.* alacritās *f.*
alarm *n.* terror *m.*, formīdō *f.*, trepidātiō *f.*; (*sound*) clāmor *m.* sound an — ad arma conclāmāre. give the — increpāre. be in a state of — trepidāre. *vt.* terrēre, perterrēre, perturbāre. **-ing** *a.* formīdolōsus.
alas *interj.* heu.
albeit *conj.* etsī, etiamsī.
alcove *n.* zōthēca *f.*
alder *n.* alnus *f.*
alderman *n.* decuriō *m.*
ale *n.* cervīsia *f.* — house *n.* caupōna *f.*, taberna *f.*
alert *a.* prōmptus, alacer, vegetus.
alertness *n.* alacritās *f.*
alien *a.* externus. — to abhorrēns ab. *n.* peregrīnus.
alienate *vt.* aliēnāre, abaliēnāre, āvertere, āvocāre.
alienation *n.* aliēnātiō *f.*
alight *vi.* (*from horse*) dēscendere, dēsilīre; (*bird*) īnsīdere.
alight *a.* be — ārdēre. set — accendere.
alike *a.* pār, similis. *ad.* aequē, pariter.
alive *a.* vīvus. be — vīvere.
all *a.* omnis; (*together*) ūniversus, cūnctus; (*whole*) tōtus. — but paene. — for studiōsus (*gen.*). — in cōnfectus. — of tōtus. — over with āctum dē (*abl.*). — the best men optimus quisque. — the more eō plūs, tantō plūs. at — ullō modō, quid. not at — haudquāquam. *n.* fortūnae *f.pl.*
allay *vt.* sēdāre, mītigāre, [lēnīre.
allegation *n.* adfirmātiō *f.*; (*charge*) īnsimulātiō *f.*
allege *vt.* adfirmāre, praetendere; (*in excuse*) excūsāre.
allegiance *n.* fidēs *f.* owe — to in fidē esse (*gen.*). swear — to in verba iūrāre (*gen.*).
allegory *n.* allēgoria *f.*, immūtāta ōrātiō *f.*
alleviate *vt.* mītigāre, adlevāre, sublevāre.
alleviation *n.* levātiō *f.*, levāmentum *n.*
alley *n.* (*garden*) xystus *m.*; (*town*) angiportus *m.* [*n.*
alliance *n.* societās *f.*, foedus
allied *a.* foederātus, socius; (*friends*) coniūnctus.
alligator *n.* crocodīlus *m.*
allocate *vt.* adsignāre, impertīre.
allot *vt.* adsignāre, distribuere. be -ted obtingere.
allotment *n.* (*land*) adsignātiō *f.*
allow *vt.* sinere, permittere (*dat.*), concēdere (*dat.*), patī; (*admit*) fatērī, concēdere; (*approve*) comprobāre. it is -ed licet. — for ratiōnem habēre (*gen.*).
allowance *n.* venia *f.*, indulgentia *f.*; (*pay*) stīpendium *n.*; (*food*) cibāria *n.pl.*; (*for travel*) viāticum *n.* make — for indulgēre (*dat.*), ignōscere (*dat.*).
alloy *n.* admixtum *n.* excūsāre.
allude *vi.* — to dēsignāre, attingere, significāre.
allure *vt.* adlicere, pellicere.
allurement *n.* blanditiā *f.*, blandīmentum *n.*, illecebra *f.*
alluring *a.* blandus. **-ly** *ad.* blandē.
allusion *n.* mentiō *f.*, indicium *n.*
alluvial *a.* — land adluviō *f.*
ally *n.* socius *m.* *vt.* sociāre, coniungere.
almanac *n.* fāstī *m.pl.*
almighty *a.* omnipotēns.
almond *n.* (*nut*) amygdalum *n.*; (*tree*) amygdala *f.*

almost *ad.* paene, ferē, fermē, propemodum.
alms *n.* stipem (*no nom.*) *f.*
aloe *n.* aloē *f.*
aloft *a.* sublīmis. *ad.* sublīme.
alone *a.* sōlus, sōlitārius, ūnus. *ad.* sōlum.
along *pr.* secundum (*acc.*), praeter (*acc.*). *ad.* porrō. all — iamdūdum, ab initiō. — with ūnā cum.
alongside *ad.* bring — adpellere. come — ad crepīdinem accēdere.
aloof *ad.* procul. stand — sē removēre. *a.* sēmōtus.
aloofness *n.* sōlitūdō *f.*, sēcessus *m.*
aloud *ad.* clārē, māgnā vōce.
alphabet *n.* elementa *n.pl.*
already *ad.* iam. [īdem.
also *ad.* etiam, et, quoque;
altar *n.* āra *f.*
alter *vt.* mūtāre, commūtāre; (*order*) invertere.
alteration *n.* mūtātiō *f.*, commūtātiō *f.*
altercation *n.* altercātiō *f.*, iūrgium *n.*
alternate *a.* alternus. *vt.* variāre. **-ly** *ad.* invicem.
alternation *n.* vicem (*no nom.*) *f.*, vicissitūdō *f.*
alternative *a.* alter, alius. *n.* optiō *f.*
although *conj.* quamquam, etsī, etiamsī, quamvīs.
altitude *n.* altitūdō *f.*
altogether *ad.* omnīnō; (*emphasis*) plānē, prōrsus.
altruism *n.* beneficentia *f.*
alum *n.* alūmen *n.*
always *ad.* semper.
amalgamate *vt.* miscēre, coniungere.
amalgamation *n.* coniūnctiō *f.*, temperātiō *f.*
amanuensis *n.* librārius *m.*
amass *vt.* cumulāre, coacervāre.
amateur *n.* idiōta *m.*
amatory *a.* amātōrius.
amaze *vt.* obstupefacere. be -d obstupēscere.
amazement *n.* stupor *m.* in — attonitus, stupefactus.
ambassador *n.* lēgātus *m.*
amber *n.* sūcinum *n.*
ambidextrous *a.* utrīusque manūs compos.
ambiguity *n.* ambiguitās *f.*; (*rhet.*) amphibolia *f.*
ambiguous *a.* ambiguus, anceps, dubius. **-ly** *ad.* ambiguē.
ambition *n.* glōria *f.*, laudis studium.
ambitious *a.* glōriae cupidus, laudis avidus.
amble *vi.* ambulāre.
ambrosia *n.* ambrosia *f.*
ambrosial *a.* ambrosius.
ambuscade *n.* īnsidiae *f.pl.*
ambush *n.* īnsidiae *f.pl.* *vt.* īnsidiārī (*dat.*).
ameliorate *vt.* corrigere, meliōrem reddere.
amelioration *n.* prōfectus *m.*
amenable *a.* facilis, docilis.
amend *vt.* corrigere, ēmendāre.
amendment *n.* ēmendātiō *f.*
amends *n.* (*apology*) satisfactiō *f.* make — for expiāre. make — to satisfacere (*dat.*).
amenity *n.* (*scenery*) amoenitās *f.*; (*comfort*) commodum *n.*
amethyst *n.* amethystus *f.*
amiability *n.* benignitās *f.*, suāvitās *f.*
amiab/le *a.* benignus, suāvis. **-ly** *ad.* benignē, suāviter.
amicab/le *a.* amīcus, cōmis. **-ly** *ad.* amīcē, cōmiter.
amid, amidst *pr.* inter (*acc.*).
amiss *ad.* perperam, secus, incommodē. take — aegrē ferre.
amity *n.* amīcitia *f.*
ammunition *n.* tēla *n.pl.*
amnesty *n.* venia *f.*
among, amongst *pr.* inter (*acc.*), apud (*acc.*).
amorous *a.* amātōrius, amāns. **-ly** *ad.* cum amōre.

amount *vi.* — to efficere; (*fig.*) esse. *n.* summa *f.*
amours *n.* amōrēs *m.pl.*
amphibious *a.* anceps.
amphitheatre *n.* amphitheātrum *n.*
ample *a.* amplus, satis.
amplification *n.* amplificātiō *f.*
amplify *vt.* amplificāre.
amplitude *n.* amplitūdō *f.*, cōpia *f.*
amputate *vt.* secāre, amputāre.
amuck *ad.* run — bacchārī.
amulet *n.* amulētum *n.*
amus/e *vt.* dēlectāre, oblectāre. **-ing** *a.* rīdiculus, facētus.
amusement *n.* oblectāmentum *n.*, dēlectātio *f.* for — animī causā.
an, *see* **a.**
anaemic *a.* exsanguis.
analogous *a.* similis.
analogy *n.* prōportiō *f.*, comparātiō *f.*
analyse *vt.* excutere, perscrūtārī.
analysis *n.* explicātiō *f.*
anapaest *n.* anapaestus *m.*
anarchical *a.* sēditiōsus.
anarchy *n.* reī pūblicae perturbātiō, lēgēs nullae *f.pl.*, licentia *f.*
anathema *n.* exsecrātiō *f.*; (*object*) pestis *f.*
ancestor *n.* proavus *m.*; (*pl.*) māiōrēs *m.pl.*
ancestral *a.* patrius.
ancestry *n.* genus *n.*, origō *f.*
anchor *n.* ancora *f.* lie at — in ancorīs stāre. weigh — ancoram tollere. *vi.* ancoram iacere.
anchorage *n.* statiō *f.*
ancient *a.* antīquus, prīscus, vetustus. — history, — world antīquitās *f.* from, in — times antīquitus. the -s veterēs.
and *conj.* et, atque, ac, -que. — . . . not nec, neque.
anecdote *n.* fābella *f.*
anent *pr.* dē (*abl.*).
anew *ad.* dēnuō, ab integrō.
angel *n.* angelus *m.*
angelic *a.* angelicus; (*fig.*) dīvīnus, eximius.
anger *n.* īra *f.* *vt.* inrītāre.
angle *n.* angulus *m.* *vi.* hāmō piscārī.
angler *n.* piscātor *m.*
angr/y *a.* īrātus. be — īrāscī. **-ily** *ad.* īrātē.
anguish *n.* cruciātus *m.*, dolor *m.*; (*mind*) angor *m.*
angular *a.* angulātus.
animadversion *n.* reprehēnsiō *f.*
animadvert *vt.* reprehendere, notāre.
animal *n.* animal *n.*; (*domestic*) pecus *f.*; (*wild*) fera *f.*
animate *vt.* animāre. **-d** *a.* excitātus, vegetus.
animation *n.* ārdor *m.*, alacritās *f.*
animosity *n.* invidia *f.*, inimīcitia *f.*
ankle *n.* tālus *m.*
annalist *n.* annālium scrīptor.
annals *n.* annālēs *m.pl.*
annex *vt.* addere.
annexation *n.* adiectiō *f.*
annihilate *vt.* dēlēre, exstinguere, perimere.
annihilation *n.* exstinctiō *f.*, interneciō *f.*
anniversary *n.* diēs anniversārius; (*public*) sollemne *n.*
annotate *vt.* adnotāre.
annotation *n.* adnotātiō *f.*
announce *vt.* nūntiāre; (*officially*) dēnūntiāre, prōnūntiāre; (*election result*) renūntiāre.
announcement *n.* (*official*) dēnūntiātiō *f.*; (*news*) nūntius *m.*
announcer *n.* nūntius *m.*
annoy *vt.* inrītāre, vexāre. be -ed with aegrē ferre.
annoyance *n.* molestia *f.*, vexātiō *f.*; (*felt*) dolor *m.*
annoying *a.* molestus.

annual *a.* annuus, anniversārius. **-ly** *ad.* quotannis.
annuity *n.* annua *n.pl.*
annul *vt.* abrogāre, dissolvere, tollere.
annulment *n.* abrogātiō *f.*
anoint *vt.* ungere, illinere.
anomalous *a.* novus.
anomaly *n.* novitās *f.*
anon *ad.* mox.
anonymous *a.* incertī auctōris. **-ly** *ad.* sine nōmine.
another *a* alius; (*second*) alter. of — aliēnus. one after — alius ex aliō. one — inter sē, alius alium. in — place alibī. to — place aliō. in — way aliter. at — time aliās.
answer *vt.* respondēre (*dat.*); (*by letter*) rescrībere (*dat.*); (*agree*) respondēre, congruere. — a charge crīmen dēfendere. — for (*surety*) praestāre; (*account*) ratiōnem referre; (*substitute*) īnstar esse (*gen.*). *n.* respōnsum *n.*; (*to a charge*) dēfēnsiō *f.* — to the name of vocārī. give an — respondēre.
answerable *a.* reus. I am — for ratiō mihī reddenda est (*gen.*).
ant *n.* formīca *f.*
antagonism *n.* simultās *f.*, inimīcitia *f.* [hostis *m.*
antagonist *n.* adversārius *m.*,
antarctic *a.* antarcticus.
antecedent *a.* antecēdēns, prior.
antediluvian *a.* prīscus, horridus, Deucaliōnēus.
antelope *n.* dorcas *f.*
anterior *a.* prior.
ante-room *n.* vestibulum *n.*
anthology *n.* excerpta *n.pl.* make an — excerpere.
anthropology *n.* rēs hūmānae *f.pl.*
anticipate *vt.* (*expect*) exspectāre; (*forestall*) antevenīre, occupāre, (*in thought*) animō praecipere.
anticipation *n.* exspectātiō *f.*, spēs *f*; praesūmptiō *f.*
antics *n.* gestus *m.*, ineptiae *f.pl.*
anticyclone *n* serēnitās *f.*
antidote *n.* remedium *n.*, medicāmen *n.*
antipathy *n.* fastīdium *n.*, odium *n.*; (*things*) repugnantia *f.*
antiphon/al *a.* alternus.
antiphony *n.* alterna *n. pl.*
antipodes *n.* contrāria pars terrae.
antiquarian *a.* historicus.
antiquary *n.* antīquārius *m.*
antiquated *a.* prīscus, obsolētus.
antique *a.* antīquus, prīscus.
antiquity *n.* antīquitās *f.*, vetustas *f.*, veterēs *m.pl.*
antithesis *n.* contentiō *f.*, contrārium *n.*
antlers *n.* cornua *n.pl.*
anvil *n.* incūs *f.*
anxiety *n.* sollicitūdō *f.*, metus *m*, cūra *f.*
anxious *a.* sollicitus, anxius; avidus.
any *a.* ullus; (*interrog.*) ecquī; (*after* sī, nisi, num, nē) quī; (*indef.*) quīvīs, quīlibet. hardly — nullus ferē.
anybody, anyone *pro.* aliquis; (*indef.*) quīvīs, quīlibet; (*after* sī, nisi, num, nē) quis; (*interrog.*) ecquis, numquis; (*after neg.*) quisquam. hardly — nēmō ferē.
anyhow *ad.* ullō modō, quōquō modō.
anything *pro.* aliquid; quidvīs, quidlibet; (*interrog.*) ecquid, numquid; (*after neg.*) quicquam; (*after* sī, nisi, num, nē) quid. hardly — nihil ferē.
anywhere *ad.* usquam, ubīvīs.
apace *ad.* citō, celeriter.
apart *ad.* seōrsum, sēparātim. *a.* diversus. be six feet — sex pedēs distāre. set — sēpōnere. stand — distāre.

joking — remōtō iocō — from praeter (*acc*).
apartment *n.* cubiculum *n.*, conclāve *n.* [ignāvus.
apathetic *a.* lentus, languidus,
apathy *n.* lentitūdō *f.*, languor *m.*, ignāvia *f.*
ape *n.* sīmia *f.* *vt.* imitārī.
aperture *n.* hiātus *m.*, forāmen *n.*, rīma *f.*
apex *n.* fastīgium *n.*
aphorism *n.* sententia *f.*
apiary *n.* alveārium *n.*
apiece *ad.* in singulōs. **two** — bīnī.
aplomb *n* cōnfīdentia *f.*
apocryphal *a* commentīcius.
apologetic *a.* cōnfitēns, veniam petēns.
apologize *vi.* veniam petere, sē excūsāre.
apology *n.* excūsātiō *f.*
apophthegm *n.* sententia *f.*
apoplectic *a.* apoplēcticus.
apoplexy *n.* apoplēxis *f.*
apostle *n.* apostolus *m.*
apothecary *n.* medicāmentārius *m.*
appal *vt.* perterrēre, cōnsternere.
appalling *a.* dīrus.
apparatus *n.* īnstrūmenta *n.pl.*, ōrnāmenta *n.pl.*
apparel *n.* vestis *f.*, vestīmenta *n.pl.*
apparent *a.* manifestus, apertus, ēvidēns. **-ly** *ad.* speciē, ut vidētur. [speciēs *f.*
apparition *n.* vīsum *n.*,
appeal *vi.* (*to magistrate*) appellāre; (*to people*) prōvocāre ad; (*to gods*) invocāre, testārī; (*to senses*) placēre (*dat.*). *n.* appellātiō *f.*, prōvocātiō *f.*, testātiō *f.*
appear *vi.* (*in sight*) apparēre; (*in court*) sistī; (*in public*) prōdīre; (*at a place*) adesse, advenīre; (*seem*) vidērī.
appearance *n.* (*coming*) adventus *m.*; (*look*) aspectus *m.*, faciēs *f.*; (*semblance*) speciēs *f.*; (*thing*) vīsum *n.* **for the sake of -s** in speciem; (*formula*) dicis causā. **make one's** — prōcēdere, prōdīre.
appeasable *a.* plācābilis.
appease *vt.* plācāre, lēnīre, mītigāre, sēdāre.
appeasement *n.* plācātiō *f.*; (*of enemy*) pācificātiō *f.*
appellant *n.* appellātor *m.*
appellation *n.* nōmen *n.*
append *vt.* adiungere, subicere. [adiūnctum *n.*
appendage *n.* appendix *f.*,
appertain *vi.* pertinēre.
appetite *n.* adpetītus *m.*; (*for food*) fāmēs *f.*
applaud *vt.* plaudere; (*fig.*) laudāre.
applause *n.* plausus *m.*; (*fig.*) adsēnsiō *f.*, adprobātiō *f.*
apple *n.* mālum *n.* — **tree** mālus *f.* — **of my eye** ocellus meus. **upset the — cart** plaustrum percellere.
appliance *n.* māchina *f.*, īnstrūmentum *n.*
applicable *a.* aptus, commodus. **be** — pertinēre.
applicant *n.* petītor *m.*
application *n.* (*work*) industria *f.*, (*mental*) intentiō *f.*; (*asking*) petītiō *f.*; (*med.*) fōmentum *n.*
apply *vt.* adhibēre, admovēre; (*use*) ūtī (*abl.*). — **oneself to** sē adplicāre, incumbere in (*acc.*). *vi.* pertinēre; (*to a person*) adīre (*acc.*); (*for office*) petere.
appoint *vt.* (*magistrate*) creāre, facere, cōnstituere; (*commander*) praeficere; (*guardian, heir*) īnstituere; (*time*) dīcere, statuere; (*for a purpose*) dēstināre.
appointment *n.* cōnstitūtum *n.*; (*duty*) mandātum *n.*; (*office*) magistrātus *m.* **have an — with** cōnstitūtum habēre cum. **keep an — ad** cōnstitūtum venīre.

apportion *vt.* dispertīre, dīvidere; (*land*) adsignāre.
apposite *a.* aptus, appositus.
appraise *vt.* aestimāre. [*f.*
appraisement *n.* aestimātiō
appreciable *a.* haud exiguus.
appreciate *vt.* aestimāre.
appreciation *n.* aestimātiō *f.*
apprehend *vt.* (*person*) comprehendere; (*idea*) intellegere, mente comprehendere; (*fear*) metuere, timēre.
apprehension *n.* comprehēnsiō *f.*; metus *m.*, formīdō *f.*
apprehensive *a.* anxius, sollicitus. be — of metuere.
apprentice *n.* discipulus *m.*, tīrō *m.* **-ship** *n.* tīrōcinium *n.*
apprise *vt.* docēre, certiōrem facere.
approach *vt.* adpropinquāre (*dat.*), accēdere ad; (*person*) adīre. *vi.* (*time*) adpropinquāre, adpetere. *n.* (*act*) accessus *m.*, aditus *m.*; (*time*) adpropinquātiō *f.*; (*way*) aditus *m.* make —es to adīre ad, ambīre, petere.
approachable *a.* (*place*) patēns; (*person*) facilis.
approbation *n.* adprobātiō *f.*, adsēnsiō *f.*
appropriate *a.* aptus, idōneus, proprius. **-ly** *ad.* aptē, commodē. [adsūmere.
appropriate *vt.* adsciscere,
approval *n.* adprobātiō *f.*, adsēnsus *m.*, favor *m.*
approve *vt.* & *i.* adprobāre, comprobāre, adsentīrī (*dat.*); (*law*) scīscere. **—d** *a.* probātus, spectātus.
approximate *a.* propinquus. **-ly** *ad.* prope, propemodum; (*number*) ad (*acc.*). *vi.* — to accēdere ad.
appurtenances *n.* instrūmenta *n.pl.*, apparātus *m.*
apricot *n.* armēniacum *n.* — tree *n.* armēniaca *f.*
April *m.* mēnsis Aprīlis *m.* of — Aprīlis.
apron *n.* operīmentum *n.*
apropos of quod attinet ad.
apse *n.* apsis *f.*
apt *a.* aptus, idōneus; (*pupil*) docilis, prōmptus. — to prōnus, prōclīvis ad. be — to solēre. **-ly** *ad.* aptē.
aptitude *n.* ingenium *n.*, facultās *f.*
aquarium *n.* piscīna *f.*
aquatic *a.* aquātilis.
aqueduct *n.* aquae ductus *m.*
aquiline *a.* (*nose*) aduncus.
arable land *n.* arvum *n.*
arbiter *n.* arbiter *m.*
arbitrar/y *a.* libīdinōsus (*act*); (*ruler*) superbus. **-ily** *ad.* ad libīdinem, licenter.
arbitrate *vi.* dīiūdicāre, disceptāre. [dīiūdicātiō *f.*
arbitration *n.* arbitrium *n.*,
arbitrator *n.* arbiter *m.*, disceptātor *m.*
arbour *n.* umbrāculum *n.*
arbutus *n.* arbutus *f.*
arc *n.* arcus *m.*
arcade *n.* porticus *f.*
arch *n.* fornix *m.*, arcus *m.* *vt.* arcuāre. **-ed** *a.* fornicātus.
arch *a.* lascīvus, vafer.
archaeologist *n.* antīquitātis investīgātor *m.*
archaeology *n.* antīquitātis investīgātiō *f.*
archaic *a.* prīscus.
archaism *n.* verbum obsolētum *n.* [*m.*
archbishop *n.* archiepiscopus
archer *n.* sagittārius *m.*
archery *n.* sagittāriōrum ars *f.*
architect *n.* architectus *m.*
architecture *n.* architectūra *f.*
architrave *n.* epistylium *n.*
archives *n.* tabulae (pūblicae) *f.pl.*
arctic *a.* arcticus, septentriōnālis. *n.* septentriōnēs *m.pl.*
ardent *a.* ārdēns, fervidus, vehemēns. **-ly** *ad.* ārdenter, ācriter, vehementer.

ardour *n.* ārdor *m.*, fervor *m.*
arduous *a.* difficilis, arduus.
area *n.* regiō *f.*; (*math.*) superficiēs *f.*
arena *n.* harēna *f.*
argonaut *n.* argonauta *m.*
argosy *n.* onerāria *f.*
argue *vi.* (*discuss*) disserere, disceptāre; (*dispute*) ambigere; (*reason*) argūmentārī. *vt.* (*prove*) arguere.
argument *n.* (*discussion*) contrōversia *f.*, disputātiō *f.*; (*reason*) ratiō; (*proof, theme*) argūmentum.
argumentation *n.* argūmentātiō *f.*
argumentative *a.* lītigiōsus.
aria *n.* canticum *n.*
arid *a.* āridus, siccus.
aright *ad.* rectē, vērē.
arise *vi.* exorīrī, coorīrī, exsistere. — **from** nāscī ex, proficīscī ab.
aristocracy *n.* optimātēs *m.pl.*, nōbilēs *m.pl.*; (*govt.*) optimātium dominātus *m.*
aristocrat *n.* optimās *m.*
aristocratic *a.* patricius, generōsus.
arithmetic *n.* numerī *m.pl.*, arithmētica *n.pl.*
ark *n.* arca *f.*
arm *n.* bracchium *n.*, (*upper*) lacertus *m.*; (*sea*) sinus *m.*; (*weapon*) tēlum *n.* **-s** (*mil.*) arma *n.pl.* **by force of -s** vī et armīs. **under -s** in armīs. *vt.* armāre. *vi.* arma capere.
armament *n.* bellī apparātus *m.*; cōpiae *f.pl.*
armed *a.* armātus. **light — troops** levis armātūra *f.*, vēlitēs *m.pl.*
armistice *n.* indutiae *f.pl.*
armlet *n.* armilla *f.*
armour *n.* arma *n.pl.*; (*kind of*) armātūra *f.*
armourer *n.* (armōrum) faber *m.* [*n.*
armoury *n.* armāmentārium
arm-pit *n.* āla *f.*
army *n.* exercitus *m.*; (*in battle*) aciēs *f.*; (*on march*) agmen *n.*
aroma *n.* odor *m.*
aromatic *a.* frāgrāns.
around *ad.* circum, circā. *pr.* circum (*acc.*).
arouse *vt.* suscitāre, ērigere, excitāre.
arraign *vt.* accūsāre.
arrange *vt.* (*in order*) compōnere, ōrdināre, dīgerere, dispōnere; (*agree*) pacīscī.
arrangement *n.* ōrdō *m.* collocātiō *f.*, dispositiō *f.*; pactum *n.*, cōnstitūtum *n.*
arrant *a.* summus.
array *n.* vestis *f.*, habitus *m.*; (*mil.*) aciēs *f.* *vt.* vestīre, exōrnāre; (*mil.*) īnstruere.
arrears *n.* residuae pecūniae *f.pl.*, reliqua *n.pl.*
arrest *vt.* comprehendere, adripere; (*attention*) in sē convertere; (*movement*) morārī, tardāre. *n.* comprehēnsiō *f.*
arrival *n.* adventus *m.*
arrive *vi.* advenīre, pervenīre.
arrogance *n.* superbia *f.*, adrogantia *f.*, fastus *m.*
arrogant *a.* superbus, adrogāns. **-ly** *ad.* superbē, adroganter.
arrogate *vt.* adrogāre.
arrow *n.* sagitta *f.*
arsenal *n.* armāmentārium *n.*
arson *n.* incēnsiōnis crīmen *n.*
art *n.* ars *f.*, artificium *n.* **fine -s** ingenuae artēs.
artery *n.* artēria *f.*
artful *a.* callidus, vafer, astūtus. **-ly** *ad.* callidē, astūtē. [dolus *m.*
artfulness *n.* astūtia *f.*,
artichoke *n.* cinara *f.*
article *n.* rēs *f.*, merx *f.*; (*clause*) caput *n.*; (*term*) condiciō *f.*
articulate *a.* explānātus, distinctus. *vi.* explānāre, exprimere. **-ly** *ad.* explānātē, clārē.

articulation *n.* prōnūntiātiō *f.* [dolus *m.*
artifice *n.* ars *f.*, artificium *n.*,
artificer *n.* artifex *m.*, opifex *m.*, faber *m.*
artificial *a.* (*work*) artificiōsus; (*appearance*) fūcātus. **-ly** *ad.* arte, manū.
artillery *n.* tormenta *n.pl.*
artisan *n.* faber *m.*, opifex *m.*
artist *n.* artifex *m.*; pictor *m.*
artistic *a.* artificiōsus, ēlegāns. **-ally** *ad.* artificiōsē, ēleganter.
artless *a.* (*work*) inconditus; (*person*) simplex. **-ly** *ad.* inconditē; simpliciter, sine dolō.
artlessness *n.* simplicitās *f.*
as *ad.* (*before a., ad.*) tam; (*after* aequus, īdem, similis) ac, atque; (*correlative*) quam, quālis, quantus. *conj.* (*comp.*) ut, sīcut, velut, quemadmodum; (*cause*) cum, quōniam, quippe quī; (*time*) dum, ut. *rel. pro.* quī, quae, quod. — being utpote. — follows ita. — for quod attinet ad. — if quasi, tamquam, velut. — it were ut ita dīcam. — yet adhūc.
as *n.* (*coin*) as *m.*
ascend *vt.* & *i.* ascendere.
ascendancy *n.* praestantia *f.*, auctōritās *f.*
ascendant *a.* surgēns, potēns. be in the — praestāre.
ascent *n.* ascēnsus *m.*; (*slope*) clīvus *m.*
ascertain *vt.* comperīre, cognōscere. [austērus.
ascetic *a.* nimis abstinēns,
asceticism *n.* dūritia.
ascribe *vt.* adscrībere, attribuere, adsignāre.
ash *n.* (*tree*) fraxinus *f.* *a.* fraxineus.
ashamed *a.* I am — pudet mē.
ashen *a.* pallidus.
ashes *n.* cinis *m.*
ashore *ad.* (*motion*) in lītus; (*rest*) in lītore. go — ēgredī.
aside *ad.* sēparatim, sē- (*in cpd.*).
ask *vt.* (*question*) rogāre, quaerere; (*request*) petere, poscere. — for petere.
askance *ad.* oblīquē. look — at līmis oculis aspicere, invidēre (*dat.*).
askew *ad.* prāvē.
aslant *ad.* oblīquē.
asleep *a.* sōpītus. be — dormīre. fall — obdormīre, somnum inīre. half — sēmisomnus.
asp *n.* aspis *f.*
asparagus *n.* asparagus *m.*
aspect *n.* (*place*) aspectus *m.*; (*person*) vultus *m.*; (*circs.*) status *m.* have a southern — ad merīdiem spectāre. there is another — to the matter aliter sē rēs habet.
aspen *n.* pōpulus *f.*
asperity *n.* acerbitās *f.*
asperse *vt.* maledīcere (*dat.*), calumniārī.
aspersion *n.* calumnia *f.* cast -s on calumniārī, īnfāmiā aspergere.
asphalt *n.* bitūmen *n.*
asphodel *n.* asphodelus *m.*
asphyxia *n.* strangulātiō *f.*
asphyxiate *vt.* strangulāre.
aspirant *n.* petītor *m.*
aspirate *n.* (*gram.*) aspīrātiō *f.*
aspiration *n.* spēs *f.*, (*pol.*) ambitiō *f.*
aspire *vi.* — to adfectāre, petere, spērāre.
ass *n.* asinus *m.*, asellus *m.*; (*fig.*) stultus.
assail *vt.* oppugnāre, adorīrī, aggredī.
assailable *a.* expugnābilis.
assailant *n.* oppugnātor *m.*
assassin *n.* sīcārius *m.*, percussor *m.*
assassinate *vt.* interficere, occīdere, iugulāre.
assassination *n.* caedēs *f.*, parricīdium *n.*
assault *vt.* oppugnāre, adorīrī

aggredī; (*speech*) invehī in (*acc.*). *n.* impetus *m.*, oppugnātiō *f.*; (*personal*) vīs *f.*
assay *vt.* (*metal*) spectāre; temptāre, cōnārī.
assemble *vt.* convocāre, congregāre, cōgere. *vi.* convenīre, congregārī.
assembly *n.* coetus *m.*, conventus *m.*; (*plebs*) concilium *n.*; (*Roman people*) comitia *n.pl.*; (*troops*) cōntiō; (*things*) congeriēs *f.*
assent *vi.* adsentīrī, adnuere. *n.* adsēnsus *m.*
assert *vt.* adfirmāre, adsevērāre, dīcere.
assertion *n.* adfirmātiō *f.*, adseverātiō *f.*, dictum *n.*, sententia *f.*
assess *vt.* cēnsēre, aestimāre. — damages lītem aestimāre.
assessment *n.* cēnsus *m.*, aestimātiō *f.*
assessor *n.* cēnsor *m.*; (*assistant*) cōnsessor *m.*
assets *n.* bona *n.pl.*
assiduity *n.* dīligentia *f.*, sēdulitās *f.*, industria *f.*
assiduous *a.* dīligēns, sēdulus, industrius.
assign *vt.* tribuere, attribuere; (*land*) adsignāre; (*in writing*) perscrībere; (*task*) dēlēgāre; (*reason*) adferre.
assignation *n.* cōnstitūtum [*n.*
assignment *n.* adsignātiō *f.*, perscrīptiō *f.*; (*task*) mūnus *n.*, pēnsum *n.*
assimilate *vt.* aequāre; (*food*) concoquere; (*knowledge*) concipere.
assist *vt.* adiuvāre, succurrere (*dat.*), adesse (*dat.*).
assistance *n.* auxilium *n.*, opem (*no nom.*), *f.* come to the — of subvenīre (*dat.*). be of — to auxiliō esse (*dat.*).
assistant *n.* adiūtor *m.*, minister *m.*
assize *n.* conventus *m.* hold -s conventūs agere.
associate *vt.* cōnsociāre, coniungere. *vi.* rem inter sē cōnsociāre. — with familiāriter ūtī (*abl.*). *n.* socius *m.*, sodālis *m.*
association *n.* societās *f.*; (*club*) sodālitās *f.*
assort *vt.* dīgerere, dispōnere. *vi.* congruere.
assortment *n.* (*of goods*) variae mercēs *f.pl.*
assuage *vt.* lēnīre, mītigare, sēdāre.
assume *vt.* (*for oneself*) adsūmere, adrogāre; (*hypothesis*) pōnere; (*office*) inīre.
assumption *n.* (*hypothesis*) sūmptiō *f.*, positum *n.*
assurance *n.* (*given*) fidēs *f.*, pignus *n.*; (*felt*) fīdūcia *f.*; (*boldness*) cōnfīdentia *f.*
assure *vt.* cōnfirmāre, prōmittere (*dat.*). **-d** *a.* (*person*) fīdēns; (*fact*) explōrātus, certus.
assuredly *ad.* certō, certē, profectō, sānē.
astern *ad.* ā puppī; (*movement*) retrō. — of post.
asthma *n.* anhēlitus *m.*
astonish *vt.* obstupefacere. **-ed** *a.* attonitus, stupefactus. be -ed at admīrārī. [mīrus.
astonishing *a.* mīrificus,
astonishment *n.* stupor *m.*, admīrātiō *f.*
astound *vt.* obstupefacere.
astray *a.* vagus. go — errāre, aberrāre, deerrāre.
astride *a.* vāricus.
astrologer *n.* Chaldaeus *m.*, mathēmaticus *m.*
astrology *n.* Chaldaeōrum dīvīnātiō *f.*
astronomer *n.* astrologus *m.*
astronomy *n.* astrologia *f.*
astute *a.* callidus, vafer.
astuteness *n.* calliditās *f.*
asunder *ad.* sēparātim, dis- (*in cpd.*).
asylum *n.* asȳlum *n.*
at *pr.* in (*abl.*), ad (*acc.*);

(*time*) *abl.*; (*towns, small islands*) *loc.* — the house of apud (*acc.*).
atheism *n.* deōs esse negāre.
atheist *n.* atheos *m.* be an — deōs esse negāre.
athirst *a.* sitiens; (*fig.*) avidus.
athlete *n.* athlēta *m.*
athletic *a.* rōbustus, lacertōsus. **-s** *n.* athlētica *n.pl.*
athwart *pr.* trāns (*acc.*).
atlas *n.* orbis terrārum dēscrīptiō *f.*
atmosphere *n.* āēr *m.*
atom *n.* atomus *f.*, corpus indīviduum *n.*
atone *vi.* — for expiāre.
atonement *n.* expiātiō *f.*, piāculum *n.*
atrocious *a.* immānis, nefārius, scelestus. **-ly** *ad.* nefāriē, scelestē.
atrociousness *n.* immānitās [*f.*
atrocity *n.* nefas *n.*, scelus *n.*, flāgitium *n.*
atrophy *vi.* marcēscere.
attach *vt.* adiungere, adfīgere, illigāre; (*word*) subicere. **-ed** to amāns (*gen.*).
attachment *n.* vinculum *n.*; amor *m.*, studium *n.*
attack *vt.* oppugnāre, adorīrī, aggredī; (*speech*) însequī, invehī in (*acc.*); (*disease*) ingruere in (*acc.*). *n.* impetus *m.*, oppugnātiō *f.*, incursus *m.*
attacker *n.* oppugnātor *m.*
attain *vt.* adsequī, adipīscī, cōnsequī. — to pervenīre ad.
attainable *a.* impetrābilis, in prōmptū.
attainder, bill of *n.* prīvilēgium *n.*
attainment *n.* adeptiō *f.*; (*pl.*) doctrīna *f.*, ērudītiō *f.*
attaint *vt.* māiestātis condemnāre.
attempt *vt.* cōnārī, temptāre; (*with effort*) mōlīrī. *n.* cōnātus *m.*, inceptum *n.*; (*risk*) periculum *n.* first -s rudīmenta *n.pl.*
attend *vt.* (*meeting*) adesse (*dat.*), interesse (*dat.*); (*person*) prōsequī, comitārī; (*master*) appārēre (*dat.*); (*invalid*) cūrāre. *vi.* animum advertere, animum attendere. — to (*task*) adcūrāre. — upon prōsequī, adsectārī. — the lectures of audīre. not — aliud agere. — first to praevertere (*dat.*). well -ed frequēns. thinly -ed infrequēns.
attendance *n.* (*courtesy*) adsectātiō *f.*; (*med.*) cūrātiō *f.*; (*service*) apparitiō *f.* constant — adsiduitās *f.* full — frequentia *f.* poor — infrequentia *f.* dance — on haerēre (*dat.*).
attendant *n.* famulus *m.*, minister *m.*; (*on candidate*) sectātor *m.*; (*on nobleman*) adsectātor; (*on magistrate*) apparitor *m.*
attention *n.* animadversiō *f.*, animī attentiō *f.*; (*to work*) cūra *f.*; (*respect*) observantia *f.* attract — digitō mōnstrārī. call — to indicāre. pay — to animadvertere, observāre; ratiōnem habēre (*gen.*) —! hōc age!
attentive *a.* intentus; (*to work*) dīligēns. **-ly** *ad.* intentē, dīligenter.
attenuate *vt.* attenuāre.
attest *vt.* cōnfirmāre, testārī.
attestation *n.* testificātiō *f.*
attestor *n.* testis *m.*
attic *n.* cēnāculum *n.*
attire *vt.* vestīre. *n.* vestis *f.*, habitus *m.*
attitude *n.* (*body*) gestus *m.*, status *m.*, habitus *m.*; (*mind*) ratiō *f.*
attorney *n.* āctor *m.*; advocātus *m.*
attract *vt.* trahere, attrahere, adlicere.
attraction *n.* vīs attrahendī; illecebra *f.*, invītāmentum *n.*
attractive *a.* suāvis, venustus, lepidus. **-ly** *ad.* suāviter, venustē, lepidē.

attractiveness *n.* venustās *f.*, lepōs *m.*
attribute *vt.* tribuere, attribuere, adsignāre. *n.* proprium *n.*
attrition *n.* attrītus *m.*
attune *vt.* modulārī.
auburn *a.* flāvus.
auction *n.* auctiō *f.*; (*public*) hasta *f.* **hold an —** auctiōnem facere. **sell by —** sub hastā vēndere.
auctioneer *n.* praecō *m.*
audacious *a.* audāx; protervus. **-ly** *ad.* audācter, protervē. [temeritās *f.*
audacity *n.* audācia *f.*,
audib/le *a.* **be —** exaudīrī posse. **-ly** *ad.* clārā vōce.
audience *n.* audītōrēs *m.pl.*; (*interview*) aditus *m.* **give an — to** admittere.
audit *vt.* īnspicere. *n.* ratiōnum īnspectiō *f.*
auditorium *n.* cavea *f.*
auditory *a.* audītōrius.
auger *n.* terebra *f.*
augment *vt.* augēre, adaugēre. *vi.* crēscere, augērī.
augmentation *n.* incrēmentum *n.*
augur *n.* augur *m.* **-'s staff** lituus *m.* **-ship** *n.* augurātus *m.* *vi.* augurārī; (*fig.*) portendere.
augural *a.* augurālis.
augur/y *n.* augurium *n.*, auspicium *n.*; ōmen *n.* **take -ies** augurārī. **after taking -ies** augurātō.
august *a.* augustus.
August *n.* mēnsis Augustus, Sextīlis. **of —** Sextīlis.
aunt *n.* (*paternal*) amita *f.*, (*maternal*) mātertera *f.*
auspices *n.* auspicium *n.* **take —** auspicārī. **after taking —** auspicātō. **without taking —** inauspicātō.
auspicious *a.* faustus, fēlīx. **-ly** *ad.* fēlīciter, prosperē.
austere *a.* austērus, sevērus, dūrus. **-ly** *ad.* sevērē.
austerity *n.* sevēritās *f.*, dūritia *f.*
authentic *a.* vērus, certus.
authenticate *vt.* recognōscere. [fidēs *f.*
authenticity *n.* auctōritās *f.*,
author *n.* auctor, inventor; scrīptor. **-ess** *n.* auctor *f.*
authoritative *a.* fīdus; imperiōsus.
authority *n.* auctōritās *f.*, potestās *f.*, iūs *n.*; (*mil.*) imperium *n.* (*lit.*) auctor *m.*, scrīptor *m.* **enforce —** iūs suum exsequī. **have great —** multum pollēre. **on Caesar's —** auctōre Caesare. **an — on** perītus (*gen.*).
authorize *vt.* potestātem facere (*dat.*), mandāre; (*law*) sancīre.
autobiography *n.* dē vītā suā scrīptus liber *m.*
autochthonous *a.* indigena.
autocracy *n.* imperium singulāre *n.*, tyrannis *f.*
autocrat *n.* tyrannus *m.*, dominus *m.*
autocratic *a.* imperiōsus.
autograph *n.* manus *f.* chīrographum *n.*
automatic *a.* necessārius. **-ally** *ad.* necessāriō.
autonomous *a.* līber.
autonomy *n.* lībertās *f.*
Autumn *n.* autumnus *m.*
autumnal *a.* autumnālis.
auxiliary *a.* auxiliāris. *n.* adiūtor *m.*; (*pl.*) auxilia *n.pl.*, auxiliāriī *m.pl.*
avail *vi.* valēre. *vt.* prōdesse (*dat.*). **— oneself of** ūtī (*abl.*). *n.* ūsus *m.* **of no —** frustrā.
available *a.* ad manum, in prōmptū.
avalanche *n.* montis ruīna *f.*
avarice *n.* avāritia *f.*, cupiditās *f.* [**-ly** *ad.* avārē.
avaricious *a.* avārus, cupidus.
avaunt *interj.* apage.
avenge *vt.* ulcīscī, vindicāre.
avenger *n.* ultor *m.*, vindex *m.*

avenue *n.* xystus *m.*; (*fig.*) aditus *m.*, iānua *f.*
aver *vt.* adfirmāre, adsevērāre.
average *n.* medium *n.* on the — ferē.
averse *a.* āversus (*ab.*). be — to abhorrēre ab.
aversion *n.* odium *n.*, fastīdium *n.*
avert *vt.* arcēre, dēpellere; (*by prayer*) dēprecārī.
aviary *n.* aviārium *n.*
avid *a.* avidus. **-ly** *ad.* avidē.
avidity *n.* aviditās *f.*
avoid *vt.* vītāre, fugere, dēclīnāre; (*battle*) dētrectāre.
avoidance *n.* fuga *f.*, dēclīnātiō *f.*
avow *vt.* fatērī, cōnfitērī. **-ed** *a.* apertus. **-edly** *ad.* apertē, palam.
avowal *n.* cōnfessiō *f.*
await *vt.* exspectāre; (*future*) manēre.
awake *vt.* suscitāre, exsuscitare. *vi.* expergīscī. *a.* vigil.
awaken *vt.* exsuscitāre.
award *vt.* tribuere; (*law*) adiūdicāre. *n.* (*decision*) arbitrium *n.*, iūdicium *n.*; (*thing*) praemium *n.*
aware *a.* gnārus. be — scīre. become — of percipere.
away *ad.* ā-, ab- (*in cpd.*). be — abesse. far — procul, longē. make — with dē mediō tollere.
awe *n.* formīdō *f.*, reverentia *f.*, rēligiō *f.* stand in — of verērī. (*gods*) venerārī.
awe-struck *a.* stupidus.
awful *a.* terribilis, formīdolōsus, dīrus. **-ly** *ad.* formīdolōsē.
awhile *ad.* aliquamdiū, aliquantisper, parumper.
awkward *a.* incallidus, inconcinnus; (*to handle*) inhabilis. (*fig.*) molestus. **-ly** *ad.* incallidē, imperitē.
awkwardness *n.* imperitia *f.*, īnscitia *f.*
awl *n.* sūbula *f.*
awning *n.* vēlum *n.*
awry *a.* prāvus, dissidēns.
axe *n.* secūris *f.* battle — bipennis *f.*
axiom *n.* prōnūntiātum *n.*, sententia *f.*
axiomatic *a.* ēvidēns, manifestus.
axis *n.* axis *m.*
axle *n.* axis *m.*
aye *ad.* semper. for — in aeternum.
azure *a.* caeruleus.

B

baa *vi.* bālāre. *n.* bālātus *m.*
babble *vi.* garrīre, blaterāre.
babbler *n.* garrulus *m.*
babbling *a.* garrulus.
babe *n.* īnfāns *m.*, *f.*
babel *n.* dissonae vōcēs *f.pl.*
baboon *n.* sīmia *f.*
baby *n.* īnfāns. **-hood** *n.* īnfantia *f.*
Bacchanalian *a.* Bacchicus.
Bacchante *n.* Baccha *f.*
bachelor *n.* caelebs *m.*; (*degree*) baccalaureus *m.*
back *n.* tergum *n.*; (*animal*) dorsum; (*head*) occipitium *n.* at one's — ā tergō. behind one's — (*fig.*) clam (*acc.*). put one's — up stomachum movēre (*dat.*). turn one's — on sē āvertere ab. *a.* āversus, posticus. *ad.* retrō, retrōrsum, re- (*in cpd.*). *vt.* obsecundāre (*dat.*), adesse (*dat.*). — water inhibēre rēmis, inhibēre nāvem. *vi.* — out of dētrectāre, dēfugere.
backbite *vt.* obtrectāre (*dat.*), maledīcere (*dat.*).
backbone *n.* spīna *f.*
back-door *n.* posticum *n.*
backer *n.* fautor *m.*
background *n.* recessus *m.*, umbra *f.*
backing *n.* fidēs *f.*, favor *m.*
backslide *vi.* dēscīscere.

backward *a.* āversus; (*slow*) tardus; (*late*) sērus.
backwardness *n.* tarditās *f.*, pigritia *f.*
backwards *ad.* retrō, retrōrsum.
bacon *n.* lārdum *n.*
bad *a.* malus, prāvus, improbus, turpis. go— corrumpī. be — for obesse (*dat.*), nocēre (*dat.*). **-ly** *ad.* male, prāvē, improbē, turpiter.
badge *n.* insigne *n.*, infula *f.*
badger *n.* mēles *f.* *vt.* sollicitāre
badness *n.* prāvitās *f.*, nēquitia *f.*, improbitās *f.*
baffle *vt.* ēlūdere, fallere, frustārī.
bag *n.* saccus *m.*, folliculus *m.*; hand — mantica *f.*
bagatelle *n.* nūgae *f.pl.*, floccus *m.*
baggage *n.* impedimenta *n.pl.*, vāsa *n.pl.*, sarcinae *f.pl.* — train impedimenta *n.pl.* without — expeditus.
bail *n.* vadimōnium *n.*; (*person*) vas *m.* become — for spondēre prō (*abl.*). accept — for vadārī. keep one's — vadimōnium obīre. *vt.* spondēre prō (*abl.*).
bailiff *n.* (*pol.*) apparitor *m.*; (*private*) vilicus *m.*
bait *n.* esca *f.*, illecebra *f.* *vt.* lacessere.
bake *vt.* coquere, torrēre. — house pistrina *f.*
baker *n.* pistor *m.*
bakery *n.* pistrina *f.*
balance *n.* (*scales*) libra *f.*, trutina *f.*; (*equilibrium*) librāmentum *n.*; (*money*) reliqua *n.pl.* — sheet ratiō acceptī et expēnsī. *vt.* librāre; (*fig.*) compēnsāre. the account -s ratiō cōnstat.
balcony *n.* podium *n.*, Maeniānum *n.*
bald *a.* calvus; (*style*) āridus, iēiūnus.
baldness *n.* calvitium *n.*; (*style*) iēiūnitās *f.*
bale *n.* fascis *m.* — out *vt.* exhaurīre.
baleful *a.* fūnestus, perniciōsus, tristis.
balk *n.* tignum *n.* *vt.* frustrārī, dēcipere.
ball *n.* globus *m.*; (*play*) pila *f.*; (*wool*) glomus *n.* (*dance*) saltātiō *f.*
ballad *n.* carmen *n.*
ballast *n.* saburra *f.*
ballet *n.* saltātiō *f.*
ballot *n.* suffrāgium *n.* — box [urna *f.*
balm *n.* unguentum *n.*; (*fig.*) sōlātium *n.*
balmy *a.* lēnis, suāvis.
balsam *n.* balsamum *n.*
balustrade *n.* cancellī *m.pl.*
bamboozle *vt.* cōnfundere.
ban *vt.* interdīcere (*dat.*), vetāre. *n.* interdictum *n.*
banal *a.* trītus.
banana *n.* ariēna *f.*; (*tree*) pāla *f.*
band *n.* vinculum *n.*, redimīculum *n.*; (*head*) infula *f.*; (*men*) caterva *f.*, manus *f.*, grex *f.* *vi.* — together cōnsociārī.
bandage *n.* fascia *f.*, infula *f.* *vt.* obligāre, adligāre.
band-box *n.* out of a — (*fig.*) dē capsulā.
bandeau *n.* redimīculum *n.*
bandit *n.* latrō *m.*
bandy *vt.* iactāre. — words altercārī *a.* vārus.
bane *n.* venēnum *n.*, pestis *f.*, perniciēs *f.*
baneful *a.* perniciōsus, pestifer.
bang *vt.* pulsāre. *n.* fragor *m.*
bangle *n.* armilla *f.*
banish *vt.* pellere, expellere, ēicere; (*law*) aquā et ignī interdīcere (*dat.*); (*temporarily*) relēgāre; (*feeling*) abstergēre.
banishment *n.* (*act*) aquae et ignis interdictiō *f.*; relēgātiō *f.*; (*state*) exsilium *n.*, fuga *f.*
bank *n.* (*earth*) agger *m.*; (*river*) rīpa *f.*; (*money*) argentāria *f.*

banker *n.* argentārius *m.*; (*public*) mēnsārius *m.*
bankrupt *a.* be — solvendō nōn esse. declare oneself — bonam cōpiam ēiūrāre. go — dēcoquere. *n.* dēcoctor *m.*
banner *n.* vexillum *n.*
banquet *n.* cēna *f.*, epulae *f.pl.*; (*religious*) daps *f.* *vi.* epulārī.
banter *n.* cavillātiō *f.* *vi.* cavillārī.
baptism *n.* baptisma *n.*
baptize *vt.* baptizāre.
bar *n.* (*door*) sera *f.*; (*gate*) claustrum *n.*; (*metal*) later *m.*; (*wood*) asser *m.*; (*lever*) vectis *m.*; (*obstacle*) impedīmentum *n.*; (*law-court*) cancellī *m.pl.*; (*barristers*) advocātī *m.pl.*; (*profession*) forum *n.* of the — forēnsis. practise at the — causās agere.
bar *vt.* (*door*) obserāre; (*way*) obstāre (*dat.*), interclūdere, prohibēre; (*exception*) excipere, exclūdere.
barb *n.* acūleus *m.*, dēns *m.*, hāmus *m.*
barbarian *n.* barbarus *m.* *a.* barbarus.
barbarism *n.* barbaria *f.*
barbarity *n.* saevitia *f.*, ferōcia *f.*, immānitās *f.*, inhūmānitās *f.*
barbarous *a.* barbarus, saevus, immānis, inhūmānus. **-ly** *ad.* barbarē, inhūmānē.
barbed *a.* hāmātus.
barber *n.* tōnsor *m.* **—'s shop** tōnstrīna *f.*
bard *n.* vātēs *m.*, *f.*; (*Gallic*) bardus *m.*
bare *a.* nūdus; (*mere*) merus. lay — nūdāre, aperīre, dētegere. *vt.* nūdāre. **-ly** *ad.* vix.
barefaced *a.* impudēns.
barefoot *a.* nūdīs pedibus.
bargain *n.* pactum *n.*, foedus *n.* make a — pacīscī. make a bad — male emere. into the — grātiīs. *vi.* pacīscī.
barge *n.* linter *f.*
bark *n.* cortex *m.*; (*dog*) lātrātus *m.*; (*ship*) nāvis *f.*, ratis *f.* *vi.* lātrāre.
barley *n.* hordeum *n.* of — hordeāceus.
barn *n.* horreum *n.*
barrack *vt.* obstrepere (*dat.*).
barracks *n.* castra *n.pl.*
barrel *n.* cūpa *f.*
barren *a.* sterilis.
barrenness *n.* sterilitās *f.*
barricade *n.* claustrum *n.*, mūnīmentum *n.* *vt.* obsaepīre, obstruere. — off intersaepīre.
barrier *n.* impedīmentum *n.*; (*race-course*) carcer *n.*
barrister *n.* advocātus *m.*, patrōnus *m.*, causidicus *m.*
barrow *n.* ferculum *n.*; (*mound*) tumulus *m.*
barter *vi.* mūtāre. *vi.* mercēs mūtāre. *n.* mūtātiō *f.*, commercium *n.*
base *a.* turpis, vīlis; (*birth*) humilis, ignōbilis; (*coin*) adulterīnus. **-ly** *ad.* turpiter.
base *n.* fundāmentum *n.*; (*statue*) basis *f.*; (*hill*) rādīcēs *f.pl.*; (*mil.*) castra *n.pl.*
baseless *a.* falsus, inānis.
basement *n.* basis *f.*; (*storey*) īmum tabulātum *n.*
baseness *n.* turpitūdō *f.*
bashful *a.* pudīcus verēcundus.
bashfulness *n.* pudor *m.*, verēcundia *f.*
basic *a.* prīmus.
basin *n.* alveolus *m.*, pelvis *f.* wash- aquālis *m.*
basis *n.* fundāmentum *n.*
bask *vi.* aprīcārī. **-ing** *n.* aprīcātiō *f.*
basket *n.* corbis *f.*, fiscus *m.*; (*for bread*) canistrum *n.*; (*for wool*) quasillum *n.*
bas-relief *n.* toreuma *n.*
bass *a.* (*voice*) gravis.
bastard *a.* nothus.
bastinado *n.* fustuārium *n.*
bastion *n.* prōpugnāculum *n.*

bat *n.* vespertiliō *m.*; (*games*) clāva *f.*
batch *n.* numerus *m.*
bath *n.* balneum *n.*; (*utensil*) lābrum *n.*, lavātiō *f.* public -s balneae *f.pl.* Turkish — Lacōnicum *n.* -room balneāria *n.pl.* cold — frigidārium *n.* hot — calidārium *n.* — superintendent balneātor *m.* *vt.* lavāre. [perluī.
bathe *vt.* lavāre. *vi.* lavārī,
batman *n.* cālō *m.*
baton *n.* virga *f.*, scīpiō *m.*
battalion *n.* cohors *f.*
batter *vt.* quassāre, pulsāre, verberāre.
battering-ram *n.* ariēs *m.*
battery *n.* (*assault*) vīs *f.*
battle *n.* pugna *f.*, proelium *n.*, certāmen *n.* a — was fought pugnatum est. pitched — iūstum proelium. line of — aciēs *f.* drawn — anceps proelium. *vi.* pugnāre, contendere. — order aciēs *f.* — axe bipennis *f.*
battlement *n.* pinna *f.*
bawl *vt.* vōciferārī, clāmitāre.
bay *n.* (*sea*) sinus *m.*; (*tree*) laurus *f.*, laurea *f.* of — laureus. at — interclūsus. *a.* (*colour*) spādīx. *vi.* (*dog*) lātrāre.
be *vi.* esse; (*circs.*) versārī; (*condition*) sē habēre. — at adesse (*dat.*). — amongst interesse (*dat.*). — in inesse (*dat.*). consul-to — cōnsul dēsignātus. how are you? quid agis? so — it estō.
beach *n.* lītus *n.*, acta *f.* *vt.* (*ship*) subdūcere.
beacon *n.* ignis *m.*
bead *n.* pilula *f.*
beadle *n.* appāritor *m.*
beak *n.* rōstrum *n.* **-ed** *a.* rōstrātus.
beaker *n.* cantharus *m.*, scyphus *m.*
beam *n.* (*wood*) trabs *f.*, tignum *n.* (*balance*) iugum *n.*; (*light*) radius *m.*; (*ship*) latus *n.* on the — ā latere. *vi.* fulgēre; (*person*) adrīdēre.
beaming *a.* hilaris.
bean *n.* faba *f.*
bear *n.* ursus *m.*, ursa *f.* Great — septentriōnēs *m.pl.*, Arctos *f.* Little — septentriō minor, Cynosūra *f.* -'s ursīnus.
bear *vt.* (*carry*) ferre, portāre; (*endure*) ferre, tolerāre, patī; (*produce*) ferre, fundere; (*child*) parere. — down upon appropinquāre. — off ferre. — out arguere. — up under obsistere (*dat.*), sustinēre. — upon innītī (*dat.*); (*refer*) pertinēre ad. — with indulgēre (*dat.*). — oneself sē gerere. I cannot — to addūcī nōn possum ut.
bearable *a.* tolerābilis.
beard *n.* barba *f.* **-ed** *a.* barbātus. *vt.* ultrō lacessere.
beardless *a.* imberbis.
bearer *n.* bāiulus *m.*; (*letter*) tabellārius *m.*; (*litter*) lecticārius *m.*; (*news*) nūntius *m.*
bearing *n.* (*person*) gestus *m.*, vultus *m.* (*direction*) regiō *f.* have no — on nihil pertinēre ad. I have lost my — s ubi sim nesciō. [*m.*
bear's-breech *n.* acanthus
beast *n.* bestia *f.*; (*large*) bēlua *f.*; (*wild*) fera *f.*; (*domestic*) pecus *f.*; (*of burden*) iūmentum *n.*
beastliness *n.* foeditās *f.*, stuprum *n.*
beastly *a.* foedus.
beat *n.* ictus *m.*; (*heart*) palpitātiō *f.*; (*music*) percussiō *f.* (*oars, pulse*) pulsus *m.*
beat *vt.* ferīre, percutere, pulsāre; (*the body in grief*) plangere; (*punish*) caedere, verberāre; (*conquer*) vincere, superāre. *vi.* palpitāre, micāre. — back repellere. — in perfringere. — out excutere; (*metal*) extundere. — the air lītus arāre. — a retreat re-

ceptui canere. — about the bush circuitiōne ūti be -en vāpulāre. dead — cōnfectus.
beating *n.* verbera *n.pl.*; (*defeat*) clādes *f.*; (*time*) percussiō *f.* get a — vāpulāre.
beatitude *n.* beātitūdō *f.*, fēlīcitās *f.*
beau *n.* nitidus homō *m.*; (*lover*) amāns *m.* [mōsus.
beauteous *a.* pulcher, fōr-
beautiful *a.* pulcher, formōsus; (*looks*) decōrus; (*scenery*) amoenus. **-ly** *ad.* pulchrē.
beautify *vt.* exōrnāre decorāre.
beauty *n.* fōrma *f.*, pulchritūdō *f.*, amoenitās *f.*
beaver *n.* castor *m.* fiber *m.*; (*helmet*) buccula *f.*
becalmed *a.* ventō dēstitūtus.
because *conj.* quod, quia, quōniam quippe qui. — of propter (*acc.*).
beck *n.* nūtus *m.*
beckon *vt.* innuere vocāre.
become *vi.* fieri. what will — of me? quid me fiet? *vt.* decēre, convenire in (*acc.*).
becoming *a.* decēns, decōrus. **-ly** *ad* decōrē, convenienter.
bed *n.* cubile *n.*, lectus *m.*, lectulus *m.* go to — cubitum ire. make a — lectum sternere. be — ridden lectō tenērī. camp — grabātus *m* flower — pulvinus *m.* marriage — lectus geniālis *m.* river — alveus *m.* **-room** *n.* cubiculum *n.* **-clothes** *n.* strāgula *n.pl.* **-post** *n.* fulcrum *n.* **-stead** *n* sponda *f.*
bedaub *vt.* illinere, oblinere.
bedding *n.* strāgula *n.pl.*
bedeck *vt.* ōrnāre, exōrnāre.
bedew *vt.* inrōrāre.
bedim *vt.* obscūrāre.
bedraggled *a.* sordidus, madidus.
bee *n* apis *f.* **-hive** *n.* alvus *f.* **-keeper** *n.* apiārius *m.* **queen** — rēx *m.*
beech *n.* fāgus *f.* *a.* fāginus.
beef *n.* būbula *f.* [*n.*
beer *n.* cervisia *f.*, fermentum
beet *n.* bēta *f.*
beetle *n.* (*insect*) scarabaeus *m.*, (*implement*) fistūca *f*
beetling *a.* imminēns mināx.
befall *vi. t.* & accidere ēvenire (*dat.*); (*good*) contingere (*dat.*).
befit *vt.* decēre, convenire in (*acc.*).
before *ad.* ante, anteā, antehāc. *pr.* ante (*acc.*); (*place*) prō (*abl.*); (*presence*) apud (*acc.*), cōram (*abl.*). *conj.* antequam, priusquam.
beforehand *ad.* ante, anteā; prae (*in cpd.*).
befoul *vt.* inquināre, foedāre.
befriend *vt.* favēre (*dat.*), adiuvāre; (*in trouble*) adesse (*dat.*).
beg *vt.* ōrāre obsecrāre, poscere ab, petere ab — for petere. *vi.* mendicāre.
beget *vt.* gignere prōcreāre, generāre. [creātor *m.*
begetter *n.* generātor *m.*,
beggar *m.* mendicus *m.*
beggarly *a.* mendicus, indigēns.
beggary *n.* mendicitās *f.*, indigentia *f.*
begin *vi. t.* & incipere, coepisse; (*speech*) exōrdiri; (*plan*) instituere, incohāre; (*time*) inire. — with incipere ab.
beginning *n.* initium *n.*, principium *n.*, exōrdium *n.*, inceptiō *f.*; (*learning*) rudimenta *n.pl.* elementa *n.pl.*; (*origin*) origō *f.*, fōns *m.* at the — of spring ineunte vēre.
begone *interj.* apage tē āmovē.
begotten *a.* genitus nātus.
begrime *vt.* inquināre, lutō aspergere. **-d** *a.* luteus.
begrudge *vt.* invidēre (*dat.*).
beguile *vt.* dēcipere, fallere.
behalf *n.* on — of prō (*abl.*). on my — meō nōmine.

behave *vi.* sē gerere, sē praebēre (*with a.*). well -d bene mōrātus.
behaviour *n.* mōrēs *m.pl.*
behead *vt.* dētruncāre, secūrī percutere.
behest *n.* iussum *n.*
behind *ad.* pōne, post, ā tergō. *pr.* post (*acc.*), pōne (*acc.*).
behindhand *ad.* sērō. be — parum prōficere.
behold *vt* aspicere, cōnspicere intuērī. *interj.* ecce, ēn. [strictus, obligātus.
beholden *a.* obnoxius, ob-
behoof *n.* ūsus *m.*
behove *vt* oportēre.
being *n.* (*life*) animātiō *f.*; (*nature*) nātūra *f.*; (*person*) homō *m.f.*
bejewelled *a.* gemmeus, gemmātus.
belabour *vt.* verberāre. caedere.
belated *a.* sērus.
belch *vi.* ructāre, ēructāre.
beldam *n.* anus *f.*
beleaguer *vt.* obsidēre, circumsedēre. [pugnāre.
belie *vt.* abhorrēre ab re-
belief *n.* fidēs *f.*, opiniō *f.*; (*opinion*) sententia *f.* to the best of my — ex animī meī sententiā. past — incrēdibilis.
believe *vt.* & *i.* (*thing*) crēdere; (*person*) crēdere (*dat.*); (*suppose*) crēdere, putāre, arbitrārī, opīnārī. — in gods deōs esse crēdere. make — simulāre.
believer *n.* deōrum cultor *m.*; Christiānus *m.*
belike *ad.* fortasse.
belittle *vt.* obtrectāre.
bell *n.* tintinnābulum *n.*; (*public*) campāna *f.*
belle *n.* fōrmōsa *f.*, pulchra *f.*
belles-lettres *n.* litterae *f.pl.*
bellicose *a.* ferōx.
belligerent *a.* bellī particeps.
bellow *vi.* rūdere, mūgīre. *n.* mūgītus *m.*
bellows *n.* follis *m.*
belly *n.* abdōmen *n.*, venter *m.*; (*sail*) sinus *m.* *vi.* tumēre.
belong *vi.* esse (*gen.*), proprium esse (*gen.*), inesse (*dat.*). (*concern*) attinēre, pertinēre.
belongings *n.* bona *n.pl.*
beloved *a* cārus, dīlectus grātus.
below *ad.* īnfrā, subter. *a.* īnferus. *pr.* īnfrā (*acc.*), sub (*abl.*, *acc.*).
belt *n.* zōna *f.*; (*sword*) balteus *m.*
bemoan *vt.* dēplōrāre, lāmentārī. [stupidus.
bemused *a.* stupefactus,
bench *n.* subsellium *n.*; (*rowing*) trānstrum *n.*; (*law*) iūdicēs *m.pl.* seat on the — iūdicātus. *m.*
bend *vt.* flectere, curvāre, inclīnāre; (*bow*) intendere; (*course*) tendere, flectere; (*mind*) intendere. *vi.* sē inflectere; (*person*) sē dēmittere. — back reflectere. — down dēflectere; sē dēmittere. *n.* flexus *m.*, ānfrāctus *m.*
beneath *ad.* subter. *pr.* sub (*acc.*, *abl.*). [*f.pl.*
benediction *n.* bonae precēs
benedictory *a.* faustus.
benefaction *n.* beneficium *n.*, dōnum *n.*
benefactor *n.* patrōnus *m.* be a — bene merērī (dē).
beneficence *n.* beneficentia *f.*, līberālitās *f.*
beneficent *a.* beneficus.
beneficial *a.* ūtilis, salūbris.
benefit *n.* beneficium *n.*; (*derived*) fructus *m.* have the — of fruī (*abl.*). *vt.* prōdesse (*dat.*), ūsuī esse (*dat.*).
benevolence *n.* benevolentia *f.* benignitās *f.*
benevolent *a.* benevolus, benignus. -ly *ad.* benevolē, benignē.
benighted *a.* nocte oppressus; (*fig.*) ignārus, indoctus.

benign *a.* benignus, cōmis.
bent *n.* (*mind*) inclīnātiō *f.* ingenium *n.* *a.* curvus, flexus; (*mind*) attentus. be — on studēre (*dat.*).
benumb *vt.* stupefacere. **-ed** stupefactus, torpidus. **be -d** torpēre.
bequeath *vt.* lēgāre.
bequest *n.* lēgātum *n.*
bereave *vt.* orbāre; prīvāre.
bereavement *n.* damnum *n.*
bereft *a.* orbus, orbātus prīvātus.
berry *n.* bāca *f.*
berth *n.* statiō *f.* **give a wide — to** dēvītāre
beryl *n.* bēryllus *m.*
beseech *vt.* implōrāre, ōrāre, obsecrāre.
beseem *vt.* decēre. [sedēre.
beset *vt.* obsidēre, circum-
beside *pr.* ad (*acc.*), apud (*acc.*); (*close*) iuxtā (*acc.*) — **the point** nihil ad rem. **be — oneself** nōn esse apud sē.
besides *ad.* praetereā, accēdit quod; (*in addition*) īnsuper. *pr.* praeter (*acc.*).
besiege *vt.* obsidēre, circumsedēre.
besieger *n.* obsessor *m.*
besmear *vt.* illinere.
besmirch *vt.* maculāre.
besom *n.* scōpae *f.pl.*
besotted *a.* stupidus.
bespatter *vt.* aspergere.
bespeak *vt.* (*order*) imperāre; (*denote*) significāre.
besprinkle *vt.* aspergere.
best *a.* optimus. **the — part** māior pars. *n.* flōs *m.*, rōbur *n.* **do one's —** prō virīlī parte agere. **do one's — to** operam dare ut. **have the — of it** vincere. **make the — of** (*a situation*) aequō animō accipere. **to the — of one's ability** prō virīlī parte. **to the — of my knowledge** quod sciam. *ad.* optimē.
bestial *a.* foedus.
bestir *vt* movēre. **— oneself** expergīscī.
bestow *vt.* dōnāre. tribuere, dare. cōnferre. [(*abl.*).
bestride *vt.* (*horse*) sedēre in
bet *n.* pignus *n.* *vt.* oppōnere. *vi.* pignore contendere.
betake *vt.* cōnferre, recipere.
bethink *vt.* **— oneself** sē colligere. **— onself of** respicere.
betide *vi.* accidere, ēvenīre.
betimes *ad.* mātūrē, tempestīvē.
betoken *vt.* significāre; (*foretell*) portendere.
betray *vt.* prōdere trādere; (*feelings*) arguere. **without -ing one's trust** salvā fidē.
betrayal *n.* prōditiō *f.*
betrayer *n.* prōditor *m.*; (*informer*) index *m.*
betroth *vt.* spondēre, dēspondēre.
betrothal *n.* spōnsālia *n.pl.*
better *a.* melior. **it is — to** praestat (*inf.*). **get the — of** vincere, superāre. **I am —** (*in health*) melius est mihi. **I had — go** praestat īre. **get —** convalēscere. **think — of** sententiam mūtāre dē. *ad.* melius. *vt.* corrigere. **— oneself** prōficere.
betterment *n.* prōfectus *m.*
between *pr.* inter (*acc.*).
betwixt *pr.* inter (*acc.*).
beverage *n.* pōtiō *f.*
bevy *n.* manus *f.*, grex *f.*
bewail *vt.* dēflēre. lāmentārī, dēplōrāre.
beware *vt.* cavēre
bewilder *vt.* cōnfundere, perturbāre. **-ed** attonitus.
bewilderment *n.* perturbātiō *f.*, admīrātiō *f.*
bewitch *vt.* fascināre; (*fig.*) dēlēnīre.
beyond *ad.* ultrā, suprā. *pr.* ultrā (*acc.*), extrā (*acc.*); (*motion*) trāns (*acc.*); (*amount*) ultrā, suprā (*acc.*). **go, pass —** excēdere, ēgredī.

bezel *n.* pāla *f.*
bias *n.* inclīnātiō *f.*; (*party*) favor *m.* *vt.* inclīnāre. **-sed** prōpēnsior.
bibber *n.* pōtor *m.*, pōtātor *m.*
Bible *n.* litterae sacrae *f.pl.*
bibulous *a.* bibulus.
bicephalous *a.* biceps.
bicker *vi.* altercārī, iūrgāre.
bid *vt.* iubēre; (*guest*) vocāre, invitāre. *vi.* (*at auction*) licērī. — **for** licērī. — **good day** salvēre iubēre. **he -s fair to make progress** spēs est eum prōfecturum esse.
biddable *a.* docilis.
bidding *n.* iussum *n.*; (*auction*) licitātiō *f.*
bide *vt.* manēre, opperīrī.
biennial *a.* biennālis.
bier *n.* ferculum *n.*
bifurcate *vi.* sē scindere. [*n.*
bifurcation *n.* (*road*) trivium
big *a.* māgnus, grandis, amplus; (*with child*) gravida. **very** — permāgnus. **talk** — glōriārī.
bight *n.* sinus *m.*
bigness *n.* māgnitūdō *f.*, amplitūdō *f.*
bigot *n.* nimis obstinātus fautor *m.* **-ed** *a.* contumāx.
bigotry *n.* contumācia *f.*, nimia obstinātio *f.*
bile *n.* bīlis *f.*, fel *n.*
bilge-water *n.* sentīna *f.*
bilk *vt.* fraudāre.
bill *n.* (*bird*) rōstrum *n.*; (*implement*) falx *f.*; (*law*) rogātiō *f.*, lēx *f.*; (*money*) syngrapha *f.*; (*notice*) libellus *m.*, titulus *m.* **introduce a** — populum rogāre, lēgem ferre. **carry a** — lēgem perferre.
billet *n.* hospitium *n.* *vt.* in hospitia dīvidere.
bill-hook *n.* falx *f.*
billow *n.* fluctus *m.*
billowy *a.* undōsus.
billy-goat *n.* caper *m.*
bin *n.* lacus *m.*
bind *vt.* adligāre, dēligāre, vincīre; (*by oath*) adigere; (*by obligation*) obligāre, obstringere; (*wound*) obligāre. — **fast** dēvincīre. — **together** conligāre. — **over** vadārī.
binding *n.* compāgēs *f.* *a.* (*law*) ratus. **it is** — **on** oportet.
bindweed *n.* convolvulus *m.*
biographer *n.* vitae nārrātor *m.*
biography *n.* vīta *f.*
bipartite *a.* bipartītus.
biped *n.* bipēs *m.*
birch *n.* bētula *f.*; (*flogging*) virgae ulmeae *f.pl.*
bird *n.* avis *f.* **-catcher** *n.* auceps *m.* **-lime** *n.* viscum *n.* **-s of a feather** parēs cum paribus facillimē congregantur. **kill two -s with one stone** ūnō saltū duōs aprōs capere, dē eādem fidēliā duōs parietēs dealbāre. **-'s-eye view of** dēspectus in (*acc.*).
birth *n.* (*act*) partus *m.*; (*origin*) genus *n.* **low** — ignōbilitās *f.* **high** — nōbilitās *f.* **by** — nātū, ortū.
birthday *n.* nātālis *m.* — **party** *n.* nātālicia *n.pl.*
birthplace *n.* locus nātālis *m.*; (*fig.*) incūnābula *n.pl.*
birthright *n.* patrimōnium.
bisect *vt.* dīvidere.
bishop *n.* episcopus *m.*
bison *n.* ūrus *m.*
bit *n.* pars *f.*; (*food*) frustum *n.*; (*broken off*) fragmentum *n.*; (*horse*) frēnum *n.* — **by** — minūtātim. **a** — *ad.* aliquantulum. **a** — **sad** tristior.
bitch *n.* canis *f.*
bite *vt.* mordēre; (*frost*) ūrere. *n.* morsus *m.* **with a** — mordicus.
biting *a.* mordāx.
bitter *a.* acerbus, amārus, asper. **-ly** *ad.* acerbē, asperē.
bittern *n.* būtiō *m.*, ardea *f.*
bitterness *n.* acerbitās *f.*
bitumen *n.* bitūmen *n.*

bivouac *n.* excubiae *f.pl.* *vi.* excubāre.
bizarre *a.* insolēns.
blab *vt.* & *i.* garrire, effūtīre.
black *a.* (*dull*) āter, (*glossy*) niger.; (*dirt*) sordidus. (*eye*) līvidus, (*looks*) trux. — and blue līvidus. — list prōscriptiō *f.* — magic magicae artēs *f.pl.* — mark nota *f.* *n.* ātrum *n.*, nigrum *n.* dressed in — ātrātus; (*in mourning*) sordidātus.
blackberry *n.* mōrum *n.*
blackbird *n.* merula *f.*
blacken *vt.* nigrāre, nigrum reddere.; (*character*) īnfāmāre, obtrectāre (*dat.*).
blackguard *n.* scelestus, scelerātus *m.*
blacking *n.* ātrāmentum *n.*
blackmail *n.* minae. *vt.* minis cōgere.
blacksmith *n.* faber *m.*
bladder *n.* vēsica *f.*
blade *n.* (*grass*) herba *f.*; (*oar*) palma *f.*; (*sword*) lāmina *f.*
blame *vt.* reprehendere, culpāre. I am to — reus sum. *n.* reprehēnsiō *f.*, culpa *f.*
blameless *a.* innocēns. **-ly** *ad.* innocenter.
blamelessness *n.* innocentia *f.*, integritās *f.*
blameworthy *a.* accūsābilis, nocēns.
blanch *vi.* exalbēscere, pallēscere.
bland *a.* mītis, lēnis.
blandishment *n.* blanditiae [*f.pl.*
blank *a.* vacuus, pūrus; (*look*) stolidus.
blanket *n.* lōdix *f.* wet — nimium sevērus.
blare *vi.* canere, stridere. *n.* clangor *m.*, stridor *m.*
blarney *n.* lēnōcinium *n.*
blaspheme *vi.* maledicere.
blasphemous *a.* maledicus, impius.
blasphemy *n.* maledicta *n.pl.*, impietās *f.*
blast *n.* flātus *m.*, inflātus *m.* *vt.* disicere, discutere; (*crops*) rōbīgine adficere.
blatant *a.* raucus.
blaze *n.* flamma *f.*, ignis *m.*, fulgor *m.* *vi.* flāgrāre, ārdēre, fulgēre. — up exārdēscere. *vt.* — a broad pervulgāre.
blazon *vt.* prōmulgāre.
bleach *vt.* candidum reddere.
bleak *a.* dēsertus, tristis, inamoenus.
blearedness *n.* lippitūdō *f.*
blear-eyed *a.* lippus.
bleat *vi.* bālāre. *n.* bālātus *m.*
bleed *vi.* sanguinem fundere. *vt.* sanguinem mittere (*dat.*). my heart -s animus mihi dolet.
bleeding *a.* crūdus, sanguineus. *n.* sanguinis missiō *f.*
blemish *n.* macula *f.*, vitium *n.* *vt.* maculāre, foedāre.
blend *vt.* miscēre, immiscēre, admiscēre. *n.* coniūnctiō *f.*
bless *vt.* beāre; laudāre; (*eccl.*) benedīcere. — with augēre (*abl.*). — my soul ! ita me dī ament !
blessed *a.* beātus, fortūnātus; (*emperors*) dīvus.
blessing *n.* (*thing*) commodum *n.*, bonum *n.*; (*eccl.*) benedictiō *f.*
blight *n.* rōbīgō *f.*, ūrēdō *f.* *vt.* rōbīgine adficere; (*fig.*) nocēre (*dat.*).
blind *a.* caecus; (*in one eye*) luscus; (*fig.*) ignārus, stultus; (*alley*) nōn pervius; (*forces*) necessārius. turn a — eye to cōnīvēre in (*abl.*) *vt.* excaecāre, caecāre; (*fig.*) occaecāre; (*with light*) praestringere.
blindfold *a.* capite obvolūtō.
blindly *ad.* temerē.
blindness *n.* caecitās *f.*; (*fig*) temeritās *f.*, īnsipientia *f.*
blink *vi.* nictāre.
bliss *n.* fēlīcitās *f.*, laetitia *f.*
blissful *a.* fēlīx, beātus, laetus. **-ly** *ad.* fēlīciter, beātē.

blister *n.* pustula *f.*
blithe *a.* hilaris, laetus. **-ly** *ad.* hilare, laetē.
blithesome *a.* hilaris.
blizzard *n.* hiems *f.*
bloated *a.* tumidus, turgidus.
blob *n.* gutta *f.*, particula *f.*
block *n.* (*wood*) stipes *m.*, caudex *m.*; (*stone*) massa *f.*; (*houses*) īnsula *f.* — **letter** quadrāta littera. **stumbling** — offēnsiō *f.*
block *vt* claudere, obstruere, interclūdere. — **the way** obstāre.
blockade *n.* obsidiō *f.* **raise a** — obsidiōnem solvere. *vt.* obsidēre, interclūdere.
blockhead *n.* caudex *m.*, bārō *m.*, truncus *m.*
blockhouse *n.* castellum *n.*
blond *a.* flāvus.
blood *n.* sanguis *m.*; (*shed*) cruor *m.*; (*murder*) caedēs *f.*; (*kin*) genus *n.* **let** — sanguinem mittere. **staunch** — sanguinem supprimere. **-stained** cruentus. **bad** — simultās *f.* **in cold** — cōnsultō. **own flesh and** — cōnsanguineus. **-vessel** *n.* vēna *f.* [*tory*) incruentus.
bloodless *a.* exsanguis; (*vic-*
bloodshed *n.* caedēs *f.*
bloodshot *a.* sanguineus.
bloodsucker *n.* hirūdō *f.*
bloodthirsty *a.* sanguinārius.
bloody *a.* cruentus.
bloom *n.* flōs *m.* **in** — flōrēns. *vi.* flōrēre flōrēscere, vigēre.
blossom *n.* flōs *m.* *vi.* efflōrēscere, flōrēre.
blot *n.* macula *f.*; (*erasure*) litūra *f.* *vt.* maculāre. — **out** dēlēre, oblitterāre.
blotch *n.* macula *f.* **-ed** *a.* maculōsus.
blow *vt.* & *i.* (*wind*) flāre; (*breath*) anhēlāre; (*instrument*) canere; (*flower*) efflōrēscere; (*nose*) ēmungere. —**over** (*storm*) —cadere; (*fig.*) abīre. — **out** extinguere. — **up** īnflāre; (*destroy*) discutere, disturbāre. *n.* ictus *m.*; (*on the cheek*) alapa *f.*; (*fig.*) plāga *f.*; (*misfortune*) calamitās *f.* **aim a** — **at** petere. **come to -s** ad manūs venīre.
blowy *a.* ventōsus.
bludgeon *n.* fustis *m.*
blue *a.* caeruleus. **black and** — līvidus. **true** — fīdissimus. — **blood** nōbilitās *f.*
bluff *n.* rūpēs *f.*, prōmunturium *n.* *a.* inurbānus. *vt.* fallere, dēcipere, verba dare. (*dat.*), impōnere (*dat.*).
blunder *vi.* errāre, offendere. *n.* error *m.* errātum *n.*; (*in writing*) mendum *n.*
blunt *a.* hebes; (*manners*) horridus, rūsticus, inurbānus. **be** — hebēre. *vt.* hebetāre, obtundere, retundere. **-ly** *ad.* līberius, plānē et apertē.
blur *n.* macula *f.* *vt.* obscūrāre.
blurt *vt.* — **out** ēmittere.
blush *vi.* rubēre, ērubēscere. *n.* rubor *m.*
bluster *vi.* dēclāmitāre, lātrāre.
boa *n.* boa *f.*
Boadicea *n.* Boudicca *f.*
boar *n.* verrēs *m.*; (*wild*) aper *m.*
board *n.* tabula *f.*; (*table*) mēnsa *f.*; (*food*) vīctus *m.*; (*committee*) concilium *n.* (*judicial*) quaestiō *f.*, (*of ten men*) decemvirī *m.pl.*; (*gaming*) abacus *m.*, alveus *m.* **on** — **in** nāvī. **go on** — nāvem cōnscendere. **go by the** — intercidere, perīre. **above** — sine fraude. *vt.* (*building*) contabulāre; (*ship*) cōnscendere; (*person*) vīctum praebēre (*dat.*). *vi.* — **with** dēvertere ad.
boarder *m.* hospes *m.*
boast *vi.* glōriārī, sē iactāre. — **of** glōriārī dē (*abl.*) *n.* glōria *f.*, glōriātiō *f.*, iactātiō *f.*
boastful *a.* glōriōsus. **-ly** *ad.* glōriōsē.

boasting *n.* glōriātiō *f.* *a.* glōriōsus.
boat *n.* linter *f.*, scapha *f.* cymba; *f.* (*ship*) nāvis *f.* be in the same — *fig.*) in eādem nāvī esse.
boatman *n.* nauta *m.*
boatswain *n.* hortātor *m.*
bobbin *n.* fūsus *m.*
bode *vt.* portendere, praesāgīre.
bodiless *a.* sine corpore.
bodily *a.* corporeus.
bodkin *n.* acus *f.*
body *n.* corpus *n.*; (*dead*) cadāver *n.*; (*small*) corpusculum *n.*; (*person*) homō *m.*, *f.*; (*of people*) globus *m.*, numerus *m.*; (*of troops*) manus *f.*, caterva *f.*; (*of cavalry*) turma *f.*; (*of officials*) collēgium *n.*; (*heavenly*) astrum *n.* in a — ūniversī, frequentēs.
bodyguard *n.* custōs *m.*, stīpātōrēs *m.pl.*; (*emperor's*) praetōriānī *m.pl.*
bog *n.* palūs *f.*
boggle *vi.* tergiversārī, haesitāre.
boggy *a.* palūster.
bogus *a.* falsus, fictus.
bogy *n.* mōnstrum *n.*
Bohemian *a.* līberior, solūtior, libīdinōsus.
boil *vt.* coquere; (*liquid*) fervefacere. — down dēcoquere. *vi.* fervēre, effervēscere; (*sea*) exaestuāre; (*passion*) exārdēscere, aestuāre. — over effervēscere. *n.* (*med.*) fūrunculus *m.*
boiler *n.* cortīna *f.*
boiling *a.* (*hot*) fervēns.
boisterous *a.* (*person*) turbulentus, vehemēns; (*sea*) turbidus, agitātus; (*weather*) procellōsus, violentus. **-ly** *ad.* turbidē, turbulentē.
boisterousness *n.* tumultus *m.*, violentia *f.*
bold *a.* audāx, fortis, intrepidus; (*impudent*) impudēns, protervus; (*language*) līber; (*headland*) prōminēns. make — audēre. **-ly** *ad.* audācter, fortiter, intrepidē; impudenter.
boldness *n.* audācia *f.*, cōnfīdentia *f.*; impudentia *f.*, petulantia *f.*; (*speech*) lībertās *f.*
bole *n.* truncus *m.*
bolster *n.* pulvīnus *m.* *vt.* — up sustinēre, cōnfirmāre.
bolt *n.* (*door*) claustrum *n.*, pessulus *m.*, sera *f.*; (*missile*) tēlum *n.*, sagitta *f.*; (*lightning*) fulmen *n.* make a — for it sē prōripere, aufugere. a— from the blue rēs subita, rēs inopīnāta. *vt.* (*door*) obserāre, obdere.
bombard *vt.* tormentīs verberāre; (*fig.*) lacessere.
bombast *n.* ampullae *f.pl.*
bombastic *a.* tumidus, inflātus. be — ampullārī.
bond *n.* vinculum *n.*, catēna *f.*, compes *f.*; (*of union*) cōpula *f.*, iugum *n.*, nōdus *m.*; (*document*) syngrapha *f.*; (*agreement*) foedus *n.* *a.* servus, addictus.
bondage *n.* servitūs *f.*, famulātus *m.*
bone *n.* os *n.*; (*fish*) spīna *f.* *vt.* exossāre.
boneless *a.* exos.
bonfire *n.* ignis festus *m.*
bonhomie *n.* festīvitās *f.*
bon mot *n.* dictum *n.*, sententia *f.*
bonny *a.* pulcher bellus.
bony *a.* osseus.
boo *vt.* explōdere.
book *n.* liber *m.*; (*small*) libellus *m.*; (*scroll*) volūmen *n.* (*modern form*) cōdex *m.* **-s** (*bus.*) rationēs *f.pl.* tabulae *f.pl.*, bring to — in iūdicium vocāre.
book-binder *m.* glūtinātor *m.*
book-case *n.* librārium *n.*, pēgma *n.*
bookish *a.* litterārum studiōsus.
book-keeper *n.* āctuārius *m.*
book-seller *n.* librārius *m.*, bibliopōla *m.*
book-shop *n.* bibliothēca *f.*, librāria taberna *f.*

book-worm *n.* tinea *f.*
boom *n.* (*spar*) longurius *m.*; (*harbour*) ōbex *m.*, *f.* *vi.* resonāre.
boon *n.* bonum *n.*, beneficium *n.*, dōnum *n.* *a.* festivus. — companion sodālis *m.*, compōtor *m.*
boor *n.* agrestis *m.*, rūsticus *m.*
boorish *a.* agrestis, rūsticus, inurbānus. **-ly** *ad.* rūsticē.
boost *vt.* efferre; (*wares*) vēnditāre.
boot *n.* calceus *m.*; (*mil.*) caliga *f.*; (*rustic*) pērō *m.*; (*tragic*) cothurnus *m.* *vi.* prōdesse. to — insuper, praetereā.
booted *a.* calceātus, caligātus.
booth *n.* taberna *f.*
bootless *a.* inūtilis, vānus. **-ly** *ad.* frustrā.
booty *n.* praeda *f.*, spolia *n.pl.*
border *n.* ōra *f.*, margō *f.*; (*country*) fīnis *m.*; (*dress*) limbus *m.* *vt.* praetexere, margināre; fīnire. *vi.* — on adiacēre (*dat.*) imminēre (*dat.*), attingere; (*fig.*) fīnitimum esse (*dat.*).
bordering *a.* fīnitimus.
bore *vt.* perforāre, perterbrāre; (*person*) obtundere, fatigāre. — out exterebrāre. *n.* terebra *f.*; (*hole*) forāmen *n.*; (*person*) homō importūnus *m.*, ineptus *m.*
boredom *n.* lassitūdō *f.*
borer *n.* terebra *f.*
born *a.* nātus. be — nāsci.
borough *n.* mūnicipium *n.*
borrow *vt.* mūtuārī.
borrowed *a.* mūtuus; (*fig.*) aliēnus.
borrowing *n.* mūtuātiō *f.*; (*to pay a debt*) versūra *f.*
bosky *a.* nemorōsus.
bosom *n.* sinus *m.*; (*fig.*) gremium *n.* — friend familiāris *m.*, *f.*, sodālis *m.* be a — friend of ab latere esse (*gen.*).
boss *n.* bulla *f.*; (*shield*) umbō *m.*
botanist *n.* herbārius *m.*
botany *n.* herbāria *f.*
botch *vt.* male sarcire, male gerere.
both *pro.* ambō, uterque. *ad.* — . . . and et . . . et, cum . . . tum.
bother *n.* negōtium *n.* *vt.* vexāre, molestus esse (*dat.*). *vi.* operam dare.
bothersome *a.* molestus.
bottle *n.* lagoena *f.*, amphora *f.* *vt.* (*wine*) diffundere.
bottom *n.* fundus *m.*; (*ground*) solum *n.*; (*ship*) carina *f.* the — of īmus. be at the — of (*cause*) auctōrem esse. go to the — pessum īre, perīre. send to the — pessum dare. from the — funditus, ab īnfimō.
bottomless *a.* profundus, fundō carēns.
bottommost *a.* īnfimus.
bough *n.* rāmus *m.*
boulder *n.* saxum *n.*
boulevard *n.* platea *f.*
bounce *vi.* salire, resultāre.
bound *n.* fīnis *m.*, modus *m.*, terminus *m.*; (*leap*) saltus *m.* set -s to modum facere (*dat.*). *vt.* fīnire, dēfīnire, termināre. *vi.* salire, saltāre. *a.* adligātus, obligātus, obstrictus. be — to (*duty*) dēbēre. it is — to happen necesse est ēveniat. be — for tendere in (*acc.*). be storm — tempestāte tenērī.
boundary *n.* fīnis *m.*; (*of fields*) terminus *m.*; (*fortified*) līmes *m.* — stone terminus *m.*
boundless *a.* immēnsus, īnfīnītus.
boundlessness *n.* īnfīnitās *f.*, immēnsum *n.*
bounteous, bountiful *a.* largus, līberālis, benignus. **-ly** *ad.* largē, līberāliter, cōpiōsē.
bounteousness, bounty *n.* largitās *f.*, līberālitās *f.*; (*store*) cōpia *f.*

bouquet *n.* corollārium *n.*; (*of wine*) flōs *m.*
bourn *n.* fīnis *m.*
bout *n.* certāmen *n.*; (*drinking*) cōmissātiō *f.*
bovine *a.* būbulus; (*fig.*) stolidus.
bow *n.* arcus *m.*; (*ship*) prōra *f.*; (*courtesy*) salūtātiō *f.* have two strings to one's — duplicī spē ūtī. rain — arcus *m.* *vi.* flectere, inclīnāre. *vi.* caput dēmittere.
bowels *n.* alvus *f.*; (*fig.*) viscera *n.pl.*
bower *n.* umbrāculum *n.*, trichila *f*
bowl *n.* (*cooking*) catina *f.*; (*drinking*) calix *m.*; (*mixing wine*) crātēra *f.*; (*ball*) pila *f.* *vt.* volvere. — over prōruere.
bow-legged *a.* valgus.
bowler *n.* (*game*) dator *m.*
bowman *n.* sagittārius *m.*
bowstring *n.* nervus *m.*
box *n.* arca *f.*, capsa *f.*; (*for clothes*) cista *f.*; (*for medicine*) pyxis *f.*; (*for perfume*) alabaster *m.*; (*tree*) buxus *f.*; (*wood*) buxum *n.*; (*blow on ears*) alapa *f.* *vt.* inclūdere. — the ears of alapam dūcere (*dat.*), colaphōs infringere (*dat.*). *vi.* (*fight*) pugnīs certāre.
boxer *n.* pugil *m.*
boxing *n.* pugilātiō *f.* — **glove** *n.* caestus *m.*
boy *n.* puer *m.* become a — again repuerāscere.
boycott *vt.* repudiāre.
boyhood *n.* pueritia *f.* from — ā puerō.
boyish *a.* puerīlis. **-ly** *ad.* puerīliter.
brace *n.* (*building*) fībula *f.*; (*strap*) fascia *f.*; (*pair*) pār *n.* *vt.* adligāre; (*strengthen*) firmāre.
bracelet *n.* armilla *f.*
bracing *a.* (*air*) salūbris.
bracken *n.* filix *f.*
bracket *n.* uncus *m.*
brackish *a.* amārus.
brad *n.* clāvulus *m.*
bradawl *n.* terebra *f.*
brag *vi.* glōriārī, sē iactāre.
braggart *n.* glōriōsus *m.*
braid *vt.* nectere.
brain *n.* cerebrum *n.*; ingenium *n.*
brainless *a.* sōcors, stultus.
brainy *a.* ingeniōsus.
brake *n.* (*wood*) dūmētum *n.*; (*on wheel*) sufflāmen *n.*
bramble *n.* rubus *m.*
bran *n.* furfur *n.*
branch *n.* rāmus *m.*; (*kind*) genus *n.* *vi.* — out rāmōs porrigere.
branching *a.* rāmōsus.
brand *n.* (*fire*) torris *m.*, fax *f.*; (*mark*) nota *f.*; (*sword*) ēnsis *m.*; (*variety*) genus *n.* *vt.* (*mark*) inūrere; (*stigma*) notāre. — new recēns.
brandish *vt.* vibrare.
brass *n.* orichalcum *n.*
bravado *n.* ferōcitās *f.* out of — per speciem ferōcitātis.
brave *a.* fortis, ācer. *vt.* adire, patī. **-ly** *ad.* fortiter, ācriter.
bravery *n.* fortitūdō *f.*, virtūs *f.*
bravo *interj.* bene, euge, macte.
brawl *n.* rixa *f.*, iūrgium *n.* *vi.* rixārī.
brawn *n.* lacertī *m.pl.*
brawny *a.* lacertōsus, rōbūstus.
bray *vi.* rūdere.
brazen *a.* aēneus; (*fig.*) impudēns.
brazier *n.* foculus *m.*
breach *n.* (*in wall*) ruīna *f.*; (*of friendship*) dissēnsiō *f.* *vt.* perfringere. — of trust mala fidēs. commit a — of promise prōmissīs nōn stāre. — of the peace iūrgium *n.*, tumultus, *m.*
bread *n.* pānis *m.*
breadth *n.* lātitūdō *f.* in — in lātitūdinem (*acc.*).
break *vt.* frangere, perfringere. — down infringere, dirūere. — in (*animal*) domāre. —

in pieces dirumpere. — off abrumpere dēfringere; (*action*) dirimere. — open effringere, solvere. — through interrumpere. — up dissolvere, interrumpere. — one's word fidem fallere, violāre. without -ing the law salvīs lēgibus. *vi.* rumpī, frangī; (*day*) illūcēscere; (*strength*) dēficere. — off dēsinere. — into intrāre — out ērumpere; (*sore*) recrūdēscere; (*trouble*) exārdēscere. — up dīlābī, dissolvī; (*meeting*) dimittī. — through inrumpere. — with dissidēre ab. *n.* intermissiō *f.*, intervallum *n.* day — prīma lūx *f.*, dīlūculum *n.*
breakable *a.* fragilis.
breakage *n.* frāctum *n.*
breakdown *n.* (*activity*) mora *f.*; (*health*) dēbilitās *f.*
breaker *n.* fluctus *m.*
breakfast *n.* ientāculum *n.*, prandium *n.* *vi.* ientāre, prandēre.
breakwater *n.* mōlēs *f.*
bream *n.* sparulus *m.*
breast *n.* pectus *n.*; (*woman's*) mamma *f.* make a clean — of cōnfitērī. **-plate** *n.* lōrīca *f.* **-work** *n.* lōrīca *f.*, pluteus *m.*
breath *n.* spīritus *m.*, anima *f.*; (*bad*) hālitus *m.*; (*quick*) anhēlitus *m.*; (*of wind*) aura *f.*, adflātus *m.* below one's — mussitāns. catch one's — obstipēscere. hold one's — animam comprimere, continēre. take a — spīritum dūcere. take one's — away exanimāre. waste one's — operam perdere. out of — exanimātus.
breathable *a.* spīrābilis.
breathe *vt.* & *i.* spīrāre, respīrāre; (*quickly*) anhēlāre. — again respīrāre. — in spīritum dūcere. — out exspīrāre, exhālāre. — upon īnspīrāre (*dat.*), adflāre (*dat.*). — one's last animam agere, efflāre.
breathing *n.* hālitus *m.*, respīrātiō *f.* **-space** *n.* respīrātiō *f.*
breathless *a.* exanimātus.
breeches *n.* brācae *f.pl.*
breed *n.* genus *n.* *vt.* generāre, prōcreāre; (*raise*) ēducāre, alere; (*fig.*) adferre, efficere. well-bred generōsus.
breeder *n.* (*animal*) mātrix *f.*; (*man*) generātor *m.*; (*fig.*) nūtrīx *f.*
breeding *n.* (*act*) fētūra *f.*; (*manners*) mōrēs *m.pl.* good — hūmānitās *f.*
breeze *n.* aura *f.*, flātus *m.*
breezy *a.* ventōsus; (*manner*) hilaris.
brevity *n.* brevitās *f.*
brew *vt.* coquere. *vi.* (*fig.*) parārī, imminēre
bribe *vt.* corrumpere. *vi.* largīrī. *n.* pecūnia *f.*, mercēs *f.*
briber *n.* corruptor *m.*, largītor *m.* [largītiō *f.*
bribery *n.* ambitus *m.*,
brick *n.* later *m.* *a.* latericius. **-work** *n.* latericium *n.*
bridal *a.* nūptiālis; (*bed*) geniālis. *n.* nūptiae *f.pl.*
bride *n.* nūpta *f.*
bridegroom *m.* marītus *m.*
bridge *n.* pōns *m.* *vt.* pontem impōnere (*dat.*).
bridle *n.* frēnum *n.* *vt.* frēnāre, īnfrēnāre.
brief *a.* brevis. to be — nē longum sit, nē multa. **-ly** *ad.* breviter, paucīs verbīs.
briefness *n.* brevitās *f.*
brier *n.* veprēs *m.*, sentis *m.*
brig *n.* Liburna *f.*
brigade *n.* legiō *f.*; (*cavalry*) turma *f.*
brigadier *n.* lēgātus *m.*
brigand *n.* latrō *m.*, praedō *m.*
brigandage *n.* latrōcinium *n.*
brigantine *n.* Liburna *f.*
bright *a.* clārus, lūculentus; (*sky*) serēnus; (*intellect*) ingeniōsus; (*manner*) hilaris, laetus. be — lūcēre, splendēre. **-ly** *ad.* clārē.

brightness *n.* fulgor *m.*, candor *m.*; (*sky*) serēnitās *f.*
brighten *vt.* illūstrāre; laetificāre. *vi.* lūcēscere; (*person*) hilarem fierī.
brilliance *n.* splendor *m.*, fulgor *m.*; (*style*) nitor *m.*, lūmen *n.*, īnsignia *n.pl.*
brilliant *a.* clārus, illūstris, splendidus; (*fig.*) īnsignis, praeclārus, lūculentus. **–ly** *ad.* splendidē, praeclārē, lūculentē.
brim *m.* lābrum *n.*, margō *f.* fill to the — explēre.
brimstone *n.* sulfur *n.*
brindled *a.* varius.
brine *n.* salsāmentum *n.*
bring *vt.* ferre; (*person*) dūcere; (*charge*) intendere; (*to a place*) adferre, addūcere, advehere, dēferre; (*to a destination*) perdūcere; (*to a worse state*) redigere. — **about** efficere. — **before** dēferre ad, referre ad. — **back** (*thing*) referre; (*person*) redūcere. — **down** dēdūcere, dēferre. — **forth** (*from store*) dēprōmere; (*child*) parere; (*crops*) ferre, ēdere. — **forward** (*for discussion*) iactāre, iacere; (*reason*) adferre. — **home** (*bride*) dēdūcere; (*in triumph*) dēportāre. — **home to** pervincere. — **in** invehere, indūcere, intrōdūcere; (*import*) importāre; (*revenue*) reddere. — **off** (*success*) reportāre. — **on** inferre, importāre; (*stage*) indūcere. — **out** efferre; (*book*) ēdere; (*play*) dare; (*talent*) ēlicere. — **over** perdūcere, trādūcere. — **to bear** adferre. — **to light** nūdāre, dētegere. — **to pass** perficere, peragere. — **to land** (*ship*) appellere, applicāre. — **together** contrahere, cōgere; (*enemies*) conciliāre. — **up** (*child*) ēducāre, tollere; (*troops*) admovēre; (*topic*) prōferre. — **upon oneself** sibī cōnsciscere, sibī contrahere.
brink *n.* ōra *f.*, margō *f.*
briny *a.* salsus.
brisk *a.* alacer, vegetus, ācer. **–ly** *ad.* ācriter.
briskness *n.* alacritās *f.*
bristle *n.* sēta *f.* *vi.* horrēre, horrēscere.
bristly *a.* horridus, hirsūtus.
brittle *a.* fragilis.
broach *vt.* (*topic*) in medium prōferre.
broad *a.* lātus; (*accent*) lātus; (*joke*) inurbānus; (*daylight*) multus. **–ly** *ad.* lātē. **pronounce** — dīlātāre.
broadcast *vt.* dissēmināre.
broaden *vt.* dīlātāre.
broad-sword *n.* gladius *m.*
brocade *n.* Attalica *n.pl.*
brochure *n.* libellus *m.*
brogue *n.* pērō *m.*
broil *n.* rixa *f.*, iūrgium *n.* *vt.* torrēre.
broiling *a.* torridus.
broken *a.* frāctus; (*fig.*) cōnfectus; (*speech*) infrāctus. **be** — **winded** īlia dūcere. — **hearted** dolōre cōnfectus.
broker *n.* institor *m.*
bronze *n.* aes *n.* *a.* aēneus, aerātus.
brooch *n.* fībula *f.*
brood *n.* fētus *m.*; (*fig.*) gēns *f.* *vi.* incubāre (*dat.*); (*fig.*) incubāre (*dat.*), fovēre. — **over** meditārī. [patī.
brook *n.* rīvus *m.* *vt.* ferre,
brooklet *n.* rīvulus *m.*
broom *n.* (*plant*) genista *f.*; (*brush*) scōpae *f.pl.*
broth *n.* iūs *n.*
brother *n.* frāter *m.*; (*full*) germānus *m.* — **and sister** marītus *m.pl.*
brotherhood *n.* frāternitās *f.*
brother-in-law *n.* lēvir *m.*, uxōris frāter *m.*, sorōris marītus *m.*
brotherly *a.* frāternus.
brow *n.* frōns *f.*; (*eye*) supercilium *n.*; (*hill*) dorsum *n.*

browbeat *vt.* obiūrgāre, exagitāre.
brown *a.* fulvus, spādīx; (*skin*) adūstus.
browse *vi.* pāscī, dēpāscī.
bruise *vt.* atterere, frangere, contundere. *n.* vulnus *n.*
bruit *vt.* pervulgāre.
brunt *n.* vīs *f.* **bear the — of** exhaurīre.
brush *n.* pēniculus *m.*; (*artist's*) pēnicillus *m.*; (*quarrel*) rixa *f.* *vt.* verrere, dētergēre; (*teeth*) dēfricāre. **— aside** aspernārī, neglegere. **— up** (*fig.*) excolere.
brushwood *n.* virgulta *n.pl.*; (*for cutting*) sarmenta *n.pl.*
brusque *a.* parum cōmis.
brutal *a.* atrōx, saevus, inhūmānus. **-ly** *ad.* atrōciter, inhūmānē.
brutality *n.* atrōcitās *f.*, saevitia *f.*
brute *n.* bēlua *f.*, bestia *f.*
brutish *a.* stolidus.
bubble *n* bulla *f.* *vi.* bullāre. **— over** effervēscere. **— up** scatēre.
buccaneer *n.* praedō *m.*, pīrāta *m.*
buck *n.* cervus *m.* *vi.* exsultāre.
bucket *n.* situla *f.*, fidēlia *f.*
buckle *n.* fībula *f.* *vt.* fībulā nectere. **— to** accingī.
buckler *n.* parma *f.*
buckram *n.* carbasus *m.*
bucolic *a.* agrestis. **-s** *n.* būcolica *n.pl.*
bud *n.* gemma *f.*, flōsculus *m.* *vi.* gemmāre.
budge *vi.* movērī, cēdere.
budget *n.* pūblicae pecūniae ratiō *f.* *vi.* **— for** prōvidēre (*dat.*).
buff *a.* lūteus.
buffalo *n.* ūrus *m.*
buffet *n.* (*blow*) alapa *f.*; (*fig.*) plāga *f.*; (*sideboard*) abacus *m.* *vt.* iactāre, tundere.
buffoon *n.* scurra *m.*, balatrō *m.*
buffoonery *n.* scurrilitās *f.*
bug *n.* cīmex *m.*
bugbear *n.* terricula *n.pl.*, terror *m.*
bugle *n.* būcina *f.*
bugler *n.* būcinātor *m.*
build *vt.* aedificāre, struere; (*bridge*) facere; (*road*) mūnīre. **— on** (*add*) adstruere; (*hopes*) pōnere. **— up** exstruere; (*to block*) inaedificāre; (*knowledge*) īnstruere. **— on sand** in aquā fundāmenta pōnere. **— castles in the air** spem inānem pāscere.
build *n.* statūra *f.*
builder *n.* aedificātor *m.*, structor *m.*
building *n.* (*act*) aedificātiō *f.*; (*structure*) aedificium *n.*
bulb *n.* bulbus *m.*
bulge *vi.* tumēre, tumēscere, prōminēre. *vi.* tuberculum *n.*; (*of land*) locus prōminēns *m.*
bulk *n* māgnitūdō *f.*, amplitūdō *f.*; (*mass*) mōlēs *f.*; (*most*) plērīque, māior pars.
bulky *a.* amplus, grandis.
bull *n.* taurus *m.* **-'s** taurīnus. **take the — by the horns rem** fortiter adgredī.
bulldog *n.* Molossus *m.*
bullet *n.* glāns *f.*
bulletin *n.* libellus *m.*
bullion *n.* aurum īnfectum *n.*, argentum īnfectum *n.*
bullock *n.* iuvencus *m.*
bully *n.* obiūrgātor *m.* patruus *m.* *vt.* obiūrgāre, exagitāre.
bulrush *n.* scirpus *m.*
bulwark *n.* prōpugnāculum *n.*; (*fig.*) arx *f.*
bump *n.* (*swelling*) tuber *n.*, tuberculum *n.*; (*knock*) ictus *m.* *vi.* **— against** offendere.
bumper *n.* plēnum pōculum *n.* *a.* plēnus, māximus.
bumpkin *n.* rūsticus *m.*
bumptious *a* adrogāns.
bunch *n.* fasciculus *m.*; (*of berries*) racēmus *m.*
bundle *n.* fascis *m.*; (*of hay*) manipulus *m.* *vt.* obligāre.

bung *n.* obtūrāmentum *n.* *vt.* obtūrāre.
bungle *vt.* male gerere.
bunk *n.* lectus *m.*, lectulus *m.*
buoy *n.* cortex *m.* *vt.* sublevāre.
buoyancy *n.* levitās *f.*
buoyant *a.* levis; (*fig.*) hilaris.
bur *n.* lappa *f.*
burden *n.* onus *n.* beast of — iūmentum *n.* *vt.* onerāre.
burdensome *a.* gravis, molestus.
bureau *n.* scrīnium *n.*
burgeon *vi.* gemmāre.
burgess, burgher *n.* mūniceps *m.*
burgh *n.* mūnicipium *n.*
burglar *n.* fūr *m.*
burglary *n.* fūrtum *n.*
burial *n.* fūnus *n.*, humātiō *f.*, sepultūra *f.*
burin *n.* caelum *n.*
burlesque *n.* imitātiō *f.* *vt.* per iocum imitārī.
burly *a.* crassus.
burn *vt.* incendere, ūrere; (*to ashes*) cremāre. *vi.* ārdēre, flagrāre. — up ambūrere, combūrere, exūrere. be -ed down dēflagrāre. — out *vi.* exstinguī. — the midnight oil lūcubrāre. *n.* (*med.*) ambūstum *n.*
burning *a.* igneus.
burnish *vt.* polīre.
burrow *n.* cuniculus *m.* *vi.* dēfodere.
burst *vt.* rumpere, dīrumpere. *vi.* rumpī dīrumpī. — in inrumpere. — into tears in lacrimās effundī. — out ērumpere, prōrumpere. — out laughing cachinnum tollere. — through perrumpere per (*acc.*). — upon offerrī (*dat.*), invādere. *n.* ēruptiō *f.*; (*noise*) fragor *m.* — of applause clāmōrēs *m.pl.* with a — of speed citātō gradū, citātō equō.
bury *vt.* sepelīre, humāre; (*ceremony*) efferre; (*hiding*) condere; (*things*) dēfodere; (*fig.*) obruere. — the hatchet amīcitiam reconciliāre.
bush *n.* frutex *m.*, dūmus *m.* beat about the — circuitiōne ūtī.
bushel *n.* medimnus *m.*
bushy *a.* fruticōsus; (*thick*) dēnsus; (*hair*) hirsūtus.
business *n.* negōtium *n.*; (*occupation*) ars *f.*, quaestus *m.*; (*public life*) forum *n.*; (*matter*) rēs *f.* it is your — tuum est. make it one's — to id agere ut. you have no — to nōn tē decet (*inf.*). mind one's own — suum negōtium agere. — days diēs fāstī *m.pl.* — man negōtiātor *m.*
buskin *n.* cothurnus *m.*
bust *n.* imāgō *f.*
bustle *vi.* trepidāre, festīnāre. — about discurrere.
bus/y *a.* negōtiōsus, occupātus; (*active*) operōsus, impiger, strēnuus. keep — *vt.* exercēre. — oneself with pertractāre, studēre (*dat.*). **-ily** *ad.* strēnuē, impigrē.
busybody *n.* be a — aliēnīs negōtiīs sē immiscēre.
but *conj.* sed, at; (*2nd place*) autem, tamen. *ad.* modo. *pr.* praeter (*acc.*). nothing — nihil nisī. — that, — what quīn. not — what nihilōminus.
butcher *n.* lanius *m.* *vt.* trucīdāre. **-'s shop** *n.* laniēna *f.* [occīdiō *f.*
butchery *n.* strāgēs *f.*,
butler *n.* prōmus *m.*
butt *n.* (*cask*) cadus *m.*; (*of ridicule*) lūdibrium *n.* *vi.* arietāre. — in interpellāre.
butter *n.* būtyrum *n.*
butterfly *n.* pāpiliō *m.*
buttock *n.* clūnis *m.*, *f.*
button *n.* bulla *f.*
buttonhole *vt.* (*fig.*) dētinēre, prēnsāre. [*vt.* fulcīre.
buttress *n.* antērides *f.pl.*

buxom *a.* nitidus.
buy *vt.* emere. — **back** redimere. — **off** redimere. — **up** coemere. — **provisions** obsōnāre.
buyer *n.* emptor *m.*; (*at auctions*) manceps *m.*
buzz *n.* strīdor *m.*, susurrus *m.* *vi.* strīdere. susurrāre.
buzzard *n.* būteō *m.*
by *pr.* (*near*) ad (*acc.*), apud (*acc.*); (*along*) secundum (*acc.*); (*past*) praeter (*acc.*). (*agent*) ā, ab (*abl.*); (*instrument*) *abl.*; (*time*) ante (*acc.*); (*oath*) per (*acc.*). *ad.* prope iuxtā. — **and** — mox. **be** — adesse, adstāre.
bygone *a.* praeteritus.
bypath, byway *n.* dēverticulum *n.*, trāmes *m.*, sēmita *f.*
bystander *n.* arbiter *m.*; (*pl.*) circumstantēs *m.pl.*
byword *n.* prōverbium *n.*

C

cabal *n.* factiō *f.*
cabbage *n.* brassica *f.*, caulis *m.* [cubiculum *n.*
cabin *n.* casa *f.*; (*ship*)
cabinet *n.* armārium *n.*
cable *n.* fūnis *m.*; (*anchor*) ancorāle *n.*
cache *n.* thēsaurus *m.*
cachet *n.* nota *f.*
cackle *vi.* strepere. *n.* strepitus *m.* clangor *m.*
cacophonous *a.* dissonus.
cacophony *n.* vōcēs dissonae *f.pl.*
cadaverous *a.* cadāverōsus.
cadence *n.* clausula numerōsa *f.*, numerus *m.*
cadet *n.* (*son*) nātū minor; (*mil.*) contubernālis *m.*
cage *n.* cavea *f.* *vt.* inclūdere.
caitiff *n.* ignāvus *m.*
cajole *vt.* blandīrī, dēlēnīre.
cajolery *n.* blanditiae *f.pl.*
cake *n.* placenta *f.*
calamitous *a.* exitiōsus, calamitōsus.
calamity *n.* calamitās *f.*, malum *n.*; (*mil.*) clādēs *f.*
calculate *vt.* ratiōnem dūcere, inīre.
calculation *n.* ratiō *f.*
calculator *n.* ratiōcinātor *m.*
calendar *n.* fāstī *m.pl.*
calends *n.* Kalendae *f.pl.*
calf *n* (*animal*) vitulus *m.*, vitula *f.*; (*leg*) sūra *f.*
calibre *n.* (*fig.*) ingenium *n.*, auctōritās *f.*
call *vt.* vocāre; (*name*) appellāre. nōmināre; (*aloud*) clāmāre; (*to a place*) advocāre, convocāre. — **aside** sēvocāre. — **down** (*curse*) dētestārī. — **for** postulāre, requīrere. — **forth** ēvocāre, excīre, ēlicere. — **in** advocāre. — **on** (*for help*) implōrāre; (*visit*) salūtāre. — **off** āvocāre. revocāre. — **out** exclāmāre. — **up** (*dead*) excitāre, ēlicere; (*mil.*) ēvocāre. *n.* vōx *f.*, clāmor *m.*; (*summons*) invītātiō *f.*; (*visit*) salūtātiō *f.*
caller *n.* salūtātor *m.*
calling *n.* ars *f.*, quaestus *m.*
callous *a.* dūrus. **become** — obdūrēscere.
callow *a.* rudis.
calm *a.* tranquillus, placidus; (*mind*) aequus. *vi.* — **down** (*fig.*) dēfervēscere. *vt.* sēdāre, tranquillāre. *n.* tranquillitās *f.* **dead** — (*at sea*) malacia *f.* **-ly** *ad.* tranquillē, placidē; aequō animō.
calumniate *vt.* obtrectāre, crīminārī; (*falsely*) calumniārī.
calumniator *n.* obtrectātor *m.*
calumnious *a.* crīminōsus.
calumny *n.* opprobria *n.pl.*, obtrectātiō *f.*
calve *vi.* parere.
cambric *n.* linteum *n.*
camel *n.* camēlus *m.*
camouflage *n.* dissimulātiō *f.* *vt.* dissimulāre.

camp *n.* castra *n.pl.* summer — aestiva *n.pl.* winter — hiberna *n.pl.* in — sub pellibus. pitch — castra pōnere. strike — castra movēre. *a.* castrēnsis. *vi.* tendere.
camp-bed *n.* grabātus *m.*
camp-followers *n.* lixae *m.pl.*
campaign *n.* stipendium *n.*, bellum *n.*; (*rapid*) expeditiō *f.* *vi.* bellum gerere, stipendium merēre.
campaigner *n.* miles *m.* old — veterānus *m.*; (*fig.*). veterātor *m.*
can *n.* hirnea *f.*
can *vi.* posse; (*know how*) scire. -not nōn posse, nequire. I -not but facere nōn possum quin (*subj.*), nōn possum nōn (*inf.*).
canaille *n.* vulgus *n.*, plebs *f.*
canal *n.* fossa nāvigābilis *f.*, euripus *m.*
cancel *vt.* indūcere, abrogāre.
cancellation *n.* (*writing*) litūra *f.*; (*law*) abrogātiō *f.*
cancer *n.* cancer *m.*; (*fig.*) carcinōma *n.*, ulcus *n.*
cancerous *a.* (*fig.*) ulcerōsus.
candelabrum *n.* candēlābrum *n.*
candid *a.* ingenuus, apertus, liber, simplex. **-ly** *ad.* ingenuē.
candidate *n.* petitor *m.* be a — for petere.
candidature *n.* petitiō *f.*
candle *n.* candēla *f.* **-stick** *n.* candēlābrum *n.*
candour *n.* ingenuitās *f.*, simplicitās *f.*, lībertās *f.*
cane *n.* (*reed*) harundō *f.*; (*for walking, punishing*) virga *f.* *vt.* verberāre.
canine *a.* canīnus.
canister *n.* capsula *f.*
canker *n.* (*plants*) rōbīgō *f.*; (*fig.*) aerūgō *f.*, carcinōma *n.* *vt.* corrumpere. [*m.*
cannibal *n.* anthrōpophagus
cannon *n.* tormentum *n.*
canny *a.* prūdens, prōvdus, cautus, circumspectus.
canoe *n.* linter *f.*
canon *n.* nōrma *f.*, rēgula *f.*; (*eccl.*) canonicus *m.*
canopy *n.* aulaeum *n.*
cant *n.* fūcus *m.*, fūcāta verba *n.pl.* *vt.* obliquāre. [tūnus.
cantankerous *a.* impor-
cantankerousness *n.* importūnitās *f.*
canter *n.* lēnis cursus *m.* *vi.* lēniter currere.
canticle *n.* canticum *n.*
canto *n.* carmen *n.*
canton *n.* pāgus *m.*
canvas *n.* carbasus *m.*, linteum *n.* *a.* carbaseus. under — sub pellibus.
canvass *vi.* ambire; *vt.* prēnsāre, circumire.
canvassing *n.* ambitus *m.*, ambitiō *f.*
cap *n.* pilleus *m.*; (*priest's*) galērus *m.*, apex *m.*
capability *n.* facultās *f.*, potestās *f.*
capab/le *a.* capāx, doctus, peritus. **-ly** *ad.* bene, doctē.
capacious *a.* capāx, amplus.
capacity *n.* capācitās *f.*, amplitūdō *f.*; (*mind*) ingenium.
caparison *n.* ephippium *n.*
cape *n.* (*geog.*) prōmunturium *n.*; (*dress*) chlamys *f.*
caper *vi.* saltāre; (*animal*) lascivire. *n.* saltus *m.* **-ing** *n.* lascivia *f.*
capercailzie *n.* tetraō *m.*
capital *a.* (*chief*) praecipuus, princeps; (*excellent*) ēgregius; (*law*) capitālis. convict of a — offence capitis damnāre. *n.* (*town*) caput *n.*, (*money*) sors *f.*; (*class*) negōtiātorēs *m.pl.* make — out of ūti.
capitalist *n.* faenerātor *m.*
capitation tax *n.* capitum exāctiō *f.*
capitulate *vi.* sē dēdere. troops who have -d dēditicii *m.pl.*

capitulation *n.* dēditiō *f.*
capon *n.* capō *m.*
caprice *n.* libīdō *f.*, incōnstantia *f.*
capricious *a.* incōnstāns, levis. **-ly** *ad.* incōnstanter, leviter.
capriciousness *n.* incōnstantia *f.*, libīdō *f.*
capsize *vt.* ēvertere. *vi.* ēvertī.
captain *m.* dux *m.*, praefectus *m.*, princeps *m.*; (*mil.*) centuriō *m.*; (*naval*) nāvarchus *m.*; (*of merchant ship*) magister *m.* *vt.* praeesse (*dat.*), dūcere.
captaincy *n.* centuriātus *m.*
caption *n.* caput *n.*
captious *a.* mōrōsus; (*question*) captiōsus. **-ly** *ad.* mōrōsē.
captiousness *n.* mōrōsitās *f.*
captivate *vt.* capere, dēlēnīre, adlicere.
captive *n.* captīvus *m.*
captivity *n.* captīvitās *f.*, vincula *n.pl.*
captor *n.* (*by storm*) expugnātor *m.*; victor *m.*
capture *n.* (*by storm*) expugnātiō *f.* *vt.* capere.
car *n.* currus *m.*
caravan *n.* commeātus *m.* [*n.*
caravanserai *n.* dēversōrium
carbuncle *n.* (*med.*) fūrunculus *m.*; (*stone*) acaustus *m.*
carcass *n.* cadāver *n.*
card *n.* charta *f.*; (*ticket*) tessera *f.*; (*wool*) pecten *n.* *vt.* pectere.
cardamom *n.* amōmum *n.*
cardinal *a.* praecipuus. — point cardō *m.* *n.* (*eccl.*) cardinālis.
care *n.* cūra *f.*; (*anxiety*) sollicitūdō *f.*; (*attention*) dīligentia *f.*; (*charge*) custōdia *f.* take — cavēre. take — of cūrāre. *vi.* cūrāre. — for (*look after*) cūrāre; (*like*) amāre. I don't — nīl moror. I don't — a straw for floccī nōn faciō, pendō. I don't — about mittō, nihil moror. for all I — per mē.
career *n.* curriculum *n.*; (*pol.*) cursus honōrum; (*completed*) rēs gestae *f.pl.* *vi.* ruere, volāre.
carefree *a.* sēcūrus.
careful *a.* (*cautious*) cautus; (*attentive*) dīligēns, attentus; (*work*) accūrātus. **-ly** *ad.* cautē; dīligenter, attentē; accūrātē.
careless *a.* incautus, neglegēns. **-ly** *ad.* incautē, neglegenter.
carelessness *n.* incūria *f.*, neglegentia *f.*
caress *vt.* fovēre, blandīrī. *n.* blandīmentum *n.*, amplexus *m.*
cargo *n.* onus *n.*
caricature *n.* (*picture*) gryllus *m.*; (*fig.*) imāgō dētorta *f.* *vt.* dētorquēre.
carking *a.* molestus, gravis.
carmine *n.* coccum *n.* *a.* coccineus.
carnage *n.* strāgēs *f.*, caedēs *f.*
carnal *a.* corporeus; (*pleasure*) libīdinōsus.
carnival *n.* fēriae *f.pl.*
carol *n.* carmen *n.* *vi.* cantāre.
carouse *vi.* perpōtāre, cōmissārī. *n.* cōmissātiō *f.*
carp *vi.* obtrectāre. — at carpere, rōdere. [lignārius *m.*
carpenter *n.* faber *m.*,
carpet *n.* tapēte *n.*
carriage *n.* (*conveying*) vectūra *f.*; (*vehicle*) vehiculum *n.*; (*for journeys*) raeda *f.*, petorritum *n.*; (*for town*) carpentum *n.*, pīlentum *n.*; (*deportment*) gestus *m.*, incessus *m.* — and pair bīgae *f.pl.* — and four quadrīgae *f.pl.*
carrier *n.* vector *m.*; (*porter*) bāiulus *m.* letter — tabellārius *m.*
carrion *n.* cadāver *n.*
carrot *n.* carōta *f.*
carry *vt.* portāre, vehere, ferre, gerere; (*law*) perferre; (*by

assault) expugnāre. — away auferre, āvehere; (*by force*) rapere; (*with emotion*) efferre. — all before one ēvincere. — along (*building*) dūcere. — back revehere, referre. — down dēportāre, dēvehere. — in invehere, intrōferre. — off auferre, asportāre, āvehere; (*by force*) abripere, ēripere; (*prize*) ferre, reportāre; (*success*) bene gerere. — on gerere; (*profession*) exercēre. — out efferre, ēgerere, ēvehere; (*task*) exsequī. — over trānsportāre, trānsferre. — the day vincere. — one's point pervincere. — through perferre. — to adferre, advehere. — up subvehere. *vi.* (*sound*) audīrī. — on pergere; (*flirt*) lascīvīre.

cart *n.* plaustrum *n.* put the — before the horse praeposterum dīcere. *vt.* plaustrō vehere.

cart-horse *n.* iūmentum *n.*

carve *vt.* sculpere; (*on surface*) caelāre; (*meat*) secāre. — out exsculpere.

carver *n.* caelātor *m.*

carving *n.* caelātūra *f.*

cascade *n.* cataracta *m.*

case *n.* (*instance*) exemplum *n.*, rēs *f.*; (*legal*) āctiō *f.*, līs *f.* causa *f.*; (*plight*) tempus *n.*; (*gram.*) cāsus *m.*; (*receptacle*) thēca *f.*, involucrum *n.* in — sī; (*to prevent*) nē. in any — utut est rēs. in that — ergō. such is the — sīc sē rēs habet. civil — causa prīvāta. criminal — causa pūblica. win a — causam, lītem obtinēre. lose a — causam, lītem āmittere.

casement *n.* fenestra *f.*

cash *n.* nummī *m.pl.*; (*ready*) numerātum *n.*, praesēns pecūnia *f.* pay — ex arcā absolvere, repraesentāre. — payment repraesentātiō *f.* — box arca *f.*

cashier *n.* dispēnsātor *m.* *vt.* (*mil.*) exauctōrāre.

cask *n.* cūpa *f.*

casket *n.* arcula *f.*, pyxis *f.*

casque *n.* galea *f.*, cassis *f.*

cast *vt.* iacere; (*account*) inīre; (*eyes*) conicere; (*lots*) conicere; (*covering*) exuere; (*metal*) fundere. — ashore ēicere. — away prōicere. — down dēicere; (*humble*) abicere. — in one's teeth exprobrāre. — lots sortīrī. — off abicere, exuere. — out prōicere, ēicere, pellere. *n.* iactus *m.*; (*mould-ing*) typus *m.*, fōrma *f.* with a — in the eye paetus.

castanet *n.* crotalum *n.*

castaway *n.* ēiectus *m.*

caste *n.* ōrdō *m.*

castellated *a.* turrītus.

castigate *vt.* animadvertere, castigāre. [*f.*, castīgātiō *f.*

castigation *n.* animadversiō

castle *n.* arx *f.*, castellum *n.*

castrate *vt.* castrāre.

casual *a.* fortuītus; (*person*) neglegēns. **-ly** *ad.* temerē.

casualty *n.* infortūnium *n.*; (*pl.*) occīsī *m.pl.*

casuist *n.* sophistēs *m.*

cat *n.* fēlēs *f.*

catachresis *n.* abūsiō *f.*

cataclysm *n.* dīluvium *n.*, ruīna *f.*

catalogue *n.* index *m.*

catapult *n.* catapulta *f.*, ballista *f.*

cataract *n.* cataracta *f.*

catarrh *n.* gravēdō *f.* liable to — gravēdinōsus.

catastrophe *n.* calamitās *f.*, ruīna *f.* [exitiōsus.

catastrophic *a.* calamitōsus,

catch *vt.* capere, dēprehendere, excipere; (*disease*) contrahere, nancīscī; (*fire*) concipere, comprehendere; (*meaning*) intellegere. — at captāre. — out dēprehendere. — up with adsequī. — birds aucupārī. — fish piscārī. *n.* bolus *m.*

categorical *a.* (*statement*) plānus. **-ly** *ad.* sine exceptiōne.

category *n.* numerus *m.*, [genus *n.*

cater *vi.* obsōnāre.

cateran *n.* praedātor *m.*

caterer *n.* obsōnātor *m.*

caterpillar *m.* ērūca *f.*

caterwaul *vi.* ululāre.

catgut *n.* chorda *f.*

catharsis *n.* pūrgātiō *f.*

cathedral *n.* aedēs *f.*

catholic *a.* generālis.

catkin *n.* iūlus *m.*

cattle *n* (*collectively*) pecus *n.*; (*singly*) pecus *f.*; (*for plough*) armenta *n.pl.* — **breeder** *n.* pecuārius *m.* — **thief** *n.* abāctor *m.*

cauldron *n.* cortīna *f.*

cause *n.* causa *f.*; (*person*) auctor *m.*; (*law*) causa *f.*; (*party*) partēs *f.pl.* **give — for** māteriam dare (*gen.*). **make common — with** facere cum, stāre ab. **plead a —** causam dīcere. **in the — of** prō (*abl.*). **without —** iniūriā. *vt.* efficere, facere, facessere (*with* ut); cūrāre (*with gerundive*); (*feelings*) movēre, inicere, ciēre.

causeless *a.* vānus, sine causā.

causeway *n.* agger *m.*

caustic *a.* (*fig.*) mordāx.

cauterize *vt.* adūrere.

caution *n.* (*wariness*) cautiō *f.*, prūdentia *f.*; (*warning*) monitum *n.* *vt.* monēre, admonēre.

cautious *a.* cautus, prōvidus, prūdens. **-ly** *ad.* cautē, prūdenter.

cavalcade *n.* pompa *f.*

cavalier *n.* eques *m.* *a.* adrogāns. **-ly** *ad.* adroganter.

cavalry *n.* equitēs *m.pl.*, equitātus *m.* *a.* equester. **— man** eques *m.* **troop of —** turma *f.*

cave *n.* spēlunca *f.*, caverna *f.* **— in** *vi.* concidere, conlābī. [*f.*

cavern *n.* spēlunca *f.*, caverna

cavil *vi.* cavillārī. **— at** carpere, cavillārī. *n.* captiō *f.*, cavillātiō *f.*

cavity *n.* caverna *f.*, cavum *n.*

cavort *vi.* saltāre.

caw *vi.* cornīcārī.

cease *vi.* dēsinere, dēsistere.

ceaseless *a.* adsiduus, perpetuus. **-ly** *ad.* adsiduē, perpetuō.

cedar *n.* cedrus *f.* *a.* cedrinus.

cede *vt.* cēdere, concēdere.

ceiling *n.* tēctum *n.*; (*panelled*) lacūnar *n.*, laqueārium *n.*

celebrate *vt.* (*rite*) celebrāre, agitāre; (*in crowds*) frequentāre; (*person, theme*) laudāre, celebrāre, dīcere. **-d** *a.* praeclārus, illūstris, nōtus. **the —** ille.

celebration *n.* celebrātiō *f.*; (*rite*) sollemne *n.*

celebrity *n.* celebritās *f.*, fāma *f.*; (*person*) vir illūstris.

celerity *n.* celeritās *f.*, vēlōcitās *f.*

celery *n.* apium *n.*

celestial *a.* caelestis; dīvīnus.

celibacy *n.* caelibātus *m.*

celibate *n.* caelebs *m.*

cell *n.* cella *f.*

cellar *n.* cella *f.*

cellarer *n.* prōmus *m.*

cement *n.* ferrūmen *n.* *vt.* coagmentāre.

cemetery *n.* sepulchrētum *n.*

cenotaph *n.* tumulus honōrārius, tumulus inānis *m.* [*f.*

censer *n.* tūribulum *n.*, acerra

censor *n.* cēnsor *m.* *vt.* cēnsēre. [obtrectātor.

censorious *a.* cēnsōrius,

censorship *n.* cēnsūra *f.*

censure *n.* reprehēnsiō *f.*, animadversiō *f.*, (*censor's*) nota *f.* *vt.* reprehendere, animadvertere, increpāre; notāre.

census *n.* cēnsus *m.*

cent *n.* **one per —** centēsima *f.* **12 per —** per annum centēsima *f.* (*i.e. monthly*).

centaur *n.* centaurus *m.*

centaury *n.* (*plant*) centaurēum *n.*
centenarian *n.* centum annōs nātus *m.*, nāta *f.* [annus *m.*
centenary *n.* centēsimus
centesimal *a.* centēsimus.
centipede *n.* centipeda *f.*
central *a.* medius.
centralize *vt.* in ūnum locum cōnferre; (*power*) ad ūnum dēferre.
centre *n.* centrum *n.*, media pars *f.* **the — of** medius.
centuple *a.* centuplex.
centurion *n.* centuriō *m.*
century *n.* (*mil.*) centuria *f.*; (*time*) saeculum *n.*
ceramic *a.* fictilis.
cereal *n.* frūmentum *n.*
ceremonial *a.* sollemnis. *n.* rītus *m.*
ceremonious *a.* (*rite*) sollemnis; (*person*) officiōsus. **-ly** *ad.* sollemniter; officiōsē.
ceremon/y *n.* caerimōnia *f.*, rītus *m.*; (*politeness*) officium *n.*; (*pomp*) apparātus *m.* **master of -ies** dēsignātor *m.*
cerise *n.* coccum *n.* *a.* coccineus.
certain *a.* (*sure*) certus; (*future*) explōrātus; (*indef.*) quīdam. **be —** (*know*) prō certō scīre. **-ly** *ad.* certē, certō, sine dubiō; (*yes*) ita, māximē; (*concessive*) quidem.
certainty *n.* (*thing*) certum *n.*, (*belief*) fidēs *f.* **for a —** prō certō explōrātē. **regard as a —** prō explōrātō habēre.
certificate *n.* testimōnium *n.*
certify *vt.* (*writing*) recognōscere; (*fact*) adfirmāre, testificārī.
cerulean *a.* caeruleus.
cessation *n.* fīnis *m.*; (*from labour*) quiēs *f.*; (*temporary*) intermissiō *f.*; (*of hostilities*) indutiae *f.pl.*
chafe *vt.* ūrere; (*fig.*) inrītāre. *vi.* stomachārī.
chaff *n.* palea *f.* *vt.* lūdere.
chaffinch *n.* fringilla *f.*
chagrin *n.* dolor *m.*, stomachus *m.* *vt.* stomachum facere (*dat.*), sollicitāre.
chain *n.* catēna *f.*; (*for neck*) torquis *m.*; (*sequence*) seriēs *f.* (*pl.*) vincula *n.pl.* *vt.* vincīre.
chair *n.* sella *f.*; (*of office*) sella curūlis *f.*; (*sedan*) sella gestātōria *f.*, lectīca *f.*; (*teacher's*) cathedra *f.*
chairman *n.* (*at meeting*) magister *m.*; (*of debate*) disceptātor *m.*
chalet *n.* cāsa *f.*
chalice *n.* calix *m.*
chalk *n.* crēta *f.*
chalky *a.* crētōsus.
challenge *n.* prōvocātiō *f.* *vt.* prōvocāre, lacessere; (*statement*) in dubium vocāre; (*fig.*) invītāre, dēposcere.
challenger *n.* prōvocātor *m.*
chamber *n.* conclāve *n.*; (*bed*) cubiculum *n.*; (*bridal*) thalamus *m.*; (*parliament*) cūria *f.*
chamberlain *n.* cubiculārius *m.*
chambermaid *m.* serva *f.*, [ancilla *f.*
chameleon *n.* chamaeleōn *f.*
chamois *n.* rūpicapra *f.*
champ *vt.* mandere.
champaign *n.* ager *m.*
champion *n.* prōpugnātor *m.* patrōnus *m.*; (*winner*) victor *m.* *vt.* favēre (*dat.*), adesse (*dat.*).
chance *n.* fors *f.*, fortūna *f.*, cāsus *m.*; (*opportunity*) occāsiō *f.*; (*prospect*) spēs *f.* **game of —** ālea f. **by —** cāsū, fortuītō. **have an eye to the main —** forō ūtī. **on the — of** sī forte. *a.* fortuītus. *vi.* accidere, ēvenīre. **— upon** incidere in, invenīre. *vt.* perīclitārī.
chancel *n.* absis *f.*
chancellor *n.* cancellārius *m.*
chancy *a.* dubius, perīculōsus.
chandelier *n.* candēlābrum *n.*
chandler *n.* candēlārum propōla *m.*

change *n.* mūtātiō *f.*, commūtātiō *f.*, permūtātiō *f.*; (*pol.*) rēs novae *f.pl.*; (*alternation*) vicēs *f.pl.*, vicissitūdō *f.*; (*money*) nummī minōrēs *m.pl.* *vt.* mūtāre, commūtāre, permūtāre. *vi.* mūtārī. — **hands** abaliēnarī. — **places** ōrdinem permūtāre, inter sē loca permūtare. [mūtābilis.
changeable *a.* incōnstāns,
changeableness *n.* incōnstantia *f.*, mūtābilitās *f.*
changeful *a.* varius.
changeless *a.* cōnstāns, immūtābilis.
changeling *a.* subditus *m.*
channel *n.* canālis *m.*; (*sea*) fretum *n.*; (*irrigation*) rīvus *m.*; (*groove*) sulcus *m.*
chant *vt.* cantāre, canere. *n* cantus *m.* [turbātiō *f.*
chaos *n.* chaos *n.*; (*fig.*) per-
chaotic *a.* perturbātus.
chap *n.* rīma *f.*; (*man*) homō *m.*
chapel *n.* sacellum *n.*, aedicula *f.*
chaplain *n.* diāconus *m.*
chaplet *n.* corōna *f.*, sertum *n.*
chapman *n.* caupō *m.*
chapter *n.* caput *n.*
chaps *n.* (*animal*) mālae *f.pl.*
char *vt.* ambūrere.
character *n.* (*inborn*) indolēs *f.*, ingenium *n.*, nātūra *f.*; (*moral*) mōrēs *m.pl.*; (*reputation*) existimātiō *f.*; (*kind*) genus *n.*; (*mark*) signum *n.*, littera *f.*; (*theat.*) persōna *f.*, partēs *f.pl.* **sustain a** — persōnam gerere. **I know his** — sciō quālis sit.
characteristic *a.* proprius. *n.* proprium *n.* **-ally** *ad.* suō mōre.
characterize *vt.* dēscrībere; proprium esse (*gen.*).
charcoal *n.* carbō *m.*
charge *n.* (*law*) accūsātiō *f* crīmen *n.*; (*mil.*) impetus *m.*, dēcursus *m.*; (*cost*) impēnsa *f.*; (*task*) mandātum *n.*, onus *n.*; (*trust*) cūra *f.*, tūtēla *f.* **bring a — against** lītem intendere (*dat.*). **entertain a — against** nōmen recipere (*gen.*). **give in** — in custōdiam trādere. **put in — of** praeficere (*dat.*). **be in — of** praesse (*dat.*). *vt.* (*law*) accūsāre, (*falsely*) īnsimulāre; (*mil.*) incurrere in (*acc.*), signa īnferre in (*acc.*); (*duty*) mandāre; (*cost*) ferre, īnferre; (*empty space*) complēre; (*trust*) committere; (*speech*) hortārī. — **to the account of** expēnsum ferre (*dat.*).
chargeable *a.* obnoxius.
charger *n.* (*dish*) lānx *f.*; (*horse*) equus *m.*
chariot *n.* currus *m.*; (*races*) quadrigae *f. pl.*; (*war*) essedum *n.*
charioteer *n.* auriga *m.*; (*war*) essedārius *m.*
charitab/le *a.* benevolus, benignus. **-ly** *ad.* benevolē, benignē.
charity *n.* amor *m.*, benignitās *f.*; līberālitās *f.*
charlatan *n.* planus *m.*
charm *n.* (*spell*) carmen *n.*; (*amulet*) bulla *f.*; (*fig.*) blanditiae *f.pl.*, dulcēdō *f.*, illecebra *f.*; (*beauty*) venus *f.*, lepōs *m.* *vt.* (*magic*) fascināre; (*delight*) dēlectāre, dēlēnīre.
charming *a.* venustus, lepidus; (*speech*) blandus; (*scenery*) amoenus. **-ly** *ad.* venustē, blandē.
chart *n.* tabula *f.*
charter *n.* diplōma *n.* *vt.* condūcere.
char/y *a.* (*cautious*) cautus; (*sparing*) parcus. **-ily** *ad.* cautē, parcē.
chase *vt.* (*hunt*) vēnārī; (*pursue*) īnsequī; (*engrave*) caelāre. — **away** pellere, abigere. *n.* vēnātus *m.*, vēnātiō *f.*; (*pursuit*) īnsectātiō *f.*
chaser *n.* (*in metal*) caelātor *m.*
chasm *n.* hiātus *m.*

chaste *a.* castus, pudīcus; (*style*) pūrus.
chasten *vt.* castīgāre, corrigere.
chastener *n.* castīgātor *m.*, corrēctor *m.*
chastise *vt.* castīgāre, animadvertere.
chastisement *n.* castīgātiō *f.*, poena *f.*
chastity *n.* castitās *f.*, pudīcitia *f.*
chat *vi.* colloquī, sermōcinārī. *n.* sermō *m.*, colloquium *n.*
chatelaine *n.* domina *f.*
chattels *n.* bona *n.pl.*, rēs mancipī.
chatter *vi.* garrīre; (*teeth*) crepitāre. *n.* garrulitās *f.* loquācitās *f.* **—box** *n.* lingulāca *m.*, *f.*
chatterer *n.* garrulus *m.*, loquāx *m*
chattering *a.* garrulus, loquāx. *n.* garrulitās *f.*, loquācitās *f.*; (*teeth*) crepitus *m.*
cheap *a.* vīlis. hold — parvī aestimāre. buy — bene emere. **-ly** *ad.* vīliter, parvō pretiō.
cheapen *vt.* pretium minuere (*gen.*).
cheapness *n.* vīlitās *f.*
cheat *vt.* dēcipere, fraudāre, dēfraudāre, frustrārī. *n.* fraudātor *m.*
check *vt.* cohibēre, coercēre; (*movement*) impedīre, inhibēre; (*rebuke*) reprehendere; (*test*) probāre. *n.* impedīmentum *n.*, mora *f.*; (*mil.*) offēnsiō *f.*; (*rebuke*) reprehēnsiō *f.*; (*test*) probātiō *f.*; (*ticket*) tessera *f.*
checkmate *n.* incitae calcēs *f.pl.* *vt.* ad incitās redigere.
cheek *n.* gena *f.*, (*pl.*) mālae *f.pl.*; (*impudence*) ōs *n.* how have you the — to say ? quō ōre dīcis ? — **bone** *n.* maxilla *f.*
cheeky *a.* impudēns.
cheep *vi.* pīpilāre.
cheer *vt.* hilarāre, exhilarāre; hortārī; (*in sorrow*) cōnsōlārī. *vi.* clāmāre, adclāmāre. — **up** ! bonō animō es ! *n.* (*shout*) clāmor *m.*, plausus *m.*; (*food*) hospitium *n.*; (*mind*) animus *m.*
cheerful *a.* alacer, hilaris, laetus. **-ly** *ad.* hilare, laetē.
cheerfulness *n.* hilaritās *f.*
cheerless *a.* tristis, maestus. **-ly** *ad.* triste.
cheer/y *a.* hilaris. **-ily** *ad.* hilare.
cheese *n.* cāseus *m.*
chef *n.* coquus *m.*
cheque *n.* perscrīptiō *f.*, syngrapha *f.*
chequer *vt.* variāre. **-ed** *a.* varius; (*mosaic*) tessellātus.
cherish *vt.* fovēre, colere.
cherry *n.* (*fruit*) cerasum *n.*; (*tree*) cerasus *f.*
chess *n.* latrunculī *m.pl.* — board *n.* abacus *m.*
chest *n.* (*box*) arca *f.*, arcula *f.*; (*body*) pectus *n.* — **of drawers** armārium *n.*
chestnut *n.* castanea *f.* *a.* (*colour*) spādīx.
chevalier *n.* eques *m.*
chevaux-de-frise *n.* ēricius *m.*
chew *vt.* mandere.
chic *a.* expolītus, concinnus.
chicanery *n.* (*law*) calumnia *f.*; (*fig.*) dolus *m.*
chick *n.* pullus *m.*
chicken *n.* pullus *m.* don't count your —s before they're hatched adhūc tua messis in herbā est. — **hearted** *a.* timidus, ignāvus.
chick-pea *n.* cicer *n.*
chide *vt.* reprehendere, increpāre, obiūrgāre.
chief *n.* prīnceps *m.*, dux *m.* *a.* praecipuus, prīmus. — **point** caput *n.* **-ly** *ad.* in prīmīs praesertim, potissimum.
chieftain *n.* prīnceps *m.*, rēgulus *m.*
chiffonier *n.* abacus *m.*
chilblain *n.* perniō *m.*
child *n.* īnfāns *m.*, *f.*; puer *m.*, puerulus *m.*, puella *f.*; fīlius *m.*, fīlia *f.*; (*pl.*) līberī *m.pl.*

-bed *n.* puerperium *n.* **-birth** *n.* partus *m.* **-'s play** lūdus *m.*
childhood *n.* pueritia *f.* from — ā puerō.
childish *a.* puerīlis. **-ly** *ad.* puerīliter.
childless *a.* orbus.
childlessness *n.* orbitās *f.*
childlike *a.* puerīlis.
chill *n.* frigus *n.* *a.* frigidus. *vt.* refrīgerāre.
chilly *a.* frīgidus, frīgidior.
chime *vi.* sonāre, canere. — in interpellāre; (*fig.*) cōnsonāre. *n.* sonus *m.*
chimera *n.* chimaera *f.*; (*fig.*) somnium *n.*
chimerical *a.* commentīcius.
chimney *n.* camīnus *m.*
chin *n.* mentum *n.*
china *n.* fictilia *n.pl.*
chine *n.* spīna *f.*; (*beef*) tergum *n.*
chink *n.* rīma *f.*; (*sound*) tinnītus *m.* *vi.* crepāre, tinnīre.
chip *n.* assula *f.*, fragmentum *n.* *vt.* dolāre.
chirp *vi.* pīpilare.
chirpy *a.* hilaris.
chisel *n.* scalprum *n.*, scalpellum *n.* *vt.* sculpere.
chit *n.* (*child*) pūsiō *m.*, puerulus *m.*
chit-chat *n.* sermunculī *m. pl.*
chitterlings *n.* hillae *f.pl.*
chivalrous *a.* generōsus.
chivalry *n.* virtūs *f.*; (*men*) iuventūs *f.*; (*class*) equitēs *m.pl.*
chive *n.* caepe *n.* [refertus.
chock *n.* cuneus *m.* **-full** *a.*
choice *n.* dēlēctus *m.*, ēlēctiō *f.*; (*of alternatives*) optiō *f.* *a.* lēctus, eximius, exquīsītus.
choiceness *n.* ēlegantia *f.*, praestantia *f.*
choir *n.* chorus *m.*
choke *vt.* suffocāre; (*emotion*) reprimere (*passage*) obstruere.
choler *n.* bīlis *f.*; (*anger*) īra *f.*, stomachus *m.*
choleric *a.* īrācundus.
choose *vt.* legere, ēligere, dēligere; (*alternative*) optāre; (*for office*) dēsignāre; (*with inf.*) velle, mālle.
chop *vt.* concīdere. — off praecīdere. *n.* (*meat*) offa *f.*
chopper *n.* secūris *f.*
choppy *a.* (*sea*) asper.
choral *a.* symphōniacus.
chord *n.* (*string*) nervus *m.*, chorda *f.*
chortle *vi.* cachinnāre.
chorus *n.* (*singers*) chorus *m.*; (*song*) concentus *m.*, symphōnia *f.* in — unā vōce.
christen *vt.* baptizāre.
Christian *a.* Christiānus.
Christianity *n.* Christiānismus *m.*
chronic *a.* inveterātus. become — inveterāscere.
chronicle *n.* annālēs *m.pl.*, ācta pūblica *n.pl.* *vt.* in annālēs referre. [scrīptor *m.*
chronicler *n.* annālium
chronological *a.* in — order servātō temporum ōrdine. make a — error temporibus errāre.
chronology *n.* temporum ratiō *f.*, temporum ōrdō *m.* [*n.*
chronometer *n.* hōrologium
chubby *a.* pinguis.
chuck *vt.* conicere. — out extrūdere.
chuckle *vi.* rīdēre. *n.* rīsus *m.*
chum *n.* sodālis *m.*
church *n.* ecclēsia *f.*
churl *n.* rūsticus *m.*
churlish *a.* difficilis, importūnus; avārus. **-ly** *ad.* rūsticē, avārē.
churlishness *n.* mōrōsitās *f.*, avāritia *f.*
chute *n.* (*motion*) lāpsus *m* (*place*) dēclīve *n.*
cicada *n.* cicāda *f.*
cicatrice *n.* cicātrīx *f.*
cincture *n.* cingulum *n.*
cinder *n.* cinis *m.*
cipher *n.* numerus *m.*, nihil *n.*;

(*code*) notae *f.pl.* in — per notās.
circle *n.* orbis *m.*, circulus *m.*, gȳrus *m.* form a — in orbem cōnsistere. *vi.* sē circumagere, circumīre.
circlet *n.* infula *f.*
circuit *n.* ambitus *m.*, circuitus *m.*; (*assizes*) conventus *m.*
circuitous *a.* longus. a — route circuitus *m.*, (*speech*) ambāgēs *f.pl.*
circular *a.* rotundus.
circulate *vt.* (*news*) pervulgāre. *vi.* circumagi; (*news*) circumferri, percrēbrēscere.
circulation *n.* ambitus *m.* be in — in manibus esse. go out of — obsolēscere.
circumcise *vt.* circumcīdere.
circumference *n.* ambitus *m.*
circumlocution *n.* ambāgēs *f.pl.*, circuitiō *f.*
circumnavigate *vt.* circumvehī.
circumscribe *vt.* circumscrībere; (*restrict*) coercēre, fīnīre.
circumspect *a.* cautus, prūdēns. **-ly** *ad.* cautē, prūdenter.
circumspection *n.* cautiō *f.*, prūdentia *f.*, circumspectiō *f.*
circumstance *n.* rēs *f.* -s rērum status *m.*; (*wealth*) rēs *f.* as -s arise ē rē nātā. under the -s cum haec ita sint, essent. under no —s nēquāquam.
circumstantial *a.* adventīcius; (*detailed*) accūrātus. — evidence coniectūra *f.* **-ly** *ad.* accūrātē, subtīliter.
circumvallation *n.* circummūnītiō *f.*
circumvent *vt.* circumvenīre, fallere.
circus *n.* circus *m.*
cistern *n.* lacus *m.*, cisterna *f.*
citadel *n.* arx *f.*
citation *n.* (*law*) vocātiō *f.*; (*mention*) commemorātiō *f.*
cite *vt.* in iūs vocāre; (*quote*) commemorāre, prōferre.
cithern *n.* cithara *f.*
citizen *n.* cīvis *m.*, *f.*; (*of provincial town*) mūniceps *m.* fellow — cīvis *m.*, *f.* Roman -s Quirītes *m.pl.* *a.* cīvīlis, cīvicus.
citizenship *n.* cīvitās *f.* deprived of — capite dēminūtus. loss of — capitis dēminūtiō *f.*
citron *n.* (*fruit*) citrum *n.*; (*tree*) citrus *f.*
city *n.* urbs *f.*, oppidum *n.*
civic *a.* cīvīlis, cīvicus.
civil *a.* (*of citizens*) cīvīlis; (*war*) cīvīlis, intestīnus, domesticus; (*manners*) urbānus, cōmis, officiōsus; (*law-suit*) prīvātus.
civilian *n.* togātus *m.*
civility *n.* urbānitās *f.*, cōmitās *f.*; (*act*) officium *n.*
civilization *n.* exculta hominum vīta *f.*, cultus atque hūmānitās.
civilize *vt.* excolere, expolīre, ad hūmānum cultum dēdūcere.
clad *a.* vestītus.
claim *vt.* (*for oneself*) adrogāre, adserere; (*something due*) poscere, postulāre, vindicāre; (*at law*) petere; (*statement*) adfirmāre. *n.* postulātiō *f.*, postulātum *n.*; (*at law*) petītiō *f.*, vindiciae *f.pl.*
claimant *n.* petītor *m.*
clam *n.* chāma *f.*
clamber *vi.* scandere.
clammy *a.* ūmidus, lentus.
clamorous *a.* vōciferāns.
clamour *n.* strepitus *m.*, clāmōrēs *m.pl.* *vi.* — against obstrepere (*dat.*).
clamp *n.* cōnfībula *f.*
clan *n.* gēns *f.* **-sman** *n.* gentīlis *m.*
clandestine *a.* fūrtīvus. **-ly** *ad.* clam, fūrtim.
clang *n.* clangor *m.*, crepitus *m.* *vi.* increpāre.
clangour *n.* clangor *m.*
clank *n.* crepitus *m.* *vi.* crepitāre.

clap *vi.* plaudere, applaudere. — eyes on cōnspicere. — in prison in vincula conicere. *n.* plausus *m.*; (*thunder*) fragor *m.*
clapper *n.* plausor *m.*
claptrap *n.* iactātiō *f.*
claque *n.* plausōrēs *m.pl.*, operae *f.pl.*
clarify *vt.* pūrgāre; (*knowledge*) illūstrāre. *vi.* liquēre.
clarinet *n.* tībia *f.*
clarion *n.* lituus *m.*, cornū *n.*
clarity *n.* perspicuitās *f.*
clash *n.* concursus *m.*; (*sound*) strepitus *m.*, crepitus *m.*; (*fig.*) discrepantia *f.* *vi.* concurrere; (*sound*) increpāre; (*fig.*) discrepāre. *vt.* cōnflīgere.
clasp *n.* fībula *f.*; (*embrace*) amplexus *m.* *vt.* implicāre; amplectī, complectī. — together interiungere.
class *n.* (*pol.*) ōrdō *m.*, classis *f.*; (*kind*) genus *n.*; (*school*) classis *f.* *vt.* dēscrībere. — as in numerō (*gen. pl.*) referre, repōnere, habēre.
classic *n.* scrīptor classicus *m.*; (*pl.*) scrīptōrēs Graecī et Rōmānī.
classical *a.* classicus. — literature litterae Graecae et Rōmānae.
classify *vt.* dēscrībere, in ōrdinem redigere.
class-mate *n.* condiscipulus [*m.*
clatter *n.* crepitus *m.* *vi.* increpāre.
clause *n.* (*gram.*) incīsum *n.*, membrum *n.*; (*law*) caput *n.*; (*will*) ēlogium *n.* in short -s incīsim.
claw *n.* unguis *m.*, ungula *f.* *vt.* (unguibus) lacerāre.
clay *n.* argilla *f.* made of — fictilis.
clayey *a.* argillāceus.
claymore *n.* gladius *m.*
clean *a.* mundus; (*fig.*) pūrus, castus. — slate novae tabulae *f.pl.* make a — sweep of omnia tollere. show a — pair of heels sē in pedēs conicere. my hands are — innocēns sum. *ad.* prōrsus, tōtus. *vt.* pūrgāre.
cleanliness *n.* munditia *f.*
cleanly *a.* mundus, nitidus. *ad.* mundē, pūrē.
cleanse *vt.* pūrgāre, abluere dētergēre.
clear *a.* clārus; (*liquid*) limpidus; (*space*) apertus, pūrus; (*sound*) clārus; (*weather*) serēnus; (*fact*) manifestus, perspicuus; (*language*) illūstris dīlūcidus; (*conscience*) rēctus, innocēns. it is — liquet. — of līber (*abl.*) expers (*gen.*). be — about rēctē intellegere. keep — of ēvitāre. the coast is — arbitrī absunt. *vt.* (*of obstacles*) expedīre, pūrgāre; (*of a charge*) absolvere; (*self*) pūrgāre; (*profit*) lucrārī. — away āmovēre, tollere. — off (*debt*) solvere, exsolvere. — out ēluere, dētergēre. — up (*difficulty*) illūstrāre, ēnōdāre, explicāre. *vi.* — off facessere. — up (*weather*) disserēnāscere.
clearance *n.* pūrgātiō *f.*; (*space*) intervallum *n.*
clearing *n.* (*in forest*) lūcus *m.*
clearly *ad.* clārē; manifestē, apertē, perspicuē; (*with clause*) vidēlicet.
clearness *n.* clāritās *f.*; (*weather*) serēnitās *f.*; (*mind*) acūmen *n.*; (*style*) perspicuitās *f.*
clear-sighted *a.* sagāx, [perspicāx.
cleavage *n.* discidium *n.*
cleave *vt.* (*cut*) findere, discindere. *vi.* (*cling*) — to haerēre (*dat.*), adhaerēre (*dat.*).
cleaver *n.* dolabra *f.*
cleft *n.* rīma *f.*, hiātus *m.* *a.* fissus, discissus.
clemency *n.* clēmentia *f.*, indulgentia *f.* with — clēmenter.
clement *a.* clēmēns, misericors. [cors.
clench *vt.* (*nail*) retundere; (*hand*) comprimere.

clerk *n.* scrība *m.*; (*of court*) lēctor *m.*
clever *a.* callidus, ingeniōsus doctus, astūtus. **-ly** *ad.* doctē, callidē, ingeniōsē.
cleverness *n.* calliditās *f.*, sollertia *f.*
clew *n.* glomus *n.*
cliché *n.* verbum trītum *n.*
client *n.* cliēns *m.*, *f.*; (*lawyer's*) cōnsultor *m.* body of **-s** clientēla *f.*
clientship *n.* clientēla *f.*
cliff *n.* rūpēs *f.*, scopulus *m.*
climate *n.* caelum *n.*
climax *n.* (*rhet.*) gradātiō *f.*; (*fig.*) culmen *n.*
climb *vt.* & *i.* scandere, ascendere. — down dēscendere. *n.* ascēnsus *m.*
climber *n.* scandēns *m.*
clime *n.* caelum *n.*, plāga *f.*
clinch *vt.* cōnfirmāre.
cling *vi.* adhaerēre. —together cohaerēre.
clink *vi.* tinnīre. *n.* tinnītus *m.*
clip *vt.* tondēre; praecīdere.
clippers *n.* forfex *f.*
clique *n.* factiō *f.*
cloak *n.* (*rain*) lacerna *f.*; (*travel*) paenula *f.*; (*mil.*) sagum *n.*; (*Greek*) pallium *n.*; (*fig.*) involūcrum *n.*; (*pretext*) speciēs *f.* *vt.* tegere, dissimulāre.
clock *n.* hōrologium *n.*; (*sun*) sōlārium *n.*; (*water*) clepsydra *f.* ten o' — quarta hōra.
clockwise *ad.* dextrōvorsum, dextrōrsum.
clod *n.* glaeba *f.*
clog *n.* (*shoe*) sculpōnea *f.*; (*fig.*) impedīmentum *n.* *vt.* impedīre.
cloister *n.* porticus *f.* **-ed** *a.* (*fig.*) umbrātilis.
close *a.* (*shut*) clausus; (*tight*) artus; (*narrow*) angustus; (*near*) propinquus; (*compact*) refertus, dēnsus; (*stingy*) parcus; (*secret*) obscūrus; (*weather*) crassus. — together dēnsus, refertus. at — quarters comminus. be — at hand īnstāre. keep — to adhaerēre. — to prope (*acc.*), iuxtā (*acc.*). *ad.* prope iuxtā. *n.* angiportus *m.*
close *vt.* claudere, operīre; (*finish*) perficere, fīnīre, conclūdere, termināre; (*ranks*) dēnsāre. *vi.* claudī; conclūdī, terminārī; (*time*) exīre; (*wound*) coīre; (*speech*) perōrāre. — with (*fight*) manum cōnserere, signa cōnferre; (*deal*) pacīscī; (*offer*) accipere. *n.* fīnis *m.* terminus *m.*; (*action*) exitus *m.*; (*sentence*) conclūsiō *f.* at the — of summer aestāte exeunte.
close fisted *a.* tenāx.
closely *ad.* prope; (*attending*) attentē; (*associating*) coniūnctē. follow — īnstāre (*dat.*).
closeness *n.* propinquitās *f.*; (*weather*) gravitās *f.*, crassitūdō *f.*; (*with money*) parsimōnia *f.*; (*friends*) coniūnctiō *f.*; (*manner*) cautiō *f.* [*vt.* inclūdere.
closet *n.* cubiculum *n.*, cella *f.*
clot *n.* (*blood*) concrētus sanguis *m.* *vi.* concrēscere.
cloth *n.* textile *n.*; (*piece*) pannus *m.*; (*linen*) linteum *n.*; (*covering*) strāgulum *n.*
clothe *vt.* vestīre.
clothes *n.* vestis *f.*, vestītus *m.*, vestīmenta *n.pl.* bed — strāgula *n.pl.*
clothier *n.* vestiārius *m.*
clothing *n.* vestis *f.*, vestītus *m.*, vestīmenta *n.pl.*
clotted *a.* concrētus.
cloud *n.* nūbēs *f.*; (*storm*) nimbus *m.*; (*dust*) globus *m.*; (*disfavour*) invidia *f.* *vt.* nūbibus obdūcere; (*fig.*) obscūrāre. **-ed** *a.* obnūbilus.
cloudiness *n.* nūbilum *n.*
cloudless *a.* pūrus, serēnus.
cloudy *a.* obnūbilus.
clout *n.* pannus *m.*
clover *n.* trifolium *n.*
cloven *a.* (*hoof*) bifidus.
clown *n.* (*boor*) rūsticus *m.*; (*comic*) scurra *m.*

clownish *a.* rūsticus, inurbānus.
clownishness *n.* rūsticitās *f.*
cloy *vt.* satiāre. **-ing** *a.* pūtidus.
club *n.* (*stick*) fustis *m.*, clāva *f.*; (*society*) sodālitās *f.* *vi.* — together in commūne cōnsulere, pecūniās cōnferre.
club-footed *a.* scaurus.
cluck *vi.* singultīre. *n.* singultus *m.*
clue *n.* indicium *n.*, vestigium *n.*
clump *n.* massa *f.*; (*earth*) glaeba *f.*; (*trees*) arbustum *n.*; (*willows*) salictum *n.*
clumsiness *n.* inscītia *f.*
clums/y *a.* (*person*) inconcinnus, ineptus; (*thing*) inhabilis; (*work*) inconditus. **-ily** *ad.* ineptē, inēleganter; inconditē, infabrē.
cluster *n.* cumulus *m.*; (*grapes*) racēmus *m.*; (*people*) corōna *f.* *vi.* congregārī.
clutch *vt.* prehendere, adripere. — at captāre *n.* comprehēnsiō *f.* from one's -es ē manibus. in one's -es in potestāte.
clutter *n.* turba *f.* *vt.* impedīre, obstruere.
coach *n.* currus *m.*, raeda *f.*, pīlentum *n.*; (*trainer*) magister *m.* *vt.* ēdocēre, praecipere (*dat.*). [raedārius *m.*
coachman *n.* auriga *m.*,
coadjutor *n.* adiūtor *m.*
coagulate *vt.* cōgere. *vi.* concrēscere.
coagulation *n.* concrētiō *f.*
coal *n.* carbō *m.* carry -s to Newcastle in silvam ligna ferre.
coalesce *vi.* coīre, coalēscere.
coalition *n.* coitiō *f.*, cōnspīrātiō *f.*
coarse *a.* (*quality*) crassus; (*manners*) rūsticus, inurbānus; (*speech*) infacētus. **-ly** *ad.* inurbānē, inēleganter.
coarseness *n.* crassitūdō *f.*; rūsticitās *f.*
coast *n.* lītus *n.*, ōra *f.* *vi.* — along legere, praetervehī.
coastal *a.* lītorālis, maritimus.
coastline *n.* lītus *n.*
coat *n.* pallium *n.*; (*animals*) pellis *f.* great — abolla *f.* *vt.* indūcere, inlinere.
coating *n.* corium *n.*
coax *vt.* blandīrī, dēlēnīre.
coaxing *a.* blandus. *n.* blanditiae *f.pl.*
cob *n.* (*horse*) mannus *m.*; (*swan*) cygnus *m.*
cobble *n.* lapis *m.* *vt.* sarcīre.
cobbler *n.* sūtor *m.*
cobweb *n.* arāneum *n.*
cock *n.* gallus *m.*, gallus gallīnāceus *m.*; (*other birds*) mās *m.*; (*tap*) epitonium *n.*; (*hay*) acervus *m.* — crow gallī cantus *m.* *vt.* ērigere.
cockatrice *n.* basiliscus *m.*
cockchafer *n.* scarabaeus *m.*
cockerel *n.* pullus *m.*
cockroach *m.* blatta *f.*
cocksure *a.* cōnfīdēns.
cod *n.* callarias *m.*
coddle *vt.* indulgēre (*dat.*), permulcēre. [notae *f.pl.*
code *n.* fōrmula *f.*; (*secret*)
codicil *n.* cōdicillī *m.pl.*
codify *vt.* in ōrdinem redigere.
coequal *a.* aequālis.
coerce *vt.* cōgere.
coercion *n.* vīs *f.*
coeval *a.* aequālis.
coffer *n.* arca *f.*, cista *f.*; (*public*) fiscus *m.*
coffin *n.* arca *f.*
cog *n.* dēns *m.*
cogency *n.* vīs *f.*, pondus *n.*
cogent *a.* gravis, validus.
cogitate *vi.* cōgitāre, meditārī.
cogitation *n.* cōgitātiō *f.*, meditātiō *f.*
cognate *a.* cognātus.
cognition *n.* cognitiō *f.*
cognizance *n.* cognitiō *f.* take — of cognōscere.
cognizant *a.* gnārus.

cohabit *vi.* cōnsuēscere.
cohabitation *n.* cōnsuētūdō *f.*
coheir *n.* cohērēs *m., f.*
cohere *vi.* cohaerēre; (*statement*) congruere.
coherence *n.* coniūnctiō *f.*; (*fig.*) convenientia *f.*
coherent *a.* congruēns.
cohesion *n.* coagmentātiō *f.*
cohesive *a.* tenāx.
cohort *n.* cohors *f.*
coif *n.* calautica *f.*
coign *n.* angulus *m.*
coil *n.* spīra *f.* *vt.* glomerāre.
coin *n.* nummus *m.* *vt.* cūdere; (*fig.*) fingere.
coinage *n.* monēta *f.*; (*fig.*) fictum *n.*
coincide *vi.* concurrere; (*opinion*) cōnsentīre.
coincidence *n.* concursus *m.*; cōnsēnsus *m.* by a — cāsū.
coincidental *a.* fortuītus.
coiner *n.* (*of money*) signātor [*m.*
col *n.* iugum *n.*
colander *n.* cōlum *n.*
cold *a.* frīgidus; (*icy*) gelidus. very — perfrīgidus. be, feel — algēre, frīgēre. get — algēscere, frīgēscere. *n.* frīgus *n.*; (*felt*) algor *m.*; (*malady*) gravēdō *f.* catch — algēscere, frīgus colligere. catch a — gravēdinem contrahere. have a — gravēdine labōrāre.
coldish *a.* frīgidulus, frīgidior.
coldly *ad.* (*manner*) sine studiō.
coldness *n.* frīgus *n.*, algor *m.*
colic *n.* tormina *n.pl.*
collar *n.* collāre *n.*
collarbone *n.* iugulum *n.*
collate *vt.* cōnferre, comparāre.
collateral *a.* adiūnctus; (*evidence*) cōnsentāneus.
collation *n.* collātiō *f.*; (*meal*) prandium *n.*, merenda *f.*
colleague *n.* collēga *m.*
collect *vt.* colligere, cōgere, congerere; (*persons*) congregāre, convocāre; (*taxes*) exigere; (*something due*) recipere. — oneself animum colligere. cool and -ed aequō animō. *vi.* convenīre, congregārī.
collection *n.* (*persons*) coetus *m.*, conventus *m.*; (*things*) congeriēs *f.* (*money*) exāctiō *f.*
collective *a.* commūnis. **-ly** *ad.* commūniter. [*m.*
collector *m.* (*of taxes*) exāctor
college *n.* collēgium *n.*
collide *vi.* concurrere, cōnflīctārī.
collier *m.* carbōnārius *m.*
collision *n.* concursus *m.*
collocation *n.* collocātiō *f.*
collop *n.* offa *f.*
colloquial *a.* cottīdiānus.
colloquy *n.* sermō *m.*, colloquium *n.*
collude *vi.* praevāricārī.
collusion *n.* praevāricātiō *f.*
collusive *a.* praevāricātor.
colonel *n.* lēgātus.
colonial *a.* colōnicus. *n.* colōnus *m.*
colonist *n.* colōnus *m.*
colonization *n.* dēductiō *f.*
colonize *vt.* colōniam dēdūcere, cōnstituere in (*acc.*).
colonnade *n.* porticus *f.*
colony *n.* colōnia *f.*
colossal *a.* ingēns, vastus.
colossus *n.* colossus *m.*
colour *n.* color *m.*; (*paint*) pigmentum *n.*; (*artificial*) fūcus *m.*; (*complexion*) color *m.*; (*pretext*) speciēs *f.* take on a — colōrem dūcere. under — of per speciem (*gen.*). local — māteria dē regiōne sūmpta. — sergeant signifer *m.* *vt.* colōrāre; (*dye*) īnficere, fūcāre; (*fig.*) praetendere (*dat.*). *vi.* rubēre, ērubēscere.
colourable *a.* speciōsus.
coloured *a.* (*naturally*) colōrātus; (*artificially*) fūcātus.
colourful *a.* fūcōsus, varius.
colouring *n.* pigmentum *n.*; (*dye*) fūcus *m.*
colourless *a.* perlūcidus; (*person*) pallidus; (*fig.*) īnsulsus.
colours *n.* (*mil.*) signum *n.*,

vexillum *n.*; (*pol.*) partēs *f.pl.* sail under false — aliēnō nōmine ūtī. with flying — māximā cum gloriā.
colt *n.* equuleus *m.*, equulus *m.*
coltsfoot *n.* farfarus *m.*
column *n.* columna *f.*; (*mil.*) agmen *n.*
coma *n.* sopor *m.*
comb *n.* pecten *m.*; (*bird*) crista *f.*; (*loom*) pecten *m.*; (*honey*) favus *m.* *vt.* pectere.
combat *n.* pugna *f.*, proelium *n.*, certāmen *n.* *vi.* pugnāre, dimicāre, certāre. *vt.* pugnāre cum (*abl.*), obsistere (*dat.*).
combatant *n.* pugnātor *m.* *a.* pugnāns. non — imbellis.
combative *a.* ferōx, pugnāx.
combination *n.* coniūnctiō *f.*, cōnfūsiō *f.*; (*persons*) cōnspirātiō *f.*; (*illegal*) coniūrātiō *f.*
combine *vt.* coniungere, iungere. *vi.* coīre, coniungī. *n.* societās *f.*
combustible *a.* ignī obnoxius.
combustion *n.* dēflāgrātiō *f.*, incendium *n.*
com/e *vi.* venīre, advenīre; (*after a journey*) dēvenīre; (*interj.*) age! how -s it that . . .? quī fit ut . . .? — across invenīre, offendere. — after sequī, excipere, succēdere (*dat.*). — again revenīre, redīre. — away abscēdere; (*when pulled*) sequī. — back revenīre, redīre. — between intervenīre, intercēdere. — down dēvenīre, dēscendere; (*from the past*) trādī, prōdī. — forward prōcēdere, prōdīre. — from (*origin*) dēfluere. — in inīre, introīre; (*revenue*) redīre. — near accēdere ad (*acc.*), appropinquāre (*dat.*). — nearer and nearer adventāre. — of (*family*) ortum esse ab, ex (*abl.*). — off ēvādere, discēdere. — on prōcēdere; (*progress*) prōficere; (*interj.*) age, agite. — on the scene intervenīre, supervenīre, adesse. — out exīre, ēgredī; (*hair, teeth*) cadere; (*flower*) flōrēscere; (*book*) ēdī; — over trānsīre; (*feeling*) subīre, occupāre. — to advenīre ad, in (*acc.*); (*person*) adīre; (*amount*) efficere. — to nought ad nihilum recidere. — to pass ēvenīre, fierī. — together convenīre, coīre. — up subīre, succēdere; (*growth*) prōvenīre. — upon invenīre. he is -ing to animus eī redit.
comedian *n.* (*actor*) cōmoedus *m.*; (*writer*) cōmicus *m.*
comedienne *n.* mīma *f.*
comedy *n.* cōmoedia *f.*
comeliness *n.* decor *m.*, decōrum *n.*
comely *a.* decōrus, pulcher.
comestibles *n.* vīctus *m.*
comet *n.* comētēs *m.*
comfort *vt.* sōlārī, cōnsōlārī, adlevāre. *n.* sōlācium *n.*, cōnsōlātiō *f.*; (*pl.*) commoda *n.pl.*
comfortab/le *a.* commodus. make oneself — corpus cūrāre. **-ly** *ad.* commodē.
comforter *n.* cōnsōlātor *m.*
comfortless *a.* incommodus. be — sōlātiō carēre.
comic *a.* cōmicus; facētus. *n.* scurra *m.*
comical *a.* facētus, rīdiculus.
coming *a.* futūrus. *n.* adventus *m.*
comity *n.* cōmitās *f.*
command *vt.* iubēre, imperāre (*dat.*); (*be in* —) praeesse (*dat.*), dūcere; (*feelings*) regere; (*resources*) fruī (*abl.*); (*view*) prōspectāre. *n.* (*mil.*) imperium *n.*; (*sphere*) prōvincia *f.*; (*order*) imperium *n.*, iussum *n.*, mandātum *n.* be in — of praeesse (*dat.*). put in — of praeficere (*dat.*). — of language fācundia *f.*
commandant *n.* praefectus *m.*

commandeer *vt.* pūblicāre.
commander *n.* dux *m.*, praefectus *m.* — in chief imperātor *m.*
commandment *n.* mandātum *n.*
commemorate *vt.* celebrāre, memoriae trādere.
commemoration *n.* celebrātiō *f.*
commence *vt.* incipere, exōrdīrī, initium facere (*gen.*).
commencement *n.* initium *n.*, exōrdium *n.*, prīncipium *n.*
commend *vt.* laudāre; (*recommend*) commendāre, (*entrust*) mandāre. — oneself sē probāre.
commendable *a.* laudābilis, probābilis.
commendation *n.* laus *f.*, commendātiō *f.*
commendatory *a.* commendātīcius.
commensurable *a.* pār.
commensurate *a.* congruēns, conveniēns.
comment *vi.* dīcere, scrībere. — on interpretārī; (*with notes*) adnotāre. *n.* dictum *n.*, sententia *f.* [*m.pl.*
commentary *n.* commentāriī
commentator *n.* interpres *m.*
commerce *n.* mercātūra *f.*, commercium *n.* engage in — mercātūrās facere, negōtiārī.
commercial *a.* — dealings commercium *n.* — traveller īnstitor *m.*
commination *n.* minae *f.pl.*
comminatory *a.* minājx.
commingle *vt.* intermiscēre.
commiserate *vi.* miserērī (*gen.*).
commiseration *n.* misericordia *f.*; (*rhet.*) commiserātiō *f.*
commissariat *n.* rēs frūmentāria *f.*, commeātus *m.*; (*staff*) frūmentāriī *m.pl.*
commissary *n.* lēgātus *m.*; reī frūmentāriae praefectus *m.*
commission *n.* (*charge*) mandātum *n.*; (*persons*) triumvirī *m.pl.*, decemvirī *m.pl.*, etc.; (*abroad*) lēgātiō *f.* get a — (*mil.*) tribūnum fierī. standing — (*law*) quaestiō perpetua *f.* *vt.* mandāre, adlēgāre.
commissioner *n.* lēgātus *m.* three -s triumvirī *m.pl.* ten -s decemvirī *m.pl.*
commit *vt.* (*charge*) committere, mandāre; (*crime*) admittere; (*to prison*) conicere; (*to an undertaking*) obligāre, obstringere. — to memory memoriae trādere. — to writing litterīs mandāre. — an error errāre. — a theft fūrtum facere.
commitment *n.* mūnus *n.*, officium *n.*
committee *n.* dēlēctī *m.pl.*
commodious *a.* capāx.
commodity *n.* merx *f.*, rēs *f.*
commodore *n.* praefectus classis *m.*
common *a.* (*for all*) commūnis; (*ordinary*) vulgāris, cottīdiānus; (*repeated*) frequēns, crēber; (*inferior*) nēquam. — law mōs māiōrum *m.* — man homō plēbēius *m.* — people plēbs *f.*, vulgus *n.* — sense prūdentia *f.* — soldier gregārius mīles *m.* *n.* compāscuus ager *m.*, prātum *n.*
commonalty *n.* plēbs *f.* [*m.*
commoner *n.* homō plēbēius
commonly *ad.* ferē, vulgō.
commonplace *n.* trītum prōverbium *n.*; (*rhet.*) locus commūnis *m.* *a.* vulgāris, trītus. [diāria *n.pl.*
commons *n.* plēbs *f.*; (*food*)
commonwealth *n* cīvitās *f.*, rēs pūblica *f.*
commotion *n.* perturbātiō *f.*, tumultus *m.* cause a — tumultuārī.
communal *a.* commūnis.
commune *n.* pāgus *m.* *vi.* colloquī, sermōnēs cōnferre.

communicate *vt.* commūnicāre; (*information*) nūntiāre patefacere. *vi.* — **with** commūnicāre (*dat.*), commercium habēre (*gen.*), agere cum (*abl.*).
communication *n.* (*dealings*); commercium *n.* (*information*) litterae *f.pl.*, nūntius *m.*; (*passage*) commeātus *m.* **cut off the -s of** interclūdere.
communicative *a.* loquāx.
communion *n.* societās *f.*
communiqué *n.* litterae *f.pl.* praedicātiō *f.*
communism *n.* bonōrum aequātiō *f.*
community *n.* cīvitās *f.*, commūne *n.*; (*participation*) commūniō *f.*
commutation *n.* mūtātiō *f.*
commute *vt.* mūtāre, commūtāre.
compact *n.* foedus *n.*, conventum *n.* *a.* dēnsus. *vt.* dēnsāre.
companion *n.* socius *m.*, comes *m.*, *f.*; (*intimate*) sodālis *m.*; (*at school*) condiscipulus *m.*; (*in army*) commīlitō *m.*, contubernālis *m.*
companionable *a.* facilis, commodus.
companionship *n.* sodālitās *f.*, cōnsuētūdō *f.*; (*mil.*) contubernium *n.*
company *n.* societās *f.*, cōnsuētūdō *f.*; (*gathering*) coetus *m.*, conventus *m.*; (*guests*) cēnantēs *m.pl.*; (*commercial*) societās *f.*; (*magistrates*) collēgium *n.*; (*mil.*) manipulus *m.*; (*theat.*) grex *m.*, caterva *f.* — **of ten** decuria *f.*
comparable *a.* comparābilis, similis.
comparative *a.* māgnus, sī cum aliīs cōnfertur. **-ly** *ad.* ut in tālī tempore, ut in eā regiōne, ut est captus hominum. — **few** perpaucī, nūllus ferē.
compare *vt.* comparāre, cōnferre. **-d with** ad (*acc.*).
comparison *n.* comparātiō *f.*, collātiō *f.*; (*rhet.*) similitūdō *f.* **in — with** prō (*abl.*).
compartment *n.* cella *f.*, pars *f.*
compass *n.* ambitus *m.*, spatium *n.*, modus *m.* **pair of -es** circinus *m.* *vt.* circumdare, cingere; (*attain*) cōnsequī.
compassion *n.* misericordia *f.*
compassionate *a.* misericors, clēmēns. **-ly** *ad.* clēmenter.
compatibility *n.* convenientia *f.*
compatib/le *a.* congruēns, conveniēns. **be —** congruere. **-ly** *ad* congruenter, convenienter.
compatriot *n.* cīvis *m.*, populāris *m.*
compeer *n.* pār *m.* aequālis [*m.*
compel *vt.* cōgere.
compendious *a.* brevis. **-ly** *ad.* summātim.
compendium *n.* epitomē *f.*
compensate *vt.* compēnsāre, satisfacere (*dat.*).
compensation *n.* compēnsātiō *f.*; pretium *n.*, poena *f.*
compete *vi.* certāre, contendere.
competence *n.* facultās *f.*; (*law*) iūs *n.*; (*money*) quod sufficit.
competent *a.* peritus, satis doctus, capāx; (*witness*) locuplēs. **it is —** licet.
competition *n.* certāmen *n.*, contentiō *f.*
competitor *n.* competitor *m.*, aemulus *m.*
compilation *n.* collectānea *n.pl.*, liber *m.*
compile *vt.* compōnere.
compiler *n.* scrīptor *m.*
complacency *n.* amor suī *m.*
complacent *a.* suī contentus.
complain *vi.* querī, conquerī. — **of** (*person*) nōmen dēferre (*gen.*).

complainant *n.* accūsātor *m.*, petītor *m.*
complaint *n.* questus *m.*, querimōnia *f.*; (*law*) crīmen *n.*; (*med.*) morbus *m.*, valētūdō *f.*
complaisance *n.* cōmitās *f.*, obsequium *n.*, indulgentia *f.*
complaisant *a.* cōmis, officiōsus, facilis.
complement *n.* complēmentum *n.*; numerus suus *m.* make up the — of complēre.
complete *vt.* (*amount, time*) complēre, explēre; (*work*) cōnficere, perficere, absolvere, peragere. *a.* perfectus, absolūtus, integer; (*victory*) iūstus; (*amount*) explētus. **-ly** *ad.* funditus, omninō, absolūtē, plānē.
completeness *n.* integritās *f.*; (*perfection*) perfectiō *f.*
completion *n.* (*process*) absolūtiō *f.*, cōnfectiō *f.*; (*end*) fīnis *m.* bring to — absolvere.
complex *a.* implicātus, multiplex.
complexion *n.* color *m.*
complexity *n.* implicātiō *f.*
compliance *n.* accommodātiō *f.*, obsequium *n.*, obtemperātiō *f.*
compliant *a.* obsequēns, facilis.
complicate *vt.* implicāre, impedīre. **-d** *a.* implicātus, involūtus, impedītus.
complication *n.* implicātiō *f.*
complicity *n.* cōnscientia *f.*
compliment *n.* blandimentum *n.*, honōs *m.*; (*pl. as greeting*) salūs *f.* *vt.* blandīrī, laudāre. — on grātulārī (*dat.*) dē (*abl.*).
complimentary *a.* honōrificus, blandus.
comply *vi.* obsequī (*dat.*), obtemperāre (*dat.*); mōrem gerere (*dat.*), mōrigerārī (*dat.*).
component *n.* elementum *n.*, pars *f.*
comport *vt* gerere.
compose *vt.* (*art*) compōnere, condere, pangere; (*whole*) efficere, cōnflāre; (*quarrel*) compōnere, dirimere; (*disturbance*) sēdāre. be -d of cōnsistere ex (*abl.*), cōnstāre ex (*abl.*). **-d** *a.* tranquillus, placidus.
composer *n.* auctor *m.*, scrīptor *m.*
composite *a.* multiplex.
composition *n.* (*process*) compositiō *f.*, scrīptūra *f.*; (*product*) opus *n.*, poēma *n.*, carmen *n.*; (*quality*) structūra *f.*
composure *n.* sēcūritās *f.*, aequus animus *m.*; (*face*) tranquillitās *f.*
compound *vt.* miscēre; (*words*) duplicāre, iungere. *vi.* (*agree*) pacīscī. *a.* compositus. — interest anatocismus *m.* *n.* (*word*) iūnctum verbum *n.*; (*area*) saeptum *n.*
comprehend *vt.* intellegere, comprehendere; (*include*) continēre, complectī.
comprehensible *a.* perspicuus.
comprehension *n.* intellegentia *f.*, comprehēnsiō *f.*
comprehensive *a.* capāx. be — lātē patēre, multa complectī.
compress *vt.* comprimere, coartāre. *n.* fōmentum *n.*
compression *n.* compressus *m.*
comprise *vt.* continēre, complectī, comprehendere.
compromise *n.* (*by one side*) accommodātiō; (*by both sides*) comprōmissum *n.* *vi.* comprōmittere. *vt* implicāre, in suspiciōnem vocāre. be -d in suspiciōnem venīre.
comptroller *n.* moderātor *m.*
compulsion *n.* necessitās *f.*, vīs *f.* under — coāctus.
compulsory *a.* necesse, lēge imperātus. use — measures vim adhibēre.
compunction *n.* paenitentia *f.*
computation *n.* ratiō *f.*
compute *vt.* computāre, ratiōnem dūcere.

comrade *n.* socius *m.*, contubernālis *m.*
comradeship *n.* contubernium *n.*
con *vt.* studēre (*dat.*); (*ship*) regere.
concatenation *n.* seriēs *f.*
concave *a.* concavus.
conceal *vt.* cēlāre, abdere, abscondere; (*fact*) dissimulāre.
concealment *n.* occultātiō *f.*; (*place*) latebrae *f.pl.*; (*of facts*) dissimulātiō *f.* in — abditus, occultus. be in — latēre, latitāre. go into — dēlitēscere.
concede *vt.* concēdere.
conceit *n.* (*idea*) nōtiō *f.*; (*wit*) facētiae *f.pl.*; (*pride*) superbia *f.*, adrogantia *f.*, vānitās *f.* [gāns.
conceited *a.* glōriōsus, adro-
conceitedness *n.* adrogantia *f.*, vānitās *f.*
conceive *vt.* concipere, comprehendere, intellegere.
concentrate *vt.* (*in one place*) cōgere, congregāre; (*attention*) intendere, dēfīgere. **-d** *a.* dēnsus. [intentiō *f.*
concentration *n.* animī
concept *n.* nōtiō *f.*
conception *n.* conceptus *m.*; (*mind*) intellegentia *f.*, īnfōrmātiō *f.* (*idea*) nōtiō *f.*, cōgitātiō *f.*, cōnsilium *n.*
concern *vt.* (*refer*) attinēre ad (*acc.*), interesse (*gen.*); (*worry*) sollicitāre. it **-s** me meā rēfert, meā interest. as far as I am **-ed** per mē. *n.* rēs *f.*, negōtium *n.*; (*importance*) mōmentum *n.*; (*worry*) sollicitūdō *f.*, cūra *f.*; (*regret*) dolor *m.*
concerned *a.* sollicitus, anxius. be — dolēre. be — about molestē ferre.
concerning *pr.* dē (*abl.*).
concernment *n.* sollicitūdō *f.*
concert *n.* (*music*) concentus *m.*; (*agreement*) cōnsēnsus *m.* in — ex compositō, ūnō animō. *vt.* compōnere; (*plan*) inīre.

concession *n.* concessiō *f.* by the — of concessū (*gen.*). make a — concēdere, tribuere.
conciliate *vt.* conciliāre.
conciliation *n.* conciliātiō *f.*
conciliator *m.* arbiter *m.*
conciliatory *a.* pācificus.
concise *a.* brevis; (*style*) dēnsus. **-ly** *ad.* breviter.
conciseness *n.* brevitās *f.*
conclave *n.* sēcrētus cōnsessus *m.*
conclude *vt.* (*end*) termināre, fīnīre, cōnficere; (*settle*) facere, compōnere, pangere; (*infer*) īnferre, colligere.
conclusion *n.* (*end*) fīnis *m.*; (*of action*) exitus *m.*; (*of speech*) perōrātiō *f.*; (*inference*) coniectūra *f.*; (*decision*) placitum *n.*, sententia *f.* in — dēnique. try — s with contendere cum.
conclusive *a.* certus, manifestus, gravis. **-ly** *ad.* sine dubiō.
concoct *vt.* coquere; (*fig.*) cōnflāre. [ātiō *f.*
concoction *n.* (*fig.*) māchin-
concomitant *a.* adiūnctus.
concord *n.* concordia *f.*; (*music*) harmonia *f.*
concordant *a.* concors.
concordat *n.* pactum *n.*, foedus *n.*
concourse *n.* frequentia *f.*, celebrātiō *f.*; (*moving*) concursus *m.* [— rē.
concrete *a.* concrētus. in the
concretion *n.* concrētiō *f.*
concubine *n.* concubīna *f.*
concupiscence *n.* libīdō *f.*
concur *vi.* (*time*) concurrere; (*opinion*) cōnsentīre, adsentīre.
concurrence *n.* (*time*) concursus *m.*; (*opinion*) cōnsēnsus *m.*
concurrent *a.* (*time*) aequālis; (*opinion*) cōnsentāneus. be — concurrere, cōnsentīre. **-ly** *ad.* simul, ūnā.
concussion *n.* ictus *m.*
condemn *vt.* damnāre, con-

damnāre; (*disapprove*) improbāre. — to death capitis damnāre. — for treason dē māiestāte damnāre.
condemnation *n.* damnātiō *f.* condemnātiō *f.*
condemnatory *a.* damnātōrius.
condense *vt.* dēnsāre; (*words*) premere.
condescend *vi.* dēscendere, sē submittere. **-ing** *a.* cōmis.
condescension *n.* cōmitās *f.*
condign *a.* meritus, dignus.
condiment *n.* condimentum *n.*
condition *n.* (*of body*) habitus *m.*; (*external*) status *m.* condiciō *f.*, rēs *f.*; (*in society*) locus *m.*, fortūna *f.*; (*of agreement*) condiciō *f.*, lēx *f.* -s of sale mancipī lēx *f.* on — that eā lēge ut (*subj.*). in — (*animals*) nitidus. *vt.* fōrmāre, regere.
conditional *a.* the assistance is — on eā condiciōne succurritur ut (*subj.*). **-ly** *ad.* sub condiciōne.
conditioned *a.* (*character*) mōrātus.
condole *vi.* — with cōnsōlārī.
condolence *n.* cōnsōlātiō *f.*
condonation *n.* venia *f.*
condone *vt.* condōnāre, ignōscere (*dat.*).
conduce *vi.* condūcere (ad), prōficere (ad).
conducive *a.* ūtilis, accommodātus.
conduct *vt.* dūcere; (*escort*) dēdūcere; (*to a place*) addūcere, perdūcere; (*business*) gerere, administrāre; (*self*) gerere. *n.* mōrēs *m.pl.*; (*past*) vīta *f.*, facta *n.pl.*; (*business*) administrātiō *f.* safe — praesidium *n.*
conductor *m.* dux *m.*, ductor *m.*
conduit *n.* canālis *m.*, aquae ductus *m.*
cone *n.* cōnus *m.*
coney *n.* cuniculus *m.* [*n.*
confabulation *n.* colloquium
confabulate *vi.* colloquī.
confection *n.* cuppēdō *f.*
confectioner *n.* cuppēdinārius *m.*
confectionery *n.* dulcia *n.pl.*
confederacy *n.* foederātae cīvitātēs *f.pl.*, societās *f.*
confederate *a.* foederātus. *n.* socius. *vi.* coniūrāre, foedus facere.
confederation *n.* societās *f.*
confer *vt.* cōnferre, tribuere. *vi.* colloquī, sermōnem cōnferre. — about agere dē (*abl.*).
conference *n.* colloquium *n.*, congressus *m.*
conferment *n.* dōnātiō *f.*
confess *vt.* fatērī, cōnfitērī.
confessedly *ad.* manifestō.
confession *n.* cōnfessiō *f.*
confidant *n.* cōnscius *m.*
confide *vi.* fīdere (*dat.*), cōnfīdere (*dat.*). *vt.* crēdere, committere.
confidence *n.* fidēs *f.* fīdūcia *f.* self — cōnfīdentia *f.* fīdūcia *f.* have — in fīdere (*dat.*), cōnfīdere (*dat.*). inspire — in fidem facere (*dat.*). tell in — tūtīs auribus dēpōnere.
confident *a.* fīdens. — in frētus (*abl.*). be — that certō scīre, prō certō habēre. self — fīdens. **-ly** *ad.* fīdenter.
confidential *a.* arcānus, intimus. **-ly** *ad.* inter nōs.
confiding *a.* crēdulus.
configuration *n.* figūra *f.*, fōrma *f.*
confine *vt.* (*prison*) inclūdere, in vincula conicere; (*limit*) termināre, circumscrībere; (*restrain*) coercēre, cohibēre; (*to bed*) dētinēre. be -d (*women*) parturīre.
confinement *n.* custōdia *f.*, vincula *n.pl.*, inclūsiō *f.*; (*women*) puerperium *n.*
confines *n.* fīnēs *m.pl.*
confirm *vt.* (*strength*) corrō-

borāre, firmāre; (*decision*) sancīre, ratum facere; (*fact*) adfirmāre, comprobāre. **-ed** *a.* ratus
confirmation *n.* cōnfirmātiō *f.*, adfirmātiō *f.*
confiscate *vt.* pūblicāre.
confiscation *n.* pūblicātiō *f.*
conflagration *n.* incendium *n.*, dēflāgrātiō *f.*
conflict *n.* (*physical*) concursus *m.*; (*hostile*) certāmen *n.*, proelium *n.*, (*verbal*) contentiō *f.*, contrōversia *f.*; (*contradiction*) repugnantia *f.*, discrepantia *f.* *vi.* inter sē repugnāre. **-ing** *a.* contrārius.
confluence *n.* cōnfluēns *m.*
confluent *a.* cōnfluēns.
conform *vt.* accommodāre. *vi.* sē cōnfōrmāre (ad), obsequī (*dat.*), mōrem gerere (*dat.*).
conformab/le *a.* accommodātus, conveniēns. **-ly** *ad.* convenienter
conformation *n.* structūra *f.* confōrmātiō *f.*
conformity *n.* convenientia *f.*, cōnsēnsus *m.*
confound *vt.* (*mix*) cōnfundere, permiscēre; (*amaze*) obstupefacere; (*thwart*) frustrārī; (*suppress*) opprimere, obruere. — **you!** dī tē perduint. **-ed** *a.* miser, sacer nefandus. **-edly** *ad.* mīrum quantum nefāriē.
confraternity *n.* frāternitās *f.*
confront *vt.* sē oppōnere (*dat.*), obviam īre (*dat.*) sē cōram offerre.
confuse *vt.* permiscēre, perturbāre. **-d** *a.* perturbātus. **-dly** *ad.* perturbātē, prōmiscuē.
confusion *n.* perturbātiō *f.*; (*shame*) rubor *m.*
confutation *n.* refūtātio *f.*
confute *vt.* refūtāre, redarguere, convincere.
congé *n.* commeātus *m.*
congeal *vt.* congelāre, dūrāre. *vi.* concrēscere. **-ed** *a.* concrētus.
congenial *a.* concors, congruēns, iūcundus.
congeniality *n.* concordia *f.*, mōrum similitūdō *f.*
congenital *a.* nātivus.
conger *n.* conger *m.*
congested *a.* refertus, dēnsus; (*with people*) frequentissimus.
congestion *n.* congeriēs *f.*; frequentia *f.*
conglomerate *vt.* glomerāre.
conglomeration *n.* congeriēs *f.*, cumulus *m.*
congratulate *vt.* grātulārī (*dat.*).
congratulation *n.* grātulātiō [*f.*
congratulatory *a.* grātulābundus.
congregate *vt.* congregāre, cōgere. *vi* convenīre, congregārī.
congregation *n.* conventus *m.*, coetus *m.*
congress *n.* conventus *m.*, cōnsessus *m.*, concilium *n.*; senātus *m.*
congruence, congruity *n.* convenientia *f.*
congruent, congruous *a.* conveniēns, congruēns. **-ly** *ad.* convenienter, congruenter.
conical *a.* turbinātus.
coniferous *a.* cōnifer.
conjectural *a.* opīnābilis. **-ly** *ad.* coniectūrā.
conjecture *n.* coniectūra *f.* *vt.* conicere, augurārī.
conjoin *vt.* coniungere. **-t** *a.* coniūnctus. **-tly** *ad.* coniūnctē, ūnā.
conjugal *a.* coniugālis.
conjugate *vt.* dēclīnāre.
conjugation *n.* (*gram.*) dēclīnātiō *f.*
conjunct *a.* coniūnctus.
conjunction *n.* coniūnctiō *f.*, concursus *m.* [cāsus *m.*
conjuncture *n.* tempus *n.*,
conjuration *n.* obtestātiō *f.*; (*magic*) cantus *m.*

conjure *vt.* (*entreat*) obtestārī, obsecrāre; (*spirits*) ēlicere, ciēre. *vi.* praestigiīs ūtī.
conjurer *n.* praestigiātor *m.*
conjuring *n.* praestigiae *f.pl.*
connate *a.* innātus, nātūrā insitus.
connect *vt.* iungere, coniungere, cōpulāre, connectere. **-ed** *a.* coniūnctus; (*unbroken*) continēns; (*by marriage*) adfīnis. be **-ed** with contingere. be closely **-ed** with inhaerēre (*dat.*), cohaerēre cum (*abl.*). **-edly** *ad.* coniūnctē, continenter.
connection *n.* coniūnctiō *f.*, contextus *m.*, seriēs *f.*; (*kin*) necessitūdō *f.*; (*by marriage*) adfīnitās *f.* — between . . and ratiō (*gen.*) . . . cum (*abl.*). I have no — with you nīl mihī tēcum est.
connivance *n.* venia *f.* dissimulātiō *f.*
connive *vi.* connīvēre in (*abl.*), dissimulāre.
connoisseur *n.* intellegēns *m.*
connotation *n.* vīs *f.*, significātiō *f.*
connote *vt.* significāre.
connubial *a.* coniugālis.
conquer *vt.* vincere, superāre.
conquerable *a.* superābilis, expugnābilis.
conqueror *n.* victor *m.*
conquest *n.* victōria *f.*; (*town*) expugnātiō *f.*; (*prize*) praemium *n.*, praeda *f.* the — of Greece Graecia capta.
consanguineous *a.* cōnsanguineus.
consanguinity *n.* cōnsanguinitās *f.*
conscience *n.* cōnscientia *f.* guilty — mala cōnscientia. have a clear — nullīus culpae sibi cōnscium esse. have no — nullam rēligiōnem habēre.
conscientious *a.* probus, rēligiōsus. **-ly** *ad.* bonā fidē, rēligiōsē.
conscientiousness *n.* fidēs *f.*, rēligiō *f.*
conscious *a.* sibi cōnscius; (*aware*) gnārus; (*physically*) mentis compos. be — sentīre. **-ly** *ad.* sciēns.
consciousness *n.* animus *m.*; (*of action*) cōnscientia *f.* he lost — animus eum relīquit.
conscript *n.* tīrō *m.* *vt.* cōnscrībere.
conscription *n.* dēlēctus *m.*, (*of wealth*) pūblicātiō *f.*
consecrate *vt.* dēdicāre, cōnsecrāre; (*self*) dēvovēre. **-d** *a.* sacer.
consecration *n.* dēdicātiō *f.*, cōnsecrātiō *f.*; (*self*) dēvōtiō *f.*
consecutive *a.* deinceps, continuus. **-ly** *ad.* deinceps, ōrdine.
consensus *n.* cōnsēnsus *m.*
consent *vi.* adsentīre (*dat.*), adnuere (*inf.*); (*together*) cōnsentīre. *n.* (*one side*) adsēnsus *m.*; (*all*) cōnsēnsus *m.* by common — omnium cōnsēnsū.
consequence *n.* ēventus *m.*, exitus *m.*; (*logic*) conclūsiō *f.*; (*importance*) mōmentum *n.*, auctōritās *f.* it is of — interest. what will be the — of? quō ēvādet?
consequent *a.* cōnsequēns. **-ly** *ad.* itaque, igitur, proptereā.
consequential *a.* cōnsentāneus; (*person*) adrogāns. [*f.*
conservation *n.* cōnservātiō
conservative *a.* reī pūblicae cōnservandae studiōsus; (*estimate*) mediocris. — party optimātēs *m.pl.*
conservator *m.* custōs *m.*, cōnservātor *m.*
conserve *vt.* cōnservāre, servāre.
consider *vt.* cōnsīderāre, contemplārī; (*reflect*) sēcum volūtāre, meditari, dēlīberāre; (*deem*) habēre, dūcere; (*respect*) respicere, observāre.

considerab/le *a.* aliquantus, nōnnullus; (*person*) illūstris. **-ly** *ad.* aliquantum; (*with comp.*) aliquantō, multō.
considerate *a.* hūmānus, benignus. **-ly** *ad.* hūmānē, benignē.
consideration *n.* cōnsīderātiō *f.*, contemplātiō *f.*, dēlīberātiō *f.*; (*respect*) respectus *m.*, ratiō *f.*; (*importance*) mōmentum; (*reason*) ratiō *f.*; (*pay*) pretium *n.* for a — mercēde, datā mercēde. in — of propter (*acc.*), prō (*abl.*). on no — nēquāquam. with — cōnsultō. without — temerē. take into — ad cōnsilium dēferre. show — for respectum habēre (*gen.*).
considered *a.* (*reasons*) exquīsītus.
considering *pr.* prō (*abl.*), propter (*acc.*). *conj.* ut, quōniam.
consign *vt.* mandāre, committere.
consist *vi.* cōnstāre. — in cōnstāre ex (*abl.*), continērī (*abl.*), positum esse in (*abl.*). — with congruere (*dat.*), convenīre (*dat.*).
consistence *n.* firmitās *f.*
consistency *n.* cōnstantia *f.*
consistent *a.* cōnstāns; (*with*) cōnsentāneus, cōngruens; (*of movement*) aequābilis. be — cohaerēre. **-ly** *ad.* constanter
consolable *a.* cōnsōlābilis.
consolation *n.* cōnsōlātiō *f.*; (*thing*) sōlācium *n.*
consolatory *a.* cōnsōlātōrius.
console *vt.* cōnsōlārī.
consoler *n.* cōnsōlātor *m.*
consolidate *vt.* (*liquid*) cōgere; (*strength*) corrōborāre; (*gains*) obtinēre. *vi.* concrēscere.
consolidation *n.* concrētiō *f.*; cōnfirmātiō *f.*
consonance *n.* concentus *m.*
consonant *a.* cōnsonus, haud absonus. *n.* cōnsonāns *f.*
consort *n.* cōnsors *m.*, *f.*, socius *m.*; (*married*) coniunx *m.*, *f.* *vi.* — with familiāriter ūtī (*abl.*) coniūnctissimē vīvere cum (*abl.*).
conspectus *n.* summārium *n.*
conspicuous *a.* ēminēns, īnsignis, manifestus. be — ēminēre. **-ly** *ad.* manifestō, palam, ante oculōs.
conspiracy *n.* coniūrātiō *f.*
conspirator *n.* coniūrātus *m.*
conspire *vi.* coniūrāre; (*for good*) cōnspīrāre.
constable *n.* lictor *m.*
constancy *n.* cōnstantia *f.*, firmitās *f.* with — cōnstanter.
constant *a.* cōnstāns; (*faithful*) fīdus fidēlis; (*continuous*) adsiduus. **-ly** *ad.* adsiduē, saepe, crēbrō.
constellation *n.* sīdus *n.*
consternation *n.* trepidātiō *f.*, pavor *m.* throw into — perterrēre, cōnsternere.
constituency *n.* suffrāgātōrēs *m.pl.*
constituent *a.* — part elementum *n.* *n.* (*voter*) suffrāgātor *m.*
constitute *vt.* creāre, cōnstituere; esse.
constitution *n.* nātūra *f.*, status *m.*, (*body*) habitus *m.*; (*pol.*) cīvitātis fōrma *f.*, reī pūblicae status *m.*, lēgēs *f.pl.*
constitutional *a.* lēgitimus, iūstus. **-ly** *ad.* ē rē pūblicā.
constrain *vt.* cōgere.
constraint *n.* vīs *f.* under — coāctus. without — suā sponte.
constrict *vt.* comprimere, cōnstringere.
constriction *n.* contractiō *f.*
construct *vt.* aedificāre, exstruere.
construction *n.* aedificātiō *f.*; (*method*) structūra *f.*; (*meaning*) interpretātiō *f.* put a wrong — on in malam partem interpretārī.
construe *vt.* interpretārī.

consul *n.* cōnsul *m.* — elect cōnsul dēsignātus. ex — cōnsulāris *m.*
consular *a.* cōnsulāris.
consulship *n.* cōnsulātus *m.* stand for the — cōnsulātum petere. hold the — cōnsulātum gerere. in my — mē cōnsule.
consult *vt.* cōnsulere. — the interests of cōnsulere (*dat.*). *vi.* dēlīberāre, cōnsiliārī.
consultation *n.* (*asking*) cōnsultātiō *f.*; (*discussion*) dēlīberātiō *f.*
consume *vt.* cōnsūmere, absūmere; (*food*) edere.
consumer *n.* cōnsūmptor *m.*
consummate *a.* summus, perfectus. *vt.* perficere, absolvere.
consummation *n.* absolūtiō *f.*; fīnis *m.*, ēventus *m.*
consumption *n.* cōnsūmptiō *f.*; (*disease*) tābēs *f.*, phthisis *f.*
consumptive *a.* pulmōnārius.
contact *n.* tāctus *m.*, contāgiō *f.* come in — with contingere.
contagion *n.* contāgiō *f.*
contagious *a.* tābificus. be — contāgiīs vulgārī.
contain *vt.* capere, continēre; (*self*) cohibēre.
container *n.* vās *n.*
contaminate *vt.* contāmināre, inficere.
contamination *n.* contāgiō *f.*, lābēs *f.*
contemn *vt.* contemnere, [spernere.
contemplate *vt.* contemplārī, intuērī; (*action*) in animō habēre; (*prospect*) spectāre.
contemplation *n.* contemplātiō *f.*; (*thought*) cōgitātiō *f.*
contemplative *a.* cōgitāns, meditāns. in a — mood cōgitātiōnī dēditus.
contemporaneous *a.* aequālis. **-ly** *ad.* simul.
contemporary *a.* aequālis.
contempt *n.* contemptiō *f.* be an object of — contemptuī esse. treat with — contemptum habēre, conculcāre.
contemptible *a.* contemnendus, abiectus, vīlis.
contemptuous *a.* fastīdiōsus. **-ly** *ad.* contemptim, fastīdiōsē.
contend *vi.* certāre, contendere; (*in battle*) dīmicāre, pugnāre; (*in words*) adfirmāre, adseverāre.
contending *a.* contrārius.
content *a.* contentus. *n.* aequus animus *m.* *vt.* placēre (*dat.*) satisfacere (*dat.*). be —ed satis habēre.
contentedly *ad.* aequō animō.
contention *n.* certāmen *n.*; contrōversia *f.*; (*opinion*) sententia *f.*
contentious *a.* pugnāx, lītigiōsus. **-ly** *ad.* pugnāciter.
contentiousness *n.* contrōversiae studium *n.*
contentment *n.* aequus animus *m.*
contents *n.* quod inest, quae insunt; (*of speech*) argūmentum *n.*
conterminous *a.* adfīnis.
contest *n.* certāmen *n.*, contentiō *f.* *vt.* (*law*) lēge agere dē (*abl.*); (*office*) petere; (*dispute*) repugnāre (*dat.*), resistere (*dat.*).
contestable *a.* contrōversus.
contestant *n.* petītor *m.*, aemulus *m.*
context *n.* contextus *m.*
contiguity *n.* vīcīnia *f.*, propinquitās *f.*
contiguous *a.* vīcīnus, adiacēns. be — to adiacēre (*dat.*), contingere.
continence *n.* continentia *f.*, abstinentia *f.*
continent *a.* continēns, abstinēns *n.* continēns *f.* **-ly** *ad.* continenter, abstinenter.
contingency *n.* cāsus *m.*, rēs *f.*
contingent *a.* fortuītus. *n.* (*mil.*) numerus *m.*

continual *a.* adsiduus, perpetuus. **-ly** *ad.* adsiduē, semper.
continuance *n.* perpetuitās *f.*, adsiduitās *f.*
continuation *n.* continuātiō *f.*; (*of a command*) prōrogātiō *f.*; (*of a story*) reliqua pars *f.*
continue *vt.* continuāre; (*time*) prōdūcere; (*command*) prōrogāre. *vi.* (*action*) pergere; (*time*) manēre; (*endurance*) perstāre, dūrāre.
continuity *n.* continuātiō *f.*; (*of speech*) perpetuitās *f.*
continuous *a.* continuus, continēns, perpetuus. **-ly** *ad.* perpetuō, continenter.
contort *vt.* contorquēre, dētorquēre.
contortion *n.* distortiō *f.*
contour *n.* fōrma *f.*
contraband *a.* interdictus, vetitus.
contract *n.* pactum *n.*, mandātum *n.*, conventum *n.*; (*pol.*) foedus *n.* **trial for a breach of —** mandātī iūdicium. *vt.* (*narrow*) contrahere, addūcere; (*short*) dēminuere; (*illness*) contrahere; (*agreement*) pacīscī; (*for work*) locāre; (*to do work*) condūcere. *vi.* pacīscī.
contraction *n.* contractiō *f.*; (*word*) compendium *n.*
contractor *n.* redemptor *m.*, conductor *m.*
contradict *vt.* (*person*) contrādīcere (*dat.*), refrāgārī (*dat.*); (*statement*) īnfitiās īre (*dat.*); (*self*) repugnāre (*dat.*).
contradiction *n.* repugnantia *f.*, īnfitiae *f.pl.*
contradictory *a.* repugnāns, contrārius. **be —** inter sē repugnāre.
contradistinction *n.* oppositiō *f.*
contradistinguish *vt.* discernere.
contraption *n.* māchina *f.*
contrariety *n.* repugnantia *f.*
contrariwise *ad.* ē contrāriō.
contrary *a.* contrārius, adversus; (*person*) difficilis, mōrōsus. **— to** contrā (*acc.*), praeter (*acc.*). *n.* contrārium *n.* **on the —** ē contrāriō, contra; (*retort*) immo.
contrast *n.* discrepantia *f.* *vt.* comparāre, oppōnere. *vi.* discrepāre.
contravene *vt.* (*law*) violāre; (*statement*) contrādīcere (*dat.*).
contravention *n.* violātiō *f.*
contribute *vt.* cōnferre, adferre, contribuere. *vi.* **— towards** cōnferre ad (*acc.*) adiuvāre. **— to the cost** impēnsās cōnferre.
contribution *n.* conlātiō *f.*; (*money*) stipem (*no nom.*) *f.*
contributor *n.* quī cōnfert.
contributory *a.* adiūnctus.
contrite *a.* paenitēns.
contrition *n.* paenitentia *f.*
contrivance *n.* māchinātiō *f.*, excōgitātiō *f.*; (*thing*) māchina *f.*; (*idea*) cōnsilium *n.*; (*deceit*) dolus *m.*
contrive *vt.* māchinārī, excōgitāre, struere; (*to do*) efficere ut.
contriver *n.* māchinātor *m.*, artifex *m.*, auctor *m.*
control *n.* (*restraint*) frēnum *n.*; (*power*) moderātiō *f.* potestās *f.*, imperium *n.* **have — of** praeesse (*dat.*). **self —** temperantia *f.* **out of —** impotēns. *vt.* moderārī (*dat.*), imperāre (*dat.*).
controller *n.* moderātor *m.*
controversial *a.* concertātōrius.
controversy *n.* contrōversia *f.*, disceptātiō *f.*
controvert *vt.* redarguere, impugnāre, in dubium vocāre.
contumacious *a.* contumāx, pervicāx. **-ly** *ad.* contumāciter, pervicāciter.
contumacy *n.* contumācia *f.*, pervicācia *f*

contumelious *a.* contumēliōsus. **-ly** *ad.* contumēliōsē.
contumely *n.* contumēlia *f.*, opprobrium *n.*
contusion *n.* sūgillātiō *f.*
conundrum *n.* aenigma *n.*
convalesce *vi.* convalēscere.
convalescence *n.* melior valētūdō *f.*
convalescent *a.* convalēscēns.
convene *vt.* convocāre.
convenience *n.* opportūnitās *f.*, commoditās *f.*; (*thing*) commodum *n.* at your — commodō tuō.
convenient *a.* idōneus, commodus, opportūnus. be — convenīre. very — percommodus. **-ly** *ad.* opportūnē, commodē.
conventicle *n.* conventiculum [*n.*
convention *n.* (*meeting*) conventus *m.*; (*agreement*) conventum *n.*; (*custom*) mōs *m.*, iūsta *n.pl.*
conventional *a.* iūstus, solitus.
conventionality *n.* mōs *m.*, cōnsuētūdō *f.*
converge *vi.* in medium vergere, in eundem locum tendere.
conversant *a.* perītus, doctus, exercitātus. be — with versārī in (*abl.*).
conversation *n.* sermō *m.*, colloquium *n.*
converse *n.* sermō *m.*, colloquium *n.*; (*opposite*) contrārium *n.* *vi.* colloquī, sermōnem cōnferre. *a.* contrārius. **-ly** *ad.* ē contrāriō, contrā.
conversion *n.* mūtātiō *f.*; (*moral*) mōrum ēmendātiō *f.*
convert *vt.* mūtāre, convertere; (*to an opinion*) dēdūcere. *n.* discipulus *m.*
convertible *a.* commūtābilis.
convex *a.* convexus.
convexity *n.* convexum *n.*
convey *vt.* vehere, portāre, convehere; (*property*) abaliēnāre; (*knowledge*) commūnicāre; (*meaning*) significāre. — across trānsmittere, trādūcere, trānsvehere. — away auferre, āvehere. — down dēvehere, dēportāre. — into importāre, invehere. — to advehere, adferre. — up subvehere.
conveyance *n.* vehiculum *n.*; (*property*) abaliēnātiō *f.*
convict *vt.* (*prove guilty*) convincere; (*sentence*) damnāre. *n.* reus *m.*
conviction *n.* (*law*) damnātiō *f.*; (*argument*) persuāsiō *f.*; (*belief*) fidēs *f.* carry — fidem facere. have a — persuāsum habēre.
convince *vt.* persuādēre (*dat.*). I am firmly -d mihi persuāsum habeō.
convincing *a.* (*argument*) gravis; (*evidence*) manifestus. **-ly** *ad.* manifestō. [festīvus.
convivial *a.* convīvālis,
conviviality *n.* festīvitās *f.*
convocation *n.* conventus *m.*
convoke *vt.* convocāre.
convolution *n.* spīra *f.*
convoy *n.* praesidium *n.* *vt.* prōsequī.
convulse *vt.* agitāre. be -d with laughter sē in cachinnōs effundere.
convulsion *n.* (*med.*) convulsiō *f.*; (*pol.*) tumultus *m.*
convulsive *a.* spasticus.
coo *vi.* gemere.
cook *vt.* coquere. *n.* coquus *m.*
cookery *n.* ars coquināria *f.*
cool *a.* frīgidus; (*conduct*) impudens; (*mind*) impavidus, lentus. *n.* frīgus *n.* *vt.* refrīgerāre; (*passion*) restinguere, sēdāre. *vi.* refrīgēscere, refrīgerārī, dēfervēscere. **-ly** *ad.* aequō animō; impudenter.
coolness *n.* frīgus *n.*; (*mind*) aequus animus *m.*; impudentia *f.*

coop *n.* hara *f.*; (*barrel*) cūpa *f.* *vt.* inclūdere.
co-operate *vi.* operam cōnferre. — with adiuvāre, socium esse (*gen.*).
co-operation *n.* cōnsociātiō *f.*; auxilium *n.*, opera *f.*
co-operative *a.* (*person*) officiōsus.
co-operator *n.* socius *m.*
co-opt *vt.* cooptāre.
coot *n.* fulica *f.*
copartner *n.* socius *m.*
copartnership *n.* societās *f.*
cope *vi.* — with contendere cum (*abl.*). able to — with pār (*dat.*). unable to — with impār (*dat.*).
copier *n.* librārius *m.*
coping *n.* fastigium *n.*
copious *a.* cōpiōsus, largus, plēnus, abundāns. **-ly** *ad.* cōpiōsē, abundanter.
copiousness *n.* cōpia *f.*, ūbertās *f.*
copper *n.* aes *n.* *a.* aēneus. **-smith** *n.* faber aerārius *m.*
coppice, copse *n.* dūmētum *n.*, virgultum *n.*
copy *n.* exemplar *n.* *vt.* imitārī; (*writing*) exscrībere, trānscrībere.
copyist *n.* librārius *m.*
coquet *vi.* lascīvīre.
coquetry *n.* lascīvia *f.*
coquette *n.* lascīva *f.*
coracle *n.* linter *f.*
coral *n.* cūrālium *n.*
cord *n.* fūniculus *m.*
cordage *n.* fūnēs *m.pl.*
cordial *a.* cōmis, festīvus, amīcus; (*greetings*) multus. **-ly** *ad.* cōmiter, libenter, ex animō. [studium *n.*
cordiality *n.* cōmitās *f.*,
cordon *n.* corōna *f.*
core *n.* (*fig.*) nucleus *m.*
cork *n.* sūber *n.*; (*bark*) cortex *m.*
corn *n.* frūmentum *n.* *a.* frūmentārius. **-dealer** frūmentārius *m.* **-field** seges *f.* price of — annōna *f.* (*on the foot*) clāvus *m.*
cornel *n.* (*tree*) cornus *f.*
corner *n.* angulus *m.*
cornet *n.* cornū *n.*
cornice *n.* corōna *f.*
coronet *n.* diadēma *n.*
corporal *a.* corporeus. — punishment verbera *n.pl.*
corporation *n.* collēgium *n.*; (*civic*) magistrātūs *m.pl.*
corporeal *a.* corporeus.
corps *n.* manus *f.*
corpse *n.* cadāver *n.* [*n.*
corpulence *n.* obēsum corpus
corpulent *a.* obēsus, pinguis.
corpuscle *n.* corpusculum *n.*
corral *n.* praesēpe *n.*
correct *vt.* corrigere, ēmendāre; (*person*) castīgāre. *a.* vērus; (*language*) integer; (*style*) ēmendātus. **-ly** *ad.* bene, vērē.
correction *n.* ēmendātiō *f.*; (*moral*) corrēctiō *f.*; (*punishment*) castīgātiō *f.*
correctness *n.* (*fact*) vēritās *f.*; (*language*) integritās *f.*; (*moral*) probitās *f.*
corrector *n.* ēmendātor *m.*, corrēctor *m.*
correspond *vi.* (*agree*) respondēre (*dat.*), congruere (*dat.*); (*by letter*) inter sē scrībere.
correspondence *n.* similitūdō *f.*; epistulae *f.pl.*
correspondent *n.* epistulārum scrīptor *m.*
corresponding *a.* pār. **-ly** *ad.* pariter.
corridor *n.* porticus *f.*
corrigible *a.* ēmendābilis.
corroborate *vt.* cōnfirmāre.
corroboration *n.* cōnfirmātiō *f.*
corrode *vt.* ērōdere, edere.
corrosive *a.* edāx.
corrugate *vt.* rūgāre. **-d** *a.* rūgōsus.
corrupt *vt.* corrumpere, dēprāvāre; (*text*) vitiāre. *a.*

corruptus, vitiātus; (*person*) prāvus, vēnālis; (*text*) vitiātus.
corrupter *n.* corruptor *m.*
corruptible *a.* (*matter*) dissolūbilis; (*person*) vēnālis.
corruption *n.* (*of matter*) corruptiō *f.*; (*moral*) corruptēla *f.*, dēprāvātiō *f.*; (*bribery*) ambitus *m.*
corsair *n.* pīrāta *m.*
corse *n.* cadāver *n.*
corselet *n.* lōrīca *f.*
cortège *n.* pompa *f.*
coruscate *vi.* fulgēre.
coruscation *n.* fulgor *m.*
Corybant *n.* Corybas *m.* **-ic** *a.* Corybantius.
cosmetic *n.* medicāmen *n.*
cosmic *a.* mundānus.
cosmopolitan *a* mundānus.
cosmos *n.* mundus *m.*
cost *vt.* emī, stāre (*abl.*). it — me dear māgnō mihi stetit, male ēmī. it — me a talent talentō mihi stetit, talentō ēmī. it — me my freedom lībertātem perdidi. *n.* pretium *n.*, impēnsa *f.* — of living annōna *f.* to your — incommodō tuō, dētrimentō tuō. at the — of one's reputation violātā fāmā, nōn salvā existimātiōne. I sell at — price quantī ēmī vēndō.
costliness *n.* sūmptus *m.* cāritās *f.*
costly *a.* cārus; (*furnishings*) lautus, sūmptuōsus.
costume *n.* habitus *m.*
cosy *a.* commodus.
cot *n.* lectulus *m.*
cote *n.* columbārium *n.*
cottage *n.* casa *f.*, tugurium *n.*
cottager *n.* rūsticus *m.*
cotton *n.* (*tree*) gossympinus *f.*; (*cloth*) xylinum *n.*
couch *n.* lectus *m.* *vi.* recumbere. *vt.* (*lance*) intendere; (*words*) exprimere, reddere.
cough *n.* tussis *f.* *vi.* tussīre.
council *n.* concilium *n.*; (*small*) cōnsilium *n.* [*m.*
councillor *n.* (*town*) dēcuriō
counsel *n.* (*debate*) cōnsultātiō *f.*; (*advice*) cōnsilium *n.*; (*law*) advocātus *m.*, patrōnus *m.* take — cōnsiliārī, dēlīberāre. take — of cōnsulere. *vt.* suādēre (*dat.*).
counsellor *n.* cōnsiliārius *m.*
count *vt.* numerāre, computāre — as dūcere, habēre. — amongst pōnere in (*abl.*). — up ēnumerāre. — upon cōnfīdere (*dat.*). be -ed among in numerō esse (*gen.*). *vi.* aestimārī, habērī. *n.* ratiō *f.*; (*in indictment*) caput *n.*; (*title*) comes *m.*
countenance *n.* faciēs *f.*, vultus *m.*, ōs *n.*; (*fig.*) favor *m.* put out of — conturbāre. *vt.* favēre (*dat.*), indulgēre (*dat.*).
counter *n.* (*for counting*) calculus *m.*; (*for play*) tessera *f.*; (*shop*) mēnsa *f.* *a.* contrārius. *ad.* contrā, obviam. *vt.* obsistere (*dat.*), respondēre (*dat.*).
counteract *vt.* obsistere (*dat.*), adversārī (*dat.*); (*malady*) medērī (*dat.*).
counter-attack *vt.* in vicem oppugnāre, adgredī.
counter-attraction *n.* altera illecebra *f.*
counterbalance *vt.* compēnsāre, exaequāre.
counter-clockwise *ad.* sinistrōrsus.
counterfeit *a.* falsus, fūcātus, adsimulātus, fictus. *vt.* fingere, simulāre, imitārī.
countermand *vt.* renūntiāre.
counterpane *n.* lōdīx *f.*, strāgulum *n.*
counterpart *n.* pār *m.*, *f.*, *n.*
counterpoise *n.* aequum pondus *n.* *vt.* compēnsāre, exaequāre. [*f.*
countersign *n.* (*mil.*) tessera
counting-table *n.* abacus *m.*
countless *a.* innumerābilis.
countrified *a.* agrestis, rūsticus.
country *n.* (*region*) regiō *f.*

terra *f.*; (*territory*) fīnēs *m.pl.*; (*native*) patria *f.*; (*not town*) rūs *n.*; (*open*) agrī *m.pl.* — side agrī *m.pl.*, rūs *n.* — man agricola *m.* fellow — man populāris *m.*, cīvis *m.* of our — nostrās. live in the — rūsticārī. living in the — rūsticātiō *f.* — house vīlla *f.* — town mūnicipium *n.*

couple *n.* pār *n.* a — of duō. *vt.* cōpulare, coniungere.

couplet *n.* distichon *n.*

courage *n.* fortitūdō *f.*, animus *m.*; (*mil.*) virtūs *f.* have the — to audēre. lose — animōs dēmittere. take — bonō animō esse.

courageous *a.* fortis, ācer. **-ly** *ad.* fortiter, ācriter.

courier *n.* tabellārius *m.*

course *n.* (*movement*) cursus *m.*; (*route*) iter *n.*; (*sequence*) seriēs *f.*; (*career*) dēcursus; (*for races*) stadium *n.*, circus *m.*; (*of dinner*) ferculum *n.*; (*of stones*) ōrdō *m.*; (*of water*) lāpsus *m.* of — certē, sānē, scīlicet. as a matter of — continuō. in due — mox. in the — of inter (*acc.*), in (*abl.*). keep on one's — cursum tenēre. be driven off one's — dēicī. second — secunda mēnsa.

court *n.* (*space*) ārea *f.*; (*of house*) ātrium; (*of king*) aula *f.*; (*suite*) cohors *f.*, comitēs *m.pl.*; (*law*) iūdicium *n.*, iūdicēs *m.pl.* pay — to ambīre, īnservīre (*dat.*). hold a — forum agere. bring into — in iūs vocāre. *vt.* colere, ambīre; (*danger*) sē offerre (*dat.*); (*woman*) petere.

courteous *a.* cōmis, urbānus, hūmānus. **-ly** *ad.* cōmiter, urbānē.

courtesan *n.* meretrīx *f.*

courtesy *n.* (*quality*) cōmitās *f.*, hūmānitās *f.*; (*act*) officium *n.*

courtier *n.* aulicus *m.*; (*pl.*) [aula *f.*

courtly *a.* officiōsus.

cousin *n.* cōnsobrīnus *m.*, cōnsobrīna *f.*

cove *n.* sinus *m.*

covenant *n.* foedus *n.*, pactum *n.* *vi.* pacīscī.

cover *vt.* tegere, operīre; (*hide*) vēlāre; (*march*) claudere. — over obdūcere. — up obtegere. *n.* integumentum, operculum *n.*; (*shelter*) latebrae *f.pl.*, suffugium *n.*; (*pretence*) speciēs *f.* under — of sub (*abl.*), sub speciē (*gen.*). take — dēlitēscere.

covering *n.* integumentum *n.*, involucrum *n.*, operculum *n.*; (*of couch*) strāgulum *n.*

coverlet *n.* lōdīx *f.*

covert *a.* occultus; (*language*) oblīquus. *n.* latebra *f.*, perfugium *n.*; (*thicket*) dūmētum *n.* **-ly** *ad.* occultē, sēcrētō.

covet *vt.* concupīscere, expetere.

covetous *a.* avidus, cupidus. **-ly** *ad.* avidē, cupidē.

covetousness *n.* aviditās *f.*, cupiditās *f.*

covey *n.* grex *f.*

cow *n.* vacca *f.* *vt.* terrēre.

coward *n.* ignāvus *m.*

cowardice *n.* ignāvia *f.*

cowardly *a.* ignāvus.

cower *vi.* subsīdere.

cow-herd *m.* bubulcus *m.*

cowl *n.* cucullus *m.*

coxcomb *n.* crista *f.*; (*fig.*) nūgātor *m.*

coxswain *n.* rēctor *m.*

coy *a.* pudens, verēcundus. **-ly** *ad.* pudenter, modestē.

coyness *n.* pudor *m.*, verēcundia *f.*

cozen *vt.* fallere, dēcipere

crab *n.* cancer *m.*

crabbed *a.* mōrōsus, difficilis.

crack *n.* (*chink*) rīma *f.*; (*sound*) crepitus *m.* *vt.* findere, frangere; (*whip*) crepitāre (*abl.*) *vi.* (*open*) fatīscere; (*sound*) crepāre crepitāre.

crackle *vi.* crepitāre.
crackling *n.* crepitus *m.*
cradle *n.* cūnae *f.pl.*; (*fig.*) incūnābula *n.pl.*
craft *n.* ars *f.*; (*deceit*) dolus *m.*; (*boat*) nāvigium *n.*
craftsman *n.* artifex *m.*, faber *m.* [artificium *n.*
craftsmanship *n.* ars *f.*,
craft/y *a.* callidus, sollers; dolōsus. **-ily** *ad.* callidē, sollerter; dolōsē.
crag *n.* rūpēs *f.*, scopulus *m.*
cram *vt* farcīre, refercīre; (*with food*) sagināre.
cramp *n.* convulsiō *f.*; (*tool*) cōnfībula *f.* *vt.* coercēre, coartāre.
crane *n.* (*bird*) grus *f.*; (*machine*) māchina *f.*, trochlea *f.* [ineptus *m.*
crank *n.* uncus *m.*; (*person*)
crannied *a.* rīmōsus.
cranny *n.* rīma *f.*
crash *n.* (*fall*) ruīna *f.*; (*noise*) fragor *m.* *vi.* ruere; strepere.
crass *a.* crassus. — **stupidity** mera stultitia.
crate *n.* crātēs *f.pl.*
crater *n.* crātēr *m.*
cravat *n.* fōcāle *n.*
crave *vt.* (*desire*) concupīscere, adpetere, exoptāre; (*request*) ōrāre, obsecrāre.
craven *a.* ignāvus.
craving *n.* cupīdō *f.*, dēsīderium *n.*, adpetītiō *f.*
crawl *vi.* (*animal*) serpere; (*person*) rēpere.
crayfish *n.* commarus *m.*
craze *n.* libīdō *f.* *vt.* mentem aliēnāre.
craziness *n.* dēmentia *f.*
crazy *a.* dēmēns, fatuus.
creak *vi.* crepāre. **-ing** *n.* crepitus *m.*
cream *n.* spūma lactis *f.*; (*fig.*) flōs *m.*
crease *n.* rūga *f.* *vt.* rūgāre.
create *vt.* creāre, facere, gignere.
creation *n.* (*process*) fabricātiō *f.*; (*result*) opus *n.*; (*human*) hominēs *m.pl.*
creative *a.* (*nature*) creātrix; (*mind*) inventor, inventrix.
creator *n.* creātor *m.*, auctor *m.*, opifex *m.*
creature *n.* animal *n.*; (*person*) homō *m.*, *f.*
credence *n.* fidēs *f.*
credentials *n.* litterae commendātīciae *f.pl.*; (*fig.*) auctōritās *f.*
credibility *n.* fidēs *f.*; (*source*) auctōritās *f.*
credible *a.* crēdibilis; (*witness*) locuplēs.
credit *n.* (*belief*) fidēs *f.*; (*repute*) existimātiō *f.*; (*character*) auctōritās *f.*, grātia *f.*; (*bus.*) fidēs *f.* **be a — to** decus esse (*gen.*). **it is to your —** tibi laudī est. **give — for** laudem tribuere (*gen.*). **have —** fidē stāre. *vt.* crēdere (*dat.*); (*with money*) acceptum referre (*dat.*).
creditab/le *a.* honestus, laudābilis. **-ly** *ad.* honestē, cum laude.
creditor *n.* crēditor *m.*
credulity *n.* crēdulitās *f.*
credulous *a.* crēdulus.
creed *n.* dogma *n.*
creek *n.* sinus *m.*
creel *n.* vīdulus *m.*
creep *vi.* (*animal*) serpere; (*person*) rēpere; (*flesh*) horrēre.
cremate *vt.* cremāre.
crescent *n.* lūna *f.* — **shaped** lūnātus.
cress *n.* nasturtium *n.*
crest *n.* crista *f.* — **fallen** *a.* dēmissus.
crested *a.* cristātus.
crevasse *n.* hiātus *m.*
crevice *n.* rīma *f.*
crew *n.* nautae *m.pl.*, rēmigēs *m.pl.*, grex *f.*, turba *f.*
crib *n.* (*cot*) lectulus *m.*; (*manger*) praesēpe *n.*
cricket *n.* gryllus *m.*
crier *n.* praecō *m.*

crime *n.* scelus *n.*, facinus *n.*, flāgitium *n.*
criminal *a.* scelestus, facinorōsus flāgitiōsus. *n.* reus *m.* **-ly** *ad.* scelestē, flāgitiōsē.
criminality *n.* scelus *n.*
crimson *n.* coccum *n.* *a.* coccineus.
cringe *vi.* adūlārī, adsentārī.
crinkle *n.* rūga *f.*
cripple *vt.* dēbilitāre, mūtilāre; (*fig.*) frangere. *a.* claudus.
crisis *n.* discrīmen *n.*
crisp *a.* fragilis; (*manner*) alacer; (*hair*) crispus.
criss-cross *a.* in quīncūncem dispositus.
criterion *n.* index *m.*, indicium *n.* take as a — referre ad (*acc.*).
critic *n.* iūdex *m.*; (*literary*) criticus, grammaticus *m.*; (*adverse*) castīgātor *m.*
critical *a.* (*mind*) accūrātus, ēlegāns; (*blame*) cēnsōrius, sevērus; (*danger*) perīculōsus, dubius. — moment discrīmen. **-ly** *ad.* accūrātē, ēleganter; sevērē; cum perīculō.
criticism *n.* iūdicium *n.*; (*adverse*) reprehēnsiō *f.*
criticize *vt.* iūdicāre; reprehendere, castīgāre.
croak *vi.* (*raven*) crōcīre; (*frog*) coaxāre.
croaking *n.* cantus *m.* *a.* raucus.
crock *n.* olla *f.*
crockery *n.* fictilia *n.pl.*
crocodile *n.* crocodīlus *m.* weep — tears lacrimās cōnfingere.
crocus *n.* crocus *m.*
croft *n.* agellus *m.*
crone *n.* anus *f.*
crony *n.* sodālis *m.*
crook *n.* pedum *n.* *vt.* incurvāre.
crooked *a.* incurvus, aduncus; (*deformed*) prāvus; (*winding*) flexuōsus; (*morally*) perversus. **-ly** *ad.* perversē, prāvē.
crookedness *n.* prāvitās *f.*
croon *vt.* & *i.* cantāre.
crop *n.* (*grain*) seges *f.* messis *f.*; (*tree*) fructus *m.*; (*bird*) ingluviēs *f.* *vt.* (*reap*) metere; (*graze*) carpere, tondēre. *vi.* — up intervenīre.
cross *n.* (*mark*) decussis *m.*; (*torture*) crux *f.* *a.* trānsversus, oblīquus; (*person*) acerbus, īrātus. *vt.* trānsīre; (*water*) trāicere; (*mountain*) trānscendere; (*enemy*) obstāre (*dat.*), frustrārī. — out (*writing*) expungere. *vi.* trānsīre. — over (*on foot*) trānsgredī; (*by sea*) trānsmittere.
cross-bar *n.* iugum *n.*
cross-bow *n.* scorpiō *m.*
cross-examination *n.* interrogātiō *f.*
cross-examine *vt.* interrogāre, percontārī.
cross-grained *a.* (*fig.*) mōrōsus.
crossing *n.* trānsitus *m.*; (*over water*) trāiectus *m.*
cross purpose *n.* be at -s dīversa spectāre.
cross-question *vt* interrogāre
cross-roads *n.* quadrivium *n.*
cross-wise *ad.* ex trānsversō. divide — decussāre.
crotchety *a.* mōrōsus, difficilis.
crouch *vi.* subsīdere, sē submittere.
crow *n.* cornīx *f.* as the — flies rēctā regiōne. cock — gallī cantus *m.* *vi.* cantāre; (*fig.*) exsultāre, gestīre.
crow-bar *n.* vectis *m.*
crowd *n.* turba *f.*, concursus *m.*, frequentia *f.*; (*small*) grex *m.* in -s gregātim. *vi.* frequentāre, celebrāre. *vt.* (*place*) complēre; (*person*) stīpāre. **-ed** *a.* frequēns.
crown *n.* corōna *f.*; (*royal*) diadēma *n.*; (*of head*) vertex *m.*; (*fig.*) apex *m.*, flōs *m.*

the — of summus. *vt.* corōnāre; (*fig.*) cumulāre, fastigium impōnere (*dat.*).
crucial *a.* gravissimus, māximī mōmentī. — moment discrimen *n.*
crucifixion *n.* crucis supplicium *n.*
crucify *vt.* crucī suffigere.
crude *a.* crūdus; (*style*) dūrus, inconcinnus. **-ly** *ad.* dūrē, asperē.
crudity *n.* asperitās *f.*
cruel *a.* crūdēlis, saevus, atrōx. **-ly** *ad.* crūdēliter, atrōciter.
cruelty *n.* crūdēlitās *f.* saevitia *f.*, atrōcitās *f.*
cruise *n.* nāvigātiō *f.* *vi.* nāvigāre.
cruiser *n.* speculātōria nāvis *f.*
crumb *n.* mīca *f.*
crumble *vi.* corruere, putrem fierī. *vt.* putrefacere, friāre.
crumbling *a.* putris.
crumple *vt.* rūgāre.
crunch *vt.* dentibus frangere.
crupper *n.* postilēna *f.*
crush *vt.* frangere, contundere, obterere; (*fig.*) adflīgere, opprimere, obruere. *n.* turba *f.*, frequentia *f.*
crust *n.* crusta *f.*; (*bread*) frustum *n.*
crusty *a.* (*fig.*) stomachōsus.
crutch *n.* baculum *n.*
cry *vt.* & *i.* clāmāre, clāmitāre; (*weep*) flēre; (*infant*) vāgīre. — down dētrectāre. — out exclāmāre, vōciferārī. — out against adclāmāre, reclāmāre. — up laudāre, vēnditāre. *n.* clāmor *m.*, vōx *f.*; (*child's*) vāgītus *m.*; (*of grief*) plōrātus *m.*
cryptic *a.* arcānus.
crystal *n.* crystallum *n.* *a.* crystallinus.
cub *n.* catulus *m.*
cube *n.* cubus *m.*
cubit *n.* cubitum *n.*
cuckoo *n.* coccyx *m.*
cucumber *n.* cucumis *m.*
cud *n.* chew the — rūminārī.
cudgel *n.* fustis *m.* *vt.* verberāre.
cue *n.* signum *n.*, indicium *n.*
cuff *n.* (*blow*) alapa *f.*
cuirass *n.* lōrīca *f.*
culinary *a.* coquīnārius.
cull *vt.* legere, carpere, dēlībāre.
culminate *vi.* ad summum fastigium venīre.
culmination *n.* fastigium *n.*
culpability *n.* culpa *f.*, noxa *f.*
culpable *a.* nocēns.
culprit *n.* reus *m.*
cultivate *vt.* (*land*) colere, subigere; (*mind*) excolere; (*interest*) fovēre, studēre (*dat.*).
cultivation *n.* cultus *m.*, cultūra *f.*
cultivator *n.* cultor *m.*, agricola *m.*
cultural *a.* hūmānior.
culture *n.* hūmānitās *f.*, bonae artēs *f.pl.*
cultured *a.* doctus, litterātus.
culvert *n.* cloāca *f.*
cumber *vt.* impedīre, obesse (*dat.*); (*load*) onerāre.
cumbersome, cumbrous *a.* molestus, gravis.
cumulative *a.* alius ex aliō. be — cumulārī.
cuneiform *a.* cuneātus.
cunning *a.* callidus, astūtus. *n.* ars *f.*, astūtia *f.*, calliditās *f.* **-ly** *ad.* callidē, astūtē.
cup *n.* pōculum *n.* drink the — of (*fig.*) exanclāre, exhaurīre. in one's —s ēbrius, pōtus.
cupboard *n.* armārium *n.*
Cupid *n.* Cupīdō *m.*, Amor *m.*
cupidity *n.* avāritia *f.*
cupola *n.* tholus *m.*
cupping-glass *n.* cucurbita *f.*
cur *n.* canis *m.*
curable *a.* sānābilis.
curative *a.* salūbris.
curator *m.* custōs *m.*
curb *vt.* frēnāre, īnfrēnāre; (*fig.*) coercēre, cohibēre. *n.* frēnum *n.*

curdle *vt.* cōgere. *vi.* concrēscere.
curds *n.* concrētum lac *n.*
cure *vt.* sānāre, medērī (*dat.*). *n.* remedium *n.*; (*process*) sānātiō *f.*
curio *n.* dēliciae *f.pl.*
curiosity *n.* studium *n.*; (*thing*) mīrāculum *n.*
curious *a.* (*inquisitive*) cūriōsus, cupidus; (*artistic*) ēlābōrātus; (*strange*) mīrus, novus. **-ly** *ad.* cūriōsē; summā arte; mīrum in modum.
curl *n.* (*natural*) cirrus *m.*; (*artificial*) cincinnus *m.* *vt.* (*hair*) crispāre. *vi.* (*smoke*) volvī.
curling-irons *n.* calamistrī *m.pl.*
curly *a.* crispus.
currency *n.* (*coin*) monēta *f.*; (*use*) ūsus *m.* gain — (*rumour*) percrēbrēscere.
current *a.* vulgātus, ūsitātus; (*time*) hīc. *n.* flūmen *n.* with the — secundō flūmine. against the — adversō flūmine. **-ly** *ad.* vulgō.
curriculum *n.* īnstitūtiō *f.*
currier *n.* coriārius *m.*
curry *vt.* (*favour*) aucupārī.
curse *n.* exsecrātiō *f.*, maledictum *n.*; (*formula*) exsecrābile carmen *n.*; (*fig.*) pestis *f.*; (*interj.*) malum ! *vt.* exsecrārī, maledīcere (*dat.*).
cursed *a.* exsecrātus, sacer; scelestus.
cursor/y *a.* brevis. **-ily** *ad.* breviter, strictim.
curt *a.* brevis.
curtail *vt.* minuere, contrahere.
curtailment *n.* dēminūtiō *f.*, contractiō *f.*
curtain *n.* aulaeum *n.* *vt.* vēlāre.
curule *a.* curūlis.
curve *n.* flexus *m.*, arcus *m.* *vt.* flectere, incurvāre, arcuāre.
cushion *n.* pulvīnus *m.*
custodian *n.* custōs *m.*
custody *n.* custōdia *f.*, tūtēla *f.*; (*prison*) carcer *m.* hold in — custōdīre.
custom *n.* mōs *m.*, cōnsuētūdō *f.*; (*national*) īnstitūtum *n.*; (*pl.*) portōria *n.pl.* **-s-officer** *n.* portitor *m.*
customar/y *a.* solitus ūsitātus; (*rite*) sollemnis. it is — mōs est. **-ily** *ad.* plērumque, dē mōre, vulgō.
customer *n.* emptor *m.*
cut *vt.* secāre, caedere, scindere; (*corn*) metere; (*branch*) amputāre; (*acquaintance*) āversārī; (*hair*) dētondēre. — away abscindere, resecāre. — down caedere, succīdere. — into incīdere. — off abscīdere, praecīdere; (*exclude*) exclūdere; (*intercept*) interclūdere, intercipere. — out excīdere, exsecāre; (*omit*) ōmittere. — round circumcīdere. — short praecīdere; (*speech*) incīdere, interrumpere. — through intercīdere. — up concīdere. — out for aptus ad, nātus ad (*acc.*). *n.* volnus *n.* short — via compendiāria *f.*
cutlass *n.* gladius *m.*
cutlery *n.* cultrī *m.pl.*
cutter *n.* sector *m.*; (*boat*) lembus *m.*
cut-throat *n.* sīcārius *m.*
cutting *n.* (*plant*) propāgō *f.* *a.* acūtus; (*fig.*) acerbus, mordāx.
cuttle-fish *n.* sēpia *f.*
cyclamen *n.* baccar *n.*
cycle *n.* orbis *m.*
cyclone *n.* turbō *f.*
cylinder *n.* cylindrus *m.*
cymbal *n.* cymbalum *n.*
cynic *n.* (*philos.*) cynicus *m.*
cynical *a.* mordāx, acerbus. **-ly** *ad.* mordāciter, acerbē.
cynicism *n.* acerbitās *f.*
cynosure *n.* cynosūra *f.*
cypress *n.* cypressus *f.*.

D

dabble *vi.* — in gustāre, leviter attingere.
dactyl *n.* dactylus *m.*
dactylic *a.* dactylicus.
dagger *n.* sīca *f.*, pugiō *f.*
daily *a.* diūrnus, cottīdiānus. *ad.* cottīdiē, in diēs.
daintiness *n.* munditia *f.*, concinnitās *f.*, (*squeamish*) fastīdium *n.*
daint/y *a.* mundus, concinnus, mollis; fastīdiōsus. *n.* (*pl.*) cuppēdia *n.pl.* **-ily** *ad.* molliter, concinnē; fastīdiōsē.
dais *n.* suggestus *m.*
daisy *n.* bellis *f.*
dale *n.* vallis *f.*
dalliance *n.* lascīvia *f.*
dally *vi.* lūdere; morārī.
dam *n.* mōlēs *f.*, agger *m.*; (*animal*) māter *f.* *vt.* obstruere, exaggerāre.
damage *n.* damnum *n.*, dētrīmentum *n.*, malum *n.*; (*inflicted*) iniūria *f.*; (*law*) damnum *n.* assess **-s** lītem aestimāre. *vt.* laedere, nocēre (*dat.*); (*by evidence*) laedere; (*reputation*) violāre.
damageable *a.* fragilis.
dame *n.* mātrōna *f.*, domina *f.*
damn *vt.* damnāre, exsecrārī.
damnab/le *a.* dētestābilis, improbus. **-ly** *ad.* improbē.
damnation *n.* malum *n.*
damp *a.* ūmidus. *n.* ūmor *m.* *vt.* madefacere; (*enthusiasm*) restinguere, dēmittere.
damsel *n.* puella *f.*, virgō *f.*
damson *n.* Damascēnum *n.*
dance *vi.* saltāre. *n.* saltātiō *f.*; (*religious*) tripudium *n.*
dancer *n.* saltātor *m.*, saltātrix *f.*
dandruff *n.* porrigō *f.*
dandy *n.* dēlicātus *m.*
danger *n.* perīculum *n.*, discrīmen *n.*
dangerous *a.* perīculōsus, dubius; (*in attack*) infestus. **-ly** *ad.* perīculōsē.
dangle *vt.* suspendere *vi.* pendēre.
dank *a.* ūmidus.
dapper *a.* concinnus, nitidus.
dapple *vt.* variāre, distinguere. **-d** *a.* maculōsus, distinctus.
dare *vt.* audēre; (*challenge*) prōvocāre. I — say haud sciō an. [**-ly** *ad.* audācter.
daring *n.* audācia *f.* *a.* audāx.
dark *a.* obscūrus, opācus; (*colour*) fuscus, āter; (*fig.*) obscūrus. it is getting — advesperāscit. keep — silēre. *n.* tenebrae *f.pl.*; (*mist*) cālīgō *f.* keep in the — cēlāre.
darken *vt.* obscūrāre, occaecāre.
darkish *a.* subobscūrus.
darkling *a.* obscūrus.
darkness *n.* tenebrae *f.pl.*; (*mist*) cālīgō *f.*
darksome *a.* obscūrus.
darling *a.* cārus, dīlēctus. *n.* dēliciae *f.pl.*, voluptās *f.*
darn *vt.* resarcīre.
darnel *n.* lolium *n.*
dart *n.* iaculum *n.* *vi.* ēmicāre, sē conicere. *vt.* iaculārī, iacere.
dash *vt.* adflīgere; (*hope*) frangere. — against inlīdere, incutere. — down dēturbāre. — out ēlīdere. — to pieces discutere. — to the ground prōsternere. *vi.* currere, sē incitāre, ruere. *n.* impetus *m.*; (*quality*) ferōcia *f.*
dashing *a.* ferōx, animōsus.
dastardly *a.* ignāvus.
date *n.* (*fruit*) palmula *f.*; (*time*) tempus *n.*, diēs *m.* out of — obsolētus. become out of — exolēscere. to — adhūc. be up to — praesentī mōre ūtī. *vt.* (*letter*) diem adscrībere; (*past event*) repetere. *vi.* initium capere.
dative *n.* datīvus *m.*
daub *vt.* inlinere.
daughter *n.* fīlia *f.*; (*little*)

filiola *f*. **-in-law** *n*. nurus *f*. **grand** — *n*. neptis *f*. **step** — *n*. privigna *f*.
daunt *vt*. terrēre, perterrēre.
dauntless *a*. impavidus, intrepidus. **-ly** *ad*. impavidē, intrepidē.
dawdle *vi*. cessāre, cunctārī.
dawdler *n*. cunctātor *m*.
dawn *n*. aurōra *f*., dīlūculum *n*.; (*fig*.) orīgō *f*. at — prīmā lūce. *vi*. dīlūcēscere. day -s diēs illūcēscit. it — s upon me mente concipiō.
day *n*. diēs *m*., *f*.; (*period*) aetās *f*. — about alternīs diēbus. — by — in diēs. by — *a*. diūrnus. *ad*. interdiū. during the — interdiū. every — cottīdiē. from — to — in diēs, diem dē diē. late in the — multō diē. next — postrīdiē. one — some — ōlim. the — after *ad*. postrīdiē. *conj*. postrīdiē quam. the — after to-morrow perendiē. the — before *ad*. prīdiē. *conj*. prīdiē quam. the — before yesterday nūdius tertius. the present — haec ætās. time of — hōra. twice a — bis (in) diē: — s of old præteritum tempus. better — s to come posteritās. better — s rēs prosperae. evil — s rēs adversae. three -s trīduum *n*. two -s biduum *n*. to — hodiē. win the — vincere.
day-book *n*. adversāria *n.pl*.
day-break *n*. aurōra *f*., prīma lūx *f*.
daylight *n*. diēs *m*.
daytime *n*. diēs *m*. in the — interdiū.
day-star *n*. lūcifer *m*.
daze *vt*. obstupefacere. *n*. stupor *m*.
dazzle *vt*. praestringere.
dazzling *a*. splendidus, nitēns.
deacon *n*. diāconus *m*. **-ess** *n*. diāconissa *f*.
dead *a*. mortuus; (*in battle*) occīsus; (*lit*). frīgidus; (*place*) iners, sōlitārius; (*senses*) hebes. half — sēmivīvus, intermortuus. — of night nox intempesta *f*. — body cadāver *n*. — calm malacia *f*. — certainty rēs certissima. — loss mera iactūra — weight mōlēs. be — to nōn sentīre. in — earnest sēriō ac vērō. rise from the — revīvīscere. *ad*. prōrsus, omninō.
dead-beat *a*. cōnfectus.
deaden *vt*. (*senses*) hebetāre, obtundere; (*pain*) restinguere.
deadlock *n*. incitae *f.pl*. reach a — ad incitās redigī.
deadly *a*. fūnestus, exitiōsus, exitiābilis; (*enmity*) implācābilis; (*pain*) acerbissimus.
deaf *a*. surdus. become — obsurdēscere. be — to nōn audīre, obdūrēscere contrā.
deafen *vt*. (*with noise*) obtundere.
deafness *n*. surditās *f*.
deal *n*. (*amount*) cōpia *f*. a good — aliquantum *n*., bona pars *f*. (*wood*) abiēs *f*. *a*. abiēgnus. *vt*. (*blow*) dare, infligere; (*share*) dīvidere, partīrī. *vi*. agere, negōtiārī. — with (*person*) agere cum (*abl*.); (*matter*) tractāre.
dealer *n*. (*wholesale*) negōtiātor *m*., mercātor *m*.; (*retail*) caupō *m*. double — fraudātor *m*. [negōtium *n*., rēs *f*.
dealings *n*. commercium *n*.,
dean *n*. decānus *m*.
dear *a*. (*love*) cārus, grātus; (*cost*) cārus, pretiōsus. my — Quintus mī Quinte; (*beginning of letter from Marcus*) Marcus Quintō salūtem. — me! (*sorrow*) hei! (*surprise*) ehem! buy — male emere. sell — bene vēndere. **-ly** *ad*. (*love*) valdē, ārdenter; (*value*) magnī.
dearness *n*. cāritās *f*.
dearth *n*. inopia *f*., pēnūria *f*.
death *n*. mors *f*.; (*natural*) obitus *m*.; (*violent*) nex *f*.,

interitus *m.* condemn to — capitis damnāre. put to — interficere. give the — blow to interimere. on one's — bed moriēns, moribundus.
deathless *a.* immortālis.
deathly *a.* pallidus.
debar *vt.* prohibēre, exclūdere.
debase *vt.* dēprāvāre, corrumpere; (*coin*) adulterāre; (*self*) prōsternere, dēmittere.
debasement *n.* dēdecus *n.*; (*coin*) adulterium *n.*
debatable *a.* ambiguus, dubius.
debate *vt.* disputāre, disceptāre. *n.* contrōversia *f.*, disceptātiō *f.*, altercātiō *f.*
debater *n.* disputātor *m.*
debauch *vt.* corrumpere, pellicere. *n.* cōmissātiō *f.* **-ed** *a.* perditus, prāvus.
debauchee *n.* cōmissātor *m.*
debaucher *n.* corruptor *m.*
debauchery *n.* luxuria *f.*, stuprum *n.*
debilitate *vt.* dēbilitāre.
debility *n.* īnfirmitās *f.*
debit *n.* expēnsum *n.* *vt.* in expēnsum referre.
debonair *a.* urbānus, cōmis.
debouch *vi.* exīre.
debris *n.* rūdus *n.*
debt *n.* aes aliēnum *n.*; (*booked*) nōmen *n.*; (*fig.*) dēbitum *n.* be in — in aere aliēnō esse. pay off — aes aliēnum persolvere. run up — aes aliēnum contrahere. collect -s nōmina exigere. abolition of -s novae tabulae *f.pl.*
debtor *n.* dēbitor *m.*
decade *n.* decem annī *m.pl.*
decadence *n.* occāsus *m.*
decadent *a.* dēgener, dēterior.
decamp *vi.* (*mil.*) castra movēre; (*fig.*) discēdere, aufugere.
decant *vt.* dēfundere, diffundere.
decanter *n.* lagoena *f.*
decapitate *vt.* dētruncāre.
decay *vi.* dīlābī, perīre, putrēscere; (*fig.*) tābēscere, senēscere. *n.* ruīna *f.*, lāpsus *m.*; (*fig.*) occāsus *m.*, dēfectiō *f.*
decease *n.* mors *f.*, excessus *m.*, obitus *m.* *vi.* mortem obīre. **-d** *a.* mortuus.
deceit *n.* fraus *f.*, fallācia *f.*, dolus *m.*
deceitful *a.* fallāx, fraudulentus, dolōsus. **-ly** *ad.* fallāciter, dolōsē.
deceive *vt.* dēcipere, fallere, circumvenīre, fraudāre.
deceiver *n.* fraudātor *m.*
December *n.* mēnsis December *m.* of — December.
decemvir *n.* decemvir *m.* of the -s decemvirālis.
decemvirate *n.* decemvirātus *m.*
decency *n.* honestum *n.*, decōrum *n.*, pudor *m.*
decent *a.* honestus, pudēns. **-ly** *ad.* honestē, pudenter.
deception *n.* fraus *f.*, fallācia *f.*
deceptive *a.* fallāx, fraudulentus.
decide *vt.* & *i.* (*dispute*) dīiūdicāre, dēcernere, dīrimere; (*to do*) statuere, cōnstituere (*inf.*). I have -d mihī certum est. — the issue dēcernere.
decided *a.* certus, firmus. **-ly** *ad.* certē, plānē.
deciduous *a.* cadūcus.
decimate *vt.* decimum quemque occīdere.
decipher *vt.* expedīre, ēnōdāre.
decision *n.* (*of judge*) iūdicium *n.*; (*of council*) dēcrētum *n.*; (*of senate*) auctōritās *f.*; (*of referee*) arbitrium *n.*; (*personal*) sententia *f.*; (*quality*) cōnstantia *f.*
decisive *a.* certus. — moment discrīmen *n.* **-ly** *ad.* sine dubiō.
deck *vt.* ōrnāre, exōrnāre. *n.* (*ship*) pōns *m.* with a — cōnstrātus.
decked *a.* ōrnātus; (*ship*) cōnstrātus.

declaim *vt.* & *i.* dēclāmāre, prōnūntiāre.
declamation *n.* dēclāmātiō *f.*
declamatory *a.* dēclāmātōrius.
declaration *n.* adfirmātiō *f.*, adseverātiō *f.*; (*formal*) professiō *f.*; (*of war*) dēnūntiātiō *f.*
declare *vt.* adfirmāre, adseverāre; (*secret*) aperīre, expōnere; (*proclamation*) dēnūntiāre, ēdīcere; (*property in census*) dēdicāre; (*war*) indīcere.
declension *n.* dēclīnātiō *f.*
declination *n.* dēclīnātiō *f.*
decline *n.* (*slope*) dēclīve *n.*, dēiectus *m.*; (*of age*) senium *n.*; (*of power*) dēfectiō *f.*; (*of nation*) occāsus *m.* *vi.* inclīnāre, occidere; (*fig.*) ruere, dēlābī, dēgenerāre. *vt.* dētrectāre, recūsare; (*gram.*) dēclīnāre.
declivity *n.* dēclīve *n.*, dēiectus *m.*
decode *vt.* expedīre, ēnōdāre.
decompose *vt.* dissolvere. *vi.* putrēscere. **-d** *a.* putridus.
decomposition *n.* dissolūtiō *f.*
decorate *vt.* adōrnāre, decorāre.
decoration *n.* ōrnāmentum *n.*; (*medal*) īnsigne *n.*
decorous *a.* pudēns, modestus, decōrus. **-ly** *ad.* pudenter, modestē.
decorum *n.* pudor *m.*, honestum *n.*
decoy *n.* illecebra *f.* *vt.* adlicere, inescāre.
decrease *n.* dēminūtiō *f.*, dēcessiō *f.* *vt.* dēminuere, extenuāre. *vi.* dēcrēscere.
decree *n.* (*of magistrate*) dēcrētum *n.*, ēdictum *n.*; (*of senate*) cōnsultum *n.*, auctōritās *f.*; (*of people*) scītum *n.* *vt.* ēdīcere, dēcernere; (*people*) scīscere, iubēre. **the senate -s** placet senātuī.
decrepit *a.* īnfirmus, dēbilis, dēcrepitus.
decrepitude *n.* īnfirmitās *f.*, dēbilitās *f.*
decry *vt.* obtrectāre, reprehendere.
decurion *n.* decuriō *m.*
dedicate *vt.* dēdicāre, cōnsecrāre; (*life*) dēvovēre.
dedication *n.* dēdicātiō *f.*; dēvōtiō *f.*
dedicatory *a.* commendātīcius.
deduce *vt.* colligere, conclūdere.
deduct *vt.* dēmere, dētrahere.
deduction *n.* (*inference*) conclūsiō *f.*, cōnsequēns *n.*; (*subtraction*) dēductiō *f.*, dēminūtiō *f.*
deed *n.* factum *n.*, facinus *n.*; (*legal*) tabulae *f.pl.*; (*pl.*) rēs gestae *f.pl.*
deem *vt.* dūcere, cēnsēre, habēre.
deep *a.* altus, profundus; (*discussion*) abstrūsus; (*sleep*) artus; (*sound*) gravis; (*width*) lātus. **three —** (*mil.*) ternī in lātitūdinem. *n.* altum *n.* **-est** *a.* īmus. **-ly** *ad.* altē; graviter; (*inside*) penitus; (*very*) valdē, vehementer.
deepen *vt.* dēfodere, altiōrem reddere; (*fig.*) augēre. *vi.* altiōrem fierī; (*fig.*) crēscere.
deer *n.* cervus *m.*, cerva *f.*; (*fallow*) dāma *f.*
deface *vt.* dēfōrmāre, foedāre. **-d** *a.* dēfōrmis.
defacement *n.* dēfōrmitās *f.*
defalcation *n.* peculātus *m.*
defamation *n.* calumnia *f.*, opprobrium *n.*
defamatory *a.* contumēliōsus, probrōsus.
defame *vt.* īnfāmāre, obtrectāre, calumniārī.
default *vi.* dēesse; (*money*) nōn solvere. *n.* dēfectiō *f.*, culpa *f.* **let judgment go by —** vadimōnium dēserere, nōn respondēre.
defaulter *n.* reus *m.*
defeat *vt.* vincere, superāre; (*completely*) dēvincere; (*plan*)

frustrari, disicere. *n.* clādes *f.*; (*at election*) repulsa *f.*, offēnsiō *f.*; (*of plan*) frustrātiō *f.*
defeatism *n.* patientia *f.*
defeatist *n.* imbellis *m.*
defect *n.* vitium *n.*
defection *n.* dēfectiō *f.*, sēditiō *f.*
defective *a.* mancus, vitiōsus.
defence *n.* praesidium *n.*, tūtēla *f.*; (*pl.*) mūnimenta *n.pl.*, mūnītiōnēs *f.pl.*; (*legal*) patrōcinium *n.*; (*speech*) dēfēnsiō *f.* **speak in —** dēfendere.
defenceless *a.* inermis, indēfēnsus. **leave —** nūdāre.
defend *vt.* dēfendere, tuērī, custōdīre.
defendant *n.* reus *m.*
defender *n.* dēfēnsor *m.*, prōpugnātor *m.*; (*law*) patrōnus *m.*
defensible *a.* iūstus.
defensive *a.* dēfēnsiōnis causā. **be on the —** sē dēfendere. **-ly** *ad.* dēfendendō.
defer *vt.* differre, prōlātāre. *vi.* mōrem gerere (*dat.*). **I — to you in this** hōc tibī tribuō.
deference *n.* obsequium *n.* observantia *f.* **show — to** observāre, īnservīre (*dat.*).
deferential *a.* observāns, officiōsus.
deferment *n.* dīlātiō *f.*, prōlātiō *f.*
defiance *n.* ferōcia *f.*, minae [*f.pl.*]
defiant *a.* ferōx, mināx. **-ly** *ad.* ferōciter, mināciter.
deficiency *n.* vitium *n.*; (*lack*) pēnūria *f.*, inopia *f.*
deficient *a.* vitiōsus, inops. **be —** dēesse, dēficere.
deficit *n.* lacūna *f.*
defile *n.* faucēs *f.pl.*, angustiae *f.pl.* *vt.* inquināre, contāmināre.
defilement *n.* sordēs *f.*, foeditās *f.*
define *vt.* (*limits*) fīnīre, dēfīnīre, termināre; (*meaning*) explicāre.
definite *a.* certus dēfīnītus. **-ly** *ad.* dēfīnītē; prōrsus.
definition *n.* dēfīnītiō *f.*, explicātiō *f.*
definitive *a.* dēfīnītīvus.
deflate *vt.* laxāre.
deflect *vt.* dēdūcere, dēclīnāre. *vi.* dēflectere, dēgredī.
deflection *n.* dēclīnātiō *f.*, flexus *m.*
deform *vt.* dēfōrmāre. **-ed** *a.* dēfōrmis, distortus.
deformity *n.* dēfōrmitās *f.*, prāvitās *f.*
defraud *vt.* fraudāre dē[fraudāre].
defrauder *n.* fraudātor *m.*
defray *vt.* solvere, suppeditāre.
deft *a.* habilis. **-ly** *ad.* habiliter.
defunct *a.* mortuus.
defy *vt.* contemnere, spernere, adversārī (*dat.*); (*challenge*) prōvocāre, lacessere.
degeneracy *n.* dēprāvātiō *f.*
degenerate *a.* dēgener. *vi.* dēgenerāre, dēscīscere.
degradation *n.* īnfāmia *f.*, ignōminia *f.*, nota *f.*
degrade *vt.* notāre, abicere; (*from office*) movēre.
degrading *a.* turpis, indignus.
degree *n.* gradus; (*social*) locus *m.* **in some —** aliquā ex parte. **by -s** gradātim, sēnsim.
deification *n.* apotheōsis *f.*
deif/y *vt.* cōnsecrāre, inter deōs referre. **-ied** *a.* (*emperor*) dīvus.
deign *vi.* dignārī.
deity *n.* deus *m.*
dejected *a.* adflīctus, dēmissus **-ly** *ad.* animō dēmissō.
dejection *n.* maestitia *f.*
delay *vt.* dēmorārī, dētinēre, retardāre. *vi.* cunctārī, cessāre. *n.* mora *f.*, cunctātiō *f.*
delayer *n.* morātor *m.*, cunctātor *m.*
delectable *a.* iūcundus, [amoenus.]
delegate *vt.* lēgāre, mandāre, committere *n.* lēgātus *m.*

delegation *n.* lēgātiō *f.* lēgātī *m.pl.*
delete *vt.* dēlēre.
deleterious *a.* perniciōsus, noxius.
deletion *n.* (*writing*) litūra *f.*
deliberate *vi.* dēlīberāre, cōnsulere. *a.* (*act*) cōnsīderātus; (*intention*) certus; (*manner*) cōnsīderātus; (*speech*) lentus. **-ly** *ad.* dē industriā.
deliberation *n.* dēlīberātiō *f.*
deliberative *a.* dēlīberātīvus.
delicacy *n.* (*judgment*) subtīlitās *f.*, ēlegantia *f.*; (*manners*) mollitia *f.*, luxus *m.*; (*health*) valētūdō *f.*; (*food*) cuppēdia *n.pl.*
delicate *a.* mollis; (*health*) īnfirmus; (*shape*) gracilis; (*feelings*) hūmānus. **-ly** *ad.* molliter; hūmānē.
delicious *a.* suāvis, lautus.
delight *n.* voluptās *f.*, gaudium *n.*, dēlectātiō *f.* *vt.* dēlectāre, oblectāre, iuvāre. *vi.* gaudēre, dēlectārī.
delightful *a.* iūcundus, dulcis, festīvus; (*scenery*) amoenus. **-ly** *ad.* iūcundē, suāviter.
delimitation *n.* dēfīnītiō *f.*
delineate *vt.* dēscrībere, dēpingere.
delineation *n.* dēscrīptiō *f.*
delinquency *n.* culpa *f.*, dēlictum *n.*, noxa *f.*
delinquent *n.* nocēns *m.*, *f.*, reus *m.*
delirious *a.* dēlīrus, āmēns, furiōsus. be — furere, dēlīrāre.
delirium *n.* furor *m.*, āmentia [*f.*
deliver *vt.* (*from*) līberāre, exsolvere, ēripere; (*to*) dēferre, trādere, dare; (*blow*) intendere; (*message*) referre; (*speech*) habēre. — up dēdere, trādere. be -ed of parere.
deliverance *n.* līberātiō *f.*
deliverer *n.* līberātor *m.*
delivery *n.* (*of things due*) trāditiō *f.*; (*of speech*) āctiō *f.* prōnūntiātiō *f.*; (*of child*) partus *m.*
dell *n.* convallis *f.*
delude *vt.* dēcipere, frustrārī, dēlūdere.
deluge *n.* ēluviō *f.* *vt.* inundāre.
delusion *n.* error *m.*, fraus *f.*
delusive *a.* fallāx, inānis.
delve *vt.* fodere.
demagogue *n.* plēbicola *m.*
demand *vt.* poscere, postulāre, imperāre; (*urgently*) efflāgitāre, exposcere; (*thing due*) exigere; (*answer*) quaerere. — back repetere. *n.* postulātiō *f.*, postulātum *n.*
demarcation *n.* līmes *m.*
demean *vt.* (*self*) dēmittere.
demeanour *n.* gestus *m.*, mōs *m.*, habitus *m.* [ōsus.
demented *a.* dēmēns, furi-
demerit *n.* culpa *f.*. vitium *n.*
demesne *n.* fundus *m.*
demigod *n.* hērōs *m.*
demise *n.* obitus *m.* *vt.* lēgāre.
democracy *n.* cīvitās populāris *f.* [*m.*, *f.*
democrat *n.* homō populāris
democratic *a.* populāris.
demolish *vt.* dēmōlīrī, dīruere, dēstruere; (*argument*) discutere.
demolition *n.* ruīna *f.*, ēversiō *f.*
demon *n.* daemōn *m.*
demonstrate *vt.* (*show*) mōnstrāre, ostendere, indicāre; (*prove*) dēmōnstrāre.
demonstration *n.* exemplum *n.*; (*proof*) dēmōnstrātiō *f.*
demonstrative *a.* (*manner*) vehemēns; (*rhet.*) dēmōnstrātīvus.
demoralization *n.* corruptiō *f.*, dēprāvātiō *f.*
demoralize *vt.* corrumpere, dēprāvāre, labefactāre.
demote *vt.* locō movēre.
demur *vi.* gravārī, recūsāre. *n.* mora *f.*, dubitātiō *f.*

demure *a.* modestus, verēcundus. **-ly** *ad.* modestē, verēcundē.
demureness *n.* modestia *f.*, verēcundia *f.*, pudor *m.*
demurrer *n.* (*law*) exceptiō *f.*
den *n.* latibulum *n.*, latebra *f.*; (*of vice*) lustrum *n.*
denial *n.* īnfitiātiō *f.*, negātiō *f.*
denigrate *vt.* obtrectāre, calumniārī.
denizen *n.* incola *m.*, *f.*
denominate *vt.* nōmināre, appellāre.
denomination *n.* nōmen *n.*; (*religious*) secta *f.*
denote *vt.* notāre, significāre.
denouement *n.* exitus *m.*
denounce *vt.* dēferre, incūsāre.
denouncer *n.* dēlātor *m.*
dense *a.* dēnsus; (*crowd*) frequēns; (*person*) stolidus.
density *n.* crassitūdō *f.*; (*crowd*) frequentia *f.*
dent *n.* nota *f.*
dentate *a.* dentātus.
denture *n.* dentēs *m.pl.*
denudation *n.* spoliātiō *f.*
denude *vt.* spoliāre, nūdāre.
denunciation *n.* (*report*) indicium *n.*, dēlātiō *f.*; (*threat*) minae *f.pl.*
deny *vt.* īnfitiārī, īnfitiās īre, negāre, abnuere; (*on oath*) abiūrāre. — oneself genium dēfraudāre.
depart *vi.* discēdere, abīre, exīre, ēgredī.
department *n.* (*district*) regiō *f.*, pars *f.*; (*duty*) prōvincia *f.*, mūnus *n.*
departure *n.* discessus *m.*, abitus *m.*, digressus *m.*, exitus *m.*; (*change*) mūtātiō *f.*; (*death*) obitus *m.*
depend *vi.* pendēre; (*be dependent*) pendēre ex (*abl.*), nītī (*abl.*); (*rely*) fīdere, cōnfīdere. **-ing on** frētus (*abl.*).
dependable *a.* fīdus.
dependant *n.* cliēns *m.*, *f.*
dependence *n.* clientēla *f.*; (*reliance*) fīdūcia *f.*
dependency *n.* prōvincia *f.*
dependent *a.* subiectus, obnoxius.
depict *vt.* dēscrībere, dēpingere; (*to the life*) expingere.
deplete *vt.* dēminuere.
depletion *n.* dēminūtiō *f.*
deplorab/le *a.* turpis, nefandus, pessimus. **-ly** *ad.* turpiter, pessimē, miserē.
deplore *vt.* dēplōrāre, dēflēre, conquerī.
deploy *vt.* explicāre. [dāre.
depopulate *vt.* vastāre, nū-
depopulation *n.* vastātiō *f.*, sōlitūdō *f.*
deport *vt.* (*banish*) dēportāre; (*self*) gerere.
deportation *n.* exsilium *n.*
deportment *n.* gestus *m.*, habitus *m.*
depose *vt.* dēmovēre, dēpellere; (*evidence*) testārī.
deposit *n.* fīdūcia *f.*, dēpositum *n.* *vt.* dēpōnere, mandāre.
depositary *n.* sequester *m.*
deposition *n.* (*law*) testimōnium *n.*, indicium *n.*
depository *n.* apothēca *f.*
depot *n.* (*for arms*) armāmentārium *n.*; (*for trade*) emporium *n.* [rumpere. **-d** *a.* prāvus.
deprave *vt.* dēprāvāre, cor-
depravity *n.* dēprāvātiō *f.*, turpitūdō *f.*
deprecate *vt.* abōminārī, dēprecārī.
deprecation *n.* dēprecātiō *f.*
depreciate *vt.* obtrectāre, dētrectāre.
depreciation *n.* obtrectātiō *f.*; (*price*) vīlitās *f.*
depredation *n.* praedātiō *f.*, dīreptiō *f.*
depress *vt.* dēprimere; (*mind*) adflīgere, frangere. **be -ed** iacēre, animum dēspondēre.
depressing *a.* maestus, tristis.
depression *n.* (*place*) cavum

n.; (*mind*) tristitia *f.*, sollicitūdō *f.* [spoliātiō *f.*
deprivation *n.* prīvātiō *f.*,
deprive *vt.* prīvāre, spoliāre.
depth *n.* altitūdō *f.*; (*place*) profundum *n.*, gurges *m.*
deputation *n.* lēgātiō *f.*, lēgātī *m.pl.*
depute *vt.* lēgāre, mandāre.
deputy *n.* lēgātus *m.*; (*substitute*) vicārius *m.*
derange *vt.* conturbāre. **-d** *a.* īnsānus, mente captus.
derangement *n.* perturbātiō *f.*; (*mind*) īnsānia *f.*, dēmentia *f.*
derelict *a.* dēsertus.
dereliction *n.* (*of duty*) neglegentia *f.*
deride *vt.* dērīdēre, inlūdere.
derision *n.* rīsus *m.*, irrīsiō *f.*
derisive *a.* mordāx.
derivation *n.* origō *f.*
derive *vt.* dūcere, trahere; (*advantage*) capere, parāre; (*pleasure*) dēcerpere, percipere. be -d dēfluere.
derogate *vi.* dērogāre, dētrahere. — **from** imminuere, obtrectāre.
derogation *n.* imminūtiō *f.*, obtrectātiō *f.*
derogatory *a.* indignus. — remarks obtrectātiō *f.*
derrick *n.* trochlea *f.*
descant *vt.* disserere. *n.* cantus *m.*
descend *vi.* dēscendere; (*water*) dēlābī; (*from heaven*) dēlābī; (*by inheritance*) pervenīre, prōdī; (*morally*) dēlābī, sē dēmittere. **be -ed from** orīrī ex (*abl.*).
descendant *n.* prōgeniēs *f.*; (*pl.*) minōrēs *m.pl.*, posterī *m.pl.*
descent *n.* dēscensus *m.*; (*slope*) clīvus *m.*, dēiectus *m.*; (*birth*) genus *n.*; (*hostile*) dēcursus *m.*, incursiō *f.* **make a — upon** inrumpere in (*acc.*), incursāre in (*acc.*).
describe *vt.* dēscrībere; (*tell*) nārrāre; (*portray*) dēpingere, exprimere.
description *n.* dēscriptiō *f.*; (*tale*) nārrātiō *f.*; (*kind*) genus *n.* [prōspectāre.
descry *vt.* cernere, cōnspicere,
desecrate *vt.* prōfānāre, exaugurāre.
desecration *n.* exaugurātiō *f.*, violātiō *f.*
desert *vt.* dēserere, dērelinquere, dēstituere. *vi.* dēscīscere, dēficere. *a.* dēsertus, sōlitārius. *n.* (*place*) sōlitūdō *f.*, loca dēserta *n.pl.*; (*merit*) meritum *n.*
deserter *n.* dēsertor *m.*; (*mil.*) trānsfuga *m.*
desertion *n.* dēfectiō *f.*, trānsfugium *n.*
deserve *vt.* merērī. — **well of** bene merērī dē (*abl.*). **-d** *a.* meritus. **-dly** *ad.* meritō.
deserving *a.* dignus.
desiccate *vt.* siccāre.
desiderate *vt.* dēsīderāre.
design *n.* (*drawing*) adumbrātiō *f.*; (*plan*) cōnsilium *n.*, prōpositum *n.* by — cōnsultō. *vt.* adumbrāre; in animō habēre.
designate *vt.* dēsignāre, mōnstrāre; (*as heir*) scrībere; (*as official*) dēsignāre. *a.* dēsignātus.
designation *n.* nōmen *n.*, titulus *m.* [cōnsultō.
designedly *ad.* dē industriā,
designer *n.* auctor *m.*, inventor *m.*
designing *a.* vafer, dolōsus.
desirable *a.* optābilis, expetendus, grātus.
desire *n.* cupīdō *f.*; (*uncontrolled*) libīdō *f.*; (*natural*) adpetītiō *f.* *vt.* cupere; (*much*) exoptāre, expetere; (*command*) iubēre.
desirous *a.* cupidus, avidus, studiōsus.
desist *vi.* dēsistere.
desk *n.* scrīnium *n.*

desolate *a.* dēsertus, sōlitārius; (*place*) vastus. *vt.* vastāre.
desolation *n.* sōlitūdō *f.*, vastitās *f.*; (*process*) vastātiō *f.*
despair *vi.* dēspērāre, animum dēspondēre. *n.* dēspērātiō *f.*
despairingly *ad.* dēspēranter.
despatch *vt.* mittere, dīmittere; (*finish*) absolvere, perficere; (*kill*) interficere. *n.* (*letter*) litterae *f.pl.*; (*speed*) celeritās *f.*
desperado *n.* homō dēspērātus *m.*
desperate *a.* (*hopeless*) dēspērātus; (*wicked*) perditus; (*dangerous*) perīculōsus. **-ly** *ad.* dēspēranter.
desperation *n.* dēspērātiō *f.*
despicab/le *a.* dēspectus, abiectus, turpis. **-ly** *ad.* turpiter.
despise *vt.* contemnere, dēspicere, spernere.
despiser *n.* contemptor *m.*
despite *n.* malevolentia *f.*, odium *n.*
despoil *vt.* spoliāre, nūdāre.
despoiler *n.* spoliātor *m.*, praedātor *m.*
despond *vi.* animum dēspondēre, dēspērāre.
despondency *n.* dēspērātiō *f.*
despondent *a.* abiectus, adflictus, dēmissus. be — animum dēspondēre. **-ly** *ad.* animō dēmissō.
despot *n.* dominus *m.*, rēx *m.*
despotic *a.* imperiōsus, superbus. **-ally** *ad.* superbē.
despotism *n.* dominātiō *f.*, superbia *f.*, rēgnum *n.*
dessert *n.* secunda mēnsa *f.*
destination *n.* fīnis *m.*
destine *vt.* dēstināre, dēsignāre. -d to be futūrus.
destiny *n.* fātum *n.* of — fātālis.
destitute *a.* inops, pauper, prīvātus. — of expers (*gen.*).
destitution *n.* inopia *f.*, egestās *f.*
destroy *vt.* dēlēre, ēvertere, dīrimere, perdere.
destroyer *n.* ēversor *m.*
destructible *a.* fragilis.
destruction *n.* exitium *n.*, ēversiō *f.*, excidium *n.*
destructive *a.* exitiābilis, perniciōsus. **-ly** *ad.* perniciōsē.
desuetude *n.* dēsuētūdō *f.*
desultor/y *a.* varius, incōnstāns. **-ily** *ad.* carptim.
detach *vt.* abiungere, sēiungere, āmovēre, sēparāre.
detachment *n.* (*mil.*) manus *f.*, cohors *f.*; (*mind*) integer animus *m.* līber animus.
detail *n.* (*pl.*) singula *n.pl.* in — singillātim. *vt.* exsequī.
detain *vt.* dēmorārī, dētinēre, distinēre, morārī.
detect *vt.* dēprehendere, patefacere.
detection *n.* dēprehēnsiō *f.*
detective *n.* inquīsītor *m.*
detention *n.* retentiō *f.*, (*prison*) vincula *n.pl.*
deter *vt.* dēterrēre, absterrēre, impedīre.
deteriorate *vi.* dēgenerāre.
deterioration *n.* dēprāvātiō *f.*, lāpsus *m.*
determinate *a.* certus, fīnītus.
determination *n.* obstinātiō *f.*, cōnstantia *f.*; (*intention*) prōpositum *n.*, sententia *f.*
determine *vt.* (*fix*) fīnīre; (*decide*) statuere, cōnstituere.
determined *a.* obstinātus; (*thing*) certus. I am — to mihi certum est (*inf.*). **-ly** *ad.* cōnstanter.
deterrent *n.* act as a — to dēterrēre.
detest *vt.* ōdisse, dētestārī.
detestable *a.* dētestābilis, odiōsus.
detestation *n.* odium *n.*, invidia *f.*
dethrone *vt.* rēgnō dēpellere.
detour *n.* circuitus *m.* make a — iter flectere; (*mil.*) agmen circumdūcere.

detract *vi.* — from dērogāre, dētrahere.
detraction *n.* obtrectātiō *f.*
detractor *n.* obtrectātor *m.*, invidus *m.*
detriment *n.* damnum *n.*, dētrimentum *n.*
detrimental *a.* damnōsus. be — to dētrimentō esse (*dat.*).
devastate *vt.* vastāre, populārī.
devastation *n.* vastātiō *f.*, populātiō *f.*; (*state*) vastitās *f.*
develop *vt.* ēvolvere, explicāre; (*person*) ēducāre, alere. *vi.* crēscere. — into ēvādere in (*acc.*).
development *n.* explicātiō *f.*; (*of men*) ēducātiō *f.*; (*of resources*) cultus *m.*; (*of events*) exitus *m.*
deviate *vi.* dēcēdere dē viā, aberrāre, dēclīnāre; (*speech*) dēgredī.
deviation *n.* dēclīnātiō *f.*; (*from truth*) error *m.*; (*in speech*) digressus *m.*
device *n.* (*plan*) cōnsilium *n.*; (*machine*) māchina *f.*; (*emblem*) īnsigne *n.*
devil *n.* diabolus *m.* go to the — abī in malam crucem! talk of the — lupus in fābulā!
devilish *a.* scelestus, impius.
devil-may-care *a.* praeceps, lascīvus.
devilment *n.* malitia *f.*
devilry *n.* magicae artēs *f.pl.*
devious *a.* dēvius, errābundus.
devise *vt.* excōgitāre, commentārī, fingere.
devoid *a.* vacuus, expers. be — of carēre (*abl.*).
devolve *vi.* obtingere, obvenīre. *vt.* dēferre, committere.
devote *vt.* dēdicāre; (*attention*) dēdere, trādere; (*life*) dēvovēre. **-d** *a.* dēditus, studiōsus; (*victim*) dēvōtus, sacer. be — to studēre (*dat.*), incumbere (*dat.*).
devotee *n.* cultor *m.*
devotion *n.* amor *m.*, studium *n.*; rēligiō *f.*
devour *vt.* dēvorāre, cōnsūmere; (*fig.*) haurīre.
devout *a.* pius, rēligiōsus. **-ly** *ad.* piē, rēligiōsē.
dew *n.* rōs *m.*
dewlap *n.* palear *n.*
dewy *a.* rōscidus.
dexterity *n.* ars *f.*, sollertia *f.*
dexterous *a.* sollers, habilis. **-ly** *ad.* sollerter, habiliter.
diabolical *a.* scelestus, nefārius.
diadem *n.* diadēma *n.*
diagnose *vt.* discernere, diiūdicāre.
diagnosis *n.* iūdicium *n.*
diagonal *a.* oblīquus.
diagram *n.* fōrma *f.*
dial *n.* sōlārium *n.*
dialect *n.* dialectus *f.*, sermō [*m.*
dialectic *n.* ars disserendī *f.*, dialecticē *f.* *a.* dialecticus.
dialectician *n.* dialecticus *m.*
dialogue *n.* dialogus *m.*, colloquium *n.*
diameter *n.* diametros *f.*
diamond *n.* adamās *m.*
diaphanous *a.* perlūcidus.
diaphragm *n.* praecordia *n.pl.*
diary *n.* ephēmeris *f.*
diatribe *n.* convīcium *n.*
dice *n.* tālus *m.*, tessera *f.* game of — ālea *f.*
dictate *vt.* dictāre. *n.* praeceptum *n.* **-s** of nature nātūrae iūdicia *n.pl.*
dictation *n.* dictāta *n.pl.*; (*fig.*) arbitrium *n.*
dictator *n.* dictātor *m* **-'s** dictātōrius.
dictatorial *a.* imperiōsus, superbus.
dictatorship *n.* dictātūra *f.*
diction *n.* (*enunciation*) ēlocūtiō *f.*; (*words*) ōrātiō *f.*
dictionary *n.* verbōrum thēsaurus *m.*
die *n.* signum *n.* the — is cast iacta alea est. *vi.* morī, perīre, obīre; (*in battle*) cadere, occum-

bere. — off dēmorī. — out ēmorī. be dying to exoptāre.
diet *n.* (*food*) diaeta *f.*; (*meeting*) conventus *m.*
differ *vi.* differe, discrepāre, dissentīre.
difference *n.* discrepantia *f.*, dissimilitūdō *f.*; (*of opinion*) dissēnsiō *f.* there is a — interest.
different *a.* dīversus, varius, dissimilis. in — directions dīversī. they say — things alius aliud dīcit. **-ly** *ad.* dīversē, variē, alius aliter.
differentiate *vt.* discernere.
difficult *a.* difficilis, arduus. very — perdifficilis, perarduus.
difficulty *n.* difficultās *f.*, labor *m.*, negōtium *n.* with — difficulter, aegrē. be in — labōrāre.
diffidence *n.* diffīdentia *f.*; (*shyness*) pudor *m.* with — modestē.
diffident *a.* diffīdēns; (*shy*) modestus, verēcundus. **-ly** *ad.* modestē.
diffuse *vt.* diffundere, dispergere. be -d diffluere. *a.* fūsus, diffūsus, cōpiōsus. **-ly** *ad.* diffūsē, cōpiōsē.
diffuseness *n.* cōpia *f.*
dig *vt.* fodere; (*nudge*) fodicāre. — up effodere, ēruere.
digest *vt.* coquere, concoquere. *n.* summārium *n.*
digestion *n.* concoctiō *f.* with a bad — crūdus.
digger *n.* fossor *m.*
dignified *a.* gravis, augustus.
dignify *vt.* honōrāre, honestāre. [*f.*, amplitūdō *f.*
dignity *n.* gravitās *f.*, māiestās
digress *vi.* dēvertere, digredī, dēclīnāre.
digression *n.* dēclīnātiō *f.*, digressus *m.*
dike *n.* (*ditch*) fossa *f.*; (*mound*) agger *m.*
dilapidated *a.* ruīnōsus.
dilapidation *n.* ruīna *f.*
dilate *vi.* dīlātāre; (*speech*) plūra dīcere.
dilatoriness *n.* mora *f.*, cunctātiō *f.*
dilator/y *a.* tardus, lentus, segnis. **-ily** *ad.* tardē, cunctanter.
dilemma *n.* nōdus *m.*, angustiae *f.pl.* be in a — haerēre. be on the horns of a — auribus tenēre lupum.
diligence *n.* dīligentia *f.*, industria *f.*, cūra *f.*
diligent *a.* dīligēns, industrius, sēdulus. **-ly** *ad.* dīligenter, sēdulō.
dill *n.* anēthum *n.*
dilly-dally *vi.* cessāre.
dilute *vt.* dīluere, temperāre.
dim *a.* obscūrus; (*fig.*) hebes. *vt.* obscūrāre; hebetāre. **-ly** *ad.* obscūrē.
dimension *n.* modus *m.*; (*pl.*) amplitūdō, *f.* māgnitūdō *f.*
diminish *vt.* minuere, imminuere, extenuāre, īnfringere. *vi.* dēcrēscere.
diminution *n.* imminūtiō *f.*, dēminūtiō *f.*
diminutive *a.* parvulus, exiguus. *n.* (*word*) dēminūtum *n.* [*f.*
diminutiveness *n.* exiguitās
dimness *n.* tenebrae *f.pl.*, cālīgō *f.*
dimple *n.* gelasīnus *m.*
din *n.* fragor *m.*, strepitus *m.* make a —strepere. *vt.* obtundere.
dine *vi.* cēnāre.
diner *n.* convīva *m.*
dinghy *n.* scapha *f.*
dingy *a.* sordidus; (*colour*) fuscus.
dining-room *n.* cēnātiō *f.*
dinner *n.* cēna *f.* — party convīvium *n.* [per (*acc.*).
dint *n.* ictus *m.* by — of
dip *vt.* imbuere, mergere. *vi.* mergī. — into (*study*) perstringere.
diploma *n.* diplōma *n.*

diplomacy *n.* (*embassy*) lēgātiō *f.*; (*tact*) iūdicium *n.*, sagācitās *f.*
diplomat *n.* lēgātus *m.*
diplomatic *a.* sagāx, circumspectus.
diptych *n.* tabellae *f.pl.*
dire *a.* dīrus, horridus.
direct *vt.* regere, dīrigere; (*attention*) attendere, admovēre, advertere; (*course*) tendere; (*business*) administrāre, moderārī; (*letter*) īnscrībere; (*order*) imperāre (*dat.*), iubēre; (*to a place*) viam mōnstrāre (*dat.*); (*weapon*) intendere. *a.* rēctus, dīrēctus; (*person*) simplex; (*language*) apertus. *ad.* rēctā.
direction *n.* (*of going*) cursus *m.*, iter *n.*; (*of looking*) pars *f.*, regiō *f.*; (*control*) administrātiō *f.*, regimen *n.*; (*order*) praeceptum *n.*, iussum *n.* in the — of Rome Rōmam versus. in all -s passim, undique. in both -s utrōque.
directly *ad.* (*place*) rēctā; (*time*) prōtinus, continuō, statim; (*language*) apertē. *conj.* simulac.
directness *n.* (*fig.*) simplicitās [*f.*
director *n.* dux *m.*, gubernātor *m.*, moderātor *m.*
direful *a.* dīrus, horridus.
dirge *n.* nēnia *f.*
dirk *n.* pūgiō *m.*
dirt *n.* sordēs *f.*; (*mud*) lūtum *n.*
dirty *a.* sordidus, foedus; (*speech*) inquinātus. *vt.* foedāre, inquināre.
disability *n.* vitium *n.*
disable *vt.* dēbilitāre, imminuere. **-d** *a.* mutilus, dēbilis.
(*dat.*).
disabuse *vt.* errōrem dēmere
disaccustom *vt.* dēsuēfacere.
disadvantage *n.* incommodum *n.*, dētrīmentum *n.*
disadvantageous *a.* incommodus, inīquus. **-ly** *ad.* incommodē.
disaffected *a.* aliēnātus, sēditiōsus.
disaffection *n.* aliēnātiō *f.* sēditiō *f.*
disagree *vi.* discrepāre, dissentīre, dissidēre.
disagreeab/le *a.* molestus, incommodus, iniūcundus. **-ly** *ad.* molestē, incommodē.
disagreement *n.* discordia *f.*, dissēnsiō *f.*, discrepantia *f.*
disallow *vt.* improbāre, abnuere, vetāre.
disappear *vi.* dēperīre, perīre, abīre, diffugere, ēvānēscere.
disappearance *n.* dēcessiō *f.*, fuga *f.*
disappoint *vt.* dēcipere spē dēicere, frustārī. be **-ed** in a hope ā spē dēcidere, dē spē dēicī.
disappointment *n.* frustrātiō *f.*, malum *n.*
disapprobation *n.* reprehēnsiō *f.*, improbātiō *f.*
disapproval *n.* improbātiō *f.*
disapprove *vt.* & *i.* improbāre, reprehendere.
disarm *vt.* exarmāre, dearmāre; (*fig.*) mītigāre.
disarrange *vt.* turbāre, cōnfundere. **-d** *a.* incompositus.
disarrangement *n.* turbātiō *f.* [*vt.* perturbāre.
disarray *n.* perturbātiō *f.*
disaster *n.* calamitās *f.*, cāsus *m.*; (*mil.*) clādēs *f.*
disastrous *a.* īnfēlīx, exitiōsus, calamitōsus.
disavow *vt.* diffitērī, īnfitiārī.
disavowal *n.* īnfitiātiō *f.*
disband *vt.* dīmittere.
disbelief *n.* diffīdentia *f.*, suspīciō *f.*
disbelieve *vt.* diffīdere (*dat.*).
disburden *vt.* exonerāre.
disburse *vt.* ērogāre, expendere.
disbursement *n.* impēnsa *f.*
disc *n.* orbis *m.* [prōicere.
discard *vt.* mittere, pōnere,
discern *vt.* cōnspicere, dispi-

cere, cernere; (*fig.*) intellegere.
discernment *n.* iūdicium *n.*, intellegentia *f.*, sagācitās *f.*
discharge *vt.* (*load*) exonerāre; (*debt*) exsolvere; (*duty*) fungī (*abl.*), exsequī; (*officer*) exauctōrāre; (*troops*) missōs facere, dīmittere; (*weapon*) iacere, iaculārī; (*prisoner*) absolvere; (*from body*) ēdere, reddere. *vi.* (*river*) effundī, īnfluere. *n.* (*bodily*) dēfluxiō *f.*; (*mil.*) missiō *f.*, dīmissiō *f.*; (*of a duty*) perfūnctiō *f.*
disciple *n.* discipulus *m.*
discipline *n.* (*mil.*) modestia *f.*; (*punishment*) castīgātiō *f.*; (*study*) disciplīna *f.* *vt.* coercēre, castīgāre. **-d** *a.* modestus.
disclaim *vt.* renūntiāre, repudiāre, rēicere.
disclaimer *n.* repudiātiō *f.*
disclose *vt.* aperīre, patefacere, indicāre.
disclosure *n.* indicium *n.*
discoloration *n.* dēcolōrātiō *f.*
discolour *vt.* dēcolōrāre. **-ed** *a.* dēcolor.
discomfit *vt.* vincere, conturbāre, dēprehendere.
discomfiture *n.* clādēs *f.*; (*pol.*) repulsa *f.*
discomfort *n.* molestia *f.*, incommodum *n.*
disconcert *vt.* conturbāre, percellere. **-ing** *a.* molestus.
disconnect *vt.* abiungere, sēiungere. **-ed** *a.* dissolūtus, abruptus. **-edly** *ad.* dissolūtē.
disconsolate *a.* maestus, dēmissus. **-ly** *ad.* animō dēmissō.
discontent *n.* offēnsiō *f.*, fastīdium *n.*, taedium *n.*
discontented *a.* invidus, fastīdiōsus, parum contentus **-ly** *ad.* invītus, inīquō animō.
discontinuance *n.* intermissiō *f.*
discontinue *vt.* intermittere. *vi.* dēsistere, dēsinere.
discord *n.* discordia *f.*; (*music*) dissonum *n.* [*f.*, dissēnsiō *f.*
discordance *n.* discrepantia
discordant *a.* discors, discrepāns; (*music*) dissonus, absonus.
discount *vt.* dētrahere; (*fig.*) praetermittere. *n.* dēcessiō *f.* be at a — iacēre.
discountenace *vt.* improbāre.
discourage *vt.* dēhortārī, dēterrēre. be **-d** animum dēmittere, animō dēficere.
discouragement *n.* animī abiectiō *f.*; (*cause*) incommodum *n.*
discourse *n.* sermō *m.*; (*lecture*) ōrātiō *f.* *vi.* conloquī, disserere, disputāre.
discourteous *a.* inurbānus, asper, inhūmānus. **-ly** *ad.* inhūmānē, rūsticē.
discourtesy *n.* inhūmānitās *f.*, acerbitās *f.*
discover *vt.* invenīre, reperīre; (*detect*) dēprehendere; (*reveal*) aperīre, patefacere.
discoverer *n.* inventor *m.*
discovery *n.* inventum *n.*
discredit *vt.* notāre, fidem imminuere (*gen.*). *n.* invidia *f.*, lābēs *f.* be in — iacēre.
discreditab/le *a.* inhonestus, turpis. **-ly** *ad.* inhonestē, turpiter.
discreet *a.* prūdēns, sagāx, cautus. **-ly** *ad.* prūdenter, sagāciter, cautē.
discrepancy *n.* discrepantia *f.*, dissēnsiō *f.*
discretion *n.* prūdentia *f.*; (*tact*) iūdicium *n.*; (*power*) arbitrium *n.*, arbitrātus *m.* at your — arbitrātū tuō. surrender at — in dēditiōnem venīre, sine ullā pactiōne sē tradere. years of — adulta aetās *f.*
discretionary *a.* liber.
discriminate *vt.* & *i.* discernere, internōscere, distinguere.

discriminating *a.* perspicāx, sagāx.
discrimination *n.* discrimen *n.*, iūdicium *n.*
discursive *a.* vagus, loquāx. be — excurrere.
discuss *vt.* agere, disputāre, disceptāre dē (*abl.*).
discussion *n.* disceptātiō *f.*, disputātiō *f.*
disdain *vt.* contemnere, aspernārī, fastīdīre. *n.* contemptiō *f.*, fastīdium *n.*
disdainful *a.* fastīdiōsus, superbus. **-ly** *ad.* fastīdōsē, superbē.
disease *n.* morbus *m.*
diseased *a.* aeger, aegrōtus.
disembark *vi.* ēgredi, *vt.* expōnere.
disembarkation *n.* ēgressus [*m.*
disembarrass *vt.* expedīre.
disembodied *a.* sine corpore.
disembowel *vt.* exenterāre.
disencumber *vt.* exonerāre.
disengage *vt.* expedīre, līberāre; (*mind*) abstrahere, abdūcere. **-d** *a.* vacuus, ōtiōsus.
disentangle *vt.* expedīre, explicāre, exsolvere.
disfavour *n.* invidia *f.*
disfigure *vt.* dēfōrmāre, foedāre. **-d** *a.* dēfōrmis.
disfigurement *n.* dēfōrmātiō *f.*
disfranchise *vt.* cīvitātem adimere (*dat.*). **-d** *a.* capite dēminūtus.
disfranchisement *n.* capitis dēminūtiō *f.*
disgorge *vt.* ēvomere.
disgrace *n.* dēdecus *n.*, ignōminia *f.*, infāmia *f.* *vt.* dēdecorāre, dēdecorī esse (*dat.*).
disgraceful *a.* ignōminiōsus flāgitiōsus, turpis. — thing flāgitium *n.* **-ly** *ad.* turpiter, flāgitiōsē.
disgruntled *a.* mōrōsus, invidus.
disguise *n.* integumentum *n.*; (*fig.*) speciēs *f.*, simulātiō *f.* in — mūtātā veste. *vt.* obtegere, involvere; (*fact*) dissimulāre. — oneself vestem mūtāre.
disgust *vt.* displicēre (*dat.*), fastīdium movēre (*dat.*). be **-ed** stomachārī. I am **-ed** mē taedet, mē piget. *n.* fastīdium *n.*, taedium *n.*
disgusting *a.* taeter, foedus, dēfōrmis. **-ly** *ad.* foedē.
dish *n.* lanx *f.*; (*course*) ferculum *n.*
dishearten *vt.* percellere. be **-ed** animō dēficere, animum dēmittere. [passus.
dishevelled *a.* solūtus,
dishonest *a.* perfidus, inīquus, improbus. **-ly** *ad.* improbē, dolō malō.
dishonesty *n.* mala fidēs *f.*, perfidia *f.*, fraus *f.*
dishonour *n.* dēdecus *n.*, ignōminia *f.*, turpitūdō *f.* *vt.* dēdecorāre.
dishonourable *a.* ignōminiōsus, indecōrus, turpis. **-ly** *ad.* turpiter, inhonestē.
disillusion *vt.* errōrem adimere. (*dat.*).
disinclination *n.* odium *n.*
disinclined *a.* invītus, āversus.
disinfect *vt.* pūrgāre.
disingenuous *a.* dolōsus, fallāx. **-ly** *ad.* dolōsē.
disinherit *vt.* abdicāre, exhērēdāre. **-ed** *a.* exhērēs.
disintegrate *vt.* dissolvere. *vi.* dīlābī, dissolvi.
disinter *vt.* effodere, ēruere.
disinterested *a.* grātuītus, favōris expers. **-ly** *ad.* sine favōre.
disinterestedness *n.* innocentia *f.*, integritās *f.*
disjoin *vt.* sēiungere.
disjointed *a.* parum cohaerēns.
disk *n.* orbis *m.*
dislike *n.* odium *n.*, offēnsiō *f.*, invidia *f.* *vt.* ōdisse. I — mihī displicet, mē piget (*gen.*).

dislocate *vt.* extorquēre. **-d** *a.* luxus.
dislodge *vt.* dēmovēre, dēicere, dēpellere, dētrūdere.
disloyal *a.* īnfīdus, īnfidēlis; (*to gods, kin, country*) impius. **-ly** *ad.* īnfidēliter.
disloyalty *n.* perfidia *f.*, īnfidēlitās *f.*; impietās *f.*
dismal *a.* fūnestus, maestus. **-ly** *ad.* miserē.
dismantle *vt.* nūdāre; (*building*) dīruere.
dismay *n.* pavor *m.*, formīdō *f.* *vt.* terrēre perturbāre.
dismember *vt.* discerpere.
dismiss *vt.* dīmittere; (*troops*) missōs facere; (*from service*) exauctōrāre; (*fear*) mittere, pōnere.
dismissal *n.* missiō *f.*, dīmissiō *f.*
dismount *vi.* dēgredī, (ex equō) dēscendere.
disobedience *n.* contumācia [*f.*
disobedient *a.* contumāx. **-ly** *ad.* contrā iussa.
disobey *vt.* nōn pārēre (*dat.*), aspernārī.
disoblige *vt.* displicēre (*dat.*), offendere.
disobliging *a.* inofficiōsus, difficilis. **-ly** *ad.* contrā officium.
disorder *n.* turba *f.*, cōnfūsiō *f.*; (*med.*) morbus *m.*; (*pol.*) mōtus *m.*, tumultus *m.* *vt.* turbāre, miscēre, sollicitāre.
disorderly *a.* immodestus, inōrdinātus, incompositus; (*pol.*) turbulentus, sēditiōsus. in a —manner nullō ōrdine, temerē.
disorganize *vt.* dissolvere, perturbāre.
disown *vt.* (*statement*) īnfitiārī; (*thing*) abnuere, repudiāre; (*heir*) abdicāre.
disparage *vt.* obtrectāre, dētrectāre.
disparagement *n.* obtrectātiō *f.*, probrum *n.*
disparager *n.* obtrectātor *m.*, dētrectātor *m.*
disparate *a.* dispār.
disparity *n.* discrepantia *f.*, dissimilitūdō *f.*
dispassionate *a.* studiī expers. **-ly** *ad.* sine īrā et studiō.
dispatch, *see* **despatch**.
dispel *vt.* dispellere, discutere.
dispensation *n.* (*distribution*) partītiō *f.*; (*exemption*) venia *f.*; (*of heaven*) sors *f.* by divine — dīvīnitus.
dispense *vt.* dispertīrī, dīvidere. *vi.* — with ōmittere, praetermittere, repudiāre.
dispersal *n.* dīmissiō *f.*, diffugium *n.*
disperse *vt.* dispergere, dissipāre, disicere. *vi.* diffugere, dīlābī.
dispirited *a.* dēmissō animō. be — animō dēficere, animum dēmittere.
displace *vt.* locō movēre.
display *n.* ostentātiō *f.*, iactātiō *f.* for — per speciem. *vt.* exhibēre, ostendere, prae sē ferre.
displease *vt.* displicēre (*dat.*), offendere. be -d aegrē ferre, stomachārī, indignārī.
displeasing *a.* ingrātus, odiōsus.
displeasure *n.* invidia *f.*, offēnsiō *f.*, odium *n.*
disport *vt.* — oneself lūdere.
disposal *n.* (*sale*) vēnditiō *f.*; (*power*) arbitrium *n*.
dispose *vt.* (*troops*) dispōnere; (*mind*) inclīnāre, addūcere. *vi.* — of abaliēnāre, vēndere; (*get rid*) tollere; (*argument*) refellere. **-d** *a.* adfectus, inclīnātus, prōnus. well — benevolus, bonō animō.
disposition *n.* animus *m.*, adfectiō *f.*, ingenium *n.*, nātūra *f.*; (*of troops*) dispositiō *f.*
dispossess *vt.* dētrūdere [spoliāre.

disproportion *n.* inconcinnitās. *f.*
disproportionate *a.* impār, inconcinnus. **-ly** *ad.* inaequāliter.
disprove *vt.* refūtāre, redarguere, refellere.
disputable *a.* dubius, ambiguus.
disputation *n.* disputātiō *f.*
dispute *n.* altercātiō *f.*, contrōversia *f.*; (*violent*) iūrgium *n.* beyond — certissimus. *vi.* altercārī, certāre, rixārī. *vt.* negāre, in dubium vocāre.
disqualification *n.* impedimentum *n.*
disqualify *vt.* impedīre.
disquiet *n.* sollicitūdō *f.* *vt.* sollicitāre.
disquisition *n.* disputātiō *f.*
disregard *n.* neglegentia *f.*, contemptiō *f.* *vt.* neglegere, contemnere, ōmittere.
disrepair *n.* vitium *n.* in — male sartus.
disreputable *a.* inhonestus, īnfāmis.
disrepute *n.* īnfāmia *f.*
disrespect *n.* neglegentia *f.*, contumācia *f.*
disrespectful *a.* contumāx, īnsolēns. **-ly** *ad.* īnsolenter.
disrobe *vt.* nūdāre, vestem exuere (*dat.*). *vi.* vestem exuere. [dīvellere.
disrupt *vt.* dīrumpere,
disruption *n.* discidium *n.*
dissatisfaction *n.* molestia *f.*, aegritūdō *f.*, dolor *m.*
dissatisfied *a.* parum contentus. I am — with mē taedet (*gen.*).
dissect *vt.* incīdere; (*fig.*) investigāre.
dissemble *vt.* & *i.* dissimulāre; mentīrī.
dissembler *n.* simulātor *m.*
disseminate *vt.* dīvulgāre, dissēmināre.
dissension *n.* discordia *f.*, dissēnsiō *f.*; (*violent*) iūrgium *n.*
dissent *vi.* dissentīre, dissidēre. *n.* dissēnsiō *f.*
dissertation *n.* disputātiō *f.*
disservice *n.* iniūria *f.*, incommodum *n.*
dissimilar *a.* dispār, dissimilis.
dissimilarity *n.* discrepantia *f.*, dissimilitūdō *f.*
dissident *a.* discors. [lātiō *f.*
dissimulation *n.* dissimu-
dissipate *vt.* dissipāre, diffundere, disperdere. **-d** *a.* dissolūtus, lascīvus, luxuriōsus.
dissipation *n.* dissipātiō *f.*; (*vice*) luxuria *f.*, licentia *f.*
dissociate *vt.* dissociāre, sēiungere.
dissociation *n.* sēparātiō *f.*, discidium *n.*
dissoluble *a.* dissolūbilis.
dissolute *a.* dissolūtus, perditus, libīdinōsus. **-ly** *ad.* libīdinōsē, luxuriōsē.
dissoluteness *n.* luxuria *f.*
dissolution *n.* dissolūtiō *f.*, discidium *n.*
dissolve *vt.* dissolvere; (*ice*) liquefacere; (*meeting*) dīmittere; (*contract*) dirimere. *vi.* liquēscere; (*fig.*) solvī.
dissonance *n.* dissonum *n.*
dissonant *a.* dissonus.
dissuade *vt.* dissuādēre (*dat.*), dēhortārī.
dissuasion *n.* dissuāsiō *f.*
distaff *n.* colus *f.*
distance *n.* intervallum *n.*, spatium *n.*; (*long way*) longinquitās *f.* at a — (*far*) longē; (*within sight*) procul; (*fight*) ēminus. at a — of spatiō (*gen.*). within striking —intrā iactum tēlī.
distant *a.* longinquus; (*measure*) distāns; (*person*) parum familiāris. be — abesse.
distaste *n.* fastīdium *n.*
distasteful *a.* molestus, iniūcundus.
distemper *n.* morbus *m.*
distend *vt.* distendere.

distil *vt.* & *i.* stillāre.

distinct *a.* (*different*) dīversus; (*separate*) distinctus; (*clear*) clārus, argūtus; (*marked*) distinctus; (*sure*) certus; (*well-drawn*) expressus. **-ly** *ad.* clārē, distinctē, certē, expressē.

distinction *n.* discrīmen *n.*; (*dissimilarity*) discrepantia *f.*; (*public status*) amplitūdō *f.*; (*honour*) honōs *m.*, decus *n.*; (*mark*) īnsigne *n.* there is a — interest. without — prōmiscuē.

distinctive *a.* proprius, īnsignītus. **-ly** *ad.* propriē, īnsignītē.

distinguish *vt.* distinguere, internōscere, dīiūdicāre, discernere; (*honour*) decorāre, ōrnāre. — oneself ēminēre.

distinguished *a.* īnsignis, praeclārus, ēgregius, amplissimus.

distort *vt.* dētorquēre; (*fig.*) dēprāvāre. **-ed** *a.* distortus.

distortion *n.* distortiō *f.*; dēprāvātiō *f.*

distract *vt.* distrahere, distinēre, āvocāre; (*mind*) aliēnāre. **-ed** *a.* āmēns, īnsānus.

distraction *n.* (*state*) indīligentia *f.*; (*cause*) invītāmentum *n.*; (*madness*) furor *m.*, dēmentia *f.* to —efflīctim.

distraught *a.* āmēns, dēmēns.

distress *n.* labor *m.*, dolor *m.*, aegrimōnia *f.*, aerumna *f.* be in — labōrāre. *vt.* adflīgere, sollicitāre. **-ed** *a.* adflīctus, sollicitus.

distressing *a.* tristis, miser, acerbus.

distribute *vt.* distribuere, dīvidere, dispertīre.

distribution *n.* partītiō *f.*, distribūtiō *f.*

district *n.* regiō *f.*, pars *f.*

distrust *n.* diffīdentia *f.* *vt.* diffīdere (*dat.*), nōn crēdere (*dat.*).

distrustful *a.* diffīdēns. **-ly** *ad.* diffīdenter.

disturb *vt.* turbāre, conturbāre; (*mind*) sollicitāre.

disturbance *n.* turba *f.*, perturbātiō *f.*; (*pol.*) mōtus *m.*, tumultus *m.*

disturber *n.* turbātor *m.*

disunion *n.* discordia *f.*, discidium *n.*

disunite *vt.* dissociāre, sēiungere.

disuse *n.* dēsuētūdō *f.* fall into — obsolēscere.

disused *a.* dēsuētus, obsolētus.

disyllabic *a.* disyllabus.

ditch *n.* fossa *f.*, scrobis *m.*

dithyramb *n.* dithyrambus *m.*

dithyrambic *a.* dithyrambicus.

dittany *n.* dictamnum *n.*

ditty *n.* carmen *n.*, cantilēna *f.*

diurnal *a.* diūrnus.

divagate *vi.* dīgredī.

divan *n.* lectus *m.*, lectulus *m.*

dive *vi.* dēmergī.

diver *n.* ūrīnātor *m.*

diverge *vi.* dēvertere, dīgredī; (*road*) sē scindere; (*opinions*) discrepāre.

divergence *n.* dīgressiō *f.*; discrepantia *f.*

divers *a.* complūrēs.

diverse *a.* varius, dīversus.

diversify *vt.* variāre.

diversion *n.* (*of water*) dērīvātiō *f.*; (*of thought*) āvocātiō *f.*; (*to amuse*) oblectāmentum *n.* create a — (*mil.*) hostēs distringere. for a — animī causā.

diversity *n.* varietās *f.*, discrepantia *f.*

divert *vt.* dēflectere, āvertere; (*attention*) āvocāre, abstrahere; (*water*) dērīvāre; (*to amuse*) oblectāre, placēre (*dat.*).

diverting *a.* iūcundus; (*remark*) facētus.

divest *vt.* exuere, nūdāre. — oneself of (*fig.*) pōnere, mittere.

divide *vt.* dividere; (*troops*) didūcere. — among partīrī, distribuere. — from sēparāre ab, sēiungere ab. — out dispertīrī, dividere. *vi.* discēdere, sē scindere; (*senate*) in sententiam īre. be -d (*opinions*) discrepāre.
divination *n.* dīvīnātiō *f.*; (*from birds*) augurium *n.*; (*from entrails*) haruspicium *n.*
divine *a.* dīvīnus. *vt.* dīvīnāre, augurārī, hariolārī. by — intervention dīvīnitus. -ly *ad.* dīvīnē.
diviner *n.* dīvīnus *m.*, augur *m.*, haruspex *m.*
divinity *n.* (*status*) dīvīnitās *f.*; (*god*) deus *m.*, dea *f.*
divisible *a.* dīviduus.
division *n.* (*process*) dīvīsiō *f.*, partītiō *f.*; (*variance*) discordia *f.*, dissēnsiō *f.*; (*section*) pars *f.*; (*grade*) classis *f.* (*of army*) legiō *f.*; (*of time*) discrīmen *n.*; (*in senate*) discessiō *f.*
divorce *n.* dīvortium *n.*, repudium *n.* *vt.* (*wife*) nūntium mittere (*dat.*); (*things*) dīvellere, sēparāre.
divulge *vt.* aperīre, patefacere, ēvulgāre, ēdere.
dizziness *n.* vertīgō *f.*
dizzy *a.* vertīginōsus; (*fig.*) attonitus.
do *vt.* facere, agere; (*duty*) fungī (*abl.*); (*wrong*) admittere. — away with tollere; (*kill*) interimere. — one's best to id agere ut (*subj.*). — without repudiāre. how — you — ? quid agis? I have nothing to — with you mihī tēcum nihil est commercī. it has nothing to — with me nihil est ad mē. that will — iam satis est. well-to — beātus. be -ne fierī. have -ne with dēfungī (*abl.*).
docile *a.* docilis.
docility *n.* docilitās *f.*
dock *n.* (*ships*) nāvāle *n.*; (*law*) cancellī *m.pl.* *vt.* praecīdere. — yard *n.* nāvālia *n.pl.*
doctor *n.* medicus *m.*; (*univ.*) doctor *m.* *vt.* cūrāre.
doctrine *n.* dogma *n.*, dēcrētum *n.*; (*system*) ratiō *f.*
document *n.* litterae *f.pl.*, tabula *f.*
dodge *vt.* dēclīnāre, ēvādere. *n.* dolus *m.*
doe *n.* cerva *f.*
doer *n.* āctor *m.*, auctor *m.*
doff *vt.* exuere.
dog *n.* canis *m.*, *f.* — star Canīcula *f.* — 's canīnus. *vt.* īnsequī, īnstāre (*dat.*).
dogged *a.* pertināx. -ly *ad.* pertināciter. [ceptum *n.*
dogma *n.* dogma *n.*, prae-
dogmatic *a.* adrogāns. -ally *ad.* adroganter.
doing *n.* factum *n.*
dole *n.* sportula *f.* *vt.* — out dispertīrī, dividere.
doleful *a.* lūgubris, flēbilis, maestus. -ly *ad.* flēbiliter.
dolefulness *n.* maestitia *f.*, miseria *f.*
doll *n.* pūpa *f.*
dolorous *a.* lūgubris, maestus.
dolour *n.* maestitia *f.*, dolor *m.*
dolphin *n.* delphīnus *m.*
dolt *n.* stīpes *m.*, caudex *m.*
domain *n.* ager *m.*; (*king's*) rēgnum *n.*
dome *n.* tholus *m.*, testūdō *f.*
domestic *a.* domesticus, familiāris; (*animal*) mānsuētus. *n.* famulus *m.*, servus *m.*, famula *f.*, ancilla *f.*; (*pl.*) familia *f.*
domesticate *vt.* mānsuēfacere. -d *a.* mānsuētus.
domesticity *n.* larēs suī *m.pl.*
domicile *n.* domicilium *n.*, domus *f.* [potēns.
dominant *a.* superior, prae-
dominate *vt.* dominārī in (*acc.*), imperāre (*dat.*); (*view*) dēspectāre.
domination *n.* dominātiō *f.*, dominātus *m.*

domineer *vi.* dominārī, rēgnāre.
dominion *n.* imperium *n.*, rēgnum *n.* [*m.*
don *vt.* induere. *n.* scholasticus
donate *vt.* dōnāre.
donation *n.* dōnum *n.*
donkey *n.* asellus *m.*
donor *n.* dōnātor *m.*
doom *n.* fātum *n.* *vt.* damnāre.
door *n.* (*front*) iānua *f.*; (*back*) posticum *n.*; (*double*) forēs *f.pl.* folding -s valvae *f.pl.* in -s domī, intus. out of -s forīs, (*to*) forās. next — to iuxtā (*acc.*).
door-keeper *n.* iānitor *m.*
door-post *n.* postis *m.*
door-way *n.* ōstium *n*
dormant *a.* sōpītus. lie — iacēre.
dormitory *n.* cubiculum *n.*
dormouse *n.* glīs *m.*
dose *n.* pōculum *n.*
dot *n.* pūnctum *n.*
dotage *n.* senium *n.*
dotard *n.* senex dēlīrus *m.*
dote *vi.* dēsipere. — upon dēamāre. [-ly *ad.* perditē.
doting *a.* dēsipiēns, peramāns.
double *a.* duplex; (*amount*) duplus; (*meaning*) ambiguus. *n.* duplum *n.* *vt.* duplicāre; (*promontory*) superāre; (*fold*) complicāre. *vi.* duplicārī; (*mil.*) currere.
double-dealing *a.* fallāx, dolōsus. *n.* fraus *f.*, dolus *m.*
doublet *n.* tunica *f.*
doubly *ad.* bis, dupliciter.
doubt *n.* dubium *n.*; (*hesitancy*) dubitātiō *f.*; (*distrust*) suspiciō *f.* give one the benefit of the — innocentem habēre. no — sānē. there is no — that nōn dubium est quīn (*subj.*). *vt.* dubitāre; (*distrust*) diffīdere (*dat.*), suspicārī.
doubtful *a.* dubius, incertus; (*result*) anceps; (*word*) ambiguus. -ly *ad.* dubiē; (*hesitation*) dubitanter.
doubtless *ad.* scīlicet, nimirum.
doughty *a.* fortis, strēnuus.
dove *n.* columba *f.* — **cote** columbārium *n.*
dowdy *a.* inconcinnus.
dower *n.* dōs *f.* *vt.* dōtāre.
dowerless *a.* indōtātus.
down *n.* plūmae *f.pl.* lānūgō *f.*; (*thistle*) pappus *m.*
down *ad.* deōrsum. be — iacēre. — with! perea(n)t. up and — sūrsum deōrsum. *pr.* dē (*abl.*). — from dē (*abl.*). — stream secundō flūmine. [maestus.
downcast *a.* dēmissus,
downfall *n.* ruīna *f.*; (*fig.*) occāsus *m.*
down-hearted *a.* dēmissus, frāctus animī.
down-hill *a.* dēclīvis; (*fig.*) prōclīvis. *ad.* in præceps.
downpour *n.* imber *m.*
downright *a.* dīrēctus; (*intensive*) merus.
downtrodden *a.* subiectus, oppressus.
downward *a.* dēclīvis, prōclīvis. -s *ad.* deōrsum.
downy *a.* plūmeus.
dowry *n.* dōs *f.*
doyen *n.* pater *m.*
doze *vi.* dormītāre.
dozen *n.* duodecim.
drab *a.* sordidior.
drachma *n.* drachma *f.*
draft *n.* (*writing*) exemplum *n.*; (*mil.*) dīlēctus *m.*; (*money*) syngrapha *f.*; (*literary*) silva *f.* *vt.* scrībere; (*mil.*) mittere.
drag *vt.* trahere. *vi.* (*time*) trahī. *n.* harpagō *m.*; (*fig.*) impedīmentum *n.*
dragnet *n.* ēverriculum *n.*
dragon *n.* drācō *m.*
dragoon *n.* eques *m.*
drain *n.* cloāca *f.* *vt.* (*water*) dērīvāre; (*land*) siccāre; (*drink*) exhaurīre; (*resources*) exhaurīre.
drainage *n.* dērīvātiō *f.*
drake *n.* anas *m.*

drama *n.* fābula *f.* the — scaena *f.*
dramatic *a.* scaenicus.
dramatist *n.* fābulārum scrīptor *m.* [compōnere.
dramatize *vt.* ad scaenam
drape *vt.* vēlāre.
drapery *n.* vestīmenta *n.pl.*
drastic *a.* vehemēns, efficāx.
draught *n.* (*air*) aura *f.*; (*drink*) haustus *m.*; (*net*) bolus *m.* — animal iūmentum *n.*
draughts *n.* latrunculī *m.pl.*
draw *vt.* dūcere, trahere; (*bow*) addūcere; (*inference*) colligere; (*picture*) scrībere, pingere; (*sword*) stringere, dēstringere; (*tooth*) eximere; (*water*) haurīre. — aside sēdūcere. — away āvocāre. — back retrahere. *vi.* recēdere. — near adpropinquāre. — off dētrahere; (*water*) dērivāre. — out ēdūcere; (*lengthen*) prōdūcere. — over obdūcere. — taut addūcere. — together contrahere. — up (*mil.*) īnstruere; (*document*) scrībere.
drawback *n.* scrūpulus *m.* this was the only — hōc ūnum dēfuit.
drawing *n.* dēscrīptiō *f.*; (*art*) graphicē *f.*; (*pl.*) līneāmenta *n.pl.*
drawing-room *n.* sellāria *f.*
drawl *vi.* lentē dīcere.
drawling *a.* lentus in dīcendō.
dray *n.* plaustrum *n.*
dread *n.* formīdō *f.*, pavor *m.*, horror *m.* *a.* dīrus. *vt.* expavēscere, extimēscere, formīdāre.
dreadful *a.* terribilis, horribilis, formīdolōsus, dīrus. **-ly** *ad.* vehementer, atrōciter.
dream *n.* somnium *n.* *vt.* & *i.* somniāre.
dreamy *a.* somniculōsus.
dreariness *n.* (*place*) vastitās *f.*; (*mind*) tristitia *f.*
dreary *a.* (*place*) vastus; (*person*) tristis.
dregs *n.* faex *f.*; (*of oil*) amurca *f.* drain to the — exhaurīre.
drench *vt.* perfundere.
dress *n.* vestis *f.*, vestītus *m.*, vestīmenta *n.pl.*; (*style*)habitus *m.* *vt.* vestīre; (*wound*) cūrāre; (*tree*) amputāre. *vi.* induī. [*n.*
dressing *n.* (*med.*) fōmentum
drift *n.* (*motion*) mōtus *m.*; (*snow*) agger *m.*; (*language*) vīs *f.* I see the — of your speech videō quōrsum ōrātiō tua tendat. *vi.* fluitāre; (*fig.*) lābī, ferrī.
drill *n.* terebra *f.*; (*mil.*) exercitātiō *f.* *vt.* (*hole*) terebrāre; (*mil.*) exercēre; (*pupil*) īnstruere.
drink *vt.* & *i.* bibere, pōtāre. — a health propīnāre, Graecō mōre bibere. — deep of exhaurīre. — in haurīre. — up ēpōtāre. *n.* pōtiō *f.*
drinkable *a.* pōtulentus.
drinker *n.* pōtor *m.*
drinking-bout *n.* pōtātiō *f.*
drip *vi.* stillāre, dēstillāre.
drive *vt.* agere; (*force*) cōgere. — away abigere; (*fig.*) pellere, prōpulsāre. — back repellere. — home dēfīgere. — in, into īnfīgere in (*acc.*); (*flock*) cōgere in (*acc.*). — off dēpellere. — out exigere, expellere, exturbāre. — through trānsfīgere. *vi.* vehī — away āvehī. — back revehī. — in invehī. — round circumvehī. — past praetervehī. what are you driving at? quōrsum tua spectat ōrātiō? *n.* gestātiō *f.*
drivel *vi.* dēlīrāre.
drivelling *a.* dēlīrus, ineptus. *n.* ineptiae *f.pl.*
driver *n.* aurīga *m.*
drizzle *vi.* rōrāre.
droll *a.* facētus, ioculāris.
drollery *n.* facētiae *f.pl.*
dromedary *n.* dromas *m.*
drone *n.* (*bee*) fūcus *m.*; (*sound*) bombus *m.* *vi.* fremere.

droop *vi.* dēmittī; (*flower*) languēscere; (*mind*) animum dēmittere.
drooping *a.* languidus.
drop *n.* gutta *f.* *vi.* cadere; (*liquid*) stillāre. *vt.* mittere; (*anchor*) iacere; (*hint*) ēmittere; (*liquid*) instillāre; (*work*) dēsistere ab (*abl.*). *vi.* — behind cessāre. — in vīsere supervenīre. — out excidere.
dropsical *a.* hydrōpicus.
dropsy *n.* hydrōps *m.*, aqua intercus *f.*
dross *n.* scōria *f.*; (*fig.*) faex *f.*
drought *n.* siccitās *f.*
drouth *n.* sitis *f.*
drove *n.* grex *f.*
drover *n.* bubulcus *m.*
drown *vt.* mergere, obruere; (*noise*) obscūrāre. *vi.* aquā perīre.
drowse *vi.* dormitāre.
drowsiness *n.* sopor *m.*
drows/y *a.* sēmisomnus, somniculōsus. **-ily** *ad.* somniculōsē.
drub *vt.* pulsāre, verberāre.
drudge *n.* mediastīnus *m.* *vi.* labōrāre.
drudgery *n.* labor *m.*
drug *n.* medicāmentum *n.* *vt.* medicāre. [*m.pl.*
Druids *n.* Druidae, Druidēs
drum *n.* tympanum *n.*
drummer *n.* tympanista *m.*
drunk *a.* pōtus, ēbrius, tēmulentus.
drunkard *n.* ēbriōsus *m.*
drunken *a.* ēbriōsus, tēmulentus.
drunkenness *n.* ēbrietās *f.*
dry *a.* siccus, āridus; (*thirst*) sitiēns; (*speech*) āridus, frīgidus; (*joke*) facētus. be — ārēre. *vt.* siccāre. *vi.* ārēscere. — up exārēscere.
dryad *n.* dryas *f.*
dry-rot *n.* rōbīgō *f.*
dual *a.* duplex.
duality *n.* duplex nātūra *f.*
dubiety *n.* dubium *n.*
dubious *a.* dubius, incertus; (*meaning*) ambiguus. **-ly** *ad.* dubiē; ambiguē.
duck *n.* anas *f.* *vt.* dēmergere. *vi.* dēmergī, sē dēmittere.
duckling *n.* anaticula *f.*
duct *n.* ductus *m.*
dudgeon *n.* dolor *m.*, stomachus *m.*
due *a.* dēbitus, meritus, iūstus. be — dēbērī. be — to orīrī ex, fierī (*abl.*). *n.* iūs *n.*, dēbitum *n.*; (*tax*) vectīgal *n.*; (*harbour*) portōrium *n.* give every man his — suum cuique tribuere. *ad.* rēctā.
duel *n.* certāmen *n.*
dug *n.* ūber *n.*
duke *n.* dux *m.*
dulcet *a.* dulcis.
dulcimer *n.* sambūca *f.*
dull *a.* hebes; (*weather*) subnūbilus; (*language*) frīgidus; (*mind*) tardus. be — hebēre. become — hebēscere. *vt.* hebetāre, obtundere retundere.
dullard *n.* stolidus *m.*
dulness *n.* (*mind*) tarditās *f.*, stultitia *f.*
duly *ad.* rītē, ut pār est.
dumb *a* mūtus. be struck — obmūtēscere.
dun *n.* flāgitātor *m.* *vt.* flāgitāre. *a.* fuscus.
dunce *n.* bārō *m.*
dune *n.* tumulus *m.*
dung *n.* fimus *m.* [*n.*
dungeon *n.* carcer *m.*, rōbur
dupe *vt.* dēlūdere, fallere. *n.* crēdulus *m.*
duplicate *n.* exemplar *n.* *vt.* duplicāre.
duplicity *n.* fraus *f.*, perfidia *f.*
durability *n.* firmitās *f.*, firmitūdō *f.*
durab/le *a.* firmus, perpetuus. **-ly** *ad.* firmē.
duration *n.* spatium *n.*; (*long*) diūturnitās *f.*
duresse *n.* vīs *f.* [(*acc.*).
during *pr.* inter (*acc.*) per

dusk *n.* crepusculum *n.*, vesper *m.*
dusky *a.* fuscus.
dust *n.* pulvis *m.* **throw — in the eyes of** tenebrās offundere (*dat.*). *vt.* dētergēre.
dusty *a.* pulverulentus.
dutiful *a.* pius, officiōsus. **-ly** *ad.* piē, officiōsē.
dutifulness *n.* pietās *f.*
duty *n.* (*moral*) officium *n.*; (*task*) mūnus *n.*; (*tax*) vectīgal *n.* **be on —** (*mil.*) statiōnem agere, excubāre. **do one's —** officiō fungī. **do — for** (*pers.*) in locum sufficī (*gen.*); (*thing*) adhibērī prō (*abl.*). **it is my—** dēbeō, mē oportet, meum est. **it is the — of a commander** ducis est. **sense of —** pietās *f.* **— call** salūtātiō *f.* **— free** immūnis.
duumvir *n.* duumvir *m.*
dwarf *n.* nānus *m.*
dwell *vi.* habitāre. **— in** incolere. **— upon** (*theme*) commorārī in (*abl.*).
dweller *n.* incola *m.*
dwelling *n.* domus *f.*, domicilium *n.*; (*place*) sēdēs *f.*
dwindle *vi.* dēcrēscere, extenuārī.
dye *n.* fūcus *m.*, color *m.* *vt.* inficere, fūcāre.
dyer *n.* infector *m.*
dying *a.* moribundus, moriēns.
dynasty *n.* domus (rēgia) *f.*
dyspepsy *n.* crūditās *f.*
dyspeptic *a.* crūdus.

E

each *a.* & *pro.* quisque; (*of two*) uterque. **— other** inter sē. **one —** singulī.
eager *a.* avidus, cupidus, ācer. **-ly** *ad.* avidē, cupidē, ācriter.
eagerness *n.* cupīdō *f.*, ārdor *m.*, studium *n.*
eagle *n.* aquila *f.*
ear *n.* auris *f.*; (*of corn*) spica *f.* **give —** aurem praebēre, auscultāre. **go in at one — and out at the other** surdīs auribus nārrārī. **prick up one's -s** aurēs ērigere. **with long -s** aurītus.
earl *n.* comes *m.*
early *a.* (*in season*) mātūrus; (*in day*) mātūtīnus; (*at beginning*) prīmus; (*in history*) antīquus. *ad.* (*in day*) māne; (*before time*) mātūrē, temperī. **— in life** ab ineunte aetāte.
earn *vt.* merērī, cōnsequī. **— a living** victum quaerere, quaestum facere.
earnest *a.* (*serious*) sērius; (*eager*) ācer, sēdulus. *n.* pignus *n.*; (*money*) arrabō *m.* **in —** sēdulō, ēnīxē. **-ly** *ad.* sēriō, graviter, sēdulō.
earnestness *n.* gravitās *f.*, studium *n.*
earnings *n.* quaestus *m.*
ear-ring *n.* elenchus *m.*
earth *n.* (*planet*) tellūs *f.*; (*inhabited*) orbis terrārum *m.*; (*land*) terra *f.*; (*soil*) solum *n.*, humus *f.*; (*fox's*) latibulum *n.* **where on — ?** ubi gentium ? **of the —** terrestris.
earthen *a.* (*ware*) fictilis; (*mound*) terrēnus.
earthenware *n.* fictilia *n.pl.* *a.* fictilis.
earthly *a.* terrestris.
earthquake *n.* terrae mōtus [*m.*
earthwork *n.* agger *m.*
earthy *a.* terrēnus.
ease *n.* facilitās *f.*; (*leisure*) ōtium *n.* **at —** ōtiōsus; (*in mind*) sēcūrus. **ill at —** sollicitus. *vt.* laxāre, relevāre; (*pain*) mītigāre.
easiness *n.* facilitās *f.*
east *n.* oriēns *m.*, sōlis ortus *m.* **— wind** eurus *m.*
easter *n.* pascha *f.* [tālis.
easterly, eastern *a.* orien-
eastward *ad.* ad orientem.
eas/y *a.* facilis; (*manner*) adfābilis, facilis; (*mind*) sēcūrus; (*speech*) expedītus; (*dis*

cipline) remissus. —circumstances dīvitiae *f.pl.*, abundantia *f.* **-ily** *ad.* facile; (*gladly*) libenter; (*at leisure*) ōtiōsē. not — nōn temerē.
eat *vt.* edere, vescī (*abl.*). — away rōdere. — up exedere.
eatable *a.* esculentus.
eating *n.* cibus *m.* — house *n.* popīna *f.*
eaves *n.* suggrunda *f.* — dropper *n.* sermōnis auceps.
ebb *n.* dēcessus *m.*, recessus *m.* at — tide minuente aestū. be at a low — (*fig.*) iacēre. *vi.* recēdere.
ebony *n.* ebenus *f.*
ebullient *a.* fervēns.
ebullition *n.* fervor *m.*
eccentric *a.* īnsolēns.
eccentricity *n.* īnsolentia *f.*
echo *n.* imāgō *f.* *vt.* & *i.* resonāre.
eclipse *n.* dēfectus *m.*, dēfectiō *f.* *vt.* obscūrāre. be -d dēficere, labōrāre.
eclogue *n.* ecloga *f.*
economic *a.* quaestuōsus, sine iactūrā. **-al** *a.* (*person*) frūgī, parcus. **-ally** *ad.* nullā iactūrā factā.
economics *n.* reī familiāris dispēnsātiō *f.*
economize *vi.* parcere.
economy *n.* frūgālitās *f.*
ecstasy *n.* alacritās *f.*, furor *m.*
ecstatic *a.* gaudiō ēlātus.
eddy *n.* vertex *m.* *vi.* volūtārī.
edge *n.* ōra *f.*, margō *f.*; (*of dish*) labrum *n.*; (*of blade*) aciēs *f.* take the — off obtundere. on — (*fig.*) suspēnsō animō. *vt.* (*garment*) praetexere; (*blade*) acuere. *vi.* — in sē īnsinuāre.
edging *n.* limbus *m.*
edible *a.* esculentus.
edict *n.* ēdictum *n.*, dēcrētum [*n.*
edification *n.* ērudītiō *f.*
edifice *n.* aedificium *n.*
edify *vt.* ērudīre.
edit *vt.* recognōscere, recēnsēre.
edition *n.* ēditiō *f.*
educate *vt.* ērudīre, īnfōrmāre. — in īnstituere ad (*acc.*).
education *n.* doctrīna *f.*; (*process*) īnstitūtiō *f.*
eel *n.* anguilla *f.*
eerie *a.* mōnstruōsus.
efface *vt.* dēlēre, tollere.
effect *n.* (*result*) ēventus *m.*; (*impression*) vīs *f.*, effectus *m.*; (*show*) iactātiō *f.*; (*pl.*) bona *n.pl.* for — iactātiōnis causā. in — rē vērā. to this — in hanc sententiam. without — inritus. *vt.* efficere, facere, patrāre.
effective *a.* valēns, validus; (*rhet.*) gravis, ōrnātus. **-ly** *ad.* validē, graviter, ōrnātē.
effectiveness *n.* vīs *f.*
effectual *a.* efficāx, idōneus **-ly** *ad.* efficāciter. [sequī
effectuate *vt.* efficere, cōn
effeminacy *n.* mollitiēs *f.*
effeminate *a.* mollis, effēminātus. **-ly** *ad.* molliter effēminātē.
effervesce *vi.* effervēscere.
effete *a.* effētus.
efficacious *a.* efficāx. **-ly** *ad.* efficāciter.
efficacy *n.* vīs *f.*
efficiency *n.* virtūs *f.*, perītia *f.*
efficient *a.* capāx, perītus; (*logic*) efficiēns. **-ly** *ad.* perītē, bene.
effigy *n.* simulacrum *n.*, effigiēs *f.*
effloresce *vi.* flōrēscere.
efflorescence *n.* (*fig.*) flōs *m.*
effluvium *n.* hālitus *m.*
effort *n.* opera *f.*, cōnātus *m.*; (*of mind*) intentiō *f.* make an — ēnītī.
effrontery *n.* audācia *f.*, impudentia *f.*
effulgence *n.* fulgor *m.*
effulgent *a.* splendidus.
effusive *a.* officiōsus.
egg *n.* ōvum *n.* lay an —

ōvum parere. *vt.* impellere, instigāre.
egoism *n.* amor suī *m.*
egoist *n.* suī amāns *m.*
egotism *n.* iactātiō *f.*
egotist *n.* glōriōsus *m.*
egregious *a.* singulāris.
egress *n.* exitus *m.*
eight *num.* octō. — **hundred** octingentī. — **hundredth** octingentēsimus. — **each** octōnī. — **times** octiēns.
eighteen *num.* duodēvīgintī. **-th** duodēvīcēsimus.
eighth *a.* octāvus.
eightieth *a.* octōgēsimus.
eighty *num.* octōgintā. — **each** octōgēnī. — **times** octōgiēns.
either *pro.* alteruter, uterlibet, utervīs. *conj.* aut, vel.
ejaculate *vt.* & *i.* exclāmāre.
ejaculation *n.* clāmor *m.*
eject *vt.* ēicere, expellere.
ejection *n.* expulsiō *f.*
eke out *vt.* parcendō prōdūcere.
elaborate *vt.* ēlabōrāre. *a.* ēlabōrātus, exquīsītus. **-ly** *ad.* summō labōre, exquīsītē.
elan *n.* ferōcia *f.*
elapse *vi.* abīre, intercēdere. **allow to —** intermittere. **a year has -d since** annus est cum (*indic.*).
elated *a.* ēlātus. **be —** efferrī.
elation *n.* laetitia *f.*
elbow *n.* cubitum *n.*
elder *a.* nātū māior, senior. *n.* (*pl.*) patrēs *m.pl.*; (*tree*) sambūcus *f.*
elderly *a* aetāte prōvectus.
eldest *a.* nātū māximus.
elecampane *n.* inula *f.*
elect *vt.* ēligere, dēligere; (*magistrate*) creāre; (*colleague*) co-optāre. *a.* dēsignātus; (*special*) lēctus.
election *n.* (*pol.*) comitia *n.pl.*
electioneering *n.* ambitiō *f.*
elector *n.* suffrāgātor *m.*
elegance *n.* ēlegantia *f.*, lepōs *m.*, munditia *f.*, concinnitās *f.*
elegant *a.* ēlegāns, concinnus, nitidus. **-ly** *ad.* ēleganter, concinnē.
elegiac *a.* — **verse** elegī *m.pl.*, versūs alternī *m.pl.*
elegy *n.* elegīa *f.*
element *n.* elementum *n.*; (*pl.*) initia *n.pl.*, prīncipia *n.pl.* **out of one's —** peregrīnus.
elementary *a* prīmus.
elephant *n.* elephantus *m.*, elephās *m.*
elevate *vt.* efferre, ērigere. **-d** *a.* ēditus, altus.
elevation *n.* altitūdō *f.*; (*style*) ēlātiō *f.*
eleven *num.* ūndecim. — **each** ūndēnī. — **times** ūndeciēns.
eleventh *a.* ūndecimus.
elf *n.* deus *m.* [ēruere.
elicit *vt.* ēlicere; (*with effort*)
elide *vt.* ēlīdere.
eligible *a.* idōneus, aptus.
eliminate *vt.* tollere, āmovēre.
elite *n.* flōs *m.*, rōbur *n.*
elk *n.* alcēs *f.*
ell *n.* ulna *f.*
ellipse *n.* (*rhet.*) dētractiō *f.*; (*oval*) ōvum *n.*
elm *n.* ulmus *f.* *a.* ulmeus.
elocution *n.* prōnūntiātiō *f.*
elongate *vt.* prōdūcere.
elope *vi.* aufugere.
eloquence *n.* ēloquentia *f.*; (*natural*) fācundia *f.*, dīcendī vīs *f.*
eloquent *a.* ēloquēns; (*natural*) fācundus; (*fluent*) disertus. **-ly** *ad.* fācundē, disertē.
else *ad.* aliōquī, aliter. **or —** aliōquī. **who —** quis alius.
elsewhere *ad.* alibī; (*to*) aliō.
elucidate *vt.* ēnōdāre, illūstrāre.
elucidation *n.* ēnōdātiō *f.*, explicātiō *f.*
elude *vt.* ēvītāre, frustrārī, fallere.
elusive *a.* fallāx.
emaciated *a.* macer.
emaciation *n.* maciēs *f.*

emanate *vi.* mānāre; (*fig.*) ēmānāre, orīrī.
emanation *n.* exhālātiō *f.*
emancipate *vt.* ēmancipāre, manū mittere, līberāre.
emancipation *n.* lībertās *f.*
emasculate *vt.* ēnervāre, dēlumbāre.
embalm *vt.* condīre.
embankment *n.* agger *m.*, mōlēs *f.*
embargo *n.* interdictum *n.*
embark *vi.* cōnscendere, nāvem cōnscendere. — **upon** (*fig.*) ingredī. *vt.* impōnere.
embarkation *n.* cōnscēnsiō *f.*
embarrass *vt.* (*by confusing*) perturbāre; (*by obstructing*) impedīre; (*by revealing*) dēprehendere. **be — ed** haerēre.
embarrassing *a.* incommodus, intempestīvus.
embarrassment *n.* (*in speech*) haesitātiō *f.*; (*in mind*) sollicitūdō *f.*; (*in business*) angustiae *f.pl.*, difficultās *f.*; (*cause*) molestia *f.*, impedīmentum *n.*
embassy *n.* lēgātiō *f.*
embedded *a.* dēfīxus.
embellish *vt.* adōrnāre, exōrnāre, decorāre.
embellishment *n.* decus *n.*, exōrnātiō *f.*, ōrnāmentum *n.*
embers *n.* cinis *m.*, favilla *f.*
embezzle *vt.* pecūlārī dēpecūlārī.
embezzlement *n.* pecūlātus *m.*
embezzler *n.* pecūlātor *m.*
embitter *vt.* exacerbāre.
emblazon *vt.* īnsignīre.
emblem *n.* īnsigne *n.*
embodiment *n.* exemplar *n.*
embody *vt.* repraesentāre; (*mil.*) cōnscrībere.
embolden *vt.* cōnfirmāre.
emboss *vt.* imprimere, caelāre.
embrace *vt.* amplectī, complectī; (*items*) continēre, comprehendere; (*party*) sequī; (*opportunity*) adripere. *n.* amplexus *m.*, complexus *m.*
embroider *vt.* acū pingere.
embroidery *n.* vestis picta *f.*
embroil *vt.* miscēre, implicāre.
emend *vt.* ēmendāre, corrigere.
emendation *n.* ēmendātiō *f.*, corrēctiō *f.*
emerald *n.* smaragdus *m.*
emerge *vi.* ēmergere, exsistere.
emergency *n.* tempus *n.*, discrīmen *n.* *a.* subitārius.
emigrate *vi.* migrāre, ēmigrāre.
emigration *n.* migrātiō *f.*
eminence *n.* (*ground*) tumulus *m.*, locus ēditus *m.*; (*rank*) praestantia *f.*, amplitūdō *f.*
eminent *a.* ēgregius, ēminēns, īnsignis, amplus. **-ly** *ad.* ēgregiē, prae cēteris, in prīmīs.
emissary *n.* lēgātus *m.*
emit *vt.* ēmittere.
emmet *n.* formīca *f.*
emolument *n.* lucrum *n.*, ēmolumentum *n.*
emotion *n.* animī mōtus *m.*, commōtiō *f.*, adfectus *m.*
emotional *a.* (*person*) mōbilis; (*speech*) flexanimus.
emperor *n.* prīnceps *m.*, imperātor *m.*
emphasis *n.* pondus *n.*; (*words*) impressiō *f.*
emphasize *vt.* exprimere.
emphatic *a.* gravis. **-ally** *ad.* adsevēranter, vehementer.
empire *n.* imperium *n.*
employ *vt.* ūtī (*abl.*); (*for purpose*) adhibēre; (*person*) exercēre. **-ed** *a.* occupātus.
employee *n.* (*pl.*) operae *f.pl.*
employer *n.* redēmptor *m.*
employment *n.* (*act*) ūsus *m.*; (*work*) quaestus *m.*
empower *vt.* permittere (*dat.*), potestātem facere (*dat.*).
emptiness *n.* inānitās *f.*
empty *a.* inānis, vacuus; (*fig.*) vānus, inritus. *vt.* exhaurīre, exinānīre. *vi.* (*river*) īnfluere.

emulate *vt.* aemulārī.
emulation *n.* aemulātiō *f.*
emulous *a.* aemulus. **-ly** *ad.* certātim.
enable *vt.* potestātem facere (*dat.*).; efficere ut (*subj.*).
enact *vt.* dēcernere, ēdīcere, scīscere; (*part*) agere.
enactment *n.* dēcrētum *n.* lēx *f.*
enamoured *a.* amāns. be — of dēamāre.
encamp *vi.* castra pōnere, tendere.
encampment *n.* castra *n.pl.*
encase *vt.* inclūdere.
enchant *vt.* fascināre; (*fig.*) dēlectāre.
enchantment *n.* fascinātiō *f.*; blandimentum *n.*
enchantress *n.* sāga *f.*
encircle *vt.* cingere, circumdare, amplectī.
enclose *vt.* inclūdere, saepīre.
enclosure *n.* saeptum *n.*, māceria *f.*
encomium *n.* laudātiō *f.*
encompass *vt.* cingere, circumdare, amplectī.
encounter *vt.* obviam īre (*dat.*), occurrere (*dat.*); (*in battle*) concurrere cum (*abl.*), congredī cum. *n.* occursus *m.*, concursus *m.*
encourage *vt.* cōnfirmāre, cohortārī, sublevāre, favēre (*dat.*).
encouragement *n.* hortātiō *f.*, favor *m.*, auxilium *n.*
encroach *vi.* invādere. — upon occupāre; (*fig.*) imminuere.
encrust *vt.* incrustāre.
encumber *vt.* impedīre, onerāre.
encumbrance *n.* impedimentum *n.*, onus *n.*
end *n.* fīnis *m.*; (*aim*) prōpositum *n.*; (*of action*) ēventus *m.*, exitus *m.*; (*of speech*) perōrātiō *f.* — to — continuī at a loose — vacuus, ōtiōsus. for two days on — biduum continenter. in the — dēnique. the — of extrēmus; (*time*) exāctus. put an — to fīnem facere (*dat.*).] fīnem impōnere (*dat.*). to the — that eō cōnsiliō ut (*subj.*). to what —? quō ?, quōrsum ? *vt.* fīnīre, cōnficere; (*mutual dealings*) dirimere. *vi.* dēsinere; (*event*) ēvādere; (*sentence*) cadere, (*speech*) perōrāre; (*time*) exīre. — up as ēvādere. — with dēsinere in (*acc.*).
endanger *vt.* periclitārī, in discrīmen addūcere.
endear *vt.* dēvincīre.
endearing *a.* blandus.
endearment *n.* blanditiae *f.pl.*
endeavour *vt.* cōnārī, ēnītī. *n.* cōnātus *m.*
ending *n.* fīnis *m.*, exitus *m.*
endive *n.* intubum *n.*
endless *a.* īnfīnītus; (*time*) aeternus, perpetuus. **-ly** *ad.* sine fīne, īnfīnītē.
endorse *vt.* ratum facere.
endow *vt.* dōnāre, īnstruere. **-ed** *a.* praeditus.
endowment *n.* dōnum *n.*
endurance *n.* patientia *f.*
endure *vi.* dūrāre, permanēre. *vt.* ferre, tolerāre, patī.
enemy *n.* (*public*) hostis *m.*, hostēs *m.pl.*; (*private*) inimīcus *m.* greatest — inimīcissimus *m.* — territory hosticum *n.*
energetic *a.* impiger, nāvus, strēnuus; (*style*) nervōsus. **-ally** *ad.* impigrē, nāviter, strēnuē.
energy *n.* impigritās *f.*, vigor *m.*, incitātiō *f.*; (*mind*) contentio *f.*; (*style*) nervī *m.pl.*
enervate *vt.* ēnervāre, ēmollīre.
enervation *n.* languor *m.*
enfeeble *vt.* īnfirmāre, dēbilitāre.
enfold *vt.* involvere, complectī.
enforce *vt.* (*law*) exsequī; (*argument*) cōnfirmāre.

enfranchise *vt.* cīvitāte dōnāre; (*slave*) manū mittere.
engag/e *vt.* (*affection*) dēvincīre; (*attention*) distinēre, occupāre; (*enemy*) manum cōnserere cum (*abl.*); (*hire*) condūcere; (*promise*) spondēre, recipere. be -d in versārī in (*abl.*). *vi.* — in ingredī, suscipere. **-ing** *a.* blandus.
engagement *n.* (*bus.*) occupātiō *f.*; (*mil.*) pugna *f.*, certāmen *n.*; (*agreement*) spōnsiō *f.* keep an — fidem praestāre. break an — fidem fallere. I have an — at your house prōmīsī ad tē.
engender *vt.* ingenerāre, ingignere.
engine *n.* māchina *f.*
engineer *n.* māchinātor *m.* *vt.* mōlīrī.
engraft *vt.* īnserere.
engrave *vt.* īnsculpere, incīdere, caelāre.
engraver *n.* sculptor *m.*, caelātor *m.* [caelātūra *f.*
engraving *n.* sculptūra *f.*,
engross *vt.* distringere, occupāre. -ed in tōtus in (*abl.*).
engulf *vt.* dēvorāre, obruere.
enhance *vt.* amplificāre, augēre, exaggerāre.
enigma *n.* aenigma *n.*, ambāgēs *f.pl.*
enigmatic *a.* ambiguus, obscūrus. **-ally** *ad.* per ambāgēs, ambiguē.
enjoin *vt.* imperāre (*dat.*), iniungere (*dat.*).
enjoy *vt.* fruī (*abl.*); (*advantage*) ūtī (*abl.*); (*pleasure*) percipere, dēcerpere. — oneself dēlectārī, geniō indulgēre.
enjoyable *a.* iūcundus.
enjoyment *n.* frūctus *m.*; dēlectātiō *f.*, voluptās *f.*
enlarge *vt.* augēre, amplificāre, dīlātāre; (*territory*) prōpāgāre. — upon amplificāre.
enlargement *n.* amplificātiō *f.*, prōlātiō *f.*
enlighten *vt.* inlūstrāre; docēre, ērudīre.
enlightenment *n.* ērudītiō *f.*, hūmānitās *f.*
enlist *vt.* scrībere, cōnscrībere; (*sympathy*) conciliāre. *vi.* nōmen dare.
enliven *vt.* excitāre.
enmesh *vt.* impedīre, implicāre.
enmity *n.* inimīcitia *f.*, simultās *f.*
ennoble *vt.* honestāre, excolere.
ennui *n.* taedium *n.*
enormity *n.* immānitās *f.*; (*deed*) scelus *n.*, nefās *n.*
enormous *a.* immānis, ingēns. **-ly** *ad.* immēnsum.
enough *a.* satis (*gen.*). *ad.* satis. more than — satis superque. I have had — of mē taedet (*gen.*).
enquire *vi.* quaerere, percontārī. — into cognōscere, inquīrere in (*acc.*).
enquiry *n.* percontātiō *f.*; (*legal*) quaestiō *f.*
enrage *vt.* inrītāre, incendere.
enrapture *vt.* dēlectāre.
enrich *vt.* dītāre locuplētāre. — with augēre (*abl.*).
enrol *vt.* adscrībere, scrībere. *vi.* nōmen dare.
enshrine *vt.* dēdicāre; (*fig.*) sacrāre.
enshroud *vt.* involvere.
ensign *n.* signum *n.*, īnsigne *n.*; (*officer*) signifer *m.*
enslave *vt.* in servitūtem redigere.
enslavement *n.* servitūs *f.*
ensnare *vt.* dēcipere, inlaqueāre, inrētīre.
ensue *vi.* īnsequī.
ensure *vt.* praestāre. — that efficere ut (*subj.*).
entail *vt.* adferre.
entangle *vt.* impedīre, implicāre, inrētīre.
entanglement *n.* implicātiō *f.*

enter *vi.* inīre, ingredī, intrāre; (*riding*) invehī. — **into** introīre in (*acc.*). — **upon** inīre, ingredī. *vt.* (*place*) intrare; (*account*) ferre, indūcere; (*mind*) subīre.
enterprise *n.* inceptum *n.*; (*character*) prōmptus animus *m.*
enterprising *a.* prōmptus, strēnuus.
entertain *vt.* (*guest*) invītāre, excipere; (*state of mind*) habēre, concipere; (*to amuse*) oblectāre.
entertainer *n.* acroāma *n.*
entertainment *n.* hospitium *n.*; oblectāmentum *n.*; acroāma *n.*
enthral *vt.* capere.
enthusiasm *n.* studium *n.* fervor *m.*
enthusiastic *a.* studiōsus, fervidus. **-ally** *ad.* summō studiō.
entice *vt.* inlicere, ēlicere, invītāre.
enticement *n.* illecebra *f.*, lēnōcinium *n.*
entire *a.* integer, tōtus, ūniversus. **-ly** *ad.* omnīnō, funditus, penitus.
entitle *vt.* (*book*) īnscrībere. **be -d to** merērī, dignum esse quī (*subj.*), iūs habēre (*gen.*).
entity *n.* rēs *f.*
entomb *vt.* humāre, sepelīre.
entrails *n.* intestīna *n.pl.*, exta *n.pl.*
entrance *n.* aditus *m.*, introitus *m.*; (*act*) ingressiō *f.*; (*of house*) vestibulum *n.*; (*of harbour*) ōstium *n.*
entrance *vt.* fascināre, cōnsōpīre, capere.
entreat *vt.* implōrāre, obsecrāre; (*successfully*) exōrāre.
entreaty *n.* precēs *f.pl.*
entrust *vt.* committere, crēdere, mandāre; (*for keeping*) dēpōnere.
entry *n.* introitus *m.*, aditus *m.* **make an** — (*book*) in tabulās referre.
entwine *vt.* implicāre, involvere.
enumerate *vt.* numerāre, dīnumerāre.
enunciate *vt.* ēdīcere; (*word*) exprimere.
envelop *vt.* implicāre, involvere.
envelope *n.* involucrum *n.*
enviable *a.* beātus.
envious *a.* invidus, invidiōsus. **-ly** *ad.* invidiōsē.
environment *n.* vīcīnia *f.* **our** — ea in quibus versāmur.
envoy *n.* lēgātus *m.*
envy *n.* invidia *f.* *vt.* invidēre (*dat.*).
enwrap *vt.* involvere.
ephemeral *a.* brevis.
ephor *n.* ephorus *m.*
epic *a.* epicus. *n.* epos *n.*
epicure *n.* dēlicātus *m.*
epigram *n.* sententia *f.*; (*poem*) epigramma *n.*
epilepsy *n.* morbus comitiālis *m.*
epilogue *n.* epilogus *m.*
episode *n.* ēventum *n.*
epistle *n.* epistula *f.*, litterae *f.pl.*
epitaph *n.* epigramma *n.*, titulus *m.*
epithet *n.* adsūmptum *n.*
epitome *n.* epitomē *f.*
epoch *n.* saeculum *n.*
equable *a.* aequālis; (*temper*) aequus.
equal *a.* aequus, pār. **be** — **to** aequāre; (*task*) sufficere (*dat.*). *n.* pār *m.*, *f.* *vt.* aequāre, adaequāre. **-ly** *ad.* aequē, pariter.
equality *n.* aequālitās *f.*
equalize *vt.* adaequāre, exaequāre.
equanimity *n.* aequus animus *m.*
equate *vt.* aequāre.
equator *n.* aequinoctiālis circulus *m.*
equestrian *a.* equester.
equidistant *a.* **be** — aequō spatiō abesse, idem distāre.

equilibrium *n.* lībrāmentum *n.*
equine *a.* equīnus.
equinoctial *a.* aequinoctiālis.
equinox *n.* aequinoctium *n.*
equip *vt.* armāre, īnstruere, ōrnāre.
equipment *n.* arma *n.pl.*, īnstrūmenta *n.pl.*, adparātus *m.*
equipoise *n.* lībrāmentum *n.*
equitab/le *a.* aequus, iūstus. **–ly** *ad.* iūstē, aequē.
equity *n.* aequum *n.*, aequitās *f.*
equivalent *a.* pār, idem īnstar (*gen*).
equivocal *a.* anceps, ambiguus. **–ly** *ad.* ambiguē.
equivocate *vi.* tergiversārī.
era *n.* saeculum *n.*
eradicate *vt.* ēvellere, exstirpāre.
erase *vt.* dēlēre, indūcere.
erasure *n.* litūra *f.*
ere *conj.* priusquam.
erect *vt.* ērigere; (*building*) exstruere; (*statue*) pōnere. *a.* ērēctus.
erection *n.* (*process*) exstructiō *f.*; (*product*) aedificium *n.*
erode *vt.* rōdere.
erotic *a.* amātōrius.
err *vi.* errāre, peccāre.
errand *n.* mandātum *n.*
errant *a.* vagus.
erratic *a.* incōnstāns.
erroneous *a.* falsus. **–ly** *ad.* falsō, perperam.
error *n.* error *m.*; (*moral*) peccātum *n.*; (*writing*) mendum *n.*
erstwhile *ad.* ōlim, quondam.
erudite *a.* doctus.
erudition *n.* doctrīna *f.*, ērudītiō *f.*
erupt *vi.* ērumpere.
eruption *n.* ēruptiō *f.*
escapade *n.* ausum *n.*
escape *vi.* effugere, ēvādere. *vt.* fugere, ēvītāre; (*memory*) excidere ex (*abl.*). — the notice of fallere, praeterīre. *n.* effugium *n.*, fuga *f.* way of — effugium *n.*
eschew *vt.* vītāre.
escort *n.* praesidium *n.*; (*private*) dēductor *m.* *vt.* comitārī, prōsequī; (*out of respect*) dēdūcere.
especial *a.* praecipuus. **–ly** *ad.* praecipuē, praesertim, māximē, in prīmīs.
espionage *n.* inquīsītiō *f.*
espouse *vt.* (*wife*) dūcere; (*cause*) fovēre.
espy *vt.* cōnspicere, cōnspicārī.
essay *n.* cōnātus *m.*; (*test*) perīculum *n.*; (*literary*) libellus *m.* *vt.* cōnārī, incipere.
essence *n.* vīs *f.*, nātūra *f.*
essential *a.* necesse, necessārius. **–ly** *ad.* necessāriō.
establish *vt.* īnstituere, condere; (*firmly*) stabilīre. **–ed** *a* firmus, certus. be — cōnstāre. become — (*custom*) inveterāscere.
establishment *n.* (*act*) cōnstitūtiō *f.*; (*domestic*) familia *f.*
estate *n.* fundus *m.*, rūs *n.*; (*in money*) rēs *f.*; (*rank*) ōrdō *m.*
esteem *vt.* aestimāre, respicere. *n.* grātia *f.*, opīniō *f.*
estimable *a.* optimus.
estimate *vt.* aestimāre, ratiōnem inīre (*gen.*). *n.* aestimātiō *f.*, iūdicium *n.*
estimation *n.* opīniō *f.*, sententia *f.*
estrange *vt.* aliēnāre abaliēnāre.
estrangement *n.* aliēnātiō *f.*, discidium *n.*
estuary *n.* aestuārium *n.*
eternal *a.* aeternus, perennis. **–ly** *ad.* semper, aeternum.
eternity *n.* aeternitās *f.*
etesian winds *n.* etēsiae *f.pl.*
ether *n.* (*sky*) aethēr *m.*
ethereal *a.* aetherius, caelestis.

ethic, -al *a.* mōrālis. **-s** *n.* mōrēs *m.pl.*, officia *n.pl.*
etymology *n.* verbōrum notātiō *f.*
eulogist *n.* laudātor *m.*
eulogize *vt.* laudāre, conlaudāre.
eulogy *n.* laudātiō *f.*
eunuch *n.* eunūchus *m.*
euphony *n.* sonus *m.*
evacuate *vt.* (*place*) exinānīre; (*people*) dēdūcere.
evacuation *n.* discessiō *f.*
evade *vt.* dēclīnāre, dēvītāre, ēlūdere.
evanescent *a.* fluxus.
evaporate *vt.* exhālāre. *vi.* exhālārī.
evaporation *n.* exhālātiō *f.*
evasion *n.* tergiversātiō *f.*
evasive *a.* ambiguus.
eve *n.* vesper *m.*; (*before festival*) pervigilium *n.* **on the — of** prīdiē (*gen.*).
even *a.* aequus, aequālis; (*number*) pār. *ad.* et, etiam; (*tentative*) vel. **— if** etsī, etiamsī. **— so** nihilōminus. **— yet** etiamnum. **not — nē . . . quidem.** *vt.* aequāre.
evening *n.* vesper *m.* *a.* vespertīnus. **— is drawing on** invesperāscit. **— star** *n.* Vesper *m.*, Hesperus *m.*
evenly *ad.* aequāliter, aequābiliter.
evenness *n.* aequālitās *f.*, aequābilitās *f.* [tempus *n.*
eventide *n.* vespertīnum
event *n.* ēventum *n.*; (*outcome*) ēventus *m.*
eventually *ad.* mox, aliquandō, tandem.
eventuality *n.* cāsus *m.*
ever *ad.* unquam; (*after* sī, nisī, num, nē) quandō; (*always*) semper; (*after interrog.*) -nam. tandem. **— so** nimium, nimium quantum. **best —** omnium optimus. **for —** in aeternum.
verlasting *a.* aeternus, immortālis.
evermore *ad.* semper, in aeternum.
every *a.* quisque, omnis. **— four years** quintō quōque annō. **— now and then** interdum. **— other day** alternīs diebus. **-body -one** *pro.* quisque, omnēs *m.pl.* **-day** cottīdiē. *a.* cottīdiānus. **-thing** omnia *n.pl.* **your health is — to me** meā māximē interest tē valēre. **-where** *ad.* ubique, passim.
evict *vt.* dēicere, dētrūdere.
eviction *n.* dēiectiō *f.*
evidence *n.* testimōnium *n.*, indicium *n.*; (*person*) testis *m.*, *f.*; (*proof*) argūmentum *n.* **on the — of** fidē (*gen.*). **collect — against** inquīrere in (*acc.*). **turn King's —** indicium profitērī.
evident *a.* manifestus, ēvidēns, clārus. **it is —** appāret. **it is self — ante pedēs positum est.** **-ly** *ad.* manifestō, clārē.
evil *a.* malus, improbus, scelerātus. **— eye** fascinum *n.* *n.* malum *n.*, improbitās *f.* **-doer** *n.* scelerātus *m.*, maleficus *m.* **-minded** *a.* malevolus.
evince *vt.* praestāre.
evoke *vt.* ēvocāre, ēlicere.
evolution *n.* seriēs *f.*, prōgressus *m.*; (*mil.*) dēcursus *m.*, dēcursiō *f.*
evolve *vt.* explicāre, ēvolvere. *vi.* crēscere.
ewe *n.* ovis *f.*
ewer *n.* hydria *f.*
exacerbate *vt.* exacerbāre, exasperāre.
exact *vt.* exigere. *a.* accūrātus; (*person*) dīligēns; (*number*) exāctus. **-ly** *ad.* accūrātē; (*reply*) ita prōrsus.
exaction *n.* exāctiō *f.*
exactitude, exactness *n.* cūra *f.*, dīligentia *f.*
exaggerate *vt.* augēre, in māius extollere.

exalt *vt.* efferre, extollere; laudāre.
exaltation *n.* ēlātiō *f.*
examination *n.* inquīsītiō *f.*, scrūtātiō *f.*; (*of witness*) interrogātiō *f.*; (*test*) probātiō *f.*
examine *vt.* investīgāre, scrūtārī; (*witness*) interrogāre; (*case*) quaerere dē (*abl.*); (*candidate*) probāre.
examiner *n.* scrūtātor *m.*
example *n.* exemplum *n.*, documentum *n.* for — exemplī grātiā. make an — of animadvertere in (*acc.*).
exasperate *vt.* exacerbāre, inrītāre.
exasperation *n.* inrītātiō *f.*
excavate *vt.* fodere.
excavation *n.* fossiō *f.*
excavator *n.* fossor *m.*
exceed *vt.* excēdere, superāre.
exceedingly *ad.* nimis, valdē, nimium quantum.
excel *vt.* praestāre (*dat.*), exsuperāre. *vi.* excellere.
excellence *n.* praestantia *f.* virtūs *f.*
excellent *a.* ēgregius, praestāns, optimus. **-ly** *ad.* ēgregiē, praeclārē.
except *vt.* excipere. *pr.* praeter (*acc.*). *ad.* nisi. *conj.* praeterquam, nisi quod.
exception *n.* exceptiō *f.* make an — of excipere. take — to gravārī quod. with the — of praeter (*acc.*).
exceptional *a.* ēgregius, eximius. **-ly** *ad.* ēgregiē, eximiē.
excerpt *vt.* excerpere. *n.* excerptum *n.*
excess *n.* immoderātiō *f.*, intemperantia *f.* *a.* supervacāneus. be in — superesse.
excessive *a.* immoderātus, immodestus, nimius. **-ly** *ad.* immodicē, nimis.
exchange *vt.* mūtāre, permūtāre. *n.* permūtātiō *f.*; (*of currencies*) collybus *m.*
exchequer *n.* aerārium *n.*; (*emperor's*) fiscus *m.*
excise *n.* vectīgālia *n.pl.* *vt.* excīdere.
excision *n.* excīsiō *f.*
excitable *a.* mōbilis.
excite *vt.* excitāre, concitāre; (*to action*) incitāre, incendere; (*to hope*) ērigere, exacuere; (*emotion*) movēre, commovēre.
excitement *n.* commōtiō *f.*
exclaim *vt.* exclāmāre. — against adclāmāre (*dat.*).
exclamation *n.* clāmor *m.*, exclāmātiō *f.*
exclude *vt.* exclūdere.
exclusion *n.* exclūsiō *f.*
exclusive *a.* proprius. **-ly** *ad.* sōlum.
excogitate *vt.* excōgitāre.
excrescence *n.* tūber *n.*
excruciating *a.* acerbissimus.
exculpate *vt.* pūrgāre, absolvere.
excursion *n.* iter *n.*; (*mil.*) excursiō *f.*
excuse *n.* excūsātiō *f.*; (*false*) speciēs *f.* *vt.* excūsāre, ignōscere (*dat.*); (*something due*) remittere. plead in — excūsāre. put forward as an — praetendere.
execrable *a.* dētestābilis, sacer, nefārius.
execrate *vt.* dētestārī, exsecrārī.
execration *n.* dētestātiō *f.*, exsecrātiō *f.*
execute *vt.* efficere, patrāre, exsequī; (*behead*) secūrī percutere.
execution *n.* effectus *m.*; (*penalty*) supplicium *n.*, mors *f.*
executioner *n.* carnifex *m.*
exemplar *n.* exemplum *n.*
exempt *a.* immūnis, liber. *vt.* līberāre.
exemption *n.* (*from tax*) immūnitās *f.*; (*from service*) vacātiō *f.*
exercise *n.* exercitātiō *f.*, ūsus *m.*; (*school*) dictāta *n.pl.* *vt.* exercēre, ūtī (*abl.*); (*mind*) acuere.
exert *vt.* extendere, intendere.

ūtī (*abl.*). — oneself mōlīrī ēnītī, sē intendere.
exertion *n.* mōlīmentum *n.*; (*mind*) intentiō *f.* [vapor *m.*
exhalation *n.* exhālātiō *f.*
exhale *vt.* exhālāre, exspīrāre.
exhaust *vt.* exhaurīre; (*tire*) dēfatīgāre, cōnficere.
exhaustion *n.* dēfatīgātiō *f.*
exhaustive *a.* plēnus.
exhibit *vt.* exhibēre, ostendere, expōnere; (*on stage*) ēdere.
exhibition *n.* expositiō *f.*, ostentātiō *f.*
exhilarate *vt.* exhilarāre.
exhort *vt.* hortārī, cohortārī.
exhortation *n.* hortātiō *f.*, hortāmen *n.*
exhume *vt.* ēruere.
exigency *n.* necessitās *f.*
exile *n.* exsilium *n.*, fuga *f.*; (*temporary*) relēgātiō *f.*; (*person*) exsul *m.* live in — exsulāre. *vt.* in exsilium pellere, dēportare; (*temporarily*) relēgāre.
exist *vi.* esse.
existence *n.* vīta *f.*
exit *n.* exitus *m.*, ēgressus *m.*
exodus *n.* discessus *m.*
exonerate *vt.* absolvere.
exorbitant *a.* nimius, immoderātus.
exotic *a.* peregrīnus.
expand *vt.* extendere, dīlātāre.
expanse *n.* spatium *n.*, lātitūdō *f.* [ficāre.
expatiate *vi.* — upon ampli-
expatriate *vt.* extermināre. *n.* extorris *m.*
expect *vt.* exspectāre, spērāre.
expectancy, expectation *n.* spēs *f.*, exspectātiō *f.*
expediency *n.* ūtile *n.*, ūtilitās *f.*
expedient *a.* ūtilis, commodus. it is — expedit. *n.* modus *m.*, ratiō *f.* -ly *ad.* commodē.
expedite *vt.* mātūrāre.
expedition *n.* (*mil.*) expedītiō *f.*
expeditious *a.* prōmptus, celer. -ly *ad.* celeriter.
expel *vt.* pellere, expellere, ēicere. [pendere.
expend *vt.* impendere, ex-
expenditure *n.* impēnsae *f.pl.* sūmptus *m.*
expense *n.* impēnsae *f.pl.*, impendia *n.pl.* at my — meō sūmptū. at the public — dē pūblicō.
expensive *a.* cārus, pretiōsus; (*furnishings*) lautus. -ly *ad.* sūmptuōsē, māgnō pretiō.
experience *n.* ūsus *m.*, experientia *f.* *vt.* experīrī, patī. -d *a.* perītus, expertus.
experiment *n.* experīmentum *n.* *vi.* — with experīrī.
expert *a.* perītus, sciēns. -ly *ad.* perītē, scienter.
expertness *n.* perītia *f.*
expiate *vt.* expiāre, luere. *f.*;
expiatio *f.* (*act*) expiātiō (*penalty*) piāculum *n.*
expiatory *a.* piāculāris.
expiration *n.* (*breath*) exspīrātiō *f.*; (*time*) exitus *m.*
expire *vi.* exspīrāre; (*die*) animam agere, animam efflāre; (*time*) exīre.
expiry *n.* exitus *m.*, fīnis *m.*
explain *vt.* explicāre, expōnere, explānāre, interpretārī; (*lucidly*) ēnōdāre; (*in detail*) ēdisserere.
explanation *n.* explicātiō *f.*, ēnōdātiō *f.*, interpretātiō *f.*
explicit *a.* expressus, apertus. -ly *ad.* apertē. [dīrumpī.
explode *vt.* discutere. *vi.*
exploit *n.* factum *n.*, ausum *n.*; (*pl.*) rēs gestae *f.pl.* *vt.* ūtī (*abl.*), fruī (*abl.*).
explore *vt.* & *i.* explōrāre, scrūtārī.
explorer *n.* explōrātor *m.*
explosion *n.* fragor *m.*
exponent *n.* interpres *m.*, auctor *m.* [exportātiō *f.*
export *vt.* exportāre. *n.*
exportation *n.* exportātiō *f.*

expose *vt.* dētegere, dēnūdāre, patefacere; (*child*) expōnere; (*to danger*) obicere; (*mil.*) nūdare; (*for sale*) prōpōnere. **–d** *a.* apertus, obnoxius.
exposition *n.* explicātiō *f.*, interpretātiō *f.*
expostulate *vi.* expostulāre, conquerī.
expostulation *n.* expostulātiō *f.*
exposure *n.* (*of child*) expositiō *f.*; (*of guilt*) dēprehēnsiō *f.*; (*to hardship*) patientia *f.*
expound *vt.* expōnere, interpretārī.
expounder *n.* interpres *m.*
express *vt.* (*in words*) exprimere, dēclārāre, ēloquī; (*in art*) effingere. *a.* expressus; (*speed*) celerrimus. **–ly** *ad.* plānē, nōminātim.
expression *n.* significātiō *f.*; (*word*) vōx *f.*, verbum *n.*; (*face*) vultus *m.*
expressive *a.* significāns. — of index (*gen.*). be very — māximam vim habēre. **–ly** *ad.* significanter.
expressiveness *n.* vīs *f.*
expulsion *n.* expulsiō *f.* ēiectiō *f.*
expunge *vt.* dēlēre.
expurgate *vt.* pūrgāre.
exquisite *a.* ēlegāns, exquīsītus, eximius; (*judgment*) subtīlis. **–ly** *ad.* ēleganter, exquīsītē.
ex-service *a.* ēmeritus.
extant *a.* superstes. be — exstāre.
extempore *ad.* ex tempore, subitō. *a.* extemporālis.
extemporize *vi.* subita dīcere.
extend *vt.* extendere, dīlātāre; (*hand*) porrigere; (*line*) dūcere; (*office*) prōrogāre; (*territory*) propāgāre. *vi.* patēre, porrigī. — into incurrere in (*acc.*).
extension *n.* prōductiō *f.*, prōlātiō *f.*; (*of office*) prōrogātiō *f.*; (*of territory*) propāgātiō *f.*; (*extra*) incrēmentum *n.*
extensive *a.* effūsus, amplus, lātus. **–ly** *ad.* lātē.
extent *n.* spatium *n.*, amplitūdō *f.* to a large — māgnā ex parte. to some — aliquā ex parte. to this — hāctenus.
extenuate *vt.* levāre, mitigāre.
exterior *a.* externus, exterior. *n.* speciēs *f.*
exterminate *vt.* occīdiōne occīdere, interimere.
extermination *n.* occīdiō *f.*, interneciō *f.*
external *a.* externus. **–ly** *ad.* extrīnsecus.
extinct *a.* mortuus; (*custom*) obsolētus.
extinction *n.* exstinctiō *f.*, interitus *m.*
extinguish *vt.* exstinguere, restinguere.
extinguisher *n.* exstinctor *m.*
extirpate *vt.* exstirpāre, excīdere.
extol *vt.* laudāre, laudibus efferre.
extort *vt.* extorquēre, exprimere.
extortion *n.* (*offence*) rēs repetundae *f.pl.*
extortionate *a.* inīquus, rapāx.
extra *ad.* īnsuper, praetereā. *a.* additus.
extract *vt.* excerpere, extrahere. *n.* make **–s** excerpere.
extraction *n.* ēvulsiō *f.*; (*descent*) genus *n.*
extraneous *a.* adventīcius, aliēnus.
extraordinar/y *a.* extraōrdinārius; (*strange*) mīrus, novus; (*outstanding*) eximius, īnsignis. **–ily** *ad.* mīrificē, eximiē.
extravagance *n.* intemperantia *f.*; (*language*) immoderātiō *f.*, luxuria *f.*; (*spending*) sūmptus *m.*
extravagant *a.* immoderātus, immodestus; (*spending*) sūmptuōsus, prōdigus.

extreme *a.* extrēmus, ultimus. **-ly** valdē, vehementer.
extremity *n.* extrēmum *n.*, fīnis *m.*; (*distress*) angustiae *f.pl.* the — of extrēmus.
extricate *vt.* expedīre, absolvere. — oneself ēmergere.
extrinsic *a.* extrārius, externus.
exuberance *n.* ūbertās *f.*, luxuria *f.*
exuberant *a.* ūber, laetus, luxuriōsus. **-ly** *ad.* ūbertim.
exude *vt.* exsūdāre. *vi.* mānāre.
exult *vi.* exsultārī, laetārī, gestīre.
exultant *a.* laetus. **-ly** *ad.* laetē.
exultation *n.* laetitia *f.*
eye *n.* oculus *m.*; (*needle*) forāmen *n.* cast -s on oculōs conicere in (*acc.*). have an — to spectāre. in your -s iūdice tē. keep one's -s on oculōs dēfīgere in (*abl.*). lose an — alterō oculō capī. see — to — cōnsentīre. set -s on cōnspicere. shut one's -s to cōnīvēre in (*abl.*). take one's -s off oculōs dēicere ab (*abl.*). one -d *a.* luscus. up to the -s in tōtus in (*abl.*). with a cast in the — paetus. with sore -s lippus. sore -s lippitūdō *f.* with one's -s open sciēns. *vt.* intuērī, aspicere.
eyeball *n.* pūpula *f.*
eyebrow *n.* supercilium *n.*
eyelash *n.* palpebrae pilus *m.*
eyelid *n.* palpebra *f.*
eyeshot *n.* oculōrum coniectus *m.*
eyesight *n.* aciēs *f.*, oculī *m.pl.*
eyesore *n.* turpe *n.* it is an— to me oculī meī dolent.
eye-tooth *n.* dēns canīnus *m.*
eye-wash *n.* sycophantia *f.*
eye-witness *n.* arbiter *m.* be an — of interesse (*dat.*).

F

fable *n.* fābula *f.*, apologus *m.*
fabled *a.* fābulōsus.
fabric *n.* (*built*) structūra *f.*; (*woven*) textile *n.*
fabricate *vt.* fabricārī; (*fig.*) comminīscī, fingere. **-d** *a.* commentīcius.
fabrication *n.* (*process*) fabricātiō *f.*; (*thing*) commentum *n.*
fabricator *n.* auctor *m.*
fabulous *a.* commentīcius, fictus. **-ly** *ad.* incrēdibiliter.
facade *n.* frōns *f.*
face *n.* faciēs *f.*, ōs *n.*; (*aspect*) aspectus *m.*; (*impudence*) ōs *n.* — to — cōram. how shall I have the — to go back? quō ōre redībō? in the — of (*abl.*). on the — of it ad speciem, prīmō aspectū. put a bold — on fortem sē praebēre. save — factum pūrgāre. set one's — against adversārī (*dat.*). *vt.* spectāre ad (*acc.*); (*danger*) obviam īre (*dat.*), sē oppōnere (*dat.*). *vi.* (*place*) spectāre, vergere. — about (*mil.*) signa convertere.
facetious *a.* facētus, salsus. **-ly** *ad.* facētē, salsē.
facetiousness *n.* facētiae *f.pl.*, salēs *m.pl.*
facile *a.* facilis.
facilitate *vt.* expedīre.
facility *n.* facilitās *f.*; (*pl.*) opportūnitās *f.*
facing *a.* adversus. *pr.* adversus (*acc.*).
facsimile *n.* exemplār *n.*
fact *n.* rēs *f.*, vērum *n.* as a matter of — enimvērō. in — rē vērā; (*conj.*) etenim; (*climax*) dēnique. the — that quod.
faction *n.* factiō *f.*
factious *a.* factiōsus, sēditiōsus. **-ly** *ad.* sēditiōsē.
factor *n.* prōcūrātor *m.*
factory *n.* officīna *f.*
faculty *n.* facultās *f.*, vīs *f.*

fad *n.* libīdō *f.*
fade *vi.* dēflōrēscere, marcēscere. **-d** *a.* marcidus.
faggot *n.* sarmentum *n.*
fail *vi.* dēficere, dēesse; (*fig.*) cadere, dēcidere; (*in business*) forō cēdere. — **to come** nōn venīre. *vt.* dēficere, dēstituere.
failing *n.* culpa *f.*, vitium *n.*
failure *n.* (*of supply*) dēfectiō *f.*; (*in action*) offēnsiō *f.*; (*at election*) repulsa *f.*
fain *ad.* libenter.
faint *a.* (*body*) languidus, dēfessus; (*impression*) hebes, levis; (*courage*) timidus; (*colour* pallidus. — **hearted** timidus, **be** — languēre; hebēre. *vi.* intermorī, animō linquī. **I feel** — animō male est. **-ly** *ad.* languidē; leviter.
faintness *n.* dēfectiō *f.*, languor *m.*; levitās *f.*
fair *a.* (*appearance*) pulcher, fōrmōsus; (*hair*) flāvus; (*skin*) candidus; (*weather*) serēnus; (*wind*) secundus; (*copy*) pūrus; (*dealings*) aequus; (*speech*) speciōsus, blandus; (*ability*) mediocris; (*reputation*) bonus. — **and square** sine fūcō ac ac fallāciīs. —**play** aequum et bonum *n.* **-ly** *ad.* iūre, iūstē; mediocriter. *n.* nūndinae *f.pl.*
fairness *n.* aequitās *f.*
fairy *n.* nympha *f.*
faith *n.* fidēs *f.* **in good** — bonā fidē. [*ad.* fidēliter.
faithful *a.* fidēlis, fīdus. **-ly**
faithfulness *n.* fidēlitās *f.*
faithless *a.* īnfidēlis, īnfīdus, perfidus. **-ly** *ad.* īnfidēliter.
faithlessness *n.* īnfidēlitās *f.*
fake *vt.* simulāre.
falchion *n.* falx *f.*
falcon *n.* falcō *m.*
fall *vi.* cadere; (*gently*) lābī; (*morally*) prōlābī; (*dead*) concidere, occidere. (*fortress*) expugnārī, capī. —**at** accidere. — **away** dēficere, dēsciscere. — **back** recidere; (*mil.*) pedem referre. — **between** intercidere. — **behind** cessāre: — **by the way** intercidere. — **down** dēcidere, dēlābī; (*building*) ruere, corruere. — **due** cadere. — **flat** sē prōsternere; (*speech*) frigēre. — **forward** prōlābī. — **foul of** incurrere in (*acc.*). — **headlong** sē praecipitāre. — **in, into** incidere. — **in with** occurrere (*dat.*). — **off** dēcidere; (*fig.*) dēsciscere. — **on** incumbere in (*acc.*), incidere in (*acc.*). — **out** excidere; (*event*) ēvenīre; (*hair*) dēfluere. —**short** of deesse ad. — **to** (*by lot*) obtingere obvenīre (*dat.*). — **to the ground** (*case*) iacēre. — **upon** invādere, ingruere in (*acc.*); (*one's neck*) in collum invādere. *n.* cāsus *m.*; (*building*) ruīna *f.*; (*moral*) lāpsus *m.*; (*season*) autumnus *m.* **the** — **of Capua** Capua capta.
fallacious *a.* captiōsus, fallāx. **-ly** *ad.* fallāciter.
fallacy *n.* captiō *f.* [solēre.
fallible *a.* **be** — errāre
fallow *a.* (*land*) novālis. *n.* novāle *n.* **lie** — cessāre.
false *a.* falsus, fictus. **-ly** *ad.* falsō.
falsehood *n.* falsum *n.*, mendācium *n.* **tell a** — mentīrī.
falsify *vt.* vitiāre, interlinere.
falter *vi.* (*speech*) haesitāre; (*gait*) titubāre.
faltering *a.* (*speech*) īnfrāctus; (*gait*) titubāns. *n.* haesitātiō *f.*
fame *n.* fāma *f.*, glōria *f.*, nōmen *n.* **-d** *a.* illūstris, praeclārus.
familiar *a.* (*friend*) intimus; (*fact*) nōtus; (*manner*) cōmis. — **spirit** genius *m.* **be** — **with** nōvisse. **be on** — **terms with** familiāriter ūtī (*abl.*). **-ly** *ad.* familiāriter.
familiarity *n.* ūsus *m.*, cōnsuētūdō *f.*

familiarize *vt.* adsuēfacere.
family *n.* domus *f.*, gēns *f.* *a.* domesticus, familiāris. — property rēs familiāris *f.*
famine *n.* famēs *f.*
famished *a.* famēlicus.
famous *a.* illūstris, praeclārus, nōbilis. make — nōbilitāre. the — ille.
fan *n.* flābellum *n.*; (*winnowing*) vannus *f.* *vt.* ventilāre. — the flames of (*fig.*) īnflammāre.
fanatic *n.* (*religious*) fānāticus *m.*
fanciful *a.* (*person*) incōnstāns; (*idea*) commentīcius.
fancy *n.* (*faculty*) mēns *f.*; (*idea*) opīnātiō *f.*; (*caprice*) libīdō *f.* take a — to amāre incipere. — oneself sē amāre. *vt.* animō fingere, imāginārī, sibi prōpōnere. — you thinking . . . ! tē crēdere . . . ! *a.* dēlicātus.
fancy-free *a.* sēcūrus, vacuus.
fane *n.* fānum *n.*
fang *n.* dēns *m.*
fantastic *a.* commentīcius, mōnstruōsus.
fantasy *n.* imāginātiō *f.*; (*contemptuous*) somnium *n.*
far *a.* longinquus. *ad.* longē, procul; (*with comp.*) multō. as — as *pr.* tenus (*abl.*); *ad.* usque; *conj.* quātenus; (*know*) quod. be — from longē abesse ab. by — longē. how — ? quātenus ? quousque ? so — hāctenus, eātenus; (*limited*) quādam tenus. thus — hāctenus. — and wide lātē. —be it from me to say equidem dīcere nōlim. — from thinking . . . I adeō nōn crēdō . . . ut.
farce *n.* mīmus *m.*
farcical *a.* rīdiculus.
fare *vi.* sē habēre, agere. *n.* vectūra *f.*; (*boat*) naulum *n.*; (*food*) cibus *m.*
farewell *interj.* valē, valēte. say — to valēre iubēre.
far-fetched *a.* quaesītus, arcessītus, altē repetītus.
farm *n.* fundus *m.*, praedium *n.* *vt.* (*soil*) colere; (*taxes*) redimere. — out locāre.
farmer *n.* agricola *m.*; (*of taxes*) pūblicānus *m.*
farming *n.* agricultūra *f.*
far-sighted *a.* prōvidus, prūdēns.
farrow *vt.* parere. *n.* fētus *m.*
farther *ad.* longius, ultrā. *a.* ulterior.
farthest *a.* ultimus, extrēmus. *ad.* longissimē.
farthing *n.* as *m.* to the last — ad assem.
fasces *n.* fascēs *m.pl.*
fascinate *vt.* dēlēnīre, capere.
fascination *n.* dulcēdō *f.*, dēlēnīmenta *n.pl.*, lēnōcinia *n.pl.*
fashion *n.* mōs *m.*, ūsus *m.*; (*manner*) modus *m.*, ratiō *f.*; (*shape*) fōrma *f.* *vt.* fingere, fōrmāre. after the — of ritū (*gen.*). come into — in mōrem venīre. go out of — obsolēscere.
fashionab/le *a.* ēlegāns. it is — mōris est. **-ly** *ad.* ēleganter.
fast *a.* (*firm*) firmus; (*quick*) celer. make — dēligāre. *ad.* firmē; celeriter. be — asleep artē dormīre. *vi.* iēiūnum esse, cibō abstinēre. *n.* iēiūnium *n.*
fasten *vt.* fīgere, ligāre. — down dēfīgere. — on inligāre. — to adligāre. — together conligāre, cōnfīgere.
fastening *n.* iūnctūra *f.*
fastidious *a.* dēlicātus, ēlegāns. **-ly** *ad.* fastīdiōsē.
fastidiousness *n.* fastīdium [*n.*
fasting *n.* iēiūnium *n.*, inedia *f.* *a.* iēiūnus.
fastness *n.* arx *f.*, castellum *n.*
fat *a.* pinguis, opīmus. grow — pinguēscere. *n.* adeps *m.*, *f.*
fatal *a.* (*deadly*) fūnestus, exitiābilis; (*fated*) fātālis. **-ly**

ad. be — **wounded** vulnere perire.
fatality *n.* fātum *n.*, cāsus *m.*
fate *n.* fātum *n.*, fortūna *f.* sors *f.* **-s** (*goddesses*) Parcae *f.pl.*
fated *a.* fātālis.
fateful *a.* fātālis; fūnestus.
father *n.* pater *m.*; (*fig.*) auctor *m.* **-in-law** *n.* socer *m.* *vt.* gignere. — **upon** addicere. tribuere.
fatherland *n.* patria *f.*
fatherless *a.* orbus.
fatherly *a.* paternus.
fathom *n.* sex pedēs *m.pl.* *vt.* (*fig.*) exputāre.
fathomless *a.* profundus.
fatigue *n.* fatīgātio *f.*, dēfatīgātiō *f* *vt.* fatīgāre, dēfatīgāre.
fatness *n.* pinguitūdō *f.*
fatten *vt.* sagināre.
fatty *a.* pinguis.
fatuity *n.* īnsulsitās *f.*, ineptiae *f.pl.* [ineptus.
fatuous *a.* fatuus, īnsulsus,
fault *n.* culpa *f.*, vitium *n.*; (*written*) mendum *n.* **count as a** — vitiō vertere. **find** — **with** incūsāre. **it is not your** — **that** nōn per tē stat quōminus (*subj.*).
faultiness *n.* vitium *n.*
faultless *a.* ēmendātus, integer. **-ly** *ad.* ēmendātē.
fault/y *a.* vitiōsus, mendōsus. **-ily** *ad.* vitiōsē, mendōsē.
faun *n.* faunus *m.*
fauna *n.* animālia *n.pl.*
favour *n.* grātia *f.*, favor *m.*; (*done*) beneficium *n.* **win** — **with** grātiam inīre apud. **by your** — bonā veniā tuā. *vt.* favēre (*dat.*), indulgēre (*dat.*).
favourab/le *a.* faustus, prosperus, secundus. **-ly** *ad.* faustē, fēlīciter benignē.
favourer *n.* fautor *m.*
favourite *a.* dīlectus, grātissimus. *n.* dēliciae *f.pl.*
favouritism *n.* indulgentia *f.*, studium *n.*
fawn *n.* hinnuleus *m.* *a.* (*colour*) gilvus. *vi.* — **upon** adūlārī.
fawning *a.* blandus. *n.* adūlātiō *f.*
fear *n.* timor *m.*, metus *m.*, formīdō *f.* *vt.* timēre, metuere, formīdāre, verērī.
fearful *a.* timidus; horrendus, terribilis, formīdōlosus. **-ly** *ad.* timidē; formīdolōsē.
fearless *a.* impavidus, intrepidus. **-ly** *ad.* impavidē, intrepidē. [audācia *f.*
fearlessness *n.* fīdentia *f.*,
fearsome *a.* formīdolōsus.
feasible *a.* it is — fierī potest.
feast *n.* epulae *f.pl.*, (*private*) convīvium *n.*; (*public*) epulum *n.*; (*religious*) daps *f.*; (*festival*) festus diēs *m.* *vi.* epulārī, convīvārī; (*fig.*) pāscī. *vt.* — **one's eyes on** oculōs pāscere (*abl.*).
feat *n.* factum *n.*, facinus *n.*
feather *n.* penna *f.*; (*downy*) plūma *f.* **birds of a** — **flock together** parēs cum paribus facillimē congregantur.
feathered *a.* pennātus.
feathery *a.* plūmeus.
feature *n.* līneāmentum *n.*; (*fig.*) proprium *n.*
February *n.* mēnsis Februārius *m.* **of** — Februārius.
fecund *a.* fertilis, fēcundus.
fecundity *n.* fertilitās *f.*, fēcunditās *f.*
federal *a.* sociālis, foederātus.
federate *vi.* societātem facere. **-d** *a.* foederātus.
federation *n.* societās *f.*, foederātae cīvitātēs *f.pl.*
fee *n.* honōs *n.*, mercēs *f.*
feeb/le *a.* imbēcillus, īnfirmus, dēbilis. **-ly** *ad.* īnfirmē.
feebleness *n.* imbēcillitās *f.*, īnfirmitās *f.*
feed *vt.* alere, pāscere. *vi.* pāscī. — **on** vescī (*abl.*). *n.* pābulum *n.*
feel *vt.* sentīre; (*with hand*) tractāre, tangere; (*emotion*)

capere, adficī (*abl.*); (*opinion*) cēnsēre, sentīre. — one's way pedetemptim prōgredī. *vi.* sentīre. I — glad gaudeō.
feeling *n.* sēnsus *m.*, tāctus *m.*; (*mind*) animus *m.*, adfectus *m.*; (*pity*) misericordia *f.* good — voluntās *f.* ill — invidia *f.*
feign *vt.* simulāre, fingere.
feignedly *ad.* simulātē, fictē.
feint *n.* simulātiō *f.*
felicitate *vt.* grātulārī (*dat.*).
felicitation *n.* grātulātiō *f.*
felicitous *a.* fēlīx, aptus.
felicity *n.* fēlīcitās *f.*
feline *a.* fēlīnus.
fell *vt.* (*tree*) succīdere; (*enemy*) sternere, caedere. *a.* dīrus, crūdēlis, atrōx. *n.* mōns *m.*; (*skin*) pellis *f.*
fellow *n.* socius *m.*, aequālis *m.*; (*contemptuous*) homō *m.* — citizen cīvis *m.*, *f.* — countryman cīvis *m.*, *f.*, populāris *m.*, *f.* — feeling misericordia *f.* — slave cōnservus *m.* — soldier commīlitō *m.* — student condiscipulus *m.*
fellowship *n.* societās *f.*, sodālitās *f.*
felon *n.* nocēns *m.* [ātus.
felonious *a.* scelestus, sceler-
felony *n.* scelus *n.*, noxa *f.*
felt *n.* coāctum *n.*
female *a.* muliebris. *n.* fēmina *f.*
feminine *a.* muliebris.
fen *n.* palūs *f.*
fence *n.* saepēs *f.* sit on the — quiēscere, medium sē gerere. *vt.* saepīre. — off intersaepīre. *vi.* bātuere, rudibus lūdere.
fencing *n.* rudium lūdus *m.* — master lānista *m.*
fend *vt.* arcēre. *vi.* prōvidēre.
fennel *n.* ferula *f*
fenny *a*, paluster.
ferment *n.* fermentum *n.*; (*fig.*) aestus *m.* *vt.* fermentāre; (*fig.*) excitāre, accendere. *vi.* fervēre.
fermentation *n.* fervor *m.*
fern *n.* filix *f.*
ferocious *a.* ferōx, saevus, truculentus. **-ly** *ad.* truculentē.
ferocity *n.* ferōcitās *f.*, saevitia *f.*
ferret *n.* vīverra *m.* *vt.* — out rīmārī, ēruere.
ferry *n.* trāiectus *m.*; (*boat*) cymba *f.*, pontō *m.* *vt.* trānsvehere.
ferryman *n.* portitor *m.*
fertile *a.* fertilis, fēcundus.
fertility *n.* fertīlitās *f.*, fēcunditās *f.* [ficāre.
fertilize *vt.* fēcundāre, laeti-
fervent *a.* fervidus, ārdēns. **-ly** *ad.* ārdenter.
fervid *a.* fervidus.
fervour *n.* ārdor *m.*, fervor *m.*
festal *a.* festus.
fester *vi.* exulcerārī.
festival *n.* diēs festus *m.*, sollemne *n.*
festive *a.* (*time*) festus; (*person*) festīvus.
festivity *n.* hilaritās *f.*, (*event*) sollemne *n.* [ōnāre.
festoon *n.* sertum *n.* *vt.* cor-
fetch *vt.* arcessere, addūcere; (*price*) vēnīre (*gen.*). — out dēprōmere. — water aquārī.
fetching *a.* lepidus, blandus.
fetid *a.* foetidus, pūtidus.
fetter *n.* compes *f.*, vinculum *n.* *vt.* compedēs inicere (*dat.*), vincīre; (*fig.*) impedīre.
fettle *n.* habitus *m.*, animus *m.*
feud *n.* simultās *f.*, inimīcitia *f.*
fever *n.* febris *f.*
feverish *a.* febrīculosus; (*fig.*) sollicitus.
few *a.* paucī. very — perpaucī. how — ? quotus quisque ?
fewness *n.* paucitās *f.*
fiancé *n.* spōnsus *m.*
fiasco *n.* calamitās *f.* be a — frīgēre.
fiat *n.* ēdictum *n.*
fibre *n.* fibra *f.*
fickle *a.* incōnstāns, levis, mōbilis.

fickleness *n.* incōnstantia *f.* levitās *f.*, mōbilitās *f.*
fiction *n.* fābula *f.*, commentum *n.*
fictitious *a.* fictus, falsus, commentīcius; (*character*) persōnātus. **-ly** *ad.* fictē.
fidelity *n.* fidēlitās *f.*, fidēs *f.*
fidget *vi.* sollicitārī.
field *n.* ager *m.*, (*ploughed*) arvum *n.*; (*of grain*) seges *f.*; (*mil.*) campus *m.*, aciēs *f.*; (*scope*) campus *m.*, locus *m.* in the — (*mil.*) mīlitiae. hold the — vincere, praevalēre. — of vision cōnspectus *m.*
fiend *n.* diabolus *m.*
fiendish *a.* nefārius, improbus.
fierce *a.* saevus, ācer, atrōx; (*look*) torvus. **-ly** *ad.* ācriter, atrōciter, saevē.
fierceness *n.* saevitia *f.*, atrōcitās *f.*
fieriness *n.* ārdor *m.*, fervor [*m.*
fiery *a.* igneus, flammeus; (*fig.*) ārdēns, fervidus.
fife *n.* tībia *f.*
fifteen *num.* quīndecim. — each quīndēnī. — times quīndeciēns.
fifteenth *a.* quīntus decimus.
fifth *a.* quīntus. *n.* quīnta pars *f.*
fiftieth *a.* quīnquāgēsimus.
fifty *num.* quīnquāgintā.
fig *n.* fīcus *f.*; (*tree*) fīcus *f* of — fīculnus. not care a — for floccī nōn facere.
fight *n.* pugna *f.*, proelium *n.* *vi.* pugnāre, dīmicāre. — it out dēcernere, dēcertāre. — to the end dēpugnāre. *vt.* (*battle*) committere; (*enemy*) pugnāre cum (*abl.*).
fighter *n.* pugnātor *m.*
fighting *n.* dīmicātiō *f.*
figment *n.* commentum *n.*
figurative *a.* trānslātus. in — language trānslātīs per similitūdinem verbīs. use **-ly** trānsferre.
figure *n.* figūra *f.*, fōrma *f.*; (*in art*) signum *n.*; (*of speech*) figūra *f.*, trānslātiō *f.*; (*pl.*, *on pottery*) sigilla *n.pl.* — head (*of ship*) īnsigne *n.* *vt.* figūrāre, fōrmāre; (*art*) fingere, effingere. — to oneself sibi prōpōnere. **-d** *a.* sigillātus.
filament *n.* fibra *f.*
filch *vt.* fūrārī, surripere.
file *n.* (*tool*) līma *f.*; (*line*) ōrdō *m.*, agmen *n.*; (*of papers*) fasciculus *m.*, (*pl.*) tabulae *f.pl.* in single — simplicī ōrdine. the rank and — gregāriī mīlitēs. *vt.* līmāre.
filial *a.* pius.
filigree *n.* diatrēta *n.pl.*
fill *vt.* implēre, explēre, complēre; (*office*) fungī (*abl.*). — up supplēre.
fillet *n.* īnfula *f.*, vitta *f.* *vt.* (*fish*) exossāre.
fillip *n.* stimulus *m.*
filly *n.* equula *f.*
film *n.* membrāna *f.*
filter *n.* cōlum *n.* *vt.* dēliquāre. *vi.* percōlārī.
filth *n.* sordēs *f.*, caenum *n.*
filthiness *n.* foeditās *f.*, impūritās *f.*
filth/y *a.* foedus, impūrus; (*speech*) inquinātus. **-ily** *ad.* foedē, inquinātē.
fin *n.* pinna *f.*
final *a.* ultimus, postrēmus, extrēmus. **-ly** *ad.* dēnique, tandem.
finance *n.* rēs nummāria *f.*; (*state*) vectīgālia *n.pl.*
financial *a.* aerārius.
financier *n.* faenerātor *m.*
finch *n.* fringilla *f.*
find *vt.* invenīre, reperīre; (*supplies*) parāre; (*verdict*) iūdicāre; (*pleasure*) capere. — fault with incūsāre. — guilty damnāre. — out comperīre, cognōscere.
finder *n.* inventor *m.*
finding *n.* iūdicium *n.*, sententia *f.*
fine *n.* (*law*) multa *f.*, damnum

n. in — dēnique. *vt.* multāre. *a.* (*thin*, tenuis, subtīlis; (*refined*) ēlegāns, mundus, decōrus; (*beautiful*) pulcher, venustus; (*showy*) speciōsus; (*of weather*) serēnus. **-ly** *ad.* pulchrē, ēleganter, subtīliter.
fineness *n.* tenuitās *f.*; ēlegantia *f.*; pulchritūdō *f.*; speciēs *f.*; serēnitās *f.*
finery *n.* ōrnātus *m.*, munditiae *f.pl.* [argūtiae *f.pl.*
finesse *n.* astūtia *f.*, ars *f.*,
finger *n.* digitus *m.* fore — index *m.* — tips extrēmī digitī. a —'s breadth trānsversus digitus. not lift a — (*in effort*) nē manum quidem vertere. *vt.* pertractāre.
finish *n.* fīnis *m.*; (*art*) perfectiō *f.* *vt.* fīnīre, perficere; (*with art*) perficere, expolīre. — off transigere, peragere, absolvere. *vi.* dēsinere. **—ing-post** mēta *f.* **—ing-touch** manus extrēma.
finite *a.* circumscrīptus.
fir *n.* abiēs *f.* of — abiēgnus.
fire *n.* ignis *m.*; (*conflagration*) incendium *n.*; (*in hearth*) focus *m.*; (*fig.*) ārdor *m.*, calor *m.*, impetus *m.* be on — ārdēre, flagrārē. catch — flammam concipere, ignem comprehendere. set on — accendere, incendere. *vt.* incendere; (*fig.*) īnflammāre; (*missile*) iaculārī.
fire-brand *n.* fax *f.*
fire-brigade *n.* vigilēs *m.pl.*
fire-place *n.* focus *m.*
fire-side *n.* focus *m.*
firewood *n.* lignum *n.*
firm *n.* societās *f.* *a.* firmus, stabilis; (*mind*) cōnstāns. stand—perstāre. **-ly** *ad.* firmē, cōnstanter.
firmament *n.* caelum *n.*
firmness *n.* firmitās *f.*, firmitūdō *f.*; cōnstantia *f.*
first *a.* prīmus, prīnceps; (*of two*) prior. *ad.* prīmum. at — prīmō, principiō. at — hand ipse, ab ipsō. come in — vincere. give — aid to ad tempus medērī (*dat.*). I was the — to see prīmus vīdī. **-ly** *ad.* prīmum.
first-class *a.* classicus.
first-fruits *n.* prīmitiae *f.pl.*
first-rate *a.* eximius, lūculentus. [*n.*
firth *n.* aestuārium *n.*, fretum
fiscal *a.* vectīgālis, aerārius.
fish *n.* piscis *m.* *vi.* piscārī; (*fig.*) expiscārī. **-pond** *n.* piscīna *f.* **-market** *n.* forum piscārium *n.* [cātor *m.*
fisher, fisherman *n.* pis-
fishery, fishing *n.* piscātus *m.* *a.* piscātōrius.
fishing-rod *n.* harundō *f.*
fishmonger *n.* piscārius *m.*
fissile *a.* fissilis.
fissure *n.* rīma *f.*
fist *n.* pugnus *m.*
fit *n.* (*med.*) convulsiō *f.*: (*of anger, illness*) impetus *m.* by -s and starts temerē, carptim. *vt.* aptāre, accommodāre; (*dress*) sedēre (*dat.*). — out armāre, īnstruere. *a.* aptus, idōneus, dignus. I see — to mihi vidētur. **-ly** *ad.* dignē, aptē.
fitful *a.* dubius, incōnstāns. **-ly** *ad.* incōnstanter.
fitness *n.* convenientia *f.*
fitting *n.* adparātus *m.*, īnstrūmentum *n.* *a.* idōneus, dignus. it is — convenit, decet. **-ly** *ad.* dignē, convenienter.
five *num.* quīnque. — each quīnī. — times quīnquiēns. — years quīnquennium *n.*, lūstrum *n.* — sixths quīnque partēs.
five hundred *num.* quīngentī. — each quīngēnī. — times quīngentiēns. — th *a.* quīngentēsimus.
fix *vt.* fīgere; (*time*) dīcere, cōnstituere; (*decision*) statuere.

n. angustiae *f.pl.* put in a — dēprehendere.
fixed *a.* fixus; (*attention*) intentus; (*decision*) certus; (*star*) inerrāns. be firmly — in insīdere (*dat.*). **-ly** *ad.* intentē.
fixity *n.* stabilitās *f.*; (*of purpose*) cōnstantia *f.*
fixture *n.* (*pl.*) adfīxa *n.pl.*
flabbergast *vt.* obstupefacere.
flabbiness *n.* mollitia *f.*
flabby *a.* flaccidus, mollis.
flag *n.* vexillum *n.* — officer praefectus classis *m.* — ship nāvis imperātōria *f.* *vi.* flaccēre, flaccēscere, languēscere.
flagellate *vt.* verberāre.
flagon *n.* lagoena *f.*
flagrant *a.* manifestus; flāgitiōsus. **-ly** *ad.* flāgitiōsē.
flail *n.* fustis *m.*
flair *n.* iūdicium *n.* [nix *f.*
flake *n.* squāma *f.*; (*pl., snow*)
flame *n.* flamma *f.* *vi.* flagrāre, exārdēscere.
flaming *a.* flammeus. [*m.*
flamingo *n.* phoenicopterus
flank *n.* latus *n.* on the — ab latere, ad latus. *vt.* latus tegere (*gen.*).
flap *n.* flābellum *n.*; (*dress*) lacinia *f.* *vt.* plaudere (*abl.*).
flare *n.* flamma *f.*, fulgor *m.* *vi.* exārdēscere, flagrāre.
flash *n.* fulgor *m.*; (*lightning*) fulgur *n.*; (*time*) mōmentum *n.* *vi.* fulgēre; (*motion*) micāre.
flashy *a.* speciōsus.
flask *n.* ampulla *f.*
flat *a.* plānus; (*ground*) aequus; (*on back*) supīnus; (*on face*) prōnus; (*music*) gravis; (*style*) āridus, frigidus. fall — (*fig.*) frigēre. *n.* (*land*) plānitiēs *f.*; (*sea*) vadum *n.*; (*house*) tabulātum *n.* **-ly** *ad.* prōrsus.
flatness *n.* plānitiēs *f.*
flatten *vt.* aequāre, complānāre.
flatter *vt.* adūlārī (*dat.*), adsentārī (*dat.*), blandīrī (*dat.*).
flatterer *n.* adsentātor *m.*
flattering *a.* blandus. **-ly** *ad.* blandē.
flattery *n.* adūlātiō *f.*, adsentātiō *f.*, blanditiae *f.pl.*
flatulence *n.* īnflātiō *f.*
flatulent *a.* īnflātus.
flaunt *vt.* iactāre. *vi.* iactāre, glōriārī.
flaunting *n.* iactātiō *f.* *a.* glōriōsus. **-ly** *ad.* glōriōsē.
flavour *n.* gustātus *m.*, sapor *m.* *vt.* imbuere, condīre.
flavouring *n.* conditiō *f.*
flavourless *a.* īnsulsus.
flaw *n.* vitium *n.*
flawless *a.* ēmendātus.
flax *n.* līnum *n.*
flaxen *a.* flāvus.
flay *vt.* dēglūbere.
flea *n.* pūlex *m.*
fleck *n.* macula *f.* *vt.* variāre.
fledged *a.* pennātus.
flee *vi.* fugere, effugere; (*for refuge*) cōnfugere.
fleece *n.* vellus *n.* *vt.* tondēre; (*fig.*) spoliāre.
fleecy *a.* lāneus. [celer.
fleet *n.* classis *f.* *a.* vēlōx,
fleeting *a.* fugāx.
fleetness *n.* vēlōcitās *f.*, celeritās *f.*
flesh *n.* cārō *f.*; (*fig.*) corpus *n.* in the — vīvus. one's own — and blood cōnsanguineus. put on — pinguēscere.
fleshiness *n.* corpus *n.*
fleshliness *n.* libīdō *f.*
fleshly *a.* libīdinōsus.
fleshy *a.* pinguis.
flexibility *n.* lentitia *f.*
flexible *a.* flexibilis, lentus.
flicker *vi.* coruscāre. **-ing** *a.* tremulus.
flight *n.* (*flying*) volātus *m.*; (*fleeing*) fuga *f.*; (*steps*) scāla *f.* put to — fugāre, in fugam conicere. take to — sē in fugam dare, terga vertere.
flightiness *n.* mōbilitās *f.*

flighty *a.* mōbilis, incōnstāns.
flimsy *a.* tenuis, pertenuis.
flinch *vi.* recēdere.
fling *vt.* iacere, conicere; (*missile*) intorquēre. — away abicere, prōicere. — open patefacere. — in one's teeth obicere (*dat.*). — to the ground prōsternere. *vi.* sē incitāre. *n.* iactus *m.*
flint *n.* silex *m.*
flinty *a.* siliceus.
flippancy *n.* lascīvia *f.*
flippant *a.* lascīvus, protervus. **-ly** *ad.* petulanter.
flirt *vi.* lūdere, lascīvīre. *n.* lascīvus *m.*, lascīva *f.*
flit *vi.* volitāre.
flitch *n.* succīdia *f.*
float *vi.* innāre, fluitāre; (*in air*) volitāre. — down dēfluere.
flock *n.* grex *m.*; (*wool*) floccus *m.* *vi.* concurrere, congregārī, cōnfluere. — in adfluere. [caedere.
flog *vt.* verberāre, virgīs
flogging *n.* verbera *n.pl.*
flood *n.* (*deluge*) ēluviō *f.*; (*river*) torrēns *m.*; (*tide*) accessus *m.*; (*fig.*) flūmen *n.* *vt.* inundāre.
flood-gate *n.* cataracta *f.*
floor *n.* solum *n.*; (*paved*) pavīmentum *n.*; (*storey*) tabulātum *n.*; (*threshing*) ārea *f.* *vt.* contabulāre. be -ed (*in argument*) iacēre.
flora *n.* herbae *f.pl.*
floral *a.* flōreus.
florid *a.* flōridus.
flotilla *n.* classicula *f.*
flounce *vi.* sē conicere. *n.* īnstita *f.*
flounder *vi.* volūtāre; (*in speech*) haesitāre.
flour *n.* fārīna *f.*
flourish *vi.* flōrēre, vigēre. *vt.* vibrāre, iactāre. *n.* (*rhet.*) calamistrī *m.pl.*; (*music*) clangor *m.* [(*dat.*).
flout *vt.* aspernārī, inlūdere
flow *vi.* fluere, mānāre; (*tide*) accēdere. — back recēdere. — between interfluere. — down dēfluere. — into īnfluere in (*acc.*). — out prōfluere, ēmānāre. — through permānāre. — past praeterfluere. — together cōnfluere. — towards adfluere. *n.* flūmen *n.*, cursus *m.*; (*tide*) accessus *m.*; (*words*) flūmen *n.*
flower *n.* flōs *m.*, flōsculus *m.* *vi.* flōrēre, flōrēscere.
floweret *n.* flōsculus *m.*
flowery *a* flōridus.
flowing *a.* prōfluēns. — with abundāns (*abl.*). **-ly** *ad.* prōfluenter.
flown *a.* īnflātus.
fluctuate *vi.* aestuāre, fluctuāre. **-ing** *a.* incōnstāns, incertus.
fluctuation *n.* aestus *m.*, dubitātiō *f.*
fluency *n.* fācundia *f.*, verbōrum cōpia *f.*
fluent *a.* disertus, prōfluēns. **-ly** *ad.* disertē, prōfluenter.
fluid *a.* liquidus. *n.* liquor *m.*
fluidity *n.* liquor *m.*
fluke *n.* (*anchor*) dēns *m.*; (*luck*) fortuītum *n.*
flurry *n.* trepidātiō *f.* *vt.* sollicitāre, turbāre.
flush *n.* rubor *m.* in the first — of victory victōriā ēlātus. *vi.* ērubēscere *a.* (*full*) abundāns; (*level*) aequus.
fluster *n.* trepidātiō *f.* *vt.* turbāre, sollicitāre.
flute *n.* tībia *f.* play the — tībiā canere.
fluted *a.* striātus.
flute-player *n.* tībīcen *m.*
flutter *n.* tremor *m.*; (*fig.*) trepidātiō *f.* *vi.* (*heart*) palpitāre; (*mind*) trepidāre; (*bird*) volitāre.
fluvial *a.* fluviātilis.
flux *n.* fluxus *m.* be in a state of — fluere.
fly *n.* musca *f.* *vi.* volāre; (*flee*) fugere. — apart dissilīre.

— at involāre in (*acc.*). — away āvolāre. — from fugere. — in the face of obviam īre (*dat.*). — out ēvolāre. — to advolāre *ad.* (*acc.*) — up ēvolāre, subvolāre. let — at immittere in (*acc.*).
flying *a.* volucer, volātilis; (*time*) fugāx. [*vt.* parere.
foal *n.* equuleus *m.*, equulus *m.*
foam *n.* spūma *f.* *vi.* spūmāre; (*with rage*) saevīre.
foaming *a.* spūmeus.
focus *vt.* (*mind*) intendere.
fodder *n.* pābulum *n.*
foe *n.* hostis *m.*; (*private*) inimīcus *m.*
fog *n.* cālīgō *f.*, nebula *f.*
foggy *a.* cālīginōsus, nebulōsus.
foible *n.* vitium *n.*
foil *n.* (*metal*) lāmina *f.*; (*sword*) rudis *f.* *vt.* ēlūdere, ad inritum redigere.
foist *vt.* inculcāre, interpōnere.
fold *n.* sinus *m.*; (*sheep*) ovīle *n.* *vt.* plicāre, complicāre; (*hands*) comprimere; (*sheep*) inclūdere. — back replicāre. — over plicāre. — together complicāre. — up in involvere in (*abl.*).
folding-doors *n.* valvae *f.pl.*
foliage *n.* frondēs *f.pl.*
folk *n.* hominēs *m.pl.* *a.* patrius.
follow *vt.* sequī; (*calling*) facere; (*candidate*) adsectārī; (*enemy*) īnsequī; (*example*) imitārī; (*instructions*) pārēre (*dat.*); (*predecessor*) succēdere (*dat.*); (*road*) pergere (*speaker*) intellegere. — closely īnsequī. — hard on the heels of īnsequī, īnsistere (*dat.*), īnstāre (*dat.*). — out exsequī. — to the grave exsequī. — up subsequī, īnsistere (*dat.*). *vi.* (*time*) īnsequī; (*inference*)sequī. as -s ita, in hunc modum.
follower *n.* comes *m.*; (*of candidate*) adsectātor *m.*; (*of model*) imitātor *m.*; (*of teacher*) auditor *m.*
following *a.* īnsequēns, proximus, posterus. *n.* adsectātōrēs *m.pl.*
folly *n.* stultitia *f.*, dēmentia *f.*, īnsipientia *f.*
foment *vt.* fovēre; (*fig.*) augēre.
fomentation *n.* fōmentum *n.*
fond *a.* amāns, studiōsus; ineptus. **-ly** *ad.* amanter; ineptē.
fondle *vt.* fovēre, mulcēre. [*n.*
food *n.* cibus *m.*; (*fig.*) pābulum
fool *n.* stultus *m.*, ineptus *m.*; (*jester*) scurra *m.* make a — of ludibriō habēre. play the — dēsipere. *vt.* dēcipere, lūdere. — away disperdere. *vi.* dēsipere.
foolery *n.* ineptiae *f.pl.*, nūgae *f.pl.*
foolhardy *a.* temerārius.
foolish *a.* stultus, ineptus, īnsipiēns. **-ly** *ad.* stultē, ineptē.
foolishness *n.* stultitia *f.* īnsipientia *f.*
foot *n.* pēs *m.*; (*mil.*) peditātus *m.* a — long pedālis. on — pedes. set — on īnsistere (*dat.*). set on — īnstituere. the — of īmus. *vt.* (*bill*) solvere. — it saltāre, pedibus īre.
football *n.* follis *m.*
footing *n.* locus *m.*, status *m.* keep one's — īnsistere. on an equal — ex aequō.
footman *n.* pedisequus *m.*
footpad *n.* grassātor *m.* [*m.*
foot-path *n.* sēmita *f.* trāmes
footprint *n.* vestigium *n.*
foot-soldier *n.* pedes *m.*
footstep *n.* vestigium *n.* follow in the -s of vestigiis ingredī (*gen.*).
foppish *a.* dēlicātus.
for *pr.* (*advantage*) *dat.*; (*duration*) *acc.*; (*after noun*) *gen.*; (*price*) *abl.*; (*behalf*) prō (*abl.*);

(*cause*) propter (*acc.*), causā (*gen.*), (*after neg.*) prae (*abl.*); (*feelings*) erga (*acc.*); (*lieu*) prō (*abl.*); (*purpose*) ad, in (*acc.*).; (*time fixed*) in (*acc.*). *conj.* nam (1*st word*), enim (2*nd word*); (*with pro.*) quippe quī.
forage *n.* pābulum *n.* *vi.* pābulārī, frūmentārī.
forager *n.* pābulātor *m.*, frūmentātor *m.*
foraging *n.* pābulātiō *f.*, frūmentātiō *f.*
forasmuch as *conj.* quōniam.
foray *n.* incursiō *f.*
forbear *vi.* parcere (*dat.*), supersedēre (*inf.*).
forbearance *n.* venia *f.*, indulgentia *f.*
forbears *n.* māiōrēs *m.pl.*
forbid *vt.* vetāre, interdīcere (*dat.*). Heaven — ! dī meliōra !
forbidding *a.* tristis.
force *n.* vīs *f.*; (*pl., mil.*) cōpiae *f.pl.* *vt.* cōgere, impellere; (*way*) rumpere, mōlīrī; (*growth*) festīnāre. — down dētrūdere. — out extrūdere, expellere, exturbāre. — upon inculcāre. — a way in intrōrumpere, inrumpere.
forced *a.* (*march*) māgnus; (*style*) quaesītus.
forceful *a.* validus.
forceps *n.* forceps *m., f.*
forci/ble *a.* validus; (*fig.*) gravis. **-ly** *ad.* vī, violenter; (*fig.*) graviter. [trānsīre.
ford *n.* vadum *n.* *vt.* vadō
fore *a.* prior. to the — praestō. *ad.* — and aft in longitūdinem.
forearm *n.* bracchium *n.* *vt.* be -ed praecavēre.
forebode *vt.* ōminārī, portendere; prasentīre.
foreboding *n.* praesēnsiō *f.*; ōmen *n.*
forecast *n.* praedictiō *f.* *vt.* praedīcere, prōvidēre.
fore-court *n.* vestibulum *n.*
forefathers *n.* māiōrēs *m.pl.*
forefinger *n.* index *m.* [*n.pl.*
foreground *n.* ēminentia
forehead *n.* frōns *f.*
foreign *a.* peregrīnus, externus; (*goods*) adventīcius. — to aliēnus ab. — ways peregrīnitās *f.* [advena *m.*
foreigner *n.* peregrīnus *m.*,
foreknow *vt.* praenōscere.
foreknowledge *n.* prōvidentia *f.*
foreland *n.* prōmunturium *n.*
foremost *a* prīmus, prīnceps.
forenoon *n.* antemerīdiānum tempus *n*
forensic *a.* forēnsis.
forerunner *n.* praenūntius *m.*
foresee *vt.* praevidēre.
foreshadow *vt.* praemonēre.
foresight *n.* prōvidentia *f.*
forest *n.* silva *f.*
forester *n.* silvicola *m.*
forestall *vt.* occupāre, antevenīre.
foretaste *vt.* praegustāre.
foretell *vt.* praedīcere, vāticinārī.
forethought *n.* prōvidentia *f.*
forewarn *vt.* praemonēre.
foreword *n.* praefātio *f.*
forfeit *n.* multa *f.*, damnum *n.* *vt.* āmittere, perdere, multārī (*abl.*); (*bail*) dēserere.
forfeiture *n.* damnum *n.*
forgather *vi.* congregārī, convenīre.
forge *n.* fornāx *f.* *vt.* fabricārī, excūdere; (*document*) subicere; (*will*) suppōnere; (*signature*) imitārī; (*money*) adulterīnōs nummōs percutere. **-d** *a.* falsus, adulterīnus, commentīcius.
forger *n.* (*of will*) subiector *m.*
forgery *n.* falsum *n.*, commentum *n.*
forg/et *vt.* oblīvīscī (*gen.*); (*thing learnt*) dēdiscere. be **-otten** memoriā cadere, ex animō effluere.
forgetful *a.* immemor; (*by habit*) oblīviōsus.

forgetfulness *n.* oblīviō *f.*
forgive *vt.* ignōscere (*dat.*), veniam dare (*dat.*).
forgiveness *n.* venia *f.*
forgo *vt.* dīmittere, renūntiāre; (*rights*) dēcēdere dē iūre.
fork *n.* furca *f.*; (*small*) furcula *f.*; (*road*) trivium *n.*
forlorn *a.* inops, dēstitūtus, exspēs.
form *n.* fōrma *f.*, figūra *f.*; (*of procedure*) fōrmula *f.*; (*condition*) vigor *m.*; (*etiquette*) mōs *m.*; (*seat*) scamnum *n.*; (*school*) schola *f.* (*hare's*) latibulum *n.* *vt.* fōrmāre, fingere, efficere; (*mil.*) īnstruere; (*plan*) inīre, capere.
formal *a.* iūstus; (*rite*) sollemnis. **-ly** *ad.* ritē.
formality *n.* iūsta *n.pl.*, rītus *m.* **as a —** dicis causā. **with due —** rītē.
formation *n.* fōrma *f.*, figūra *f.*; (*process*) cōnfōrmātiō *f.* **in —** (*mil.*) īnstructus.
former *a.* prior, prīstinus, vetus. **the —** ille. **-ly** *ad.* anteā, ōlim, quondam.
formidab/le *a.* formīdolōsus. **-ly** *ad.* formīdolōsē.
formula *n.* fōrmula *f.*; (*dictated*) praefātiō *f.*
formulate *vt.* compōnere.
forsake *vt.* dērelinquere, dēstituere, dēserere.
forsooth *ad.* scīlicet, sānē.
forswear *vt.* pēierāre, abiūrāre.
fort *n.* castellum *n.*
forth *ad.* forās; (*time*) posthāc.
forthwith *ad.* extemplō, statim.
fortieth *a.* quadragēsimus.
fortification *n.* (*process*) mūnītiō *f.*; (*place*) mūnīmentum *n.*, arx *f.*
fortify *vt.* mūnīre, ēmūnīre; (*fig.*) cōnfirmāre.
fortitude *n.* fortitūdō *f.*
fortnight *n.* quīndecim diēs *m.pl.*
fortnightly *ad.* quīnto decimō quōque diē.
fortress *n.* arx *f.*, castellum *n.*
fortuitous *a.* fortuītus. **-ly** *ad.* fortuītō, cāsū.
fortunate *a.* fēlīx, fortūnātus. **-ly** *ad.* fēlīciter, bene.
fortune *n.* fortūna *f.*, fors *f.*; (*wealth*) rēs *f.*, dīvitiae *f.pl.* **good —** fēlīcitās *f.*, secundae rēs *f.pl.* **bad —** adversae rēs *f.pl.* **make one's —** rem facere, rem quaerere. **tell -s** hariolārī. **-teller** *n.* hariolus *m.*, sāga f. **— hunter** *n.* captātor *m.*
forty *num.* quadrāgintā. **— each** quadrāgēnī. **— times** quadrāgiēns.
forum *n.* forum *n.*
forward *a.* (*person*) protervus, audāx; (*fruit*) praecox. *ad.* porrō, ante. **bring —** prōferre. **come —** prōdīre. *vt.* (*letter*) perferre; (*cause*) adiuvāre, favēre (*dat.*). [alacritās *f.*
forwardness *n.* audācia *f.*
forwards *ad.* porrō, prōrsus. **backwards and —** rursum prōrsum, hūc illūc.
fosse *n.* fossa *f.*
foster *vt.* alere, nūtrīre; (*fig.*) fovēre. **— child** alumnus *m.*, alumna *f.* **— father** altor *m.*, ēducātor *m.* **— mother** altrīx *f.*, nūtrīx *f.*
foul *a.* foedus; (*speech*) inquinātus. **fall — of** inruere in (*acc.*). **— mouthed** maledicus. **-ly** *ad.* foedē, inquinātē.
foulness *n.* foeditās *f.*
found *vt.* condere, fundāre, īnstituere; (*metal*) fundere.
foundation *n.* fundāmenta *n.pl.*
founder *n.* fundātor *m.*, conditor *m.* *vi.* submergī, naufragium facere.
foundling *n.* expositīcia *f.*
fount *n.* fōns *m.*
fountain *n.* fōns *m.* **— head** *n.* fōns *m.*, origō *f*

four *num.* quattuor. — each quaternī. — times quater. — days quadriduum *n.* — years quadriennium *n.*
fourfold *a.* quadruplex. *ad.* quadrifāriam.
four hundred *num.* quadringentī. — each quadringēnī. — times quadringentiēns. —th *a.* quadringentēsimus.
fourteen *num.* quattuordecim — each quaternī dēnī. — times quater deciēns.
fourteenth *a.* quartus decimus.
fourth *a.* quartus. *n.* quadrāns *m.* three -s dōdrāns *m.*, trēs partēs *f.pl.*
fowl *n.* avis *f.*; gallīna *f.*
fowler *n.* auceps *m.*
fowling *n.* aucupium *n.*
fox *n.* vulpes *f.* -'s vulpīnus.
foxy *a.* astūtus, vafer.
fracas *n.* rixa *f.*
fraction *n.* pars *f.*
fractious *a.* difficilis.
fracture *n.* frāctum os *n.* *vt.* frangere.
fragile *a.* fragilis.
fragility *n.* fragilitās *f.*
fragment *n.* fragmentum *n.*
fragrance *n.* odor *m.*
fragrant *a.* suāvis. **-ly** *ad.* suāviter.
frail *a.* fragilis, īnfirmus, dēbilis.
frailty *n.* dēbilitās *f.*; (*moral*) error *m.*
frame *vt.* fabricārī, fingere, effingere; (*document*) compōnere. *n.* fōrma *f.*; (*of mind*) adfectiō *f.*, habitus *m.* in a — of mind animātus.
framer *n.* fabricātor *m.*, opifex *m.*; (*of law*) lātor *m.*
framework *n.* compāgēs *f.*
franchise *n.* suffrāgium *n.*, cīvitās *f.*
frank *a.* ingenuus, apertus; (*speech*) līber. **-ly** *ad.* ingenuē apertē; līberē.
frankincense *n.* tūs *n.*
frankness *n.* ingenuitās *f.*; (*speech*) lībertās *f.*
frantic *a.* furēns, furiōsus, dēlīrus. **-ally** *ad.* furenter.
fraternal *a.* frāternus. **-ly** *ad.* frāternē.
fraternity *n.* frāternitās *f.*; (*society*) sodālitās *f.*; (*guild*) collēgium *n.*
fraternize *vi.* amīcitiam iungere.
fratricide *n.* frātricīda *m.*; (*act*) frātris parricīdium *n.*
fraud *n.* fraus *f.*, dolus *m.*, falsum *n.*; (*criminal*) dolus malus *m.*
fraudulence *n.* fraus *f.*
fraudulent *a.* fraudulentus, dolōsus. **-ly** *ad.* dolōsē, dolō malō.
fraught *a.* plēnus.
fray *n.* pugna *f.*, rixa *f.* *vt.* terere.
freak *n.* mōnstrum *n.*; (*caprice*) libīdō *f.*
freckle *n.* lentīgō *f.*
freckly *a.* lentīginōsus.
free *a.* līber; (*disengaged*) vacuus; (*generous*) līberālis; (*from cost*) grātuītus; (*from duty*) immūnis; (*from encumbrance*) expedītus. be — from vacāre (*abl.*). I am still — to integrum est mihi (*inf.*). set — absolvere, līberāre; (*slave*) manū mittere. *ad.* grātīs, grātuītō. *vt.* līberāre, expedīre, exsolvere.
freebooter *n.* praedō *m.*
free-born *a.* ingenuus.
freedman *n.* lībertus *m.*
freedom *n.* lībertās *f.*; (*from duty*) immūnitās *f.*
freehold *n.* praedium līberum *n.* *a.* immūnis.
freely *ad.* līberē; (*lavishly*) cōpiōsē, largē; (*frankly*) apertē; (*voluntarily*) ultrō, suā sponte.
freeman *n.* cīvis *m.*
free-will *n.* voluntās *f.* of one's own — suā sponte.
freez/e *vt.* gelāre, glaciāre.

vi. concrēscere. it is -ing gelat. -ing *a.* gelidus.
freight *n.* vectūra *f.*; (*cargo*) onus *n.* *vt.* onerāre.
freighter *n.* nāvis onerāria *f.*
frenzied *a.* furēns, furiōsus, fānāticus.
frenzy *n.* furor *m.*, īnsania *f.*
frequency *n.* adsiduitās *f.*
frequent *a.* frequēns, crēber. *vt.* frequentāre, commeāre in (*acc.*). **-ly** *ad.* saepe, saepenumerō, frequenter.
fresh *a.* (*new*) recēns, novus; (*vigorous*) integer; (*water*) dulcis; (*wind*) ācer. **-ly** *ad.* recenter.
freshen *vt.* renovāre. *vi.* (*wind*) incrēbrēscere.
freshman *n.* tīrō *m.*
freshness *n.* novitās *f.*, viriditās *f.*
fret *vi.* maerēre, angī. *vt.* sollicitāre.
fretful *a.* mōrōsus, querulus.
fretfulness *n.* mōrōsitās *f.*
fretted *a.* laqueātus.
friable *a.* puter.
friction *n.* trītus *m.*
friend *n.* amīcus *m.*, familiāris *m.*, *f.*, hospes *m.*, sodālis *m.* make -s with sē cōnferre ad amīcitiam (*gen.*).
friendless *a.* sine amīcīs.
friendliness *n.* cōmitās *f.*, officium *n.*
friendly *a.* cōmis, facilis, benignus. on — terms familiāriter.
friendship *n.* amīcitia *f.*, familiāritās *f.*
frigate *n.* liburna *f.*
fright *n.* horror *m.*, pavor *m.*, terror *m.* take — extimēscere, expavēscere.
frighten *vt.* terrēre, exterrēre, perterrēre. — away absterrēre. — off dēterrēre. — the life out of exanimāre.
frightful *a.* horribilis, immānis; (*look*) taeter. **-ly** *ad.* foedē.
frigid *a.* frigidus.
frigidity *n.* frīgus *n.*
frill *n.* fimbriae *f.pl.* (*rhet.*) calamistrī *m.pl.*
fringe *n.* fimbriae *f.pl.*
frisk *vi.* lascīvīre, exsultāre.
frisky *a.* lascīvus.
fritter *vt.* — away dissipāre; (*time*) extrahere.
frivolity *n.* levitās *f.*
frivolous *a.* levis, inānis. **-ly** *ad.* ināniter.
fro *ad.* to and — hūc illūc.
frock *n.* stola *f.*
frog *n.* rāna *f.*
frolic *n.* lūdus *m.* *vi.* lūdere, lascīvīre.
frolicsome *a.* lascīvus, hilaris.
from *pr.* ab (*abl.*), ā (*before consonants*); (*out*) ē, ex (*abl.*); (*cause*) propter (*acc.*); (*prevention*) quōminus, quīn.
front *n.* frōns *f.* in — ā fronte, adversus.
frontier *n.* līmes *m.*, cōnfīnia *n.pl.* [*n.pl.*
frontlet *n.* (*horse*) frontālia
frost *n.* gelū *n.* be — bitten vī frigoris ambūrī.
frosty *a.* gelidus, glaciālis.
froth *n.* spūma *f.* *vi.* spūmās agere.
frothy *a.* spūmeus.
froward *a.* contumāx.
frown *n.* frontis contractiō *f.* *vi.* frontem contrahere.
frozen *a.* glaciālis.
fructify *vt.* fēcundāre.
frugal *a.* parcus, frūgī. **-ly** *ad.* parcē, frūgāliter.
frugality *n.* frūgālitās *f.*, parsimōnia *f.*
fruit *n.* fructus *m.*; (*tree*) māla *n.pl.*; (*pl.*, *of earth*) frūgēs *f.pl.*; (*berry*) bāca *f.*; (*fig.*) fructus *m.*
fruiterer *m.* pōmārius *m.*
fruitful *a.* fēcundus, fructuōsus. **-ly** *ad.* ferāciter.
fruitfulness *n.* fēcunditās *f.*, ūbertās *f.*
fruition *n.* fructus *m.*

fruitless *a.* inūtilis, vānus. **-ly** *ad.* nēquīquam, frustrā.
fruit-tree *n.* pōmum *n.*
frustrate *vt.* frustrārī, ad inritum redigere.
frustration *n.* frustrātiō *f.*
fry *vt.* frīgere.
frying-pan *n.* sartāgō *f.* out of the — into the fire incidit in Scyllam quī vult vitāre Charybdim.
fuel *n.* fōmes *m.*
fugitive *a.* fugitīvus. *n.* fugitīvus *m.*, trānsfuga *m.*; (*from abroad*) extorris *m.*
fulfil *vt.* (*duty*) explēre, implēre; (*promise*) praestāre; (*order*) exsequī, perficere.
fulfilment *n.* absolūtiō *f.*
full *a.* plēnus, refertus, explētus; (*entire*) integer; (*amount*) solidus; (*brother*) germānus; (*measure*) iūstus; (*meeting*) frequēns; (*style*) cōpiōsus. at — length porrēctus. at — speed citātō gradū, citātō equō. **-y** *ad.* plēnē, penitus, funditus.
fuller *n.* fullō *m.*
full-grown *a.* adultus.
fullness *n.* (*style*) cōpia *f.*; (*time*) mātūritās *f.*
fulminate *vi.* intonāre.
fulminations *n.* fulmina *n.pl.*
fulsome *a.* fastīdiōsus, pūtidus.
fumble *vi.* haesitāre.
fume *n.* fūmus *m.*, hālitus *m.* *vi.* stomachārī.
fumigate *vt.* suffīre.
fun *n.* iocus *m.*, lūdus *m.* for — animī causā. make — of inlūdere, dēlūdere, lūdibriō habēre.
function *n.* officium *n.*, mūnus *n.*
fund *n.* cōpia *f.*; (*pl.*) sors *f.*, pecūniae *f.pl.*
fundamental *a.* prīmus. *n.* prīncipium *n.*, elementum *n.*
funeral *n.* fūnus *n.*, exsequiae *f.pl.* *a.* fūnebris. — pile rogus *m.* — rites exsequiae *f.pl.*, īnferia *f.pl.*
funereal *a.* fūnebris, lūgubris.
funnel *n.* īnfundibulum *n.*
funny *a.* ioculāris, rīdiculus.
fur *n.* pellis *m.*
furbelow *n.* īnstita *f.*
furbish *vt.* expolīre. — up interpolāre.
furious *a.* saevus, vehemēns, perīrātus. **-ly** *ad.* furenter, saevē, vehementer.
furl *vt.* (*sail*) legere.
furlong *n.* stadium *n.*
furlough *n.* commeātus *m.*
furnace *n.* fornāx *f.*
furnish *vt.* praebēre, suppeditāre; (*equip*) īnstruere, ōrnāre.
furniture *n.* supellex *f.*
furrow *n.* sulcus *m.* *vt.* sulcāre.
furry *a.* villōsus.
further *a.* ulterior. *ad.* ultrā, porrō; amplius. *vt.* adiuvāre, cōnsulere (*dat.*).
furtherance *n.* prōgressus *m.*; (*means*) īnstrūmentum *n.*
furthermore *ad.* praetereā, porrō.
furthest *a.* ultimus. *ad.* longissimē.
furtive *a.* fūrtīvus, clandestīnus. **-ly** *ad.* clam, fūrtim.
fury *n.* furor *m.*, saevitia *f.*; īra *f.*; (*pl.*) Furiae *f.pl.*
fuse *vt.* fundere; (*together*) coniungere.
fusion *n.* coniūnctiō *f.*
fuss *n.* importūnitās *f.*, querimōnia *f.* *vi.* conquerī, sollicitārī.
fussy *a.* importūnus, incommodus.
fusty *a.* mūcidus.
futile *a.* inānis, inūtilis, futtilis.
futility *n.* vānitās *f.* futtilitās *f.*
future *a.* futūrus, posterus. *n.* posterum *n.*, reliquum *n.* in — posthāc. for the — in posterum.
futurity *n.* posterum tempus *n.*, posteritās *f.*

G

gabble *vi.* garrire.
gable *n.* fastigium *n.*
gadfly *n.* tabānus *m.*
gag *vt.* ōs praeligāre (*dat.*), ōs obvolvere (*dat.*).
gage *n.* pignus *n.*
gaiety *n.* laetitia *f.*, hilaritās *f.*, festīvitās *f.*
gain *n.* lucrum *n.*, quaestus *m.* *vt.* (*profit*) lucrārī; (*thing*) parāre, cōnsequī, capere; (*case*) vincere; (*place*) pervenīre ad; (*possession of*) potīrī (*gen.*); (*victory*) reportāre. — over conciliāre. — ground incrēbrēscere.
gainful *a.* quaestuōsus.
gainsay *vt.* contrādīcere (*dat.*).
gait *n.* incessus *m.*, ingressiō *f.*
gaiters *n.* ocreae *f.pl.*
gala *n.* diēs festus *m.*
galaxy *n.* circulus lacteus *m.*
gale *n.* ventus *m.*
gall *n.* fel *n.*, bīlis *m.* — bladder *n.* fel *n.* *vt.* ūrere.
gallant *a.* fortis, audāx; (*courteous*) officiōsus. -ly *ad.* fortiter; officiōsē.
gallantry *n.* virtūs *f.*; urbānitās *f.*
gallery *n.* porticus *f.*
galley *n.* nāvis āctuāria *f.*; (*cook's*) culīna *f.*
galling *a.* amārus, mordāx.
gallon *n.* congius *m.*
gallop *n.* cursus *m.* at the — citātō equō, admissō equō. *vi.* admissō equō currere.
gallows *n.* īnfēlīx arbor *m.*, furca *f.* — bird *n.* furcifer *m.*
galore *ad.* adfatim.
gamble *n.* ālea *f.* *vi.* āleā lūdere.
gambler *n.* āleātor *m.*
gambling *n.* ālea *f.*
gambol *n.* lūsus *m.* *vi.* lūdere, lascīvīre, exsultāre.
game *n.* lūdus *m.*; (*with dice*) ālea *f.*; (*hunt*) praeda *f.* public -s lūdī *m.pl.* Olympic -s Olympia *n.pl.* play the —rēctē facere. the -'s up āctum est. *a.* animōsus.
gamester *n.* āleātor *m.*
gammon *n.* perna *f.*
gander *n.* ānser *m.*
gang *n.* grex *m.*, caterva *f.*
gangster *n.* grassātor *m.*
gangway *n.* forus *m.*
gaol *n.* carcer *m.*
gaoler *n.* custōs *m.*
gap *n.* hiātus *m.*, lacūna *f.*
gape *vi.* hiāre, inhiāre; (*opening*) dēhiscere.
garb *n.* habitus *m.*, amictus *m.* *vt.* amicīre.
garbage *n.* quisquiliae *f.pl.*
garden *n.* hortus *m.*; (*public*) hortī *m.pl.*
gardener *n.* hortulānus *m.*; (*ornamental*) topiārius *m.*
gardening *n.* hortī cultūra *f.*; (*ornamental*) topiāria *f.*
gargle *vi.* gargarissāre.
garish *a.* speciōsus, fūcātus.
garland *n.* sertum *n.*, corōna *f.* *vt.* corōnāre.
garlic *n.* ālium *n.*
garment *n.* vestis *f.*, vestīmentum *n.*
garner *n.* horreum *n.*
garnish *vt.* ōrnāre, decorāre.
garret *n.* cēnāculum *n.*
garrison *n.* praesidium *n.*, dēfēnsōrēs *m.pl.* *vt.* praesidiō mūnīre, praesidium collocāre in (*abl.*).
garrotte *vt.* laqueō gulam frangere (*dat.*).
garrulity *n.* garrulitās *f.*
garrulous *a.* garrulus, loquāx.
gas *n.* vapor *m.*
gash *n.* vulnus *n.* *vt.* caedere, lacerāre.
gasp *n.* anhēlitus *m.*, singultus *m.* *vi.* anhēlāre.
gastronomy *n.* gula *f.*
gate *n.* porta *f.*
gather *vt.* colligere, cōgere; (*fruit*) legere; (*inference*) colligere, conicere. *vi.* congregārī.
gathering *n.* conventus *m.*, coetus *m.*

gauche *a.* inconcinnus, illepidus.
gaud/y *a.* speciōsus, fūcātus, lautus. **-ily** *ad.* splendidē, speciōsē.
gauge *n.* modulus *m.* *vt.* mētīrī.
gaunt *a.* macer.
gauntlet *n.* manica *f.*
gauze *n.* Coa *n.pl.*
ga/y *a.* hilaris, festīvus, laetus. **-ily** *ad.* hilare, festīvē.
gaze *vi.* intuērī. — at intuērī, adspectāre, contemplārī.
gazelle *n.* oryx *m.*
gazette *n.* ācta diūrna *n.pl.*, ācta pūblica *n.pl.*
gear *n.* īnstrūmenta *n.pl.*; (*ship's*) armāmenta *n.pl.*
gelding *n.* cantērius *m.*
gelid *a.* gelidus.
gem *n.* gemma *f.*
gender *n.* genus *n.*
genealogical *a.* dē stirpe. — table stemma *n.*
genealogist *n.* geneālogus *m.*
genealogy *n.* geneālogia *f.*
general *a.* generālis, ūniversus; (*usual*) vulgāris, commūnis. in — omnīnō. *n.* dux *m.*, imperātor *m.* **-ly** *ad.* ferē, plērumque; (*discuss*) īnfīnītē.
generalissimo *n.* imperātor *m.* [plērīque *m.pl.*
generality *n.* vulgus *n.*,
generalize *vi.* ūniversē loquī.
generalship *n.* ductus *m.*
generate *vt.* gignere, generāre.
generation *n.* aetās *f.*, saeculum *n.*
generic *a.* generālis. **-ally** *ad.* genere.
generosity *n.* līberālitās *f.*, largitās *f.*
generous *a.* līberālis, largus, benignus. **-ly** *ad.* līberāliter, largē, benignē. [*n.*
genesis *n.* origō *f.*, principium
genial *a.* cōmis, hilaris. **-ly** *ad.* cōmiter, hilare.
geniality *n.* cōmitās *f.*, hilaritās *f.*

genitive *n.* genitīvus *m.*
genius *n.* (*deity*) genius *m.*; (*talent*) ingenium *n.*, indolēs *f.* of — ingeniōsus.
genre *n.* genus *n.*
genteel *a.* urbānus, polītus.
gentility *n.* urbānitās *f.*, ēlegantia *f.*
gent/le *a.* (*birth*) ingenuus; (*manner*) hūmānus, indulgēns, mītis; (*slope*) lēnis, mollis; (*thing*) placidus, lēnis. **-ly** *ad.* lēniter, molliter, placidē.
gentleman *n.* vir *m.*, ingenuus *m.*, vir honestus *m.* **-ly** *a.* ingenuus, līberālis, honestus.
gentleness *n.* hūmānitās *f.*, indulgentia *f.*, lēnitās *f.*
gentlewoman *n.* ingenua *f.*, mulier honesta *f.*
gentry *n.* ingenuī *m.pl.*, optimātēs *m.pl.*; (*contempt*) hominēs *m.pl.*
genuine *a.* vērus, germānus, sincērus. **-ly** *ad.* germānē, sincērē.
genuineness *n.* fidēs *f.*
geographical *a.* geōgraphicus. — position situs *m.*
geography *n.* geōgraphia *f.*
geometrical *a.* geōmetricus.
geometry *n.* geōmetria *f.*
Georgics *n.* Geōrgica *n.pl.*
germ *n.* germen *n.*, sēmen *n.*
germane *a.* adfīnis.
germinate *vi.* gemmāre.
gesticulate *vi.* sē iactāre, gestū ūtī.
gesticulation *n.* gestus *m.*
gesture *n.* gestus *m.*, mōtus *m.*
get *vt.* adipīscī, nancīscī, parāre; (*malady*) contrahere; (*request*) impetrāre; (*return*) capere; (*reward*) ferre; (*something done*) cūrāre (*with gerundive*); (*someone to do*) persuādēre (*dat.*), addūcere. — by heart ēdiscere. — in repōnere. — the better of superāre. go and — arcessere. *vi.* fierī. — about (*rumour*)

palam fierī, percrēbrēscere. — away effugere. — at (*intent*) spectāre. — behind cessāre. — off absolvī. — on prōficere. — out effugere, ēvādere. — out of hand lascīvīre. — out of the way dē viā dēcēdere. — rid of abicere, tollere. — to pervenīre ad. — together congregārī. — up exsurgere.
get-up *n.* ōrnātus *m.*
ghastliness *n.* pallor *m.*
ghastly *a.* pallidus; (*sight*) taeter.
ghost *n.* larva *f.*, īdōlon *n.*; (*pl.*) mānēs *m.pl.* give up the — animam agere, efflāre.
giant *n.* Gigās *m.*
gibberish *n.* barbaricus sermō *m.*
gibbet *n.* furca *f.*
gibe *vi.* inrīdēre.
giddiness *n.* vertīgō *f.*
giddy *a.* vertīginōsus; (*fig.*) levis.
gift *n.* dōnum *n.*; (*small*) mūnusculum *n.*; (*pl.*, *mind*) ingenium *n.*
gifted *a.* ingeniōsus.
gig *n.* cisium *n.*
gigantic *a.* ingēns, immānis.
gild *vt.* inaurāre.
gill *n.* (*measure*) quartārius *m.*; (*fish*) branchia *f.*
gilt *a.* aurātus.
gimlet *n.* terebra *f.*
gin *n.* pedica *f.*, laqueus *m.*
ginger *n.* zingiberī *n.*
gingerly *ad.* pedetemptim.
giraffe *n.* camēlopardālis *f.*
gird *vt.* circumdāre. — on accingere. — oneself cingī. — up succingere.
girder *n.* tignum *n.*
girdle *n.* cingulus *m.* *vt.* cingere.
girl *n.* puella *f.*, virgō *f.*
girlhood *n.* aetās puellāris *f.*
girlish *a.* puellāris.
girth *n.* ambitus *m.*, amplitūdō *f.*
gist *n.* firmāmentum *n.*
give *vt.* dare, dōnāre, tribuere; (*thing due*) reddere. — away largīrī; (*bride*) in matrimōnium collocāre; (*secret*) prōdere. — back reddere, restituere. — in (*name*) profitērī. — off ēmittere. — out (*orders*) ēdere; (*sound*) ēmittere. — up dēdere, trādere; (*hope of*) dēspērāre; (*rights*) dēcēdere dē, renūntiāre. — way cēdere; (*mil.*) inclīnāre. *vi.* labāre. — in sē victum fatērī; (*mil.*) manūs dare. — out (*fail*) dēficere; (*pretend*) ferre. — up dēsistere.
giver *n.* dator *m.*
glacial *a.* glaciālis.
glad *a.* laetus, alacer, hilaris. be — gaudēre. **-ly** *ad.* laetē, libenter.
gladden *vt.* exhilarāre, oblectāre.
glade *n.* saltus *m.*
gladiator *m.* gladiātor *m.*
gladiatorial *a.* gladiātōrius. present a — show gladiātōrēs dare.
gladness *n.* laetitia *f.*, alacritās *f.*, gaudium *n.*
gladsome *a.* laetābilis, laetus.
glamorous *a.* venustus.
glamour *n.* venustās *f.*
glance *n.* aspectus *m.* *vi.* oculōs conicere. — at aspicere; (*fig.*) attingere, perstringere. — off stringere.
glare *n.* fulgor *m.* *vi.* fulgēre. — at torvīs oculīs intuērī.
glaring *a.* (*look*) torvus; (*fault*) manifestus. be — ante pedēs positum esse.
glass *n.* vitrum *n.*; (*mirror*) speculum *n.*
glassy *a.* vitreus.
glaze *vt.* vitrō obdūcere.
gleam *n.* fulgor *m.*, lūx *f.* *vi.* fulgēre, lūcēre. **-ing** *a.* splendidus, nitidus.
glean *vi.* spīcās legere.
gleaning *n.* spīcilegium *n.*
glebe *n.* fundus *m.*
glee *n.* hilaritās *f.*, gaudium *n.*
gleeful *a.* hilaris, festīvus, laetus. **-ly** *ad.* hilare, laetē.

glen *n.* vallis *f.*
glib *a.* prōfluēns, fācundus. **-ly** *ad.* prōfluenter.
glide *n.* lāpsus *m.* *vi.* lābī. — **away** ēlābī.
glimmer *vi.* sublūcēre. *n.* a — **of hope** spēcula *f.*
glimpse *n.* aspectus *m.* *vt.* cōnspicārī.
glint *vi.* renīdēre.
glisten *vi.* fulgēre, nitēre.
glitter *vi.* micāre.
gloaming *n.* crepusculum *n.*
gloat *vi.* — **over** inhiāre, animō haurīre, oculōs pāscere (*abl.*).
globe *n.* globus *m.*, sphaera *f.*; (*inhabited*) orbis terrārum *m.*
globular *a.* globōsus.
globule *n.* globulus *m.*, pilula *f.*
gloom *n.* tenebrae *f.pl.*; tristitia *f.*
gloomy *a.* tenebricōsus; tristis, dēmissus.
glorify *vt.* illūstrāre, extollere, laudāre.
glorious *a.* illūstris, praeclārus, splendidus. **-ly** *ad.* praeclārē, splendidē.
glory *n.* laus *f.*, glōria *f.*, decus *n.* *vi.* glōriārī, sē iactāre.
gloss *n.* nitor *m.* *vt.* — **over** (*fig.*) dissimulāre.
glossy *a.* nitidus.
glove *n.* manica *f.*
glow *n.* (*light*) lūmen *n.*; (*heat*) ārdor *m.*; (*passion*) calor *m.* *vi.* lūcēre, ārdēre, calēre, candēre.
glowing *a.* candēns, ārdēns, calidus.
glue *n.* glūten *n.* *vt.* glūtināre.
glum *a.* tristis, maestus.
glut *vt.* explēre, saturāre. *n.* satietās *f.* abundantia *f.*
glutton *n.* ganeō *m.*, helluō *m.*
gluttonous *a.* edāx, vorāx, avidus.
gluttony *n.* gula *f.*, edācitās *f.*
gnarled *a.* nōdōsus.
gnash *vt.* & *i.* frendere. — **one's teeth** dentibus frendere.
gnat *n.* culex *m.*
gnaw *vt.* rōdere. — **away** ērōdere.
gnawing *a.* mordāx.
go *vi.* īre, vādere; (*depart*) abīre, discēdere; (*event*) ēvādere; (*mechanism*) movērī. — **about** incipere, adgredī. — **after** īnsequī. — **away** abīre, discēdere. — **back** redīre, regredī. — **before** anteīre, praeīre. — **by** praeterīre; (*rule*) sequī, ūtī (*abl.*). — **down** dēscendere, (*storm*) cadere; (*star*) occidere. — **for** petere. — **forward** prōgredī. — **in** intrāre, ingredī. — **in for** (*profession*) facere, exercēre. — **off** abīre. — **on** pergere; (*event*) agī. — **out** exīre, ēgredī; (*fire*) extinguī. — **over** trānsīre; (*to enemy*) dēsciscere; (*preparation*) meditarī; (*reading*) legere; (*work done*) retractāre. — **round** circumīre, ambīre. — **through** percurrere; penetrāre; (*suffer*) perferre. — **to** adīre, petere. — **up** ascendere. — **with** comitārī. — **without** carēre (*abl.*). sē abstinēre (*abl.*). *n.* vīs *f.*, ācrimōnia *f.*
goad *n.* stimulus *m.* *vt.* pungere; (*fig.*) stimulāre.
go-ahead *a.* impiger.
goal *n.* fīnis *m.*, mēta *f.*
goat *n.* caper *m.*, capra *f.*
gobble *vt.* dēvorāre.
go-between *n.* internūntius *m.*, internūntia *f.*; (*bribery*) sequester *m.*
goblet *n.* pōculum *n.*, scyphus *m.*
god *n.* deus *m.*
goddess *n.* dea *f.*
godhead *n.* dīvīnitās *f.*, nūmen *n.*
godless *a.* impius.
godlike *a.* dīvīnus.
godliness *n.* pietās *f.*, rēligiō *f.*
godly *a.* pius.
godsend *n.* quasi caelō dēmissus.
going *n.* itiō *f.*; (*way*) iter *n.*;

(*departure*) profectiō *f.*, discessus *m.*
goitre *n.* strūma *n.*
gold *n.* aurum *n.* *a.* aureus.
golden *a.* aureus; (*hair*) flāvus.
gold-leaf *n.* bractea *f.*
gold-mine *n.* aurāria *f.*
goldsmith *n.* aurārius *m.*, aurifex *m.*
good *a.* bonus, probus; (*fit*) idōneus aptus; (*considerable*) māgnus. — day! salvē, salvēte! — looks fōrma *f.*, pulchritūdō *f.* — nature facilitās *f.*, cōmitās *f.* — for-nothing nēquam. *n.* bonum *n.*, commodum *n.*; (*pl.*) bona *n.pl.*, rēs *f.*, (*for sale*) merx *f.* do — to prōdesse (*dat.*). make — supplēre, praestāre. seem — vidērī. *interj.* bene.
good-bye *interj.* valē, valēte. say — to valēre iubēre.
goodly *a.* pulcher; (*size*) amplus.
good-humoured *a.* cōmis.
good-looking *a.* pulcher.
good-natured *a.* facilis, benignus, benevolus.
goodness *n.* bonitās *f.*; (*character*) virtūs *f.*, probitās *f.*, pietās *f.*
good-tempered *a.* mītis, lēnis.
goodwill *n.* benevolentia *f.*, favor *m.*, grātia *f.*
goose *n.* ānser *m.*, *f.* — flesh horror *m.*
gore *n.* cruor *m.* *vt.* cornibus cōnfodere.
gorge *n.* faucēs *f.pl.*, gula *f.*; (*geog.*) angustiae *f.pl.* *vt.* — oneself sē ingurgitāre.
gorgeous *a.* lautus, splendidus. **-ly** *ad.* lautē, splendidē.
gorgeousness *n.* lautitia *f.*
gormandize *vi.* helluārī.
gory *a.* cruentus.
gospel *n.* ēvangelium *n.*
gossip *n.* (*talk*) sermunculus *m.*, rūmusculus *m.*, fāma *f.*; (*person*) linguläca *f.* *vi.* garrīre.
gouge *vt.* ēruere.
gourd *n.* cucurbita *f.*
gourmand *n.* helluō *m.*, gāneō *m.*
gout *n.* podagra *f.*, articulāris morbus *m.*
gouty *a.* arthrīticus.
govern *vt.* (*subjects*) regere; (*state*) administrāre, gubernāre; (*emotion*) moderārī (*dat.*), cohibēre.
governess *n.* ēducātrīx *f.*
government *n.* gubernātiō *f.*, administrātiō *f.*; (*men*) magistrātūs *m.pl.*
governor *n.* gubernātor *m.*, moderātor *m.*; (*province*) prōcōnsul *m.*, prōcūrātor *m.*
gown *n.* (*men*) toga *f.*; (*women*) stola *f*
grab *vt.* adripere, corripere.
grace *n.* grātia *f.*, lepōs *m.*, decor *m.*; (*favour*) grātia *f.*, venia *f.*; (*of gods*) pāx *f.* be in the good -s of in grātiā esse apud (*acc.*). with a bad — invītus. *vt.* decorāre, ōrnāre.
graceful *a.* decōrus, venustus, lepidus. **-ly** *ad.* venustē, lepidē.
graceless *a.* illepidus, impudēns.
gracious *a.* benignus, prōpitius, misericors. **-ly** *ad.* benignē, līberāliter.
graciousness *n.* benignitās *f.*, līberālitās *f.*
gradation *n.* gradus *m.*
grade *n.* gradus *m.*
gradient *n.* clīvus *m.*
gradual *a.* lēnis. **-ly** *ad.* gradātim, sēnsim, paulātim.
graft *n.* surculus *m.*; (*pol.*) ambitus *m.* *vt.* īnserere.
grafting *n.* īnsitiō *f.*
grain *n.* frūmentum *n.*; (*seed*) grānum *n.* against the — invītā Minervā.
grammar *n.* grammatica *f.*
grammarian *n.* grammaticus *m.*
granary *n.* horreum *n.*
grand *a.* (*person*) amplus,

illūstris, ēgregius; (*way of life*) lautus, māgnificus; (*language*) grandis, sublīmis.
granddaughter *n.* neptis *f.* great — prōneptis *f.*
grandeur *n.* māiestās *f.*, māgnificentia *f.*; (*style*) granditās *f.*
grandfather *n.* avus *m.* great — proavus *m.* great-great- — abavus. of a — avītus.
grandiloquence *n.* māgniloquentia *f.*
grandiloquent *a.* grandiloquus, tumidus.
grandiose *a.* māgnificus.
grandmother *n.* avia *f.* great — proavia *f.*
grandsire *n.* avus *m.*
grandson *n.* nepōs *m.* great — prōnepōs *m.* great-great — abnepōs *m.*
grant *vt.* dare, concēdere, tribuere; (*admit*) fatērī. *n.* concessiō *f.*
grape *n.* ūva *f.*
graphic *a.* expressus. give a — account of ante oculōs ponere, oculīs subicere.
grapnel *n.* manus ferrea *f.*, harpagō *f.*
grapple *vi.* luctārī.
grappling-iron *n.* manus ferrea *f.*
grasp *vt.* prēnsāre, comprehendere; (*with mind*) complectī, adsequī, percipere, intellegere. — at captāre, adpetere. *n.* manus *f.*, comprehēnsiō *f.*; (*mind*) captus *m.*
grasping *a.* avārus, rapāx.
grass *n.* herba *f.*
grass-hopper *n.* gryllus *m.*
grassy *a.* herbōsus.
grate *n.* focus *m.* *vt.* atterere. — upon offendere.
grateful *a.* grātus. feel — grātiam habēre. **-ly** *ad.* grātē.
gratification *n.* voluptās *f.*
gratify *vt.* mōrem gerere (*dat.*), mōrigerārī (*dat.*), grātificārī (*dat.*).
gratifying *a.* iūcundus.
gratis *ad.* grātuītō, grātīs.
gratitude *n.* grātia *f.* feel — grātiam habēre. show — grātiam referre.
gratuitous *a.* grātuitus. **-ly** *ad.* grātuītō.
gratuity *n.* stips *f.*; (*mil.*) dōnātīvum *n.*
grave *n.* sepulchrum *n.* *a.* gravis, austērus. *vt.* scalpere. **-ly** *ad.* graviter, sevērē.
gravel *n.* glārea *f.*
gravitate *vi.* vergere.
gravity *n.* (*person*) sevēritās *f.*, tristitia *f.*; (*circs.*) gravitās *f.*, mōmentum *n.*; (*physics*) nūtus *m.* by force of — nūtū suō.
gray *a.* rāvus; (*hair*) cānus.
graze *vi.* pāscī. *vt.* (*cattle*) pāscere; (*by touch*) stringere.
grazing *n.* pāstus *m.*
grease *n.* arvina *f.* *vt.* ungere.
greasy *a.* pinguis, ūnctus.
great *a.* māgnus, grandis, ingēns, amplus; (*fame*) īnsignis, praeclārus. as — as tantus . . . quantus. — deal plūrimum. — many plūrimī. how — quantus. very — permāgnus. **-ly** *ad.* multum, māgnopere.
greatcoat *n.* lacerna *f.*
greave *n.* ocrea *f.*
greed *n.* avāritia *f.*
greed/y *a.* avārus, cupidus. **-ily** *ad.* avārē, cupidē.
green *a.* viridis; (*unripe*) crūdus. be — virēre.
greenness *n.* viriditās *f.*
greens *n.* olus *n.*
greet *vt.* salūtāre.
greeting *n.* salūs *f.*, salūtātiō *f.*
grey *a.* rāvus; (*hair*) cānus.
greyhound *n.* vertagus *m.*
grief *n.* dolor *m.*, maeror *m.*, lūctus *m.* come to — perīre.
grievance *n.* querimōnia *f.*; iniūria *f.*
grieve *vi.* dolēre, maerēre, lūgēre.

grievous *a.* tristis, lūctuōsus; molestus, gravis, acerbus. **-ly** *ad.* graviter, valdē.
griffin *n.* gryps *m.*
grim *a.* trux, truculentus; atrōx.
grimace *n.* ōris dēprāvātiō *f.* make a — ōs dūcere.
grime *n.* sordēs *f.*, lutum *n.*
grimy *a.* sordidus, lutulentus.
grin *n.* rīsus *m.* *vi.* adrīdēre.
grind *vt.* contundere; (*corn*) molere; (*blade*) acuere. — down (*fig.*) opprimere. — stone *n.* cōs *f.*
grip *vt.* comprehendere, arripere. *n.* comprehēnsiō *f.* come to -s with in complexum venīre (*gen.*).
gripe *n.* tormina *n.pl.*
grisly *a.* horridus, dīrus.
grist *n.* (*fig.*) ēmolumentum *n.*
grit *n.* harēna *f.*
groan *n.* gemitus *m.* *vi.* gemere, ingemere.
groin *n.* inguen *n.*
groom *n.* agāsō *m.*
groove *n.* canālis *m.*, stria *f.*
grope *vi.* praetentāre.
gross *a.* crassus, pinguis; (*morally*) turpis, foedus. **-ly** *ad.* foedē, turpiter; (*very*) valdē.
grossness *n.* crassitūdō *f.*; turpitūdō *f.*
grotto *n.* spēlunca *f.*, antrum [*n.*
ground *n.* (*bottom*) solum *n.*; (*earth*) terra *f.*, humus *f.*; (*cause*) ratiō *f.*, causa *f.*; (*sediment*) faex *f.* on the — humī. gain — prōficere; (*rumour*) incrēbrēscere. lose — cēdere; (*mil.*) inclīnāre. *vt.* īnstituere. *vi.* (*ship*) sīdere.
grounding *n.* īnstitūtiō *f.*
groundless *a.* vānus, inānis. **-ly** *ad.* frustrā, temerē.
grounds *n.* faex *f.*; (*property*) praedium *n.*; (*reason*) causa *f.* I have good — for doing nōn sinē causā faciō, iūstīs dē causīs faciō.
groundwork *n.* fundāmentum *n.*
group *n.* globus *m.*, circulus *m.* *vt.* dispōnere.
grouse *n.* (*bird*) tetraō *m.*; (*complaint*) querēla *f.* *vi.* querī.
grove *n.* nemus *n.*, lūcus *m.*
grovel *vi.* serpere, sē prōsternere, sē advolvere.
grovelling *a.* humilis, abiectus.
grow *vi.* crēscere, glīscere; (*spread*) percrēbrēscere; (*become*) fierī. — old senēscere. — up adolēscere, pūbēscere. let — (*hair*) prōmittere. *vt.* (*crops*) colere; (*beard*) dēmittere. **-n-up** *a.* adultus, grandis.
growl *n.* fremitus *m.* *vi.* fremere.
growth *n.* incrēmentum *n.*, auctus *m.*
grub *n.* vermiculus *m.*
grudge *n.* invidia *f.* *vt.* invidēre (*dat.*); (*thing*) gravārī.
grudgingly *ad.* invītus, gravātē.
gruesome *a.* taeter.
gruff *a.* acerbus, asper.
grumble *vi.* querī, mussāre. *n.* querēla *f.*
grumpy *a.* mōrōsus, querulus.
grunt *n.* grunnītus *m.* *vi.* grunnīre.
guarantee *n.* (*money*) spōnsiō *f.*; (*promise*) fidēs *f.*; (*person*) praes *m.* *vt.* spondēre, praestāre.
guarantor *n.* spōnsor *m.*
guard *n.* custōdia *f.*, praesidium *n.*; (*person*) custōs *m.* be on one's — cavēre. keep — statiōnem agere. — house *n.* custōdia *f.* off one's — imprūdēns, inopīnāns. be taken off one's — dē gradū dēicī. *vt.* custōdīre, dēfendere; (*keep*) cōnservāre. — against cavēre.
guarded *a.* cautus. **-ly** *ad.* cautē.
guardian *n.* custōs *m.*; (*of*

minors) tūtor *m.* — spirit genius *m.* [tūtēla *f.*
guardianship *n.* custōdia *f.*,
gudgeon *n.* gōbius *m.*
guerdon *n.* praemium *n.*, mercēs *f.*
guess *n.* coniectūra *f.* *vt.* dīvīnāre conicere.
guest *n.* hospes *m.*, hospita *f.*; (*at dinner*) convīva *m.* uninvited — umbra *f.* -'s hospitālis.
guffaw *n.* cachinnus *m.* *vi.* cachinnāre.
guidance *n.* moderātiō *f.* under the — of God dūcente deō.
guide *n.* dux *m.*, ductor *m.*; (*in policy*) auctor *m.* *vt.* dūcere; (*steer*) regere; (*control*) moderārī.
guild *n.* collēgium *n.*
guile *n.* dolus *m.*, fraus *f.*
guileful *a.* dolōsus, fraudulentus. **-ly** *ad.* dolōsē.
guileless *a.* simplex, innocēns. **-ly** *ad.* sine fraude.
guilt *n.* culpa *f.*, scelus *n.*
guiltless *a.* innocēns, insōns. **-ly** *ad.* integrē.
guilty *a.* nocēns, sōns. find — damnāre.
guise *n.* speciēs *f.*
guitar *n.* fidēs *f.pl.* play the — fidibus canere. [hiātus *m.*
gulf *n.* sinus *m.*; (*chasm*)
gull *n.* mergus *m.* *vt.* dēcipere.
gullet *n.* gula *f.*, guttur *n.*
gullible *a.* crēdulus.
gulp *vt.* dēvorāre, haurīre.
gum *n.* gummi *n.*; (*mouth*) gingīva *f.*
gumption *n.* prūdentia *f.*
gurgle *vi.* singultāre.
gush *vi.* sē prōfundere, ēmicāre. *n.* scatūrīginēs *f.pl.*
gust *n.* flāmen *n.*, impetus *m.*
gusty *a.* ventōsus.
gusto *n.* studium *n.*
gut *n.* intestīnum *n.* *vt.* exenterāre; (*fig.*) extergēre.
gutter *n.* canālis *m.*
guzzle *vi.* sē ingurgitāre.
gymnasium *n.* gymnasium *n.*, palaestra *f.* head of a — gymnasiarchus *m.*
gymnastic *a.* gymnicus. **-s** *n.* palaestra *f.*
gyrate *vi.* volvī.

H

habit *n.* mōs *m.*, cōnsuētūdō *f.*; (*dress*) habitus *m.*, vestītus *m.* be in the — of solēre.
habitable *a.* habitābilis.
habitation *n.* domus *f.*, domicilium *n.*; (*place*) sēdēs *f.*
habitual *a.* ūsitātus. **-ly** *ad.* ex mōre, persaepe.
habituate *vt.* adsuēfacere, insuēscere.
hack *vt.* caedere, concīdere. *n.* (*horse*) caballus *m.*
hackneyed *a.* trītus.
Hades *n.* īnferī *m.pl.*
haft *n.* manubrium *n.*
hag *n.* anus *f.*
haggard *a.* ferus.
haggle *vi.* altercārī.
hail *n.* grandō *f.* *vi.* it **-s** grandinat. *vt.* salūtāre, adclāmāre. *interj.* avē, avēte; salvē, salvēte. I — from Rome Rōma mihi patria est.
hair *n.* capillus *m.*, crīnis *m.*, (*single*) pilus *m.*; (*animals*) sēta *f.*, villus *n.* deviate a -'s breadth from trānsversum digitum discēdere ab. split **-s** cavillārī.
hair-dresser *n.* tōnsor *m.*
hairless *a.* (*head*) calvus; (*body*) glaber.
hairpin *n.* crīnāle *n.*
hair-splitting *a.* captiōsus. *n.* cavillātiō *f.*
hairy *a.* pilōsus.
halberd *n.* bipennis *f.*
halcyon *n.* alcēdō *f.* — days alcēdōnia *n.pl.*
hale *a.* validus, rōbustus. *vt.* trahere, rapere.

half *n.* dīmidium *n.*, dīmidia pars *f.* *a.* dīmidius, dīmidiātus. — as much again sesquī. well begun is — done dīmidium factī quī coepit habet.
half-asleep *a.* sēmisomnus.
half-baked *a.* (*fig.*) rudis.
half-dead *a.* sēmianimis, sēmivīvus.
half-full *a.* sēmiplēnus.
half-hearted *a.* incūriōsus, sōcors. — ly *ad.* sine studiō.
half-hour *n.* sēmihōra *f.*
half-moon *n.* lūna dīmidiāta [*f.*
half-open *a.* sēmiapertus.
half-pound *n.* sēlibra *f.*
half-way *a.* medius. — up the hill in mediō colle.
half-yearly *a.* sēmestris.
hall *n.* ātrium *n.*; (*public*) exedra *f.*
hallo *interj.* heus.
hallow *vt.* sacrāre.
hallucination *n.* error *m.*, somnium *n.*
halo *n.* corōna *f.*
halt *vi.* insistere, cōnsistere. *vt.* sistere. *n.* come to a — cōnsistere, agmen cōnstituere. *a.* claudus.
halter *n.* capistrum *n.*; (*fig.*) laqueus *m.*
halve *vt.* bipartīre.
ham *n.* perna *f.*
hamlet *n.* vīcus *m.*
hammer *n.* malleus *m.* *vt.* tundere. — out excūdere.
hamper *n.* corbis *f.* *vt.* impedīre; (*with debt*) obstringere.
hamstring *vt.* poplitem succīdere (*dat.*).
hand *n.* manus *f.* left — laeva *f.*, sinistra *f.* right — dextra *f.* an old — veterātor *m.* at — praestō, ad manum. be at — adesse. at first — ipse. at second — ab aliō. on the one — . . . on the other et . . . et, quidem . . . at. near at — in expeditō, inibī. the matter in — quod nunc īnstat, quae in manibus sunt. fight — to — manum cōnserere, comminus pugnāre. get out of — lascīvīre. have a — in interesse (*dat.*). have one's -s full satis agere. lay -s on manum adferre, inicere (*dat.*). live from — to mouth ad hōram vīvere. pass from — to — per manūs trādere. take in — suscipere. -s (*workmen*) operae *f.pl.* *vt.* trādere, porrigere. — down trādere, prōdere. — over dēferre, reddere.
hand-bill *n.* libellus *m.*
handbook *n.* ars *f.*
handcuffs *n.* manicae *f.pl.*
handful *n.* manipulus *m.*
handicap *n.* impedīmentum *n.*
handicraft *n.* artificium *n.*, ars operōsa *f.*
handiness *n.* habilitās *f.*; commoditās *f.*
handiwork *n.* opus *n.*, [manus *f.*
handkerchief *n.* sūdārium *n.*
handle *n.* (*cup*) ānsa *f.*; (*knife*) manubrium *n.*; (*fig.*) ānsa *f.*, occāsiō *f.* *vt.* tractāre.
handling *n.* tractātiō *f.*
handmaid *n.* famula *f.*
handsome *a.* fōrmōsus, pulcher; (*gift*) līberālis. -ly *ad.* pulchrē; līberāliter.
handsomeness *n.* pulchritūdō *f.*, fōrma *f.*
handwriting *n.* manus *f.*
hand/y *a.* (*to use*) habilis; (*near*) praestō. -ily *ad.* habiliter.
hang *vt.* suspendere; (*head*) dēmittere; (*wall*) vestīre. *vi.* pendēre. — back gravārī, dubitāre. — down dēpendēre. — on to haerēre (*dat.*). — over imminēre (*dat.*), impendēre (*dat.*). go and be -ed abī in malam crucem!
hanger-on *n.* cliēns *m.*, *f.*, assecla *m.*, *f.*
hanging *n.* (*death*) suspendium *n.*; (*pl.*) aulaea *n.pl.* *a.* pendulus.
hangman *n.* carnifex *m.*

hanker *vi.* — after appetere, exoptāre.
hap *n.* fors *f.*
haphazard *a.* fortuītus.
hapless *a.* miser, īnfēlīx.
haply *ad.* fortasse.
happen *vi.* accidere, ēvenīre, contingere, fierī. as usually -s ut fit. — upon incidere in (*acc.*).
happiness *n.* fēlīcitās *f.*
happ/y *a.* fēlīx, beātus; (*in some respect*) fortūnātus. **-ily** *ad.* fēlīciter, beātē, bene.
harangue *n.* cōntiō *f.* *vt.* cōntiōnārī, hortārī.
harass *vt.* vexāre, lacessere, exagitāre, sollicitāre.
harassing *a.* molestus.
harbinger *n.* praenūntius *m.*
harbour *n.* portus *m.* *vt.* recipere. — dues portōria *n.pl.*
hard *a.* dūrus; (*circs.*) asper, inīquus; (*task*) difficilis, arduus; (*of hearing*) surdaster. grow — dūrēscere. — cash præsēns pecūnia. *ad.* sēdulō, valdē. — by prope, iuxtā. I am — put to it to do aegerrimē faciō.
harden *vt.* dūrāre. *vi.* dūrēscere; (*fig.*) obdūrēscere. become -ed obdūrēscere.
hard-fought *a.* atrōx.
hard-hearted *a.* crūdēlis, dūrus, inhūmānus.
hardihood *n.* audācia *f.*
hardiness *n.* rōbur *n.*; dūritia *f.*
hardly *ad.* vix, aegrē; (*severely*) dūriter, acerbē. — any nullus ferē.
hardness *n.* dūritia *f.*; (*fig.*) asperitās *f.*, inīquitās *f.*; (*difficulty*) difficultās *f.*; (*of hearing*) surditās *f.*
hardship *m.* labor *m.*, malum *n.*, iniūria *f.*
hard-working *a.* industrius, nāvus, sēdulus.
hard/y *a.* dūrus, rōbustus, sevērus. **-ily** *ad.* sevērē.
hare *n.* lepus *m.*
hark *interj.* auscultā, auscultāte. *vi.* — back to repetere.
harm *n.* iniūria *f.*, damnum *n.*, malum *n.*, dētrīmentum *n.* come to — dētrīmentum capere, accipere. *vt.* laedere, nocēre (*dat.*).
harmful *a.* damnōsus, noxius. **-ly** *ad.* male.
harmless *a.* innocēns. **-ly** *ad.* innocenter; (*escape*) salvus, incolumis, inviolātus.
harmonious *a.* cōnsonus, canōrus; (*fig.*) concors; (*things*) congruēns. **-ly** *ad.* modulātē; concorditer; convenienter.
harmonize *vi.* concinere, cōnsentīre, congruere.
harmony *n.* concentus *m.*; (*fig.*) concordia *f.*, cōnsēnsus *m.*
harness *n.* arma *n.pl.* *vt.* infrēnāre, iungere.
harp *n.* fidēs *f.pl.* play the — fidibus canere. *vi.* — on (*fig.*) cantāre, dictitāre. be always -ing on the same thing cantilēnam eandem canere.
harpist *n.* fidicen *m.*, fidicina *f.*
harpoon *n.* iaculum *n.*
harpy *n.* Harpyia *f.*
harrow *n.* rastrum *n.* *vt.* occāre
harrower *n.* occātor *m.*
harrowing *a.* horrendus.
harry *vt.* vexāre, dīripere.
harsh *a.* dūrus, acerbus, asper; (*person*) inclēmēns, sevērus. **-ly** *ad.* acerbē, asperē; sevērē.
harshness *n.* acerbitās *f.*, asperitās *f.*; crūdēlitās *f.*
hart *n.* cervus *m.*
harvest *n.* messis *f.* *vt.* metere, dēmetere.
harvester *n.* messor *m.*
hash *n.* farrāgō *f.* *vt.* comminuere.
haste *n.* festīnātiō *f.*, properātiō *f.* in — festīnanter. in hot — incitātus. make — festīnāre.
hasten *vt.* mātūrāre, adcele-

rāre. *vi.* festīnāre, properāre, mātūrāre.
hastiness *n.* temeritās *f.*; (*temper*) īrācundia *f.*
hast/y *a.* properus, celer; (*action*) incōnsultus, temerārius; (*temper*) īrācundus, ācer. over — praeproperus. **-ily** *ad.* properē, raptim; temerē, incōnsultē; īrācundē.
hat *n.* petasus *m.*
hatch *vt.* exclūdere, parere.
hatchet *n.* dolabra *f.*
hate *n.* odium *n.*, invidia *f.* *vt.* ōdisse.
hateful *a.* odiōsus, invīsus. **-ly** *ad.* odiōsē.
hatred *n.* odium *n.*
haughtiness *n.* fastus *m.*, adrogantia *d.* superbia *f.*
haught/y *a.* adrogāns, superbus, īnsolēns. **-ily** *ad.* adroganter, superbē, īnsolenter.
haul *vt.* trahere. *n.* bolus *m.*
haulage *n.* vectūra *f.*
haulm *n.* culmus *m.*
haunch *n.* femur *n.*
haunt *vt.* frequentāre. *n.* locus *m.*; (*animals*) lustrum *n.*
have *vt.* habēre, tenēre; (*get done*) cūrāre (*gerundive*). **I —** a house est mihī domus. **I —** to go mihī abeundum est. **—it out with** rem dēcernere cum. **— on** gerere, gestāre, induī. **I had better go** melius est īre, praestat īre. **I had rather** mālim, māllem.
haven *n.* portus *m.*; (*fig.*) perfugium *n.* [*f.*, ruīna *f.*
havoc *n.* exitium *n.*, vastātiō
hawk *n.* accipiter *m.* *vt.* (*wares*) circumferre.
hawker *n.* īnstitor *m.*
hawser *n.* fūnis *m.*
hay *n.* faenum *n.* **make — while the sun shines** forō ūtī.
hazard *n.* perīculum *n.*, discrīmen *n.*, ālea *f.* *vt.* perīclitārī, in āleam dare.
hazardous *a.* perīculōsus.
haze *n.* nebula *f.*
hazel *n.* corylus *f.* [certus.
hazy *a.* nebulōsus; (*fig.*) in-
he *pro.* hic, ille, is.
head *n.* caput *n.*; (*person*) dux *m.*, prīnceps *m.*; (*composition*) caput *n.*; (*mind*) animus *m.*, ingenium *n.* **— first** praeceps. **— over heels** cernuus. **off one's —** dēmēns. **be at the — of** dūcere, praeesse (*dat.*). **come to a —** caput facere; (*fig.*) in discrīmen addūcī. **give one his —** indulgēre (*dat.*), habēnās immittere (*dat.*). **keep one's —** praesentī animō ūtī. **lose one's —** suī compotem nōn esse. **shake one's —** abnuere. *vt.* dūcere, praeesse (*dat.*). **— off** intercipere. *vi.* (*in a direction*) tendere.
headache *n.* capitis dolor *m.*
heading *n.* caput *n.*
headland *n.* prōmunturium *n.*
headlong *a.* praeceps. *ad.* in praeceps. **rush —** sē praecipitāre. [tōrium *n.*
headquarters *n.* (*mil.*) prae-
headship *n.* prīncipātus *m.*
headsman *n.* carnifex *m.*
headstrong *a.* impotēns, pervicāx.
headway *n.* prōfectus *m.*
heady *a.* incōnsultus; (*wine*) vehemēns.
heal *vt.* sānāre, medērī (*dat.*). *vi.* sānēscere. **— over** obdūcī.
healer *n.* medicus *m.*
healing *a.* salūbris.
health *n.* valētūdō *f.*, salūs *f.* **state of —** valētūdō *f.* **ill —** valētūdō *f.* **be in good —** valēre. **drink the — of** propīnāre (*dat.*).
healthful *a.* salūbris.
healthiness *n.* sānitās *f.*
healthy *a.* sānus, integer; (*conditions*) salūber.
heap *n.* acervus *m.*, cumulus *m.* **in -s** acervātim. *vt.* acervāre. **— up** adcumulāre, coacervāre, congerere.
hear *vt.* audīre; (*case*) cognō-

scere. — clearly exaudīre. — in secret inaudīre.
hearer *m.* audītor *m.*
hearing *n.* (*sense*) audītus *m.*; (*act*) audītiō *f.*; (*of case*) cognitiō *f.* get a — sibi audientiam facere. hard of — surdaster. without a — indictā causā.
hearken *vi.* auscultāre.
hearsay *n.* fāma *f.*, rūmor *m.*
heart *n.* cor *n.*; (*emotion*) animus *m.*, pectus *n.*; (*courage*) animus *m.*; (*interior*) viscera *n.pl.* by — memoriā, memoriter. learn by — ēdiscere. the — of the matter rēs ipsa. lose — animum dēspondēre. take to — graviter ferre.
heart-ache *n.* dolor *m.*, angor *m.*
heart-broken *a.* animī frāctus, aeger. be — animō labōrāre.
heart-burning *n.* invidia *f.*
heart-felt *a.* sincērus.
hearth *n.* focus *m.* — and home ārae et focī. [vigor *m.*
heartiness *n.* studium *n.*,
heartless *a.* dūrus, inhūmānus, crūdēlis. **-ly** *ad.* inhūmānē.
heartlessness *n.* inhūmānitās *f.*, crūdēlitās *f.*
heart/y *a.* studiōsus, vehemēns; (*health*) rōbustus; (*feeling*) sincērus. **-ily** *ad.* vehementer, valdē.
heat *n.* ārdor *m.*, calor *m.*; (*emotion*) ārdor *m.*, aestus *m.*; (*race*) missus *m.* *vt.* calefacere, fervefacere; (*fig.*) accendere. become **-ed** incalēscere.
heatedly *ad.* ferventer, ārdenter.
heath *n.* inculta loca *n.pl.*
heath-cock *n.* attagēn *m.*
heathen *n.* pāgānus *m.*
heather *n.* ericē *f.*
heave *vt.* tollere; (*missile*) conicere; (*sigh*) dūcere. *vi.* tumēre, fluctuāre.
heaven *n.* caelum *n.*, dī *m.pl.* — forbid! dī meliōra. from — dīvīnitus. in **-'s** name prō deum fidem! be in the seventh — digitō caelum attingere.
heavenly *a.* caelestis, dīvīnus.
heaviness *n.* gravitās *f.*, pondus *n.*; (*of spirit*) maestitia *f.*
heav/y *a.* gravis; (*air*) crassus; (*spirit*) maestus; (*shower*) māgnus, dēnsus. **-ily** *ad.* graviter
heckle *vt.* interpellāre.
heckler *n.* interpellātor *m.*
hectic *a.* violēns, ācer, fervidus.
hector *vt.* obstrepere (*dat.*).
hedge *n.* saepēs *f.* *vt.* saepīre. — off intersaepīre. *vi.* tergiversārī.
hedgehog *n.* echīnus *m.*, ēricius *m.*
heed *vt.* cūrāre, respicere. *n.* cūra *f.*, opera *f.* pay — animum attendere. take — cavēre.
heedful *a.* attentus, cautus dīligēns. **-ly** *ad.* attentē, cautē.
heedfulness *n.* cūra *f.*, dīligentia *f.*
heedless *a.* incautus, immemor, neglegēns. **-ly** *ad.* incautē, neglegenter, temerē.
heedlessness *n.* neglegentia *f.*
heel *n.* calx *f.* take to one's **-s** sē in pedēs conicere. *vi.* sē inclīnāre.
hegemony *n.* principātus *m.*
heifer *n.* būcula *f.*
height *n.* altitūdō *f.*; (*person*) prōcēritās *f.*; (*hill*) collis *m.*, iugum *n.*; (*fig.*) fastīgium *n.* the — of summus.
heighten *vt.* augēre, exaggerāre.
heinous *a.* atrōx, nefārius. **-ly** *ad.* atrōciter, nefāriē.
heinousness *n.* atrōcitās *f.*
heir *n.* hērēs *m.* sole — hērēs ex asse.
heiress *n.* hērēs *f.*

heirship *n.* hērēditās *f.*
hell *n.* Tartarus *m.*, īnferī *m.pl.*
hellebore *n.* elleborus *m.*
hellish *a.* īnfernus, scelestus.
helm *n.* gubernāculum *n.*, clāvus *m.*
helmet *n.* galea *f.*
helmsman *n.* gubernātor *m.*
helots *n.* Hīlōtae *m.pl.*
help *n.* auxilium *n.*, subsidium *n.* *vt.* adiuvāre, auxiliārī, subvenīre (*dat.*), succurrere (*dat.*) *vi.* prōdesse. **I cannot — facere** nōn possum quīn (*subj.*). **it can't be -ed** fierī nōn potest aliter. **so — me God** ita me dī ament.
helper *n.* adiūtor *m.*, adiūtrix *f.*
helpful *a.* ūtilis. **be — to** auxiliō esse (*dat.*).
helpless *a.* inops.
helplessness *n.* inopia *f.*
hem *n.* ōra *f.*, limbus *m.* *vt.* **— in** interclūdere, circumsedēre.
hemlock *n.* cicūta *f.*
hemp *n.* cannabis *f.*
hen *n.* gallīna *f.*
hence *ad.* hinc; (*consequence*) igitur ideō. **— forth, — forward** dehinc, posthāc, ex hōc tempore.
her *a.* suus, ēius.
herald *n.* praecō *m.*; (*pol.*) fētiālis *m.* *vt.* praenūntiāre.
herb *n.* herba *f.*, olus *n.*
herbage *n.* herbae *f.pl.*
herd *n.* grex *f.*, armentum *n.* *vi.* congregārī.
herdsman *n.* pāstor *m.*
here *ad.* hīc. **be —** adesse. **— and there** passim. **here . . . there** alibī . . . alibī. **from —** hinc. **— is** ecce (*acc.*).
hereabouts *ad.* hīc ferē.
hereafter *ad.* posthāc posteā.
hereat *ad.* hīc.
hereby *ad.* ex hōc, hinc.
hereditary *a.* hērēditārius, patrius.
heredity *n.* genus *n.*
herein *ad.* hīc. **— after** *ad.* īnfrā.
hereof *ad.* ēius reī.
heretofore *ad.* quondam, antehāc.
hereupon *ad* hīc, quō factō.
herewith *ad.* cum hōc, ūnā.
heritable *a.* hērēditārius.
heritage *n.* hērēditās *f.*
hermaphrodite *n.* androgynus *m.*
hermit *n.* homō sōlitārius *m.*
hero *n.* vir fortissimus *m.*; (*demigod*) hērōs *m.*
heroic *a.* fortissimus, māgnanimus; (*epic*) hērōicus; (*verse*) hērōus. **-ally** *ad.* fortissimē, audācissimē.
heroism *n.* virtūs *f.*, fortitūdō *f.*
heron *n.* ardea *f.*
hers *pro.* suus, ēius. [sē.
herself *pro.* ipsa *f.*; (*reflexive*)
hesitancy *n.* dubitātiō *f.*
hesitant *a.* incertus, dubius.
hesitate *vi.* dubitāre, haesitāre.
hesitating *a.* dubius. **-ly** *ad.* cunctanter.
hesitation *n.* dubitātiō *f.* **with —** dubitanter.
heterogeneous *a.* dīversus, aliēnigenus.
hew *vt.* dolāre, caedere. **— down** excīdere, interscindere.
hexameter *n.* hexameter *m.*
heyday *n.* flōs *m.*
hiatus *n.* hiātus *m.*
hiccup *n.* singultus *m.* *vi.* singultīre.
hide *vt.* cēlāre, abdere, abscondere, occultāre. **— away** abstrūdere. **— from** cēlāre (*acc.*). *vi.* sē abdere, latēre. **— away** dēlitēscere. *n.* pellis *f.*, corium *n.*
hideous *a.* foedus, dēfōrmis, turpis. **-ly** *ad.* foedē.
hideousness *n.* foeditās *f.*, dēfōrmitās *f.*
hiding *n.* (*place*) latebra *f.*
hie *vi.* festīnāre.

hierarchy *n.* ōrdinēs *m.pl.*
high *a.* altus, excelsus; (*ground*) ēditus; (*pitch*) acūtus; (*rank*) amplus; (*price*) cārus; (*tide*) māximus; (*wind*) māgnus. — living luxuria *f.* — treason māiestās *f.* — and mighty superbus. on — sublīmis. *ad.* altē. **-ly** *ad.* (*value*) māgnī; (*intensity*) valdē. — strung trepidus.
high-born *a.* nōbilis, generōsus.
high-class *a.* (*goods*) lautus.
high-flown *a.* īnflātus tumidus.
high-handed *a.* superbus, īnsolēns. **-ly** *ad.* superbē, licenter.
high-handedness *n.* licentia *f.*, superbia *f.*
highland *a.* montānus. **-s** *n.* montāna *n.pl.*
highlander *n.* montānus *m.*
high-minded *a.* generōsus.
high-spirited *a.* ferōx, animōsus.
highway *n.* via *f.*
highwayman *n.* grassātor *m.*, latrō *m.*
hilarious *a.* festīvus, hilaris. **-ly** *ad.* festīvē, hilare.
hilarity *n.* festīvitās *f.*, hilaritās *f.*
hill *n.* collis *m.*, mōns *m.*; (*slope*) clīvus *m.*
hillock *n.* tumulus *m.*
hilly *a.* montuōsus, clīvōsus.
hilt *n.* manubrium *n.*, capulus *m.*
himself *pro.* ipse; (*reflexive*) sē.
hind *n.* cerva *f.*
hinder *a.* posterior.
hinder *vt.* impedīre, obstāre (*dat.*), morārī.
hindmost *a.* postrēmus; (*in column*) novissimus.
hindrance *n.* impedīmentum *n.*, mora *f.*
hinge *n.* cardō *f.*
hint *n.* indicium *n.*, suspiciō *f.* throw out a — inicere. *vt.* subicere, significāre.
hip *n.* coxendīx *f.*
hippodrome *n.* spatium *n.*
hire *vt.* condūcere. — out locāre. *n.* conductiō *f.*, locātiō *f.*; (*wages*) mercēs *f.*
hired *a.* mercennārius, conductus.
hireling *n.* mercennārius *m.*
hirsute *a.* hirsūtus.
his *a.* suus, ēius.
hiss *vi.* sībilāre. *vt.* — off (*stage*) explōdere, exsībilāre. *n.* sībilus *m.*
historian *n.* historicus *m.*, rērum scrīptor *m.*
historical *a.* historicus.
history *n.* historia *f.* the — of Rome rēs Rōmānae *f.pl.* since the beginning of — post hominum memoriam. ancient antīquitās *f.*
histrionic *a.* scaenicus.
hit *n.* ictus *m.*, plāga *f.* a — ! (*in duel*) habet ! *vt.* ferīre, īcere, percutere. — against offendere. — upon invenīre.
hitch *n.* mora *f.* *vt.* implicāre. — up succingere.
hither *ad.* hūc. — and thither hūc illūc. *a.* citerior.
hitherto *ad.* adhūc, hāctenus, hūcusque.
hive *n.* alveārium *n.*
hoar *a.* cānus. *n.* pruīna *f.*
hoard *n.* thēsaurus *m.*, acervus *m.* *vt.* condere, recondere.
hoar-frost *n.* pruīna *f.*
hoarse *a.* raucus, fuscus. **-ly** *ad.* raucā vōce.
hoary *a.* cānus.
hoax *n.* fraus *f.*, fallācia *f.*, lūdus *m.* *vt.* dēcipere, fallere.
hobble *vi.* claudicāre.
hobby *n.* studium *n.*
hob-nob *vi.* familiāriter ūtī (*abl.*).
hocus-pocus *n.* tricae *f.pl.*
hoe *n.* sarculum *n.* *vt.* sarrīre.
hog *n.* sūs *m.*, porcus *m.* -'s porcinus.
hogshead *n.* dōlium *n.*
hoist *vt.* tollere; (*sail*) dare.
hold *n.* (*grasp*) comprehēnsiō

f.; (*power*) potestās *f.*; (*ship*) alveus *m.* gain a — over obstringere, sibid ēvincīre. get — of potīrī (*abl.*). keep hold of retinēre. lose — of ōmittere. take — of prehendere, comprehendere. *vt.* tenēre, habēre; (*possession*) obtinēre, possidēre; (*office*) gerere, fungī (*abl.*); (*capacity*) capere; (*meeting*) habēre. — one's own with parem esse (*dat.*). — over differre, prōlātāre. — water (*fig.*) stāre. *vi.* manēre, dūrāre; (*opinion*) dūcere, existimāre, adfirmāre. — back *vt.* retinēre, inhibēre. *vi.* gravārī, dubitāre. — cheap parvī facere. — fast *vt.* retinere, amplectī. *vi.* haerēre — good valēre. — out *vt.* porrigere, extendere; (*hope*) ostendere. *vi* dūrāre, perstāre. — together cohaerēre — up tollere; (*falling*) sustinēre; (*movement*) obstāre (*dat.*), morārī. — with adsentīre (*dat.*).

holdfast *n.* fībula *f.*

holding *n.* (*land*) agellus *m.*

hole *n.* forāmen *n.*, cavum *n.* make a — in pertundere, perforāre.

holiday *n.* festus diēs *m.*; (*pl.*) fēriae *f.pl.* on — fēriātus.

holiness *n.* sanctitās *f.*

hollow *a.* cavus, concavus, (*fig.*) inānis, vānus. *n.* cavum *n.*, caverna *f.* *vt.* excavāre.

hollowness *n.* (*fig.*) vānitās *f.*

holly *n.* aquifolium *n.*

holm-oak *n.* īlex *f.*

hol/y *a.* sanctus. **-ily** *ad.* sanctē.

homage *n.* observantia *f.*, venerātiō *f.* pay — to venerārī, colere.

home *n.* domus *f.*; (*town country*) patria *f.* at — domī. from — domō. *a.* domesticus. *ad.* domum.

homeless *a.* profugus.

homely *a.* simplex, rūsticus; (*speech*) plēbēius.

homestead *n.* fundus *m.*

homwards *ad.* domum.

homicide *n.* (*act*) homicīdium *n.*, caedēs *f.*; (*person*) homicīda *m.*

homily *n.* sermō *m.*

homogeneous *a.* aequābilis.

homologous *a.* cōnsimilis.

hone *n.* cōs *f.* *vt.* acuere.

honest *a.* probus, frūgī, integer. **-ly** *ad.* probē. integrē.

honesty *n.* probitās *f.*, fidēs *f.*

honey *n.* mel *n.*

honey-comb *n.* favus *m.*

honeyed *a.* mellītus, mulsus.

honorarium *n.* stips *f.*

honorary *a.* honōrārius.

honour *n.* honōs *m.*; (*repute*) honestās *f.*, existimātiō *f.*; (*chastity*) pudor *m.*; (*trust*) fidēs *f.*, (*rank*) dignitās *f.*; (*award*) decus *n.*, īnsigne *n.*; (*respect*) observantia *f.* do — to honestāre. *vt.* honōrāre, decorāre; (*respect*) observāre, colere.

honourab/le *a.* honestus, probus; (*rank*) illūstris, praeclārus. **-ly** *ad.* honestē.

hood *n.* cucullus *m.*

hoodwink *vt.* verba dare (*dat.*).

hoof *n.* ungula *f.*

hook *n.* uncus *m.*, hāmus *m.* *vt.* hāmō capere.

hooked *a.* aduncus, hāmātus.

hoop *n.* circulus *m.*; (*toy*) trochus *m.*

hoopoe *n.* epops *m.*

hoot *vi.* obstrepere. — off (*stage*) explōdere.

hop *n.* saltus *m.* catch on the — in ipsō articulō opprimere. *vi.* salīre.

hope *n.* spēs *f.* give up — spem dēpōnere, dēspērāre. past — dēspērātus. entertain -s spem habēre. *vt.* spērāre.

hopeful *a.* bonae speī. be —

aliquam spem habēre. **-ly** *ad.* nōn sine spē.
hopeless *a.* dēspērātus. **-ly** *ad.* dēspēranter.
hopelessness *n.* dēspērātiō *f.*
horde *n.* multitūdō *f.*
horizon *n.* fīniēns *m.*
horizontal *a.* aequus, lībrātus. **-ly** *ad.* ad lībram.
horn *n.* cornū *n.*; (*shepherd's*) būcina *f.*
hornbeam *n.* carpinus *f.*
horned *a.* corniger.
hornet *n.* crabrō *m.* **stir up a -'s nest** crabrōnēs irrītāre.
horny *a.* corneus.
horoscope *n.* sīdus nātālicium [*n.*
horrib/le *a.* horrendus, horribilis, dīrus, foedus. **-ly** *ad.* foedē.
horrid *a.* horribilis.
horrify *vt.* terrēre, perterrēre.
horror *n.* horror *m.*, terror *m.*; odium *n.*
horse *n.* equus *m.*; (*cavalry*) equitēs *m.pl.* **flog a dead —** asellum currere docēre. **spur a willing —** currentem incitāre **ride on — back** in equō vehī. **fight on — back** ex equō pugnāre. **-'s** equīnus.
horseman *n.* eques *m.*
horse-radish *n.* armoracia *f.*
horse-soldier *n.* eques *m.*
horticulture *n.* hortōrum cultus *m.*
hospitab/le *a.* hospitālis. **-ly** *ad.* hospitāliter.
hospital *n.* valētūdinārium *n.*
hospitality *n.* hospitālitās *f.*, hospitium *n.*
host *n.* hospes *m.*; (*inn*) caupō *m.*; (*number*) multitūdō *f.*; (*mil.*) exercitus *m.*
hostage *n.* obses *m.*, *f.*
hostelry *n.* taberna *f.*, dēversōrium *n.*
hostile *a.* hostīlis, īnfēnsus, inimīcus. **in a — manner** īnfensē, hostīliter, inimīcē.
hostility *n.* inimīcitia *f.*; (*pl.*) bellum *n.*

hot *a.* calidus, fervidus, aestuōsus; (*boiling*) fervēns; (*fig.*) ārdēns. **be —** calēre, fervēre, ārdēre. **get —** calēscere. **be white —** excandēscere. **— tempered** *a.* īrācundus. **-ly** *ad.* ārdenter, ācriter.
hotch-potch *n.* farrāgō *f.*
hotel *n.* dēversōrium *n.*
hot-headed *a.* ārdēns, temerārius, praeceps.
hough *n.* poples *m.* [(*dat.*).
hound *n.* canis *m.* *vt.* īnstāre
hour *n.* hōra *f.*
hourly *ad.* in hōrās.
house *n.* domus *f.*, aedēs *f.pl.*; (*country*) vīlla *f.*; (*family*) domus *f.*, gēns *f.* **at the — of** apud (*acc.*). **full —** frequēns senātus, frequēns theātrum. *vt.* hospitiō accipere, recipere; (*things*) condere.
household *n.* familia *f.*, domus *f.* *a.* familiāris, domesticus.
householder *n.* paterfamiliās *m.*, dominus *m.*
housekeeping *n.* reī familiāris cūra *f.*
housemaid *n.* ancilla *f.*
house-top *n.* fastīgium *n.*
housewife *n.* māterfamiliās *f.*, domina *f.*
housing *n.* hospitium *n.*; (*horse*) ōrnāmenta *n.pl.*
hovel *n.* gurgustium *n.*
hover *vi.* pendēre; (*fig.*) impendēre.
how *ad.* (*interrog.*) quōmodō, quō pactō; (*exclam.*) quam. **— many** quot. **— much** quantum. **— often** quotiēns.
howbeit *ad.* tamen.
however *ad.* tamen, nihilōminus; utcumque, quōquō modō. **— much** quamvīs, quantumvīs. **— great** quantuscumque.
howl *n.* ululātus *m.* *vi.* ululāre; (*wind*) fremere.
howsoever *ad.* utcumque.
hub *n.* axis *m.*

hubbub *n.* tumultus *m.*
huckster *n.* institor *m.*, propōla *m.*
huddle *n.* turba *f.* *vi.* conglobāri. [gregāri.
hue *n.* color *m.* — and cry clāmor *m.*
huff *n.* offēnsiō *f.* *vt.* offendere.
hug *n.* complexus *m.* *vt.* complectī.
huge *a.* ingēns, immānis, immēnsus, vastus. **-ly** *ad.* vehementer.
hugeness *n.* immānitās *f.*
hulk *n.* alveus *m.*
hull *n.* alveus *m.*
hum *n.* murmur *n.*, fremitus *m.* *vi.* murmurāre, fremere.
human *a.* hūmānus. — being homō *m.*, *f.* — nature hūmānitās *f.*
humane *a.* hūmānus, misericors. **-ly** *ad.* hūmānē, hūmāniter.
humanism *n.* litterae *f.pl.*
humanist *n.* homō litterātus *m.* [misericordia *f.*
humanity *n.* hūmānitās *f.*;
humanize *vt.* excolere.
humanly *ad.* hūmānitus.
humb/le *a.* humilis, modestus. *vt.* dēprimere; (*oneself*) summittere. **-ly** *ad.* summissē, modestē.
humbleness *n.* humilitās *f.*
humbug *n.* tricae *f.pl.*
humdrum *a.* vulgāris; (*style*) pedester.
humid *a.* ūmidus, madidus. be — madēre.
humidity *n.* ūmor *m.*
humiliate *vt.* dēprimere, dēdecorāre.
humiliation *n.* dēdecus *n.*
humility *n.* modestia *f.*, animus summissus *m.*
humorist *n.* homō facētus *m.*
humorous *a.* facētus, ioculāris, rīdiculus. **-ly** *ad.* facētē.
humour *n.* facētiae *f.pl.*; (*disposition*) ingenium *n.*; (*mood*) libīdō *f.* be in a bad — sibi displicēre. I am in the — for libet (*inf.*). *vt.* indulgēre (*dat.*), mōrem gerere (*dat.*), mōrigerārī (*dat.*).
hump *n.* gibbus *m.*
hunchback *n.* gibber *m.*
hundred *num.* centum. — each centēnī. — times centiēns.
hundredth *a.* centēsimus
hundredweight *n.* centumpondium *n.*
hunger *n.* famēs *f.* *vi.* ēsurīre.
hungr/y *a.* ēsuriēns, iēiūnus, avidus. be — ēsurīre. **-ily** *ad.* avidē.
hunt *n.* vēnātiō *f.*, vēnātus *m.* *vt.* vēnārī, indāgāre, exagitāre.
hunter *n.* vēnātor *m.*
hunting *n.* vēnātiō *f.*; (*fig.*) aucupium *n.* **-spear** *n.* vēnābulum *n.*
huntress *n.* vēnātrix *f.*
huntsman *n.* vēnātor *m.*
hurdle *n.* crātēs *f.*; (*obstacle*) obex *m.*, *f.*
hurl *vt.* conicere, ingerere, iaculārī.
hurly-burly *n.* turba *f.*, tumultus *m.*
hurrah *interj.* euax, iō.
hurricane *n.* procella *f.*
hurried *a.* praeproperus, praeceps, trepidus. **-ly** *ad.* properātō, cursim festīnanter.
hurry *vt.* adcelerāre, mātūrāre. *vi.* festīnāre, properāre. — along *vt.* rapere. — away *vi.* discēdere properāre. — about *vi.* discurrere. — on *vt.* mātūrāre. — up *vi.* properāre. *n.* festīnātiō *f.* in a — festīnanter, raptim.
hurt *n.* iniūria *f.*, damnum *n.*; vulnus *n.* *vt.* laedere, nocēre (*dat.*). it **-s** dolet.
hurtful *a.* nocēns, damnōsus. **-ly** *ad.* nocenter, damnōsē.
hurtle *vi.* volāre, sē praecipitāre.
husband *n.* vir *m.*, marītus *m.* *vt.* parcere (*dat.*).
husbandman *n.* agricola *m.*

husbandry *n.* agrī cultūra *f.*; (*economy*) parsimōnia *f.*
hush *n.* silentium *n.* *vt.* silentium facere (*dat.*), lēnīre. *vi.* tacēre, silēre. — up comprimere, cēlāre. *interj.* st !
hushed *a.* tacitus.
husk *n.* folliculus *m.*, siliqua *f.* *vt.* dēglūbāre.
husky *a.* fuscus, raucus.
hustle *vt.* trūdere, īnstāre (*dat.*).
hut *n.* casa *f.*, tugurium *n.*
hutch *n.* cavea *f.*
hyacinth *n.* hyacinthus *m.*
hybrid *n.* hibrida *m.*, *f.*
hydra *n.* hydra *f.*
hyena *n.* hyaena *f.*
hygiene *n.* salūbritās *f.*
hygienic *a.* salūbris.
hymeneal *a.* nūptiālis
hymn *n.* carmen *n.* *vt.* canere.
hyperbole *n.* superlātiō *f.*
hypercritical *a.* Aristarchus *m.*
hypocaust *n.* hypocaustum *n.*
hypocrisy *n.* simulātiō *f.*, dissimulātiō *f.*
hypocrite *n.* simulātor *m.*, dissimulātor *m.*
hypocritical *a.* simulātus, fictus.
hypothesis *n.* positum *n.*, sūmptiō *f.*, coniectūra *f.*
hypothetical *a.* sūmptus.

I

I *pro.* ego.
iambic *a.* iambēus.
iambus *n.* iambus *m.*
ibis *n.* ībis *f.*
ice *n.* glaciēs *f.*
icicle *n.* stīria *f.*
icon *n.* simulacrum *n.*
icy *a.* glaciālis, gelidus.
idea *n.* nōtiō *f.*, nōtitia *f.*, imāgō *f.*; (*Platonic*) fōrma *f.*; (*expressed*) sententia *f.* conceive the — of īnfōrmāre.
ideal *a.* animō comprehēnsus; (*perfect*) perfectus, optimus. *n.* specimen *n.*, speciēs *f.*, exemplar *n.*
identical *a.* īdem, cōnsimilis.
identify *vt.* agnōscere.
identity *n.* establish the — of cognōscere quis sit.
Ides *n.* Īdūs *f.pl.*
idiocy *n.* animī imbēcillitās *f.*
idiom *n.* proprium *n.*, sermō *m.*
idiomatic *a.* proprius. **-ally** *ad.* sermōne suō, sermōne propriō.
idiosyncrasy *n.* proprium *n.*, libīdō *f.*
idiot *n.* excors *m.*
idiotic *a.* fatuus, stultus. **-ally** *ad.* stultē, ineptē.
id/le *a.* ignāvus, dēses, iners; (*unoccupied*) ōtiōsus, vacuus; (*useless*) inānis, vānus. be — cessāre, dēsidēre. lie — (*money*) iacēre. *vi.* cessāre. **-ly** *ad.* ignāvē; ōtiōsē; frustrā, nēquīquam.
idleness *n.* ignāvia *f.*, dēsidia *f.*, inertia *f.*; ōtium *n.*
idler *n.* cessātor *m.*
idol *n.* simulacrum *n.*; (*person*) dēliciae *f.pl.*
idolater *n.* falsōrum deōrum cultor *m.*
idolatry *n.* falsōrum deōrum cultus *m.*
idolize *vt* venerārī.
idyll *n.* carmen Theocritēum *n.*
if *conj.* sī; (*interrog.*) num, utrum. — ever sī quandō. — not nisi. — only dum, dummodo. — . . . or sīve . . . sīve. as — quasi, velut. but — sīn, quodsī. even — etiamsī.
igneous *a.* igneus.
ignite *vt.* accendere, incendere. *vi.* ignem concipere.
ignoble *a.* (*birth*) ignōbilis; (*repute*) illīberālis, turpis.
ignominious *a.* ignōminiōsus, īnfāmis, turpis. **-ly** *ad.* turpiter.

ignominy *n.* ignōminia *f.*, īnfāmia *f.*, dēdecus *n.*
ignoramus *n.* idiōta *m.*, indoctus *m.*
ignorance *n.* īnscītia *f.*, ignōrātiō *f.*
ignorant *a.* ignārus, indoctus; (*of something*) īnscītus, rudis; (*unaware*) īnscius. be — of nescīre, ignōrāre. **-ly** *ad.* īnscienter, īnscītē, indoctē.
ignore *vt.* praetermittere.
ilex *n.* īlex *f.*
Iliad *n.* Īlias *f.*
ill *a.* aeger, aegrōtus, invalidus; (*evil*) malus. be — aegrōtāre. fall — in morbum incidere. — at ease sollicitus. — will invidia *f.* *ad.* male, improbē. *n.* malum *n.*, incommodum *n.*, aerumna *f.*, damnum *n.*
ill-advised *a.* incōnsultus.
ill-bred *a.* agrestis, inurbānus. [invidus.
ill-disposed *a.* malevolus,
illegal *a.* illicitus, vetitus. **-ly** *ad.* contrā lēgēs.
ill-fated *a.* īnfēlīx.
ill-favoured *a.* turpis.
ill-gotten *a.* male partus.
ill-health *n.* valētūdō *f.*
illicit *a.* vetitus.
illimitable *a.* īnfīnītus.
illiteracy *n.* litterārum īnscītia *f.*
illiterate *a.* illitterātus, inērudītus.
ill-natured *a.* malevolus, malignus. [tūdō *f.*
illness *n.* morbus *m.*, valē-
illogical *a.* absurdus.
ill-omened *a.* dīrus, īnfaustus.
ill-starred *a.* īnfēlīx.
ill-tempered *a.* īrācundus, amārus, stomachōsus.
ill-timed *a.* immātūrus, intempestīvus.
ill-treat *vt.* malefacere (*dat.*).
illuminate *vt.* illūmināre, illūstrāre.
illumination *n.* lūmina *n.pl.*
illusion *n.* error *m.*, somnium *n.* optical — oculōrum lūdibrium *n.*
illusive, illusory *a.* fallāx.
illustrate *vt.* illūstrāre; (*with instances*) exemplō cōnfirmāre.
illustration *n.* exemplum *n.*
illustrious *a.* illūstris, īnsignis, praeclārus. **-ly** *ad.* praeclārē.
image *n.* imāgō *f.*, effigiēs *f.*; (*idol*) simulacrum *n.*; (*verbal*) figūra *f.*, similitūdō *f.*
imagery *n.* figūrae *f.pl.*
imaginary *a.* commentīcius, fictus. [opīnātiō *f.*
imagination *n.* cōgitātiō *f.*,
imaginative *a.* ingeniōsus.
imagine *vt.* animō fingere, animum indūcere, ante oculōs pōnere; (*think*) opīnārī, arbitrārī.
imbecile *a.* animō imbēcillus, fatuus, mente captus.
imbecility *n.* animī imbēcillitās *f.*
imbibe *vt.* adbibere; (*fig.*) imbuī (*abl.*).
imbrue *vt.* īnficere.
imbue *vt.* imbuere, īnficere, tingere.
imitable *a.* imitābilis.
imitate *vt.* imitārī.
imitation *n.* imitātiō *f.*; (*copy*) imāgō *f.*
imitator *n.* imitātor *m.*, imitātrix *f.*, aemulātor *m.*
immaculate *a.* integer, ēmendātus. **-ly** *ad.* integrē, sine vitiō.
immaterial *a.* indifferēns.
immature *a.* immātūrus.
immeasurable *a.* immēnsus, īnfīnītus.
immediate *a.* īnstāns, praesēns; (*neighbour*) proximus. **-ly** *ad.* statim, extemplō, cōnfestim.
immemorial *a.* antiquissimus. from time — post hominum memoriam.
immense *a.* immēnsus, im-

mānis, ingēns, vastus. **-ly** *ad.* vehementer.
immensity *n.* immēnsum *n.*, māgnitūdō *f.*
immerse *vt.* immergere, [mergere.
immigrant *n.* advena *m.*
immigrate *vi.* migrāre.
imminent *a.* īnstāns, praesēns. be — imminēre, impendēre.
immobile *a.* fixus, immōbilis.
immoderate *a.* immoderātus, immodestus. **-ly** *ad.* immoderātē, immodestē.
immodest *a.* impudīcus, inverēcundus.
immolate *vt.* immolāre.
immoral *a.* prāvus, corruptus, turpis. **-ly** *ad.* prāvē, turpiter.
immorality *n.* corruptī mōrēs *m.pl.*, turpitūdō *f.*
immortal *a.* immortālis, aeternus. **-ly** *ad.* aeternum.
immortality *n.* immortālitās *f.*
immortalize *vt.* in astra [tollere.
immovable *a.* fixus, immōbilis.
immune *a.* immūnis, vacuus.
immunity *n.* immūnitās *f.*, vacātiō *f.*
immure *vt.* inclūdere.
immutability *n.* immūtābilitās *f.*
immutable *a.* immūtābilis.
imp *n.* puer improbus *m.*
impact *n.* ictus *m.*, incussus *m.*
impair *vt.* imminuere, corrumpere.
impale *vt.* induere, īnfīgere.
impalpable *a.* tenuissimus.
impart *vt.* impertīre, commūnicāre; (*courage*) addere.
impartial *a.* aequus, medius. **-ly** *ad.* sine favōre. [*f.*
impartiality *n.* aequābilitās
impassable *a.* invius; (*mountains*) inexsuperābilis; (*fig.*) inexplicābilis. [*f.pl.*
impasse *n.* mora *f.*, incitae
impassioned *a.* ārdēns, fervidus.
impassive *a.* rigidus, sēnsū carēns.
impatience *n.* aviditās *f.*; (*of anything*) impatientia *f.*
impatient *a.* trepidus, avidus; impatiēns. **-ly** *ad.* aegrē.
impeach *vt.* diem dīcere (*dat.*), accūsāre.
impeachment *n.* accūsātiō *f.*, crīmen *n.*
impeccable *a.* ēmendātus.
impecunious *a.* pauper.
impede *vt.* impedīre, obstāre (*dat.*). [tum *n.*
impediment *n.* impedīmen-
impel *vt.* impellere, incitāre.
impend *vi.* impendēre, imminēre, īnstāre.
impenetrable *a.* impenetrābilis; (*country*) invius, impervius.
impenitent *a.* I am — nīl mē paenitet.
imperative *a.* necessārius.
imperceptib/le *a.* tenuissimus, obscūrus. **-ly** *ad.* sēnsim.
imperfect *a.* imperfectus, vitiōsus. **-ly** *ad.* vitiōsē.
imperfection *n.* vitium *n.*
imperial *a.* imperātōrius, rēgius.
imperil *vt.* in discrimen addūcere, labefactāre.
imperious *a.* imperiōsus, superbus. **-ly** *ad.* superbē.
imperishable *a.* immortālis, aeternus. [(*gen.*).
impersonate *vt.* partēs agere
impertinence *n.* importūnitās *f.*, protervitās *f.*
impertinent *a.* importūnus, protervus, ineptus. **-ly** *ad* importūnē, ineptē, protervē.
imperturbable *a.* immōtus gravis. [impenetrābilis.
impervious *a.* impervius.
impetuosity *n.* ārdor *m.*, violentia *f.*, vīs *f.*
impetuous *a.* violēns, fervidus, effrēnātus. **-ly** *ad.* effrēnātē.

impetus *n.* impetus *m.*
impiety *n.* impietās *f.*
impinge *vi.* incidere.
impious *a.* impius, profānus. it is — nefas est. **-ly** *ad.* impiē.
impish *a.* improbus.
implacab/le *a.* implācābilis, inexōrābilis, dūrus. **-ly** *ad.* dūrē.
implant *vt.* īnserere, ingignere.
implement *n.* īnstrūmentum *n.* *vt.* implēre, exsequī.
implicate *vt.* implicāre, impedīre.
implication *n.* indicium *n.*
implicit *a.* tacitus; absolūtus. **-ly** *ad.* absconditē; (*trust*) omnīnō, summā fidē.
implore *vt.* implōrāre, obsecrāre.
impl/y *vt.* significāre, continēre. be **-ied** inesse.
impolite *a.* inurbānus, illepidus. **-ly** *ad.* inurbānē.
impolitic *a.* incōnsultus, imprūdēns.
imponderable *a.* levissimus.
import *vt.* importāre, invehere; (*mean*) velle. *n.* significātiō *f.*; (*pl.*) importātīcia *n.pl.*
importance *n.* gravitās *f.*, mōmentum *n.*; (*rank*) dignitās *f.*, amplitūdō *f.*, auctōritās *f.* it is of great — to me meā māgnī rēfert.
important *a.* gravis, magnī mōmentī. it is — interest, rēfert. more, most — antiquior, antīquissimus.
importation *n.* invectiō *f.*
importunate *a.* molestus.
importune *vt.* flāgitāre, īnstāre (*dat.*).
impose *vt.* impōnere; (*by order*) indīcere, iniungere. — upon illūdere, fraudāre, abūtī (*abl.*).
imposing *a.* māgnificus, lautus.
imposition *n.* fraus *f.*; (*tax*) tribūtum *n.*
impossible *a.* it is — fierī nōn potest.
impost *n.* tribūtum *n.*, vectīgal *n.*
impostor *n.* planus *m.*, fraudātor *m.*
imposture *n.* fraus *f.*, fallācia *f.*
impotence *n.* īnfirmitās *f.*
impotent *a.* īnfirmus, dēbilis; (*with rage*) impotēns. **-ly** *ad.* frustrā; (*rage*) impotenter.
impound *vt.* inclūdere; (*confiscate*) pūblicāre.
impoverish *vt.* in inopiam redigere.
impracticable *a.* be — fierī nōn posse.
imprecate *vt.* exsecrārī.
imprecation *n.* exsecrātiō *f.*
impregnable *a.* inexpugnābilis.
impregnate *vt.* imbuere, inficere.
impress *vt.* imprimere; (*on mind*) īnfīgere; (*person*) permovēre; (*mil.*) invītum scrībere.
impression *n.* (*copy*) exemplar *n.*; (*mark*) signum *n.*; (*feeling*) impulsiō *f.*; (*belief*) opīnātiō *f.* make an — of exprimere. make an — on commovēre. have the — opīnārī.
impressionable *a.* crēdulus.
impressive *a.* gravis. **-ly** *ad.* graviter.
impressiveness *n.* gravitās [*f.*
imprint *n.* impressiō *f.*, signum *n.* *vt.* imprimere; (*on mind*) īnfīgere, inūrere.
imprison *vt.* inclūdere, in vincula conicere.
imprisonment *n.* custōdia *f.*, vincula *n.pl.*
improbable *a.* incrēdibilis, haud vērisimilis.
impromptu *ad.* ex tempore.
improper *a.* indecōrus, ineptus. **-ly** *ad.* prāvē, per peram.

impropriety *n.* culpa *f.*, offēnsa *f.*
improve *vt.* ēmendāre, corrigere; (*mind*) excolere. *vi.* prōficere, meliōrem fierī.
improvement *n.* ēmendātiō *f.*, prōfectus *m.*
improvident *a.* imprōvidus; (*with money*) prōdigus. **–ly** *ad.* imprōvidē; prōdigē.
improvise *vt.* ex tempore compōnere, excōgitāre. [*f.*
imprudence *n.* imprūdentia
imprudent *a.* imprūdēns. **–ly** *ad.* imprūdenter.
impudence *n.* impudentia *f.*, audācia *f.*
impudent *a.* impudēns, audāx. **–ly** *ad.* impudenter, protervē.
impugn *vt.* impugnāre, in dubium vocāre.
impulse *n.* impetus *m.*, impulsus *m.*
impulsive *a.* praeceps, violentus. **–ly** *ad.* impetū quōdam animī.
impulsiveness *n.* impetus *m.*, violentia *f.*
impunity *n.* impūnitās *f.* with — impūne.
impure *a.* impūrus, incestus, inquinātus. **–ly** *ad.* impūrē, incestē, inquinātē.
impurity *n.* impūritās *f.*, sordēs *f.pl.*
imputation *n.* crimen *n.*
impute *vt.* attribuere, adsignāre. **— as a fault** vitiō vertere.
in *pr.* in (*abl.*); (*with motion*) in (*acc.*); (*authors*) apud (*acc.*); (*time*) *abl.* **— doing this** dum hoc faciō. **— my youth** adulēscēns **— that** quod. *ad.* (*rest*) intrā; (*motion*) intrō.
inaccessible *a.* inaccessus.
inaccuracy *n.* neglegentia *f.* incūria *f.*; (*error*) mendum *n.*
inaccurate *a.* parum diligēns, neglegēns. **–ly** *ad.* neglegenter.
inaction *n.* inertia *f.*
inactive *a.* iners, quiētus be — cessāre.
inactivity *n.* inertia *f.*, ōtium *n.*
inadequate *a.* impār, parum idōneus. **–ly** *ad.* parum. [*f.*
inadvertency *n.* imprūdentia
inadvertent *a.* imprūdēns. **–ly** *ad.* imprūdenter.
inane *a.* inānis, vānus; ineptus, stultus. **–ly** *ad* ineptē.
inanimate *a.* inanimus.
inanity *n.* ineptiae *f.pl.*, stultitia *f.*
inapplicable *a.* be — nōn valēre.
inappropriate *a.* aliēnus, parum aptus.
inarticulate *a.* infāns.
inartistic *a.* sine arte, dūrus, inēlegāns.
inasmuch as *conj.* quōniam, cum (*subj.*).
inattention *n.* incūria *f.* neglegentia *f.*
inattentive *a.* neglegēns. **–ly** *ad.* neglegenter.
inaudible *a.* be — audīrī nōn posse.
inaugurate *vt.* inaugurāre, cōnsecrāre.
inauguration *n.* cōnsecrātiō *f.*
inauspicious *a.* infaustus, infēlix. **–ly** *ad.* malis ōminibus.
inborn *a.* innātus.
incalculable *a.* inaestimābilis.
incantation *n.* carmen *n.*
incapable *a.* inhabilis, indocilis. be — nōn posse.
incapacitate *vt.* dēbilitāre.
incapacity *n.* inertia *f.*, inscītia *f.*
incarcerate *vt.* inclūdere, in vincula conicere.
incarnate *a.* hūmānā speciē indūtus.
incautious *a.* incautus, temerārius. **–ly** *ad.* incautē.
incendiary *a.* incendiārius.

incense *n.* tūs *n.* *vt.* inrītāre, stomachum movēre (*dat.*). be -d stomacharī.
incentive *n.* incitāmentum *n.*, stimulus *m.*
inception *n.* initium *n.*, exōrdium *n.*
incessant *a.* adsiduus. **-ly** *ad.* adsiduē.
incest *n.* incestus *m.*
inch *n.* digitus *m.*, ūncia *f.*
incident *n.* ēventum *n.*, cāsus *m.*, rēs *f.*
incidental *a.* fortuītus. **-ly** *ad.* cāsū.
incipient *a.* prīmus.
incisive *a.* ācer.
incite *vt.* īnstīgāre, impellere, hortārī, incitāre.
incitement *n.* invītāmentum *n.*, stimulus *m.*
inciter *n.* īnstimulātor *m.*
incivility *n.* importūnitās *f.*, inhūmānitās *f.*
inclemency *n.* (*weather*) intemperiēs *f.*
inclement *a.* asper, tristis.
inclination *n.* inclīnātiō *f.*, animus *m.*, libīdō *f.*; (*slope*) clīvus *m.*
incline *vt.* inclīnāre; (*person*) indūcere. *vi.* inclīnāre, incumbere. — towards sē adclīnāre *ad.* *n.* adclīvitās *f.*, clīvus *m.*
inclined *a.* inclīnātus, prōpēnsus. I am — to think haud sciō an.
include *vt.* inclūdere, continēre, complectī.
incognito *ad.* clam.
incoherent *a.* interruptus. be — non cohaerēre.
income *n.* fructus *m.*, mercēs *f.*
incommensurate *a.* dispār.
incommode *vt.* molestiam adferre (*dat.*).
incomparable *a.* singulāris, eximius.
incompatibility *n.* discrepantia *f.*, repugnantia *f.*
incompatible *a.* īnsociābilis, repugnāns. be — with dissidēre ab, repugnāre (*dat.*).
incompetence *n.* inertia *f.*, īnscītia *f.*
incompetent *a.* iners, īnscītus.
incomplete *a.* imperfectus.
incomprehensible *a.* incrēdibilis.
inconceivable *a.* incrēdibilis.
inconclusive *a.* inānis.
incongruous *a.* absonus, aliēnus.
inconsiderable *a.* exiguus.
inconsiderate *a.* imprōvidus, incōnsultus.
inconsistency *n.* discrepantia *f.*, incōnstantia *f.*
inconsistent *a.* incōnstāns. be — discrepāre. be — with abhorrēre ab, repugnāre (*dat.*). **-ly** *ad.* incōnstanter.
inconsolable *a.* nōn cōnsōlābilis.
inconspicuous *a.* obscūrus. be — latēre.
inconstancy *n.* incōnstantia *f.*, levitās *f.*
inconstant *a.* incōnstāns, levis, mōbilis. **-ly** *ad.* incōnstanter.
incontestable *a.* certus.
incontinence *n.* incontinentia *f.*
incontinent *a.* intemperāns.
inconvenience *n.* incommodum *n.* *vt.* incommodāre.
inconvenient *a.* incommodus. **-ly** *ad.* incommodē.
incorporate *vt.* īnserere, adiungere.
incorrect *a.* falsus. be — nōn cōnstāre. **-ly** *ad.* falsō, perperam.
incorrigible *a.* improbus, perditus.
incorruptibility *n.* integritās.
increasingly *ad.* magis magisque.
incorruptible *a.* incorruptus.
increase *n.* incrēmentum *n.*, additāmentum *n.*, auctus *m.* *vt.* augēre, amplificāre. *vi.* crēscere, incrēscere.

incredib/le *a.* incrēdibilis. **-ly** *ad.* incrēdibiliter.
incredulous *a.* incrēdulus.
increment *n.* incrēmentum *n.*
incriminate *vt.* crīminārī.
inculcate *vt.* inculcāre, înfīgere.
incumbent *a.* **it is — on** oportet.
incur *vt.* subīre; (*guilt*) admittere.
incurable *a.* īnsānābilis.
incursion *n.* incursiō *f.*
indebted *a.* obnoxius. **be —** dēbēre.
indecency *n.* obscēnitās *f.*
indecent *a.* obscēnus, impudīcus. **-ly** *ad.* obscēnē.
indecision *n.* dubitātiō *f.*
indecisive *a.* anceps, dubius. **the battle is —** ancipitī Marte pugnātur. **-ly** *ad.* incertō ēventū.
indecorous *a.* indecōrus.
indeed *ad.* profectō, sānē; (*concessive*) quidem; (*interrog.*) itane vērō?; (*reply*) certē, vērō; (*with pro.*) dēmum; (*with a., ad., conj.*) adeō.
indefatigable *a.* impiger.
indefensible *a.* **be —** dēfendī nōn posse; (*belief*) tenērī nōn posse; (*offence*) excūsārī nōn posse.
indefinite *a.* incertus, ambiguus, īnfīnītus. **-ly** *ad.* ambiguē; (*time*) in incertum.
indelicate *a.* pūtidus, indecōrus.
independence *n.* lībertās *f.*
independent *a.* liber, suī iūris.
indescribable *a.* inēnārrābilis.
indestructible *a.* perennis.
indeterminate *a.* incertus.
index *n.* index *m.*
indicate *vt.* indicāre, significāre.
indication *n.* indicium *n.*, signum *n.*
indict *vt.* diem dīcere (*dat.*), accūsāre, nōmen dēferre (*gen.*).
indictment *n.* accūsātiō *f.*
indifference *n.* neglegentia *f.*, languor *m.*
indifferent *a.* (*manner*) neglegēns, frīgidus, sēcūrus: (*quality*) mediocris. **-ly** *ad* neglegenter; mediocriter; (*without distinction*) promiscuē, sine discrīmine.
indigence *n.* indigentia *f.*, egestās *f.*
indigenous *a.* indigena.
indigent *a.* indigēns, egēnus.
indigestible *a.* crūdus.
indigestion *n.* crūditās *f.*
indignant *a.* indignābundus, īrātus. **be —** indignārī. **-ly** *ad.* īrātē.
indignation *n.* indignātiō *f.*, dolor *m.*
indignity *n.* contumēlia *f.*, indignitās *f.*
indigo *n.* Indicum *n.*
indirect *a.* oblīquus. **-ly** *ad.* oblīquē, per ambāgēs.
indirectness *n.* ambāgēs *f.pl.*
indiscipline *n.* lascīvia *f.*, licentia *f.*
indiscreet *a.* incōnsultus, imprūdēns. **-ly** *ad.* incōnsultē, imprūdenter.
indiscretion *n.* imprūdentia *f.*; (*act*) culpa *f.*
indiscriminate *a.* prōmiscuus. **-ly** *ad.* prōmiscuē, sine discrīmine.
indispensable *a.* necesse necessārius.
indisposed *a.* īnfirmus, aegrōtus, (*will*) āversus, aliēnātus. **be —** aegrōtāre; abhorrēre, aliēnārī.
indisposition *n.* īnfirmitās *f.*, valētūdō *f.*
indisputab/le *a.* certus, manifestus. **-ly** *ad.* certē, sine dubiō.
indissoluble *a.* indissolūbilis.
indistinct *a.* obscūrus, obtūsus.; (*speaker*) balbus. **-ly** *ad.* obscūrē. **pronounce —** opprimere. **speak —** balbutīre.
individual *a.* proprius. *n.*

homō *m.*, *f.*, prīvātus *m.*; (*pl.*) singulī *m.pl.* **-ly** *ad.* singulātim, prīvātim.
individuality *n.* proprium *n.*
indivisible *a.* indīviduus.
indolence *n.* dēsidia *f.* ignāvia *f.*, inertia *f.*
indolent *a.* dēses, ignāvus, iners. **-ly** *ad.* ignāvē.
indomitable *a.* indomitus.
indoor *a.* umbrātilis. **-s** *ad.* intus; (*motion*) intrā.
indubitab/le *a.* certus. **-ly** *ad.* sine dubiō.
induce *vt.* indūcere, addūcere, persuādēre (*dat.*).
inducement *n.* illecebra *f.*, praemium *n.*
induction *n.* (*logic*) inductiō *f.*
indulge *vt.* indulgēre (*dat.*).
indulgence *n.* indulgentia *f.*, venia *f.*; (*favour*) grātia *f.*
indulgent *a.* indulgēns, lēnis. **-ly** *ad.* indulgenter.
industrious *a.* industrius, impiger, dīligēns. **-ly** *ad.* industriē.
industry *n.* industria *f.*, dīligentia *f.*, labor *m.*
inebriated *a.* ēbrius.
inebriation *n.* ēbrietās *f.*
ineffable *a.* eximius.
ineffective *a.* inūtilis, invalidus. **-ly** *ad.* ināniter.
ineffectual *a.* irritus.
inefficient *a.* īnscītus, parum strēnuus.
inelegant *a.* inēlegāns, inconcinnus. **-ly** *ad.* inēleganter.
inept *a.* ineptus. **-ly** *ad.* ineptē.
inequality *n.* dissimilitūdō *f.*, inīquitās *f.*
inert *a.* iners, sōcors, immōbilis. **-ly** *ad.* tardē, lentē.
inertia *f.* inertia *f.*
inestimable *a.* inaestimābilis.
inevitabl/e *a.* necessārius. **-ly** *ad.* necessāriō.
inexact *a.* parum subtīlis.
inexhaustible *a.* perennis.
inexorable *a.* inexōrābilis.
inexpediency *n.* inūtilitās *f.*, incommodum *n.*
inexpedient *a.* inūtilis. **it is** — nōn expedit.
inexpensive *a.* vīlis.
inexperience *n.* imperītia *f.*, īnscītia *f.* **-d** *a.* imperītus, rudis, īnscītus.
inexpert *a.* imperītus.
inexpiable *a.* inexpiābilis.
inexplicable *a.* inexplicābilis, inēnōdābilis.
inexpressible *a.* inēnārrābilis.
inextricable *a.* inexplicābilis.
infallible *a.* certus, errōris expers.
infamous *a.* īnfāmis, flāgitiōsus. **-ly** *ad.* flāgitiōsē.
infamy *n.* īnfāmia *f.*, flāgitium *n.*, dēdecus *n.*
infancy *n.* īnfantia *f.*; (*fig.*) incūnābula *n.pl.*
infant *n.* īnfāns *m.*, *f.*
infantile *a.* puerīlis.
infantry *n.* peditēs *m.pl.*, peditātus *m.*
infatuate *vt.* īnfatuāre. **-d** *a.* dēmēns.
infatuation *n.* dēmentia *f.*
infect *vt.* īnficere.
infection *n.* contāgiō *f.*
infer *vt.* īnferre, colligere.
inference *n.* conclūsiō *f.*
inferior *a.* (*position*) īnferior; (*quality*) dēterior.
infernal *a.* īnfernus.
infest *vt.* frequentāre.
infidel *a.* impius.
infidelity *n.* perfidia *f.*, īnfidēlitās *f.*
infiltrate *vi.* sē īnsinuāre.
infinite *a.* īnfīnītus, immēnsus. **-ly** *ad.* longē, immēnsum.
infinitesimal *a.* minimus.
infinity *n.* īnfīnitās *f.*
infirm *a.* īnfirmus, invalidus.
infirmary *n.* valētūdinārium *n.*
infirmity *n.* morbus *m.*
inflame *vt.* accendere, incendere, īnflammāre. **be -d** exārdēscere.

inflammation *n.* (*med.*) inflātiō *f.*
inflate *vt.* inflāre. **-d** *a.* (*fig.*) inflātus, tumidus.
inflexible *a.* rigidus.
inflexion *n.* (*gram.*) flexūra *f.*; (*voice*) flexiō *f.*
inflict *vt.* infligere, incutere; (*burden*) impōnere; (*penalty*) sūmere. **be -ed with** labōrāre ex.
infliction *n.* poena *f.*; malum [*n.*
influence *n.* (*physical*) impulsiō *f.*, mōmentum *n.*; (*moral*) auctōritās *f.*; (*partial*) grātia *f.* **have —** valēre. **have great —** with plūrimum posse apud. **under the — of** instinctus (*abl.*). *vt.* impellere, movēre.
influential *a* gravis, potēns; grātiōsus.
influenza *n.* gravēdō *f.*
inform *vt.* docēre, certiōrem facere. **— against** nōmen dēferre (*gen.*).
informant *n.* index *m.*, auctor *m.*
information *n.* indicium *n.*, nūntius *m.*
informer *n.* index *m.*, dēlātor *m.* **turn —** indicium profitērī.
infrequent *a.* rārus. **-ly** *ad.* rārō.
infringe *vt.* violāre, imminuere.
infringement *n.* violātiō *f.*
infuriate *vt.* efferāre. **-d** *a.* furibundus.
infuse *vt.* infundere; (*fig.*) inicere.
ingenious *a.* ingeniōsus, callidus; (*thing*) artificiōsus. **-ly** *ad.* callidē, summā arte.
ingenuity *n.* ars *f.*, artificium *n.*, acūmen *n*
ingenuous *a.* ingenuus, simplex. **-ly** *ad.* ingenuē, simpliciter.
ingenuousness *n.* ingenuitās *f.*
ingle *n.* focus *m.*
inglorious *a.* inglōrius, ignōbilis, inhonestus. **-ly** *ad.* sine glōriā, inhonestē.
ingot *n.* later *m.*
ingrained *a.* insitus.
ingratiate *vt.* **— oneself with** grātiam inīre ab, sē insinuāre in familiāritātem (*gen.*). **— oneself into** sē insinuāre in (*acc.*). [mus *m.*
ingratitude *n.* ingrātus animus *m.*
ingredient *n.* pars *f.*
inhabit *vt.* incolere, habitāre in (*abl.*).
inhabitable *a.* habitābilis.
inhabitant *n.* incola *m.*, *f.*
inhale *vt.* haurīre.
inharmonious *a.* dissonus.
inherent *a.* insitus. **be — in** inhaerēre (*dat.*), inesse (*dat.*). **-ly** *ad.* nātūrā.
inherit *vt.* excipere.
inheritance *n.* hērēditās *f.*, patrimōnium *n.* **divide an —** herctum ciēre. **come into an —** hērēditātem adīre.
inheritor *n.* hērēs *m.*, *f.*
inhibit *vt.* prohibēre, inhibēre.
inhospitable *a.* inhospitālis.
inhuman *a.* inhūmānus, immānis, crūdēlis. **-ly** *ad.* inhūmānē, crūdēliter.
inhumanity *n.* inhūmānitās *f.*, crūdēlitās *f.*
inimical *a.* inimīcus.
inimitable *a* singulāris, eximius.
iniquitous *a.* inīquus, improbus, nefārius. [*n.*
iniquity *n.* scelus *n.*, flāgitium
initial *a.* prīmus.
initiate *vt.* initiāre; (*with knowledge*) imbuere.
initiative *n.* initium *n.* **take the —** initium capere, facere; occupāre (*inf.*).
inject *vt.* inicere.
injudicious *a.* incōnsultus, imprūdēns.
injunction *n.* iussum *n.*, praeceptum *n.*
injure *vt.* laedere, nocēre (*dat.*).

injurious *a.* damnōsus, nocēns.
injury *n.* iniūria *f.*, damnum *n.*; (*bodily*) vulnus *n.*
injustice *n.* iniūria *f.*, inīquitās *f.*
ink *n.* ātrāmentum *n.*
inkling *n.* audītiō *f.*, suspiciō *f.*
inland *a.* mediterrāneus. further — interior.
inlay *vt.* īnserere.
inlet *n.* sinus *m.*, aestuārium *n.*
inly *ad.* penitus.
inmate *n.* inquilīnus *m.*
inmost *a.* intimus.
inn *n.* dēversōrium *n.*
innate *a.* innātus, īnsitus.
inner *a.* interior. — **most** *a.* intimus.
innkeeper *n.* caupō *m.*
innocence *n.* innocentia *f.*
innocent *a.* innocēns, īnsōns; (*character*) integer, castus. **-ly** *ad.* innocenter integrē, castē.
innocuous *a.* innoxius.
innovate *vt.* novāre.
innovation *n.* novum *n.*, nova rēs *f.*
innovator *n.* novārum rērum auctor *m.*
innuendo *n.* verbum inversum *n.*
innumerable *a.* innumerābilis.
inoffensive *a.* innocēns. **-ly** *ad.* innocenter.
inopportune *a.* intempestīvus. **-ly** *ad.* intempestīvē.
inordinate *a.* immodicus, immoderātus. **-ly** *ad.* immoderātē.
inquest *n.* quaestiō *f.* hold an — on quaerere dē.
inquire *vi.* exquīrere, rogāre. — into inquīrere in (*acc.*), investīgāre.
inquir/y *n.* quaestiō *f.*, investīgātiō *f.*; (*asking*) interrogātiō *f.* make — exquīrere. make -ies about inquīrere in (*acc.*). hold an — on quaerere dē, quaestiōnem īnstituere dē.
inquisition *n.* inquīsītiō *f.*
inquisitive *a.* cūriōsus.
inquisitiveness *n.* cūriōsitās *f.*
inquisitor *n.* inquīsītor *m.*
inroad *n.* incursiō *f.*, impressiō *f.* make an — incursāre.
insane *a.* īnsānus, mente captus. be — īnsānīre.
insanity *n.* īnsānia *f.*, dēmentia *f.*
insatiab/le *a.* īnsatiābilis, inexplēbilis, īnsaturābilis. **-ly** *ad.* īnsaturābiliter.
inscribe *vt.* īnscrībere.
inscription *n.* epigramma *n.*; (*written*) īnscrīptiō *f.*
inscrutable *a.* obscūrus.
insect *n.* bestiola *f.*
insecure *a.* īnstabilis, intūtus.
insecurity *n.* pericula *n.pl.*
insensate *a.* ineptus, stultus.
insensible *a.* torpidus; (*fig.*) dūrus.
insensitive *a.* dūrus.
inseparab/le *a.* coniūnctus. be the — companion of ab latere esse (*gen.*). **-ly** *ad.* coniūnctē.
insert *vt.* īnserere, immittere, interpōnere.
insertion *n.* interpositiō *f.*
inshore *ad.* prope lītus.
inside *ad.* intus; (*motion*) intrō. *a.* interior. *n.* pars interior. *pr.* intrā (*acc.*). get right — sē īnsinuāre in (*acc.*). turn — out excutere. on the — interior.
insidious *a.* īnsidiōsus, subdolus. **-ly** *ad.* īnsidiōsē.
insight *n.* intellegentia *f.*, cognitiō *f.*
insignia *n.* īnsignia *n.pl.*
insignificance *n.* levitās *f.*
insignificant *a.* levis, exiguus, nullīus mōmentī; (*position*) humilis.
insincere *a.* simulātus, fūcōsus. **-ly** *ad.* simulātē.
insincerity *n* simulātiō *f.*, fraus *f.*
insinuate *vt.* īnsinuāre; (*hint*) significāre. *vi.* sē īnsinuāre.

insinuating *a.* blandus.
insinuation *n.* ambigua verba *n.pl.*
insipid *a.* īnsulsus, frigidus.
insipidity *n.* īnsulsitās *f.*
insist *vi.* īnstāre. — on postulāre.
insistence *n.* pertināćia *f.*
insistent *a.* pertināx.
insolence *n.* īnsolentia *f.*, contumācia *f.*, superbia *f.*
insolent *a.* īnsolēns, contumāx, superbus. **-ly** *ad.* īnsolenter.
insoluble *a.* inexplicābilis.
insolvency *n.* reī familiāris naufragium *n.*
insolvent *a.* be — solvendō nōn esse.
inspect *vt.* īnspicere; (*mil.*) recēnsēre.
inspection *n.* cognitiō *f.*; (*mil.*) recēnsiō *f.*
inspector *n.* cūrātor *m.*
inspiration *n.* adflātus *m.*, īnstinctus *m.*
inspire *vt.* īnstinguere, incendere.
instability *n.* mōbilitās *f.*
install *vt.* inaugurāre.
instalment *n.* pēnsiō *f.*
instance *n.* exemplum *n.* for — exemplī causā, grātiā. at the — admonitū. at my — mē auctōre. *vt.* memorāre.
instant *a.* īnstāns, praesēns. *n.* temporis pūnctum *n.*, mōmentum *n.* **-ly** *ad.* īlicō, extemplō.
instantaneous *a.* praesēns. **-ly** *ad.* continuō, īlicō.
instead of *pr.* prō (*abl.*), locō (*gen.*). (*with verb*) nōn . . . sed.
instigate *vt.* īnstigāre, impellere.
instigation *n.* impulsus *m.*, stimulus *m.* at my — mē auctōre.
instigator *n.* īnstimulātor *m.*, auctor *m.*
instil *vt.* imbuere, adspīrāre, inicere.
instinct *n.* nātūra *f.*, ingenium *n.*, sēnsus *m.*
instinctive *a.* nātūrālis. **-ly** *ad.* nātūrā, ingeniō suō.
institute *vt.* īnstituere, inaugurāre.
institution *n.* īnstitūtum *n.*; societās *f.*
instruct *vt.* docēre, īnstituere, īnstruere; (*order*) praecipere (*dat.*).
instruction *n.* doctrīna *f.*, disciplīna *f.*; praeceptum *n.* give -s dēnūntiāre, praecipere.
instructor *n.* doctor *m.*, praeceptor *m.*
instructress *n.* magistra *f.*
instrument *n.* īnstrūmentum *n.*; (*music*) fidēs *f.pl.*; (*legal*) tabulae *f.pl.*
instrumental *a.* ūtilis.
instrumentalist *n.* fidicen *m.*, fidicina *f.*
instrumentality *n.* opera *f.*
insubordinate *a.* turbulentus, sēditiōsus.
insubordination *n.* intemperantia *f.*, licentia *f.*
insufferable *a.* intolerandus, intolerābilis.
insufficiency *n.* inopia *f.*
insufficient *a.* minor. be — nōn sufficere. **-ly** *ad.* parum.
insulate *vt.* sēgregāre.
insult *n.* iniūria *f.*, contumēlia *f.*, probrum *n.* *vt.* maledīcere (*dat.*), contumēliam impōnere (*dat.*).
insulting *a.* contumēliōsus. **-ly** *ad.* contumēliōsē.
insuperable *a.* inexsuperābilis.
insupportable *a.* intolerandus, intolerābilis.
insurance *n.* cautiō *f.*
insure *vi.* cavēre.
insurgent *n.* rebellis *m.*
insurmountable *a.* inexsuperābilis.
insurrection *n.* mōtus *m.*, sēditiō *f.*
intact *a.* integer, intāctus, incolumis.
integrity *n.* integritās *f.*, innocentia *f.*, fidēs *f.*

intellect *n.* ingenium *n.*, mēns *f.*, animus *m.*
intellectual *a.* ingeniōsus.
intelligence *n.* intellegentia *f.*, acūmen *n.*; (*mil.*) nūntius *m.*
intelligent *a.* ingeniōsus, sapiēns, argūtus. **-ly** *ad.* ingeniōsē, sapienter.
intelligible *a.* perspicuus, apertus.
intemperance *n.* intemperantia *f.*, licentia *f.*
intemperate *a.* intemperāns, intemperātus. **-ly** *ad.* intemperanter.
intend *vt.* (*with inf.*) in animō habēre, velle.; (*with object*) dēstināre.
intense *a.* ācer, nimius. **-ly** *ad.* valdē, nimium.
intensif/y *vt.* augēre, amplificāre. be **-ied** ingravēscere.
intensity *n.* vīs *f.*
intensive *a.* ācer, multus, adsiduus. **-ly** *ad.* summō studiō.
intent *a.* ērēctus, intentus. be — on animum intendere in (*acc.*). *n.* cōnsilium *n.* with — cōnsultō.
intention *n.* cōnsilium *n.*, prōpositum *n.* it is my — mihi in animō est. with the — of eā mente, eō cōnsiliō ut (*subj.*). [dē industriā.
intentionally *ad.* cōnsultō,
inter *vt.* humāre.
intercalary *a.* intercalāris.
intercalate *vt.* intercalāre.
intercede *vi.* intercēdere, dēprecārī.
intercept *vt.* excipere, intercipere; (*cut off*) interclūdere.
intercession *n.* dēprecātiō *f.*; (*tribune's*) intercessiō *f.*
intercessor *n.* dēprecātor *m.*
interchange *vt.* permūtāre. *n.* permūtātiō *f.*, vicissitūdō *f.*
intercourse *n.* commercium *n.*, ūsus *m.*, cōnsuētūdō *f.*
interdict *n.* interdictum *n.* *vt.* interdīcere (*dat.*), vetāre.
interest *n.* (*advantage*) commodum *n.*; (*study*) studium *n.*; (*money*) fænus *n.*, ūsūra *f.* compound — anatocismus *m.* rate of — fænus *n.* — at 12 per cent (per annum) centēsimae *f.pl.* it is of — interest. it is in my **-s** meā interest. consult the **-s** of cōnsulere (*dat.*). take an — in animum intendere (*dat.*). *vt.* dēlectāre, capere; (*audience*) tenēre. — oneself in studēre (*dat.*).
interested *a.* attentus; (*for gain*) ambitiōsūs. [novus.
interesting *a.* iūcundus,
interfere *vi.* intervenīre: (*with*) sē interpōnere (*dat.*), sē admiscēre ad; (*hinder*) officere (*dat.*).
interference *n.* interventus *m.*, intercessiō *f.*
interim *n.* in the — interim, intereā.
interior *a.* interior. *n.* pars interior *f.*; (*country*) interiōra *n.pl.*
interject *vt.* exclāmāre.
interjection *n.* interiectiō *f.*
interlace *vt.* intexere.
interlard *vt.* variāre.
interlock *vt.* implicāre.
interloper *n.* interpellātor *m.*
interlude *n.* embolium *n.* [*n.*
intermarriage *n.* cōnūbium
intermediary *a.* medius. *n.* internūntius *m.*
intermediate *a.* medius.
interment *n.* humātiō *f.*
interminable *a.* sempiternus, longus.
intermingle *vt.* intermiscēre. *vi.* sē immiscēre.
intermission *n.* intercapēdō *f.*, intermissiō *f.*
intermittent *a.* interruptus. **-ly** *ad.* interdum.
intern *vt.* inclūdere.
internal *a.* internus; (*pol.*) domesticus. **-ly** *ad.* intus, domī.
international *a.* — **law** iūs gentium.

internecine *a.* internecīvus.
interplay *n.* vicēs *f.pl.*
interpolate *vt.* interpolāre.
interpose *vt.* interpōnere. *vi.* intercēdere.
interposition *n.* intercessiō *f.*
interpret *vt.* interpretārī.
interpretation *n.* interpretātiō *f.*
interpreter *n.* interpres *m., f.*
interregnum *n.* interrēgnum *n.*
interrogate *vt.* interrogāre, percontārī.
interrogation *n.* interrogātiō *f.*, percontātiō *f.*
interrupt *vt.* (*action*) intercipere; (*speaker*) interpellāre; (*talk*) dirimere; (*continuity*) intermittere.
interrupter *n.* interpellātor [*m.*
interruption *n.* interpellātiō *f.*; intermissiō *f.*
intersect *vt.* dividere, secāre.
intersperse *vt.* distinguere.
interstice *n.* rīma *f.*
intertwine *vt.* intexere, implicāre.
interval *n.* intervallum *n.*, spatium *n.* **after an —** spatiō interpositō. **after an — of a year** annō interiectō. **at — s** interdum. **at frequent — s** identidem. **leave an —** intermittere.
intervene *vt.* intercēdere, intervenīre.
intervention *n.* intercessiō *f.*, interventus *m.* **by the — of** intercursū. (*gen.*).
interview *n.* colloquium *n.*, aditus *m.* *vt.* convenīre.
interweave *vt.* implicāre, intexere.
intestate *a.* intestātus. *ad.* intestātō.
intestine *a.* intestīnus; (*pol.*) domesticus. *n.* (*pl.*) intestīna *n.pl.*; (*victim's*) exta *n.pl.*
intimacy *n.* familiāritās *f.*
intimate *a.* familiāris. **be an — friend of** ab latere esse (*gen.*). **a very — friend** perfamiliāris *m., f.* **-ly** *ad.* familiāriter. *vt.* dēnūntiāre.
intimation *n.* dēnūntiātiō *f.*; (*hint*) indicium *n.*
intimidate *vt.* minārī (*dat.*), terrōrem inicere (*dat.*).
intimidation *n.* metus *m.*, minae *f.pl.*
into *pr.* in (*acc.*). intrā (*acc.*).
intolerab/le *a.* intolerandus, intolerābilis. **-ly** *ad.* intoleranter.
intolerance *n.* impatientia *f.*
intolerant *a.* impatiēns, intolerāns.
intone *vt.* cantāre.
intonation *n.* sonus *m.*, flexiō *f.*
intoxicate *vt.* ēbrium reddere.
intoxicated *a.* ēbrius.
intoxication *n.* ēbrietas *f.*
intractable *a.* indocilis, difficilis.
intransigent *a.* obstinātus.
intrepid *a.* intrepidus, impavidus.
intrepidity *n.* audācia *f.*, fortitūdō *f.*
intricacy *n.* implicātiō *f.*
intricate *a.* implicātus, involūtus. **-ly** *ad.* implicitē.
intrigue *n.* factiō *f.*, artēs *f.pl.*, fallācia *f.* *vi.* māchinārī, fallāciīs ūtī.
intriguing *a.* factiōsus; blandus.
intrinsic *a.* vērus, innātus. **-ally** *ad.* per sē.
introduce *vt.* indūcere, inferre, importāre; (*acquaintance*) commendāre; (*custom*) instituere.
introduction *n.* exōrdium *n.*, prooemium *n.*; (*of person*) commendātiō *f.* **letter of —** litteræ commendātīciae *f.pl.*
intrude *vi.* sē interpōnere, intervenīre.
intruder *n.* interpellātor m., advena *m.*; (*fig.*) alienus *m.*
intrusion *n.* interpellātiō *f.*

intuition *n.* sēnsus *m.*, cognitiō *f.*
inundate *vt.* inundāre.
inundation *n.* ēluviō *f.*
inure *vt.* dūrāre, adsuēfacere.
invade *vt.* invādere.
invalid *a.* aeger, dēbilis; (*null*) inritus.
invalidate *vt.* infirmāre.
invaluable *a.* inaestimābilis.
invariab/le *a.* cōnstāns, immūtābilis. **–ly** *ad.* semper.
invasion *n.* incursiō *f.*
invective *n.* convīcium *n.*
inveigh *vi.* — against invehī in (*acc.*), īnsectārī.
inveigle *vt.* illicere, pellicere.
invent *vt.* fingere, comminīscī, invenīre.
invention *n.* inventum *n.*; (*faculty*) inventiō *f.*
inventor *n.* inventor *m.*, auctor *m.*
inverse *a.* inversus. **–ly** *ad.* inversō ōrdine.
invert *vt.* invertere.
invest *vt.* (*in office*) inaugurāre: (*mil.*) obsidēre, circumsedēre; (*money*) locāre.
investigate *vt.* investīgāre, indāgāre; (*case*) cognōscere.
investigation *n.* investīgātiō *f.*, indāgātiō *f.*; (*case*) cognitiō *f.*
investment *n.* (*mil.*) obsessiō *f.*; (*money*) locāta pecūnia *f.*
inveterate *a.* inveterātus, vetus. become — inveterāscere.
invidious *a.* invidiōsus. **–ly** *ad.* invidiōsē.
invigorate *vt.* recreāre, reficere.
invincible *a.* invictus.
inviolab/le *a.* inviolātus; (*person*) sacrōsanctus. **–ly** *ad.* inviolātē.
inviolate *a.* integer.
invisible *a.* caecus. be — vidērī nōn posse.
invitation *n.* invītātiō *f.* at the — of invītātū (*gen.*).
invite *vt.* invītāre, vocāre.
inviting *a.* suāvis, blandus. **–ly** *ad.* blandē, suāviter.
invocation *n.* testātiō *f.*
invoke *vt.* invocāre, testārī.
involuntar/y *a.* coāctus. **–ily** *ad.* īnscienter, invītus.
involve *vt.* implicāre, involvere. be **–d** in inligārī (*abl.*)
invulnerable *a.* inviolābilis. be — vulnerārī nōn posse.
inward *a.* interior. **–ly** *ad.* intus. **–s** *ad.* intrōrsus.
inweave *vt.* intexere.
inwrought *a.* intextus.
irascibility *n.* īrācundia *f.*
irascible *a.* īrācundus.
irate *a.* īrātus.
ire *n.* īra *f.*
iris *n.* hyacinthus *m.*
irk *vt.* incommodāre. I am **–ed** mē piget.
irksome *a.* molestus.
irksomness *n.* molestia *f.*
iron *n.* ferrum *n.* *a.* ferreus. — **mine** *n.* ferrāria *f.* — tipped ferrātus.
ironical *a.* inversus. **–ly** *ad.* inversīs verbīs.
ironmonger *n.* negōtiātor ferrārius *m.*
ironmongery *n.* ferrāmenta [*n.pl.*
irony *n.* illūsiō *f.*, verbōrum inversiō *f.*, dissimulātiō *f.*
irradiate *vt.* illūstrāre.
irrational *a.* absurdus, ratiōnis expers; (*animal*) brūtus. **–ly** *ad.* absurdē, sine ratiōne.
irreconcilable *a.* repugnāns, īnsociābilis.
irrefutable *a.* certus, invictus.
irregular *a.* incompositus; (*ground*) inaequālis; (*meeting*) extraōrdinārius; (*troops*) tumultuārius. **–ly** *ad.* nūllō ōrdine; (*elected*) vitiō.
irregularity *n.* inaequālitās *f.*; (*conduct*) prāvitās *f.*, licentia *f.*; (*election*) vitium *n.*
irrelevant *a.* aliēnus.
irreligion *n.* impietās *f.*
irreligious *a.* impius.

irremediable *a.* īnsānābilis.
irreparable *a.* inrevocābilis.
irreproachable *a.* integer, innocēns.
irresistible *a.* invictus.
irresolute *a.* dubius, anceps. **-ly** *ad.* dubitanter.
irresolution *n.* dubitātiō *f.*
irresponsibility *n.* licentia *f.*
irresponsible *a.* lascīvus, levis.
irretrievable *a.* inrevocābilis.
irreverence *n.* impietās *f.*
irreverent *a.* impius. **-ly** *ad.* impiē.
irrevocable *a.* inrevocābilis.
irrigate *vt.* inrigāre.
irrigation *n.* inrigātiō *f.*
irritability *n.* īrācundia *f.*
irritable *a* īrācundus.
irritate *vt.* inrītāre, stomachum movēre (*dat.*).
irritation *n.* īrācundia *f.* stomachus *m.*
island *n.* īnsula *f.*
islander *n.* īnsulānus *m.*
isle *n.* īnsula *f.*
isolate *vt.* sēgregāre, sēparāre.
isolation *n.* sōlitūdō *f.*
issue *n.* (*result*) ēventus *m.*, exitus *m.*; (*children*) prōlēs *f.*; (*question*) rēs *f.*; (*book*) ēditiō *f.* **decide the —** dēcernere, dēcertāre. **the point at —** quā dē rē agitur. *vt.* distribuere; (*book*) ēdere; (*announcement*) prōmulgāre; (*coin*) ērogāre. *vi.* ēgredī, ēmānāre; (*result*) ēvādere, ēvenīre.
isthmus *n.* isthmus *m.*
it *pro.* hōc id.
itch *n.* (*disease*) scabiēs *f.*; (*fig.*) cacoēthes *n.* *vi.* prūrīre.
item *n* nōmen *n.*, rēs *f.*
iterate *vt.* iterāre.
itinerant *a.* vagus, circumforāneus.
itinerary *n.* iter *n.*
its *a.* suus, ēius.
itself *pro.* ipse, ipsa, ipsum.
ivory *n.* ebur *n.* *a.* eburneus.
ivy *n.* hedera *f.*

J

jabber *vi.* blaterāre.
jackdaw *n.* grāculus *m.*
jaded *a.* dēfessus, fatīgātus.
jagged *a.* serrātus.
jail *n.* carcer *m.*
jailer *n.* custōs *m.*, carcerārius *m.*
jam *vt.* comprimere; (*way*) obstruere.
jamb *n.* postis *m.*
jangle *vi.* crepitāre; rixārī.
janitor *n* iānitor *m.*
January *n.* mēnsis Iānuārius *m.* **of —** Iānuārius.
jar *n.* urna *f.*; (*for wine*) amphora *f.*; (*for water*) hydria *f.*; (*sound*) offēnsa *f.*; (*quarrel*) rixa *f.* *vi.* offendere.
jasper *n.* iaspis *f.*
jaundice *n.* morbus arquātus.
jaundiced *a.* ictericus.
jaunt *n.* **take a —** excurrere.
jauntiness *n.* hilaritās *f.*
jaunt/y *a.* hilaris, festīvus. **-ily** *ad.* hilare, festīvē.
javelin *n.* iaculum *n.*, pīlum *n.* **throw the —** iaculārī.
jaw *n.* māla *f.*; (*pl.*) faucēs *f.pl.*
jay *n.* grāculus *m.*
jealous *a.* invidus. **be — of** invidēre (*dat.*).
jealousy *n.* invidia *f.*
jeer *n.* irrīsiō *f.* *vi.* irrīdēre. **— at** illūdere.
jejune *a.* iēiūnus, exīlis.
jeopardize *vt.* in periculum addūcere.
jeopardy *n.* perīculum *n.*
jerk *n.* subitus mōtus *m.*
jest *n.* iocus *m.*
jester *n.* scurra *m.*
jet *n.* (*mineral*) gagātēs *m.*; (*of water*) saltus *m.* *vi.* salīre.
jetsam *n.* ēiectāmenta *n.pl.*
jettison *vt.* ēicere.
jetty *n.* mōlēs *f.*
Jew *n.* Iūdaeus.
jewel *n.* gemma *f.*
Jewish *a.* Iūdaicus.
jig *n.* tripudium *n.*
jilt *vt.* repudiāre.

jingle *n.* nēnia *f.* *vi.* crepitāre, tinnīre.
job *n.* opus *n.*
jocose, jocular *a.* facētus, ioculāris. **-ly** *ad.* facētē, per iocum.
jocoseness, jocularity *n.* facētiae *f.pl.*
jocund *a.* hilaris, festīvus.
jog *vt.* fodicāre; (*fig.*) stimulāre. *vi.* ambulāre.
join *vt.* iungere, coniungere, cōpulāre. *vi.* coniungī, sē coniungere. — in interesse (*dat.*), sē immiscēre (*dat.*).
joiner *n.* faber *m.*
joint *a.* commūnis. *n.* commissūra *f.*; (*of body*) articulus *m.*, nōdus *m.* — by — articulātim. **-ly** *ad.* ūnā, coniūnctē.
jointed *a.* geniculātus.
joint-heir *n.* cohērēs *m.*, *f.*
joist *n.* tignum *n.*
joke *n.* iocus *m.* *vi.* iocārī, lūdere.
joking *n.* iocus *m.* — apart remōtō iocō. **-ly** *ad.* per iocum.
jollity *n.* hilaritās *f.*, festīvitās [*f.*
jolly *a.* hilaris, festīvus.
jolt *vt.* iactāre.
jolting *n.* iactātiō *f.*
jostle *vt.* agitāre, offendere.
jot *n.* minimum *n.* not a — nihil. not care a — nōn floccī facere.
journal *n.* ācta diūrna *n.pl.*
journey *n.* iter *n.*
journeyman *n.* opifex *m.*
Jove *n.* Iuppiter *m.*
jovial *a.* hilaris. **-ly** *ad.* hilare.
joviality *n.* hilaritās *f.*
jowl *n.* māla *f.* cheek by — iuxtā.
joy *n.* gaudium *n.*, laetitia *f.*, alacritās *f.*
joyful, joyous *a.* laetus hilaris. **-ly** *ad.* laetē, hilare.
joyfulness *n.* gaudium *n.*, laetitia *f.*
joyless *a.* tristis, maestus.
jubilant *a.* laetus, gaudiō exsultāns.
judge *n.* iūdex *m.*, arbiter *m.* *vt.* iūdicāre; (*think*) existimāre, cēnsēre. — between diiūdicāre.
judgment *n.* iūdicium *n.*, arbitrium *n.*; (*opinion*) sententia *f.*; (*punishment*) poena *f.* (*wisdom*) iūdicium *n.* in my — meō animō, meō arbitrātū. pass — on statuere dē. sit in — iūdicium exercēre. [*n.*
judgment-seat *n.* tribūnal
judgeship *n.* iūdicātus *m.*
judicature *n.* iūrisdictiō *f.*; (*men*) iūdicēs *m.pl.*
judicial *a.* iūdiciālis; (*law*) iūdiciārius.
judiciary *n* iūdicēs *m.pl.*
judicious *a.* prūdēns, cōnsīderātus. **-ly** *ad.* prūdenter.
jug *n.* hydria *f.*, urceus *m.*
juggler *n.* praestīgiātor *m.*
juggling *n.* praestīgiae *f.pl*
juice *n.* liquor *m.*, sūcus *m.*
juicy *a.* sūcī plēnus.
July *n.* mēnsis Quīnctīlis, Iūlius *m.* of — Quīnctīlis, Iūlius.
jumble *n.* congeriēs *f* *vt.* cōnfundere.
jump *n.* saltus *m.* *vi.* salīre. —at (*opportunity*) captāre, adripere, amplectī. — down dēsilīre. — on to īnsilīre in (*acc.*).
junction *n.* coniūnctiō *f.*
juncture *n.* tempus *n.*
June *n.* mēnsis Iūnius. of — Iūnius.
junior *a.* iūnior, nātū minor.
juniper *n* iūniperus *f.*
juridical *a.* iūdiciārius.
jurisconsult *n.* iūriscōnsultus *m.*
jurisdiction *n.* iūrisdictiō *f.*, diciō *f.* exercise — iūs dīcere.
jurisprudence *n.* iūrisprūdentia *f.*
jurist *n.* iūriscōnsultus *m.*
juror *n.* iūdex *m.*
jury *n.* iūdicēs *m.pl.*

just *a.* iūstus, aequus. *ad.* (*exactly*) prōrsus; (*only*) modo; (*time*) commodum, modo; (*with ad.*) dēmum, dēnique; (*with pro.*) adeō dēmum, ipse. — as (*comparison*) — aequē ac, perinde ac, quemadmodum. — before (*time*) cum māximē, sub (*acc.*). — now modo, nunc. — so ita prōrsus, sānē. only — vix. **-ly** *ad.* iūstē aequē; iūre, meritō.
justice *n.* iūstitia *f.*, aequitās *f.*, iūs *n.*; (*person*) praetor *m.* administer — iūs reddere.
justiciary *n.* praetor *m.*
justifiab/le *a.* iūstus. **-ly** *ad.* iūre.
justification *n.* pūrgātiō *f.* excūsātiō *f.*
justify *vt.* excūsāre pūrgāre.
jut *vi.* prōminēre, excurrere.
jutting *a.* prōiectus.
juvenile *a.* iuvenīlis, puerīlis.

K

keel *n.* carīna *f.*
keen *a.* ācer; (*mind*) acūtus argūtus; (*sense*) sagāx; (*pain*) acerbus. **-ly** *ad.* ācriter, sagāciter, acūtē, acerbē.
keenness *n.* (*scent*) sagācitās *f.*; (*sight*) aciēs *f.*; (*pain*) acerbitās *f.*; (*eagerness*) studium *n.*, ārdor *m.*
keep *vt.* servāre tenēre, habēre; (*celebrate*) agere, celebrāre; (*guard*) custōdīre; (*obey*) observāre; (*preserve*) cōnservāre; (*rear*) alere, pāscere; (*store*) condere. — apart distinēre. — away arcēre. — back dētinēre, reservāre. — down comprimere; (*exuberance*) dēpāscere. — in cohibēre, claudere. — in with grātiam sequī (*gen.*). — off arcēre, dēfendere. — house domī sē retinēre. — secret cēlāre. — together continēre. — up sustinēre, cōnservāre. — up with subsequī. — waiting dēmorārī. *vi.* dūrāre, manēre. *n.* arx *f.*
keeper *n.* custōs *m.*
keeping *n.* custōdia *f.* in — with prō (*abl.*). be in — with convenīre (*dat.*).
keg *n.* cadus *m.*
ken *n.* cōnspectus *m.*
kennel *n.* stabulum *n.*
kerb *n.* crepīdō *f.* [*m.*
kernel *n.* grānum *n.*, nucleus
kettle *n.* lebēs *f.*
key *n.* clāvis *f.*; (*fig.*) claustra *n.pl.*, iānua *f.* — position cardō *m.*
kick *vi.* calcitrāre. *vt.* calce ferīre.
kid *n.* haedus *m.* **-'s** *a.* haedīnus.
kidnap *vt.* surripere.
kidnapper *n.* plagiārius *m.*
kidney *n.* rēn *m.* — bean *n.* phasēlus *m.*
kill *vt.* interficere, interimere; (*in battle*) occīdere; (*murder*) necāre, iugulāre; (*time*) perdere.
killer *n.* interfector *m.*
kiln *n.* fornāx *f.*
kin *n.* cognātī *m.pl.*, propinquī *m.pl.* next of — proximī *m.pl.*
kind *a.* bonus, benignus, benevolus. *n.* genus *n.* of such a — tālis. what — of quālis. **-ly** *ad.* benignē *a.* cōmis.
kindle *vt.* incendere, succendere, īnflammāre.
kindliness *n.* cōmitās *f.*, hūmānitās *f.*
kindling *n.* (*fuel*) fōmes *m.*
kindness *n.* benignitās *f.*, benevolentia *f.*; (*act*) beneficium *n.*, officium *n.*, grātia *f.*
kindred *n.* necessitūdō *f.*, cognātiō *f.*; propinquī *m.pl.*, cognātī *m.pl.* *a.* cognātus, adfīnis.
kine *n.* bovēs *m.*, *f.pl.*
king *n.* rēx *m.*

kingdom *n.* rēgnum *n.*
kingfisher *n.* alcēdō *f.*
kingly *a.* rēgius, rēgālis.
kingship *n.* rēgnum *n.*
kink *n.* vitium *n.*
kinsfolk *n.* cognātī *m.pl.*, necessāriī *m.pl.*
kinsman *n.* cognātus *m.*, propinquus *m.*, necessārius *m.*
kinswoman *n.* cognāta *f.*, propinqua *f.*, necessāria *f.*
kismet *n.* fātum *n.*
kiss *n.* ōsculum *n.* *vt.* ōsculārī.
kit *n.* (*mil.*) sarcina *f.*
kitchen *n* culīna *f.* — **garden** *n.* hortus *m.*
kite *n.* mīluus *m.* **–'s** *a.* mīluīnus.
knack *n.* calliditās *f.*, artificium *n.* have the — of callēre.
knapsack *n.* sarcina *f.*
knave *n.* veterātor *m.*
knavish *a.* improbus. **-ly** *ad.* improbē.
knead *vt.* depsere, subigere.
knee *n.* genū *n.*
kneel *vi.* genibus nītī.
knife *n.* culter *m.*; (*surgeon's*) scalprum *n.*
knight *n.* eques *m.* *vt.* in ōrdinem equestrem recipere.
knighthood *n.* ōrdō equester *m.*
knightly *a.* equester.
knit *vt.* texere; (*brow*) contrahere.
knob *n.* bulla *f.*
knock *vt.* ferīre, percutere. — at pulsāre. — against offendere. — down dēicere, adflīgere; (*at auction*) addīcere. — off dēcutere; (*work*) dēsistere ab. — out ēlīdere, excutere; (*unconscious*) exanimāre; (*fig.*) dēvincere. — up suscitāre. *n.* pulsus *m.*, ictus *m.*
knock-kneed *a.* vārus.
knoll *n.* tumulus *m.*
knot *n.* nōdus *m.* *vt.* nectere.
knotty *a.* nōdōsus. — point nōdus *m.*
know *vt.* scīre; (*person* nōvisse. — all about explōrātum habēre. — again agnōscere. — how to scīre. not — ignōrāre, nescīre. let me — fac sciam, fac mē certiōrem. *n.* in the — cōnscius.
knowing *a.* prūdēns, callidus. **-ly** *ad.* cōnsultō, sciēns.
knowledge *n* scientia *f.*, doctrīna *f.*; (*practical*) experientia *f.*; (*of something*) cognitiō *f.* [doctus.
knowledgeable *a.* gnārus,
known *a.* nōtus. make — dēclārāre. well — nōtus; (*saying*) trītus.
knuckle *n.* articulus *m.* — **bone** *n.* tālus *m.*
kotow *vi.* adulārī.
kudos *n.* glōria *f.*, laus *f.*

L

label *n.* titulus *m.* *vt.* titulō īnscrībere.
laboratory *n.* officīna *f.*
laborious *a.* labōriōsus, operōsus. **-ly** *ad.* operōsē.
laboriousness *n.* labor *m.*
labour *n.* labor *m.*, opera *f.*; (*work done*) opus *n.*; (*work allotted*) pēnsum *n.*; (*workmen*) operae *f.pl.* be in — parturīre. *vi.* labōrāre, ēnītī. — at ēlabōrāre. — under a delusion errōre fallī.
laboured *a.* adfectātus.
labourer *n.* operārius *m.*; (*pl.*) operae *f.pl.*
labyrinth *n.* labyrinthus *m.*
lace *n.* texta rēticulāta *n.pl.*; (*shoe*) ligula *f.* *vt.* nectere.
lacerate *vt.* lacerāre.
laceration *n.* lacerātiō *f.*
lack *n.* inopia *f.*, dēfectiō *f.* *vt.* egēre (*abl.*), carēre (*abl.*).
lackey *n.* pedisequus *m.*
laconic *a.* brevis. **-ally** *ad.* ūnō verbō, paucīs verbīs.
lacuna *n.* lacūna *f.*

lad *n.* puer *m.*
ladder *n.* scāla *f.*
lade *vt.* onerāre. **-n** *a.* onustus, onerātus.
lading *n.* onus *n.*
ladle *n.* trulla *f.*
lady *n.* domina *f.*, mātrōna *f.* mulier *f.*
ladylike *a.* līberālis, honestus.
lag *vi.* cessāre.
laggard *n.* cessātor *m.*
lagoon *n.* stagnum *n.*
lair *n.* latibulum *n.*
lake *n.* lacus *m.*
lamb *n.* agnus *m.*; (*flesh*) agnīna *f.* ewe — agna *f.*
lame *a.* claudus; (*argument*) inānis. be — claudicāre.
lameness *n.* claudicātiō *f.*
lament *n.* lāmentātiō *f.* lāmentum *n.* *vt.* lūgēre, lāmentārī; (*regret*) dēplōrāre.
lamentab/le *a.* lāmentābilis, miserābilis. **-ly** *ad.* miserābiliter.
lamentation *n.* lāmentātiō *f*
lamp *n.* lucerna *f.*, lychnus *m.*
lampoon *n.* satura *f.* *vt.* carmine dēstringere.
lance *n.* hasta *f.*, lancea *f.*
lancer *n.* hastātus *m.*
lancet *n.* scalpellum *n.*
land *n.* terra *f.*; (*country*) terra *f.*, regiō *f.*; (*territory*) fīnēs *m.pl.*; (*native*) patria *f.*; (*property*) praedium *n.*, ager *m.*; (*soil*) solum *n.* *vt.* expōnere. *vi.* ēgredī. *a.* terrēnus terrestris.
landfall *n.* adpulsus *m.*
landing-place *n.* ēgressus *m.*
landlady *n.* caupona *f.*
landlord *n.* dominus *m.*; (*inn*) caupō *m.*
landmark *n.* lapis *m.* be a — ēminēre.
landscape *n.* agrōrum prōspectus *m.*
landslide *n.* terrae lābēs *f.*, lāpsus *m.*
landwards *ad.* terram versus.
lane *n.* (*country*) sēmita *f.*; (*town*) angiportus *m*

language *n.* lingua *f.*; (*style*) ōrātiō *f.*, sermō *m.*; (*diction*) verba *n.pl.* bad — maledicta *n.pl.*
languid *a.* languidus, remissus **-ly** *ad.* languidē.
languish *vi.* languēre, languēscere; (*with disease*) tābēscere.
languor *n.* languor *m.*
lank, lanky *a.* exīlis, gracilis.
lantern *n.* lanterna *f.*
lap *n.* gremium *n.*, sinus *m.* *vt.* lambere; (*cover*) involvere.
lapse *n.* (*time*) lāpsus *m.*; (*mistake*) errātum *n* after the — of a year interiectō annō. *vi.* lābī; (*agreement*) inritum fierī; (*property*) revertī.
larceny *n.* fūrtum *n.*
larch *n.* larix *f.* *a.* larignus.
lard *n.* adeps *m.*, *f.*
larder *n.* cella penāria *f.*
large *a.* māgnus, grandis, amplus. at — solūtus. very — permāgnus. **-ly** *ad.* plērumque.
largesse *n.* largitiō *f.*; (*mil.*) dōnātīvum *n.*; (*civil*) congiārium *n.* give — largīrī.
lark *n.* alauda *f.*
lascivious *a.* libīdinōsus. **-ly** *ad.* libīdinōsē.
lasciviousness *n.* libīdō *f.*
lash *n.* flagellum *n.*, lōrum *n.*; (*eye*) cilium *n.* *vt.* verberāre; (*tie*) adligāre; (*with words*) castīgāre.
lashing *n.* verbera *n.pl.*
lass *n.* puella *f.*
lassitude *n.* languor *m.*
last *a.* ultimus, postrēmus, suprēmus; (*in line*) novissimus; (*preceding*) proximus. at — tandem, dēmum. for the — time postrēmum. *n.* fōrma *f.* let the cobbler stick to his — nē sūtor suprā crepidam. *vi.* dūrāre, permanēre.
lasting *a.* diūtinus, diūturnus.
lastly *ad.* postrēmō, dēnique.
latch *n.* pessulus *m.*
latchet *n.* corrigia *f.*

late *a.* sērus; (*date*) recēns; (*dead*) dēmortuus; (*emperor*) dīvus. — at night multā nocte. till — in the day ad multum diem. *ad.* sērō. too — sērō. too — to sērius quam quī (*subj.*). of — nūper. **-r** *a.* posterior. *ad.* posteā, posthāc, mox. **-st** *a.* novissimus. **-ly** *ad.* nūper.
latent *a.* occultus, latitāns.
lath *n.* tigillum *n.*
lathe *n.* tornus *m.*
lather *n.* spūma *f.*
Latin *a.* Latīnus. speak — Latīnē loquī. understand — Latīnē scīre. translate into — Latīnē reddere.
Latinity *n.* Latīnitās *f.*
latitude *n.* (*geog.*) caelum *n.*; (*scope*) lībertās *f.*
latter *a.* posterior. the — hic. **-ly** *ad.* nūper.
lattice *n.* trānsenna *f.*
laud *n.* laus *f.* *vt.* laudāre.
laudable *a.* laudābilis, laude dignus.
laudatory *a.* honōrificus.
laugh *n.* rīsus *m.*; (*loud*) cachinnus *m.* *vi.* rīdēre, cachinnāre. — at (*joke*) rīdēre; (*person*) dērīdēre. — up one's sleeve in sinū gaudēre.
laughable *a.* rīdiculus.
laughing-stock *n.* lūdibrium *n.*
laughter *n.* rīsus *m.*
launch *vt.* (*missile*) contorquēre; (*ship*) dēdūcere. *vi.* — out into ingredī in (*acc.*). *n.* celōx *f.*, lembus *m.*
laureate *a.* laureātus.
laurel *n.* laurus *m.* *a.* laureus.
lave *vt.* lavāre.
lavish *a.* prōdigus, largus. *vt.* largīrī, profundere. **-ly** *ad.* prōdigē, effūsē.
lavishness *n.* largitās *f.*
law *n.* lēx *f.*; (*system*) iūs *n.*; (*divine*) fās *n.* civil — iūs cīvīle. constitutional — iūs pūblicum. international — iūs gentium. go to — lēge agere, lītigāre. break the — lēges violāre. pass a — (*magistrate*) lēgem perferre; (*people*) lēgem iubēre.
law-abiding *a.* bene mōrātus.
law-court *n.* iūdicium *n.*; (*building*) basilica *f.*
lawful *a.* lēgitimus, (*morally*) fās. **-ly** *ad.* lēgitimē, lēge.
law-giver *n.* lēgum scrīptor *m.*
lawless *a.* exlēx. **-ly** *ad.* licenter.
lawlessness *n.* licentia *f.*
lawn *n.* prātulum *n.*
law-suit *n.* līs *f.*, āctiō *f.*
lawyer *n.* iūrisconsultus *m.*, causidicus *m.*
lax *a.* dissolūtus, remissus.
laxity *n.* dissolūtiō *f.*
lay *vt.* pōnere, locāre; (*ambush*) collocāre, tendere; (*disorder*) sēdāre; (*egg*) parere; (*foundation*) iacere, (*hands*) inicere; (*plan*) capere, inīre; (*trap*) tendere; (*wager*) facere. — aside pōnere; (*in store*) repōnere. — by repōnere. — down dēpōnere; (*rule*) statuere. — hold of prehendere, adripere. — in condere. — a motion before referre ad. — on impōnere. — open patefacere; (*to attack*) nūdāre. — out (*money*) impendere, ērogāre; (*camp*) mētārī. — siege to obsidēre. — to heart in pectus dēmittere. — up recondere. — upon iniungere, impōnere. — violent hands on vim adferre, adhibēre (*dat.*). whatever they could — hands on quod cuique in manum vēnisset. — waste vastāre. *n.* carmen *n.*, melos *n.*
lay *a.* (*eccl.*) lāicus.
layer *n.* corium *n.*; (*stones*) ōrdō *m.*; (*plant*) propāgō *f.*
lay-out *n.* dēsignātiō *f.*
laze *vi.* ōtiārī.
laziness *n.* ignāvia *f.*, dēsidia *f.*, pigritia *f.*

laz/y *a.* ignāvus, dēsidiōsus, piger. **-ily** *ad.* ignāvē, ōtiōsē.
lea *n.* prātum *n.*
lead *vt.* dūcere, (*life*) agere; (*wall*) perdūcere; (*water*) dērivāre. — astray in errōrem indūcere. — away abdūcere. — back redūcere. — down dēdūcere. — in intrōdūcere. — out ēdūcere. — the way dūcere, praeīre. — up to tendere ad. spectare ad, the road -s via fert.
lead *n.* plumbum *n.* *a.* plumbeus.
leaden *a.* (*colour*) līvidus.
leader *n.* dux *m.*, ductor *m.*
leadership *n.* ductus *m.*
leading *a.* prīmus, prīnceps, praecipuus.
lea/f *n.* folium *n.*, frōns *f.*; (*paper*) scheda *f.* put forth -ves frondēscere.
leaflet *n.* libellus *m.*
leafy *a.* frondōsus.
league *n.* foedus *n.*, societās *f.*; (*distance*) tria mīlia passuum. *vi.* coniūrāre, foedus facere. **-d** *a.* foederātus.
leak *n.* rīma *f.* *vi.* mānāre, rimās agere.
leaky *a.* rīmōsus.
leal *a.* fidēlis.
lean *a.* macer, exilis, gracilis. *vi.* nītī. — back sē reclīnāre. — on innītī in (*abl.*), incumbere (*dat.*). — over inclīnāre.
leaning *n.* prōpēnsiō *f.* *a.* inclīnātus.
leanness *n.* gracilitās *f.*, maciēs *f.*
leap *n.* saltus *m.* *vi.* salīre; (*for joy*) exsultāre. — down dēsilīre. — on to īnsilīre in (*acc.*).
leap-year *n.* annus bissextīlis *m.*
learn *vt.* discere; (*news*) accipere, audīre; (*by heart*) ēdiscere.
learned *a.* doctus, ērudītus, litterātus. **-ly** *ad.* doctē.
learner *n.* tīrō *m.*, discipulus *m.*
learning *n.* doctrīna *f.*, ērudītiō *f.*, litterae *f.pl.*
lease *n.* (*taken*) conductiō *f.*; (*given*) locātiō *f.* *vt.* condūcere; locāre.
leash *n.* cōpula *f.*
least *a.* minimus. *ad.* minimē. at — saltem. to say the — ut levissimē dīcam. not in the — haudquāquam.
leather *n.* corium *n.*, alūta *f.*
leathery *a.* lentus.
leave *n.* (*of absence*) commeātus *m.*; (*permission*) potestās *f.*, venia *f.* ask — veniam petere. give — potestātem facere. obtain — impetrāre. by your — pace tuā, bonā tuā veniā. *vt.* relinquere, dēserere; (*legacy*) lēgāre. — alone nōn tangere, manum abstinēre ab. — behind relinquere. — in the lurch dēstituere, dērelinquere. — off dēsinere, dēsistere ab; (*temporarily*) intermittere; (*garment*) pōnere. — out praetermittere ōmittere. *vi.* discēdere, abīre.
leaven *n.* fermentum *n.*
leavings *n.* rēliquiae *f.pl.*
lecherous *a.* salāx.
lecture *n.* acroāsis *f.*, audītiō *f.* *vi.* docēre, scholam habēre.
lecturer *n.* doctor *m.*
lecture-room *n.* audītōrium *n.*
ledge *n.* līmen *n.*
ledger *n.* cōdex acceptī et expēnsī.
lee *n.* pars ā ventō tūta.
leech *n.* hirūdō *f.*
leek *n.* porrum *n.*
leer *vi.* līmīs oculīs intuērī.
lees *n.* faex *f.*; (*of oil*) amurca *f.*
left *a.* sinister, laevus. *n.* sinistra *f.*, laeva *f.* on the — ā laevā, ad laevam, ā sinistrā.
leg *n.* crūs *n.*; (*of table*) pēs *m.*
legacy *n.* lēgātum *n.* —hunter *n.* captātor *m.*
legal *a.* lēgitimus. **-ly** *ad.* secundum lēgēs, lēge.
legalize *vt.* sancīre.
legate *n.* lēgātus *m.*
legation *n.* lēgātiō *f.*

legend *n.* fābula *f.*; (*inscription*) titulus *m.*
legendary *a.* fābulōsus.
legerdemain *n.* praestigiae *f.pl.*
legging *n.* ocrea *f.*
legible *a.* clārus.
legion *n.* legiō *f.* men of the 10th — decumānī *m.pl.*
legionary *n.* legiōnārius *m.*
legislate *vi.* lēgēs scrībere, lēgēs facere.
legislation *n.* lēgēs *f.pl.*, lēgēs scrībendae.
legislator *n.* lēgum scrīptor *m.*
legitimate *a.* lēgitimus. **-ly** *ad.* lēgitimē.
leisure *n.* ōtium *n.* **at —** ōtiōsus, vacuus. **have — for** vacāre (*dat.*).
leisured *a.* ōtiōsus.
leisurely *a.* lentus.
lend *vt.* commodāre, mūtuum dare; (*at interest*) faenerārī; (*ear*) praebēre, admovēre. — **a ready ear** aurēs patefacere. — **assistance** opem ferre.
length *n.* longitūdō *f.*; (*time*) diūturnitās *f.* **at —** tandem, dēmum; (*speech*) cōpiōsē.
lengthen *vt.* extendere; (*time*) prōtrahere; (*sound*) prōdūcere.
lengthwise *ad.* in longitūdinem.
lengthy *a.* longus, prōlixus.
leniency *n.* clēmentia *f.*
lenient *a.* clēmēns, mītis. **-ly** *ad.* clēmenter.
lentil *n.* lēns *f.*
leonine *a.* leōnīnus.
leopard *n.* pardus *m.*
less *a.* minor. *ad.* minus. — **than** (*num.*) intrā (*acc.*). **much —, still —** nēdum.
lessee *n.* conductor *m.*
lessen *vt.* minuere, imminuere, dēminuere. *vi.* dēcrēscere.
lesson *n.* documentum *n.*, (*pl.*) dictāta *n.pl.* **be a — to** documento esse (*dat.*). **give -s** scholās habēre. **give -s in** docēre.
lessor *n.* locātor *m.*
lest *conj.* nē.
let *vt.* (*allow*) sinere; (*lease*) locāre; (*imper.*) fac. **— alone** ōmittere; (*mention*) nē dīcam. **— blood** sanguinem mittere. **— down** dēmittere. **— fall** ā manibus mittere; (*word*) ēmittere. **— fly** ēmittere. **— go** mittere, āmittere; (*ship*) solvere. **— in** admittere. **— loose** solvere. **— off** absolvere, ignōscere (*dat.*). **— oneself go** geniō indulgēre. **— out** ēmittere. **— slip** āmittere, ōmittere.
lethal *a.* mortifer.
lethargic *a.* veternōsus.
lethargy *n.* veternus *m.*
letter *n.* epistula *f.*, litterae *f.pl.*; (*of alphabet*) littera *f.* **the — of the law** scrīptum *n.* **to the —** ad praescrīptum. **by —** per litterās. **-s** (*learning*) litterae *f.pl.* **man of -s** scrīptor *m.*
lettered *a.* litterātus.
lettuce *n.* lactūca *f.*
levee *n.* salūtātiō *f.*
level *a.* aequus, plānus. *n.* plānitiēs *f.*; (*instrument*) lībra *f.* **do one's — best** prō virīlī parte agere. **put on a — with** exaequāre cum. *vt.* aequāre, adaequāre, inaequāre; (*to the ground*) solō aequāre, sternere; (*weapon*) intendere. **-led** *a.* (*weapon*) īnfestus.
level-headed *a.* prūdēns.
lever *n.* vectis *m.*
levity *n.* levitās *f.*; (*fun*) iocī *m.pl.*, facētiae *f.pl.*
levy *vt.* (*troops*) scrībere; (*tax*) exigere. *n.* dīlectus *m.*
lewd *a.* impudīcus.
lewdness *n.* impudīcitia *f.*
liable *a.* obnoxius. **render —** obligāre.
liaison *n.* cōnsuētūdō.
liar *n.* mendāx *m.*
libation *n.* lībāmentum *n.* **pour a —** lībāre.
libel *n.* probrum *n.*, calumnia *f.* *vt.* calumniārī.

libellous *a.* probrōsus, fāmōsus.
liberal *a.* līberālis; (*in giving*) largus, benignus. — education bonae artēs *f.pl.* **-ly** *ad.* līberāliter, largē, benignē.
liberality *n.* līberālitās *f.*, largitās *f.*
liberate *vt.* līberāre; (*slave*) manū mittere.
liberation *n.* līberātiō *f.*
liberator *n.* līberātor *m.*
libertine *n.* libīdinōsus *m.*
liberty *n.* lībertās *f.*; (*excess*) licentia *f.* I am at — to mihī licet (*inf.*). I am still at — to integrum est mihī (*inf.*), take a — with licentius ūtī (*abl.*). familiārius sē gerere in (*acc.*).
libidinous *a.* libīdinōsus.
librarian *n.* librārius *m.*
library *n.* bibliothēca *f.*
licence *n.* (*permission*) potestās *f.*; (*excess*) licentia *f.*
license *vt.* potestātem dare (*dat.*).
licentious *a.* dissolūtus.
licentiousness *n.* libīdō *f.*, licentia *f.*
lick *vt.* lambere.
lictor *n.* lictor *m.*
lid *n.* operculum *n.*
lie *n.* mendācium *n.* give the — to redarguere. tell a — mentīrī. *vi.* mentīrī.
lie *vi.* iacēre; (*place*) situm esse; (*consist*) continērī. as far as in me -s quantum in mē est. — at anchor stāre. — between interiacēre. — down cubāre, discumbere. — heavy on premere. — hid latēre. — in wait īnsidiārī. — low dissimulāre. — on incumbere (*dat.*).
lief *ad.* libenter.
lien *n.* nexus *m.*
lieu *n.* in — of locō (*gen.*).
lieutenant *n.* decuriō *m.*
life *n.* vīta *f.*; (*in danger*) salūs *f.*, caput *n.*; *biography* vīta. *f.* (*breath*) anima *f.*; (*rhet.*) sanguis *m.*; (*time*) aetās *f.* come to — again revīvīscere. draw to the — exprimere. for — aetātem. matter of — and death capitāle *n.* prime of — flōs aetātis. way of — mōrēs *m.pl.*
life-blood *n.* sanguis *m.*
life-giving *a.* almus, vītalis.
life-guard *n.* custōs *m.*; (*emperor's*) praetōriānus *m.*
lifeless *a.* exanimis; (*style*) exsanguis.
lifelike *a.* expressus.
life-long *a.* perpetuus
lifetime *n.* aetās *f.*
lift *vt.* tollere, sublevāre. — up efferre, attollere.
light *n.* lūx *f.*, lūmen *n.*; (*painting*) lūmen *n.* bring to — in lūcem prōferre. see in a favourable — in meliōrem partem interpretārī. throw — on lūmen adhibēre (*dat.*). *vt.* accendere, incendere; (*illuminate*) illūstrāre, illūmināre. be lit up collūcēre. *vi.* — upon invenīre, offendere. *a.* illūstris; (*movement*) agilis; (*weight*) levis. grow — illūcēscere, dīlūcēscere. make — of parvī pendere.
light-armed *a.* expedītus.
lighten *vi.* fulgurāre. *vt.* levāre.
lighter *n.* linter *f.*
light-fingered *a.* tagāx.
light-footed *a.* celer, pernīx.
light-headed *a.* levis, volāticus. [laetus.
light-hearted *a.* hilaris,
lightly *ad.* leviter; perniciter.
lightness *n.* levitās *f.*
lightning *n.* fulgur *n.*; (*striking*) fulmen *n.* be hit by — dē caelō percutī. of — fulgurālis.
like *a.* similis, pār. — this ad hunc modum. *ad.* similiter, sicut, ritū (*gen.*). *vt.* amāre. I — mihī placet, mē iuvat. I — to libet (*inf.*). I don't

— nil moror, mihi displicet. look — similem esse, referre.
likelihood *n.* vēri similitūdō *f.*
likely *a.* vēri similis. *ad.* sānē.
liken *vt.* comparāre, aequiperāre.
likeness *n.* imāgō *f.*, instar *n.*, similitūdō *f.*
likewise *ad.* item; (*also*) etiam.
liking *n.* libīdō *f.*, grātia *f.* to one's — ex sententiā.
lily *n.* līlium *n.*
limb *n.* membrum *n.*, artus *m.*
lime *n.* calx *f.*; (*tree*) tilia *f.* bird — viscum *n.* quick — calx viva. slaked — calx exstincta.
limelight *n.* celebritās *f.* enjoy the — mōnstrārī digitō.
limestone *n.* calx *f.*
limit *n.* fīnis *m.*, terminus *m.*, modus *m.* mark the -s of dēterminare. *vt.* fīnīre, dēfinīre termināre; (*restrict*) circumscribere.
limitation *n.* modus *m.*
limp *a.* mollis, flaccidus. *vi.* claudicāre.
limpid *a.* limpidus.
linden *n.* tilia *f.*
line *n.* līnea *f.*; (*battle*) aciēs *f.*; (*limit*) modus *m.*; (*outline*) līneāmentum *n.*; (*writing*) versus *m.* in a straight — ē regiōne. — of march agmen *n.* read beween the —s dissimulātā dispicere. ship of the — nāvis longa. write a — pauca scrībere. *vt.* (*street*) saepīre.
lineage *n.* genus *n.*, stirps *f.*
lineal *a.* (*descent*) gentīlis.
lineaments *n.* līneāmenta *n.pl.*, ōris ductūs *m.pl.*
linen *n.* linteum *n.* *a.* linteus.
liner *n.* nāvis *f.*
linger *vi.* cunctārī, cessāre, dēmorārī.
lingering *a.* tardus. *n.* cunctātiō *f.*
linguist *n.* be a — complūrēs linguās callēre.
link *n.* ānulus *m.*; (*fig.*) nexus *m.*, vinculum *n.* *vt.* coniungere.
lintel *n.* līmen superum *n.*
lion *n.* leō *m.* —'s leōnīnus. —'s share māior pars.
lioness *n.* leaena *f.*
lip *n.* lābrum *n.* be on everyone's -s in ōre omnium hominum esse, per omnium ōra ferrī. pay — service to verbō tenus obsequī (*dat.*).
liquefy *vt.* liquefacere.
liquid *a.* liquidus. *n.* liquor *m.*
liquidate *vt.* persolvere.
liquor *n.* liquor *m.*; vīnum *n.*
lisp *vi.* balbūtīre.
lisping *a.* blaesus.
lissom *a.* agilis.
list *n.* index *m.*, tabula *f.*; (*ship*) inclīnātiō *f.* *vt.* scrībere. *vi.* (*lean*) sē inclīnāre; (*listen*) auscultāre; (*wish*) cupere.
listen *vi.* auscultāre. — to auscultāre, audīre.
listener *n.* audītor *m.*, auscultātor *m.*
listless *a.* languidus.
listlessness *n.* languor *m.*
literally *ad.* ad verbum.
literary *a.* (*man*) litterātus. — pursuits litterae *f.pl.*, studia *n.pl.*
literature *n.* litterae *f.pl.*
lithe *a.* mollis, agilis.
litigant *n.* lītigātor *m.*
litigate *vi.* lītigāre.
litigation *n.* līs *f.*
litigious *a.* lītigiōsus.
litter *n.* (*carriage*) lectīca *f.*; (*brood*) fētus *m.*; (*straw*) strāmentum *n.*; (*mess*) strāgēs *f.* *vt.* sternere; (*young*) parere.
little *a.* parvus, exiguus; (*time*) brevis. very — perexiguus, minimus. — boy puerulus *m.* *n.* paulum *n.* aliquantulum *n.* for a — paulisper, parumper. — or nothing vix quicquam. *ad.* paulum, nōnnihil; (*with comp.*) paulō. — by — paulātim, sēnsim, gradātim. think — of parvī aestimāre.

littleness *n.* exiguitās *f.*
littoral *n.* lītus *n.*
live *vi.* vīvere, vītam agere; (*dwell*) habitāre. — down (*reproach*) ēluere. — on (*food*) vescī (*abl.*). *a.* vīvus.
livelihood *n.* victus *m.*
liveliness *n.* alacritās *f.*, hilaritās *f.*
livelong *a.* tōtus.
lively *a.* alacer, hilaris.
liven *vt.* exhilarāre.
liver *n.* iecur *n.*
livery *n.* vestis famulāris *f.*
livid *a.* līvidus. be — līvēre.
living *a.* vīvus. *n.* victus *m.*; (*earning*) quaestus *m.*
lizard *n.* lacerta *f.*
lo *interj.* ecce.
load *n.* onus *n.* *vt.* onerāre.
loadstone *n.* magnēs *m.*
loaf *n.* pānis *m.* *vi.* grassārī.
loafer *n.* grassātor *m.*
loam *n.* lutum *n.*
loan *n.* mūtuum *n.*, mūtua pecūnia *f.*
loathe *vt.* fastīdīre, ōdisse.
loathing *n.* fastīdium *n.*
loathsome *a.* odiōsus, taeter.
lobby *n.* vestibulum *n.*
lobe *n.* fibra *f.*
lobster *n.* astacus *m.*
local *a.* indigena, locī.
locality *n.* locus *m.*
locate *vt.* reperīre. be -d situm esse.
location *n.* situs *m.*
loch *n.* lacus *m.*
lock *n.* (*door*) sera *f.*; (*hair*) coma *f.* *vt.* obserāre.
locomotion *n.* mōtus *m.*
locust *n.* locusta *f.*
lodge *n.* casa *f.* *vi.* dēversārī. *vt.* īnfīgere; (*complaint*) dēferre.
lodger *n.* inquilīnus *m.*
lodging *n.* hospitium *n.*, dēversōrium *n.*
loft *n.* cēnāculum *n.*
loftiness *n.* altitūdō *f.*, sublīmitās *f.*
lofty *a.* excelsus, sublīmis.
log *n.* stipes *m.*; (*fuel*) lignum *n.*
loggerhead *n.* be at -s rixārī.
logic *n.* dialecticē *f.*
logical *a.* dialecticus, ratiōne frētus. **-ly** *ad.* ex ratiōne.
logician *n.* dialecticus *m.*
loin *n.* lumbus *m.*
loiter *vi.* grassārī, cessāre.
loiterer *n.* grassātor *m.*, cessātor *m.*
loll *vi.* recumbere.
lone *a.* sōlus, sōlitārius.
loneliness *n.* sōlitūdō *f.*
lonely, lonesome *a.* sōlitārius.
long *a.* longus; (*hair*) prōmissus; (*syllable*) prōductus; (*time*) longus, diūturnus. in the — run aliquandō. to make a — story short nē longum sit, nē longum faciam. *ad.* diū. — ago iamprīdem, iamdūdum. as — as *conj.* dum. before — mox. for — diū. how — quamdiū, quōusque. I have — been wishing iam prīdem cupiō. not — after haud multō post. no -er nōn iam. *vi.* — for dēsīderāre, exoptāre, expetere. — to gestīre.
longevity *n.* vīvācitās *f.*
longing *n.* dēsīderium *n.*, cupīdō *f.* *a.* avidus. **-ly** *ad.* avidē.
longitudinally *ad.* in longitūdinem.
long-lived *a.* vīvāx.
long-suffering *a.* patiēns.
long-winded *a.* verbōsus, longus.
longwise *ad.* in longitūdinem.
look *n.* aspectus *m.*; (*expression*) vultus *m.* — s speciēs *f.* good — s fōrma *f.*, pulchritūdō *f.* *vi.* aspicere; (*seem*) vidērī, speciem praebēre. — about circumspicere. — after prōvidēre (*dat.*), cūrāre. — at aspicere, intuērī; (*with mind*) contemplārī. — back respicere. — down on dēspectāre; (*fig.*)

dēspicere. — for quaerere. — forward to exspectāre. — here heus tu, ehodum. — into īnspicere, intrōspicere. — out prōspicere; (*beware*) cavēre. — round circumspicere. — through perspicere. — to ratiōnem habēre (*gen.*); (*leader*) spem pōnere in (*abl.*). — towards spectāre ad. — up suspicere. — up to suspicere. — upon habēre.
looker-on *n.* arbiter *m.* [*n.*
looking-glass *n.* speculum
look-out *n.* (*place*) specula *f.*; (*man*) vigil *m.*, excubiae *f.pl.*
loom *n.* tēla *f.* *vi.* in cōnspectum sē dare.
loop *n.* orbis *m.*, sinus *m.*
loop-hole *n.* fenestra *f.*
loose *a.* laxus, solūtus, remissus; (*morally*) dissolūtus. let — on immittere in (*acc.*). *vt.* (*undo*) solvere; (*slacken*) laxāre. -ly *ad.* solūtē, remissē.
loosen *vt.* solvere; (*structure*) labefacere.
looseness *n.* dissolūtiō *f.*, dissolūtī mōrēs *m.pl.*
loot *n.* praeda *f.*, rapīna *f.*
lop *vt.* amputāre.
lop-sided *a.* inaequālis.
loquacious *a.* loquāx.
loquacity *n.* loquācitās *f.*
lord *n.* dominus *m.* *vi.* — it dominārī.
lordliness *n.* superbia *f.*
lordly *a.* superbus; (*rank*) nōbilis. [imperium *n.*
lordship *n.* dominātiō *f.*,
lore *n.* litterae *f.pl.*, doctrīna *f.*
lose *vt.* āmittere, perdere. — an eye alterō oculō capī. — heart animum dēspondēre. — one's way deerrāre. be lost perīre, interīre. *vi.* (*in contest*) vincī.
loss *n.* damnum *n.*, dētrīmentum *n.* be at a — haerēre, haesitāre. suffer — damnum accipere, facere. -es (*in battle*) caesī *m.pl.*
lost *a.* āmissus, absēns. be — perīre, interīre. give up for — dēplōrāre.
lot *n.* sors *f.* be assigned by — sorte obvenīre. draw a — sortem dūcere. draw -s for sortīrī. a — of multus, plūrimus.
loth *a.* invītus. [ālea *f.*
lottery *n.* sortēs *f.pl.*; (*fig.*)
lotus *n.* lōtos *f.*
loud *a.* clārus, māgnus. -ly *ad.* māgnā vōce.
loudness *n.* māgna vōx *f.*
lounge *vi.* ōtiārī.
louse *n.* pedis *m.*, *f.*
lout *n.* agrestis *m.*
lovable *a.* amābilis.
love *n.* amor *m.* be hopelessly in — dēperīre. fall in — with adamāre. *vt.* amāre, dīligere. I — to mē iuvat (*inf.*). — affair amor *m.*
loveless *a.* amōre carēns.
loveliness *n.* grātia *f.*, venustās *f.*
lovely *a.* amābilis, venustus.
love-poem *n.* carmen amātōrium *n.*
lover *n.* amāns *m.*, amātor *m.*
lovesick *a.* amōre aeger.
loving *a.* amāns. -ly *ad.* amanter.
low *a.* humilis; (*birth*) ignōbilis; (*price*) vīlis; (*sound*) gravis; (*spirits*) dēmissus; (*voice*) dēmissus. at — water aestūs dēcessū. be — iacēre. lay — interficere. — lying *a.* dēmissus. be — sedēre. *vi.* mūgīre.
lower *a.* īnferior. the — world īnferī *m.pl.* of the — world īnfernus. *ad.* īnferius. *vt.* dēmittere, dēprimere. *vi.* (*cloud*) obscūrārī, mināri.
lowering *a.* mināx.
lowest *a.* īnfimus, īmus.
lowing *n.* mūgītus *m.*
lowland *a.* campestris. -s *n.* campī *m.pl.*
lowliness *n.* humilitās *f.*

lowly *a.* humilis, obscūrus.
lowness *n.* humilitās *f.*; (*spirit*) tristitia *f.*
loyal *a.* fidēlis, fīdus; (*citizen*) bonus. **-ly** *ad.* fidēliter.
loyalty *n.* fidēs *f.*, fidēlitās *f.*
lubber *n.* agrestis *m.*
lubricate *vt* ungere.
lucid *a.* clārus, perspicuus. **-ly** *ad.* clārē, perspicuē.
lucidity *n.* perspicuitās *f.*
luck *n.* fortūna *f.*, fors *f.* good — fēlicitās *f.* bad — infortūnium *n.*
luckless *a.* infēlix.
luck/y *a.* fēlix, fortūnātus; (*omen*) faustus. **-ily** *ad.* fēliciter, faustē, prosperē.
lucrative *a.* quaestuōsus.
lucre *n.* lucrum *n.*, quaestus *m.*
lucubration *n.* lūcubrātiō *f.*
ludicrous *a.* rīdiculus. **-ly** *ad.* rīdiculē.
lug *vt.* trahere.
luggage *n.* impedimenta *n.pl.*, sarcina *f.*
lugubrious *a.* lūgubris, maestus.
lukewarm *a.* tepidus; (*fig.*) segnis, neglegēns. be — tepēre. **-ly** *ad.* segniter, neglegenter.
lukewarmness *n.* tepor *m.*; (*fig.*) neglegentia *f.*, incūria *f.*
lull *vt.* sōpīre; (*storm*) sēdāre. *n.* intermissiō *f.*
lumber *n.* scrūta *n.pl.* [*n.*
luminary *n.*, lūmen *n.*, astrum
luminous *a.* lūcidus, illūstris.
lump *n.* massa *f.*; (*on body*) tuber *n.*
lumpish *a.* hebes, crassus, stolidus.
lunacy *n.* īnsānia *f.*
lunar *a.* lūnāris.
lunatic *n.* īnsānus *m.*
lunch *n.* prandium *n.* *vi.* prandēre.
lung *n.* pulmō *m.*; (*pl.*, *rhet.*) latera *n.pl.*
lunge *n.* ictus *m.* *vi.* prōsilīre.
lurch *n.* leave in the — dērelinquere, dēstituere. *vi.* titubāre.
lure *n.* esca *f.* *vt.* allicere, illicere.
lurid *a.* lūridus.
lurk *vi.* latēre, latitāre, dēlitēscere.
lurking-place *n.* latebra *f.*
luscious *a.* praedulcis.
lush *a.* luxuriōsus.
lust *n.* libīdō *f.* *vi.* libīdine flagrāre, concupīscere.
lustful *a.* libīdinōsus. [*m.pl.*
lustiness *n.* vigor *m.*, nervī
lustration *n.* lūstrum *n.*
lustre *n.* fulgor *m.*, splendor *m.*
lustrous *a.* illūstris.
lust/y *a.* validus, lacertōsus. **-ily** *ad.* validē, strēnuē.
lute *n.* cithara *f.*, fidēs *f.pl.* **-player** *n.* citharista *m.*, citharistria *f.*, fidicen *m.*, fidicina *f.*
luxuriance *n.* luxuria *f.*
luxuriant *a.* luxuriōsus.
luxuriate *vi.* luxuriārī.
luxurious *a.* sūmptuōsus, lautus. **-ly** *ad.* sūmptuōsē, lautē.
luxury *n.* luxuria *f.*, luxus *m.*; (*pl.*) lautitiae *f.pl.*
lye *n.* lixivia *f.* [lynceus.
lynx *n.* lynx *m.*, *f.* -eyed
lyre *n.* lyra *f.*, fidēs *f.pl.* play the — fidibus canere.
lyric *a.* lyricus. *n.* carmen *n.*
lyrist *n.* fidicen *m.*, fidicina *f.*

M

mace *n.* scīpiō *m.*
machination *n.* dolus *m.*
machine *n.* māchina *f.*
mackerel *n.* scomber *m.*
mad *a.* īnsānus, furiōsus, vēcors, dēmēns. be — īnsānīre furere. **-ly** *ad.* īnsānē, furiōsē, dēmenter.
madam *n.* domina *f.*
madden *vt.* furiāre, mentem aliēnāre (*dat.*).

maelstrom *n.* vertex *m.*
madness *n.* īnsānia *f.*, furor *m.*, dēmentia *f.*; (*animals*) rabiēs *f.*
magazine *n.* horreum *n.*, apothēca *f.*
maggot *n.* vermiculus *m.*
magic *a.* magicus. *n.* magicae artēs *f.pl.* [ficus *m.*
magician *n.* magus *m.*, vene-
magistracy *n.* magistrātus *m.*
magistrate *n.* magistrātus *m.*
magnanimity *n.* māgnanimitās *f.*, līberalitās *f.*
magnanimous *a.* generōsus, līberālis, māgnanimus.
magnet *n.* magnēs *m.*
magnificence *n.* māgnificentia *f.*, adparātus *m.*
magnificent *a.* māgnificus, amplus, splendidus. **-ly** *ad.* māgnificē, amplē, splendidē.
magnify *vt.* amplificāre, exaggerāre.
magnitude *n.* māgnitūdō *f.*
magpie *n.* pica *f.*
maid *n.* virgō *f.*; (*servant*) ancilla *f.*
maiden *n.* virgō *f.*
maidenhood *n.* virginitās *f.*
maidenly *a.* virginālis.
mail *n.* (*armour*) lōrica *f.*; (*letters*) epistulæ *f.pl.*
maim *vt.* mutilāre. **-ed** *a.* mancus.
main *a.* princeps, primus. — point caput, *n.* *n.* (*sea*) altum *n.*, pelagus *n.* with might and — manibus pedibusque, omnibus nervis.
mainland *n.* continēns *f.*
mainly *ad.* praecipuē, plērumque.
maintain *vt.* (*keep*) tenēre, servāre; (*keep up*) sustinēre; (*keep alive*) alere, sustentāre; (*argue*) adfirmāre, dēfendere.
maintenance *n.* (*food*) alimentum *n.*
majestic *a.* augustus, māgnificus. **-ally** *ad.* augustē.
majesty *n.* māiestās *f.*
major *a.* māior. — **domo** *n.* ātriēnsis *m.*
majority *n.* māior pars *f.*, plērique. have attained one's — sui iūris esse.
make *vt.* facere, fingere; (*appointment*) creāre; (*bed*) sternere; (*cape*) superāre; (*compulsion*) cōgere; (*consequence*) efficere; (*craft*) fabricārī, (*harbour*) capere; (*living*) quaerere; (*sum*) efficere; (*with a.*) reddere; (*with verb*) cōgere. — away with tollere, interimere. — good supplēre, resarcire. — light of parvi facere. — much of māgni aestimāre, multum tribuere, (*dat.*). — for petere. — out arguere. — over dēlēgāre, trānsferre. — up (*loss*) supplēre; (*total*) efficere; (*story*) fingere. be made fierī.
make-believe *n.* simulātiō *f.*
maker *n.* fabricātor *m.*, auctor *m.*
make-up *n.* medicāmina *n.pl.*
maladministration *n.* (*charge*) repetundae *f.pl.*
malady *n.* morbus *m.*
malcontent *a.* novārum rērum cupidus.
male *a.* mās, māsculus.
malediction *n.* exsecrātiō *f.*
malefactor *n.* nocēns *m.*, reus *m.* [*f.*
malevolence *n.* malevolentia
malevolent *a.* malevolus, malignus. **-ly** *ad.* malignē.
malformation *n.* dēprāvātiō *f.*
malice *n.* invidia *f.*, malevolentia *f.* bear — towards invidēre (*dat.*).
malicious *a.* invidiōsus, malevolus, malignus. **-ly** *ad.* malignē.
malign *a.* malignus, invidiōsus. *vt.* obtrectāre.
malignant *a.* malevolus.
maligner *n.* obtrectātor *m.*
malignity *n.* malevolentia *f.*

malleable *a.* ductilis.
mallet *n.* malleus *m.*
mallow *n.* malva *f.*
malpractices *n.* dēlicta *n.pl.*
maltreat *vt.* laedere, vexāre.
malversation *n.* peculātus *m.*
man *n.* (*human being*) homō *m., f.*; (*male*) vir *m.*; (*mil.*) mīles *m.*; (*chess*) latrunculus *m.* to a — omnēs ad unum. old — senex *m.* young — adulēscēns *m.* — of war nāvis longa *f.* *vt.* (*ship*) complēre; (*walls*) praesidiō firmāre.
manacle *n.* manicae *f.pl.* *vt.* manicās inicere (*dat.*).
manage *vt.* gerere, gubernāre, administrāre; (*horse*) moderārī; (*with verb*) posse.
manageable *a.* tractābilis, habilis.
management *n.* administrātiō *f.*, cūra *f.*; (*finance*) dispēnsātiō *f.*
manager *n.* administrātor *m.*, moderātor *m.*; dispēnsātor *m.*
mandate *n.* mandātum *n.*
mane *n.* iuba *f.*
manful *a.* virīlis, fortis. **-ly** *ad.* virīliter, fortiter.
mange *n.* scabiēs *f.*
manger *n.* praesēpe *n.*
mangle *vt.* dīlaniāre, lacerāre.
mangy *a.* scaber. [virīlis *f.*
manhood *n.* pūbertās *f.*, toga
mania *n.* īnsānia *f.*
maniac *n.* furiōsus *m.*
manifest *a.* manifestus, apertus, clārus. *vt.* dēclārāre, aperīre. **-ly** *ad.* manifestō, apertē.
manifestation *n.* speciēs *f.*
manifesto *n.* ēdictum *n.*
manifold *a.* multiplex, varius.
manikin *n.* homunciō *m.*, homunculus *m.*
manipulate *vt.* tractāre.
manipulation *n.* tractātiō *f.*
mankind *n.* hominēs *m.pl.*, genus hūmānum *n.*
manliness *n.* virtūs *f.*
manly *a.* fortis, virīlis.
manner *n.* modus *m.*, ratiō *f.*; (*custom*) mōs *m.*, ūsus *m.*; (*pl.*) mōrēs *m.pl.* after the — of ritū, mōre (*gen.*). good **-s** hūmānitās *f.*, modestia *f.*
mannered *a.* mōrātus.
mannerism *n.* mōs *m.*
mannerly *a.* bene mōrātus, urbānus.
manoeuvre *n.* (*mil.*) dēcursus *m.*, dēcursiō *f.*; (*fig.*) dolus *m.* *vi.* dēcurrere; (*fig.*) māchinārī.
manor *n.* praedium *n.*
mansion *n.* domus *f.*
manslaughter *n.* homicidium *n.*
mantle *n.* pallium *n.*; (*women's*) palla *f.*
manual *a.* — labour opera *f.* *n.* libellus *m.*, ars *f.*
manufacture *n.* fabrica *f.* *vt.* fabricārī.
manumission *n.* manūmissiō *f.*
manumit *vt.* manū mittere, ēmancipāre.
manure *n.* fimus *m.*, stercus *n.* *vt.* stercorāre.
manuscript *n.* liber *m.*, cōdex *m.*
many *a.* multī. as — as tot . . . quot. how — quot. so — tot. in — places multifāriam. a good — complūrēs. too — nimis multī. the — vulgus *n.* very — permultī, plūrimī.
map *n.* tabula *f.* *vt.* — out dēscrībere, dēsignāre.
maple *n.* acer *n.* *a.* acernus.
mar *vt.* corrumpere, dēfōrmāre.
marauder *n.* praedātor *m.*, dēpopulātor *m.* [moreus.
marble *n.* marmor *n.* *a.* mar-
March *n.* mēnsis Martius *m.* of — Martius.
march *n.* iter *n.* line of — agmen *n.* by forced **-es** māgnīs itineribus. on the — ex itinere, in itinere. quick — plēnō gradū. a regular day's — iter iūstum *n.* *vi.* iter facere, incēdere, īre.

— out exīre. — on signa prōferre, prōgredī. *vt.* dūcere. — out ēdūcere. — in intrōdūcere.
mare *n.* equa *f.*
margin *n.* margō *f.*; (*fig.*) discrimen *n.*
marigold *n.* caltha *f.*
marine *a.* marīnus. *n.* mīles classicus *m.*
mariner *n.* nauta *m.*
marital *a.* marītus.
maritime *a.* maritimus.
marjoram *n.* amāracus *m.*
mark *n.* nota *f.*; (*of distinction*) īnsigne *n.*; (*target*) scopos *m.*; (*trace*) vestīgium *n.* beside the — nihil ad rem. it is the — of a wise man to sapientis est (*inf.*). be wide of the — errāre. *vt.* notāre, dēsignāre; (*observe*) animadvertere, animum attendere. — out (*site*) mētārī, dēsignāre; (*for purpose*) dēnotāre.
marked *a.* īnsignis, manifestus. **-ly** *ad.* manifestō.
marker *n.* index *m.*
market *n.* macellum *n.* — day nūndinae *f.pl.* — place forum *n.* — town emporium *n.* — prices annōna *f.* cattle — forum boārium *n.* fish — forum piscārium *n.*
marketable *a.* vēndibilis.
marking *n.* macula *f.*
marmoreal *a.* marmoreus.
maroon *vt.* dērelinquere.
marriage *n.* mātrimōnium *n.*, coniugium *n.*; (*ceremony*) nūptiae *f.pl.* give in — collocāre. — bed lectus geniālis *m.*
marriageable *a.* nūbilis.
marrow *n.* medulla *f.*
marry *vt.* (*a wife*) dūcere, in mātrimōnium dūcere; (*a husband*) nūbere (*dat.*).
marsh *n.* palūs *f.*
marshal *n.* imperātor *m.* *vt.* instruere.
marshy *a.* palūster.
mart *n.* forum *n.*
marten *n.* mēlēs *f.*
martial *a.* bellicōsus, ferōx.
martyr *n.* dēvōtus *m.*; (*eccl.*) martyr *m.,f.*
marvel *n.* mīrāculum *n.*, portentum *n.* *vi.* mīrārī. — at admīrārī.
marvellous *a.* mīrus, mīrificus, mīrābilis. **-ly** *ad.* mīrē, mīrum quantum.
masculine *a.* mās, virīlis.
mash *n.* farrāgō *f.* *vt.* commiscēre, contundere.
mask *n.* persōna *f.* *vt.* persōnam induere (*dat.*); (*fig.*) dissimulāre.
mason *n.* structor *m.*
masonry *n.* lapidēs *m.pl.*, caementum *n.*
masquerade *n.* simulātiō *f.* *vi.* vestem mūtāre. —as speciem sibi induere (*gen.*), persōnam ferre (*gen.*).
mass *n.* mōlēs *f.*; (*of small things*) congeriēs *f.*; (*of people*) multitūdō *f.*; (*eccl.*) missa *f.* the -es vulgus *n.*, plēbs *f.* *vt.* congerere, coacervāre.
massacre *n.* caedēs *f.*, interneciō *f.* *vt.* trucīdāre.
massive *a.* ingēns, solidus.
massiveness *n.* mōlēs *f.*, soliditās *f.*
mast *n.* mālus *m.*
master *n.* dominus *m.*; (*school*) magister *m.* be — of dominārī in (*abl.*); (*skill*) perītum esse (*gen.*). become — of potīrī (*abl.*). be one's own — suī iūris esse. not — of impotēns (*gen.*). a past — veterātor *m.* *vt.* dēvincere; (*skill*) ēdiscere; (*passion*) continēre.
masterful *a.* imperiōsus.
masterly *a.* doctus, perītus.
masterpiece *n.* praeclārum opus *n.*
mastery *n.* dominātiō *f.*, imperium *n.*, arbitrium *n.*
masticate *vt.* mandere.
mastiff *n.* Molossus *m.*

mat *n.* storea *f.*
match *n.* (*person*) pār *m.*, *f.*; (*marriage*) nūptiae *f.pl.*; (*contest*) certāmen *n.* a — for pār (*dat.*). no — for impār (*dat.*). *vt.* exaequāre, adaequāre. *vi.* congruere.
matchless *a.* singulāris, ūnicus.
mate *n.* socius *m.*; (*married*) coniunx *m.*, *f.* *vi.* coniungī.
material *a.* corporeus; (*significant*) haud levis. *n.* māteriēs *f.*; (*literary*) silva *f.* **-ly** *ad.* māgnopere.
materialize *vi.* ēvenīre.
maternal *a.* māternus.
mathematical *a.* mathēmaticus.
mathematician *n.* mathēmaticus *m.*, geōmetrēs *m.*
mathematics *n.* numerī *m.pl.*
matin *a.* mātūtīnus.
matricide *n.* (*act*) mātricīdium *n.*; (*person*) mātricīda *m.*
matrimony *n.* mātrimōnium *n.*
matrix *n.* fōrma *f.*
matron *n.* mātrōna *f.*
matter *n.* māteria *f.*, corpus *n.*; (*affair*) rēs *f.*; (*med.*) pūs *n.* subject — argūmentum *n.*, māteria *f.* what is the — with you? quid tibī est? *vi.* it -s interest, rēfert.
matting *n.* storea *f.*
mattock *n.* dolābra *f.*
mattress *n.* culcita *f.*
mature *a.* mātūrus; (*age*) adultus. *vi.* mātūrēscere.
maturity *n.* mātūritās *f.*; (*age*) adulta aetās *f.*
maul *n.* fistūca *f.* *vt.* contundere, dīlaniāre.
maw *n.* ingluviēs *f.*
mawkish *a.* pūtidus. **-ly** *ad.* pūtidē.
maxim *n.* dictum *n.*, praeceptum *n.*, sententia *f.*
maximum *a.* quam māximus, quam plūrimus.

May *n.* mēnsis Māius *m.* of — Māius.
may *vi.* posse. I — licet mihī.
mayor *n.* praefectus *m.*
maze *n.* labyrinthus *m.*
mead *n.* (*drink*) mulsum *n.*; (*land*) prātum *n.*
meagre *a.* exilis, iēiūnus. **-ly** *ad.* exiliter, iēiūnē.
meagreness *n.* exilitās *f.*
meal *n.* (*flour*) farīna *f.*; (*repast*) cibus *m.*
mealy-mouthed *a.* blandiloquus.
mean *a.* humilis, abiectus; (*birth*) ignōbilis; (*average*) medius, mediocris. *n.* modus *m.*, mediocritās *f.* *vt.* dīcere, significāre; (*word*) valēre; (*intent*) velle, in animō habēre. **-ly** *ad.* abiectē, humiliter.
meander *vi.* sinuōsō cursū fluere.
meaning *n.* significātiō *f.*, vis *f.*, sententia *f.* what is the — of quid sibī vult, quōrsum spectat.
meanness *n.* humilitās *f.*; (*conduct*) illīberālitās *f.*, avāritia *f.*
means *n.* instrūmentum *n.*; (*of doing*) facultās *f.*; (*wealth*) opēs *f.pl.* by — of per (*acc.*). by all — māximē. by no — nullō modō, haudquāquam. of small — pauper.
meantime, meanwhile *ad.* intereā, interim.
measles *n.* boa *f.*
measure *n.* modus *m.*, mēnsūra *f.*; (*rhythm*) numerī *m.pl.*; (*plan*) cōnsilium *n.*; (*law*) rogātiō *f.*, lēx *f.* beyond — nimium. in some — aliquā ex parte. take -s cōnsulere take the — of quālis sit cognōscere. without — immoderātē. *vt.* mētīrī. — out dīmētīrī; (*land*) mētārī.
measured *a.* moderātus.
measureless *a.* infīnītus, immēnsus.
measurement *n.* mēnsūra *f.*

meat *n.* carō *f.* [faber *m.*
mechanic *n.* opifex *m.*,
mechanical *a.* mēchanicus. — device māchinātiō *f.*
mechanics *n.* māchinālis scientia *f.*
mechanism *n.* māchinātiō *f.*
medal *n.* insigne *n.*
meddle *vi.* sē interpōnere.
meddlesome *a.* cūriōsus.
mediate *vi.* intercēdere. — between compōnere, conciliāre.
mediator *n.* intercessor *m.*, dēprecātor *m.*
medical *a.* medicus.
medicate *vt.* medicāre. [bris.
medicinal *a.* medicus, salū-
medicine *n.* (*art*) medicīna *f.*; (*drug*) medicāmentum *n.* — chest narthēcium *n.*
mediocre *a.* mediocris.
mediocrity *n.* mediocritās *f.*
meditate *vi.* meditārī, cōgitāre, sēcum volūtāre.
meditation *n.* cōgitātiō *f.*, meditātiō *f.*
medium *n.* internūntius *m.*; (*means*) modus *m.* *a.* mediocris.
medley *n.* farrāgō *f.* [*n.*
meed *n.* mercēs *f.*, praemium
meek *a.* mītis, placidus. **-ly** *ad.* summissō animō.
meet *a.* idōneus, aptus. *n.* conventus *m.* *vi.* convenīre. *vt.* obviam īre (*dat.*), occurrere (*dat.*); (*fig.*) obīre. — with invenīre, excipere.
meeting *n.* conventus *m.*
melancholic *a.* melancholicus.
melancholy *n.* ātra bīlis *f.*; tristitia *f.*, maestitia *f.* *a.* tristis, maestus.
mêlée *n.* turba *f.*, concursus *m.*
mellifluous *a.* mulsus.
mellow *a.* mītis; (*wine*) lēnis. become — mītēscere. make — mitigāre.
mellowness *n.* mātūritās *f.*
melodious *a.* canōrus, numerōsus. **-ly** *ad.* numerōsē.
melody *n.* melos *n.*, modī *m.pl.*
melt *vt.* liquefacere, dissolvere; (*fig.*) movēre. *vi.* liquēscere, dissolvī; (*fig.*) commovērī. — away dēliquēscere.
member *n.* membrum *n.*; (*person*) socius *m.*
membrane *n.* membrāna *f.*
memento *n.* monumentum *n.*
memoir *n.* commentārius *m.*
memorable *a.* memorābilis, commemorābilis.
memorandum *n.* hypomnēma *n.*
memorial *n.* monumentum *n.*
memorize *vt.* ēdiscere.
memory *n.* memoria *f.* from — memoriter.
menace *n.* minae *f.pl.* *vt.* minārī, minitārī; (*things*) imminēre (*dat.*).
menacing *a.* mināx. **-ly** *ad.* mināciter.
menage *n.* familia *f.*
mend *vt.* sarcīre, reficere. *vi.* meliōrem fierī; (*health*) convalēscere.
mendacious *a.* mendāx.
mendacity *n.* mendācium *n.*
mendicant *n.* mendīcus *m.*
mendicity *n.* mendīcitās *f.*
menial *a.* servīlis, famulāris. *n.* servus *m.*, famulus *m.*
menstrual *a.* mēnstruus.
mensuration *n.* mētiendī ratiō *f.*
mental *a.* cōgitātiōnis, mentis. **-ly** *ad.* cōgitātiōne, mente.
mentality *n.* animī adfectus *m.*, mēns *f.*
mention *n.* mentiō *f.* *vt.* memorāre, mentiōnem facere (*gen.*); (*casually*) inicere; (*briefly*) attingere. omit to — praetermittere.
mentor *n.* auctor *m.*, praeceptor *m.*
mercantile *a.* mercātōrius.
mercenary *a.* mercennārius, vēnālis. *n.* mercennārius mīles *m.*

merchandise *n.* mercēs *f.pl.*
merchant *n.* mercātor *m.*
merchantman *n.* nāvis onerāria *f.*
merciful *a.* misericors, clēmens. **-ly** *ad.* clēmenter.
merciless *a.* immisericors, inclēmens, inhūmānus. **-ly** *ad.* inhūmānē.
mercurial *a.* hilaris.
mercy *n.* misericordia *f.*, clēmentia *f.*, venia *f.* at the — of obnoxius (*dat.*), in manū (*gen.*).
mere *n.* lacus *m.* *a* merus, ipse. **-ly** *ad.* sōlum, tantum, dumtaxat.
meretricious *a.* meretricius. — attractions lēnōcinia *n.pl.*
merge *vt.* cōnfundere. *vi.* cōnfundī.
meridian *n.* merīdiēs *m.* *a.* merīdiānus.
merit *n.* meritum *n.*, virtūs *f.* *vt.* merērī.
meritorious *a.* laudābilis. **-ly** *ad.* optimē.
merle *n.* merula *f.*
mermaid *n.* nympha *f.*
merriment *n.* hilaritās *f.*, festīvitās *f.*
merr/y *a.* hilaris, festīvus. make — lūdere. **-ily** *ad.* hilare, festīvē.
merry-making *n.* lūdus *m.*, festīvitās *f.*
mesh *n.* macula *f.*
mess *n.* (*dirt*) sordēs *f.*, squālor *m.*; (*trouble*) turba *f.*; (*food*) cibus *m.*; (*mil.*) contubernālēs *m.pl.*
messmate *n.* contubernālis *m.*
message *n.* nūntius *m.*
messenger *n.* nūntius *m.*
metal *n.* metallum *n.* *a.* ferreus, aereus.
metamorphose *vt.* mūtāre, trānsfōrmāre. [*f.*
metamorphosis *n.* mūtātiō
metaphor *n.* trānslātiō *f.*
metaphorical *a.* trānslātus. **-ly** *ad.* per trānslātiōnem.
metaphysics *n.* dialectica *n.pl.*
mete *vt.* mētīrī.
meteor *n.* fax caelestis *f.*
meteorology *n.* prognōstica *n.pl.* [videor esse.
methinks *vi.* — I am mihi
method *n.* ratiō *f.*, modus *m.*
methodical *a.* dispositus; (*person*) dīligēns. **-ly** *ad.* dispositē.
meticulous *a.* accūrātus. **-ly** *ad.* accūrātē.
meticulousness *n.* cūra *f.*
metonymy *n.* immūtātiō *f.*
metre *n.* numerī *m.pl.*, modī *m.pl.*
metropolis *n.* urbs *f.*
mettle *n.* ferōcitās *f.*, virtūs *f.*
mettlesome *a.* ferōx, animōsus.
mew *n.* (*bird*) larus *m.*; (*pl.*) stabula *n.pl.* *vi.* vāgīre.
miasma *n.* hālitus *m.*
mid *a.* medius. *pr.* inter (*acc.*).
midday *n.* merīdiēs *m.* *a.* merīdiānus.
middle *a.* medius. *n.* medium *n.* in the — medius, in mediō.
middling *a.* mediocris.
midge *n.* culex *m.*
midget *n.* pūmiliō *m.*, *f.*
midland *a.* mediterrāneus.
midnight *n.* media nox *f.*
midriff *n.* praecordia *n.pl.*
midst *n.* medium *n.* in the — medius. in the — of inter (*acc.*). through the — of per medium. [*n.* *a.* sōlstitiālis.
midsummer *n.* sōlstitium
midway *ad.* medius.
midwife *n.* obstetrix *f.*
midwinter *n.* brūma *f.* *a.* brūmālis.
mien *n.* aspectus *m.*, vultus *m.*
might *n.* vīs *f.*, potentia *f.* with — and main omnibus nervīs, manibus pedibusque.
might/y *a.* ingēns, validus. **-ily** *ad.* valdē, magnopere.
migrate *vi.* abīre, migrāre.
migration *n.* peregrīnātiō *f.*

migratory *a.* advena.
mild *a.* mītis, lēnis, clēmēns. **-ly** *ad.* lēniter, clēmenter.
mildness *n.* clēmentia *f.*, mānsuētūdō *f.*; (*weather*) caelī indulgentia *f.*
mildew *n.* rōbīgō *f.*
mile *n.* mīlle passūs *m.pl.*; (*pl.*) mīlia passuum.
milestone *n.* lapis *m.*, mīliārium *n.*
militant *a.* ferōx.
military *a.* mīlitāris. — service mīlitia *f.* *n.* mīlitēs *m.pl.*
militate *vi.* — against repugnāre (*dat.*), facere contrā (*acc.*).
militia *n.* mīlitēs *m.pl.*
milk *n.* lac *n.* *vt.* mulgēre.
milk-pail *n.* mulctra *f.*
milky *a.* lacteus.
mill *n.* pistrīnum *n.*
milled *a.* (*coin*) serrātus.
millennium *n.* mīlle annī *m.pl.*
miller *n.* pistor *m.*
millet *n.* milium *n.*
million *num.* deciēs centēna mīlia *n.pl.*
millionaire *n.* rēx *m.* [*m.*
millstone *n.* mola *f.*, molāris
mime *n.* mīmus *m.*
mimic *n.* imitātor *m.*, imitātrīx *f.* *vt.* imitārī.
mimicry *n.* imitātiō *f.*
minatory *a.* mināx.
mince *vt.* concīdere. not — words plānē apertēque dīcere. *n.* minūtal *n.*
mind *n.* mēns *f.*, animus *m.*, ingenium *n.*; (*opinion*) sententia *f.*; (*memory*) memoria *f.* be in one's right — mentis suae esse. be of the same — eadem sentīre. be out of one's mind īnsānīre. bear in — meminisse (*gen.*), memorem esse (*gen.*). call to — memoriā repetere, recordārī. have a — to libet. make up one's — animum indūcere, animō obstināre, statuere. put in — of admonēre (*gen.*). speak one's — sententiam suam aperīre. to one's — ex sententiā. *vt.* cūrāre, attendere. — one's own business suum negōtium agere. *vi.* gravārī. I don't — nīl moror. never — mitte.
minded *a.* animātus.
mindful *a.* memor.
mine *n.* metallum *n.*; (*mil.*) cunīculus *m.*, (*fig.*) thēsaurus *m.* *vi.* fodere; (*mil.*) cunīculum agere. *pro.* meus.
miner *n.* fossor *m.*
mineral *n.* metallum *n.*
mingle *vt.* miscēre, commiscēre, *vi.* sē immiscēre.
miniature *n.* minima pictūra *f.*
minimize *vt.* dētrectāre.
minimum *n.* minimum *n.* *a.* quam minimus.
minion *n.* cliēns *m.*, *f.*; dēlicātus *m.*
minister *n.* administer *m.* *vi.* ministrāre, servīre. [*n.*
ministry *n.* mūnus *n.*, officium
minor *a.* minor. *n.* pupillus *m.*, pupilla *f.*
minority *n.* minor pars *f.* in one's — nōndum suī iūris.
Minotaur *n.* Mīnōtaurus *m.*
minstrel *n.* fidicen *m.*
minstrelsy *n.* cantus *m.*
mint *n.* (*plant*) menta *f.*; (*money*) Monēta *f.* *vt.* cūdere.
minute *n.* temporis mōmentum *n.* *a.* minūtus, exiguus, subtīlis. **-ly** *ad.* subtīliter.
minuteness *n.* exiguitās *f.*, subtīlitas *f.*
minutiae *n.* singula *n.pl.*
minx *n.* lascīva *f.*
miracle *n.* mīrāculum *n.*, mōnstrum *n.*
miraculous *a.* mīrus, mīrābilis. **-ly** *ad.* dīvīnitus.
mirage *n.* falsa speciēs *f.*
mire *n.* lutum *n.*
mirror *n.* speculum *n.* *vt.* reddere.

mirth *n.* hilaritās *f.*, laetitia *f.*
mirthful *a.* hilaris, laetus. **-ly** *ad.* hilare, laetē.
miry *a.* lutulentus.
misadventure *n.* infortūnium *n.*, cāsus *m.*
misapply *vt.* abūtī (*abl.*). (*words*) invertere.
misapprehend *vt.* male intellegere.
misapprehension *n.* error [*m.*
misappropriate *vt.* intervertere.
misbecome *vt.* dēdecēre.
misbegotten *a.* nothus.
misbehave *vi.* male sē gerere.
miscalculate *vi.* errāre, fallī.
miscalculation *n.* error *m.*
miscall *vt.* maledīcere (*dat.*).
miscarriage *n.* abortus *m.*; (*fig.*) error *m.*
miscarry *vi.* abortrī; (*fig.*) cadere, inritum esse.
miscellaneous *a.* prōmiscuus, varius.
miscellany *n.* farrāgō *f.*
mischance *n.* infortūnium *n.*
mischief *n.* malum *n.*, facinus *n.*, maleficium *n.*; (*children*) lascīvia *f.*
mischievous *a.* improbus, maleficus; lascīvus.
misconceive *vt.* male intellegere.
misconception *n.* error *m.*
misconduct *n.* dēlictum *n.*, culpa *f.*
miscontruction *n.* prāva interpretātiō *f.* [pretārī.
misconstrue *vt.* male inter-
miscreant *n.* scelerātus *m.*
misdeed *n.* maleficium *n.*, dēlictum *n.*
misdemeanour *n.* peccātum *n.*, culpa *f.*
miser *n.* avārus *m.*
miserab/le *a.* miser, infēlix. make oneself — sē cruciāre. **-ly** *ad.* miserē.
miserliness *n.* avāritia *f.*
miserly *a.* avārus. [*f.*
misery *n.* miseria *f.*, aerumna
misfortune *n.* malum *n.* infortūnium *n.*, incommodum *n.*, rēs adversae *f.pl.*
misgiving *n.* suspiciō *f.*, cūra *f.* have **-s** parum cōnfīdere.
misgovern *vt.* male regere.
misgovernment *n.* prāva administrātiō *f.*
misguide *vt.* fallere, dēcipere.
misguided *a.* dēmēns.
mishap *n.* infortūnium *n.*
misinform *vt.* falsa docēre.
misinterpret *vt.* male interpretārī.
misinterpretation *n.* prāva interpretātiō *f.*
misjudge *vt.* male iūdicāre.
mislay *vt.* āmittere.
mislead *vt.* dēcipere, indūcere, auferre.
mismanage *vt.* male gerere.
misnomer *n.* falsum nōmen *n.*
misogamy *n.* nūptiārum odium *n.* [*n.*
misogyny *n.* mulierum odium
misplace *vt.* in aliēnō locō collocāre. **-d** *a.* (*fig.*) vānus.
misprint *n.* mendum *n.*
mispronounce *vt.* prāvē appellāre.
misquote *vt.* perperam prōferre.
misrepresent *vt.* dētorquēre, invertere; (*person*) calumniārī.
misrepresentation *n.* calumnia *f.*
misrule *n.* prāva administrātiō *f.*
miss *vt.* (*aim*) aberrāre (*abl.*); (*loss*) requīrere, dēsīderāre; (*notice*) praetermittere. *n.* error *m.*; (*girl*) virgō *f.*
misshapen *a.* distortus, dēfōrmis.
missile *n.* tēlum *n.*
missing *a.* absēns. **be** — dēesse, dēsīderārī.
mission *n.* lēgātiō *f.*
missive *n.* litterae *f.pl.*
misspend *vt.* perdere, dissipāre.

misstatement *n.* falsum *n.*, mendācium *n.*
mist *n.* nebula *f.*
mistake *n.* error *m.*; (*writing*) mendum *n.* full of -s mendōsus. *vt.* — for habēre prō (*abl.*). be -n errāre, fallī.
mistletoe *n.* viscum *n.*
mistranslate *vt.* prāvē reddere.
mistress *n.* domina *f.*; (*school*) magistra *f.*; (*lover*) amīca *f.*
mistrust *n.* diffīdentia *f.*, suspīciō *f.* *vt.* diffīdere (*dat.*)
mistrustful *a.* diffīdēns. **-ly** *ad.* diffīdenter.
misty *a.* nebulōsus.
misunderstand *vt.* male intellegere. *vi.* errāre.
misunderstanding *n.* error *m.*; (*quarrel*) discidium *n.*
misuse *n.* malus ūsus *m.* *vt.* abūtī (*abl.*).
mite *n.* parvulus *m.*; (*insect*) vermiculus *m.*
mitigate *vt.* mītigāre, lēnīre.
mitigation *n.* mītigātiō *f.*
mix *vt.* miscēre. — in admiscēre. — together commiscēre get -ed up with admiscērī cum, sē interpōnere (*dat.*).
mixed *a.* prōmiscuus.
mixture *n.* (*act*) temperātiō *f.*; (*state*) dīversitās *f.*
mnemonic *n.* artificium memoriae *n.*
moan *n.* gemitus *m.* *vi.* gemere.
moat *n.* fossa *f.*
mob *n.* vulgus *n.*, turba *f.* *vt.* circumfundī in (*acc.*).
mobile *a.* mōbilis, agilis.
mobility *n.* mōbilitās *f.*, agilitās *f.*
mobilize *vt.* (*mil.*) ēvocāre.
mock *vt.* irrīdēre, lūdibriō habēre, lūdificārī; (*ape*) imitārī. — at inlūdere. *n.* lūdibrium *n.* *a.* simulātus, fictus.
mocker *n.* dērīsor *m.*
mockery *n.* lūdibrium *n.*, irrīsus *m.*
mode *n.* modus *m.*, ratiō *f.*
model *n.* exemplar *n.*, exemplum *n.* *vt.* fingere.
modeller *n.* fictor *m.*
moderate *a.* (*size*) modicus: (*conduct*) moderātus. *vt.* temperāre; (*emotion*) temperāre (*dat.*). *vi.* mītigārī. **-ly** *ad.* modicē, moderātē, mediocriter.
moderation *n.* moderātiō *f.*, modus *m.*; (*mean*) mediocritās *f.*
moderator *n.* praefectus *m.*
modern *a.* recēns.
modernity *n.* haec aetās *f.*
modest *a.* pudīcus, verēcundus. **-ly** *ad.* verēcundē, pudenter.
modesty *n.* pudor *m.*, verēcundia *f.*
modicum *n.* paullulum *n.*, aliquantulum *n.*
modification *n.* mūtātiō *f.*
modify *vt.* immūtāre; (*law*) derogāre aliquid dē.
modulate *vt.* (*voice*) inflectere.
modulation *n.* flexiō *f.* inclīnātiō *f.*
moiety *n.* dīmidia pars *f.*
moist *a.* ūmidus.
moisten *vt.* ūmectāre, rigāre.
moisture *n.* ūmor *m.*
molar *n.* genuīnus *m.*
mole *n.* (*animal*) talpa *f.*; (*on skin*) naevus *m.*; (*pier*) mōlēs *f.*
molecule *n.* corpusculum *n.*
molehill *n.* make a mountain out of a — ē rīvō flūmina māgna facere, arcem facere ē cloācā.
molest *vt.* sollicitāre, vexāre.
molestation *n.* vexātiō *f.*
mollify *vt.* mollīre, lēnīre.
molten *a.* liquefactus.
moment *n.* temporis mōmentum *n.*, temporis pūnctum *n.* for a — parumper. in a — iam. without a —'s delay nullā interpositā morā. be of great — māgnō mōmentō esse. it is of — interest.
momentary *a.* brevis.

momentous *a.* gravis, māgnī mōmentī.
momentum *n.* impetus *m.*
monarch *n.* rēx *m.*, tyrannus *m.*
monarchical *a.* rēgius.
monarchy *n.* rēgnum *n.*
monastery *n.* monastērium *n.*
monetary *a.* pecūniārius.
money *n.* pecūnia *f.*; (*cash*) nummī *m.pl.* for — mercēde. ready — nummī, praesēns pecūnia. make — rem facere, quaestum facere.
money-bag *n.* fiscus *m.*
moneyed *a.* nummātus, pecūniōsus. [*m.*
money-lender *n.* faenerātor
money-making *n.* quaestus *m.*
mongoose *n.* ichneumōn *m.*
mongrel *n.* hibrida *m.*
monitor *n.* admonitor *m.*
monk *n.* monachus *m.*
monkey *n.* sīmia *f.*
monkshood *n.* aconītum *n.*
monograph *n.* libellus *m.*
monologue *n.* ōrātiō *f.*
monopolize *vt.* absorbēre, sibī vindicāre.
monopoly *n.* arbitrium *n.*
monosyllabic *a.* monosyllabus.
monosyllable *n.* monosyllabum *n.*
monotonous *a.* aequābilis.
monotony *n.* taedium *n.*
monster *n.* mōnstrum *n.*, portentum *n.*, bēlua *f.*
monstrosity *n.* mōnstrum *n.*
monstrous *a.* immānis, mōnstruōsus; improbus.
month *n.* mēnsis *m.*
monthly *a.* mēnstruus. [*n.*
monument *n.* monumentum
monumental *a.* ingēns.
mood *n.* adfectiō *f.*, adfectus *m.*, animus *m.*; (*gram.*) modus *m.* I am in the mood — for libet (*inf.*)
moody *a.* mōrōsus, tristis.
moon *n.* lūna *f.* half- lūna dīmidiāta. full — lūna plēna. new — interlūnium *n.* by — light ad lūnam.
moonshine *n.* somnia *n.pl.*
moonstruck *a.* lūnāticus.
moor *vt.* religāre *n.* tesqua *n.pl.*
moorings *n.* ancorae *f.pl.*
moot *n.* conventus *m.* it is a — point discrepat. *vt.* iactāre.
mop *n.* pēniculus *m.* *vt.* dētergēre.
mope *vi.* maerēre.
moral *a.* honestus, probus; (*opposed to physical*) animī; (*philos.*) mōrālis. *n.* documentum *n.*; (*pl.*) mōrēs *m.pl.* -**ly** *ad.* honestē.
morale *n.* animus *m.* — is low iacet animus.
morality *n.* bonī mōrēs *m.pl.*, virtūs *f.* [serere.
moralize *vi.* dē officiīs dis-
morass *n.* palūs *f.*
moratorium *n.* mora *f*
morbid *a.* aeger.
mordant *a.* mordāx.
more *a.* plūs. *ad.* plūs, magis, amplius; (*extra*) ultrā. — than three feet amplius trēs pedēs. — and — magis magisque. nay — immo. — or less ferē. no — (*time*)nōn diūtius, nunquam posteā. [praetereā.
moreover *ad.* tamen, autem,
moribund *a.* moribundus.
morning *n.* māne *n.* early in the — bene māne. this — hodiē māne. good — salvē. *a.* mātūtīnus. — call salūtātiō *f.* — watch tertia vigilia *f.*
moron *n.* sōcors *m.*
morose *a.* acerbus, tristis.
moroseness *n.* acerbitās *f.*, tristitia *f.*
morrow *n.* posterus diēs *m.*
morsel *n.* offa *f.*
mortal *a.* mortālis, hūmānus; (*wound*) mortifer. *n.* mortālis *m.*, *f.*, homō *m.*, *f.* poor — homunculus *m.* -**ly** *ad.* be

— wounded mortiferum vulnus accipere.
mortality *n.* mortālitās *f.*; (*death*) mors *f.* the — was high plūrimī periērunt.
mortar *n.* mortārium *n.*
mortgage *n.* pignus *n.*, fīdūcia *f.* *vt.* obligāre.
mortification *n.* dolor *m.*, angor *m.*
mortif/y *vt.* mordēre, vexāre; (*lust*) coercēre. *vi.* putrēscere. be -ied at aegrē ferre.
mortise *vt.* immittere.
mosaic *n.* emblēma *n.*, lapilli *m.pl.* *a.* tessellātus.
mosquito *n.* culex *m.* [*n.*
mosquito-net *n.* cōnōpēum
moss *n.* muscus *m.*
mossy *a.* muscōsus.
most *a.* plūrimus, plērusque. for the — part māximam partem. *ad.* māximē, plūrimum. **-ly** *ad.* plērumque, ferē.
mote *n.* corpusculum *n.*
moth *n.* tinea *f.*
mother *n.* māter *f.* **-in-law** *n.* socrus *f.* — tongue patrius sermō *m.* — wit Minerva *f.* of a — māternus.
motherless *a.* mātre orbus.
motherly *a.* māternus.
motif *n.* argūmentum *n.*
motion *n.* mōtus *m.*; (*for law*) rogātiō *f.*; (*in debate*) sententia *f.* propose a — ferre. set in — movēre. *vt.* innuere.
motionless *a.* immōbilis.
motive *n.* causa *f.*, ratiō *f.* I know your — in asking sciō cūr rogēs.
motley *a.* versicolor, varius.
mottled *a.* maculōsus.
motto *n.* sententia *f.*
mould *n.* fōrma *f.*; (*soil*) humus *f.*; (*fungus*) mūcor *m.* *vt.* fingere, fōrmāre.
moulder *vi.* putrēscere. *n.* fictor *m.*
mouldering *a.* puter.
mouldiness *n.* situs *m.*
mouldy *a.* mūcidus.
moult *vi.* pennas exuere. [*m.*
mound *n.* agger *m.*, tumulus
mount *n.* mōns *m.*; (*horse*) equus *m.* *vt.* scandere, cōnscendere, ascendere. *vi.* ascendere. — up ēscendere.
mountain *n.* mōns *m.*
mountaineer *n.* montānus *m.*
mountainous *a.* montuōsus.
mountebank *n.* planus *m.*
mourn *vi.* maerēre, lūgēre. *vt.* dēflēre, lūgēre.
mourner *n.* plōrātor *m.*; (*hired*) praefica *f.*
mournful *a.* (*cause*) lūctuōsus, acerbus; (*sound*) lūgubris, maestus. **-ly** *ad.* maestē.
mourning *n.* maeror *n.*, lūctus *m.*; (*dress*) sordēs *f.pl.* in — fūnestus. be in — lūgere. put on — vestem mūtāre, sordēs suscipere. wearing — ātrātus.
mouse *n.* mūs *m.* [*n.*
mouse-trap *n.* mūscipulum
mouth *n.* ōs *n.*; (*river*) ōstium *n.*
mouthful *n.* bucca *f.*
mouthpiece *n.* interpres *m.*
movable *a.* mōbilis. *n.* (*pl.*) rēs *f.pl.*, supellex *f.*
move *vt.* movēre; (*emotion*) commovēre. — backwards and forwards reciprocāre. — out of the way dēmovēre. — up admovēre. *vi.* movērī; (*residence*) dēmigrāre; (*proposal*) ferre, cēnsēre. — into immigrāre in (*acc.*). — on prōgredī.
movement *n.* mōtus *m.*; (*process*) cursus *m.*; (*society*) societās *f.*
mover *n.* auctor *m.*
moving *a.* flēbilis, flexanimus.
mow *vt.* secāre, dēmetere.
mower *n.* faenisex *m.*
much *a.* multus. *ad.* multum; (*with comp.*) multō. as — as tantum quantum. so — tantum. — less nēdum. too — nimis. *n.* multum *n.*

muck *n.* stercus *n.*
mud *n.* lutum *n.*
muddle *n.* turba *f.* *vt.* turbāre.
muffle *vt.* involvere. — **up** obvolvere. **-d** *a.* surdus.
mug *n.* pōculum *n.*
mulberry *n.* mōrum *n.*; (*tree*) mōrus *f.*
mulct *vt.* multāre.
mule *n.* mūlus *m.*
muleteer *n.* mūliō *m.*
mulish *a.* obstinātus.
mullet *n.* mullus *m.* [varius.
multifarious *a.* multiplex,
multiform *a.* multifōrmis.
multiply *vt.* multiplicāre. *vi.* crēscere.
multitude *n.* multitūdō *f.*
multitudinous *a.* crēberrimus.
mumble *vt.* (*words*) opprimere. *vi.* murmurāre.
munch *vt.* mandūcāre.
mundane *a.* terrestris.
municipal *a.* mūnicipālis. [*n.*
municipality *n.* mūnicipium
munificence *n.* largitās *f.*
munificent *a.* largus, mūnificus. **-ly** *ad.* mūnificē. [*m.*
munitions *n.* belli adparātus
mural *a.* mūrālis.
murder *n.* parricīdium *n.*, caedēs *f.* **charge with** — inter sīcāriōs accūsāre. **trial for** — quaestiō inter sīcāriōs. *vt.* interficere, iūgulāre, necāre.
murderer *n.* sīcārius *m.*, homicīda *m.*, parricīda *m.*, percussor *m.*
murderess *n.* interfectrix *f.*
murderous *a.* cruentus.
murky *a.* tenebrōsus.
murmur *n.* murmur *n.*; (*angry*) fremitus *m.* *vi.* murmurāre; fremere.
murmuring *n.* admurmur-
muscle *n.* torus *m.* [ātiō *f.*
muscular *a.* lacertōsus.
muse *vi.* meditārī. *n.* Mūsa *f.*
mushroom *n.* fungus *m.*, bōlētus *m.*

music *n.* (*art*) mūsica *f.*; (*sound*) cantus *m.*, modī *m.pl.*
musical *a.* (*person*) mūsicus; (*sound*) canōrus.
musician *n.* mūsicus *m.*; (*strings*) fidicen *m.*; (*wind*) tībīcen *m.*
muslin *n.* sindōn *f.*
must *n.* (*wine*) mustum *n.* *vi.* dēbēre. **I — go** mē oportet īre, mihī eundum est.
mustard *n.* sināpi *n.*
muster *vt.* convocāre, cōgere; (*review*) recēnsēre. *vi.* convenīre, coīre. *n.* conventus *m.*; (*review*) recēnsiō *f.*
muster-roll *n.* album *n.*
mustiness *n.* situs *m.*
musty *a.* mūcidus.
mutability *n.* incōnstantia *f.*
mutable *a.* incōnstāns, mūtābilis.
mute *a.* mūtus.
mutilate *vt.* mūtilāre, truncāre. **-d** *a.* mūtilus, truncus.
mutilation *n.* lacerātiō *f.*
mutineer *n.* sēditiōsus *m.*
mutinous *a.* sēditiōsus.
mutiny *n.* sēditiō *f.* *vi.* sēditiōnem facere.
mutter *vi.* mussitāre.
mutton *n.* carō ovilla *f.*
mutual *a.* mūtuus. **-ly** *ad.* mūtuō, inter sē.
muzzle *n.* ōs *n.*, rōstrum *n.*; (*guard*) fiscella *f.* *vt.* fiscella capistrāre.
my *a.* meus.
myriad *n.* decem mīlia; (*any large no.*) sēscentī.
myrmidon *n.* satelles *m.*
myrrh *n.* murra *f.*
myrtle *n.* myrtus *f.* *a.* myrteus. **-grove** *n.* myrtētum *n.*
myself *pro.* ipse, egomet; (*reflexive*) mē.
mysterious *a.* arcānus, occultus. **-ly** *ad.* occultē.
mystery *n.* arcānum *n.*; (*rites*) mystēria *n.pl.*; (*fig.*) latebra *f.* [ticus.
mystic, mystical *a.* mys-

mystification *n.* fraus *f.*, ambāgēs *f.pl.*
mystify *vt.* fraudāre, cōnfundere.
myth *n.* fābula *f.*
mythical *a.* fābulōsus.
mythology *n.* fābulae *f.pl.*

N

nabob *n.* rēx *m.*
nadir *n.* fundus *m.*
nag *n.* caballus *m.* *vt.* obiūrgitāre.
naiad *n.* nāias *f.*
nail *n.* clāvus *m.*; (*finger*) unguis *m.* hit the — on the head rem acū tangere. *vt.* clāvis adfīgere.
naive *a.* simplex. **-ly** *ad.* simpliciter.
naiveté *n.* simplicitās *f.*
naked *a.* nūdus. **-ly** *ad.* apertē.
name *n.* nōmen *n.*; (*repute*) existimātiō *f.*; (*term*) vocābulum *n.* by — nōmine. have a bad — male audīre. have a good — bene audīre. in the — of verbīs (*gen.*); (*oath*) per. *vt.* appellāre, vocāre, nōmināre; (*appoint*) dīcere.
nameless *a.* nōminis expers, sine nōmine.
namely *ad.* nempe, dīcō.
namesake *n.* gentīlis *m.*, *f.*
nanny-goat *n.* capra *f.*
nap *n.* brevis somnus *m.*; (*cloth*) villus *n.*
napkin *n.* linteum *n.*
narcissus *n.* narcissus *m.*
narcotic *a.* somnifer.
nard *n.* nardus *f.*
narrate *vt.* nārrāre, ēnārrāre.
narration *n.* nārrātiō *f.*
narrative *n.* fābula *f.*
narrator *n.* nārrātor *m.*
narrow *a.* angustus. *vt.* coartāre. *vi.* coartārī. **-ly** *ad.* aegrē, vix.
narrowness *n.* angustiae *f.pl.*
narrows *n.* angustiae *f.pl.*
nasal *a.* nārium.
nascent *a.* nāscēns.
nastiness *n.* foeditās *f.*
nast/y *a.* foedus, taeter, impūrus. **-ily** *ad.* foedē.
natal *a.* nātālis.
nation *n.* populus *m.*; (*foreign*) gēns *f.*
national *a.* pūblicus, cīvīlis; (*affairs*) domesticus.
nationality *n.* cīvitās *f.*
native *a.* indigena; (*speech*) patrius. — land patria *f.* *n.* indigena *m.*, *f.*
nativity *n.* ortus *m.*
natural *a.* nātūrālis; (*innate*) nātīvus, genuīnus, īnsitus. **-ly** *ad.* nātūrāliter, secundum nātūram; (*of course*) scīlicet, certē.
naturalization *n.* cīvitās *f.*
naturalize *vt.* cīvitāte dōnāre. **-d** *a.* (*person*) cīvitāte dōnātus; (*thing*) īnsitus.
nature *n.* nātūra *f.*, rērum nātūra *f.*, (*character*) indolēs *f.*, ingenium *n.*; (*species*) genus *n.* course of — nātūra *f.* good — facilitās *f.*, benignitās *f.* I know the — of sciō quālis sit.
naught *n.* nihil *n.* set at — parvī facere.
naughty *a.* improbus.
nausea *n.* nausea *f.*; (*fig.*) fastīdium *n.*
nauseate *vt.* fastīdium movēre (*dat.*). be **-d** with fastīdīre.
nauseous *a.* taeter.
nautical *a.* nauticus, maritimus.
naval *a.* nāvālis.
navel *n.* umbilīcus *m.*
navigable *a.* nāvigābilis.
navigate *vt.* & *i.* nāvigāre.
navigation *n.* rēs nautica *f.*; (*sailing*) nāvigātiō *f.*
navigator *n.* nauta *m.*, gubernātor *m.*
navy *n.* classis *f.*, cōpiae nāvālēs *f.pl.*
nay *ad.* nōn. — more immo.
near *ad.* prope. — by iuxtā

a. propinquus. *pr.* prope (*acc.*). ad (*acc.*). lie — adiacēre (*dat.*). *vt.* adpropinquāre (*dat.*). **-er** *a.* propior. **-est** *a.* proximus.
nearly *ad.* paene, prope fermē.
neat *a.* nitidus, mundus, concinnus; (*wine*) pūrus. **-ly** *ad.* mundē, concinnē.
neatherd *n.* bubulcus *m.*
neatness *n.* munditia *f.*
nebulous *a.* nebulōsus; (*fig.*) incertus.
necessar/y *a.* necessārius, necesse. **-ies** *n.* rēs ad vivendum necessāriae *f.pl.* **-ily** *ad.* necessāriō, necesse.
necessitate *vt.* cōgere (*inf.*), efficere ut (*subj.*).
necessitous *a.* egēnus, pauper.
necessity *n.* necessitās *f.*; (*thing*) rēs necessāria *f.*; (*want*) paupertās *f.*, egestās *f.*
neck *n.* collum *n.* **-cloth** *n.* fōcāle *n.* [*m.*
necklace *n.* monīle *n.*, torquis
nectar *n.* nectar *n.*
need *n.* (*necessity*) necessitās *f.*; (*want*) egestās *f.*, inopia *f.*, indigentia *f.*; (*pl.*) necessitātēs *f.pl.* there is — of opus est (*abl.*). there is no — to nihil est quod, cūr (*subj.*). *vt.* egēre (*abl.*), indigēre (*abl.*). I — opus est mihi (*abl.*).
needful *a.* necessārius.
needle *n.* acus *f.*
needless *a.* vānus, inūtilis. **-ly** *ad.* frustrā, sine causā.
needs *ad.* necesse.
needy *a.* egēns, inops, pauper.
nefarious *a.* nefārius, scelestus.
negation *n.* negātiō *f.*, infitiātiō *f.*
negative *a.* negāns. *n.* negātiō *f.* answer in the — negāre. *vt.* vetāre, contrādīcere (*dat.*).
neglect *n.* neglegentia *f.*, incūria *f.*; (*of duty*) dērelictiō *f.* *vt.* neglegere, ōmittere.
neglectful *a.* neglegens, immemor.
negligence *n.* neglegentia *f.*, incūria *f.*
negligent *a.* neglegēns, indīligēns. **-ly** *ad.* neglegenter, indīligenter.
negligible *a.* levissimus, minimī mōmentī.
negotiate *vi.* agere dē. *vt.* (*deal*) peragere; (*difficulty*) superāre. [pactum *n.*
negotiation *n.* āctiō *f.*,
negotiator *n.* lēgātus *m.*, conciliātor *m.*
negro *n.* Aethiops *m.*
neigh *vi.* hinnīre.
neighbour *n.* vīcīnus *m.*, fīnitimus *m.*
neighbourhood *n.* vīcīnia *f.*, vīcīnitās *f.*
neighbouring *a.* vīcīnus, fīnitimus, propinquus.
neighbourly *a.* hūmānus, amīcus.
neighing *n.* hinnītus *m.*
neither *ad.* neque, nec; nēve, neu. *pro.* neuter.
neophyte *n.* tīrō *m.*
nephew *n.* frātris fīlius *m.*, sorōris fīlius *m.*
nereid *n.* Nērēis *f.*
nerve *n.* nervus *m.* (*fig.*) audācia *f.*; (*pl.*) pavor *m.*, trepidātiō *f.* have the — to audēre. *vt.* cōnfirmāre.
nervous *a.* diffīdēns, sollicitus, trepidus. **-ly** *ad.* trepidē.
nervousness *n.* sollicitūdō *f.*, diffīdentia *f.*
nest *n.* nīdus *m.* *vi.* nīdificāre.
nestle *vi.* recubāre.
nestling *n.* pullus *m.*
net *n.* rēte *n.* **drag** — *n.* ēverriculum *n.* *vt.* inrētīre.
nether *a.* inferior. **—most** *a.* īnfimus, īmus.
netting *n.* rēticulum *m.*
nettle *n.* urtīca *f.* *vt.* inrītāre, ūrere.
neuter *a.* neuter.
neutral *a.* medius. be —

neutrī partī sē adiungere, medium sē gerere.
neutralize *vt.* compēnsāre.
never *ad.* nunquam.
nevertheless *ad.* nihilōminus, at tamen.
new *a.* novus, integer, recēns. **-ly** *ad.* nūper, modo.
new-comer *n.* advena *m.*, *f.*
new-fangled *a.* novus, inaudītus.
newness *n.* novitās *f.*
news *n.* nūntius *m.* **what — ?** quid novī ?
newt *n.* lacerta *f.*
next *a.* proximus; (*time*) īnsequēns. **— day** *ad.* postrīdiē. *ad.* dēinde, dēinceps. **— to** iuxtā. **come — to** excipere.
nibble *vi.* rōdere.
nice *a.* bellus, dulcis; (*exact*) accūrātus; (*particular*) fastīdiōsus. **-ly** *ad.* bellē, probē.
nicety *n.* subtīlitās *f.*
niche *n.* aedicula *f.*
nick *n.* **in the — of time** in ipsō articulō temporis.
nickname *n.* cognōmen *n.*
niece *n.* frātris fīlia *f.*, sorōris fīlia *f.* [ālitās *f.*, avāritia *f.*
niggardliness *n.* illīber-
niggardly *a.* illīberālis, parcus, avārus.
nigh *ad.* prope.
night *n.* nox *f.* **by —** noctū. **all —** pernox. **spend the —** pernoctāre. **be awake all —** pervigilāre. *a.* nocturnus.
night-bird *n.* noctua *f.*
nightfall *n.* prīmae tenebrae *f.pl.* **at —** sub noctem.
nightingale *n.* luscinia *f.*
nightly *a.* nocturnus. *ad.* noctū.
nightmare *n.* incubus *m.*
night-work *n.* lūcubrātiō *f*
nimb/le *a.* agilis, pernīx. **-ly** *ad.* perniciter.
nimbleness *n.* agilitās *f.*, pernīcitās *f.*; (*mind*) argūtiae *f.pl.*
nine *num.* novem. **— each** novēnī. **— times** noviēns. **— days'** novendiālis. **— hundred** *num.* nōngentī. **— hundredth** *a.* nōngentēsimus.
nineteen *num.* ūndēvīgintī. **— each** ūndēvīcēnī. **— times** deciēns et noviēns. **-th** *a.* ūndēvīcēsimus.
ninetieth *a.* nōnāgēsimus.
ninety *num.* nōnāgintā. **— each** nōnāgēnī. **— times** nōnāgiēns.
ninth *a.* nōnus.
nip *vt.* vellicāre; (*frost*) ūrere.
nippers *n.* forceps *m.*
nipple *n.* papilla *f.*
no *ad.* nōn; (*correcting*) immo. **say —** negāre. *a.* nullus. **— one** nēmō *m.*
nobility *n.* nōbilitās *f.*; (*persons*) optimātēs *m.pl.*, nōbilēs *m.pl.*
nob/le *a.* nōbilis; (*birth*) generōsus; (*appearance*) decōrus. **-ly** *ad.* nōbiliter, praeclārē.
nobleman *n.* prīnceps *m.*, optimās *m.*
nobody *n.* nēmō *m.*
nocturnal *a.* nocturnus.
nod *n.* nūtus *m.* *vi.* nūtāre; (*sign*) adnuere; (*sleep*) dormītāre.
noddle *n.* caput *n.*
node *n.* nōdus *m.*
noise *n.* strepitus *m.*, sonitus *m.*; (*loud*) fragor *m.* **make a —** increpāre, strepere. *vt.* **— abroad** ēvulgāre. **be -d abroad** percrēbrēscere.
noiseless *a.* tacitus. **-ly** *ad.* tacitē.
noisome *a.* taeter, gravis.
nois/y *a.* clāmōsus. **-ily** *ad.* cum strepitū.
nomadic *a.* vagus. [*n.pl.*
nomenclature *n.* vocābula
nominally *ad.* nōmine, verbō.
nominate *vt.* nōmināre, dīcere; (*in writing*) scrībere.
nomination *n.* nōminātiō *f.*

nominative *a.* nōminātīvus.
nominee *n.* nōminātus *m.* [*f.*
non-appearance *n.* absentia
nonce *n.* for the — semel.
nonchalance *n.* aequus animus *m.*
nonchalantly *ad.* aequō animō.
non-combatant *a.* imbellis.
non-committal *a.* circumspectus.
nondescript *a.* īnsolitus.
none *a.* nullus. *pro.* nēmō *m.*
nonentity *n.* nihil *n.*, nullus.
nones *n.* Nōnae *f.pl.*
non-existent *a.* quī nōn est.
nonplus *vt.* ad incitās redigere.
non-resistance *n.* patientia *f.*
nonsense *n.* nūgae *f.pl.*, ineptiae *f.pl.*
nonsensical *a.* ineptus, absurdus.
nook *n.* angulus *m.*
noon *n.* merīdiēs *m.* *a.* merīdiānus.
noose *n.* laqueus *m.*
nor *ad.* neque, nec; nēve, neu.
norm *n.* nōrma *f.*
normal *a.* solitus. **-ly** *ad.* plērumque.
north *n.* septentriōnēs *m.pl.* *a.* septentriōnālis. — pole arctos *f.* — wind aquilō *m.*
northerly, northern *a.* septentriōnālis.
north-east *ad.* inter septentriōnēs et orientem.
northwards *ad.* ad septentriōnēs versus.
north-west *ad.* inter septentriōnēs et occidentem. *a.* — wind Cōrus *m.*
nose *n.* nāsus *m.*, nārēs *f.pl.* blow the — ēmungere. lead by the — labiīs ductāre. *vi.* scrūtārī.
nostril *n.* nāris *f.*
not *ad.* nōn, haud. — at all haudquāquam. — as if nōn quod, nōn quō. — but what nōn quīn. — even nē . . quidem. — so very nōn ita. that nōn quō. and — neque. does —, did — (*interrog.*) nonne. if . . — nisi. that — (*purpose*) nē; (*fear*) nē nōn.
notability *n.* vir praeclārus *m.*
notab/le *a.* īnsignis, īnsignītus. **-ly** *ad.* īnsignītē.
notary *n.* scrība *m.*
notation *n.* notae *f.pl.*
notch *n.* incīsūra *f.* *vt.* incīdere.
note *n.* (*mark*) nota *f.*; (*comment*) adnotātiō *f.*; (*letter*) litterulae *f.pl.*; (*sound*) vōx *f.* make a — of in commentāriōs referre. *vt.* notāre; (*observe*) animadvertere.
note-book *n.* pugillārēs *m.pl.*
noted *a.* īnsignis, praeclārus.
noteworthy *a.* memorābilis.
nothing *n.* nihil, nīl *n.* — but merus, nīl nisī. come to — in inritum cadere. for — frustrā; (*gift*) grātis, grātuītō. good for — nēquam. think — of nihilī facere.
notice *n.* (*official*) prōscrīptiō *f.*; (*private*) libellus *m.* attract — cōnspicī. escape the — latēre. escape the — of fallere. give — of dēnūntiāre. take — of animadvertere. *vt.* animadvertere, cōnspicere.
noticeab/le *a.* cōnspicuus, īnsignis. **-ly** *ad.* īnsignītē.
notification *n.* dēnūntiātiō *f.*
notify *vt.* (*event*) dēnūntiāre, indicāre; (*person*) renūntiāre (*dat.*), certiōrem facere.
notion *n.* nōtio *f.*, īnfōrmātiō *f.*; suspiciō *f.*
notoriety *n.* īnfāmia *f.*
notorious *a.* fāmōsus, īnfāmis; (*thing*) manifestus. **-ly** *ad.* manifestō.
notwithstanding *ad.* nihilōminus, tamen. *pr.* — the danger in tantō discrīmine.
nought *n.* nihil, nīl, *n.*
noun *n.* nōmen *n.*
nourish *vt.* alere, nūtrīre.

nourisher *n.* altor *m.*, altrīx *f.*
nourishment *n.* cibus *m.*, alimenta *n.pl.*
novel *a.* novus, inaudītus. *n.* fābella *f.*
novelty *n.* rēs nova *f.*; novitās *f.*, īnsolentia *f.*
November *n.* mēnsis November. of — November.
novice *n.* tīrō *m.*
now *ad.* nunc; (*past*) iam. — and then interdum. just — nunc; (*lately*) dūdum, modo. — . . — modo . . . modo. *conj.* at, autem.
nowadays *ad.* nunc, hodiē.
nowhere *ad.* nusquam.
nowise *ad.* nullō modō, haudquāquam.
noxious *a.* nocēns, noxius.
nuance *n.* color *m.*
nucleus *n.* sēmen *n.*
nude *a.* nūdus.
nudge *vt.* fodicāre.
nudity *n.* nūdātum corpus *n.*
nugget *n.* massa *f.*
nuisance *n.* malum *n.*, incommodum *n.*
null *a.* inritus.
nullify *vt.* inritum facere; (*law*) abrogāre.
numb *a.* torpēns, torpidus. be — torpēre. become — torpēscere.
number *n.* numerus *m.* a — of complūrēs, aliquot. a great — multitūdō *f.*, frequentia *f.* a small — īnfrequentia *f.* in large -s frequentēs. *vt.* numerāre, ēnumerāre.
numberless *a.* innumerābilis.
numbness *n.* torpor *m.*
numerous *a.* frequēns, crēber, plūrimī.
nun *n.* monacha *f.*
nuptial *a.* nūptiālis. **-s** *n.* nūptiae *f.pl.*
nurse *n.* nūtrīx *f.* *vt.* (*child*) nūtrīre; (*sick*) cūrāre; (*fig.*) fovēre. [alumna *f.*
nursling *n.* alumnus *m.*,
nursery *n.* (*children*) cubiculum *n.*; (*plants*) sēminārium *n.*
nurture *n.* ēducātiō *f.*
nut *n.* nux *f.* — shell *n.* putāmen *n.* — tree *n.* nux. *f.*
nutriment, nutrition *n.* alimenta *n.pl.*
nutritious *a.* salūbris.
nymph *n.* nympha *f.*

O

o *interj.* ō!
oaf *n.* agrestis *m.*
oak *n.* quercus *f.*; (*evergreen*) īlex *f.*; (*timber*) rōbur *n.* *a.* quernus, īlignus, rōboreus. — forest quercētum *n.*
oakum *n.* stuppa *f.*
oar *n.* rēmus *m.*
oarsman *n.* rēmex *m.*
oaten *a.* avēnāceus.
oath *n.* iūsiūrandum *n.*; (*mil.*) sacrāmentum *n.*; (*imprecation*) exsecrātiō *f.* false — periūrium *n.* take an — iūrāre. take an — of allegiance to in verba iūrāre (*gen.*).
oats *n.* avēna *f.*
obduracy *n.* obstinātus animus *m.*
obdurate *a.* obstinātus, pervicāx. **-ly** *ad.* obstinātē.
obedience *n.* oboedientia *f.*, obsequium *n.*
obedient *a.* oboediēns, obsequēns. be — to pārēre (*dat.*), obtemperāre (*dat.*), obsequī (*dat.*). **-ly** *ad.* oboedienter.
obeisance *n.* obsequium *n.* make — to adōrāre.
obelisk *n.* obeliscus *m.*
obese *a.* obēsus, pinguis.
obesity *n.* obēsitās *f.*, pinguitūdō *f.*
obey *vt.* pārēre (*dat.*), obtemperāre (*dat.*), oboedīre (*dat.*). — orders dictō pārēre.
obituary *n.* mortēs *f.pl.*
object *n.* rēs *f.*; (*aim*) fīnis *m.*, prōpositum *n.* be an — of

hate odiō esse. with what — quō cōnsiliō. *vi.* recūsāre, gravārī. but, it is -ed at enim. — to improbāre.
objection *n.* recūsātiō *f.*, mora *f.* I have no — nīl moror.
objectionable *a.* invīsus, iniūcundus.
objective *a.* externus. *n.* prōpositum *n.*, fīnis *m.*
objurgate *vt.* obiūrgāre, culpāre.
oblation *n.* dōnum *n.*
obligation *n.* (*legal*) dēbitum *n.*; (*moral*) officium *n.* lay under an — obligāre, obstringere.
obligatory *a.* dēbitus, necessārius.
oblige *vt.* (*force*) cōgere; (*contract*) obligāre, obstringere; (*compliance*) mōrem gerere (*dat.*), mōrigerārī (*dat.*). I am -d to (*action*) dēbeō (*inf.*); (*person*) amāre, grātiam habēre (*dat.*).
obliging *a.* cōmis, officiōsus. -ly *ad.* cōmiter, officiōsē.
oblique *a.* oblīquus. -ly *ad.* oblīquē. [*f.*
obliquity *n.* (*moral*) prāvitās
obliterate *vt.* dēlēre, oblitterāre.
obliteration *n.* litūra *f.*
oblivion *n.* oblīviō *f.*
oblivious *a.* oblīviōsus, immemor.
oblong *a.* oblongus.
obloquy *n.* vituperātiō *f.*, opprobrium *n.*
obnoxious *a.* invīsus.
obol *n.* obolus *m.* [pūrus.
obscene *a.* obscaenus, im-
obscenity *n.* obscaenitās *f.* impūritās *f.*
obscure *a.* obscūrus, caecus. *vt.* obscūrāre, officere (*dat.*). -ly *ad.* obscūrē; (*speech*) per ambāgēs.
obscurity *n.* obscūritās *f.*; (*speech*) ambāgēs *f.pl.*
obsequies *n.* exsequiae *f.pl.*
obsequious *a.* officiōsus, ambitiōsus. -ly *ad.* officiōsē.
obsequiousness *n.* adsentātiō *f.*
observance *n.* observantia *f.*; (*rite*) rītus *m.* [gēns.
observant *a.* attentus, dīli-
observation *n.* observātiō *f.*, animadversiō *f.*; (*remark*) dictum *n.*
observe *vt.* animadvertere, contemplārī; (*see*) cernere, cōnspicere; (*remark*) dicere; (*adhere to*) cōnservāre, observāre.
observer *n.* spectātor *m.*, contemplātor *m.*
obsess *vt.* occupāre. I am -ed by tōtus sum in (*abl.*).
obsession *n.* studium *n.*
obsolescent *a.* be — obsolēscere.
obsolete *a.* obsolētus. become — exolēscere.
obstacle *n.* impedīmentum *n.*, mora *f.*
obstinacy *n.* pertinācia *f.*, obstinātus animus *m.*
obstinate *a.* pertināx, obstinātus. -ly *ad.* obstinātō animō.
obstreperous *a.* clāmōsus, ferus.
obstruct *vt.* impedīre, obstruere, obstāre (*dat.*); (*pol.*) intercēdere (*dat.*); (*fig.*) officere (*dat.*).
obstruction *n.* impedīmentum *n.*; (*pol.*) intercessiō *f.*
obstructionist *n.* intercessor *m.*
obtain *vt.* adipīscī, nancīscī, cōnsequī; (*by request*) impetrāre. *vi.* tenēre, obtinēre.
obtrude *vi.* sē inculcāre. *vt.* ingerere.
obtrusive *a.* importūnus, molestus.
obtuse *a.* hebes, stolidus. -ly *ad.* stolidē.
obtuseness *n.* stupor *m.*
obverse *a.* obversus.

obviate *vt.* tollere, praevertere.
obvious *a.* ēvidēns, manifestus, apertus. **-ly** *ad.* ēvidenter, apertē, manifestō. it is — appāret.
occasion *n.* occāsiō *f.*, locus *m.*; (*reason*) causa *f.* *vt.* movēre, facessere, auctōrem esse (*gen.*).
occasional *a.* fortuītus. **-ly** *ad.* interdum, nōnnunquam.
occidental *a.* occidentālis.
occult *a.* arcānus.
occupancy *n.* possessiō *f.*
occupant *n.* habitātor *m.*, possessor *m.*
occupation *n.* quaestus *m.*, occupātiō *f.*
occupier *n.* possessor *m.*
occupy *vt.* possidēre; (*mil.*) occupāre; (*space*) complēre; (*attention*) distinēre, occupāre.
occur *vi.* ēvenīre, accidere; (*to mind*) occurrere, in mentem venīre.
occurrence *n.* ēventum *n.*
ocean *n.* mare *n.*, ōceanus *m.*
October *n.* mēnsis Octōber *m.* of — Octōber.
ocular *a.* oculōrum. give— proof of ante oculōs pōnere, videntī dēmōnstrāre.
odd *a.* (*number*) impār, (*moment*) subsecīvus; (*appearance*) novus, īnsolitus. **-ly** *ad.* mīrum in modum.
oddity *n.* novitās *f.*; (*person*) homō rīdiculus *m.*
odds *n.* praestantia *f.* be at — with dissidēre cum. the — are against us imparēs sumus. the — are in our favour superiōrēs sumus.
ode *n.* carmen *n.*
odious *a.* invīsus, odiōsus.
odium *n.* invidia *f.*
odorous *a.* odōrātus.
odour *n.* odor *m.*
of *pr.* *gen.*; (*origin*) ex, dē; (*cause*) *abl.* all — us nōs omnēs. the city — Rome urbs Rōma.
off *ad.* procul; (*prefix*) ab-. — and on interdum. — with you aufer tē. come — ēvādere. well — beātus. well — for abundāns(*abl.*).
offal *n.* quisquiliae *f.pl.*
offence *n.* offēnsiō *f.*; (*legal*) dēlictum *n.* commit an — dēlinquere.
offend *vt.* laedere, offendere. be -ed aegrē ferre. *vi.* dēlinquere. — against peccāre in (*acc.*), violāre.
offender *n.* reus *m.*
offensive *a.* odiōsus; (*smell*) gravis; (*language*) contumēliōsus. take the — bellum īnferre. **-ly** *ad.* odiōsē; graviter.
offer *vt.* offerre, dare, praebēre; (*hand*) porrigere; (*violence*) adferre; (*honour*) dēferre; (*with verb*) profitērī, pollicērī. *n.* condiciō *f.*
offering *n.* dōnum *n.*; (*to the dead*) īnferiae *f.pl.*
off-hand *a.* neglegēns, incūriōsus.
office *n.* (*pol.*) magistrātus *m.*, mūnus *n.*, honōs *m.*; (*kindness*) officium *n.*; (*place*) mēnsa *f.*
officer *n.* praefectus *m.*
official *a.* pūblicus. *n.* adiūtor *m.*, minister *m.* **-ly** *ad.* pūblicē.
officiate *vi.* operārī, officiō [fungī.
officious *a.* molestus. **-ly** *ad.* molestē.
officiousness *n.* occursātiō *f.*
offing *n.* in the — procul.
offscourings *n.* purgāmenta *n.pl.*
offset *vt.* compēnsāre.
offspring *n.* prōgeniēs *f.*, līberī *m.pl.*; (*animal*) fētus *m.*
often *ad.* saepe, saepenumerō. as — as quotiēns. how — quotiēns. so — totiēns. very — persaepe.
ogle *vi.* — at līmīs oculīs intuērī.
ogre *n.* mōnstrum *n.*

oh *interj.* (*joy, surprise*) ōh! (*sorrow*) prō!
oil *n.* oleum *n.* *vt.* ungere.
oily *a.* oleōsus.
ointment *n.* unguentum *n.*
old *a.* (*person*) senex; (*thing*) vetus; (*ancient*) antīquus, prīscus. — age senectūs *f.* — man senex *m.* — woman anus *f.* be ten years — decem annōs habēre. ten years — decem annōs nātus. two years — bīmus. good — antīquus. good — days antīquitās *f.* grow — senēscere. of — quondam.
olden *a.* prīscus, prīstinus.
older *a.* nātū māior, senior.
oldest *a.* nātū māximus.
old-fashioned *a.* antīquus obsolētus.
oldness *n.* vetustās *f.*
oligarchy *n.* paucōrum dominātiō *f.*, optimātium factiō *f.*
olive *n.* olea *f.* — orchard olīvētum *n.*
Olympiad *n.* Olympias *f.*
Olympic *a.* Olympicus. — Games Olympia *n.pl.* win an — victory Olympia vincere.
omen *n.* ōmen *n.*, auspicium *n.* announce a bad — obnūntiāre. obtain favourable -s litāre.
ominous *a.* īnfaustus, mināx.
omission *n.* praetermissiō *f.*, neglegentia *f.*
omit *vt.* ōmittere, praetermittere.
omnipotence *n.* īnfīnīta potestās *f.*
omnipotent *a.* omnipotēns.
on *pr.* (*place*) in (*abl.*), in- (*prefix*,; (*time*) *abl.*; (*coast of*) ad (*acc.*); (*subject*) dē (*abl.*); (*side*) ab (*abl.*). *ad.* porrō, usque. and so — ac deinceps. — hearing the news nūntiō accepto.
once *ad.* semel; (*past*) ōlim, quondam. at — extemplō, statim; (*together*) simul. for — aliquandō. — and for all semel. — more dēnuō, iterum. — upon a time ōlim, quondam.
one *num.* ūnus. *pro.* quīdam. — and the same ūnus. — another inter sē, alius alium. — or the other alteruter. — day ōlim. — each singulī. — would have thought crēderēs. be — of in numerō esse (*gen.*). be at — idem sentīre. it is all — nihil interest. the — alter, hic. this is the — hōc illud est.
one-eyed *a.* luscus.
oneness *n.* ūnitās *f.*
onerous *a.* gravis.
oneself *pro.* ipse; (*reflexive*) sē.
one-sided *a.* inaequālis, inīquus.
onion *n.* caepe *n.*
onlooker *n.* spectātor *m.*
only *a.* ūnus, sōlus; (*son*) ūnicus. *ad.* sōlum, tantum, modo; (*with clause*) nōn nisī, nīl nisī, nihil aliud quam; (*time*) dēmum. if — sī modo; (*wish*) utinam.
onrush *n.* incursus *m.*
onset *n.* impetus *m.*
onslaught *n.* incursus *m.* make an — on (*words*) invehī in (*acc.*).
onus *n.* officium *n.*
onward, onwards *ad.* porrō.
onyx *n.* onyx *m.*
ooze *vi.* mānāre, stillāre
opaque *a.* haud perlūcidus.
open *a.* apertus; (*wide*) patēns, hiāns; (*ground*) pūrus, apertus; (*question*) integer. lie — patēre. stand — hiāre. stand -mouthed at inhiāre (*dat.*). throw — adaperīre, patefacere. in the — air sub dīvō. it is — to me to mihi integrum est (*inf.*). while the question is still — rē integrā. *vt.* aperīre, patefacere; (*book*) ēvolvere; (*letter*) resolvere; (*speech*) exōrdīrī; (*with ceremony*) inaugurāre; (*will*) resignāre.

vi. aperīrī, hiscere; (*sore*) recrūdēscere. — out extendere, pandere. — up (*country*) aperīre.
open-handed *a.* largus, mūnificus.
open-handedness *n.* largitās *f.*
open-hearted *a.* ingenuus.
opening *n.* forāmen *n.*, hiātus *m.*; (*ceremony*) cōnsecrātiō *f.*, (*opportunity*) occāsiō *f.*, ānsa *f.* *a.* prīmus.
openly *ad.* palam, apertē.
operate *vi.* rem gerere. *vt.* movēre.
operation *n.* opus *n.*, āctiō *f.*; (*med.*) sectiō *f.*
operative *a.* efficāx.
ophthalmia *n.* lippitūdō *f.*
opiate *a.* somnifer.
opine *vi.* opīnārī, exīstimāre.
opinion *n.* sententia *f.*; (*of person*) exīstimātio *f.* public — fāma *f.* in my — meō iūdiciō, meō animō.
opponent *n.* adversārius *m.*, hostis *m.*
opportune *a.* opportūnus, tempestīvus. **-ly** *ad.* opportūnē.
opportunity *n.* occāsiō *f.*; (*to act*) facultās. *f.*
oppose *vt.* (*barrier*) obicere; (*contrast*) oppōnere. *vi.* adversārī (*dat.*), resistere (*dat.*), obstāre (*dat.*). be -d to adversārī (*dat.*); (*opinion*) dīversum esse ab.
opposite *a.* (*facing*) adversus; (*contrary*) contrārius, dīversus. *pr.* contrā (*acc.*), adversus (*acc.*). directly — ē regione (*gen.*). *ad.* ex adversō.
opposition *n.* repugnantia *f.*; (*party*) factiō adversa *f.*
oppress *vt.* opprimere, adflīgere; (*burden*) premere, onerāre. [servitūs *f.*
oppression *n.* iniūria *f.*,
oppressive *a.* gravis, inīquus. become more — ingravēscere.
oppressor *n.* tyrannus *m.*
opprobrious *a.* turpis. **-ly** *ad.* turpiter. [ignōminia *f.*
opprobrium *n.* dēdecus *n.*,
optical *a.* oculōrum.
optimism *n.* spēs *f.*
option *n.* optiō *f.*, arbitrium *n.* I have no — nōn est arbitriī meī.
optional *a.* it is — for you optiō tua est.
opulence *n.* opēs *f.pl.*, cōpia *f.*
opulent *a.* dīves, cōpiōsus.
or *conj.* aut, vel, -ve; (*after* utrum) an. — else aliōquin. — not (*direct*) annōn; (*indirect*) necne.
oracle *n.* ōrāculum *n.*
oracular *a.* fātidicus. (*fig.*) obscūrus.
oral *a.* give an — message vōce nūntiāre. **-ly** *ad.* vōce, verbīs.
oration *n.* ōrātiō *f.*
orator *n.* ōrātor *m.*
oratorical *a.* ōrātōrius.
oratory *n.* ēloquentia *f.*, rhētoricē *f.*; (*for prayer*) sacellum *n.* of — dīcendī, ōrātōrius.
orb *n.* orbis *m.*
orbit *n.* orbis *m.*, ambitus *m.*
orchard *n.* pōmārium *n.*
ordain *vt.* ēdīcere, sancīre.
ordeal *n.* labor *m.*
order *n.* (*arrangement*) ōrdō *m.*; (*class*) ōrdō *m.*; (*battle*) aciēs *f.*; (*command*) iussum *n.*, imperātum *n.*; (*money*) perscrīptiō *f.* in — dispositus; (*succession*) deinceps. in — that ut. in — that not nē. put in — dispōnere, ōrdināre. by — of iussū (*gen.*). out of — incompositus. without -s from iniussū (*gen.*). *vt.* (*arrange*) dispōnere, ōrdināre. (*command*) iubēre, imperāre (*dat.*).
orderly *a.* ōrdinātus; (*conduct*) modestus. *n.* accēnsus *m.*
ordinance *n.* ēdictum *n.*, institūtum *n.*

ordinar/y *a.* ūsitātus, solitus, cottīdiānus. **-ily** *ad.* plērumque, ferē.
ordnance *n.* tormenta *n.pl.*
ordure *n.* stercus *m.*
ore *n.* aes *n.* iron — ferrum īnfectum *n.*
oread *n.* oreas *f.*
organ *n.* (*bodily*) membrum *n.*; (*musical*) organum *n.*, hydraulus *m.*
organic *a.* nātūrālis. **-ally** *ad.* nātūrā.
organization *n.* ōrdinātiō *f.*, structūra *f.*
organize *vt.* ōrdināre, īnstituere, adparāre.
orgy *n.* cōmissātiō *f.*; (*pl.*) orgia *n.pl.*
orient *n.* oriēns *m.*
oriental *a.* Asiāticus.
orifice *n.* ōstium *n.*
origin *n.* origō *f.*, prīncipium *n.*; (*source*) fōns *m.*; (*birth*) genus *n.*
original *a.* prīmus, prīstinus; (*lit.*) proprius. *n.* exemplar *n.* **-ly** *ad.* prīncipiō, antīquitus.
originate *vt.* īnstituere, auctōrem esse (*gen.*). *vi.* exorīrī. — in innāscī in (*abl.*), initium dūcere ab.
originator *n.* auctor *m.*
orisons *n.* precēs *f.pl.*
ornament *n.* ōrnāmentum *n.*; (*fig.*) decus *n.* *vt.* ōrnāre, decorāre.
ornamental *a.* decōrus. be — decorī esse. **-ly** *ad.* ōrnātē.
ornate *a.* ōrnātus. **-ly** *ad.* ōrnātē.
orphan *n.* orbus *m.*, orba *f.*
orphaned *a* orbātus.
orthodox *a.* antīquus. [*f.*
orthography *n.* orthographia
oscillate *vi.* reciprocāre.
osculate *vt.* ōsculārī.
osier *n.* vīmen *n.* *a.* vīmineus.
osprey *n.* haliaeetos *m.*
ostensib/le *a.* speciōsus. **-ly** *ad.* per speciem.
ostentation *n.* iactātiō *f.*, ostentātiō *f.*
ostentatious *a.* glōriōsus, ambitiōsus. **-ly** *ad.* glōriōsē.
ostler *n.* agāsō *m.*
ostrich *n.* strūthiocamēlus *m.*
other *a.* alius; (*of two*) alter. one or the — alteruter. every — year tertiō quōque annō. of -s aliēnus.
otherwise *ad.* aliter; (*if not*) aliōquī.
otter *n.* lutra *f.*
ought *vi.* dēbēre. I — mē oportet. I — to have said dēbuī dīcere.
ounce *n.* ūncia *f.* two -s sextāns *m* three -s quadrāns *m.* four -s triēns *m.* five -s quīncūnx *m.* six -s sēmis *m.* seven -s septūnx *m.* eight -s bēs *m.* nine -s dōdrāns *m.* ten -s dextāns *m.* eleven -s deūnx *m.*
our *a.* noster. **-selves** *pro.* ipsī; (*reflexive*) nōs.
oust *vt.* extrūdere, ēicere.
out *ad* (*rest*) forīs; (*motion*) forās. — of dē, ex (*abl.*); (*cause*) propter (*acc.*); (*beyond*) extrā, ultrā (*acc.*). be — (*book*) in manibus esse; (*calculation*) errāre; (*fire*) exstīnctum esse; (*secret*) palam esse.
outbreak *n* initium *n.*, ēruptiō *f.*
outburst *n.* ēruptiō *f.*
outcast *n.* profugus *m.*
outcome *n.* ēventus *m.*, exitus *m.*
outcry *n.* clāmor *m.*, adclāmātiō *f.* raise an — against obstrepere (*dat.*).
outdistance *vt.* praevertere.
outdo *vt.* superāre.
outdoor *a.* sub dīvō.
outer *a.* exterior. **-most** *a.* extrēmus.
outfit *n.* īnstrūmenta *n.pl.*; vestīmenta *n.pl.*
outflank *vt.* circumīre.
outgrow *vt.* excēdere ex.

outing *n.* excursiō *f.*
outlandish *a.* barbarus.
outlaw *n.* prōscrīptus *m.* *vt.* prōscrībere, aquā et ignī interdīcere (*dat.*).
outlawry *n.* aquae et ignis interdictiō *f.*
outlay *n.* impēnsa *f.*, sūmptus [*m.*
outlet *n.* ēmissārium *n.*, exitus *m.*
outline *n.* ductus *m.*, adumbrātiō *f.* *vt.* adumbrāre.
outlive *vt.* superesse (*dat.*).
outlook *n.* prōspectus *m.*
outlying *a.* longinquus, exterior.
outnumber *vt.* numerō superiōrēs esse, multitūdine superāre.
outpost *n.* statiō *f.*
outpouring *n.* effūsiō *f.*
output *n.* fructus *m.*
outrage *n.* flāgitium *n.*, iniūria *f.* *vt.* laedere, violāre.
outrageous *a.* flāgitiōsus, indignus. **-ly** *ad.* flāgitiōsē.
outrider *n.* praecursor *m.*
outright *ad.* penitus, prōrsus; semel.
outrun *vt.* praevertere.
outset *n.* initium *n.*
outshine *vt.* prælūcēre (*dat.*).
outside *a.* externus. *ad.* extrā, forīs; (*motion to*) forās. — in inversus. from — extrīnsecus. *n.* exterior pars *f.*; (*show*) speciēs *f.* at the — summum, ad summum. on the — extrīnsecus. *pr.* extrā (*acc.*).
outsider *n.* aliēnus *m.*; (*pol.*) novus homō *m.*
outskirts *n.* suburbānus ager *m.* on the — suburbānus.
outspoken *a.* līber.
outspokenness *n.* lībertās *f.*
outspread *a.* patulus.
outstanding *a.* ēgregius, īnsignis, singulāris; (*debt*) residuus.
outstep *vt.* excēdere.
outstretched *a.* passus, porrēctus, extentus.
outstrip *vt.* praevertere.
outvote *vt.* suffrāgiīs superāre.
outward *a.* externus. — form speciēs *f.* *ad.* domō, forās.
outweigh *vt.* praeponderāre.
outwit *vt.* dēcipere circumvenīre.
outwork *n.* prōpugnāculum *n.*, bracchium *n.*
outworn *a.* exolētus.
oval *a.* ōvātus. *n.* ōvum *n.*
ovation *n.* (*triumph*) ovātiō *f.* receive an — cum laudibus excipī.
oven *n.* furnus *m.*, fornāx *f.*
over *pr.* (*above*) super (*abl.*), suprā (*acc.*); (*across*) super (*acc.*); (*extent*) per (*acc.*); (*time*) inter (*acc.*). — and above super (*acc.*), praeter (*acc.*). all — per. — against adversus (*acc.*). *ad.* suprā; (*excess*) nimis; (*done*) cōnfectus. — again dēnuō. — and above īnsuper. — and — identidem. be left — superesse, restāre. it is all — with āctum est dē.
overall *a.* tōtus. *ad.* ubīque, passim.
overawe *vt.* formīdinem inicere (*dat.*).
overbalance *vi.* titubāre.
overbearing *a.* superbus.
overboard *ad.* ē nāvī, in mare. throw — excutere, iactāre.
overbold *a.* importūnus.
overburden *vt.* praegravāre.
overcast *a.* nūbilus. [*f.*
overcoat *n.* paenula *f.*, lacerna
overcome *vt.* superāre, vincere.
over-confidence *n.* cōnfīdentia *f.*
over-confident *a.* cōnfīdēns.
overdo *vt.* modum excēdere in (*abl.*). -ne *a.* (*style*) pūtidus.
overdraw *vt.* (*style*) exaggerāre.
overdue *a.* (*money*) residuus.
overestimate *vt.* māiōris aestimāre.
overflow *n.* ēluviō *f.* *vi.*

abundāre, redundāre. *vt.* inundāre.
overgrown *a.* obsitus. be — luxuriāre.
overhang *vt.* & *i.* impendēre imminēre (*dat.*).
overhaul *vt.* reficere.
overhead *ad.* insuper.
overhear *vt.* excipere, auscultāre.
overjoyed *a.* nimiō gaudiō ēlātus.
overladen *a.* praegravātus.
overland *ad.* terrā.
overlap *vt.* implicāre.
overlay *vt.* indūcere.
overload *vt.* (*fig.*) obruere.
overlook *vt.* (*place*) dēspectāre, imminēre (*dat.*); (*knowledge*) ignōrāre; (*notice*) neglegere, praetermittere; (*fault*) ignōscere (*dat.*).
overlord *n.* dominus *m.*
overmaster *vt.* dēvincere.
overmuch *ad.* nimis, plūs aequō.
overnight *a.* nocturnus. *ad.* noctū.
overpower *vt.* superāre domāre, obruere, opprimere.
overpraise *vt.* in māius extollere.
overrate *vt.* māiōris aestimāre.
overreach *vt.* circumvenire.
overriding *a.* praecipuus.
overrule *vt.* rescindere.
overrun *vt.* pervagārī; (*fig.*) obsidēre.
oversea *a.* trānsmarinus.
oversee *vt.* præesse (*dat.*)
overseer *n.* cūrātor *m.* custōs *m.*
overset *vt.* ēvertere.
overshadow *vt.* officere (*dat.*).
overshoot *vt.* excēdere.
oversight *n.* neglegentia *f.*
overspread *vt.* offendere (*dat.*), obdūcere.
overstep *vt.* excēdere.
overt *a.* apertus. **-ly** *ad.* palam.
overtake *vt.* cōnsequī; (*surprise*) opprimere, dēprehendere.
overtax *vt.* (*fig.*) abūti (*abl.*).
overthrow *vt.* ēvertere; (*destroy*) prōfligāre, dēbellāre. *n.* ēversiō *f.*, ruina *f.*
overtop *vt.* superāre.
overture *n.* exōrdium *n.* make -s to temptāre, agere cum, lēgātōs mittere ad.
overturn *vt.* ēvertere.
overweening *a.* superbus, adrogāns, insolēns.
overwhelm *vt.* obruere, dēmergere.
overwhelming *a.* insignis, vehementissimus. **— ly** *ad.* mīrum quantum.
overwork *vi.* plūs aequō labōrāre. *vt.* cōnficere. *n.* immodicus labor *m.*
overwrought *a.* (*emotion*) ēlātus; (*style*) ēlabōrātus.
owe *vt.* dēbēre.
owing *a.* be — dēbērī. — to (*person*) per; (*cause*) propter.
owl *n.* būbō *m.*
own *a.* proprius. my — meus. have of one's —domī habēre. hold one's — parem esse. *vt.* possidēre, habēre; (*admit*) fatērī, cōnfitērī.
owner *n.* dominus *m.*, possessor *m.*
ownership *n.* possessiō *f.*, mancipium *n.*
ox *n.* bōs *m.*
ox-herd *n.* bubulcus *m.*
oyster *n.* ostrea *f.*

P

pace *n.* passus *m.*; (*speed*) gradus *m.* keep — gradum cōnferre. *vi.* incēdere. — up and down spatiārī, inambulāre.
pacific *a.* pācificus; (*quiet*) placidus.
pacification *n.* pācificātiō *f.*
pacifist *n.* imbellis *m.*

pacify *vt.* (*anger*) plācāre; (*rising*) sēdāre.
pack *n.* (*mil.*) sarcina *f.*; (*animals*) grex *m.*; (*people*) turba *f.* *vt.* (*kit*) colligere; (*crowd*) stipāre. — together coartāre. — up colligere, compōnere. *vi.* vāsa colligere. send —ing missum facere. *a.* (*animal*) clītellārius.
package *n.* fasciculus *m.*, sarcina *f.*
packet *n.* fasciculus *m.*; (*ship*) nāvis āctuāria *f.*
pack-horse *n.* iūmentum *n.*
pack-saddle *n.* clītellae *f.pl.*
pact *n.* foedus *n.*, pactum *n.*
pad *n.* pulvillus *m.*
padding *n.* tōmentum *n.*
paddle *n.* rēmus *m.* *vi.* rēmigāre.
paddock *n.* saeptum *n.*
paean *n.* paeān *m.*
pagan *a.* pāgānus.
page *n.* (*book*) pāgina *f.*; (*boy*) puer *m.* [culum *n.*
pageant *n.* pompa *f.*, spectā-
pageantry *n.* adparātus *m.*
pail *n.* situla *f.*
pain *n.* dolor *m.*; (*pl.*) opera *f.* be in — dolēre. take -s operam dare. take -s with (*art*) ēlabōrāre. *vt.* dolōre adficere.
painful *a.* acerbus; (*work*) labōriōsus. **-ly** *ad.* acerbē, labōriōsē.
painless *a.* dolōris expers. **-ly** *ad.* sine dolōre.
painlessness *n.* indolentia *f.*
painstaking *a.* dīligēns, operōsus. **-ly** *ad* dīligenter, summā cūrā.
paint *n.* pigmentum *n.*; (*cosmetic*) fūcus *m.* *vt.* pingere, (*red*) fūcāre; (*in words*) dēpingere; (*portrait*) dēpingere.
painter *n.* pictor *m.*
painting *n.* pictūra *f.*
paint-brush *n.* pēnicillus *m.*
pair *n.* pār *n.* *vt.* coniungere, compōnere.
palace *n.* rēgia *f.*
palatable *a.* suāvis, iūcundus.
palate *n.* palātum *n.*
palatial *a.* rēgius.
palaver *n.* colloquium *n.*, sermunculī *m.pl.*
pale *n.* pālus *m.*, vallus *m.* beyond the — extrāneus. *a.* pallidus. look — pallēre. grow — pallēscere. — brown subfuscus. — green subviridis. *vi.* pallēscere.
paleness *n.* pallor *m.* [*m.*
palimpsest *n.* palimpsēstus
paling *n.* saepēs *f.*
palisade *n.* (*mil.*) vallum *n.*
palish *a.* pallidulus. [*vi.* taedet.
pall *n.* (*funeral*) pallium *n.*
pallet *n.* grabātus *m.*
palliasse *n.* strāmentum *n.*
palliate *vt.* extenuāre, excūsāre.
palliation *n.* excūsātiō *f.*
palliative *n.* lēnīmentum *n.*
pallid *a.* pallidus.
pallor *n.* pallor *m.*
palm *n.* (*hand*) palma *f.*; (*tree*) palma *f.* *vt.* — off impōnere.
palmy *a.* flōrēns.
palpab/le *a.* tractābilis; (*fig.*) manifestus. **-ly** *ad.* manifestō, propalam.
palpitate *vi.* palpitāre, micāre.
palpitation *n.* palpitātiō *f.*
palsied *a.* membrīs captus.
palsy *n.* paralysis *f.*
paltry *a.* vīlis, frīvolus.
pamper *vt.* indulgēre (*dat.*). **-ed** *a.* dēlicātus.
pamphlet *n.* libellus *m.*
pan *n.* patina *f.*, patella *f.*; (*frying*) sartāgō *f.*; (*of balance*) lanx *f.*
pancake *n.* laganum *n.*
pander *n.* lēnō *m.* *vi.* — to lēnōcinārī (*dat.*).
panegyric *n.* laudātiō *f.*
panegyrist *n.* laudātor *m.*
panel *n.* (*wall*) abacus *m.*; (*ceiling*) lacūnār *n.*; (*judges*) decuria *f.*

panelled *a.* laqueātus.
pang *n.* dolor *m.*
panic *n.* pavor *m.* — **stricken** *a.* pavidus.
panniers *n.* clītellae *f.pl.*
panoply *n.* arma *n.pl.*
panorama *n.* prōspectus *m.*
Pan-pipe *n.* fistula *f.*
pant *vi.* anhēlāre.
panther *n.* panthēra *f.*
panting *n.* anhēlitus *m.*
pantomime *n.* mīmus *m.*
pantry *n.* cella penāria *f.*
pap *n.* mamma *f.*
paper *n.* charta *f.* **news** — *n.* ācta diūrna *n.pl.*
papyrus *n.* papyrus *f.*
par *n.* on a — with pār (*dat.*).
parable *n.* parabolē *f.*
parade *n.* pompa *f.*; (*show*) adparātus *m.* *vt.* trādūcere, iactāre *vi.* pompam dūcere, incēdere.
paradox *n.* verba sēcum repugnantia, (*pl.*) paradoxa *n.pl.*
paragon *n.* exemplar *n.*, specimen *n.*
paragraph *n.* caput *n.*
parallel *a.* parallēlus; (*fig.*) cōnsimilis.
paralyse *vt.* dēbilitāre; (*with fear*) percellere. be -d torpēre.
paralysis *n.* dēbilitās *f.*; (*fig.*) torpēdō *f.*
paramount *a.* princeps, summus.
paramour *n.* adulter *m.*
parapet *n.* lōrīca *f.* [*m.*
paraphernalia *n.* adparātus
paraphrase *vt.* vertere.
parasite *n.* parasītus *m.*
parasol *n.* umbella *f.*
parboiled *a.* subcrūdus.
parcel *n.* fasciculus *m.* *vt.* — out distribuere dispertīre.
parch *vt.* torrēre. **-ed** *a.* torridus, āridus. be — ārēre.
parchment *n* membrāna *f.*
pardon *n.* venia *f.* *vt.* ignōscere (*dat.*); (*offence*) condōnāre.
pardonable *a.* ignōscendus.
pare *vt.* dēglūbere; (*nails*) resecāre.
parent *n.* parēns *m.*, *f.*, genitor *m.*, genetrix *f.* [*n.*
parentage *n.* stirps *f.*, genus
parental *a.* patrius.
parenthesis *n.* interclūsiō *f.*
parings *n.* praesegmina *n.pl.*
parish *n.* (*eccl.*) paroecia *f.*
parity *n.* aequālitās *f.*
park *n.* hortī *m.pl.*
parlance *n.* sermō *m.*
parley *n.* colloquium *n.* *vi.* colloquī, agere.
parliament *n.* senātus *m.* house of — cūria *f.*
parliamentary *a.* senātōrius.
parlour *n.* exedrium *n.*
parlous *a.* difficilis, perīculōsus.
parochial *a.* mūnicipālis.
parody *n.* carmen ioculāre *n.* *vt.* calumniārī.
parole *n.* fidēs *f.*
paronomasia *n.* agnōminātiō *f.*
paroxysm *n.* accessus *m.*
parricide *n.* (*doer*) parricīda *m.*; (*deed*) parricīdium *n.*
parrot *n.* psittacus *m.*
parry *vt.* ēlūdere, prōpulsāre.
parsimonious *a.* parcus. **-ly** *ad.* parcē.
parsimony *n.* parsimōnia *f.*, frūgālitās *f.*
part *n.* pars *f.*; (*play*) partēs *f.pl.*, persōna *f.*; (*duty*) officium *n.* -s loca *n.pl.*; (*ability*) ingenium *n.* for my — equidem. for the most — māximam partem. on the — of ab. act the — of persōnam sustinēre, partēs agere. have no — in expertem esse (*gen.*). in — partim. it is the — of a wise man sapientis est. play one's — officiō satisfacere. take — in interesse (*dat.*), participem esse (*gen.*). take in good — in bonam partem accipere. take someone's — adesse alicui, dēfendere ali-

quem. from all -s undique. in foreign -s peregrē. in two -s bifāriam; (*mil.*) bipartītō. in three -s trifāriam; (*mil.*) tripartītō. of -s ingeniōsus. *vt.* dīvidere, sēparāre, dirimere. — company dīversōs discēdere. *vi.* dīgredī, discēdere; (*things*) dissilīre. — with renūntiāre.
partake *vi.* interesse, participem esse. — of gustāre.
partial *a.* (*biased*) inīquus, studiōsus; (*incomplete*) mancus. be — to favēre (*dat.*), studēre (*dat.*). win a — victory aliquā ex parte vincere. **-ly** *ad.* partim, aliquā ex parte.
partiality *n.* favor *m.*, studium *n.*
participant *n.* particeps *m.*, *f.*
participate *vi.* interesse, participem esse.
participation *n.* societās *f.*
particle *n.* particula *f.*
parti-coloured *a.* versicolor, varius.
particular *a.* (*own*) proprius; (*special*) praecipuus; (*exact*) dīligēns, accūrātus; (*fastidious*) fastīdiōsus. a — person quīdam. *n.* rēs *f.* with full -s subtīliter. give all the -s omnia exsequī. in — praesertim. **-ly** *ad.* praecipuē, praesertim, in prīmīs, māximē.
particularity *n.* subtīlitās *f.*
particularize *vt.* singula exsequī.
parting *n.* dīgressus *m.* discessus *m.* *a.* ultimus.
partisan *n.* fautor *m.*, studiōsus *m.*
partisanship *n.* studium *n.*
partition *n.* (*act*) partītiō *f.*; (*wall*) pariēs *m.*; (*compartment*) loculāmentum *n.* *vt.* dīvidere.
partly *ad.* partim, ex parte.
partner *n.* socius *m.*; (*in office*) collēga *f.*
partnership *n.* societās *f.* form a — societātem inīre.
partridge *n.* perdix *m.*, *f.*
parturition *n.* partus *m.*
party *n.* (*pol.*) factiō *f.*, partēs *f.pl.*; (*entertainment*) convīvium *n.*; (*mil.*) manus *f.*; (*individual*) homō *m.*, *f.*; (*associate*) socius *m.*, cōnscius *m.* — spirit studium *n.*
parvenu *n.* novus homō *m.*
pass *n.* (*hill*) saltus *m.*; (*narrow*) angustiae *f.pl.*, faucēs *f.pl.*; (*crisis*) discrīmen *n.*; (*document*) diplōma *n.*; (*fighting*) petītiō *f.* things have come to such a — in eum locum ventum est, adeō rēs rediit. *vi.* īre, praeterīre; (*time*) trānsīre; (*property*) pervenīre. — away abīre; (*die*) morī, perīre; (*fig.*) dēfluere. — by praeterīre. — for habērī prō (*abl.*). — off abīre. — on pergere. — over trānsīre. come to — fierī, ēvenīre. let — intermittere, praetermittere. *vt.* praeterīre; (*riding*) praetervehī; (*by hand*) trādere; (*law*) iubēre; (*limit*) excēdere; (*sentence*) interpōnere, dīcere; (*test*) satisfacere (*dat.*); (*time*) dēgere, agere. — accounts ratiōnēs ratās habēre. — a decree dēcernere. — off ferre. — over praeterīre, mittere; (*fault*) ignōscere (*dat.*). — round trādere. — through trānsīre.
passab/le *a.* (*place*) pervius; (*standard*) mediocris. **-ly** *ad.* mediocriter.
passage *n.* iter *n.*, cursus *m.*; (*land*) trānsitus *m.*; (*sea*) trānsmissiō *f.*; (*book*) locus *m.* of — (*bird*) advena.
passenger *n.* vector *m.*
passer-by *n.* praeteriēns *m.*
passing *n.* obitus *m.* *a.* admodum.
passion *n.* animī mōtus *m.*, permōtiō *f.*, ārdor *m.*; (*anger*) īra *f.*; (*lust*) libīdō *f.*
passionate *a.* ārdēns, impotēns, ācer; īrācundus. **-ly** *ad.* vehementer, ārdenter;

īrācundē. be — in love amōre ārdēre.
passive *a.* iners.
passiveness *n.* inertia *f.*, patientia *f.*
passport *n.* diplōma *n.*
password *n.* tessera *f.*
past *a.* praeteritus; (*recent*) proximus. *n.* praeterita *n.pl.* *pr.* praeter (*acc.*); (*beyond*) ultrā (*acc.*).
paste *n.* glūten *n.* *vt.* glūtināre.
pastime *n.* lūdus *m.*, oblectāmentum *n.*
pastoral *a.* pastōrālis; (*poem*) būcolicus.
pastry *n.* crustum *n.*
pasture *n.* pāstus *m.*, pāscuum *n.* *vt.* pāscere.
pat *vt.* dēmulcēre. *a.* opportūnus. [sarcīre.
patch *n.* pannus *m.* *vt.* re-
patchwork *n.* centō *m.*
pate *n.* caput *n.*
patent *a.* apertus, manifestus. *n.* prīvilēgium *n.* **-ly** *ad.* manifestō.
paternal *a.* paternus.
path *n.* sēmita *f.*, trāmes *m.*
pathetic *a.* miserābilis. **-ally** *ad.* miserābiliter.
pathfinder *n.* explōrātor *m.*
pathless *a.* āvius.
pathos *n.* misericordia *f.*; (*rhet.*) dolor *m.*
pathway *n.* sēmita *f.*
patience *n.* patientia *f.*
patient *a.* patiēns. *n.* aeger *m.* **-ly** *ad.* patienter, aequō animō.
patois *n.* sermō *m.*
patrician *a.* patricius. *n.* patricius *m.*
patrimony *n.* patrimōnium *n.*
patriot *n.* amāns patriae *m.*
patriotic *a.* pius, amāns patriae. **-ally** *ad* prō patriā.
patriotism *n.* amor patriae *m.* [circumīre.
patrol *n.* excubiae *f.pl.* *vi.*
patron *n.* patrōnus *m.*, fautor *m.*
patronage *n.* patrōcinium *n.*
patroness *n.* patrōna *f.*, fautrīx *f.* [fovēre.
patronize *vt.* favēre (*dat.*),
patronymic *n.* nōmen *n.*
patter *vi.* crepitāre. *n.* crepitus *m.*
pattern *n.* exemplar *n.*, exemplum *n.*, nōrma *f.*; (*ideal*) specimen *n.*; (*design*) figūra *f.*
paucity *n.* paucitās *f.*
paunch *n.* abdōmen *n.*, venter *m.*
pauper *n.* pauper *m.*
pause *n.* mora *f.*, intervallum *n.* *vi.* īnsistere, intermittere.
pave *vt.* sternere. — the way (*fig.*) viam mūnīre.
pavement *n.* pavīmentum *n.*
pavilion *n.* tentōrium *n.*
paw *n.* pēs *m.* *vt.* pede pulsāre.
pawn *n.* (*chess*) latrunculus *m.*; (*bus.*) pignus *n.*, fīdūcia *f.* *vt.* oppignerāre [*m.*
pawnbroker *n.* pignerātor
pay *n.* mercēs *f.*; (*mil.*) stīpendium *n.*; (*workman*) manupretium *n.* *vt.* solvere, pendere; (*debt*) exsolvere; (*in full*) persolvere; (*honour*) persolvere; (*mil.*) stīpendium numerāre (*dat.*); (*penalty*) dare, luere. — down numerāre. — for condūcere. — off dissolvere, exsolvere. — out, expendere; (*publicly*) ērogāre. — up dēpendere. — a compliment to laudāre. — respects to salūtāre. *vi.* respondēre. it **-s** expedit.
payable *a.* solvendus.
pay-master *n.* (*mil.*) tribūnus aerārius *m.*
payment *n.* solūtiō *f.*; (*money*) pēnsiō *f.*
pea *n.* pīsum *n.* like as two **-s** tam similis quam lac lactī est.
peace *n.* pāx *f.* — and quiet ōtium *n.* breach of the — vīs *f.* establish — pācem conciliāre. hold one's — re-

ticēre. sue for — pācem petere.
peaceab/le *a.* imbellis, placidus. **-ly** *ad.* placidē.
peaceful *a.* tranquillus, placidus, pācātus. **-ly** *ad.* tranquillē.
peacemaker *n.* pācificus *m.*
peace-offering *n.* piāculum *n.*
peach *n.* Persicum *n.*
peacock *n.* pāvō *m.*
peak *n.* apex *m.*, vertex *m.*
peal *n.* (*bell*) sonitus *m.*; (*thunder*) fragor *m.* *vi.* sonāre.
pear *n.* pirum *n.*; (*tree*) pirus *f.*
pearl *n.* margarita *f.*
pearly *a.* gemmeus; (*colour*) candidus.
peasant *n.* agricola *m.*, colōnus *m.*
peasantry *n.* agricolae *m.pl.*
pebble *n.* calculus *m.*
pebbly *a.* lapidōsus.
peccadillo *n.* culpa *f.*
peck *n.* (*measure*) modius *m.* *vt.* vellicāre.
peculate *vi.* pecūlārī.
peculation *n.* pecūlātus *m.*
peculiar *a.* (*to one*) proprius; (*strange*) singulāris. **-ly** *ad.* praecipuē, praesertim.
peculiarity *n.* proprietās *f.*, nota *f.*
pecuniary *a.* pecūniārius.
pedagogue *n.* magister *m.*
pedant *n.* scholasticus *m.*
pedantic *a.* nimis dīligenter. **-ally** *ad.* dīligentior.
pedantry *n.* nimia dīligentia *f.*
peddle *vt.* circumferre.
pedestal *n.* basis *f.*
pedestrian *a.* pedester. *n.* pedes *m.*
pedigree *n.* stirps *f.*, stemma *n.* *a.* generōsus.
pediment *n.* fastīgium *n.*
pedlar *n.* īnstitor *m.*, circumforāneus *m.*
peel *n.* cortex *m.* *vt.* glūbere.
peep *vi.* dispicere. *n.* aspectus *m.* at — of day prīmā lūce.
peer *vi.* — at intuērī. *n.* pār *m.*; (*rank*) patricius *m.*
peerless *a.* ūnicus, ēgregius.
peevish *a.* stomachōsus, mōrōsus. **-ly** *ad.* stomachōsē, mōrōsē.
peevishness *n.* stomachus *m.*, mōrōsitās *f.*
peg *n.* clāvus *m.* put a round — in a square hole bovi clītellās impōnere. *vt.* clāvis dēfigere.
pelf *n.* lucrum *n.*
pellet *n.* globulus *m.*
pell-mell *ad.* prōmiscuē, turbātē.
pellucid *a.* perlūcidus.
pelt *n.* pellis *f.* *vt.* petere. *vi.* violenter cadere.
pen *n.* calamus *m.*, stilus *m.*; (*cattle*) saeptum *n.* *vt.* scrībere.
penal *a.* poenālis.
penalize *vt.* poenā adficere, multāre.
penalty *n.* poena *f.*, damnum *n.*; (*fine*) multa *f.* pay the — poenās dare.
penance *n.* supplicium *n.*
pencil *n.* graphis *f.*
pending *a.* sub iūdice. *pr.* inter (*acc.*).
penetrable *a.* pervius.
penetrate *vt.* penetrāre.
penetrating *a.* ācer, acūtus; (*mind*) perspicāx.
penetration *n.* (*mind*) acūmen *n.*
peninsula *n.* paenīnsula *f.*
penitence *n.* paenitentia *f.*
penitent *a.* I am — mē paenitet.
penknife *n.* scalpellum *n.*
penmanship *n.* scrīptiō *f.*, manus, *f.*
pennant *n.* vexillum *n.*
penny *n.* dēnārius *m.*
pension *n.* annua *n.pl.*
pensioner *n.* ēmeritus *m.*
pensive *a.* attentus.
pensiveness *n.* cōgitātiō *f.*
pent *a.* inclūsus.
penthouse *n.* (*mil.*) vinea *f.*

penurious *a.* parcus, avārus, tenāx.
penuriousness *n.* parsimōnia *f.*, tenācitās *f.*
penury *n.* egestās *f.*, inopia *f.*
people *n.* hominēs *m.pl.*; (*nation*) populus *m.*, gēns *f.* common — plēbs *f.* *vt.* frequentāre. **-d** *a.* frequēns.
pepper *n.* piper *n.*
peradventure *ad.* fortasse.
perambulate *vi.* spatiārī, inambulāre.
perceive *vt.* sentīre percipere, intellegere.
perceptible *a.* be — sentīrī posse, audīrī posse.
perception *n.* sēnsus *m.*
perch *n.* (*bird's*) pertica *f.*; (*fish*) perca *f.* *vi.* īnsīdere.
perchance *ad.* fortasse, forsitan (*subj.*).
percolate *vi.* permānāre.
percussion *n.* ictus *m.*
perdition *n.* exitium *n.*
peregrinate *vi.* peregrīnārī.
peregrination *n.* peregrīnātiō *f.*
peremptor/y *a.* imperiōsus. **-ily** *ad.* praecīsē, prō imperiō.
perennial *a.* perennis.
perfect *a.* perfectus, absolūtus; (*entire*) integer; (*faultless*) ēmendātus. *vt.* perficere, absolvere. **-ly** *ad.* perfectē, ēmendātē; (*quite*) plānē.
perfection *n.* perfectiō *f.*, absolūtiō *f.*
perfidious *a.* perfidus, perfidiōsus. **-ly** *ad.* perfidiōsē.
perfidy *n.* perfidia *f.*
perforate *vt.* perforāre, terebrāre.
perforation *n.* forāmen *n.*
perforce *ad.* per vim, necessāriō.
perform *vt.* perficere, peragere; (*duty*) exsequī, fungī (*abl.*); (*play*) agere.
performance *n.* (*process*) exsecūtiō *f.*, fūnctiō *f.*; (*deed*) factum *n.*; (*stage*) fābula *f.*
performer *n.* āctor *m.*; (*music*) tībīcen *m.*, fidicen *m.*; (*stage*) histriō *m.*
perfume *n.* odor *m.*, unguentum *n.* *vt.* odōrāre.
perfumer *n.* uguentārius [*m.*
perfumery *n.* unguenta *n.pl.*
perfunctor/y *a.* neglegēns. **-ily** *ad.* neglegenter.
perhaps *ad.* fortasse, forsitan (*subj.*) nescio an (*subj.*); (*tentative*) vel; (*interrog.*) an.
peril *n.* perīculum *m.*, discrīmen *n.*
perilous *a.* perīculōsus. **-ly** *ad.* perīculōsē.
perimeter *n.* ambitus *m.*
period *n.* tempus *n.*, spatium *n.*; (*history*) aetās *f.*; (*end*) terminus *m.*; (*sentence*) complexiō *f.*, ambitus *m.*
periodic *a.* (*style*) circumscrīptus. **-al** *a.* status. **-ally** *ad.* certīs temporibus, identidem.
peripatetic *a.* vagus; (*sect*) peripatēticus.
periphery *n.* ambitus *m.*
periphrasis *n.* circuitus *m.*
perish *vi.* perīre, interīre.
perishable *a.* cadūcus, fragilis, mortālis.
peristyle *n.* peristȳlium *n.*
perjure oneself *vi.* pēierāre.
perjured *a.* periūrus.
perjurer *n.* periūrus *m.*
perjury *n.* periūrium *n.* commit — pēierāre.
permanence *n.* cōnstantia *f.*, stabilitās *f.*
permanent *a.* stabilis, diūturnus, perpetuus. **-ly** *ad.* perpetuō.
permeable *a.* penetrābilis.
permeate *vt.* penetrāre. *vi.* permānāre.
permissible *a.* licitus, concessus. it is — licet.
permission *n.* potestās *f.* ask — veniam petere. give — veniam dare, potestātem facere. by — of permissū

(*gen.*). with your kind — bonā tuā veniā. without your — tē invītō.
permit *vt.* sinere, permittere (*dat.*). I am — tēd licet mihi.
pernicious *a.* perniciōsus, exitiōsus.
perorate *vi.* perōrāre.
peroration *n.* perōrātiō *f.*, epilogus *m.*
perpendicular *a.* dīrēctus. **-ly** *ad.* ad perpendiculum, ad lineam. [mittere.
perpetrate *vt.* facere, ad-
perpetual *a.* perpetuus, perennis, sempiternus. **-ly** *ad.* perpetuō.
perpetuate *vt.* continūare, perpetuāre.
perpetuity *n.* perpetuitās *f.*
perplex *vt.* sollicitāre, cōnfundere. **-ing** *a.* ambiguus, perplexus.
perplexity *n.* haesitātiō *f.*
perquisite *n.* peculium *n.*
persecute *vt.* īnsectārī, exagitāre.
persecution *n.* īnsectātiō *f.*
persecutor *n.* īnsectātor *m.*
perseverance *n.* persevērantia *f.*, cōnstantia *f.*
persevere *vi.* persevērāre, perstāre. — in tenēre.
persist *vi.* īnstāre, perstāre, persevērāre.
persistence, persistency *n.* pertinācia *f.*, persevērantia *f.*
persistent *a.* pertināx. **-ly** *ad.* pertināciter, persevēranter.
person *n.* homō *m.*, *f.*; (*counted*) caput *n.*; (*character*) persōna *f.*; (*body*) corpus *n.* in — ipse, praesēns.
personage *n.* vir *m.*
personal *a.* prīvātus, suus. — property peculium *n.* **-ly** *ad.* ipse, cōram.
personality *n.* nātūra *f.*; (*person*) vir ēgregius *m.*
personate *vt.* persōnam gerere (*gen.*). [poeia *f.*
personification *n.* prosōpo-
personify *vt.* hūmānam nātūram tribuere (*dat.*).
personnel *n.* membra *n.pl.*, socii *m.pl.* [*f.*
perspective *n.* scaenographia
perspicacious *a.* perspicāx, acūtus.
perspicacity *n.* perspicācitās *f.*, acūmen *n.*
perspicuity *n.* perspicuitās *f.*
perspicuous *a.* perspicuus.
perspiration *n.* sūdor *m.*
perspire *vi.* sūdāre.
persuade *vt.* persuādēre (*dat.*); (*by entreaty*) exōrāre.
persuasion *n.* persuāsiō *f.*
persuasive *a.* blandus. **-ly** *ad.* blandē.
pert *a.* procāx, protervus. **-ly** *ad.* procāciter, protervē.
pertain *vi.* pertinēre, attinēre.
pertinacious *a.* pertināx. **-ly** *ad.* pertināciter.
pertinacity *n.* pertinācia *f.*
pertinent *a.* appositus. be — ad rem pertinēre. **-ly** *ad.* appositē.
perturb *vt.* perturbāre.
perturbation *n.* animī perturbātiō *f.*, trepidātiō *f.*
peruke *n.* capillāmentum *n.*
perusal *n.* perlēctiō *f.*
peruse *vt.* perlegere; (*book*) ēvolvere.
pervade *vt.* permānāre per, complēre; (*emotion*) perfundere.
pervasive *a.* crēber.
perverse *a.* perversus, prāvus. **-ly** *ad.* perversē.
perversion *n.* dēprāvātiō *f.*
perversity *n.* perversitās *f.*
pervert *vt.* dēprāvāre; (*words*) dētorquēre; (*person*) corrumpere.
perverter *n.* corruptor *m.*
pessimism *n.* dēspērātiō *f.*
pest *n.* pestis *f.*
pester *vt.* sollicitāre. [pestis *f.*
pestilence *n.* pestilentia *f.*,
pestilential *a.* pestilēns, nocēns.

pestle *n.* pistillum *n.*
pet *n.* dēliciae *f.pl.* *vt.* in dēliciīs habēre, dēlēnīre.
petard *n.* be hoist with his own — suō sibī gladiō iugulārī.
petition *n.* precēs *f.pl.*; (*pol.*) libellus *m.* *vt.* ōrāre.
petrif/y *vt.* (*fig.*) dēfīgere. be -ied stupēre, obstupēscere.
pettifogger *n.* lēgulēius *m.*
pettiness *n.* levitās *f.*
pettish *a.* stomachōsus.
petty *a.* levis, minūtus.
petulance *n.* protervitās *f.*
petulant *a.* protervus, petulāns. **-ly** *ad.* petulanter.
pew *n.* subsellium *n.*
phalanx *n.* phalanx *f.* [*n.pl.*
phantasy *n.* commenticia
phantom *n.* simulacrum *n.*, īdōlon *n.*
phase *n.* (*pl.*) vicēs *f.pl.*
pheasant *n.* phāsiānus *m.*
phenomenal *a.* eximius, singulāris.
phenomenon *n.* rēs *f.*, novum *n.*, spectāculum *n.*
philander *vi.* lascīvīre.
philanthropic *a.* hūmānus, beneficus. **-ally** *ad.* hūmānē.
philanthropy *n.* hūmānitās *f.*, beneficia *n.pl.*
Philippic *n.* Philippica *f.*
philologist *n.* grammaticus *m.*
philology *n.* grammatica *n.pl.*
philosopher *n.* philosophus *m.*, sapiēns *m.*
philosophical *a.* philosophus; (*temperament*) aequābilis.
philosophize *vi.* philosophārī.
philosophy *n.* philosophia *f.*, sapientia *f.*
philtre *n.* philtrum *n.*
phlegm *n.* pituīta *f.*; (*temper*) lentitūdō *f.*
phlegmatic *a.* lentus.
phoenix *n.* phoenīx *m.*
phrase *n.* locūtiō *f.*; (*gram.*) incīsum *n.*
phraseology *n.* verba *n.pl.*, ōrātiō *f.*
physic *n.* medicāmentum *n.*; (*pl.*) physica *n.pl.* [corporis.
physical *a.* physicus; (*of body*)
physician *n.* medicus *m.*
physicist *n.* physicus *m.*
physique *n.* corpus *n.*, vīrēs *f.pl.*
piazza *n.* forum *n.*
pick *n.* (*tool*) dolabra *f.*; (*best part*) lēctī *m.pl.*, flōs *m.* *vt.* (*choose*) legere; (*pluck*) carpere. — out ēligere, excerpere. — up colligere.
picked *a.* ēlēctus, dēlēctus.
pickaxe *n.* dolabra *f.*
picket *n.* (*mil.*) statiō *f.*
pickle *n.* muria *f.* *vt.* condīre.
picture *n.* pictūra *f.*, tabula *f.* *vt.* dēpingere; (*to oneself*) ante oculōs pōnere. [amoenus.
picturesque *a.* (*scenery*)
pie *n.* crustum *n.*
piebald *a.* bicolor, varius.
piece *n.* pars *f.*; (*broken off*) fragmentum *n.*; (*food*) frustum *n.*; (*coin*) nummus *m.*; (*play*) fābula *f.* break in -s comminuere. fall to -s dīlābī take to — dissolvere. tear in -s dīlaniāre.
piecemeal *ad.* membrātim, minūtātim.
pied *a.* maculōsus.
pier *n.* mōlēs *f.*
pierce *vt.* perfodere; (*bore*) perforāre; (*fig.*) pungere.
piercing *a.* acūtus.
piety *n.* pietās *f.*, rēligiō *f.*
pig *n.* porcus *m.*, sūs *m.*, *f.* buy a — in a poke spem pretiō emere. -'s suillus.
pigeon *n.* columba *f.* wood — palumbēs *f.*
pig-headed *a.* pervicāx.
pigment *n.* pigmentum *n.*
pig-sty *n.* hara *f.*
pike *n.* dolō *m.*, hasta *f.*
pikeman *n.* hastātus *m.*

pile *n.* acervus *m.*, cumulus *m.*; (*funeral*) rogus *m.*; (*building*) mōlēs *f.*; (*post*) sublica *f.* *vt.* cumulāre, congerere. — up exstruere, adcumulāre, coacervāre.
pile-driver *n.* fistūca *f.*
pilfer *vt.* fūrārī, surripere.
pilferer *n.* fūr *m.*, fūrunculus *m.*
pilgrim *n.* peregrīnātor *m.*
pilgrimage *n.* peregrīnātio *f.*
pill *n.* pilula *f.*
pillage *n.* rapīna *f.*, dēpopulātiō *f.*, expīlātiō *f.* *vt.* dīripere, dēpopulārī, expīlāre.
pillager *n.* expīlātor *m.*, praedātor *m.*
pillar *n.* columen *n.*, columna *f.*
pillory *n.* furca *f.*
pillow *n.* pulvīnus *n.*, culcita *f.*
pilot *n.* gubernātor *n.*, ductor *m.* *vt.* regere, gubernāre.
pimp *n.* lēnō *m.*
pimple *n.* pustula *f.*
pin *n.* acus *f.* *vt.* adfīgere.
pincers *n.* forceps *m.*, *f.*
pinch *vt.* pervellere, vellicāre; (*shoe*) ūrere; (*for room*) coartāre.
pine *n.* pīnus *f.* pitch — picea *f.* *vi.* tābēscere. — away intābēscere. — for dēsīderāre.
pinion *n.* penna *f.*
pink *a.* rubicundus.
pinnace *n.* lembus *m.*
pinnacle *n.* fastīgium *n.*
pint *n.* sextārius *m.*
pioneer *n.* antecursor *m.*
pious *a.* pius, rēligiōsus. **-ly** *ad.* piē, rēligiōsē.
pip *n.* grānum *n.*
pipe *n.* (*music*) fistula *f.*, tībia *f.*; (*water*) canālis *m.* Pan **-s** fistula *f.* *vi.* fistulā canere.
piper *n.* tībīcen *m.*
pipkin *n.* olla *f.*
piquancy *n.* sāl *m.*, vīs *f.*
piquant *a.* salsus, argūtus.
pique *n.* offēnsio *f.*, dolor *m.* *vt.* offendere.
piracy *n.* latrōcinium *n.*
pirate *n.* pīrāta *m.*, praedō *m.*
piratical *a.* pīrāticus.
piscatorial *a.* piscātōrius.
piston *n.* embolus *m.*
pit *n.* fovea *f.*, fossa *f.*; (*theat.*) cavea *f.*
pitch *n.* pix *f.*; (*sound*) sonus *m.* *vt.* (*camp*) pōnere; (*tent*) tendere; (*missile*) conicere. — black piceus.
pitcher *n.* hydria *f.*
pitchfork *n.* furca *f.*
pitch-pine *n.* picea *f.*
piteous *a.* miserābilis, flēbilis. **-ly** *ad.* miserābiliter.
pitfall *n.* fovea *f.*
pith *n.* medulla *f.*
pithy *a.* (*style*) dēnsus. — saying sententia *f.*
pitiable *a.* miserandus.
pitiful *a.* miser, miserābilis; misericors. **-ly** *ad.* miserē, miserābiliter.
pitiless *a.* immisericors, immītis. **-ly** *ad.* crūdēliter.
pittance *n.* (*food*) dēmēnsum *n.*; (*money*) stips *f.*
pity *n.* misericordia *f.* take — on miserērī (*gen.*). it is a — that male accidit quod. *vt.* miserērī (*gen.*). I — mē miseret (*gen.*).
pivot *n.* cardō *m.*
placability *n.* plācābilitās *f.*
placable *a.* plācābilis.
placard *n.* libellus *m.*
placate *vt.* plācāre.
place *n.* locus *m.* in another — alibī. in the first — prīmum. in — of locō (*gen.*). to this — hūc. out of — intempestīvus. give — to cēdere (*dat.*). take — fierī, accidere. take the — of in locum (*gen.*) succēdere. *vt.* pōnere, locāre, collocāre. — beside adqōnere. — over (*in charge*) praepōnere. — round circumdare. — upon impōnere.
placid *a.* placidus, tranquillus, quiētus. **-ly** *ad.* placidē, quiētē.

placidity *n.* tranquillitās *f.*, sedātus animus *m.*
plagiarism *n.* fūrtum *n.*
plagiarize *vt.* fūrārī.
plague *n.* pestilentia *f.*, pestis *f.*
plain *a.* (*lucid*) clārus, perspicuus; (*unadorned*) subtīlis, simplex; (*frank*) sincērus; (*ugly*) invenustus. *n.* campus *m.* plānitiēs *f.* of the — campester. **-ly** *ad.* perspicuē; simpliciter; sincērē.
plainness *n.* perspicuitās *f.*; simplicitās *f.*
plaint *n.* querella *f.*
plaintiff *n.* petītor *m.*
plaintive *a.* flēbilis, queribundus. **-ly** *ad.* flēbiliter.
plait *vt.* implicāre, nectere.
plan *n.* cōnsilium *n.*; (*of a work*) fōrma *f.*, dēsignātiō *f.*; (*of living*) ratiō *f.*; (*intent*) prōpositum *n.*; (*drawing*) dēscrīptiō *f.* *vt.* (*a work*) dēsignāre, dēscrībere; (*intent*) cōgitāre, meditārī; (*with verb*) in animō habēre (*inf.*).
plane *n.* (*surface*) plānitiēs *f.*; (*tree*) platanus *f.*; (*tool*) runcīna *f.* *a.* aequus, plānus. *vt.* runcīnāre.
planet *n.* stēlla errāns *f.*
plank *n.* tabula *f.*
plant *n.* herba *f.*, planta *f.* *vt.* (*tree*) serere; (*field*) cōnserere; (*colony*) dēdūcere; (*feet*) pōnere. — firmly īnfīgere.
plantation *n.* arbustum *n.*
planter *n.* sator *m.*, colōnus *m.*
plaque *n.* tabula *f.*
plaster *n.* albārium *n.*, tectōrium *n.*; (*med.*) emplastrum *n.* — of Paris gypsum *n.* *vt.* dealbāre.
plasterer *n.* albārius *m.*
plastic *a.* ductilis, fūsilis.
plate *n.* (*dish*) catillus *m.*; (*silver*) argentum *n.*; (*layer*) lāmina *f.* *vt.* indūcere.
platform *n.* suggestus *m.*
platitude *n.* trīta sententia *f.*
platter *n.* patella *f.*, lanx *f.*
plaudit *n.* plausus *m.* [*f.*
plausibility *n.* vērisimilitūdō
plausible *a.* speciōsus, vērī similis.
play *n.* lūdus *m.*; (*theat.*) fābula *f.*; (*voice*) inclīnātiō *f.*; (*scope*) campus *m.*; (*hands*) gestus *m.* — on words agnōminātiō *f.* fair — aequum et bonum. **-bill** *n.* ēdictum *n.* **-ground** *n.* ārea *f.* *vi.* lūdere; (*fountain*) scatēre. *vt.* (*music*) canere; (*instrument*) canere (*abl.*); (*game*) lūdere (*abl.*); (*part*) agere. — the part of agere. — a trick on lūdificārī, impōnere (*dat.*).
player *n.* lūsor *m.*; (*at dice*) āleātor *m.*; (*on flute*) tībīcen *m.*; (*on lyre*) fidicen *m.*; (*on stage*) histriō *m.*
playful *a.* lascīvus; (*words*) facētus. **-ly** *ad.* per lūdum, per iocum.
playfulness *n.* lascīvia *f.*; facētiae *f.pl.*
playmate *n.* collūsor *m.*
playwright *n.* fābulārum scrīptor *m.*
plea *n.* causa *f.*; (*in defence*) dēfēnsiō *f.*, excūsātiō *f.*
plead *vi.* causam agere, causam ōrāre, causam dīcere; (*in excuse*) dēprecārī, excūsāre. — with obsecrāre. [*m.*
pleader *n.* āctor *m.*, causidicus
pleasant *a.* iūcundus, dulcis, grātus; (*place*) amoenus. **-ly** *ad.* iūcundē, suāviter.
pleasantry *n.* facētiae *f.pl.*, iocus *m.*
please *vt.* placēre (*dat.*), dēlectāre. try to — īnservīre (*dat.*). just as you — quod commodum est. if you — sīs. be -d with oneself sibī placēre. *ad.* amābō.
pleasing *a.* grātus, iūcundus. be — to cordī esse (*dat.*).
pleasurable *a.* iūcundus.
pleasure *n.* voluptās *f.*;

(*decision*) arbitrium *n*. it is my — libet. derive — voluptātem capere. *vt*. grātificārī (*dat*.). [*m.pl*.
pleasure grounds *n*. hortī
pleasure-loving *a*. dēlicātus.
plebeian *a*. plēbēius. *n*. the -s plēbs *f*.
plebiscite *n*. suffrāgium *n*.
plectrum *n*. plēctrum *n*.
pledge *n*. pignus *n*. *vt*. obligāre. — oneself prōmittere, spondēre. — one's word fidem obligāre, fidem interpōnere.
Pleiads *n*. Plēiades *f.pl*.
plenary *a*. īnfīnītus. [*m*.
plenipotentiary *n*. lēgātus
plenitude *n*. cōpia *f*., mātūritās *f*.
plenteous, plentiful *a*. cōpiōsus, largus. **-ly** *ad*. cōpiōsē, largē.
plenty *n*. cōpia *f*., abundantia *f*.; (*enough*) satis.
pleonasm *n*. redundantia *f*.
pleurisy *n*. lateris dolor *m*.
pliable, pliant *a*. flexibilis, mollis, lentus.
pliers *n*. forceps *m*., *f*.
plight *n*. habitus *m*., discrimen *n*. *vt*. spondēre.
plod *vi*. labōrāre, operam, īnsūmere.
plot *n*. coniūrātiō *f*., īnsidiae *f.pl*.; (*land*) agellus; (*play*) argūmentum *n*. *vi*. coniūrāre, mōlīrī.
plotter *n*. coniūratus *m*.
plough *n*. arātrum *n*. *vt*. arāre; (*sea*) sulcāre. — up exarāre.
ploughing *n*. arātiō *f*.
ploughman *n*. arātor *m*.
ploughshare *n*. vōmer *m*.
pluck *n*. fortitūdō *f*. *vt*. carpere, legere. — out ēvellere. — up courage animum recipere, animō adesse.
plucky *a*. fortis.
plug *n*. obtūrāmentum *n*. *vt*. obtūrāre.
plum *n*. prūnum *n*. — **tree** *n*. prūnus *f*.
plumage *n*. plūmae *f.pl*.
plumb *n*. perpendiculum *n*. *a*. dīrēctus. *ad*. ad perpendiculum. *vt*. (*building*) ad perpendiculum exigere; (*depth*) scrūtārī. [bārius *m*.
plumber *n*. artifex plum-
plumb-line *n*. līnea *f*., perpendiculum *n*.
plume *n*. crista *f*. *vt*. — oneself on iactāre, prae sē ferre.
plummet *n*. perpendiculum *n*.
plump *a*. pinguis.
plumpness *n*. nitor *m*.
plunder *n*. (*act*) rapīna *f*.; (*booty*) praeda *f*. *vi*. praedārī. *vt*. dīripere, expīlāre.
plunderer *n*. praedātor *m*., spoliātor *m*.
plundering *n*. rapīna *f*. *a*. praedābundus.
plunge *vt*. mergere, dēmergere; (*weapon*) dēmittere. *vi*. mergī, sē dēmergere.
plural *a*. plūrālis.
plurality *n*. multitūdō *f*., plūrēs *pl*.
ply *vt*. exercēre.
poach *vt*. surripere.
pocket *n*. sinus *m*. — **money** peculium *n*.
pod *n*. siliqua *f*.
poem *n*. poēma *n*., carmen *n*.
poesy *n*. poēsis *f*.
poet *n*. poēta *m*.
poetess *n*. poētria *f*.
poetic, -al *a*. poēticus. **-ally** *ad*. poēticē.
poetry *n*. (*art*) poētica *f*.; (*poems*) poēmata *n.pl*., carmina *n.pl*.
poignancy *n*. acerbitās *f*.
poignant *a*. acerbus, acūtus. **-ly** *ad*. acerbē, acūtē.
point *n*. (*dot*) pūnctum *n*.; (*place*) locus *m*.; (*item*) caput *n*.; (*sharp end*) aciēs *f*.; (*of sword*) mucrō *m*.; (*of epigram*) acūleī *m.pl*. — of honour

officium *n.* — of view sententia *f.* beside the — ab rē. to the — ad rem. from this — hinc. to that — eō. up to this — hāctenus, adhūc. without — īnsulsus. in — of fact nempe. make a — of doing consulto facere. on the — of death moritūrus. on the — of happening inibī. I was on the — of saying in eō erat ut dīcerem. matters have reached such a — eō rēs recidit. come to the — ad rem redīre. the — at issue is illud quaeritur. the main — cardō *m.*, caput *n.* turning — articulus temporis *m.* *vt.* acuere, exacuere; (*aim*) intendere; (*punctuate*) distinguere. — out indicāre, mōnstrāre.

point-blank *a.* simplex. *ad.* præcīsē.

pointed *a.* acūtus; (*criticism*) acūleātus; (*wit*) salsus. **-ly** *ad.* apertē, dīlūcidē.

pointer *n.* index *m.*

pointless *a.* īnsulsus, frīgidus. **-ly** *ad.* īnsulsē.

poise *n.* lībrāmen *n.*; (*fig.*) urbānitās *f.* *vt.* lībrāre.

poison *n.* venēnum *n.* *vt.* venēnō necāre; (*fig.*) īnficere. **-ed** *a.* venēnātus.

poisoner *n.* venēficus *m.*

poisoning *n.* venēficium *n.*

poisonous *a.* noxius.

poke *vt.* trūdere, fodicāre.

polar *a.* septentriōnālis.

pole *n.* asser *m.*, contus *m.*; (*astr.*) polus *m.*

pole-axe *n.* bipennis *f.*

polemic *n.* contrōversia *f.*

police *n.* lictōrēs *m.pl.*; (*night*) vigilēs *m.pl.*

policy *n.* ratiō *f.*, cōnsilium *n.* honesty is the best — ea māximē condūcunt quae sunt rēctissima.

polish *n.* (*appearance*) nitor *m.*; (*character*) urbānitās *f.*; (*lit.*) līma *f.* *vt.* polīre; (*fig.*) expolīre. **-ed** *a.* polītus, mundus; (*person*) excultus, urbānus; (*style*) līmātus.

polite *a.* urbānus, hūmānus, cōmis. **-ly** *ad.* urbānē, cōmiter.

politeness *n.* urbānitās *f.*, hūmānitās *f.*, cōmitās *f.*

politic *a.* prūdēns, circumspectus.

political *a.* cīvīlis, pūblicus. — life rēs pūblica *f.*

politician *n.* magistrātus *m.*

politics *n.* rēs pūblica *f.* take up — ad rem pūblicam accēdere.

polity *n.* reī pūblicae fōrma *f.*

poll *n.* caput *n.*; (*voting*) comitia *n.pl.* — tax tribūtum in singula capita impositum. *vi.* suffrāgia inīre.

pollute *vt.* inquināre, contāmināre.

pollution *n.* corruptēla *f.*

poltroon *n.* ignāvus *m.*

poltroonery *n.* ignāvia *f.*

pomegranate *n.* mālum Pūnicum *n.*

pomp *n.* adparātus *m.*

pomposity *n.* māgnificentia *f.*, glōria *f.*

pompous *a.* māgnificus, glōriōsus. **-ly** *ad.* māgnificē, glōriōsē. [centia *f.*

pompousness *n.* māgnifi-

pond *n.* stagnum *n.*, lacūna *f.*

ponder *vi.* sēcum reputāre. *vt.* animō volūtāre, in mente agitāre.

ponderous *a.* gravis, ponderōsus. **-ly** *ad.* graviter.

poniard *n.* pugiō *m.*

pontiff *n.* pontifex.

pontifical *a.* pontificālis, pontificius.

pontoon *n.* pontō *m.*

pony *n.* mannus *m.*

pooh-pooh *vt.* dērīdēre.

pool *n.* lacūna *f.*, stagnum *n.* *vt.* cōnferre.

poop *n.* puppis *f.*

poor *a.* pauper, inops; (*meagre*) exīlis; (*inferior*) improbus;

(*pitiable*) miser. — little misellus.
poorly *a.* aeger, aegrōtus. *ad.* parum, tenuiter.
pop *n.* crepitus *m.* *vi.* ēmicāre.
pope *n.* pāpa *m.*
poplar *n.* pōpulus *f.*
poppy *n.* papāver *n.*
populace *n.* vulgus *n.*, plēbs *f.*
popular *a.* grātus, grātiōsus; (*party*) populāris. **-ly** *ad.* vulgō.
popularity *n.* populi favor *m.*, studium *n.*
populate *vt.* frequentāre.
population *n.* populus *m.*, cīvēs *m.pl.*
populous *a.* frequēns.
porcelain *n.* fictilia *n.pl.*
porch *n.* vestibulum *n.*
porcupine *n.* hystrix *f.*
pore *n.* forāmen *n.* *vi.* — over scrūtārī, incumbere in (*acc.*).
pork *n.* porcīna *f.*
porous *a.* rārus.
porridge *n.* puls *f.*
port *n.* portus *m.* *a.* (*side*) laevus, sinister.
portage *n.* vectūra *f.*
portal *n.* porta *f.*
portcullis *n.* cataracta *f.*
portend *vt.* portendere.
portent *n.* mōnstrum *n.*, portentum *n.*
portentous *a.* mōnstruōsus.
porter *n.* iānitor *m.*; (*carrier*) bāiulus *m.*
portico *n.* porticus *f.*
portion *n.* pars *f.*; (*marriage*) dōs *f.*; (*lot*) sors *f.*
portliness *n.* amplitūdō *f.*
portly *a.* amplus, opīmus.
portmanteau *n.* mantica *f.*
portrait *n.* imāgō *f.*, effigiēs *f.*
portray *vt.* dēpingere, exprimere, effingere.
pose *n.* status *m.*, habitus *m.* *vt.* pōnere. *vi.* habitum sūmere.
poser *n.* nōdus *m.*
posit *vt.* pōnere.
position *n.* (*geog.*) situs *m.*; (*body*) status *m.*, gestus *m.*; (*rank*) dignitās *f.*; (*office*) honōs *m.*; (*mil.*) locus *m.* be in a — to habēre (*inf.*). take up a — (*mil.*) locum capere.
positive *a.* certus. be — about adfirmāre. **-ly** *ad.* certō, adfirmātē, rē vērā.
posse *n.* manus *f.*
possess *vt.* possidēre, habēre; (*take*) occupāre, potīrī (*abl.*).
possession *n.* possessiō *f.*; (*pl.*) bona *n.pl.*, fortūnae *f.pl.* take — of potīrī (*abl.*) occupāre, manum inicere (*dat.*); (*inheritance*) obīre; (*emotion*) invādere, incēdere (*dat.*). self — aequus animus.
possessor *n.* possessor *m.*, dominus *m.*
possibility *n.* facultās *f.* there is a — fierī potest.
possib/le *a.* it is — fierī potest. as big as — quam māximus. **-ly** *ad.* fortasse.
post *n.* pālus *m.*; (*mil.*) statiō *f.*; (*office*) mūnus *n.*; (*courier*) tabellārius *m.* leave one's — locō cēdere, signa relinquere. *vt.* (*troops*) locāre, collocāre; (*at intervals*) dispōnere. (*letter*) dare, tabellāriō dare; (*entry*) in cōdicem referre. be **-d** (*mil.*) in statiōne esse.
postage *n.* vectūra *f.*
poster *n.* libellus *m.*
posterior *a.* posterior.
posterity *n.* posterī *m.pl.*; (*time*) posteritās *f.*
postern *n.* postīcum *n.* [tāte.
post-haste *ad.* summā celeri-
posthumous *a.* postumus. **-ly** *ad.* (*born*) patre mortuō, (*published*) auctōre mortuō.
postpone *vt.* differre, prōferre.
postponement *n.* dīlātiō *f.*
postscript *n.* add a — adscrībere, subicere.
postulate *vt.* sūmere. *n.* sūmptiō *f.*

posture *n.* gestus *m.*, status *m.*
pot *n.* olla *f.*, matella *f.*
pot-bellied *a.* ventriōsus.
potency *n.* vīs *f.*
potent *a.* efficāx, valēns. **-ly** *ad.* efficienter.
potentate *n.* dynastēs *m.*, tyrannus *m.*
potential *a.* futūrus. **-ly** *ad.* ut fierī posse vidētur. — an emperor capāx imperiī.
potentiality *n.* facultās *f.*
potion *n.* pōtiō *f.*
pot-pourri *n.* farrāgō *f.*
potsherd *n.* testa *f.*
pottage *n.* iūs *n.* [figulāris.
potter *n.* figulus *m.* **-'s**
pottery *n.* fictilia *n.pl.*
pouch *n.* pēra *f.*, sacculus *m.*
poultice *n.* fōmentum *n.*, emplastrum *n.*
poultry *n.* gallīnae *f.pl.*
pounce *vi.* involāre, īnsilīre.
pound *n.* lībra *f.* five **-s** (*weight*) of gold aurī quīnque pondō. *vt.* conterere; pulsāre.
pour *vt.* fundere. — forth effundere. — in īnfundere. — on superfundere. — out effundere. *vi.* fundī, fluere. — down ruere, sē praecipitāre.
pouring *a.* (*rain*) effūsus.
poverty *n.* paupertās *f.*, egestās *f.*, inopia *f.*; (*style*) iēiūnitās *f.*
powder *n.* pulvis *m.*
powdery *a.* pulvereus.
power *n.* potestās *f.*; (*strength*) vīrēs *f.pl.*; (*excessive*) potentia *f.*; (*supreme*) imperium *n.*; (*divine*) nūmen *n.*; (*legal*) auctōritās *f.*; (*of father*) manus *f.* as far as is in my — quantum in mē est. have great — multum valēre, posse. have of — attorney cognitōrem esse. it is still in my — to integrum est mihi (*inf.*).
powerful *a.* validus, potēns. **-ly** *ad.* valdē.
powerless *a.* impotēns, imbēcillus. be — nihil valēre.
powerlessness *n.* imbēcillitas *f.*
practicable *a.* in apertō. be — fierī posse.
practical *a.* (*person*) habilis. — joke lūdus *m.* — knowledge ūsus *m.* **-ly** *ad.* ferē, paene.
practice *n.* ūsus *m.*, exercitātiō *f.*; (*rhet.*) meditātiō *f.*; (*habit*) consuētūdō *f.*, mōs *m.* corrupt **-s** malae artēs.
practise *vt.* (*occupation*) exercēre, facere; (*custom*) factitāre; (*rhet.*) meditārī. *vi.* (*med.*) medicīnam exercēre; (*law*) causās agere.
practised *a.* exercitātus, perītus. [cus *m.*
practitioner *n.* (*med.*) medi-
praetor *n.* praetor *n.* **-'s** praetōrius.
praetorian *a.* praetōrius. — guards praetōriānī *m.pl.*
praetorship *n.* praetūra *f.*
praise *n.* laus *f.* *vt.* laudāre.
praiser *n.* laudātor *m.*
praiseworthy *a.* laudābilis, laude dignus.
prance *vi.* exsultāre.
prank *n.* lūdus *m.*
prate *vi.* garrīre.
prating *a.* garrulus.
pray *vi.* deōs precārī, deōs venerārī. *vt.* precārī, ōrāre. — for petere, precārī. — to adōrāre.
prayer *n.* precēs *f.pl.*
prayerful *a.* supplex.
preach *vt.* & *i.* docēre, praedicāre.
preacher *n.* ōrātor *m.*
preamble *n.* exōrdium *n.*
prearranged *a.* cōnstitūtus.
precarious *a.* dubius, perīculōsus. [*n.*
precariousness *n.* discrīmen
precaution *n.* cautiō *f.*, prōvidentia *f.* take **-s** cavēre, praecavēre.
precede *vt.* praeīre (*dat.*), anteīre (*dat.*), antecēdere.
precedence *n.* prīmārius

locus *m.* give — to cēdere (*dat.*). take — (*thing*) antīquius esse; (*person*) prīmās agere.
precedent *n.* exemplum *n.*; (*law*) praeiūdicium *n.* breach of — īnsolentia *f.* in defiance of — īnsolenter.
preceding *a.* prior, superior.
precept *n.* praeceptum *n.*
preceptor *n.* doctor *m.*, magister *m.*
precinct *n.* terminus *m.*, templum *n.*
precious *a.* cārus; (*style*) pūtidus. — stone gemma *f.*
precipice *n.* locus praeceps *m.*, rūpēs *f.*
precipitancy, precipitation *n.* festīnātiō *f.*
precipitate *vt.* praecipitāre. *a.* praeceps; praeproperus.
precipitous *a.* dēruptus, praeceps, praeruptus.
precise *a.* certus, subtīlis; (*person*) accūrātus. **-ly** *ad.* dēmum.
precision *n.* cūra *f.*
preclude *vt.* exclūdere, prohibēre.
precocious *a.* praecox.
precocity *n.* festīnāta mātūritās *f.*
preconceive *vt.* praecipere. **-d** idea praeiūdicāta opīniō *f.* [*f.*
preconception *n.* praeceptiō
preconcerted *a.* ex compositō factus.
precursor *n.* praenūntius *m.*
predatory *a.* praedātōrius.
predecessor *n.* dēcessor *m.* my — cui succēdō.
predestination *n.* fātum *n.*, necessitās *f.*
predestine *vt.* dēvovēre.
predetermine *vt.* praefīnīre.
predicament *n.* angustiae *f.pl.*, discrīmen *n.*
predicate *n.* attribūtum *n.*
predict *vt.* praedīcere, augurārī.
prediction *n.* praedictiō *f.*
predilection *n.* amor *m.*, studium *n.*
predispose *vt.* inclīnāre, praeparāre. [*f.*
predisposition *n.* inclīnātiō
predominance *n.* potentia *f.*, praestantia *f.*
predominant *a.* praepotēns, praecipuus. **-ly** *ad.* plērumque.
predominate *vi.* pollēre, dominārī. [*f.*
pre-eminence *n.* praestantia
pre-eminent *a.* ēgregius, praecipuus, excellēns. **-ly** *ad.* ēgregiē, praecipuē, excellenter.
preface *n.* prooemium *n.*, praefātiō *f.* *vi.* praefārī.
prefect *n.* praefectus *m.*
prefecture *n.* praefectūra *f.*
prefer *vt.* (*charge*) dēferre; (*to office*) anteferre; (*choice*) antepōnere (*acc.* & *dat.*), posthabēre (*dat.* & *acc.*); (*with verb*) mālle.
preferab/le *a.* potior. **-ly** *ad.* potius.
preference *n.* favor *m.* give — to antepōnere, praeoptāre. in — to potius quam.
preferment *n.* honōs *m.*, dignitās *f.*
prefix *vt.* praetendere. *n.* praepositiō *f.*
pregnancy *n.* graviditās *f.*
pregnant *a.* gravida.
prejudge *vt.* praeiūdicāre.
prejudice *n.* praeiūdicāta opīniō *f.*; (*harmful*) invidia *f.*, incommodum *n.* without — cum bonā veniā. *vt.* obesse (*dat.*). be **-d** against invidēre (*dat.*), male opīnārī dē (*abl.*).
prejudicial *a.* damnōsus. be — to obesse (*dat.*), nocēre (*dat.*), officere (*dat.*), dētrīmentō esse (*dat.*).
preliminary *a.* prīmus. *n.* prōlūsiō *f.*; (*pl.*) praecurrentia *n.pl.*
prelude *n.* prooemium *n.*
premature *a.* immātūrus;

(*birth*) abortivus. **-ly** *ad.* ante tempus.
premeditate *vt.* praecōgitāre, praemeditārī. **-d** *a.* praemeditātus.
premier *a.* prīnceps, praecipuus.
premise *n.* (*major*) prōpositiō *f.*; (*minor*) adsūmptiō *f.*; (*pl.*) aedēs *f.pl.*, domus *f.*
premium *n.* praemium *n.* be at a — male emī.
premonition *n.* monitus *m.*
preoccupation *n.* sollicitūdō *f.*
preoccupied *a.* sollicitus, districtus.
preordain *vt.* praefīnīre.
preparation *n.* (*process*) adparātiō *f.*, comparātiō *f.*; (*product*) adparātus *m.*; (*of speech*) meditātiō *f.* make **-s** for īnstruere, exōrnāre, comparāre.
prepare *vt.* parāre, adparāre, comparāre; (*speech*) meditārī; (*with verb*) parāre.
preponderance *n.* praestantia *f.*
preponderate *vi.* praepollēre, vincere.
preposition *n.* praepositiō *f.*
prepossess *vt.* commendāre (*dat.* & *acc.*), praeoccupāre.
prepossessing *a.* suāvis, iūcundus.
prepossession *n.* favor *m.*
preposterous *a.* absurdus.
prerogative *n.* iūs *n.*
presage *n.* ōmen *n.* *vt.* ōmināri, portendere.
prescience *n.* prōvidentia *f.*
prescient *a.* prōvidus.
prescribe *vt.* imperāre; (*med.*) praescrībere; (*limit*) fīnīre.
prescription *n.* (*med.*) compositiō *f.*; (*right*) ūsus *m.*
presence *n.* praesentia *f.*; (*appearance*) aspectus *m.* — of mind praesēns animus *m.* in the — of cōram (*abl.*). in my — mē praesente.
present *a.* praesēns, īnstāns. be — adesse. be — at interesse (*dat.*). *n.* praesēns tempus *n.*; (*gift*) dōnum *n.* at — in praesentī, nunc. for the — in praesēns. *vt.* dōnāre, offerre; (*on stage*) indūcere; (*in court*) sistere. — itself occurrere.
presentable *a.* spectābilis.
presentation *n.* dōnātiō *f.*
presentiment *n.* augurium *n.*
presently *ad.* mox.
preservation *n.* cōnservātiō *f.*
preserve *vt.* cōnservāre, tuērī; (*food*) condīre.
preside *vi.* praesidēre (*dat.*).
presidency *n.* praefectūra *f.*
president *n.* praefectus *m.*
press *n.* prēlum *n.* *vt.* premere; (*crowd*) stīpāre; (*urge*) īnstāre (*dat.*). — for flāgitāre. — hard (*pursuit*) īnsequī, īnstāre (*dat.*), īnsistere (*dat.*). — out exprimere. — together comprimere.
pressing *a.* īnstāns, gravis.
pressure *n.* pressiō *f.*, nīsus *m.*
prestige *n.* auctōritās *f.*, opīniō *f.*
presumably *ad.* sānē.
presume *vt.* sūmere, conicere. *vi.* audēre, confīdere. I — opīnor, crēdō.
presuming *a.* adrogāns.
presumption *n.* coniectūra *f.*; (*arrogance*) adrogantia *f.*, licentia *f.*
presumptuous *a.* adrogāns, audāx. **-ly** *ad.* adroganter, audacter.
presuppose *vt.* praesūmere.
pretence *n.* simulātiō *f.*, speciēs *f.* under — of per speciem (*gen.*). under false **-s** dolō malō.
pretend *vt.* simulāre, fingere. — that . . . not dissimulāre.
pretender *n.* captātor *m.*
pretension *n.* postulātum *n.* make **-s** to adfectāre, sibi adrogāre.
pretentious *a.* adrogāns, glōriōsus.

pretext *n.* speciēs *f.* under — of per speciem (*gen.*).
prettiness *n.* pulchritūdō *f.*, lepōs *m.*
prett/y *a.* formōsus, pulcher, bellus. *ad.* admodum, satis. **-ily** *ad.* pulchrē, bellē.
prevail *vi.* vincere; (*custom*) tenēre, obtinēre. — **upon** persuādēre (*dat.*); (*by entreaty*) exōrāre. **-ing** *a.* vulgātus.
prevalent *a.* vulgātus. **be** — obtinēre. **become** — incrēbrēscere.
prevaricate *vi.* tergiversārī.
prevarication *n.* tergiversātiō *f.*
prevaricator *n.* veterātor *m.*
prevent *vt.* impedīre, prohibēre.
prevention *n.* impedītiō *f.*
previous *a.* prior, superior. **-ly** *ad.* anteā, antehāc.
prevision *n.* prōvidentia *f.*
prey *n.* praeda *f.* *vi.* — **upon** insectārī; (*fig.*) vexāre, carpere.
price *n.* pretium *n.*; (*of corn*) annōna *f.* **at a high** — māgnī. **at a low** — parvī. *vt.* pretium cōnstituere (*gen.*).
priceless *a.* inaestimābilis.
prick *vt.* pungere; (*goad*) stimulāre. — **up the ears** aurēs adrigere.
prickle *n.* aculeus *m.*
prickly *a.* aculeātus, horridus.
pride *n.* superbia *f.*, fastus *m.*; (*boasting*) glōria *f.*; (*object*) decus *n.*; (*best part*) flōs *m.* *vt.* — **oneself on** iactāre, prae sē ferre.
priest *n.* sacerdōs *m.*; (*especial*) flāmen *m.* **high** — pontifex *m.*, antistēs *m.*
priestess *n.* sacerdōs *f.* **high** — antistita *f.*
priesthood *n.* sacerdōtium *n.*, flāminium *n.*
prig *n.* homō fastīdiōsus *m.*
priggish *a.* fastīdiōsus.
prim *a.* modestior.
primar/y *a.* prīmus, praecipuus. **-ily** *ad.* prīncipiō; praecipuē.
prime *a.* prīmus, ēgregius. — **mover** auctor *m.* *n.* flōs *m.* **in one's**— flōrēns. *vt.* instruere, ērudīre.
primeval *a.* prīscus.
primitive *a.* prīstinus, incultus.
primordial *a.* prīscus.
prince *n.* rēgulus *m.*; rēgis fīlius *m.*
princely *a.* rēgālis.
princess *n.* rēgis fīlia *f.*
principal *a.* praecipuus, prīnceps, māximus. *n.* (*person*) prīnceps *m.*, *f.*; (*money*) sors *f.* **-ly** *ad.* in prīmīs, māximē, māximam partem.
principle *n.* prīncipium *n.*; (*rule*) fōrmula *f.*, ratiō *f.*; (*character*) fidēs *f.* (*pl.*) īnstitūta *n.pl.*, disciplīna *f.* **first -s** elementa *n.pl.*, initia *n.pl.*
print *n.* nota *f.*, signum *n.*; (*foot*) vestīgium *n.* *vt.* imprimere
prior *a.* prior, potior.
priority *n.* **give** — **to** praevertere (*dat.*).
prise *vt.* sublevāre. — **open** vectī refringere.
prison *n.* carcer *m.*, vincula *n.pl.* **put in** — in vincula conicere.
prisoner *n.* reus *m.*; (*for debt*) nexus *m.*; (*of war*) captīvus *m.* — **at the bar** reus *m.*, rea *f.* **take** — capere.
pristine *a.* prīscus, prīstinus, vetus.
privacy *n.* sēcrētum *n.*
private *a.* (*individual*) prīvātus; (*home*) domesticus; (*secluded*) sēcrētus. *n.* (*mil.*) gregārius mīles *m.* **-ly** *ad.* clam, sēcrētō.
privation *n.* inopia *f.*, egestās *f.*
privet *n.* ligustrum *n.*
privilege *n.* iūs *n.*, immūnitās *f.*
privileged *a.* immūnis.

priv/y *a.* sēcrētus. — to cōnscius (*gen.*). **-ily** *ad.* sēcrētō.
prize *n.* praemium *n.*; (*captured*) praeda *f.* — money manubiae *f.pl.* *vt.* māgnī aestimāre.
pro- Athenian *a.* rērum Athēniēnsium studiōsus.
probability *n.* vērī similitūdō *f.*
probab/le *a.* vērī similis. more — vērō propior. **-ly** *ad.* fortasse.
probation *n.* probātiō *f.*
probationer *n.* tīrō *m.*
probe *vt.* īnspicere, scrūtārī.
probity *n.* honestās *f.*, integritās *f.*
problem *n.* quaestiō *f.* the — is illud quaeritur.
problematical *a.* dubius, anceps.
procedure *n.* ratiō *f.*, modus *m.*; (*law*) fōrmula *f.*
proceed *vi.* pergere, prōgredī; (*narrative*) īnsequī. — against persequī, lītem intendere (*dat.*). — from orīrī, proficīscī ex.
proceedings *n.* ācta *n.pl.*
proceeds *n.* fructus *m.*, reditus *m.*
process *n.* ratiō *f.*; (*law*) āctiō *f.* in the — of time post aliquod tempus.
procession *n.* pompa *f.*; (*fig.*) agmen *n.*
proclaim *vt.* ēdīcere, prōnūntiāre, praedicāre, dēclārāre.
proclamation *n.* ēdictum *n.*
proclivity *n.* prōpēnsiō *f.*
proconsul *n.* prōcōnsul *m.*
proconsular *a.* prōcōnsulāris. [sulātus *m.*
proconsulship *n.* prōcōn-
procrastinate *vt.* differre, prōferre. *vi.* cunctārī.
procrastination *n.* prōcrāstinātiō *f.*, mora *f.*
procreate *vt.* generāre, prōcreāre.
procreation *n.* prōcreātiō *f.*
procreator *n.* generātor *m.*
procumbent *a.* prōnus.
procurator *n.* prōcūrātor *m.*
procure *vt.* parāre, adipīscī, adquīrere; (*by request*) impetrāre.
procurer *n.* lēnō *m.*
prod *vt.* stimulāre.
prodigal *a.* prōdigus. *n.* nepōs *m.* **-ly** *ad.* effūsē.
prodigality *n.* effūsiō *f.*
prodigious *a.* ingēns, immānis.
prodigy *n.* prōdigium *n.*, portentum *n.*; (*fig.*) mīrāculum *n.*
produce *vt.* ēdere; (*young*) parere; (*crops*) ferre; (*play*) dare, docēre; (*line*) prōdūcere; (*in court*) sistere; (*into view*) prōferre; (*from store*) prōmere, dēprōmere. *n.* fructus *m.*; (*of earth*) frūgēs *f.pl.*; (*in money*) reditus *m.*
product *n.* opus *n.* — of fructus (*gen.*).
production *n.* opus *n.*
productive *a.* fēcundus, ferāx, fructuōsus.
productivity *n.* fēcunditās, ūbertās *f.*
proem *n.* prooemium *n.*
profanation *n.* violātiō *f.*
profane *a.* profānus, impius. *vt.* violāre, polluere. **-ly** *ad.* impiē.
profanity *n.* impietās *f.*
profess *vt.* profitērī, prae sē ferre. — to be profitērī sē.
profession *n.* professiō *f.*; (*occupation*) ars *f.*, haeresis *f.*
professor *n.* doctor *m.*
proffer *vt.* offerre, pollicērī.
proficiency *n.* prōgressus *m.*, perītia *f.* attain — prōficere.
proficient *a.* perītus.
profile *n.* ōris līneāmenta *n.pl.*; (*portrait*) oblīqua imāgō *f.*
profit *n.* lucrum *n.*, ēmolumentum *n.*, fructus *m.* make a — out of quaestuī habēre. *vt.* prōdesse (*dat.*). *vi.* — by

fruī (*abl.*). ūtī (*abl.*); (*opportunity*) arripere.
profitab/le *a.* fructuōsus, ūtilis. **–ly** *ad.* ūtiliter.
profligacy *n.* flāgitium *n.*, perditī mōrēs *m.pl.*
profligate *a.* perditus, dissolūtus. *n.* nepōs *m.*
profound *a.* altus; (*discussion*) abstrūsus. **–ly** *ad.* penitus.
profundity *n.* altitūdō *f.*
profuse *a.* prōdigus, effūsus. **–ly** *ad.* effūsē.
profusion *n.* abundantia *f.*, adfluentia *f.* in — abundē.
progenitor *n.* auctor *m.*
progeny *n.* prōgeniēs *f.*, prōlēs *f.*
prognostic *n.* signum *n.*
prognosticate *vt.* ōminārī, augurārī, praedīcere.
prognostication *n.* ōmen *n.*, praedictiō *f.*
programme *n.* libellus *m.*
progress *n.* prōgressus *m.* make — prōficere. *vi.* prōgredī.
progression *n.* prōgressus *m.*
progressively *ad.* gradātim.
prohibit *vt.* vetāre, interdīcere (*dat.*).
prohibition *n.* interdictum *n.*
project *n.* prōpositum *n.* *vi.* ēminēre, exstāre; (*land*) excurrere. *vt.* prōicere.
projectile *n.* tēlum *n.*
projecting *a.* ēminēns.
projection *n.* ēminentia *f.*
proletarian *a.* plēbēius.
proletariat *n.* plēbs *f.*
prolific *a.* fēcundus.
prolix *a.* verbōsus, longus.
prolixity *n.* redundantia *f.*
prologue *n.* prologus *m.*
prolong *vt.* dūcere, prōdūcere; (*office*) prōrogāre.
prolongation *n.* (*time*) propāgātiō *f.*; (*office*) prōrogātiō *f.*
promenade *n.* ambulātiō *f.* *vi.* inambulāre, spatiārī.
prominence *n.* ēminentia *f.*
prominent *a.* ēminēns, īnsignis. be — ēminēre.
promiscuous *a.* prōmiscuus. **–ly** *ad.* prōmiscuē.
promise *n.* prōmissum *n.* break a — fidem fallere. keep a — fidem praestāre. make a — fidem dare. a youth of great — summae speī adulēscēns. *vt.* prōmittere, pollicērī; (*in marriage*) dēspondēre. — in return reprōmittere. *vi.* — well bonam spem ostendere.
promising *a.* bonae speī.
promissory note *n.* syngrapha *f.*
promontory *n* prōmunturium *n.*
promote *vt.* favēre (*dat.*); (*growth*) alere; (*in rank*) prōdūcere.
promoter *n.* auctor *m.*, fautor *m.*
promotion *n.* dignitās *f.*
prompt *a.* alacer, prōmptus. *vt.* incitāre, commovēre; (*speaker*) subicere. **–ly** *ad.* extemplō, citō.
prompter *n.* monitor *m.*
promptitude *n.* alacritās *f.*, celeritās *f.*
promulgate *vt.* prōmulgāre, palam facere. [gātiō *f.*
promulgation *n.* prōmul-
prone *a.* prōnus; (*mind*) inclīnātus.
prong *n.* dēns *m.*
pronounce *vt.* ēloquī, appellāre; (*oath*) interpōnere; (*sentence*) dīcere, prōnūntiāre. **–d** *a.* manifestus, īnsignis.
pronouncement *n.* ōrātiō *f.*, adfirmātiō *f.* [*f.*
pronunciation *n.* appellātiō
proof *n.* documentum *n.*, argūmentum *n.*; (*test*) probātiō *f.* *a.* immōtus, impenetrābilis.
prop *n.* adminiculum *n.*, firmāmentum *n.* *vt.* fulcīre.
propaganda *n.* documenta *n.pl.*

propagate *vt.* propāgāre.
propagation *n.* propāgātiō *f.*
propel *vt.* incitāre, prōpellere.
propensity *n.* inclīnātiō *f.*
proper *a.* idōneus, decēns, decōrus; rēctus. it is — decet. **-ly** *ad.* decōrē; rēctē.
property *n.* rēs *f.*, rēs mancipī, bona *n.pl.*; (*estate*) praedium *n.*; (*attribute*) proprium *n.*; (*slave's*) peculium *n.* private — rēs familiāris *f.*
prophecy *n.* vāticinātiō *f.*, praedictiō *f.*
prophesy *vt.* vāticinārī, praedīcere. [*m.*
prophet *n.* vātēs *m.*, fātidicus
prophetess *n.* vātēs *f.*
prophetic *a.* dīvīnus, fātidicus. **-ally** *ad.* dīvīnitus.
propinquity *n.* (*place*) vīcīnitās *f.*; (*kin*) propinquitās *f.*
propitiate *vt.* plācāre.
propitiation *n.* plācātiō *f.*, litātiō *f.*
propitious *a.* fēlīx, faustus; (*god*) praesēns.
proportion *n.* mēnsūra *f.* in — prō portiōne, prō ratā parte. in — to prō (*abl.*).
proportionately *ad.* prō portiōne, prō ratā parte.
proposal *n.* condiciō *f.*
propose *vt.* (*motion*) ferre, rogāre; (*penalty*) inrogāre; (*candidate*) rogāre magistrātum. [*m.*
proposer *n.* auctor *m.*, lātor
proposition *n.* (*offer*) condiciō *f.*; (*plan*) cōnsilium *n.*, prōpositum *n.*; (*logic*) prōnūntiātum *n.*
propound *vt.* expōnere, in medium prōferre.
propraetor *n.* prōpraetor *m.*
proprietor *n.* dominus *m.*
propriety *n.* decōrum *n.*; (*conduct*) modestia *f.* with — decenter.
propulsion *n.* impulsus *m.*
prorogation *n.* prōrogātio *f.*
prorogue *vt.* prōrogāre.
prosaic *a.* pedester.
proscribe *vt.* prōscrībere.
proscription *n.* prōscrīptiō *f.*
prose *n.* ōrātiō *f.*, ōrātiō solūta *f.*
prosecute *vt.* (*task*) exsequī, gerere; (*at law*) accūsāre, lītem intendere (*dat.*).
prosecution *n.* exsecūtiō *f.*; (*at law*) accūsātiō *f.*; (*party*) accūsātor *m.*
prosecutor *n.* accūsātor *m.*
prosody *n.* numerī *m.pl.*
prospect *n.* prōspectus *m.*; (*fig.*) spēs *f.* *vi.* explōrāre.
prospective *a.* futūrus, spērātus.
prosper *vi.* flōrēre, bonā fortūnā ūtī. *vt.* fortūnāre.
prosperity *n.* fortūna *f.*, rēs secundae *f.pl.*, fēlīcitās *f.*
prosperous *a.* fēlīx, fortūnātus, secundus. **-ly** *ad.* prosperē.
prostrate *a.* prōstrātus, adflīctus. lie — iacēre. *vt.* prōsternere, dēicere. — oneself prōcumbere, sē prōicere. [*m.*
prostration *n.* frāctus animus
prosy *a.* longus.
protagonist *n.* prīmārum partium āctor *m.*
protect *vt.* tuērī, dēfendere, custōdīre.
protection *n.* tūtēla *f.*, praesidium *n.*; (*law*) patrōcinium *n.*; (*pol.*) fidēs *f.* put oneself under the — of in fidem venīre (*gen.*). take under one's — in fidem recipere.
protector *n.* patrōnus *m.*, dēfēnsor *m.*, custōs *m.*
protectress *n.* patrōna *f.*
protégé *n.* cliēns.
protest *n.* obtestātiō *f.*; (*pol.*) intercessiō *f.* *vi.* obtestārī, reclāmāre; (*pol.*) intercēdere.
protestation *n.* adsevērātiō *f.*
prototype *n.* archetypum *n.*
protract *vt.* dūcere, prōdūcere.
protrude *vi.* prōminēre.

protruding *a.* exsertus.
protuberance *n.* ēminentia *f.*, tūber *n.*
protuberant *a.* ēminēns, turgidus.
proud *a.* superbus, adrogāns, însolēns. be — superbīre. be — of iactāre. **-ly** *ad.* superbē.
prove *vt.* dēmōnstrāre, arguere, probāre; (*test*) experīrī. *vi.* (*person*) se praebēre; (*event*) ēvādere. — oneself sē praebēre, sē praestāre. **-d** *a.* expertus. not **-n** nōn liquet.
provenance *n.* origō *f.*
provender *n.* pābulum *n.*
proverb *n.* prōverbium *n.*
proverbial *a.* trītus. become — in prōverbium venīre.
provide *vt.* parāre, praebēre. — for prōvidēre (*dat.*). the law -s lēx iubet. — against praecavēre. **-d that** *conj.* dum, dummodo.
providence *n.* prōvidentia *f.*; Deus *m.*
provident *a.* prōvidus, cautus. **-ly** *ad.* cautē.
providential *a.* dīvīnus; secundus. **-ly** *ad.* dīvīnitus.
providing *conj.* dum, dummodo.
province *n.* prōvincia *f.*
provincial *a.* prōvinciālis; (*contemptuous*) oppidānus, mūnicipālis.
provision *n.* parātus *m.*; (*pl.*) cibus *m.*, commeātus *m.*, rēs frūmentāria *f.* make — for prōvidēre (*dat.*). make — cavēre.
provisionally *ad.* ad tempus.
proviso *n.* condiciō *f.* with this — hāc lēge.
provocation *n.* inrītāmentum *n.*, offēnsiō *f.*
provocative *a.* (*language*) molestus, invidiōsus.
provoke *vt.* inrītāre, lacessere; (*to action*) excitāre. [estus.
provoking *a.* odiōsus, mol-
provost *n.* praefectus *m.*
prow *n.* prōra *f.*
prowess *n.* virtūs *f.*
prowl *vi.* grassārī, vagārī.
proximate *a.* proximus.
proximity *n.* propinquitās *f.*, vīcīnia *f.*
proxy *n.* vicārius *m.*
prude *n.* fastīdiōsa *f.*
prudence *n.* prūdentia *f.*
prudent *a.* prūdēns, cautus, sagāx. **-ly** *ad.* prūdenter, cautē.
prudery *n.* fastīdiōsa quaedam pudīcitia *f.*
prudish *a.* fastīdiōsus.
psychology *n.* animī ratiō. *f.*
prune *vt.* amputāre.
pruner *n.* putātor *m.*
pruning-hook *n.* falx *f.*
pry *vi.* inquīrere. — into scrūtārī. [*n.*
pseudonym *n.* falsum nōmen
Ptolemy *n.* Ptolemaeus *m.*
puberty *n.* pūbertās *f.*
public *a.* pūblicus; (*speech*) forēnsis. — life rēs pūblica *f.*, forum *n.* in — forīs. appear in — in medium prōdīre. make — in mediō pōnere, forās perferre. make a — case of in medium vocāre. act for the — good in medium cōnsulere. be a — figure in lūce versārī, digitō mōnstrārī. *n.* vulgus *n.*, hominēs *m.pl.*
publican *n.* (*taxes*) pūblicānus *m.*; (*inn*) caupō *m.*
publication *n.* ēditiō *f.*, prōmulgātiō *f.*; (*book*) liber *m.*
publicity *n.* lūx *f.*, celebritās *f.*
publicly *ad.* palam; (*by the state*) pūblicē.
publish *vt.* ēvulgāre, dīvulgāre; (*book*) ēdere.
pucker *vt.* corrūgāre.
puerile *a.* puerīlis.
puerility *n.* ineptiae *f.pl.*
puff *n.* aura *f.* *vt.* inflāre. **-ed up** *a.* inflātus, tumidus. *vi.* anhēlāre.
pugilism *n.* pugilātus *m.*

pugilist *n.* pugil *m.*
pugnacious *a.* pugnāx.
pugnacity *n.* ferōcitās *f.*
puissance *n.* potentia *f.*, virēs *f.pl.*
puissant *a.* potēns.
pull *n.* tractus *m.*; (*of gravity*) contentiō *f.* *vt.* trahere, tractāre. — **apart** distrahere. — **at** vellicāre. — **away** āvellere. — **back** retrahere. — **down** dēripere, dētrahere; (*building*) dēmōlīrī. — **off** āvellere. — **out** ēvellere, extrahere. — **through** *vi.* pervincere; (*illness*) convalēscere. — **up** (*plant*) ēruere; (*movement*) coercēre. — **to pieces** dīlaniāre.
pullet *n.* pullus gallīnāceus *m.*
pulley *n.* trochlea *f.*
pulmonary *a.* pulmōneus.
pulp *n.* carō *f.*
pulpit *n.* suggestus *m.*
pulsate *vi.* palpitāre, micāre.
pulse *n.* (*plant*) legūmen *n.*; (*of blood*) vēnae *f.pl.* **feel the** — vēnās temptāre.
pulverize *vt.* contundere.
pumice-stone *n.* pūmex *m.*
pummel *vt.* verberāre.
pump *n.* antlia *f.* *vt.* haurīre. — **out** exhaurīre.
pumpkin *n.* cucurbita *f.*
pun *n.* agnōminātiō *f.*
punch *n.* ictus *m.* *vt.* pertundere, percutere.
punctilious *a.* rēligiōsus.
punctiliousness *n.* rēligiō *f.*
punctual *a.* accūrātus, dīligēns. **-ly** *ad.* ad hōram, ad tempus.
punctuality *n.* dīligentia *f.*
punctuate *vt.* distinguere. [*f.*
punctuation *n.* interpūnctiō
puncture *n.* pūnctiō *f.* *vt.* pungere.
pundit *n.* scholasticus *m.*
pungency *n.* ācrimōnia *f.*; (*in debate*) aculeī *m.pl.*
pungent *a.* ācer, mordāx.
punish *vt.* pūnīre, animadvertere in (*acc.*). **be -ed** poenās dare.
punishable *a.* poenā dignus.
punisher *n.* vindex *m.*, ultor *m.*
punishment *n.* poena *f.*, supplicium *n.*; (*censors'*) animadversiō *f.* **capital** — capitis supplicium *n.* **corporal** — verbera *n.pl.* **inflict** — **on** poenā adficere, poenam capere dē (*abl.*), supplicium sūmere dē (*abl.*). **submit to** — poenam subīre. **undergo** — poenās dare, pendere, solvere.
punitive *a.* ulcīscendī causā.
punt *n.* pontō *m.*
puny *a.* pusillus.
pup *n.* catulus *m.* *vi.* parere.
pupil *n.* discipulus *m.*, discipula *f.*; (*eye*) aciēs *f.*, pūpula *f.*
pupillage *n.* tūtēla *f.*
puppet *n.* pūpa *f.*
puppy *n.* catulus *m.*
purblind *a.* luscus.
purchase *n.* emptiō *f.*; (*formal*) mancipium *n.* *vt.* emere.
purchaser *n.* emptor *m.*; (*at auction*) manceps *m.*
pure *a.* pūrus, integer; (*morally*) castus; (*mere*) merus. **-ly** *ad.* pūrē, integrē; (*solely*) sōlum, nīl nisi; (*quite*) omnīnō, plānē.
purgation *n.* pūrgātiō *f.*
purge *vt.* pūrgāre, expūrgāre.
purification *n.* lūstrātiō *f.*, pūrgātiō *f.*
purify *vt.* pūrgāre, expūrgāre.
purist *n.* fastīdiōsus *m.* [*f.*
purity *n.* integritās *f.*, castitās
purlieus *n.* vīcīnia *f.*
purloin *vt.* surripere, fūrārī.
purple *n.* purpura *f.* *a.* purpureus.
purport *n.* sententia *f.*; (*of words*) vīs *f.* **what is the** — **of ?** quō spectat ? quid vult ? *vt.* velle spectāre ad.
purpose *n.* prōpositum *n.*, cōnsilium *n.*, mēns *f.* **for**

that — eō. for the — of ad (*acc.*), ut (*subj.*), eā mente ut, eō cōnsiliō ut (*subj.*). on — cōnsultō, dē industriā. to the — ad rem. to what — quō, quōrsum. to no — frustrā, nēquīquam. without achieving one's — rē īnfectā. *vt.* in animō habēre, velle.
purposeful *a.* intentus.
purposeless *a.* inānis.
purposely *ad.* cōnsultō, dē industriā.
purr *n.* murmur *n.* *vi.* murmurāre.
purse *n.* marsupium *n.*, crumēna *f.* privy — fiscus *m.* *vt.* adstringere.
pursuance *m.* exsecūtiō *f.* in — of secundum (*acc.*).
pursue *vt.* īnsequī, īnsectārī; (*closely*) īnstāre (*dat.*) īnsistere (*dat.*); (*aim*) petere; (*course*) īnsistere.
pursuer *n.* īnsequēns *m.*; (*law*) accūsātor *m.*
pursuit *n.* īnsectātiō *f.*; (*hunt*) vēnātiō *f.*; (*ambition*) studium *n.* [obsōnāre.
purvey *vt.* parāre; (*food*)
purveyance *n.* prōcūrātiō *f.*
purveyor *n.* obsōnātor *m.*
purview *n.* prōvincia *f.*
pus *n.* pūs *n.*
push *n.* pulsus *m.*, impetus *m.* *vt.* impellere, trūdere, urgēre. — away āmovēre. — back repellere. — down dēprimere, dētrūdere. — forward prōpellere. — in intrūdere. — on incitāre. — through perrumpere.
pushing *a.* cōnfīdēns.
pusillanimity *n.* ignāvia *f.*, timor *m.* [timidus.
pusillanimous *a.* ignāvus,
pustule *n.* pustula *f.*
put *vt.* (*in a state*) dare; (*in a position*) pōnere; (*in words*) reddere; (*argument*) pōnere; (*spur*) subdere; (*to some use*) adhibēre. — an end to fīnem facere (*dat.*). — a question to interrogāre. — against adpōnere. — among intericere. — aside sēpōnere. — away pōnere, dēmovēre; (*store*) repōnere. — back repōnere. — beside adpōnere. — between interpōnere. — by condere. — down dēpōnere; (*revolt*) opprimere. — forth extendere; (*growth*) mittere. — forward ostentāre; (*plea*) adferre. — in immittere, īnserere; (*ship*) adpellere. — off differre. — on impōnere; (*clothes*) induī; (*play*) dare. — out ēicere; (*eye*) effodere; (*fire*) exstinguere; (*money*) pōnere; (*tongue*) exserere; (*to sea*) solvere. — out of the way dēmovēre. — over superimpōnere. — to adpōnere; (*flight*) dare in (*acc.*); (*sea*) solvere. — together cōnferre. — under subicere. — up (*for sale*) prōpōnere; (*lodge*) dēvertere, dēversārī apud. — up with ferre, patī. — upon impōnere.
putrefaction *n.* pūtor *m.*
putrefy *vi.* putrēscere.
putrid *a.* putridus.
puzzle *n.* nōdus *m.* *vt.* impedīre, sollicitāre. be -d haerēre. [plexus.
puzzling *a.* ambiguus, per-
pygmy *n.* pygmaeus *m.*
pyramid *n.* pȳramis *f.*
pyramidal *a.* pȳramidātus.
pyre *n.* rogus *m.*
python *n.* pȳthōn *m.*

Q

quack *n.* (*doctor*) circulātor *m.* *vi.* tetrinnīre.
quadrangle *n.* ārea *f.* [*f.*
quadruped *n.* quadrupēs *m.*,
quadruple *a.* quadruplex.
quaestor *n.* quaestor *m.* -'s quaestōrius.

quaestorship *n.* quaestūra *f.*
quaff *vt.* ēpōtāre, haurīre.
quagmire *n.* palūs *f.*
quail *n.* (*bird*) coturnīx *f.* *vi.* pāvēscere, trepidāre.
quaint *a.* novus, īnsolitus.
quaintness *n.* īnsolentia *f.*
quake *vi.* horrēre, horrēscere. *n.* (*earth*) mōtus *m.*
quaking *n.* horror *m.*, tremor *m.* *a.* tremulus.
qualification *n.* condiciō *f.*; (*limitation*) exceptiō *f.*
qualified *a.* (*for*) aptus, idōneus, dignus; (*in*) perītus, doctus.
qualify *vi.* prōficere. *vt.* temperāre, mītigāre.
quality *n.* nātūra *f.*, vīs *f.*; (*pl.*) ingenium *n.*, indolēs *f.*; (*rank*) locus *m.*, genus *n.* I know the — of sciō quālis sit.
qualm *n.* rēligiō *f.*, scrūpulus *m.* [be in a — haerēre.
quandary *n.* angustiae *f.pl.*
quantity *n.* cōpia *f.*, numerus *m.*; (*metre*) vōcum mēnsiō *f.* a large — multum *n.*, plūrimum *n.* a small — aliquantulum *n.*
quarrel *n.* dissēnsiō *f.*, contrōversia *f.*; (*violent*) rixa *f.*, iūrgium *n.* *vi.* rixārī, altercārī.
quarrelsome *a.* pugnāx, lītigiōsus.
quarry *n.* lapicīdinae *f.pl.*, metallum *n.*; (*prey*) praeda *f.* *vt.* excīdere.
quart *n.* duo sextāriī *m.pl.*
quartan *n.* (*fever*) quartāna *f.*
quarter *n.* quarta pars *f.*, quadrāns *m.*; (*sector*) regiō *f.*; (*direction*) pars *f.*, regiō *f.*; (*respite*) missiō *f.* -s castra *n.pl.*: (*billet*) hospitium *n.* three -s dōdrāns *m.*, trēs partēs *f.pl.* come to close -s manum cōnserere; (*armies*) signa cōnferre. winter -s hīberna *n.pl.* *vt.* quadrifidam dīvidere; (*troops*) in hospitia dīvidere.
quarter-deck *n.* puppis *f.*
quarterly *a.* trimestris. *ad.* quartō quōque mēnse.
quartermaster *n.* (*navy*) gubernātor *m.*; (*army*) castrōrum praefectus *m.*
quarterstaff *n.* rudis *f.*
quash *vt.* comprimere; (*decision*) rescindere.
quatrain *n.* tetrastichon *n.*
quaver *n.* tremor *m.* *vi.* tremere.
quavering *a.* tremebundus.
quay *n.* crepīdō *f.*
queasy *a.* fastīdiōsus. [*m.*
queen *n.* rēgīna *f.*; (*bee*) rēx
queer *a.* īnsolēns, rīdiculus.
quell *vt.* opprimere, domāre, dēbellāre.
quench *vt.* exstinguere, restinguere; (*thirst*) sēdāre, explēre.
querulous *a.* querulus, querībundus.
query *n.* interrogātiō *f.* *vt.* in dubium vocāre. *vi.* rogāre.
quest *n.* investīgātiō *f.* go in — of investīgāre, anquīrere.
question *n.* interrogātiō *f.*; (*at issue*) quaestiō *f.*, rēs *f.*; (*in doubt*) dubium *n.* ask a — rogāre, quaerere, scīscitārī, percontārī. call in — in dubium vocāre, addubitāre. out of the — indignus. be the out of the — improbārī, fierī nōn posse. the — is illud quaeritur. there is no — that nōn dubium est quīn (*subj.*). without — sine dubiō. *vt.* interrogāre; (*closely*). percontārī; (*doubt*) in dubium vocāre. *vi.* dubitāre.
questionable *a.* incertus, dubius.
questioner *n.* percontātor *m.*
questioning *n.* interrogātiō *f.*
queue *n.* agmen *n.*
quibble *n.* captiō *f.* *vi.* cavillārī.
quibbler *n.* cavillātor *m.*
quibbling *a.* captiōsus.
quick *a.* (*speed*) celer, vēlōx,

citus; (*to act*) alacer, impiger; (*to perceive*) sagāx; (*with hands*) facilis; (*living*) vīvus. be — properāre, festīnāre. cut to the — ad vīvum resecāre; (*fig.*) mordēre. **-tempered** *a.* īrācundus.
quicken *vt.* adcelerāre; (*with life*) animāre.
quickening *a.* vītālis.
quickly *ad.* celeriter, citō; (*haste*) properē; (*mind*) acūtē.
quickness *n.* celeritās *f.*, vēlōcitās *f.*; (*to act*) alacritās *f.*; (*to perceive*) sagācitās *f.*, sollertia *f.*
quicksand *n.* syrtis *f.*
quick-witted *a.* acūtus, sagāx, perspicāx. [ōtium *n.*
quiescence *n.* inertia *f.*,
quiescent *a.* iners, ōtiōsus.
quiet *a.* tranquillus, quiētus, placidus; (*silent*) tacitus. be — quiēscere; silēre. *n.* quiēs *f.*, tranquillitās *f.*; silentium *n.*; (*peace*) pāx *f.* *vt.* pācāre, compōnere. **-ly** *ad.* tranquillē, quiētē; tacitē, per silentium; aequō animō.
quietness *n.* tranquillitās *f.*; silentium *n.*
quill *n.* penna *f.*
quince *n.* cydōnium *n.*
quinquennial *a.* quinquennālis. [mis *f.*
quinquereme *n.* quinquerē-
quinsy *n.* angina *f.* [vis *f.*
quintessence *n.* flōs *m.*,
quip *n.* sāl *m.*, facētiae *f.pl.*
quirk *n.* captiuncula *f.*; (*pl.*) trīcae *f.pl.*
quit *vt.* relinquere. *a.* līber, solūtus; (*pl.*) parēs.
quite *ad.* admodum, plānē, prōrsus. not — minus, parum; (*time*) nōndum.
quiver *n.* pharetra *f.* *vi.* tremere, contremere.
quivering *a.* tremebundus, tremulus.
quoit *n.* discus *m.*
quota *n.* pars *f.*, rata pars *f.*
quotation *n.* (*act*) commemorātiō *f.*; (*passage*) locus *m.*
quote *vt.* prōferre, commemorāre.
quoth *vt.* inquit.

R

rabbit *n.* cuniculus *m.*
rabble *n.* turba *f.*; (*class*) vulgus *n.*, plēbēcula *f.*
rabid *a.* rabidus. **-ly** *ad.* rabidē.
race *n.* (*descent*) genus *n.*, stirps *f.*; (*people*) gēns *f.*, nōmen *n.*; (*contest*) certāmen *n.*; (*fig.*) cursus *m.*, curriculum *n.*; (*water*) flūmen *n.* run a — cursū certāre. run the — (*fig.*) spatium dēcurrere. *vi.* certāre, contendere.
race-course *n.* (*foot*) stadium *n.*; (*horse*) spatium *n.*
racer *n.* cursor *m.*
racial *a.* gentīlis.
rack *n.* (*torture*) tormentum *n.*; (*shelf*) pluteus *m.* be on the — (*fig.*) cruciārī. *vt.* torquēre, cruciāre. — off (*wine*) diffundere.
racket *n.* (*noise*) strepitus *m.*
racy *a.* (*style*) salsus.
radiance *n.* splendor *m.*, fulgor *m.*
radiant *a.* splendidus, nitidus. **-ly** *ad.* splendidē.
radiate *vi.* fulgēre; (*direction*) dīversōs tendere. *vt.* ēmittere.
radical *a.* īnsitus, innātus; (*thorough*) tōtus. *n.* novārum rērum cupidus *m.* **-ly** *ad.* omninō, penitus, funditus.
radish *n.* rādīx *f.*
radius *n.* radius *m.*
raffish *a.* dissolūtus.
raffle *n.* ālea *f.* *vt.* āleā vēndere.
raft *n.* ratis *f.*
rafter *n.* trabs *f.*, tignum *n.*
rag *n.* pannus *m.*
rage *n.* īra *f.*, furor *m.* be all

the — in ōre omnium esse. spend one's — exsaevīre. *vi.* furere, saevīre; (*furiously*) dēbacchārī.
ragged *a.* pannōsus.
raid *n.* excursiō *f.*, incursiō *f.*, impressiō *f.* make a — excurrere. *vt.* incursiōnem facere in (*acc.*).
rail *n.* longurius *m.* *vt.* saepīre. *vi.* — at maledīcere (*dat.*), convīcia facere (*dat.*). [*m.pl.*
railing *n.* saepēs *f.*, cancellī
raillery *n.* cavillātiō *f.*
raiment *n.* vestis *f.*
rain *n.* pluvia *f.*, imber *m.* *vi.* pluere.
rainbow *n.* arcus *m.*
rainy *a.* pluvius.
raise *vt.* tollere, ēlevāre; (*army*) cōgere, cōnscrībere; (*children*) ēducāre; (*cry*) tollere; (*from dead*) excitāre; (*laugh*) movēre; (*money*) cōnflāre; (*price*) augēre; (*siege*) exsolvere; (*structure*) exstruere. (*to higher rank*) ēvehere. — up ērigere, sublevāre.
raisin *n.* astaphis *f.*
rajah *n.* dynastēs *m.*
rake *n.* rastrum *n.*; (*person*) nepōs *m.* *vt.* rādere. — in conrādere. — up (*fig.*) ēruere.
rakish *a.* dissolūtus.
rally *n.* conventus *m.* *vt.* (*troops*) in ōrdinem revocāre; (*with words*) hortārī; (*banter*) cavillārī. *vi.* sē colligere.
ram *n.* ariēs *m.*; (*battering*) ariēs *m.* *vt.* — down fistūcāre. — home (*fact*) inculcāre.
ramble *n.* errātiō *f.* *vi.* vagārī, errāre.
rambling *a.* vagus; (*plant*) errāticus; (*speech*) fluēns.
ramification *n.* rāmus *m.*
rammer *n.* fistūca *f.*
rampage *vi.* saevīre.
rampant *a.* ferōx. [*n.*
rampart *n.* agger *m.*, vallum
ranch *n.* lātifundium *n.*
rancid *a.* pūtidus.
rancour *n.* odium *n.*, acerbitās *f.*, invidia *f.*
random *a.* fortuītus. *at* — temerē.
range *n.* ōrdō *m.*, seriēs *f.*; (*mountain*) iugum *n.*; (*of weapon*) iactus *m.* within — intrā tēlī iactum. come within — sub ictum venīre. *vt.* ōrdināre. *vi.* ēvagārī, pervagārī; (*in speech*) excurrere.
rank *n.* (*line*) ōrdō *m.*; (*class*) ōrdō *m.*; (*position*) locus *m.*, dignitās *f.* — and file gregāriī mīlitēs *m.pl.* keep the -s ōrdinēs observāre. leave the -s ōrdine ēgredī, ab signīs discēdere. reduce to the -s in ōrdinem redigere. *vt.* numerāre. *vi.* in numerō habērī.
rank *a.* luxuriōsus; (*smell*) gravis, foetidus.
rankle *vi.* exulcerāre.
rankness *n.* luxuriēs *f.*
ransack *vt.* dīripere, spoliāre.
ransom *n.* redemptiō *f.*, pretium *n.* *vt.* redimere.
rant *vi.* latrāre. [*m.*
ranter *n.* rabula *m.*, lātrātor
rap *n.* ictus *m.* *vt.* ferīre.
rapacious *a.* rapāx. avidus. **-ly** *ad.* avidē.
rapacity *n.* rapācitās *f.*, aviditās *f.*
rape *n.* raptus *m.*
rapid *a.* rapidus, vēlōx, citus, incitātus. **-ly** *ad.* rapidē, vēlōciter, citō.
rapidity *n.* celeritās *f.*, vēlōcitās *f.*, incitātiō *f.*
rapine *n.* rapīna *f.*
rapt *a.* intentus. [*f.*
rapture *n.* laetitia *f.*, alacritās
rare *a.* rārus; (*occurrence*) īnfrequēns; (*quality*) singulāris. **-ly** *ad.* rārō.
rarefy *vt.* extenuāre.
rarity *n.* rāritās *f.*; (*thing*) rēs īnsolita *f.* [*m.*
rascal *n.* furcifer *m.*, scelestus
rascality *n.* scelus *n.*

rascally *a.* improbus.
rash *a.* temerārius, audāx, incōnsultus. **-ly** *ad.* temerē, incōnsultē.
rashness *n.* temeritās *f.*, audācia *f.*
rat *n.* mūs *m.*, *f.*
rate *n.* (*cost*) pretium *n.*; (*standard*) nōrma *f.*; (*tax*) vectīgal *n.*; (*speed*) celeritās *f.* at any — (*concessive*) utique, saltem; (*adversative*) quamquam, tamen. *vt.* (*value*) aestimāre; (*scold*) increpāre, obiūrgāre.
rather *ad.* potius, satius; (*somewhat*) aliquantum; (*with comp.*) aliquantō; (*correcting*) immo. — sad tristior. I would — mālō. I — think haud sciō an.
ratification *n.* (*formal*) sanctiō *f.*
ratify *vt.* ratum facere, sancīre; (*law*) iubēre.
rating *n.* taxātiō *f.*, aestimātiō *f.*; (*navy*) nauta *m.*; (*scolding*) obiūrgātiō *f.*
ratiocinate *vi.* ratiōcinārī. [*f.*
ratiocination *n.* ratiōcinātiō
ration *n.* dēmēnsum *n.* (*pl.*) cibāria *n.pl.*, diāria *n.pl.*
rational *a.* animō praeditus. be — sapere. **-ly** *ad.* ratiōne.
rationality *n.* ratiō *f.*
rattle *n.* crepitus *m.*; (*toy*) crotalum *n.* *vi.* crepitāre, increpāre.
raucous *a.* raucus.
ravage *vt.* dēpopulārī, vastāre, dīripere.
rave *vi.* furere, īnsānīre; (*fig.*) bacchārī, saevīre.
raven *n.* cornix *f.*
ravenous *a.* rapāx, vorāx. **-ly** *ad.* avidē. [*m*
ravine *n.* faucēs *fpl.*, hiātus
raving *a.* furiōsus, īnsānus. *n.* furor *m.*
ravish *vt.* rapere; (*joy*) efferre.
raw *a.* crūdus; (*person*) rudis, agrestis.
ray *n.* radius *m.* the first — of hope appeared prīma spēs adfulsit.
raze *vt.* excīdere, solō aequāre.
razor *n.* novācula *f.*
reach *n.* (*space*) spatium *n.*; (*mind*) captus *m.*; (*weapon*) ictus *m.* out of — of extrā (*acc.*). within — ad manum. *vt.* attingere; (*space*) pertinēre ad; (*journey*) pervenīre ad.
react *vi.* adficī. — to ferre.
reaction *n.* what was his — to quo animō tulit.
read *vt.* legere; (*a book*) ēvolvere; (*aloud*) recitāre. — over perlegere. **well** — *a.* litterātus.
reader *n.* lēctor *m.*
readiness *n.* facilitās *f.* in — ad manum, in prōmptū, in expeditō. [dāre.
readjust *vt.* dēnuō accommo-
read/y *a.* parātus, prōmptus; (*manner*) facilis; (*money*) praesēns. get, make — parāre, expedīre, adōrnāre. **-ily** *ad.* facile, libenter, ultrō.
reading *n.* lēctiō *f.*
reaffirm *vt.* iterum adfirmāre.
real *a.* vērus, germānus. — estate fundus *m.*, solum *n.* **-ly** *ad.* vērē, rēvērā, profectō; (*interrog.*) itane vērō ?
realism *n.* vēritās *f.*
realistic *a.* vērī similis.
reality *n.* rēs *f.*, rēs ipsa *f.*, vērum *n.* in — rēvērā.
realize *vt.* intellegere, animadvertere; (*aim*) efficere, peragere; (*money*) redigere.
realm *n.* rēgnum *n.*
reap *vt.* metere. — the reward of fructum percipere ex.
reaper *n.* messor *m.*
reappear *vi.* revenīre.
rear *vt.* alere, ēducāre; (*structure*) exstruere. *vi.* sē ērigere. *n.* tergum *n.*; (*mil.*) novissima aciēs *f.*, novissimum agmen *n.* in the — ā tergō bring up the — agmen claudere, agmen

cōgere. *a.* postrēmus, novissimus.
rearguard *n.* novissimum agmen *n.*, novissimi *m.pl.*
rearrange *vt.* ōrdinem mūtāre (*gen.*).
reason *n.* (*faculty*) mēns *f.*, animus *m.*, ratiō *f.*; (*sanity*) sānitās *f.*; (*argument*) ratiō *f.*; (*cause*) causa *f.*; (*moderation*) modus *m.* **by — of** propter (*acc.*). **for this —** idcircō, ideō, proptereā. **in —** aequus, modicus. **with good —** iūre. **without —** temerē, sine causā. **without good —** frustrā, iniūriā. **give a — for** ratiōnem adferre (*gen.*). **I know the — for** sciō cūr, quamobrem (*subj.*). **there is no — for** nōn est cūr, nihil est quod (*subj.*). **lose one's —** īnsānīre. *vi.* ratiōcinārī, disserere.
reasonab/le *a.* aequus, iūstus; (*person*) modestus; (*amount*) modicus. **–ly** *ad.* ratiōne, iūstē; modicē.
reasoning *n.* ratiō *f.*, ratiōcinātiō *f*
reassemble *vt.* colligere, cōgere.
reassert *vt.* iterāre.
reassume *vt.* recipere.
reassure *vt.* firmāre, cōnfirmāre.
rebate *vt.* dēdūcere.
rebel *n.* rebellis *m.* *a.* sēditiōsus. *vi.* rebellāre, dēscīscere.
rebellion *n.* sēditiō *f.*, mōtus *m.*
rebellious *a.* sēditiōsus.
rebound *vi.* resilīre.
rebuff *n.* repulsa *f.* *vt.* repellere, āversārī. [rare.
rebuild *vt.* renovāre, restau-
rebuke *n.* reprehēnsiō *f.*, obiūrgātiō *f.* *vt.* reprehendere, obiūrgāre, increpāre.
rebut *vt.* refūtāre, redarguere.
recalcitrant *a.* invītus.
recall *n.* revocātiō *f.*, reditus *m.* *vt.* revocāre; (*from exile*) redūcere; (*to mind*) reminīscī (*gen.*) recordārī (*gen.*).
recant *vt.* retractāre.
recantation *n.* receptus *m.*
recapitulate *vt.* repetere, summātim dīcere. [rātiō *f.*
recapitulation *n.* ēnume-
recapture *vt.* recipere.
recast *vt.* reficere, retractāre.
recede *vi.* recēdere.
receipt *n.* (*act*) acceptiō *f.*; (*money*) acceptum *n.*; (*written*) apocha *f.*
receive *vt.* accipere, capere; (*in turn*) excipere.
receiver *n.* receptor *m.*
recent *a.* recēns. **–ly** *ad.* nūper recēns.
receptacle *n.* receptāculum *n.*
reception *n.* aditus *m.*, hospitium *n.*
receptive *a.* docilis.
recess *n.* recessus *m.*, angulus *m.*; (*holiday*) fēriae *f.pl.*
recharge *vt.* replēre.
recipe *n.* compositiō *f.*
recipient *n.* quī accipit.
reciprocal *a.* mūtuus. **–ly** *ad.* mūtuō, inter sē. [dere.
reciprocate *vt.* referre, red-
reciprocity *n.* mūtuum *n.*
recital *n.* nārrātiō *f.*, ēnumerātiō *f.*; (*lit.*) recitātiō *f.*
recitation *n.* recitātiō *f.*
recite *vt.* recitāre; (*details*) ēnumerāre.
reciter *n.* recitātor *m.*
reck *vt.* ratiōnem habēre (*gen.*).
reckless *a.* temerārius, incautus, praeceps. **–ly** *ad.* incautē, temerē.
recklessness *n.* temeritās *f.*, neglegentia *f.*
reckon *vt.* (*count*) computāre, numerāre; (*think*) cēnsēre, dūcere. **— on** cōnfīdere (*dat.*). **— up** dīnumerāre; (*cost*) aestimāre. **— with** contendere cum.
reckoning *n.* ratiō *f.*
reclaim *vt.* repetere; (*from error*) revocāre.

recline *vi.* recumbere; (*at table*) accumbere; (*plur.*) discumbere.
recluse *n.* homō sōlitārius *m.*
recognition *n.* cognitiō *f.*
recognizance *n.* vadimōnium *n.*
recognize *vt.* agnōscere; (*approve*) accipere; (*admit*) fatērī.
recoil *vi.* resilīre. — **from** refugere. — **upon** recidere in (*acc.*).
recollect *vt.* reminīscī (*gen.*).
recollection *n.* memoria *f.*, recordātiō *f.*
recommence *vt.* renovāre, redintegrāre.
recommend *vt.* commendāre; (*advise*) suādēre (*dat.*).
recommendation *n.* commendātiō *f.*; (*advice*) cōnsilium *n.* **letter of** — litterae commendātīciae.
recompense *vt.* remūnerārī, grātiam referre (*dat.*). *n.* praemium *n.* remūnerātiō *f.*
reconcile *vt.* compōnere, reconciliāre **be -d** in grātiam redīre.
reconciliation *n.* reconciliātiō *f.*, grātia *f.*
recondite *a.* reconditus, [abstrūsus.
recondition *vt.* reficere.
reconnaissance *n.* explōrātiō *f.*
reconnoitr/e *vt.* & *i.* explōrāre. **without -ing** inexplōrātō.
reconquer *vt.* recipere.
reconsider *vt.* reputāre, retractāre.
reconstruct *vt.* restituere, renovāre.
reconstruction *n.* renovātiō *f.*
record *n.* monumentum *n.*; (*lit.*) commentārius *m.*; (*pl.*) tabulae *f.pl.*, fāstī *m.pl.*, ācta *n.pl.* **break the** — priōrēs omnēs superāre. *vt.* in commentārium referre; (*history*) perscrībere, nārrāre.
recount *vt.* nārrāre, commemorāre.
recourse *n.* **have — to** (*for safety*) cōnfugere *ad*; (*as expedient*) dēcurrere ad.
recover *vt.* recipere, recuperāre; (*loss*) reparāre. — **oneself** sē colligere. — **one's senses** ad sānitātem revertī. *vi.* convalēscere.
recovery *n.* recuperātiō *f.*; (*from illness*) salūs *f.*
recreate *vt.* recreāre.
recreation *n.* requiēs *f.*, remissiō *f.*, lūdus *m.*
recriminate *vi.* in vicem accūsāre.
recrimination *n.* mūtua accūsātiō *f.*
recruit *n.* tīrō *m.* *vt.* (*mil.*) cōnscrībere; (*strength*) reficere. **-ing officer** conquīsītor *m.*
rectify *vt.* corrigere, ēmendāre.
rectitude *n.* probitās *f.*
recumbent *a.* supīnus.
recuperate *vi.* convalēscere.
recur *vi.* recurrere, redīre.
recurrence *n.* reditus *m.*, reversiō *f.*
recurrent *a.* adsiduus.
red *a.* ruber **-haired** rūfus.
redden *vi.* ērubēscere. *vt.* rutilāre.
reddish *a.* subrūfus.
redeem *vt.* redimere, līberāre.
redeemer *n.* līberātor *m.*
redemption *n.* redemptiō *f.*
red-handed *a.* **catch — in** manifestō scelere dēprehendere.
red-lead *n.* minium *n.*
redness *n.* rubor *m.*
redolent *a.* **be — of** redolēre.
redouble *vt.* ingemināre.
redoubt *n.* prōpugnāculum *n.*
redoubtable *a.* īnfestus, formīdolōsus.
redound *vi.* redundāre. **it -s to my credit** mihi honōrī est.
redress *n.* remedium *n.* **demand —** rēs repetere. *vt.* restituere.

reduce *vt.* minuere, attenuāre; (*to a condition*) redigere, dēdūcere; (*mil.*) expugnāre. — to the ranks in ōrdinem cōgere.
reduction *n.* imminūtiō *f.*; (*mil.*) expugnātiō *f.*
redundancy *n.* redundantia *f.*
redundant *a.* redundāns. be — redundāre.
reduplication *n.* gemīnātiō *f.*
re-echo *vt.* reddere, referre. *vi.* resonāre.
reed *n* harundō *f.*
reedy *a.* harundineus.
reef *n.* saxa *n.pl.* *vt.* (*sail*) subnectere.
reek *n.* fūmus *m.* *vi.* fūmāre.
reel *vi.* vacillāre, titubāre.
re-enlist *vt.* rescrībere.
re-establish *vt.* restituere.
refashion *vt.* reficere.
refer *vt.* (*person*) dēlēgāre; (*matter*) rēicere, remittere. *vi.* — to spectāre ad; (*in speech*) attingere, perstringere.
referee *n.* arbiter *m.*
reference *n.* ratiō *f.*; (*in book*) locus *m.*
refine *vt.* excolere, expolīre; (*metal*) excoquere.
refined *a.* hūmānus, urbānus, polītus.
refinement *n.* hūmānitās *f.*, cultus *m.*, ēlegantia *f.*
refit *vt.* reficere.
reflect *vt.* reddere, repercutere. *vi.* meditārī. — upon cōnsīderāre, sēcum reputāre; (*blame*) reprehendere.
reflection *n.* (*of light*) repercussus *m.*; (*image*) imāgō *f.*; (*thought*) meditātiō *f.*, cōgitātiō *f.*; (*blame*) reprehēnsiō *f.* cast -s on maculīs aspergere, vitiō vertere. with due — cōnsīderātē. without — incōnsultē.
reflux *n.* recessus *m.*
reform *n.* ēmendātiō *f.* *vt.* (*lines*) restituere; (*error*) corrigere, ēmendāre, meliōrem facere. *vi.* sē corrigere.
reformation *n.* corrēctiō *f.*
reformer *n.* corrēctor *m.*, ēmendātor *m.*
refract *vt.* īnfringere.
refractory *a.* contumāx.
refrain *vi.* temperāre, abstinēre (*dat.*), supersedēre (*inf.*).
refresh *vt.* recreāre, renovāre, reficere; (*mind*) integrāre. **-ed** *a.* requiētus. [dus.
refreshing *a.* dulcis, iūcun-
refreshment *n.* cibus *m.*
refuge *n.* perfugium *n.*; (*secret*) latebra *f.* take — with perfugere ad (*acc.*).
refugee *n.* profugus *m.*
refulgence *n.* splendor *m.*
refulgent *a.* splendidus.
refund *vt.* reddere.
refusal *n.* recūsātiō *f.*, dētrectātiō *f.*
refuse *n.* pūrgāmenta *n.pl.*; (*fig.*) faex *f.* *vt.* (*request*) dēnegāre; (*offer*) dētrectāre, recūsāre; (*with verb*) nōlle.
refutation *n.* refūtātiō *f.*, reprehēnsiō *f.*
refute *vt.* refellere, redarguere, revincere.
regain *vt.* recipere.
regal *a* rēgius, rēgālis. **-ly** *ad.* rēgāliter.
regale *vt.* excipere, dēlectāre. — oneself epulārī.
regalia *n.* īnsignia *n.pl.*
regard *n.* respectus *m.*, ratiō *f.*; (*esteem*) grātia *f.* with — to ad (*acc.*) quod attinet ad. *vt.* (*look*) intuērī, spectāre; (*deem*) habēre, dūcere. send -s to salūtem dīcere (*dat.*).
regarding *pr.* dē (*abl.*).
regardless *a.* neglegēns, immemor.
regency *n.* interrēgnum *n.*
regent *n.* interrēx *m.*
regicide *n.* (*person*) rēgis interfector *m.*; (*act*) rēgis caedēs *f.*
regime *n.* administrātiō *f.*
regimen *n.* victus *m.*
regiment *n.* legiō *f.*

region *n.* regiō *f.*, tractus *m.*
register *n.* tabulae *f.pl.*, album *n.* *vt.* in tabulās referre, perscrībere; (*emotion*) ostendere, sūmere.
registrar *n.* tabulārius *m.*
registry *n.* tabulārium *n.*
regret *n.* dolor *m.*; (*for past*) dēsīderium *n.*; (*for fault*) paenitentia *f.* *vt.* dolēre. **I** — me paenitet, me piget (*gen.*).
regretful *a.* maestus. **-ly** *ad.* dolenter.
regrettable *a.* īnfēlīx, īnfortūnātus.
regular *a.* (*consistent*) cōnstāns; (*orderly*) ōrdinātus; (*habitual*) solitus, adsiduus; (*proper*) iūstus, rēctus. **-ly** *ad.* ōrdine; cōnstanter; iūstē, rēctē.
regularity *n.* moderātiō *f.*, ōrdō *m.*; (*consistency*) cōnstantia *f.*
regulate *vt.* ōrdināre, dīrigere; (*control*) moderārī.
regulation *n.* lēx *f.*, dēcrētum [*n.*
rehabilitate *vt.* restituere.
rehearsal *n.* meditātiō *f.*
rehearse *vt.* meditārī.
reign *n.* rēgnum *n.*; (*emperor's*) prīncipātus *m.* **in the — of Numa** rēgnante Numā. *vi.* rēgnāre; (*fig.*) dominārī.
reimburse *vt.* rependere.
rein *n.* habēna *f.* **give full — to** habēnās immittere. *vt.* īnfrēnāre.
reindeer *n.* rēnō *m.*
reinforce *vt.* firmāre, cōnfirmāre.
reinforcement *n.* subsidium *n.*; (*pl.*) novae cōpiae *f.pl.*
reinstate *vt.* restituere, redūcere.
reinstatement *n.* restitūtiō *f.* reductiō *f.*; (*to legal privileges*) postlīminium *n.*
reinvigorate *vt.* recreāre.
reiterate *vt.* dictitāre, iterāre.
reiteration *n.* iterātiō *f.*
reject *vt.* rēicere; (*with scorn*) respuere, aspernārī.
rejection *n.* rēiectiō *f.*, repulsa *f.*
rejoice *vi.* gaudēre, laetārī. *vt.* dēlectāre.
rejoicing *n.* gaudium *n.*
rejoin *vt.* redīre ad. *vi.* respondēre.
rejoinder *n.* respōnsum *n.*
rejuvenate *vt.* **be -d** repuerāscere.
rekindle *vt.* suscitāre.
relapse *vi.* recidere.
relate *vt.* (*tell*) nārrāre, commemorāre, expōnere; (*compare*) cōnferre. *vi.* pertinēre.
related *a.* propinquus; (*by birth*) cognātus; (*by marriage*) adfīnis; (*fig.*) fīnitimus.
relation *n.* (*tale*) nārrātiō *f.*; (*connection*) ratiō *f.*; (*kin*) necessārius *m.*, cognātus *m.*, adfīnis *m.*
relationship *n.* necessitūdō *f.*; (*by birth*) cognātiō *f.*; (*by marriage*) adfīnitās *f.*; (*connection*) vīcīnitās *f.*
relative *a.* cum cēteris comparātus. *n.* propinquus *m.*, cognātus *m.*, adfīnis *m.*, necessārius *m.* **-ly** *ad.* ex comparātiōne.
relax *vt.* laxāre, remittere. *vi.* languēscere.
relaxation *n.* remissiō *f.*, requiēs *f.*, lūdus *m.*
relay *n.* **-s of horses** dispositī equī *m.pl.*
release *vt.* solvere exsolvere, līberāre, expedīre; (*law*) absolvere. *n.* missiō *f.*, līberātiō *f.*
relegate *vt.* relēgāre.
relent *vi.* concēdere, plācārī, flectī.
relentless *a.* immisericors, inexōrābilis; (*things*) improbus.
relevant *a.* ad rem.
reliability *n.* fīdūcia *f.*
reliable *a.* fīdus.
reliance *n.* fīdūcia *f.*, fidēs *f.*
reliant *a.* frētus.

relic *n.* rēliquiae *f.pl.*

relief *n.* levātiō *f.*, levāmen *n.*, adlevāmentum *n.*; (*aid*) subsidium *n.*; (*turn of duty*) vicēs *f.pl.*; (*art*) ēminentia *f.*; (*sculpture*) toreuma *n.* bas — anaglypta *n.pl.* in — ēminēns, expressus. throw into — exprimere, distinguere.

relieve *vt.* levāre, sublevāre; (*aid*) subvenīre (*dat.*); (*duty*) succēdere (*dat.*), excipere; (*art*) distinguere.

religion *n.* rēligiō *f.*, deōrum cultus *m.*

religious *a.* rēligiōsus, pius. — feeling rēligiō *f.* **-ly** *ad.* rēligiōsē.

relinquish *vt.* relinquere; (*office*) sē abdicāre (*abl.*).

relish *n.* sapor *m.*; (*sauce*) condīmentum *n.*; (*zest*) studium *n.* *vt.* dēlectārī (*abl.*).

reluctance *n.* with — invītus.

reluctant *a.* invītus. **-ly** *ad.* invītus, gravātē.

rely *vi.* fīdere (*dat.*), cōnfīdere (*dat.*). **-ing** *a.* frētus (*abl.*).

remain *vi.* manēre, morārī; (*left over*) restāre, superesse.

remainder *n.* reliquum *n.*

remaining *a.* reliquus. the — cēterī *pl.*

remains *n.* rēliquiae *f.pl.*

remand *vt.* (*law*) ampliāre.

remark *n.* dictum *n.* *vt.* dīcere; (*note*) observāre.

remarkab/le *a.* īnsignis, ēgregius, memorābilis. **-ly** *ad.* īnsignītē, ēgregiē.

remediable *a.* sānābilis.

remedy *n.* remedium *n.* *vt.* medērī (*dat.*), sānāre.

remember *vt.* meminisse (*gen.*); (*recall*) recordārī (*gen.*), reminīscī (*gen.*).

remembrance *n.* memoria *f.*, recordātiō *f.* [monefacere.

remind *vt.* admonēre, com-

reminder *n.* admonitiō *f.*, admonitum *n.*

reminiscence *n.* recordātiō *f.*

remiss *a.* dissolūtus, neglegēns.

remission *n.* venia *f.*

remissness *n.* neglegentia *f.*

remit *vt.* remittere; (*fault*) ignōscere (*dat.*); (*debt*) dōnāre; (*punishment*) condōnāre; (*question*) referre.

remittance *n.* pecūnia *f.*

remnant *n.* fragmentum *n.*; (*pl.*) rēliquiae *f.pl.*

remonstrance *n.* obtestātiō *f.*, obiūrgātiō *f.*

remonstrate *vi.* reclāmāre. — with obiūrgāre. — about expostulāre.

remorse *n.* paenitentia *f.*, cōnscientia *f.*

remorseless *a.* immisericors.

remote *a.* remōtus, reconditus. **-ly** *ad.* procul.

remoteness *n.* longinquitās *f.*

removal *n.* āmōtiō *f.*; (*going*) migrātiō *f.*

remove *vt.* āmovēre, dēmere, eximere; (*out of the way*) dēmovēre. *vi.* migrāre, dēmigrāre.

remunerate *vt.* remūnerārī.

remuneration *n.* mercēs *f.*, praemium *n.*

rend *vt.* scindere, dīvellere.

render *vt.* reddere; (*music*) interpretārī; (*translation*) vertere; (*thanks*) referre.

rendering *n.* interpretātiō *f.*

rendez-vous *n.* cōnstitūtum *n.*

renegade *n.* dēsertor *m.*

renew *vt.* renovāre, integrāre, īnstaurāre.

renewal *n.* renovātiō *f.*; (*ceremony*) īnstaurātiō *f.*

renounce *vt.* renūntiāre, mittere, repudiāre.

renovate *vt.* renovāre, reficere.

renown *n.* fāma *f.*, glōria *f.*

renowned *a.* praeclārus, īnsignis, nōtus.

rent *n.* (*tear*) fissum *n.*; (*pay*) mercēs *f.* *vt.* (*hire*) condūcere; (*lease*) locāre.

renunciation *n.* cessiō *f.*, repudiātiō *f.*
repair *vt.* reficere, sarcīre. *vi.* sē recipere. *n.* keep in good — tuērī. in bad — ruinōsus.
reparable *a.* ēmendābilis.
reparation *n.* satisfactiō *f.*
repartee *n.* facetiae *f.pl.*, salēs *m.pl.*
repast *n.* cēna *f.*, cibus *m.*
repay *vt.* remūnerārī, grātiam referre (*dat.*); (*money*) repōnere.
repayment *n.* solūtiō *f.*
repeal *vt.* abrogāre. *n.* abrogātiō *f.*
repeat *vt.* iterāre; (*lesson*) reddere; (*ceremony*) instaurāre; (*performance*) referre.
repeatedly *ad.* identidem, etiam atque etiam.
repel *vt.* repellere, dēfendere.
repellent *a.* iniūcundus.
repent *vi.* I — mē paenitet.
repentance *n.* paenitentia *f.*
repentant *a.* paenitēns.
repercussion *n.* ēventus *m.*
repertory *n.* thēsaurus *m.*
repetition *n.* iterātiō *f.*
repine *vi.* conquerī.
replace *vt.* repōnere, restituere. — by substituere.
replacement *n.* supplēmentum *n.*
replenish *vt.* replēre, supplēre.
replete *a.* plēnus.
repletion *n.* satietās *f.*
replica *n.* apographon *n.*
reply *vi.* respondēre. *n.* respōnsum *n.*
report *n.* (*talk*) fāma *f.*, rūmor *m.*; (*repute*) opīniō *f.*; (*account*) renūntiātiō *f.*, litterae *f.pl.*; (*noise*) fragor *m.* make a — renūntiāre. *vt.* referre, dēferre, renūntiāre.
repose *n.* quiēs *f.*, requiēs *f.* *vt.* repōnere, pōnere. *vi.* quiēscere.
repository *n.* horreum *n.*
reprehend *vt.* reprehendere, culpāre.
reprehensible *a.* accūsābilis, improbus.
reprehension *n.* reprehēnsiō [*f.*, culpa *f.*
represent *vt.* dēscrībere, effingere, exprimere imitārī; (*character*) partēs agere (*gen.*), persōnam gerere (*gen.*); (*case*) prōpōnere; (*substitute for*) vicārium esse (*gen.*).
representation *n.* imāgō *f.*, imitātiō *f.* make -s to admonēre.
representative *n.* lēgātus *m.*
repress *vt.* reprimere, cohibēre.
repression *n.* coercitiō *f.*
reprieve *n.* mora *f.*, venia *f.* *vt.* veniam dare (*dat.*).
reprimand *vt.* reprehendere, increpāre. *n.* reprehēnsiō *f.*
reprisals *n.* ultiō *f.*
reproach *vt.* exprobāre, obicere (*dat.*). *n.* exprobrātiō *f.*, probrum *n.*; (*cause*) opprobrium *n.*
reproachful *a.* contumēliōsus.
reprobate *a.* perditus.
reproduce *vt.* propāgāre; (*likeness*) referre.
reproduction *n.* prōcreātiō *f.*; (*likeness*) imāgō *f.*
reproductive *a.* genitalis.
reproof *n.* reprehēnsiō *f.*, obiūrgātiō *f.*
reprove *vt.* reprehendere, increpāre, obiūrgāre.
reptile *n.* serpēns *f.*
republic *n.* lībera rēs pūblica *f.*, cīvitās populāris *f.*
republican *a.* populāris.
repudiate *vt.* repudiāre.
repudiation *n.* repudiātiō *f.*
repugnance *n.* fastīdium *n.*, odium *n.* [versus.
repugnant *a.* invīsus, ad-
repulse *n.* dēpulsiō *f.*; (*at election*) repulsa *f.* *vt.* repellere, āversārī, prōpulsāre.
repulsion *n.* repugnantia *f.*
repulsive *a.* odiōsus, foedus.

reputable *a.* honestus.
reputation *n.* fāma *f.*, existimātiō *f.*; (*for something*) opīniō *f.* (*gen.*). have a — nōmen habēre.
repute *n.* fāma *f.*, existimātiō *f.* bad — īnfāmia *f.* **-d** *a.* I am — to be dīcor esse.
request *n.* rogātiō *f.*, postulātum *n.* obtain a — impetrāre. *vt.* rogāre, petere; (*urgently*) dēposcere.
require *vt.* (*demand*) imperāre, postulāre; (*need*) egēre (*abl.*); (*call for*) requīrere.
requirement *n.* postulātum *n.*, necessārium *n.*
requisite *a.* necessārius.
requisition *n.* postulātiō *f.* *vt.* imperāre.
requital *n.* grātia *f.*, vicēs *f.pl.*
requite *vt.* grātiam referre (*dat.*), remūnerārī.
rescind *vt.* rescindere, abrogāre.
rescript *n.* rescrīptum *n.*
rescue *vt.* ēripere, expedīre, servāre. *n.* salūs *f.* come to the — of subvenīre (*dat.*).
research *n.* investīgātiō *f.*
resemblance *n.* similitūdō *f.*, imāgō *f.*, īnstar *n.*
resemble *vt.* similem esse (*dat.*), referre.
resent *vt.* aegrē ferre, indignārī.
resentful *a.* īrācundus.
resentment *n.* dolor *m.*, indignātiō *f.*
reservation *n.* (*proviso*) exceptiō *f.*
reserve *vt.* servāre; (*store*) recondere; (*in a deal*) excipere. *n.* (*mil.*) subsidium *n.*; (*disposition*) pudor *m.*, reticentia *f.*; (*caution*) cautiō *f.* in — in succenturiātus. without — palam.
reserved *a.* (*place*) adsignātus; (*disposition*) taciturnus, tēctus. **-ly** *ad.* circumspectē.
reservoir *n.* lacus *m.*
reside *vi.* habitāre. — in incolere.
residence *n.* domicilium *n.* domus *f.*
resident *n.* incola *m.*, *f.*
residual *a.* reliquus.
residue, residuum *n.* reliqua pars *f.*
resign *vt.* cēdere; (*office*) abdicāre. — oneself acquiēscere. *vi.* sē abdicāre.
resignation *n.* abdicātiō *f.*; (*state of mind*) patientia *f.*, aequus animus *m.*
resigned *a.* patiēns. be — to aequō animō ferre.
resilience *n.* mollitia *f.*
resilient *a.* mollis.
resist *vt.* resistere (*dat.*), adversārī (*dat.*), repugnāre (*dat.*).
resistance *n.* repugnantia *f.* offer — obsistere (*dat.*).
resistless *a.* invictus.
resolute *a.* fortis, cōnstāns. **-ly** *ad.* fortiter, cōnstanter.
resolution *n.* (*conduct*) fortitūdō *f.*, cōnstantia *f.*; (*decision*) dēcrētum *n.*, sententia *f.* (*into parts*) sēcrētiō *f.*
resolve *n.* fortitūdō *f.*, cōnstantia *f.* *vt.* dēcernere, cōnstituere; (*into parts*) dissolvere. the senate -s placet senātuī.
resonance *n.* sonus *m.*
resonant *a.* canōrus.
resort *n.* locus celeber *m.* last — ultimum auxilium *n.* *vi.* frequentāre, ventitāre; (*have recourse*) dēcurrere, dēscendere, cōnfugere.
resound *vi.* resonāre, personāre.
resource *n.* subsidium *n.*; (*means*) modus *m.*; (*pl.*) opēs *f.pl.*, cōpiae *f.pl.*
resourceful *a.* versūtus, callidus.
resourcefulness *n.* calliditās *f.*, versūtus animus *m.*
respect *n.* (*esteem*) honōs *m.*, observantia *f.*; (*reference*) ratiō *f.* out of — honōris causā. pay one's -s to salūtāre. show — for observāre. in

every — ex omnī parte, in omnī genere. in — of ad (acc.), ab (abl.). vt. honōrāre, observāre, verērī.
respectability n. honestās f.
respectab/le a. honestus, līberālis, frūgī. **-ly** ad. honestē.
respectful a. observāns. **-ly** ad. reverenter.
respectfulness n. observantia f.
respective a. suus (with quisque). **-ly** ad. alius . . . alius.
respiration n. respīrātiō f., spīritus m.
respire vi. respīrāre.
respite n. requiēs f., intercapēdō f., intermissiō f.
resplendence n. splendor m.
resplendent a. splendidus, illūstris. **-ly** ad. splendidē.
respond vi. respondēre.
response n. respōnsum n.
responsibility n. auctōritās f., cūra f.
responsible a. reus; (witness) locuplēs. be — for praestāre.
responsive a. (pupil) docilis; (character) facilis.
rest n. quiēs f., ōtium n.; (after toil) requiēs f.; (remainder) reliqua pars f. be at — requiēscere. set at — tranquillāre. the — of reliquus; (pl.) cēterī. vi. requiēscere, acquiēscere. — on nītī (abl.) innītī in (abl.). vt. (hope) pōnere in (abl.). [sēdēs f.
resting-place n. cubīle n.,
restitution n. satisfactiō f. make — restituere. demand — rēs repetere.
restive a. contumāx.
restless a. inquiētus, sollicitus. be — fluctuārī.
restlessness n. sollicitūdō f.
restoration n. renovātiō f.; (of king) reductiō f.
restore vt. reddere, restituere; (to health) recreāre; (to power) redūcere; (damage) reficere, redintegrāre.
restorer n. restitūtor m.
restrain vt. coercēre, comprimere, cohibēre.
restraint n. moderātiō f., temperantia f., frēnī m.pl. self — modestia f. with — abstinenter.
restrict vt. continēre, circumscrībere. **-ed** a. artus. — to proprius (gen.).
restriction n. modus m., fīnis m.; (limitation) exceptiō f.
result n. ēventus m., ēventum n., exitus m. the — is that quō fit ut. vi. ēvenīre, ēvādere.
resultant a. cōnsequēns.
resume vt. repetere.
resuscitate vt. excitāre, suscitāre.
retail vt. divēndere, vēndere.
retailer n. caupō m.
retain vt. retinēre, tenēre, cōnservāre.
retainer n. satelles m.
retake vt. recipere.
retaliate vi. ulcīscī.
retaliation n. ultiō f.
retard vt. retardāre, remorārī.
retention n. cōnservātiō f.
retentive a. tenāx.
reticence n. taciturnitās f.
reticent a. taciturnus.
reticulated a. rēticulātus.
retinue n. satellitēs m.pl., comitātus m.
retire vi. recēdere, abscēdere; (from office) abīre; (from province) dēcēdere; (mil.) pedem referre, sē recipere.
retired a. ēmeritus; (place) remōtus.
retirement n. (act) recessus m., dēcessus m.; (state) sōlitūdō f., otium n. life of — vita prīvāta. [cundus.
retiring a. modestus, verē-
retort vt. respondēre, referre. n. respōnsum n.
retouch vt. retractāre.
retrace vt. repetere, iterāre.

retract *vt.* revocāre, renūntiāre.
retreat *n.* (*mil.*) receptus *m.*; (*place*) recessus *m.*, sēcessus *m.* sound the — receptuī canere. *vi.* sē recipere, pedem referre.
retrench *vt.* minuere, recīdere.
retrenchment *n.* parsimōnia *f.*
retribution *n.* poena *f.*
retributive *a.* ultor, ultrīx.
retrieve *vt.* reparāre, recipere.
retrograde *a.* (*fig.*) dēterior.
retrogression *n.* regressus *m.*
retrospect *n.* in — respicientī.
retrospective *a.* be — retrōrsum sē referre. **-ly** *ad.* retrō.
return *n.* reditus *m.*; (*pay*) remūnerātiō *f.*; (*profit*) fructus *m.*, pretium *n.*; (*statement*) professiō *f.* make a — of profitērī. in — in vicem, vicissim. *vt.* reddere, restituere, referre. *vi.* redīre, revenīre, revertī; (*from province*) dēcēdere.
reunion *n.* convīvium *n.*
reunite *vt.* reconciliāre.
reveal *vt.* aperīre, patefacere.
revel *n.* cōmissātiō *f.*, bacchātiō *f.*; (*pl.*) orgia *n.pl.* *vi.* cōmissārī, bacchārī. — in luxuriārī.
revelation *n.* patefactiō *f.*
reveller *n.* cōmissātor *m.*
revelry *n.* cōmissātiō *f.*
revenge *n.* ultiō *f.* take — on vindicāre in (*acc.*). *vt.* ulcīscī.
revengeful *a.* ulcīscendī cupidus.
revenue *n.* fructus *m.*, reditus *m.*, vectīgālia *n.pl.*
reverberate *vi.* resonāre.
reverberation *n.* repercussus *m.*
revere *vt.* venerārī, colere.
reverence *n.* venerātiō *f.*; (*feeling*) rēligiō *f.*
reverent *a.* rēligiōsus, pius. **-ly** *ad.* rēligiōsē.
reverie *n.* meditātiō *f.*, somnium *n.*
reversal *n.* abrogātiō *f.*
reverse *a.* contrārius. *n.* contrārium *n.*; (*mil.*) clādēs *f.* *vt.* invertere; (*decision*) rescindere.
reversion *n.* reditus *m.*
revert *vi.* redīre, revertī.
review *n.* recognitiō *f.*, recēnsiō *f.* *vt.* (*mil.*) recēnsēre.
revile *vt.* maledīcere (*dat.*).
revise *vt.* recognōscere, corrigere; (*lit.*) līmāre.
revision *n.* ēmendātiō *f.*; (*lit.*) līma *f.*
revisit *vt.* revīsere.
revival *n.* renovātiō *f.*
revive *vt.* recreāre, excitāre. *vi.* revīvīscere, renāscī.
revocation *n.* revocātiō *f.*
revoke *vt.* renūntiāre, īnfectum reddere.
revolt *n.* sēditiō *f.*, dēfectiō *f.* *vi.* dēficere, rebellāre.
revolting *a.* taeter, obscēnus.
revolution *n.* (*movement*) conversiō *f.*; (*change*) rēs novae *f.pl.* effect a — rēs novāre.; (*revolt*) mōtus *m.*
revolutionary *a.* sēditiōsus, novārum rērum cupidus.
revolve *vi.* volvī, versārī, convertī. *vt.* (*in mind*) volūtāre.
revulsion *n.* mūtātiō *f.*
reward *n.* praemium *n.*, mercēs *f.* *vt.* remūnerārī, compēnsāre.
rhapsody *n.* carmen *n.*; (*epic*) rhapsōdia *f.*
rhetoric *n.* rhētorica *f.* of — rhētoricus. exercise in — dēclāmātiō *f.* practise — dēclāmāre. teacher of — rhētōr *m.*
rhetorical *a.* rhētoricus, dēclāmātōrius. **-ly** rhētoricē.
rhetorician *n.* rhētōr *m.*, dēclāmātor *m.*
rhinoceros *n.* rhīnocerōs *m.*
rhyme *n.* homoeoteleuton *n.* without — or reason temerē.
rhythm *n.* numerus *m.*, modus *m.*

rhythmical *a.* numerōsus.
rib *n.* costa *f.*
ribald *a.* obscēnus.
ribaldry *n.* obscēnitās *f.*
ribbon *n.* īnfula *f.*
rice *n.* oryza *f.*
rich *a.* dīves, locuplēs; (*fertile*) ūber, opīmus; (*food*) pinguis. **-ly** *ad.* opulentē, largē, lautē.
riches *n.* dīvitiae *f.pl.*, opēs *f.pl.*
richness *n.* ūbertās *f.*, cōpia *f.*
rid *vt.* līberāre. get — of dēpōnere, dēmovēre, exuere.
riddle *n.* aenigma *n.*; (*sieve*) cribrum *n.* *vt.* (*with wounds*) cōnfodere.
ride *vi.* equitāre, vehī. — a horse in equō vehī. — at anchor stāre. — away abequitāre, āvehī. — back revehī. — between interequitāre. — down dēvehī. — into invehī. — off āvehī. — out ēvehī. — past praetervehī. — round circumvehī (*dat.*), circumequitāre. — up and down perequitāre. — up to adequitāre ad, advehī ad.
rider *n.* eques *m.*
ridge *n.* iugum *n.*
ridicule *n.* lūdibrium *n.*, irrīsus *m.* *vt.* irrīdēre, illūdere, lūdibriō habēre.
ridiculous *a.* rīdiculus, dērīdiculus. **-ly** *ad.* rīdiculē.
riding *n.* equitātiō *f.*
rife *a.* frequēns.
riff-raff *n.* faex populī *f.*
rifle *vt.* expīlāre, spoliāre.
rift *n.* rīma *f.*
rig *vt.* (*ship*) armāre, ōrnāre. *n.* habitus *m.*
rigging *n.* rudentēs *m.pl.*
right *a.* rēctus; (*just*) aequus, iūstus; (*true*) rēctus, vērus; (*proper*) lēgitimus, fās; (*hand*) dexter. you are — vēra dīcis. if I am — nisi fallor. in the — place in locō. at the — time ad tempus. at — angles ad parēs angulōs. on the — ā dextrā. all — rēctē. it is all — bene est. — hand dextra *f.* *ad.* rēctē, bene, probē; (*justifiably*) iūre. — on rēctā. *n.* (*legal*) iūs *n.*; (*moral*) fās *n.* *vt.* (*replace*) restituere; (*correct*) corrigere; (*avenge*) ulcīscī.
righteous *a.* iūstus, sanctus, pius. **-ly** *ad.* iūstē, sanctē, piē. [pietās *f.*
righteousness *n.* sanctitās *f.*,
rightful *a.* iūstus, lēgitimus. **-ly** *ad.* iūstē, lēgitimē.
right-hand *a.* dexter. — man comes *m.*
rightly *ad.* rēctē, bene; iūre.
right-minded *a.* sānus.
rigid *a.* rigidus. **-ly** *ad.* rigidē, sevērē.
rigidity *n.* rigor *m.*; (*strictness*) sevēritās *f.*
rigmarole *n.* ambāgēs *f.pl.*
rigorous *a.* dūrus; (*strict*) sevērus. **-ly** *ad.* dūriter, sevērē.
rigour *n.* dūritia *f.*; sevēritās *f.*
rile *vt.* inrītāre, stomachum movēre (*dat.*).
rill *n.* rīvulus *m.*
rim *n.* labrum *n.*
rime *n.* pruīna *f.*
rind *n.* cortex *m.*
ring *n.* ānulus *m.*; (*circle*) orbis *m.*; (*of people*) corōna *f.*; (*motion*) gȳrus *m.* *vt.* circumdare; (*bell*) movēre. *vi.* tinnīre, sonāre. [ōrus.
ringing *n.* tinnītus *m.* *a.* can-
ring-leader *n.* caput *n.*, dux *m.*
ringlet *n.* cincinnus *m.*
rinse *vt.* colluere.
riot *n.* tumultus *m.*, rixa *f.* run — exsultāre, luxuriārī. tumultuārī, turbās efficere; (*revel*) bacchārī.
rioter *n.* cōmissātor *m.*
riotous *a.* tumultuōsus, sēditiōsus; (*debauched*) dissolūtus. — living cōmissātiō *f.*, luxuria *f.* **-ly** *ad.* tumultuōsē; luxuriōsē.

rip *vt.* scindere.
ripe *a.* mātūrus. of — judgment animī mātūrus.
ripen *vt.* mātūrāre. *vi.* mātūrēscere.
ripeness *n.* mātūritās *f.*
ripple *n.* unda *f.* *vi.* trepidāre.
rise *vi.* orīrī, surgere; (*hill*) ascendere; (*wind*) cōnsurgere; (*passion*) tumēscere; (*voice*) tollī; (*in size*) crēscere; (*in rank*) ascendere; (*in revolt*) coorīrī, arma capere. — and fall (*tide*) reciprocāre. — above superāre. — again resurgere. — in (*river*) orīrī ex (*abl.*). — out ēmergere. — up exsurgere. *n.* ascēnsus *m.*; (*slope*) clīvus *m.*; (*increase*) incrēmentum *n.*; (*start*) ortus *m.* give — to parere.
rising *n.* (*sun*) ortus *m.*; (*revolt*) mōtus *m.* *a.* (*ground*) ēditus.
risk *n.* periculum *n.* run a — periculum subīre, ingredī. *vt.* periclitārī, in āleam dare.
risky *a.* periculōsus.
rite *n.* rītus *m.*
ritual *n.* caerimōnia *f.*
rival *a.* aemulus. *n.* aemulus *m.*, rīvālis *m.* *vt.* aemulārī.
rivalry *n.* aemulātiō *f.*
river *n.* flūmen *n.*, fluvius *m.* *a.* fluviātilis. — bed alveus *m.*
river-side *n.* rīpa *f.*
rivet *n.* clāvus *m.* *vt.* (*attention*) dēfīgere.
rivulet *n.* rīvulus *m.*, rīvus *m.*
road *n.* via *f.*, iter *n.* on the — in itinere, ex itinere. off the — dēvius. make a — viam mūnīre.
roadstead *n.* statiō *f.*
roam *vi.* errāre, vagārī. — at large ēvagārī.
roar *n.* fremitus *m.* *vi.* fremere.
roast *vt.* torrēre. *a.* assus. *n.* assum *n.*
rob *vt.* spoliāre, exspoliāre, expīlāre; (*of hope*) dēicere dē.
robber *n.* latrō *m.*, fūr *m.*; (*highway*) grassātor *m.*
robbery *n.* latrōcinium *n.*
robe *n.* vestis *f.*; (*woman's*) stola *f.*; (*of state*) trabea *f.* *vt.* vestīre.
robust *a.* rōbustus, fortis.
robustness *n.* rōbur *n.*, firmitās *f.*
rock *n.* saxum *n.*; (*steep*) rūpēs *f.*, scopulus *m.* *vt.* agitāre. *vi.* agitārī, vacillāre.
rocky *a.* saxōsus, scopulōsus.
rod *n.* virga *f.*; (*fishing*) harundō *f.*
rodomontade *n.* māgniloquentia *f.*, ampullae *f.pl.*
roe *n.* (*deer*) capreolus *m.*, caprea *f.*; (*fish*) ōva *n.pl.*
rogue *n.* veterātor *m.*
roguery *n.* nēquitia *f.*, scelus [*n.*
roguish *a.* improbus, malus.
role *n.* partēs *f.pl.*
roll *n.* (*book*) volūmen *n.*; (*movement*) gȳrus *m.*; (*register*) album *n.* call the — of legere. answer the — call ad nōmen respondēre. *vt.* volvere. *vi.* volvī, volūtārī. — down *vt.* dēvolvere. *vi.* dēfluere. — over *vt.* prōvolvere. *vi.* prōlābī. — up *vt.* convolvere.
roller *n.* (*agr.*) cylindrus *m.*; (*for moving*) phalangae *f. pl.*; (*in book*) umbilīcus *m.*
rolling *a.* volūbilis.
rollicking *a.* hilaris.
romance *n.* fābula *f.*; amor *m.*
romantic *a.* fābulōsus; amātōrius.
romp *vi.* lūdere.
roof *n.* tēctum *n.*; (*of mouth*) palātum *n.* *vt.* tegere, integere.
rook *n.* corvus *m.*
room *n.* conclāve *n.*; (*small*) cella *f.*; (*bed*) cubiculum *n.*; (*dining*) cēnāculum *n.*; (*dressing*) apodytērium *n.*; (*space*) locus *m.* make — for locum dare (*dat.*), cēdere (*dat.*).
roominess *n.* laxitās *f.*
roomy *a.* capāx.

roost *vi.* stabulārī.
rooster *n.* gallus gallīnāceus [*m.*
root *n.* rādīx *f.* take — coalēscere. *vt.* — out ērādīcāre.
rooted *a.* (*fig.*) dēfixus. deeply — (*custom*) inveterātus. be — in īnsidēre (*dat.*). become deeply — inveterāscere.
rope *n.* fūnis *m.*; (*thin*) restis *f.*; (*ship's*) rudēns *m.* tight — extentus fūnis. tight — walker fūnambulus *m.* know the -s perītum esse.
rose *n.* rosa *f.*
rosemary *n.* rōs marīnus *m.*
rostrum *n.* rōstra *n.pl.*, suggestus *m.*
rosy *a.* roseus, purpureus.
rot *n.* tābēs *f.* *vi.* putrēscere, pūtēscere. *vt.* putrefacere.
rotate *vi.* volvī, sē convertere.
rotation *n.* conversiō *f.*; (*succession*) ōrdō *m.*, vicissitūdō *f.* in — ōrdine. move in — in orbem īre.
rote *n.* by — memoriter.
rotten *a.* putridus.
rotund *a.* rotundus.
rotundity *n.* rotunditās *f.*
rouge *n.* fūcus *m.* *vt.* fūcāre.
rough *a.* asper; (*art*) incultus, rudis; (*manners*) agrestis, inurbānus; (*stone*) impolītus; (*treatment*) dūrus, sevērus; (*weather*) atrōx, procellōsus. — draft (*lit.*) silva *f.* *vi.* — it dūram vītam vīvere.
rough-and-ready *a.* fortuītus.
roughen *vt.* asperāre, exasperāre.
rough-hew *vt.* dolāre.
roughly *ad.* asperē, dūriter; (*with numbers*) circiter.
roughness *n.* asperitās *f.*
round *a.* rotundus; (*spherical*) globōsus; (*cylindrical*) teres. *n.* (*circle*) orbis *m.*; (*motion*) gȳrus *m.*; (*series*) ambitus *m.* go the -s (*mil.*) vigiliās circumīre. *vt.* (*cape*) superāre. — off rotundāre; (*sentence*) conclūdere. — up compellere. *ad.* circum, circā. go — ambīre. *pr.* circum (*acc.*), circā (*acc.*).
roundabout *a.* — story ambāgēs *f.pl.*; — route circuitus *m.*, ānfrāctus *m.*
roundly *ad.* (*speak*) apertē, līberē.
rouse *vt.* excīre, excitāre; (*courage*) adrigere.
rousing *a.* vehemēns.
rout *n.* fuga *f.*; (*crowd*) turba *f.* *vt.* fugāre, fundere.
route *n.* cursus *m.*, iter *n.*
routine *n.* ūsus *m.*, ōrdō *m.*
rove *vi.* errāre, vagārī.
rover *n.* vagus *m.*; (*sea*) pīrāta *m.*
row *n.* (*line*) ōrdō *m.*; (*noise*) turba *f.*, rixa *f.* *vi.* (*boat*) rēmigāre. *vt.* rēmīs incitāre.
rowdy *a.* turbulentus.
rower *n.* rēmex *m.*
rowing *n.* rēmigium *n.*
royal *a.* rēgius, rēgālis. **-ly** *ad.* rēgiē, rēgāliter.
royalty *n.* (*power*) rēgnum *n.*; (*persons*) rēgēs *m pl.*, domus rēgia *f.*
rub *vt.* fricāre, terere. — away conterere. — hard dēfricāre. — off dētergēre. — out dēlēre. — up expolīre.
rubbing *n.* trītus *m.*
rubbish *n.* quisquiliae *f.pl.*; (*talk*) nūgae *f.pl.*
rubble *n.* rūdus *n.*
rubicund *a.* rubicundus.
rudder *n.* gubernāculum *n.*, clāvus *m.*
ruddy *a.* rubicundus, rutilus.
rude *a.* (*uncivilized*) barbarus, dūrus, inurbānus; (*insolent*) asper, importūnus. **-ly** *ad.* horridē, rusticē; petulanter.
rudeness *n.* barbariēs *f.*; petulantia *f.*, importūnitās *f.*
rudiment *n.* elementum *n.*, initium *n.*
rudimentary *a.* prīmus, incohātus.
rue *n.* (*herb*) rūta *f.* *vt.* I — mē paenitet (*gen.*).
rueful *a.* maestus.

ruffian *n.* grassātor *m.*
ruffle *vt.* agitāre; (*temper*) sollicitāre, commovēre.
rug *n.* strāgulum *n.*
rugged *a.* horridus, asper.
ruggedness *n.* asperitās *f.*
ruin *n.* ruīna *f.*; (*fig.*) exitium *n.*, perniciēs *f.* go to — pessum īre, dīlābī. *vt.* perdere, dēperdere, pessum dare; (*moral*) corrumpere, dēprāvāre. be **-ed** perīre.
ruined *a.* ruīnōsus.
ruinous *a.* exitiōsus, damnōsus.
rule *n.* (*instrument*) rēgula *f.*, amussis *f.*; (*principle*) nōrma *f.*, lēx *f.*, praeceptum *n.*; (*government*) dominātiō *f.*, imperium *n.* ten-foot — decempeda *f.* as a — ferē. lay down **-s** praecipere. make it a — to īnstituere (*inf.*). — of thumb ūsus *m.* *vt.* regere, moderārī. *vi.* rēgnāre, dominārī; (*judge*) ēdīcere; (*custom*) obtinēre. — over imperāre (*dat.*).
ruler *n.* (*instrument*) rēgula *f.*; (*person*) dominus *m.*, rēctor *m.*
ruling *n.* ēdictum *n.*
rumble *vi.* mūgīre.
rumbling *n.* mūgītus *m.*
ruminate *vi.* rūminārī.
rummage *vi.* — through rīmārī.
rumour *n.* fāma *f.*, rūmor *m.*
rump *n.* clūnis *f.*
run *vi.* currere; (*fluid*) fluere, mānāre; (*road*) ferre; (*time*) lābī. — about discurrere, cursāre. — across incidere in (*acc.*). — after sectārī. — aground offendere. — away aufugere, terga vertere; (*from*) fugere, dēfugere. — down dēcurrere, dēfluere. *vt.* (*in words*) obtrectāre. — high (*fig.*) glīscere. — into incurrere in (*acc.*), īnfluere in (*acc.*). — off with abripere, abdūcere. — on pergere. — out (*land*) excurrere; (*time*) exīre; (*supplies*) dēficere. — over *vt.* (*with car*) obterere; (*details*) percurrere. — riot luxuriārī. — through (*course*) dēcurrere; (*money*) disperdere. — short dēficere. — up to adcurrere ad. — up against incurrere in (*acc.*). — wild lascīvīre. *vt.* gerere, administrāre. *n.* cursus *m.*
runaway *a.* fugitīvus.
rung *n.* gradus *m.*
runner *n.* cursor *m.*
running *n.* cursus *m.* *a.* (*water*) vīvus.
rupture *n.* (*fig.*) dissidium *n.* *vt.* dīrumpere.
rural *a.* rūsticus, agrestis.
ruse *n.* fraus *f.*, dolus *m.*
rush *n.* (*plant*) cārex *f.*, iuncus *m.*; (*movement*) impetus *m.* *vi.* currere, sē incitāre, ruere. — forward sē prōripere. — in inruere, incurrere. — out ēvolāre, sē effundere. *a.* iunceus.
russet *a.* flāvus.
rust *n.* (*iron*) ferrūgō *f.*; (*copper*) aerūgō *f.* *vi.* rōbīginem trahere.
rustic *a.* rūsticus, agrestis.
rusticate *vi.* rūsticārī. *vt.* relēgāre.
rusticity *n.* mōrēs rūsticī *m.pl.*
rustle *vi.* increpāre, crepitāre. *n.* crepitus *m.*
rusty *a.* rōbīginōsus.
rut *n.* orbita *f.*
ruthless *a.* inexōrābilis, crūdēlis. **-ly** *ad.* crūdēliter.
rye *n.* secāle *n.*

S

sabbath *n.* sabbata *n.pl.*
sable *a.* āter, niger.
sabre *n.* acīnacēs *m.*
sacerdotal *a.* sacerdōtālis.
sack *n.* saccus *m.*; (*mil.*) dīreptiō *f.* *vt.* dīripere, expīlāre.
sackcloth *n.* cilicium *n.*

sacred *a.* sacer, sanctus. **-ly** *ad.* sanctē.
sacredness *n.* sanctitās *f.*
sacrifice *n.* sacrificium *n.*, sacrum *n.*; (*act*) immolātiō *f.*; (*victim*) hostia *f.*; (*fig.*) iactūra *f.* *vt.* immolāre, sacrificāre, mactāre; (*fig.*) dēvovēre, addicere. *vi.* sacra facere; (*give up*) prōicere.
sacrificer *n.* immolātor *m.*
sacrilege *n.* sacrilegium *n.*
sacrilegious *a.* sacrilegus.
sacristan *n.* aedituus.
sacrosanct *a.* sacrōsanctus.
sad *a.* maestus, tristis; (*thing*) tristis. **-ly** *ad.* maestē.
sadden *vt.* dolōre adficere.
saddle *n.* strātum *n.* *vt.* sternere; (*fig.*) impōnere.
saddle-bags *n.* clītellae *f. pl.*
sadness *n.* tristitia *f.*, maestitia *f.*
safe *a.* tūtus; (*out of danger*) incolumis, salvus; (*to trust*) fīdus. — and sound salvus. *n.* armārium *n.* **-ly** *ad.* tūtō, impūne.
safe-conduct *n.* fidēs pūblica.
safeguard *n.* cautiō *f.*, prōpugnāculum *n.* *vt.* dēfendere.
safety *n.* salūs *f.*, incolumitās *f.*
saffron *n.* crocus *m.* *a.* croceus.
sag *vi.* dēmittī.
sagacious *a.* prūdēns, sagāx, acūtus. **-ly** *ad.* prūdenter, sagāciter. [sagācitās *f.*
sagacity *n.* prūdentia *f.*,
sage *n.* sapiēns *m.*; (*herb*) salvia *f.* *a.* sapiēns. **-ly** *ad.* sapienter.
sail *n.* vēlum *n.* set — vēla dare, nāvem solvere. shorten — vēla contrahere. *vi.* nāvigāre. — past legere, praetervehī.
sailing *n.* nāvigātiō *f.*
sailor *n.* nauta *m.*
sail-yard *n.* antenna *f.*
saint *n.* vir sanctus *m.*
sainted *a.* beātus.
saintly *a.* sanctus.
sake *n.* for the — of grātiā (*gen.*), causā (*gen.*), propter (*acc.*); (*behalf*) prō (*abl.*).
salacious *a.* salāx.
salad *n.* morētum *n*
salamander *n.* salamandra *f.*
salary *n.* mercēs *f.*
sale *n.* vēnditiō *f.*; (*formal*) mancipium *n.*; (*auction*) hasta *f.* for — vēnālis. be for — prōstāre. offer for — vēnum dare.
saleable *a.* vēndibilis.
salient *a.* ēminēns. — points capita *n.pl.*
saline *a.* salsus.
saliva *n.* salīva *f.*
sallow *a.* pallidus.
sally *n.* ēruptiō *f.*; (*wit*) facētiae *f.pl.* *vi.* ērumpere, excurrere.
salmon *n.* salmō *m.*
salon *n.* ātrium *n.*
salt *n.* sal *m.* *a.* salsus.
salt-cellar *n.* salīnum *n.*
saltpetre *n.* nitrum *n.*
salt-pits *n.* salinae *f.pl.*
salty *a.* salsus.
salubrious *a.* salūbris. **-ly** *ad.* salūbriter. [*f.*
salubriousness *n.* salūbritās
salutary *a.* salūtāris, ūtilis.
salutation *n.* salūs *f.*
salute *vt.* salūtāre.
salvage *vt.* servāre, ēripere.
salvation *n.* salūs *f.*
salve *n.* unguentum *n.*
salver *n.* scutella *f.*
same *a.* īdem. — as īdem ac. all the — nihilōminus. one and the — ūnus et īdem. from the — place indidem. in the — place ibīdem. to the — place eōdem. at the — time simul, eōdem tempore; (*adversative*) tamen. it is all the — to me meā nōn interest.
sample *n.* exemplum *n.*, specimen *n.* *vt.* gustāre.
sanctify *vt.* cōnsecrāre.
sanction *n.* comprobātiō *f.*, auctōritās *f.* *vt.* ratum facere.

sanctity *n.* sanctitās *f.*
sanctimony *n.* falsa rēligiō *f.*
sanctuary *n.* fānum *n.*, dēlubrum *n.*; (*for men*) asȳlum *n.*
sand *n.* harēna *f.*
sandal *n.* (*outdoors*) crepida *f.*; (*indoors*) solea *f.*
sandalled *a.* crepidātus, soleātus.
sandstone *n.* tōfus *m.*
sand-pit *n.* harēnāria *f.*
sandy *a.* harēnōsus.; (*colour*) flāvus.
sane *a.* sānus.
sangfroid *n.* aequus animus *m.*
sanguinary *a.* cruentus.
sanguine *a.* laetus.
sanitary *a.* salūbris.
sanity *n.* mēns sāna *f.*
sap *n.* sūcus *m.* *vt.* subruere.
sapience *n.* sapientia *f.*
sapient *a.* sapiēns.
sapling *n.* surculus.
sapper *n.* cunīculārius *m.*
sapphire *n.* sapphīrus *f.*
sarcasm *n.* acūlei *m.pl.*, dicācitās *f.*
sarcastic *a.* dicāx, acūleātus.
sardonic *a.* amārus.
sash *n.* cingulum *n.*
satchel *n.* loculus *m.*
sate *vt.* explēre, satiāre.
satellite *n.* satelles *m.*
satiate *vt.* explēre, satiāre, saturāre.
satiety *n.* satietās *f.*
satire *n.* satura *f.*; (*pl., of Horace*) sermōnēs *m.pl.*
satirical *a.* acerbus.
satirist *n.* saturārum scrīptor *m.*
satirize *vt.* perstringere, notāre.
satisfaction *n.* (*act*) explētiō *f.*; (*feeling*) voluptās *f.*; (*penalty*) poena *f.* demand — rēs repetere.
satisfactor/y *a.* idōneus, grātus. **-ily** *ad.* ex sententiā.
satisf/y *vt.* satisfacere (*dat.*); (*desire*) explēre. **be -ied** satis habēre, contentum esse.
satrap *n.* satrapēs *m.*
saturate *vt.* imbuere.
satyr *n.* satyrus *m.*
sauce *n.* condīmentum *n.*; (*fish*) garum *n.*
saucer *n.* patella *f.*
sauc/y *a.* petulāns. **-ily** *ad.* petulanter.
saunter *vi.* ambulāre.
sausage *n.* tomāculum *n.*, hillae *f.pl.*
savage *a.* ferus, efferātus; (*cruel*) atrōx, inhūmānus. **-ly** *ad.* ferōciter, inhūmānē.
savagery *n.* ferōcitās *f.*, inhūmānitās *f.*
savant *n.* vir doctus *m.*
save *vt.* servāre. — up reservāre. *pr.* praeter (*acc.*).
saving *a.* parcus. — clause exceptiō *f.* *n.* compendium *n.*; (*pl.*) peculium *n.*
saviour *n.* līberātor *m.*
savory *n.* thymbra *f.*
savour *n.* sapor *m.*; (*of cooking*) nīdor *m.* *vi.* sapere. — of olēre, redolēre.
savoury *a.* conditus.
saw *n.* (*tool*) serra *f.*; (*saying*) prōverbium *n.* *vt.* serrā secāre.
sawdust *n.* scobis *f.*
say *vt.* dīcere. — that . . . not negāre. — no negāre. he -s (*quoting*) inquit. he -s yes āit. they — ferunt.
saying *n.* dictum *n.*
scab *n.* (*disease*) scabiēs *f.*; (*over wound*) crusta *f.*
scabbard *n.* vāgīna *f.*
scabby *a.* scaber.
scaffold, -ing *n.* fala *f.*
scald *vt.* ūrere.
scale *n.* (*balance*) lanx *f.*; (*fish, etc.*) squāma *f.*; (*gradation*) gradūs *m.pl.*; (*music*) diagramma *n.* *vt.* scālīs ascendere.
scallop *n.* pecten *m.*
scalp *n.* capitis cutis *f.*
scalpel *n.* scalpellum *n.*
scamp *n.* verberō *m.*

scamper *vi.* currere.
scan *vt.* contemplārī; (*verse*) mētīrī.
scandal *n.* īnfāmia *f.*, opprobrium *n.*; (*talk*) calumnia *f.*
scandalize *vt.* offendere.
scandalous *a.* flāgitiōsus, turpis.
scansion *n.* syllabārum ēnārrātiō *f.*
scant *a.* exiguus, parvus.
scantiness *n.* exiguitās *f.*
scant/y *a.* exiguus, tenuis, exīlis; (*number*) paucus. **-ily** *ad.* exiguē, tenuiter.
scapegoat *n.* piāculum *n.*
scar *n.* cicātrīx *f.*
scarce *a.* rārus. make oneself — sē āmovēre, dē mediō recēdere. *ad.* vix, aegrē.
scarcely *ad.* vix, aegrē. — anyone nēmō ferē.
scarcity *n.* inopia *f.*, angustiae *f.pl.*
scare *n.* formīdō *f.* *vt.* terrēre. — away absterrēre.
scarecrow *n.* formīdō *f.*
scarf *n.* fōcāle *n.*
scarlet *n.* coccum *n.* *a.* coccinus.
scarp *n.* rūpēs. *f.*
scathe *n.* damnum *n.*
scatter *vt.* dispergere, dissipāre; (*violently*) disicere. *vi.* diffugere. **-ed** *a.* rārus.
scatter-brained *a.* dēsipiēns.
scene *n.* spectāculum *n.*; (*place*) theātrum *n.*
scenery *n.* locī faciēs *f.*, speciēs *f.*; (*beautiful*) amoenitās *f.*
scent *n.* odor *m.*; (*sense*) odōrātus *m.* keen — sagācitās *f.* *vt.* odōrārī; (*perfume*) odōribus perfundere.
scented *a.* odōrātus.
sceptic *n.* Pyrrhōnēus *m.*
sceptical *a.* incrēdulus.
sceptre *n.* scēptrum *n.*
schedule *n.* tabulae *f.pl.*, ratiō *f.*
scheme *n.* cōnsilium *n.*, ratiō *f.* *vt.* māchinārī, mōlīrī.
schemer *n.* māchinātor *m.*
schism *n.* discidium *n.*, sēcessiō *f.*
scholar *n.* vir doctus *m.*, litterātus *m.*; (*pupil*) discipulus *m.*
scholarly *a.* doctus, litterātus.
scholarship *n.* litterae *f.pl.*, doctrīna *f.*
scholastic *a.* umbrātilis.
school *n.* (*elementary*) lūdus *m.*; (*advanced*) schola *f.*; (*high*) gymnasium *n.*; (*sect*) secta *f.*, domus *f.* *vt.* īnstituere.
schoolboy *n.* discipulus *m.*
school-fellow *n.* condiscipulus *m.*
schoolmaster *n.* magister *m.*
schoolmistress *n.* magistra *f.*
science *n.* doctrīna *f.*, disciplīna *f.*, ars *f.*
scimitar *n.* acinacēs *m.*
scintillate *vi.* scintillāre.
scion *n.* prōgeniēs *f.*
scissors *n.* forfex *f.*
scoff *vi.* irrīdēre. — at dērīdēre.
scoffer *n.* irrīsor *m.*
scold *vt.* increpāre, obiūrgāre.
scolding *n.* obiūrgātiō *f.*
scoop *n.* trulla *f.* *vt.* — out excavāre.
scope *n.* (*aim*) fīnis *m.*; (*room*) locus, campus *m.* ample — laxus locus.
scorch *vt.* exūrere, torrēre. **-ed** *a.* torridus.
score *n.* (*mark*) nota *f.*; (*total*) summa *f.*; (*reckoning*) ratiō *f.*; (*number*) vīgintī. *vt.* notāre. *vi.* vincere.
scorn *n.* contemptiō *f.* *vt.* contemnere, spernere.
scorner *n.* contemptor *m.*
scornful *a.* fastīdiōsus. **-ly** *ad.* contemptim.
scorpion *n.* scorpiō *m.*, nepa *f.*
scot-free *a.* immūnis, impūnītus.
scoundrel *n.* furcifer *m.*
scour *vt.* (*clean*) tergēre; (*range*) percurrere.
scourge *n.* flagellum *n.*; (*fig.*)

pestis *f*. *vt*. verberāre, virgīs caedere.
scout *n*. explōrātor *m*., speculātor *m*. *vi*. explōrāre, speculārī. *vt*. spernere, repudiāre.
scowl *n*. frontis contractiō *f*. *vi*. frontem contrahere.
scraggy *a*. strigōsus.
scramble *vi*. — for certātim captāre. — up scandere.
scrap *n*. frustum *n*.
scrape *vt*. rādere, scabere. — off abrādere.
scraper *n*. strigil *f*.
scratch *vt*. rādere; (*head*) perfricāre. — out exsculpere, ērādere.
scream *n*. clāmor *m*., ululātus *m*. *vi*. clāmāre, ululāre.
screech *n*. ululātus *m*. *vi*. ululāre.
screen *n*. obex *m*., *f*.; (*from sun*) umbra *f*.; (*fig*.) vēlāmentum *n*. *vt*. tegere.
screw *n*. clāvus *m*.; (*of wine-press*) cochlea *f*.
scribble *vt*. properē scrībere.
scribe *n*. scrība *m*.
script *n*. scrīptum *n*.; (*handwriting*) manus *f*.
scroll *n*. volūmen *n*.
scrub *vt*. dētergēre, dēfricāre.
scruple *n*. rēligiō *f*., scrūpulus *m*.
scrupulous *a*. rēligiōsus; (*careful*) dīligēns. **-ly** *ad*. rēligiōsē, dīligenter.
scrupulousness *n*. rēligiō *f*.; dīligentia *f*.
scrutinize *vt*. scrūtārī, intrōspicere in (*acc*.), excutere.
scrutiny *n*. scrūtātiō *f*.
scud *vi*. volāre.
scuffle *n*. rixa *f*. [rēmus *m*.
scull *n*. calvāria *f*.; (*oar*)
scullery *n*. culīna *f*.
sculptor *m*. fictor, sculptor *m*.
sculpture *n*. ars fingendī *f*.; (*product*) statuae *f.pl*. *vt*. sculpere.
scum *n*. spūma *f*.
scurf *n*. porrīgō *f*.
scurrility *n*. maledicta *n.pl*.
scurrilous *a*. maledicus.
scurvy *a*. (*fig*.) turpis, improbus.
scythe *n*. falx *f*.
sea *n*. mare *n*. open — altum *n*. put to — solvere. be at — nāvigāre; (*fig*.) in errōre versārī. *a*. marīnus; (*coast*) maritimus.
sea-board *n*. lītus *n*.
sea-faring, *a*. maritimus, nauticus.
sea-fight *n*. nāvāle proelium *n*.
sea-gull *n*. larus *m*.
seal *n*. (*animal*) phōca *f*.; (*stamp*) signum *n*. *vt*. signāre. — up obsignāre.
seam *n*. sūtūra *f*.
seaman *n*. nauta *m*.
seamanship *n*. scientia et ūsus nauticārum rērum.
seaport *n*. portus *m*.
sear *vt*. adūrere, torrēre.
search *n*. investīgātiō *f*. *vi*. investīgāre, explōrāre. *vt*. excutere, scrūtārī. — for quaerere, exquīrere, investīgāre. — into inquīrere, anquīrere. — out explōrāre, indāgāre.
searcher *n*. inquīsītor *m*.
searching *a*. acūtus, dīligēns.
seashore *n*. lītus *n*.
seasick *a*. be — nauseāre.
seasickness *n*. nausea *f*.
seaside *n*. mare *n*.
season *n*. annī tempus *n*., tempestās *f*.; (*right time*) tempus *n*., opportūnitās *f*. in — tempestīvē. *vt*. condīre.
seasonab/le *a*. tempestīvus. **-ly** *ad*. tempestīvē.
seasoned *a*. (*food*) condītus; (*wood*) dūrātus.
seasoning *n*. condīmentum *n*.
seat *n*. sēdēs *f*.; (*chair*) sedīle *n*.; (*home*) domus *f*., domicilium *n*. keep one's — (*riding*) in equō haerēre. *vt*. collocāre. — oneself īnsidēre.

seated *a.* be — sedēre. deep — (*fig.*) inveterātus.
seaweed *n.* alga *f.*
seaworthy *a.* ad nāvigandum ūtilis.
secede *vi.* sēcēdere.
secession *n.* sēcessiō *f.*
seclude *vt.* sēclūdere, abstrūdere. **-d** *a.* sēcrētus, remōtus.
seclusion *n.* sōlitūdō *f.*, sēcrētum *n.*
second *a.* secundus, alter. a — time iterum. *n.* temporis pūnctum *n.*; (*person*) fautor *m.* — sight hariolātiō *f.* *vt.* favēre (*dat.*), adesse (*dat.*). [terior.
secondary *a.* inferior, dē-
seconder *n.* fautor *m.*
second-hand *a.* aliēnus, trītus.
secondly *ad.* deinde.
secrecy *n.* sēcrētum *n.*, silentium *n.*
secret *a.* occultus, arcānus; (*stealth*) fūrtīvus. *n.* arcānum *n.* keep — dissimulāre, cēlāre. in — clam. be — latēre. **-ly** *ad.* clam, occultē.
secretary *n.* scrība *m.*, ab epistolīs, ā manū.
secrete *vt.* cēlāre, abdere.
secretive *a.* tēctus.
sect *n.* secta *f.*, schola *f.*, domus *f.*
section *n.* pars *f.*
sector *n.* regiō *f.*
secular *a.* profānus.
secure *a.* tūtus. *vt.* (*mil.*) firmāre, ēmūnīre; (*fasten*) religāre; (*obtain*) parāre, nancīscī. **-ly** *ad.* tūtō.
security *n.* salūs *f.*, impūnitās *f.*; (*money*) cautiō *f.*, pignus *n.*, spōnsiō *f.* sense of — sēcūritās *f.* give good — satis dare. on good — (*loan*) nōminibus rēctis cautus. stand — for praedem esse prō (*abl.*).
sedan *n.* lectīca *f.*
sedate *a.* placidus, temperātus, gravis. **-ly** *ad.* placidē.
sedateness *n.* gravitās *f.*
sedge *n.* ulva *f.*
sediment *n.* faex *f.*
sedition *n.* sēditiō *f.*, mōtus *m.*
seditious *a.* sēditiōsus. **-ly** *ad.* sēditiōsē.
seduce *vt.* illicere, pellicere.
seducer *n.* corruptor *m.*
seduction *n.* corruptēla *f.*
seductive *a.* blandus. **-ly** *ad.* blandē.
sedulity *n.* dīligentia *f.*
sedulous *a.* dīligēns, sēdulus. **-ly** *ad.* dīligenter, sēdulō.
see *vt.* vidēre, cernere; (*suddenly*) cōnspicārī; (*performance*) spectāre; (*with mind*) intellegere. go and — vīsere, invīsere. — to vidēre, cōnsulere (*dat.*). — through dispicere. — that you are vidē ut sīs, fac sīs. — that you are not vidē nē sīs, cavē sīs.
seed *n.* sēmen *n.*; (*in a plant*) grānum *n.*; (*in fruit*) acinum *n.*; (*fig.*) stirps *f.*, prōgeniēs *f.*
seedling *n.* surculus *m.*
seed-time *n.* sēmentis *f.*
seeing that *conj.* quoniam, siquidem.
seek *vt.* petere, quaerere.
seeker *n.* indāgātor *m.*
seem *vi.* vidērī.
seeming *a.* speciōsus. *n.* speciēs *f.* **-ly** *ad.* ut vidētur.
seemly *a.* decēns, decōrus. it is — decet.
seep *vi.* mānāre, percōlārī.
seer *n.* vātēs *m.*, *f.*
seethe *vi.* fervēre.
segregate *vt.* sēcernere, sēgregāre.
segregation *n.* sēparātiō *f.*
seize *vt.* rapere, corripere, adripere, prehendere; (*mil.*) occupāre; (*illness*) adficere; (*emotion*) invādere, occupāre.
seizure *n.* ēreptiō *f.*, occupātiō *f.*
seldom *ad.* rārō.
select *vt.* ēligere, excerpere, dēligere. *a.* lēctus, ēlēctus.

selection *n.* ēlēctiō *f.*, dēlēctus *m.*; (*lit.*) ecloga *f.*
self *n.* ipse; (*reflexive*) sē. a second — alter idem.
self-centred *a.* glōriosus.
self-confident *a.* cōnfīdēns.
self-conscious *a.* pudibundus.
self-control *n.* temperantia *f.*
self-denial *n.* abstinentia *f.*
self-evident *a.* manifestus.
self-governing *a.* liber.
self-government *n.* libertās *f.*
self-important *a.* adrogāns.
self-interest *n.* ambitiō *f.*
selfish *a.* inhūmānus, avārus. be — suā causā facere. **-ly** inhūmānē, avārē.
selfishness *n.* inhūmānitās *f.*, incontinentia *f.*, avāritia *f.*
self-made *a.* (*man*) novus.
self-possessed *a.* aequō animō.
self-reliant *a.* cōnfīdēns.
self-respect *n.* pudor *m.*
self-sacrifice *n.* dēvōtiō *f.*
selfsame *a.* ūnus et idem.
sell *vt.* vēndere; (*in lots*) dīvēndere. be sold vēnīre.
seller *n.* vēnditor *m.*
selvage *n.* limbus *m.*
semblance *n.* speciēs *f.*, imāgō *f.*
semicircle *n.* hēmicyclium *n.*
senate *n.* senātus *m.* hold a meeting of the — senātum habēre. decree of the — senātus cōnsultum *n.* — house *n.* cūria *f.*
senator *n.* senātor *m.*; (*provincial*) decuriō *m.*; (*pl.*) patrēs *m.pl.*
senatorial *a.* senātōrius.
send *vt.* mittere. — across trānsmittere. — away dīmittere. — back remittere. — for arcessere; (*doctor*) adhibēre. — forth ēmittere. — forward praemittere. — in immittere, intrōmittere. — out ēmittere; (*in different directions*) dīmittere. — out of the way ablēgāre. — up submittere.
senile *a.* senīlis.
senility *n.* senium *n.*
senior *a.* nātū māior; (*thing*) prior.
sensation *n.* sēnsus *m.*; (*event*) rēs nova *f.* lose — obtorpēscere. create a — hominēs obstupefacere.
sensational *a.* novus, prōdigiōsus.
sense *n.* (*faculty*) sēnsus *m.*; (*wisdom*) prūdentia *f.*; (*meaning*) vīs *f.*, sententia *f.* common — prūdentia *f.* be in one's -s apud sē esse, mentis suae esse. out of one's -s dēmēns. recover one's -s resipīscere. what is the — of quid sibi vult? *vt.* sentīre.
senseless *a.* absurdus, ineptus, īnsipiēns. **-ly** *ad.* īnsipienter.
senselessness *n.* īnsipientia *f.*
sensibility *n.* sēnsus *m.*
sensib/le *a.* prūdēns, sapiēns. **-ly** *ad.* prūdenter, sapienter.
sensitive *a.* mollis, inrītābilis, patibilis.
sensitiveness *n.* mollitia *f.*
sensual *a.* libīdinōsus. **-ly** *ad.* libīdinōsē.
sensuality *n.* libīdō *f.*, voluptās *f.*
sentence *n.* (*judge*) iūdicium *n.*, sententia *f.*; (*gram.*) sententia *f.* pass — iūdicāre. execute — lēge agere. *vt.* damnāre. — to death capitis damnāre.
sententious *a.* sententiōsus. **-ly** *ad.* sententiōsē.
sentient *a.* patibilis.
sentiment *n.* (*feeling*) sēnsus *m.*; (*opinion*) sententia *f.*; (*emotion*) mollitia *f.*
sentimental *a.* mollis, flēbilis. **-ly** *ad.* molliter.
sentimentality *n.* mollitia *f.*
sentinel, sentry *n.* custōs *m.*, vigil *m.*; (*pl.*) statiōnēs *f.pl.*

excubiae *f.pl.* be on — duty in statiōne esse. [ābilis.
separable *a.* dīviduus, sēpar-
separate *vt.* sēparāre, dīvidere, disiungere; (*forcibly*) dirimere, dīvellere. *vi.* digredī. *a.* sēparātus, sēcrētus. **-ly** *ad.* sēparātim, seōrsum.
separation *n.* sēparātiō *f.*; (*violent*) discidium *n.*
September *n.* mēnsis September *m.* of — September.
sepulchral *a.* fūnebris.
sepulchre *n.* sepulcrum *n.*
sepulture *n.* sepultūra *f.*
sequel *n.* exitus *m.*, quae sequuntur.
sequence *n.* seriēs *f.*, ōrdō *m.*
sequestered *a.* sēcrētus.
ser nade *vt.* occentāre.
serene *a.* tranquillus, sēcūrus. **-ly** *ad.* tranquillē.
serenity *n.* sēcūritās *f.*
serf *n.* servus *m.*
serfdom *n.* servitūs *f.*
sergeant *n.* signifer *m.*
series *n.* seriēs *f.*, ōrdō *m.*
serious *a.* gravis, sērius, sevērus. **-ly** *ad.* graviter, sēriō, sevērē.
seriousness *n.* gravitās *f.*
sermon *n.* ōrātiō *f.*
serpent *n.* serpēns *f.*
serpentine *a.* tortuōsus.
serrated *a.* serrātus.
serried *a.* cōnfertus.
servant *n.* (*domestic*) famulus *m.*, famula *f.*; (*public*) minister *m.*, ministra *f.* family **-s** familia *f.* — **maid** ancilla *f.*
serve *vt.* servīre (*dat.*); (*food*) ministrāre, adpōnere; (*interest*) condūcere (*dat.*). *vi.* (*mil.*) stīpendia merēre, mīlitāre; (*suffice*) sufficere. — as esse prō (*abl.*). — in the cavalry equō merēre. — in the infantry pedibus merēre. having -d one's time ēmeritus. — a sentence poenam subīre. — well bene merērī dē (*abl.*).
service *n.* (*status*) servitium *n.*, famulātus *m.*; (*work*) ministerium *n.*; (*help*) opera *f.*; (*by an equal*) meritum *n.*, beneficium *n.*; (*mil.*) mīlitia *f.*, stīpendia *n.pl.* be of — to prōdesse (*dat.*), bene merērī dē. I am at your — adsum tibi complete one's — stīpendia ēmerērī.
serviceable *a.* ūtilis.
servile *a.* servīlis; (*fig.*) abiectus, humilis.
servility *n.* adūlātiō *f.*
servitude *n.* servitūs *f.*
session *n.* conventus *m.* be in — sedēre.
sesterce *n.* sēstertius *m.* 10 -s decem sēstertiī. 10,000 -s dēna sēstertia *n.pl.* 1,000,000 -s deciēs sēstertium.
set *vt.* pōnere, locāre, statuere, sistere; (*bone*) condere; (*course*) dīrigere; (*example*) dare; (*limit*) impōnere; (*mind*) intendere; (*music*) modulārī; (*sail*) dare; (*sentries*) dispōnere; (*table*) instruere; (*trap*) parāre. *vi.* (*astr.*) occidere. — about incipere. — against oppōnere. — apart sēpōnere. — aside sēpōnere. — down (*writing*) perscrībere. — eyes on cōnspicere. — foot on ingredī. — forth expōnere, ēdere. — free līberāre. — in motion movēre. — in order compōnere, dispōnere. — off (*decoration*) distinguere; (*art*) illūmināre. — on (*to attack*) immittere. — on foot īnstituere. — on fire incendere. — one's heart on exoptāre. — out *vi.* proficīscī. — over praeficere, impōnere. — up statuere; (*fig.*) cōnstituere.
set *a.* (*arrangement*) status; (*purpose*) certus (*rule*) praescrīptus; (*speech*) compositus. of — purpose cōnsultō. *n.* (*persons*) numerus *m.*; (*things*) congeriēs *f.*; (*current*) cursus *m.*
set-back *n.* repulsa *f.*

settee *n.* lectulus *m.*
setting *n.* (*astr.*) occāsus *m.*; (*event*) locus *m.*
settle *n.* sella *f.* *vt.* statuere; (*annuity*) praestāre; (*business*) trānsigere; (*colony*) dēdūcere; (*debt*) exsolvere; (*decision*) cōnstituere; (*dispute*) dēcīdere, compōnere. *vi.* (*abode*) cōnsīdere; (*agreement*) cōnstituere, convenīre; (*sediment*) dēsīdere. — in īnsīdere (*dat.*).
settled *a.* certus, explōrātus.
settlement *n.* (*of a colony*) dēductiō *f.*; (*colony*) colōnia *f.*; (*of dispute*) dēcīsiō *f.*, compositiō *f.*; (*to wife*) dōs *f.*
settler *n.* colōnus *m.*
set to *n.* pugna *f.*
seven *num.* septem. — each septēnī. — times septiēns. — hundred *num.* septingentī. — **hundredth** *a.* septingentēsimus.
seventeen *num.* septendecim. **-th** *a.* septimus decimus.
seventh *a.* septimus. for the — time septimum.
seventieth *a.* septuāgēsimus.
seventy *num.* septuāgintā. — each septuāgēnī. — times septuāgiēns.
sever *vt.* incīdere, sēparāre, dīvidere.
several *a.* complūrēs, aliquot. **-ly** *ad.* singulī.
severe *a.* gravis, sevērus, dūrus; (*style*) austērus; (*weather*) asper; (*pain*) ācer, gravis. **-ly** *ad.* graviter, sevērē.
severity *n.* gravitās *f.*; asperitās *f.*; sevēritās *f.*
sew *vt.* suere. — up cōnsuere. — up in īnsuere in (*acc.*).
sewer *n.* cloāca *f.*
sex *n.* sexus *m.*
shabbiness *n.* sordēs *f.pl.*
shabb/y *a.* sordidus. **-ily** *ad.* sordidē.
shackle *n.* compes *f.*, vinculum *n.* *vt.* impedīre, vincīre.
shade *n.* umbra *f.*; (*colour*) color *m.*; (*pl.*) mānēs *m.pl.* put in the — officere (*dat.*). *vt.* opācāre, umbram adferre (*dat.*).
shadow *n.* umbra *f.*
shadowy *a.* obscūrus; (*fig.*) ināṅis.
shady *a.* umbrōsus, opācus.
shaft *n.* (*missile*) sagitta *f.*; (*of spear*) hastīle *n.*; (*of cart*) tēmō *m.*; (*of light*) radius *m.*; (*excavation*) puteus *m.*
shaggy *a.* hirsūtus.
shake *vt.* quatere, agitāre; (*structure*) labefacere, labefactāre; (*belief*) īnfirmāre; (*resolution*) labefactāre, commovēre. — hands with dextram dare (*dat.*). *vi.* quatī, agitārī, tremere, horrēscere. — off dēcutere, excutere. — out excutere.
shaking *n.* tremor *m.*
shaky *a.* īnstābilis, tremebundus.
shall *vi. fut. indic.*
shallot *n.* caepa Ascalōnia *f.*
shallow *a.* brevis, vadōsus; (*fig.*) levis. **-s** *n.* brevia *n.pl.*, vada *n.pl.*
shallowness *n.* vada *n.pl.*; (*fig.*) levitās *f.*
sham *a.* fictus, falsus, fūcōsus. *n.* simulātiō *f.*, speciēs *f.* *vt.* simulāre.
shambles *n.* laniēna *f.*
shame *n.* (*feeling*) pudor *m.*; (*cause*) dēdecus *n.*, ignōminia *f.* it is a — flāgitium est. *vt.* rubōrem incutere (*dat.*). *interj.* prō pudor!
shamefaced *a.* verēcundus.
shameful *a.* ignōminiōsus, turpis. **-ly** *ad.* turpiter.
shameless *a.* impudēns. **-ly** *ad.* impudenter. [dentia *f.*
shamelessness *n.* impu-
shank *n.* crūs *n.*
shape *n.* fōrma *f.*, figūra *f.* *vt.* fōrmāre, fingere; (*fig.*) īnfōrmāre. *vi.* — well prōficere.

shapeless *a.* īnfōrmis, dēfōrmis.

shapelessness *n.* dēfōrmitās *f.*

shapeliness *n.* fōrma *f.*

shapely *a.* fōrmōsus.

shard *n.* testa *f.*

share *n.* pars *f.*; (*plough*) vōmer *m.* go -s with inter sē partīrī. *vt.* (*give*) partīrī, impertīre; (*have*) commūnicāre, participem esse (*gen.*).

sharer *n.* particeps *m.*, *f.*, socius *m.*

shark *n.* volpēs marīna *f.*

sharp *a.* acūtus; (*fig.*) ācer, acūtus. **-ly** *ad.* ācriter, acūtē.

sharpen *vt.* acuere; (*fig.*) exacuere.

sharpness *n.* aciēs *f.*; (*mind*) acūmen *n.*, argūtiae *f.pl.*; (*temper*) acerbitās *f.*

shatter *vt.* quassāre, perfringere, adflīgere; (*fig.*) frangere.

shave *vt.* rādere. — off abrādere.

shavings *n.* rāmenta *n.pl.*

she *pro.* haec, ea, illa.

sheaf *n.* manipulus *m.*

shear *vt.* tondēre, dētondēre.

shears *n.* forficēs *f.pl.*

sheath *n.* vāgīna *f.*

sheathe *vt.* recondere.

shed *vt.* fundere; (*blood*) effundere, (*one's own*) profundere; (*tears*) effundere; (*covering*) exuere. — light on (*fig.*) lūmen adhibēre (*dat.*).

sheen *n.* nitor *m.*

sheep *n.* ovis *f.*; (*flock*) pecus *n.*

sheep-fold *n.* ovīle *n.*

sheepish *a.* pudibundus. **-ly** *ad.* pudenter.

sheer *a.* (*absolute*) merus; (*steep*) praeruptus.

sheet *n.* (*cloth*) linteum *n.*; (*metal*) lāmina *f.*; (*paper*) carta *f.*, scheda *f.*; (*sail*) pēs *m.*; (*water*) aequor *n.*

shelf *n.* pluteus *m.*, pēgma *n.*

shell *n.* concha *f.*; (*egg*) putāmen *n.*; (*tortoise*) testa *f.*

shell-fish *n.* conchȳlium *n.*

shelter *n.* suffugium *n.*, tegmen *n.*; (*refuge*) perfugium *n.*, asȳlum *n.*; (*lodging*) hospitium *n.*; (*fig.*) umbra *f.* *vt.* tegere, dēfendere; (*refugee*) excipere. *vi.* latēre. — behind (*fig.*) dēlitēscere in (*abl.*).

sheltered *a.* (*life*) umbrātilis.

shelve *vt.* differre. *vi.* sē dēmittere.

shelving *a.* dēclīvis.

shepherd *n.* pastor *m.*

shield *n.* scūtum *n.*; (*small*) parma *f.*; (*fig.*) praesidium *n.* *vt.* prōtegere, dēfendere.

shift *n.* (*change*) mūtātiō *f.*; (*expedient*) ars *f.* dolus *m.* make — to efficere ut. in -s per vicēs. *vt.* mūtāre; (*move*) movēre. *vi.* mūtārī; discēdere.

shiftless *a.* iners, inops.

shifty *a.* vafer, versūtus.

shilling *n.* solidus *m.*

shimmer *vi.* micāre. *n.* tremulum lūmen *n.*

shin *n.* tībia *f.*

shine *vi.* lūcēre fulgēre; (*reflecting*) nitēre; (*fig.*) ēminēre. — forth ēlūcēre, ēnitēre. — upon adfulgēre (*dat.*). *n.* nitor *m.*

shingle *n.* lapillī *m.pl.*, glārea *f.*

shining *a.* lūcidus splendidus; (*fig.*) illūstris.

shiny *a.* nitidus.

ship *n.* nāvis *f.* admiral's — nāvis praetōria. decked — nāvis tēcta, nāvis cōnstrāta. merchant — nāvis onerāria. war — nāvis longa. *vt* (*cargo*) impōnere; (*to a place*) nāvī invehere.

ship-owner *n.* nāviculārius *m.*

shipping *n.* nāvēs *f.pl.*

shipwreck *n.* naufragium *n.* suffer — naufragium facere.

shipwrecked *a.* naufragus.

shirk *vt.* dēfugere, dētrectāre.

shirt *n.* subūcula *f.*

shiver *n.* horror *m.* *vi.* horrēre, tremere. *vt.* perfringere, comminuere.

shivering *n.* horror *m.*
shoal *n.* (*fish*) exāmen *n.*; (*water*) vadum *n.*; (*pl.*) brevia *n.pl.*
shock *n.* impulsus *m.*; (*battle*) concursus *m.*, cōnflictus *m.*; (*hair*) caesariēs *f.*; (*mind*) offēnsiō *f.* *vt.* percutere, offendere.
shocking *a.* atrōx, dētestābilis, flāgitiōsus.
shoddy *a.* vīlis.
shoe *n.* calceus *m.*
shoemaker *n.* sūtor *m.*
shoot *n.* surculus *m.*; (*vine*) pampinus *m.* *vi.* frondēscere; (*movement*) volāre. — up ēmicāre. *vt.* (*missile*) conicere, iaculārī; (*person*) iaculārī, trānsfīgere.
shop *n.* taberna *f.*
shore *n.* lītus *n.*, ōra *f.* *vt.* fulcīre.
short *a.* brevis; (*broken*) curtus; (*amount*) exiguus. — cut via compendiāria *f.* — of (*number*) intrā (*acc.*). be — of indigēre (*abl.*). cut — interpellāre. in — ad summam, dēnique. very — perbrevis. fall — of nōn pervenīre ad, abesse ab. run — dēficere. to cut a long story — nē multīs morer, nē multa. **-ly** *ad.* (*time*) brevī; (*speech*) breviter.
shortage *n.* inopia *f.*
short-coming *n.* dēlictum *n.*, culpa *f.*
shorten *vt.* curtāre, imminuere, contrahere; (*sail*) legere.
shorthand *n.* notae *f.pl.* — **writer** *n.* āctuārius *m.*
short-lived *a.* brevis.
shortness *n.* brevitās *f.*, exiguitās *f.*; (*difficulty*) angustiae *f.pl.*
short-sighted *a.* (*fig.*) imprōvidus, imprūdēns.
short-sightedness *n.* imprūdentia *f.*
short-tempered *a.* īrācundus.
shot *n.* ictus *m.*; (*range*) iactus *m.*
should *vi.* (*duty*) dēbēre.
shoulder *n.* humerus *m.*; (*animal*) armus *m.* *vt.* (*burden*) suscipere.
shout *n.* clāmor *m.*, adclāmātiō *f.* *vt.* & *i.* clāmāre, vōciferārī. — down obstrepere (*dat.*). — out exclāmāre.
shove *vt.* trūdere, impellere.
shovel *n.* rutrum *n.*
show *n.* speciēs *f.*; (*entertainment*) lūdī *m.pl.*, spectāculum *n.*; (*stage*) lūdicrum *n.* for — in speciem. put on a — spectācula dare. *vt.* mōnstrāre, indicāre, ostendere, ostentāre. — off *vi.* sē iactāre; *vt.* ostentāre.
shower *n.* imber *m.* *vt.* fundere, conicere.
showery *a.* pluvius.
showiness *n.* ostentātiō *f.*
showing off *n.* iactātiō *f.*
showy *a.* speciōsus.
shred *n.* fragmentum *n.* in -s minūtātim. tear to -s dīlaniāre. *vt.* concīdere.
shrew *n.* virāgō *f.*
shrewd *a.* acūtus, ācer, sagāx. **-ly** *ad.* acūtē, sagāciter.
shrewdness *n.* acūmen *n.*, sagācitās *f.*
shriek *n.* ululātus *m.* *vi.* ululāre.
shrill *a.* acūtus, argūtus.
shrine *n.* fānum *n.*, dēlubrum *n.*
shrink *vt.* contrahere. *vi.* contrahī. — from abhorrēre ab, refugere ab, dētrectāre.
shrivel *vt.* corrūgāre. *vi.* exārēscere.
shroud *n.* integumentum *n*; (*pl.*) rudentēs *m. pl.* *vt.* involvere.
shrub *n.* frutex *m.*
shrubbery *n.* fruticētum *n.*
shudder *n.* horror *m.* *vi.* exhorrēscere. — at horrēre.
shuffle *vt.* miscēre. *vi.* claudicāre; (*fig.*) tergiversārī.

shun *vt.* vītāre, ēvītāre, dēfugere.
shut *vt.* claudere; (*with cover*) operīre; (*hand*) comprimere. — in inclūdere. — off interclūdere. — out exclūdere. — up inclūdere. [*n.*
shutter *n.* foricula *f.*, lūmināre
shuttle *n.* radius *m.*
shy *a.* timidus, pudibundus, verēcundus. **-ly** *ad.* timidē, verēcundē.
shyness *n.* verēcundia *f.*
sibyl *n.* sibylla *f.*
sick *a.* aeger, aegrōtus. **be** — aegrōtāre. **feel** — nauseāre. **I am** — of mē taedet (*gen.*).
sicken *vt.* fastīdium movēre (*dat.*). *vi.* nauseāre, aegrōtāre.
sickle *n.* falx *f.*
sickly *a.* invalidus.
sickness *n.* nausea *f.*; (*illness*) morbus *m.*, aegritūdō *f.*
side *n.* latus *n.*; (*direction*) pars *f.*; (*faction*) partēs *f.pl.*; (*kin*) genus *n.* **on all -s** undique. **on both -s** utrimque. **on one** — unā ex parte. **on our** — ā nōbis. **be on the** — **of** stāre ab, sentīre cum. **on the far** — **of** ultrā (*acc.*). **on this** — hinc. **on this** — **of** cis (*acc.*), citrā (*acc.*). *vi.* — **with** stāre ab, facere cum.
sideboard *n.* abacus *m.*
sidelong *a.* oblīquus.
sideways *ad.* oblīquē, **in** oblīquum.
sidle *vi.* oblīquō corpore incēdere.
siege *n.* obsidiō *f.*, oppugnātiō *f.* **lay** — **to** obsidēre. — **works** *n.* opera *n.pl.*
siesta *n.* merīdiātiō *f.* **take a** — merīdiāre.
sieve *n.* crībrum *n.*
sigh *n.* suspīrium *n.*; (*loud*) gemitus *m.* *vi.* suspīrāre, gemere.
sight *n.* (*sense*) vīsus *m.*; (*process*) aspectus *m.*; (*range*) cōnspectus *m.*; (*thing seen*) spectāculum *n.*, speciēs *f.* **at** — ex tempore. **at first** — prīmō aspectū. **in** — in cōnspectū. **come in** — in cōnspectum sē dare. **in the** — **of** in oculīs (*gen.*). **catch** — **of** cōnspicere. **lose** — **of** ē cōnspectū āmittere; (*fig.*) oblīvīscī (*gen.*) *vt.* cōnspicārī.
sightless *a.* caecus.
sightly *a.* decōrus.
sign *n.* signum *n.*, indicium *n.*; (*distinction*) īnsigne *n.*; (*mark*) nota *f.*; (*trace*) vestīgium *n.*; (*proof*) documentum *n.*; (*portent*) ōmen *n.*; (*Zodiac*) signum *n.* **give a** — innuere. *vi.* signum dare, innuere. *vt.* subscrībere (*dat.*); (*as witness*) obsignāre.
signal *n.* signum *n.* **give the** — **for retreat** receptuī canere. *vi.* signum dare. *a.* īnsignis, ēgregius. **-ly** *ad.* ēgregiē.
signalize *vt.* nōbilitāre.
signature *n.* nōmen *n.*, manus *f.*, chīrographum *n.*
signet *n.* signum *n.*
significance *n.* interpretātiō *f.*, significātiō *f.*, vīs *f.*; (*importance*) pondus *n.*
significant *a.* gravis, clārus.
signification *n.* significātiō *f.*
signify *vt.* significāre, velle; (*omen*) portendere. **it does not** — nōn interest.
silence *n.* silentium *n.* **in** — per silentium. *vt.* comprimere; (*argument*) refūtāre.
silent *a.* tacitus; (*habit*) taciturnus. **be** — silēre, tacēre. **be** — **about** silēre, tacēre. **become** — conticēscere. **-ly** *ad.* tacitē.
silhouette *n.* adumbrātiō *f.*
silk *n.* bombȳx *m.*; (*clothes*) sērica *n.pl.* *a.* bombȳcinus, sēricus.
silken *a.* bombȳcinus.
sill *n.* līmen *n.*
silliness *n.* stultitia *f.*, ineptiae *f.pl.*

silly *a.* fatuus, ineptus. be — dēsipere.
silt *n.* līmus *m.*
silvan *a.* silvestris, agrestis.
silver *n.* argentum *n.* *a.* argenteus.
silver-mine *n.* argentāria *f.*
silver-plate *n.* argentum *n.* **-d** *a.* argentātus.
silvery *a.* argenteus.
similar *a.* similis. **-ly** *ad.* similiter.
similarity *n.* similitūdō *f.*
simile *n.* similitūdō *f.*
simmer *vi.* lēniter fervēre.
simper *vi.* molliter subrīdēre.
simp/le *a.* simplex; (*mind*) fatuus; (*task*) facilis. **-ly** *ad.* simpliciter; (*merely*) sōlum, tantum.
simpleton *n.* homō ineptus *m.*
simplicity *n.* simplicitās *f.*; (*mind*) stultitia *f.*
simplify *vt.* faciliōrem reddere.
simulate *vt.* simulāre.
simulation *n.* simulātiō *f.*
simultaneously *ad.* simul, ūnā, eōdem tempore.
sin *n.* peccātum *n.*, nefas *n.*, dēlictum *n.* *vi.* peccāre.
since *ad.* abhinc. long — iamdūdum. *conj.* (*time*) ex quō tempore, postquam; (*reason*) cum, quōniam. — he quippe quī. *pr.* ab (*abl.*), ex (*abl.*), post (*acc.*). ever — usque ab.
sincere *a.* sincērus, simplex, apertus. **-ly** *ad.* sincērē, ex animō.
sincerity *n.* fidēs *f.*, simplicitās *f.*
sinew *n.* nervus *m.*
sinewy *a.* nervōsus.
sinful *a.* improbus, impius, incestus. **-ly** *ad.* improbē, impiē.
sing *vt.* canere, cantāre. — of canere.
singe *vt.* adūrere.
singer *n.* cantor *m.*
singing *n.* cantus *m.* *a.* canōrus.
single *a.* ūnus, sōlus, ūnicus; (*unmarried*) caelebs. *vt.* — out ēligere, excerpere.
single-handed *a.* ūnus.
singly *ad.* singillātim, singulī.
singular *a.* singulāris; (*strange*) novus. **-ly** *ad.* singulāriter, praecipuē.
sinister *a.* īnfaustus, malevolus.
sink *vi.* dēsīdere; (*in water*) dēmergī. — in inlābī, īnsīdere. *vt.* dēprimere, mergere; (*well*) fodere; (*fig.*) dēmergere.
sinless *a.* integer, innocēns, castus.
sinner *n.* peccātor *m.*
sinuous *a.* sinuōsus.
sip *vt.* gustāre, lībāre.
siphon *n.* siphō *m.*
sir *n.* (*to master*) ere; (*to equal*) vir optime; (*title*) eques *m.*
sire *n.* pater *m.*
siren *n.* sīrēn *f.*
sirocco *n.* Auster *m.*
sister *n.* soror *f.* **-'s** sorōrius.
sisterhood *n.* germānitās *f.*; (*society*) sorōrum societās *f.*
sister-in-law *n.* glōs *f.*
sisterly *a.* sorōrius.
sit *vi.* sedēre. — beside adsidēre (*dat.*). — down cōnsīdere. — on īnsidēre (*dat.*); (*eggs*) incubāre. — at table accumbere. — up (*at night*) vigilāre.
site *n.* situs *m.*; (*for building*) ārea *f.*
sitting *n.* sessiō *f.*
situated *a.* situs.
situation *n.* situs *m.*; (*circs.*) status *m.*, condiciō *f.*
six *num.* sex. — each sēnī. — or seven sex septem. — times sexiēns.
six hundred *num.* sēscentī. — each sēscēnī. — times sēscentiēns. **-th** *a.* sēscentēsimus.
sixteen *num.* sēdecim. — each sēnī dēnī. — times sēdeciēns. **-th** *a.* sextus decimus.

sixth *a.* sextus. for the — time sextum.
sixtieth *a.* sexāgēsimus.
sixty *num.* sexāgintā. — each sexāgēni. — times sexāgiēns.
size *n.* māgnitūdō *f.*, amplitūdō *f.*; (*measure*) mēnsūra *f.*, fōrma *f.*
skate *vi.* per glaciem lābi. — on thin ice (*fig.*) incēdere per ignēs suppositōs cineri dolōsō.
skein *n.* glomus *n.*
skeleton *n.* ossa *n.pl.*
sketch *n.* adumbrātiō *f.*, dēscrīptiō *f.* *vt.* adumbrāre, īnfōrmāre.
skewer *n.* verū *n.*
skiff *n.* scapha *f.*, lēnunculus *m.*
skilful *a.* peritus, doctus, scitus; (*with hands*) habilis. **-ly** *ad.* peritē, doctē; habiliter.
skill *n.* ars *f.*, peritia *f.*, sollertia *f.*
skilled *a.* peritus, doctus.
skim *vt.* dēspūmāre. — over (*fig.*) legere, perstringere.
skin *n.* cutis *f.*; (*animal*) pellis *f.* *vt.* pellem dētrahere (*dat.*).
skinflint *n.* avārus *m.*
skinny *a.* macer.
skip *vi.* exsultāre. *vt.* praeterīre.
skipper *n.* magister *m.*
skirmish *n.* leve proelium *n.* *vi.* vēlitārī.
skirmisher *n.* vēles *m.*, excursor *m.*
skirt *n.* īnstita *f.*; (*border*) limbus *m.* *vt.* contingere (*dat.*); (*motion*) legere.
skittish *a.* lascīvus.
skulk *vi* latēre, dēlitēscere.
skull *n.* caput *n.*
sky *n.* caelum *n.* of the — caelestis.
skylark *n.* alauda *f.*
slab *n.* tabula *f.*
slack *a.* remissus, laxus; (*work*) piger, neglegēns.
slacken *vt.* remittere, dētendere. *vi.* laxārī.
slackness *n.* remissiō *f.*; pigritia *f.*
slag *n.* scōria *f.*
slake *vt.* restinguere, sēdāre.
slam *vt.* adflīgere.
slander *n.* maledicta *n.pl.*, obtrectātiō*f.*; (*law*) calumnia *f.* *vt.* maledicere (*dat.*), īnfāmāre, obtrectāre (*dat.*).
slanderer *n.* obtrectātor *m.*
slanderous *a.* maledicus.
slang *n.* vulgāria verba *n.pl.*
slant *vi.* in trānsversum īre.
slanting *a.* oblīquus, trānsversus. **-ly** *ad.* oblīquē, ex trānsversō.
slap *n.* alapa *f.* *vt.* palmā ferīre.
slap-dash *a.* praeceps, temerārius.
slash *vt.* caedere. *n.* ictus *m.*
slate *n.* (*roof*) tēgula *f.*; (*writing*) tabula *f.* *vt.* increpāre.
slatternly *a.* sordidus, incōmptus.
slaughter *n.* caedēs *f.*, strāgēs *f.* *vt.* trucīdāre.
slaughter-house *n.* laniēna *f.*
slave *n.* servus *m.*; (*domestic*) famulus *m.*; (*home-born*) verna *m.* be a — to īnservīre (*dat.*). household -s familia *f.*
slavery *n.* servitūs *f.*
slavish *a.* servīlis. **-ly** *ad.* servīliter.
slay *vt.* interficere, occīdere.
slayer *n.* interfector *m.*
sleek *a.* nitidus, pinguis.
sleep *n.* somnus *m.* go to — obdormīscere. *vi.* dormīre. — off *vt.* ēdormīre.
sleeper *n.* dormitor *m.*
sleepiness *n.* sopor *m.*
sleepless *a.* īnsomnis, vigil.
sleeplessness *n.* īnsomnia *f.*
sleepy *a.* somniculōsus. be — dormītāre.
sleeve *n.* manica *f.*
sleight of hand *n.* praestigiae *f.pl.*
slender *a.* gracilis, exīlis.
slenderness *n.* gracilitās *f.*

slice *n.* frustum *n.* *vt.* secāre.
slide *n.* lāpsus *m.* *vi.* lābī.
slight *a.* levis, exiguus, parvus. *n* neglegentia *f.* *vt.* neglegere, offendere. **-ly** *ad.* leviter, paululum.
slightingly *ad.* contemptim.
slightness *n.* levitās *f.*
slim *a.* gracilis.
slime *n.* līmus *m.*
slimness *n.* gracilitās *f.*
slimy *a.* līmōsus, mūcōsus.
sling *n.* funda *f.* *vt.* mittere, iaculārī.
slinger *n.* funditor *m.*
slink *vi.* sē subducere.
slip *n.* lāpsus *m.*; (*mistake*) offēnsiuncula *f.*; (*plant*) surculus *m.* *vi.* lābī. — away ēlābī, dīlābī. — out ēlābī; (*word*) excidere. give the — to ēlūdere. let — āmittere, ēmittere; (*opportunity*) ōmittere. there's many a — twixt the cup and the lip inter ōs et offam multa interveniunt.
slipper *n.* solea *f.*
slippery *a.* lūbricus.
slipshod *a.* neglegēns.
slit *n.* rīma *f.* *vt.* findere, incīdere.
sloe *n.* spīnus *m.*
slope *n.* dēclīve *n.*, clīvus *m.*; (*steep*) dēiectus *m.* *vi.* sē dēmittere, vergere.
sloping *a.* dēclīvis, dēvexus; (*up*) adclīvis.
slot *n.* rīma *f*
sloth *n.* inertia *f.*, segnitia *f.*, dēsidia *f.*, ignāvia *f.*
slothful *a.* ignāvus, iners, segnis. **-ly** *ad.* ignāvē, segniter.
slouch *vi.* languidē incēdere.
slough *n.* (*skin*) exuviae *f.pl.*; (*bog*) palūs *f.*
slovenliness *n.* ignāvia *f.*, sordēs *f.pl.*
slovenly *a.* ignāvus, sordidus.
slow *a.* tardus, lentus; (*mind*) hebes. **-ly** *ad.* tardē, lentē.
slowness *n.* tarditās *f.*
sludge *n.* līmus *m.*
slug *n.* līmāx *f.*
sluggard *n.* homō ignāvus *m.*
sluggish *a.* piger, segnis; (*mind*) hebes. **-ly** *ad.* pigrē, segniter.
sluggishness *n.* pigritia *f.*, [inertia *f.*
sluice *n.* cataracta *f.*
slumber *n.* somnus *m.*, sopor *m.* *vi.* dormīre.
slump *n.* vīlis annōna *f.*
slur *n.* nota *f.* cast — on dētrectāre. *vt.* — words balbūtīre.
sly *a.* astūtus, vafer, callidus. on the — ex opīnātō. **-ly** *ad.* astūtē, callidē.
slyness *n.* astūtia *f.*
smack *n.* (*blow*) ictus *m.*; (*with hand*) alapa *f.*; (*boat*) lēnunculus *m.*; (*taste*) sapor *m.* *vt.* ferīre. *vi.* — of olēre, redolēre.
small *a.* parvus, exiguus. how — quantulus, quantillus. so — tantulus. very — perexiguus, minimus. a — meeting of īnfrequēns. — talk sermunculus *m.*
smallness *n.* exiguitās *f.*, brevitās *f.*
smart *a.* (*action*) ācer, alacer; (*dress*) concinnus, nitidus; (*pace*) vēlōx; (*wit*) facētus, salsus. *n.* dolor *m.* *vi.* dolēre; (*fig.*) ūrī, morderī. **-ly** *ad.* ācriter; nitidē; vēlōciter; facētē.
smartness *n.* alacritās *f.*; (*dress*) nitor *m.*; (*wit*) facētiae *f.pl.*, sollertia *f.*
smash *n.* ruīna *f.* *vt.* frangere, comminuere.
smattering *n.* get a — of odōrārī, prīmīs labrīs attingere. with a — of imbūtus (*abl.*).
smear *vt.* oblinere, ungere.
smell *n.* (*sense*) odōrātus *m.*; (*odour*) odor *m.*; (*of cooking*) nīdor *m.* *vt.* olfacere, odōrārī. *vi.* olēre.

smelly *a.* olidus.
smelt *vt.* fundere.
smile *n.* rīsus *m.* *vi.* subrīdēre. — at adrīdēre (*dat.*). — upon rīdēre ad.; (*fig.*) secundum esse (*dat.*].
smiling *a.* laetus.
smirk *vi.* subrīdēre.
smite *vt.* ferīre, percutere.
smith *n.* faber *m.*
smithy *n.* fabrica *f.*
smock *n.* tunica *f.*
smoke *n.* fūmus *m.* *vi.* fūmāre.
smoke *a.* fūmōsus.
smooth *a.* lēvis; (*skin*) glaber; (*talk*) blandus; (*sea*) placidus; (*temper*) aequus; (*voice*) lēvis, teres. *vt.* sternere, līmāre. **-ly** *ad.* lēviter, lēniter.
smoothness *n.* lēvitās *f.*, lēnitās *f.*
smother *vt.* opprimere, suffocāre.
smoulder *vi.* fūmāre.
smudge *n.* macula *f.*
smug *a.* suī contentus.
smugness *n.* amo. suī.
smuggle *vt.* fūrtim importāre.
smut *n.* fūlīgō.
snack *n.* cēnula *f.* take a — gustāre. [scrūpulus *m.*
snag *n.* impedīmentum *n.*,
snail *n.* cochlea *f.*
snake *n.* anguis *m.*, serpēns *f.*
snaky *a.* vīpereus.
snap *vt.* rumpere, praerumpere. — the fingers digitīs concrepāre. *vi.* rumpī, dissilīre. — at mordēre. — up corripere.
snare *n.* laqueus *m.*, plaga *f.*, pedica *f.* *vt.* inrētīr .
snarl *n.* gannītus *m.* *vi.* gannīre.
snatch *vt.* rapere, ēripere, adripere. — at captāre.
sneak *n.* perfidus *m.* *vi.* conrēpere. — in sē īnsinuāre. — out ēlābī.
sneaking *a.* humilis, fūrtīvus.
sneer *n.* irrīsiō *f.* *vi.* irrīdēre, dērīdēre.
sneeze *n.* sternūtāmentum *n.* *vi.* sternuere.
sniff *vt.* odōrārī.
snip *vt.* praecīdere, secāre.
snob *n.* homō ambitiōsus *m.*
snood *n.* mitra *f*
snooze *vi.* dormītāre.
snore *vi.* stertere.
snoring *n.* rhoncus *m.*
snort *n.* fremitus *m.* *vi.* fremere.
snout *n.* rōstrum *n.*
snow *n.* nix *f.* *vi.* ningere. -ed under nive obrutus.
snowy *a.* nivālis; (*colour*) niveus.
snub *vt.* neglegere, praeterīre.
snub-nosed *a.* sīmus.
snuff *n.* (*candle*) fungus *m.*
snug *a.* commodus. **-ly** *ad.* commodē.
so *ad.* (*referring back*) sīc; (*referring forward*) ita; (*with a. & ad.*) tam; (*with verb*) adeō; (*consequence*) ergō, itaque, igitur. **so-so** sīc. — as to ut. — be it estō. — big tantus. — far usque adeō, adhūc. — far as quod. — far from adeō nōn. — little tantillus. — long as dum. — many tot. — much *a.* tantus. *ad.* tantum; (*with comp.*) tantō. — often totiēns. — that ut. — that . . . not (*purpose*) nē; (*result*) ut nōn. and — on deinceps. not — very haud ita. say — id dīcere.
soak *vt.* imbuere, madefacere.
soaking *a.* madidus.
soap *n.* sapō *m.*
soar *vi.* in sublīme ferrī, subvolāre. — above superāre.
sob *n.* singultus *m.* *vi.* singultāre.
sober *a.* sobrius; (*conduct*) modestus; (*mind*) sānus. **-ly** *ad.* sobriē, modestē.
sobriety *n.* modestia *f.*, continentia *f.*
so-called *a.* quī dīcitur.

sociability *n.* facilitās *f.*
sociab/le *a.* facilis, cōmis. **-ly** *ad.* faciliter, cōmiter.
social *a.* sociālis, commūnis.
socialism *n.* populāris ratiō *f.*
socialist *n.* homō populāris *m., f.*
society *n.* societās *f.* (*class*) optimātēs *m.pl.*; (*being with*) convictus *m.* cultivate the — of adsectārī. secret — sodālitās *f.*
sod *n.* caespes *m.*, glaeba *f.*
soda *n.* nitrum *n.*
sodden *n.* madidus.
soever *ad.* -cumque.
sofa *n.* lectus *m.*
soft *a.* mollis; (*fruit*) mītis; (*voice*) submissus; (*character*) dēlicātus; (*words*) blandus. **-ly** *ad.* molliter, lēniter; blandē.
soften *vt.* mollīre; (*body*) ēnervāre; (*emotion*) lēnīre, mītigāre. *vi.* mollēscere, mītēscere.
soft-hearted *a.* misericors.
softness *n.* mollitia *f.*, mollitiēs *f.*
soil *n.* sōlum *n.*, humus *f.* *vt.* inquināre, foedāre.
sojourn *n.* commorātiō *f.*, mānsiō *f.*. *vi.* commorārī.
sojourner *n.* hospes *m.*, hospita *f.*
solace *n.* sōlātium *n.*, levātiō *f.* *vt.* sōlārī, cōnsōlārī.
solar *a.* sōlis.
solder *n.* ferrūmen *n.* *vt.* ferrūmināre.
soldier *n.* mīles *m.* be a — mīlitāre. common — manipulāris *m.*, gregārius mīles *m.* fellow — commīlitō *m.* foot — pedes *m.* old — veterānus *m.* *vi.* mīlitāre.
soldierly *a.* mīlitāris.
soldiery *n.* mīles *m.*
sole *a.* sōlus, ūnus, ūnicus. *n.* (*foot*) planta *f.*; (*fish*) solea *f.* **-ly** *ad.* sōlum, tantum, modō.
solecism *n.* soloecismus *m.*
solemn *a.* gravis; (*religion*) sanctus. **-ly** *ad.* graviter; rītē.
solemnity *n.* gravitās *f.*; sanctitās *f.*
solemnize *vt.* agere.
solicit *vt.* flāgitāre, obsecrāre.
solicitation *n.* flāgitātiō *f.*
solicitor *n.* advocātus *m.*
solicitous *a.* anxius, trepidus. **-ly** *ad.* anxiē, trepidē. [*f.*
solicitude *n.* cūra *f.*, anxietās
solid *a.* solidus; (*metal*) pūrus; (*food*) firmus; (*argument*) firmus; (*character*) cōnstāns, spectātus. become — concrēscere. make — cōgere. **-ly** *ad.* firmē, cōnstanter.
solidarity *n.* societās *f.*
solidify *vt.* cōgere. *vi.* concrēscere.
solidity *n.* soliditās *f.*
soliloquize *vi.* sēcum loquī.
soliloquy *n.* ūnius ōrātiō *f.*
solitary *a.* sōlus, sōlitārius; (*instance*) ūnicus; (*place*) dēsertus.
solitude *n.* sōlitūdō *f.*
solo *n.* canticum *n.*
solstice *n.* (*summer*) sōlstitium *n.*: (*winter*) brūma *f.* [mālis.
solstitial *a.* sōlstitiālis, brū-
soluble *a.* dissolūbilis.
solution *n.* (*of puzzle*) ēnōdātiō *f.*
solve *vt.* ēnōdāre, explicāre.
solvency *n.* solvendī facultās *f.*
solvent *a.* be — solvendō esse.
sombre *a.* obscūrus; (*fig.*) tristis.
some *a.* aliquī; (*pl.*) nonnullī, aliquot. — . . . other alius . . . alius. for — time aliquamdiū. with — reason nōn sine causā. *pr.* aliquis; (*pl.*) nonnullī, sunt quī (*subj.*), erant quī (*subj.*).
somebody *pr.* aliquis. — or other nescioquis.
somehow *ad.* quōdammodō, nescio quōmodō.
someone *pr.* aliquis. — or other nescioquis. — else alius.

something *pr.* aliquid. — or other nescioquid. — else aliud.
sometime *ad.* aliquandō; (*past*) quondam.
sometimes *ad.* interdum, nonnumquam. — . . . — modo . . . modo.
somewhat *ad.* aliquantum, nōnnihil, paulum; (*with comp.*) paulō, aliquantō.
somewhere *ad.* alicubi; (*to*) aliquō. — else alibī; (*to*) aliō. from — alicunde. from — else aliunde.
somnolence *n.* somnus *m.*
somnolent *a.* sēmisomnus.
son *n.* filius *m.* small — fīliolus *m.* — **in-law** *n.* gener *m.*
song *n.* carmen *n.*, cantus *m.*
sonorous *a.* sonōrus, canōrus.
soon *ad.* brevi, citō. as — as ut prīmum, cum prīmum, simulāc. as — as possible quam prīmum. too — praemātūrē, ante tempus.
sooner *ad.* prius, mātūrius; (*preference*) libentius, potius. — or later sērius ōcius. no — said than done dictum factum.
soonest *ad.* mātūrissimē.
soot *n.* fūligō *f.*
soothe *vt.* dēlēnīre, permulcēre.
soothing *a.* lēnis, blandus. **-ly** *ad.* blandē.
soothsayer *n.* hariolus *m.*, vātēs *m.*, *f.*, haruspex *m.*
sooty *a.* fūmōsus.
sop *n.* offa *f.*; (*fig.*) dēlēnīmentum *n.*
sophism *n.* captiō *f.*
sophist *n.* sophistēs *m.*
sophistical *a.* acūleātus, captiōsus.
sophisticated *a.* lepidus, urbānus.
sophistry *n.* captiō *f.*
soporific *a.* sopōrifer, somnifer.
soprano *a.* acūtus.
sorcerer *n.* veneficus *m.*
sorceress *n.* venefica *f.*, saga *f.*
sorcery *n.* veneficium *n.*; (*means*) venēna *n.pl.*, carmina *n.pl.*
sordid *a.* sordidus. (*conduct*) illīberālis. **-ly** *ad.* sordidē.
sordidness *n.* sordēs *f.pl.*; illīberālitās *f.*
sore *a.* molestus, gravis, acerbus. feel — dolēre. *n.* ulcus *n.* **-ly** *ad.* graviter, vehementer. [*n.*
sorrel *n.* lapathus *f.*, lapathum
sorrow *n.* dolor *m.*, aegritūdō *f.*; (*outward*) maeror *m.*; (*for death*) lūctus *m.* *vi.* dolēre, maerere, lūgēre.
sorrowful *a.* maestus, tristis. **-ly** *ad.* maestē.
sorry *a.* paenitēns; (*poor*) miser. I am — for (*remorse*) mē paenitet, mē piget (*gen.*); (*pity*) mē miseret (*gen.*).
sort *n.* genus *n.* a — of quīdam. all -s of omnēs. the — of tālis. this — of huiusmodi. the common — plēbs *f.* I am not the — of man to nōn is sum quī. I am out of —s mihi displiceō. *vt.* digerere, compōnere; (*votes*) diribēre.
sortie *n.* excursiō *f.*, excursus *m.*, ēruptiō *f.* make a — ērumpere, excurrere.
sot *n.* ēbriōsus *m.* [entus.
sottish *a.* ēbriōsus, tēmul-
sottishness *n.* vīnolentia *f.*
soul *n.* anima *f.*, animus *m.*; (*essence*) vis *f.*; (*person*) caput *n.* not a — nēmō ūnus. the — of (*fig.*) medulla *f.*
soulless *a.* caecus, dūrus.
sound *n.* sonitus *m.*, sonus *m.*; (*articulate*) vōx *f.*; (*confused*) strepitus *m.*; (*loud*) fragor *m.*; (*strait*) fretum *n.* *vt.* (*signal*) canere; (*instrument*) inflāre; (*depth*) scrūtārī, temptāre; (*person*) animum temptāre (*gen.*). *vi.* canere, sonāre; (*seem*) vidērī. — a retreat

receptui canere. *a.* sānus, salūbris; (*health*) firmus; (*sleep*) artus; (*judgment*) exquisitus; (*argument*) vērus. safe and — salvus, incolumis. **-ly** *ad.* (*beat*) vehementer; (*sleep*) artē; (*study*) penitus, diligenter.
soundness *n.* sānitās *f.*, integritās *f.*
soup *n.* iūs *n.*
sour *a.* acerbus, amārus, acidus. turn — acēscere; (*fig.*) coacēscere. *vt.* (*fig.*) exacerbāre.
source *n.* fōns *m.*; (*river*) caput *n.*; (*fig.*) fōns *m.*, origō *f.* have its — in orīrī ex; (*fig.*) proficīscī ex.
sourness *n.* acerbitās *f.*; (*temper*) mōrōsitās *f.*
souse *vt.* immergere.
south *n.* merīdiēs *f.* *a.* austrālis. *ad.* ad merīdiem. — wind auster *m.* **-east** *ad.* inter sōlis ortum et merīdiem.
southerly *a.* ad merīdiem versus.
southern *a.* austrālis.
south-west *ad.* inter occāsum sōlis et merīdiem.
souvenir *n.* monumentum *n.*
sovereign *n.* rēx *m.*, rēgīna *f.* *a.* prīnceps, summus.
sovereignty *n.* rēgnum *n.*, imperium *n.*, prīncipātus *m.*; (*of the people*) māiestās *f.*
sow *n.* scrōfa *f.*, sūs *f.*
sow *vt.* serere; (*field*) cōnserere. *vi.* sementem facere.
sower *n.* sator *m.*
sowing *n.* sementis *f.*
spa *n.* aquae *f.pl.*
space *n.* (*extension*) spatium *n.*; (*not matter*) ināne *n.*; (*room*) locus *m.*; (*distance*) intervallum *n.*; (*time*) spatium *n.* open — ārea *f.* leave a — of intermittere. *vt.* — out dispōnere.
spacious *a.* amplus, capāx.
spaciousness *n.* amplitūdō *f.*
spade *n.* pāla *f.*, rūtrum *n.*
span *n.* (*measure*) palmus *m.*; (*extent*) spatium *n.* *vt.* iungere.
spangle *n.* bractea *f.* **-d** *a.* distinctus.
spar *n.* tignum *n.*
spare *vt.* parcere (*dat.*); (*to give*) suppeditāre. — time for vacāre (*dat.*). *a.* exīlis; (*extra*) subsecīvus. [parcē.
sparing *a.* parcus. **-ly** *ad.*
spark *n.* scintilla *f.*; (*fig.*) igniculus *m.* [micāre.
sparkle *vi.* scintillāre, nitēre,
sparrow *n.* passer *m.*
sparse *a.* rārus.
spasm *n.* convulsiō *f.*
spasmodically *ad.* interdum.
spatter *vt.* aspergere.
spawn *n.* ōva *n.pl.*
speak *vt.* & *i.* loquī; (*make speech*) dīcere, contiōnārī, ōrātiōnem habēre. — out ēloquī. — to adloquī; (*converse*) colloquī cum. — well of bene dīcere (*dat.*). it **-s** for itself rēs ipsa loquitur.
speaker *n.* ōrātor *m.*
speaking *n.* art of — dīcendī ars *f.* practise public — dēclāmāre. *a.* likeness — vīvida imāgō.
spear *n.* hasta *f.*
spearman *n.* hastātus *m.*
special *a.* praecipuus, proprius. **-ly** *ad.* praecipuē, praesertim.
speciality *n.* proprium *n.*
species *n.* genus *n.*
specific *a.* certus.
specification *n.* dēsignātiō *f.*
specify *vt.* dēnotāre, dēsignāre.
specimen *n.* exemplar *n.*, exemplum *n.*
specious *a.* speciōsus. **-ly** *ad.* speciōsē.
speciousness *n.* speciēs *f.*
speck *n.* macula *f.*
speckled *a.* maculīs distinctus.
spectacle *n.* spectāculum *n.*
spectacular *a.* spectābilis.
spectator *n.* spectātor *m.*
spectral *a.* larvālis.

spectre *n.* larva *f.*
speculate *vi.* cōgitāre, coniectūrās facere; (*bus.*) forō ūtī.
speculation *n.* cōgitātiō *f.*, coniectūra *f.*; (*bus.*) ālea *f.*
speculator *n.* contemplātor *m.*; (*bus.*) āleātor *m.*
speech *n.* ōrātiō *f.*; (*language*) sermō *m.*, lingua *f.*; (*to people or troops*) cōntiō *f.* **make a —** ōrātiōnem, cōntiōnem habēre.
speechless *a.* ēlinguis, mūtus.
speed *n.* celeritās *f.*, cursus *m.*, vēlōcitās *f.* **at full —** māgnō cursū, incitātus; (*riding*) citātō equō. *vt.* adcelerāre, mātūrāre. *vi.* properāre, festīnāre.
speed/y *a.* celer, vēlōx, citus. **-ily** *ad.* celeriter, citō.
spell *n.* carmen *n.* **be — bound** obstipēscere.
spelt *n.* far *n.*
spend *vt.* impendere, īnsūmere; (*public money*) ērogāre; (*time*) agere, cōnsūmere, terere; (*strength*) effundere. **— itself** (*storm*) dēsaevīre. **— on** īnsūmere (*acc.* & *dat.*).
spendthrift *n.* nepōs *m.*, prōdigus *m.*
sphere *n.* globus *m.*; (*of action*) prōvincia *f.*
spherical *a.* globōsus.
sphinx *n.* sphinx *f.*
spice *n.* condīmentum *n.*; (*pl.*) odōrēs *m.pl.* *vt.* condīre.
spicy *a.* odōrātus; (*wit*) salsus.
spider *n.* arānea *f.* **-'s web** arāneum *n.*
spike *n.* dēns *m.*, clāvus *m.*
spikenard *n.* nardus *m.*
spill *vt.* fundere, profundere. *vi.* redundāre.
spin *vt.* (*thread*) nēre, dēdūcere; (*top*) versāre. **— out** (*story*) prōdūcere. *vi.* circumagī, versārī.
spindle *n.* fūsus *m.*
spine *n.* spīna *f.*
spineless *a.* ēnervātus.
spinster *n.* virgō *f.*
spiral *a.* intortus. *n.* spīra *f.*
spire *n.* cōnus *m.*
spirit *n.* (*life*) anima *f.*; (*intelligence*) mēns *f.*; (*soul*) animus *m.*; (*vivacity*) spīritus *m.*, vigor *m.*, vīs *f.*; (*character*) ingenium *n.*; (*intention*) voluntās *f.*; (*of an age*) mōrēs *m.pl.*; (*ghost*) anima *f.*; (*pl.*) mānēs *m.pl.* **full of —** alacer, animōsus.
spirited *a.* animōsus, ācer.
spiritless *a.* iners, frāctus, timidus.
spiritual *a.* animī.
spit *n.* verū *n.* *vi.* spuere, spūtāre. **— on** cōnspūtāre. **— out** exspuere.
spite *n.* invidia *f.*, malevolentia *f.*, līvor *m.* **in — of me** mē invītō. **in — of the difficulties** in his angustiīs. *vt.* incommodāre, offendere.
spiteful *a.* malevolus, malignus, invidus. **-ly** *ad.* malevolē, malignē.
spitefulness *n.* malevolentia [*f.*
spittle *n.* spūtum *n.*
splash *n.* fragor *m.* *vt.* aspergere.
spleen *n.* splēn *m.*; (*fig.*) [stomachus *m.*
splendid *a.* splendidus, lūculentus; (*person*) amplus. **-ly** *ad.* splendidē, optimē.
splendour *n.* splendor *m.*, fulgor *m.*; (*fig.*) lautitia *f.*, adparātus *m.*
splenetic *a.* stomachōsus.
splice *vt.* iungere.
splint *n.* ferula *f.*
splinter *n.* fragmentum *n.*, assula *f.* *vt.* findere.
split *vt.* findere. *vi.* dissilīre. *a.* fissus. *n.* fissum *n.*; (*fig.*) dissidium *n.*
splutter *vi.* balbūtīre.
spoil *n.* praeda *f.*; (*pl.*) spolia *n.pl.*, exuviae *f.pl.* *vt.* (*rob*) spoliāre; (*mar*) corrumpere. *vi.* corrumpī.
spoiler *n.* spoliātor *m.*; corruptor *m.*

spoke *n.* radius *m.* put a — in one's wheel inicere scrūpulum (*dat.*).
spokesman *n.* interpres *m.*, ōrātor *m.*
spoliation *n.* spoliātiō *f.*, dīreptiō *f.*
spondee *n.* spondēus *m.*
sponge *n.* spongia *f.*
sponsor *n.* spōnsor *m.*; (*fig.*) auctor *m.*
spontaneity *n.* impulsus *m.*, voluntās *f.*
spontaneous *a.* voluntārius. **-ly** *ad.* suā sponte, ultrō.
spoon *n.* cochlear *n.*
spoor *n.* vestīgia *n.pl.*
sporadic *a.* rārus. **-ally** *ad.* passim.
sport *n.* lūdus *m.*; (*in Rome*) campus *m.* (*fun*) iocus *m.*; (*ridicule*) lūdibrium *n.* make — of illūdere (*dat.*). *vi.* lūdere.
sportive *a.* lascīvus.
sportiveness *n.* lascīvia *f.*
sportsman *n.* vēnātor *m.*
sportsmanlike *a.* honestus, generōsus.
spot *n.* macula *f.*; (*place*) locus *m.*; (*dice*) pūnctum *n.* on the — īlicō. *vt.* maculāre; (*see*) animadvertere.
spotless *a.* integer, pūrus; (*character*) castus.
spotted *a.* maculōsus.
spouse *n.* coniunx *m.*, *f.*
spout *n.* (*of jug*) ōs *n.*; (*pipe*) canālis *m.* *vi.* ēmicāre.
sprain *vt.* intorquēre.
sprawl *vi.* sē fundere. **-ing** *a.* fūsus.
spray *n.* aspergō *f.* *vt.* aspergere.
spread *vt.* pandere, extendere; (*news*) dīvulgāre; (*infection*) vulgare. *vi.* patēre; (*rumour*) mānāre, incrēbrēscere; (*feeling*) glīscere.
spreadeagle *vt.* dispandere.
spreading *a.* (*tree*) patulus.
spree *n.* cōmissātiō *f.*
sprig *n.* virga *f.*
sprightliness *n.* alacritās *f.*
sprightly *a.* alacer, hilaris.
spring *n.* (*season*) vēr *n.*; (*water*) fōns *m.*; (*leap*) saltus *m.* *vi.* (*grow*) crēscere, ēnāscī; (*leap*) salīre. — from orīrī ex, proficīscī ex. — on to īnsillīre in (*acc.*). — up exorīrī, exsilīre. *vt.* — a leak rīmās agere. — a surprise on admīrātiōnem movēre (*dat.*). *a.* vērnus.
springe *n.* laqueus *m.*
sprinkle *vt.* aspergere. — on īnspergere (*dat.*).
sprint *vi.* currere.
sprout *n.* surculus *m.* *vi.* fruticārī.
spruce *a.* nitidus, concinnus.
sprung *a.* ortus, oriundus.
spume *n.* spūma *f.*
spur *n.* calcar *n.* — of a hill prōminēns collis. on the — of the moment ex tempore. *vt.* incitāre. — the willing horse currentem incitāre.
spurious *a.* falsus, fūcōsus, fictus.
spurn *vt.* spernere, aspernārī, respuere.
spurt *vi.* ēmicāre; (*run*) sē incitāre. *n.* impetus *m.*
spy *n.* speculātor *m.*, explōrātor *m.* *vi.* speculārī. *vt.* cōnspicere. — out explōrāre.
squabble *n.* iūrgium *n.* *vi.* rixārī.
squad *n.* (*mil.*) decuria.
squadron *n.* (*cavalry*) āla *f.*, turma *f.*; (*ships*) classis *f.*
squalid *a.* sordidus, dēfōrmis.
squall *n.* procella *f.*
squally *a.* procellōsus.
squalor *n.* sordēs *f.pl.*, squālor *m.*
squander *vt.* dissipāre, dispergere, effundere.
squanderer *n.* prōdigus *m.*
square *n.* quadrātum *n.*; (*town*) ārea *f.* *vt.* quadrāre; (*account*) subdūcere. *vi.* cōnstāre, congruere. *a.* quadrātus.
squash *vt.* conterere, contundere.

squat *vi.* subsīdere. *a.* brevis atque obēsus.

squatter *n.* (*on land*) agripeta [*m.*

squawk *vi.* crōcīre.

squeak *n.* strīdor *m.* *vi.* strīdēre.

squeal *n.* vāgītus *m.* *vi.* vāgīre.

squeamish *a.* fastīdiōsus. feel — nauseāre, fastīdīre.

squeamishness *n.* fastīdium *n.*, nausea *f.*

squeeze *vt.* premere, comprimere. — out exprimere.

squint *a.* perversus. *n.* person with a — strabō *m.* *vi.* strabōnem esse.

squinter *n.* strabō *m.*

squinting *a.* paetus.

squire *n.* armiger *m.*; (*landed*) dominus *m.*

squirm *vi.* volūtārī.

squirrel *n.* sciūrus *m.*

squirt *vt.* ēicere, effundere. *vi.* ēmicāre.

stab *n.* ictus *m.*, vulnus *n.* *vt.* fodere, ferīre, percutere.

stability *n.* stabilitās *f.*, firmitās *f.*, cōnstantia *f.*

stabilize *vt.* stabilīre, firmāre.

stable *a.* firmus, stabilis. *n.* stabulum *n.*, equīle *n.* shut the — door after the horse is stolen clipeum post vulnera sūmere.

stack *n.* acervus *m.* *vt.* congerere, cumulāre.

stadium *n.* spatium *n.*

staff *n.* scīpiō *m.*, virga *f.*; (*augur's*) lituus *m.*; (*officers*) contubernālēs *m.pl.*

stag *n.* cervus *m.*

stage *n.* pulpitum *n.*, proscēnium *n.*; (*theatre*) scēna *f.*, theātrum *n.*; (*scene of action*) campus *m.*; (*of journey*) iter *n.*; (*of progress*) gradus *m.* *a.* scēnicus. *vt.* (*play*) dare, docēre.

stage-fright *n.* horror *m.*

stagger *vi.* titubāre. *vt.* obstupefacere.

stagnant *a.* iners.

stagnate *vi.* (*fig.*) cessāre, refrīgēscere. [torpor *m.*

stagnation *n.* cessātiō *f.*,

stagy *a.* scēnicus.

staid *a.* sevērus, gravis.

stain *n.* macula *f.*, lābēs *f.*; (*fig.*) dēdecus *n.*, ignōminia *f.* *vt.* maculāre, foedāre, contāmināre. — with īnficere (*abl.*).

stainless *a.* pūrus, integer.

stair *n.* scālae *f.pl.*, gradus *m.pl.*

staircase *n.* scālae *f.pl.*

stake *n.* pālus *m.*, stipes *m.*; (*pledge*) pignus *n.* be at — agī, in discrīmine esse. *vt.* (*wager*) dēpōnere.

stale *a.* obsolētus, effētus.; (*wine*) vapidus.

stalemate *n.* reach a — ad incitās redigī.

stalk *n.* (*corn*) calamus *m.*; (*plant*) stipes *m.* *vi.* incēdere. *vt.* vēnārī, īnsidiārī (*dat.*).

stall *n.* (*animal*) stabulum *n.*; (*seat*) subsellium *n.*; (*shop*) taberna *f.* *vt.* stabulāre.

stallion *n.* equus *m.*

stalwart *a.* ingēns, rōbustus, fortis.

stamina *n.* patientia *f.*

stammer *n.* haesitātiō *f.* *vi.* balbūtīre.

stammering *a.* balbus.

stamp *n.* fōrma *f.*; (*mark*) nota *f.*, signum *n.*; (*of feet*) supplōsiō *f.* *vt.* imprimere; (*coin*) ferīre, signāre, (*fig.*) inūrere. — one's feet pedem supplōdere. — out exstinguere.

stampede *n.* discursus *m.*; (*fig.*) pavor *m.* *vi.* discurrere.; (*fig.*) expavēscere.

stance *n.* status *m.*

stanchion *n.* columna *f.*

stand *n.* (*position*) statiō *f.*; (*platform*) suggestus *m.* make a — resistere, restāre. *vi.* stāre; (*remain*) manēre; (*matters*) sē habēre. *vt.* statuere;

(*tolerate*) ferre, tolerāre. — against resistere (*dat.*). — aloof abstāre. — by adsistere (*dat.*); (*friend*) adesse (*dat.*); (*promise*) praestāre. — convicted manifestum tenērī. — down concēdere. — for (*office*) petere; (*meaning*) significāre; (*policy*) postulāre. — in awe of in metū habēre. — in need of indigēre (*abl.*). — on insistere in (*abl.*). — on end horrēre. — on one's dignity gravitātem suam tuērī. — out ēminēre, exstāre; (*against*) resistere (*dat.*); (*to sea*) in altum prōvehī. — out of the way of dēcēdere (*dat.*). — over (*case*) ampliāre. — still cōnsistere, insistere. — to reason sequī. — trial reum fierī. — up surgere, cōnsurgere. — up for dēfendere, adesse (*dat.*). — up to respōnsāre (*dat.*).

standard *n.* (*mil.*) signum *n.*; (*measure*) nōrma *f.* — author scrīptor classicus *m.* up to — iūstus. judge by the — of referre ad. [*m.*

standard-bearer *n.* signifer

standing *a.* perpetuus. *n.* status *m.*; (*social*) locus *m.*, ōrdō *m.* of long — inveterātus. be of long — inveterāscere.

stand-offish *a.* tēctus.

standstill *n.* be at a — haerēre, frīgēre. bring to a — ad incitās redigere. come to a — insistere.

stanza *n.* tetrastichon *n.*

staple *n.* uncus *m.* *a.* praecipuus.

star *n.* stēlla *f.*, astrum *n.* shooting -s acontiae *f.pl.*

starboard *a.* dexter.

starch *n.* amylum *n.*

stare *n.* obtūtus *m.* *vi.* intentis oculis intuērī, stupēre. — at contemplārī.

stark *a.* rigidus; simplex. *ad.* plānē, omnīnō.

starling *n.* sturnus *m.*

starry *a.* stēllātus.

start *n.* initium *n.*; (*movement*) saltus *m.*; (*journey*) profectiō *f.* by fits and -s carptim. have a day's — of diē antecēdere. *vt.* incipere, instituere; (*game*) excitāre; (*process*) movēre. *vi.* (*with fright*) resilīre; (*journey*) proficīscī. — up exsilīre. [*m.pl.*

starting-place *n.* carcerēs

startle *vt.* excitāre, terrēre.

starvation *n.* famēs *f.*

starve *vi.* fame cōnficī; (*cold*) frīgēre. *vt.* fame ēnecāre.

starveling *n.* famēlicus *m.*

state *n.* (*condition*) status *m.*, condiciō *f.*; (*pomp*) adparātus *m.*; (*pol.*) cīvitās *f.*, rēs pūblica *f.* — of health valētūdō *f.* — of mind adfectiō *f.* the — of affairs is ita sē rēs habet. I know the — of affairs quō in locō rēs sit sciō of the — pūblicus. *a.* pūblicus. *vt.* adfirmāre, expōnere, profitērī. — one's case causam dīcere.

stateliness *n.* māiestās *f.*, gravitās *f.*

stately *a.* gravis, grandis, nōbilis.

statement *n.* adfirmātiō *f.*, dictum *n.*; (*witness*) testimōnium *n.*

statesman *n.* vir reī pūblicae gerendae peritus *m.*, cōnsilī pūblicī auctor *m.*

statesmanlike *a.* prūdēns.

statesmanship *n.* cīvīlis prūdentia *f.*

static *a.* stabilis.

station *n.* locus *m.*; (*mil.*) statiō *f.*; (*social*) locus *m.*, ōrdō *m.* *vt.* collocāre, pōnere; (*in different places*) dispōnere.

stationary *a.* immōtus, statārius, stabilis.

statistics *n.* cēnsus *m.*

statuary *n.* fictor *m.*

statue *n.* statua *f.*, signum *n.*, imāgō *f.*

statuette *n.* sigillum *n.*
stature *n.* fōrma *f.*, statūra *f.*
status *n.* locus *m.* restore the — quo ad integrum restituere.
statutable *a.* lēgitimus.
statute *n.* lēx *f.*
staunch *vt.* (*blood*) sistere. *a.* fīdus, cōnstāns.
stave *vt.* perrumpere, perfringere. — off arcēre.
stay *n.* firmāmentum *n.*; (*fig.*) columen *n.*; (*sojourn*) mānsiō *f.*, commorātiō *f.* *vt.* (*prop*) fulcīre; (*stop*) dētinēre, dēmorārī. *vi.* manēre, commorārī.
stead *n.* locus *m.* stand one in good — prōdesse (*dat.*).
steadfast *a.* firmus, stabilis, cōnstāns. **-ly** *ad.* cōnstanter. — at home tenēre sē domī.
steadfastness *n.* firmitās *f.*, cōnstantia *f.*
steadiness *n.* stabilitās *f.*; (*fig.*) cōnstantia *f.*
stead/y *a.* stabilis, firmus; (*fig.*) gravis, cōnstāns. **-ily** *ad.* firmē, cōnstanter.
steak *n.* offa *f.*
steal *vt.* surripere, fūrārī. *vi.* — away sē subdūcere. — over subrēpere (*dat.*). — into sē īnsinuāre in (*acc.*). — a march on occupāre.
stealing *n.* fūrtum *n.*
stealth *n.* fūrtum *n.* by — fūrtim, clam.
stealth/y *a.* fūrtīvus, clandestīnus. **-ily** *ad.* fūrtim, clam.
steam *n.* aquae vapor *m.*, fūmus *m.* *vi.* fūmāre.
steed *n.* equus *m.*
steel *n.* ferrum *n.*, chalybs *m.* *a.* ferreus. *vt.* dūrāre. — oneself obdūrēscere.
steely *a.* ferreus.
steelyard *n.* statēra *f.*
steep *at.* arduus, praeceps, praeruptus; (*slope*) dēclīvis. *vt.* imbuere.
steeple *n.* turris *f.*
steepness *n.* arduum *n.*
steer *vi.* gubernāre, regere, dīrigere. *n.* iuvencus *m.*
steering *n.* gubernātiō *f.*
steersman *n* gubernātor *m.*
stellar *a.* stēllārum.
stem *n.* stīpes *m.*, truncus *m.*; (*ship*) prōra *f.* *vt.* adversārī (*dat.*). — the tide of (*fig.*) obsistere (*dat.*).
stench *n.* foetor *m.*
stenographer *n.* exceptor *m.*, āctuārius *m.*
stenography *n.* notae *f.pl.*
stentorian *a.* (*voice*) ingēns.
step *n.* gradus *m.*; (*track*) vestigium *n.*; (*of stair*) gradus *m.* — by — gradātim. flight of -s gradus *m.pl.* take a — gradum facere. take -s to ratiōnem inīre ut, vidēre ut. march in — in numerum īre. out of — extrā numerum. *vi.* gradī, incēdere. — aside dēcēdere. — back regredī. — forward prōdīre. — on īnsistere (*dat.*).
step-daughter *n.* prīvigna *f.*
step-father *n.* vītricus *m.*
step-mother *n.* noverca *f.*
step-son *n.* prīvignus *m.*
stereotyped *a.* trītus.
sterile *a.* sterilis.
sterility *n.* sterilitās *f.*
sterling *a.* integer, probus, gravis.
stern *a.* dūrus, sevērus; (*look*) torvus. *n.* puppis *f.* **-ly** *ad.* sevērē, dūriter.
sternness *n.* sevēritās *f.*
stew *vt.* coquere.
steward *n.* prōcūrātor *m.*; (*of estate*) vīlicus *m.*
stewardship *n.* prōcūrātiō *f.*
stick *n.* (*for beating*) fustis *m.*; (*for walking*) baculum *n.* *vi.* haerēre. — at nothing ad omnia dēscendere. — fast in inhaerēre (*dat.*), inhaerēscere in (*abl.*). — out ēminēre. — to adhaerēre (*dat.*). — up ēminēre. — up for dēfendere. *vt.* (*with glue*) conglūtināre;

(*with point*) fīgere — into īnfīgere. — top on praefīgere.
stickler *n* dīligēns (*gen.*).
sticky *a.* lentus, tenāx.
stiff *a.* rigidus; (*difficult*) difficilis. be — rigēre. **-ly** *ad.* rigidē. [*vi.* rigērs.
stiffen *vt.* rigidum facere.
stiff-necked *a.* obstinātus.
stiffness *n.* rigor *m.*
stifle *vt.* suffocāre; (*fig.*) opprimere, restinguere.
stigma *n.* nota *f.*
stigmatize *vt.* notāre.
stile *n.* saepēs *f.*
still *a.* immōtus, tranquillus, quiētus; tacitus. *vt.* lēnīre, sēdāre. *ad.* etiam, adhūc, etiamnum; (*past*) etiam tum; (*with comp.*) etiam; (*adversative*) tamen, nihilōminus. [*n.*
stillness *n.* quiēs *f.*; silentium
stilly *a.* tacitus.
stilted *a.* (*language*) īnflātus.
stilts *n.* grallae *f.pl.*
stimulant *n.* stimulus *m.*
stimulate *vt.* stimulāre, acuere, exacuere, excitāre.
stimulus *n.* stimulus *m.*
sting *n.* aculeus *m.*; (*wound*) ictus *m.*; (*fig.*) aculeus *m.*, morsus *m.* *vt.* pungere, mordēre.
stinginess *n.* avāritia *f.*, sordēs *f.pl.*, tenācitās *f.*
stinging *a.* (*words*) aculeātus, mordāx.
sting/y *a.* sordidus, tenāx. **-ily** *ad.* sordidē.
stink *n.* foetor *m.* *vi.* foetere. — of olēre.
stinking *a.* foetidus.
stint *n.* modus *m.* without — abundē. *vt.* circumscrībere.
stipend *n.* mercēs *f.*
stipulate *vt.* pacīscī, stipulārī.
stipulation *n.* condiciō *f.*, pactum *n.*
stir *n.* tumultus *m.* *vt.* movēre, agitāre; (*fig.*) commovēre. — up excitāre, incitāre. *vi.* movērī.
stirring *a.* impiger, tumultuōsus; (*speech*) ārdēns.
stitch *vt.* suere. *n.* sūtūra *f.*; (*in side*) dolor *m.*
stock *n.* stirps *f.*, genus *n.*, gēns *f.*; (*equipment*) īnstrūmenta *n.pl.*; (*supply*) cōpia *f.*; (*investment*) pecūniae *f.pl.* live — rēs pecuāria *f.* **-in-trade** īnstrūmenta *n.pl.* *vt.* īnstruere. *a.* commūnis, trītus.
stockade *n.* vallum *n.*
stock-dove *n.* palumbēs *m.*, *f.*
stocks *n.* (*ship*) nāvālia *n.pl.*; (*torture*) compedēs *f.pl.*
stock-still *a.* plānē immōtus.
stocky *a.* brevis atque obēsus.
stodgy *a.* crūdus, īnsulsus.
stoic *n.* Stōicus *m.* *a.* Stōicus.
stoical *a.* dūrus, patiēns. **-ly** *ad.* patienter.
stoicism *n.* Stōicōrum ratiō *f.*, Stōicōrum disciplīna *f.*
stoke *vt.* agitāre.
stole *n.* stola *f.* [stolidē.
stolid *a.* stolidus. **-ly** *ad.*
stolidity *n.* īnsulsitās *f.*
stomach *n.* stomachus *m.* *vt.* patī, tolerāre.
stone *n.* lapis *m.*, saxum *n.*; (*precious*) gemma *f.*, lapillus *m.*; (*of fruit*) acinum *n.* leave no — unturned omnia experīrī. kill two birds with one — ūnō saltū duōs aprōs capere. hewn — saxum quadrātum. unhewn — caementum *n.* *vt.* lapidibus percutere. *a.* lapideus. — blind plānē caecus. — deaf plānē surdus.
stonecutter *n.* lapicīda *m.*
stony *a.* (*soil*) lapidōsus; (*path*) scrūpōsus; (*feeling*) dūrus, ferreus.
stool *n.* sēdēcula *f.*
stoop *vi.* sē dēmittere. — to dēscendere in (*acc.*).
stop *n.* mora *f.*; (*punctuation*) pūnctum *n.* come to a — īnsistere. put a — to comprimere, dirimere. *vt.* sistere, inhibēre, fīnīre; (*hole*) obtū-

rāre. — up occlūdere, interclūdere. *vi.* dēsinere, dēsistere; (*motion*) insistere.
stop-gap *n.* tībīcen *m.*
stoppage *n.* interclūsiō *f.*, impedīmentum *n.*
stopper *n.* obtūrāmentum *n.*
store *n.* cōpia *f.*; (*place*) horreum *n.*; (*for wine*) apothēca *f.* be in — for manēre. set great — by māgnī aestimāre. *vt.* condere, repōnere. — away recondere. — up repōnere, congerere.
store-house *n.* (*fig.*) thēsaurus *m.*
store-keeper *n.* cellārius *m.*
store-ship *n.* nāvis frūmentāria *f.*
storey *n.* tabulātum *n.*
stork *n.* cicōnia *f.*
storm *n.* tempestās *f.*, procella *f.* take by — expugnāre. *vt.* (*mil.*) expugnāre. *vi.* saevīre. — at insectārī, invehī in (*acc.*).
storm-bound *a.* tempestāte dētentus.
stormer *n.* expugnātor *m.*
storming *n.* expugnātiō *f.*
stormy *a.* turbidus, procellōsus; (*fig.*) trubulentus.
story *n.* fābula *f.*, nārrātiō *f.*; (*short*) fābella *f.*; (*untrue*) mendācium *n.* **-teller** *n.* nārrātor *m.*; (*liar*) mendāx *m.*
stout *a.* pinguis; (*brave*) fortis; (*strong*) validus, rōbustus; (*material*) firmus. **-ly** *ad.* fortiter. [mus.
stout-hearted *a.* māgnani-
stove *n.* camīnus *m.*, fornāx *f.*
stow *vt.* repōnere, condere. — away *vi.* in nāvī dēlitēscere.
straddle *vi.* vāricāre.
straggle *vi.* deerrāre, pālārī.
straggler *n.* pālāns *m.*
straggling *a.* dispersus, rārus.
straight *a.* rēctus, dīrēctus; (*fig.*) apertus, vērāx. in a — line rēctā, ē regiōne. set — dīrigere. *ad.* dīrēctō, rēctā.
straighten *vt.* corrigere, extendere.
straightforward *a.* simplex, dīrēctus; (*easy*) facilis.
straightforwardness *n.* simplicitās *f.*
straightness *n.* (*fig.*) integritās *f.*
straightway *ad.* statim, extemplō.
strain *n.* contentiō *f.*; (*effort*) labor *m.*; (*music*) modī *m.pl.*; (*breed*) genus *n.* *vt.* intendere, contendere; (*injure*) nimiā contentiōne dēbilitāre; (*liquid*) dēliquāre, percōlāre. *vi.* ēnītī, vīrēs contendere. [sītus.
strained *a.* (*language*) arces-
strainer *n.* cōlum *n.*
strait *a.* angustus. *n.* fretum *n.*; (*pl.*) angustiae *f.pl.*
straiten *vt.* coartāre, contrahere. **-ed circumstances** angustiae *f.pl.*
strait-laced *a.* tristis, sevērus.
strand *n.* lītus *n.*; (*of rope*) fīlum *n.* *vt.* (*ship*) ēicere.
strange *a.* novus, īnsolitus; (*foreign*) peregrīnus; (*another's*) aliēnus; (*ignorant*) rudis, expers. **-ly** *ad.* mīrē, mīrum in modum.
strangeness *n.* novitās *f.*, īnsolentia *f.*
stranger *n.* (*from abroad*) peregrīnus *m.*; (*visiting*) hospes *m.*, hospita *f.*; (*not of the family*) externus *m.*; (*unknown*) ignōtus *m.*
strangle *vt.* strangulāre, laqueō gulam frangere.
strap *n.* lōrum *n.*, habēna *f.*
strapping *a.* grandis.
stratagem *n.* cōnsilium *n.*, fallācia *f.*
strategic *a.* (*action*) prūdēns; (*position*) idōneus.
strategist *n.* artis bellicae peritus *m.*
strategy *n.* ars imperātōria *f.*; cōnsilia *n.pl.*

straw *n.* (*stalk*) culmus *m.*; (*collective*) strāmentum *n.* **not care a — for** floccī nōn facere. *a.* strāmenticius.
strawberry *n.* frāgum *n.* **-tree** *n.* arbutus *m.*
stray *vi.* aberrāre, deerrāre. *a.* errābundus.
streak *n.* līnea *f.*, macula *f.*; (*light*) radius *m.*; (*character*) vēna *f.* *vt.* maculāre.
stream *n.* flūmen *n.*, fluvius *m.* **down —** secundō flūmine. **up —** adversō flūmine. *vi.* fluere, sē effundere. **— into** īnfluere in (*acc.*). [*m.*
streamlet *n.* rīvus *m.*, rīvulus
street *n.* via *f.*, platea *f.*
strength *n.* vīrēs *f.pl.*; (*of material*) firmitās *f.*; (*fig.*) rōbur *n.*, nervī *m.pl.*; (*mil.*) numerus *m.* **know the enemy's —** quot sint hostēs scīre. **on the — of** frētus (*abl.*).
strengthen *vt.* firmāre, corrōborāre; (*position*) mūnīre.
strenuous *a.* impiger, strēnuus, sēdulus. **-ly** *ad.* impigrē, strēnuē.
strenuousness *n.* industria *f.*
stress *n.* (*words*) ictus *m.*; (*meaning*) vīs *f.*; (*importance*) mōmentum *n.*; (*difficulty*) labor *m.* **lay great — on** in māgnō discrīmine pōnere. *vt.* exprimere.
stretch *n.* spatium *n.*, tractus *m.* **at a —** sine ullā intermissiōne. *vt.* tendere, intendere; (*length*) prōdūcere, extendere; (*facts*) in māius crēdere. **— a point** indulgēre. **— before** obtendere. **— forth** porrigere. **— oneself** (*on ground*) sternī. **— out** porrigere, extendere. *vi.* extendī, patēscere.
strew *vt.* (*things*) sternere; (*place*) cōnsternere.
stricken *a.* saucius.
strict *a.* (*defined*) ipse, certus; (*severe*) sevērus, rigidus; (*accurate*) dīligēns. **-ly** *ad.* sevērē; dīligenter. **— speaking** scīlicet, immo. [dīligentia *f.*
strictness *n.* sevēritās *f.*;
stricture *n.* vituperātiō *f.*
stride *n.* passus *m.* **make great -s** (*fig.*) multum prōficere. *vi.* incēdere, ingentēs gradūs ferre.
strident *a.* asper.
strife *n.* discordia *f.*, pugna *f.*
strike *vt.* ferīre, percutere; (*instrument*) pellere, pulsāre; (*sail*) subdūcere; (*tent*) dētendere; (*mind*) venīre in (*acc.*); (*camp*) movēre; (*fear into*) incutere in (*acc.*). **— against** offendere. **— out** dēlēre. **— up** (*music*) incipere. **— a bargain** pacīscī. **be struck** vāpulāre. *vi.* (*work*) cessāre.
striking *a.* īnsignis, īnsignītus, ēgregius. **-ly** *ad.* īnsignītē.
string *n.* (*cord*) resticula *f.*; (*succession*) seriēs *f.*; (*instrument*) nervus *m.*; (*bow*) nervus *m.* **have two -s to one's bow** duplicī spē ūtī. *vt.* (*bow*) intendere; (*together*) coniungere.
stringency *n.* sevēritās *f.*
stringent *a.* sevērus.
strip *vt.* nūdāre, spoliāre, dēnūdāre. **— off** exuere; (*leaves*) stringere, dēstringere. *n.* lacinia *f.*
stripe *n.* virga *f.*; (*on tunic*) clāvus *m.*; (*pl.*) verbera *n.pl.*
striped *a.* virgātus.
stripling *n.* adulēscentulus *m.*
strive *vi.* nītī, ēnītī, contendere; (*contend*) certāre.
stroke *n.* ictus *m.*; (*lightning*) fulmen *n.*; (*oar*) pulsus *m.*; (*pen*) līnea *f.* **— of luck** fortūna secunda *f.* *vt.* mulcēre, dēmulcēre.
stroll *vi.* deambulāre, spatiārī.
strong *a.* fortis, validus; (*health*) rōbustus, firmus; (*material*) firmus; (*smell*) gravis (*resources*) pollēns, potēns; (*feeling*) ācer, māgnus; (*lan-*

guage) vehemēns probrōsus. be — valēre. be twenty — vigintī esse numerō. **-ly** *ad.* validē, vehementer, ācriter, graviter.
strong-box *n.* arca *f.*
stronghold *n.* arx *f.*
strong-minded *a.* pertināx, cōnstans.
strop *n.* lōrum *n.*
strophe *n.* stropha *f.*
structure *n.* aedificium *n.*; (*form*) structūra *f.*; (*arrangement*) compositiō *f.*
struggle *n.* (*effort*) cōnātus *m.*; *fight*) pugna *f.*, certāmen *n.* *vi.* nītī, contendere; (*fight*) luctārī. — upwards ēnītī.
strut *vi.* māgnificē incēdere.
stubble *n.* stipula *f.*
stubborn *a.* pertināx, pervicāx, **-ly** *ad.* pertināciter, pervicāciter.
stubbornness *n.* pertinācia *f.*, pervicācia f.
stucco *n.* gypsum *n.*
stud *n.* clāvus *m.*; (*horses*) equī *m.pl.*
studded *a.* distinctus.
student *n.* discipulus *m.* be a — of studēre (*dat.*).
studied *a.* meditātus, accūrātus; (*language*) exquīsītus.
studio *n.* officīna *f.*
studious *a.* litterīs dēditus litterārum studiōsus; (*careful*) attentus. **-ly** *ad.* dē industriā.
study *vt.* studēre (*dat.*); (*prepare*) meditārī — under audīre, *n.* studium *n.*; (*room*) bibliothēca *f.*
stuff *n.* māteria *f.*; (*cloth*) textile *n.* *vt.* farcīre, refercīre; (*with food*) sagināre.
stuffing *n.* sagīna *f.*; (*of cushion*) tōmentum *n.*
stultify *vt.* ad inritum redigere.
stumble *vi.* offendre. — upon incidere in (*acc.*), offendere. [siō *f.*
stumbling-block *n.* offēn-
stump *n.* stipes *m.*
stun *vt.* stupefacere; (*fig.*) obstupefacere, cōnfundere.
stunned *a.* attonitus.
stunt *vt.* corporis auctum inhibēre, **-ed** *a.* curtus.
stupefaction *n.* stupor *m.*
stupef/y *vt.* obstupefacere. be **-ied** stupēre, obstupēscere.
stupendous *a.* mīrus, mīrificus.
stupid *a.* stultus, hebes, ineptus. **-ly** *ad.* stultē, ineptē.
stupidity *n.* stultitia *f.*
stupor *n.* stupor *m.*
sturdiness *n.* rōbur *n.*, firmitās *f.*
sturd/y *a.* fortis, rōbustus, **-ily** *ad.* fortiter.
sturgeon *n.* acipēnser *m.*
stutter *vi.* balbūtīre. **-ing** *a.* balbus.
sty *n.* hara *f.*
style *n.* (*kind*) genus *n.*, ratiō *f.*; (*of dress*) habitus *m.*; (*of prose*) ēlocūtiō *f.*, ōrātiō *f.*; (*pen*) stilus *m.* *vt.* appellāre.
stylish *a.* ēlegāns, lautus, expolītus. **-ly** *ad.* ēleganter.
suasion *n.* suāsiō *f.*
suave *a.* blandus, urbānus.
suavity *n.* urbānitās *f.*
subaltern *n.* succenturiō *m.*
subdivide *vt.* dividere.
subdivision *n.* pars *f.*, mōmentum *n.*
subdue *vt.* subigere, dēvincere, domāre; (*fig.*) cohibēre. **-d** *a.* dēmissus, summissus.
subject *n.* (*person*) cīvis *m.*, *f.*; (*matter*) rēs *f.*; (*theme*) locus *m.* argūmentum *n.* **-matter** *n.* māteria *f.* a. subiectus. — to obnoxius (*dat.*), *vt.* subicere; obnoxium reddere.
subjection *n.* servitūs *f.*
subjective *a.* proprius.
subjoin *vt.* subicere, subiungere. [lāre.
subjugate *vt.* subigere, dēbel-
sublime *a.* sublīmis, ēlātus. excelsus. **-ly** *ad.* excelsē.

sublimity *n.* altitūdō *f.*, ēlātiō *f.*
submarine *a.* submersus.
submerge *vt.* dēmergere; (*flood*) inundāre. *vi.* sē dēmergere.
submersed *a.* submersus.
submission *n.* obsequium *n.*, servitium *n.*; (*fig.*) patientia *f.*
submissive *a.* submissus, docilis, obtemperāns. **-ly** *ad.* submissē, oboedienter, patienter.
submit *vi.* sē dēdere. — to pārēre (*dat.*), obtemperāre (*dat.*), patī, subīre. *vt.* (*proposal*) referre.
subordinate *a.* subiectus, secundus. *vt.* subiungere, subicere.
suborn *vt.* subicere, subōrnāre.
subpoena *n.* *vt.* testimōnium dēnūntiāre (*dat.*).
subscribe *vt.* (*name*) subscrībere; (*money*) cōnferre.
subscription *n.* collātiō *f.*
subsequent *a.* sequēns, posterior. **-ly** *ad.* posteā, mox.
subserve *vt.* subvenīre (*dat.*), commodāre. [*n.*
subservience *n.* obsequium
subservient *a.* obsequēns; (*thing*) ūtilis, commodus.
subside *vi.* dēsīdere, resīdere; (*fever*) dēcēdere; (*wind*) cadere; (*passion*) dēfervēscere.
subsidence *n.* lābēs *f.*
subsidiary *a.* subiectus, secundus.
subsidize *vt.* pecūniās suppeditāre (*dat.*).
subsidy *n.* pecūniae *f.pl.*, vectigal *n.*
subsist *vi.* cōnstāre, sustentārī.
subsistence *n.* vīctus *m.*
substance *n.* (*matter*) rēs *f.*, corpus *n.*; (*essence*) nātūra *f.*; (*gist*) summa *f.*; (*reality*) rēs *f.*; (*wealth*) opēs *f.pl.*
substantial *a.* solidus; (*real*) vērus; (*important*) gravis; (*rich*) opulentus, dīves. **-ly** *ad.* rē; māgnā ex parte.
substantiate *vt.* cōnfirmāre.
substitute *vt.* subicere, repōnere, substituere. *n.* vicārius *m.* [*n.*
substratum *n.* fundāmentum
subterfuge *n.* latebra *f.*, perfugium *n.* [rāneus.
subterranean *a.* subter-
subt/le *a.* (*fine*) subtīlis; (*shrewd*) acūtus, astūtus. **-ly** *ad.* subtīliter; acūtē, astūtē.
subtlety *n.* subtīlitās *f.*; acūmen *n.*, astūtia *f.*
subtract *vt.* dētrahere, dēmere; (*money*) dēdūcere.
subtraction *n.* dētractiō *f.*, dēductiō *f.*
suburb *n.* suburbium *n.*
suburban *a.* suburbānus.
subvention *n.* pecūniae *f.pl.*
subversion *n.* ēversiō *f.*, ruīna *f.*
subversive *a.* sēditiōsus.
subvert *vt.* ēvertere, subruere.
subverter *n.* ēversor *m.*
succeed *vi.* (*person*) rem bene gerere; (*activity*) prosperē ēvenīre. — in obtaining impetrāre. *vt.* īnsequī, excipere, succēdere (*dat.*).
success *n.* bonus ēventus *m.*, rēs bene gesta *f.*
successful *a.* fēlīx; (*thing*) secundus. be — rem bene gerere; (*play*) stāre. **-ly** *ad.* fēlīciter, prosperē, bene.
succession *n.* (*coming next*) successiō *f.*; (*line*) seriēs *f.*, ōrdō *m.* alternate — vicissitūdō *f.* in — deinceps, ex ōrdine.
successive *a.* continuus, perpetuus. **-ly** *ad.* deinceps, ex ōrdine; (*alternately*) vicissim.
successor *n.* successor *m.*
succinct *a.* brevis, pressus. **-ly** *ad.* breviter, pressē.
succour *n.* auxilium *n.*,

subsidium *n.* *vt.* subvenire (*dat.*), succurrere (*dat.*), opem ferre (*dat.*).
succulence *n.* sūcus *m.*
succulent *a.* sūcidus.
succumb *vi.* succumbere, dēficere.
such *a.* tālis, ēiusmodī, hūiusmodī; (*size*) tantus. at — a time id temporis.
such-like *a.* hūiusmodī, ēiusdem generis.
suck *vt.* sūgere. — in sorbēre. — up exsorbēre, ēbibere.
sucker *n.* surculus *m.*
sucking *a.* (*child*) lactēns.
suckle *vt.* nūtricārī, mammam dare (*dat.*).
suckling *n.* lactēns *m.*, *f.*
sudden *a.* subitus, repentīnus. **-ly** *ad.* subitō, dērepente.
sue *vt.* in iūs vocāre, lītem intendere (*dat.*). — for rogāre, petere, ōrāre.
suffer *vt.* patī, ferre, tolerāre; (*injury*) accipere; (*loss*) facere; (*permit*) patī, sinere. *vi.* dolōre adficī. — from labōrāre ex, adficī (*abl.*). — for poenās dare (*gen.*).
sufferable *a.* tolerābilis.
sufferance *n.* patientia *f.*, tolerantia *f.*
suffering *n.* dolor *m.*
suffice *vi.* sufficere, suppetere.
sufficiency *n.* satis.
sufficient *a.* idōneus, satis (*gen*). **-ly** *ad.* satis.
suffocate *vt.* suffocāre.
suffrage *n.* suffrāgium *n.*
suffuse *vt.* suffundere.
sugar *n.* saccharon *n.*
suggest *vt.* admonēre, inicere, subicere. — itself occurrere.
suggestion *n.* admonitiō *f.* at the — of admonitū (*gen.*). at my — mē auctōre.
suicidal *a.* fūnestus.
suicide *n.* mors voluntāria *f.* commit — mortem sibī cōnsciscere.
suit *n.* (*law*) līs *f.*, āctiō *f.*; (*clothes*) vestītus *m.* *vt.* convenīre (*dat.*), congruere (*dat.*); (*dress*) sedēre (*dat.*), decēre. it -s decet. to — me dē meā sententiā.
suitab/le *a.* aptus, idōneus. **-ly** *ad.* aptē, decenter.
suitability *n.* convenientia *f.*
suite *n.* comitēs *m.pl.*, comitātus *m.*
suitor *n.* procus *m.*, amāns *m.*
sulk *vi.* aegrē ferre, mōrōsum esse.
sulky *a.* mōrōsus, tristis.
sullen *a.* tristis, mōrōsus.
sullenness *n.* mōrōsitās *f.*
sully *vt.* īnfuscāre, contāmināre.
sulphur *n.* sulfur *n.*
sultriness *n.* aestus *m.*
sultry *a.* aestuōsus.
sum *n.* summa *f.* — of money pecūnia *f.* *vt.* subdūcere, computāre. — up summātim dēscrībere. to — up ūnō verbō, quid plūra ?
summarize *vt.* summātim dēscrībere.
summar/y *n.* summārium *n.*, epitomē *f.* *a.* subitus, praesēns. **-ily** *ad.* strictim, summātim; sine morā.
summer *n.* aestās *f.* *a.* aestīvus.
summit *n.* vertex *m.*, culmen *n.*; (*fig.*) fastigium *n.* the — of summus.
summon *vt.* arcessere; (*meeting*) convocāre; (*witness*) citāre. — up courage animum sūmere.
summons *n.* (*law*) vocātiō *f.* *vt.* in iūs vocāre, diem dīcere (*dat.*).
sumptuary *a.* sūmptuārius.
sumptuous *a.* sūmptuōsus, adparātus, māgnificus, lautus. **-ly** *ad.* sūmptuōsē, māgnificē.
sun *n.* sōl *m.* *vt.* — oneself apricārī.
sunbeam *n.* radius *m.*
sunburnt *a.* adūstus.

sunder *vt.* sēparāre, dīvidere.
sundial *n.* sōlārium *n.*
sundry *a.* dīversī, complūrēs.
sunlight *n.* sōl *m.*
sunlit *a.* apricus.
sunny *a.* apricus, serēnus.
sunrise *n.* sōlis ortus *m.*
sunset *n.* sōlis occāsus *m.*
sunshade *n.* umbella *f.*
sunshine *n.* sōl *m.*
sup *vi.* cēnāre.
superabundance *n.* abundantia *f.*
superabundant *a.* nimius. **-ly** *ad.* satis superque.
superannuated *a.* ēmeritus.
superb *a.* māgnificus. **-ly** *ad.* māgnificē.
supercilious *a.* adrogāns, superbus. **-ly** *ad.* adroganter, superbē.
superciliousness *n.* adrogantia *f.*, fastus *m.*
supererogation *n.* of — ultrō factus.
superficial *a.* levis. acquire a — knowledge of prīmīs labrīs gustare. **-ly** *ad.* leviter, strictim.
superficiality *n.* levitās *f.*
superfluity *n.* abundantia *f.*
superfluous *a.* supervacāneus, nimius. be — redundāre.
superhuman *a.* dīvīnus, hūmānō māior.
superimpose *vt.* superimpōnere.
superintend *vt.* prōcūrāre, praeesse (*dat.*).
superintendence *n.* cūra *f.*
superintendent *n.* cūrātor *m.*, praefectus *m.*
superior *a.* melior, amplior. be — praestāre, superāre. *n.* prīnceps *m.*, praefectus *m.*
superiority *n.* praestantia *f.* have the — superāre; (*in numbers*) plūrēs esse.
superlative *a.* ēgregius, optimus.
supernatural *a.* dīvīnus. **-ly** *ad.* dīvīnitus.
supernumerary *a.* adscrīptīcius. — soldiers accēnsī *m.pl.*
superscription *n.* titulus *m.*
supersede *vt.* succēdere (*dat.*), in locum succēdere (*gen.*) — gold with silver prō aurō argentum suppōnere.
superstition *n.* rēligiō *f.*, superstitiō *f.*
superstitious *a.* rēligiōsus, superstitiōsus. [succēdere.
supervene *vi.* īnsequī,
supervise *vt.* prōcūrāre.
supervision *n.* cūra *f.*
supervisor *n.* cūrātor *m.*
supine *a.* supīnus; (*fig.*) neglegēns, segnis. **-ly** *ad.* segniter. [cēnātus.
supper *n.* cēna *f.* after —
supperless *a.* iēiūnus.
supplant *vt.* praevertere.
supple *a.* flexibilis, mollis.
supplement *n.* appendix *f.* *vt.* amplificāre.
supplementary *a.* additus.
suppleness *n.* mollitia *f.*
suppliant *n.* supplex *m.*, *f.*
supplicate *vt.* supplicāre, obsecrāre.
supplication *n.* precēs *f.pl.*
supply *n.* cōpia *f.*; (*pl.*) commeātus *m.* *vt.* suppeditāre, praebēre; (*loss*) supplēre.
support *n.* firmāmentum *n.*; (*help*) subsidium *n.*, adiūmentum *n.*; (*food*) alimenta *n pl.*; (*of party*) favor *m.*; (*of needy*) patrōcinium *n.* lend — to rumours alimenta rūmōribus addere. *vt.* fulcīre; (*living*) sustinēre, sustentāre; (*with help*) adiuvāre, opem ferre (*dat.*); (*at law*) adesse (*dat.*). —ing cast adiūtōrēs *m.pl.*
supportable *a.* tolerābilis.
supporter *n.* fautor *m.*; (*at trial*) advocātus *m.*; (*of proposal*) auctor *m.*
suppose *vi.* (*assume*) pōnere; (*think*) existimāre, opīnārī, crēdere. — it is true fac vērum esse.

supposedly *ad.* ut fāma est.
supposing *conj.* sī; (*for the sake of argument*) sī iam.
supposition *n.* opīniō *f.* on this — hōc positō.
supposititious *a.* subditus, subditīvus.
suppress *vt.* opprimere, comprimere; (*knowledge*) cēlāre, reticēre; (*feelings*) coercēre, reprimere. [reticentia *f.*
suppression *n.* (*of fact*)
supremacy *n.* imperium *n.*, dominātus *m.*, prīncipātus *m.*
supreme *a.* summus. be — dominārī. — command imperium *n.* **-ly** *ad.* ūnicē. plānē.
sure *a.* certus; (*fact*) explōrātus; (*friend*) fīdus. be — of compertum habēre. feel — persuāsum habēre, haud scīre an. make — of (*fact*) comperīre; (*action*) efficere ut. to be — quidem. — enough rē vērā. **-ly** *ad.* certō, certē; (*tentative*) scīlicet, sānē. — you do not think? num putās?
surety *n.* (*person*) vās *m.*, praes *m.*, spōnsor *m.*; (*deposit*) fīdūcia *f.* be — for spondēre prō.
surf *n.* fluctus *m.*
surface *n.* superficiēs *f.* — of the water summa aqua.
surfeit *n.* satietās *f.* *vt.* satiāre, explēre.
surge *n.* aestus *m.*, fluctus *m.* *vi.* tumēscere.
surgeon *n.* chīrūrgus *m.*
surgery *n.* chīrūrgia *f.*
surliness *n.* mōrōsitās *f.*
surl/y *a.* mōrōsus, difficilis. **-ily** *ad.* mōrōsē.
surmise *n.* coniectūra *f.* *vi.* suspicārī, conicere, augurārī.
surmount *vt.* superāre.
surmountable *a.* superābilis.
surname *n.* cognōmen *n.*
surpass *vt.* excellere, exsuperāre, antecēdere.
surpassing *a.* excellēns.
surplus *n.* reliquum *n.*; (*money*) pecūniae residuae *f.pl.*
surprise *n.* admīrātiō *f.*; (*cause*) rēs inopīnāta *f.* take by — dēprehendere. *a.* subitus. *vt.* dēprehendere; (*mil.*) opprimere. be -d dēmīrārī. be -d at admīrārī.
surprising *a.* mīrus, mīrābilis. **-ly** *ad.* mīrē, mīrābiliter.
surrender *vt.* dēdere, trādere, concēdere. *vi.* sē dēdere. — unconditionally to sē suaque omnia potestātī permittere (*gen.*) *n.* dēditiō *f.*; (*legal*) cessiō *f.* unconditional — permissiō *f.*
surreptitious *a.* fūrtīvus. **-ly** *ad.* fūrtim, clam. get in — inrēpere in (*acc.*).
surround *vt.* circumdare, cingere.
surrounding *a.* circumiectus. **-s** *n.* vīcīnia *f.*
survey *vt.* contemplārī. cōnsīderāre; (*land*) mētārī. *n.* contemplātiō *f.*; (*land*) mēnsūra *f.*
surveyor *n.* fīnītor *m.*, agrimēnsor *m.*, mētātor *m.*
survival *n.* salūs *f.*
survive *vi.* superāre. *vt.* superesse (*dat.*).
survivor *n.* superstes *m.*, *f.*
susceptibility *n.* mollitia *f.*
susceptible *a.* mollis.
suspect *vt.* suspicārī. be -ed in suspiciōnem venīre.
suspend *vt.* suspendere; (*activity*) differre; (*person*) locō movēre. be -ed pendēre.
suspense *n.* dubitātiō *f.* be in — animī pendēre. haerēre.
suspicion *n.* suspiciō *f.* direct — to suspiciōnem adiungere ad.
suspicious *a.* (*suspecting*) suspiciōsus; (*suspected*) dubius, anceps.
sustain *vt.* (*weight*) sustinēre; (*life*) alere, sustentāre; (*hard-*

ship) ferre, sustinēre; (*the part of*) agere.
sustenance *n.* alimentum *n.*, victus *m.*
sutler *n.* lixa *m.*
suzerain *n.* dominus *m.*
swaddling-clothes *n.* incūnābula *n.pl.*
swagger *vi.* sē iactāre. [*m.*
swaggerer *n.* homō glōriōsus
swallow *n.* hirundō *f.* *vt.* dēvorāre. — up absorbēre.
swamp *n.* palūs *f.* *vt.* opprimere.
swampy *a.* ūlīginōsus.
swan *n.* cycnus *m.* -'s cycnēus.
swank *vi.* sē iactāre.
sward *n.* caespes *m.*
swarm *n* exāmen *n.*; (*fig.*) nūbēs *f.* *vi.* — round circumfundī.
swarthy *a.* fuscus, aquilus.
swathe *vt.* conligāre.
sway *n.* dīciō *f.*, imperium *n.* bring under one's — suae diciōnis facere. *vt.* regere. *vi.* vacillāre.
swear *vi.* iūrāre. — allegiance to iūrāre in verba (*gen.*).
sweat *n.* sūdor *m.* *vi.* sūdāre.
sweep *vt.* verrere. — away rapere. — out ēverrere.
sweet *a.* dulcis, suāvis. **-ly** *ad.* dulciter, suāviter.
sweeten *vt.* dulcem reddere.
sweetheart *n.* dēliciae *f.pl.*
sweetness *n.* dulcitūdō *f.*, suāvitās *f.*
sweet-tempered *a.* suāvis, cōmis.
swell *n.* tumor *m.* *vi.* tumēre, tumēscere; (*fig.*) glīscere. *vt.* inflāre.
swelling *a.* tumidus. *n.* tumor *m.*
swelter *vi.* aestū labōrāre.
swerve *vi.* dēclīnāre, dēvertere. *n.* dēclīnātiō *f.*
swift *a.* celer, vēlōx, incitātus. **-ly** *ad.* celeriter, vēlōciter.
swiftness *n.* celeritās *f.*, vēlōcitās *f.*
swill *vt.* (*rinse*) colluere; (*drink*) ēpōtāre.
swim *vi.* nāre, innāre; (*place*) natāre. — across trānāre. — ashore ēnāre. — to adnāre.
swimming *n.* natātiō *f.*
swindle *vt.* circumvenīre, verba dare (*dat.*). *n.* fraus *f.*
swine *n.* sūs *m.*, *f.*
swineherd *n.* subulcus *m.*
swing *n.* (*motion*) oscillātiō *f.* *vi.* oscillāre. *vt.* lībrāre.
swinish *a.* obscēnus.
swirl *n.* vertex *m.* *vi.* volūtārī.
switch *n.* virga *f.* *vt.* flectere, torquēre.
swivel *n.* cardō *f.*
swollen *a.* tumidus, turgidus, inflātus. [termorī.
swoon *n.* dēfectiō *f.* *vi.* in-
swoop *n.* impetus *m.* *vi.* lābī. — down on involāre in (*acc.*).
sword *n.* gladius *m.* put to the — occīdere. with fire and — ferrō ignīque.
swordsman *n.* gladiātor *m.*
sworn *a.* iūrātus.
sybarite *n.* dēlicātus *m.*
sycophancy *n.* adsentātiō *f.*, adūlātiō *f.*
sycophant *n.* adsentātor *m.*, adūlātor *m.*
syllable *n.* syllaba *f.*
syllogism *n.* ratiōcinātiō *f.*
sylvan *a.* silvestris. [*n.*
symbol *n.* signum *n.*, īnsigne
symmetrical *a.* concinnus, aequus. [aequitās *f.*
symmetry *n.* concinnitās *f.*,
sympathetic *a.* concors, misericors. **-ally** *ad.* misericorditer.
sympathize *vi.* cōnsentīre. — with miserērī (*gen.*).
sympathy *n.* concordia *f.*, consēnsus *m.*; misericordia *f.*
symphony *n.* concentus *m.*
symptom *n.* signum *n.*, indicium *n.*
syndicate *n.* societās *f.*
synonym *n.* verbum idem dēclārāns *n.*

synonymous *a.* idem dēclārāns.
synopsis *n.* summārium *n.*
syringe *n.* clystēr *m.*
system *n.* ratiō *f.*, fōrmula *f.*; (*philos.*) disciplīna *f.*
systematic *a.* ōrdinātus, cōnstāns. **-ally** *ad.* ratiōne, ōrdine.
systematize *vt.* in ōrdinem redigere.

T

tabernacle *n.* tabernāculum *n.*
table *n.* mēnsa *f.*; (*inscribed*) tabula *f.* (*list*) index *m.* **at —** inter cēnam. **turn the -s on** pār parī referre.
tablet *n.* tabula *f.*, tabella *f.*
taboo *n.* rēligiō *f.*
tabulate *vt.* in ōrdinem redigere.
tacit *a.* tacitus. **-ly** *ad.* tacitē.
taciturn *a.* taciturnus.
taciturnity *n.* taciturnitās *f.*
tack *n.* clāvulus *m.*; (*of sail*) pēs *m.* *vt.* **— on** adsuere. *vi.* (*ship*) reciprocārī, nāvem flectere. [*vt.* adgredī.
tackle *n.* armāmenta *n.pl.*
tact *n.* iūdicium *n.*, commūnis sēnsus *m.*, hūmānitās *f.*
tactful *a.* prūdēns, hūmānus. **-ly** *ad.* prūdenter, hūmāniter.
tactless *a.* ineptus. **-ly** *ad.* ineptē.
tactician *n.* reī mīlitāris perītus *m.*
tactics *n.* rēs mīlitāris *f.*, bellī ratiō *f.*
tadpole *n.* rānunculus *m.*
tag *n.* appendicula *f.*
tail *n.* cauda *f.* **turn —** terga vertere.
tailor *n.* vestītor *m.*
taint *n.* lābēs *f.*, vitium *n.* *vt.* inquināre, contāmināre, īnficere.
take *vt.* capere, sūmere; (*auspices*) habēre; (*disease*) contrahere; (*experience*) ferre; (*fire*) concipere. (*meaning*) accipere, interpretārī; (*in the act*) dēprehendere; (*person*) dūcere. **— after** similem esse (*dat.*, *gen.*). **— away** dēmere, auferre, adimere, abdūcere. **— back** recipere. **— down** dētrahere; (*in writing*) exscrībere. **— for** habēre prō. **— hold of** prehendere. **— in** (*as guest*) recipere; (*information*) percipere, comprehendere; (*with deceit*) dēcipere. **— in hand** incipere, suscipere. **— off** dēmere; (*clothes*) exuere. **— on** suscipere. **— out** eximere, extrahere; (*from store*) prōmere. **— over** excipere. **— place** fierī, accidere. **— the field** in aciem dēscendere. **— to** sē dēdere (*dat.*), amāre. **— to oneself** suscipere. **— up** sūmere, tollere; (*task*) incipere, adgredī ad; (*in turn*) excipere; (*room*) occupāre. **— upon oneself** recipere, sibī sūmere.
taking *a.* grātus. *n.* (*mil.*) expugnātiō *f.*
tale *n.* fābula *f.*, fābella *f.*
talent *n.* (*money*) talentum *n.*; (*ability*) ingenium *n.*, indolēs *f.*
talented *a.* ingeniōsus.
talk *n.* sermō *m.*; (*with another*) colloquium *n.* **common —** fāma *f.* **be the — of the town** in ōre omnium esse. *vi.* loquī; (*to one*) colloquī cum. **— down to** ad intellectum audientis dēscendere. **— over** cōnferre, disserere dē.
talkative *a.* loquāx.
talkativeness *n.* loquācitās *f.*
tall *a.* prōcērus, grandis.
tallness *n.* prōcēritās *f.*
tallow *n.* sēbum *n.*
tally *n.* tessera *f.* *vi.* congruere.
talon *n.* unguis *m.*
tamarisk *n.* myrīca *f.*
tambourine *n.* tympanum *n.*

tame *vt.* domāre, mānsuēfacere. *a.* mānsuētus; (*character*) ignāvus; (*language*) īnsulsus, frīgidus. **-ly** *ad.* ignāvē, lentē.
tameness *n.* mānsuētūdō *f.*; (*fig.*) lentitūdō *f.*
tamer *n.* domitor *m.*
tamper *vi.* — with (*person*) sollicitāre; (*writing*) interpolāre.
tan *vt.* imbuere. **-ned** *a.* (*by sun*) adūstus.
tang *n.* sapor *m.*
tangible *a.* tāctilis.
tangle *n.* nōdus *m.* *vt.* implicāre.
tank *n.* lacus *m.*
tanner *n.* coriārius *m.*
tantalize *vt.* lūdere.
tantamount *a.* pār, īdem.
tantrum *n.* īra *f.*
tap *n.* epitonium *n.*; (*touch*) plāga *f.* *vt.* (*cask*) relinere; (*hit*) ferīre.
tape *n.* taenia *f.*
taper *n.* cēreus *m.* *vi.* fastīgārī.
tapestry *n.* aulaea *n.pl.*
tar *n.* pix *f.*
tardiness *n.* tarditās *f.*, segnitia *f.*
tard/y *a.* tardus, lentus. **-ily** *ad.* tardē, lentē.
tare *n.* lolium *n.*
targe *n.* parma *f.*
target *n.* scopus *m.*
tariff *n.* portōrium *n.*
tarn *n.* lacus *m.*
tarnish *vt.* īnfuscāre, inquināre. *vi.* īnfuscārī.
tarry *vi.* morārī, commorārī, cunctārī.
tart *a.* acidus, asper. *n.* scriblīta *f.* **-ly** *ad.* acerbē.
tartness *n.* asperitās *f.*
task *n.* pēnsum *n.*, opus *n.* take to — obiūrgāre.
task-master *n* dominus *m.*
tassel *n.* fimbriae *f.pl.*
taste *n.* (*sense*) gustātus *m.*; (*flavour*) sapor *m.*; (*artistic*) iūdicium *n.*, ēlegantia *f.*; (*for rhetoric*) aurēs *f.pl.* of — doctus. in good — ēlegāns. *vt.* gustāre, dēgustāre. *vi.* sapere. — of resipere.
tasteful *a.* ēlegāns. **-ly** *ad.* ēleganter.
tastefulness *n.* ēlegantia *f.*
tasteless *a.* īnsulsus, inēlegāns. **-ly** *ad.* īnsulsē, inēleganter.
tastelessness *n.* īnsulsitās *f.*
taster *n.* praegustātor *m.*
tasty *a.* dulcis.
tattered *a.* pannōsus.
tatters *n.* pannī *m.pl.*
tattoo *vt.* compungere.
taunt *n.* convīcium *n.*, probrum *n.* *vt.* exprobrāre, obicere (*dat. of pers., acc. of charge*).
taunting *a.* contumēliōsus. **-ly** *ad.* contumēliōsē.
taut *a.* intentus. draw — addūcere.
tavern *n.* taberna *f.*, hospitium *n.*
tawdry *a.* vīlis.
tawny *a.* fulvus.
tax *n.* vectīgal *n.*, tribūtum *n.* a 5 per cent — vīcēsima *f.* free from — immūnis. *vt.* vectīgal impōnere (*dat.*); (*strength*) contendere. — with (*charge*) obicere (*acc.* & *dat.*), īnsimulāre.
taxable *a.* vectīgālis.
taxation *n.* vectīgālia *n.pl.*
tax-collector *n.* exāctor *m.*
tax-farmer *n.* pūblicānus *m.*
tax-payer *n.* assiduus *m.*
teach *vt.* docēre, ērudīre, īnstituere; (*thoroughly*) ēdocēre; (*pass.*) discere. — your grandmother sūs Minervam.
teachable *a.* docilis.
teacher *n.* magister *m.*, magistra *f.*, doctor *m.*; (*philos.*) praeceptor *m.*; (*of literature*) grammaticus *m.*; (*of rhetoric*) rhētor *m.*
teaching *n.* doctrina *f.*, disciplīna *f.*
team *n.* (*animals*) iugum *n.*
tear *n.* lacrima *f.* shed -s

lacrimās effundere. *vt.* scindere. — **down** revellere. — **in pieces** dīlaniāre, discerpere, lacerāre. — **off** abscindere, dēripere. — **open** rescindere. — **out** ēvellere. — **up** convellere.
tearful *a.* flēbilis.
tease *vt.* lūdere, inrītāre.
teat *n.* mamma *f.*
technical *a.* (*term*) proprius.
technique *n.* ars *f.*
tedious *a.* longus, lentus, odiōsus. **-ly** *ad.* molestē.
tedium *n.* taedium *n.*, molestia *f.*
teem *vi.* abundāre.
teeming *a.* fēcundus, refertus.
teens *n.* **in one's** — adulescentulus.
teethe *vi.* dentīre.
tell *vt.* (*story*) nārrāre; (*person*) dīcere (*dat.*); (*number*) ēnumerāre; (*difference*) intellegere; (*order*) iubēre. *vi.* valēre. — **the difference between** discernere. **I cannot** — nesciō.
telling *a.* validus.
temerity *n.* temeritās *f.*
temper *n.* animus *m.*, ingenium *n.*; (*bad*) īra *f.* īrācundia *f.*; (*of metal*) temperātiō *f.*. *vt.* temperāre; (*fig.*) moderārī (*dat.*).
temperament *n.* animī habitus *m.*, animus *m.*
temperamental *a.* incōnstāns.
temperance *n.* temperantia *f.*, continentia *f.*
temperate *a.* temperātus, moderātus, sobrius. **-ly** *ad.* moderātē.
temperature *n.* calor *m.*, frīgus *n.* **mild** — temperiēs *f.*
tempest *n.* tempestās *f.*, procella *f.*
tempestuous *a.* procellōsus.
temple *n.* templum *n.*, aedēs *f.*; (*head*) tempus *n.*
temporal *a.* hūmānus, profānus.
temporar/y *a.* brevis. **-ily** *ad.* ad tempus.
temporize *vi.* temporis causā facere, tergiversārī.
tempt *vt.* sollicitāre, pellicere, invītāre.
temptation *n.* illecebra *f.*
tempter *n.* impulsor *m.*
ten *num.* decem. — **each** dēnī. — **times** deciēns.
tenable *a.* inexpugnābilis, stabilis, certus.
tenacious *a.* tenāx, firmus. **-ly** *ad.* tenāciter.
tenacity *n.* tenācitās *f.*
tenant *n.* inquilīnus *m.*, habitātor *m.*; (*on land*) colōnus *m.*
tenantry *n.* colōnī *m.pl.*
tend *vi.* spectāre, pertinēre. *vt.* cūrāre, colere.
tendency *n.* inclīnātiō *f.*, voluntās *f.*
tender *a.* tener, mollis. *vt.* dēferre, offerre. **-ly** *ad.* indulgenter.
tender-hearted *a.* misericors.
tenderness *n.* indulgentia *f.*, mollitia *f.*
tendon *n.* nervus *m.*
tendril *n.* clāviculus *m.*
tenement *n.* habitātiō *f.* **block of -s** īnsula *f.*
tenet *n.* dogma *n.*, dēcrētum *n.*
tennis-court *n.* sphaeristērium *n.*
tenor *n.* (*course*) tenor *m.*; (*purport*) sententia *f.*
tense *a.* intentus. *n.* tempus *n.*
tension *n.* intentiō *f.*
tent *n.* tabernāculum *n.*; (*general's*) praetōrium *n.*
tentacle *n.* bracchium *n.*
tentatively *ad.* experiendō.
tenterhooks *n.* **on** — animī suspēnsus.
tenth *a.* decimus. **for the** — **time** decimum. **men of the** — **legion** decumānī *m.pl.*
tenuous *a.* rārus.
tenure *n.* possessiō *f.*
tepid *a.* tepidus. **be** — tepēre.

tergiversation *n.* tergiversātiō *f.*
term *n.* (*limit*) terminus *m.*; (*period*) spatium *n.*; (*word*) verbum *n.* **-s** *n.* condiciō *f.*, lēx *f.* propose — condiciōnem ferre. be on good — in grātiā esse. we come to — inter nōs convenit. *vt.* appellāre, nuncupāre.
terminate *vt.* termināre, fīnīre. *vi.* dēsinere; (*words*) cadere.
termination *n.* fīnis *m.*, terminus *m.* [*pl.*
terminology *n.* vocābula *n.*
terrain *n.* ager *m.*
terrestrial *a.* terrestris.
terrib/le *a.* terribilis, horribilis, horrendus. **-ly** *ad.* horrendum in modum.
terrific *a.* formīdolōsus; vehemēns.
terrify *vt.* terrēre, perterrēre, exterrēre. **-ing** *a.* formīdolōsus. [*m.pl.*
territory *n.* ager *m.*, fīnēs
terror *n.* terror *m.*, formīdō *f.*, pavor *m.* object of — terror *m.* be a — to terrōrī esse (*dat.*).
terrorize *vt.* metum inicere (*dat.*).
terse *a.* pressus, brevis. **-ly** *ad.* pressē.
terseness *n.* brevitās *f.*
tessellated *a.* tessellātus.
test *n.* experīmentum *n.*, probātiō *f.*; (*standard*) obrussa *f.* put to the — experīrī, perīclitārī. stand the — spectārī. *vt.* experīrī, probāre, spectāre.
testament *n.* testāmentum *n.*
testamentary *a.* testāmentārius.
testator *n.* testātor *m.*
testify *vt.* testificārī.
testifying *n.* testificātiō *f.*
testimonial *n.* laudātiō *f.*
testimony *n.* testimōnium *n.*
test/y *a.* difficilis, stomachōsus. **-ily** *ad.* stomachōsē.
tether *n.* retināculum *n.*, vinculum *n.* *vt.* religāre.
tetrarch *n.* tetrarchēs *m.*
tetrarchy *n.* tetrarchia *f.*
text *n.* verba *n.pl.*
text-book *n.* ars *f.*
textile *a.* textilis.
textual *a.* verbōrum.
texture *n.* textus *m.*
than *conj.* quam; *abl.* other — alius ac.
thank *vt.* grātiās agere (*dat.*). — you bene facis. no, — you benignē. [grātē.
thankful *a.* grātus. **-ly** *ad.*
thankfulness *n.* grātia *f.*
thankless *a.* ingrātus. **-ly** *ad.* ingrātē.
thanks *n.* grātiae *f.pl.*, grātēs *f.pl.* return — grātiās agere, grātēs persolvere. — to you operā tuā, beneficiō tuō.
thanksgiving *n.* grātulātiō *f.*; (*public*) supplicātiō *f.*
that *pro.* (*demonstr.*) ille; (*rel.*) quī. *conj.* (*statement*) *acc.* & *inf.*; (*command, purpose, result*) ut; (*fearing*) nē; (*emotion*) quod. oh — utinam.
thatch *n.* culmus *m.*, strāmentum *n.* *vt.* tegere, integere.
thaw *vt.* dissolvere. *vi.* liquēscere, tabēscere.
the *art. not expressed*; (*emphatic*) ille; (*with comp.*) quō . . . eō.
theatre *n.* theātrum *n.*
theatrical *a.* scēnicus.
theft *n.* fūrtum *n.* [suus.
their *a.* eōrum; (*ref. to subject*)
theme *n.* māteria *f.*, argūmentum *n.*
themselves *pro.* ipsī; (*reflexive*) sē.
then *ad.* (*time*) tum, tunc; (*succession*) deinde, tum, posteā; (*consequence*) igitur, ergō. now and — interdum. only — tum dēmum.
thence *ad.* inde.
thenceforth *ad.* inde, posteā, ex eō tempore.

theologian *n.* theologus *m.*
theology *n.* theologia *f.*
theorem *n.* prōpositum *n.*
theoretical *a.* contemplātīvus.
theory *n.* ratiō *f.* — and practice ratiō atque ūsus
there *ad.* ibī, illīc; (*thither*) eō, illūc. from — inde, illinc. here and — passim. — is est; (*interj.*) ecce.
thereabout(s) *ad.* circā. circiter, prope.
thereafter *ad.* deinde, posteā.
thereby *ad.* eā rē, hōc factō.
therefore *ad.* itaque, igitur, ergō, idcircō.
therein *ad.* inibī, in eō.
thereof *ad.* ēius, ēius reī.
thereon *ad.* īnsuper, in eō.
thereupon *ad.* deinde, statim, inde.
therewith *ad.* cum eō.
thesis *n.* prōpositum *n.*
thews *n.* nervī *m.pl.*
they *pro.* iī, hī, illī.
thick *a.* dēnsus; (*air*) crassus. **-ly** *ad.* dēnsē. — populated frequēns. [crēscere.
thicken *vt.* dēnsāre. *vi.* con-
thickening *n.* concrētiō *f.*
thicket *n.* dūmētum *n.*
thick-headed *a.* stupidus, hebes.
thickness *n.* crassitūdō *f.*
thick-set *a.* brevis atque obēsus.
thick-skinned *a.* be — callēre. become — occallēscere.
thief *n.* fūr *m.*
thieve *vt.* fūrārī, surripere.
thievery *n.* fūrtum *n.*
thievish *a.* fūrāx.
thigh *n.* femur *n.*
thin *a.* exīlis, gracilis, tenuis; (*attendance*) īnfrequēns. *vt.* attenuāre, extenuāre. — out rārefacere. — down dīluere.
thine *a.* tuus.
thing *n.* rēs *f.* as —s are nunc, cum haec ita sint.
think *vi.* cōgitāre; (*opinion*) putāre, exīstimāre, arbitrārī, rērī, crēdere. as I — meā sententiā. — about cōgitāre dē. — highly of māgnī aestimāre. — nothing of nihilī facere. — out excōgitāre. — over reputāre, in mente agitāre.
thinker *n.* philosophus *m.*
thinking *a.* sapiēns. *n.* cōgitātiō *f.* [rārē.
thinly *ad.* exīliter, tenuiter;
thinness *n.* exīlitās *f.*, gracilitās *f.*; (*person*) maciēs *f.*; (*number*) exiguitās *f.*, īnfrequentia *f.*; (*air*) tenuitās *f.*
thin-skinned *a.* inrītābilis.
third *a.* tertius. for the — time tertium. *n.* tertia pars *f.*, triēns *m.* two -s duae partēs, bēs *m.*
thirdly *ad.* tertiō.
thirst *n.* sitis *f.* *vi.* sitīre. — for sitīre.
thirst/y *a.* sitiēns. **-ily** *ad.* sitienter.
thirteen *num.* tredecim. — each ternī dēnī. — times terdeciēns.
thirteenth *a.* tertius decimus.
thirtieth *a.* trīcēsimus.
thirty *num.* trīgintā. — each trīcēnī. — times trīciēns.
this *pro.* hīc.
thistle *n.* carduus.
thither *ad.* eō, illūc.
thole *n.* scalmus *n.*
thong *n.* lōrum *n.*, habēna *f.*
thorn *n.* spīna *f.*, sentis *m.*
thorny *a.* spīnōsus.
thorough *a.* absolūtus, germānus; (*work*) accūrātus. **-ly** *ad.* penitus, omnīnō, funditus.
thoroughbred *a.* generōsus.
thoroughfare *n.* via *f.*
thoroughness *n.* cūra *f.*, dīligentia *f.*
thou *pro.* tū.
though *conj.* etsī, etiamsī, quamvīs, quamquam.
thought *n.* (*faculty*) cōgitātiō *f.*, mēns *f.*, animus *m.*; (*an*

idea) cōgitātum *n.*, nōtiō *f.*; (*design*) cōnsilium *n.*, prōpositum *n.*; (*expressed*) sententia *f.*; (*heed*) cautiō *f.*, prōvidentia *f.*; (*rhet.*) inventiō *f.* second -s posteriōrēs cōgitātiōnēs.

thoughtful *a.* cōgitābundus; prōvidus. **-ly** *ad.* prōvidē.

thoughtless *a.* incōnsiderātus, incōnsultus, imprōvidus, immemor. **-ly** *ad.* temerē, incōnsultē.

thoughtlessness *n.* incōnsiderantia *f.*, imprūdentia *f.*

thought-reader *n.* coniector *m.*

thousand *num.* mīlle; (*pl.*) mīlia *n.pl.* — each mīllēnī. — times mīlliēns.

thousandth *a.* mīllēsimus.

thrall *n.* servus *m.*

thraldom *n.* servitūs *f.*

thrash *vt.* verberāre.

thrashing *n.* verbera *n.pl.*

thread *n.* fīlum *n.* hang by a — (*fig.*) fīlō pendēre. *vt.* — one's way sē īnsinuāre.

threadbare *a.* trītus, obsolētus.

threat *n.* minae *f.pl.*, minātiō *f.*

threaten *vt.* minārī (*dat. of pers.*) dēnūntiāre. *vi.* imminēre, impendēre.

threatening *a.* mināx, imminēns. **-ly** *ad.* mināciter.

three *num.* trēs. — each ternī. — times ter. — days triduum *n.* — years triennium *n.* — quarters trēs partēs *f. pl.*, dōdrāns *m.*

three-cornered *a.* triangulus, triquetrus.

threefold *a.* triplex.

three hundred *num.* trecentī. — each trecēnī. — times trecentiēns. **-th** *a.* trecentēsimus.

three-legged *a.* tripēs.

thresh *vt.* terere, exterere.

threshing-floor *n.* ārea *f.*

threshold *n.* līmen *n.*

thrice *ad.* ter.

thrift *n.* frūgālitās *f.*, parsimōnia *f.*

thrift/y *a.* parcus, frūgī. **-ily** *ad.* frūgāliter.

thrill *n.* horror *m.* *vt.* percellere, percutere. *vi.* trepidāre.

thrilling *a.* mīrābilis.

thrive *vi.* vigēre, valēre, crēscere.

thriving *a.* valēns, vegetus; (*crops*) laetus.

throat *n.* faucēs *f.pl.*, guttur *n.* cut the — of iugulāre.

throaty *a.* gravis, raucus.

throb *vi.* palpitāre micāre. *n.* pulsus *m.*

throe *n.* dolor *m.* be in the -s of labōrāre ex.

throne *n.* solium *n.*; (*power*) rēgnum *n.*

throng *n.* multitūdō *f.*, frequentia *f.* *vt.* celebrāre. — round stīpāre, circumfundī (*dat.*).

throttle *vt.* strangulāre.

through *pr.* per (*acc.*); (*cause*) propter (*acc.*), *abl.* *ad.* — and — penitus. carry — exsequī, peragere. go — trānsīre. run — percurrere. be — with perfūnctum esse (*abl.*).

throughout *ad.* penitus, omnīnō. *pr.* per (*acc.*).

throw *n.* iactus *m.*, coniectus *m.* *vt.* iacere, conicere. — about iactāre. — across trāicere. — away abicere; (*something precious*) prōicere. — back rēicere. — down dēturbāre, dēicere. — into inicere. — off excutere, exsolvere. — open patefacere. — out ēicere, prōicere. — over inicere; (*fig.*) dēstituere. — overboard iactūram facere (*gen.*). — to (*danger*) obicere. — up ēicere; (*building*) exstruere. — a bridge over pontem inicere (*dat.*), pontem faciendum cūrāre in (*abl.*) —

light on (*fig.*) lūmen adhibēre (*dat.*). — **a rider** equitem excutere. [iactus *m.*
throwing *n.* coniectiō *f.*,
thrum *n.* licium *n.*
thrush *n.* turdus *m.*
thrust *vt.* trūdere, pellere, impingere. — **at** petere. — **away** dētrūdere. — **forward** prōtrūdere. — **home** dēfīgere. — **into** īnfīgere, impingere. — **out** extrūdere.
thud *n.* gravis sonitus *m.* [*m.*
thug *n.* percussor *m.* sīcārius
thumb *n.* pollex *m.* **have under one's** — in potestāte suā habēre.
thump *n.* plāga *f.* *vt.* tundere, pulsāre.
thunder *n.* tonitrus *m.* *vi.* tonāre, intonāre.
thunderbolt *n.* fulmen *n.*
thunderer *n.* tonāns *m.*
thunder-struck *a.* attonitus.
thus *ad.* (*referring back*) sic, (*referring forward*) ita. — **far** hāctenus.
thwack *vt.* verberāre.
thwart *vt.* obstāre (*dat.*), officere (*dat.*), remorārī, frustrārī. *n.* (*boat's*) trānstrum *n.*
thy *a.* tuus.
thyme *n.* thymum *n.*; (*wild*) serpyllum *n.*
tiara *n.* diadēma *n.*
ticket *n.* tessera *f.*
tickle *vt.* titillāre.
tickling *n.* titillātiō *f.*
ticklish *a.* lūbricus. [*n.*
tidal *a.* — **waters** aestuārium
tide *n.* aestus *m.*; (*time*) tempus *n.* **ebb** — aestūs recessus *m.* **flood** — aestūs accessus *m.* **turn of the** — commūtātiō aestūs. **the** — **will turn** (*fig.*) circumagētur hic orbis.
tidiness *n.* concinnitās *f.*, munditia *f.*
tidings *n.* nūntius *m.*
tid/y *a.* concinnus, mundus. **-ily** *ad.* concinnē, mundē.
tie *n.* (*bond*) vinculum *n.*, cōpula *f.*; (*kin*) necessitūdō *f.* *vt.* ligāre; (*knot*) nectere. — **fast** dēvincīre, cōnstringere. — **on** illigāre. — **to** adligāre. — **together** colligāre. — **up** adligāre; (*wound*) obligāre.
tier *n.* ōrdō *m.*
tiff *n.* dissēnsiō *f.*
tiger *n.* tigris *m.*, *more usu.* *f.*
tight *a.* strictus, astrictus, intentus; (*close*) artus. **draw** — intendere, addūcere. **-ly** *ad.* artē.
tighten *vt.* adstringere, contendere.
tigress *n.* tigris *f.*
tile *n.* tegula *f.*, imbrex *f.*, **later** *n.*
till *conj.* dum, dōnec. *pr.* usque ad (*acc.*), in (*acc.*). **not** — dēmum. *n.* arca *f.* *vt.* colere.
tillage *n.* cultus *m.*
tiller *n.* (*agr.*) cultor *m.*; (*ship*) clāvus *m.*, gubernāculum *n.*
tilt *vt.* inclīnāre.
tilth *n.* cultus *m.*, arvum *n.*
timber *n.* (*for building*) māteria *f.*; (*firewood*) lignum *n.*
timbrel *n.* tympanum *n.*
time *n.* tempus *n.*; (*lifetime*) aetās *f.*; (*interval*) intervallum *n.*, spatium *n.*; (*of day*) hōra *f.*; (*leisure*) ōtium *n.*; (*rhythm*) numerus *m.* **another** — aliās. **at -s** aliquandō. interdum. **at all -s** semper. **at any** — umquam. **at one** — . . . **at another** aliās . . . aliās. **at that** — tunc, id temporis. **at the right** — ad tempus, mātūrē, tempestīvē. **at the same** — simul; tamen. **at the wrong** — intempestīvē. **beating** — percussiō *f.* **convenient** — opportūnitās *f.* **for a** — aliquantisper, parumper. **for a long** — diū. **for some** — aliquamdiū. **for the** — **being** ad tempus. **from** — **to** — interdum, identidem. **have a good** — geniō indulgēre. **have**

— for vacāre (*dat.*). in — ad tempus, tempore. in a short — brevī. in good — tempestīvus. in the — of apud (*acc.*). keep — (*marching*) gradum cōnferre; (*music*) modulārī. many -s saepe, saepenumerō. pass, spend — tempus sūmere, dēgere. several -s aliquotiēns. some — aliquandō. waste — tempus terere. what is the — ? quota hōra est ? — expired *a.* ēmeritus.
time-honoured *a.* antīquus.
timeliness *n.* opportūnitās *f.*
timely *a.* opportūnus, tempestīvūs, mātūrus.
timid *a.* timidus. **-ly** *ad.* timidē.
timidity *n.* timiditās *f.*
timorous *a.* timidus. **-ly** *ad.* timidē.
tin *n.* stannum *n.*, plumbum album *n.* *a.* stanneus.
tincture *n.* color *m.*, sapor *m.* *vt.* īnficere.
tinder *n.* fōmes *m.*
tinge *vt.* imbuere, īnficere, tingere.
tingle *vi.* horrēre.
tingling *n.* horror *m.* [*m.*
tinkle *vi.* tinnīre. *n.* tinnītus
tinsel *n.* bractea *f.*; (*fig.*) speciēs *f.*, fūcus *m.*
tint *n.* color *m.* *vt.* colōrāre.
tiny *a.* minūtus, pusillus, perexiguus.
tip *n.* apex *m.*, cacūmen *n.*, extrēmum *n.* the — of prīmus, extrēmus. *vt.* praefīgere. — over invertere.
tipple *vi.* pōtāre.
tippler *n.* pōtor *m.*, ēbrius *m.*
tipsy *a.* tēmulentus.
tiptoes *n.* on — suspēnsō gradū.
tirade *n.* obiūrgātiō *f.*, dēclāmātiō *f.*
tire *vt.* fatigāre. — out dēfatīgāre. *vi.* dēfetīscī, fatīgārī. I — of mē taedet (*gen.*).
tired *a.* fessus, lassus. — out dēfessus. I am — of mē taedet.
tiresome *a.* molestus, difficilis.
tiring *a.* labōriōsus, operōsus.
tiro *n.* tīrō *m.*, rudis *m.*
tissue *n.* textus *m.*
tit *n.* give — for tat pār parī respondēre.
Titan *n.* Tītān *m.*
titanic *a.* immānis.
titbit *n.* cuppēdium *n.*
tithe *n.* decuma *f.* — gatherer decumānus *m.*
titillate *vt.* titillāre.
titillation *n.* titillātiō *f.*
title *n.* (*book*) īnscrīptiō *f.*, index *m.*; (*inscription*) titulus *m.*; (*person*) nōmen *n.*, appellātiō *f.*; (*claim*) iūs *n.*, vindiciae *f.pl.* assert one's — to vindicāre. give a — to īnscrībere.
titled *a.* nōbilis.
title-deed *n.* auctōritās *f.*
titter *n.* rīsus *m.* *vi.* rīdēre.
tittle-tattle *n.* sermunculus *m.*
titular *a.* nōmine.
to *pr.* ad (*acc.*), in (*acc.*); (*attitude*) erga (*acc.*); (*giving*) *dat.* (*towns, small islands,* domus, rūs) *acc.* *conj.* (*purpose*) ut. *ad.* come — animum recipere. — and fro hūc illūc.
toad *n.* būfō *m.*
toady *n.* adsentātor *m.*, parasītus. *m.* *vt.* adsentārī (*dat.*).
toadyism *n.* adsentātiō *f.*
toast *n.* drink a — propīnāre. *vt.* torrēre; (*drink*) propīnāre (*dat.*).
today *ad.* hodiē. -'s hodiernus.
toe *n.* digitus *m.* big — pollex *m.*
toga *n.* toga *f.*
together *ad.* ūnā, simul. bring — cōgere, congerere. come — convenīre, congregārī. put — cōnferre, compōnere.
toil *n.* labor *m.*; (*snare*) rēte *n.* *vi.* labōrāre. — at ēlabōrāre in (*abl.*).
toilet *n.* (*lady's*) cultus *m.*

toilsome *a.* labōriōsus, operōsus.
toil-worn *a.* labōre cōnfectus.
token *n.* insigne *n.*, signum *n.*, indicium *n.*
tolerab/le *a.* tolerābilis, patibilis; (*quality*) mediocris; (*size*) modicus. **-ly** *ad.* satis, mediocriter.
tolerance *n.* patientia *f.*, tolerantia *f.*
tolerant *a.* indulgēns, tolerāns. **-ly** *ad.* indulgenter.
tolerate *vt.* tolerāre, ferre, indulgēre (*dat.*).
toleration *n.* patientia *f.*; (*freedom*) lībertās *f.*
toll *n.* vectīgal *n.*; (*harbour*) portōrium *n.*
toll-collector *n.* exāctor *m.*; portitor *m.*
tomb *n.* sepulcrum *n.*
tombstone *n.* lapis *m.*
tome *n.* liber *m.*
tomorrow *ad.* crās. **-'s** crāstinus. the day after — perendiē. put off till — in crāstinum differre.
tone *n.* sonus *m.*, vōx *f.*; (*painting*) color *m.*
tongs *n.* forceps *m.*, *f.*
tongue *n.* lingua *f.*; (*shoe*) ligula *f.* on the tip of one's — in prīmōribus labrīs.
tongue-tied *a.* ēlinguis, īnfāns.
tonnage *n.* amphorae *f.pl.*
tonsils *n.* tōnsillae *f.pl.*
tonsure *n.* rāsūra *f.*
too *ad.* (*also*) etiam, īnsuper; (*excess*) nimis, *comp. a.* — far extrā modum. — much nimium. — long nimium diū. — great to māior quam quī (*subj.*).
tool *n.* īnstrūmentum *n.*; (*agr.*) ferrāmentum *n.*; (*person*) minister *m.*
tooth *n.* dēns *m.* — and nail tōtō corpore atque omnibus unguibus. cast in one's teeth exprobrāre, obicere. cut teeth dentīre. in the teeth of obviam (*dat.*), adversus (*acc.*). with the teeth mordicus.
toothache *n.* dentium dolor *m.*
toothed *a.* dentātus.
toothless *a.* ēdentulus.
toothpick *n.* dentiscalpium *n.*
toothsome *a.* suāvis, dulcis.
top *n.* vertex *m.*, fastīgium *n.*; (*tree*) cacūmen *n.*; (*toy*) turbō *m.* from — to toe ab īmīs unguibus usque ad verticem summum. the — of summus. *vt.* exsuperāre. — up supplēre. *a.* superior, summus.
tope *vi.* pōtāre.
toper *n.* pōtor *m.*
topiary *a.* topiārius. *n.* topiārium opus *n.*
topic *n.* rēs *f.*; (*rhet.*) locus *m.* — of conversation sermō *m.*
topical *a.* hodiernus.
topmost *a.* summus.
topography *n.* dēscrīptiō.
topple *vi.* titubāre. — over prōlābī.
topsail *n.* dolō *m.*
topsyturvy *ad.* praeposterē. turn — sūrsum deōrsum versāre, permiscēre.
tor *n.* mōns *m.*
torch *n.* fax *f.*, lampas *f.*
torment *n.* cruciātus *m.*; (*mind*) angor *m.* *vt.* cruciāre; (*mind*) discruciāre, excruciāre, angere.
tormentor *n.* tortor *m.*
tornado *n.* turbō *m.*
torpid *a.* torpēns. be — torpēre. grow — obtorpēscere.
torpor *n.* torpor *m.*, inertia *f.*
torrent *n.* torrēns *m.*
torrid *a.* torridus.
torsion *n.* tortus *m.*
torso *n.* truncus *m.*
tortoise *n.* testūdō *f.* **-shell** *n.* testūdō *f.*
tortuous *a.* flexuōsus.
torture *n.* cruciātus *m.*, supplicium *n.* instrument of — tormentum *n.* *vt.* torquēre, cruciāre, excruciāre.
torturer *n.* tortor *m.*, carnifex *m.*

toss *n.* iactus *m.* *vt.* iactāre, excutere. — **about** agitāre. **be -ed** (*at sea*) fluitāre.
total *a.* tōtus, ūniversus. *n.* summa *f.* **-ly** *ad.* omnīnō, plānē.
totality *n.* ūniversitās *f.*
totter *vi.* lābāre, titubāre. **make** — labefactāre.
tottering *n.* titubātiō *f.*
touch *n.* tāctus *m.* **a — of** aliquantulum (*gen.*). **finishing — manus** extrēma *f.* *vt.* tangere, attingere; (*feelings*) movēre, tangere. *vi.* inter sē contingere. — **at** nāvem appellere ad. — **on** (*topic*) attingere, perstringere. — **up** expolīre.
touch-and-go *a.* anceps. *n.* discrīmen *n.*
touching *a.* (*place*) contiguus; (*emotion*) flexanimus. *pr.* quod attinet ad (*acc.*).
touchstone *n.* (*fig.*) obrussa *f.*
touchy *a.* inrītābilis, stomachōsus.
tough *a.* dūrus.
toughen *vt.* dūrāre.
toughness *n.* dūritia *f.*
tour *n.* iter *n.*; (*abroad*) peregrīnātiō *f.*
tourist *n.* viātor *m.*, peregrīnātor *m.*
tournament *n.* certāmen *n.*
tow *n.* stuppa *f.* **of** — stuppeus. *vt.* adnexum trahere, remulcō trahere.
toward(s) *pr.* ad (*acc.*) versus, (*after noun, acc.*); (*feelings*) in (*acc.*), erga (*acc.*); (*time*) sub (*acc.*).
towel *n.* mantēle *n.*
tower *n.* turris *f.* *vi.* ēminēre.
towered *a.* turrītus.
town *n.* urbs *f.*, oppidum *n.* **country** — mūnicipium *n.* *a.* urbānus.
town-councillor *n.* decuriō [*m.*
townsman *n.* oppidānus *m.*
tow-rope *n.* remulcum *n.*
toy *n.* crepundia *n.pl.* *vi.* lūdere.

trace *n.* vestīgium *n.*, indicium *n.* *vt.* investīgāre; (*draw*) dēscrībere. — **out** dēsignāre.
track *n.* (*mark*) vestīgium *n.*; (*path*) callis *m.*, sēmita *f.*; (*of wheel*) orbita *f.*; (*of ship*) cursus *m.* *vt.* investīgāre, indāgāre.
trackless *a.* invius.
tract *n.* (*country*) tractus *m.*, regiō *f.*; (*book*) libellus *m.*
tractable *a.* tractābilis, facilis, docilis.
trade *n.* mercātūra *f.*, mercātus *m.*; (*a business*) ars *f.*, quaestus *m.* **freedom of** — commercium *n.* *vi.* mercātūrās facere, negōtiārī. — **in** vēndere, vēnditāre. [ātor *m.*
trader *n.* mercātor *m.*, negōti-
tradesman *n.* opifex *m.*
tradition *n.* fāma *f.*, mōs māiōrum *m.*, memoria *f.*
traditional *a.* ā māiōribus trāditus, patrius. **-ly** *ad.* mōre māiōrum.
traduce *vt.* calumniārī, obtrectāre (*dat.*).
traducer *n.* calumniātor *m.*, obtrectātor *m.*
traffic *n.* commercium *n.*; (*on road*) vehicula *n.pl.* *vi.* mercātūrās facere. — **in** vēndere, vēnditāre.
tragedian *n.* (*author*) tragoedus *m.*; (*actor*) āctor tragicus *m.*
tragedy *n.* tragoedia *f.*; (*fig.*) calamitās *f.*, malum *n.*
tragic *a.* tragicus; (*fig.*) tristis. **-ally** *ad.* tragicē; male.
tragicomedy *n.* tragicocōmoedia *f.*
trail *n.* vestīgia *n.pl.* *vt.* trahere. *vi.* trahī.
train *n.* (*line*) agmen *n.*, ōrdō *m.*; (*of dress*) īnstita *f.*; (*army*) impedīmenta *n.pl.*; (*followers*) comitēs *m.pl.*, satellitēs *m.pl.*, cohors *f.* *vt.* īnstituere, īnstruere, docēre, adsuēfacere; (*weapon*) dīrigere.

trainer *n.* (*sport*) lanista *m.*, aliptēs *m.*
training *n.* disciplīna *f.*, īnstitūtiō *f.*; (*practice*) exercitātiō *f.*
trait *n.* līneāmentum *n.*
traitor *n.* prōditor *m.*
traitorous *a.* perfidus, perfidiōsus. **-ly** *ad.* perfidiōsē.
trammel *vt.* impedīre.
tramp *n.* (*man*) planus *m.*; (*of feet*) pulsus *m.* *vi.* gradī.
trample *vi.* — on obterere, prōterere, prōculcāre.
trance *n.* stupor *m.*; (*prophetic*) furor *m.*
tranquil *a.* tranquillus, placidus, quiētus, sēdātus. **-ly** *ad.* tranquillē, placidē, tranquillō animō.
tranquility *n.* tranquillitās *f.*, quiēs *f.*, pāx *f.*
tranquillize *vt.* pācāre, [sēdāre.
transact *vt.* agere, gerere, trānsigere.
transaction *n.* rēs *f.*, negōtium *n.*
transactor *n.* āctor *m.*
transalpine *a.* trānsalpīnus.
transcend *vt.* superāre, excēdere.
transcendence *n.* praestantia [*f.*
transcendent *a.* eximius, ēgregius, excellēns. **-ly** *ad.* eximiē, ēgregiē, ūnicē.
transcendental *a.* dīvīnus.
transcribe *vt.* dēscrībere, trānscrībere.
transcriber *n.* librārius *m.*
transcript *n.* exemplar *n.*, exemplum *n.*
transfer *n.* trānslātiō *f.*; (*of property*) aliēnātiō *f.* *vt.* trānsferre; (*troops*) trādūcere; (*property*) abaliēnāre; (*duty*) dēlēgāre.
transference *n.* trānslātiō *f.*
transfigure *vt.* trānsfōrmāre.
transfix *vt.* trānsfīgere, trāicere, trānsfodere; (*mind*) obstupefacere. **be -ed** stupēre, stupēscere.
transform *vt.* commūtāre, vertere.
transformation *n.* commūtātiō *f.*
transgress *vt.* violāre, perfringere. *vi.* dēlinquere.
transgression *n.* dēlictum *n.*
transgressor *n.* violātor *m.*
transience *n.* brevitās *f.*
transient *a.* fluxus, cadūcus, brevis.
transit *n.* trānsitus *m.*
transition *n.* mūtātiō *f.*; (*speech*) trānsitus *m.*
transitory *a.* brevis, fluxus.
translate *vt.* vertere, reddere. — into Latin Latīnē reddere.
translation *n.* a Latin — of Homer Latīnē redditus Homērus.
translator *n.* interpres *m.*
translucent *a.* perlūcidus.
transmarine *a.* trānsmarīnus.
transmission *n.* missiō *f.*
transmit *vt.* mittere; (*legacy*) trādere, prōdere.
transmutable *a.* mūtābilis.
transmutation *n.* mūtātiō *f.*
transmute *vt.* mūtāre, commūtāre.
transom *n.* trabs *f.*
transparency *n.* perlūcida nātūra *f.*
transparent *a.* perlūcidus; (*fig.*) perspicuus. **-ly** *ad.* perspicuē.
transpire *vi.* (*get known*) ēmānāre, dīvulgārī; (*happen*) ēvenīre.
transplant *vt.* trānsferre.
transport *n.* vectūra *f.*; (*ship*) nāvis onerāria *f.*; (*emotion*) ēlātiō *f.*, summa laetitia *f.* *vt.* trānsportāre, trānsvehere, trānsmittere. **be -ed** (*fig.*) efferrī, gestīre.
transportation *n.* vectūra *f.*
transpose *vt.* invertere; (*words*) trāicere.
transposition *n.* (*words*) trāiectiō *f.*
transverse *a.* trānsversus.

obliquus. **-ly** *ad.* in trānsversum, obliquē.
trap *n.* laqueus *m.*; (*fig.*) insidiae *f.pl.* *vt.* dēcipere, excipere; (*fig.*) inlaqueāre.
trappings *n.* ōrnāmenta *n.pl.*, insignia *n.pl.*; (*horse's*) phalerae *f.pl.*
trash *n.* nūgae *f.pl.*
trashy *a.* vīlis.
travail *n.* labor *m.* sūdor *m.*; (*woman's*) puerperium *n.* *vi.* labōrāre, sūdāre; parturīre.
travel *n.* itinera *n.pl.*; (*foreign*) peregrīnātiō *f.* *vi.* iter facere; (*abroad*) peregrīnārī; — through peragrāre. — to contendere ad, in (*acc.*), proficīscī in (*acc.*).
traveller *n.* viātor *m.*; (*abroad*) peregrīnātor *m.* commercial — īnstitor *m.*
traverse *vt.* peragrāre, lūstrāre.
travesty *n.* perversa imitātiō *f.* *vt.* perversē imitārī.
tray *n.* ferculum *n.*
treacherous *a.* perfidus, perfidiōsus; (*ground*) lūbricus. **-ly** *ad.* perfidiōsē.
treachery *n.* perfidia *f.*
tread *vi.* incēdere, ingredī. — on īnsistere (*dat.*). *n.* gradus *m.*, incessus *m.*
treadle *n.* (*loom*) īnsilia *n.pl.*
treadmill *n.* pistrīnum *n.*
treason *n.* māiestās *f.* perduelliō *f.* be charged with — māiestātis accūsārī. be guilty of high — against māiestātem minuere, laedere (*gen.*).
treasonable *a.* perfidus, perfidiōsus.
treasure *n.* gāza *f.*, thēsaurus *m.*; (*person*) dēliciae *f.pl.* *vt.* māximī aestimāre dīligere, fovēre. — up condere, congerere.
treasure-house *n.* thēsaurus *m.*
treasurer *n.* aerārī praefectus *m.*; (*royal*) dioecētēs *m.*
treasury *n.* aerārium *n.*; (*emperor's*) fiscus *m.*
treat *n.* convīvium *n.*, dēlectātiō *f.* *vt.* (*in any way*) ūtī (*abl.*), habēre, tractāre, accipere; (*patient*) cūrāre; (*topic*) tractāre; (*with hospitality*) invītāre. — with agere cum. — as a friend amīcī locō habēre.
treatise *n.* liber *m.*
treatment *n.* tractātiō *f.*; (*med.*) cūrātiō *f*
treaty *n.* foedus *n.* make a — foedus ferīre.
treble *a.* triplus; (*voice*) acūtus. *n.* acūtus sonus *m.* *vt.* triplicāre.
tree *n.* arbor *f.*
trek *vi.* migrāre. *n.* migrātiō *f.*
trellis *n.* cancellī *m.pl.*
tremble *vi.* tremere, horrēre.
trembling *n.* tremor *m.*, horror *m.* *a.* tremulus.
tremendous *a.* immānis, ingēns, vastus. **-ly** *ad.* immāne quantum.
tremor *n.* tremor *m.*
tremulous *a.* tremulus.
trench *n* fossa *f.*
trenchant *a.* ācer. **-ly** *ad.* ācriter.
trend *n.* inclīnātiō *f.* *vi.* [vergere.
trepidation *n.* trepidātiō *f.*
trespass *n.* dēlictum *n.* *vi.* dēlinquere. — on (*property*) invādere in (*acc.*); (*patience, time, etc.*) abūtī (*abl.*).
trespasser *n.* quī iniussū dominī ingreditur.
tress *n.* crīnis *m.*
trial *n.* (*essay*) experientia *f.*; (*test*) probātiō *f.*; (*law*) iūdicium *n.* quaestiō *f.*; (*trouble*) labor *m.*, aerumna *f.* make — of experīrī, periculum facere (*gen.*). be brought to — in iūdicium venīre. put on — in iūdicium vocāre. hold a — on quaestiōnem habēre dē (*abl.*).
triangle *n.* triangulum *n.*

triangular *a.* triangulus, triquetrus. [nātiō *f.*
tribe *n.* tribus *m.*; (*barbarian*)
tribulation *n.* aerumna *f.*
tribunal *n.* iūdicium *n.*
tribune *n.* tribūnus *m.*: (*platform*) rōstra *n. pl.*
tribuneship, **tribunate** *n.* tribūnātus *m.*
tribunician *a.* tribūnicius.
tributary *a.* vectīgālis. *n.* be a — of (*river*) īnfluere in (*acc.*).
tribute *n.* tribūtum *n.*, vectīgal *n.*; (*verbal*) laudātiō *f.* pay a — to laudāre.
trice *n.* in a — mōmentō temporis.
trick *n.* dolus *m.*, fallācia *f.*, fraus *f.*, īnsidiae *f.pl.*, ars *f.*; (*conjurer's*) praestīgiae *f.pl.*; (*habit*) mōs *m.* *vt.* fallere, dēcipere, ēlūdere; (*with words*) verba dare (*dat.*) — out ōrnāre, distinguere.
trickery *n.* dolus *m.*, fraus *f.*, fallāciae *f.pl.*
trickle *n.* guttae *f.pl.* *vi.* mānāre, dēstillāre.
trickster *n.* fraudātor *m.*, veterātor *m.*
tricky *a.* lūbricus, difficilis.
trident *n.* tridēns *m.*, fuscina *f.*
tried *a.* probātus, spectātus.
triennial *a.* trietēricus. **-ly** *ad.* quartō quōque annō.
trifle *n.* nūgae *f.pl.*, paululum *n.* *vi.* lūdere, nūgārī. — with lūdere.
trifling *a.* levis, exiguus. **-ly** *ad.* leviter.
trig *a.* lepidus, concinnus.
trigger *n.* manulea *f.*
trim *a.* nitidus, concinnus. *vt.* putāre, tondēre; (*lamp*) oleum īnstillāre (*dat.*). *vi.* temporibus servīre. **-ly** *ad.* concinnē.
trimness *n.* nitor, munditia *f.*
trinket *n.* crepundia *n.pl.*
trip *n.* iter *n.* *vt.* supplantāre. *vi.* lābī, titubāre. — along currere. — over incurrere in (*acc.*).
tripartite *a.* tripartītus.
tripe *n.* omāsum *n.*
trip/le *a.* triplex, triplus. *vt.* triplicāre. **-ly** *ad.* trifāriam.
tripod *n.* tripus *m.*
trireme *n.* trirēmis *f.*
trite *a.* trītus.
triumph *n.* triumphus *m.*; (*victory*) victōria *f.* *vi.* triumphāre; vincere. — over dēvincere.
triumphal *a.* triumphālis.
triumphant *a.* victor; laetus.
triumvir *n.* triumvir *m.*
triumvirate *n.* triumvirātus *m.*
trivial *a.* levis, tenuis.
triviality *n.* nūgae *f.pl.*
trochaic *a.* trochaicus.
trochee *n.* trochaeus *m.*
troop *n.* grex *f.*, caterva *f.*; (*cavalry*) turma *f.*; (*pl.*) cōpiae *f.pl.* *vi.* cōnfluere, congregārī.
trooper *n.* eques *m.*
trope *n.* figūra *f.*, trānslātiō *f.*
trophy *n.* tropaeum *n.* set up a — tropaeum pōnere.
tropic *n.* sōlstitiālis orbis *m.*; (*pl.*) loca fervida *n.pl.*
tropical *a.* tropicus.
trot *vi.* tolūtim īre.
troth *n.* fidēs *f.*
trouble *n.* incommodum *n.*, malum *n.*, molestia *f.*, labor *m.*; (*effort*) opera *f.*, negōtium *n.*; (*disturbance*) turba *f.*, tumultus *m.* take the — to operam dare ut. be worth the — operae pretium esse. *vt.* (*disturb*) turbāre: (*make uneasy*) sollicitāre, exagitāre; (*annoy*) incommodāre, molestiam exhibēre (*dat.*). — oneself about cūrāre, respicere. be -d with labōrāre ex.
troubler *n.* turbātor *m.*
troublesome *a.* molestus, incommodus, difficilis.
troublesomeness *n.* molestia *f*

troublous *a.* turbidus, turbulentus.
trough *n.* alveus *m.*
trounce *vt.* castīgāre.
troupe *n.* grex *f.*, caterva *f.*
trousered *a.* brācātus.
trousers *n.* brācae *f.pl.*
trow *vi.* opīnārī.
truant *a.* tardus. *n.* cessātor *m.* play — cessāre, nōn compārēre.
truce *n.* indutiae *f.pl.*
truck *n.* carrus *m.* **have no — with** nihil commercī habēre cum.
truckle *vi.* adsentārī.
truculence *n.* ferōcia *f.*, asperitās *f.*
truculent *a.* truculentus, ferōx. **-ly** *ad.* ferōciter.
trudge *vi.* rēpere. pedibus incēdere.
tru/e *a.* vērus; (*genuine*) germānus, vērus; (*loyal*) fīdus, fidēlis; (*exact*) rēctus, iūstus. **-ly** *ad.* rēvērā, profectō, vērē.
truism *n.* verbum trītum *n.*
trump up *vt.* ēmentīrī, cōnfingere. [*a.* vīlis.
trumpery *n.* nūgae *f.pl.*
trumpet *n.* tuba *f.*, būcina *f.*
trumpeter *n.* būcinātor *m.* tubicen *m.*
truncate *vt.* praecīdere.
truncheon *n.* fustis *m.*, scīpiō *m.*
trundle *vt.* volvere.
trunk *n.* truncus *m.*; (*elephant's*) manus *f.*; (*box*) cista *f.*
truss *n.* fascia *f.* *vt.* colligāre.
trust *n.* fidēs *f.*, fīdūcia *f.* **breach of —** mala fidēs. **held in —** fīdūciārius. **put — in** fidem habēre (*dat.*). *vt.* fīdere (*dat.*), crēdere (*dat.*); (*entrust*) committere, concrēdere.
trustee *n.* tūtor *m.*
trusteeship *n.* tūtēla *f.*
trustful *a.* crēdulus, fīdēns. **-ly** *ad.* fīdenter. [*f.*
trustiness *n.* fidēs *f.*, fidēlitās
trusting *a.* fīdēns. **-ly** *ad.* fīdenter.
trustworthiness *n.* fidēs *f.*, integritās *f.*
trustworth/y *a.* fīdus, certus; (*witness*) locuplēs; (*authority*) certus, bonus. **-ily** *ad.* fidēliter.
trust/y *a.* fīdus fidēlis. **-ily** *ad.* fidēliter.
truth *n.* vēritās *f.*, vērum *n.* **in —** rē vērā. [vērē.
truthful *a.* vērāx. **-ly** *ad.*
truthfulness *n.* fidēs *f.*
try *vt.* (*attempt*) cōnārī; (*test*) experīrī, temptāre; (*harass*) exercēre; (*judge*) iūdicāre, cognōscere. **— for** petere, quaerere.
trying *a.* molestus.
tub *n.* alveus *m.*, cūpa *f.*
tubby *a.* obēsus.
tube *n.* fistula *f.*
tufa *n.* tōfus *m.*
tuft *n.* crista *f.*
tug *vt.* trahere, tractāre.
tuition *n.* īnstitūtiō *f.*
tumble *vi.* concidere, corruere, prōlābī. *n.* cāsus *m.*
tumbledown *a.* ruīnōsus.
tumbler *n.* pōculum *n.*
tumid *a.* tumidus īnflātus.
tumour *n.* tūber *n.*
tumult *n.* tumultus *m.*, turba *f.*; (*fig.*) perturbātiō *f.*
tumultuous *a.* tumultuōsus, turbidus. **-ly** *ad.* tumultuōsē.
tumulus *n.* tumulus *m.*
tun *n.* dolium *n.*
tune *n.* modī *m.pl.*, carmen *n.* **keep in —** concentum servāre. **out of —** absonus, dissonus; (*strings*) incontentus. *vt.* (*strings*) intendere.
tuneful *a.* canōrus. **-ly** *ad.* numerōsē.
tunic *n.* tunica *f.* **wearing a —** tunicātus.
tunnel *n.* cunīculus *m.*
tunny *n.* thunnus *m.*
turban *n.* mitra *f.*, mitella *f.*
turbid *a.* turbidus.

turbot *n.* rhombus *m.*
turbulence *n.* tumultus *m.*
turbulent *a.* turbulentus, turbidus. **-ly** *ad.* turbulentē, turbidē.
turf *n.* caespes *m.*
turgid *a.* turgidus, īnflātus. **-ly** *ad.* īnflātē.
turgidity *n.* (*rhet.*) ampullae *f.pl.*
turmoil *n.* turba *f.*, tumultus *m.*; (*mind*) perturbātiō *f.*
turn *n.* (*motion*) conversiō *f.*; (*bend*) flexus *m.*, ānfrāctus *m.*; (*change*) commūtātiō *f.*, vicissitūdō *f.*; (*walk*) spatium *n.*; (*of mind*) adfectus *m.*; (*of language*) sententia *f.*, cōnfōrmātiō *f.* bad — iniūria *f.* good — beneficium *n.* — of the scale mōmentum *n.* take a — for the worse in pēiōrem partem vertī. in -s invicem, vicissim, alternī. in one's — locō, ōrdine. *vt.* vertere, convertere, flectere; (*change*) vertere, mūtāre; (*direct*) intendere, dīrigere; (*translate*) vertere, reddere; (*on a lathe*) tornāre. — the edge of retundere. — the head mentem exturbāre. — the laugh against rīsum convertere in (*acc.*). — the scale (*fig.*) mōmentum habēre. — the stomach nauseam facere. — to account ūtī (*abl.*), in rem suam convertere. *vi.* versārī, circumagī; (*change*) vertere, mūtārī; (*crisis*) pendēre; (*direction*) convertī; (*scale*) prōpendēre. — king's (queen's) evidence indicium profitērī. — against *vt.* aliēnāre ab. *vi.* dēscīscere ab. — aside *vt.* dēflectere, dēclīnāre. *vi.* dēvertere, sē dēclīnāre. — away *vt.* āvertere, dēpellere. *vi.* āversārī, discēdere. — back *vi.* revertī. — down *vt.* invertere; (*proposal*) rēicere. — into *vi.* vertere in (*acc.*), mūtārī in (*acc.*). — out *vt.* ēicere, expellere. *vi.* cadere, ēvenīre, ēvādere. — outside in excutere. — over *vt.* ēvertere; (*book*) ēvolvere; (*in mind*) volūtāre, agitāre. — round *vt.* circumagere. *vi.* convertī. — up retorquēre; (*earth*) versāre; (*nose*) corrūgāre. *vi.* adesse, intervenīre. — upside down invertere.
turncoat *n.* trānsfuga *m.*
turned *a.* well — teres. — up repandus.
turning *n.* flexus *m.*, ānfrāctus *m.*
turning-point *n.* discrīmen *n.*, mēta *f.*
turnip *n.* rāpum *n.*
turpitude *n.* turpitūdō *f.*
turquoise *n.* callais *f.* *a.* callainus.
turret *n.* turris *f.*
turreted *a.* turrītus.
turtle *n.* testūdō *f.* turn — invertī. — **dove** *n.* turtur *m.*
tusk *n.* dēns *m.*
tussle *n.* luctātiō *f.* *vi.* luctārī.
tutelage *n.* tūtēla *f.*
tutelary *a.* praeses.
tutor *n.* praeceptor *m.*, magister *m.* *vt.* docēre, praecipere (*dat.*).
tutorship *n.* tūtēla *f.*
twaddle *n.* nūgae *f.pl.*
twang *n.* sonus *m.* *vi.* increpāre.
tweak *vi.* vellicāre.
tweezers *n.* forceps *m.*, *f.*, volsella *f.*
twelfth *a.* duodecimus. *n.* duodecima pars *f.*, ūncia *f.* eleven -s deūnx *m.* five -s quīncūnx *m.* seven -s septūnx *m.*
twelve *num.* duodecim. — each duodēnī. — times duodeciēns.
twelvemonth *n.* annus *m.*
twentieth *a.* vīcēsimus. *n.* vīcēsima pars *f.*; (*tax*) vīcēsima *f.*

twenty *num.* vīgintī. — each vīcēnī. — times vīciēns.
twice *ad.* bis. — as much duplus, bis tantō. — a day bis diē, bis in diē.
twig *n.* virga *f.*, rāmulus *m.*
twilight *n.* (*morning*) dīlūculum *n.*; (*evening*) crepusculum *n.*
twin *a.* geminus. *n.* geminus [*m.*, gemina *f.*
twine *n.* resticula *f.* *vt.* nectere, implicāre, contexere. *vi.* sē implicāre. — round complectī.
twinge *n.* dolor *m.*
twinkle *vi.* micāre.
twirl *vt.* intorquēre, contorquēre. *vi.* circumagī.
twist *vt.* torquēre, intorquēre. *vi.* torquērī.
twit *vt.* obicere (*dat.*).
twitch *vt.* vellicāre. *vi.* micāre.
twitter *vi.* pīpilāre.
two *num.* duo. — each bīnī. — days biduum *n.* — years biennium *n.* — years old bīmus. — by — bīnī. — feet long bipedālis. in — parts bifāriam, bipartītō.
two-coloured *a.* bicolor.
two-edge *a.* anceps.
twofold *a.* duplex, anceps.
two-footed *a.* bipēs.
two-headed *a.* biceps.
two-horned *a.* bicornis.
two hundred *num.* ducentī. — each ducēnī. — times ducentiēns. **-th** *a.* ducentēsimus.
two-oared *a.* birēmis.
two-pronged *a.* bidēns, bifurcus.
two-way *a.* bivius.
type *n.* (*pattern*) exemplar *n.*; (*kind*) genus *n.*
typhoon *n.* turbō *m.*
typical *a.* proprius, solitus. **-ly** *ad.* dē mōre, ut mōs est.
typify *vt.* exprimere.
tyrannical, **tyrannous** *a.* superbus, crūdēlis. **-ly** *ad.* superbē, crūdēliter.
tyrannize *vi.* dominārī, rēgnāre.
tyranny *n.* dominātiō *f.*, [rēgnum *n.*
tyrant *n.* rēx *m.*, crūdēlis dominus *m.*; (*Greek*) tyrannus *m.*
tyro *n.* tīrō *m.*, rudis *m.*

U

ubiquitous *a.* omnibus locīs praesēns.
ubiquity *n.* ūniversa prae- [sentia *f.*
udder *n.* ūber *n.*
ugliness *n.* foeditās *f.*, dēfōrmitās *f.*, turpitūdō *f.*
ugly *a.* foedus, dēfōrmis, turpis.
ulcer *n.* ulcus *n.*, vomica *f.*
ulcerate *vi.* ulcerārī.
ulcerous *a.* ulcerōsus.
ulterior *a.* ulterior.
ultimate *a.* ultimus, extrēmus. **-ly** *ad.* tandem, ad ultimum.
umbrage *n.* offēnsiō *f.* take — at indignē ferre, patī.
umbrageous *a.* umbrōsus.
umbrella *n.* umbella *f.*
umpire *n.* arbiter *m.*, disceptātor *m.*
unabashed *a.* intrepidus, impudēns.
unabated *a.* integer.
unable *a.* impotēns. be — nōn posse, nequīre.
unacceptable *a.* ingrātus.
unaccompanied *a.* sōlus.
unaccomplished *a.* īnfectus, imperfectus; (*person*) indoctus.
unaccountab/le *a.* inexplicābilis. **-ly** *ad.* sine causā, repente.
unaccustomed *a.* insuētus, īnsolitus.
unacquainted *a.* ignārus (*gen.*), imperītus (*gen.*).
unadorned *a.* inōrnātus, incōmptus; (*speech*) nūdus, ēnucleātus.
unadulterated *a.* sincērus, integer.

unadvisedly *ad.* imprūdenter, incōnsultē.
unaffected *a.* simplex, candidus. **-ly** *ad.* simpliciter.
unaided *a.* sine auxiliō, nūdus.
unalienable *a.* proprius.
unalloyed *a.* pūrus.
unalterable *a.* immūtābilis.
unaltered *a.* immūtātus.
unambiguous *a.* apertus, certus.
unambitious *a.* humilis, modestus.
unanimity *n.* cōnsēnsiō *f.*, ūnanimitās *f.*
unanimous *a.* concors, ūnanimus. be — idem omnēs sentīre. **-ly** *ad.* ūnā vōce, omnium cōnsēnsū.
unanswerab/le *a.* necessārius. **-ly** *ad.* sine contrōversia.
unappreciative *a.* ingrātus.
unapproachable *a.* inaccessus; (*person*) difficilis.
unarmed *a.* inermis.
unasked *a.* ultrō, suā sponte.
unassailable *a.* inexpugnābilis. [columis.
unassailed *a.* intāctus, in-
unassuming *a.* modestus, dēmissus. — manners modestia *f.* **-ly** *ad.* modestē.
unattached *a.* liber.
unattempted *a.* intentātus. leave — praetermittere.
unattended *a.* sōlus, sine comitibus.
unattractive *a.* invenustus.
unauthentic *a.* incertō auctōre.
unavailing *a.* inūtilis, inānis.
unavenged *a.* inultus.
unavoidab/le *a.* necessārius. **-ly** *ad.* necessāriō.
unaware *a.* īnscius, ignārus. **-s** *ad.* inopīnātō, dē imprōvisō.
unbalanced *a.* turbātus.
unbar *vt.* reserāre.
unbearab/le *a.* intolerābilis, intolerandus. **-ly** *ad.* intoleranter.
unbeaten *a.* invictus.
unbecoming *a.* indecōrus, inhonestus. it is — dēdecet.
unbeknown *a.* ignōtus.
unbelief *n.* diffīdentia *f.*
unbelievab/le *a.* incrēdibilis. **-ly** *ad.* incrēdibiliter.
unbelieving *a.* incrēdulus.
unbend *vt.* remittere, laxāre. *vi.* animum remittere, aliquid dē sevēritāte remittere. **-ing** *a.* inexōrābilis, sevērus.
unbiassed *a.* integer, incorruptus, aequus.
unbidden *a.* ultrō, sponte.
unbind *vt.* solvere, resolvere.
unblemished *a.* pūrus, integer.
unblushing *a.* impudēns. **-ly** *ad.* impudenter.
unbolt *vt.* reserāre.
unborn *a.* nōndum nātus.
unbosom *vt.* patefacere, effundere.
unbound *a.* solūtus.
unbounded *a.* infīnītus, immēnsus.
unbridled *a.* infrēnātus; (*fig.*) effrēnātus, indomitus, impotēns.
unbroken *a.* integer; (*animal*) intractātus; (*friendship*) inviolātus; (*series*) perpetuus, continuus.
unburden *vt.* exonerāre. — oneself of aperīre, patefacere.
unburied *a.* inhumātus, īnsepultus.
unbusinesslike *a.* iners.
uncalled-for *a.* supervacāneus. [ōsus.
uncanny *a.* mīrus, mōnstru-
uncared-for *a.* neglectus.
unceasing *a.* perpetuus, adsiduus. **-ly** *ad.* perpetuō, adsiduē.
unceremonious *a.* agrestis, inurbānus. **-ly** *ad.* inurbānē.
uncertain *a.* incertus, dubius, anceps. be — dubitāre, pen-

dēre. **-ly** *ad.* incertē, dubitanter.
uncertainty *n.* incertum *n.*; (*state*) dubitātiō *f.*
unchangeable *a.* immūtābilis; (*person*) cōnstāns.
unchanged *a.* immūtātus, idem. remain — permanēre.
uncharitab/le *a.* inhūmānus, malignus. **-ly** *ad.* inhūmānē, malignē.
uncharitableness *n.* inhūmānitās *f.*
unchaste *a.* impudicus, libidinōsus. **-ly** *ad.* impudicē.
unchastity *n.* incestus *m.*, libīdō *f.*
unchecked *a.* līber, indomitus.
uncivil *a.* inurbānus, importūnus, inhūmānus. **-ly** *ad.* inurbānē.
uncivilized *a.* barbarus, incultus, ferus.
uncle *n.* (*paternal*) patruus *m.*; (*maternal*) avunculus *m.*
unclean *a.* immundus; (*fig.*) impūrus, obscēnus. **-ly** *ad.* impūrē.
uncleanness *n.* sordēs *f.pl.*; (*fig.*) impūritās *f.*, obscēnitās *f.*
unclose *vt.* aperīre.
unclothe *vt.* nūdāre, vestem dētrahere (*dat.*). **-d** *a.* nūdus.
unclouded *a.* serēnus.
uncoil *vt.* explicāre, ēvolvere.
uncomeliness *n.* dēfōrmitās *f.*
uncomely *a.* dēfōrmis, turpis.
uncomfortab/le *a.* incommodus, molestus. **-ly** *ad.* incommodē.
uncommitted *a.* vacuus.
uncommon *a.* rārus, insolitus, inūsitātus; (*eminent*) ēgregius, singulāris, eximius. **-ly** *ad.* rārō; ēgregiē, ūnicē.
uncommonness *n.* insolentia *f.*
uncommunicative *a.* tēctus, taciturnus.
uncomplaining *a.* patiēns.
uncompleted *a.* imperfectus.
uncompromising *a.* dūrus, rigidus.
unconcern *n.* sēcūritās *f.*
unconcerned *a.* sēcūrus, ōtiōsus. **-ly** *ad.* lentē.
uncondemned *a.* indemnātus.
unconditional *a.* absolūtus. **-ly** *ad.* nullā condiciōne.
uncongenial *a.* ingrātus.
unconnected *a.* sēparātus, disiūnctus; (*style*) dissolūtus.
unconquerable *a.* invictus.
unconquered *a.* invictus.
unconscionab/le *a.* improbus. **-ly** *ad.* improbē.
unconscious *a.* — of inscius (*gen.*), ignārus (*gen.*). become — sōpīrī, animō linquī.
unconsciousness *n.* sopor *m.*
unconsecrated *a.* profānus.
unconsidered *a.* neglectus.
unconstitutional *a.* illicitus. **-ly** *ad.* contrā lēgēs, contrā rem pūblicam.
uncontaminated *a.* pūrus, incorruptus, integer.
uncontrollab/le *a.* impotēns, effrēnātus. **-ly** *ad.* effrēnātē.
uncontrolled *a.* līber, solūtus.
unconventional *a.* insolitus, solūtus.
unconvicted *a.* indemnātus.
unconvincing *a.* incrēdibilis, nōn vērī similis.
uncooked *a.* crūdus.
uncorrupted *a.* incorruptus, integer.
uncouple *vt.* disiungere.
uncouth *a.* horridus, agrestis, inurbānus. **-ly** *ad.* inurbānē.
uncouthness *n.* inhūmānitās *f.*, rūsticitās *f.*
uncover *vt.* detegere, aperīre, nūdāre.
uncritical *a.* indoctus., crēdulus.
uncultivated *a.* incultus; (*fig.*) agrestis, rūsticus impolitus.
uncultured *a.* agrestis, rudis.
uncut *a.* intōnsus.
undamaged *a.* integer, inviolātus.

undaunted *a.* intrepidus, fortis.

undecayed *a.* incorruptus.

undeceive *vt.* errōrem tollere (*dat.*), errōrem ēripere (*dat.*).

undecided *a.* dubius, anceps; (*case*) integer.

undecked *a.* (*ship*) apertus.

undefended *a.* indēfēnsus, nūdus.

undefiled *a.* integer, incontāminātus.

undemonstrative *a.* taciturnus.

undeniab/le *a.* certus. **-ly** *ad.* sine dubiō.

undependable *a.* inconstāns, mōbilis.

under *ad.* īnfrā, subter. *pr.* sub (*abl.*), īnfrā (*acc.*); (*number*) intrā (*acc.*); (*motion*) sub (*acc.*). — **age** impūbēs. — **arms** in armīs. — **colour, pretext of** speciē (*gen.*) per speciem (*gen.*). — **my leadership** mē duce. — **the circumstances** cum haec ita sint. **labour** — labōrāre ex.

undercurrent *n.* **an — of** lātens.

underestimate *vt.* minōris aestimāre.

undergarment *n.* subūcula *f.*

undergo *vt.* subīre, patī, ferre.

underground *a.* subterrāneus. *ad.* sub terrā.

undergrowth *n.* virgulta *n.pl.*

underhand *a.* clandestinus, fūrtīvus. *ad.* clam, fūrtim.

underline *vt.* subscrībere.

underling *n.* minister *m.*, satelles *m.*, *f.*

undermine *vt.* subruere; (*fig.*) labefacere, labefactāre.

undermost *a.* īnfimus.

underneath *ad.* īnfrā. *pr.* sub (*abl.*), īnfrā (*acc.*); (*motion*) sub (*acc.*).

underprop *vt.* fulcīre.

underrate *vt.* obtrectāre, extenuāre, minōris aestimāre.

understand *vt.* intellegere, comprehendere; (*be told*) accipere, comperīre; (*in a sense*) interpretārī. — **Latin** Latīnē scīre.

understandable *a.* crēdibilis.

understanding *a.* sapiēns, perītus. *n.* intellegentia *f.*; (*faculty*) mēns *f.*, intellectus *m.*; (*agreement*) cōnsēnsus *m.*; (*condition*) condiciō *f.*

undertake *vt.* suscipere, sūmere, adīre ad; (*business*) condūcere; (*case*) agere, dēfendere.; (*promise*) recipere, spondēre.

undertaker *n.* dissignātor *m.*

undertaking *n.* inceptum *n.*, inceptiō *f.*

undervalue *vt.* minōris aestimāre.

underwood *n.* virgulta *n.pl.*

underworld *n.* īnferī *m.pl.*

undeserved *a.* immeritus, iniūstus. **-ly** *ad.* immeritō, indignē.

undeserving *a.* indignus.

undesigned *a.* fortuītus. **-ly** *ad.* fortuītō, temerē.

undesirable *a.* odiōsus, ingrātus.

undeterred *a.* immōtus.

undeveloped *a.* immātūrus.

undeviating *a.* dīrēctus.

undigested *a.* crūdus.

undignified *a.* levis, inhonestus.

undiminished *a.* integer.

undiscernible *a.* invīsus, obscūrus.

undisciplined *a.* lascīvus, immoderātus; (*mil.*) inexercitātus.

undiscovered *a.* ignōtus.

undisguised *a.* apertus. **-ly** *ad.* palam, apertē.

undismayed *a.* impavidus, intrepidus.

undisputed *a.* certus.

undistinguished *a.* ignōbilis, inglōrius.

undisturbed *a.* tranquillus, placidus.

undo *vt.* (*knot*) expedīre, resolvere; (*sewing*) dissuere; (*fig.*) īnfectum reddere. **-ne**

a. infectus; (*ruined*) perditus. be — perīre, disperīre. **hopelessly** — dēperditus.
undoing *n.* ruīna *f.*
undoubted *a.* certus. **-ly** *ad.* sine dubiō, plānē.
undress *vt.* exuere, vestem dētrahere (*dat.*). **-ed** *a.* nūdus.
undu/e *a.* nimius immoderātus, inīquus. **-ly** *ad.* nimis, plūs aequō.
undulate *vi.* fluctuāre.
undulation *n.* spīra *f.*
undutiful *a.* impius. **-ly** *ad.* impiē.
undutifulness *n.* impietās *f.*
undying *a.* immortālis, aeternus.
unearth *vt.* ēruere, dētegere.
unearthly *a.* mōnstruōsus, dīvīnus, hūmānō māior.
unemployment *n.* cessātiō *f.*
uneasiness *n.* sollicitūdō *f.*, perturbātiō *f.*
uneas/y *a.* sollicitus, anxius, inquiētus. **-ily** *ad.* aegrē.
uneducated *a.* illitterātus, indoctus, rudis. **be** — litterās nescīre.
unemployed *a.* ōtiōsus.
unencumbered *a.* expedītus, līber.
unending *a.* perpetuus, sempiternus.
unendowed *a.* indōtātus.
unendurable *a.* intolerandus, intolerābilis.
unenjoyable *a.* iniūcundus, molestus.
unenlightened *a.* rudis, inērudītus.
unenterprising *a.* iners.
unenviable *a.* nōn invidendus
unequal *a.* impār, dispār. **-ly** *ad.* inaequāliter, inīquē.
unequalled *a.* ūnicus, singulāris.
unequivocal *a.* apertus, plānus. [certē.
unerring *a.* certus. **-ly** *ad.*
unessential *a.* adventīcius, uspervacāneus.
uneven *a.* impār; (*surface*) asper inīquus, inaequābilis. **-ly** *ad.* inīquē, inaequāliter.
unevenness *n.* inīquitās *f.*, asperitās *f.* [cognitus.
unexamined *a.* (*case*) in-
unexampled *a.* inaudītus, ūnicus, singulāris
unexceptionable *a.* ēmendātus; (*authority*) certissimus.
unexpected *a.* imprōvīsus, inopīnātus, īnspērātus. **-ly** *ad.* dē imprōvīsō, ex īnspērātō, inopīnātō, necopīnātō.
unexplored *a.* inexplōrātus.
unfading *a.* perennis, vīvus.
unfailing *a.* perennis, certus, perpetuus. **-ly** *ad.* semper.
unfair *a.* inīquus, iniūstus. **-ly** *ad.* inīquē, iniūstē.
unfairness *n.* inīquitās *f.*, iniūstitia *f.*
unfaithful *a.* īnfidēlis, īnfīdus. perfidus. **-ly** *ad.* īnfidēliter.
unfaithfulness *n.* īnfidēlitās *f.*
unfamiliar *a.* novus, ignōtus, īnsolēns; (*sight*) invīsitātus.
unfamiliarity *n.* īnsolentia *f.*
unfashionable *a.* obsolētus.
unfasten *vt.* solvere, refīgere.
unfathomable *a.* īnfīnītus, profundus.
unfavourab/le *a.* inīquus, adversus, importūnus. **-ly** *ad.* inīquē, male. **be** — **disposed** āversō animō esse.
unfed *a.* iēiūnus.
unfeeling *a.* dūrus, crūdēlis, ferreus. **-ly** *ad.* crūdēliter.
unfeigned *a.* sincērus, vērus, simplex. **-ly** *ad.* sincērē, vērē.
unfilial *a.* impius.
unfinished *a.* īnfectus, imperfectus. [aliēnus.
unfit *a.* inūtilis, incommodus,
unfix *vt.* refīgere. [firmus.
unflinching *a.* impavidus,
unfold *vt.* explicāre, ēvolvere; (*story*) expōnere, ēnārrāre.
unfolding *n.* explicātiō *f.*
unforeseen *a.* imprōvīsus.

unforgettable *a.* memorābilis.
unforgiving *a.* implācābilis.
unformed *a.* īnfōrmis.
unfortified *a.* immūnītus, nūdus.
unfortunate *a.* īnfēlīx, īnfortūnātus. **-ly** *ad* īnfēlīciter, male. — you did not come male accidit quod nōn vēnistī.
unfounded *a.* inānis, vānus.
unfrequented *a.* dēsertus.
unfriendliness *n.* inimīcitia *f.*
unfriendly *a.* inimīcus, malevolus. in an — manner inimīcē.
unfruitful *a.* sterilis; (*fig.*) inānis, vānus.
unfruitfulness *n.* sterilitās *f.*
unfulfilled *a.* īnfectus, inritus.
unfurl *vt.* explicāre, pandere.
unfurnished *a.* nūdus.
ungainly *a.* agrestis, rūsticus.
ungallant *a.* inurbānus, parum cōmis.
ungenerous *a.* illīberālis. — conduct illīberālitās *f.*
ungentlemanly *a.* illīberālis.
ungirt *a.* discinctus.
ungodliness *n.* impietās *f.*
ungodly *a.* impius.
ungovernable *a.* impotēns, indomitus.
ungovernableness *n.* impotentia *f*
ungraceful *a.* inconcinnus, inēlegāns. **-ly** *ad.* inēleganter
ungracious *a.* inhūmānus, petulāns, importūnus. **-ly** *ad.* acerbē.
ungrammatical *a.* barbarus. be — soloecismum facere.
ungrateful *a.* ingrātus.
ungrudging *a.* largus, nōn invītus. **-ly** *ad.* sine invidiā.
unguarded *a.* intūtus; (*word*) incautus, incōnsultus. **-ly** *ad.* temerē, incōnsultē.
unguent *n.* unguentum *n.*
unhallowed *a.* profānus, impius.
unhand *vt.* mittere.
unhandy *a.* inhabilis.
unhappiness *n.* miseria *f.*, tristitia *f.*, maestitia *f.*
unhapp/y *a.* īnfēlīx, miser, tristis. **-ily** *ad.* īnfēlīciter, miserē.
unharmed *a.* incolumis, integer, salvus.
unharness *vt.* disiungere.
unhealthiness *n.* valētūdō *f.*; (*climate*) gravitās *f.*
unhealthy *a.* invalidus, aeger; (*climate*) gravis, pestilens.
unheard *a.* inaudītus; (*law*) indictā causā. — of inaudītus.
unheeded *a.* neglectus.
unheeding *a.* immemor, sēcūrus.
unhelpful *a.* difficilis, invītus.
unhesitating *a.* audāx, prōmptus. **-ly** *ad.* sine dubitātiōne.
unhewn *a.* rudis.
unhindered *a.* expedītus.
unhinged *a.* mente captus.
unhistorical *a.* fictus, commentīcius.
unholiness *n.* impietās *f.*
unholy *a.* impius.
unhonoured *a.* inhonōrātus.
unhoped-for *a.* īnspērātus.
unhorse *vt.* excutere, equō dēicere.
unhurt *a.* integer, incolumis.
unicorn *n.* monocerōs *m.*
uniform *a.* aequābilis aequālis. *n.* īnsignia *n.pl.*; (*mil.*) sagum *n.* in — sagātus. put on — saga sūmere. **-ly** *ad.* aequābiliter, ūnō tenōre.
uniformity *n.* aequābilitās *f.*, cōnstantia *f.*
unify *vt.* coniungere.
unimaginative *a.* hebes, stolidus.
unimpaired *a.* integer, incolumis, illībātus.
unimpeachable *a.* (*character*) integer; (*style*) ēmendātus.
unimportant *a.* levis, nullīus mōmentī.
uninformed *a.* indoctus, ignārus.

uninhabitable *a.* inhabitābilis.
uninhabited *a.* dēsertus.
uninitiated *a.* profānus; (*fig.*) rudis.
uninjured *a.* integer, incolumis.
unintelligent *a.* insipiēns, tardus, excors.
unintelligib/le *a.* obscūrus. **-ly** *ad.* obscūrē.
unintentionally *ad.* imprūdēns, temerē.
uninteresting *a.* frīgidus, āridus.
uninterrupted *a.* continuus, perpetuus. **-ly** *ad.* continenter, sine ullā intermissiōne.
uninvited *a.* invocātus. — guest umbra *f.*
uninviting *a.* iniūcundus, invenustus.
union *n.* coniūnctiō *f.*; (*social*) cōnsociātiō *f.*, societās *f.*; (*pol.*) foederātae cīvitātēs *f.pl.*; (*agreement*) concordia *f.*, cōnsēnsus *m.*; (*marriage*) coniugium *n.*
unique *a.* ūnicus, ēgregius, singulāris.
unison *n.* concentus *m.*; (*fig.*) concordia *f.*, cōnsēnsus *m.*
unit *n.* ūniō *f.*
unite *vt.* coniungere, cōnsociāre, cōpulāre. *vi.* coīre; cōnsentīre, cōnspīrāre; (*rivers*) cōnfluere.
unity *n.* (*concord*) concordia *f.*, cōnsēnsus *m.*
universal *a.* ūniversus, commūnis. **-ly** *ad.* ūniversus, omnis; (*place*) ubīque.
universe *n.* mundus *m.*, rērum nātūra *f.*
university *n.* acadēmia *f.*
unjust *a.* iniūstus, inīquus. **-ly** *ad.* iniūstē, iniūriā.
unjustifiable *a.* indignus, inexcūsābilis.
unkempt *a.* horridus.
unkind *a.* inhūmānus, inīquus. **-ly** *ad.* inhūmānē, asperē.
unkindness *n.* inhūmānitās *f.*
unknowingly *ad.* imprūdēns, īnscius.
unknown *a.* ignōtus, incognitus; (*fame*) obscūrus.
unlawful *a.* vetitus, iniūriōsus. **-ly** *ad.* iniūriōsē, iniūriā.
unlearn *vt.* dēdiscere.
unlearned *a.* indoctus, inēruditus.
unless *conj.* nisi.
unlettered *a.* illitterātus.
unlike *a.* dissimilis, dispār.
unlikely *a.* nōn vērisimilis.
unlimited *a.* īnfīnītus, immēnsus.
unload *vt.* exonerāre, deonerāre; (*from ship*) expōnere.
unlock *vt.* reserāre, reclūdere.
unlooked-for *a.* īnspērātus, inexpectātus.
unloose *vt.* solvere, exsolvere.
unlovely *a.* invenustus.
unluck/y *a.* īnfēlīx, īnfortūnātus; (*day*) āter. **-ily** *ad.* īnfēlīciter.
unmake *vt.* īnfectum reddere.
unman *vt.* mollīre, frangere, dēbilitāre.
unmanageable *a.* inhabilis.
unmanly *a.* mollis, ēnervātus, muliebris.
unmannerliness *n.* importūnitās *f.*, inhūmānitās *f.*
unmannerly *a.* importūnus, inhūmānus.
unmarried *a.* (*man*) caelebs; (*woman*) vidua.
unmask *vt.* nūdāre, dētegere.
unmatched *a.* ūnicus, singulāris.
unmeaning *a.* inānis.
unmeasured *a.* īnfīnītus, immoderātus.
unmeet *a.* parum idōneus.
unmelodious *a.* absonus, absurdus.
unmentionable *a.* īnfandus.
unmentioned *a.* indictus. leave — ōmittere.
unmerciful *a.* immisericors, inclēmēns. **-ly** *ad.* inclēmenter.

unmerited *a.* immeritus, indignus.
unmindful *a.* immemor.
unmistakab/le *a.* certus, manifestus. **–ly** *ad.* sine dubiō, certē.
unmitigated *a.* merus.
unmixed *a.* pūrus.
unmolested *a.* intāctus.
unmoor *vt.* solvere.
unmoved *a.* immōtus.
unmusical *a.* absonus, absurdus.
unmutilated *a.* integer.
unnatural *a.* (*event*) mōnstruōsus; (*feelings*) impius, inhūmānus; (*style*) arcessītus, pūtidus. **–ly** *ad.* contrā nātūram; impiē, inhūmānē; pūtidē. [ābilis.
unnavigable *a.* innāvig-
unnecessar/y *a.* inūtilis, supervacāneus. **–ily** *ad.* nimis. [gere.
unnerve *vt.* dēbilitāre, fran-
unnoticed *a.* be — latēre, fallere.
unnumbered *a.* innumerus.
unobjectionable *a.* honestus, culpae expers.
unobservant *a.* tardus.
unobserved *a.* be — latēre, fallere. [pūrus.
unobstructed *a.* apertus,
unobtrusive *a.* verēcundus. be — fallere.
unobtrusiveness *n.* verēcundia *f.*
unoccupied *a.* vacuus, ōtiōsus.
unoffending *a.* innocēns.
unofficial *a.* prīvātus.
unorthodox *a.* abnōrmis.
unostentatious *a.* modestus, verēcundus. **–ly** *ad.* nullā iactātiōne.
unpaid *a.* (*services*) grātuītus; (*money*) dēbitus.
unpalatable *a.* amārus; (*fig.*) iniūcundus, īnsuāvis.
unparalleled *a.* ūnicus, inaudītus.
unpardonable *a.* inexcūsābilis.
unpatriotic *a.* impius.
unpitying *a.* immisericors, ferreus.
unpleasant *a.* iniūcundus, ingrātus, īnsuāvis, gravis, molestus. **–ly** *ad.* iniūcundē, ingrātē, graviter.
unpleasantness *n.* iniūcunditās *f.*, molestia *f.*
unpleasing *a.* ingrātus, invenustus.
unploughed *a.* inarātus.
unpoetical *a.* pedester.
unpolished *a.* impolītus; (*person*) incultus, agrestis, inurbānus; (*style*) inconditus, rudis.
unpopular *a.* invidiōsus, invīsus. [odium *n.*
unpopularity *n.* invidia *f.*,
unpractised *a.* inexercitātus, imperītus.
unprecedented *a.* īnsolēns, novus, inaudītus.
unprejudiced *a.* integer, aequus.
unpremeditated *a.* repentīnus, subitus.
unprepared *a.* imparātus.
unprepossessing *a.* invenustus, illepidus.
unpretentious *a.* modestus, verēcundus.
unprincipled *a.* improbus, levis, prāvus. [sterilis.
unproductive *a.* īnfēcundus,
unprofitab/le *a.* inūtilis, vānus. **–ly** *ad.* frustrā, ab rē.
unpropitious *a.* īnfēlīx, adversus. **–ly** *ad.* malīs ōminibus.
unprotected *a.* indēfēnsus, intūtus, nūdus.
unprovoked *a.* ultrō (*ad.*).
unpunished *a.* impūnītus. *ad.* impūne.
unqualified *a.* nōn idōneus; (*unrestricted*) absolūtus.
unquestionab/le *a.* certus. **–ly** *ad.* facile, certē.
unquestioning *a.* crēdulus.

unravel *vt.* retexere; (*fig.*) ēnōdāre, explicāre.
unready *a.* imparātus.
unreal *a.* falsus, vānus.
unreality *n.* vānitās *f.*
unreasonab/le *a.* iniquus, importūnus. **–ly** *ad.* iniquē.
unreasonableness *n.* iniquitās *f.*
unreasoning *a.* stolidus, temerārius.
unreclaimed *a.* (*land*) incultus.
unrefined *a.* impolītus, inurbānus, rudis.
unregistered *a.* incēnsus.
unrelated *a.* aliēnus.
unrelenting *a.* implācābilis, inexōrābilis.
unreliab/le *a.* incertus, levis. **–ly** *ad.* leviter.
unrelieved *a.* perpetuus, adsiduus.
unremitting *a.* adsiduus.
unrequited *a.* inultus, inānis.
unreservedly *ad.* apertē, sine ullā exceptiōne.
unresponsive *a.* hebes.
unrest *n.* inquiēs *f.*, sollicitūdō *f.*
unrestrained *a.* līber, impotēns, effrēnātus, immoderātus.
unrestricted *a.* līber, absolūtus.
unrevenged *a.* inultus.
unrewarded *a.* inhonōrātus.
unrewarding *a.* ingrātus, vānus.
unrighteous *a.* iniūstus, impius. **–ly** *ad.* iniūstē, impiē.
unrighteousness *n.* impietās *f.*
unripe *a.* immātūrus, crūdus.
unrivalled *a.* ēgregius, singulāris, ūnicus.
unroll *vt.* ēvolvere, explicāre.
unromantic *a.* pedester.
unruffled *a.* immōtus, tranquillus.
unruliness *n.* licentia *f.*, impotentia *f.*
unruly *a.* effrēnātus, impotēns, immoderātus.
unsafe *a.* perīculōsus, dubius; (*structure*) īnstābilis.
unsaid *a.* indictus.
unsatisfactory *a.* parum idōneus, malus. **–ily** *ad.* nōn ex sententiā, male.
unsatisfied *a.* parum contenus.
unsavoury *a.* insuāvis, taeter.
unscathed *a.* incolumis, integer.
unschooled *a.* indoctus, inēruditus.
unscrupulous *a.* improbus, impudēns. **–ly** *ad.* improbē, impudenter.
unscrupulousness *n.* improbitās *f.*, impudentia *f.*
unseal *vt.* resignāre, solvere.
unseasonab/le *a.* intempestīvus, importūnus. **–ly** *ad.* intempestīvē, importūnē.
unseasonableness *n.* incommoditās *f.*
unseasoned *a.* (*food*) nōn conditus: (*wood*) viridis.
unseat *vt.* (*rider*) excutere.
unseaworthy *a.* īnfirmus.
unseeing *a.* caecus.
unseemly *a.* indecōrus.
unseen *a.* invīsus; (*ever before*) invīsitātus.
unselfish *a.* innocēns, probus, līberālis. **–ly** *ad.* līberāliter.
unselfishness *n.* innocentia *f.*, līberālitās *f.*
unserviceable *a.* inūtilis.
unsettle *vt.* ad incertum revocāre, turbāre, sollicitāre.
unsettled *a.* incertus, dubius; (*mind*) sollicitus, suspēnsus; (*times*) turbidus.
unsew *vt.* dissuere.
unshackle *vt.* expedīre, solvere.
unshaken *a.* immōtus, firmus, stabilis.
unshapely *a.* dēfōrmis.
unshaven *a.* intōnsus.
unsheathe *vt.* dēstringere, stringere.
unshod *a.* nūdīs pedibus.
unshorn *a.* intōnsus.

unsightliness *n.* dēfōrmitās *f.*, turpitūdō *f.*
unsightly *a.* foedus, dēfōrmis.
unskilful *a.* indoctus, īnscītus, incallidus. **-ly** *ad.* indoctē, īnscītē, incallidē.
unskilfulness *n.* īnscītia *f.*, imperītia *f.*
unskilled *a.* imperītus, indoctus.
unslaked *a.* (*lime*) vīvus; (*thirst*) inexplētus.
unsociable *a.* īnsociābilis, difficilis.
unsoiled *a.* integer, pūrus.
unsolicited *a.* voluntārius. *ad.* ultrō.
unsophisticated *a.* simplex, ingenuus.
unsound *a.* īnfirmus; (*mind*) īnsānus; (*opinion*) falsus, perversus.
unsoundness *n.* īnfirmitās *f.*; īnsānitās *f.*; prāvitās *f.*
unsparing *a.* inclēmēns, immisericors; (*lavish*) prōdigus. **-ly** *ad.* inclēmenter; prōdigē.
unspeakab/le *a.* īnfandus, incrēdibilis. **-ly** *ad.* incrēdibiliter.
unspoilt *a.* integer.
unspoken *a.* indictus, tacitus.
unspotted *a.* integer, pūrus.
unstable *a.* instabilis; (*fig.*) incōnstāns, levis.
unstained *a.* pūrus, incorruptus, integer.
unstatesmanlike *a.* illīberālis.
unsteadiness *n.* (*fig.*) incōnstantia *f.*
unstead/y *a.* īnstabilis; (*fig.*) incōnstāns. **-ily** *ad.* incōnstanter. walk — titubāre.
unstitch *vt.* dissuere.
unstring *vt.* retendere.
unstudied *a.* simplex.
unsubdued *a.* invictus.
unsubstantial *a.* levis, inānis.
unsuccessful *a.* īnfēlīx; (*effort*) inritus. be — offendere. I am — mihi nōn succēdit. **-ly** *ad.* īnfēlīciter. rē īnfectā.
unsuitab/le *a.* incommodus, aliēnus, importūnus. it is — dēdecet. **-ly** *ad.* incommodē, ineptē.
unsuitableness *n.* incommoditās *f.*
unsuited *a.* parum idōneus.
unsullied *a.* pūrus, incorruptus.
unsure *a.* incertus, dubius.
unsurpassable *a.* inexsuperābilis.
unsurpassed *a.* ūnicus, singulāris.
unsuspected *a.* latēns, nōn suspectus. be — latēre, in suspiciōnem nōn venīre.
unsuspecting *a.* imprōvidus, imprūdēns.
unsuspicious *a.* nōn suspicāx, crēdulus.
unswerving *a.* cōnstāns.
unsworn *a.* iniūrātus.
unsymmetrical *a.* inaequālis.
untainted *a.* incorruptus, integer.
untamable *a.* indomitus.
untamed *a.* indomitus, ferus.
untaught *a.* indoctus, rudis.
unteach *vt.* dēdocēre.
unteachable *a.* indocilis.
untenable *a.* inānis, īnfirmus.
unthankful *a.* ingrātus. **-ly** *ad.* ingrātē.
unthankfulness *n.* ingrātus animus *m.*
unthinkable *a.* incrēdibilis.
unthinking *a.* incōnsīderātus, imprōvidus.
unthrift/y *a.* prōdigus, profūsus. **-ily** *ad.* prōdigē.
untidiness *n.* neglegentia *f.*
untid/y *a.* neglegēns, inconcinnus, squālidus. **-ily** *ad.* neglegenter.
untie *vt.* solvere.
until *conj.* dum, dōnec. *pr.* usque ad (*acc.*), in (*acc.*). — now adhūc.
untilled *a.* incultus.
untimely *a.* intempestīvus, immātūrus, importūnus.

untiring *a.* impiger; (*effort*) adsiduus.
unto *pr.* ad (*acc*), in (*acc.*).
untold *a.* innumerus.
untouched *a.* intāctus, integer.
untoward *a.* adversus, malus.
untrained *a.* inexercitātus, imperītus, rudis.
untried *a.* intemptātus, inexpertus; (*trial*) incognitus.
untrodden *a.* āvius.
untroubled *a.* tranquillus, placidus, quiētus; (*mind*) sēcūrus.
untrue *a.* falsus, fictus; (*disloyal*) īnfīdus, īnfidēlis.
untrustworthy *a.* infīdus, mōbilis. [falsum *n.*
untruth *n.* mendācium *n.*,
untruthful *a.* mendāx, falsus. **–ly** *ad.* falsō, falsē.
untuneful *a.* absonus.
unturned *a.* leave no stone — nihil intemptātum relinquere, omnia experīrī.
untutored *a.* indoctus, incultus.
unused *a.* (*person*) īnsuētus, īnsolitus; (*thing*) integer.
unusual *a.* īnsolitus, inūsitātus, īnsolēns, novus. **–ly** *ad.* īnsolenter, praeter cōnsuētūdinem.
unusualness *n.* īnsolentia *f.*, novitās *f.*
unutterable *a.* īnfandus, inēnārrābilis.
unvarnished *a.* (*fig.*) simplex, nūdus. [facere.
unveil *vt.* (*fig.*) aperīre, pate-
unversed *a.* ignārus (*gen.*), imperītus (*gen.*).
unwanted *a.* supervacāneus.
unwariness *n.* imprūdentia *f.*
unwarlike *a.* imbellis.
unwarrantab/le *a.* inīquus, iniūstus. **–ly** *ad.* iniūriā.
unwar/y *a.* imprūdēns, incautus, incōnsultus. **–ily** *ad.* imprūdenter, incautē, incōnsultē.
unwavering *a.* stabilis, immōtus.
unwearied, unwearying *a.* indēfessus, adsiduus.
unweave *vt.* retexere.
unwedded *a.* (*man*) caelebs; (*woman*) vidua.
unwelcome *a.* ingrātus.
unwell *a.* aeger, aegrōtus.
unwept *a.* indēflētus.
unwholesome *a.* pestilēns, gravis.
unwieldy *a.* inhabilis.
unwilling *a.* invītus. be — nolle. **–ly** *ad.* invītus.
unwind *vt.* ēvolvere, retexere.
unwise *a.* stultus, īnsipiēns, imprūdēns. **–ly** *ad.* īnsipienter, imprūdenter.
unwittingly *ad.* imprūdēns, īnsciēns.
unwonted *a.* īnsolitus, inūsitātus.
unworthiness *n.* indignitās *f.*
unworth/y *a.* indignus. **–ily** *ad.* indignē.
unwounded *a.* intāctus, integer.
unwrap *vt.* ēvolvere, explicāre.
unwritten *a.* nōn scrīptus. — law mōs *m.*
unwrought *a.* īnfectus, rudis.
unyielding *a.* dūrus, firmus, inexōrābilis.
unyoke *vt.* disiungere.
up *ad.* sūrsum. — and down sūrsum deōrsum. — to usque ad (*acc.*), tenus (*abl.*, *after noun*). — stream adversō flūmine. bring — subvehere; (*child*) ēducāre. climb — ēscendere. come — to aequāre. lift — ērigere, sublevāre. from childhood — ā puerō. it is all — with āctum est dē. well — in gnārus (*gen.*), perītus (*gen*). what is he — to? quid struit? *pr.* (*motion*) in (*acc.*). *n.* -s and downs (*fig.*) vicissitūdinēs *f.pl.*).
upbraid *vt.* exprobrāre (*dat. pers.*, *acc. charge*), obicere

(*dat.* & *acc.*), increpāre, castigāre.
upbringing *n.* ēducātiō *f.*
upheaval *n.* ēversiō *f.*
upheave *vt.* ēvertere.
uphill *a.* acclīvis. *ad.* adversō colle, in adversum collem.
uphold *vt.* sustinēre, tuērī, servāre.
upholstery *n.* supellex *f.*
upkeep *n.* impēnsa *f.*
upland *a.* montānus.
uplift *vt.* extollere, sublevāre.
upon *p.* in (*abl.*), super (*abl.*); (*motion*) in (*acc.*), super (*acc.*); (*dependence*) ex (*abl.*). — this quō factō.
upper *a.* superior. gain the — hand superāre, vincere.
uppermost *a.* suprēmus, summus.
uppish *a.* superbus.
upright *a.* rēctus, ērēctus; (*character*) integer, probus, honestus. **-ly** *ad.* rēctē; integrē.
uprightness *n.* integritās *f.*
uproar *n.* tumultus *m.*
uproarious *a.* tumultuōsus. **-ly** *ad.* tumultuōsē.
uproot *vt.* ērādīcāre, exstirpāre, ēruere.
upset *vt.* ēvertere, invertere. — the apple-cart plaustrum percellere. *a.* (*fig.*) perturbātus.
upshot *n.* ēventus *m.*
upside-down *ad.* turn — ēvertere, invertere; (*fig.*) miscēre.
upstart *n.* novus homō *m.* *a.* repentīnus.
upward(s) *ad.* sūrsum. — of (*number*) amplius.
urban *a.* urbānus, oppidānus.
urbane *a.* urbānus, cōmis. **-ly** *ad.* urbānē, cōmiter.
urbanity *n.* urbānitās *f.*
urchin *n.* (*boy*) puerulus *m.*; (*animal*) echīnus *m.*
urge *vt.* urgēre, impellere; (*speech*) hortārī, incitāre; (*advice*) suādēre; (*request*) sollicitāre. *n.* impulsus *m.*; dēsīderium *n.*
urgency *n.* necessitās *f.*
urgent *a.* praesēns, gravis. be — instāre. **-ly** *ad.* graviter.
urn *n.* urna *f.*
usage *n.* mōs *m.*, īnstitūtum *n.*, ūsus *m.*
use *n.* ūsus *m.*; (*custom*) mōs *m.*, cōnsuētūdō *f.* be of — ūsuī esse, prōdesse, condūcere. out of — dēsuētus. go out of — exolēscere. in common — ūsitātus. it's no — nīl agis, nīl agimus. *vt.* ūtī (*abl.*); (*improperly*) abūtī; (*for a purpose*) adhibēre; (*word*) ūsurpāre. — up cōnsūmere, exhaurīre. -d to adsuētus (*dat.*). I -d to do faciēbam.
useful *a.* ūtilis. be — ūsuī esse. **-ly** *ad.* ūtiliter.
usefulness *n.* ūtilitās *f.*
useless *a.* inūtilis; (*thing*) inānis, inritus. be — nihil valēre. **-ly** *ad.* inūtiliter, frustrā.
uselessness *n.* inānitās *f.*
usher *n.* (*court*) appāritor *m.*; (*theatre*) dēsignātor *m.* *vt.* — in indūcere, intrōdūcere.
usual *a.* ūsitātus, solitus. as — ut adsolet, ut fert cōnsuētūdō, ex cōnsuētūdine. out of the — īnsolitus, extrā ōrdinem. **-ly** *ad.* ferē, plērumque. he — comes venīre solet.
usufruct *n.* ūsus et fructus *m.*
usurer *n.* faenerātor *m.*
usurp *vt.* occupāre, invādere in (*acc.*).
usurpation *n.* occupātō *f.*
usury *n.* faenerātiō *f.*, ūsūra *f.* practise — faenerārī.
utensil *n.* īnstrūmentum *n.*, vās *n.*
utility *n.* ūtilitās *f.*, commodum *n.*
utilize *vt.* ūtī (*abl.*); (*for a purpose*) adhibēre.
utmost *a.* extrēmus, summus. at the — summum. do one's

— omnibus viribus contendere.
utter *a.* tōtus, extrēmus, summus. **-ly** *ad.* funditus, omninō.
utter *vt.* ēmittere, ēdere, ēloqui prōnūntiāre.
utterance *n.* dictum *n.*; (*process*) prōnūntiātiō *f.*
uttermost *a.* extrēmus, ultimus.

V

vacancy *n.* inānitās *f.*; (*office*) vacuitās *f.* there is a — locus vacat. elect to fill a — sufficere.
vacant *a.* inānis, vacuus. be — vacāre.
vacate *vt.* vacuum facere.
vacation *n.* fēriae *f.pl.*
vacillate *vi.* vacillāre, dubitāre.
vacillation *n.* dubitātiō *f.*
vacuity *n.* inānitās *f.*
vacuous *a.* vacuus.
vacuum *n.* ināne *n.*
vagabond *n.* grassātor *m.* *a.* vagus.
vagary *n.* libīdō *f.*
vagrancy *n.* errātiō *f.*
vagrant *n.* grassātor *m.*, vagus *m.*
vague *a.* incertus, dubius. **-ly** *ad.* incertē.
vain *n.* vānus, inānis, inritus; (*person*) glōriōsus. in — frustrā. **-ly** *ad.* frustrā, nēquiquam.
vainglorious *a.* glōriōsus.
vainglory *n.* glōria *f.*, iactantia *f.*
vale *n.* vallis *f.*
valet *n.* cubiculārius *m.*
valiant *a.* fortis, ācer. **-ly** *ad.* fortiter, ācriter.
valid *a.* ratus; (*argument*) gravis, firmus.
validity *n.* vis *f.*, auctōritās *f.*
valley *n.* vallis *f.*
valorous *a.* fortis.
valour *n.* virtūs *f.*
valuable *a.* pretiōsus.
valuation *n.* aestimātiō *f.*
value *n.* pretium *n.*; (*fig.*) vis *f.*, honor *m.* *vt.* aestimāre; (*esteem*) dīligere. — highly māgni aestimāre. — little parvī aestimāre, parvī facere.
valueless *a.* vīlis, minimī pretī.
valuer *n.* aestimātor *m.*
van *n.* (*in battle*) prīma aciēs *f.*; (*on march*) prīmum agmen *n.*
vanish *vi.* diffugere, ēvānēscere, dīlābī.
vanity *n.* (*unreality*) vānitās *f.*; (*conceit*) glōria *f.*
vanquish *vt.* vincere, superāre, dēvincere.
vanquisher *n.* victor *m.*
vantage *n.* (*ground*) locus superior *m.*
vapid *a.* vapidus, insulsus. **-ly** *ad.* insulsē.
vaporous *a.* nebulōsus.
vapour *n.* vapor *m.*, nebula *f.*; (*from earth*) exhālātiō *f.*
variable *a.* varius, mūtābilis.
variableness *n.* mūtābilitās *f.*, incōnstantia *f.*
variance *n.* discordia *f.*, dissēnsiō *f.*, discrepantia *f.* at — discors. be at — dissidēre, inter sē discrepāre. set at — aliēnāre.
variant *a.* varius.
variation *n.* varietās *f.*, vicissitūdō *f.*
variegate *vt.* variāre. **-d** *a.* varius.
variety *n.* varietās *f.*; (*number*) multitūdō *f.*; (*kind*) genus *n.* a — of diversī.
various *a.* varius, diversus. **-ly** *ad.* variē.
varlet *n.* verberō *m.*
varnish *n.* pigmentum *n.*; (*fig.*) fūcus *m.* **-ed** *a.* (*fig.*) fūcātus.
vary *vt.* variāre, mūtāre; (*decorate*) distinguere. *vi.* mūtārī.

vase *n.* vās *n.*
vassal *n.* ambāctus *m.*; (*fig.*) cliēns *m.*
vast *a.* vastus, immānis, ingēns, immēnsus. **-ly** *ad.* valdē.
vastness *n.* māgnitūdō *f.*, immēnsitās *f.*
vat *n.* cūpa *f.*
vault *n.* (*arch*) fornix *f.*; (*jump*) saltus *m.* *vi.* salīre.
vaulted *a.* fornicātus.
vaunt *vt.* iactāre, ostentāre. *vi.* sē iactāre, glōriārī.
vaunting *n.* ostentātiō *f.*, glōria *f.* *a.* glōriōsus.
veal *n.* vitulīna *f.*
vedette *n.* excursor *m.*
veer *vi.* sē vertere, flectī.
vegetable *n.* holus *n.*
vehemence *n.* vis *f.*, violentia *f.*; (*passion*) ārdor *m.*, impetus *m.*
vehement *a.* vehemēns, violentus, ācer. **-ly** *ad.* vehementer, ācriter.
vehicle *n.* vehiculum *n.*
veil *n.* rīca *f.*; (*bridal*) flammeum *n.*; (*fig.*) integumentum *n.* *vt.* vēlāre, tegere.
vein *n.* vēna *f.*
vellum *n.* membrāna *f.*
velocity *n.* celeritās *f.*, vēlōcitās *f.*
venal *a.* vēnālis.
vend *vt.* vēndere.
vendor *n.* caupō *m.*
vendetta *n.* simultās *f.*
veneer *n.* (*fig.*) speciēs *f.*, fūcus *m.*
venerable *a.* gravis, augustus.
venerate *vt.* colere, venerārī.
veneration *n.* venerātiō *f.*, cultus *m.*
venerator *n.* cultor *m.*
vengenace *n.* ultiō *f.*, poena *f.* take — on ulcīscī, vindicāre in (*acc.*). take — for ulcīscī, vindicāre.
vengeful *a.* ultor.
venial *a.* ignōscendus.
venison *n.* dāma *f.*, ferīna *f.*
venom *n.* venēnum *n.*; (*fig.*) vīrus *n.*
venomous *a.* venēnātus.
vent *n.* spīrāculum *n.*; (*outlet*) exitus *m.* give — to profundere, ēmittere. *vt.* ēmittere; (*feelings on*) profundere in (*acc.*), ērumpere in (*acc.*).
ventilate *vt.* perflāre; (*opinion*) in medium prōferre, vulgāre.
ventilation *n.* perflāre.
venture *n.* perīculum *n.*; (*gamble*) ālea *f.* at a — temerē. *vi.* audēre. *vt.* perīclitārī, in āleam dare.
venturesome *a.* audāx, temerārius.
venturesomeness *n.* audācia *f.*, temeritās *f.*
veracious *a.* vērāx, vēridicus.
veracity *n.* vēritās *f.*, fidēs *f.*
verb *n.* verbum *n.*
verbally *ad.* per colloquia; (*translate*) ad verbum, verbum prō verbo.
verbatim *ad.* ad verbum, totidem verbīs.
verbiage *n.* verba *n.pl.*
verbose *a.* verbōsus.
verbosity *n.* loquendī prōfluentia *f.*
verdant *a.* viridis.
verdict *n.* sententia *f.*, iūdicium *n.* deliver a — sententiam prōnūntiāre. give a — in favour of causam adiūdicāre (*dat.*).
verdigris *n.* aerūgō *f.*
verdure *n.* viriditās *f.*
verge *n.* ōra *f.* the — of extrēmus. on the — of (*fig.*) prope (*acc.*). *vi.* vergere.
verification *n.* cōnfirmātiō *f.*
verify *vt.* cōnfirmāre, comprobāre.
verily *ad.* profectō, certē.
verisimilitude *n.* vērī similitūdō *f.*
veritab/le *a.* vērus. **-ly** *ad.* vērē.
verity *n.* vēritās *f.*
vermilion *n.* sandix *f.*

vermin *n.* bestiolae *f.pl.*
vernacular *a.* patrius. *n.* patrius sermō *m.*
vernal *a.* vērnus.
versatile *a.* versūtus, varius.
versatility *n.* versātile ingenium *n.*
verse *n.* (*line*) versus *m.*; (*poetry*) versus *m.pl.*, carmina *n.pl.*
versed *a.* instructus, peritus, exercitātus.
versification *n.* ars versūs faciendī.
versify *vt.* versū inclūdere. *vi.* versūs facere.
version *n.* (*of story*) fōrma *f.* give a Latin — of Latīnē reddere.
vertex *n.* vertex *m.*, fastīgium [*n.*
vertical *a.* rēctus, dīrēctus. **-ly** *ad.* ad līneam, rēctā līneā, ad perpendiculum.
vertigo *n.* vertīgō *f.*
vervain *n.* verbēna *f.*
verve *n.* ācrimōnia *f.*
very *a.* ipse. *ad.* admodum, valdē, vehementer; *sup.* at that — moment tum māximē. not — nōn ita.
vessel *n.* (*receptacle*) vās *n.*; (*ship*) nāvigium *n.*
vest *n.* subūcula *f.* *vt.* — power in imperium dēferre (*dat.*). -ed interests nummī locātī *m.pl.*
vestal *a.* vestālis. *n.* virgō vestālis *f.*
vestibule *n.* vestibulum *n.*
vestige *n.* vestīgium *n.*, indicium *n.*
vestment *n.* vestīmentum *n.*
vesture *n.* vestis *f.*
vetch *n.* vicia *f.*
veteran *a.* veterānus. *n.* (*mil.*) veterānus *m.*; (*fig.*) veterātor *m.*
veto *n.* interdictum *n.*; (*tribune's*) intercessiō *f.* *vt.* interdīcere (*dat.*); (*tribune*) intercēdere (*dat.*).
vex *vt.* vexāre, sollicitāre, stomachum movēre (*dat*). be -ed aegrē ferre, stomachārī.
vexation *n.* (*caused*) molestia *f.*; (*felt*) dolor *m.*, stomachus *m.*
vexatious *a.* odiōsus, molestus. **-ly** *ad.* molestē.
vexed *a.* īrātus; (*question*) anceps.
via *pr.* per (*acc.*).
viaduct *n.* pōns *m.*
viands *n.* cibus *m.*
vibrate *vi.* vībrāre, tremere.
vibration *n.* tremor *m.*
vicarious *a.* vicārius.
vice *n.* (*general*) prāvitās *f.*, perditī mōrēs *m.pl.*; (*particular*) vitium *n.*, flāgitium *n.*; (*clamp*) fībula *f.*
viceroy *n.* prōcūrātor *m.* [*f.*
vicinity *n.* vīcīnia *f.*, vīcīnitās
vicious *a.* prāvus, vitiōsus, flāgitiōsus; (*temper*) contumāx. **-ly** *ad.* flāgitiōsē; contumāciter
vicissitude *n.* vicissitūdō *f.*; (*pl.*) vicēs *f.pl.*
victim *n.* victima *f.*, hostia *f.*; (*fig.*) piāculum *n.*; (*exploited*) praeda *f.* be the — of labōrāre ex. fall a — to morī (*abl.*); (*trickery*) circumvenīrī (*abl.*).
victimize *vt.* nocēre (*dat.*), circumvenīre.
victor *n.* victor *m.*
victorious *a.* victor (*m.*), victrīx (*f.*). be — vincere.
victory *n.* victōria *f.* win a — victōriam reportāre. win a — over vincere, superāre. — message laureātae litterae *f.pl.* — parade triumphus *m.*
victual *vt.* rem frūmentāriam suppeditāre (*dat.*).
victualler *n.* caupō *m.*; (*mil.*) frūmentārius *m.*
victuals *n.* cibus *m.*; (*mil.*) frūmentum *n.*, commeātus *m.*
vie *vi.* certāre, contendere. — with aemulārī.
view *n.* cōnspectus *m.*; (*from far*) prōspectus *m.*; (*from high*) dēspectus *m.*; (*opinion*) sententia *f.* exposed to — in

mediō. entertain a — sentīre. in — of propter (*acc.*). in my — meā sententiā, meō iūdiciō. end in — prōpositum *n.* have in — spectāre. point of — iūdicium *n.* with a — to eō cōnsiliō ut. *vt.* inspicere, spectāre, intuērī.
vigil *n.* pervigilium *n.* keep a — vigilāre.
vigilance *n.* vigilantia *f.*, diligentia *f.*
vigilant *a.* vigilāns, dīligēns. **-ly** *ad.* vigilanter, dīligenter.
vigorous *a.* ācer, vegetus, integer; (*style*) nervōsus. **-ly** *ad.* ācriter, strēnuē.
vigour *n.* vīs *f.*, nervī *m.pl.*, integritās *f.*
vile *a.* turpis, impūrus, abiectus. **-ly** *ad.* turpiter, impūrē.
vileness *n.* turpitūdō *f.*, impūritās *f.*
vilification *n.* obtrectātiō *f.*, calumnia *f.*
vilify *vt.* obtrectāre, calumniārī, maledīcere (*dat.*).
villa *n.* villa *f.*
village *n.* pāgus *m.*, vīcus *m.* in every — pāgātim.
villager *n.* pāgānus *m.*, vīcānus *m.*
villain *n.* furcifer *m.*, scelerātus *m.*
villainous *a.* scelestus, scelerātus, nēquam. **-ly** *ad.* scelestē.
villainy *n.* scelus *n.*, nēquitia *f.*
vindicate *vt.* (*right*) vindicāre; (*action*) pūrgāre; (*belief*) arguere; (*person*) dēfendere, prōpugnāre prō (*abl.*).
vindication *n.* dēfēnsiō *f.*, pūrgātiō *f.*
vindicator *n.* dēfēnsor *m.*, prōpugnātor *m.*
vindictive *a.* ultor, ulcīscendī cupidus.
vine *n.* vītis *f.* wild — labrusca *f.*
vine-dresser *n.* vinitor *m.*
vinegar *n.* acētum *n.* [*n.*
vineyard *n.* vīnea *f.*, vīnētum
vintage *n.* vindēmia *f.*
vintner *n.* vīnārius *m.*
violate *vt.* violāre.
violation *n.* violātiō *f.*
violator *n.* violātor *m.*
violence *n.* violentia *f.*, vīs *f.*, iniūria *f.* do — to violāre. offer — to vim īnferre (*dat.*).
violent *a.* violentus, vehemēns; (*passion*) ācer, impotēns. — death nex *f.* **-ly** *ad.* vehementer, per vim.
violet *n.* viola *f.*
viper *n.* vīpera *f.*
viperous *a.* (*fig.*) malignus.
virgin *n.* virgō *f.* *a.* virginālis.
virginity *n.* virginitās *f.*
virile *a.* virīlis.
virility *n.* virtūs *f.*
virtually *ad.* rē vērā, ferē.
virtue *n.* virtūs *f.*, honestum *n.*; (*woman's*) pudīcitia *f.*; (*power*) vīs *f.*, potestās *f.* by — of *abl.*, ex (*abl.*).
virtuous *a.* honestus, probus, integer. **-ly** *ad.* honestē.
virulence *n.* vīs *f.*, vīrus *n.*
virulent *a.* acerbus.
virus *n.* vīrus *n.*
visage *n.* ōs *n.*, faciēs *f.*
vis-à-vis *pr.* exadversus (*acc.*)
viscosity *n.* lentor *m.*
viscous *a.* lentus, tenāx.
visib/le *a.* ēvidēns, cōnspicuus, manifestus. be — appārēre. **-ly** *ad.* manifestō.
vision *n.* (*sense*) vīsus *m.*; (*power*) aspectus *m.*; (*apparition*) vīsum *n.*, vīsiō *f.*; (*whim*) somnium *n.*
visionary *a.* vānus. *n.* somniāns *m.*
visit *n.* adventus *m.*; (*formal*) salūtātiō *f.*; (*long*) commorātiō *f.* pay a — to invīsere. *vt.* vīsere. — occasionally intervīsere. go to — invīsere.
visitation *n.* (*to inspect*) recēnsiō *f.*; (*to punish*) animadversiō *f.*

visitor *n.* hospes *m.*, hospita *f.*; (*formal*) salūtātor *m.*
visor *n.* buccula *f.*
vista *n.* prōspectus *m.*
visual *a.* oculōrum. **-ly** *ad.* oculīs.
visualize *vt.* animō cernere, ante oculōs pōnere.
vital *a.* (*of life*) vītālis; (*essential*) necessārius, māximī mōmenti. **-ly** *ad.* praecipuē, imprīmīs.
vitality *n.* vīs *f.*; (*style*) sanguis *m.*
vitals *n.* viscera *n.pl.*
vitiate *vt.* corrumpere, vitiāre.
vitreous *a.* vitreus.
vitrify *vt.* in vitrum excoquere.
vituperate *vt.* vituperāre, obiūrgāre.
vituperation *n.* vituperātiō *f.*, maledicta *n.pl.*
vituperative *a.* maledicus.
vivacious *a.* alacer, vegetus, hilaris. **-ly** *ad.* hilare.
vivacity *n.* alacritās *f.*, hilaritās *f.*
vivid *a.* vīvidus, ācer. **-ly** *ad.* ācriter.
vivify *vt.* animāre.
vixen *n.* vulpēs *f.*
vocabulary *n.* verbōrum cōpia *f.*
vocal *a.* — music vōcis [cantus *m.*
vocation *n.* officium *n.*, mūnus *n.*
vociferate *vt.* & *i.* vōciferārī, clāmāre. [clāmor *m.*
vociferation *n.* vōciferātiō *f.*,
vociferous *a.* vōciferāns. **-ly** *ad.* māgnīs clāmōribus.
vogue *n.* mōs *m.* be in — flōrēre, in honōre esse.
voice *n.* vōx *f.* *vt.* exprimere, ēloquī.
void *a.* inānis, vacuus. — of expers (*gen.*). null and — inritus. *n.* ināne *n.* *vt.* ēvomere, ēmittere.
volatile *a.* levis, mōbilis.
volatility *n.* levitās *f.*
volition *n.* voluntās *f.*
volley *n.* imber *m.*
volubility *n.* volūbilitās *f.*
voluble *a.* volūbilis.
volume *n.* (*book*) liber *m.*; (*mass*) mōlēs *f.*; (*of sound*) māgnitūdō *f.*
voluminous *a.* cōpiōsus.
voluntar/y *a.* voluntārius; (*unpaid*) grātuītus. **-ily** *ad.* ultrō, suā sponte.
volunteer *n.* (*mil.*) ēvocātus *m.* *vt.* ultrō offerre. *vi.* (*mil.*) nōmen dare.
voluptuary *n.* dēlicātus *m.*, homō voluptārius *m.*
voluptuous *a.* voluptārius, mollis, dēlicātus, luxuriōsus. **-ly** *ad.* molliter, dēlicātē, luxuriōsē.
voluptuousness *n.* luxuria *f.*, libīdō *f.*
vomit *vt.* vomere, ēvomere. — up ēvomere.
voracious *a.* vorāx, edāx. **-ly** *ad.* avidē.
voracity *n.* edācitās *f.*, gula *f.*
vortex *n.* vertex *m.*, turbō *m.*
votary *n.* cultor *m.*
vote *n.* suffrāgium *n.*; (*opinion*) sententia *f.* — for (*candidate*) suffrāgārī (*dat.*); (*senator's motion*) discēdere in sententiam (*gen.*). *vi.* (*election*) suffrāgium ferre; (*judge*) sententiam ferre; (*senator*) cēnsēre. take a — (*senate*) discessiōnem facere. *vt.* (*senate*) dēcernere. — against (*bill*) antīquāre.
voter *n.* suffrāgātor *m.*
votive *a.* vōtīvus.
vouch *vi.* spondēre. — for praestāre, testificārī.
voucher *n.* (*person*) auctor *m.*; (*document*) auctōritās *f.*
vouchsafe *vt.* concēdere.
vow *n.* vōtum *n.*; (*promise*) fidēs *f.* *vt.* vovēre; (*promise*) spondēre.
vowel *n.* vōcālis *f.*
voyage *n.* nāvigātiō *f.*, cursus *m.* *vi.* nāvigāre.
vulgar *a.* (*common*) vulgāris;

(*low*) plēbēius, sordidus, insulsus. **-ly** *ad.* vulgō; īnsulsē.
vulgarity *n.* sordēs *f.pl.*, īnsulsitās *f.*
vulnerable *a.* nūdus; (*fig.*) obnoxius. **be —** vulnerārī posse.
vulture *n.* vultur *m.*; (*fig.*) vulturius *m.*

W

wad *n.* massa *f.*
wade *vi.* per vada īre. **— across** vadō trānsīre.
waft *vt.* ferre, vehere.
wag *n.* facētus homō *m.*, ioculātor *m.* *vt.* movēre, mōtāre, agitāre. *vi.* movērī, agitārī.
wage *n.* mercēs *f.*; (*pl.*) mercēs *f.*, manupretium *n.*; (*fig.*) pretium *n.*, praemium *n.* *vt.* gerere. **— war on** bellum īnferre (*dat.*).
wager *n.* spōnsiō *f.* *vi.* spōnsiōnem facere. *vt.* dēpōnere, oppōnere.
waggery *n.* facētiae *f.pl.*
waggish *a.* facētus rīdiculus.
waggle *vt.* agitāre, mōtāre.
wagon *n.* plaustrum *n.*, carrus *m.*
waif *n.* inops *m.*, *f.*
wail *n.* ēiulātus *m.* *vi.* ēiulāre, dēplōrāre, lāmentārī.
wailing *n.* plōrātus *m.*, lāmentātiō *f.*
waist *n.* medium corpus *n.* **hold by the —** medium tenēre.
wait *n.* **have a long —** diū exspectāre. **lie in —** īnsidiārī. *vi.* manēre, opperīrī, exspectāre. **— for** exspectāre. **— upon** (*accompany*) adsectārī, dēdūcere; (*serve*) famulārī (*dat.*); (*visit*) salūtāre. [*m.*
waiter *n.* famulus *m.*, minister
waive *vt.* dēpōnere, remittere.
wake *vt.* excitāre, suscitāre. *vi.* expergīscī.
wake *n.* vestīgia *n.pl.* **in the —** pōne, ā tergō. **follow in the — of** vestīgiīs īnstāre (*gen.*).
wakeful *a.* vigil.
wakefulness *n.* vigilantia *f.*
waken *vt.* excitāre. *vi.* expergīscī.
walk *n.* (*act*) ambulātiō *f.*, deambulātiō *f.*; (*gait*) incessus *m.*; (*place*) ambulātiō *f.*, xystus *m.* **— of life** status *m.* **go for a —** spatiārī, deambulāre. *vi.* ambulāre, īre, gradī; (*with dignity*) incēdere. **— about** inambulāre. **— out** ēgredī.
wall *n.* mūrus *m.*; (*indoors*) pariēs *m.*; (*afield*) māceria *f.*; (*pl., of town*) moenia *n.pl.* *vt.* mūnīre, saepīre. **— up** inaedificāre.
wallet *n.* pēra *f.*
wallow *vi.* volūtārī.
walnut *n.* iūglāns *f.*
wan *a.* pallidus.
wand *n.* virga *f.*
wander *vi.* errāre, vagārī; (*in mind*) ālūcinārī. **— over** pervagārī.
wanderer *n.* errō *m.*, vagus *m.*
wandering *a.* errābundus, vagus. *n.* errātiō *f.*, error *m.*
wane *vi.* dēcrēscere, senēscere.
want *n.* inopia *f.*, indigentia *f.*, egestās *f.*, pēnūria *f.*; (*craving*) dēsīderium *n.* **in —** inops. **be in —** egēre. *vt.* (*lack*) carēre (*abl.*), egēre (*abl.*), indigēre (*abl.*); (*miss*) dēsīderāre; (*wish*) velle.
wanting *a.* (*missing*) absēns; (*defective*) vitiōsus, parum idōneus. **be —** deesse, dēficere. *pr.* sine (*abl.*).
wanton *a.* lascīvus, libīdinōsus. *vi.* lascīvīre. **-ly** *ad.* lascīvē, libīdinōsē.
war *n.* bellum *n.* **civil —** bellum cīvīle, domesticum, intestīnum. **regular —** iūstum bellum. **fortunes of —** fortūna bellī. **outbreak of —** exortum bellum. **be at — with** bellum

gerere cum. declare — bellum indīcere. discontinue — bellum dēpōnere. end — (*by agreement*) compōnere; (*by victory*) cōnficere. enter — bellum suscipere. give the command of a — bellum mandāre. make — bellum īnferre. prolong a — bellum trahere. provoke — bellum movēre. wage — bellum gerere. wage — on bellum īnferre (*dat.*). *vi.* bellāre.

warble *vi.* canere, cantāre.

warbling *a.* garrulus, canōrus. *n.* cantus *m.*

war-cry *n.* clāmor *m.*

ward *n.* custōdia *f.*; (*person*) pupillus *m.*, pupilla *f.*; (*of town*) regiō *f.* *vt.* — off arcēre, dēfendere, prōpulsāre.

warden *n.* praefectus *m.*

warder *n.* custōs *m.*

wardrobe *n.* vestiārium *n.*

wardship *n.* tūtēla *f.*

warehouse *n.* apothēca *f.*

wares *n.* merx *f.*, merces *f.pl.*

warfare *n.* bellum *n.*

wariness *n.* circumspectiō *f.*, cautiō *f.*

warlike *a.* ferōx, bellicōsus.

warm *a.* calidus; (*fig.*) ācer, studiōsus. be — calēre. become — calefierī, incalēscere. keep — *vt.* fovēre. — baths thermae *f.pl.* *vt.* calefacere, tepefacere, fovēre. *vi.* calefierī. **-ly** *ad.* (*fig.*) ferventer, studiōsē.

warmth *n.* calor *m.*

warn *vt.* monēre, admonēre.

warning *n.* (*act*) monitiō *f.*; (*particular*) monitum *n.*; (*lesson*) documentum *n.*, exemplum *n.*

warp *n.* stāmina *n.pl.* *vt.* dēprāvāre, īnflectere. **-ed** *a.* (*fig.*) prāvus. [praestāre.

warrant *n.* auctōritās *f.* *vt.*

warranty *n.* cautiō *f.*

warrior *n.* bellātor *m.*, bellātrīx *f.*, mīles *m.*

wart *n.* verrūca *f.*

war/y *a.* prōvidus, cautus, prūdēns. **-ily** *ad.* prōvidenter, cautē.

wash *vt.* lavāre; (*of rivers, sea*) adluere. — away dīluere. — clean abluere. — out (*fig.*) ēluere. *vi.* lavārī.

wash-basin *n.* aquālis *m.*

washing *n.* lavātiō *f.*

wasp *n.* vespa *f.*

waspish *a.* acerbus, stomachōsus.

waste *n.* dētrīmentum *n.*, intertrīmentum *n.*; (*extravagance*) effūsiō *f.*; (*of time*) iactūra *f.*; (*land*) sōlitūdō *f.*, vastitās *f.* *a.* dēsertus, vastus. lay — vastāre, populārī. *vt.* cōnsūmere, perdere, dissipāre; (*time*) terere, absūmere; (*with disease*) absūmere. *vi.* — away tābēscere, intābēscere.

wasteful *a.* prōdigus, profūsus; (*destructive*) damnōsus, perniciōsus. **-ly** *ad.* prōdigē.

wasting *n.* tābēs *f.*

wastrel *n.* nebulō *m.*

watch *n.* (*being awake*) vigilia *f.*; (*sentry*) statiō *f.*, excubiae *f.pl.* keep — excubāre. keep — on, over custōdīre, invigilāre (*dat.*). set — vigiliās dispōnere. at the third — ad tertiam būcinam. *vt.* (*guard*) custōdīre; (*observe*) intuērī, observāre, spectāre. — for observāre, exspectāre; (*enemy*) īnsidiārī (*dat.*). — closely adservāre.

watcher *n.* custōs *m.*

watchful *a.* vigilāns. **-ly** *ad.* vigilanter.

watchfulness *n.* vigilantia *f.*

watchman *n.* custōs *m.*, vigil *m.*

watch-tower *n.* specula *f.*

watchword *n.* tessera *f.*, signum *n.*

water *n.* aqua *f.* deep — gurges *m.* fresh — aqua dulcis. high — māximus aestus. running — aqua prōfluēns. still — stagnum *n.* fetch — aquārī. fetching — aquātiō *f.* cold — frīgida *f.* hot — calida *f.* troubled -s (*fig.*) turbidae res. *vt.* (*land*) inrigāre; (*animal*) adaquāre.

water-carrier *n.* aquātor *m.*; (*Zodiac*) Aquārius *m.*

water-clock *n.* clepsydra *f.*

waterfall *n.* cataracta *f.*

watering *n.* aquātiō *f.* **-place** *n.* (*spa*) aquae *f.pl.*

water-pipe *n.* fistula *f.*

watershed *n.* aquārum dīvortium *n.*

water-snake *n.* hydrus *m.*

water-spout *n.* prēstēr *m.*

watery *a.* aquōsus, ūmidus.

wattle *n.* crātēs *f.*

wave *n.* fluctus *m.* *vt.* agitāre, iactāre. *vi.* fluctuāre.

waver *vi.* dubitāre, fluctuārī, nūtāre, vacillāre, labāre.

wavering *a.* dubius, incōnstāns. *n.* dubitātiō *f.*, fluctuātiō *f.*

wavy *a.* undātus; (*hair*) crispus.

wax *n.* cēra *f.* *vt.* cērāre. *vi.* crēscere.

waxen *a.* cēreus.

waxy *a.* cērōsus.

way *n.* via *f.*; (*route*) iter *n.*; (*method*) modus *m.*, ratiō *f.*; (*habit*) mōs *m.*; (*ship's*) impetus *m.* all the — to, from usque ad, ab. by the — (*parenthesis*) etenim. get in the — of intervenīre (*dat.*). impedīre. get under — nāvem solvere. give — (*structure*) labāre; (*mil.*) cēdere. give — to indulgēre (*dat.*). go out of one's — to do ultrō facere. have one's — imperāre. in a — quōdam modō. in this — ad hunc modum. it is not my — to nōn meum est (*inf.*). lose one's — deerrare. make — dē viā dēcēdere. make — for cēdere (*dat.*) make one's — into sē īnsinuāre in (*acc.*). on the — inter viam, in itinere. out of the — āvius, dēvius; (*fig.*) reconditus. pave the — for praeparāre. put out of the — tollere. right of — iter. stand in the — of obstāre (*dat.*). that — illāc. this — hāc. -s and means opēs *f.pl.*, reditūs *m.pl.*

wayfarer *n.* viātor *m.*

waylay *vt.* īnsidiārī (*dat.*).

wayward *a.* protervus, incōnstāns, levis.

waywardness *n.* libīdō *f.*, levitās *f.*

we *pro.* nōs.

weak *a.* dēbilis, īnfirmus, imbēcillus; (*health*) invalidus; (*argument*) levis,tenuis; (*senses*) hebes. **-ly** *ad.* īnfirmē.

weaken *vt.* dēbilitāre, īnfirmāre; (*resistance*) frangere, labefactāre. *vi.* imminuī, labāre.

weakling *n.* imbēcillus *m.*

weakly *a.* invalidus, aeger.

weak-minded *a.* mollis.

weakness *n.* dēbilitās *f.*, īnfirmitās *f.*; (*of argument*) levitās *f.*; (*of mind*) mollitia *f.*, imbēcillitās *f.*; (*flaw*) vitium *n.* have a — for delectārī (*abl.*).

weal *n.* salūs *f.*, rēs *f.*; (*mark of blow*) vībex *f.* the common — rēs pūblica *f.*

wealth *n.* dīvitiae *f.pl.*, opēs *f.pl.* a — of cōpia *f.*, abundantia *f.*

wealthy *a.* dīves opulentus, locuplēs, beātus. make — locuplētāre, dītāre. very — praedīves.

wean *vt.* lacte dēpellere; (*fig.*) dēdocēre.

weapon *n.* tēlum *n.*

wear *n.* (*dress*) habitus *m.* — and tear intertrīmentum *n.* *vt.* gerere, gestāre; (*rub*) terere, conterere. — out cōnficere. *vi.* dūrāre. — off minuī.

weariness *n.* fatīgātiō *f.*, lassitūdō *f.*; (*of*) taedium *n.*
wearisome *a.* molestus, operōsus, labōriōsus.
wear/y *a.* lassus, fessus, dēfessus, fatīgātus. *vt.* fatīgāre. **-ily** *ad.* cum lassitūdine, languidē.
weasel *n.* mustēla *f.*
weather *n.* tempestās *f.*, caelum *n.* fine — serēnitās *f.* *vt.* superāre.
weather-beaten *a.* tempestāte dūrātus.
weave *vt.* texere.
weaver *n.* textor *m.*, textrix *f.*
web *n.* (*on loom*) tēla *f.*; (*spider's*) arāneum *n.*
wed *vt.* (*a wife*) dūcere; (*a husband*) nūbere (*dat.*).
wedding *n.* nūptiae *f.pl.*
wedge *n.* cuneus *m.* *vt.* cuneāre.
wedlock *n.* mātrimōnium *n.*
weed *n.* inūtilis herba *f.* *vt.* runcāre.
weedy *a.* exīlis.
week *n.* hebdomas *f.*
ween *vt.* arbitrārī, putāre.
weep *vi.* flēre, lacrimārī. — for dēflēre, dēplōrāre. [*f.pl.*
weeping *n.* flētus *m.*, lacrimae
weevil *n.* curculiō *m.*
weft *n.* subtēmen *n.*; (*web*) tēla *f.*
weigh *vt.* pendere, exāmināre; (*anchor*) tollere; (*thought*) ponderāre. — down dēgravāre, opprimere. — out expendere. *vi.* pendere.
weight *n.* pondus *n.*; (*influence*) auctōritās *f.*, mōmentum *n.*; (*burden*) onus *n.* have great — (*fig.*) multum valēre. he is worth his — in gold aurō contrā cōnstat.
weightiness *n.* gravitās *f.*
weight/y *a.* gravis. **-ily** *ad.* graviter.
weir *n.* mōlēs *f.*
weird *a.* mōnstruōsus. *n.* fātum *n.*
welcome *a.* grātus, exspectātus, acceptus. *n.* salūtātiō *f.* *vt.* excipere, salvēre iubēre. *interj.* salvē, salvēte.
welfare *n.* salūs *f.*
welkin *n.* caelum *n.*
well *n.* puteus *m.*; (*spring*) fōns *m.* *vi.* scatēre. *a.* salvus, sānus, valēns. be — valēre. *ad.* bene, probē; (*transition*) age. *interj.* (*concession*) estō; (*surprise*) heia. — and good estō. — begun is half done dīmidium factī quī coepit habet. — done! probē! — met opportūnē venis. — off beātus, fortūnātus. you are — off bene est tibī. — on in years aetāte prōvectus. all is — bene habet. as — etiam. as — as cum . . . tum, et . . . et. let — alone quiēta nōn movēre. take — in bonam partem accipere. wish — favēre (*dat.*). you may — say iūre dīcis. you might as — say illud potius dīcās.
well-advised *a.* prūdēns.
well-behaved *a.* modestus.
well-being *n.* salūs *f.*
well-bred *a.* generōsus, līberālis. [amīcus.
well-disposed *a.* benevolus,
well-informed *a.* ērudītus.
well-judged *a.* ēlegāns.
well-knit *a.* dēnsus.
well-known *a.* nōtus, nōbilis.
well-nigh *ad.* paene.
well-read *a.* litterātus.
well-timed *a.* opportūnus.
well-to-do *a.* beātus, dīves.
well-tried *a.* probātus.
well-turned *a.* rotundus.
well-versed *a.* perītus, expertus.
well-wisher *n.* amīcus *m.*, benevolēns *m.*
well-worn *a.* trītus.
welter *n.* turba *f.* *vi.* miscērī, turbārī; (*wallow*) volūtārī.

wench *n.* muliercula *f.*
wend *vt.* — **one's way** īre, sē ferre.
west *n.* occidēns *m.*, sōlis occāsus *m.* *a.* occidentālis. — wind Favōnius *m.*
westerly, western *a.* occidentālis.
westwards *ad.* ad occidentem.
wet *a.* ūmidus, madidus. **be** — madēre. — **weather** pluvia *f.* *vt.* madefacere.
wet-nurse *n.* nūtrix *f.*
wether *n.* vervēx *m.*
whack *n.* ictus *m.*, plāga *f.* *vt.* pulsāre, verberāre.
whale *n.* bālaena *f.*
wharf *n.* crepīdō *f.*
what *pro.* (*interrog.*) quid; (*a.*) quī; (*rel.*) id quod, ea quae.
whatever, whatsoever *pro.* quidquid, quodcumque; (*a.*) quīcumque.
wheat *n.* trīticum *n.*
wheaten *a.* trīticeus.
wheedle *vt.* blandīrī, pellicere.
wheedling *a.* blandus. *n.* blanditiae *f.pl.*
wheel *n.* rota *f.* *vt.* flectere, circumagere. *vi.* sē flectere, circumagī.
wheel-barrow *n.* pabō *m.*
wheeze *vi.* anhēlāre.
whelm *vt.* obruere.
whelp *n.* catulus *m.*
when *ad.* (*interrog.*) quandō, quō tempore. *conj.* (*time*) cum, ubī.
whence *ad.* unde.
whenever *conj.* quotiēns, utcumque; (*as soon as*) simulāc.
where *ad.* ubī; (*to*) quō. — **. . . from** unde.
whereabouts *n.* locus *m.* **your** — quō in locō sīs.
whereas *conj.* quōniam; (*contrast*) *not expressed.*
whereby *ad.* quō pāctō, quō.
wherefore *ad.* (*interrog.*) quārē, cūr; (*rel.*) quamobrem, quāpropter.
wherein *ad.* in quō, in quā.
whereof *ad.* cūius, cūius reī.
whereon *ad.* in quō, in quā.
whereupon *ad.* quō factō.
wherever *conj.* ubiubi, quācumque.
wherewith *ad.* quī, cum quō.
wherry *n.* linter *f.*
whet *vt.* acuere; (*fig.*) exacuere.
whether *conj.* (*interrog.*) utrum; (*single question*) num; (*condition*) sīve, seu.
whet-stone *n.* cōs *f.*
whey *n.* serum *n.*
which *pro.* (*interrog.*) quis; (*of two*) uter. (*rel.*) quī. *a.* quī; (*of two*) uter.
whichever *pro.* quisquis, quīcumque; (*of two*) utercumque.
whiff *n.* odor *m.*
while *n.* spatium *n.*, tempus *n.* **for a** — parumper. **a little** — paulisper. **a long** — diū. **it is worth** — expedit, operae pretium est. **once in a** — interdum. *conj.* dum. *vt.* — **away** dēgere, fallere.
whilst *conj.* dum.
whim *n.* libīdō *f.*, arbitrium *n.*
whimper *n.* vāgītus *m.* *vi.* vāgīre.
whimsical *a.* facētus, īnsolēns. **-ly** *ad.* facētē.
whimsy *n.* dēliciae *f.pl.*, facētiae *f.pl.*
whine *n.* quirītātiō *f.* *vi.* quirītāre.
whinny *n.* hinnītus *m.* *vi.* hinnīre.
whip *n.* flagellum *n.*, flagrum *n.* *vt.* flagellare, verberare.
whirl *n.* turbō *m.* *vt.* intorquēre, contorquēre. *vi.* contorquērī.
whirlpool *n.* vertex *m.*
whirlwind *n.* turbō *m.*
whisper *n.* susurrus *m.* *vt.* & *i.* susurrāre, īnsusurrāre. — **to** ad aurem admonēre, in aurem dīcere.

whistle *n.* (*instrument*) fistula *f.*; (*sound*) sībilus *m.* *vi.* sībilāre.
white *a.* albus; (*shining*) candidus; (*complexion*) pallidus; (*hair*) cānus. turn — exalbēscere. *n.* album *n.*; (*of egg*) albūmen *n.*
whiten *vt.* dealbāre. *vi.* albēscere.
whiteness *n.* candor *m.*
whitewash *n.* albārium *n.* *vt.* dealbāre.
whither *ad.* quō. -soever quōcumque.
whitish *a.* albulus.
whizz *n.* strīdor *m.* *vi.* strīdere, increpāre.
who *pro.* quis; (*rel.*) quī.
whoever *pro.* quisquis, quīcumque.
whole *a.* tōtus, cūnctus; (*unhurt*) integer, incolumis; (*healthy*) sānus. *n.* tōtum *n.*, summa *f.*, ūniversitās *f.* on the — plērumque.
whole-hearted *a.* studiōsissimus. -ly *ad.* ex animō.
wholesale *a.* māgnus, cōpiōsus. — business negōtiātiō *f.* — dealer mercātor *m.*, negōtiātor *m.*
wholesome *a.* salūtāris, salūbris.
wholesomeness *n.* salūbritās *f.*
wholly *ad.* omninō, tōtus.
whoop *n.* ululātus *m.* *vi.* uluāre.
whose *pro.* cūius.
why *ad.* cūr, qūarē, quamobrem.
wick *n.* mergulus *m.*
wicked *a.* improbus, scelestus; (*to gods, kin, country*) impius. -ly *ad.* improbē, scelestē, impiē.
wickedness *n.* improbitās *f.*, scelus *n.*, impietās *f.* [*n.*
wicker *a.* vīmineus. *n.* vīmen
wide *a.* lātus, amplus. be — of aberrāre ab. *ad.* lātē. far and — longē lātēque. -ly *ad.* lātē; (*among people*) vulgō.
widen *vt.* laxāre, dīlātāre.
wide-spread *a.* effūsus, vulgātus.
widow *n.* vidua *f.*
widowed *a.* viduus, orbus.
widower *n.* viduus. *m.*
widowhood *n.* viduitās *f.*
width *n.* lātitūdō *f.*, amplitūdō *f.*
wield *vt.* tractāre, gestāre, ūtī (*abl.*).
wife *n.* uxor *f.*
wifely *a.* uxōrius.
wig *n.* capillāmentum *n.*
wild *a.* ferus, indomitus; (*plant*) agrestis; (*land*) incultus; (*temper*) furibundus, impotens, āmēns; (*shot*) temerārius. — state feritās *f.* -ly *ad.* saevē.
wilderness *n.* sōlitūdō *f.*, loca dēserta *n.pl.*
wildness *n.* feritās *f.*
wile *n.* dolus *m.*, ars *f.*, fraus *f.*
wilful *a.* pervicāx, contumāx; (*action*) cōnsultus. -ly *ad.* contumāciter; cōnsultō.
wilfulness *n.* pervicācia *f.*, libīdō *f.*
wiliness *n.* astūtia *f.*
will *n.* (*faculty*) voluntās *f.*, animus *m.*; (*intent*) cōnsilium *n.*; (*decision*) arbitrium *n.*; (*of gods*) nūtus *m.*; (*document*) testāmentum *n.* — and pleasure libīdō *f.* against one's — invītus. at — ad libīdinem suam. good — studium *n.* ill — invidia *f.* with a — summō studiō. without making a — intestātus, intestātō. *vt.* velle, *fut.*; (*legacy*) lēgāre. as you — ut libet.
willing *a.* libēns, parātus. be — velle. not be — nōlle. -ly *ad.* libenter.
willingness *n.* voluntās *f.*
willow *n.* salix *f.* *a.* salignus.
willowy *a.* gracilis.

wilt *vi.* flaccēscere.
wil/y *a.* astūtus, vafer, callidus. **-ily** *ad.* astūtē, vafrē.
wimple *n.* mitra *f.*
win *vt.* ferre, obtinēre; (*after effort*) auferre; (*victory*) reportāre; (*fame*) cōnsequī, adsequī; (*friends*) sibī conciliāre. **— the day** vincere. **— over** dēlēnire, conciliāre. *vi.* vincere.
wince *vi.* resilīre.
winch *n.* māchina *f.*, sucula *f.*
wind *n.* ventus *m.*; (*north*) aquilō *m.*, (*south*) auster *m.*, (*east*) eurus *m.*, (*west*) favōnius *m.* **I get — of** subolet mihi. **run before —** ventō sē dare. **take the — out of one's sails** suō sibī gladiō iugulāre. **there is something in the —** nescio-quid olet. **which way the — blows** quōmodo sē rēs habeat.
wind *vt.* torquēre. **— round** intorquēre. *vi.* flectī, sinuāre. **— up** (*speech*) perōrāre.
wind-bag *n.* verbōsus *m.*
winded *a.* anhēlāns.
windfall *n.* repentīnum bonum *n.*
winding *a.* flexuōsus, tortuōsus. *n.* flexiō *f.*, flexus *m.*; (*pl., speech*) ambāgēs *f.pl.*
windlass *n.* māchina *f.*, sucula *f.*
window *n.* fenestra *f.*
windpipe *n.* aspera artēria *f*
windward *a.* ad ventum conversus. *ad.* **to —** ventum versus.
windy *a.* ventōsus.
wine *n.* vīnum *n.*; (*new*) mustum *n.*; (*undiluted*) merum *n.*
wine-bibber *n.* vīnōsus *m.*
wine-cellar *n.* apothēca *f.*
wine-merchant *n.* vīnārius *m.*
wine-press *n.* prēlum *n.*
wing *n.* āla *f.*; (*mil.*) cornū *n.*, āla *f.* **take —** ēvolāre. **take under one's —** patrōnum fierī (*gen.*), clientem habēre. **in** custōdiam recipere.
winged *a.* ālātus, pennātus, volucer.
wink *n.* nictus *m.* *vi.* nictāre. **— at** cōnīvēre (*dat.*).
winner *n.* victor *m.*
winning *a.* blandus, iūcundus. **-ly** *ad.* blandē, iūcundē.
winning-post *n.* mēta *f.*
winnings *n.* lucra *n.pl.*
winnow *vt.* ventilāre; (*fig.*) excutere.
winnowing-fan *n.* vannus *f.*
winsome *a.* blandus, suāvis.
winter *n.* hiems *f.*; (*mid*) brūma *f.* *a.* hībernus. **— quarters** hīberna *n.pl.* *vi.* hībernāre.
wintry *a.* hiemālis, hībernus.
wipe *vt.* dētergēre. **— away** abstergēre. **— dry** siccāre. **— off** dētergēre. **— out** dēlēre. **— the nose** ēmungere.
wire *n.* fīlum aēneum *n.*
wiry *a.* nervōsus.
wisdom *n.* sapientia *f.*; (*in action*) prūdentia *f.*; (*in judgment*) cōnsilium *n.*
wise *a.* sapiēns, prūdēns. **-ly** *ad.* sapienter, prūdenter.
wish *n.* optātum *n.*, vōtum *n.*; (*for something missing*) dēsīderium *n.*; (*pl., greeting*) salūs *f.* *vt.* optāre, cupere, velle. **— for** exoptāre, expetere, dēsīderāre. **— good-day** salvēre iubēre. **as you —** ut libet. **I — I could** utinam possim.
wishful *a.* cupidus.
wishing *n.* optātiō *f.*
wisp *n.* manipulus *m.*
wistful *a.* dēsīderī plēnus. **-ly** *ad.* cum dēsīderiō.
wistfulness *n.* dēsīderium *n.*
wit *n.* (*humour*) facētiae *f.pl.*, salēs *m.pl.*; (*intellect*) argūtiae *f.pl.*, ingenium *n.* **caustic —** dicācitās *f.* **be at one's wits' end** valdē haerēre. **be out of one's -s** dēlīrāre. **have one's -s about one** prūdentem esse. **to —** nempe, dīcō.

witch *n.* sāga *f.*, strīga *f.*
witchcraft *n.* venēficium *n.*, magicae artēs *f.pl.*
with *pr.* (*person*) cum (*abl.*); (*thing*) *abl.*; (*in company*) apud (*acc.*); (*fight*) cum (*abl.*), contrā (*acc.*). be angry — īrāscī (*dat.*). begin — incipere ab. rest — esse penes (*acc.*). end — dēsinere in (*acc.*). what do you want — me ? quid mē vīs ?
withdraw *vt.* dēdūcere, dētrahere; (*fig.*) āvocāre; (*words*) retractāre. *vi.* dēcēdere, abscēdere, sē recipere, sē subdūcere. [*m.*
withdrawal *n.* (*mil.*) receptus
wither *vt.* torrēre. *vi.* dēflōrēscere.
withered *a.* marcidus.
withhold *vt.* abstinēre, retinēre, supprimere.
within *ad.* intus, intrā; (*motion*) intrō. *pr.* intrā (*acc.*), in (*abl.*).
without *ad.* extrā, forīs. from — extrīnsecus. be — vacāre (*abl.*), carēre (*abl.*). *pr.* sine (*abl.*), expers (*gen.*). I admire — fearing ita laudō ut nōn timeam. — breaking the law salvīs lēgibus. you cannot see — admiring vidēre nōn potes quīn laudēs. you cannot appreciate — seeing for yourself aestimāre nōn potes nisi ipse vīderis.
withstand *vt.* resistere (*dat.*), obsistere (*dat.*); (*attack*) ferre, sustinēre.
withy *n.* vīmen *n.*
witless *a.* excors, ineptus, stultus.
witness *n.* (*person*) testis *m.*, *f.*; (*to a document*) obsignātor *m.*; (*spectator*) arbiter *m.*; (*evidence*) testimōnium *n.* call as — antestārī. bear — testificārī. call to — testārī. *vt.* testificārī; (*see*) vidēre, intuērī.
witnessing *n.* testificātiō *f.*
witticism *n.* dictum *n.*; (*pl.*) facētiae *f.pl.*
wittingly *ad.* sciēns.
witt/y *a.* facētus, argūtus, salsus; (*caustic*) dicāx. **-ily** *ad.* facētē, salsē.
wizard *n.* magus *m.*, venēficus *m.* [*f.pl.*
wizardry *n.* magicae artēs
wizened *a.* marcidus.
woad *n.* vitrum *n.*
wobble *vi.* titubāre; (*structure*) labāre.
woe *n.* lūctus *m.*, dolor *m.*, aerumna *f.*; (*pl.*) mala *n.pl.*, calamitātēs *f.pl.* — to vae (*dat.*).
woeful *a.* tristis, maestus, aerumnōsus. **-ly** *ad.* triste, miserē.
wolf *n.* lupus *m.*, lupa *f.* -'s lupīnus.
woman *n.* fēmina *f.*, mulier *f.* old — anus *f.* married — mātrōna *f.* -'s muliebris.
womanish *a.* muliebris, effēminātus.
womanly *a.* muliebris.
womb *n.* uterus *m.*
wonder *n.* admīrātiō *f.*; (*of a thing*) admīrābilitās *f.*; (*thing*) mīrāculum *n.*, mīrum *n.*, portentum *n.* *vi.* mīrārī — at admīrārī, dēmīrārī.
wonderful *a.* mīrus, mīrābilis, admīrābilis. **-ly** *ad.* mīrē, mīrābiliter, mīrum quantum.
wonderfulness *n.* admīrābilitās *f.*
wondering *a.* mīrābundus.
wonderment *n.* admīrātiō *f.*
wondrous *a.* mīrus, mīrābilis.
wont *n.* mōs *m.*, cōnsuētūdō *f.*
wonted *a.* solitus.
woo *vt.* petere.
wood *n.* silva *f.*, nemus *n.*; (*material*) lignum *n.* gather lignārī. touch — ! absit verbō invidia. *a.* ligneus.
woodcutter *n.* lignātor *m.*
wooded *a.* silvestris, saltuōsus.

wooden *a.* ligneus.
woodland *n.* silvae *f.pl.* *a.* silvestris.
woodman *n.* lignātor *m.*
wood-nymph *n.* dryas *f.*
woodpecker *n.* pīcus *m.*
wood-pigeon *n.* palumbēs *m., f.*
woodwork *n.* tigna *n. pl.*
wood-worker *n.* faber tignārius *m.*
woody *a.* silvestris, silvōsus.
wooer *n.* procus *m.*
woof *n.* subtēmen *n.*
wool *n.* lāna *f.*
woollen *a.* lāneus.
woolly *a.* lānātus.
word *n.* verbum *n.*; (*spoken*) vōx *f.*; (*message*) nūntius *m.*; (*promise*) fidēs *f.*; (*term*) vocābulum *n.* **— for —** ad verbum, verbum ē verbō. **a — with you!** paucīs tē volō! **break one's —** fidem fallere. **bring back —** renūntiāre. **by — of mouth** ōre. **fair -s** blanditiae *f.pl.* **give one's —** fidem dare. **have a — with** colloquī cum. **have -s with** iūrgāre cum. **have a good — for** laudāre. **in a —** ūnō verbō, dēnique. **keep one's —** fidem praestāre. **of few -s** taciturnus. **take at one's —** crēdere (*dat.*).
wording *n.* verba *n.pl.*
wordy *a.* verbōsus.
work *n.* (*energy*) labor *m.*, opera *f.*; (*task*) opus *n.*; (*thing done*) opus *n.*; (*book*) liber *m.*; (*trouble*) negōtium *n.* **-s** (*mil.*) opera *n.pl.*; (*mechansim*) māchinātiō *f.*; (*place*) officīna *f.* *vi.* labōrāre. *vt.* (*men*) exercēre; (*metal*) fabricārī; (*soil*) subigere; (*results*) efficere. **— at, out** ēlabōrāre. **— in** admiscēre. **— off** exhaurīre. **— up** (*emotion*) efferre. **— one's way up** prōficere. *vi.* gerī.
workaday *a.* cottīdiānus.
workhouse *n.* ergastulum *n.*
working *n.* (*mechanism*) māchinātiō *f.*; (*soil*) cultus *m.*
workman *n.* (*unskilled*) operārius *m.*; (*skilled*) opifex *m.*, faber *m.*; (*pl.*) operae *f.pl.*
workmanship *n.* ars *f.*, artificium *n.*
workshop *n.* fabrica *f.*, officīna *f.*
world *n.* (*universe*) mundus *m.*; (*earth*) orbis terrārum *m.*; (*nature*) rērum nātūra *f.*; (*mankind*) hominēs *m.pl.*; (*masses*) vulgus *n.* **of the —** mundānus. **man of the —** homō urbānus *m.* **best in the —** rērum optimus, omnium optimus. **where in the —** ubī gentium.
worldliness *n.* quaestūs studium *n.*
worldly *a.* quaestuī dēditus.
worm *n.* vermis *m.* *vi.* **— one's way** sē īnsinuāre.
worm-eaten *a.* vermiculōsus.
wormwood *n.* absinthium *n.*
worn *a.* trītus.
worried *a.* sollicitus, anxius.
worry *n.* cūra *f.*, sollicitūdō *f.* *vi.* sollicitārī. *vt.* vexāre, sollicitāre; (*of dogs*) lacerāre.
worse *a.* pēior, dēterior. **grow —** ingravēscere. **make matters —** rem exasperāre. *ad.* pēius, dēterius.
worsen *vi.* ingravēscere, dēteriōrem fierī.
worship *n.* venerātiō *f.*, deōrum cultus *m.*; (*rite*) sacra *n.pl.*, rēs dīvīnae *f.pl.* *vt.* adōrāre, venerārī, colere.
worst *a.* pessimus, dēterrimus. **— enemy** inimīcissimus *m.* **endure the —** ultima patī. *vt.* vincere.
worsted *n.* lāna *f.*
worth *n.* (*value*) pretium *n.*; (*moral*) dignitās *f.*, frūgālitās *f.*, virtūs *f.*; (*prestige*) auctōritās *f.* *a.* dignus. **for all one's —** prō virīlī parte. **how much is it — ?** quanti vēnit? **it is —**

a lot multum valet. it is — doing operae pretium est.
worthiness *n.* dignitās *f*
worthless *a.* (*person*) nēquam; (*thing*) vīlis, inānis.
worthlessness *n.* levitās *f.*, nēquitia *f.*; vīlitās *f.*
worth/y *a.* dignus; (*person*) frūgī, honestus. — of dignus (*abl.*). **-ily** *ad.* dignē, meritō.
wound *n.* vulnus *n.* *vt.* vulnerāre; (*feelings*) offendere.
wounded *a.* saucius.
wrangle *n.* iūrgium *n.*, rixa *f.* *vi.* iūrgāre, rixārī, altercārī.
wrap *vt.* involvere, obvolvere. — round intorquēre. — up involvere.
wrapper *n.* involucrum *n.* [*n.*
wrapping *n.* integumentum
wrath *n.* īra *f.*, īrācundia *f.*
wrathful *a.* īrātus. **-ly** *ad.* īrācundē.
wreak *vt.* — vengeance on saevīre in (*acc.*), ulcīscī.
wreath *n.* corōna *f.*, sertum *n.*
wreathe *vt.* (*garland*) torquēre; (*object*) corōnāre.
wreck *n.* naufragium *n.* *vt.* frangere; (*fig.*) perdere. be **-d** naufragium facere.
wreckage *n.* fragmenta *n.pl.*
wrecked *a.* (*person*) naufragus; (*ship*) frāctus.
wrecker *n.* perditor *m.*
wren *n.* rēgulus *m.*
wrench *vt.* intorquēre, extorquēre. — away ēripere. — open effringere.
wrest *vt.* extorquēre.
wrestle *vi.* luctārī.
wrestler *n.* luctātor *m.*, athlēta *m.*
wrestling *n.* luctātiō *f.*
wretch *n.* scelerātus *m.*, nēquam homō *m.* poor — miser homō *m.*
wretched *a.* īnfēlīx, miser; (*pitiful*) flēbilis. **-ly** *ad.* miserē.
wretchedness *n.* miseria *f.*; maestitia *f.*
wriggle *vi.* sē torquēre.
wriggling *a.* sinuōsus.
wright *n.* faber *m.*
wring *vt.* torquēre. — from extorquēre.
wrinkle *n.* rūga *f.* *vt.* corrūgāre.
wrinkled *a.* rūgōsus.
wrist *n.* prīma palmae pars *f.*
writ *n.* (*legal*) auctōritās *f.*
write *vt.* scrībere; (*book*) cōnscrībere. — off indūcere. — on īnscrībere (*dat.*). — out exscrībere, dēscrībere. — out in full perscrībere.
writer *n.* (*lit.*) scrīptor *m.*, auctor *m.*; (*clerk*) scrība *m.*
writhe *vi.* torquērī.
writing *n.* (*act*) scrīptiō *f.*; (*result*) scrīptum *n.*
wrong *a.* falsus, perversus, prāvus; (*unjust*) iniūstus, inīquus. be —, go — errāre. *n.* iniūria *f.*, culpa *f.*, noxa *f.*, malum *n.* do — peccāre, dēlinquere. right and — (*moral*) honesta ac turpia *n.pl.* *vt.* laedere, nocēre (*dat.*); (*by deceit*) fraudāre. **-ly** *ad.* falsō, dēprāvātē, male, perperam.
wrongdoer *n.* maleficus *m.*, scelerātus *m.*
wrongdoing *n.* scelus *n.*
wrongful *a.* iniūstus, iniūriosus, inīquus. **-ly** *ad.* iniūriā, iniūstē, inīquē.
wrong-headed *a.* perversus.
wrong-headedness *n.* perversitās *f.*
wroth *a.* īrātus.
wrought *a.* factus.
wry *a.* dētortus. make a — face ōs dūcere.
wryness *n.* prāvitās *f.*

Y

yacht *n.* phasēlus *m.*
yard *n.* (*court*) ārea *f.*; (*measure*) trēs pedēs.
yard-arm *n.* antenna *f.*

yarn *n.* fīlum *n.*; (*story*) fābula *f.*
yawn *n.* hiātus *m.* *vi.* hiāre, ōscitāre; (*chasm*) dehiscere.
ye *pro.* vōs.
yean *vt.* parere.
year *n.* annus *m.* **every** — quotannīs. **for a** — in annum. **half** — sēmēstre spatium *n.* **this** -'s hōrnus. **twice a** — bis annō. **two** -s biennium *n.* **three** -s triennium *n.* **four** -s quadriennium *n.* **five** -s quinquennium *n.*
yearly *a.* annuus, anniversārius. *ad.* quotannīs.
yearn *vi.* — **for** dēsīderāre, exoptāre.
yearning *n.* dēsīderium *n.*
yeast *n.* fermentum *n.*
yell *n.* clāmor *m.*; (*of pain*) ēiulātiō *f.* *vi.* clāmāre, eiulāre.
yellow *a.* flāvus; (*pale*) gilvus; (*deep*) fulvus; (*gold*) luteus; (*saffron*) croceus.
yelp *n.* gannītus *m.* *vi.* gannīre.
yeoman *n.* colōnus *m.*
yes *ad.* ita (est), māximē; (*correcting*) immo.
yesterday *ad.* herī. *n.* hesternus diēs *m.* -'s hesternus. **the day before** — nūdius tertius.
yet *ad.* (*contrast*) tamen, nihilōminus, attamen; (*time*) adhūc, etiam; (*with comp.*) etiam. **and** — atquī, quamquam. **as** — adhūc. **not** — nōndum.
yew *n.* taxus *f.*
yield *n.* fructus *m.* *vt.* (*crops*) ferre, efferre; (*pleasure*) adferre; (*concession*) dare, concēdere; (*surrender*) dēdere. *vi.* cēdere; (*surrender*) sē dēdere, sē trādere. — **to the wishes of** mōrem gerere (*dat.*), obsequī (*dat.*).
yielding *a.* (*person*) facilis, obsequēns; (*thing*) mollis. *n.* cessio *f.*; dēditiō *f.*
yoke *n.* iugum *n.* *vt.* iungere, coniungere.
yoke-fellow *n.* cōnsors *m., f.*; (*married*) coniunx *m., f.*
yokel *n.* agrestis *m.*
yolk *n.* vitellus *m.*
yonder *ad.* illic. *a.* ille, iste.
yore *n.* **of** — quondam, ōlim.
you *pro.* tū, vōs.
young *a.* iuvenis, adulēscēns; (*child*) parvus. **-er** iūnior, nātū minor. **-est** nātū minimus. *n.* fētus *m.*, pullus *m.*, catulus *m.*
youngster *n.* puer *m.*
your *a.* tuus, vester.
yourself *pro.* ipse.
youth *n.* (*age*) iuventūs *f.*, adulescentia *f.*; (*person*) iuvenis *m.*, adulēscēns *m.*; (*collective*) iuventūs *f.*
youthful *a.* iuvenīlis, puerīlis. **-ly** *ad.* iuvenīliter.

Z

zeal *n.* studium *n.*, ārdor *m.*
zealot *n.* studiōsus *m.*, fautor *m.*
zealous *a.* studiōsus, ārdēns. **-ly** *ad.* studiōsē, ārdenter.
zenith *n.* vertex *m.*
zephyr *n.* Favōnius *m.*
zero *n.* nihil *n.*
zest *n.* (*taste*) sapor *m.*; (*fig.* gustātus *m.*, impetus *m.*
zigzag *n.* ānfrāctus *m.* *a.* tortuōsus.
zither *n.* cithara *f.*
zodiac *n.* signifer orbis *m.*
zone *n.* cingulus *m.*

GEOGRAPHICAL NAMES

The following list of geographical names and their adjectives includes both ancient and medieval Latin forms. The former are printed in Roman type, the latter in Italics. Medieval place-names tend to have a variety of Latin forms, but only one has been selected in each case; occasionally both the ancient and the medieval forms have been given. Modern names which have a ready-made Latin form (*e.g.* America) have been omitted, and many names not included in this selection can be easily Latinised on the analogy of those which do appear.

AACHEN	*Aquīsgrānum* **n.**	*a.* *Aquīsgrānēnsis*
ABERDEEN	*Aberdōnia f.*	*a.* *Aberdōnēnsis*
ABERGAVENNY	Gobannium *n.*	
ABERYSTWITH	*Aberistyvium n.*	
ADIGE, R.	Athesis *m.*	
ADRIATIC	Mare superum *n.*	*a.* Hadriāticus
AEGEAN	Mare Aegaeum *n.*	*a.* Aegaeus
AFGHANISTAN	Ariāna *f.*	*a.* Ariānus
AFRICA	Libya *f.*, Africa *f.*	*a.* Libycus, Africānus
AISNE, R.	Axona *m.*	
AIX-EN-PROVENCE	Aquae Sextiae *f.pl.*	*a.* *Aquēnsis*
AIX-LA-CHAPELLE	*Aquīsgrānum n.*	*a.* *Aquisgrānēnsis*
AIX-LES-BAINS	Aquae Grātiānae *f.pl.*	
AJACCIO	*Adiacium n.*	*a.* *Adiacēnsis*
ALDBOROUGH	Isurium (*n.*) Brigantum	
ALEXANDRIA	Alexandrēa, Alexandrīa *f.*	*a.* Alexandrīnus
ALGIERS	*Algerium n.*	*a.* *Algerīnus*
ALPS	Alpēs *f.pl.*	*a.* Alpīnus
ALSACE	*Alsatia f.*	
AMALFI	Amalphis *f.*	*a.* Amalphitānus
AMBLESIDE	Galava *f.*	
AMIENS	*Ambiānum n.*	*a.* *Ambiānēnsis*
AMSTERDAM	*Amstelodamum n.*	*a.* *Amstelodamēnsis*
ANCASTER	Causennae *f.pl.*	
ANGERS	*Andegāvum n.*	*a.* Andegāvēnsis
ANGLESEY	Mona *f.*	
ANJOU	Andegāvēnsis ager *m.*	
ANKARA	Ancyra *f.*	*a.* Ancyrānus
ANIENE, R.	Aniō *m.*	*a.* Aniēnus
ANTIBES	Antipolis *f.*	*a.* Antipolītānus
ANTIOCH	Antiochīa *f.*	*a.* Antiochēnus
ANTWERP	*Antwerpium n.*	*a.* *Antwerpiēnsis*

ANZIO	Antium *n.*	*a.* Antiās, Antiānus
AOSTA	Augusta Praetōria *f.*	
APENNINES	Mōns Apennīnus *m.*	
ARAGON	*Aragōnia f.*	
ARCHANGEL	*Archangelopolis f.*	
ARDENNES	Arduenna *f.*	
AREZZO	Ārētium *n.*	*a.* Ārētīnus
ARGENTEUIL	*Argentōlium n.*	
ARGYLL	*Argadia f.*	
ARLES	Arelās *f.*	*a.* Arelātēnsis
ARMAGH	Armācha *f.*	*a.* Armāchānus
ARNO, R.	Arnus *m.*	*a.* Arniēnsis
ARRAS	Atrebatēs *m.pl.*	*a.* Atrebatēnsis
ARTOIS	Atrebatēs *m.pl.*	
ASSISSI	Assīsium *n.*	*a.* Assīsiēnsis
ATHENS	Athēnae *f.pl.*	*a.* Athēniēnsis
ATLANTIC	Mare Atlanticum *n.*	
AUGSBURG	Augusta (*f.*) Vindelicōrum	*a.* Augustānus
AUTUN	Augustodūnum *n.*	*a.* Augustodūnēnsis
AUVERGNE	Arvernī *m.pl.*	*a.* Arvernus
AVENTINE	Aventīnus *m.*	
AVIGNON	Aveniō *f.*	*a.* Aveniōnēnsis
AVON, R.	Auvona *m.*	
BABYLON	Babylōn *f.*	*a.* Babylōnius
BADEN-BADEN	Aquae Aurēliae *f.pl.*	
BALEARIC IS.	Baliārēs Īnsulae *f.pl.*	*a.* Baliāricus
BALKH	Bactra *n.pl.*	*a.* Bactriānus
BALTIC	*Balticum Mare n.*	
BANGOR	*Bangertium n.*	*a. Bangertiēnsis*
BARCELONA	Barcinō *f.*	*a.* Barcinōnēnsis
BARI	Bārium *n.*	*a. Bārēnsis*
BASLE	Basilēa *f.*	*a.* Basilēēnsis
BASQUES	Vasconēs *m.pl.*	*a.* Vasconicus
BATH	Aquae (*f.pl.*) Sulis	
BAYEUX	*Augustodūrum n.*	
BAYREUTH	*Barūthum n.*	
BEAUVAIS	Bellovacī *m.pl.*	*a. Bellovacēnsis*
BEIRUT	Bērȳtus *f.*	*a.* Bērȳtius
BELGIUM	Belgae *m.pl.*	*a.* Belgicus
BERGEN	*Bergae f.pl.*	
BERLIN	*Berolīnum n.*	*a. Berolīnēnsis*
BERNE	Vērona *f.*	
BERWICK	*Barvīcum n.*	
BESANÇON	Vesontiō *m.*	*a. Bisuntīnus*
BLACK SEA	Pontus (Euxīnus) *m.*	*a.* Ponticus
BOBBIO	*Bobbium n.*	*a. Bobbiēnsis*
BOHEMIA	Boiohaemī *m.pl.*	
BOLOGNA	Bonōnia *f.*	*a.* Bonōniēnsis
BONN	*Bonna f.*	
BORDEAUX	*Burdigala f.*	*a. Burdigalēnsis*
BOULOGNE	Bonōnia *f.*	*a.* Bononiēnsis
BOURGES	Avāricum *n.*	*a.* Avāricēnsis
BRABANT	*Brabantia f.*	

BRAGANZA	Brigantia *f.*	*a.* Brigantiēnsis
BRANCASTER	Branodūnum *n.*	
BRANDENBURG	*Brandenburgia f.*	*a. Brandenburgēnsis*
BREMEN	*Brēma f.*	*a. Brēmēnsis*
BRESLAU	*Bratislavia f.*	*a. Bratislaviēnsis*
BRINDISI	Brundisium *n.*	*a.* Brundisīnus
BRITAIN	Britannia *f.*	*a.* Britannicus
BRISTOL	*Bristolium n.*	*a. Bristoliēnsis*
BRITTANY	Armoricae *f.pl*	
BRUGES	*Brugae f.pl.*	*a. Brugēnsis*
BRUNSWICK	*Brunsvīcum n.*	*a. Brunsvīcēnsis*
BRUSSELS	*Bruxellae f.pl.*	*a. Bruxellēnsis*
BUCHAREST	*Bucarestum n.*	*a. Bucarestiēnsis*
BURGOS	*Burgī m.pl.*	*a. Burgitānus*
BURGUNDY	Burgundiōnēs *m.pl.*	
CADIZ	Gādēs *f.pl.*	*a.* Gāditānus
CAEN	*Cadomum n.*	*a. Cadomēnsis*
CAERLEON	Isca *f.*	
CAERMARTHEN	Maridūnum *n.*	
CAERNARVON	Segontium *n.*	
CAERWENT	Venta (*f.*) Silurum	
CAGLIARI	Caralis *f.*	*a.* Caralītānus
CAIRO	*Cairus f.*	
CALAIS	*Calētum n.*	*a. Calētanus*
CAMBRAI	*Camerācum n.*	*a. Camerācēnsis*
CAMBRIDGE	*Cantabrigia f.*	*a. Cantabrigiēnsis*
CAMPAGNA	Campānia *f.*	*a.* Campānus
CANNES	*Canoē f.*	
CANTERBURY	Durovernum *n.*, *Cantuāria f.*	*a. Cantuāriēnsis*
CAPRI	Capreae *f.pl.*	*a.* Capreēnsis
CARLSBAD	*Aquae Carolīnae f.pl.*	
CARDIGAN	Ceretica *f.*	
CARLISLE	Luguvallium *n.*	
CARTAGENA	Carthāgō Nova *f.*	
CARTHAGE	Carthāgō *f.*	*a.* Carthāginiēnsis
CASPIAN SEA	Mare Caspium *n.*	
CEVENNES	Gebenna *f.*	*a.* Gebennicus
CEYLON	Tāprobanē *f.*	
CHAMPAGNE	*Campānia f.*	*a. Campānicus*
CHARTRES	Carnūtēs *m.pl.*	*a.* Carnōtēnus
CHELMSFORD	Caesaromagus *m.*	
CHERBURG	*Caesaris burgus m.*	
CHESTER	Deva *f.*	
CHICHESTER	Rēgnum *n.*	
CHINA	Sēres *m.pl.*	*a.* Sēricus
CIRENCESTER	Corinium (*n.*) Dobunōrum	
CLAIRVAUX	*Clāra Vallis f.*	*a. Clāravallēnsis*
CLERMONT	Nemossus *f.*	
CLUNY	*Clīniacum n.*	*a. Clīniacēnsis*
CLYDE, R.	Clōta *f.*	
COBLENZ	Cōnfluentēs *m.pl.*	
COLCHESTER	Camulodūnum *n.*	

COLOGNE	Colōnia Agrippina *f.*	*a. Colōniēnsis*
COMO, L.	Lārius *m.*	*a.* Lārius
CONSTANCE, L.	Lacus Brigantīnus *m.*	
CONSTANTINOPLE	Bȳzantium *n.*	*a.* Bȳzantīnus
COPENHAGEN	*Hafnia f.*	
CORBRIDGE	Corstopitum *n.*	
CORDOVA	Corduba *f.*	*a.* Cordubēnsis
CORFU	Corcȳra *f.*	*a.* Corcȳraeus
CORK	*Corcagia f.*	*a. Corcagiēnsis*
CORINTH	Corinthus *f.*	*a.* Corinthius
CORNWALL	*Cornubia f.*	
CRACOW	*Cracovia f.*	*a. Cracoviēnsis*
CRETE	Crēta *f.*	*a.* Crētēnsis, Crēticus
CUMBERLAND	*Cumbria f.*	
CYPRUS	Cyprus *f.*	*a.* Cyprius
CYRENE	Cȳrēnae *f.pl.*	*a.* Cȳrēnaicus
DAMASCUS	Damascus *f.*	*a.* Damascēnus
DANUBE, R. (LOWER) Ister *m.*, (UPPER) Dānuvius *m.*		
DANZIG	*Gedānum m.*	
DARDANELLES	Hellēspontus *m.*	*a.* Hellēspontius
DEE, R.	Deva *f.*	
DENMARK	Dānia *f.*	*a.* Dānicus
DERBY	*Derventiō m.*	
DEVON	*Devōnia f.*	
DNEIPER, R.	Borysthenēs *m.*	
DNEISTER, R.	Danaster *m.*	
DIJON	*Diviō f.*	*a. Diviōnēnsis*
DON, R. (RUSSIAN)	Tanais *m.*	
DONCASTER	Dānum *n.*	
DORCHESTER	Durnovāria *f.*	
DOURO, R.	Durius *m.*	
DOVER	Dubrī *m.pl.*	
DOVER, STRAITS OF	Fretum Gallicum *n.*	
DRESDEN	*Dresda f.*	*a. Dresdēnsis*
DUBLIN	*Dublīnum n.*	*a. Dublīnēnsis*
DUMBARTON	*Britannodūnum n.*	
DUNDEE	*Taodūnum n.*	
DUNSTABLE	Durocobrīvae *f.pl.*	
DURHAM	*Dunelmum n.*	*a. Dunelmēnsis*
EBRO, R.	Hibērus *m.*	
EDEN, R.	Itūna *f.*	
EDINBURGH	*Edinburgum n.*	*a. Edinburgēnsis*
EGYPT	Aegyptus *f.*	*a.* Aegyptius
ELBA	Ilva *f.*	
ELBE, R.	Albis *m.*	
ENGLAND	Anglia *f.*	*a.* Anglicus
ETNA	Aetna *f.*	*a.* Aetnaeus
EUROPE	Eurōpa	*a.* Eurōpaeus
EXETER	Isca (*f.*) Dumnoniōrum	
FIESOLE	Faesulae *f.pl.*	*a.* Faesulānus
FLANDERS	Menapiī *m.pl.*	
FLORENCE	Flōrentia *f.*	*a.* Flōrentīnus
FONTAINEBLEAU	*Bellofontānum n.*	

Forth, R.	Bodotria *f.*	
France	Gallia *f.*	*a.* Gallicus
Frankfurt	*Francofurtum n.*	
Frejus	Forum (*n.*) Iūlii	*a.* Foroiūliēnsis
Friesland	Frisiī *m.pl.*	*a.* Frīsius
Gallipoli	*Callipolis f.*	*a.* Callipolitānus
Galloway	*Gallovidia f.*	
Ganges	Gangēs *m.*	*a.* Gangēticus
Garda, L.	Bēnācus *m.*	
Garonne, R.	Garumna *f.*	
Gaul	Gallia *f.*	*a.* Gallicus
Geneva	Genāva *f.*	*a.* Genāvēnsis
Geneva, Lake of	Lemannus lacus *m.*	
Genoa	Genua *f.*	*a.* Genuēnsis
Germany	Germānia *f.*	*a.* Germānicus
Ghent	*Gandavum n.*	*a. Gandavēnsis*
Gibraltar	Calpē *f.*	*a.* Calpētānus
Gibraltar, Straits of	Fretum Gāditānum *n.*	
Girgenti	Agrigentum *n.*	*a.* Agrigentīnus
Glasgow	*Glasgua f.*	*a. Glasguēnsis*
Gloucester	Glēvum *n.*	
Gothenburg	*Gothoburgum n.*	
Graz	*Graecium n.*	
Greece	Graecia *f.*	*a.* Graecus
Greenwich	*Grenovīcum n.*	
Grenoble	Grātiānopolis *f.*	
Groningen	*Groninga f.*	
Guadalquivir, R.	Baetis *m.*	
Guadiana, R.	Anas *m.*	
Guernsey	*Sarnia f.*	
Hague, The	Haga (*f.*) Comitis	
Halle	*Halla f.*	*a. Hallēnsis*
Hamadan	Ecbatana *n.pl.*	
Hamburg	*Hamburgum n.*	*a. Hamburgēnsis*
Hanover	*Hannovera f.*	
Harwich	*Harvīcum n.*	
Havre	Grātiae Portus *m.*	
Hebrides	Ebūdae Insulae *f.pl.*	
Hexham	Axelodūnum *n.*	
Holland	Batāvī *m.pl.*	*a.* Batāvus
Ilkley	Olicāna *f.*	
Inn, R.	Aenus *m.*	
Ipswich	*Gippevīcum n.*	
Isar, R.	Isara *f.*	
Ireland	Hibernia *f.*	*a.* Hibernicus
Istanbul	Bȳzantium *n.*	*a.* Bȳzantīnus
Italy	Ītalia *f.*	*a.* Ītalicus
Iviza	Ebusus *f.*	*a.* Ebusitānus
Jersey	Caesarea *f.*	
Jerusalem	Hierosolyma *n.pl.*	*a.* Hierosolymītānus
Jutland	Chersonnēsus Cimbrica *f.*	
Kent	Cantium *n.*	
Kiel	*Chilonium n.*	

Lancaster	*Lancastria f.*	
Lanchester	Longovicium *n.*	
Land's End	Bolerium Prōmunturium *n.*	
Lausanne	Lausōnium *n.*	*a.* Lausōniēnsis
Lebanon	Libanus *m.*	
Leeds	*Ledesia f.*	
Leicester	Ratae (*f.pl.*) Coritānōrum	
Leipsig	*Lipsia f.*	*a.* Lipsiēnsis
Lerida	Ilerda *f.*	*a.* Ilerdēnsis
Leyden	Lugdūnum (*n.*) Batāvōrum	
Lichfield	*Etocētum n.*	
Limoges	Augustorītum *n.*	
Lincoln	Lindum *n.*	
Lisbon	Olisīpō *m.*	*a.* Olisīpōnēnsis
Lizard Point	Damnonium Prōmunturium *n.*	
Loire, R.	Liger *m.*	*a.* Ligericus
Lombardy	*Langobardia f.*	
London	Londinium *n.*	*a.* Londiniēnsis
Lorraine	*Lōthāringia f.*	
Lucerne	*Lūceria f.*	*a. Lūcernēnsis*
Lund	Londinium (*n.*) Gothōrum	
Lyons	Lugdūnum *n.*	*a.* Lugdūnēnsis
Madrid	*Matrītum n.*	*a. Matrītēnsis*
Maggiore, L.	Verbannus *m.*	
Main, R.	Moenus *m.*	
Mainz	Mogontiacum *n.*	
Majorca	Baliāris Māior *f.*	
Malta	Melita *f.*	
Man, Isle of	Monapia	
Manchester	*Mancunium n.*	
Marmora, Sea of	Propontis *f.*	
Marne, R.	*Māterna f.*	
Marseilles	Massilia *f.*	*a.* Massiliēnsis
Matapan	Taenarum *n.*	*a.* Taenarius
Mediterranean	Mare internum *n.*	
Melun	Melodūnum *n.*	
Merida	Ēmerita *f.*	*a.* Ēmeritēnsis
Messina	Messāna *f.*	*a.* Messānius
Metz	Dīvodūrum *n.*	
Meuse, R.	Mosa *f.*	
Milan	Mediōlānum *n.*	*a.* Mediōlānēnsis
Minorca	Baliāris Minor *f.*	
Modena	Mutina *f.*	*a.* Mutinēnsis
Mons	Montēs *m.pl.*	
Monte Casino	Casinum *n.*	*a.* Casīnās
Moray	*Moravia f.*	
Morocco	Maurētānia *f.*	*a.* Maurus
Moscow	*Moscovia f.*	
Moselle, R.	Mosella *f.*	
Munich	*Monacum n.*	*a. Monacēnsis*
Nantes	Namnētēs *m.pl.*	
Naples	Neāpolis *f.*	*a.* Neāpolītānus
Neckar, R.	Nicer *m.*	

NEWCASTLE	Pōns (*m.*) Aelii, *Novum Castrum n.*	*a. Novocastrēnsis*
NICE	Nicaea *f.*	*a.* Nicaeēnsis
NILE, R.	Nīlus *m.*	*a.* Nīlōticus
NÎMES	Nemausus *f.*	*a.* Nemausēnsis
NORWAY	*Norvēgia f.*	*a. Norvēgiānus*
NORWICH	*Nordovīcum n.*	
ODER, R.	Viadrus *m.*	
OPORTO	Portus Calēnsis *m.*	
ORANGE	Arausiō *f.*	
ORKNEYS	Orcades *f.pl.*	
ORLEANS	*Aurēliānum n.*	*a. Aurēliānēnsis*
OUDENARDE	*Aldenarda f.*	
OXFORD	*Oxonia f.*	*a. Oxoniēnsis*
PADUA	Patavium *n.*	*a.* Patavīnus
PALERMO	Panormus *m.*	*a.* Panormitānus
PARIS	Lutetia *f.*, Parīsiī *m.pl.*	*a. Parīsiēnsis*
PATRAS	Patrae *f.pl.*	*a.* Patrēnsis
PERSIAN GULF	Mare Rubrum *n.*	
PIACENZA	Placentia *f.*	*a.* Placentīnus
PO, R.	Padus	*a.* Padānus
POITIERS	Limōnum *n.*	
POLAND	*Polōnia f.*	
PORTSMOUTH	Māgnus Portus *m.*	
PORTUGAL	Lūsitānia *f.*	
POZZUOLI	Puteolī *m.pl.*	*a.* Puteolānus
PRAGUE	*Prāga f.*	*a. Prāgēnsis*
PROVENCE	Prōvincia *f*	
PYRENEES	Pȳrēnaeī montēs *m.pl.*	
RED SEA	Sinus Arābicus *m.*	
RHEIMS	Dūrocortorum *n.*	
RHINE, R.	Rhēnus *m.*	*a.* Rhēnānus
RHODES	Rhodos *f.*	*a.* Rhodius
RHONE, R.	Rhodanus *m.*	
RICHBOROUGH	Rutupiae *f.pl.*	*a.* Rutupīnus
RIMINI	Arīminum	*a.* Arīminēnsis
ROCHESTER	Dūrobrīvae *f.pl.*	
ROME	Rōma *f.*	*a.* Rōmānus
ROTTERDAM	*Roterodamum n.*	*a. Roterodamēnsis*
ROUEN	*Rothomagus f.*	*a. Rothomagēnsis*
SAAR, R.	*Sangona f.*	
ST. ALBANS	Verulamium *n.*	
ST. ANDREWS	*Andreopolis f.*	
ST. BERNARD	(GREAT) Mōns Pennīnus *m.*, (LITTLE) Alpis Grāia *f.*	
ST. GALLEN	*Sangallēnse coenobium n.*	*a. Sangallēnsis*
ST. GOTTHARD	Alpēs summae *f.pl.*	
ST. MORITZ	*Agaunum n.*	*a.* Agaunēnsis
SALISBURY	Sarisberia *f.*	
SALZBURG	*Iuvāvum n.*	*a. Salisburgēnsis*
SAÔNE, R.	Arar *m.*	
SAVOY	*Sabaudia f.*	
SCHELDT, R.	Scaldis *m.*	
SCHLESWIG	*Slesvīcum n.*	

SCILLY IS.	Cassiterides *f.pl.*	
SCOTLAND	Calēdonia *f.*	*a.* Calēdonius
SEINE, R.	Sēquana *f.*	
SEVERN, R.	Sabrina *f.*	
SEVILLE	Hispalis *f.*	*a.* Hispalēnsis
SHREWSBURY	*Salōpia f.*	
SICILY	Sicilia *f.*	*a.* Siculus
SIDRA, GULF OF	Syrtis (māior) *f.*	
SILCHESTER	Callēva (*f.*) Atrebatum	
SOISSONS	Augusta (*f.*) Suessiōnum	
SOLWAY FIRTH	Itūna (*f.*) aestuārium	
SOMME, R.	Samara *f.*	
SPAIN	Hispānia *f.*	*a.* Hispānus
STRASBOURG	Argentorātus *f.*	*a.* Argentorātēnsis
SWABIA	Suēvia *f.*	*a.* Suēvicus
SWEDEN	*Suēcia f.*	*a. Suēcicus*
SWITZERLAND	Helvētia *f.*	*a.* Helvēticus
SYRACUSE	Syrācūsae *f.pl.*	*a.* Syrācūsānus
TANGIER	Tingī *f.*	*a.* Tingitānus
TARANTO	Tarentum *n.*	*a.* Tarentīnus
TARRAGONA	Tarracō *f.*	*a.* Tarracōnēnsis
TAY, R.	*Taus m.*	
THAMES, R.	Tamesis *m.*	
THEBES	Thēbae *f.pl.*	*a.* Thēbānus
TIBER, R.	Tiberis *m.*	*a.* Tiberīnus
TIVOLI	Tībur *n.*	*a.* Tīburtīnus
TOLEDO	Tolētum *n.*	*a.* Tolētānus
TOULON	*Tolōna f.*	*a. Tolōnēnsis*
TOULOUSE	Tolōsa *f.*	*a.* Tolōsānus
TOURS	Caesarodūnum *n.*	
TREVES, TRIER	Augusta (*f.*) Treverōrum	
TRIESTE	Tergeste *n.*	*a.* Tergestīnus
TRIPOLI	Tripolis *f.*	*a.* Tripolitānus
TUNIS	Tūnēs *f.*	*a.* Tūnētānus
TURIN	Augusta (*f.*) Taurīnōrum	*a.* Taurīnus
TUSCANY	Etrūria *f.*	*a.* Etrūscus
TYRRHENAIN SEA	Mare īnferum *n.*	
UTRECHT	*Ultrāiectum n.*	*a. Ultrāiectēnsis*
VARDAR, R.	Axius *m.*	
VENICE	Venetī *m.pl.*, *Venetiae f.pl.*	*a.* Venetus
VERDUN	*Virodūnum n.*	*a. Virodūnēnsis*
VERSAILLES	*Versāliae f.pl.*	*a. Versāliēnsis*
VICHY	Aquae (*f.pl.*) Sōlis	
VIENNA	*Vindobona f.*	*a. Vindobonēnsis*
VOSGES	Vosegus *m.*	
WALES	*Cambria f.*	
WALLSEND	Segedūnum *n.*	
WARSAW	*Varsavia f.*	*a. Varsaviēnsis*
WASH, THE	Metaris (*m.*) aestuārium	
WEAR, R.	Vedra *f.*	
WESER, R.	Visurgis *m.*	
WESTMINSTER	*Westmonastērium n.*	*a. Westmonastēriēnsis*
WIESBADEN	Mattiacum *n.*	*a.* Mattiacus

Wight, Isle of	Vectis *f.*	
Winchester	Venta (*f.*) Belgārum	
Worcester	Vigornia *f.*	
Worms	*Vormatia f.*	
Wroxeter	Viroconium *n.*	
York	Eburācum *n.*	*a.* Eburācēnsis
Zuider Zee	Flēvō *m.*	
Zurich	*Turicum n.*	*a.* Tigurīnus

PERSONAL NAMES

Albert	Albertus	**Henry**	Henrīcus
Alfred	Alfrēdus	**Horace**	Horātius
Alice	Alicia	**Hugh**	Hūgō
Andrew	Andrēās	**James**	Iacōbus
Antony	Antōnius	**Joan**	Iōanna
Arthur	Arturus	**John**	Iōannēs
Basil	Basilius	**Joseph**	Iōsēphus
Beatrice	Beātrix	**Joyce**	Iocōsa
Bernard	Bernardus	**Lawrence**	Laurentius
Cecil	Caecilius	**Lewis, Louis**	Lūdovīcus
Charles	Carolus	**Louise**	Lūdovīca
Christopher	Christophorus	**Lucy**	Lūcia
icely	Caecilia	**Luke**	Lūcās
laude	Claudius	**Margaret**	Margarīta
lement	Clēmēns	**Mark**	Marcus
yril	Cyrillus	**Mary**	Maria
enis	Dionȳsius	**Matthew**	Matthaeus
orothy	Dōrothea	**Maurice**	Mauritius
dward	Eduardus	**Norman**	Normannus
llen	Helena	**Oliver**	Olivarus
mily	Aemilia	**Patrick**	Patricius
rances	Francesca	**Paul**	Paulus
rancis	Franciscus	**Peter**	Petrus
rank	Franciscus	**Philip**	Philippus
rederick	Frēderīcus	**Ralph**	Radulfus
offrey	Gaufrīdus	**Richard**	Ricardus
orge	Geōrgius	**Robert**	Robertus
llian	Iūliāna	**Stephen**	Stephanus
dfrey	Gōdefrīdus	**Thomas**	Thōmās
ace	Grātia	**Timothy**	Tīmotheus
egory	Gregorius	**Walter**	Gualtērus
y	Guidō	**William**	Gulielmus
len	Helena	**Winifred**	Winfrīda

IMPORTANT DATES IN ROMAN HISTORY

B.C.	
753	Traditional date of the founding of Rome.
510	Expulsion of the kings.
450	Twelve Tables codifying Roman Law.
390	Capture of Rome by the Gauls.
338	Final subjugation of the Latin League.
281-272	War with Tarentum and Pyrrhus.
264	First Punic War—the beginning of the long struggle against Carthage.
216	Battle of Cannae.
202	Battle of Zama.
197	Romans defeat Macedonians at Cynoscephalae.
146	Destruction of Carthage.
133	Tribunate of Tiberius Gracchus.
107-100	Marius consul.
82-79	Sulla dictator.
70	First consulate of Pompey and Crassus.
63	Catiline conspiracy during consulship of Cicero.
60	"First Triumvirate"—Caesar, Pompey and Crassus.
58-51	Caesar's campaigns in Gaul.
48	Caesar defeats Pompey at Pharsalus.
44	Assassination of Caesar.
43	"Second Triumvirate"—Octavian, Antony and Lepidus.
42	Battle of Philippi.
31	Battle of Actium.
27	Octavian takes the title "Augustus".
A.D.	
43-5	Roman annexation of Britain.
96	The Roman Empire reaches its widest extent under the Emperor Trajan.
285	Empire divided into two parts by Diocletian.
313	Constantine legalises Christianity.

THE SEVEN KINGS OF ANCIENT ROME

1 Romulus
2 Numa Pompilius
3 Tullus Hostilius
4 Ancus Marcius
5 Tarquinius Priscus
6 Servius Tullius
7 Tarquinius Superbus